VERNACULAR LITERARY THEORY
FROM THE FRENCH OF MEDIEVAL ENGLAND

Vernacular Literary Theory from the French of Medieval England

Texts and Translations, *c.* 1120–*c.* 1450

Edited and translated by

Jocelyn Wogan-Browne
Thelma Fenster
and Delbert W. Russell

D. S. BREWER

First published 2016

D. S. Brewer, Cambridge

Paperback edition 2018

ISBN 978 1 84384 429 7 hardback
ISBN 978 1 84384 490 7 paperback

D. S. Brewer is an imprint of Boydell & Brewer Ltd
PO Box 9, Woodbridge, Suffolk IP12 3DF, UK
and of Boydell & Brewer Inc.
668 Mount Hope Ave, Rochester, NY 14620–2731, USA
website: www.boydellandbrewer.com

A catalogue record for this book is available from the British Library

This publication is printed on acid-free paper

Typeset by Word and Page, Chester, UK

Printed and bound in Great Britain by
TJ International Ltd, Padstow, Cornwall

Dedicated to the memory of

Robert M. Stein

pioneer thinker, writer and teacher
in the field of medieval Europe's multilingual cultures
with gratitude for his friendship
and in recognition of scholarship's great debt to him

Contents

Maps and Illustrations

Maps

Figures

Preface

This volume presents single manuscript editions and translations of prologues, epilogues, and other excerpts from French-language texts composed or circulating in medieval England. The French-language writing of England offers an indispensable corpus for the history of French-language literature at large and for the understanding of England's literary, documentary and cultural history over some four hundred years and more. We concentrate here on literary and other texts in their most self-reflexive moments: identifying themselves, discussing their own production and strategies, interpellating their audiences, and positioning their materials. This focus provides access to the assumptions and strategies of medieval England's literary and literate corpus of work in French. Our volume is not a conventional literary history so much as an argued anthology making a case for the interest and significance of the field from which this book draws its demonstrations.

No anthology of whatever kind can include all the texts an editor or reader might wish to have. A handful of texts in the French of England have been well served in modern translations and discussion and are omitted here: others are fully translated and introduced in our French of England Translation Series (FRETS) and its occasional publication series (FRETS OPS): see https://acmrs.org/publications/catalog?field_mrts_tax_tid=14. Nevertheless, by offering direct contact with edited texts and some mappings of French-language writing in England's regional and supra-regional cultures, we hope to have provided many reasons for others to make their own further explorations.

Contributors and Acknowledgements

The volume has been long in the making and has many debts. In the first instance, the editors want warmly to thank all those who have contributed entries. Jocelyn Wogan-Browne, Thelma Fenster, and Delbert Russell are ultimately responsible for the editions and commentary: we have each edited, introduced and cross-checked each other's entries, but we have also been delighted to work with colleagues and with our former and current graduate students. Dr Cathy Hume (Lecturer in English, University of Bristol, UK) originally prepared Part VI, §3, Middle English Versions of French Entries, and contributed the *Lumere as lais* (**19**) as a post-doctoral Modern Humanities Reseach Associate to Jocelyn Wogan-Browne at the University of York. Dr Joshua Byron Smith, Assistant Professor in English at the University of Arkansas kindly undertook to prepare (**31**), for which knowledge of Welsh was a desideratum. Dr John Spence, an expert in Anglo-Norman prose chronicle writing, contributed the *Mohun Chronicle* (**42**).

We thank Dr Henry Bainton, Lecturer in Medieval Literature, University of York, UK for (**3**) and (**6**); Dr Maija Birenbaum, Assistant Professor, University of Wisconsin at Whitewater for (**37**); Dr Donna Alfano Bussell, Assistant Professor, University of Illinois at Springfield for (**11a**); Clarissa Chenovick, doctoral candidate, Fordham University, NY for (**32a** and **32b**); Dr Katharine Handel of the Oxford English Dictionary, Oxford

University Press, for (28); Dr Rebecca June, Lecturer, English Department, Fordham University, NY for (36); Dr Brenna Mead, Manager, Oblong Ridge Farm, Armenia NY for (17); Dr Jaclyn Rajsic, Lecturer in English, Queen Mary and Westfield College, University of London for (20c and 20d); Dr Karl Steel, Associate Professor, Brooklyn College and Graduate Center, City University of New York for (14). In addition we thank Dr Jade Bailey, doctoral fellow, University of Bristol, Dr Andrea Lankin, Assistant Professor, St Joseph's University, and Karen Trimnell, freelance copy-editor, for their initial graduate work on (44), (5) and (27) respectively.

For initial funding and support of French of England projects we thank the National Endowment for the Humanities, USA, Fordham University, New York, and the Modern Humanities Research Association of the UK and the University of York, UK. We owe a special debt to the generosity and vision of Maryanne Kowaleski, Joseph P. Fitzpatrick Jr Distinguished Professor in Medieval History, Fordham University, and are grateful to Dean Nancy Busch at Fordham for her support of French of England projects. Support for research assistance with the volume and the costs of many of the archive trips and digital resources needed for it has come in large measure through funds attached to the Thomas F. X. and Theresa Mullarkey Chair in Literature at Fordham, and we are much indebted to Mrs Mullarkey for her generous support of the chair, an expression of belief in the value of the humanities that has become increasingly important in recent years. We also thank the National Endowment for the Humanities, USA, for making it possible for Karen Trimnell to work on the volume; the Modern Humanities Research Association, UK for funding for Dr Cathy Hume's invaluable post-doctoral year of work on French of England volumes and conferences; Fordham University for graduate assistance from Clarissa Chenovick, Elizabeth Light, Sarah O'Brien, David Pedersen, Danielle Sottosanti, David Smigen-Rothkopf. We owe a special debt to Dr Rebecca June who has provided a great deal of meticulous research assistance. The publisher's typesetting for the volume has been done by Dr Clive Tolley, whose skill, patience and kind helpfulness we very greatly appreciate.

We are extremely grateful to the librarians at the Walsh Library at Fordham for expert help of all kinds and especially for their remarkable Inter-Library Loan Service, and we thank the Widener Library, Harvard University, the Bodleian Libraries at Oxford, especially the Taylorian Institute, and the librarians at the Dana Porter Library, University of Waterloo. We thank Zachary Rothstein-Dowden for bibliographical and other checking.

We have used manuscripts in the care of many libraries and are grateful to be able to cite our edited extracts from them. We thank All Souls College, Oxford for MS All Souls College 182 (f. 322^{r}); the Beinecke Library, Yale University, New Haven for MS 395 (ff. 153^{r}, 158^{r}–159^{r}, extracts); the Bibliothèque de l'Arsenal, Paris, for MS 3516 (f. 69^{v}, b–c); the Bibliothèque nationale de France for MSS fr. 902 (f. 97ra), fr. 1822 (ff. 84^{r-v}, 248^{vd}–249ra), fr. 19,525 (ff. 180vb–181va, 185ra–185va), fr. 24,364 (f. 1ra), fr. 24,766 (ff. 3^{ra-b}, 9ra–10rb, extracts) and MS fr. 13,513 (ff. 97^{v}–98^{v}); the Bibliothèque municipale de Tours MS 927 (ff. 217^{r}–218^{v}, 226^{v}–229^{v}, extracts); and the Biblioteca Apostolica Vaticana for MS Reg. lat. 489 (f. 26^{r}). The Bodleian Libraries, University of Oxford have been generous with their permissions: we thank the Bodleian Library for MSS Ashmole 1470 (f. 276^{r}) and 1804 (f. 42rb–42va), Ashmole Rolls 38 (membranes 1, 2, extracts), Bodley Rolls 2 (membranes 1, 5, extracts), Bodley 415 (f. 1^{r-v}), 416 (ff. 116^{v}–118^{v}, 127^{v}–128^{v}, 131^{r}–132^{r}, extracts),

Holkham misc. 40 (1^{r-v}, 3^{v}–5^{v}, extracts), English Poetry a. 1 (f. 309^{va-c} and 293^{rc}), Laud misc. 622 (f. 27^{v}), Latin misc. e.93 (ff. 3^{v}–4^{r}), Rawlinson poet. 234 (ff. 57^{r}–59^{v}), and Selden supra 38 (f. 36^{r-v}); Jesus College, Oxford, MS Jesus 29 (f. 223^{r-v}). Cited by permission of the British Library, London, are MSS Add. 4733 vol. 1 (ff. 1^{r}–2^{r}), Add. 62,929 (ff. 1^{r}–2^{r}), Add. 14,252 (ff. 101^{r}, 101^{v}, 104^{r}), Add. 38,664 (f. 3^{r-v}), Add. 45,103 (f. 215^{rb-va}), Add. 46,919 (ff. 2^{r}, 107^{ra-b}), Add. 70,513 (ff. 55^{v}–56^{r}, 147^{r}–148^{r} and 85^{v}–86^{r}, 100^{r}), Cotton Domitian A.XI (f. 3^{r-v}), Cotton Titus C.XVI (f. 132^{r-v}), Cotton Vespasian A. VII (f. 39^{r}), Egerton 745 (ff. 91^{r}, 120^{r}), Egerton 2710 (f. 2ra), Egerton 3028 (f. 64^{r-v}), Harley 222 (ff. 9^{r}–10^{r}), Harley 1121 (ff. 143vb–144vb, 149rb–151ra, extracts), Harley 3988 (ff. 1^{r}–2^{r}), Harley 4388 (ff. 1^{a}–2^{b}), Harley 4971 (f. 34^{v}), Royal 4 C.XI (f. 249rb–249va), Royal 12.C. XII (ff. 33^{r}–35^{r}, extracts), Royal 19. C. XII (ff. 1^{r}–1^{v}, 2^{r}, 3^{r}), and G.32, g.4 (early print, ff. 2^{v}–5^{r}, extracts). We thank Cheetham's Library, Manchester, for their MS 8009 (f. 191^{r}), the London Metropolitan Archives for permission to use City Corporation of London Records Office MS COL/CS/01/006 (ff. 6^{r-v}, 176^{v}–177^{r}); the Librarian and Fellows of Corpus Christi College, Cambridge for their MSS 133 (f. 1^{r}–1^{v}) and 471 (ff. 1^{r}–1^{v}, 82^{r}–83^{v}, 110^{r}–111^{r}, extracts); the Syndics of Cambridge University Library for MSS Add. 3035 (f. 149^{r-v}), Gg.1.1 (f. 8^{r}), Ee.iv.20 (ff. 167^{r}–169^{r}, extracts), Mm.6.4 (ff. 2^{r}, 2^{v}–3^{r}); the Chapter of Durham Cathedral, copyright holders of Durham Cathedral Library MS C.IV.27 (ff. 109^{v}, 116^{v}); Fondation Martin Bodmer for MS Bodmer 168 (f. 1^{r}–1^{v}) from the Bibliothèque Bodmer, Cologny-Genève, CH; Lambeth Palace, London, for Lambeth Palace Library MS 209 (f. 53^{r}); Nottingham University Library Special Collections for MS MiLM4 (ff. 57ra–60va extracts); Princeton University Library, Princeton, NJ, for Taylor Medieval MS 1 (ff. 172^{v}–173^{v}) and MS Garrett 140 (f. 2^{r-v}); St John's College, Cambridge, for their MS G.30 (f. 1^{r}); the Librarian of the Wren Library, Trinity College, Cambridge for MSS O.2.5 (ff. 123^{r}–124^{v}) and R.3.46 (ff. 122^{r}–123^{v}); the Board of Trinity College, Dublin for MS 209 (B.5.1), (ff. 111ra–112ra). Acknowledgements for reproduced images are made in the List of Illustrations.

Graduate classes and audiences at many universities and conferences have given helpful responses and feedback: we specially thank our own students whose responses in our various courses have been lively, challenging, and encouraging. To those who have waited a long time to see published versions of their work appear in this volume we are grateful both for their work and their patience. For part of their long wait, the UK government is responsible: as this volume did not meet the criteria for their 2007 Research Assessment Exercise, one of the editors risked being declared research inactive by pursuing work on the volume while employed in the UK. Gratitude, however, is due to UK taxpayers for the support their taxes give to UK higher education institutions, and to UK colleagues in medieval and post-medieval literary scholarship alike for their support of the volume as an aid in developing research and understanding of the multilingualism of English and related cultures. Large debts are also owed to medievalist colleagues for advice, suggestions, discussion and for reading of parts of the volume: we warmly thank Christopher Baswell, Carolyn Collette, Susan Crane, Mark Cruse, Simon Gaunt, Monica Green, Robert Hanning and the Columbia Meds Group, Tony Hunt, Mark Ormrod, Ad Putter, Christine Reno, Robert M. Stein†, Elizabeth Tyler, Nicholas Watson. A special debt is owed to Dr Monika Otter, Dr Andrea Tarnowski and the Dartmouth Medieval Studies

Colloquium for an invaluable 2012 session on the project. Richard Ingham, Ian Short and David Trotter† have generously shared pre-publication typescripts and offprints. We thank Michael Clanchy and John Spence for both independently suggesting the inclusion of genealogical rolls. We thank Keith Busby for his pre-paperback observations.

As always, Caroline Palmer has been the ideal commissioning editor, and we are extremely grateful for her vision and enthusiasm for French of England projects, for the professional eye and invaluable advice she brings to all she publishes, and for her friendly, firm and constructive way with authors. All in the field of medieval studies owe her an incalculable debt.

At Boydell and Brewer, Rohais Haughton has been a gracious and supportive production editor. Laura Napran has undertaken the index with meticulous patience.

Jocelyn Wogan-Browne and Thelma Fenster would particularly like to thank their collaborator Delbert Russell: securing this expert, endlessly patient, cheerful, generous colleague for working together on the volume has been one of the very best things we have done for it. We deeply regret that the much-valued colleague and friend to whose memory the volume is dedicated did not live to see more of it than the table of contents and the dedication just as it went off to anonymous press readers, whom we also thank for constructive suggestions. While the volume was in press the field of French and English language studies suffered a further blow in the early loss of Professor David Trotter of the University of Aberystwyth in Wales. His prolific brilliance as a lexicographer and his energetic leadership at the Anglo-Norman Hub has, among much else, provided the superb online *Anglo-Norman Dictionary* and the means of revising numerous entries in the *Oxford English Dictionary*, while his open, generous and highly productive practice of scholarship and shared knowledge remains a model for all.

Abbreviations

AND	*Anglo-Norman Dictionary* (http://www.anglo-norman.net)
ANTS	Anglo Norman Text Society
BL	British Library
BN	Bibliothèque nationale de France
CUL	Cambridge University Library
Dean	R. J. Dean with M. B. M. Boulton, *Anglo-Norman Literature: A Guide to Texts and Manuscripts*, ANTS OPS 3 (London, 1999).
DMF	*Dictionnaire du Moyen Français*, Centre national de la recherche scientifique 2003, 2007 http://atilf.atilf.fr/dmf/.
EETS ES	Early English Text Society Extra Series
EETS OS	Early English Text Society Original Series
EETS SS	Early English Text Society Supplementary Series
FRETS	French of England Translation Series
Godefroy	F. Godefroy, *Dictionnaire de l'ancienne langue française et de tous ses dialectes du IX*^{e} *au XV*^{e} *siècle*, 10 vols. (Paris, 1881–1902, online 2000)
ME	Middle English
MED	*Middle English Dictionary*, ed. H. Kurath and S. M. Kuhn (Ann Arbor, Michigan, 1956–2001) (http://quod.lib.umich.edu)
OE	Old English
OED	*Oxford English Dictionary*
ODNB	*Oxford Dictionary of National Biography*
OP	Order of Preachers (Dominican Friars)
OPS	Occasional Publication Series
pers. comm.	personal communication
PL	*Patrologiae cursus completus . . . Series Latina*, ed. J.-P. Migne 217 vols. (Paris, 1844–55 and online)
PTS	Plain Texts Series
T–L	A. Tobler, rev. E. Lommatzsch, *Tobler–Lommatzsch Altfranzösisches Wörterbuch* (Berlin and Wiesbaden, 1925–2008)

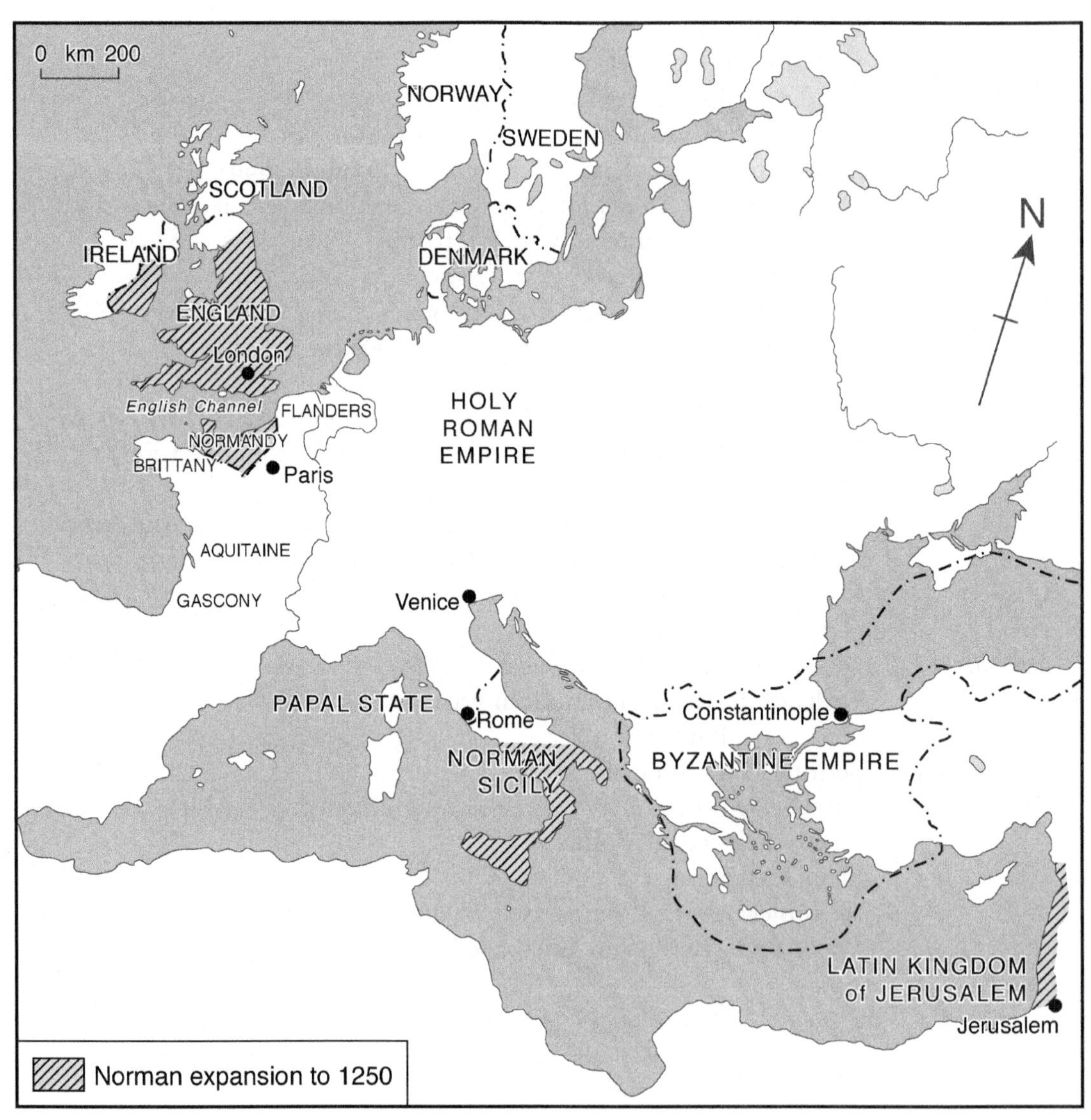

Map 1. Norman French in Europe and the Latin Kingdom of Jerusalem

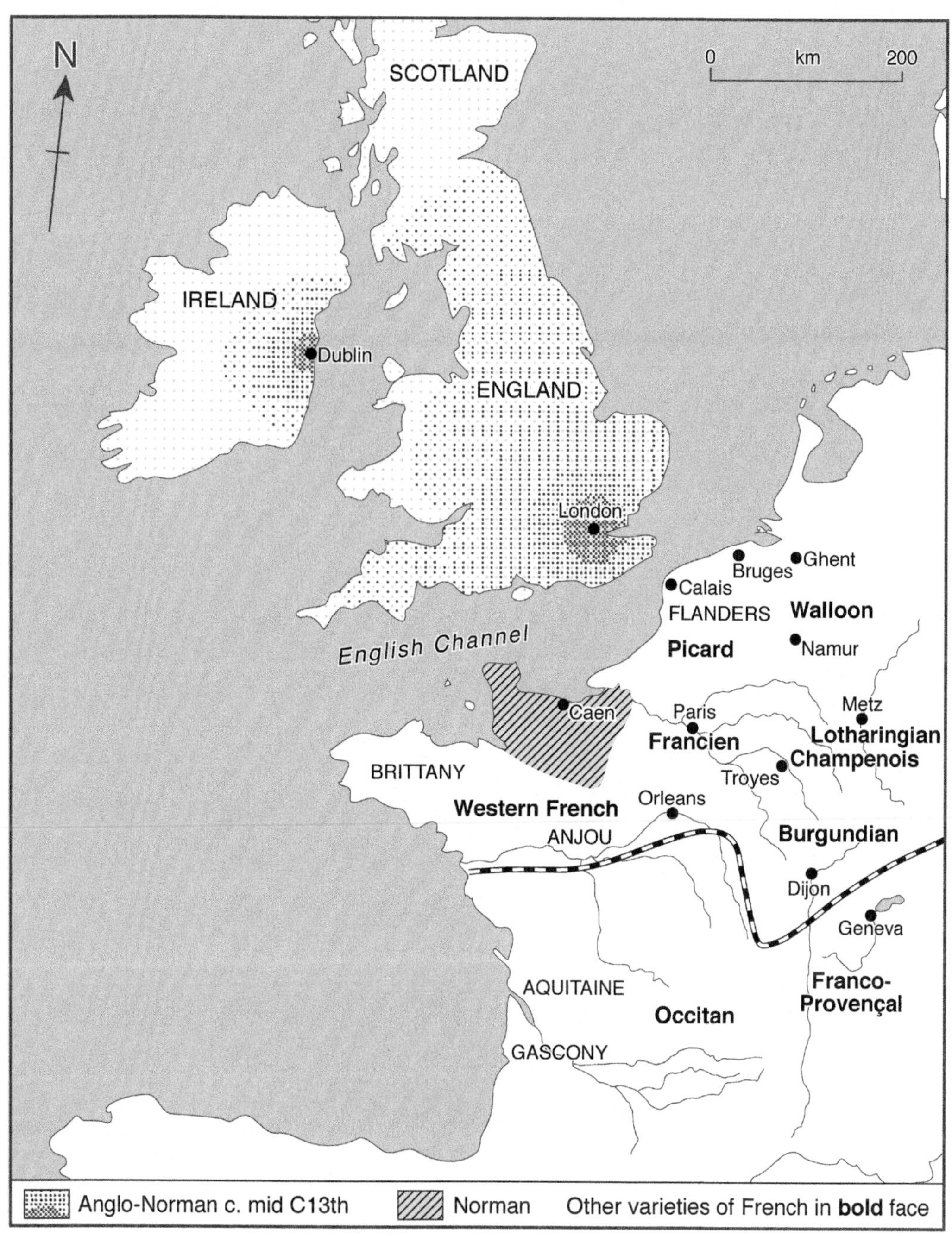

Map 2: French in England and on the north-west European coast

The distribution of Anglo-Norman in Wales, Scotland and Ireland needs more research (see p. 3, n. 9, below). A more precise geography for Anglo-Norman in England pends further research on administrative and other documents and networks (see e.g. Kowaleski 2009, Trotter 2012, Lusignan 2016) as well as continuing work on pastoral and literary texts.

General Introduction

French in and out of England

> In England and North America, the multiplicity of languages, the conflicts and mobility of power and race, and the frequent violence and repression that have characterised negotiations among them all, together make an authoritative language too touchy a point to invite rational institutionalisation. The improbability and illogic of a single, authoritative tongue lie too close to the surface; and its real instability is too plain, even on cursory examination. (Baswell 2005)

Older models of one language, one nation, one literature have increasingly come to seem inadequate for the study of England's medieval culture, in its internal dimensions as much as in its external exchanges and contacts. Recent work with multilingualism as an explicit paradigm for enquiry gives us ways to move beyond rigid associations between language and nation in the exploration of medieval European cultures. Not that multilingualism is in every circumstance a self-evident good, then or now: the medieval paradigm of the tower of Babel as a fall into mutually incomprehensible languages cast a long shadow, even if redeemed by Pentecost's endowment of the apostles with tongues of fire. The Herefordshire writer Simund de Freine observes in his late-twelfth-century French reworking of Boethius (see (38) below) that 'linguistic diversity hinders the spread of fame'.[1] To set against the richness and flexibility of lexicon, register, and allusion for multilingual speakers and writers there is much medieval commentary, serious or playful, on failures of comprehension.[2] Nevertheless, whether perceived as advantageous or problematic, multilingualism has become a newly explicit approach for literary and linguistic study.[3] In addition to new models for how we conceptualise language and new investigations into previously neglected aspects of language use in England, current scholarship's emphasis on the materiality of medieval textual culture necessarily embraces the multilingualism of medieval texts and manuscript collections on the page and in the codex, while socio-linguistic approaches to the uses and performance of text in both documentary and literary culture address the multilingualism and plurilingualism of medieval audiences.

In the light of these new approaches, it is clear that students and scholars of insular culture need to think multilingually. It may therefore seem perverse to offer a volume on the French of England rather than England's multilingualism as such. Both English and

[1] 'Ensement divers langage/ Los desturbe e sun passage', ed. Matzke 1909, vv. 945–6.

[2] For an eloquent example of an English-speaking parish priest's anguished and frustrated sense of French as exclusionary, see Short 1980, 476–8; Short 2009b, 252–4, discusses contemporary mockery of a Norman monoglot. Although, as Laura Wright has shown, medieval businesspeople in England frequently conducted their affairs in macaronic but rule-governed multilingual codes (Wright 1996, 2000, 2012, 2013 and Schendl and Wright 2011), pragmatic difficulties were doubtless also not unknown.

[3] For a classic of the multilingual and cross-disciplinary study that has always informed medieval scholarship, see Salter 2010, orig. publ. 1988.

French had important relationships with Latin as well as with British and Scandinavian languages. But it would be difficult to overstate the imbrication of English and French spoken and written cultures throughout the Middle Ages. As the two major vernaculars of England, each enriched the other. In the late eleventh and early twelfth centuries, for example, the new Anglo-Norman regime in England encountered English-language writing as a prestigious vernacular in use across a wide range of genres and functions. This contact provided a crucial stimulus to the development of French as a written vernacular literature, initially in the courts of Henry I's queens and their networks. In later-medieval England, French, by now well established as a literary language and a significant language of record, provided precedents for writing in Middle English.[4] Yet only recently has French writing in England begun to be perceived as an indispensable context for, say, the *lais* of Marie de France, while many other writers of French in England remain relatively unstudied. While some French continental literary cultures have long been acknowledged as influential for writers such as Chaucer and Gower, the role of insular French in the formation and environment of Middle English writers has been less often considered.[5] In this volume we have sought to provide a resource for expanding study of insular vernacular culture from Middle English to both the major vernaculars of medieval England.

French of England has developed further dimensions as a field in recent years. Ruth Dean's 1999 catalogue of Anglo-Norman texts and manuscripts, completed with Maureen Boulton's help, provided a new basis for the field.[6] Linguistic study of medieval English French, formerly concentrated on the twelfth and thirteenth centuries, has paid fresh attention to the later Middle Ages and found the language-death of insular French to have been exaggerated by about a century: insular French remained a living and changing language into the early fifteenth rather than the early fourteenth century.[7] When French's many professional, administrative and business uses are taken into account, the great bulk of written French in England comes from the thirteenth to the fifteenth centuries, and was produced by a much wider range of people than might be deduced from French's better known function as an elite court language. Texts we now recognise as 'literary' are part of a spectrum continuing towards instruction and information to the documentary. The boundaries between literature and literate culture are highly permeable and this enlarges the corpus of texts for attention. We include some scientific and utilitarian writing as well as pastoralia and texts of record, and one of the immediately striking features of their self-presentations is the continuity of topoi across apparently utilitarian texts, fictional and non-fictional narrative, devotion, scriptural exegesis, etc. A business handbook for French conversation (**7b**) places its own linguistic work within a gorgeously elaborated

4 For a more detailed account see 'England and French', in Part VI, §1; Ailes and Putter 2014 offer a valuable overview, as does W. Rothwell's introduction to the Anglo-Norman Dictionary at http://www.anglo-norman.net/sitedocs/main intro.shtml.

5 The question of French formation for Langland (especially as a possible translator of the werewolf romance of *Guillaume de Palerme*) has recently been re-opened (Warner 2014, 22–36); see also Marie Turner (2014), Zeeman 2008, Machan 1994. For exemplary detailed attention to French alongside English and Latin in Langland's literary environment see Galloway 2006, 372–427.

6 Referred to simply as Dean (with entry numbers immediately following).

7 Ingham 2012, 2015b, Lusignan 2004, 2016, Rothwell 1994, Trotter 2000, 2003a and b.

philosophico-cosmic setting worthy of a theological encyclopaedia; a chronicle in cogent and functional prose launches itself under Sibylline guidance through a dream exploring the making of history and its sources (**16**); a calendrical treatise locates itself against romance and *chanson de geste* (**41**).

The study of French in England also necessarily includes attention to its supra-regional character. This is no longer seen as a matter of French being 'owned' by one nation and dispersed from the north-western centre of the modern 'hexagon'-shaped French state. Medieval French developed as a pluri-local *lingua franca* in regional configurations that were both distinctive and mutually intelligible.[8] England is one of the most important of these, in that it produced a large corpus of French-language writing and in that the linguistic effects on English of its co-existence with French were very extensive. In turn, it is French, rather than English (a purely regional language throughout the Middle Ages), that is the vector for the European dissemination of texts composed in England, as well as for commercial and diplomatic exchange. Such contact is at once participation in a medieval global vernacular and a series of intra-regional encounters in specific networks and institutions, not simply a question of inter-national relations.

Finding a post-national conceptual vocabulary for languages is not easy. Our label, 'French of England', embraces 'internal' and 'external' French: that is, French-language texts composed in England (usually referred to in scholarship as Anglo-Norman), texts from England that moved into Europe and the Mediterranean, and texts that came into England from regions outside it (selective though examples from these last two categories have to be, for reasons of space). That there is a French or Frenches of England entails the idea that there are Frenches elsewhere. England, although powerful both as idea and political entity in the history of the British Isles, is of course not representative of British cultures at large. Wales, Scotland, Ireland have their own relations with French and with England: we include texts from border zones between these regions and England (the Welsh Marches in (**31**), Scotland and northern England in (**16**), and Ireland and [?] Picardy in (**33**), but do not represent French in Britain as a whole.[9]

The 'situatedness' of the vernacular text and the divisions of this volume

'Vernacular' has become a flexible term as scholars explore and test new ways of thinking about medieval languages. For the fifteenth century, for instance, David Trotter argues

[8] Gaunt 2015 (http://riviste.unimi.it/interfaces/index) and at the Medieval Francophone Literary Culture outside France Project (http://www.medievalfrancophone.ac.uk/); Busby and Putter 2010; Trotter 2013, 2003b.

[9] Further research uniting consideration of documentary multilingualism, internal and external literary traditions and cultural relations and French in Wales, Scotland and Ireland is much to be desired. On Wales see Trotter 1994. For some purposes, British French-language cultures are similar to those in England, for example, the court culture of the French-speaking William I of Scotland (r. 1165–1214) and its women patrons such as Devorguilla of Balliol (linked with the brilliant early-thirteenth-century *Roman de Fergus* set in Galloway): see Owen 1997. On Scotland see Calin 2014, esp. 9–12; on Anglo-Norman cultures in Ireland, Busby 2017; Mullally 1988, and for more recent work on multilingualism among francophone and English colonists in Ireland (33) below and Part VI, §2.8.

that the ternary system of Latin, French and English gives way to a binary opposing Latin and vernacular, whether French or English or both.[10] On the other hand, Christopher Cannon has proposed that Latin, certainly for those privileged with early literacy training, can itself be a vernacular in the sense of being both a first written language and one familiar from early childhood.[11] French, growing and developing in England throughout the Middle Ages, functioned sometimes as an alternative to Latin, sometimes, especially in paraliturgical and scriptural reading, as an access language, sometimes as the language of high literary culture, sometimes as a meritocratic language, and in numerous roles and linguistic combinations for administration, diplomacy, trade, and business.

Neither this wide range nor French's early use as a literary language in England produces general theoretical discussion in the manner of medieval Latin treatises or post-medieval theoretical treatments of literature. Many of the works excerpted here, however, deal with issues that were also important in classical and medieval Latin thought on writing and performing texts: the ethical and exemplary functions of texts, the role of their affective dimensions, the relation of form and teaching, the value of record, precedent, commemoration, the complexities of exegesis, the nature of the word and its transmission, the politics of *translatio studii et imperii*.[12] Some discussions are notably extensive (see for example *Evangiles ou Miroir* (**14**), *Lumere as lais* (**19**), Angier's *Dialogues* (**24a**), Commentaries on the Song of Songs (**26**) and on Proverbs (**39**)). We have not, however, grouped our texts thematically by such questions, but rather according to the main vectors of their 'situatednesss'. This term was originally coined for Middle English texts considered as vernacular theory, in an argument that focused on linguistic self-consciousness in vernacular texts: 'it is precisely the 'situatedness' of [English-language] discussions of language and writing in a complex cultural context – and the awarenesss of that context on the part of their writers and audiences- that gives [English] discussions their distinctiveness and makes the analysis of their theoretical implications potentially important'.[13] Such questions, unsurprisingly, are not exclusive to vernaculars and they arise with different emphases in French-language writing. But, as is common to other medieval literatures, the French-language prologue and other discussions sampled here focus strongly on the texts' socio-cultural context as created by patron, audience, and narratorial or discursive performance, on their relations to their subject matters and predecessors, on readers and audiences' activities and choices, on literary form and its codicological and other material realisation, and (less often and in a different linguistic politics than Middle English texts) on linguistic affiliations. Like its Middle English predecessor, this volume, then, deals with vernacular literary theory in a particular sense, that of textual self-consciousness and strategic interpellation of audience and circumstance: a second and currently dominant understanding of theory as 'beyond text', for all the fecund and diverse readings it can often enable, is not so immediately to the purpose here.[14]

10 Trotter 2013.

11 C. Cannon 2014, 2015. See, more generally, Somerset and Watson 2003.

12 For discussions of Latin prologues by genre, see Hamesse, ed., 2000.

13 Wogan-Browne *et al.* 1999, 316.

14 See Marion Turner ed, 2013, 3.

The demands of a particular group or community that produces, or comes into being, or is imagined as doing so, around a text is offered in most of our texts as a major rationale for composition.[15] The inscription of initial production communities and audiences, however, does not inhibit subsequent re-inventions and re-situations for texts. The mobility of medieval texts occurs historically along narrower chains of contact and more specific networks than texts in print culture, but can be extremely vigorous. 'Situatedness' is a constant engine for innovation, cultural and linguistic translation, rewriting, re-presentation and changing *mise-en-page*.

Further dimensions of 'situatedness' have been increasingly demonstrated in scholarship on the material realisation of text in manuscript culture. The choice of roll (as in **20c** and **d** below) or of codex (the majority of our entries), the planned organisation of the contents of a manuscript and their distribution within the codex, the presence – or not- of a visual program, a planned level of expenditure on script and decoration on a patron's part, or its absence, may all elucidate meaning unrealised or differently realised in other versions of the text. Equally, meaning may be realised opportunistically in the actual making of the manuscript. Matthew Paris, composer, scribe (or scribal director) and artist for his own texts in French and Latin, exemplifies an improvisatory response in the process of creating *mise-en-page* for manuscript openings. The process of book-making and the creation of meaning continue beyond the boundaries of the page in Paris's custom of supplying further information on attached small flaps of vellum or parchment.[16] His practices have something in common with those of other writers, manuscript makers, and readers in the way they anticipate, respond to, work with the materality of the codex. The specific materiality of manuscripts and all the choices and accidents that have gone into them are a constant element of medieval textual culture and an important factor in the situated nature of its interests and experiences. We incorporate this dimension by offering single manuscript editions of our texts and briefly characterising the particular manuscript and the manuscript representation of the text at large as appropriate in the headnote for each entry. The possibility of other and different realisations of the text is, of course, intrinsic to this procedure.

Some other dimensions of medieval literary and literate culture are harder to demonstrate, most notably visual, performance, and sonic dimensions. These we try to signal through links to manuscript digitisations and to audio readings of texts on the Fordham French of England website;[17] through entries specifically addressing visual discourse (**20a**, **b**, **c**, **d**), and in entries dealing with questions of voice, chant, and sound as intrinsic textual support (**8a**: 89–96, **12**: 11–13, **14**: 21–4 **21**, **26**).

Each Part in the volume highlights a different vector of 'situatedness', but this is hardly a rigid categorisation, and examples are found in texts outside as well as within each

15 Brian Stock's concept of 'textual communities' remains fundamental, and continues to apply to more recent work on larger manuscript distributions moving far beyond initial communities or on manuscripts copied as nearly identically as possible to each other (Stock 1983).

16 D. K. Connolly 2009; Baswell 2010, 169–94.

17 http://legacy.fordham.edu/academics/programs_at_fordham_/medieval_studies/french_of_england/ where readings relevant for (2), (9), (10), (15), (27) and other texts may be seen and heard under Audio-Visual Readings on the French of England site.

Part. Wace's *Roman de Rou* (3), for instance, is placed in Part I because of its eloquence regarding linguistic change as a marker of temporal and political mutability, but its discussion of patronage (3.143–66) could allow the *Rou* to be included as readily in Part II. Texts that circulate in England but come from regions outside it usually respond to these divisions, indicating some transregional commonalities to vernacular literary production. We therefore place texts from inside and outside England thematically within the volume's different parts, rather than grouping them according to their production geographies (these are listed in Part VI, §3.4). In our divisions for the volume, we have tried to identify commonalities that remain important throughout the long career of French-language writing in England, but without assuming that these categories are supra-historical. The category of authorship is a good illustration of how a continuous element of textual production can be differently conceived and practised over time. For much of the period of this book we think it an inappropriately foregrounded category and therefore do not include vernacular authorship as a free-standing thematic division of our material, but subsume it within the division thematised around patronage (see further Part II).

In our Glossary of literary terms, designed as a resource in its own right, semantic clusters support the importance of our five divisions. The terminology of the literate culture sampled in the volume both overlaps and differs from post-medieval literary discourse (see e.g. Glossary, *s.v. Deu,* God). Literary thought in the French of medieval England with its distinctive inclusions and exclusions can be explored, as is argued in the Glossary headnote, by reading across the Glossary as well as across our entries.

How far the vectors of French-language writing in England apply to medieval English is complex to gauge. When directly comparable Middle English reworkings of prologues and other material in this volume exist, they are presented in Part VI, §2. Even this small sample confirms a general sense that Middle English adaptations of French sources or analogues are as much a matter of register, occasion, and text-type as of language: consistently predictable 'French' and 'English' patterns are elusive. Some texts in both languages use comparable panoplies of authorising strategies. Some remove, some incorporate or modify the representation of the original production communities. For some purposes French and English operate in similar ways: for example, origins and authorities (social or intellectual) are invoked to legitimate texts and confer prestige in both, though this can vary in relation to the status of the two languages as vernaculars at any one time. In the fifteenth century, for instance, when French is long established and English increasingly so, it is noticeable that patrons re-appear even in English-language romance (as in the case of Sir Miles and Lady Katherine Stapleton in John Metham's *Amoryus and Cleopes* of 1449).[18] In this respect as in most others, a fuller literary history for England requires detailed attention to both French and English, and we hope this volume will help redress the balance.

[18] See Wogan-Browne *et al.* 1999, 1.8. The bulk of early-fourteenth-century English-language romance, on the other hand, is notably anonymous in relation to patrons and authors in comparison with twelfth and thirteenth-century French-language romance; see further Field 2011.

Establishment of Texts and Translations and Conventions Used

All the selections are newly edited, each from a single manuscript. In a few cases the texts given here have not been previously edited; others have been edited during the life of this project. Some have been available only in editions dating from the late-nineteenth-century archival explorations. In cases where a modern printed edition exists, we have often chosen a different manuscript from the published one in order to bring out some aspect of codicological interest, e.g., what the manuscript selection of texts or its *mise-en-page* may suggest about the text's relations with its audiences. We have sometimes left aside the 'best text' manuscript, especially if a modern edition is available, in favour of a manuscript traditionally thought of as a 'Middle English' manuscript.

Scribal word division, punctuation and paragraphing are modernised. Editorially supplied letters or words are signalled with square brackets. Where we are editing from a single manuscript text with an already published edition, variants in readings are given in the notes, as are emendations that we have introduced. Scriptural quotations are normally identified in notes to texts where they are not identified in the texts themselves. Citations are from the Vulgate version.

We normalise *i/j*, *u/v* to modern French spelling. We add modern diacritics: the cedilla when *c* precedes *a*, *o*, or *u*; an acute accent on *é* when it is a stressed vowel in the final syllable of polysyllabic words (this includes *aprés*, to distinguish it from adj., *apres* (=Mod.Fr. *âpres*), and past participles in *és*, or *ét* (but not –*ez*, or fem. –*ee*, –*ees*). We also use the acute accent in monosyllables where meaning may not be clear: *dé* = *des (*and *Dé=Dieu), lé* = *les*, and *pués* = *puis* (not 2 pres, *pouvoir*). We retain Anglo-Norman titles where possible, but use modern French titles where these have become standard in the absence of medieval titles. We use the conventional name 'Marie de France', though there is no certainty that the works ascribed to this figure are all by the same woman.

Editors of continental Old and Middle French poetry traditionally use the tréma (¨) to mark vowels in hiatus, either word-final or word-internal. Given that flexible syllable count characterises much, but not all, of England's French-language verse, it is often impossible to know whether vowels remain in hiatus or have been reduced phonetically. We use a tréma, however, to separate homographs, e.g. *oy*, 1 pret of *aver* (*avoir*), versus *oÿ*, p.p. of *oir*. We use the tréma at the rhyme where the vowel in hiatus is guaranteed by the rhyme, e.g. *plaisir / oïr*. In cases where the entire text suggests that the poet used strict syllable timing, we employ the tréma to indicate contiguous vowels that are retained in pronunciation.

Shortened bibliographic references (author's surname followed by date of publication) normally use the latest date of publication, with information about first date of publication supplied in the Bibliography.

Rubrics are not counted in the lineation. For entries combining prose and verse, verse lines are numbered in roman, prose lines in italic.

All texts, whether verse or prose, have been translated into prose.

Part I. *Faus franceis* and *dreit engleis*: On Language

Introduction

These phrases from the Nun of Barking and Marie de France, two twelfth-century women writers who thought a great deal about language and the valences and strategies of vernacular writing, effectively thematise Part I.[1] An important subset of 'situatedness' is linguistic choice, and in a multilingual translating culture, there is considerable linguistic choice available. But, like authorship, medieval language choice may work by different paradigms than our own. As David Trotter points out, 'an awareness of the differences between languages is not the same as a consciousness of the nationality of an individual word'.[2] References to 'English' within Middle English texts have often attracted intense attention because they seem to promise access to a supra-textual 'national' story, however locally situated and strategic they may be. References to French, especially given its regional and supra-regional character, have not had the same charge in scholarship on England (though they are often deployed in modern accounts of social and linguistic hierarchy). What we may identify retrospectively as a lexical switch from French to English or vice versa may not necessarily have been historically settled or even conceptualised as a switch by medieval users: much medieval lexis was interchanged between what has only subsequently become classified as French and English. Mixed language was relatively routine across a range of pragmatic text types and practised as an art in macaronic poetry and prose, and it is often more helpful to think of writers as changing or adding registers rather than switching languages.[3] Whatever the matrix language of a text may be, other languages are not precluded from being present in various ways (borrowed, alluded to, implicit in, or breaking through, as Christopher Baswell has argued, in a *pentimento* effect, etc.): other languages offer further resources and bring additional registers to the matrix language.[4]

Writing in the vernacular is differently inflected for French than for Middle English, partly because of French's social prestige, its longstanding literary uses from the twelfth century on, and its increased deployment, in the later Middle Ages, as a language of record. Yet French texts almost never deprecate English. Linguistic hierarchies between French and English were initially complicated by overlaps and disjunctions between oral and written modes. If English was the speech of peasants, it was also a written language for elite and Latinate writers: as earlier noted, the Norman Conquest exposed continental

1 For *faus franceis* see the Nun of Barking (2.7): for *dreit engleis*, Marie de France, *Laüstic*, v. 6.

2 Trotter 2013: 147–8. Since Clemence of Barking has been translated elsewhere and is the subject of some discussion (Wogan-Browne and Burgess, trans., 1996, Brown and Bussell 2012), and since Marie de France has long been the subject of intense (but until recently in some ways decontextualised) interest, they are omitted from the volume. For a recent handbook on Marie de France see Kinoshita and McCracken 2014.

3 On code-switching see Schendl and Wright 2011, Introduction, 1–14, and on literary macaronics, the essay by Putter, 281–302.

4 See Baswell 2007, M. Warren 2007a, 2007b.

French-speakers to Anglo-Saxon English as a prestigious written language alongside Latin. One consequence of this situation is that, although French could and did operate hierarchically as a language of social cachet in relation to English, it was also a language with debts to English cultural tradition. Certainly for twelfth and thirteenth-century writers, English is often a language of authentication and authority, not a low register.[5] The very act of landholding in England necessarily engaged with a past of which English was the language: *Waldef* (**6**) notes translation of early English-language narratives but for purposes of contemporary access and as a marker of change and transience rather than as a matter of social elevation out of English. French (whether in its various forms as *franceis* or *normand* or as 'the vernacular', *romanz*) is rarely proposed as superior to English (though this is possibly implied in (**25b**), *La Vie de seint Clement*).[6] Marie de France's tribute to King Alfred in the *Fables* and her use of the English verb *scieppan* (to create) for the name of the goddess of animal creation is one relatively well-known example of the response of a courtly and educated writer, who must have heard or seen echoes of English's function as a language of knowledge, record, instruction.[7] Another is Geffrei Gaimar's consciousness of English-language historiography as an elite socio-political institution as well as a source of historical material: this is clear both in his use of the Anglo-Saxon Chronicle and what he has to say about it (see **10**).[8] The romance of *Waldef* (**6**) and Piramus's *Vie seint Edmund le rei* (**27**) also claim written English sources, *Waldef* even suggesting that the *Brut*, *Tristan* and the geste of 'Aelof' (presumably the father of Horn from the *Roman de Horn*), among others, were initially in English (**6**, vv. 45–54). Adgar, author of the earliest known vernacular miracles of the Virgin, identifies himself with both an English and a French name (**11a**).

Where in Middle English texts the rhetoric of linguistic choice often deals with both French and Latin in making space for English, French writing is primarily concerned with Latin as its other. Latin literacy is so integral to the idea of writing as to be sometimes referred to as *gramaire* rather than as *latin* (**34.10**). Spoken and written distinctions are vital in assessing the valences attached to language: as Thomas O'Donnell has argued, Guernes de Pont Ste Maxence's well-known claim for the status of his French (**11b**) can be seen in the context of his awareness of Becket's written Latin biographies rather than as a put-down of the French-language writing he encountered in England (and which may in

[5] In lives of early saints, for instance, the saint's reported English utterances are often preserved in their French lives (as in St Edmund's severed head, which called out 'here!' to direct those searching for it ('[E] her, her, her sovent diseit', Russell, ed., 2014, v. 2762). For a French text using English phrases today best known from later-fourteenth-century English ('Do wel and have wel', 'Al shal be wel'), see Wogan-Browne 2013.

[6] The *Vie de seint Clement* (**25b**) claims that French will be understood by both clerics and laypeople unless they are too rustic (*vilains*) to have learned *rumanz* (vv. 41–2). It has been calculated that thirteenth-century towns were, unsurprisingly, much more heavily multilingual (and francophone) than rural areas, though Anglo-Norman was by no means confined to the south-east as was once thought: Short 2009a.

[7] *Fables*, ed. and trans. H. Spiegel 1994, Epilogue 204, vv. 11–19; *Fables* 75, v. 10; 97, v. 7.

[8] Gaimar translated his *livere engleis* i.e. the Anglo-Saxon Chronicle (also referred to as *croniches* vv. 952, 2107, 2184, 2327) in the 1130s. See further Gaunt 2015, 30–40. Guischart de Beaulieu's twelfth-century *Sermun del secle* in alexandrine *laisses* seems to have drawn on Ælfric's vernacular sermons and on the Early Middle English and Latin *Poema morale* (Hill 1977, 123–6).

fact have validated his vernacular biography for him).[9] Nevertheless although French texts often position themselves against or alongside Latin, the authority of Latin is rarely overbearing. It is rather a resource, a credential and a marker of literacy and letters from which French-language writing can depart or which it can overwrite. Deference to Latin is often an enabling springboard to valuing the vernacular, as in the mockery of self-contained academic Latinity in the anonymous Life of St Clement (**25b**), or Hue de Rotelande's *Ipomedon*:

> I do not claim that the person who set [the narrative] down in Latin did not recount it well. But there are so many more laypeople than there are educated people; if the Latin tale is not translated there will be very few to understand it (**4**.25–9).

As there is no known Latin source for this romance, Hue is probably having it both ways. (On the other hand *Waldef* (**6**) was translated into Latin in the fifteenth century: we cannot assume an impermeable wall between vernacular and Latin production of the materials we call romance.)[10] The very term *latin* as signifyng an exclusive register is played with and made into a vernacular in Old French's expanded meanings for the word: birdsong is often referred to as the birds' *latin* (*DMF, s.v.* 'latin', 2.3); for the *Roman de Horn*, professional interpreters are learned in *plusurs latins* (v. 1351), and the pupil interrogator in the *Lumere as lais* (**19**) complains that the term *contemplacion* is *un franceis latin* and needs explanation (vv. 7182–6): Judas speaks *en sun latin* to Arabs in the *Poème sur l'Ancien Testament* (**43**), v. 924.

As against Latin, French claims a function as the language of access. In the twelfth century, Hue de Rotelande's term is *romanz* (**4**.30) with its sense of 'vernacular, not Latin' as well as its meaning of 'French'. Concomitant with the thirteenth-century proliferation of documents and users of French, the topos of French (by this time often referred to as *franceis*) as a language of inclusion intensifies: French retains social cachet but is presented as open to more audiences than Latin. It is praised by a number of authors for the quality of being *apert-* 'open'. Matthew Paris says his life of St Edmund of Abingdon (composed 1247–53) offers an *escrit apert*, i.e. an open, accessible, non-specialist history (**13**.4), composed in *franceis apert*, clear, understandable French (**13**.32–3), French, in this case, translated from Paris's own Latin biography of the archbishop and courtier saint. Denis Piramus, writing in the 1190s of an earlier St Edmund (of East Anglia; see (**27**)), claims that by translating from English and Latin sources into French, he has enabled elite, middle and humble people (*Li grant, [li maien] e li mendre*, Russell, ed., 2014, v. 3280) to hear about St Edmund: similarly, Pierre d'Abernon de Fetcham claims that his text is entitled 'for Laypeople' because it is in *entendable* (comprehensible) French (**19**.156).[11] The narrator of the romance *Waldef* (**6**) says he has looked over 'the English

[9] O'Donnell 2011. Topoi on French are reviewed in Short 2013, 20–4; and see further (**2**) and (**11b**) below.

[10] In the case of *Floire et Blancheflor* (Dean 164, not excerpted here) where the romance writer claims to be translating from English into French, it is even possible that there is a silenced Latin source, not alluded to explicitly in the French text at all (Legge 1971, 334–5). Codicologically, Latin and French romance are often closely associated: see C. Cannon 2015.

[11] Piramus may be thinking specifically of the large Bury community and its lay associates (where French of various pragmatic kinds may well have been known down the social scale to estate stewards and other officials; see Ingham 2009). On his audiences see further (**27**).

story' (which may actually have been a Latin story) – *L'estoire englesche regardai* – and then translated it into French for his *amie*, who wants him to translate *apertement* (6.80, 'openly, clearly'). Robert of Greatham's influential thirteenth-century *Miroir* (14) on the Sunday Gospels claims that anyone who knows the Latin alphabet (*lettr[e]üre*) and can speak French, can read Robert's *Miroir* and teach others from it (14.21–4). Angier of St Frideswide extends the claim to *mise-en-page*: readers should be able clearly to see and move around French-language works in their books (24a.25–48).

Movements between languages are often unmarked or assumed. Interpreters' services were of course sometimes required on preaching tours within Britain.[12] But professional linguistic interpreters (*latimers*) are principally associated in Anglo-Norman texts with contact beyond Britain: the *latimiers ... bien escolé et sage* of the *Roman de Horn* (vv. 1350–2), for instance, come from Africa to Hunlaf's Brittany together with the invading pagan kings Gudolf and Egolf: John de Courcy takes a latimer with him in his expedition to Ireland, and they figure in Alexander the Great texts.[13] Nevertheless, it is clear that what happened on the ground could involve real and in some cases invidious linguistic differences.[14] What of, for instance, pastoral care at parish level? This must usually have been primarily in English, especially for parishioners whose access to other languages was restricted to the sounds (without grammatical understanding) of Latin in church. Competence in church Latin might itself vary according to the range of clerical ability and educational opportunity, as is shown in the abiding concerns of episcopal legislation with the education of priests and the Latinity tests of candidates for vacancies. But episcopal statutes do not legislate for priests to be trained in speaking French, even though French becomes the dominant vernacular of written pastoral materials from the late twelfth to the mid-fourteenth centuries.

What may be at work here is that such legislation is not perceived as necessary in a multilingual culture where written literacy is practised by specific occupational groups, and is a very particular techné, not inevitably co-extensive with reading or oral and aural literacies. As Catherine Batt points out, when the highly literate Henry, duke of Lancaster, author of the *Livre des seyntz medicines* (1354), says he is not 'a good writer', he refers to his amateur status as a physical writer of text: although it was not unknown for noblemen to write for themselves, or to make notes on wax tablets to be written up by their clerks, a duke does not normally undertake the labour of writing.[15] William of Normandy's writs, discussed below (p. 401), provide for delivery in multiple languages: so too,

12 See e.g. Archbishop Baldwin's crusade preaching, expounded to the Welsh by an interpreter (Gerald of Wales, *Itinerarium Kambriae*, ed. Dimock 1868, 14); Cate 1937, 67–89.

13 The single use of *entrepretours* in this volume is in Gray's *Scalacronica* (16.65), where it is used of historical writers to mean 'interpreters, translators' (see Glossary and *AND*, *s.v.* 'interpretur'), in effect, cultural translators. For 'latimers' see the *Roman de Horn* (ed. M. K. Pope, v. 1351); *The Deeds of the Normans In Ireland*, ed. and trans. Mullally 2002, 28–9, vv. 1–11, 423, 2993; *Roman de toute chevalerie* (for which the prologue is given in (28) below and see Foster and Short, ed., 1976–7, P85 and v. 4472.

14 See Short 1980, 476–8.

15 There may be a penitential element to this physical labour. The deficiencies Lancaster claims may constitute socio-historical evidence, but are, as Catherine Batt argues 'advisedly deployed metaphors for the writer's spiritual condition ... part of his self-construction as spiritually abject' (Batt, introd. and trans., 2014, xx and 239.22–8).

episcopal visitation of nuns (where the question of Latinity is more marked, or marked in different ways from male monasteries) provides for sending or at least announcing the results of visitations in several languages.[16] Moreover, as Felicity Riddy and Elizabeth Tyler have powerfully argued (for late-medieval female sub-cultures of nunnery and laywomen's reading and for the Latin historiographical patronage of both literate and non-literate eleventh-century queens, respectively), and as is exemplified here in St Edmund's *Mirour* (22.50–60), full Latin literacy is not a *sine qua non* of textual engagement in a culture where talk about texts and the oral matrices of much consumption and circulation of texts play a major role.[17] From the point of view of clerics engaging in public speech, language choices are expected to be circumstantial and varied, and translation to be frequently ex tempore. As Claire Waters has argued, 'clerical attempts to present Latin and vernacular, clergy and laity as opposed categories are continually undermined by the writers' obvious recognition of the fact that they must deal with a situation, preaching, whose very function was to integrate those realms', and medieval preachers and teachers are less concerned with language as such than with questions of access: focused rather on the possibilities of Pentecost than on the barriers created by Babel.[18] Preachers probably worked with notes or sermon outlines in Latin or French and with more marked (and orthographically less settled) English-language quotations and exempla written out (as with the lyrics that appear in sermon collections), but with the expectation of themselves preaching in, or using the services of colleagues to preach in, whatever language is appropriate to a particular audience.[19] One case may suggest a systematic attempt to address these issues: the *Ormulum*, a late-twelfth-century English-language pastoral work from the East Midlands (perhaps Bourne in Lincolnshire), is by an Augustinian canon with a Danish name, Orm, written at the command of a brother canon and probably superior, with a French name, Walter. Meg Worley has argued that the idiosyncratic but systematic spelling of the autograph manuscript is perhaps designed not to stabilise relations of sound and meaning for the sake of English, but to help French-speaking Augustinian canons in pastoral work with English users.[20] Certainly lack of words in *either* Latin *or* French (*propter defectum latinitatis, vel propter defectum vulgaris loquutionis*) is seen as a problem in the Dominican Humbert of Romans's influential treatise on preaching.[21]

Part I on language gives a selective focus on a few issues and possibilities. It is not designed as a history of French in England (though it follows a roughly chronological order

16 For a concise review of the multilingualism provided for in the injunctions of visiting bishops, see Power 1922, 247–50. For more recent accounts of nunnery Latinity, see Blanton, O'Mara and Stoop, ed., 2013.

17 Riddy 2003, repr. 2006, Tyler 2016. On talk, see further Fenster and Smail 2003.

18 Waters 2003, 39. As Waters points out, conceptions of language in Latin treatises on preaching are therefore as much concerned with style, genre, efficacy as with language per se, since even speaking the vernacular may not be the same thing as to speak in a community's language. See also the discussion in Reeves 2015. For a similar argument on written instruction for lay patrons by clerics, see Wogan-Browne 2005a.

19 Zink argues that the presence of Latin (in citation, aide-memoire, etc.) characterises original composition in the vernacular, whereas sermons wholly in French tend to be translated closely from works by St Bernard, Gregory the Great or Haymo of Auxerre (Zink 1976, 100, and see further Pt II, ch. 1, 85–113).

20 Worley 2003.

21 Cited in Zink 1976, 102.

from the twelfth to the fifeenth century), but suggests, rather, something of the variety of perspectives and attitudes involved in language choice. It should be noted here too (and is exemplified at greater length in Parts IV and V) that French, English and Latin are far from the only linguistic choices envisioned in the French texts of England: Greek, Hebrew, and Arabic are also invoked, often in texts which have moved through one or more European vernaculars on their way into languages of learning and into French as a prestige vernacular (see (**32a–35**) below and p. 250).[22] One historiographically authenticating language is, like Pictish in (**1**), often present in its absence: *Breton*, the language of the British (i.e. of the Welsh) is, as Sir Thomas Gray points out in his *Scalacronica* (**16**, headnote), not taken into account in Bede's foundational history of England. Welsh nevertheless returns as a language and an important connection with the insular past in many *Brut* texts (see here (**32**), *Fouke le Fitz Waryn*). Its close relative, Breton, is famously deployed as a predecessor language in Marie de France's *lais*.

Among Part I's concerns are topics important in most insular historiography, such as the notation of linguistic diversity, change and language-death in England (*De Bretaine ki ore est* (**1**), and see also the discussion of *muement de languages* in 3.12); these concerns are frequently important ways of considering conquest, settlement, and regime change. Language's mutability and transience and writing as a way of stabilising it (*Roman de Rou* (**3**); see also (**42**)) are allied concerns, as is linguistic translation as a way of coping with regime change and itself creating cultural and political change (*Waldef*, **6**.43–5). Other topics addressed include topoi of continental versus insular French and their status relative to each other and to Latin (*The Life of Edward the Confessor* (**2**), and see also **11b**, Guernes's *Life of Becket*); the cultural centrality of translation and the relative restrictedness of Latin (*Ipomedon* (**4**), where the danger of imperfectly maintained grammar in the move from Latin to French is also a subject of jest and irony, **4**.35–8). The theological implications of language access are discussed in Grosseteste's dignified account of the vernacular: not all can access the sacred languages of Hebrew, Greek, Latin and there is both necessity and validity in each person's using what they feel is their own language in praising God (*Chasteau d'amour* (**5**): see also *Lumere as lais* (**19**.159–62)).

England had an early role in the development of French-language instruction. Entry (**7a–e**) exemplifies in brief the teaching of French in various registers and kinds in which insular culture was often a pioneer: in teaching children to speak French for elite and aspirant social uses, but also for training in the registers and concerns of estate management, for business, accountancy, trade, conveyancing and the law, and for letters both polite and bureaucratic.[23] The civic uses of various registers of French in the later Middle Ages

[22] A notable example is the *Ladder of Mahomet* (*L'Eschiele Mahomet*) of *c.* 1264 (ed. Wunderli 1968, trans. Hyatte 1997), extant only in an Anglo-Norman copy from a continental French translation but initially translated from Arabic into Spanish for Alfonso X of Castile (r 1252–84) by his Jewish physician. In the *Ornatus mulierum* (**32b**) below, a complex textual lineage from the Mediterranean to French is claimed, even though the text is a translation from the Latin.

[23] For further examples, including early-modern teaching of French in the Tudor court, see the useful Appendices of prefaces to linguistic works and brief biographies of their writers in Kibbee 1991 (Kibbee's discursive account of language death for French in England has been superseded by subsequent research: see e.g. Ingham 2015b, 2012, 2010).

and the multilingual world of business, commerce and urban legal custom, sociability, identity and literary production served by French in late-medieval London are pointed to by the *Liber custumarum*'s prescriptions for mayoral election (from a treatise written by an Italian in French), and the *Puy de Londres* (**8a**) and by Gower's *Mirour de l'omme* (**8b**). With London's francophony, we are back in the world of the prose *De Bretaine ki ore est* (**1**), whose account of languages and change in 'Britain, now called England' comes from one of the many medieval legal compilations focused on London, in this case one compiled against the background of Magna Carta.

1. *De Bretaine ki ore est apelé Engletere / About Britain which is now called England* [Dean 5], Excerpts: London, British Library, MS Add. 14,252, f. 101^{r}, 101^{v}, 104^{r}

Date of composition and provenance. Late twelfth century, extant in a London compilation of 1206–16.

Author, sources and nature of text. The following account of conquest and language is taken from an anonymous prose description of Britain. The material derives ultimately from Bede's account of Britain and British multilingualism in his *Historia ecclesiastica* (*c.* 730), updated and supplemented via Henry of Huntingdon's influential *Historia Anglorum* (1130–54). *De Bretaine* begins with the exceptional fecundity and desirability of the island of Britain and with its early invasions (Roman, Pictish and Scottish, English, Danish and Norman), graphically seen as so many wounds to insular integrity. The Anglo-Saxon political and ecclesiastical organisation of Britain is then dealt with, the land's physical features, and its four major roads, before concluding with Britain's languages. Bede and Henry of Huntingdon list the languages of five groups of people: *De Bretaine* updates with a sixth, which it calls 'Norman' or 'French' (line 32), being apparently less troubled than many medieval and modern accounts by the need to differentiate French dialects. *De Bretaine* registers linguistic difference and change in other ways, noting for instance that *shire* is the English for *county* (*sire en engleis est apelé contree*, f. 102^{v}) and also that the Picts and their language are erased in some traditions and memories (lines 34–8). The very naming of the land is seen as inherently unstable: the phrase 'Britain, now called England' (*Bretaine, ki ore est apelé Engletere*) is used eight times in the short prose *De Bretaine* (a variant, *Engletere que jadis fu apelé Bretanne*, f. 102^{v}, also appears). Variations of the phrase echo through historiographical and topographical writing from the twelfth to the fifteenth centuries, a sign of the shifting complexities of linguistic, cultural, and political change in the British archipelago.

Audience and circulation. The prose *De Bretaine* is extant in a London compilation of legal, historical and civic documents carefully thought out but hastily executed in the early thirteenth century to present the long co-existence of differing peoples in Britain; traditions and models of good government from King Arthur to Prester John; and the legal rights and customs specifically of London and also of the kingdom, from the laws of Ine to those of Edward the Confessor. Hanna 2005, 56–73 and Keene 2008 show that the compilation served the interests of the barons, the mayor and other London leaders, and the canons of St Paul in their confrontation with King John; that it offers a wide and rich presentation of London as a legal, historical and commercial entity, and that it needs to be understood not simply as law or historiography but also as a work theorising and practising the value of the written record in defence of particular communities and in shaping their representation. The compilation continued to be consulted in the thirteenth and early fourteenth centuries and was one model for Andrew Horn's great London compilation, the *Liber custumarum* (8^{a}). Only this one manuscript of the prose *De*

Bretaine is known, but versions of *De Bretaine* materials were adapted in a wide range of insular writings and languages for different purposes (see further e.g. (**16**), (**42**)). Earlier French versions include a verse reworking of Henry of Huntingdon's Book I (Dean 4), made independently of the prose *De Bretaine* after 1139: the verse version precedes Gaimar's *Estoire des Engleis* (**10**) in two manuscripts and in a third where Gaimar is announced, but lacking. Apart from the London users specific to the compilation in which the prose *De Bretaine* appears, audiences for this kind of historical-topographical material must have overlapped with those for histories of the British (*Brut* texts), and, like *Brut* readers, embraced a wide range of seigneurial, gentry, urban, and professional audiences within and outside London.

MANUSCRIPT SOURCE. BL Add. 14,252 (*Leges Anglorum Londoniis collectae*) was compiled in Latin and French in the early thirteenth century: it is a small vellum manuscript (210 × 153 mm), professionally prepared. The manuscript was originally the second volume of what is now Manchester, John Rylands University Library, MS lat. 155 (digitised at http://www.earlyenglishlaws.ac.uk/laws/manuscripts/). The two were designed and formatted as a whole, though the collection of London laws was abandoned by MS Add. 14,252's second scribe, probably in 1216–17, after the making of Magna Carta (with whose aims the compilation has much in common, Keene 2008, 80–90). MS Add. 14,252 contains several legal treatises, notably the *Tractatus* on English law ascribed to Ranulf Glanville (d. 1190), and a variety of items including assizes, an intended but unrealised copy of Geoffrey of Vinsauf's *Poetria Nova*, and the customs, liberties and laws of London in Latin and French. *De Bretaine*'s role in the geographical framing of the compilation continues that of material from Geoffrey of Monmouth in the compilation's first volume, the Rylands manuscript (Keene 2008, 84–7). MS Add. 14,252 concludes with a discursive genealogy in French of the Cornhill (*blemunt*) family (*ODNB*, *s.v.* 'Gervase of Cornhill'), perhaps, as Keene speculates, in the role of 'London heroes'. An English recipe for 'metheglyn' (with Latin title) is added in a fifteenth-century hand on f. 109^{v} (current foliation).

BIBLIOGRAPHY. The prose *De Bretaine* is edited in Lagomarsini 2011, the verse *Description of England* (Dean 4) in Bell 1993. Fundamental for both texts is the account of the verse *Description* and its place in historiography in Johnson 1993. MS Add. 14,252 is partially transcribed and its contents noted in Bateson 1902a, 1902b. Hanna 2005, 44–103 and Keene 2008 give detailed accounts of the compilation and the traditions of civic writing and record in which it is located. On the legal aspects of such compilations see further O'Brien 1999, Brand 1992, Brand 2003. Colgrave and Mynors 1969 edit Bede's *Historia ecclesiastica*; for Henry of Huntingdon, see Greenway, ed. and trans., 1996, 10–30. Hanning 1966 remains fundamental to high-medieval British historiography: more recently see Otter 1991, 1996, M. Warren 2000. On Bede's foundational grouping of five languages and four peoples, see Ní Mhaonaigh 2013, Broun 2007. Short 2013, 17–44, discusses French dialect awareness, particularly as between continental France, Normandy and Britain: see also (**2**) and (**11b**). On the linguistic history of Britain see e.g. Townend 2006.

TEXT AND TRANSLATION

[f. 101^{r}]: De Bretaine ki ore est apelé Engletere e ki est si bonuree sur tuz altres idles, e ke si est plentivuse de blez e de arbres e large de bois e de riveres e de veneisuns e de oiseals covenable, e noble de bons chiens, e ço de multes manieres, de iceste Bretaine vus voil alkes escrivre, e puis vus musterai une partie de la lei de la cité de Lundres . . .

About Britain, which is now called England, and which is blessed above all other islands and which is so plentifully supplied with grain and trees, and full of forests and rivers and game and choice birds, and splendidly provided with good hunting dogs (and they are of many kinds) – I want to write you something about this Britain and then I will

[f. 101v] De Bretaigne ki est apelee Engletere ses granz travailz vus volum mustrer. Bretaigne ad suferte granz mals e multes haschies, e cinc plaies ad eue par bataille puis le cumencement de siecle. La premeraine plaie fu par les Romeins, ki as Bretuns se conbatirent, mes il s'en perirent. La secunde plaie fu par les Picteis e par les Escoz qui griefment travaillerent les Bretuns par bataille, mes il ne la tindrent pas. La tierce plaie fut par les Engleis ki par grant ahan la conquistrent en bataille e uncore la tienent. La quarte fud par les Daneis ki par bataille la guerrierent, mes puis il i perirent. La quinte fud par les Normanz ki la venquirent e conquistrent e uncores sur tut altres unt la saignurie. . . .

[f. 104r] Ore devez saveir que en Bretaigne ki ore est apelé Engletere orent ja cinc languages, e si vus dirai que[u]s il sunt: bretoneis e engleis, eschoteis, picteis e latineis. Ore i est la sime, que l'om apele normand e francés, les que[u]s sunt fait cumuns a plusurs par la doctrine des anciens escriz. E ja seit iço que li Picteis seient ore destruit e ublié, e lur language ne seit usé, e ke de plusurs a fable seit tenu, nepurquant si truve l'om d'els remenbrance es anciens escriz.

Desque ci vus avom mustré de l'establissement de Bretaigne ki ore est apelé Engletere. Ore vus volum demustrer [f. 104v] une partie des leis de la cité de Lundres e des franchises.

explain to you some part of the laws of the city of London. . . .

We wish to tell you about the great troubles of Britain now called England. Britain has suffered great evils and many inflictions of suffering and it has had five wounds of battle since the beginning of the world. The first wound was through the Romans, who fought the Britons but subsequently left. The second wound was through the Picts and the Scots who bitterly troubled the Britons with fighting, but did not hold [the land]. The third wound was through the English who inflicted great suffering in conquering it in battle and who still hold it. The fourth was through the Danes, who waged war against it, but then lost it. The fifth was through the Normans, who vanquished and conquered it and who still hold the lordship [of it] over all others. . . .

Now you may know that in Britain, which is now called England, there were formerly five languages, and I will tell you what they are: British and English, Scottish, Pictish, and Latin. Now, there is a sixth, which is called Norman and French. These have become known to many through the teaching of old writings. Even though the Picts are now defeated and forgotten, and their language is no longer used, so that many think this tongue never existed, nonetheless remembrances of the Picts are found in the old writings.

Up to this point we have set out for you how Britain, which is now called England, was established. Now we want to show you something of the laws of the city of London and its liberties.

Notes

1 **ki ore est apelé Engletere** For further examples and variations on this phrase see lines 9–10, 27–8, 40–1, and (**3**.15), (**16**.1–3), (**42**.35–6).

3 **blez** Translated here as 'grain' to distinguish the smaller European corn seed from the American maize, or corn.

5 **noble de bons chiens** Lagomarsini (2011, 326) suggests that this is a mistranslation of Henry of Huntingdon's 'delightful for its hunting grounds of wildfowl and game' (*iocunda volucrum et ferarum venatibus*, Greenway 1996, 10, 11). The dogs do, however, function as a synecdoche for the plenitude of game in the Latin text and they shift its vision from a land of untouched potential to one organised by human activity.

15–16 **mes il s'en perirent** added in margin in same hand, black rather than brown ink.

18 **travaillerent** Scribal correction of a to e

18–19 **les Bretuns . . . mes il ne la tindrent** The plural *Britons* occupy the territory of Britain in this sentence, hence the singular pronoun *la*.

27 **que en** inserted in a smaller version of same script above *saueir.*

29 **que[u]s** for MS *ques*, added in by the same correcting hand as in 15 above

30 **bretoneis** (MS *Bretoneis*) is not modern 'Breton', but 'British', i.e. Welsh. In Bede the Britons come from 'Armorica' (originally western Gaul from the Seine to the Loire rather than just the modern Brittany, Greenway 1996, 16 n. 2), but the idea of the Welsh as British descendants of the Trojans flourished (not uncontroversially) from the mid-twelfth century. Henry of Huntingdon says that he has learned from authors other than Bede that the Britons are descended from Dardanus, father of Troius (Greenway 1996, 25, 8). On Bede's omission of the Britons, see further (**19**) (*Scalacronica*, headnote) below and Tyler 2012a.

32 **normand e francés** Both forms are said to be used in England as a single language, suggesting that distinctions between the two varieties are not a matter of concern.

32 **les que[u]s** MS *ques*. Punctuated as a new sentence in the manuscript.

32–4 **Les que[u]s sunt fait cumuns . . . la doctrine des anciens escriz** In Henry of Huntingdon this refers only to Latin and the 'teaching of ancient writings' are *doctrina scripturarum*, so probably 'the scriptures' (Greenway 1996, 24, 8).

34 **Picteis** In Bede the Picts are originally from Scythia, and try first to settle in Ireland: they are given Irish wives, but redirected to northern Britain (Colgrave and Mynors 1969, i. 1, 16–19). Henry of Huntingdon adds a note on the language death of Pictish and the near fictive status of the Picts in existing records (Greenway 1996, 24–5, and n. 37). In Geoffrey of Monmouth, the Picts try to settle Caithness, but are refused British wives, leave for Ireland and are dismissed as not part of the narrative of Geoffrey's Britain (Reeve and Wright 2007, 86–7, 70: see further Ní Mhaonaigh 2013, 100–5; Broun 2007).

35–6 **lur language ne seit usé . . . a fable seit tenu** *De Bretaine* makes the Pictish language rather than (as in Henry of Huntingdon, n. 34 above) the Picts themselves the object of disbelief.

37–8 **remenbrance es anciens escriz** A claim for the value of the written record repeatedly made in historiographical writing: cf. e.g. *Scalacronica* (**16**), *Mohun Chronicle* (**42**).

43 **franchises** were liberties, or rights and privileges of towns. These were a matter of great significance, over which, in London, the city and the king frequently struggled for control: see further *Liber custumarum* (**8a**). A smaller cursive hand using light brown ink writes *suffice* in the left margin at the end of the French and the beginning of the Latin text.

2. A Nun of Barking Abbey, *Le Romanz de saint Edward, rei et confessur* [Dean 523], Verse Prologue: Baker transcript and London, British Library, MS Add. 70,513, ff. 55^{v}–56^{r}; Verse Epilogue: Bibliotheca Apostolica Vaticana, MS Reg. lat. 489, f. 26^{r}; Anonymous prose reworking: London, British Library, MS Egerton 745, ff. 91^{r}, 120^{r}

Date of composition and provenance. The verse life was written by a nun of Barking Abbey and is dated to 1163–70 (Dean 523): a continental prose translation (or *remaniement*) of the later thirteenth or early fourteenth century is extant in a manuscript in the family of Marie de St Pol, countess of Pembroke (1304–77), foundress of Pembroke College, Cambridge (1347), and active in both France and England (Russell 2009). It was perhaps commissioned by her brother Jean de Châtillon (d. 1344), count of St Pol, or his son Guy (d. 1360).

Author, sources and nature of text. The suggestion that the *Edward* author, a nun of Barking, is the same writer who gives her name as Clemence of Barking in the Barking Life of St Catherine receives confirmation in the most recent work (Russell 2012). The *Edward* life is based on the *vita* by Aelred of Rievaulx, written in 1163. Aelred's text was created, in part, to support the legitimacy of the Anglo-Norman dynasty of Henry II, an aim also reflected in *Edward*. An accomplished spiritual and political biography, *Edward* has been most often cited in modern scholarship for its supposed confession of linguistic inadequacy in its (now fragmentary) opening. In the context of the rhetorical stances of other prologues and epilogues by both male and female hagiographers, however, the anxiety is better read strategically rather than literally.

In characterising its own language as 'the false French of England' (v. 7), the prologue appears to express insecurity in moving from the learned language Latin to French. But this insecurity is expressed in a language where the feminine grammatical accords are perfectly made, and in which the subjunctive mood in vv. 1–2 correctly serves to express an untrue hypothesis: the writer is precisely not confusing the cases, and she is correctly construing her sentences. She is also keenly aware of the distinction between nominative and accusative in Latin, a distinction which she claims to disregard when she uses French. These lines could be read as subtle word play on both the process of vernacularisation, and on the role of a professed virgin in the context of medieval dynastic and genealogical concerns. The nun draws playful attention to the fact that while case distinctions between nominative and accusative (in all genders) are possible in the (male) world of clerical Latin, in the vernacular (female) linguistic context of this text there is no distinction possible between nominative and accusative feminine nouns (these case markers in medieval French are found only on masculine nouns). Similarly, as a professed virgin the author is removed from sexual congress (*Ne ne juigne part a sa part*: if I do not join one part to another, v. 2), which is a *sine qua non* in the dynastic economy of the lay world from which she has removed herself and so 'cannot do this in any fashion' (*nel puis faire en nule guise*, v. 4). The remainder of the Prologue and the Epilogue given here further show a writer aware of what she is doing in her skilful use of language.

The nun's linguistic humility topos (vv. 7–10) must also be seen in the context of the full prologue (Campsey version, vv. 12–68) which shows an independent treatment of the theological notions of divine plenitude, poverty and riches, desire and chastity, themes which will be presented in the Life. Edward's charity and chastity are linked with his desire for divine plenitude, *plenté suveraine* (v. 24), itself mirrored in the angelic desire which only grows in strength as it is consummated in divine rapture (vv. 27–8). The theological nuances are carefully expressed in the word play of the prologue and the nature of angelic desire is developed in the complex image of the gaze which both engenders and feeds this never sated, eternal desire (vv. 28–42). The repeated terms of the prologue themselves link desire, power, and the gaze with divine rapture (vv. 41–2). The nun is an innovator in redirecting courtly love from *eros* to *agape*.

In the Epilogue to the life the nun names her abbey but professes personal unworthiness to be named beside such a great saint as Edward. Allied to this theme is the topos of female unlearnedness in contrast to the male domain of clerical knowledge: the author asks that her work not be despised because it is a translation done by a woman and she asks forgiveness of the Son of Mary, for herself, and all her community's nuns. Her male/female contrasts resonate on learned and religious levels: the Son of Mary shares his maleness with the clergy, but this is divinity also of woman born. And although the nun professes intellectual humility, she is clearly learned, has translated this life from Latin, and this translation by a woman transmits the saint's power to her community. Equating intellectual and biological creation, she makes a Marian pun on the creation of the Life (vv. 31–2).

The anonymous nun in fact firmly claims her work (*soen romanz*, Epilogue v. 18); translates Latin with 'authority and verve' (MacBain 1993, 240–1), and innovates in all she does. Her humility is designed to show the elevated sanctity and power of Edward's name rather than feminine unworthiness. In choosing the richness of humility, the nun imitates St Edward the better to show the divine perfection attained by the subject of her writing.

Audience and circulation. Barking Abbey, the initial context for both the verse Life of St Edward and the Life of St Catherine, was a community of high status in the twelfth century: it had many connections with the royal court (who provided some of its abbesses) and with other major houses including the Westminster Benedictines. The level of learning and of literary sophistication is high in both works as is the awareness of secular vernacular contemporary writing. The linguistic and gender humility topoi in the prologue and epilogue of the Life of St Edward imply an audience of both nuns and learned men, as well as their courtly guests. In its Campsey manuscript version, the verse Life had an audience of Augustinian canonesses at Campsey Ash together with their patrons and guests.

The circulation of the Edward Life extended to the continent: it is included in a Picard copy of Wace's *Brut*, and a prose reworking is preserved, as noted above, in a manuscript book made for the Norman family of St Pol (Meyer 1910, 532–8; 1911). The cult of Edward was principally a royal and aristocratic cult, in which the *Edward* life continued to play a role for its exemplary, historiographic and devotional value from the late twelfth century to the early fourteenth. A second Anglo-Norman metrical life (based on the same Latin source), dated to 1236–45, is attributed to Matthew Paris (Dean 522, Fenster and Wogan-Browne 2008), who may allude to the Nun's life (Laurent 1998, 120; cited by Short 2010, 47).

Manuscript source. The metrical life and miracles has 6685 octosyllabic lines and is found in three manuscripts and one fragment; none of the manuscripts is complete. BL Add. 70,513 (the Campsey collection) lacks the first part of the prologue, and ends abruptly at line 4240; MS BAV Reg. lat. 489 lacks the beginning, lines 1–1462; MS Paris, BN fr. 1416 incorporates the text corresponding to lines 69–4482 in the middle of a Picard copy of Wace's *Brut*. Fragments of a manuscript, containing part of the prologue and 240 lines of the beginning of the text, formerly owned by A. T. Baker, are now lost (Baker, ed., 1907–8). Ten complete lines as published in Baker, ed., 1907–8 are used here for the prologue's opening: the Campsey manuscript provides the rest of the Prologue and the Vatican manuscript the Epilogue. The prose *remaniement* of the Barking metrical Life is found in BL Egerton 745 (it has only the shortened prologue of the Campsey version, and the epilogue as found in the Vatican manuscript). Details of both BL Add. 70,513 and Egerton 745 are online at http://www.bl.uk/catalogues/illuminatedmanuscripts/.

Baker's description of the lost manuscript fragment implies that the prologue was at least 50 lines long (he numbers his lines in this fashion, without explanation), and he refers to a subsequent 240 lines (which are the same, except for spelling variations, as the lines found in the Campsey manuscript) which he does not give. The fragment was from a small manuscript, 'probably 8 in. by 5 in.', used as fly leaves in a sixteenth-century book binding.

It is possible that the Vatican manuscript also originally had the extended prologue; our study of the collation of the manuscript indicates that one quire (probably 5 bifolia, if it was the same length as the remaining quires) is missing at the beginning of the volume. Judging from the ruling of the rest of the text, and from the 1462 lines missing from this copy, there would have been space for a prologue of up to an additional 108 lines in such a quire.

Bibliography. Södergård 1948 gives a critical edition of the verse life, which includes all known lines; the shortened Campsey version is available electronically (http://margot.uwaterloo.ca): see on this manuscript and its audiences Russell 2003, Wogan-Browne 2003. There is a translation in Bliss 2014. For audio-visual readings by Alice Colby-Hall see http://legacy.fordham.edu/academics/programs_at_fordham_/medieval_studies/french_of_england/audio_readings_94163.asp. On the identity of the author as Clemence of Barking see MacBain 1958, 1993; Russell 2012: a dissenting view is Bliss 2012. The verse life together with its innovative textual strategies is analysed in its larger cultural context by Wogan-Browne 1993, 1994a, 1994b, 2001, Fenster 2012, and Brown 2012. For the range of literary knowledge within Barking see Batt 1991, and for Barking's literary culture generally, Brown and Bussell 2012. On Marie de St Pol and the prose reworking of the metrical life, see Russell 2009. The prose text is partly edited in Meyer 1910, 1911. On topoi of linguistic inadequacy see Baker, ed., 1907–8 (French of England as 'debased'), Vising 1923, 26 (consciousness of linguistic isolation), MacBain 1993 (provinciality in relation to the visiting Anglo-Norman court), Short 2013, 20–2. The nun's linguistic topoi are discussed in Short 1980 and 2010, Russell 2012, Wogan-Browne 2015.

TEXTS AND TRANSLATION

2a. Verse Prologue and Epilogue

Prologue Fragment (Baker transcription)

Si joe l'ordre des cases ne gart,
Ne ne juigne part a sa part,
Certes n'en dei estre reprise
Ke nel puis faire en nule guise.
Qu'en latin est nominatif
Ço frai romanz acusatif.
Un faus franceis sai d'Angletere
Ke nel alai ailurs quere,
Mais vus ki ailurs apris l'avez,
La u mester iert, l'amendez.

If I do not keep the cases in the right order, or do not join the parts together properly, I surely should not be reproached, for I am simply not capable of doing so. What is nominative in Latin I will put in the accusative in French. I know only a faulty French of England because I have not gone elsewhere to learn it, but you who have learned French abroad, correct my language wherever it is necessary.

Prologue

(BL Add. 70,513, ff. 55va–56ra)
Ici comence le romanz de saint Edward, rei et [confessur]

Al loenge le creatur
Començ cest' ovre en son honur.
Sa valur me seit en aïe

In praise and honour of the creator I begin this work. May his great strength aid me in the translation of this life; may it please Him

De translater ci ceste vie
Que mun travail receive en gré
Et a[l] seint seit a volenté,
Le kel li bons Deus tant ama
Qu[e] il deus feiz le coruna:
En terre est primes coruné,
Et puis en ciel pur sa bunté.

to accept my work, and may this also be the will of the saint, whom God has so loved that He crowned him two times: he was first crowned on this earth, then in heaven because of his goodness.

Par la corune terriene
Conquist il la celestiene.
Poi preisa la richeise humaine,
Par ceo out la plenté suveraine,
La plenté de la grant duçur,
De la presence au creatur,
La quele li angle desirent
Et nepurquant sanz fin se mirent. [f. 55vb]
Tant lur delite l'esguarder
Que ne se poent sauler.
Faire desirent ceo qu'il unt
Et ceo desirent k'il plus unt.
Cum plus le veient, plus i tirent,
Cum plus en unt, plus en desirent.
De lur poer lur desir lur naist,
Et lur poer lur desir paist.
Il unt de l'esguarder poer
Et de l'enguard naist lur voler.
A la plenté de cest enguard
Est ja venuz li reis Edward.
En ceste plenté se delite,
Kar sa joie est en li suffite.

By his earthly kingship he earned the celestial crown. He placed little value on human wealth little human wealth, and because of this he earned heavenly plenitude, the repleteness of the great bliss of being in the presence of the creator, which is desired by the angels even as their gaze is eternally on Him. Their contemplation fills them with delight which is never sated: they desire to do what they are doing, and the more they do it the greater their desire: the more they see Him the more they are drawn to Him, the more they are drawn to him the greater is their desire. Their desire is born out of their power, and their power fulfils their desire. They are empowered by their contemplation, and in gazing on God their will to do so is born. King Edward has achieved this plenitude of contemplation. He delights in this fulness, his joy is sated by it.

Ohy! Cum grant nobilité
Et cum dublee bonurté!
Plenté out ci et plenté la,
Mes ceste out vile et cele ama.
Ceste cunuist fuitive et vaine,
Cele estable, de tuz biens plaine.
Ici fist Deus son cors regner
K'il pout tut tens son quer truver
Povre en pechié, en delit,
En veine gloire, en fol delit.
Ki si est riche cum il fu
Et si pot bien povre estre tenu
Et cil ki ci siut sa poverte,
Bien deit riche estre par deserte;
Et pur ceo riche et povre esteit
Qu[e] il ambure aver voleit:

Oh! what great nobility, and how doubly blessed is he! He experienced both earthly and divine fulness: but he held the former to be worthless, and loved the latter. The former he knew to be fleeting and vain, the latter was lasting and full of all goodness. God allowed him to rule his earthly body so that he could always find his heart impoverished with respect to sin, earthly desire, vainglory, and sensuality. Whoever is as rich as he was, yet is considered by the world to be poor, and who follows the path of this poverty, will be rich in [divine] merit. And he was thus both rich and poor, for he wished to have both: the richness of humility and the rewards of poverty.

En la richesce, humilité,
Et merite de povereté.
   Ore preium Deus ke tant est bons
Et ki par tut receit les sons,
Ki les povres n'ad en despit [f. 56ra]
Ne sul de riches n'est suffit,
Ke pur la sue grant bunté,
Senz ki nul bien n[en] est duné,
K'il de sa joie nus doint part
Ke ore ad duné a saint Edward.

Let us pray to God, who is the source of goodness and receives his own everywhere, and who does not despise the poor nor is pleased only with the rich, that by his great goodness, without which no other good is possible, that He grant to us a share of the joy He has already given to St Edward.

Epilogue

(Vatican, BAV Reg. lat. 489, f. 26*ra–b*)
(ed. Södergard, vv. 5296–5335)

Se nul de vus est desiranz, [f. 26ra]
Ki avez oï cest rumanz,
De saveir en quel liu fust fait
E ki de latin l'ait estrait,
Par tel cuvenant le savrez: [f. 26rb]
Que vus le pius Deu requerez
Que il verai merci face
A cele quil fist par sa grace.
En Berkinges, en l'abeïe,
Fu translaté ceste vie.
Pur amur saint Eduuard la fist
Une ancele al dulz Jhesu Crist.
Mais sun num n'i vult dire a ore,
Kar bien set n'est pas digne unkore
Qu'en livre seit oï ne lit
U si tres saint num ad escrit.

If any of you who has listened to my narrative wishes to know where it was composed and who translated it from Latin, you will find out on condition that you ask God that he grant true mercy to the woman who, by his grace, wrote it. This life was translated in Barking Abbey; a handmaiden of sweet Jesus Christ composed it for the love of St Edward. But she does not wish to reveal her name at present, for she knows well that her own name is not yet worthy to be heard or written in the same book where the very holy name [of St Edward] is recorded.

   Si requiert a toz les oïanz
Ki mais orrunt cest soen rumanz,
Qu'il ne seit pur ço avilé
Se femme l'ad si translaté.
Pur ço nel deit hoem pas despire
Ne le bien qu'il i ad desdire.
Mercie crie si quiert pardun
Qu'el' emprist la presumptiun
De translater ceste vie.
Desqu'ele n'est mielz acumplie
Or emblasmez sun numpueir,
Kar aquité s'ad sun vuleir.

And she requests all those listening, and those who will listen in the future to this, her own narrative in French, that they not denigrate it because it was translated by a woman. No-one should reject it on that account, nor speak pejoratively of the good it contains. She asks for pity, seeking pardon for having the presumption to undertake this translation: that it has not been better done, blame her lack of strength, for here she has accomplished her wish.

Si requierez le Fiz Marie
Pur cele sainte cumpaignie,
Od ki maint cele Deu ancele
Ki fist ceste vie nuvele.
Qu'il lur duinst sa plentive grace
E lur joie en sei si parface
Que al trespas de ceste vie
Nus mette od cele cumpaignie
U saint Eduuard ad ajusté
Par sa grace, pur sa bunté,
Ki regne e vit e regnera,
E est, e ert, e parmaindra. Amen.

Pray to the Son of Mary on behalf of the holy religious order where the handmaiden of God lives, who has produced this new Life [of St Edward]. May he grant them his full grace, and perfect their joy in him so that on leaving this life he may place us among the company where he has placed St Edward, through his grace, and his goodness, who lives and reigns, who is now and will be for evermore.

2B. Prose Prologue and Epilogue

Prose Prologue

(BL Egerton 745, f. 91*ra*)

A la loenge e a l'onneur de Dieu le tout poissant voil ci aprés raconter la vie d'un saint home noble, que Dieus ama tant que il le courouna .ii. fois. Il fu couronnés primes en terre, e puis ou ciel par ses merites. Il prisa poi les terriennes honneurs, quar il desirroit la gloire celestiele e a veoir son criateur en la joie parmanable. Laquele chose li angele desirrent, ja soit ce chose que il le voient touz jourz. Cis sains hom de qui je voil parler fu saint Edouart, jadis roys d'Engleterre.

To the praise and honour of almighty God I wish to recount here the life of a sainted nobleman, whom God loved so much that he crowned him twice. He was first crowned on earth, then in heaven as a reward for his virtues. He cared not for earthly riches, for he desired celestial glory, to see his creator in eternal bliss. This too is the desire of angels, even as they are endlessly rapt in divine contemplation. This saintly man of whom I wish to speak was St Edward, formerly king of England.

Prose Epilogue

(BL Egerton 745, f. 120*rb–va*)

Se aucuns de vous desirroit savoir qui fist cest livre en roumans, vous le sarés par [f. 120*va*] tes couvenans, que vous priez Dieu qu'il face pardon de ses pechiés a la parsonne qui le fist. Ceste vie fu translatee en l'abeie de Berkinges. Une des anceles Jhesu Crist le translata. Mais ses non n'ert mie noumés, quar ele n'est encore digne, selonc s'entente, que ses nons soit leus en sa vie de si grant home comme fu li sains roys Edouart.

If anyone among you wishes to know who wrote this book in French, you will learn it if you make this promise: that you pray to God that he pardon the sins of the one who composed it. This Life was translated in Barking Abbey. One of the handmaidens of Jesus Christ translated it. But she will not be named, for she is not yet worthy, in her own estimation, that her name be read in the Life of such a great man as saintly king Edward.

Ele requiert a touz ceus qui orrunt cest livre qu'il ne l'aient mie eu pour vil pour ce se feme le translata. Ele prie a touz ceus qui oënt ceste vie qu'il prient a Dieu que il li face pardon, en ce qu'ele fu si hardie que par presompcion ele osa translater si digne vie. Et tous ceuz qui prieront pour li et pour toute la compaignie du lieu ou ele demeure, ai[en]t la vie pardurable.

She asks all who will hear this work that they not consider it to be worthless because it was translated by a woman. She enjoins all who hear this Life to ask God to pardon her, in that she boldly had the presumptious audacity to translate such an exalted Life. And may all who will pray on behalf of her, and on behalf of all her companions in the convent where she lives, have eternal life.

Notes

Verse Prologue

1 [. . .] For the fragmentary opening lines of the text (vv. 1–12 and 41–50 in Baker's numbering, 1–10 in Södergard's), see Baker, ed., 1907–8 and Södergard 1948.

1–10 On the possible ironic meanings of this discussion of gender and syntax, see headnote. The 'false French of England' is a theme often repeated in insular literary works, but professed linguistic anxiety created by the social contrast between different dialects was a common theme in continental French writing as well. See further Short 1980, 2010.

12 **ovre en son honur** MS *ovre et sa valur*. We emend to avoid the repetition of *sa valur*, in which the scribe seems to have anticipated the words of the following line; our emendation is based on the prose translation.

13 **valur me seit en aie** MS *valur et sa aie*. We emend to make sense of the line.

17 **Le kel** MS *De kel*.

25–6 **La plenté . . . la presence au creatur** Reminiscent of 2 Pet 1:2–4, and an Anselmian treatise on the custody of the soul (Wogan-Browne 1994c, 63 n. 27)

34 **en desirent** MS *en diserent*.

36 **paist** MS *prist*, emended for rhyme.

50 **quer truver** MS *quer turner*.

62 **les sons** MS *les cens*.

Verse Epilogue

77 Barking Abbey in Essex, about eight miles from the Tower of London, was a long-established convent, newly prominent since the Conquest, and with close links with the court (see *Victoria County History Essex*, II, 117–21, Brown and Bussell 2012).

89 **nel deit hoem** The French allows both for the impersonal translation, 'no-one' and a gendered translation, 'no man', thus playing off woman translator and male critic.

92 **presumptiun** MS *presumpsitiun*.

3. Wace, *Le Roman de Rou* [Dean 2.1], Excerpt: London, British Library, MS Royal 4 C.XI, f. 249^{r-v}

Henry Bainton

Date of composition and provenance. 1160–74, perhaps at Bayeux.

Author, sources and nature of text. Wace was born in the first decade or so of the twelfth century on Jersey, but we know little for certain about his life apart from what he himself tells us in the *Roman de Rou*. There he states that he was originally from Jersey, that he was educated in Caen and in 'France' (i.e. the Île de France) and that Henry II gave him a prebend at the cathedral of Bayeux (a handful of whose charters he witnessed in the late 1160s and early 1170s). He refers to himself in the *Rou* as a *clerc lisant* (v. 180 below), a term that has been widely discussed but never finally defined. Given what Wace says about his literary activities in the *Rou*, he probably meant he was a professional technician of the written word, who produced and used written texts on behalf of those who paid him to do so. Wace's name is not found in any records after 1174, although it is not known exactly when after this he died.

Wace is best known for his *Roman de Brut*, finished in 1155, an Anglo-Norman verse reworking of Geoffrey of Monmouth's *History of the Kings of Britain*, and highly influential throughout the Middle Ages. Wace's lyric *serventeis* (v. 153 below) do not survive, but his lives of St Margaret, St Nicholas (**25a**) and his *Conception Nostre Dame* from his early career are extant in multiple manuscripts. After the *Brut*, the *Roman de Rou* is his major historiographic work. He planned it as a history of the dukes of Normandy from the time of the duchy's foundation by the Danish war-band leader Rollo ('Rou' in French) up to the reign of Henry (II) Plantagenet, duke of Normandy, count of Anjou and king of England (d. 1189). Wace never got as far as Henry II's reign, breaking off his narrative mid-way through his account of Henry I). But even in its truncated state, the *Rou* remains a lengthy and ambitious work – and as such it is a typical product of the innovative historiographical culture of the twelfth-century cross-Channel world.

Like other histories written in that world (such as Gaimar's *Estoire des Engleis*, (10)), Wace's narrative was substantially a reworking of earlier material. His principal sources were Dudo of St Quentin's early-eleventh-century *De moribus et actis Normannorum ducum* (*On the Conduct and Deeds of the Norman Dukes*) and the *Gesta Normannorum ducum*, which William of Jumièges wrote in the 1070s. Wace also adapted narrative material from the Latin histories of William of Poiters, Orderic Vitalis and William of Malmesbury and used documentary and oral information gathered in Normandy. He was possibly also influenced by the Bayeux Tapestry's account of the Norman Conquest. This wide range of sources, and the way Wace used them has given him a reputation for conscientiousness as a historian.

It is far from clear, however, that Wace thought of himself as a historian in any modern sense of that word, although he certainly presented the *Rou* as if it were a true narrative of the deeds of the Norman dukes. Wace refers to his work sometimes as an *estoire* (e.g. Holden 1970, 1:1, v. 4) and sometimes as a *geste* (e.g. Holden 1970, 1:4, v. 43); and regardless of whether or not those terms were used with any technical precision, the structure and form of his text underscores the startling degree of formal and generic flexibility accommodated by historical writing in this period. Wace had never lost his hagiographer's eye, for example, and he relates Duke Richard's encounters with the Devil (which, he says, people considered 'marvellous' [*a merveile tint*, Holden 1970 1:173, v. 338]), even while he mocks himself for having sought out the kind of 'marvels' (*merveilles*) celebrated in Breton legends (Holden 1970, 2:122, vv. 6387–93). At the same time, he also seems as content to pose as a jongleur (demanding a drink in exchange for performance, Holden 1970, 1:158, v. 4423) as he does in playing the role of the *clerc lisant* whose solemn social duty it is to preserve and perform written history for the edification of the ruling class.

Wace demonstrates considerable stylistic dexterity in the *Rou*, writing some sections in the octosyllabic rhyming couplets typical of twelfth-century vernacular romance and history, and some in alexandrine *laisses*, whose metre recalls *chanson de geste* and its invocation of remote heroic pasts. Parts of the *Rou* are notably epic in tone (such as the descriptions of the battles fought by Rollo); some are couched in terms of courtly entertainment; and others are overlain with the rhetoric of serious scholarship. The *Rou*'s use of a number of different registers should not necessarily be taken as evidence for so many 'false starts' (see e.g. Ashe 2007, 50, 68). Rather, they demonstrate Wace's nuanced experimentation with the varied modes of remembrance offered by the newly written vernacular of the francophone world. It is this concern with the written word, and with language and memory, that comes to the fore in the extract below.

Audience and circulation. It is generally assumed that Wace wrote the *Rou* for Henry II, but there is no direct evidence that Henry patronised the poem. Wace states in the extract below, for example, that Henry II had rewarded him with a prebend at Bayeux and with other gifts (vv. 173–5), but it is unclear whether he did so in payment for the *Rou* or in recognition for the *Brut*, or in return for some other service. Wace says that he had composed the *Rou* 'to the honour of the second Henry' (*pur le onur al secunt Henri*, v. 185), but dedication to a patron is not the same as a commission. Many have felt that the abrupt ending of the poem signals Henry II's dissatisfaction with the work: Wace says he is stopping writing about the dukes of Normandy because Henry II had asked one 'Beneeit' to write (*dire*) about them ('Beneeit' is almost certainly Benoît de Sainte-Maure, author of the *Histoire des ducs de Normandie*, Dean 2.2, and the *Roman de Troie*.). But as Tyson notes, there is no evidence that Henry *told* Wace to stop writing the *Rou* (1979, 198), and nowhere does Wace say that Henry had asked Benoît to write the history of the dukes of Normandy *instead* of him. So while it is certain Wace stopped writing the *Rou* as a consequence of Henry's commissioning of Benoît, we do not know what Henry thought of the *Rou* itself – if he thought anything about it at all.

What is more certain is that Wace envisaged members of the ruling family and wider aristocracy of the Plantagenet *espace* as the primary audience for his work. The *Rou*'s intense interest in the territorial and dynastic struggles between the aristocracies of north-west Europe suggests that it was directed towards an acutely politically aware society well versed in the complexities of dynastic history. This history was not just for kings and queens, in other words, but also for *baruns* and *noble dames* (vv. 147–8) – rich and powerful people with land and money (*riche gent, ki unt les rentes e le argent*, vv. 163–4). Like the king, these people participated in a culture of *noblesce* and *largesce* (vv. 166–8), in which nobility, wealth and generosity went hand-in-hand with the patronage of book production: it is only through the resources of the noble and wealthy, Wace asserts, that books are able to be made (*pur eus sunt li livre fait*, v. 165). But Wace also emphasises that, for his audience, the written word was far more than just another material product to be conspicuously consumed. This was an audience with ancestors whose deeds they should remember, and who should pay to have them remembered. Having an ancestry, Wace seems to suggest, implies the need to have a written history too, in which the audience's ancestors and their own names would be remembered because they had paid to have them written down in history books (vv. 149–50).

Despite modern consensus that the *Rou* was a 'failure', it survives in four manuscripts and was known well beyond the circle of the Plantagenet court. It appears to have circulated through most of the principal literary centres of north-west Europe. Wace's account of *translatio studii* and the role of the written word seems to have influenced the prologue to Chrétien de Troyes's *Cligès* (Freeman 1976, 98), which Chrétien probably wrote for the court of Champagne (*Cligès* circulated with the *Rou* in one of its manuscripts, Gregory and Luttrell 1993, 83–90). The *Rou* may also have been known close to the French royal court: the etymology Wace provides for the name 'Norman', for example, is also found in the *Gesta Philippi Augusti* by Rigord of Saint-Denis (Carpentier, Pon and Chauvin, ed., 2006, 204), which the latter dedicated to Philip Augustus, king of France, 1179–1223. The Artesian poet Perot de Nesle included the *Rou* in a compilation of French narratives that he assembled and epitomised in the Picard dialect in the late thirteenth century, and which is strongly associated with the house of Boulogne (Busby 2002, 1:302). The inclusion of the *Rou* in this 'global compendium of Old French narrative' (Huot 1987, 23), alongside such works as the *Roman de Troie*, the *Roman d'Alexandre* and the *Roman de Thebes*, suggests that the *Rou* was considered a canonical work of historical literature among the smartest literary circles of the later-medieval francophone world.

Manuscript source. None of the extant manuscripts is completely satisfactory; a late manuscript copy is the only one to preserve all three sections of the *Roman de Rou*, while the earliest manuscripts contain only the third section (which narrates the adulthood of Duke Richard I up to the time of Henry I). Of these partial manuscript copies, London, BL Royal 4 C.XI is the earliest and is used for the prologue below. Royal 4 C.XI contains five items copied by various hands between the late-eleventh and early-thirteenth centuries. All but the first – a late-eleventh-century copy of Jerome's commentary on the prophets – are of a directly historiographical nature, and the last three are all written in Anglo-Norman. After Jerome's commentary there follows the 'second variant version' of Geoffrey of Monmouth's *Historia regum Britanniae*, probably copied in the mid-twelfth century. The *Rou* is the third item, beginning in a new hand in the blank space left at the end of the second column of the final folio of Monmouth's *Historia*. The *Rou* is immediately followed in another hand by the *Miracle de Sardenai* (34), and a vernacular translation of the (continental) *Pseudo-Turpin Chronicle*. Linguistic, palaeographical and textual evidence suggest that the last three items were copied in the early thirteenth century (Holden 1970, 3:20; Walpole 1976, 147). The *Rou* is written in three similar hands of the early thirteenth century, each of which produced a different quire. As with the other items in the manuscript, the scribes of the *Rou* produced a carefully written, but plain, text, filling three columns per folio and 66 lines per column. The first folio is available online, at http://www.bl.uk/catalogues/illuminatedmanuscripts/TourHistoryGeneal.asp.

Two ex-libris inscriptions show that the manuscript belonged to Battle Abbey in the Middle Ages. These were probably inscribed after 1300 (Walpole 1976, 148), but it is impossible to say exactly when Battle Abbey took possession of the manuscript or even whether it was the original owner. But the number of scribes who worked at copying it – and the presence of biblical commentaries in the codex – suggests that the manuscript is the product of a monastic scriptorium. Furthermore, Battle Abbey had a strong historiographical tradition of its own: two works of history were produced there in the twelfth century (the *Brevis Relatio de Guillelmo nobilissimo comite Normannorum* and the *Battle Abbey Chronicle*), and the books Leland noted as owned by the abbey prior to dissolution included historical works copied in the twelfth and thirteenth-centuries (Ker 1964, 7–8). Marginal notes throughout the manuscript 'suggest that it was attentively read' (Walpole 1976, 152), and Latin annotations to the *Rou*, presumably made by a monk at Battle, draw attention to the *Rou*'s description of the Battle of Hastings. As the textual history of the *Rou* (and many similar works) suggests, the work's original composition for the secular nobility by no means ruled out its circulation among a monastic audience.

Bibliography. The *Rou* is edited by Holden 1970–3, and translated by Burgess 2004 (the prologue, below, begins the 'Troisième Partie', ed. Holden, 1:161–8, vv. 1–184). On its date see Holden 1970, 3:14–15; Le Saux 2005, 156. On Wace's written sources see Holden 1970, 3:101–68, and for his use of William de Jumièges, van Houts 1984, 115–24: van Houts (2004, xxxviii, xl, xlv–xlvi) discusses Wace's range and treatment of documentary and oral sources. On Wace and the Bayeux Tapestry see Bennett 1982. Gouttebroze 1991 and Broadhurst 1996 discuss the patronage of the *Rou*: for the implications of Wace as *clerc lisant* see Gouttebroze (1995, 217–30). Ashe (2007 49–55, 58, 60) discusses the *Rou* as a failure. On Wace and twelfth-century vernacular historiography see Damian-

Grint 1999, Le Saux 2005. Damian-Grint 1999 and Ashe 2007 are also important studies of insular twelfth-century vernacular historiography in general. For a text and translation of Wace's *Brut*, see Weiss 2002, and for his saints' lives see (**25a**).

TEXT AND TRANSLATION

Pur remembrer des ancesurs,
Les feiz [e] les diz e les murs –
Les felunies des feluns,
E les barnarges des baruns –
Deit l'um les livres e les gestes
E les estoires lire a festes.
Si escripture ne fust feite
E puis par clers litte e retraite,
Mult fussent choses ubliees
Ki de viez tens sunt trespassees.

In order to remember the deeds and the words and the ways of the ancestors – the crimes of the wicked and the worthy deeds of noblemen – books, histories and stories should be read aloud to people at feasts. Many things that happened long ago would have been forgotten if accounts had not been written, then read and retold by clerks.

Par lungs tens e par lungs eages
E par muement de languages,
Unt perdu lur premereins nuns
Viles plursurs e regiuns.
Engleterre Bretainne out nun,
E primes out nun Albiun;
E Lundres out nun Trinovant,
E Troie Nove out nun avant.
Everwic out nun Ebrauc,
Ki primes fu Kaer Ebrauc.
Suth Guales fu ditte Mercia,
North Guales Venedocia.
Escoce out nun jadis Albaine,
Peitou e Gascuinne, Aquitaine.
E Armoriche fu Bretainne,
E Germainne fud Alemainne,
E Culvinne out nun Agrippine,
E Terruane out nun Morine.
E Paris out nun Lutece
E Pelasge, terre de Grece,
Itaire: Puille e Lumbardie;
Constantinoble: Besancie.
Effrata out nun Beethleem,
E Gebus fu Jerusalem.
Burguinne fud Allobroga, [f. 249va]
Et Esfun out nun Cacua;
Judea fud Palestina,
E Sebaste Samaria.

With the changes in language from bygone eras of long ago, many towns and regions have lost their original names. England had the name Britain, and originally had the name Albion; and London had the name Trinovant, and before that it was called New Troy. *Everwic* [York] was called Ebrauc, which was originally Kaer Ebrauc, South Wales was called Mercia, North Wales Venedocia. Scotland was once called Albany; Poitou and Gascony were together called Aquitaine. And Brittany was Armorica, and *Alemainne* was Germania; and Cologne had the name Agrippina; and Thérouanne was called Morine, and Paris was called *Lutece*, and the land of Greece was Pelasgus. Apulia and Lombardy were *Itaire* [Italy], Constantinople was *Besemcie* [Byzantium], Bethlehem had the name Ephrata, and Jerusalem was Gebus. Burgundy was Allobroga, Palestine was Judea, and Sebaste Samaria, and Orléans was called *Genabés* [Cenabum]. Valognes had the name *Nantés* [Alauna], and Rouen had the name Rothoma, and Avranches *Ausiona*. France was Gaul, Wales was Cambria, and Normandy had the name Neustria. Neustria lost this name, and I shall tell you why.

E Orliens out nun Genabés,
Valuinnes out nun Nantés;
E Roem out nun Rothoma,
E Averanches Ausonia,
France Guale, Guales Cambrie.
E Normendie out nun Neustrie.
Neustrie perdi cest nun:
Si vus dirrai par quel reisun.

Quanque ad vers septemtriun,
Que nus Char el ciel apelum,
Seit ciel, seit eir, seit terre u mer.
Tut soelent gent north apeler,
Pur north un vent ki surt e vient,
De la u li ciels le Char tient.
Engleis dient en lur langage –
A la guise de lur usage –
'En nor[t]h alum, de north venum,
North fumes nez, en north manum'.
Autresi dient de est un vent,
De suth e de west ensement.
'Man' en engleis e en norreis
'Hume' signifie en franceis;
Justez ensemble 'north' e 'man',
E ensemble dites 'northman':
Ceo est hume de north en rumanz,
De ceo vint li nuns as normanz.
Normant soelent estre apelé
Cil ki la dunt north vient sunt né.
E en rumanz est apelee
Normendie que il unt poplee.
Neustrie aveit nun anceis,
Tant cum ele fud as Franceis.
Meis pur la gent ki de north vint,
Normendie cest nun retint,
Pur ceo que Normant la poplerent,
Ki en la terre cumverserent.
Franceis dient que 'Normendie',
Ceo est 'la gent de north mendie'.
'Normant', ceo dient en gabant,
'Sunt venu del north mendiant,
Pur ceo que il vindrent d'autre terre
Pur mieux aver e pur cunquerre'.

Everyone usually calls 'north' anything – whether in the sky, the air, on land or sea – that lies towards the constellation *Septemtrio* (which we call the 'Plough'). This name comes from the north wind which rises up and comes from the direction where the Plough appears in the heavens. The English have an expression in their language: 'We're going to the north, we came from the north; we were born in the north and we're staying in the north'. In the same way they have named winds from the east, the south and the west. In English and Norse, *man* means what *hume* means in French. Put together 'north' and 'man', and you say 'northman', or in French '*hume de north*'. And that is how the Normans' name came to them: those who were born where the north wind comes from are usually called Normans. In French, the place that they populated is called Normandy. Formerly, when it belonged to the French, it was called Neustria, but Normandy now takes this name from the people who came from the north, because the Normans now live in this land. The French say that 'Normandy' means 'the begging people of the north': the 'Normans', they say jokingly, 'came begging from the north, from another country, to conquer this one and live better'.

Des tresturnees de ces nuns
E des gestes dunt nus parluns
Poi u nient seussum dire

We would be able to say little or nothing about the transformations of these names, and about the deeds we are speaking about,

Si l'um nes eust feit escrire.
Meinte cité ad ja esté,
E meinte riche poesté
Dunt nus ore rien ne seussum,
Si en escriz rien ne en eussum.
De Thebes est grant reparlance,
E Babiloine out grant puissance,
E Troie fud de grant podnee,
E Ninive fud lunge e lee.
Ki ore irreit querant les places
A peine i truvereit les traces.
Reis fud Nabugodonosor:
Une ymage fist faire de or,
Seisante cutes de hauteur,
E sis cutes out de laur.
Ki ore vuldreit sun cors veer [f. 249vb]
N'i truvereit, al mien espeir,
Que mustrer dunt dire seust
De lui, u que os u pudre feust.
Meis par les bons clers ki escristrent,
E les gestes as livres mistrent,
Savum nus del viez tens parler,
E de oevres plusurs cunter.

if people had not had them written down. We would now know nothing about many cities and many mighty powers that once existed if we had nothing about them in writing. There is great talk of Thebes, and Babylon had great power, and Troy had great pride, and Nineveh spread far and wide. But if anyone were to go seeking these places now, they would hardly find even traces there. Nebuchadnezzar was a king who had a statue made of gold: it was sixty cubits in height and six cubits in width. But I suspect that someone wishing to see his body now wouldn't find anyone who could show or say anything about him, or where his bones or ashes lie. But we know how to talk of ancient times, and can recount many deeds, because of the good clerks who wrote, and who set their deeds down in books.

Alisandre fud reis puissanz:
Duze regnes prist en duze anz.
Mult out terre, mult out aveir,
E reis fud mult de grant poeir.
Meis si il cunquist, poi lui valut;
Envenimez fud, issi murut.
Cesar – ki tant fist e tant pout,
Ki tut le mund cunquist e out –
Unkes nuls hoem puis ne avant,
Mien escient, ne cunquist tant,
Puis fud oscis en traïsun
El Capitoile, issi lisum.
Cil dui vassal – ki tant cunquistrent,
Tant eurent terres, tanz reis pristrent –
Enprés la mort, de lur onur
Ne out chescun ne meis sa lungur.
Quel bien lur feit, quel bien lur est
De lur preie e de lur cunquest?
Ne mais tant cum l'um veit disant,
Si cum l'um le ad truvé lisant,
Que Alisandre e Cesar furent,
Tant i ad de eus que lur nuns durent,

Alexander was a mighty king: he conquered twelve kingdoms in twelve years. He was a very powerful king, with much wealth, who ruled over a large realm. But his conquests were of little use to him: he was poisoned and died. We read that Caesar, who achieved so much and exercised such power, who had conquered and ruled the whole world (I don't think any man before or since has ever conquered so much), was afterwards killed by treason in the Capitol. For each of these two warriors – who had conquered so much, ruled so many lands, and captured so many kings – their power did not endure beyond their death. What good does their booty and conquest do them now; what benefit is it for them? People only know what Alexander and Caesar were from what people say about them from what they have read, and in this way their names continue to be known. They would have been forgotten if their histories had not been written. All

E si refussent ublié
Se il ne eussent escrit esté.

Tute rien turne en declin:
Tut cheit, tut moert, tut trait a fin,
Tut funt, tut cheit: rose flaistrist,
Cheval trebuche, drap viescist,
Huem moert, fer use, fust purrist;
Tute rien faite od mein perist.
Bien entend, [e] cunuis e sai
Que tuit murrunt, e clerc e lai,
E que mult ad curte duree
Enprés la mort lur renumee.
Si par clerc ne est mis en livre,
Ne poet par el dureement vivre.
Mult soel[ei]ent estre onuré,
E mult preisé, e mult amé,
Cil ki les gestes escriveient,
E ki les estoires treiteient.
Suvent aveient des baruns
E des nobles dames beaus duns
Pur mettre lur nuns en estoire,
Que tuz tens mais fust de eus memoire.
Mais ore puis jeo lunges penser,
Livres escrire e translater,
Faire rumanz e serventeis,
Tart truverai tant seit curteis
Ki tant me duinst e mette en mein
Dunt jeo aie un meis un escrivein;
Ne ki nul autre bien me face,
Fors: 'Tant mult dit bien maistre Wace,
Vus devriez tuz tens escrire,
Ki tant savez bel e bien dire'.
A ceo me tienc, e a ceo mus;
Ja de plusurs ne en avrai plus.
Jeo parouc a la riche gent, [f. 249^{vc}]
Ki unt les rentes e le argent;
Kar pur eus sunt li livre fait
E bon dit fait e bien retrait.
Morte est ki jadis fud noblesce,
E perie est od lui largesce.
Ki ses leis ait nel puis truver,
Tant ne puis luing ne proef aler.
Ne truis gaires ki rien me dunt,
Fors li reis Henris li secunt:

that survives of them are their names – and they would have been forgotten in their turn had they not been written down.

Everything decays: everything falls into ruin, everything dies, everything comes to an end. Everything collapses, everything falls down, roses wilt, horses stumble, cloth gets old; people die, iron rusts, wood rots: every man-made thing perishes. I well understand and acknowledge and know that everyone dies, clerks and laypeople alike, and that their fame does not survive after their death if it is not set down in a book by a clerk; it cannot last for long otherwise.

Those who wrote down stories and recounted histories used to be greatly honoured and praised and loved. They often received handsome gifts from noblemen and noblewomen so that they would write their names into history – so that they would be remembered ever after. But although now I'm able to think at length, and to write and rewrite books and to compose romances and *serventeis*, it will be a long time before I find someone amenable enough to give me (and to press into my hand) what I need to hire a scribe for one month. Nor will I find anyone who might do me any favour, other than saying: 'Very well said, Master Wace – you should always write, since you know how to compose so eloquently'. So I hold my peace and keep silent: From many people, I will never receive more than this [i.e. this praise]. I appeal to the rich people, who have property and money: for it is for them that books are made, and good tales composed and performed well.

What was once nobility, however, has perished and generosity has died along with it; I can't find anyone who upholds its laws, no matter how near or far I travel. I find hardly anyone who will give me anything at all, except King Henry the second. He had a

Cil me fist duner, Deus lui rende,
A Baïeus une provende,
E meint autre dun me ad duné:
De tut lui sace Deus bon gré!
Niés fud al premerein Henri,
E pere al tierz – tuz treis les vi:
Treis reis Henriz vi e cunui,
E clerc lisant en lur tens fui.
Des Engleis furent rei tuit trei,
E tuit trei furent e duc e rei:
Rei de Engleterre la guarnie,
E duc furent de Normendie.

prebend at Bayeux given to me (God reward him!), and he gave me many other gifts. May God look kindly on him in everything! He was the nephew of the first Henry, and father to the third: I saw all three – I saw and I knew three king Henries, and was a *clerc lisant* in their time. All three were kings of the English, and all three were both duke and king: they were kings of garrisoned England, and they were dukes of Normandy.

Notes

1 The text begins with a large decorated initial letter (with space offset over eleven lines for the upper part of the letter *P*, with the descender extending another thirty lines into the bottom margin). There are two spaces for large initials (over two line spaces, but the letters are missing), marking section breaks at vv. 47 and 143; the other section breaks are editorial.

1–6 **Pur remembrer . . . festes** Wace emphasises the didactic nature of historical writing from the beginning of this prologue. Like many history-writers of this period (working in Latin and in French) Wace emphasises the exemplary nature of historical knowledge: through hearing about the good and bad deeds and words of the ancestors, the present generation can imitate the good deeds and eschew the bad. The *feiz*, *diz* and *murs* invoked by Wace map neatly onto the *facta*, *dicta* and *mores* that are commonplaces in prologues to contemporary Latin histories. For the rhetorical theory underpinning such moral didacticism, and examples from Latin historical writing, see Kempshall 2011, 151–71; for vernacular examples, see Damian-Grint 1999, 93–8.

5–6 **Deit l'um les livres e les gestes / E les estoires lire a festes** For Wace, history is not only a didactic discourse that works to shape elite conduct, but it is a fundamentally *written* discourse. As such, history-writing absolutely depends on the skills of the lettered in order to convey the social knowledge it encoded. This prologue presents an extended meditation on the role of the lettered in the preservation and propagation of such knowledge, and in this meditation Wace figures the skills of literate clerks as being social as much as technical in nature. According to Wace, clerks are responsible as much for performing books at social occasions as they are for making them in the first place. Wace's insistence on the intensely sociable means by which written history was presented to a largely illiterate audience is one of the most striking depictions of the collective nature of high-medieval memorial and literary practices. By locating books and history in the sphere of public performance, Wace gives a rare glimpse of the intersection between the social dynamics of collective cultural practices such as feasting, and the reception of literary texts. For the public performance of the written word in this period, see Bainton 2012; for the performance of historiographical texts, see Kempshall 2011, 23–9.

7–8 **Si escripture . . . par clers . . . retraite** The precise valence of *escripture* is hard to gauge: it could mean 'the technology of the written word' in an abstract sense, or it could mean 'documents', 'writings', or 'written accounts' (as translated above). We also see Wace in this couplet identifying *clers* as both technicians and performers of the written word: *lire* (of which 'litte' is the past participle) can mean both 'to read' and 'to read *out*', while *retraire* covers a wider semantic field. *Retraire* could mean 'to recopy' and 'to draw up', but also has the sense 'to tell', 'to narrate', 'to recount'.

11–46 **Par lungs tens ... reisun** As in the *Brut* (see e.g. Weiss 2002, 30–2, vv. 1175–1270, and see (1)), Wace suggests that linguistic change is a direct consequence of the political change wrought by conquest; and he suggests in turn that conquest is a marker of the instability and mortality of worldly power. Linguistic and political change, meanwhile, also demonstrate for Wace the compelling need for people to have things recorded in writing (see esp. vv. 81–4). For Wace's perspective on linguistic change, see further Paradisi 2003, 27–45.

13 **premiers** is corrected in a later, medieval hand in the manuscript to *premereins*.

17–18 **Lundres ... avant** Wace also gives these versions of London's previous names (taken from Geoffrey of Monmouth) in the *Brut*. The Trojan origins of London are directly relevant to the *Rou* too, since Dudo of St Quentin (and Wace after him) claimed that Rollo's followers were also ultimately descended from Trojan stock (see e.g. Christiansen 1998, 16; Holden 1970, 2:313–14).

21 **Suth** MS subpuncts a final *t*; **ditte Mercia** corrected to *Demetia* by a later, medieval hand in the manuscript.

40 **Nantés** MS *aiantes*. This name is not attested elsewhere, and the Roman name for what is now *Valuinnes* (Valognes) was Alauna (Nègre 1990, 53). Wace's most recent editor, Holden (1970), corrects it to *Nantés* on the basis of manuscripts B, D. But keeping the name as 'Ajantés' makes a regular octosyllable.

42 **Ausonia** There is no other record of *Ausonia* being an early name for Avranches, whose Roman name was *Abrincae* (Nègre 1990, 151).

45 **Neustrie perdi cest nun** Wace rapidly narrows the focus of the passage from Christendom as a whole to Normandy in particular, suggesting in the process that the conquest of Neustria by Rollo – and the change of its name to *Normendie* – is merely one example of the interconnected phenomena of political and linguistic change.

47 **septemtriun**, i.e. *Septentrio*, the stellar constellation (the Plough or Big Dipper).

48 **Char el ciel** Wace here gives the vernacular designation for Septentrio (literally 'the wagon in the heavens').

55–6 **En north ... manum** Evidently a proverb, but not attested elsewhere: the precise meaning is obscure.

59–60 **Man en engleis ... en franceis** Wace follows the *Gesta Normannorum ducum* in giving an etymology for the word 'Norman', although the *GND* does not mention that 'man' is both a Norse and an English word (van Houts 1992–5, 1.17). The extent of Wace's knowledge of English is a matter of some debate; and the way he provides French glosses for English words here and elsewhere has been presented as evidence that he knew English well (Mathey-Maille 2005, 405; for a more cautious approach, Le Saux 2009, 188–97). Wace's lexis certainly shows that he knew *some* English (he quotes the stereotyped exclamations of drunken English troops before the Battle of Hastings, for example, for which see Woledge 1951, 21–4), but it is unclear whether this was a result of a working knowledge of the language or a more general familiarity with it. Nevertheless, Wace shows an acute philological awareness, subtly deployed to make a wider political point: he emphasises (like Dudo and William of Jumièges before him) that the enduringly close relationship between Normandy and England was based partly on a common historical experience of Scandinavian immigration: Scandinavians figure as ancestors, allies and enemies in the history of both places as Wace presents it. The cultural connections between England and Normandy are emphasised here too, 'with the Norse and English languages mentioned in the same breath and in such a way as to suggest common origins' (Le Saux 2009, 193).

75 **Franceis dient** The first of many points in this part of the *Rou* where Wace emphasises political distinction and perennial hostility between the French and the Normans (contrast (1)).

79 **d'autre** MS *de la*. We follow Holden's emendation from MSS B and D.

81–4 **Des tresturnees . . . feit escrire** These lines concisely articulate the broad argument of this prologue: writing alone guards against the ravages of passing time, even as it provides evidence for the transience of worldly things.

89–92 **Thebes . . . Babiloine . . . Troie . . . Ninive** Thebes, Babylon, Troy and Nineveh are ancient cities (alternately classical and biblical) that were destroyed by their conquerors. I have not been able to find another instance of these four cities being associated in this way.

95–102 **Nabugodonosor . . . feust** Nebuchadnezzar was the king of Babylon who destroyed Jerusalem and was responsible for the Babylonian exile of Judah (2 Kings 24–5). He is a crucial figure in apocalyptic thought (with which Wace seems to be engaging here), because the prophet Daniel had interpreted Nebuchadnezzar's dream of a statue made from four different metals as a figure for the four empires that would succeed Nebuchadnezzar's own (Dan 2.39). Jerome's commentary on *Daniel* (which is bound with the *Rou* in this manuscript) identified these empires as those of Babylon, Persia, (Alexander's) Macedonia and Rome; and the transfer of political power between these empires became embedded in medieval apocalyptic tradition through the motif of the *translatio imperii et studii* (which stood for the shift of political power and knowledge from the East to the West, and with which authors as diverse as Otto of Friesing and Chrétien de Troyes engaged in the twelfth century). Nebuchadnezzar, therefore, was closely associated with the transience and transformation of worldly power, an association that Wace emphasises by describing the fate of the golden statue that Nebuchadnezzar had erected as a symbol of his power (Dan 3.1–11) shortly before he was driven from human society (Dan 4.30).

103–6 **par les bons clers ki escristrent . . . oevres plusurs cunter** Wace again emphasises the role of literate clerks in preserving the memory of the past.

104 **E les gestes as livres mistrent** Wace formulates clerks' relationship with historical writing here in a strikingly material way: clerks are responsible for putting accounts of deeds (*gestes*) into book form. See also vv. 141, 149.

107–30 **Alisandre . . . Cesar . . . esté** Henry of Huntingdon's treatise on contempt for the world, which is appended to his *Historia Anglorum* and circulated in Normandy in Wace's day, also uses Alexander and Caesar as figures for the fleetingness and fragility of worldly power (Greenway 1996, 616–17).

122 **ne out . . . lungur** The precise sense of this clause is unclear – but *lungur* seems to refer to the length of Alexander's and Caesar's graves: see the translations of Burgess (2004, 92) and Taylor (1837, 3).

124 **preie** MS *preies*, which Holden emends to *pris*, counts as one syllable here

125–7 **Ne mais tant . . . truvé lisant** The precise sense of the French is obscure here, and might be literally rendered 'People only [know] as much about what Alexander and Caesar were from what they find reading'.

131–42 **Tute rien . . . vivre** The trope of the world in decline is common in high-medieval historical writing, but is especially associated with the work of Henry of Huntingdon (see esp. Greenway 1996, 583–619). See also *Mohun Chronicle* (42, 14–19). Here Wace uses it to drive home the importance of written memorial technology – and consequently the role of literate clerks – to contemporary memorial culture.

145–6 **gestes escriveient . . . estoires treiteient** It is not clear whether *estoire* and *geste* were entirely semantically distinct in this period. R. H. Bloch suggested that Wace 'did not distinguish' between these 'synonyms' (1983, 98–9), but Damian-Grint argues strongly that *estoire* and *geste* have quite different referents as well as 'close links with one another and with historiography' (Damian-Grint 1997, 191). Wace did not always use these words consistently, however: here, for example, *gestes* are explicitly figured as written texts, while *estoires* seem less grounded in a specific written form. Elsewhere Wace inverts these positions and uses *estoire* specifically to mean written history (see e.g. Holden 1970, 1:87, v. 2151; 2:59, v. 4620) and *geste* to mean 'account' or 'tale' (see e.g. Holden 1970

1:4, v. 43; 1:60, v. 1360). Given Wace's different uses, it is hard to assign a stable single definition more specific than 'narrative account' (written or otherwise) to either term.

149 **Pur mettre lur nuns en estoire** Perhaps a further example of Wace's materialistic conception of clerical work: it was the duty of the clerk physically to enter names into the historical record. However, given the ambiguity of the word *estoire* – (both 'a history book' and 'a historical narrative'), the phrase could also be translated as 'to include their names in their narratives'.

152 **translater** As Damian-Grint notes, 'there is little evidence in historiographical texts of the period for a meaning of *translater* equivalent to the modern "translate". Normally, *translater* refers rather to a process of adaptation by which a text is "changed" or "moved" for the benefit of a particular audience . . . A shift from one language to another may also form a part of the process of interpretation; but such a transfer is not a primary nor even a necessary part of what the task of *translater* means' (1999, 34–4).

153 **rumanz e serventeis** *Rumanz* had the sense 'French narrative', and was not necessarily associated with the genre identified today as romance. It is being opposed to *serventeis* here because the latter were short lyrics, rather than long narrative poems.

174 **Baïeus** Tréma added to make a regular octosyllable. Holden emends to *Baieues* on the basis of MS B (C has *Baieux*, D *Baiex*).

179 **treis reis Henriz** The third king Henry is Henry the Young King, son of Henry II. The fact that the Young King appears as a king and apparently still alive at this point has been used to date the *Rou* (he was crowned in 1170 and died in 1183). Wace's claim that he 'knew and saw' three king Henries has been used to fix his own birth after Henry I's accession in 1100.

182 **rei** MS *reis* with *s* expuncted.

183 **Engleterre la guarnie** *Guarnie* could be translated as 'rich, well provisioned', and there was a longstanding historiographical tradition emphasising the fertility and richness of England: see *Description of Britain* (1). However, *garnir* has military overtones, and Wace may have been commenting on war-readiness in England in the early 1170s (which saw open warfare between supporters of Henry II and Henry the Young King, and the invasion of Northumberland by the king of the Scots; see e.g. Jordan Fantosme's verse *Chronicle*, Dean 55).

4. Hue de Rotelande, *Ipomedon* [Dean 162], Prologue: London, British Library, MS Cotton Vespasian A.VII, f. 39r

Date of composition and provenance. About 1180, near Hereford.

Author, sources and nature of text. The birthplace of Hue de Rotelande was likely Rhuddlan, site of a Norman castle on a river inlet on the north coast of Wales. What we know of Hue is gleaned from details mentioned in his two verse romances, *Ipomedon* (10,580 lines) and its sequel *Protheselaus* (12,740 lines). In *Ipomedon* Hue refers to his house at Credenhill, just outside Hereford, and implies a close acquaintance with Walter Map, a well-known writer also active at Hereford (see further (38), Simund de Freine). Hue also mentions historical events such as the siege of Rouen by Louis VII in 1174, and the resistance to the Norman invaders by the Welsh king Rhys ap Gruffydd, active in the period 1155–97. Hue dedicates *Protheselaus*, a romance set in Sicily (also a Norman kingdom), to Gilbert Fitzbaderon, fourth lord of Monmouth, who died in 1191. Although his poems show him as actively engaged with the courtly and monastic culture of Hereford, no mention of Hue is found in writing by his contemporaries.

4. Hue de Rotelande, Ipomedon

Ipomedon is set in southern Italy, and Hue draws the names of his characters from the *romans antiques*, such as the *Roman de Thèbes* and the *Roman d'Énéas*; the main theme, however, is the exploration of courtly love, using the literary conventions of the *roman arthurien*. La Fière, the princess who rules Calabria, is courted for seven years by Ipomedon, son of the king of Apulia, who adopts a series of disguises to hide his identity, but inexplicably refuses repeatedly to reveal himself to his beloved despite having won the right to do so.

What sets *Ipomedon* apart from other courtly romances, however, is that Hue de Rotelande both exploits the courtly romance conventions, and subverts them in a burlesque version of romance traditions. Hue's approach is essentially parodic and comedic, ranging from subtle irony to surprisingly obscene narrative asides. An example is the contrast between Hue's prologue and epilogue. The latter is an obvious parody of the epilogue of Thomas's *Tristan*, addressed as a greeting to courtly lovers. Hue's epilogue begins as a courtly envoi, but quickly modulates into a louche invitation for sexual dalliance to any woman, rich widow or virgin maiden, brave enough to visit him alone in his house (vv. 10,559–80).

With this final image, the audience, and the narrator, find themselves far removed from the serious and conventional tone of Hue's prologue. But re-read in light of the complete poem, the narrator's seemingly conventional stance in the prologue becomes more complicated. The prologue has two main themes: the clerical duty to share one's wisdom or learning for the benefit of all, not to hide the light of learning under a bushel; and, following from this, the obvious need to write in the vernacular, to address the largest audience possible. The terms used, however, take on multiple meanings: the narrator professes to set aside *folie* (6, 7, 14) and *enveisure* (3) in favour of *sens* (6, 8, 15, 19, 47), *grans biens* (2, 12) and remaining *sage* (9, 21). But what is the meaning of *sens*, a term well-known from Chrétien de Troyes's prologues (and much discussed by modern critics)? In hindsight, in *Ipomedon* it expands from 'wisdom' to the 'meaning of the narrative' itself and the 'artistic intention' of the author, to his (and his character's) 'manipulative intelligence' which plays with the narrator's relationship to the audience and to literary conventions. *Folie* likewise takes on new meaning, for the greatest good (*grans biens*) includes embracing comedy (*enveisure*) and the wisdom of the fool who exposes the reality behind appearances and courtly conventions. Similarly, references to Hue's Latin source (which he asserts to be surprisingly overlooked by other clerics), and the technical difficulties of translating into French, while on the surface reflecting linguistic reality, are also ironic. This is made clear in the first part of the epilogue in which Hue improbably claims (vv. 10,541–2: *De ceste estorie, ke ai ci faite, / Est cele de Tebes estraite*) that the *Roman de Thèbes* is based on his own *Ipomedon* (when the reverse is partially true, since Hue borrows the exotic elements of his tale from the *Roman de Thèbes*): what better way to underline the fact that his Latin source is a fiction, making all the more ironic his repeated insistence in the prologue that he will shorten his source (31, 42, 44) to avoid boring his audience.

Hue's audacious invocation of a Latin *auctoritas* for his comic tale, a *grant ovre* (43) which he is translating into French, and his assertion that he will only amplify the truth while remaining concise, serve to emphasise his enjoyment of the skilful manipulation of language, and his mastery of *biau motz* in the vernacular.

Audience and circulation. *Ipomedon* is extant in three manuscript copies (London, BL Cotton Vespasian A.VII, mid-fourteenth century; BL Egerton 2515, early fourteenth century; Dublin, Trinity College 523, mid-fourteenth century) and two fragments (Oxford, Bodleian Rawlinson Miscellanea D 913; private collection; see Livingston 1942), all of English origin, with the exception of one fragment (Livingston 1942) which suggests it also circulated on the Continent. As mentioned above, no references to Hue de Rotelande are known in the work of his contemporaries. The later popularity of *Ipomedon* in England is attested, however, by the three Middle English adaptations extant, and Wolfram von Eschenbach knew either the original French or the later English versions.

Manuscript source. The prologue edited below is from BL Cotton Vespasian A.VII, mid-fourteenth century, 107 folios, 230 × 150 mm, written in two columns of thirty-eight lines. The manuscript contains Guillaume le Clerc de Normandie's *Bestiaire* (ff. 2–33: (17)), the *Vision de saint Paul* by Adam de Ross (ff. 34–8), *Ipomedon* (ff. 39–106^{r}). F. 106^{v} has a list of the nobles present at the signing of the Treaty of Calais (24 Oct. 1360) by Jean II of France and Edward III, confirming the earlier Treaty of Brétigny. This ended the first phase of the Hundred Years' War. There is also a list of cities and lands ceded to Edward III by France.

Bibliography. The first edition (Kölbing 1889) is superseded by Holden's *Ipomedon* 1979, which has a useful critical introduction (7–61); see also the introduction to *Protheselaus*, Holden 1993. Holden analyses critical judgements of *Ipomedon*, and details the techniques used by Hue to make this an entertaining work that both exploits and undercuts the literary conventions of Arthurian romance. Holden discounts Legge's attempt to link Hue's work to specific dynastic marriages (Legge 1971, 86). *Ipomedon* has long attracted critical attention; Ménard 1969 (336–53 and passim) makes frequent references to it in his discussion of comic elements in medieval French romance. Thaon 1983 and Meale 1984 examine the Middle English descendants of *Ipomedon*, and see Part VI, §2.1. Among the many studies of Hue's narrative technique, Hanning 1974 is a fundamental analysis of narrative ambiguity in *Ipomedon*; Krueger 1987, 1990, Eley 2000, and Kay 2001 (65–7 and passim) extend the study of Hue's manipulation of narrative devices and of reader's expectations, and his problematic use of misogyny. On Hue as parodist see further Calin 1988 who analyses the gap between appearance and reality opened by parody; Hue uses language to demonstrate both the clerkly narrator's mastery of *sapientia* and the hero's dominance in knighly *fortitudo*. In a study of the courtly and monastic culture of Hereford, Cartlidge 2011 reviews much recent criticism of Hue's work, and examines the cultural links between Hue and Walter Map (writing in Latin), demonstrating their shared predilection for risky narrative irony which both unsettles and exhilarates the audience. On medieval perceptions of Hue as interpreted from the manuscripts of his works, see Busby 2002, vol. 2, 498.

TEXT AND TRANSLATION

Qui [a] bons countes voet entendre
Sovent il poet grans biens aprendre;
Par escuter [les] enveisures
Et retrere les aventures
Ke avyndrent a l'ancien tens
Poet l'en oÿr folie e sens.
Or lessums folie la ester
Kar de sens fet mult bien parler.
N'est de tut povre ki est sage,
Mes les uns sont de tel corage
Ne vodr[e]ient pur nule rien
Ke l'en s[e]ust par eus nul bien.
Ki si covertement se tient,
[Il] m'est avis ke fous devient,
Kar sun grant sens que lui vaudra
Kant de cest siecle departira?
Ja de cel jor n'ert mes retret

The person who wishes to be attentive to good stories can often learn much that is worthwhile. Listening to amusing tales or the recounting of events that happened long ago opens our ears both to wisdom and to folly. But let us leave folly aside for now, for it is much better to speak of wisdom. He who has wisdom is not at all poor, but there are some wise people who by disposition would not wish, at any cost, for anyone to learn good from them. In my view, anyone who behaves so secretively is foolish, for what will his great wisdom profit him when he leaves this world? His wisdom will never be spoken of after that day, if he has not done something worthy in the name of God. No-one knows where his wisdom goes, for neither he nor

Si pur Deu n'ad aucun bien fet.
Cil sen devient l'en ne seit ou,
Kar il ne autre n'avera ja pru.
  Moult me mervail de ces clers sages
Ky entendent plusurs langages,
K'il ont lesse[e] ceste estorie,
Ke nus ne ou[s]t en memorie.
Ne di pas q[e] il bien ne dit
Cil qi en latin l'ad descrit.
Mes plus i ad leis ke lettrez:
Si li latin n'est translatez
Gaires n'i erent entendanz.
Por ceo voil dire en romanz,
A plus brefment que jeo savrai,
Si entendrunt [e] clerc e lai.
Hue de Rotelande vus dit,
Ky cest' estorie vous descrit:
Ky de latin velt romanz fere,
Ne lui deit l'em a mal retrere
S'il ne poet tuz des oelz garder,
De tut en tut lé tens former.
Mes por hastiver la matire [f. 39rb]
Nos estovra par biau motz dire:
Fors la verrour n'y acrestrai,
Dirai brefment ceo que jeo en sai.
Ke grant ovre voet translater
Brefment l'estuet ou[t]re passer,
Ou si ceo noun, trop s'anoieront
Cil ki de oïr talent avront.
Ne voil tut mon sen celer mes,
Or m'escotez, si aiez pes!

anyone else will ever benefit from it.

I am amazed that these wise clerks who understand several languages have let this story go, so that no-one has related or written it. I do not say that the person who set it down in Latin did not recount it well. But there are more lay people than there are educated people: if the Latin tale is not translated, there will be very few to understand it. For this reason I wish to relate it in French, as briefly as I can, so that both clerics and laypeople will understand it. Hugh of Rutland, who wrote this narrative for us, states: 'when a person chooses to translate from Latin into French, he should not be criticised if he can not keep all the equivalences in both languages, or completely respect the tenses. But in order to move the story along, I must write with fine words; I will amplify only the truth, and what I know of it I will write succinctly. Anyone who wishes to translate a great work must treat his material with concision, for if he does not, those who want to listen to his narrative will be bored. I do not want to keep all my meaning hidden any longer: be silent now, and listen to me!'

Notes

Rejected readings: 4 *Est* 7 *Ore* 31 *brevement* 42 *brefuement* 44 *Refuement* 48 *Ore*

1 **[a]** The verbe *entendre*, in the sense 'pay attention to, be attentive to' is normally followed by the preposition *a* before the complement of the verb, and this emendation creates a regular octosyllable.

3 **[les]** This emendation emphasises the parallelism between *les enveisures* and *les aventures*, both of which occurred in times past, and are equally sources of both *folie* and *sen*. Holden (1979) emends the line by adding a syllable to *enveiseüres*.

7 **folie la ester** Holden (1979) emends: *la folie ester*; we leave the adverb *la* 'there' placed before the infinitive which it qualifies; the line would still be octosyllabic if the scribe reads *folie* with the final *–e* effaced.

11–12 **vodr[e]ient; s[e]ust** Verbal forms are frequently reduced in spelling. Here the conditional of *voleir* (expressing habitual action in the future in the past) and the imperfect subjunctive of *saveir* (expressing the hypothetical action in a noun clause dependent on a verb of volition, *vodreient*) are restored to their traditional forms.

16 **de cest siecle departira** The line is made octosyllabic by emending to remove the prefix of *departira*, or by effacing the final *-e* of *siecle*; Holden (1979) emends by removing *cest*.

24 **ou[s]t** We read as the imperfect subjunctive of *aveir*, dependent on the principal verb *me mervail*, v. 22 ('I am amazed . . . that no-one has kept it alive, retold it').

33–4 **Hue de Rotelande vus dit, Ky cest' estorie vous descrit** Both *vus* and *vous* have an ambivalent initial letter in the manuscript, which could be either *v* or *n*. Where we read *vus* and *vous*, Holden in his 1979 edition reads *nus* and *nous*, which effectively turns vv. 33–4 into an aside made by the copyist, intercalated into the narrative of the author/narrator Hue (who at vv. 30–1 says he will recount his vernacular tale briefly, a theme he takes up again at v. 39 ff.). Reading *vus* and *vous* in vv. 33–4 keeps them as part of the narrator's voice, a direct address to the audience by Hue, similar to the direct command he gives to the audience in the final line of the prologue, v. 48.

35–8 **Ky de latin . . . lé tens former** a reminder that the vernacular has simplified and reduced Latin tenses, with perhaps an allusion to the Nun of Barking's earlier, similarly sophisticated comments on language (**2**, vv. 1–6).

37–8 **tuz des oelz garder; lé tens former** Holden (1979) emends *tuz ses cas garder*; the phrase *tuz des oelz* could be read as a substantival use of the plural adjective *oelz*, meaning 'all of the equals, all of the equivalencies' with reference to the French words equivalent to the Latin words in his (putative) source: i.e. the translator has to shape his material appropriately in French, rather than attempting to give a direct equivalent in French for all the Latin terms.

39–46 **hastiver la matire . . . ou[t]re passer . . . de oïr talent avront** Hue is referring to the standard rhetorical practices of both abbreviating and amplifying Latin source material when translating into French, in order to keep the interest of his audience. He will 'urge his story along, keep up the pace' by passing over some details in Latin, to keep alive his audience's wish to listen to his story.

41 **Fors** MS *ffors*. Double *f* at the beginning of a word is a special form of majuscule *f* (Derolez 2006, 88).

47 **Ne voil tut mon sen celer mes** (he will cast aside false modesty, and show his skill) Another reference to standard rhetorical theory, in which exegesis is needed to make evident the meaning hidden in metaphorical language. Here Hue asserts he is writing plainly in the vernacular, in which the meaning will be obvious to all (but as noted above, this is not the case: his rhetorical stance in the vernacular is also designed to make interpretation difficult). On the expanded sense of *sen*, see the headnote.

5. Robert Grosseteste, *Le Chasteau d'amour* [Dean 622], Prologue: Princeton University Library, Taylor Medieval MS 1, ff. 172^{v}–173^{v}

Date of composition and provenance. 1230–53, perhaps at Oxford in the 1230s.

Author, sources and nature of text. Robert Grosseteste (*c.* 1168–1253), theologian, scholar and philosopher, wrote a large and erudite body of texts during a distinguished career as an intellectual with a particular concern for pastoral care. Born into a poor family, Grosseteste rose to become the chancellor of a young Oxford and, in the year 1235, the bishop of Lincoln. His vernacular works include a treatise on estate management addressed to the countess of Lincoln (*Les Reules*, Dean 392: subsequently also translated into Latin) and a prose prayer to his own patron saint, Margaret

(Dean 937): a prose prayer for after meals is also attributed to him (Dean 859). Although never canonised, he is frequently referred to as 'Seynt Roberd' in manuscript texts, where his authority is often borrowed for works not certainly by him and also for works very unlikely to be by him (such as *Le Miracle de Sardenai* (**34**)). Grosseteste's reputation remained high in Middle English works: as late as Wynkyn de Worde's 1508 print of the *Husbandry* treatise on estate management, 'mayster Groshede' is credited with translating the text 'out of frensshe and in to Englysshe'. Grosseteste's scientific and philosophical works and most of his theological works are in scholastic Latin: he also wrote in Latin to his sister Ivetta (her letters and replies seem not to have survived).

The *Chasteau d'amour* is a Christian theological allegory written in the vernacular so that, the prologue says, readers without Hebrew, Greek or Latin can access the praise of God. The poem is written in the typically Anglo-Norman mixture of octosyllabic and heptasyllabic rhymed couplets, with occasional shorter lines. It has no single source, but combines motifs from wide reading. Two of the text's main motifs, the Four Daughters of God (Mercy, Truth, Justice and Peace; see Ps 84.11) and the Castle of Love (the Virgin Mary embodied as fortress) have important analogues in French and Middle English. The Four Daughters allegory appears in another verse allegory (Dean 685), Jewish commentaries and Latin sermons of the twelfth century (Boulton 2013, 10) and later in Langland's *Piers Plowman*. The vernacular title *Chasteau d'amour* is not found in the extant manuscripts (Leland seems to have been the first to use it: Mackie 2003, 157) and the Latin rubric found in the manuscript used here (as in most manuscripts of the complete copies of the poem) gives a better idea of the text's scope as a treatise on fall and redemption. The *Chasteau* was famously pronounced to be Grosseteste's vernacular *summa* by Sir Richard Southern, and its allegory of the Virgin is part of a much more inclusive treatment of fundamental theological issues and doctrines.

Audience and circulation. Legge proposed that Grosseteste wrote the *Chasteau* to educate the sons of Simon de Montfort (Legge 1950, 100–1), two of whom were brought up in Grosseteste's episcopal household, but Mackie's earlier dating of the *Chasteau* challenges this, and she suggests the Franciscans at Oxford during Grosseteste's lectorship there as a more likely audience for Grosseteste in the 1230s (Mackie 2003, 154–5). Like many texts, the *Chasteau* circulated among both those with a professional interest in pastoral care and their lay constituents, and Franciscans studying at Oxford might well have found such a 'vernacular *summa*' valuable and useful, as did other religious and laypeople. Eighteen extant manuscripts suggest the importance of the text: copies were owned by Augustinian, Benedictine, Cistercian, Premonstatensian, and Carmelite houses and the female Fontevrauld community at Nuneaton, as well as by elite laypeople (Mackie 2003, 154 n. 17: Marx 1995, 160–8). Two manuscripts have scholastic annotations in Latin (Boulton 2013, 10). Lay persons owned several of these manuscripts. The Taylor manuscript used here belonged to Baroness Joan de Tateshal, while Margaret of York (1446–1503, sister of Edward IV) probably owned Brussels Bib. Roy. de Belgique MS 2806, a fifteenth-century copy of the French *Chasteau*. Manuscripts of the Anglo-Norman text are largely thirteenth century, but continued to be produced in the fourteenth and the fifteenth centuries, alongside the six fourteenth- and fifteenth-century Middle English versions of the text. The *Chasteau* gave non-Latinate readers, especially women, access to complex theological thought and the manuscript circulation suggests demand for such access.

Manuscript source. Princeton University Library, Taylor Medieval MS 1, formerly Phillips 2223, ff. 172*v*–173*v*. Taylor MS 1 was composed probably during or after the year 1280, as a miscellany for Baroness Joan de Tateshal, d. 1310. Tateshal appears twice in the manuscript's illustrations, once in her father's heraldic clothing beside a much smaller scribe at the head of her manuscript's *Manuel des pechiez* (http://ica.princeton.edu/images/princeton/t1.001r.jpg (and see (**24b**)), and once in her husband's heraldry on f. 173*r*, at the opening of the French text edited here, where she stands beside Grosseteste (http://pudl.princeton.edu/objects/tq57ns412). The convention of miniaturising the patron figure has not been adopted: Joan de Tateshal and Grosseteste are of similar height: they thus appear as co-sponsors of the French text.

The book's first text is the *Manuel des pechiez* (**24b**), a confessor's manual from which the exempla are collected together in the manuscript. There are three further Anglo-Norman texts: the verse *Roman des romans* (Dean 601), the prose *Plainte de la Vierge* (Dean 955; Bliss, Hunt, Leyser 2012, no. 6) and part of Sully's homily on the Pater noster (Dean 587). Taylor MS 1 forms a volume of vernacular religious education accessible to a female lay reader and is witness to the close relation of elite women and clerics in the production of vernacular pastoralia. The manuscript is 245 × 125 mm, narrow and easily portable. Bennett 1990 connects its shape with the *Manuel*'s prologue: 'It is called the Manual / because it should be held in the hand' (*Le* Manuel *est apelé / car en mein deit ester porté* (**24b**, vv. 41–2).

BIBLIOGRAPHY. *Le Chasteau d'amour* has been edited by Cooke 1852, repr. 1967; Murray 1918; and by Mackie 2002 in a Toronto thesis. The *Chasteau* is translated by Mackie 2003 and translated with a substantial introduction in Boulton 2013. For editions and discussion of the Middle English versions see Sajavaara 1967 (for the Vernon Middle English version, see Part VI, §2.2). On the provenances of *Chasteau* manuscripts see Mackie 2003 (154 n. 17), Marx 1995 (160–8). Bennett 1990 provides a comprehensive study of Taylor MS 1 and its patron, Joan de Tateshal: see also Kumler 2011, 45–6: the manuscript is described and some folios reproduced in colour in Skemer *et al.* 2013, 399–404, pl. 80–4 and digitised in its entirety at http://pudl.princeton.edu/objects/tq57ns412. Marx 1995 is an important study of the theology of the Devil's rights, with extensive treatment of the *Chasteau*. Whitehead 2000 discusses the implications of Mary as castle. Hunt 1982 traces the topos of the Four Daughters of God of which the *Chasteau* makes important use (as does Langland in his *Piers Plowman*: see further Marx 1995). For Grosseteste's life and works see McEvoy 2000; Southern 1992, repr. of 1986, is a charismatic, more controversial biography. On manuscript images and author portraits of Grosseteste see Bennett 1990. Maddicott 1994's study of Simon de Montfort situates Grosseteste in the circle of de Montfort associates (on his friendship with Eleanor and Simon de Montfort see 40–4). *The Electronic Grosseteste*, at www.grosseteste.com, provides full-text versions of many of Grosseteste's Latin works. For Grosseteste's letters to his sister, see Luard 1861, 43–5, Goering and Mantello 2010. For French works attributed to Grosseteste see Dean 660, 662, 670 (on confession); Dean 646 (prose treatise on the pains of Purgatory); Dean 686 (allegorical verse treatise, *Le Mariage des neuf filles du diable*).

TEXT AND TRANSLATION

[Rubric]

[f. 172*v*] Cest un treitiz que seint Robert fist eveske de Nichole, si est apelé le romanz des [*erasure*]. Il est bons, li nouns est granz: en cest treitiz pouit em trover quantque a l'ame est mester. *Hic incipit quidam tractatus in lingua romana secundum dominum Robertum Grosseteste episcopum Lincolme: De principio creationis mundi. De medio et fine. De amissione mundi per peccatum. De restauratione eiusdem per misericordiam. De rege et filio suo unico patri suo equali. De quatuor filiabus regis, scilicet de misericordia et veritate, de justitia et pace. Item: De adventu Jhesu Christi,*

This is a treatise made by St Robert, bishop of Lincoln, and it is called the romance of [erasure]. It is good and the name is illustrious: in this treatise one can find whatever is needed for the soul. *Here begins a treatise in the French tongue by Lord Robert Grosseteste, bishop of Lincoln, about the creation of the world, its beginning and end; of the loss of the world through sin and its restoration through mercy, with the king and the only Son of the Father, his equal; and of the four daughters of the king, namely Mercy and Truth, Justice and Peace. It also treats the coming of Jesus Christ: how Jesus Christ entered into a certain castle*

quomodo Jhesu Cristus intravit in quoddam castellum quod fuit corpus virginis. Et de proprietate castelli. Item: De propheta Ysaia dicente, 'Puer natus est nobis, et filius datus est nobis, cuius imperium super humerum eius, et vocabitur nomen eius admirabilis, consiliarius, deus fortis, pater futuri seculi, princeps pacis'. Quomodo fuit admirabilis, quomodo consiliarius, quomodo deus, quomodo fortis, quomodo pater futuri seculi, quomodo princeps pacis. Item: De fine seculi et de die judicii. Item: De penis inferni et de gaudio celi. Et quamvis lingua romana coram clericis saporem suavitatis non habeat, tamen pro laicis qui minus intelligunt, opusculum istud aptum est. Quia prudens lector qui novit suggere mel de petra oleumque de saxo durissimo scriptum inveniet plenum dulcedine, in quo continentur omnes articuli fidei tam divinitatis quam humanitatis.

which was the body of the Virgin; and about the properties of the castle. It also treats the prophet Isaiah's prophecy. 'Unto us a child is born, a son is given and the government shall be upon his shoulders, and his name shall be called Marvellous, Counsellor, Almighty God, Father of future ages, Prince of Peace'. In what way he was admirable. How he was counsellor. How he was God. How he was mighty. How he was father of the future ages and how he was prince of peace. It treats the end of time and the day of Judgement; it treats the pains of hell and the joy of heaven. And although the romance tongue does not have a pleasing savour to clerics, this little work is nevertheless appropriate for lay people, who know less. For the prudent reader, who knows how to draw sweetness from stone and oil from the hardest rock, may find the written text, which contains every article of faith both of divinity and of humanity, full of sweetness.

[Prologue]

Qui bien pense bien puet dire: [f. 173r]
Sanz penser ne puet suffire
De nul bon overe comencer.
Deu nus doint de lui penser
De qui, par qui, en qui sunt
Tuz les biens que sunt el mund,
Deu le Pere e Deu le Fiz
E Deu li Seint Esperiz,
Persones treis en trinité
E un soul Deu en unité,
Sanz fin e sanz commencement,
A qui honour e gloire apent.
Il nus doint ses ovres fere
E nus defende de contraire.

Whoever thinks well can speak well, and without thought one cannot be prepared to do any good work. May God grant that we think about him, from whom, through whom, in whom are all the good things that there are in the world: God the Father and God the Son and God the Holy Spirit, three persons in trinity and one God alone in unity, without end and without beginning, to whom honour and glory belong. May he grant that we do his works and may he keep us from harm.

Touz avom mester de aÿe,
Mes trestouz ne porront mie
Saver le langage en fin
De ebreu, de gru, ne de latin
Pur loer lor creatur.
Ne bouche de chanteur
Ne seit clos de Deu loer
E son seint noun nuncier!
Ke chescun en son langage

We all have need of help, and not everyone can know the languages of Hebrew, Greek or Latin, in order to praise their creator. Let not the mouth of any singer be kept from praising God, nor from declaring his holy name. So that each in his language may truly know his God and his redemption, I begin my discourse in the vernacular, for those who do not have any Latin or learning.

Le conoise sanz folage
Son Deu e sa redemption,
En romanz commence ma reison,
Pur ceus qui ne sevent mie
Ne lettrure ne clergie.

De principio creationis mundi

Del mond dirai pur quoi fu feit,
E pus coment donez esteit
A Adam nostre primer pere,
E parais en teu manere,
O tant de joie, o tant duçur,
E puis le ciel a chef de tur:
E pus coment fu perdu
Pus restorez e pus rendu. [f. 173^{v}]
Asez sovent oï avez
Coment le mond fu fez;
Pur ceo ne voil pas descrire
Fors ceo ke apent a ma matire,
Car en six jurs Deu tut crea
E au setime se reposa.

About the beginning of the creation of the world

I will speak about the world and why it was made, and then how it was given to Adam our first father, and paradise in the same way, with so much joy and honour and then heaven in the end: and how it was afterwards lost, then restored and given back. You have heard often enough how the world was created: for this reason I don't want to describe anything except what belongs to my subject matter – because God created everything in six days and on the seventh, he rested.

Notes

(*Note*: this entry was initially edited as part of an MA project by our student Andrea Lankin: we thank her for her work.)

R2–3 The scribe seems to have repeated *romanz de[s romans]*, the title of a work (see Dean 601) from elsewhere in the manuscript, erased it and then to have omitted to supply a title. Mackie points out that though the phrase *chasteu d'amur* occurs in the text, no vernacular title exists in any of the manuscripts: she suggests 'The Loss and Restoration of the Creation' (Mackie 2003, 157).

R7 ***De principio creationis mundi*** Grosseteste also wrote an entire treatise on the Hexameron, see Martin 1996.

R12 ***De quatuor filiabus regis*** (the Four Daughters of God). Derived from the four virtues of Ps 84.11; see Marx 1995.

R15 ***intravit*** … ***castellum*** Luke 10.38 Jesus's entry into Bethany, often interpreted figuratively as the Incarnation.

R17 ***De propheta Ysaia dicente*** Isa 9.6.

R28 ***saporem suavitatis*** On the importance of sweetness as an aesthetic and experiential criterion, see Carruthers 2006.

R31 ***suggere mel de petra oleumque de saxo durissimo*** Deut 32.13, influentially used by St Bernard of Clairvaux in Sermon 61 on the Song of Songs and elsewhere.

R33–4 ***omnes articuli fidei*** The articles of the faith had been declared (at Lateran IV in 1215 and at the Council of Oxford in 1222) as what all Christian parishioners ought to know and hence needed to be taught.

1–4 **Qui bien pense … penser** The obligation to communicate knowledge is a frequent topos; see e.g. Guillame le Clerc's *Le Bestiaire divin* (**17**), Adgar's *Gracial* (**11a**), Angier's *Dialogues* (**24a**).

16–19 See the prologue of Robert of Greatham's *Miroir* (**14**, vv. 79–88), for another discussion of the use of the vernacular for lay readers.

18 **ebreu . . . gru . . . latin** The three *linguae sacrae* in the titulus on Christ's cross. Grosseteste famously took pains to acquire some Greek himself (Southern 1992). Hebrew was an important language of commentary for medieval biblical scholars from Jerome's *Nomina hebraica* onwards.

20–1 **Ke bouche de chanteur . . . Deu loer** A close reminiscence of Esther 13.17. Southern (1992, 225) believes the *Chasteau* might have been sung rather than read, but see Mackie 2003, 155.

26 **commence** is either 1st or 3rd person present active indicative. The sentence could also be translated 'In the vernacular my argument begins'.

32–4 **parais . . . ciel** Both terms have specific and different meanings: *parais* refers to the garden of Eden, while *ciel* is heaven proper (*AND*, *s.v.* 'parais, paradis'; 'ciel'). See further McDannell and Lang 1988; Scafi 2006.

6. *Waldef* [Dean 155], Prologue: Cologny-Geneva, Fondation Martin Bodmer, MS Bodmer 168, f. 1*r*–*v*

Henry Bainton

Date of composition and provenance. *c.* 1190 x *c.* 1210.

Author, sources and nature of text. The author's identity is unknown. *Waldef* was written for an unnamed woman: the author translated the English *estoire* for his *douce amie*, he says, so that she could read and learn it (v. 81). The implication is that, like many high-status women in this period, *Waldef*'s dedicatee could read French, even if she could not read pre-Conquest English: by positioning himself as the polyglot mediator between an English text and a literate and francophone patroness, *Waldef*'s author undertakes a manoeuvre similar to Gaimar's in the *Estoire des Engleis* (**10**). But unlike Gaimar, the poet refuses to name himself or to reveal the name of his patroness in his prologue, although he promises to do so should he finish the work. The sole extant manuscript is incomplete, however (and although the fifteenth-century Thetford monk Johannes Bramis had access to a more complete version of the poem when he translated *Waldef*, his Latin text does not name the author or patron either). There is a possibility that the author was connected to Crowland Abbey – which was guardian of the cults of Waltheof and Guthlac – but the only evidence for this connection lies in the poem's invocation of these famous names from English history. *Waldef* and similar texts certainly had a monastic circulation (see below), but a clerical author in the service of a particular family is also a possibility.

The *Waldef* author claims that his poem of some 24,000 lines is a reworking of an English *estoire* popular among the English before the Norman Conquest (vv. 33–8). He suggests that such *gestes* and *estoires* had been translated because the peoples and languages of England changed following the Norman Conquest (vv. 43–53). He thereby implies that he is revivifying the memorial practices of the pre-Conquest *anciens*, who would listen to, and remember (*recorder*; vv. 34, 61) *gestes* about their *aventures* (vv. 53–7). *Waldef* insinuates that the English *gestes*, no longer intelligible to the francophone ruling elite of England, risked falling into oblivion if not kept alive through translation and retelling. There is, however, no suggestion here that English historiography was somehow suppressed by the Normans before being rescued by their descendants once they had 'adopted' an English identity themselves (for such a view of *Waldef*'s purposes, see e.g. Thomas 2003, 355–6, 386–9).

The *Roman de Waldef* recounts the exploits of Waldef, a legendary post-Roman king of Norfolk, and the adventures of his sons, Gudlac and Guiac. Chronologically and topographically ambitious, the poem is set in the years following the Roman occupation of Britain and narrates what happens when 'King Bede' and his son Waldef undergo exile. It tracks the fate of Waldef's sons Guiac and Gudlac, brought up at the courts of the king of Cologne and Morocco, and not re-united until they chance to encounter each other marching towards Grimsby with their armies of German and Danish followers. Eventually the brothers conquer Greece and Rome; Gudlac rules Saxony, and Guiac is elected German emperor but ends by renouncing his crown and worldly goods. The poem breaks off as Gudlac returns to England to recover his family's lands.

If an English version of *Waldef* ever existed, it is now lost – and *Waldef*'s editor trenchantly argues that by invoking an English source the *Waldef* poet was deploying a common trope of vernacular literature (Holden 1984, 18–20), rather than making a serious claim about the poem's antique authenticity. As for *Waldef*'s numerous other sources and analogues, Field notes that *Waldef's* 'range of reference goes beyond a casual plundering of commonplace motifs', and 'indicates an awareness of a large range of romance material': it 'confirms the cohesion of the Anglo-Norman literary corpus' (2000, 29). *Waldef* alludes to the legends of St Eustace, Apollonius of Tyre, Oedipus, and Hero and Leander – as well as to motifs that occur in the *Seven Sages of Rome* and the *Gesta Romanorum*. It has similarities to the Haveloc legend, Marie de France's *Milun*, *Octavian*, the *Gesta Herewardi*, *Horn*, and the tales of Gawain in the chronicle tradition.

The influence on *Waldef* of Geoffrey of Monmouth's *Historia regum Britanniae* and its vernacular tradition is mostly indirect, but profound. It is apparent in *Waldef*'s vast scale, and also in its temporal and geographical setting in the politically fragmented world of post-Roman *Bretaine* and early Europe. Unlike Gaimar's *Estoire des Engleis*, Wace's *Brut* and other texts in this tradition, however, *Waldef* does not offer founding mythologies of Britain's national communities or show any interest in the 'passage of dominion' from the Romans to the Britons to the English (the audience is referred to the *Brut*, should they wish to hear how the Romans lost their power over Britain, vv. 23–4). *Waldef*'s geographical concerns, by contrast, fluctuate between the intensely local and the global: Waldef's own sphere of influence centres on a cluster of towns lying mid-way along the Roman road from London to Great Yarmouth, but the territories ranged over by his conquering sons – cosmopolitan heroes in the mould of Boeve de Haumtone and Gui de Warewic – stretch from Denmark to Morocco and from France to Greece. England, presented not so much as a nation as a troubled – and troubling – geographical space, occupies the imaginative zone somewhere between the respective worlds of Waldef and his sons. *Waldef*'s England is always already fractured; and in tracing its shifting literary history the romance does little to idealise it as a place in which the post-Conquest elite could secure an imagined past.

AUDIENCE AND CIRCULATION. Apart from the author's claim to be writing for his *duce amie* (v. 75), nothing is known for certain about *Waldef*'s original audience or the work's patronage. *Waldef* is not concerned with the glorification of a single family or institution or their origins, though the romance's focus on the Norfolk-Suffolk border and its account of relations between the petty kings of East Anglia and their neighbours strongly suggests that it was written for a woman from that region. Candidates for *Waldef*'s patronage include the family of Roger Bigod (d. 1221), earl of Norfolk (Legge 1971, 145–6), and the Mortimers of Attleborough (Anderson 1978, 1:290–1). The patronage of Gaimar's *Estoire des Engleis* shows that such works need not have been written for members of the highest nobility, and this opens up a wider field of possibilities for *Waldef*'s audience among lesser noble and gentry circles in East Anglia. *Waldef* circulated beyond the francophone network of its original dedicatee, and like other insular romances, was translated into English at some time before the fifteenth century (Bramis used both an English and a French version of *Waldef* for his *Historia Waldei regis*, but the English version is now lost). Bramis's translation shows that Thetford Priory had access to a copy of *Waldef*, adding to the evidence supplied by monastic library catalogues that monastic and lay tastes in literature in this period converged – and there is a chance that Peterborough Abbey owned a manuscript containing *Waldef* in the late fourteenth century (see Friis-Jensen and Willoughby 2001, 173–4).

MANUSCRIPT SOURCE. Cologny-Geneva, Fondation Martin Bodmer, MS Bodmer 168. The unique manuscript of *Waldef* is a folio written in a professional late thirteenth- or early-fourteenth-century bookhand in two columns throughout the codex. Initials alternate between red and blue, with pen-flourish decorations of the opposite colour. The first column of the first folio has deteriorated, and some words are now illegible. One leaf is missing after f. 124, and f. 125 is bound after f. 118 and f. 119. *Waldef* is followed in the manuscript by *Gui de Warewic* (ff. 134^{r}–210^{v}; Dean 154), and the *chanson de geste, Otinel* (ff. 211^{r}–222^{r}; Dean 78). *Otinel* and *Gui* are written in the same hand as *Waldef*, and decorated in an identical manner. (The presence of *Otinel* in the manuscript, alongside *Gui* and *Waldef*, is a reminder that the audiences and patrons of 'insular' romances such as *Gui* and *Waldef* also had interests in 'continental' epic: see also *La Destruction de Rome* (**18**).) Line drawings of animals and human figures appear in the margins of a few folios, and the names *Margeret* and *Katerine* are written vertically in large capitals in the margins of ff. 188^{v} and 190^{v} respectively, in a medieval hand closely resembling (although not identical with) that of the scribe, and in the same ink as the marginal line drawings. The names *Jane Grey*, *Anne Grey* and *Elizebeth Matsal* appear in a very informal late-medieval hand in the margins of ff. 5^{r}, 207^{v}, and 209. Anderson suggested that *Matsal* is a contraction of Mattishall, a village 16 km from Attleborough (1978–84, 2.220), although the precise relationship between these names and the owner(s) of the manuscript remains obscure. The names do suggest, however, that *Waldef* was associated with a female readership from the time of the poem's composition to that of its subsequent medieval circulation. The *ex libris* of the eighteenth-century binding carries the name of William Fermor of Tusmore in Oxfordshire (d. 1828), and this is the first incontrovertible evidence of the manuscript's ownership. It changed hands twice more before being acquired in 1948 by the Fondation Martin Bodmer in Cologny, where it remains.

BIBLIOGRAPHY. Despite the existence of Holden's edition of *Waldef* (Holden 1984), and Anderson's stimulating survey of *Waldef*'s place in literary history (Anderson 1978–84), the romance is still underrepresented in literary studies. For detailed summaries of *Waldef*'s narrative, see Holden 1984, 7–16; Field 2000, 27–8; Anderson 1978–84, 1.283–6. A translation by Clifton, Djordjevic and Weiss for FRETS is in progress. The date of *Waldef* is discussed in Ham 1935, 178; Anderson 1978–84, 2.217; Holden 1984. For the romance's sources and allusions see Holden 1984, 23–9, Field 2000, 29–31. Field 2000 in a crucial pioneering study makes the case for more research on *Waldef*, and problematises the category of the 'Matter of England' to which *Waldef* has often been assigned. Legge 1971, 144–8 argues for the authenticity of *Waldef*'s claims to early English sources. Weiss 2002 studies *Waldef*'s vision of empire, Field 2004 its use of Arthurian allusion. On romance and *chanson de geste* in England see Short 2007a, esp. 350–61. For a brief treatment of *Waldef* and ethnic identity see Thomas 2003; for a speculative identification with Denis Piramus (**27**), see Anderson 1978–84, 2.216. For the manuscript see http://www.e-codices.unifr.ch/en/list/fmb.

TEXT AND TRANSLATION

En Bretaigne furent jadis [f. 1ra]
Plusurs rois mult poesteis,
Ki devant nus dunc i esteient,
E que les granz honurs teneient.
Bretaigne esteit dunc apelee,
Qu'ore est Engleterre clamee:
Julius Cesar la conquist,
De conquere mult s'entremist.

In Britain there were formerly many very powerful kings who were our predecessors, from whom the great nobles held their fiefs. What is now called England was then called Britain: Julius Caesar conquered it; he made great efforts to do so. Julius was the emperor of Rome; he repeatedly came with a strong army to England to conquer it, because he

Julius de Rome ert emperere;
Suvent avint ové gent fiere
En Engleterre pur conquerre,
Car il desiroit mult la terre.
Od grant esforz i vint suvent
E suvent perdi de sa gent,
Dunt il ot le quor mult iré.
Puis la conquist par poesté
Pa[r] Androgeu, un duc de Kent,
Com le Bruit conte apertement:
Come li Romein la conquistrent,
Combien de tens le treu pristrent,
Com il ierunt suvent vencu,
Com perdirent puis le treu;
Qui l'estoire savoir voldra
Lise le Brut, illoc l'orra.

intensely desired the land. He often came with fierce forces, and he often suffered losses among his men, about which his heart was heavy. Afterwards he conquered Britain by force through Androgeus, a duke of Kent, as the *Brut* clearly relates, telling how the Romans conquered Britain, how long they collected tribute, how they were often defeated, and how they then lost their power to exact tribute. Whoever would like to know the story should read the *Brut*; they will hear it there.

D'une estoire voldrai parler
Ki mult fet bien a escuter;
De verité est tute feite.
Kar des rois englois est estreite:
Com il la terre dunc tenoient,
Cum entr' euls parti l'avoient,
En quel maniere puis la tindrent
E les aventures qu'avindrent.
Ceste estoire est mult amee
E des Englés mult recordee,
Des princes, des ducs e des reis.
Mult iert amee des Engleis,
Des petites genz e des granz,
Desqu'a la prise des Normanz.
Quant li Norman la terre pristrent
Les granz estoires puis remistrent,
Qui en engleis estoient fetes,
Qui des aucuns i erent treites
Pur la gent qui dunc diverserunt [f. 1*rb*]
E les languages si changerunt.
Puis i ad asez translatees,
Qui mult sunt de plusurs amees,
Com est le Bruit, com est Tristram,
Qui tant suffri poine e hahan;
Co[m] est Aelof, li bons rois,
Qui tant en fist des granz desrois.
Ces en sunt, e altres asez
Que vus asez oïr purrez.
Ces gestes, qu'erent en engleis

I would like to speak about a history that is very worthwhile to listen to; it is based entirely on the truth. For it is composed about kings of England: how they used to hold the land, how they divided it between them, how they then ruled it, and what happened. This history is greatly loved, and often recalled, by the English – by princes, by dukes and by kings. It was greatly loved by the English – by the lesser people and the great – until the Normans' conquest. When the Normans took the land, the great histories which had been written in English survived. They were translated by some for the population which at that time changed along with the languages. Lots have been translated since, that are greatly loved by many: such is the *Brut*, such is *Tristan*, who suffered so much pain and hardship; such is *Aelof*, the good king, who fought so well. These are some of them, and there are plenty of others that you can easily hear. These histories, which used to be in English, have been translated into French. Back then the ancients had a very good custom: between them they remembered all the things that happened to them; they committed them to memory, so that those who came after them recounted them many times; they improved many of them.

Translatees sunt en franceis.
Les ancienes ça en ariere
Mult par orent bone manere:
Les aventures que lur avindrent;
Entr' euls tutes bien les retindrent
E en memoire les metoient,
Que cil q[ui] en aprés venoient
Suventes foiz les recorderent;
Plusurs suvent en amenderent.

Ceste estoire vus vuel mustrer
Del riche roi Waldef, le fier,
Com il estoit suvent traïz,
Com il perdi ses dous fiz
Quant il ierent jofne d'eé,
Com il erunt de li porté
E porté en estrange terre:
Com entr' euls avoit mortel gerre,
En quel terre furent nuriz,
Com puis devindrent bons amis.
E si vus dit les aventures
Que mult lur avindrent ja dures.

I want to tell you this history of the powerful king Waldef the valiant: how he was often betrayed, how he lost his two sons when they were young, how they were taken from him and carried off to foreign lands: how there was deadly war between them, and which land they were raised in, and how they became good friends. And the [history] also tells of the harsh misfortunes that so often befell them.

Ma duce amie m'en requist
Par la promesse qu'el' me fist,
Dunt en espoir mun quor entra.
Si me dist e mult m'en proia
Que cest' estorie translatasse,
E qu'apertement li mustrasse,
Qu'ele peust aprendre e lire;
Ne l'osoue pas contredire,
Le comandement de li fis,
Pus esguardai tuz les escriz.
L'estorie englesche regardai, [f. 1va]
En franceis la translatai.
Ne me vuel ore pas numer,
Ne le non m'amie mustrer.
Si jo le livere puis parfere
E a bon chief peusse trere,
Le nun m'amie e le mien
Saverai jo demustrer mult bien.

My sweet friend asked me to do this because of the promise she made me, because of which my heart became hopeful. She spoke about it to me so often and so entreated me to translate this history—and to present it to her clearly so that she could learn and read it—that I did not know how to refuse the order she gave. So I inspected all the writings and I examined the English history [and] I have translated it into French. I do not wish to name myself now, nor to give away my lady's name. If I can complete my book successfully I will indeed be able to reveal the name of my lady, and my own.

Notes

The first column of the manuscript is significantly deteriorated, and the digital image available on the Cologny website is possibly harder to read now than the actual manuscript was in the 1980s for *Waldef*'s editor, Holden, who himself at times relied on a transcription of this passage by Suchier in 1909. Although both Suchier and Holden were experienced editors and readers of medieval manuscripts, our reading of the digital image differs slightly in places from the readings printed by Holden. Where the manuscript is illegible we print in italics, below, the Holden-Suchier readings. Occasionally the scribe has omitted letters; we follow Holden in restoring these inside square brackets. Textual cruces are discussed in the notes below. The section break at v. 25 is indicated by a red majuscule letter, decorated in blue, two lines high; additional breaks are editorial.

4 ***E* que les granz honurs teneient** Holden reads *De qui les . . .*, but suggests that this should read *E qui les . . .*

6 ***Qu'ore est* Engleterre clamee** Gaimar notes that *Bretaine* lost its name (*perdi son nun*), and was re-named *Engleterre* after the *Engleis* who conquered it (ed. Short 2009, vv. 29–34.) The story of the conquest of Britain by the English is strikingly absent from *Waldef*.

8 **De *conquere* mult s'entremist** Conquering in *Waldef* is often not so much a single deed as the vocation of the warrior (see, for example Guiac and Gudlacs' desire to go conquering, *aler conquere*, v. 14,884). The infinitive *conquere* is here used substantively (as is common in Old French).

17 **Androgeu** Androgeous appears in Geoffrey of Monmouth's *Historia* and in Wace's *Brut* as the duke of Kent. Having fought against Caesar in his first two attempts to invade Britain, he became Caesar's ally because of a disagreement with the Kentish king.

18, 24 **Le Bruit, Le Brut** Wace's vernacular version of Geoffrey of Monmouth's *Historia*.

27–8 ***De* verité . . . des rois engleis est estreite** Note the alignment of truthful history and English royalty, and the ambiguity of the use of the verb *estraire*. *Des rois . . . estreit* could mean 'composed about' the kings or 'deriving from' the kings, or even 'descended from' the kings. On the notion of historical truth see Piramus (27) and Short 2007b.

34 **des Englés mult recordee** *Recorder* (see also v. 61) means both 'put down in writing', 'put in record' as well as 'recite' and 'recall' – and carries the notion that history can be both remembered and committed to memory in the process of its recitation.

40–2 ***Les granz estoires* . . . treites** These verses are often cited in discussions of the politics of historiographical translation in post-Conquest England. They are textually and linguistically problematic. The word supplied as 'estoires' is entirely erased in the manuscript. Secondly, we read (along with Anderson 1978–84, 2.219) as *en* the preposition supplied for v. 41 as *des* in Holden's reading. *Engleis* would then refer to the language, not to the people. Furthermore, *remistrent* is the preterite form of two different verbs: *remaindre* (to remain, survive) and *remettre* (to remake, restore, revive, reconstitute), and it has two possible subjects: *Li Normans*, and *les granz estoires*. Like Holden, we take the *estoires* to be the subject, and *remistrent* to mean 'survive'. A wholly authoritative reading and translation of this clause is not possible, which means that caution is needed before positing the Normans as the oppressors of authentic English literature, and English literature as an oppositional survivor.

43 **Pur** The initial miniscule letter *p* at the opening of the first line on f. 1*rb* is not offset in a separate column, making the line seem to be missing its first letter.

43–4 The association between political and linguistic change here is also found in Wace, *Roman de Brut* and *Roman de Rou* (3), vv. 15–80; see also (1).

47–9 **Le Brut . . . Tristram . . . Aelof** There is no evidence that any of these *gestes* had a pre-Conquest English tradition, although the first two circulated in French in England in the twelfth century, and the latter may well have done (for Wace's *Brut*, see Dean 2; for the Anglo-Norman *Tristan*, Dean 158–60; for *Aelof*, Dean 175). The fact that none of the heroes of these stories is actually English means that, like the *Beowulf* poet with his non-English hero, *Waldef* attributes literary tastes (and cultural interests) to the pre-Conquest English that are far more cosmopolitan than modern literary histories generally allow them. It also seems possible, therefore, that *Waldef*'s construction of its position with respect to 'English' literature is overlaid with a degree of irony that is obscured by the national categories of modern literary history.

47–8 **Com est Tristram . . . poine e hahan** For Tristan's hardships see e.g. the *Folie Tristan de Berne*, 'il sofri puis grant ahan' (v. 177), and the *Anglo-Norman Folie Tristan*, 'Ja sui je Tristran/ ki en tristur vif e haan' (vv. 617–18). The *Waldef*-poet's linking rhyme between Tristan and *ahan* suggests the familiarity of the association.

49 **Aelof** appears as Horn's father in Thomas's *Horn*. For the speculation that *Aalof* was the first part of a trilogy in which *Horn* was the second part, and *Hadermod* (Horn's son, whose story Thomas promises his own son would tell) the third, see Wilson 1952, 113.

50 **Qui . . . des granz desrois** Literally 'who brought about such great disarray', although elsewhere in Waldef *faire un grant desroi* is used to mean 'launch an attack', hence the looser translation here, 'fought so well'. On the licensed violence of rulers and their knights see Kaeuper 1999.

53 ***gestes*** The *Waldef* poet appears to use *geste* and *estoire* synonymously, and the *gestes* of this line seem to refer to the same texts as the *estoires* of v. 40 (and to the *Brut*, *Tristan* and *Aelof*). Despite the identification of the *Brut* as a *geste*, Field argues that 'the term *estoire* is deliberately used to associate [*Waldef's*] narrative with the work of Wace and other historians as distinct from romances, or fictional *gestes*' (Field 2000, 33; cf. Damian-Grint 1997, 198). See also (3) above.

55 **ancienes** MS *anciens* We follow Holden's emendation.

55–61 **Les ancienes . . . les recorderent** A complaint also often made in contemporary Latin and vernacular literature: history is no longer recorded for the benefit of posterity as it used to be in antiquity (for a celebrated example, see Walter Map's prologue to book 5 of *De nugis curialium*; see also the prologue to Wace's *Roman de Rou* (3); *The Mohun Chronicle* (**42**). The construction *mettre en memoire* seems to have had the precise technical sense of 'memorialise in writing', which was a feature of the ancient memorial culture lamented by Walter Map. For other such uses of *mettre en memoire*, see the *Vie de saint Audree* (Dean 566), vv. 2378–9: 'nus reconte l'estoire/ Ke saint Bede mist en mémoire'; cf. vv. 400, 658), and the epilogue to Marie's *Espurgatoire seint Patriz* (Dean 547, vv. 2297–9: 'Jo, Marie, ai mis en memoire/le livre de l'Espurgatoire/ en romanz'), and see *mettre en memorie*, Chardri (30, 8 and n.).For the senses of *recorder*, see n. to v. 34, above; and for the connection between remembrance and the (vernacular) written word, see the *Roman de Rou* (3).

60 **q[ui] en aprés** We follow Holden's emendation.

61 **recorderent** See n. to v. 34 above.

75 **Ma duce amie** Elsewhere, Waldef addresses his wife, Ernild, using these words (v. 8273), and they are typically used in lovers' addresses to one another. The *Waldef* author's description of his patroness in these terms, therefore, represents an interesting eroticisation of the relationship of patronage. I am grateful to Emma Bérat for help with this point (see Bérat 2010).

82 **Ne l'osoue** We follow Holden's emendation of MS *Ne lesoue*

84–5 **les escriz/ L'estorie englesche** The author explicitly figures the *estorie englesche* that he had translated as a *written* work. The strategy of claiming to translate an existing, English history is also used in Gaimar's *Estoire* (**10**), Piramus's *Vie seint Edmund le rei* (**27**) and Chrétien's *Guillaume d'Angleterre*. Unlike Gaimar and Chrétien, *Waldef* provides no information about the exact origin or precise location of his source.

87–92 **Ne me vuel ore pas numer . . . Saverai jo demustrer mult bien** The author never fulfils this promise to reveal his name (compare the Nun of Barking in her *Vie de saint Edward rei e confesseur* (**2**), vv. 81–4).

7. Manuals for Conversation and Composition

7a. Walter of Bibbesworth, *Tretiz de langage* [Dean 143], Prologue and Opening: London, British Library, MS Add. 46,919, f. 2^r

Date of composition and provenance. Probably composed 1240–50, by Walter of Bibbesworth for Dionysia, or Denise, de Munchensi (d. 1304?). Denise, widow of Walter Langton and daughter and heir of Nicolas of Anstey of Hertfordshire, became the second wife of Warin de Munchensi shortly after November 1234. Their son, William de Munchensi (1235–87) became one of the baronial leaders of his day. The *Tretiz,* the first known teaching vocabulary in French, is extant in either a long or a short recension in sixteen manuscripts and a fragment (Dean 285). It was also known as *Aprise de franceis*, and *Femina* or *Femme.* It was later reworked and incorporated into more extensive treatises, such as the *Femina nova* (Cambridge, Trinity College B.14.40) datable to *c.* 1415, in which the *Tretiz* receives a complete interlinear translation into English.

Author, sources and nature of text. Walter of Bibbesworth was an Essex knight associated with the manor of Bibbesworth in Hertfordshire, who later possessed three manors in Essex – Saling, Latton, and Waltham. It is in Little Dunmow, 6 miles from the last, that he is thought to have been buried (possibly at the end of the 1270s). He was born not later than 1219. His best known work is the *Tretiz*, but he also wrote a debate poem, addressed to Henry de Lacy and dealing with the crusade of 1270, in which Bibbesworth participated, and a grammatical poem of 63 couplets in punning rhyme, both found in BL Add. 46,919, ff. 92^r–93^r (and one other manuscript); and an eight-line riddle.

The *Tretiz*, comprising approx. 1140 rhyming octosyllables, was a well-known guide for teaching the French vocabulary needed for estate management, and six of the extant manuscripts include a dedicatory epistle to Denise de Munchensi. Many of the copies have English glosses. The text begins with the care of an infant, the parts of the body, moving on to the names of plants and animals, and the specialised vocabulary of daily and seasonal rural occupations (baking, brewing, sowing, reaping, etc.) and estate management. One of the favourite techniques used for introducing vocabulary is word play, involving the distinction of homonyms, or the exposition of the varieties of possible equivalents in French for a given word in English (e.g. English *reed (=red)* and French *rous, sor, goules, rouge, vermaille*, each in a specific context, Rothwell 1990, vv. 310–17). Given the nature of the text, in which the subject matter changes constantly, it lends itself easily to editorial omissions or expansions, and the extant multiple medieval copies are so varied that 'a strictly critical edition of the *Tretiz* seems scarcely possible' (Hunt 2004, *ODNB*).

The opening rubric and prefatory letter firmly situate this teaching tool as a work commissioned by a noblewoman ('because you requested me'), conscious of her role as the teacher of French to her children (specifically 'sons') for their life's role as aristocratic estate managers. Although not explicitly stated here, it is implied that this is the 'mother tongue', since it is the task of the mother. The role of women as teachers of language, and particularly of the 'mother's language' is made explicit in the Latin rubric which precedes the *Femina nova* (but which Arnould shows applies only to the *Tretiz* part of this compilation): *Lyber iste vocatur femina quia sicut femina docet infantem loqui maternam, sic docet iste liber juvenes rethorice loqui gallicum, prout infra patebit* (This book is called *Femina*, for just as a woman teaches an infant his mother tongue, this book teaches youths how to speak French, as will be evident below: Arnould 1969, 3).

The opening lines of the prologue also are directly addressed to women as expectant mothers, and advice on the physical demands of motherhood are first dealt with, since the child must survive infancy before it reaches an age when it can begin to learn language. The first words to be taught, logically, are parts of the body (see also **7b**, ii), and the first grammatical consideration is the gender distinction in possessive adjectives (and definite articles, and the first person pronoun, listed in the

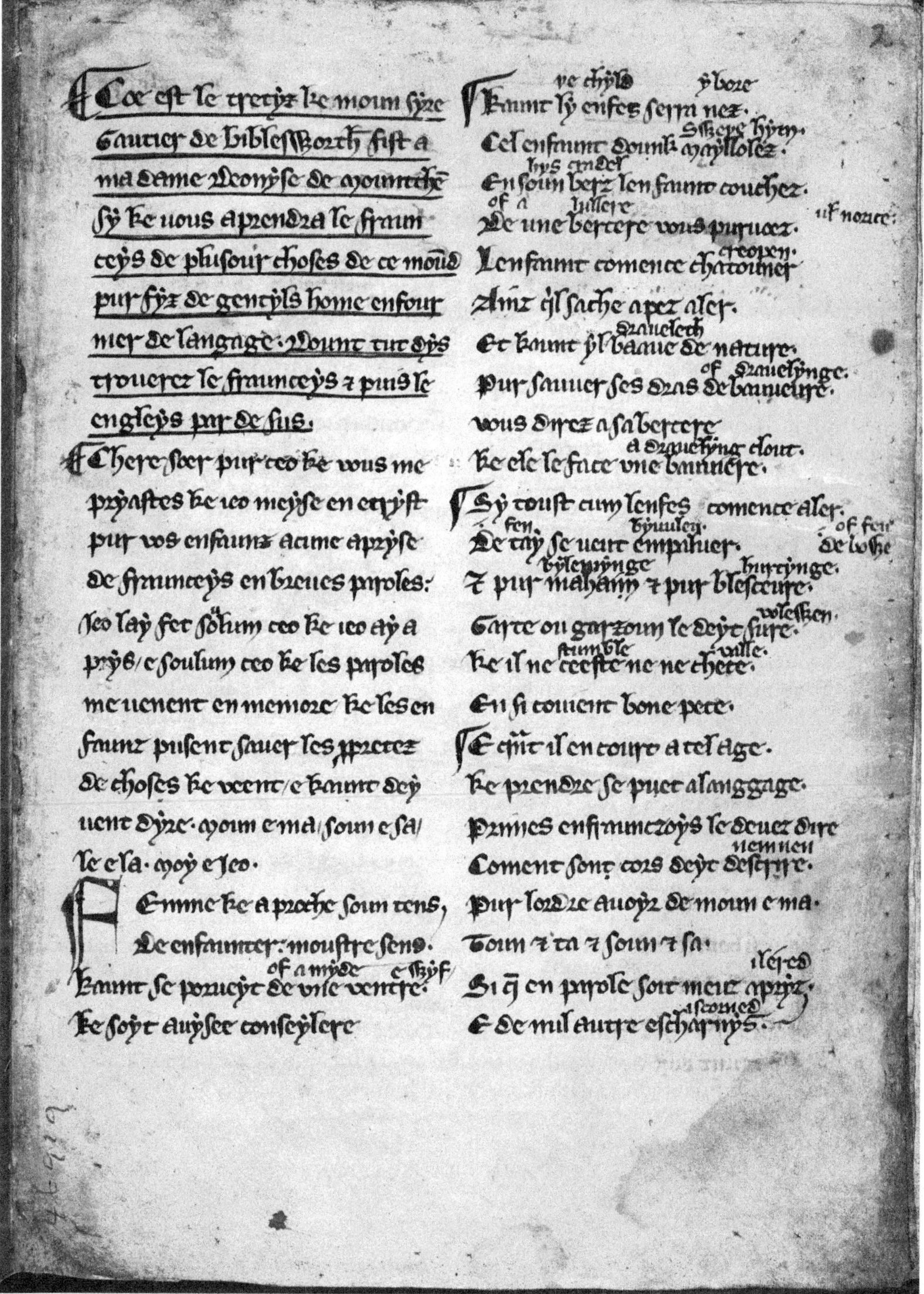

Cee est le tretiz ke moun syre
Gautier de Bibelesworth fist a
ma dame Dionyse de Mounchen-
sy ke vous aprendra le fraun
ceys de plusour choses de ce mond
pur fyz de gentyls home enfour
mer de langage. Dount tut dys
trouerez le fraunceys e puis le
engleys par de sus.
Chere soer pur ceo ke vous me
pryastes ke ieo meyse en escryst
pur vos enfaunz aeme apryse
de fraunceys en breues paroles:
ieo lay fet solum ceo ke ieo ay a
prys, e soulum ceo ke les paroles
me uenent en memore ke les en
faunz pusent sauer les propretez
de choses ke veent, e kaunt dey
uent dyre. moun e ma, soun e sa,
le e la. moy e ieo.
Femme ke aproche soun tens,
De enfaunter: moustre sens.
Kaunt se purueyt de une ventre.
Ke soyt auysee conseylere

Kaunt ly enfes serra nez.
Cel enfaunt dount maylolez.
En soun bers len faunt coucher.
De une bercere vous purueez.
Lenfaunt comence chatouner
Auant cyl sache aler.
E kaunt yl baaue de nettire
Pur sauuer ses dras de baueure.
Vous direz a sa bercere
Ke ele le face une bauuerse.
Sy toust cum lenfes comence aler
De tay se ueit empaluer.
E pur mahaym e pur blesceure.
Garte ou garzoun le deyt sure.
Ke il ne ceeste ne ne chete.
En si couient bone pece.
Echun il en course a tel age.
Ke prendre se puet a langgage.
Primes en fraunceys le deuez dire
Coment sont ceus deyt destryre.
Pur lordre auoyr de moun e ma.
Soun e ta e soun e sa.
Si qe en parole soit meuz aprys.
E de mil autre escharnys.

Fig. 1. (7a) Bibbesworth, *Tretiz*: Text and glosses in William Herebert's copy (London, BL Add. MS 46,919, f. 2r) prefatory letter), a perennial problem for students of French. A major motivation for this teaching is the need to avoid being scorned by others (v. 28) for not speaking French grammatically.

AUDIENCE AND CIRCULATION. The work was clearly popular as a teaching tool for aristocratic Anglo-Norman families, as can be seen in the number of extant manuscripts, and the later adaptations of it. Most of the manuscripts date from the early fourteenth century, with two from the fifteenth century, and all are of English origin. Denise de Munchensi was from a family with extensive landholdings (across five counties: Norfolk, Essex, Kent, Gloucestershire and Northamptonshire). She founded Waterbeach Abbey, Cambridgeshire, in 1293. The later adaptation in *Femina nova* uses both Continental French and English, and gives notes on Anglo-Norman pronunciation.

MANUSCRIPT SOURCE. BL Add. 46,919 (formerly Phillipps 8336): vellum, ff. ii+211, measuring 230 × 170 mm, with many irregular leaves. Dated to the fourteenth century and written in several hands, this important trilingual manuscript is a 'collection of treatises, poems, sermons, etc., in Anglo-Norman French (and some items in Continental French), Latin and Middle English, compiled by Fr William Herebert of Hereford (d. 1333?), who wrote or annotated considerable portions of the manuscript', including the text of the *Tretiz*. Herebert studied at both Paris and Oxford, where he became reader in divinity to the Franciscans, before retiring to the Hereford convent.

The *Tretiz*, ff. 2^{r}–14^{b}, is the first item in the collection. The opening rubric is underlined; the rubric and the introductory note have a larger reduplicated letter *C* in the margin immediately preceding the initial majuscule *C*; there is a paraph-like mark beside and above the first letters of vv. 5, 15, 21. The first line begins with a large letter *F*, two lines high (see Fig. 1).

We print the English glosses under the line; the word above which the gloss is found in the manuscript is italicised in the text.

BIBLIOGRAPHY. The *Tretiz* is edited from one manuscript by Rothwell 2009 (available at http://www.anglo-norman.net/texts/bibb-gt.pdf); this supersedes the earlier edition by Owen 1977, but does not include variants from other manuscripts. Comments and corrections to the Owen edition are given in Rothwell 1982 and Bell 1962. For the list of manuscripts, see Dean 285. There is a modern English translation by Dalby 2012. On Walter of Bibbesworth and on the Munchensi family, see Hunt 2004, *ODNB*. Dean 143, 229, 799 catalogues Bibbesworth's other works, and for a letter by Bibbesworth, see Tanqueray, ed., 1916, no. 39. Meyer 1884 gives details on BL Add. 46,919 and on the *Tretiz*; see now also the online British Library Manuscripts Catalogue and *ODNB*, Walter de Bibbesworth. The late-medieval *Femina* adaptation of the *Tretiz* (Dean 296) is edited by Rothwell 2005 (available at http://www.anglo-norman.net/texts/femina.pdf), and its sources studied by Arnould 1969. Crane 1997 discusses the socio-linguistic context and implications: Ingham 2015b is an important update regarding Bibbesworth and French instruction in England generally. For the *Tretiz* as children's literature, see Kennedy 2003; on women's language teaching see Wogan-Browne 2015. Bibbesworth's puns are discussed in Butterfield 2009, 331–2 and Knox 2013: on his glosses see Knox 2013: Ingham 2015b, 633 argues the opposite case: i.e. that the glosses are not integral to the work and are unlikely to originate with Bibbesworth himself.

TEXT AND TRANSLATION

Prologue: Rubric

Ceo est le tretyz ke moun syre Gautier de Biblesworth fist a ma dame Deonyse de Mountchensy, ke vous aprendra le fraunceys de plusour choses de ce mound, pur fiz de gentyls home enfourmer de langage. Dount

This treatise, which sir Walter of Bibbesworth wrote for Lady Denise de Munchensi, will teach you the French terms for many things in daily life useful for the language instruction of the sons of noblemen. Here you will find tutdys troverez le fraunceys e puis le engleys par desus.

first the French term, then the English term written above it.

Prologue: Prefatory letter

Chere soer, pur ceo ke vous me pryastes ke jeo meyse en ecryst pur vos enfaunz acune apryse de fraunceys en breves paroles, jeo l'ay fet soulum ceo ke je ay aprys e soulum ceo ke les paroles me venent en memore, ke les enfaunz pusent saver les propretez de choses ke veent e kaunt deyvent dyre 'moun' e 'ma', 'soun' e 'sa', 'le' e 'la', 'moy' e 'jeo'.

Dear Sister, because you requested me to put in writing for your children a briefly worded teaching text for French, I have done so according to what I myself have learned and insofar as I have been able to recall the terms from my memory, so that the children may know the proper names of things they see, and when they should say either 'moun' or 'ma', 'soun' or 'sa', 'le' or 'la', 'moy' e 'jeo'.

Opening

Femme ke aproche soun tens
De enfaunter moustre sens
Kaunt se porveyt *de une ventrere*
[of a myde wyf]
Ke soyt avysee conseylere.
Kaunt *ly enfes* sera *nez*
[þe chyld; ybore]
Cel enfaunt dounk *mayllolez*
[sweþe hym];
En *soun berz* l'enfaunt couchez
[hys cradel];
De une bercere vous purvoez
[of a lullere; *in margin: uel* norice];

A woman who is approaching the time when she will give birth shows good sense when she chooses for herself a midwife who is a wise and experienced counsellor. When the child is born, swaddle it and lay it in its cradle. Find yourself a nursemaid [for the baby].

L'enfaunt comence *chatouner*
[creopen]
Ainz qu'il sache a pez aler;
Et kaunt yl *baave* de nature
[draveleth],
Pur sauver ses dras *de bauveure*
[of dravelynge]
Vous direz a sa bercere
Ke ele le face *une bauviere*
[a dravelyng clout].

The child will begin to creep before he knows how to walk; and when he begins naturally to drool, to protect his clothing from his drooling, you will ask his nurse to make him a bib.

Sy toust cum l'enfes comence aler
De tay se veut *empaluer*
[fen; byvulen; *in margin:* of fen /de bowe];
E pur *mahain* e pur *blesceure*
[by lemynge; hurtynge],

As soon as the child begins to walk, he will want to play and soil himself in mud. And to prevent injury and wounds to either a girl or boy, one must follow them closely, so that

Garce ou garzoun, le deyt *sure*
[volewen]
Ke il ne *ceeste* ne *chece*
[stumble; valle],
Ensi covient bone pece.

they do not stumble or fall, and this state of affairs will last for a good length of time.

E quant il encourt a tel age
Ke prendre se puet a langgage,
Primes en fraunczoys le devez dire
Coment son cors deyt *descrire*
[nemnen]
Pur l'ordre avoyr de 'moun' e 'ma',
'Toun' e 'ta', e 'soun' e 'sa',
Si que en parole soit meuz *apryz*
[ilered]
E de nul autre *escharnys*
[iscorned]

And when he reaches the age when he begins to talk and learn words, you must first tell him in French the words to name parts of the body, so that he may have the proper use of 'moun' [my, *poss adj. m.*] and 'ma' [my, *poss adj. f.*], 'toun' [your, *2nd pers sg. poss. adj. m.*] and 'ta' [your, *2nd pers sg, poss adj f*], 'soun' [his, her, *poss. adj. m.*] and 'sa' [his, her, *poss. adj. f.*], so that he may be instructed in the best manner in speech, and not be scorned by others [for his ignorance].

Notes

R*1* **Ceo est le tretyz** could be interpreted with a strong sense given to the definite article, which in medieval French could have the strength of a demonstrative, approaching in this context the meaning 'This is the [famous, well-known] treatise of Walter of Bibbesworth'.

8 ***uel*** **norice** (or nurse) The second level of gloss is in Latin (*uel*), and French (*norice*). The English *lullere* corresponds to *rockere* in other manuscripts, and presumably means one who rocks or lulls the infant to sleep, as opposed to the *norice* (wetnurse).

9 **chatouner** (creep, crawl; *creopen*): the French verb is based on the image of moving on all fours like a cat.

16 **of fen / de bowe** (of mud) The second level gloss repeats the English words (*of fen*), with the French synonym (*de bowe*) written below it. *Byvulen* (soil, befoul) is an accurate synonym for *empaluer*.

17 **mahain** MS *mahaim*, with first minim stroke of final *m* expuncted. The deverbal noun *mehaing, meaing, main* is from *mehaignier, maagnier, mengnier* (wound, mutiliate); cf. modern English *maim* and Québécois *maganer* (mistreat, misuse; wear out, destroy). 'Laming' and 'hurting' seem less dramatic than *mahain* and *blesceure* (wound).

18 **sure** (follow, *volewen*) is an attested form of this verb, modern French *suivre*; in medieval French its paradigm was particularly unstable, cf. variants *sivre, siver, siouvre; siwer, siwir, siwre; suire, suier, s(e)ure*, etc. (cf. *AND s.v.* 'sivre').

22 **prendre . . . a langgage** The *Tretiz* is not directed to teaching from birth but to increasing the spoken vocabulary of children who already have some French. For a review of the longstanding discussion of whether French was formally taught and new arguments see Ingham 2015b, 632–6.

24 **son** MS *sont*, with *t* expuncted.

7b. *Manières de langage* [Dean 281–2], Prologue to 1396 *Manière*: London, British Library, MS Harley 3988, f. 1^{r}–^{v}; Dialogue from 1415 *Manière*: Oxford Bodleian Library, MS Latin misc. e. 93, ff. 3^{v}–4^{r}

Date of composition and provenance. 1396 and 1415 (or shortly after), Oxford.

Authors, sources and nature of text. Manuals for teaching spoken French with sample dialogues were composed in the late fourteenth and early fifteenth centuries in three principal recensions of 1396, 1399 and 1415. The author of the 1396 *Manière* from which the introduction is given here remains anonymous and nothing is known of the patron addressed in its text as 'Kirvyngton' (MS Harley 3988, f. 23^{r}): it contains at its fullest twenty dialogues. The *Manière* recension of *c.* 1415, also excerpted here, is by William Kingsmill, named and sometimes described as a scrivener (*Escriven*) in some of the extant manuscripts. In the early fifteenth century Kingsmill took over from Thomas Sampson the proprietorship of an Oxford 'business school' in which spoken French was part of the syllabus. Like his own successors in the school, Kingsmill built on the existing curriculum materials.

The *Manières* are rightly celebrated for their lively sample dialogues (asking the way, conversations and sociability at the inn, a visit to the market, news from the battle of Agincourt, etc.). But at the Oxford school, conversational French formed only part of a curriculum that offered administrative and business skills and basic training in less specialised aspects of common law, for all of which students needed to be able to compose charters and other documents in French as well as Latin. The school was attached to the university in some way: an Oxford statute of 1432 (presumably regulating what had been the practice for some time) rules that the school's students should attend the regular university lectures on grammar and rhetoric, and many personal and place names used in the dialogues are from Oxford and its region. Medieval England's other university, Cambridge, does not seem to have had such a school, though one late-fifteenth-century manuscript of Kingsmill's 1415 *Manière* includes precedents from local Cambridge courts (Baker and Ringrose 1996, MS CUL Add. 8391, art.3). In London the inns of court and chancery began to give more advanced instruction in the common law as the Oxford school developed its focus on basic training.

Legge 1939 reconstructs Kingsmill's course as beginning with verses for teaching French to children; followed by the 1415 *Manière de langage*; French numerals and days of the week, etc.; a *Tractatus* on French spelling by one 'T. H.', a treatise on French conjugation; a letter-writing treatise or formulary, with examples; a treatise on drafting charters; 'The Art of Pleading in French', with examples; the *Curia Baronis* (the manner of holding baronial courts). This may be imposing too standardised an order on what, the manuscripts suggest, was a moving congeries of material frequently recompiled, adapted and added to in different ways for various sub-fields of clerical work.

The *Manières*, then, teach conversational French as part of a Latin and French matrix for learning and practising professional skills. In general the *Manières* show not that French in England was dying and so needed teaching, but rather that an audience of already competent users wanted 'to acquire more finesse and social acumen through language' (Butterfield 2009, 335), and also (as suggested by the grammatical and spelling treatises often accompanying the *Manières* in their manuscripts), to formalise their written French skills (*a droit escrire*, line 21) for career purposes.

Lusignan argues that for these pioneering *Manières* there is no precedent authority, so that they lean on experience and on *usage* and *coustume* (as in legal *coutumiers* or customals) for their credentials (1987, 103–4). Prologue rhetoric also shores up the necessity and desirability of the *Manières*. The 1396 *Manière* opens grandiloquently, with topoi usually associated with theological encyclopaedias (see e.g. (**19**); cf. (**22**, 37–73)). God has created French as the language of the angels, and man, the fallen angels' replacement, is to constitute the treatise's first item and first lexical list. 'Sweet French', although not yet treated in a formal grammar textbook (as it will be in Barton's *Donait* (7e)) is dignified as a universal *lingua franca*. As an epithet for French, 'sweet' (*doulz*) would rapidly become a cliché, but medieval sweetness is rooted in the Christianisation of classical rhetoric, and is a more powerful term than it subsequently became. Among texts of the 1396 *Manière*, the fully elaborated version given here from the earliest extant manuscript lays particular emphasis on the connections of French and the socio-religious elite: proper French is associated with election to paradise.

In the dialogue from the 1415 *Manière*, the principle of beginning with the human person is recapitulated: the small boy who appears in the dialogue as a Kingsmill pupil has begun by learning how to describe his person. In advertising Kingsmill's school, the dialogue offers some of the pleasures of self-referentiality and knowingness that typify the *Manières*' conversations, and suggests, too, something of their pedagogical vitality, still evident today.

Audience and circulation. The 1396 treatise is extant in six manuscripts and the 1415 in four, while the 1399 *Manière* (not excerpted here) is nearly complete in one manuscript and fragmentary in four others. *Manières* manuscripts also participate in the wider fourteenth- and fifteenth-century teaching corpus that (by the calculations of Kristol 1990, 299) involves a hundred and one texts and forty-five manuscripts, varying in emphasis between spoken and written French language, letter writing and legal documents.

The *Manières* offer conversations and songs, dramatising French as essential to the sociability of polite society, but they also have dialogues across the classes between masters and servants (in which both groups use French), and for household officials, for tradesmen, and once for agricultural labourers. This might be to provide variety in what pupils learned, but perhaps also because, as in the apprenticeship discussed in the dialogue below, the servants of the elite and the children of burghers and artisans were educated by these means.

A certain amount of teaching to younger children or beginning students is envisaged, and the 1399 *Manière* is a cut-down version of ten dialogues and simplified vocabulary lists, entitled in its fullest manuscript *Petit livre pour enseigner les enfantz de leur entreparler comun françois* (Kristol 1995, Table 2). There are also occasional traces of cross-influence in this teaching corpus from the very successful and constantly readapted *Tretiz* by Bibbesworth for the instruction of Lady Dionysia's children (**7a**): the performed recital of parts of the body envisaged for the child in Kingsmills' dialogue perhaps owes something to Bibbesworth's use of this as a starting point for children (**7a**, vv. 23–4). But the professionalism of the Oxford courses is highlighted by the generally separate circulation of the *Tretiz*: popular as Bibbesworth's manual was, his vocabulary lists occur only four times in manuscripts together with texts used by Sampson and Kingsmill (Lusignan 1987, 98 and Appendix II).

Both kinds of spoken French teaching share an increasing inclusion of English: like Bibbesworth's *Tretiz*, which moves from glosses in its thirteenth-century version to full interlinear French and English in its fifteenth-century *Femina* version, manuscripts containing the *Manières* include English glosses and, increasingly, English translations (see e.g. Kristol 1990–1). This development is often assumed to show decreased understanding of French among the *Manière* users, but may equally testify to an increasing and diversifying concern with English as a written language and its ability to match French as a language of composition.

Manuscript source. *Manières* often occur in student collections of course texts and notes or in manuscripts compiled as reference works for students and teachers. Harley MS 3988 is a vellum manuscript (220 × 130 mm) of 67 folios from the end of the fourteenth century. The volume opens with the 1396 *Manière* copied in a single cursive hand from f. 1^r to f. 22^r, where it ends with a dialogue on going to bed and a good night prayer. On f. 22^v a letter to the patron, Kirvington, dated from Bury St Edmunds on the Eve of Pentecost, 1396 apologises for the writer, who claims to be not the most skilled (*escienteux*) in speaking and writing *doulz françois ou romance* but to have done what God's grace, in allotting him understanding and intelligence, permits. From ff. 23^r–24^v there are brief snippets of linguistic comment in a different hand (Dean 283), for example, 'he can

no more speak French than a cow can wear a saddle' (*Il ne luy avient plus a parler franceis qu'a une vache de porter une selle* (f. 24^{v}, 3–4). These are perhaps notes for further dialogues, of which one follows (*Aultre maniere*, ff. 25^{r}–26^{r}). The remaining leaves of the quire are blank, except for an *ex dono* inscription ('to Mr Parker') of 1589 on f. 27^{v} by John Thompson, *notarius*. The second major item in the manuscript (ff. 28^{r}–67^{v}) is a dictamen treatise or letter formulary in French (see (**7c**)), with numerous sample letters in order of rank, from kings to merchants, finishing with a plea to the mayor and aldermen of London. The manuscript thus contains two late-medieval tools for teaching spoken and written French, though variation in size between the folios of the two main works suggest they were collected together rather than initially planned as a compendium.

The Kingsmill dialogue from the 1415 *Manière* is taken here from Bodleian MS Lat. misc. e. 93, a small mid-fifteenth-century paper manuscript (203 × 135 mm) of ii + 56 folios, written in a single cursive hand. The acephalous *Manière* is in a separate opening quire (ff. 1^{r}–5^{r}), with the final leaf and a half blank, while the manuscript's other item is a Latin *Ars notaria* (*[T]ria sunt que pertinent ad cartas*... ff. 6^{r}–54^{r}) in which local Oxford names and institutions are used in the examples. The latter text uses a *textualis* script for its headings, but otherwise is in the same cursive hand and on the same paper as the 1415 *Manière*, suggesting a student or practitioner collecting together useful texts. Polite salutations to women are the first *Manière* item, followed by news from the battle of Agincourt: the penultimate dialogue before the one printed here is a maid-servant's account of the local textiles her master has gone to sell at the market of Woodstock (*douszeyns de mellerez* [mixed cloth] *d'Oxonford .xx. kerseyes d'Abindon*, etc., f. 3^{v}, lines 12–20).

Bibliography. The *Manières* are edited (all three recensions) in Kristol 1995. Merrilees and Sitarz-Fitzpatrick (1993, 24–6) edit the 1415 Kingsmill dialogue: Gessler 1934 edits the 1396 *Manière* (Harley MS 3988 as base). Dean 281–2 lists older editions of individual manuscripts and supplementary dialogues (283, 284): the linguistic comments in the Harley MS are Dean 283. Kristol tabulates the *Manières* manuscripts and dialogues in his 1995 edition, and lists and describes them in Kristol 1990: for a summary tabulation of manuscript contents see Lusignan 1987, 194. For Kingsmill's predecessor Thomas Sampson (*c.* 1350–*c.* 1409) and the Oxford school, see (**7c**) and Richardson 1941, I. Arnold 1937: for a successor see (**7d**). Legge 1939 discusses the university connection. Lusignan 1987, 94–118 discusses the *Manières*: for further important discussion and overview see Butterfield 2009, 323–34. On rhetoric and sweetness see Carruthers 2006.

Text and Translation

(i) Manière de langage 1396, Prologue

[f. 1^{r}] A nostre comencement nous dirons ainsi: En nom du Pere, Filz et Saint Espirit, Amen. Ci comence la maniere de language que t'enseignera bien a droit parler et escrire doulz françois selon l'usage et la coustume de France.

Primiers au comencement de nostre fait et bosoigne, nous prierons Dieu devoutement et Nostre Dame la benoite vierge Marie, sa tresdoulce mere, et toute la glorieuse compaingnie du saint reaume de paradis celestre ou Dieux mette ses amis et ses eslus, de quoi vient toute

At the beginning of this treatise we shall say: 'In the name of the Father and the Son and the Holy Ghost, Amen'. Here begins the language manual that will teach you to speak correctly and to write elegant French according to the practice and conventions of France.

At the beginning of our study, we shall devoutly pray to God and to Our Lady the blessed virgin Mary his sweet mother and all the glorious company of the holy realm of the heavenly paradise wherein God may place his friends and chosen ones, and from whence comes all knowledge, wisdom, grace

science, sapience, grace et entendement et tous manieres des vertuz, qu'il luy plaist, de sa grande misericorde et grace, tous les escoliers estudianz en cest livre ainsi abuvrer et enluminer de la rousee de sa haute sapience et entendement qu'ils pourront avoir sens naturel d'aprendre a parler, bien soner, et a droit escrire doulz françois, qu'est la plus bel et la plus gracious language et [le] plus noble parler aprés latin d'escole qui soit ou monde, et de tous gens mieulx prisee et amee que nul autre. Quar Dieux le fist si doulce et amiable principalment a l'oneur et loenge de luy mesmes. Et pour ce il peut bien comparer au parler des angels du ciel pour la grant doulceur et biaultee d'icel.

Et pour tant que homme est le plus noble et le plus digne creature que soit en cest siecle, et que Dieux a ordennee d'estre soveraine et maistre de toutes autres creatures et choses qui sont desoubz lui, pour ce je comencerai a declarer et plainement determiner de luy et des mem [f. 1v] bres de son corps et de toutes autres choses et necessairs qu'a luy appartiennent ou aviennent. Et fait a remembrer que homme est divisee en dousze parties al maniere et guise de dousze signes du ciel que les gouvernent, comme dit le sage philosophre, et les signes ont grant signeurie et domnacion de les membres susdis, quant la lune sera en aucun de eaux accordant au son membre. Et sachiez, mes tres doulz amis, que homme est une arbre bestournee; c'est a dire l'escot et les racines du quelle sont verseez contremont et la summite avec les ramsiaux en aval. Ainsi est la teste d'omme, qu'est la plus haulte et principal partie de lui, qu'est rassemblee a l'escot de l'arbre et les chiveux a les racines.

and understanding and all the virtues, that it may please him in his great mercy and grace towards all students of this book to nourish and enlighten them with the dew of his lofty wisdom and understanding, so that they can have an innate grasp of learning how to speak, accurately pronounce and correctly write elegant French, which is the most beautiful and most gracious language and the most noble speech after educated Latin in the world, better praised and loved by all peoples than any other. For God made it so sweet and gentle principally to the honour and praise of himself. And for this reason it can well be compared to the speech of the angels in heaven, given their great sweetness and beauty.

And since man is the most noble and worthy creature there is in this world, and because God has ordained him to be ruler and master of all other creatures and things beneath him, on this account I will begin with him, clearly specifying his bodily members and all the other things and requisites that pertain to or befit him. And it should be remembered that man, as the wise philosopher says, is divided into twelve types in alignment with the nature and operation of the twelve heavenly signs which govern them, and the signs have great control and power over the aforesaid members when the moon is in one of the signs and the member is governed by it. And you should also be aware, my dear friends, that man is to be thought of as an inverted tree: that is to say, the trunk and the roots are turned upwards and the top with its branches downwards. Thus the head of man, which is the highest and principal part of him, is compared to the trunk of a tree and his hair to the roots.

[*Body parts are now detailed in a topdown list from the face to the feet, followed by the naming of interior parts – entrails, brain, etc.- and concluding with the four humours.*]

7b. Manières de langage

(ii) Manière de langage 1415, Dialogue (excerpt)

[f. 3v] Sir, je vous pry, ou pensez vous chivachere ore de cy?

Dame, droit a Londrez se Dieu plest.

Sir, d'une chose je vous prioray, se j'osasse ou fuisse si hardy.

Dame, par l'amour de votre maistre et de vous, je fray ceo que je purray, savant mon estat, votre a plesir.

Sire, grant mercy, et j'ay icy un fitz de l'age de .xii. anz et solonc votre avys c'est la volunté de mon maistre et mon auxi pur luy estower a bon home de maistre en Londrez l'ou il purroit bien estre enseigné et governé en le manere d'apprentys illoques.

Dame, appellez l'enfant et lessez moy luy veier. Mon fitz, avez vous esté a l'escole?

Oy sir, par vostre congé.

A quele lieu?

Syr, a l'oscolle de Gilliam Scrivener.

Beau fitz, [f. 4r] combien de temps avez vous demurrés oveque luy?

Syr, forsque un quarter de l'an.

Cela n'est que un poy de temps. Mez qu'avez vous apris la en ycelle terme?

Sir, mon master m'a enseigné pur escrier et enditer, counter et franceis parler.

Et que avez vous apris en franceys dire?

Sir, je sçai mon nom et mon corps ben descriere.

Donques ditz moy qu'avez a nom.

J'ay a nom Johan bon enfant,
Beal et sage et bien parlant
Engloys, franceis, et bon normonde.
Benoite soit la virge que chaste l'enfant
Et le bon maistre que moy prist tant.
Jo pry a Dieu tout puissant
Nous grante le joye toudis durant.
Auxi, [f 4r, 10] sir, j'estoy hier a le fest
Oveque mon chief ou mon teste,
Mes chiveux reserfilez . . . [f. 4r, 12].

Sir, I beg you, where do you intend to ride now from here?

Lady, straight to London, if it please God.

Sir, I would ask you something if I dared, or if I were bold enough.

Lady, for the love of your lord and of you, I will do what I can, saving my estate, to please you.

Sir, thank you very much, and I have a son of twelve years and depending on what you think, my husband and I desire to place him with a good professional man in London where he can be well taught and governed in the way apprentices are there.

Lady, call the boy and let me see him. My son, have you been to school?

Yes, sir, by your leave.

And at what place?

Sir, at the school of William the Scrivener.

Fair son, how long did you stay there with him?

Sir, for a quarter of a year.

That isn't very much time. But what have you learned during that time?

Sir, my master has taught me to write and compose, to make accounts and to speak French.

And what have you learned to say in French?

Sir, I know my name and how to describe my person thoroughly.

So tell me what your name is.

I am named the good child John, handsome, wise and speaking English, French and good Norman well. Blessed be the rod which chastises the child and the good master who taught me well. I pray to God the all-powerful to grant us the joy which lasts for ever.

Also sir, I was at the feast yesterday with my head or my noggin, my hair combed . . .

[*He now lists body parts, clothes, weapons, offers to teach interlocutor 'de comune langage et d'autre maner de parlance' of beasts and agriculture (*gaynerye*) and of various classes of people from the elite to the vulgar, and the French of domestic animals and the household.*]

Notes

5–6 **la coustume de France** Overseas training and experience in France became an increasingly crucial credential in the later Middle Ages (see (**7e**)). The *Manières* deploy it in various ways. The CUL Dd.12.23 text, for instance, includes no such claim in its opening (Kristol, ed., 1995, 3).

17 **estudianz en cest livre** Kristol 1995: *toutz qui cesti libre regarderont ou enrememorunt* (3, lines 6–7).

27 **luy** MS *lur*.

27–8 **loenge de luy mesmes** *loenge* could be translated as 'praise' or 'glory': the phrasing suggests here that French should be used to praise God and/or that it is a reflection of his glory.

43–4 **comme dit le sage philosophre** unidentified, but probably Aristotle.

51 **en aval** (a gloss) '*vel contreval*' is added above. For glosses (mostly French, but with one Middle English and one Latin example) in this and two other manuscripts of the 1396 *Manières*, see Gessler 1934, 38 n. 59. On overlaps between *Manières* glosses and Bibbesworth (**7a**), see Knox 2013.

59 **si hardy** MS *sir harde* (with abbreviated *sir*) *pro* is an abbreviation: possibly intended for abbreviated form of *seigneur*).

67 **l'ou** MS *lou* On the contraction of 'la u' to one syllable, see Short, ed., 2009, 387, *Estoire des Engleis*, v. 2486n.

68 **le manere** MS *le* is blotted, but is most probably this hand's *e*.

73 **l'oscolle** Some manuscripts give *ostelle* (see Merrilees and Sitarz-Fitzpatrick 1993). The form here is perhaps a scribal compromise between *ostelle* (hostel) and *escole* (school).

77 **Cela** MS *cella*

79 **mon master** The form is not attested in *AND* but is clear in the MS.

80 **counter** can mean to calculate and also, in law, to set out the plaintiff's case (see *AND*, *s.v.* 'conter'). At twelve, the child seems unlikely to have completed Kingsmill's full course, so basic reckoning and numeracy may be the meaning here.

81 **apris en franceys** After *apris*, the words *la en ycelle terme* have been expuncted for excision.

7c. *Quant vous frez as seignours*: Dictaminal Training attributed to Thomas Sampson [Dean 317]. Cambridge University Library, MS Ee.iv.20, ff. 167ʳ–169ʳ (excerpts)

Date of composition and provenance. Later fourteenth century, Oxford.

Author, sources and nature of text. Thomas Sampson is the most important entrepreneur of notarial and general business teaching in fourteenth-century England. His career, perhaps extending from the 1340s to 1409/10, is hard to date (mentions of his name even in dated exemplary letters in his treatises are of uncertain historical status), but his school in Oxford flourished in the later half of the fourteenth century and was carried on by William Kingsmill, Simon d'O and others into the fifteenth century. An important aspect of the multi-faceted training provided by Sampson's school for clerks is letter-writing, whether for large households, offices of the crown and shires, for merchants, civic administration, etc. Italian and French dictaminal sources (in Latin) were widely influential from the twelfth century on, but English dictamen developed in particular ways in the fourteenth century, affiliating on the one hand to literary composition for those going on to university and on the other to shorter courses of study given in Sampson's and his successors' school or by the freelance teachers clustered in Oxford. Sampson was probably influenced by the *Summa de arte dictandi* (1228–9) of Guido Faba, an influential Bologna master, priest, notary and *dictamen* teacher, but perhaps indirectly through its earlier reworkings in England. Like his Italian and French precedessors in public *ars dictaminis* (cf. Brunetto Latini, a source for (**8a**)), Sampson used a mixture of precepts and examples. He is a pioneer in his systematic incorporation of French language and French documentary training alongside and intermingled with Latin forms. He composed two treatises on letter writing in French as well as several works on *dictamen* in Latin.

Sampson's letter collections are as fascinating as any other dictaminal collections of examples. As sources, however, such letters are complicated to use: while potentially rich documents of social history, they may or may not be actual letters, they may constitute pedagogical jokes and advertisements (the Oxford student writing home for more money is a favourite both of Sampson and his successors and of their modern historians), or they may use illustrious names less as a matter of record than to accrue prestige. The first model letter found in the treatise below is from one man of rank to another about the suspicion that the sender's squire has had sex (*surjeu*) with the recipient's 'wife, daughter, or maidservant'. The letter declares the squire's innocence and requests an opportunity for him to swear it to the recipient. Such a letter owes much to the literary genres of romance and fabliau, also used in Sampson and Kingsmill's *Manières de langage* (**7b**). As the first letter of the treatise, it also performs the rhetorical work of associating writing in French with elite literature and letters (French had long been used for private correspondence), and it also contributes to the meta-narrative formed by the treatise's combined elements of instruction and exemplification. This is a practical business training that pays tribute to the romance of aspiration.

Letters as such are not given here. Instead Sampson's treatment of greetings from the *salutarium* section of one of his several treatises on *dictamen* is excerpted. *Dictamen* traditionally taught that there were five parts to letters – the salutation, exordium, narration, petition, conclusion- and after the bulk of the letter, a sixth part, the sub-salutation. Like Guido Faba, nearly a third of whose influential *summa dictaminis* is devoted to the matter, Sampson gives extensive attention to salutation. The letter-writing of these treatises is of course not personal correspondence, but documents created for clients by clerks. They involve a highly articulated notion of hierarchy and a politics of access where appropriate forms of address, and cogent and clear writing according to established conventions is necessary for efficacy in petitioning, requesting favours, soliciting help, etc. Within the treatises the salutations also function as a finding device for sample letters from a king to a prince or vice versa, a lady to an archbishop, a clerk to his lord, the mayor of London, a knight to a merchant, etc.

All Sampson's *dictamen* treatises stress forms of address. A copy of his *Salutationes siue modus dictandi in gallicis* begins, 'Let all know that according to the teaching of Thomas Sampson this is the correct form for composing letters, as much in Latin as in French. And first he who is to send the letter will consider to whom he will send, since one can send to equals, to lesser, or to greater people' (*Sachent touz qe solonc l'enformacione Thomas Sampsone c'este la droite forme de feare lettres tant en latyn come en franceys. En primes cil qe mandera la letter regardera a qi il mandera come homme purra mander as owelx, mayndres ou greyndres*, CUL MS Ee.iv.20, f. 155ʳ). Sampson's *Ore fait a dire quant vous frez as seignours* (excerpted here) likewise stresses further the intricacy of such hierarchies: 'and first, when one composes a letter in the correct manner, it is necessary to consider three things: that is, who sends, and to whom, and for what reason, for there can be a greater sending to a lesser and the converse, or to a man of equal rank or estate, and so there are different forms of address for each one' (*e primes quant homme fra une lettere de droit nature il fait a regarder tres choses: ceste a savoir qi mande et a qi <et> par quelle cause qar y poet estre qe greindre mandra a meindre; vel econverso, ou homme d'owele condicione ou estat, et issint ad il a cheascun diverse salutacione*, f. 168ʳ, line 30).

In a society where justice, redress and mercy was still modelled on access to the king in his role of channelling divine justice and grace, the letter treatises' careful grades of greeting to and between kings, princes and so on downward not only add glamour but create a paradigmatic political model of the realm. This hierarchy was of course complicated by a panoply of regional and local influences and offices, but it serves as an underlying model and hence as a kind of theory as well as practice for the entire petitionary structure of public letters. It is also worth noting that Sampson's hierarchy, like that of contemporary estates writing and petitions to parliament and to the crown extends not only upwards but downwards to the *meindre* people of lower social rank (the *povers tenantz* of lines 103–4 below may be an example, though these could also be gentry landholders pleading hard).

AUDIENCE AND CIRCULATION. The treatise excerpted here is extant in four late-fourteenth-century manuscripts, and Sampson's materials are also further circulated through his successors' quarrying of them at the Oxford school (see e.g. Dean 319, 320). This treatise appears in BL Harley 4971, where the cartuary treatise of Sampson's successor, Simon d'O (**7d**) is also to be found. A second manuscript, Harley 4993, is also late fourteenth century with fifteenth-century flyleaves and a collection of similar materials. A third, Harley 3988, contains the 1396 *Manière de langage* (see (**7b**)) alongside Sampson's *Ore fait a dire* treatise. The fourth, Oxford, Magdalen College, MS 188, is fifteenth century and in addition to Sampson's formulary and other materials, includes translation exercises from French into Latin and then into English. The circulation of Sampson's specifically dictaminal works is not as wide as that of the *Manières*; this may be because government offices developed their own epistolary formularies (as in the well-known case of the poet Thomas Hoccleve, and the formulary he created in French at the Privy Seal). Nevertheless, given that Oxford was the main centre for business teaching (apart from the Inns of Court for law), Sampson's influence is probably greater than the number of extant manuscripts of his *ars dictandi* works suggests. It is significant that so much of his work was adopted by a major Benedictine abbey, as in the manuscript used here.

MANUSCRIPT SOURCE. CUL Ee.iv.20 is a substantial (312 × 244mm, writing area 300 × 230) book of 221 folios (formerly 284). The opening collection of documents (ff. 29^r–118^v) is the register of William Wyntershulle, former almoner and in 1382 chaplain to Thomas de la Mare, abbot of St Albans Abbey, Hertfordshire from 1349 to 1396. The volume as a whole (in several hands and scripts), compiles both earlier materials and additions and is the only known manuscript to contain all three of Sampson's dictaminal treatises. The book gives a vivid sense of the varied concerns of a large monastic house and of the highly developed bureaucracy of its administration: it contains not only records of the abbot's many acts, decisions, and letters, but also treatises on writing charters, wills, coroners' certificates, accounts and rents (ff. 131^r–146^v), a treatise on estate management (ff. 191^r–193^r, Dean 395), and many smaller miscellaneous items, such as a fifteenth-century English oath of office (on a tipped in half-leaf *76) for 'boteler, coke or other officer'; an account of early Anglo-Saxon law terms (f. 212^{r-v}); oaths of service for free men (*frank homme*) and *villeyn*, both given (though presumably not sworn) in French (f. 211^v); the form of inquisition for 'traylbaston', concerning homicides, robberies or other 'oppressiones ou grevaunces' (f. 113^r) and much else.

The manuscript is as much concerned with training as with records and procedures, and from f. 147^r to f. 177^r of the extant folios the book is devoted to Latin and French language arts, especially letter-writing. As well as Sampson's Latin and French treatises, there is an *Orthographia gallica* (Dean 287), and vocabularies for colours, numbers, adverbs and other parts of speech, and verb conjugations, usually with the French forms expounded in Latin (Dean 291r, 293, 298, 300, 387r). A witty French verse vocabulary on ff. 162^r–164^v (ed. Skeat 1906) set out in double columns with French and English rhyming equivalents draws on some of Bibbesworth's lexis in his *Tretiz* (**7a**).

On f. 30^r a copy of a French version of St Albans' admission to confraternity for 'monseignour Johan de Moleyns' (Marshal of Henry III) exemplifies one of the many occasions on which St Albans dealt with lay elite. There is also a treatise in French on 'Heraudie' (ff. 160^v–161^v, Dean 390) listing colours and devices, perhaps because St Albans, like many large abbeys, retained knights in its defence and had military tenants as well as elite knightly patrons. *Sir Gaweyn* and *le roy Alix*[andre] are included alongside the kings of France, Jerusalem and the (historical) *Alayn de la Zouche* (f. 161^r), exemplifying, in yet another register than that of *Brut* historiography, the operation of 'legendary' history as history for monks and laypeople alike.

7c. *Quant vous frez as seignours*

Bibliography. Hassell 1991 edits Sampson's French dictaminal treatises, including the model letters, together with Sampson's Latin treatise from CUL Ee.iv.20. Baker and Ringrose 1996 give a detailed description of CUL MS Ee.iv.20. On the Oxford Magdalen MS 188 containing Sampson's treatise see Kristol 2000. Sampson's *De modo dictandi* is edited by Camargo 1995: see also the discussion in Camargo 2007. An informative recent study of the field of clerical training is Cornelius 2010. For general accounts of medieval letter-writing see Constable 1976, Boureau 1997, and for *dictamen* in late-medieval England, Camargo 2007. Poster and Mitchell 2007 discuss the Western European tradition of instruction in letter-writing, as do Høgel and Bartoli 2015. The survey by Suggett (1946) remains valuable: on letters and petitions see 63–70. The *Epistolae* database is a valuable resource for medieval women's letters: http://epistolae.ccnmtl.columbia.edu/letters. On Hoccleve's formulary, see M. Brown 2011. Burnley 1986 is an important discussion of the interactions between dictaminal and literary styles, Dodd 2014 a valuable recent study of petitioning styles. Constable 1977 discusses the social hierarchies in *dictamen*. Some of Sampson's model letters are edited in Richardson 1942: Legge 1941 edits a fifteenth-century letter collection (which contains the treatise in (7e) among other teaching works). On the rather different tradition of private letters (mostly also in French up to the fifteenth century), see Constable 1976, Putter 2009b.

TEXT AND TRANSLATION

[f. 167r] *De modo dictandi letteras, supplicaciones, et billas cum salutatore subsequente in gallicis.*

[O]re fait a dire quant vous frez as seignours en manere de lettre quant en manere de bille, quant en manere de supplicacione, et q'est la difference parentre eux.

Sachez quant vous prieez nulle homme de socour et ne vous pleignez mye de nulle que vous ad fait grevaunce ou torte, c'est appellé un supplicacion de temperaltee. Mais si vous compleignez de nulle que vous ad tortinousment grevé et vous priez ent recoverer del roy ou de nulle ministre le roy, c'est un bille. Mez tout soit que nulle sei compleint de nulle qe tortousment lui ad ousté de sa esglise ou provendre, et prieent remedie del pape, Erchevesqe, ou evesqe, ceo serra une supplicacione appellé. De tous autres eschoses directis d'une persone a autre sount lettres faitez dont y coveymt savoir le manere de lour comencement et de reverence c'ome mettra al comencement de lez clausez et a la conclusione et subsalutacione si bien come de lour estiles. En primes c'est la manere de faire bille al roy:

On the art of writing letters, petitions, and bills with their appropriate greetings in order in French.

Now we shall explain how you are to proceed in the matter of letters, bills, and petitions, and the differences between them.

Be advised that when you are asking someone for help and you are not making a complaint about anyone who has done you harm or wrong, this is called a civil petition. But if you are complaining about someone who has illegally harmed you and you are asking the king or any minister of the king for redress, this is a bill. But should it be the case that anyone is complaining about somebody who has illegally removed him from his church or his prebendary, and they are petitioning for remedy for it from the pope, the archbishop, or bishop, this shall be called a petition. Any other subjects directed by one person to another are composed as letters, for which it is necessary to know how to begin them and the expression of respect that will be placed at the beginning of what is being stipulated, and at the end, and the concluding expressions of respect as well as their styles. And first is the correct manner of composing a bill to the king:

A nostre tresdouté et tresnoble seignour; *ou* A tres excellent et tres graciouse seignour nostre seignour le Roy. Moustre son humble et simple escoler si luy plest S. M. etcetera et sei complent de Romond Bramptone *et cetera.*

To our much honoured and very noble lord. *or* To the very excellent and very gracious lord, our lord king, his humble and simple scholar (if it please him) S. M. etc. presents and makes his complaint about Romond Brampton etc.

Et sachez qe vous n'escriveré a nully 'tres excelent et tresdoté seignour' si noun a emperoure ou roy ou prince. Et si nulle seignour d'autre terre mande a nostre seignour le roy il dirra issimt:

And be advised that you shall never write 'very excellent and very honoured lord' to anyone except an emperor or a king or a prince. And if any lord from another country writes to our lord the king he will say this:

A tres excelent et tresnoble prince *ou* excelent et noble prince le Roy d'Engletere *et cetera.*

To the very excellent and very noble prince *or* excellent and noble prince the king of England, etc.

Et a tous les autres seignours del roialme il escrivera en ceste manere.

And to all the other lords of the realm he will write in this way.

[*Instructions for the duke of Lancaster, counts, barons and knights follow*]

[f. 167r, line 20] Auxint et si al pape oue homme de seynt eglise *tunc sic*:

And so also if writing to the pope or other men of religion, *then this*:

Si al pape:

If to the pope:

Al tressentisme piere en Dieu ou al honouré ou treshonuré sire le soverayn vicar Jhesu Crist.

To the most holy father in God *or* to the honoured *or* very honoured lord, the sovereign vicar under Jesus Christ.

Si a eerchevesqe *tunc sic*:

If to an archbishop, *then this*;

A seintisme piere en Dieu et honourable seignour l'Ercevesqe de Cantirbriis.

To the most holy father in God and honourable lord, the Archbishop of Canterbury.

[*There follow instructions for the bishop of Salisbury, the abbot of Westminster, and a monk*]

[f. 167r, line 25] *vel sic* A tresreverent et tresamé homme et honourable seignour [le] Chanseler de la université d'Oxenford;

or thus To the much honoured and much loved gentleman and honourable lord, the Chancellor of the University of Oxford.

vel sic Al reverent et sage honme le Mair de Londre;

or thus To the honoured and wise personage, the Mayor of London.

vel sic A l'homme de reverente discretione et tresage, l'official de tiel lieu, *ou* til doctour ou autre grant clerc *et cetera.* [...]

or thus To the man of honoured discernment and the very wise (official of such and such a place) *or* such and such a doctor *or* other great cleric etc.

[f. 167v, line 3] Et sachez quant vous manderez as dames vous turnerez l'onour del seignour en la dame, ceo est a dire, quant vous nomerez nostre seignour le roy tresredouté, tresexcellent ou tresnoble seignour vous nomerez nostre dame la

And be advised that when you write a letter to ladies you apply the honour of the lord to the lady, that is to say, when you address our lord the king as very revered, very excellent, or very noble lord, you address our lady the queen as much revered, very

reyne tresdoté, tresexcellent ou tresnoble Reygne. Et touz jours quant nomerez le Roy, vous la nomerez reigne, quant al prince sa compaigne princesse, quant a duc, duchesse, quant a baron, baronesse quant chevalier, dame. Et touz lez seignours en lour lettres les nomerunt 'compaigne' et puis 'reigne', 'princesse' *et cetera*. Mais les chivalers et meyndres lez nomerez 'compaignes' tant solement.

Et les dames nomerent en lour lettres les seignours de lur seignourie, si bien come lour seignourie, come Philippe, par la grace de Dieu Dame d'Engleterre, d'Irlande et d'Aquitaigne *et cetera*.

N. T., compaigne al honourable Prince Edward eisné filz a noble Reigne d'Engleterre, Dame d'Irlande, Duchesse de Cornewaille et Countesse de Cestre [...].

excellent, or very noble queen. And always, just as you address the king as king, you shall address the queen as queen; just as to a prince, his consort princess, as to a duke, his duchess, as to a baron, his baroness and a knight, his lady. And all the lords in their letters will address them [first] as 'consort' and then queen, princess, etc. But in the case of knights and lesser people, you shall address them only as 'companions'.

And the ladies in their letters will use the titles of their lords, as also the name of their lordships, such as: Philippa, by the grace of God, Lady of England, Ireland and Aquitaine, etc.

N. T., consort of the honourable Prince Edward, oldest son of the noble queen of England, Lady of Ireland, Duchess of Cornwall and Countess of Chester [...].

[*Further royal and noble examples follow, down to a knight's wife, Alice Tuttebery, then follows advice on precision in thanking or reproving, with sample letters.*]

[f. 167^{v}, line 34] Et sachez qe greigndre reverence ferra homme autre foitz as femmes qe as hommes qar quant le prince nomera son piere trescher piere il dirra a sa mere treshonuree mere quar les hommes ne preignent pas si grande cure de reverence come font lez femmes [...].

[f. 168^{v}, line 21] Mes si une simple homme mande a nul seignour q'ad estile pur nul socour requeere, il ne mandra luy en manere de lettre, einz en manere de bille, feisant l'onour de estiel sanz contrere la seignourie, come a dire:

A tresgracious et tresdoté seignour le Roy moustre un simple et humble escoler, si luy pleist, Thomas Sampson;

vel sic A treshonuré et tresreverent seignour le Prince ou Duc;

vel A lour trerev[er]ent et noble seignour *vel* counte, suppliant ses povers tenantz de N.;

ou Al sentisme et honourable seignour et piere en Dieu, tiel evesqe.

And be advised that a man will sometimes pay greater respect to women than to men, for when the prince calls his father 'very dear father', he will say to his mother, 'Very honoured mother', for men do not pay so much heed to respect as women do [...].

But if a man of lowly status writes to a lord of title in order to ask for help, he should not write to him in the form of a letter, but rather in the form of a bill, using the title of honour but without bringing in the lordship, as in:

To the very gracious and very revered lord, the king presents a simple and humble school master, if it please him, Thomas Sampson;

or thus To the very honoured and very revered lord, the prince *or* duke;

or To their very revered and noble lord *or* earl, in supplication for his poor tenants of N.;

or To the most holy and honourable lord and father in God, such and such a bishop.

Et si lez dames mandent as Erchevesqes ou Evesqes

tunc sic A sentisme et treshonuré seignour et piere en Dieu, N., par div[i]ne suffrance Erchevesqe de Cantebris, la soene humble et devoute Katerine, Dame de B., sa fille espiritale, honours et toutes maners de reverences et soy mesmes toutditz prest a faire choses qe lui bien purrount vailer ou lieu tenir en bien et honour, solonc soun poar petit;

et econtra N, par divine suffrance Erchevesqe de Cantirbris, Primat de toute Engleterre a nostre treschere fille en Dieu K., salutz et nostre benisone.

Et sachez qu'en tiel manere vous frés vostre lettre et salutaciones as freres et moignes, q'ils n'ount pas estiel ne sount en la [de]gré d'abbé et priour, come vous voerés as autres amys, saluant son degré, forpris que vous nomerés lui en la dos de la lettre, moigne ou frere de tiel lieu, regardant toutditz que vous ne mandés a vostre soverangne ou ascun autre de greindre estat de vous 'salutz', qar cest parole 'salutz' signifie equitee, et lui facez compaignoun a grant deshonour de lui, et vous vous honourrez par vostre bouche demesme, le quel honour serra torné en vilaignie ou vergoigne de vous. Et pur ceo vous lui manderez honours et reverences solonc ceo que son estat demande. Et si vous soiez [f. 169r] couroucez devers un autre, vous n'en dirrez pas 'salutz' qar en cest cas vous dirrez en ceste manere:

Jeo me merveile grandement pur qoy vous vous afforcez si maliciousement d'endamager N. moun cousin, depuis q'il ne vous ad de rien offendu, come il m'ad fait a entendre *et cetera.*

And if women write to archbishops or bishops,

then thus To the most holy and much honoured lord and father in God, N., by divine sufferance Archbishop of Canterbury, his humble and devoted Katherine, Lady of B., his spiritual daughter, [sends] honour and all forms of respect and holds herself always ready to do what will serve him or maintain him well and in honour, according to her small power.

And in return N., by divine permission Archbishop of Canterbury, Primate of all England to our very dear daughter in God, K., greetings and our blessing.

And be advised that you compose your letter and greetings to friars and monks (supposing that they do not have a title or the rank of abbot or prior), as you will to other friends, acknowledging their rank, except that you will say on the back of the letter 'monk or friar of such and such a place', being careful always that to your sovereign or any other person of greater estate than yourself you do not send 'greetings', because this word 'greetings' signifies equality and makes you his equal, to his great dishonour, while you are granting honour to yourself out of your own mouth, honour which will turn into villainy or shame for you. And for this reason you will send honour and respect according to what his estate requires. And if you should be angry with someone, you will not say 'greetings', for in this case you will speak in this way:

I greatly wonder why you strive so maliciously to damage N. my kinsman, since, as he has assured me, he has done no offence to you, etc.

Notes

The orthography of the treatise is very unstable and not emended here. Some apparently erroneous spellings are probably phonetic and not errors of declension (for instance *une* for masculine nouns).

1 **frez** Hassell inserts *lettres*, but the phrase *faire lettre(s)*, compose, write letter(s), is so common that the shortened form seems possible.

20 **de reverence** Hassell emends as *de [les] reverence[s]*.

29–30 **Romond Bramptone** Hassell notes that a Romundus de Bamptone appears in a list of distrained persons on f. 146*v* of the manuscript for avoiding payment of a toll.

67 **la nomerez Reigne** Hassell emends to *vous nomerez la Reigne*

77 **Philippe** Philippa of Hainault married Edward III in 1327. After the treaty of Bretigny in 1360, Aquitaine was governed by their son Edward the Black Prince, paying homage to his father for the duchy, though the sovereignity remained disputed by France.

80–1 **compaigne al honourable Prince Edward** Joan, countess of Kent (*c.* 1328–85), married Edward (1330–76), oldest son and heir of Edward III and Philippa of Hainault, Prince of Wales and Aquitaine, in 1361, through whom she was the mother (and during his minority, the guardian) of Richard II (*ODNB* Joan *suo jure* countess of Kent).

95 **contrere** *AND* gives 'go against', but see *DMF*, *s.v.* 'contraire' 2 for the semantic field of 'rapprochement', esp. sense B (a). The underlying thought seems to be that the humble person may use only the rank of a superior, not the details of the particular lordships and properties attached to it.

112 **Katerine, Dame de B** The identity of this Lady Katherine is not known.

125 **en la [de]gré d'abbé et priour** MS *en la gré d'abbé et prior* emended to clarify a difficult reading. It is possible that the original means 'at the grace of the abbot or prior' with a sense of monks who have committed some offence.

7d. *Pur ceo que j'estoie requis*: Treatise on Conveyancing [not in Dean] Prologue: London, British Library, MS Harley 4971, f. 34*v*

Date of composition and provenance. Late fourteenth century, perhaps Oxford.

Author, sources and nature of text. The lectures on conveyancing – 'the drawing of deeds and other instruments, for the transference of property from one person to another' (*OED*) – from which this prologue is taken are ascribed to Simon of O[xford? Oseney? Offord?], *fl.* 1420, who taught business law up into the time of Henry V. From the thirteenth century onwards, letter and charter formularies, model court rolls and treatises and training in the points of oral pleading were needed in French and Latin for stewards, clerks and advocates, all of whom needed some knowledge of the law for varying purposes. In one of his own cartularies, Thomas Sampson says that his instruction is for young men intending to enter the service of lords and magnates (*pro informacione iuvencorum in servicia dominorum et magnatorum*, BL Harley 773, f. 16*r*, a manuscript which also contains instructions for jurors in French, ff. 50*r*–51*r*).

French was the common language of pleading in court and, alongside Latin, important for many legal documents, but common law training was not offered at universities in England. It was a standard topic in the courses offered by Thomas Sampson and his successors (**7b**, **7c**) at the Oxford business school or 'school of clerkship', where students trained as scriveners and administrators. Although not taught as much law as those studying at the Inns of Court, students at the Oxford school learned basic aspects of the common law, especially conveyancing, in courses that also

included practice in improving their spoken French (using *Manières* dialogues; see (**7b**)), writing and composing letters and documents in French (through, for example, letter formularies, as in (**7c**)) and basic numeracy and accountancy. The 'law French' of later-medieval England has often been viewed as a frozen technical koiné, but seems never to have been taught as a distinctive type of French: specialised legal terms were encountered and learned within the matrix of oral and written French in which students heard their lectures and did their exercises.

Nor was the need for such instruction restricted to purely clerical professions: as Thomas Sampson himself observes in his own treatise on charters, 'There are also certain records among merchants and other laypeople that are made in French' (*Auxint il y ont certaisne remembrances parentre merchantz et autres gentz lays que sont fait en franceys*, Lansdowne 560, f. 34ʳ (new foliation), lines 4–5), and he provides sample forms such as a merchant will use *en sa schope* in agreements and contracts.

Differing groups had different competences in the various languages needed for business and the professions, as Sampson himself notes: 'Although for the usual way of making charters, agreements, indentures, records and muniments there is the common cartuary in Latin, nevertheless, since I, Thomas S[ampson], teacher of this craft, have an idea that many children are very minimally educated, I will write the following discourse in French, since students with only a rudimentary literacy will be able more easily to understand the rules in French than in Latin.' (*Coment que por comen ordre de faire charters, escriptz, endentures, e[t] remembrances et munimentz agardantz [y] a la comen chartuarie en latyn, nepurquant a cause qe je Thomas S., enformer d'icel art, ay conceu qe plusours enfantz qui sunt si tenuement lettrez, je ferray la prologe devant en franceis a cause que les escolers qi sont si tenuement lettrés purront le pluys legerement entendre les reulez en fraunceys q'en latyn*, MS Lansdowne 560, new foliation 30ʳ.) On the evidence of another (fifteenth-century) manuscript Sampson was also prepared to work with English alongside French for those students who needed it (Kristol 2000).

Simon of O follows this practice in his own conveyancing lectures, as had Sampson's immediate successor William Kingsmill. The French introduction to Simon of O's lectures on charter-making and conveyancing uses several modesty topoi of authority and utility, evoking the prestigious status of literary French. But it also offers meritocratic pathways to those who need to function in *citee, borgh, ne ville* – in the cities, boroughs and towns of the realm – without the benefit of an expensive early education.

Audience and circulation. Manuscripts with selections from the Oxford business school curriculum and from the Inns of Court circulated widely. Their texts often teach polite French conversation alongside instruction in the protocols for pleading or for letter writing, charters and spelling, since both legal and administrative clerks needed to understand and perhaps themselves to speak oral French. The public for these manuscripts formed a wide, often meritocratic group, engaged in a variety of clerical, administrative and professional roles. Students heard and made notes from lectures in French, and both they and their teachers kept compilations and collections of these French resources (Baker and Ringrose 1996, xxxii–xxxiii). Simon of O's treatise is extant in BL Add. 25,238 s. xvi, in Latin and English, ff. 64–116ᵛ and Oxford Bodleian MS Rawl. A 357 (after 1421) as well as the manuscript selected here.

Manuscript source. Harley MS 4971 is a composite manuscript with added flyleaves from an earlier copy of Aristotle. Some leaves have been trimmed but in general the manuscript is 240 × 180mm. Simon of O's conveyancing treatise (ff. 34ᵛ–38ᵛ) is in the first part (ff. 4ᵛ–41ᵛ), a much thumbed miscellany in variously coloured parchments of French and Latin business-training texts of the third quarter of the fourteenth century. The texts are written in cursive hands, with frequent sub-headings, incipits and explicits in textura and occasionally elaborated opening capitals, or tall flourished top-line ascenders, but all (apart from red paraphs in the first quire) are monochrome in brown ink. The first part also includes an *Orthographia Gallica* treatise (Dean 287), vocabularies

(Dean 300), a French formulary for bills and letters (see (**7c**) and Dean 317), a treatise on a household clerk's duties (Dean 397) and some conjugations from Donatus's grammar added slightly later (Dean 293). Simon of O's lecture on conveyancing is followed by a table for how to convert *denarii* into *solidi* and *marcas* into *libris* (f. 39^{r-v}) and on f. 30^{v} a *modus tenendi curiam* (form for holding court). The manuscript is best known today for its extract from Chrétien de Troyes's *Erec et Enide* and its copy of the *Manuel des pechiez* (**24b**). Part II, ff. 42–92, contains a Latin legal formulary and statutes of Richard II's reign.

Bibliography. The lectures are unedited. On Simon of O see Richardson 1939, Baker 1999 (166–7), with a valuable overview and discussion of the legal aspects of the Oxford school's teaching, on which see also Richardson 1941. On the relations between business teachers and the university, and their different teaching subjects, see Camargo 2007. Pantin 1929 edits a dictamen treatise attributed to Simon of O. On the multilingualism of the law see Brand 2000. For a treatise on oral pleading, see *Cy poet un juvenes home ver Coment il deit parler sotylement en Court*, ed. Briggs with Jenkinson 1936, and for the developing needs of legal training in the thirteenth century, Maitland and Baildon 1891. Kingsmill's early-fifteenth-century conveyancing lectures and precedents are discussed in Baker 1999. Dean does not include legal works in French but catalogues other items in the manuscripts shared with them. Baker and Ringrose 1996 give detailed itemisation of a large corpus of law and French manuscripts with an informative introduction. On the circulation of such manuscripts see further Kristol 1990, 299; Richardson 1941, 1939. Kristol 2000 is an important study showing the flexibility of French teaching in relation to different linguistic competences and the inclusion of English.

TEXT AND TRANSLATION

[f. 34^{v}] *Iam incipiunt regule cartarum secundum novum usum*

Pur ceo que j'estoie requis par ascunz prodeshommez de faire un chartuarie pur lour enfantz enformer de faire chartes, escripts, endentures, obligacions, defesance[s], acquietancez, contuare, salutare en latyn [et] franceys ensemblement, ove altres choses bosoignables as [es]coliers pur savoir que serveront et les prodhommes et mesnés hommes d'Engletere, solo[n]c l'usage que court a yceste jour present, jeo l'ay fait solonc ceo que les condic[i]ons me veignent en memorie ou ay apprys, en priant touz prodhommes de m'avoir pour excusé si jeo le face rudement et nient clergealment par tot, qar jeo ne suy que jeofnes hommes de savoir, tot soit que jeo suy veile d'age, en contrariant a seint Daniel qu'estoit veil du savoir et juyn d'age.

Nepurquant, pur vostre benigne supportacion j'espoier de mesner a droites fyn par la grace de Dieu demostrant

Here begin the rules for drawing up charters in the new way.

Because I was requested by several men at law to make a cartuary to teach their young apprentices how to make charters, writs, indentures, bonds, annulments, and acquittals, and how to continue or begin them in Latin and French (together with other things necessary for students who will serve as estate administrators of England to know) according to the usage current at the present day, I have composed it as the relevant stipulations come to mind or as I have learned them, entreating all worthy men to hold me excused if I do this simply and not in a learned manner throughout, for I am but a man young in learning, though I am old in age (the opposite of holy Daniel, who was old in learning and young in age).

Nevertheless, through your beneficent support, I hope to bring it to a good conclusion by the grace of God, showing first

adeprimes quelle chose si est la chartre et puis de touz escriptz, endentures, et les altres avantnomez: et puis aprés d[e] lour obstacles, vices, doutes, et natures: fesanz les chartours, escripts, munimentz adeprimes en latyn et puis en franceys si overtement come par lour ensample homme ove petit enformacion plusours purra faire sanz estre de nul sage pur nounsavier repris en citee, borgh, ne ville dedeins le roialme d'Engletere, solonc l'usage del roialme, l'an du regne .ii. cent et cinquantisme primer *etcitera*.

of all what kind of thing a charter is, and then all the bills, indentures, and the other forms previously named: and then, after that, the objections, defects, difficulties, and dispositions, making the charters, writs and documents first in Latin and then in French so clearly that by their example, a man with a little instruction will be able to produce many of them without being reproached for ignorance by any wise person in city, borough, or town within the kingdom of England, according to the usage of the realm, in the two hundredth and fifty-first year of the kingdom, *etcetera*.

Notes

2 **chartuarie** A cartuary is a formulary for charters etc., as opposed to a cartulary, a collection of actual charters, but the two terms are readily confused (see *OED*, *s.v.* 'cartulary').

2 **prodeshommez** The word has a late-medieval sense of 'householder, law-worthy man' (*AND*, *s.v.* 'prudom'), but probably means here 'specialist in a given field or occupation', attested in 1260: hence men of law or teachers of law (*Trésor de la langue française informatisé* (http://www.atilf.atilf.fr/tlf.htm), *s.v.* 'prudhomme', 2a).

5 **defesance[s]** a deed annulling another document.

5 **contuare** A Latin infinitive (like the following word, *salutare*), perhaps a reduced form of *contuaere*, to ponder, weigh (Lewis and Short 1879, *s.v.* 'contueor').

6–7 **latyn [et] franceys ensemblement** could refer to bi-lingualism in the documents actually to be produced, but more probably to the capacity of the students to produce them in both languages.

7 **[es]coliers** The manuscript has a small rough patch at the beginning of the word.

8–9 **prodhommes et mesnés hommes** Synonymous terms meaning 'estate manager'; *mesnés*, 'household', is used adjectivally here, in juxtaposition to *hommes*; cf. other specialised meanings of *prudhommes* in n. to 2 above.

15 **par tot** MS *par tott* (or *tot* with otiose flourish).

17 **seint Daniel** The Old Testament prophet Daniel is associated with dream books of prognostication and insight in the Middle Ages, see e.g. Dean 384.

20 **supportacion** As with many terms associated with sponsorship of a text, this could mean anything from direct patronage to general encouragement. Its primary meaning is maintenance, upkeep (*AND*, *s.v.* 'supportation').

22 **adeprimes quelle chose** underlined and in textura script.

24 **d[e]** MS *do* Although emended here to a standard form of the definite article, MS *do* may be a slip into Latin (*do*, *dare* to give).

24–5 **lour obstacles, vices, doutes** in textura script with underlining.

27 **latyn et puis en franceys** The implication may be that once the students have learned enough Latin and French, French versions of Latin documents can be made.

28 **homme** in textura with underlining.

32–3 **l'an du regne .ii. cent et cinquantisme primer** The significance of the dating here is unclear. The two hundred and fifty-first year of the kingdom is a conceivable date if counting by the *quo warranto* provisions established by Edward I, i.e. the need for property holders to show that they held from the last year of Richard I's reign (1189), but 1440 would be late for the date of Simon of O's reworking of Thomas Sampson's conveyancing lectures.

35 **etcitera** sic MS

7e. John Barton's *Donait françois* [Dean 290], Prologue: Oxford, All Souls College, MS 182, f. 322r

DATE OF COMPOSITION AND PROVENANCE. *c.* 1400, commissioned from Paris-trained clerks (in London or Oxford [?]).

AUTHOR, SOURCES AND NATURE OF TEXT. John Barton, who claims to be the patron of the *Donait*, was a physician active *c.* 1417, and possibly the John Barton accused but cleared of heresy who subsequently wrote a *Confutatio Lollardorum* dedicated to Henry V. The nature of Barton's text is signalled by its title: Donatus was a Roman grammarian whose treatise on the parts of speech (the *Ars minor*) was, like his longer *Ars grammatica*, in use throughout the Middle Ages and beyond and formed Barton's model. Barton's *Donait* is often claimed as the first extant French grammar anywhere (as opposed to works on spoken French such as (**7a**) and (**7b**)). Although there are extant earlier short notes on verb conjugations, and there may have been some tradition of oral discussion and grammatical reflection, Barton's is the first treatise designed as a vernacular grammar. It precedes two other short works in England (the *Liber donati* of *c.* 1415, and the *Donait solum douce franceis de Paris* of *c.* 1410) and the later-fifteenth- and sixteenth-century grammars of French in France. Barton's *Donait* systematically integrates medieval grammatical knowledge with an analysis of French, adapting the categories of Latin grammatical thought to think about French as a language (Lusignan 1987, 113–15, 119). The *Donait* uses a series of questions and answers, and short examples to discuss vowels, consonants, and how they are produced, then moves to morphology and parts of speech. Barton's claim that he has commissioned the *Donait* from Parisian clerks, having himself been educated there, may indicate clerks from England educated in Paris, as much as clerks living in France. It is also possible that Barton himself wrote the treatise. In either case his use of the Parisian dialect as a credential testifies to a renewed interest in continental French also witnessed in the *Manières*. Politically, relations with continental France were intensified during the English struggle to establish and maintain an English kingdom in France and the English needed more spoken French. In textual production, linguistic and orthographic questions about the writing of vernaculars also intensified in the fifteenth century in England, and several treatises on the orthography of French preceded Barton's work.

Barton gives three reasons for having good French: communication between neighbouring England and France; the fact that the law and much else in England is in French; and that English lay letter-writing is done in French. All these, he claims, need 'correct French' (*droit françois*). By the prologue's own testimony, French is still used in England, but the treatise constructs fresh social cachet for continental French.

AUDIENCE AND CIRCULATION. Only the one incomplete manuscript text is known, but Barton is part of a strongly developing trend in the early fifteenth century and although the extant copy seems to have belonged to a successful clerk to the elite, it would be surprising if the treatise did not have a wider audience largely overlapping with that of the *Manières* (**7b**) and that for Caxton's

Dialogues in French and English (*c.* 1483; see Cooper 2007). This type of treatise, addressing or claiming elite status, but designed for the increasingly wide audience interested in French as a social accomplishment and for professional audiences interested in good French for their careers, continues to be produced in the sixteenth century: for the prologues to significant treatises by Alexander Barclay (1521), John Palgrave (1530), Gilles de Wes (1532, for Henry VIII's daughter Mary), and others, see Kibbee 1991, Appendix II; for biographies *ODNB*; for studies Machan 2009, D. Williams 2004.

Manuscript source. All Souls MS 182 is a quarto of 375 folios, written in several fifteenth-century cursive hands. The first half (ff. 1–190) contains a copy of Archbishop John Pecham's register together with a Latin letter collection of the fifteenth century (Martin 1882; Brown 1972): the second half (ff. 191–375) is a collection of French petitions, *Manière* Dialogues (see (**7b**)), proverbs and vocabulary collections and copies of treatises, including those by Bibbesworth (**7a**) and Coyfurelly (Dean 289). The *Donait*'s treatment of the verb is followed in the manuscript by part of the 1399 *Manière* known as *Petit livre pour enseigner les enfants* (see (**7b**) and Dean 282), perhaps a substitution or a *faute de mieux* completion of the chapter: the *Donait*'s final parts of speech are not extant in this, the only extant manuscript, and possibly the treatise was never completed.

According to its own inscriptions, the entire manuscript was left to All Souls in 1484 by William Elyot, former registrar of Edmund Lacy, bishop of Exeter (Legge 1941, xii). The French section of the manuscript was probably previously owned by John Stevenes (d. *c.* 1458), a clerk of Exeter diocese, notary public and successful administrator, and a chaplain of Henry V's in France. Stevenes is often mentioned in the registers of Archbishops Arundel (for whom he worked in the Canterbury diocese's administration from at least 1407–13, especially in Norwich), Stafford and Chicheley, and he was present at Oldcastle's trial in 1413 (Legge 1941, xii–xvii). This career may partly explain the range of exemplary royal and episcopal letters (and one from Christine de Pizan) collected in the formularies and treatises of the French part of All Souls MS 182.

Bibliography. The *Donait* is edited by Stengel 1879: Lusignan 1987, 111–27 is an important discussion. On Barton see *ODNB*; Kibbee 1991, 86–92. Legge 1941 edits the French letters and petitions in All Souls MS 182. For other works in the French Donatus tradition see Dean 290–4, for orthographical treatises 287–9, and for discussion, Merrilees 1993 and 1986. For the fifteenth-century status and politics of French, see Butterfield 2009, Machan 2009, D. Williams 2004. Early-modern treatises are extracted and their authors' biographies given in Kibbee 1991, Appendix.

TEXT AND TRANSLATION

[f. 322rb]: [P]our ceo que les bones gens du roiaume d'Engleterre sont enbrasez a sçavoir lire et escrire, entendre et parler droit françois afin qu'ils puissent entrecomuner bonement ove lour voisins, c'est a dire les bones gens du roiaume de France, et ainsi pour ce que les leys d'Engleterre pour le graigneur partie et aussi beaucoup de bones choses sont misez en françois, et aussi bien pres touz les s[eigneu]rs et toutes les dames en mesme roiaume d'Engleterre volentiers s'entrescrivent en romance tres necessaire je cuide estre aus Engleis de sçavoir la droite nature de françois. A le honneur de Dieu et

Because the good people of the kingdom of England are inflamed with the desire to know how to read and write, understand and speak correct French so that they can communicate well with their neighbours, that is to say the good people of the kingdom of France, and also because the greater part of the laws of England and many other valuable things have been put into French, and also because nearly all the lords and ladies of the said realm of England gladly write to each other in the vernacular, I think it very necessary for the English to know the true nature of French. To the honour of God and his sweet

de sa tresdoulce miere et toutz les saintez de paradis, je, Johan Bartoun, escolier de Paris, nee et nourie toutez voiez d'Engleterre en la conté de Cestre, j'ey baillé aus avantdiz Anglois un *Donait françois* pur les briefment entreduyr en la droit language de Paris et du pais la d'entour, laquelle language en Engliterre on appelle doulce france[is]. Et cest *Donait* je le fis la fair[e] a mes despenses et tres grande peine par pluseurs bons clercs du language avantdite. Pur ce, mes chiers enfantz et tresdoulcez puselles que avez fam d'apprendre cest *Donait*, sçachez qu'il est divisé en belcoup de chapiters si come il apperera cy avale.

mother and all the saints of paradise, I, John Barton, scholar of Paris, but nevertheless born and bred in England in the county of Chester, have made available to the aforesaid English a French *Donait* in order concisely to introduce them to the correct language of Paris and its region, the which language is called in English 'sweet French'. And I have had this *Donait* made at my own expense and great trouble by several good scholars of the aforesaid language. Wherefore, my dear children and sweet young girls who are hungry to understand this *Donait*, you should know that it is divided into many chapters as will appear below.

Notes

4 **entrecomuner** English and French people had long communicated in French as Barton's other reasons for French's importance suggest (it is the language of letters, law and *beaucoup de bones choses*): Barton is not recording a new development here so much as a new emphasis on mutual understanding.

17 **nee et nourie** Masculine but with *ee* spelling for *é*.

21 **de Paris et du pais** MS *du Paris et de pais*.

22–3 **doulce france[is]** Perhaps an intralingual name for the variety of French concerned, or possibly an appellation for the Île de France. 'Dulce' is already an epithet for France in the *Chanson de Roland*. For French as a 'sweet' language, see also *Manieres* (**7b**:5, 21, 26). On the wide range of medieval meanings for sweetness see Carruthers 2006.

23 **france[is]** MS france.

26–7 **et tresdoulcez puselles** French manuals were increasingly associated with young women during the sixteenth century, transforming the image of French into a leisure accomplishment within the private sphere (Paulsson Lash 2012).

8. London Frenches

8a. Andrew Horn, *Qui veut bone electioun faire* and *La Feste royale du Pui* [not in Dean]: *Liber custumarum*, City Corporation of London Records Office, COL/CS/01/006, f. 6r–v and ff. 176v–177r

Date of composition and provenance. Part of a compilation made at the London Guildhall, probably shortly after 1324, with continuations down to the reign of Henry V.

Author, sources and nature of text. The *Liber custumarum* is one of the largest and richest medieval English city customals (written collections of customary law, statutes, charters and other documents). The book, some of it until recently in the London Guildhall's possession,

was originally compiled by Andrew Horn (*c.* 1275–1328), a member of the fishmongers' guild and Chamberlain of the City of London from 1320 to 1328. In addition to the *Liber custumarum*, Horn left important legal, civic, and probably also historical compilations to the Guildhall in his will. As Chamberlain, Horn was responsible for the collection of city revenue (he had his own court), and had the duty of defending the customs, liberties and pastimes noted in the rolls and books of the Chamber. Defence of the city's liberties against the crown was sometimes needed (for one among several predecessor compilations made for much the same reasons as Magna Carta, see (1)), and the city's relations with the crown often had wide implications: London and its mayor Hamo Chigwell played a role in Queen Isabella's deposition of Edward II, for instance. London mayoral politics weave through the history of fourteenth-century literature, most notoriously leading to the execution of Chaucer's contemporary, Thomas Usk, author of *The Testament of Love*, a guild scrivener and adherent of two controversial mayors, Northampton and Brembre. The London Guildhall has recently been claimed as a significant institution in later-medieval literary culture: several scribes of important fourteenth-century literary manuscripts are identified as belonging to it (by Mooney and Stubbs 2013) and its compilatory practices play a role in literary production throughout the century (Bahr 2013).

The tri-lingual *Liber custumarum* contains large numbers of documents and assimilates these pragmatic records into its role as a book of London, witness to the city's rights, and concerned with the fundamental nature of those rights. The opening of the book is a ceremonious and thoughtful representation of London. It originally included Henry of Huntingdon's description of England (see (1)), with shire names given in English and 'Briton' (i.e. Welsh) as well as Latin. William FitzStephen's twelfth-century Latin description of the city follows, celebrating London's fame, wealth, and amenities, its clerical schools and their dramatic performances, its markets, trade, citizens, miracle plays, pastimes, games and historically illustrious inhabitants (Riley, II.i, 2–15). Of the prominent London citizens mentioned, the first is Brutus, founder of 'New Troy' (*Troynovant*), later London, as proclaimed in so many *Brut* texts (see e.g. (16), (42)). FitzStephen's description is immediately followed by the discussion on the election of London mayors given here, an adaptation of material from Book III of Brunetto Latini's celebrated *Tresor*.

Latini (*c.* 1220–94) is notoriously placed by Dante, his fellow Florentine citizen, among the *Inferno*'s sodomites, but was, as Dante himself recognised, a major figure and a leading example of the new professional bureaucratic and administrative writers of the thirteenth century (cf. Pierre d'Abernon de Fetcham's characterisation of himself as God's *notour e estruement*, *Lumere as lais* (19), v. 10). In the civic and consciously republican government of post-Ghibelline Florence, notaries practised commercial law, drawing up contracts and deeds, etc., and were also professional masters responsible for teaching commercial custom and documentation. After the defeat of the Guelphs in 1260, Latini was exiled: he wrote *Li Livres dou Tresor* in French in Arras. The *Tresor* is a neo-Aristotelian encyclopaedia: its first book compiles cosmology, divine and world history and a bestiary (*la nature de toutes choses ... devisee en .iii. manieres, selonc theorique*), the second (*pourquoi on doit les unes choses faire et les autres non, selon logike*) is on virtues, vices and ethics, and the third book deals with rhetoric with a concluding section (chapters 73–105) on the governance of cities.

The annual election of the mayor of London was highly contentious: demands for free election by all the citizens as opposed to election by a limited number of the wealthier male citizens resurfaced throughout the fourteenth and fifteenth centuries. Horn's role as Chamberlain offered him a central vantage point on the competing interests around the mayoralty. Perhaps as a result, his model of governance is characterised by reciprocity. The sovereign and the mayor can do nothing without securing the assent of the citizens, whose responsibility for a good choice (*bone electioun*) of London's leader is therefore all the greater. As Bahr suggests, Horn does not naively celebrate civic harmony, so much as point to its fragility and the readiness of the Crown to exploit disunity (2013, 93–7).

Horn adapted the *Tresor* carefully. He makes few lexical changes of significance (the main one is to replace the *Tresor*'s name for the ruler (the lord, *li sires*) by 'mayor or governor' (*le meire ou le governour*), but his selection and arrangements show his skill as a compiler. Horn first gives the substance of Latini's chapter on the foundation of justice and the election of the prince (*Tresor*, III.74). He uses *Tresor* III.75 for desirable qualities in a ruler, but detaches the chapter's final paragraph to form a new, separate chapter 'on the discords and struggles that arise in towns through the neglect of the guardian'. Then he selects Latini's preparations for electing the next lord and the handover to a new lord, but also incorporates *Tresor* III.97 for general principles of a lord's conduct. He then takes chapter 96's discussion of rulers who wish to be loved and rulers who wish to be feared and joins the material with the final part of Latini's chapter on the difference between a king and a tyrant.

Compilation was a highly respected literary activity, and, especially from the thirteenth century onwards, *summae*, encyclopaedias, and systematic scholastic aids proliferated, while compilation and its manuscript instantiations remained important to fourteenth-century literary production. Horn uses few specifically literary terms and does not discuss his procedures in adapting Latini, but his selections, his disposition of them and above all their placing in this particular book exemplify the eloquence and efficacy that acts of compilation could have. Following his multilingual presentation of England's administrative divisions and William Stephens's Latin encomium of the city, Horn's presentation of London's governance combines European thought and London practice in his city's main transregional vernacular, and unites principles and practice to form a text at once suasive and useful.

Equally notable in Horn's compilation are the francophone sociabilities and politics of the *Feste du Pui*, a fraternity of leading citizens and merchants (*li amorous compaignoun qui sont demoraunt e repairaunt en la bone cité de Lundres*), who elected their own 'prince' annually, held a competition for the best French lyric poem at their annual feast (*Feste du Pui*), and kept their own clerks and records in French. Horn includes a copy of the *Pui*'s founding and revised statutes. The feast and its poetic competition was the focus of the society, but members were also supposed to attend one another's weddings and funerals and generally to support each other. The London *Pui* was probably formed in imitation of that in Arras: as the Lord Edward, the future Edward I participated in the Arras *Pui* in 1263 and may have hoped to diffuse political tensions in London by encouraging a similar convivial society in London. A leading founder of the London *Pui* was most probably Henry de Waleys, mayor of London in 1273–4 and mayor of Bordeaux in 1275. While the London *Pui* excluded women and was more intensely hierarchical than that of Arras, both participate in their different ways in the new literate, record-keeping civic cultures of Europe, their cultural production as much informed by the energies, interests and networks of townsmen as of courts and noblemen. Since Latini's *Tresor* was composed in Arras in 1260, it may well be that the sociability of that town's *Pui* informs Latini's vision of civic governance and hence ultimately also Horn's account of the regulations for the city's choice of its mayor and the regulations governing the choice of London's social and cultural 'prince' and annual best song.

Audience and circulation. As a compilation, the *Liber* must have been known to and used by Guildhall and city officials, and the documents within it will also have been known to the broader public of various groups and individuals in the city in connection with whom they were originally generated. Latini's *Tresor*, Horn's source for *Qui veut bone electioun*, was widely owned both by European nobility and citizens. It is extant in at least ninety French manuscript copies (thirteenth to fifteenth centuries), as well as in subsequent translations into Italian and other languages. The *Tresor* had a continuing circulation in French in England: it is listed among the '*Libri romanizati*' of Isabella, mother of Edward III, and a copy of the *Tresor*, together with a French *Secré* (see (33)) and other texts, was included in a manuscript partly prepared by an Anglo-Norman scribe and given to Edward III by his bride Philippa of Hainault in 1326–7 (Michael 1985, 589–90). In 1393 the London moneylender Gilbert Maghfield accepted a copy of Latini's *Tresor* as security against a loan (Galloway 2011).

The *Pui* regulations detail two eras in the company's formation, its initial setting up and its later reform and more detailed regulations (from which the passage here is taken). The *Estatuz du Pui* will have been known to the members (including both local and foreign merchants) over some years and to subsequent users of the *Liber custumarum*. Cooper 2006 sees the *Pui* as a possible influence on the *Canterbury Tales*: Fisher (1964, 76–83) argues that the company may have survived long enough for Gower to direct his *Cinkante Balades* towards its poetry competition.

MANUSCRIPT SOURCE. The *Liber custumarum* manuscript (City Corporation of London Records Office, COL/CS/01/006) is more richly decorated than many contemporary 'literary' manuscripts (for a colour photogravure of f. 6r see Riley, II.i: for a plate, Sandler 1986 I, pl. 182), and was possibly worked on by the so-called Subsidiary Artist of the Queen Mary Psalter (Dennison 1990 and plates: and on the relations between the artists of the *Liber* and the Auchinleck manuscript, Hanna 2005, 79–82). The text of *Qui veut bone electioun* is written in *anglicana formata* in two columns, each column surrounded by foliate borders with trefoils, besants and small heads among the foliage, in pink, blues, rust, gilt and touches of the orange typical of East Anglia (where the Subsidiary Artist seems to have worked). An illuminated initial, seven lines high and filled with foliated scrolls, opens the work and the text's authorities – *Aristotle*, *Salamon*, *Tullie* (Cicero) and *li Apostles* are picked out in the margins (written over the broad foliate frame of the right-hand margin and outside the narrower left-hand border). The *Liber* receives a ceremonial treatment appropriate to its identity as the book of London's legal-historical and cultural identity. The *Pui* entry, deep within the manuscript at f. 176 ff., is undecorated and in a less formal hand with secretary features in the same bi-columnar text blocks.

As with the history of Horn's compilations in themselves (the *Liber custumarum* and his earlier *Liber legum antiquorum regum*), the manuscript history is complex, but its reconstruction has been indispensable to current understanding of the nature of Horn's work. Both his compiled volumes suffered dismemberment into twenty fragments and reassembly into three volumes while in the hands of the antiquary Sir Robert Cotton (1571–1631): see Riley, II.i, xvii–xxiv; Catto 1981, 376; Ker 1985. Cotton eventually returned one of the new volumes to the Guildhall (the modern *Liber custumarum*), retained one (now BL Cotton Claudius D.II) and gave one to Sir Francis Tate (now Oxford, Oriel College MS 46). These three manuscripts make up what was originally a manuscript of over 372 leaves (as reconstructed from a fifteenth-century table of contents in the Oriel manuscript by Ker 1985, 137–9). The Latini-based extracts together with the preceding shire-list from Henry of Huntingdon and FitzStephen's poem on London are all in a single quire which seems to have been inserted (probably by the Guildhall clerk John Carpenter in 1419; see Catto 1981, 397; Bahr 2013, 42–3; Mooney and Stubbs 2013, 10–15) into the *Leges anglorum* section of the *Liber legum antiquorum regum* (now Cotton Claudius D.II, f. 1a; see Riley, II.ii, 624–6; Catto 1981, 377).

BIBLIOGRAPHY. For the *Liber custumarum* see Riley, ed., 1859–62, II.i (Horn's Latini compilation is at 16–25). *Qui veut bone electioun* is translated in Riley, II.ii, 517–28. The French texts of the *Liber* are online in the *AND* Source Texts (http://www.anglo-norman.net/sources/). For the *Liber*'s text and manuscript history see Riley, II.i, ix–xxvi; Ker 1985; Catto 1981; Dennison 1990. Hanna 2005, 74–103 discusses the importance of Horn's books as physical and intellectual models for London book-making. See also Bahr 2013, D. Cannon 2003. For Horn see Catto 1981 and *ODNB*: for discussion of his will, Dennison 1990. On the details of his compilation see further Catto 1981, 388–91: Bahr 2013, 83–9. Latini's *Tresor* is edited by Carmody 1948: this is not entirely satisfactory in textual method but is based on a Picard manuscript presumably closer to Horn's exemplar than the Escorial and Venetian base manuscripts of the editions by Barrette and Baldwin 2003 and Beltrami *et al.* 2007. The *Tresor* is translated by Baldwin and Barrette 1993: on its role in northern urban cultures see Lusignan 2009, and in London, Sabapathy 2014, 1–5. The *Feste du Pui* is printed in Riley, II.i, 216–28 and translated in II.ii, 579–94. Crucial studies are Sutton 1992; Cooper 2006 (which includes an extant winning *Pui* song); Symes 2013. For the Guildhall and the politics of city and crown see Barron 2004: for its importance in literary history, see e.g. Strohm 1992 on Usk. For

Horn and the development of London legal-historical writing see Hanna 2005, Keene 2008: on London literary cultures, Meale 1995, Lindenbaum 1999, Butterfield 2006, Hanna 2011a, Gower, *Mirour de l'omme* (**8b**): on scribal cultures Mooney and Stubbs 2013, and on London's Frenches, Burnley 2003: important work on its business multilingualism is L. Wright 1996; see also Hsy 2013, 1–26. There is a translation of *Qui veut bone electioun* at http://the-orb. arlima.net/encyclop/culture/towns/florilegium/government/gvpoli01.html.

TEXT AND TRANSLATION

[f. 6ra] *Qui veut bone electioun faire de soverain governour de digneté ou de baillie, si regarde les pointz qe ensuent.*

Toutes seignories, toutes dignetés sount baillees par le sovereine pere et entre le seint establissement des choses du siecle veut il qe le governement de villes seit fermé par treis piliers. Ceo est a savoir de justice, de reverence, et de amour.

Justice deit estre ove governour, si establement fermé dedens soun quer qe il doit faire droit a chescuny et qe il ne soit ploiés a destre ne a senestere. Car Salamon dist qe juste roi n'avera jamais mescheaunce.

Reverence doit estre en burgois et en souzgis, car ceo est la seule chose eu mounde qe plus sieut les merites de foi et qe sourmounte touz sacrifices. Pur ceo dist li apostles, 'Honorez vostre seignour'.

Amour doit estre en l'un et en l'autre. Car ly soverains doit amer ses sougés de graunt quer et de clere fey, et veiller de jour et de nuit au commun profit de la ville et de tout le pueple. Tut autersi doyvent ly souzgit amer lour soverain a droit quer et od vraie entencioun, et doner lui counsail et ayde a meintenir soun office. Car a ceo q'il n'est qe un soul entre eus, il ne purroit riens faire ne acomplir saunz eus.

Et pur ceo qe le meire ou le governour est ausi come chef des cyteyns et toutes gentz desirent a avoir seyne teste (pur ceo qe quant le chief est des [f. 6rb] heitez, touz les membres en sount malades), et pur ceo deivent il sur totes choses estudier q'il eient teu governour qi les counduye a bone fyn

Whoever wishes to make a good choice of the ruling governor of territory or jurisdiction should consider the points that follow here:

All lordships and all jurisdictions are given by the sovereign Father, and in his holy ordering of the things of this world, it is his wish that the government of towns should be founded on three pillars: that is, on justice, respect, and love.

Justice ought to reside with the governor and be established with such steadfastness in his heart that he necessarily does right to each person, bending neither to the right or the left. For Solomon says that 'the just king will never meet with misfortune'.

There must be respect [for the ruler] among the citizens and subjects, for that is the one thing in the world that most closely accords with the merits of fidelity and rises above all sacrifices. It is for this reason that the Apostle said 'Honour your Lord'.

There ought to be love between the one and the other. For the sovereign ought to love his subjects with full heart and clear fidelity, and ought to be vigilant day and night about the common advantage of the town and all its people. In the same way, the subjects ought to love their ruler with true hearts and loyal intentions, and give him counsel and help in maintaining his office. For since he is only one among them, he can carry out and accomplish nothing without them.

And because the Mayor or the governor is, so to speak, like the head of the citizens, and everyone wants to have a sound head (because when the head is out of sorts all the members of the body are ill as a result), so

solom droit et solom raisoun et justice. Il ne le doivent pas eslire par sort ne par cheaunce de fortune, mais par graunde purveiaunce de counsail sage et averti. En quele electioun il deivent avoir regart a .xii. choses.

for this reason, they must above all give their attention to having a governor who will lead them to good purpose, according to right and reason and justice: they ought not to elect him by lot or the chances of fortune, but through the careful provision of sound and informed counsel. In which choice they should give consideration to twelve things.

[*Chapter II on the twelve conditions follows:*
(i) On the authority of Aristotle and Solomon, the man elected should not be too young either in years or sense.
(ii) The nobility of his heart, rather than the power of his lineage is to be considered, 'for the house must be honoured by its good lord, not the lord honoured by his house'.
(iii) He must practise justice.
(iv) He should have a good mind and sound understanding, not 'poverte de conissaunce'.
(v) He should be firm and courageous: one must be considered a worthy man for one's acts, not one's rank, and must be, not merely seem, a leader.
(vi) He must not be covetous or fond of his own will.
(vii) He must be able to speak well and wisely. Too often a single out-of-place remark destroys the value of an argument.
(viii) He should be measured in his expenditure but not niggardly (a trait that disgraces leadership).
(ix) He must not be prone to anger: anger in lordship is like a thunderclap during which truth cannot be known or just judgement given.
(x) He should be rich enough not to be corruptible, though a good poor man is generally more to be praised than a bad rich one.
(xi) He should hold no other office than this demanding one.
(xii) Above all, he should have true faith in God and his people. Without faith and truth (leauté) right cannot be maintained.
A following chapter warns that strife and hatred arise in cities if these principles are not observed and division arises among the commons. Three short chapters now give procedural details and ethical advice for the conduct of the mayoralty, before Horn turns to a discussion of how rulers work by fear or love and a final chapter on the difference between a king and a tyrant.]

Feste du Pui

[f. 176v] D'autre part, si tost com luy tresors du Pui purra a ceo suffire, soient achaté tenemenz et rentes pur la chapele et le chapelein maintenir a touz jours, et pur les povres de la compaignie sustenir e relever de poverté, solom la fourme des pri [f. 176vb] mers Estatuz du Puy.

E qe tuit lui compaignoun de Puy soient bons, natureus, et loiauz, aidant et conseillaunt chascun le autre quant il serra

Furthermore, as soon as the funds of the Pui are sufficient for this, let tenements and rents be acquired for the permanent maintenance of the chapel and the chaplain, and to support and relieve the poor of the company of their poverty, according to the formulation of the founding Statutes of the Pui.

And let all the companions of the Pui be kind and loyal, helping and advising one another when it is necessary to do so

de ceo fere requis en touz pointz et au touz lieus; ausi come confreres entrealiez par lur foy, qe de ceo fere sont il tenuz, sauve en cas qe sont encountre la pees e la corune nostre seignour le roy.

Estre ceo, qe trestut luy Estatut du Pui soient enregistré en un livre et mys en la commune houche, e qe le commun clerk du Pui eit le transecrist envers ly, ensi qe li compaignoun en puissent avoir aveyement e le transecrit a lur custages.

E por ceo qe la feste roiale du Pui est maintenue e establie principaument pur un chaunsoun reale corouner; de ci cum ele est par chansoun honoré e enhaunsiee, sont tuit luy gentil compaignoun du Pui par dreite raisoun tenuz des chaunçons roiaus avauncer a lur pouair, et especiaument cele qe est corouné par assent des compaignouns le jour de la graunt feste du Pui. Par quei il est ici purvu en droit de celes chaunçons, qe chascun prince novel le jour q'il portera la coroune et governera la feste du Pui, e si tost com il avera fait pendre son blasoun de ces armes en la sale ou la feste du Pui serra tenue qe maintenaunt face atacher desouz son blazon la chaunçoun qe estoit co [f. 177ra] rounee le jour q'il fut eslu novel prince, apertement et droitement escrite, saunz defaute. Kar nul chauntour par droit ne doit chaunçoun reale chaunter ne proffrir a la feste du Pui, desques a taunt q'il veit la chaunçoun corounee dreinement en l'an prochainement passé devaunt honouré a son dreit, en le manere avauntdite.

E qe il i eit a les chaunçouns juger eslu .ii. ou .iii. qi se conoisent en chant et en musike, pur les notes et les poinz del chaunt trier et examiner, auxi bien com la nature de la reson enditee. Kar saunz le chaunt ne doit om mie appeler une resoun endité chaunçoun, ne chaunçoun reale corounee ne doit estre saunz douçour de melodies chaunt[é].

in all matters and in all places like sworn brothers who are bound so to do, except in cases against the peace and the crown of our lord the king.

In addition, that all the Statutes of the Pui be registered in a book and put into the community's chest, and that the common clerk of the Pui hold a transcript so that the companions [of the Pui] can seek guidance and have copies at their own expense.

And because the royal feast of the Pui has been established and maintained principally in order to crown a royal song, since it is by song that it is honoured and raised in esteem, all the noble companions of the Pui are properly and rightly bound to promote royal songs to the extent of their power, and especially the song that is crowned by the companions' assent on the day of the great Feast of the Pui. Wherefore it is here provided, with respect to these songs, that each new prince on the day that he wears the crown and presides at the feast of the Pui, and as soon as he has had the blazon of his arms hung in the hall where the feast of the Pui is held, shall at once have the song that was crowned on the day that he was elected as the new prince attached under his blazon, clearly and correctly written without fail. For no singer ought by right to sing a royal song, or offer one, at the feast of the Pui until he sees that the song crowned in the immediately preceding year has been rightly honoured in the aforesaid manner.

And that for judging the songs there should be two or three who are expert in song and in music, and who can try out and evaluate the sounds and the notation of the song as well as the words composed for it. For without melody, one ought not to call a composition a song, nor should a crowned royal song be without the sweetness of sung melodies.

Notes

5 **le sovereine pere** MS *les sovereines peres* with each final *s* expuncted.

14 **Salamon dist** Cf. I Kings 1.52.

20 **li apostles** Cf. I Pet 2.17.

21–8 **Amour . . . office** 'Love' as a term for political relations has a long medieval history and refers rather to right feeling between lords and subjects than personal passion. Its earliest known insular French uses are in the Barking *Life of Edward the Confessor* (**2**): see MacBain 1988.

24 **commun profit** This term is widely used in fourteenth-century thought and literature in French and English. For an earlier use see Angier of Frideswide (**24a**: 159).

45 **Pui** From Latin *podium*: the origins of the name are disputed, but the title for the London group seems in any case to be modelled on that of Arras.

49–50 **primers Estatuz du Puy** The Pui was reformed and additional regulations devised. The earlier statutes were incorporated at the beginning of the second set (see Riley, II.i, 219–20, and on the reformation of the company, Sutton 1992).

54 **touz pointz** MS *touz I pointz* (in gutter of leaf).

57–8 **la corune nostre seignour le roy** As with the *Liber custumarum* and London's liberties in general, the privileges of the crown have always to be considered, the more so given royal participation in the Pui (Sutton 1992, Symes 2013).

60 **enregistré** *AND* gives only *registrer*, not the affixed form, but it is well represented in continental French: see *DMF*, *s.v.* 'enregistrer'.

60–1 **la commune houche** Provision for this record chest is made in the new statutes, part of their increased attention to documentation and record-keeping (in addition to the register and its copy here, see further Riley, II.i, 220 for more on the *houche* and 223 on the annual accounting roll).

70 **chaunçons roiaus** The prize songs were to be stanzaic and to be accompanied by music. For an example see Cooper 2006. The earlier statutes specify only 'songs', genre unspecified, to be judged without favour or nepotism by the old and new prince of the Pui together (Riley, II.i, 217).

82 **apertement et droitement escrite** The song is crowned, but not publicly recorded and displayed in the earlier statutes.

90 **qi se conoisent en chaunt et en musike** Together with the concern publicly to display each prize song for a year goes increased regulation of its music: the judges are to attend to both the notes and the verse of the song.

8b. John Gower, *Mirour de l'omme* [Dean 709]: Cambridge, University Library, MS Add. 3035, f. 149^{r-v} (=Macaulay vv. 27,347–60, 27,457–80)

Date of composition and provenance. Before 1379, beginning perhaps as early as the 1360s, London and Southwark.

Author, sources and nature of text. John Gower (*c.* 1330–1408) was a major court and civic writer and a contemporary of Langland and Chaucer. He had lands and connections in Kent, and possibly in Yorkshire, but lived in Southwark, south of the River Thames in London, at the priory of St Mary Overy, certainly from 1398 (he married Agnes Gundolf in the priory in January of that year), and probably for some years before. A modesty topos in the *Mirour* where Gower claims not to be a clerk, but only to have worn 'the striped sleeves' and to know little Latin and

French, suggests that he may have had some legal or civil office (*Ainz ai vestu la raye mance, Poy sai latin, poy sai romance*, ed. Macaulay 1899, vv. 21, 7674–5).

The *Mirour de l'omme* is the earliest of Gower's trilogy of major works in the three principal languages of late-fourteenth-century England: it was followed by *Vox clamantis* in Latin (*The Voice of One Crying*, 1378–81) and *Confessio amantis* (*The Lover's Confession*, English, mid-1380–90s, revised under Richard II and Henry IV). Gower wrote tri-lingually throughout his career, choosing particular languages for specific purposes. The *Mirour*, a 'massive allegory of the entry of Death into the World' (Carlson and Rigg 2011, 3) was renamed *Speculum meditantis* and then *Speculum hominis* by Gower in later life. Its 30,000 lines – 'a masterpiece in the flowing, rhetorical, passionately lofty register of the vernacular literature of ideas' (Calin 1994, 373) – offer a huge and vivid conspectus of the fallen state of humanity and of the social and natural order in which it dwells. The poem moves from the genealogy of sin to estates satire and finally to the life of the Virgin. It draws on the traditions of occupational satire and penitential manuals (especially Frère Laurens's *Somme le roi* of 1279 and Waddington's *Manuel des pechiez* (**24b**)), the Latin Bible's Ecclesiastes and other books, the fathers, the *Legenda aurea*, Cicero, and also on the apocryphal gospels for its concluding retelling of the life of the Virgin. Gower takes his complex verse form (12-line stanzas in octosyllabics, rhyming aab aab bba bba) from the influential *Vers de la mort* by the late-twelfth-century Cistercian, Hélinand de Froidmont, and writes an innovative Anglo-Norman verse-line, newly regular, both accentually and syllabically. Henry, duke of Lancaster's *Livre des seyntz medicines* (1354) may have provided a precedent for addressing a wide group of elite peers, and Gower knew Thomas of Kent's *Roman de toute chevalerie* (**28**). The scope and depth of Gower's poetic experimentation with language in the poem exceeds that of his predecessors, while the scale of the work moves beyond the considerable French satirical and doctrinal poems of the English Franciscan Nicole Bozon, or for that matter, anything in English outside Langland.

Gower's use of allegorical genealogies and marriages, like his ethical and social criticism and his apocalyptic imagery, aligns the *Mirour* with Langland's *Piers Plowman*, while his estates and occupational satire demands comparison with both Langland and Chaucer. Gower uses female allegorical *personae* to think with: there are at least eighty-six in the *Mirour*, and the poem is partly structured (as with Langland's Meed and Holy Church) around the wedding of World to the seven vices and Reason to the seven virtues. Sin's prevalence in the world is detailed through estates satire: Fraud (*Tricherie*) pervades the social order and the city, and no reassurance can be found as to the essential justice of human institutions and associations or their capacity for reform.

The *Mirour*, the least Ovidian of Gower's poems, nonetheless has a framework of love service: it is, however, love in the communal sense, with courtly love service redirected to the Virgin (cf. the *Pui de Londres*, (**8a**), lines 21–8 and n.). The extract below is preceded by the *Mirour*'s virtuoso account of Fraud in the city, after which the narrator turns from blaming the world's evil to blaming sinful mankind, and himself repents the *fols ditz d'amours* (v. 4) of his own life. He determines to sing a different song, one from the heart (*un chançon cordial*), sung softly, and (as he warns in a personal address to anyone who wants to sing together with him) beginning with the *Helas!* of sorrowful contrition, even if it is to end in spiritual joy (vv. 16–24). The passage given here thus marks the renewal of the narrator's language with a personal inflection and also positions the narration of the Virgin's life as the most redemptive service Gower's poem can offer in the face of the poem's diagnosis of humanity. As principles that emerge from the *Mirour*'s account of humanity's position in the world, the *enformacioun* offered to lay people and the *remembrance* inspired in clerks in this passage are summative terms of considerable ethical and salvific freight.

Audience and circulation. The *Mirour*, in contrast to the multiple copies of Gower's other works, is extant in a single manuscript. French may have been chosen for the *Mirour* as the *lingua franca* of the enlarged, English-controlled empire anticipated as the result of Edward III's 1360 and 1368 claims to the French crown (Yeager 2006). An elite audience at home and abroad on the

Continent could well have been among Gower's target audiences, together with the (occupationally francophone) administrators and other members of the London professional and mercantile classes. At the time of his revisions to the *Mirour* at St Mary Overy, Gower also had a francophone audience immediately before him, the Austin canons of this house. The *Mirour* may have circulated sufficiently to influence later writers: some have thought Spenser took his inspiration for his own immensely detailed iconography of virtues and vices from Gower's *Mirour* (Lowes 1914) and Gower's Satan and his engendering of Death on Sin may have contributed to Milton's *Paradise Lost* (Yeager 2009, 137–8).

Manuscript source. The extant manuscript, containing only the *Mirour*, is CUL MS Add. 3035. This is a medium-sized book (308 × 202 mm) written by a single scribe in the early fifteenth century, with contemporary rubrication, blue and red initials alternating at the head of the stanzas, and some illuminated (but not historiated) initials. The manuscript has lost leaves at beginning, end, and occasionally within the poem: about 2,000 lines are missing, including the opening 50 or 60 stanzas and the poem's conclusion. Macaulay found the text so correct as to suggest its preparation under Gower's supervision (ed., 1899, lxix): the manuscript's north-western and central French forms are commensurate with the continental aspects of Gower lexis and his wide reading in continental French sources. Nevertheless, the significance of the text's Picard traits (see Notes) and their implications for the making of the manuscript, for Gower's linguistic practice, and for the wider tendencies of late-fourteenth-century French and its audiences are matters that deserve further investigation. In format the manuscript is relatively routine for major works of doctrine and devotion: it offers a significantly monoglot presentation of the poem consonant with the status of French as an established vernacular of religious writing. Manuscripts of the *Confessio amantis*, on the other hand, are frequently elaborated with formal Latin marginal glossing, conferring authority, it has been argued, on the less established vernacular of English (see e.g. Emmerson 1999; Machan 2006, 13–15) and influenced in their presentation of narrative authority by French secular manuscripts (Butterfield 2003).

Bibliography. The *Mirour* is edited by Macaulay 1899 and Troendle 1960 and translated in Wilson 1992. For the poem in the tradition of England's French writing see Calin 1994, 372–80; for accounts free from hindsight as to the fate of Gower's literary-linguistic choices see Machan 2006, 2009, Yeager 2009. The nature of Gower's French is much discussed: Ingham 2015a and R. and M. Ingham (2015) argue for Gower's continental traits (amidst his use of predominantly Anglo-Norman phonology and grammar) as determined by the demands of his verse rather than by socio-linguistic preference. On Gower's lexis, see Merrilees and Pagan 2009. Macaulay 1899, xvi–xxxiv is still a useful overview. For Gower's French writing see Yeager 2009 (139–45 for the *Mirour*) and for his francophone audiences Yeager 2006, 2009. Lindenbaum 1999 remains a classic study of Gower and his contemporaries as city writers, see also Hsy 2013, 90–130. For Gower's use of Henry of Lancaster (Dean 696) see Yeager 2006, Batt, trans., 2014: for Gower and the *Roman de toute chevalerie* (**28**), Yeager 1990, 62–3. Dean 609 catalogues some verse by Helinand de Froidmont in England. Gower's multilingualism continues to be recognised (see Dutton *et al.* 2010, Hsy 2013, 90–116), but studies devoted to the *Mirour* remain relatively rare. For some valuable contextualising work, see Giancarlo 2007 (parliamentary procedure, legal discourse and the *Mirour*); Bestul 1993 (devotional traditions); Ladd 2010 and Galloway 2011 (anti-mercantilism); Kennedy 2009 (service, marriage and maintenance). On the *Mirour*'s metre see Duffel and Billy 2004 and the discussion in Part VI, §1.2, p. 421 below. For a study fully attentive to the *Mirour* as poetry and as significant experimental writing, see Nolan 2013. The International John Gower Society maintains an online bibliography at http://gowerbib.lib.utsa.edu/ and publishes a monograph series.

8b. John Gower, Mirour de l'omme

TEXT AND TRANSLATION

[=Macaulay, vv. 27,347–60]

Jadis trestout m'abandonoie [f. 149^{r}]
Au fol delit et veine joye
Dont ma vesture desguisay
Et les fols ditz d'amours fesoie
Dont en chantant je carolloie.
Mais ore je m'aviseray
Et tout cela je changeray,
Envers Dieu je supplieray
Q'il de sa grace me convoie:
Ma conscience accuseray,
Un autre chançon chanteray,
Que jadys chanter ne soloie.

In former years I devoted myself exclusively to wantonness and empty pleasure, cloaked by my outer clothing, and I composed the foolish songs of worldly love which I danced about singing; now, though, I will reconsider and change all that and will beg God that his grace may go with me. I will examine my conscience and sing a song very different from those I once sang.

Mais tu q'escoulter me voldras,
Escoulte que je chante bass,
Car c'est un chançon cordial;
Si tu la note bien orras,
Au commencer dolour avras
Et au fin joye espirital;
Car Conscience especial,
Qui porte le judicial,
Est de mon consail en ce cas,
Dont si tu voes en communal
Chanter oue moy ce chançonal,
Ensi chantant dirrez, Helas!

But you who are willing to listen to me, listen as I sing softly, for this is a song of the heart. If you listen well to the melody, you will be sorrowful at the beginning and spiritually joyful by the end, for Conscience, who has the right to judge, is my chief advocate in this case, so that if you want to sing this song together with me, you will say 'Alas!' as you sing.

Puisqu'il ad dit comment tout le mal dont l'en blame communement le siecle vient soulement de l'omme peccheour, dirra ore comment l'omme se refourmera et priera a Dieu.

Since it has been told how all the evil for which the world is usually blamed comes solely from sinning humanity, it will now be told how man will reform and pray to God.

[*The narrator now contemplates himself as a microcosm of sin: all seven chief vices are within him and his soul is severely wounded. He turns to the Virgin as physician and healer and someone who rewards well-meant service, however inadequate, Macaulay, vv. 27,362–456*]

[=Macaulay vv. 27,457–80]

Bien faire ou dire est a louer, [f. 149vb]
Dont l'en desert grace et loer,
Mais au bien faire endroit de moy
Je suy forein et estrangier
Qe je nen ose chalenger
Ascun merit, ou grant ou poy:
Mais, dame, pour parler de toy
Et dire j'ay assés du quoy;

To say or do good is worthy of reward and deserves pardon and praise, but I myself remain a foreigner and a stranger to doing good deeds close to home, so that I don't dare claim any merit, great or small. But, lady, I have plenty of material for speaking of you, for you, my lady, are at the foundation of the Christian religion, the mother in whom

Car tu, ma dame, au comencer
Es de la cristiene loy,
La mere, dont no droite foy
Remaint, que nous devons guarder.

dwells our true faith, which we ought to preserve.

Pour ce, ma dame, a ta plesance
Solonc ma povre suffiçance
Vuill conter ta concepcioun
Et puis ma dame, ta naiscance;
Si que l'en sache ta puissance
Qui sont du nostre nacioun:
Les clercs en scievont la leçoun
De leur latin, mais autres noun,
Par quoy en langue de romance
J'en fray la declaracioun
As lays pour enformacioun
Et a les clercs pour remembrance.

For this reason, my lady, at your pleasure and in accord with my poor abilities, I wish to talk about how you were conceived and then, my lady, about your birth, so that your power may be known by our people: clerks know it from reading their Latin, but others do not. Therefore I will make my statement of it in French: for the instruction of laypeople and as a reminder to clerks.

Notes

1–12 Gower cites Hélinand de Froidmont, the model for his demanding 12-line stanza in the *Mirour* (*Mestre Helemauns, qui fist tout pleins / Les Vers du Mort*, vv. 11,404–6), perhaps as a declaration of 'adherence to a moral theory of poetics' (see Yeager 1990, 79–83). The *Mirour* stanza is briefly discussed by Duffel and Billy 2004.

18 **au fin** is not an error in grammatical gender, but the Picard form of the definite article (*le*) in enclisis with *a* (> *au*).

20 **porte le judicial** Gower often combines legal and ethical meanings in a single term: many such puns, especially in the *Mirour*'s section on men at law, tellingly instantiate the distance between human legal practice and the religious and ethical values of justice. The *AND* gives 'be subject to judgement' here, but the meaning may be that Conscience is hearing the case rather than being tried by it. *Judicial* also (and according to J. H. Baker 1990, normally) means a judicial writ or, adjectivally, 'capable of making judgements, judicious', and is also used by Gower to mean the Last Judgement. In v. 10 above, the narrator accuses his conscience with perhaps something of legal force.

23 **oue** The MS reading (rather than *ove*) is retained here to give the single syllable required by the metre.

28 **forein et estrangier** These terms have particular resonance in the case of the city of London, where special laws for merchants and others not of the city were in operation: see e.g. *Liber custumarum* (**8a** and see (1), headnote).

35 **no** The Picard form of the possessive adjective, perhaps an authorial choice for metrical reasons.

39–40 **conter ta concepcioun . . . ta naiscance** The retelling of the Virgin's life is an act of penitence and redemption for the narrator (compare Herman de Valenciennes, *Roman de Dieu* (**15**)). According to Wilson 1992, 409 n. 143, no specific sources are known for Gower's life of Mary (and it is incomplete because of missing leaves in the manuscript), but it must have been drawn, directly or otherwise, from the usual Gospel and apocryphal sources (the New Testament, Psalms-Matthew, the Gospel of the Nativity of Mary, the Gospel of Nichodemus and the second Latin version of the *Transitus Mariae*).

42 **du nostre nacioun** Here *du* is *de* in enclisis with the Picard feminine definite article *le* (see n. to v. 18 above) in a strong form of the possessive adjective: *de la nostre nacioun*. 'Nation' is as in Latin *nacio*, 'of our people or group', rather than the modern sense of 'nation-state'. Since the choice of the Picard form here keeps the metre regular, it is probably authorial. The stressed Picard form also emphasises 'our' group as against others.

45 **langue de romance** *Romance* is Gower's usual term for the vernacular as in his *poy sai romance* (*Mirour* v. 217,675), cited above, but in context there must be a sense of 'the vernacular used by clerks and non-Latinate laypeople', i.e. the French of England. Gower's usual term for continental French is *françois* (see *Concordance*, ed. Yeager and Hinson 1997, *s.v.* 'françois', 'romance'), as in for instance, his famous declaration in his treatise for married lovers (*Traitié pour essampler les amantz marietz*) that he himself is not eloquent in French (*si jeo n'ai de françois la facounde*: 18.4:24).

Part II. *Si sa dame ne li aidast*: Authorship and the Patron

Introduction

For many works in the French of England, as in other medieval literatures, textual identity comes as much or more from patron and occasion as from what is now recognised as authorship. As A. C. Spearing has argued, it is a modern paradigm to assume an individual mind as the precondition of a text, rather than to think of stories as being always already present, and individual agency in their reshaping as an incidental rather than indispensable aspect of their existence.[1] *Translatio fabulae*, Christopher Baswell has pointed out, is important alongside *translatio studii et imperii*.[2] The *Brut*, a great, multilingual congeries of material from the twelfth to the fifteenth centuries influential for many of the texts here, is an obvious instance of a literature with and without authors, not simply in terms of whether its writers are known or anonymous but whether its various texts are produced with a model of authorship as part of their identity.

Most writers in this volume are professional writers of one or another kind, necessarily so in a culture where literacy is occupationally specific rather than, as now, a defining universal stage of socialised development through compulsory school attendance. Some of them may have produced only one or two works that might be classified as literary as part of, or as an adjunct to, their career of literate work, as monastic officers, chaplains to elite households, clerks in offices of state, etc.[3] 'Authors' in the texts here are biblical and patristic figures such as Solomon, Jerome, Gregory, and often, ultimately God (see Glossary *auctor*, *auctorité*, *auctorizer*), figures who guarantee the work as ethical and useful, to be counterposed to the pleasures of hearing about Roland and Oliver, as in (**24a**, 171).[4] Writers present themselves primarily as translators, and sometimes as compilers,

1 Spearing 2005, 1–34.

2 Baswell 2005, 173.

3 As Paul Strohm has recently argued, even Chaucer, who was made over into a vernacular *auctour* in the fifteenth century, was for much of his life known principally as a minor courtier and bureaucrat (placed as Comptroller of Customs probably through his wife's connections), and with a personal and private audience for his poetry (Strohm 2014).

4 For a concise discussion of medieval ideas of authorship see Wogan-Browne *et al.* 1999, 3–19 and the essay by A. Taylor at 353–65. Exceptionally, two thirteenth-century bishops, Robert Grosseteste (**5**) and St Edmund of Abingdon, archbishop of Canterbury (**22**), are awarded contemporary *auctor* status (by attributions of pseudonymous works and by the treatment of their texts in some manuscripts). Writers in the present volume include 7 ecclesiastics, 9 clerks of various kinds (mostly secular, including 3 probable baronial chaplains), two lay noblemen (**7a**, **16**) and one possible, Mandeville (**35**), and several cases of a name (Chardri, Johan) of unknown occupation. There are four whose roles in the creation of the text remain uncertain: in the *Enfaunces Jesu Crist* (**20b**, 39), 'Johan' may be composer, scribe, artist or all three; Waddington may have been author or scribe of the *Manuel des pechiez* (**24b**); Servais Copale may have been the scribe or co-author of *Secré de secrez* (**33**); John Barton is possibly physician and patron or perhaps author of the *Donait* (**7e**). Other writers include one possible lawyer and/or civil servant, Gower, (**8b**), one City Chamberlain, Andrew Horn (**8a**), and three professional clerics teaching for money: Thomas Sampson, William Kingsmill, Simon d'O (**7b**, **c**, **d**). There are also four

or copyists.[5] Manuscript collections of a single author's vernacular works are a rare phenomenon and almost entirely a late-medieval one.[6] As is now well recognised, none of this inhibits creativity and innovation in vernacular texts. However modestly presented their role, and however prolifically justified their work, writers of French confidently experiment in varied and changing ways from the early twelfth century onwards in England.

Patronage nevertheless has more authority in texts than most of their medieval writers do, and patronage, ecclesiastic or lay, individual or institutional, is virtually indispensable to literary production, both socio-economically and conceptually.[7] Writerly identity is often most explicitly considered as part of a relationship, actual or desired, with a patron, whose importance in this respect is true to the early Latin meanings of *auctor* as a person with authority to take action or make a decision, guarantor, surety, person who approves or authorises, person who has weight or authority, etc.[8] Herman de Valenciennes, for example, scatters many biographical details through his late-twelfth-century Marianising *Bible* or *Romanz de Dieu et de sa mere* (**15**), but the most detailed staging of his own relation to his work becomes an aspect of the text's authorising genesis in the Virgin's command to Herman as cleric.[9] Angered, injured and ill, this clerkly figure provides an occasion for the Virgin's intervention in what is closer to a Marian miracle than a demonstration of authorship. The most important aspect of the narratorial presence of 'Herman' may be his witness to a figure whose powers embrace the functions of patron, muse, and therapist, and guarantor of the truth of the authoritative subject matter she provides.

The socio-economic factors of textual production and the idea of patronage itself are constantly recurring themes in vernacular prologues, as they are in much Latin writing. But, as with the language choices discussed in Part I, invocations of a patron figure cannot simply be taken literally as social history. A dedication can express aspiration rather than constituting a record, and patrons can be added by later redactors in accordance with

monastic authors who are either not securely attached to their texts or whose particular historical identity is not known (Benedeit, *Brendan* (**9**), Thomas of Kent, *Roman de toute chevalerie*, (**28**); Jofroi de Waterford, *Secré de secrez* (**33**), and Walter de la Hove, the likely author of the *Mohun Chronicle* (**42**). There are fifteen anonymous works, though some of their writers have a specific production community, such as the Nun of Barking (**2**), or the compilers of the Crabhouse Register (**36**)).

5 The centrality of translation to medieval culture has been widely studied in recent decades, especially since the important work of Copeland 1995: for a recent account, see Campbell and Mills, ed., 2012, 1–20. For the corpus of medieval French literary translated texts see Galderisi and Agrigoroaei, 2011. For writers working as compilers or transcribers see e.g. (**8a**), (**16**), (**33**), (**35**), (**41**), also perhaps (**20b**), (**24b**).

6 For an exception see Keith Busby's argument that the extant manuscripts suggest a 'persistent and local' interest in Hue de Rotelande and attest to 'an awareness of Hue as an author' (Busby, 2002, vol. 2, 498). For an argument on Middle English texts see Spearing 2012, and on the codicological dimensions of authorship and the late-medieval perception of individual authors as responsible for particular works and oeuvres, see A. Gillespie 2006.

7 The foundational article is Short 1992: for its implications see Tyler 2009, and see Part VI, §3 for a list of patrons in this volume. We take specific accounts of patrons and their writers as at once particular to a text and simultaneously part of the meta-discourse of medieval vernacular literature and hence the lexis of patronage is included in our Glossary of literary terms.

8 For some twelfth-century textual guarantors of the matter of Britain, combining authoritative figures such as Solomon and high-ranking patrons such as Henry II, see Baumgartner 1993.

9 For further French-language writerly figures see Berthelot 1991.

their idea of appropriate historical pedigree for the text. Patrons may change and multiply depending on the audiences and versions of a text: one text may also have multiple patrons. The commissioner of a text may not actually give patronage to it: a *destinataire* or *destinateur* may be inscribed as patron but not actually have played that role. Patron figures who actually give patronage exert highly varying degrees of influence over texts: some simply send their servants to order copies; others scrutinise manuscript preparation in person and are exigent about particular effects. The representation of patrons is of course idealising, and may, moreover, present them in a manner particularly appropriate to the text, so that the patron can sometimes be thought of as produced by the text rather than the other way round. Aden Kumler has recently argued that 'portraits' of the patron are not designed as historical representations but *figurae translatae*, representations of what the patron becomes by using the text.[10] Such an argument can perhaps explain the female figures in the illustrations of the Lambeth Apocalypse (**20a**), where there is a likeness between the miniature of the patron and the representations of Mary Magdalen and the manuscript's iconically penitential female figure, but no apparent intent to represent all three figures as identical with the patroness. Figures of patronage may also change as texts are used by groups other than the community of the original patron: that the patron figure is substituted for, rather than discarded, testifies to the indispensability of the idea of patronage (see for example (**9**), *Le Voyage de saint Brendan*). Its power is further suggested by the various ways in which Gaimar (**10**), Adgar (**11a**) and Guernes (**11b**) all score off other actual or implied writers using the conventions of patronage. The many permutations here speak to the power and pervasiveness of the idea of patronage.

As the epigraph to this Part suggests, female patrons, both institutional and individual, form an important category. Our quotation, *Si sa dame ne li aidast* ('If his lady had not helped him . . .'), is taken from Gaimar's eulogy of Lady Constance Fitzgilbert, who not only provided material support but used her social networks in procuring source texts for him and who offers for his text both an aristocratic patronage circle and an image that was rapidly becoming iconic, that of the patron reading in her chamber.[11] The figure of the female patron appears so frequently (and so frequently as collaborating with her clerk or chaplain, estate steward or other writer) as to suggest a vital role for elite women in textual production of many kinds.[12] Often, wider audiences are simultaneously envisaged: there is an expectation that, authorised by a pedigree of prestigious patronage, a text will travel. The combined networks of elite female patrons and ecclesiastical writers are powerful channels for dissemination. Generic models of female patronage also figure in the self-situating of texts where the patroness figure is unidentified. *Waldef* (**6**) deploys a romance version of the patroness's command and the devotee's obedience when the anonymous writer claims to be composing at the instance of an unnamed *amie* (**6**. 75–92).

10 Kumler 2012.

11 See Short, ed. and trans., 2009 and 1994, Bérat 2010, Blacker 1997.

12 In addition to Part II's examples, see (**7a**), (**20a**), (**21**), (**39**), (**42**). For an example of a manuscript where the patron is represented as having quite literally the same stature as a textual authority (allowing for his mitre) and where she towers over her clerk/scribe as he produces a version of the *Manuel des pechiez* (**24b**) for her, see Grosseteste's *Chasteau d'amour* (**5**).

The text of *Waldef* is incomplete, and it is not known whether more would have been revealed as to this figure's identity. But she in any case invokes the powerful convention of writing at a woman's request, offers a version of the social and affective relations that might animate both the production and reception of a text, and hints, too, at the erotics of patronage, with all its pleasures of submission, service, inversion and play with relations of power.[13] Still more powerful female figures often preside: in his Life of St Faith (12), for instance, Simon of Walsingham writes not only at the bidding of his Benedictine superior but in service to the virgin martyr, St Faith, his personal patron as well as the dedicatee of a chapel in his monastery, and one of the community's important advocates at the court of heaven.

Beyond lending prestige to the text (whether historically engaged with its production or not), a patron figure can serve to exemplify the text's orientation and hence play a part in characterising the text. So, for instance, in the early-thirteenth-century *Miroir* or *Evangiles des domnees* (14) by Robert of Greatham for an unspecified Lady Aline, the patron's putative reading and listening 'to songs about heroic deeds and history' (from which she 'needs' to be converted) are central to the rationale of her chaplain's 19,000 lines of vernacular Gospel exposition (14.1–6). Lady Aline's powerful socio-economic situation is also implicitly addressed in the extended metaphors of this 600-line prologue as her chaplain asserts his capacity to give spiritual food to the seignurial patroness of the demesne lands out of which her agrarian wealth and his own living comes.

In these respects, the patron and the figure of the writer can play similar and complementary roles. Even in texts with a self-naming writer, an authorial signature functions to identify and locate the work (in topographic and socio-cultural senses), or to thematise it, rather than to simply authorise it as part of a writerly identity or as coming from an authorial canon.[14] Wace, like Chrétien de Troyes, appears to be a twelfth-century exception, but the difference in his self-presentations between the *Roman de Rou* (3) and his *Vie de seint Nicolas* (25a) is telling. Is his account of declining patronage and his own position under 'three King Henries' (3.179) a grounded literary biography, which we should use across this and his other texts to create a narrative of his life? Or is it a function of the *Rou*'s plangent topoi of transience and change? No less than for those, who, like the three Henries, wield power, transience marks the lives of those who, like Wace, create a permanent record and refresh ethical and historical custom. This writerly figure is very different from Wace's *St Nicolas* (25a), where the engaged Norman cleric puts his literate skills at the service of the wide community of different estates and talents he inscribes around the figure of the saint (freshly translated into Normandy and England by the late eleventh century). As a presentation of biography, Wace's textual appearances are comparable with Denis of Bury St Edmunds, who, in using the by-name Piramus (27.16), invokes the notion of Ovidian authorship in order to thematise himself as a repentant writer of seductive light verse.

The figure of the writer may thus serve as a thematic key or exemplary case of the text's teaching rather than functioning to identify the text. Such figures also occur within texts in a performative function, presenting and narrating in a way that cannot be reified as a

13 For discussion and further examples, see Bérat 2010.

14 Kay 1997 dismantles Chrétien and authorship.

consistent set of narrator or author 'character' traits, but is rather produced by the text's local demands. This is a familiar convention for *chanson de geste* from the twelfth century onwards, but some of the most intense narratorial performances hold together and make urgent for audiences the knowledge presented in instructional and scientific texts (see e.g. Rauf de Linham and his *Kalender*, 40). Against the thirteenth-century's increased valuation of prose, as Adrian Armstrong and Sarah Kay argue, the continuing production of verse encyclopaedias takes on a specialised function in relation to prose's newly imputed objectivity and self-sufficiency: and, verse, as the privileged medieval interface with sociality (rather than with private experience as it now is), renews its relations with knowledge in intense indications of narratorial presence and performance.[15] The vigour with which narratorial presence sutures together the *Kalender*'s diversity of Roman, Jewish and customary calendrical times and systems as authoritative and settled knowledge has no equivalent authorial self-presentation. The text offers only a name for the writer and some etymologising on the name of a patron.

In the light of these conventions and practices, an important question is that of what texts can be produced with*out* a patron. Royal and baronial chaplains and clerics, alongside monastic religious, had always had a role in the literary production of secular elites, but the intensified bureaucratic employment of clerks from the late twelfth through the thirteenth century and beyond created new clerical professions outside the church, such as the notary and the professional scribe, or the letter or petitions writer.[16] The offices of the crown and of local and civic administration supported at least the day jobs of clerical writers of a more secular kind. Royal or civic administrative service, chancery, courts, gilds, language teaching, etc. became the official occupation of many writers and the patronage of particular individuals ceased to be so strongly the *sine qua non* of textual production. Greatham's *Miroir* (14) for Lady Aline, for instance, has its detailed account of Lady Aline and her tastes dropped in its Middle English version (see Part VI, §2.3). However there is no simple universal shift from works with named patrons and specified production circles to less intensely situated works. Some Middle English works still use the full panoply of patron conventions and topoi: Osbern Bokenham's *Legendys of Holy Women* of 1445 deploys an Aristotelian *accessus* template like that of Pierre d'Abernon de Fetcham's *Lumere as lais* (19); invokes monastic and lay figures as present at his text's genesis; and represents a specific East Anglian social network of nobles, gentry and their servants as the dedicatees of his saints' lives.[17]

The mid-fourteenth century presents two major works where members of the elite groups associated with patronage become their own writers.[18] One of them, Sir Thomas

[15] Armstrong and Kay 2011 and see further Part VI, §1.2. The increase and diversity of such texts in thirteenth- and fourteenth-century England is striking: Dean lists 115 treatises and encyclopaedias in chapters on scientific, technical and medical writing and selected pastoralia, such as theological encyclopaedias, from other categories brings the total to *c.* 200 texts.

[16] See further Kerby-Fulton 2014.

[17] Camp 2012 argues that this panoply of moves for situating and recommending the *Legendys* is aimed at an offstage patron, Richard of York, who at the time had still to commit himself to supporting Bokenham's priory at Clare.

[18] Francophone pastoralia had a long career in England and it is out of a strong tradition of confessional and

Gray's *Scalacronica* (**16**), presents the occasion of writing as the leisure afforded by Gray's imprisonment in the Scottish wars (though he in fact finished much of his work after his release): this is a biographical fact of significance about Gray, but its authorising capacity perhaps depends less on Gray himself than on the way it guarantees to an elite secular lay writer a contemplative space otherwise known only to the monastic historians whom Gray represents in his dream as precedents and sources. Time in prison, so to speak, substitutes for patronage in providing the opportunity to write. Gray also includes a readily legible cypher of himself before his dream-vision prologue to his work. That this question of encoding is staged immediately prior to a dream protocol for writing seems just as pointed as, say, Chaucer's prologue to the *House of Fame*, Book I on the indeterminate significance and outcomes of dreams, and as much to do with the nature of the text as with an authorial career. (*Scalacronica* is as far as is known, Gray's only literary work). At the same time, Gray's cypher of his own name, in its combination of coterie intimacy and thematic service to his work, is inevitably suggestive for the figuration of the writer-dreamer in the great late-fourteenth-century English-language literary dream visions. His text offers a moment in which the patron's presentation of his own authorship looks both backwards and forwards in terms of the role of the writer in textual identity.

The literary history to which these and the other French-language texts of England point, then, allows authorship as a category, but frequently not as the grounding category of textual production or identity. This, as Anne Middleton showed in a magisterial study of these questions as they affect fourteenth-century authorship, does not do away with a politics of authorship within and outside texts.[19] But, as Robert Meyer-Lee notes, recent study of authorship newly conceived as enquiry into 'questions of indeterminacy, socio-cultural valence, and ideological complicity or resistance' rather than into 'artistic unity or literary greatness' has been able to pursue these issues without needing to change the texts and authors traditionally at the centre of the (Middle English) field.[20] While the present volume includes a number of authorial names, the chronological range of French-language writing in England offers for the most part a literary culture where it is more normative for texts not to require authorship, or texts where the notion of authority is distributed between the patron and the nature of the material, with the writer free to inscribe a presence in service to them and to audiences and readers. Against this background, vernacular ideas of authorship and the authority of experience in late-medieval England emerge not so much as an inevitable development but as themselves highly situated, related to text-type, questions of audience and reading publics, socio-economic locations for writing, and the specific registers of speech and writing communities, and the felt status of the selected language.[21] The generation of textual meaning continues

penitential writing (ed. and trans. in Bliss, Hunt, Leyser 2010), that Henry, duke of Lancaster produces his astonishing *Livre de seyntz medicines* (*Book of Holy Medicines*). This is translated with substantial introduction and annotation in Batt 2014. Gray's *Scalacronica* draws on an equally strong tradition, in his case that of vernacular historiography, extending from Gaimar's *Estoire des Engleis* (**10**) to the fifteenth-century *Brut remaniements* and genealogical rolls exemplified in (**20c** and **d**).

19 Middleton 1990.

20 Meyer-Lee 2013, 388.

21 See further Part VI, §1.1, pp. 411–12.

out of a production community, not from a writer alone, and is co-created by audiences, traditions, protocols and patrons.[22]

9. Benedeit, *Le Voyage de saint Brendan* [Dean 504], Prologue: Paris, Bibliothèque Nationale de France, nouv. acq. fr., MS 4503, ff. 19ᵛ–20ʳ

DATE OF COMPOSITION AND PROVENANCE. Composed most probably for Adeliza of Louvain (*c.* 1103–51) in or shortly after 1121, the year of her marriage to Henry I of England (1068/9–1135) as his second queen.

AUTHOR, SOURCES AND NATURE OF TEXT. Nothing is known of the author apart from his self-naming as *li apostolies dans Beneiz* (v. 8). The title *Dans* (from Latin *Dominus*) probably indicates a monk in this context, but no Benedict is known among the papal legates (the most likely meaning of *li apostolies*) to England or Lorraine, or among the Lotharingians Adeliza maintained in her household at Henry I's court. Benedict, monk of Gloucester (*fl.* 1150, *ODNB*), author of a life of the Welsh saint Dyfrig (Dubricius), has been thought a promising candidate (though active rather later than *Brendan*): there is also an early-twelfth-century Benedict of St Mary's Abbey, York (Sharpe 1997, 76, no.153), who contributed to the mortuary roll of Abbess Matilda of Caen (predecessor of Cecilia, sister of Adeliza's husband Henry I) in 1113, but there is no evidence to link either to *Brendan*.

St Brendan has an early existence as an abbot (d. 577 or 583) of Clonfert in Ireland, but the much loved Brendan story offers less a conventional saint's life than an early travel romance that is also a voyage of wonders and miracles, of penance and redemption, and, for all the simplicity of Brendan's curagh or coracle boat, a possible if extraordinary feat of sailing, experimentally repeated several times in the twentieth century. Careful design for a lay patron is perhaps traceable in such details as the reduction of the canonical hours sung by the birds on their paradisal island in the Anglo-Norman version or in the presentation of Brendan as an aristocrat choosing a noble vocation (vv. 19–22 below). The seven-year voyage is at once a quest and the practice of a liturgically constructed life: Brendan's monks celebrate important Christian feasts as they land each year on the island of sheep, the 'paradise of birds', and, most famously, on a whale which they take for land (often visualised in twelfth- and thirteenth-century bestiaries, and the source of the phantom island of St Brendan on Christopher Columbus's and other early-modern sea charts). Although Brendan and his monks still encounter sea serpents and a dragon and a griffin in the Anglo-Norman version, their experiences are presented as trials and purifications rather than simply as the marvels of the Latin *Navigatio Brendani*, of which the French version is a free reworking. The earliest extant manuscript of the late-eighth-century *Navigatio*, a Christianised version of an early Irish *immram* or voyage narrative with the 'Land of Promise' as its goal, is tenth century. A Latin prose *Vita Brendani* with one voyage to Britain and another in search of an island for eremitic retreat is found from the ninth century onwards, but the *Navigatio* became the most popular version, extant today in 125 manuscripts from all over Europe.

The importance of patronage in the production of early texts is clear in the textual history of the *Brendan* prologue, which is dedicated in three of the extant manuscripts to Adeliza of Louvain, but in one (the Bodleian Rawlinson D 913 fragment) to Henry I's first queen, Edith-Matilda of Scotland (1080–1118). Both queens were significant literary patrons, Matilda principally of Anglo-Latin historiography (notably of William of Malmesbury). In addition to the *Brendan*, Adeliza was the patroness of a (lost) biography of Henry I by 'David' (see (9)) and of French-language scientific and didactic writing by Philippe de Thaon, the first French poet whose identity is known. As well as a

[22] On the complexities of 'publishing' a medieval text and the author's relative lack of control over the process, see Hobbins 2009, 153–6; Kerby-Fulton 2006.

bestiary dedicated to Adeliza, Philippe composed a verse treatise on computus, (possibly) a poem on the Sibyls and perhaps a lapidary and other poems.

The change of taste brought about by Adeliza is argued (in O'Donnell 2012b) as decisive in the creation of this earliest French vernacular literature. This was not simply a matter of changing from Latin to vernacular (Queen Matilda had been taught French as were most royal women in Anglo-Saxon Britain) but of Adeliza's bringing her taste for handsome vernacular books to the established Anglo-Latin and English patronage practices of the English royal court. *Brendan*'s attribution to Matilda is less likely, for all her Scottish ancestry: not only would French-language patronage be unusual for Matilda, as not for the Lotharingian Adeliza, but the *Navigatio Brendani* first went to the Continent via Wales, Cornwall and Brittany (Kenney 1929, 412) and circulated earlier in Lorraine, Adeliza's home, than in England. The later ascription of patronage to Matilda can be explained by the fact that Matilda remained better known than her successor Adeliza (although, unless Benedict's account is a prescription for queenhood rather than a representation of it, Adeliza's role as counsellor to Henry and presider over religious law and law of the land suggests a figure memorable in her own time). Given the strong convention of illustrious patronage dedications for the new French books, as for their Latin and English predecessors, Matilda will have seemed a likely figure for the presiding patron of the Brendan narrative. The historical importance of a high-ranking inscription of patronage and hence an impressive pedigree for a poem is underlined by this probably fictive attribution.

Audience and circulation. Benedeit's is the earliest vernacular version, but Brendan's voyage was widely known and translated into many European languages, perhaps as much through Adeliza and Henry's francophone, administratively innovative and highly literate court as through the dissemination of its main source, the Latin *Navigatio Brendani*. The Anglo-Norman text is witnessed in six manuscripts (two of them fragmentary), including a large thirteenth-century continental collection (Paris, Arsenal 3516, minus the dedicatory prologue), two thirteenth-century insular manuscripts (York, Minster Library 16.K.12 and BN nouv. acq. fr. 4503) and the early-fourteenth-century BL Cotton Vespasian B.X (MS A), generally agreed to preserve the oldest forms of the text's language under scribal thirteenth-century modernisations (Short and Merrilees 1979, 10–16; Waters 1928, cxxv–ccii). This version was subsequently translated into Latin prose (extant in a manuscript of *c.* 1200, Oxford, Bodleian Library, MS Bodley 3496, from the Cistercian monastery of Valle Crucis in Wales: Waters 1928, cv–cxv), and into Latin verse (extant in the fourteenth-century Cotton Vespasian D.IX: Waters 1928, cxv–cxxv). The narrative's most recent reprises include C. S. Lewis's *Voyage of the Dawn Treader* (1952) in the Narnia series and Tim Severin's 1976–7 recreation of the voyage in a coracle (Severin 1978).

Manuscript source. BN nouv. acq. fr. 4503 is a small (194 × 130 mm) insular vellum manuscript of 74 folios, produced *c.* 1200 by several scribes. It is unilluminated but has regular formal red and blue initials. It contains Herman de Valenciennes's narrative of the Virgin's Assumption (a widely circulated section of his *Bible*; see (**15**)); a copy of the anonymous *Vie de saint Alexis* (ed. from this manuscript in Hemming 1994: the first extant copy of *c.* 1136–9 is in the psalter commissioned for Christina of Markyate, www.abdn.ac.uk/stalbanspsalter); a copy of the *Vie de sainte Catherine d'Alexandrie* by Clemence of Barking (see (**2**)); and a French prose translation of an 1177 bull of Alexander III (pope 1159–81) in favour of the Templars. This international military order followed Cistercian customs and planted some 60 foundations in England from *c.* 1120–1312.

Bibliography. The critical edition is Waters, ed., 1928 with MS Cotton Vespasian B.X (1) as base: for the BN nouv. acq. manuscript used here see Careri, Ruby and Short 2011, no. 85. Short and Merrilees, ed., 1979 offer an accessible fresh edition of the Cotton manuscript. For their text with modern French translation and website, see Short with Tixhon, 1999: http://saintbrendan.d-t-x.com/, and for an example of the bestiary whale tradition associated with the voyage see e.g. http://bestiary.ca/beasts/beast282.htm and http://bestiary.ca/manuscripts/manu556.htm (f. 86*v*). For an audio-visual reading from *Brendan*, go to http://legacy.fordham.edu/academics/programs_at_fordham_/medieval_studies/french_of_england/audio_readings_94163.asp. On the relation of Brendan and the *Navigatio* see Waters 1928, ciii–civ. Strijbosch 2000 studies sources and analogues. For English translations of the *Navigatio* and of the vernacular versions see Barron and Burgess 2002. Burgess and Strijbosch 2006 edit a collection of criticism and scholarship. On the historical and legendary Brendan, see Kenney 1929, 406–20. For Irish voyage literature, see Wooding 2000. The classic study of patronage in Anglo-Norman literature is Short 1992. Important new argument on Adeliza's patronage and early French literature is O'Donnell 2012b. On Adeliza (*c.* 1103–51), see *ODNB*, *s.v.* 'Adeliza of Louvain'. On Benedict of Gloucester, see J. B. Smith 2012.

TEXT AND TRANSLATION

Incipit vita sancti Brandani

[Da]mmë Aliz la reïne,
Pur qui vendrat lei divine,
Par quei creistrat lei de terre
E remeindrat tute guerre
Pur les armes Henri le rei,
Pur le cunseil ki ert en tei,
Salue tei mil e mil feiz
Li apostoilles dans Beneiz.
Que cumandas ço ad enpris,
Sulunc sun sens en letre mis,
[Eisi cum fud li teons cumanz,]
En letre mis e en romanz
De saint Brandan le bon abét.
Meis tu le [de]fent ne seit gabét
Quant dit que set e fait que pot:
Itel servant blasmer n'estot.
Meis cil ki pot e ne voille
Dreiz est que cil mult s'en doille.
Icil seint Deu fud nét de reis,
De naisance fud des Ireis;
Pur ço que fud de real lin
Puroc entent a noble fin.
Bien sout que la scripture dit:
'Ki de cest mund fuit le delit,
Od Deu del ciel tant en avrat
Que demander plus ne savra.'
Puroc guerpit cist reals eirs
Les fals honurs pur icels veirs:
Dras de muine, pur estre vil
En cest siecle cum [en] eissil;
Pris a l'ordre e les abiz,
Puis [fud] abés par force esliz.

[f. 19v] *Here the Life of St Brendan begins.*

Lady and Queen Alice, through whom will come divine law, by which justice will increase on earth, and all war will be prevented by King Henry's armed strength and by your own wise counsel, emissary Dom Beneit salutes you a thousandfold. He has undertaken what you ordered, and put down in writing the story of the good abbot St Brendan as best he understands it, composed in French verse, as you commanded. But defend him against mockery when he says [f. 20r] what he knows and writes what he can: a servant such as this is not to be blamed. But he who can and refuses should rightly regret it very much. Brendan, this saint of God, was born of a king and Irish by birth: because he was of royal lineage he followed a noble vocation. He well knew what scripture says: 'He who flees the delights of this world, will have more joy with God in heaven than he could ever imagine asking for'. This royal heir therefore abandoned false honours for true ones: a monk's habit, to live humbly, apart from the world as if in exile; he joined the monastic order and wore a monk's habit, then was elected abbot against his will.

Par art de lui mult i vindrent
Ki a l'ordre bien se tindrent.
Treis mil suz li par divers liu[s]
Muines aveit Bra[n]dan li piu[s],
De lui pernanz tuz essample
Par sa vertu ki iert ample.

Because of him, many were attracted to the monastic order, and they remained faithful members. The saintly Brendan had three thousand monks under him, who came from many places, all following the example of his great virtue.

Notes

1 **[Da]mme** A guide letter *d* is visible, and a space, two lines high, is left for the large initial letter, which is missing. The miniscule *a* is partly effaced, and there is a superscript *m* above the space between *m* and *e*.

4 **tute guerre** Henry I's victory over the French in the Duchy of Normandy and his peace agreements with the French crown were undone by the sudden drowning of his only son and heir William Ætheling in the White Ship disaster of 1120.

8 **Beneiz** Other manuscripts have the longer form *Benedeiz*: the author is usually known as Benedict, a convention followed here. For discussion of Benedict's soubriquet *li apostolies*, see Waters, ed., 1928, xxvi–xxvii.

11 The missing line, to rhyme with *romanz*, is supplied from the edition by Short and Merrilees 1979 (MS A). The break between f. 19^{v} and 20^{r} occurs after the first syllable of *romanz* (the poem is written as if it were prose, in a single column, with a *punctus* alone marking the line break); the line was likely dropped as the scribe changed folios. We insert the missing line arbitrarily before line 12 (cf. MS A: *Secund sun sens [e] entremis / En letre mis e en romanz / E[i]si cum fud li teons cumanz*).

14 **tu le [de]fent** It is likely the scribe simply has not graphically marked the enclisis of *tu le* > *tul.*

15–18 **dit que set . . . s'en doille** A frequent modesty topos in Anglo-Norman writings.

19 **de reis** Brendan's origins in fifth-century Kerry are obscure. Saints are often endowed with royal blood by their hagiographers, but Benedeit's emphasis here may have been designed particularly to appeal to Adeliza.

24–6 **Ki de cest mund . . . plus ne savra** Cf. Matt 6, 19–21.

27–30 **guerpit . . . essil** On the topos of fleeing the world see Johnson and Cazelles 1979.

32 **par force esliz** This was a convention of monastic modesty: when being elected, an abbot or abbess was expected to show reluctance for office.

35–6 **liu[s]: piu[s]** The scribe's dropping of final *s* suggests that it had ceased to be pronounced at the time he was copying the text.

37 **pernanz** MS *pernez*. Emended from the imperative to present participle (following MS A) for the sense.

10. Gaimar, *L'Estoire des Engleis* [Dean 1], Two extracts: Durham Cathedral Library, MS C.IV. 27, ff. 109^{v} and 116^{v}

Date of composition and provenance. 1136–7, Lincolnshire (Short 1994, 2009 xi–xii); Dalton (2007) argues for 1141–50.

Author, sources and nature of text. Geffrei Gaimar was a clerk to Lady Constance FitzGilbert and her husband Ralph, minor nobility whose chief lands were in Lincolnshire. He is the author of the earliest known historical writing in French, and he names written sources in English, French and Latin for his history of the English (Short 2009, vv. 6442–3). Lincolnshire had been part of the Danelaw, and Gaimar also drew on local traditions, presenting a wider spectrum of roles for the Danes, as of attitudes towards them, than their usual representation as demonic pagan invaders. Gaimar's use of the *Anglo-Saxon Chronicle* up to the annal for 966 has long been remarked: the particular version known to Gaimar was probably an early version of the Peterborough Chronicle. Gaimar names his patrons and indicates their clerical and baronial connections, including Baron Walter Espec of Helmsley (described by Aelred in his account of the Battle of the Standard as a great reader of chronicles: Short 1994, 334) and his nephew Nicholas Trailli, a canon of York. This information is derived from an epilogue (found in full in two of the four extant manuscripts and in shorter form in one of them) in which Gaimar gives a celebrated account of his patroness Lady Constance, without whose help, he claims, he could not have written the *Estoire*. Indicating both an elite patronage and reading circle and his own access to valuable sources, Gaimar credits his patroness with making Earl Robert of Gloucester's Latin book of Welsh materials on British kings available to him: Walter Espec had it from Earl Robert and lent it to Lady Constance's husband Ralph Fitzgilbert from whom she borrowed it (vv. 6453–8). For his part, Gaimar says, he made a copy of Earl Robert's book supplementing it from the book of Walter, Archdeacon of Oxford (another early version of Geoffrey of Monmouth?, vv. 6464–5) and making further additions based on the 'Winchester English history' (i.e. the *Anglo-Saxon Chronicle*), of which Gaimar had a text– *un livre engleis*- available to him in Washingborough, Lincolnshire (vv. 6467–9).

Gaimar's narrative as we have it begins with a reference to a previous volume written by him in which he deals with Constantine's reign as King Arthur's successor: moreover, in his epilogue, Gaimar says that his history began with Troy, and Jason's pursuit of the golden fleece (vv. 6528–30). This lost first volume, the *Estoire des Bretuns*, seems to have been superseded by Wace's *Roman de Brut*, given that a text of the *Brut* always precedes Gaimar's *Estoire des Engleis* in the extant manuscripts. The second volume, *L'Estoire des Engleis*, opens with the Lincolnshire story of Haveloc and Argentille (also circulating in the form of a *lai*, Dean 152, and in the Middle English romance of *Havelok the Dane*). After this opening, a version of the *Anglo-Saxon Chronicle* becomes Gaimar's main source up to the reign of Edgar, 959–75 (which he elaborates with the love-triangle story of Edgar, Ælfthryth and Æthelwold, vv. 3599–4094). Gaimar thereafter draws on various Latin sources and intermittently on the *Anglo-Saxon Chronicle* for his account of successive English reigns, the Danish and Norman conquests, and the death of William II (d. 1100), with which he concludes.

We give here Gaimar's account of the *Anglo-Saxon Chronicle* and his tribute to Alfred, rather than Gaimar's celebrated epilogue with its portrait of Constance Fitz-Gilbert, her patronage network and his sources (magisterially edited and discussed in the readily available Short 1994 and further in Short 2009). The Fitzgilberts' patronage was vital to the creation of the *Estoire* (and crucial to the text's combination of Lincolnshire perspectives and regional history with wider-ranging royal and seigneurial networks); but Gaimar further authorises written historiography by seeing it as a royal institution, the concern both of church and state, and the subject of regal patronage. The *Estoire* is not, he says in his concluding lines, 'fiction or fantasy' (*n'est pas . . . fable ne sunge*), but taken from an 'authentic historical source' (*de veire estoire estrait*) concerning the kings of the past . . . *ne pot el estre*, 'it cannot be otherwise' (Short 2009 354–5, A16–A21). For Gaimar, Old English historiography is not a past to be superseded, but an authorising precedent, composed in a royal vernacular.

Audience and circulation. A topic of Gaimar's well-known epilogue is the writing of biographies at the contemporary royal court. Gaimar notes that a fellow clerk, David, was commissioned by Adeliza of Louvain, queen of Henry I, to write a life of her husband, and that Lady Constance has a copy of this text which she reads in her chamber (vv. 6483–6507): if he can find a patron, Gaimar is willing to add more than David ever could on the courtliness of Henry's court, and thus to supply 'the kind of material that should be celebrated in poetry' (*d'iço devreit hom bien chanter*, v. 6517). The cultural networks from Lincolnshire to the royal court represented in the Epilogue were perhaps facilitated by Constance's ownership of land in Hampshire, as well as by the links (later replaced by bitter hatred in the civil war) between Walter Espec and Robert, earl of Gloucester. The *Estoire* thus invokes a contemporary model of royal patronage, even as it asserts the courtliness of regional magnate culture (of which one marker is competition between poets, vv. 6519–27). The *Estoire* could thus have readily circulated among regional and royal courts as well as along the monastic networks that contributed, in alliance with its secular patrons, to the book's formation, and it seems to have continued to do so at least into the early fourteenth century. The *Estoire*'s Lincoln Cathedral manuscript (see below) may have belonged to Cerne in Dorset; Hereford or the Welsh Marches has been suggested for the College of Arms manuscript; and the Royal manuscript has a fifteenth-century *ex libris* from Hagneby Abbey (close to Markby Abbey, founded by Ralph FitzGilbert).

Manuscript source. Durham Cathedral Library MS C.IV. 27 is the oldest extant manuscript, dating from the end of the twelfth or more probably the beginning of the thirteenth century (Careri, Ruby, and Short 2011, Cat. 21). In addition to Wace's *Brut* and Gaimar's *Estoire* (with the short epilogue), the manuscript includes the verse *Description of England* (see (1) and Dean 4), and Jordan Fantosme's *Chronicle* (Dean 55). The same selection of texts is found in Lincoln Cathedral Chapter Library 104 (A.4.12) of the late thirteenth century. In the early-fourteenth-century manuscript, London College of Arms Arundel XIV (150), however, the *Brut* and the *Estoire* are accompanied by the *Lai d'Haveloc* (Dean 152), Pierre Langtoft's *Règne de Edouard 1er* (Dean 66), *La Lignee des Bretuns et des Engleis* (Dean 29) and Chrétien de Troyes's Grail story, *Perceval*. In the latest extant *Estoire* manuscript, the early-fourteenth-century part of BL Royal 13. A.XXI, Gaimar's text is preceded by the Latin *Imago mundi* and a Heptarchy diagram (cf. (20c), *Genealogical Rolls*, fig. 1) as well as Wace's *Brut*. In this textual tradition modern distinctions between legendary and 'historical' origin stories for the English become moot. The Durham manuscript and its configuration of texts participates in the vigorous proliferation of insular historiography in the twelfth century, whether in French verse or Latin prose: the manuscript makes no distinctions between romance and historiography in its *mise-en-page*.

Bibliography. The study of Gaimar has been transformed by Short 2009, a magisterial edition with an authoritative facing-page translation. On the *Estoire*'s manuscripts see Short 2009, xvii–xxii. Short takes as his base the Royal manuscript, commonly reckoned the best text of the *Estoire*: for an edition based on the Durham manuscript (heavily emended with reference to Royal) see Bell 1960. Short 1994 provides essential context and commentary on Gaimar's epilogue: for studies of Gaimar and his patron, Constance Fitzgilbert, see Blacker 1997 and Bérat 2010. Gaunt 2015, 30–40 discusses the socio-political functions of Gaimar's French. The *Estoire* is frequently read as 'national' history, a view now compellingly revised in Bainton 2009. For studies of the *Estoire*'s themes and concerns see Press 1981, Gillingham 2000, 113–22, Zatta 1997, 1999: on Gaimar and the Danes see Bainton 2009. On continuities between Old English and Anglo-Norman texts see Tyler 2009. For audio-visual readings go to http://legacy.fordham.edu/academics/programs_at_fordham_/medieval_studies/french_of_england/audio_readings_94163.asp.

10. Gaimar, L'Estoire des Engleis

TEXT AND TRANSLATION

(a) An Anglo-Saxon Model for Historiography

[*Gaimar describes how, after 827, Egbert of Wessex re-orders the traditional 'heptarchy' of Anglo-Saxon kingdoms south of the Humber under his own rule*]

[L]e sist Oswald, le setme Oswi: [f. 109va]
Mais n'alot pas la terre issi,
[Ke] nuls hom [sul] né, pur la guerre
[Ne] seust cument alot la terre.
[Ne en cel tens sul ne saveit
Nuls hom ki chescon rei estait].
[M]oines, chanoines de abeïes
Escristrent de dis reis les vies,
[S]i [a]dresçast chascun sun per
Pur la veire raisun mustrer
[D]es reis – cumbien chascun regnad,
Cument ot nun, cum deviad,
[Q]uel fud ocis e quel transist,
Quels est entiers e quels purist,
[E] des evesques ensement
Firent li clerc adrescement.
[C]ronike ad nun, un livre grant,
Engleis l'alerent asemblant;
[Ore] est issi auctorizéd
Que a Vincestre [l']ait l'evesquiéd
[L]a est des reis la dreite estoire,
E les vies e les memoires.
[L]i reis Elvred l'ot en demaine.
Fermer i fist une chäaine;
[Qui] lire [i]volt, bien i gardast,
Mais de sun liu nel remuast.

Oswald [was] the sixth and Oswy the seventh: but the land as a whole did not follow that order, for because of all the wars, no man born knew the state of the land. Nor at that time did anyone even know who each king was. Monks and canons regular wrote the lives of the said kings and each conferred with his brothers to find the true record of the kings: how long each of them reigned, what their names were, how they died, which were killed, and which passed away, which remain whole and which have rotted. The clerks also compiled a similar list for the bishops. This very large book which the English have been busy compiling is called *The Chronicle*. It is currently authorised for the bishop's church at Winchester to keep it as the true history of the kings, their lives, and the record of their lives. King Alfred owned the book, and he had had a chain fastened to it. Whoever wanted to read it could easily look at it, but could not have removed it from its place.

(b) A Royal Patron

Il [Alfred] regnat bien vint e oit anz; [f. 116vb]
Poi sunt humes tels vivanz,
Kar sages fud e bon guerreier,
Bien sot [ses] enemis pleisier;
Nul mieldre clerc de lui n'esteit
Kar en s'enfance apris l'aveit.
Il fist escrivre un livre engleis
Des aventures e des leis
E des batailles de la terre

[Alfred] reigned for a good twenty-eight years. There are few men living like him, for he was wise as well as being a good military leader. He well knew how to subdue his enemies. There was no more learned cleric than he was, for he had been educated from infancy. He commanded a book to be written in English about the events, laws and battles in the land, and about the warring kings, and he had many books written which

E des reis ki firent guerre,
E meint livre fist il escrire
U li bon clerc vont suvent lire.
Deus ait merci de la sue alme
E sainte Mari[e] la duze dame!

good scholars often consult. May God and sweet Lady Mary have mercy on his soul!

Notes

(a) An Anglo-Saxon Model

Extract (a) corresponds to vv. 2311–36 in Bell 1960 and to vv. 2311–38 in Short 2009.

1 **Oswald . . . Oswi** are the last two of Gaimar's list of the kings subdued by Egbert in the creation of the Anglo-Saxon Heptarchy: Oswald (603/4–642), king of Bernicia from 634 and subsequently of the Northumbrians, was succeded by his brother Oswiu (611/12–670), *ODNB*.

5–6 **Ne en cel tens . . . ki chescun rei estait** These lines, not present in MS D, are supplied from MS R.

7 **de abeïes** Emended from MS *des abeies*.

14 **entiers . . . purist** The incorruption of a king's body was a possible sign of saintliness, and the distinction between rotting and whole bodies therefore highly significant.

17 **[C]ronike ad** emended from MS *[ ]orinke aveit*. The manuscript's verb makes this announcement of the name of Gaimar's Old English source, the *Anglo-Saxon Chronicle*, hypermetric. It is possible that this represents a deliberate elongation and slowing of the line for emphasis.

20 **a Vincestre [l]'ait** MS *a Vincestre ait*. Winchester was a royal borough and the capital of Wessex. Its major Benedictine monasteries included the Old Minster, rebuilt as the cathedral church by Bishop Æthelwold in 971 (St Swithun's), and the New Minster founded by Alfred in 899, and a nunnery (Nunnaminster).

21 **estoire** MS *estoires*, probably for eye rhyme with *memoires*, v. 22.

23 **[L]i reis Elvred** Alfred, king of Wessex (r. 871–99). For the king's management of his posterity (which probably included the early 'core' of the *Anglo-Saxon Chronicle*), see Wormald, *ODNB*, *s.v.* 'Alfred'.

24 **chäaine** emended from MS *chaine* for metre and rhyme.

(b) A Royal Patron

Extract (b) corresponds to Bell 1960, vv. 3439–52, Short 2009, vv. 3443–56.

27 **Il regnat** Alfred was born in 848/9, succeeded his brother Æthelred in 871 and died in 899 (Gaimar puts the date at 901, Bell 1960, v. 3437).

29 **sages fud e bon guerreier** On Alfred's crucial combination of Christian intellectual and north Germanic warrior, see Wormald *ODNB*, *s.v.* 'Alfred'; also Nelson 1986, 1993.

32 **Kar en s'enfance** MS *en france*: the other manuscripts agree with Asser's life of Alfred (composed in 893) that the king was taught in childhood (at the command of his mother). Their reading is taken here (especially as the line is short unless emended), but the Durham scribe may have been thinking of the tradition of educating noble children on the continent referred to in Bede.

33 **un livre engleis** Probably a reference to the *Anglo-Saxon Chronicle*, though Alfred also produced a revised law code, Gaimar may be running various aspects of the king's concerns together here in a model of good kingship.

37 **meint livre** Alfred promoted clerical learning through translations of Christian historiography and pastoralia in addition to translating Boethius and Augustine himself.

11a. Adgar/William, *Le Gracial* [Dean 558], Prologue: London, British Library, MS Add. 38,664, f. 3*r–v*

Donna Bussell

Date of composition and provenance. 1165–80?; London, St Paul's Cathedral.

Author, sources and nature of text. The author of this collection of *Miracles of the Virgin* names himself as Adgar, adding that many of those who know him still call him by his (Norman) name William, rather than by his (English) baptismal name, Adgar (Miracle XI, 34). Adgar may perhaps be the William, vicar of St Mary Magdalen's on Bread Street (1152–1200) who had a living at St Paul's but was not a canon there, or he may perhaps have been a chaplain of the nuns at Barking Abbey. Claiming that he does not want to say things only on his own authority, Adgar identifies as his source and guarantor of veracity *le livre Mestre Albri*, found in the book chest or library (*almarie*) at St Paul's Cathedral in London. A *Magister Albericus* was a canon at St Paul's between 1148 and 1162 and the compiler of a miracle collection drawing on earlier compilations by William of Malmesbury (d. 1142), Anselm, abbot of Bury (d. 1148), and Prior Dominic of Evesham (d. in or before 1150). This generation of writers in England produced a new kind of miracle collection not tied to specific cult sites or relics and perhaps fuelled by advocacy in England for the Feast of the Immaculate Conception. The Virgin, among her other powers, had become an affective focus for clerics in the aftermath of the eleventh-century tightening of clerical celibacy (see (**15**), Herman de Valenciennes's *Romanz de Dieu et de sa mere*).

Adgar's octosyllabic-verse *Gracial* is the earliest vernacular Marian miracle collection in England and, as far as is known, in Europe. The miracles are framed by a prologue and epilogue, but as with many such framed works, the collection was always unstable, or better, dynamic. Adgar himself was perhaps involved in producing some of its variant forms. BL Egerton 612 (early thirteenth century), for example, contains forty-nine miracles and names Adgar's friend Gregory as inspiration and sustainer of the work (see below). BL Add. 38,664's text is a later and shorter version of *c.* 1250–75 with 22 miracles: it is dedicated to *Dame Mahaut* in the prologue edited here.

The *Gracial* of the title invokes the connection between incarnational theology and Marian devotion: that is, the Virgin is an intermediary between her son and her supplicants, and is herself filled with grace (vv. 43–4). Adgar elaborates on the term (vv. 35–46), insisting that his audience use it for his collection (v. 46). The *Gracial*, its author, his patron and his audiences play their parts in a divinely fueled distribution of grace 'common to all people' (vv. 36, 39). Those who conceal wisdom will not be rewarded, but judged as thieves by God (vv. 11–14): they get their understanding from him and should pay it out to others (vv. 16–18). The poem is offered to God and his mother in the hope of their heavenly patronage, since, Adgar says, he eschews the rewards he might receive from a knight or a wealthy lady (vv. 51–5). He perhaps alludes to the material patronage enjoyed by Guernes de Pont-Sainte-Maxence at Barking Abbey (**11b**.27), if *Dame Mahaut* was its twelfth-century abbess, Maud. But since the manuscript witness to *Dame Mahaut* is from 1250 to 1275, this may be a case of retrospective dedication, as with *Brendan* (**9**): Barking had three abbesses named Maud between 1215 and 1275, including the daughter of King John from 1247 to 1252.

Audience and circulation. The three manuscript witnesses are textually close without direct dependence between them (Kunstmann 1982, 52–3). The smallest selection from *Le Gracial* is in

London, Dulwich College MS 22, a thirteenth- and fourteenth-century religious miscellany, which contains most of the prologue and parts of two miracles. The two major manuscripts, Egerton 612 and BL Add. 38,664, have different epilogues, suggesting that Adgar may have modified his miracle collection according to his audiences. In the Egerton 612 epilogue, Adgar asks his friend Gregory to receive his writing in the spirit of Cato's precept that a poor friend's gift must be warmly received and appreciated, while Gregory is earlier described (in Miracle XX) as Adgar's inspiration and support: *uns bels bacheler*, he is courteous and valiant, a noble, well brought-up and generous young man. Adgar's account of Gregory suggests a secular patron but could also apply to a well-born churchman. The epilogue to Add. 38,664 is brief and addresses no specific audience, but it is in this manuscript's prologue that Adgar names *Dame Mahaut* (v. 65), as pre-eminent in his text's audience. Lady Maud could have been the daughter of King Henry II, abbess of Barking Abbey 1175–98, or as noted above, another of the three thirteenth-century abbesses named Maud at Barking. This elite convent had close contact with the royal court from William the Conqueror onwards, as well as a history of writing and commissioning Latin and vernacular texts, and was about seven miles downriver from London and St Paul's. Adgar's inscribed audiences consist of both men and women (vv. 37–8, 69 below), suggesting that the *Gracial* may have been heard both by nuns and their lay patrons and relatives.

Adgar's *Gracial* collection was further revised in the thirteenth century by Everard de Gateley, a monk of Bury, and was predecessor to several other Marian collections: one witnessed in an early-fourteenth-century manuscript fragment, and a later, large collection extant in BL Royal 20 B.XIV. Continental collections sharing some of Adgar's sources also followed: in France, Gautier de Coinci's *Miracles de Nostre Dame* (1214–36), a collection by Jean le Marchant (1252–62) and others, and in Castile, the *Cantigas de Santa Maria* of Alfonso X, 'el Sabio' of Castile (1221–84).

Manuscript source. BL Add. 38,664 was copied in the second quarter of the thirteenth century. The manuscript, now worn and stained, especially on the outside leaves, is made up of vellum bifolia in gatherings of eight leaves, 240 × 152 mm. It is slim and professionally produced, in two hands, with a torn portion of leaf carefully, but not quite accurately, pieced in at the head of folio 3rb (thus preserving the line ends of column b). The two-column text on ff. 1–8 is followed by three-column text on ff. 9^{r}–16^{v}. A brief Anglo-Norman *Life of St Margaret* in 85 monorhymed quatrains occupies ff. 1–3ra. The second and last item is Adgar's *Gracial*, written on ff. 3rb–16vb by the second scribe. Though not very large, the manuscript could have been used for reading aloud (cf. prologue, v. 32); personal devotional use would also have been possible. There is no decoration or rubrication of the prologue beyond the use of enlarged initials in red and blue with occasional flourishes. Enlarged initials mark the beginning of each of the prologue's three sections: at v. 1, the work of the author and its connection with divine grace; at v. 63 an address to Lady Maud and other audience members; at v. 79 a prayer to the Virgin and request for blessing on author and audience.

Bibliography. The critical edition is Kunstmann 1982, using Egerton 612 as base manuscript with supplementation from Add. 38,664. He gives details of earlier, partial editions (Kunstmann 1982, 55) in addition to those of Neuhaus 1886 (Egerton) and 1887 (Dulwich). On Adgar's identity see Legge 1971, 190; Legge 1950, 105–6. For Master Alberic see Kunstmann 1982, 60, vv. 75–8; 327, vv. 1–3, 15–19: Alberic and the Latin miracle collections are discussed in Southern 1958, 202. On Adgar's dedicatee, Gregory, see Kunstmann 1982, 143, vv. 24–9, 328, vv. 37–42 and Legge 1971, 187–8. Bérat 2012 discusses Adgar's dual patronage and his two names. For a translation into modern French see Kunstmann 1981. Herbert 1903 discusses the then newly discovered MS 38,664 text and the prologue structure. For Everard de Gateley's revision of Adgar see Dean 560; the fragmentary miracle collection is Dean 561. Kjellmann 1977 edits the Royal MS miracle collection. The Life of St Margaret in BL Add. 38,664 (Dean 572) is edited in Reichl 1975. On the English origins of Marian miracle collections see Southern 1958, esp. 194–9, and Ziolkowski 1986 for the early-twelfth-century collection by Nigel Wireker of Christ Church, Canterbury. Latin and vernacular versions are discussed by Meale 1990. For continental collections see Iogna-Prat *et al.* 1996, and Montoya Martínez 1981. An illuminating general study of miracles is Ward 1987. On Barking's literary patronage and ecclesiastical and court connections see Levi 1925; Robertson 1996; Brown and Bussell 2012, O'Donnell 2012a, and (**2** and **11b**). For a comparison of *Le Gracial* and Marie de France's *lais* see Kay 2001, 179–215: Shea 2007 studies Adgar and attitudes to Jews. Benoit 2012 is a study with translations into modern French of some of the miracles.

TEXT AND TRANSLATION

Mut fet bien ki sun sens despent [f. 3rb]
En tel liu dunt l'en eit amendement.
Meillur uvre ne put hume fere
Que sei e autre a Deu atrere.
Qui suls i vient, mene a dreite vie,
Mieldre ki i meine cumpanie.
Pur ço, ki set se deit pener
Que plusurs puisse a Deu mener.
Ki ben set e ne s'entrem[e]t,
Mielz li venist estre mu[e]t,
Kar de Deu li ert repruvé
Pur quei sun saveir ait celé.
Si en avra mal guerredun;
Deu le fra juger a larrun.
Qui sages est ne l'a de sei;
De sul Deu l'ad, sachez en fei!
Par sei ne put grant sens aprendre;
Pur ço le deit as autres rendre,
Que de Deu del cel ne ait mal gré.
Endreit mei, m'en sui purpensé,
Que aukune chose voil treiter
Que de Deu ne aie repruver.
Uvraine ai emprise gloriuse
Dunt vul mener vie penuse,
Que m'alme en ait guerredun
E de mes pechiez veir pardun.
El nun del Pere faz l'escrit,
Del Fiz e del Saint Esperit,
De la dame sainte Marie,
Ki desuz Deu est nostre aïe.
De ses vertuz voil cunter,
Ki duces sunt a escuter.
Enz el livre puet l'em oïr
Cume l'em deit la dame servir.

He does well who applies his intelligence to learning through which one may be improved. A man can do no better work than to draw himself and others to God. The person who arrives there alone has gone the right way; better still is the person who brings company. And so, whoever knows this ought to strive to lead many others to God. The person who understands this and does not do it would have been better off mute, for God will reproach him for hiding his knowledge. He will have a poor reward for it: God will see him judged a thief. The wise person is not so of himself but has received his wisdom from God alone, take that as faith! He could not have learned great wisdom by himself. And that is why he must give it to others, so that he does not earn the ill-will of God in heaven. For my part, I am resolved to write about something for which God will not reprove me. I have undertaken a glorious work because of which I will lead a life of toil, so that my soul may have a reward for it and I may receive pardon for my sins. I compose this piece of writing in the name of the Father and of the Son and of the Holy Spirit, and in the name of holy Lady Mary, who under God is our help. I wish to tell of her miracles, which are sweet to listen to. In this book you can hear how you ought to serve the Lady.

Cest livre a nun 'Gracial',
Pur ço qu'en grace est cumunal,

This book is called *Gracial* because its grace is available to all. It is based on the

Tut estret de grace seinte
De meint humme, de femme meinte; [f. 3va]
Si est cummun a tute gent
Ki de Deu servir unt talent.
Estreite est d'icele reïne
Ki est pleine de grace fine;
De la Deu grace est replenie
Cum sa mere e sa duce am[i]e.
Pur ço est 'Graciel' numez
Cest escrit, si l'apelerez!

holy grace experienced by many a man and a woman, and is available to all who have the desire to serve God. It has been composed about that queen who is filled with true grace: she is endowed with God's grace as his mother and his beloved. That's why this writing is named *Gracial*, and thus you shall call it.

A Dampnedeu l'escrit present
E a sa mere ensement;
A lur loenge, a lur hunur
Seit le livre fet par dulçur.
Sel presentase a chevaler,
Tost me dunast un cheval cher;
A riche dame u a meschine,
Tost me dunast pelice hermine.
Mes tel dun sereit tost alé.
Al rei le faz de majesté,
E a sa mere gloriuse,
Ki tant est sainte e preciuse.
A la dame en faz present.
Deu seit a mun cumencement
E la dame sainte Marie,
De qui treiter vol par sa aïe!
Escutez, bone gent senee,
Ki en Deu estes asemblee,
E vus, dame Mahaut, premers!
A vus dirai plus volentiers
Des miracles, des grant sucurs
Ke fet Nostre Dame a plusurs,
A tuz e a tutes ki l'eiment,
E ki de bon quor la reclaiment.
Unkes ne fu hum ki l'amast
Que ele bien ne li guerredunast.
Pur ço voil jo de li treiter,
Q'a mun busuin aie luier. [f. 3vb]
Mes n'en voil treiter ne ren faire
Fors dreit sulum mun essamplaire;
Se ço ne seit essanple u dit
Ki bien se cuntenge en l'escrit.
Sainte Marie curunee,
Reine d'angles bonuree,
Mere Jesu, Nostre Seinur,

I present this writing to the Lord God and likewise to his mother; to their praise, to their honour. May this book be sweetly written. Were I to present it to a knight, he would immediately give me an expensive horse; if to a rich lady or maiden, she would at once grant me an ermine cloak. But that kind of gift would soon be gone. I am writing this for the King of Majesty and for his glorious mother, who is so holy and so precious. To the Lady I make this gift. May God be present as I begin it and the holy Lady Mary, about whom I wish to tell, with her help! Listen, good people of sense, and Lady Maud, first in that group who are brought together in God! To you I will relate most willingly the miracles and tell of the great comforts Our Lady gives to many, to all men and all women who love her, and all those of sincere heart who pray to her. For there was never a man who loved her whom she did not reward well. That's why I wish to tell you about her, so that I may have a reward for my task. I do not wish to write or do anything except strictly according to my source; may there be no exemplum or saying other than what is set out in this model. Holy Mary crowned, Blessed Queen of the angels, Mother of Jesus, Our Lord:

Entendez, dame, a cest pechur!
Preez pur mei vostre fiz cher,
84 Que de vus me duinst si treiter
Ke meindre puisse el ciel amunt
E tut cil ki lire l'orrunt.

Listen, oh Lady, to this sinner! Pray to your dear son for me that, through you, he may let me dwell in heaven above, along with all those who will hear this work read.

Notes

1 **Mut** A plain red capital *M*, 4 lines high, begins the text on f. 3rb, without the blue flourishing of some subsequent capitals in the manuscript.

2 **En** MS *Su*.

2 **liu** On this idea of 'place' as the space of composition, see Kay 2007, 4–6.

4–6 **Que sei . . . i meine cumpanie** For another version of this topos see Angier, *Dialogues* (**24a**.53–60).

9 **entrem[e]t** *e* obscured by mend in the vellum.

10 **mu[et]** *e* obscured by mending.

14 **Deu le fra juger a larrun** Cf. the unprofitable servant in the parable of the talents, Matt 25.14–30.

21 **voil** MS *uuil* is corrected by insertion of *o* above *u* in the same ink and what appears to be the same hand: *u* is expuncted; cf. *voil* in v. 75.

32 **duces** On the moral and aesthetic value of sweetness in medieval reading see Carruthers 2006.

33 **Enz al livre** suggests the audience's position, sitting before the book and listening as the reader holds the book and reads aloud.

44 **cum** MS *cume*, emended for metre; **amie** MS *ame*, we follow Kunstmann's emendation (1982, 60).

50 **dulçur** On sweetness in medieval reading see n. to 32 above.

63 **Escutez** A second red capital three lines high on f. 3va.

77–8 **Se ço ne seit . . . en l'escrit** The first of several asseverations that only the miracles contained in Master Alberic's book have been included (cf. epilogue vv. 1–15; Kunstmann 1982, 327).

79 **Sainte** Blue initial two lines high with red flourishing on f. 3va.

83 **fiz cher** MS *cher fiz* Marks above each word in a lighter ink indicate that the words should be reversed.

11b. Guernes de Pont-Ste-Maxence, *La Vie de saint Thomas Becket* [Dean 508], Two Epilogues: Paris, Bibliothèque nationale de France, fonds français, MS 13,513, ff. 97^{v}–98^{v}

Date of composition and provenance. Guernes composed two versions of the life of Becket. The first, from 1171–2, was completed immediately after the murder of the archbishop, 29 December 1170, and was based mainly on second-hand sources. A revised and improved version was written in Canterbury in 1172–4, after Guernes travelled to England to interview Becket's close associates.

Author, sources and nature of text. Little is known of Guernes, apart from the statements in his life of St Thomas. He was from Pont-Sainte-Maxence (a town north-east of Paris), he was a clerk, and he took the trouble to revise his biography of Becket on the basis of oral testimony from Becket's intimates. He comments that his French is good, since he was born in (the Île de) France.

The Becket Life has some 6180 alexandrine lines, in five-line monorhymed stanzas. It draws on several of the written Latin histories by eye witnesses to the murder (Edward Grim, William fitz Stephen, William of Canterbury), and often adds details not found in the Latin sources, no doubt drawn from Guernes's interviews about Becket. Guernes gives ample details on the political and ecclesiastical conflicts and lengthy legal arguments, with reports on documents and court proceedings, as well as the standard hagiographical elements of miracles and divine portents. Guernes continues to be used by modern historians as a source for some aspects of the conflict between Becket and Henry II. As Short (1977, 34) has shown, compared with the (now fragmentary) text of the first redaction, Guernes's changes to his revised text (on which Guernes himself often comments) increase the blame apportioned to Henry II.

In his epilogue Guernes lays claim to the excellence of his work and asserts his own superior skills as a *jongleur* (his French is good, he has used a complex verse form, his work is in demand at St Thomas's tomb). Perhaps his most striking rhetorical strategy is his repeated insistence on the truthfulness of his narrative (vv. 4, 8, 13, 15, 17, 20). Although a conventional medieval authorial assertion, his insistence serves as a reminder that he has personally researched his topic to get at the truth. Concern with the truth is especially necessary, because Guernes is writing in verse, in French, and attempting to be historically accurate, rather than entertaining (for comparable claims, see Piramus's Life of St Edmund (27)). Guernes is keenly aware of competing with the Latin prose accounts. He also stresses his method of writing and rewriting: he has revised his work over a period of two years, adding new information, removing faulty statements from the first version. This allows him both to claim authorship of the first version and to devalue pirated versions of it by declaring it inferior, not fully verified before it was stolen. In the end his truth claim effectively dismisses other lives of Thomas, in Latin or French, if they vary from his (vv. 16–20).

Whereas in the first epilogue Guernes is at pains to distinguish his work from that of his potential competitors, in the second epilogue, written in two new metrical forms, Guernes establishes his relationship with Becket's personal family, and with Becket's ecclesiastical milieu, by laying claim to two important patrons. In this epilogue's first section (vv. 26–40, in verses of sixteen syllables, with a rhyme on the eighth and another on the sixteenth syllable), Guernes lays claim to the patronage of Mary Becket, appointed Abbess of Barking in 1173 by Henry II in partial reparation for her brother's murder, and that of her convent. He inscribes Becket's female family, and women religious generally, as materially generous patronesses. Here we also see signs of the precariousness of a travelling cleric/*jongleur's* life: sometimes you win in seeking a patron, sometimes not. Guernes's risk has paid off, for himself and for Abbess Mary, who will be praised and remembered thanks to her poet's words. Lucky in St Thomas himself, his spiritual patron, Guernes has also been richly rewarded with material blessings.

In the final section of the epilogue (vv. 41–7, in 12 syllable lines, with internal rhyme at the sixth syllable, and line-end rhyme), Guernes creates his personal relationship with Becket's monastic family through the person of Prior Odo and the monks at Holy Trinity convent in Canterbury. He also completes his self-portrait as a *jongleur* welcome anywhere by observing that wherever he roams, he always comes back (home) to this convent, the best and most generous in Christendom.

AUDIENCE AND CIRCULATION. Canonised in 1173, Becket quickly became one of the best known saints across Europe, and Guernes's life of him was clearly popular (whether or not his first version was actually pirated to meet demand for copies). His revised version is extant in six manuscripts, all of English provenance, the earlier version in a single fragmentary survival. Guernes affirms that he has often performed the Life at the martyr's tomb in Canterbury (v. 3). There are two other extant Becket lives in Anglo-Norman: one by Beneit, a monk of St Albans probably composed in 1184; another, often attributed to Matthew Paris, is extant in four illustrated leaves (the 'Getty leaves'). Guernes refers in his prologue to vernacular versions other than his own by members of the church or the laity, by monks, or by a woman (Walberg 1922, 162), which suggests that some vernacular lives have been lost. Guernes's version seems to have been the most widely known vernacular version. Since Becket's shrine was one of the most popular pilgrimage sites in Europe, the potential audience for recitals by Guernes himself, and for later performances of his text by others was large. Guernes's much discussed claim that his French is good because of his continental French origin (v. 10) has often been read as evidence that the French of England was an impoverished dialect, but a relevant context is Guernes's awareness of Becket's Latin historiography. Rather than a continental cleric denigrating insular French, we could see here a writer inspired by experience of the vernacular literary culture of England to the affirmation of French biographical and historiographical writing as against Latin (O'Donnell 2011).

MANUSCRIPT SOURCE. The first epilogue (vv. 1–25) is found in all six manuscripts: the second epilogue (27–48) is extant only in BN fr. 13,513 (hereafter P). The text for both epilogues, below, is from manuscript P, dated to 1220–30 by Avril and Stirnemann (1987, 61). A small (215 × 140 mm) vellum manuscript written in England, it belonged to the Norman abbey at Saint-Evroul in the seventeenth century. It was purchased by the Bibliothèque nationale in 1839 together with two other manuscripts from the same abbey bound into the codex and also of English origin, BN fr. 13,505, a mid-thirteenth-century life of St Francis and BN fr. 14,959, a late-thirteenth-century text of Waddington's *Manuel* (**24b**). The Becket life (ff. 1–98^{r}) and epilogue (f. 98^{r-v}) are the only works in P. Walberg (1922) notes that P is written in four different hands (ff. 1–35, 35–41, 41–98, of which the fourth is a corrector). In the first section, ff. 1–35, the first and last letters of each verse are set off in vertical columns (see Legge 1971, 367–8, on this scribal practice). In the manuscript text of the extract edited here, each five-line stanza begins with a large majuscule letter in red (vv. 1, 6, 11, 16, 21), as do the two subsections of the second epilogue (26, 41). The first letter of each line is set off in a column to the left.

BIBLIOGRAPHY. Walberg's critical edition (1922) is the standard study; it includes detailed analysis of the manuscript tradition of Guernes's text and of the Latin and vernacular Becket lives (re-issued 1936 with shortened critical apparatus: this text, with variants, is now available online at the Anglo-Norman On-Line Hub (http://www.anglo-norman.net/sources). Walberg 1975 is a reprint with parts of the critical introduction and expanded study of the Becket hagiographical tradition. For the extant first redaction of Guernes's text and detailed discussion, see Short 1977. For English translations of Guernes, see Short, trans., 2013, Shirley 1975, and for a modern French translation, Gouttebroze and Queffélec 1990. The text has also been edited (with Harley 270 as base manuscript) with facing modern French translation by Thomas 2002. Legge 1971, 248–50 gives a brief contextualisation of Guernes's work. Russell 2003, 75–7 summarises the manuscript tradition. For further bibliography see Hasenohr and Zink 1992, 1350–41. J. Fox 1974 gives a brief critical overview in English. The bibliography of historical studies of Becket is extensive: for a modern biography of Becket see A. Duggan 2004 and for medieval writings on him Staunton 2006. For Beneit's Becket life (of particular interest for its staging of the copy's patron reading the life aloud to his wife), see Short 1987. Further on Guernes and literary patronage, see O'Donnell 2012a, and on Guernes's much discussed claim that his French is good because of his continental French origin see O'Donnell 2011. Van Houts 1999 discusses medieval valuations of oral and written testimony.

TEXT AND TRANSLATION

Epilogue(s) BN f. fr. 13,513

Guarniers li clerc del Punt fine ci sun sermun [f. 97v]
Del martir saint Thomas e de sa passïun,
E meinte feiz le list a la tumbe al barun;
Ci n'a mis un sul mot se la verité non.
De ses mesfez li face Jhesu li pius pardon.

Guernes, the clerk from Le Pont (Sainte-Maxence), here finishes his exposition on the passion of the martyr St Thomas. He has recited it many times at the worthy man's tomb and he has not included a single untrue word; may Jesus in his compassion grant him pardon for his sins.

Unc mes ne fu fez mieldre romanz ne trovez;
A Cantorbire fu e fet e amendez,
N'i a mis un sul mot qui ne seit veritez;
Li vers est d'une rime en cinc clauses coplez;
Mis languages est buens, car en France fui nez.

Never before was a version in French composed or created that was better than this one; it was written and revised at Canterbury; he has not put a single untrue word. The five lines linked together in each stanza keep the same rhyme, and my French is accurate, for I was born in France.

L'an secund ke li sainz fu en s'iglise ocis [f. 98r]
Comenchai cest romanz e mult m'en entremis.
Des privez saint Thomas la verité apris,
Meinte feiz en ostai ço que jo ainz escris
Pur oster la mençunge; al quart [an] fin i mis.

I began the composition of my narrative the second year after the saint was killed in his church, and I have worked hard on it. I learned the truth from St Thomas's close friends, and many times I deleted material I had previously written in order to remove inaccuracies and untruths, and in the fourth year I finished it.

Içо sachent tut cil ki ceste vie orrunt:
Que pure verité partut oïr purrunt
E ço sachent tut cil qui del saint treitié unt,
Ou romanz ou latin, e cest chemin ne vunt,
Ou el dient que jo, cuntre verité sunt.

Let all who hear this life be assured that they will hear a completely true story throughout. And all those who have also written about the saint, in Latin or in French, who do not follow the same path as me, or who say something other than what I say – they should know that they are not speaking the truth.

Ore prium Jhesu Crist le filz seinte Marie
Pur amur seint Thomas nus doinst la sue aïe,
Ke rien ne nus suffraigne a la corporal vie
E si nus esneium de seculer folie
K'al moriant aium la sue compaignie

Let us pray to Jesus Christ, the son of St Mary, that for the love of St Thomas he will give us his help, so that we shall lack nothing in our earthly lives, and that he will purge us of our worldly sins, so that at our hour of death we will be with him.

A M E N.

L'abesse suer saint Thomas, pur s'onur e pur le barun,
M'at doné palefrei e dras, ne faillent nis li esperun;
Ne getai pas mes dez sur as quant jo turnai a sa meisun!
Ne ele n'i ad mespris pas, de me[i] aura tel gueredun
E devant halz e devant bas, par tut eshalcerai sun nun:
Meillure femme tresk'a Patras en nul liu ne trovereit l'un,
E les dames m'unt fet tut gras, chescune d'eles de sun dun.
Ore lur duinst Deus tutdis a tas pain e vin e char e peisun,
E quant lur cors ert muz e kas, Deus face as almes veir pardun!
Ne dirai mes des ore: 'At las!' car servi ai seignur mult buen
De ço k'ai esté sovent las de rimeier sa passïun
Il me rent bien, neent a gas, assez me trove guarisun:
Or, argent, robe[s] en mes sas, chevals, autre possessïun.
Se nuls me dit: 'Guarniers, ou vas?' – tuz li munz est miens envirun!
Ne di si bien nun de Judas quant [il] vent a confessïun! [f. 98v]
Oede li buens priurs de seinte Terneté,
Li covenz des seignurs (Deus lur sache buen gré!)
M'unt fet mult grant sucurs, de[l] lur sovent duné,
Maintenu an e jurs e entr'els governé.
Quel part que seit mis curs, e de loing e de lé
A els est mes returs tut pur lur grant bunté
Kar unc ne vi meillurs en la crestienté.

Explicit vita sancti thome archiepiscopi et martiris canturiencis

Amen.

The abbess, St Thomas's sister, for the sake of her own honour, and that of her noble brother, provided me with a palfrey and furnishings, even down to the spurs. I did not make a losing throw of the dice when I cast my lot with her convent for help. Nor did she herself make an error, for she shall be rewarded by me when I praise her name everywhere, before those of both low and high estate. You could not find a better woman anywhere, were you to search from here to Patras, and the ladies of the abbey, each with her own gifts, have fed me very well. May God grant that they always have an abundance of bread and wine, meats and fish, and when their bodies are silent and in a casket, may God grant their souls true pardon.

From now on I shall have no reason to cry 'Alas!', for I have served a very worthy lord. Although I have often been wearied by writing his life in rhyme, St Thomas has repaid me well, – it's not a boast – by providing me with ample rewards: gold, silver, garments in my travelling bags, horses and other possessions. If anyone should ask me, 'Guarnier, where are you going?' [I'll reply:] 'The whole world around me is mine!' – and I speak well of anyone but Judas, even when he comes to confession!

Odo the worthy prior of Holy Trinity, and all the lords of the monastery (may God reward them for their generosity), have been of great help to me. They have often shared their own possessions with me, providing me hospitality among them for more than a year. Wherever my journey takes me, whether far or wide, I always return to them because of their great goodness; I have never seen better in all Christendom.

Here ends the life of St Thomas, archbishop and martyr of Canterbury

Notes

1–25 correspond to Walberg 1922, vv. 6156–80 (strophes 1232–6), while vv. 26–46 are Walberg 1922, Appendix I. Manuscript P places the epilogue after strophe 1181 (Walberg 1922, v. 5905), and omits strophes 1182–1231 (vv. 5906–6155), the passage dealing with the penance of Henry II at the tomb of Becket. All the manuscripts dating after P also put the epilogue after stanza 1181, but they then include the fifty-stanza section on Henry's penance (see Russell 2003, 75–7).

1 **Guarniers li clerc del Punt** The poet's name is found only twice in the poem proper (v. 5877 and here), and once in the second epilogue. The usual form is *Guernes*, but is uniformly *Guarniers* in P (see Walberg 1975, 82–3 on the name's forms in other medieval sources; he states that *Guernes* is a familiar form, *Guarnier* a more formal one for this relatively rare name.) Pont-Sainte-Maxence is on the Oise, on the periphery of the Île de France, between Senlis and Compiègne.

7 **a Cantorbire fu e fet e amendez** The fact that Guernes travelled to Canterbury to compose and revise his narrative demonstrates both his dedication and the fact that he was a *vagans*, or clerk/*jongleur* who travelled from place to place according to the opportunities available.

9 **cinc clauses coplez** (five lines rhyming together) *clause* initially referred to the end of the line, where the rhyming word is found; by extension, it came to refer to the group of rhyming words, or stanza.

10 **France** here means, of course, the restricted area known as the Île de France. Guernes's reference to his good French is perhaps a way of stressing that the rhymes in his five-line monorhymed stanzas are always correct if his composition is recited in the dialect of the Île de France, as opposed to (Anglo-)Norman, or another dialect.

11–15 **l'an second . . . quart** [**an**] Becket was killed in 1170. Guernes began the revised version in 1172 and completed it towards the end of 1174. The other manuscript copies have *an* in v. 15, and three of them (including H, one of the earliest) also have *quint* rather than *quart*. On the establishment of the dates, see Walberg 1975, 160–9.

26 **AMEN** is written between 25 and 26 in double-size letters, spaced apart to occupy the same length as the preceding line in the text. This is clearly an ending point in the text, but it is followed, without a break, by the second epilogue on the next line. The page is ruled uniformly.

26–40 This section of the second epilogue was printed by Hippeau 1859 in octosyllabics with alternating rhyme. The dramatic change in metrical form suggests that this epilogue was written by Guernes for a later copy of his work, dating from a period sometime after the completion of the second redaction. The fact that Guernes revised his work in 1172–4 shows that he was not loath to rewrite, so it is not inconceivable that he would have added a second epilogue to his work after some years had passed. Walberg argues, however, that this epilogue also predates 1175 (1975, 164–9), since the reference to Odo suggests he is still prior at Canterbury, and Odo was elected abbot of Battle Abbey, Hastings, in July 1175.

26 **L'abesse suer saint Thomas** Mary was appointed abbess of Barking (April 1173–Jan. 1175) by Henry II, at the request of Odo, prior of Canterbury. Becket's other sisters, Agnes and Roheise, also received amends from Henry as part of his penance (Barlow 1986, 13–14, 262).

27 **palefrei e dras** The palfrey, a fully equipped riding horse, was a sign of the owner's wealth and class.

28 **sur as** The ace, or one, was the lowest score possible when casting dice.

31 **Meillure . . . Patras** Grammatically, the form should be *meillur*, which restores the octosyllabic half-line. The Greek port city Patras here signifies the Orient in general.

32 **m'unt fet tut gras** refers literally to fattening up the recipient of these gifts: that the gifts are food is suggested by what Guernes wishes for them in exchange: ample supply of bread and wine, meat and fish.

33 **Ore** Emending to the form *or* would restore regular scansion of the half-line.

34 **lur cors ert muz e kas** Walberg 1922, 211 notes that one could read *viuz* (old) rather than *muz* (silent), but *muz* is more evocative of death; *cors* is used with a singular verb, while *almes* is used with a plural. Modern French would tend to use the singular in both contexts, while English tends to use the plural.

35 **At las** The unexpected *t* may be a dittography from the following line, where *soventlas* is found directly below *atlas*, and the form could be emended to *alas*.

41–7 **Oede li buens priurs . . . la crestienté** The change in metre corresponds to a change in subject matter. Odo was the prior of the cathedral priory, whose monks served as choral staff and chapter of the cathedral. In the twelfth century it was the largest monastery for black monks in England, with 150 members *c.* 1125. The large church and monastery of St Augustine's Abbey was situated beside Christ Church cathedral, and was often a jealous rival of the cathedral monastery (Knowles 1970, 21–3). Odo, as prior of the cathedral monastery, was in direct conflict with Thomas, who considered his election as prior to be illegal, and was on the point of deposing him when Thomas was murdered. Odo's advocacy for Mary, Becket's sister, can be seen as part of his own penance. The cathedral monks proposed prior Odo for election to the archbishopric in 1172 and again in 1184 when Odo was abbot of Battle Abbey (Barlow 1986, 249, 271–2).

47 to closing rubric Between the final line of the text and the closing rubric the manuscript has a six-line space, in which a later hand has made a number of pen trials, copying some of the preceding lines:

> kar unc ne vi meillurs en la crestienté
> vita sancti thome in galice explicit vita sancti thome martiris
> vita sancti thome in galice explicit vita sancti thome martiris
> m'unt fet mult grant sucurs de lur sovennt doné

These lines may suggest that a member of the cathedral monastery has copied repeatedly the praises to the monks. The pen trials are continued after the closing rubric:

> Explicit vita sancti thome archiepiscopi et martiris canturiencis
> Explicit vita
>
> Explicit vita sancti thome archiepiscopi
> m'unt fet mult grant sucurs de lur sovennt doné
> m'unt fet mult grant sucurs de lur sovennt doné

Whoever has written these annotations was clearly impressed by the generosity of the monks.

12. Simon of Walsingham, *La Vie de sainte Fey, virgine et martire* [Dean 570], Prologue: London, British Library, MS Add. 70,513, ff. 147^{r}–148^{r}

Date of composition and provenance. Written at Bury St Edmunds Abbey, Suffolk, early thirteenth century.

Author, sources and nature of text. The author presents himself as Simon of Walsingham, a monk at St Edmunds Abbey, who was born on St Faith's feast day. He has been asked to write a French version of the saint's life (probably in conjunction with the renovations to St Faith's chapel in the abbey at Bury, completed before 1211). Composition by monks usually requires permission or a command from a monastic superior: in this case a learned fellow monk (vv. 79–86). Baker's suggestion that this is Simon's kinsman, Thomas of Walsingham, also a monk at St Edmunds and a leader in the conflict with King John over the choice of abbot to succeed Abbot Samson after his death in 1211, has often been accepted by later critics, but it is clear that Simon is referring to Abbot Samson himself when he comments that his earthly patron is a learned monk and fellow countryman (Simon says that he was 'born and raised in the same region', v. 84), and when he playfully remarks on his patron's short physical but tall moral stature (vv. 80–1). These are all details found in the contemporary biography of Abbot Samson by Jocelin of Brakelond. His *Chronicle* portrays Samson's impeccable moral integrity and describes him as 'of medium height' (Greenway and Sayers 1989, 36), a learned and eloquent man who spoke both French and Latin, but who remained a proud Norfolkman since, when he preached to the people in English, he used 'the Norfolk dialect, for that is where he was born and brought up' (37). The county of Norfolk, seen both as St Edmund's principal cult area and the region of which the saint was most protective, was important in Bury St Edmunds' internal and external politics. Simon, from Walsingham in Norfolk, is staking his claim to this power and protection by the mention of this shared regional identity.

Simon's French version draws on all the Latin texts current at the time: the *Passio*, the *Translatio*, liturgical offices for St Faith, and the *Liber miraculorum sancte Fidis*. The Life, comprising 1242 heptasyllabic and octosyllabic lines, recounts the martyrdom of the young girl Faith at Agen, France, by Dacien, provost of the Roman emperors Maximien and Diocletian. Her suffering on a gridiron is witnessed from his hiding place by a young Christian, Capraise, and inspires his and other male martyrdoms. Many years later a bishop of Agen recovers the bodies of the martyrs and has a church built in honour of St Faith. Miracles and pilgrims ensue. A monk from Conques, a hitherto obscure monastery in the Rouergue, joins the seculars at Agen and, after ten years under cover, steals Faith's relics and takes them back to Conques. There, the fruits of this famous and successful 'sacred theft' are enshrined in a remarkable reliquary, a bejewelled and forbidding statue of the saint which remains an object of pilgrimage at Conques today.

The prologue richly deploys the humility conventions of hagiographic writing, while crafting a vernacular equivalent of sonorous liturgical recitation. The tonal range of the prologue embraces veneration as well as insider jokes, and there is extensive play on the word *fey*, both 'faith' and 'Faith'. Those who are already confirmed in the faith know that they can only be saved by faith (or Faith), and therefore will be happy to increase their faith by hearing of St Faith. By listening to the recitation (in song and story – suggesting a liturgical context to the audition of this text?) of Faith's virtues, the community of believers will be strengthened in their faith (and saved), vv. 1–10. The narrator claims to lack learning in Latin and skill in the vernacular (v. 38 and n.) but cites his own birth on Faith's feast day as impelling his special devotion and labour for his heavenly patroness. He develops the contrast between Faith's heavenly birth into eternal joy and his own earthly birth into pain and suffering, part of which is the struggle of writing this translation (*peines* in vv. 55 and 56 perhaps casts translation as the labour of giving birth). Beyond this narratorial relation to the saint, the prologue locates itself as an act of fellowship and community (another topos of saints lives: Robertson 1996, Gaunt 1995, 212–33, v. 88 and n. below). The prologue creates a shared devotional ethos in which present monastic and future audiences pray to Faith as a heavenly patroness and in which prayers for the translator are to be their reciprocation for his work in bringing the saint to them.

Audience and circulation. A text or texts of the vernacular Life must have existed in the extensive early-thirteenth-century library of St Edmunds Abbey, Bury, Suffolk (whose members are invoked in the first word of the *Vie de sainte Fey* as *Seigniurs*), but the work is now preserved only in the unique collection of verse saints' lives known as the Campsey collection. This manuscript book was written in the last part of the thirteenth century and was owned by the Augustinian canonesses at Campsey Ash (also in Suffolk) in the fourteenth century. A note in a fourteenth-century hand at the end of the manuscript indicates it was created (or perhaps bequeathed to Campsey) for mealtime reading at the convent. Nothing is known of the life's circulation outside these two influential religious houses, one male, one female. Further evidence of aristocratic women's interest in Faith's cult is to be found at Horsham St Faith in Norfolk, where a remarkable late-thirteenth-century cycle of wall-paintings shows the priory's founders, Sibyl and Robert Fitzwalter, being rescued by St Faith from robbers near Conques on their return journey to Norfolk from a pilgrimage. The Middle English lives of Faith (in the *South English Legendary*, an anonymous prose life and a verse life by Osbern Bokenham) do not draw on the *Vie de sainte Fey* but, as is usually the case with vernacular hagiographies, represent independent translations from the Latin.

Manuscript source. BL Add. 70,513, ff. 147^{rv}–156vb. This is a handsome though not de luxe manuscript of 267 folios, 250 × 175 mm. It contains thirteen French verse saints' lives with historiated initials at the beginning of seven of its texts. If used in convent reading, it was carefully handled for the purpose and remains very clean. At some point before the addition of the current first quire (containing three lives by the important Franciscan writer and preacher, Nicole Bozon, written in a slightly later hand than the other quires), the first leaf of what is now the second quire was removed, resulting in the loss of part of the prologue to the life of Thomas Becket (for this life see (**11b**)). This is the only manuscript to include texts of all three saints' lives so far known to have been composed by women in England in the twelfth and thirteenth centuries (see also (**2**)). The manuscript names Countess Isabel of Arundel as the patroness of its Life of St Edmund of Abingdon (see (**13**)): its compilatory principles, if any, remain unclear, though it remains of great importance in the literary history of, particularly, women in medieval England.

Bibliography. The Life is edited by Baker (1940–1) and by Russell on the Margot Campsey project (http://margot.uwaterloo.ca/campsey/CmpBrowserFrame_e.html). Colour reproductions of its capitals can be seen here, as also in Russell 2003, and there are two at http://www.bl.uk/catalogues/illuminatedmanuscripts/record.asp?MSID=7165. A portion of the Life is translated by Cazelles (1991, 182–203), the complete life is introduced and translated in Russell 2012. On sources for the life see Baker 1940–1, 57 and Sheingorn's translation of the *Liber miraculorum* (Sheingorn 1995). The manuscript (formerly Welbeck I C 1) is studied by Russell 2003 and its context by Wogan-Browne 2003. For the dating of the Life, see Baker 1940–1, 57 (1210–16) and Legge 1950, 9–12 (1205–10). The Life is discussed in Legge 1950, 9–12, Wogan-Browne 2001, 69–79 and E. Campbell 2004, 29–45. On Bury and Norfolk and the monastic context see Thomson 1974, esp. xl–xlvii, and Jocelin of Brakelond (Greenway and Sayers, trans., 1989): for Horsham St Faith see Rudd 1929; Park 1987, 313, pl. 1 and 2; Smith-Bernstein 2007. On sacred thefts and Faith's reliquary statue see Geary 1990: on the development of her miracles Ashley and Sheingorn 1999. For St Faith in Middle English see D'Evelyn and Foster 1970, 587, no. 102.

TEXT AND TRANSLATION

Issi cumence la vie sainte Fey, virgine et martire.[f. 147rb]

Seigniurs, vous que en Deu creez [f. 147va]
E en la fei estes fermeez,
Oï avez, si jeo ne ment,
E savez trop certeynement
Ke home en cest siecle vivant,
Veuz e jovenes, petit ne grant,
Ne serra sauf sanz ferme fei;
Ceo est veirs e bien le crei,
La bone fei nus sauvera,
E[n] la joie de cel merra.

Here begins the Life of St Faith, virgin and martyr.

Lords, you who believe in God and are confirmed in the faith: unless I lie, you have heard and know it to be true that no living being, either young or old, a child or fully grown, shall be saved without a steadfast faith. This is a truth and I fully believe it – righteous faith will save us and bring us to celestial joy .

Pur ceo, sel vus vient a pleisir,
Devez plus voluntiers oïr
De seinte Fey chanter e lire
E ses vertuz bien descrire;
Kar cum vus plus de Fei orrez
En fei plus fermé en serrez.
Pur ceo entendez ore a mey
Si vus diray de seinte Fey,
De une seintime pucele,
Bele de vis, de fei plus bele,
La seinte vie e la passiun,
E la seinte conversaciun:
Cum son seint nun e seinte vie
Ne se descordereient mie,
Mes se acorderunt plus bel
Ke ne fet la gemme en anel,
Kar de tut esteient un,
Sa seinte vie e son seint nun,
Si cum ele mesmes dist
Kant li tyranz son nun enquist,
Si cum vus orrez en avant
Si vus estes entendant.
Mes vus ki cest escrist orrez,
Pur Deu vus pri, ne me blamez [f. 147vb]
Si jeo en cest romanz mespreng,
Bien sai grant hardement enpreng,
Jeo ke ne suy guere lettré
E poverement enromancé,
E ki sui freles et pecheur
E ki mespreng nuit e jur
En dit e en fet e en penser,
Kant os de seinte Fey traiter
E en nule manere enprendre,
De ceo me devez bien reprendre.
Mes de tant dei aver pardon
Kar jeo le faz par devotion,
A l'honur de cele pucele,
Aprés Marie la plus bele.

For that reason, if you agree, you should all the more willingly hear the Life of St Faith sung and read, and her virtues described, for as you hear more about Faith you will be more steadfast in your faith. Listen to me, then, and I will tell you of St Faith, a most holy young maiden who was fair of face and even more beautiful in her faith; of her holy life and passion and her saintly conduct; of how her holy name and her saintly life were in perfect harmony, complementing each other better than a jewel in a ring, for her holy life and her saintly name were wholly one, as she herself said when the tyrant asked her name, as you yourself will hear later in my story, if you pay close attention. But you who are about to listen to my recital, I beseech you in God's name not to blame me if I make mistakes in my French narrative. I know that I am presumptuous in this undertaking, since I am unlearned and poorly skilled in the vernacular – a weak sinner who falters night and day, in thought, in deed, and in word, so when I dare to undertake to narrate in any way at all the life of St Faith, you should rightly hold me to account. But I must be forgiven, for I am doing it out of devotion, and in honour of this young maiden whose beauty is second only to that of the virgin Mary .

E vus dirray l'achesun,
E mustray [ke], par resun,
La dei honurer e cherir
E [e]speciaument servir,
Kar la nuit de sa passïun –
Ke est grant veneratïun –
Cum de ses peines s'en parti,

I will tell you my motive, and show you why I cherish, honour and especially wish to venerate Faith: on the feast night of her passion – which is a solemn veneration of the moment of her liberation from her earthly suffering – I myself was born into my earthly tribulations.

Gié a mes peines nasqui;
Al jur ke ses travailz finirent,
Est vus les mens comencirent;
Al [j]ur k'ele reçut joie e honur,
Nasqui ad peine e ad dolur;
Ele ad joie e ad leesce
E jeo ay plur e ay tristesce,
En cest travailz peines,
E pur ceo en espeir [ke] deines
K'ele me sucure en ceste vie,
En cest travail d'espeneïe –
K'en cest siecle habundez plusurs [f. 148*ra*]
E lur festes grant sucurs –
E k'ele me face par sa priere
Partir a la joie plenere
K'ele reçut cum a cest jur
Ke jeo nasqui a cest labur.
Pur ceo comançai cest escrit;
Deu doint ke jeo aye profit.
Ore vus ay dist un' achesun
Pur quei jeo dei aver pardun.
Un' autre achesun vus dirray
Pur quei cest ovre enpris ay:
Un prudome, men compaigniun,
Grant en science e en resun,
Ke est de stature petiz
Mes de vertuz bien repleniz,
Mei ad comandé e requis,
Cum a nurri de son païs,
Ke jeo cest overaine enprenge
A l'honur de Deu e a sa loenge,
De sainte Fey la Deu amye;
E jeo par amur en compaignie
Ay comencé icest escrit;
Deu doint ke turne a profit
A tuz iceus ky l'averunt
E ki entendre en voudrunt.
A cest romanz deivent entendre
Ke latin ne sievent aprendre.
Ore, seigniurs, Deu pur vus pri,
Ne mei mettez en ubli
Kant vus depriez seinte Fey,
Pur Deu suveigniez vus de mey:
Symon de Walsingham ai nun,
Serf Marie e seint Eadmun; [f. 148*rb*]

On the day that her torments ended, my own travails began; on the day that she received joy and honour, I was born into a life of pain and suffering; she now lives in rejoicing and gladness, while I live in lamentation and sadness, and the painful struggle of this translation. For this reason, I hope that you [God] will permit her to come to my aid both in this earthly struggle and in this narration which I offer as an act of penance (for there are many in this world to whom you give abundant help). Through her intercession may she usher me into the eternal joy which she herself received on the very day that I was born into the toil of this earthly life. That is why I began writing this work; may God grant that I profit from it .

Earlier I explained why I should be pardoned any errors in my narrative. I give you now another reason why I have undertaken this task. One of my companions, a worthy man, well-versed in learning and with much good sense, a man of short physical stature but filled with moral strength, requested that I, a compatriot raised in his own region, undertake this translation for the honour of God and the veneration of Faith, friend of God .

And out of my own love for our fellowship I have begun this work. May God grant that it benefit all who will have it in their possession and want to hear it read. Those who cannot learn Latin have no choice but to listen to my vernacular rendition. And now, lords, in the name of God, I beg that you not forget my name in the prayers which you offer in supplication to St Faith. I am Simon of Walsingham, a servant of St Mary in St Edmund's Abbey. When you read my

Pur Deu quant vus mun nun lisez
En vos bienfez me recevez,
Priez a Deu, mere Marie,
E seinte Fey, la Deu amie
Ke Deu pur [sa] seinte priere
Nus doune le regne de son pere.
Mes ore vus dirrai brevement,
Sulum ke latin mei aprent,
La passiun de seinte Fey,
E coment Jhesu la prist a sey

name, God grant that you include me in your blessings; pray God, Mother Mary, and St Faith, beloved of God, that Christ, through her holy intercession, grant that we all may enter the kingdom of the Father. And now I will relate briefly to you the details which I have learned from the Latin regarding the passion of St Faith, and how Jesus took her to himself in heaven .

Notes

1 **Seigniurs** The lords may be just the narrator's fellow monks, or both fellow monks and lay patrons or guests.

3 **si jeo ne ment** (unless I lie) is also a tag line which could mean 'if I am not mistaken', or more colloquially 'truth be told', 'without word of a lie'. The literal sense used in our translation, however, is a clever part of the exordium's rhetorical 'logic': 'since this cannot be denied, you too must pay special attention to my saint and my composition on her'.

5 **cest** MS *ceste* We emend inorganic final *e* (also 66, 67) to avoid grammatical ambiguity, substituting the expected masculine form for the scribal form with unexpected final *e*.

6 **petit ne grant** (a child or fully grown) Our translation is in keeping with the prologue's themes of a child saint and self-infantilising modest narrator, but the phrase could also refer to social status (commoner or noble-born). This would have particular relevance both in wealthy Bury St Edmunds and the aristocratic Campsey convent.

9 **La bone fei** The writer is using a play on words: this is both *bone Fei* (righteous Faith) and *bone fei* (the right faith). The deliberate play on the double meaning of proper name and theological virtue is used repeatedly in the prologue. Medieval manuscripts normally use lowercase letters for proper names, so the ambiguity of the oral form also remains in the written manuscript. It is the modern editor who chooses either *Fei* or *fei* for the printed text.

13 **De seinte Fey chanter e lire** The reference to singing could mean that this life was read during a liturgical celebration on Faith's feast day. The well-known early Occitan version of her life (dated to the last third of the eleventh century) is a *canso*; for a discussion of the liturgical context (including song and dance) of the Occitan version see *La Chanson de sainte Foy* (Lafont 1998, 20–43).

35–6 **mespreng: enpreng** MS *mesprenge: enprenge* the final *e* is inorganic, and we emend to prevent confusion between the indicative and subjunctive forms.

37–8 **Jeo ke ne suy guere lettré . . . enromancé** MS *Ieo ke ne say guer de letre . . .* the meaning is kept by replacing *saveir guer de letre* with *estre guere lettré*. Baker makes this emendation, which is necessary for the rhyme with *enromancé* (poorly skilled in the vernacular); on the usual sense of *enromancer* (translate into the vernacular; i.e. French) see *AND*, 233a. In this iteration of the modesty topos, Simon seems to be self-deprecating about his educational background and his skill in French. Or is this an example of (exaggerated) second language anxiety engendered by social class distinctions, to show deference to his learned superiors? Samson was trained at the University of Paris, and was reputed for his skill in both French and Latin (Greenway and Sayers 1989, 64). Simon himself was not a Master, although several of his fellow monks, including his kinsman Thomas of Walsingham, held this title, and most were probably graduates of the University of Paris. Thomson 1974, xxxvi reports that in the election dispute of 1213–15, Simon was in the faction which included all the Masters of the abbey at the time (five in total).

43 **E en nule manere enprendre** (undertake in any way at all). The phrase emphasises the modesty topos.

57–8 **finirent . . . comencirent** There is frequent fluctuation in verb paradigms in medieval French. Both *finir* and *finer* are well attested infinitive forms, but *comencir*, used here for the rhyme, is not a common variant of *comencer*.

63–4 **travailz** we take to mean the work of translation at hand, as well as the more general travails of life. Baker 1940–1 states the text is corrupt here, and suggests emendations in his notes for 63–4.

64 **[ke] deines** (that you [God] permit). The unspecified subject, whom we take to be God, is second person singular, and becomes second person plural in *habundez* 67 (you give abundant help to); the combination of plural and singular forms to refer to the same person in a single sentence is not unusual in medieval French.

66 **cest travail d'espeneïe** MS *ceste trauail depenie* Baker 1940–1 suggests the form *espenëie* as a verbal noun from *espenëir* 'to expiate'; the form *epenie* is possible, with loss of preconsonantal *s*, but we opt for a more recognisable *espeneïe*. The standard form is *espenissement*; the infinitive has collateral forms *espenir*, *–einir*, *–eneir*, *–ener*, *–enoir* (cf. *AND s.v.* 'espenir').

73 **Pur ceo comançai cest escrit** MS *Pur ceo comandai a cest escrit*. The emendation is required by the sense.

80 **Grant en science e en resun** (well-versed in learning and with much good sense). As Jocelin of Brakelond (Greenway and Sayers 1989, 31–41) demonstrates, abbot Samson, an eloquent and well-educated Master from the University of Paris, was also a remarkably able administrator, who restored the abbey's ruined finances. He preferred the active to the contemplative life, and held practical common sense in high regard.

88 **par amur en compaignie** Our translation assumes the fellowship is that of the monastic order at Bury St Edmunds. It would also be possible to read 88–9 as 'And I, out of love, have begun this work in your company', referring to the narrative as a public performance before his fellow monks.

91–3 **A tuz . . . entendre** The use of **averunt** is unexpected in this context. Baker 1940–1 asks if the meaning is *le [*sc. *l'escrit] verunt?*); the usual co-ordinate of *oïr* in this context is *lire* (cf. 12–13). But *averunt* (own, have in one's possession) here expresses the extension of the power of the textual object (saints' lives quite commonly promise that simple possession of the text can bring benefits, and texts of lives were themselves sometimes used as apotropaic objects: see Wogan-Browne 1994b). *Deivent entendre* is also subject to interpretation: it could mean 'should', 'must', or, as translated, 'have no choice but to hear'.

95 **Deu pur vus pri** A more usual word order would be *pur Deu vus pri*.

99–100 **Symun de Walsingham ai nun, Serf Marie a seint Eadmun** MS *seinte admun* Bury St Edmunds, Suffolk, was one of the most powerful and wealthy of the Benedictine abbeys in England, built in honour of Edmund, king of East Anglia, martyred 869. Benedictine monks replaced the secular priests in the eleventh century and the abbey flourished until the Dissolution. Walsingham, Simon's birthplace in Norfolk, is about twenty-five miles from Horsham St Faith, Norfolk, where an alien priory dedicated to St Faith was founded in 1105, becoming an early centre for the cult of St Faith in England (Wogan-Browne 2001, 70). No direct connection is known to have existed between Simon and Horsham St Faith, however. The reference to being *serf Marie* suggests Simon was attached in some capacity to the parish church dedicated to St Mary; this church was within the precincts of the abbey. (There were seventy to eighty monks at the abbey *c.* 1207; in 1260 there were 80 monks, 21 chaplains, 111 servants (see Knowles and Hadcock 1971, 61)). Three men from Walsingham, monks Simon and Thomas, along with clerk Stephen, son of Roger of Walsingham, were among those sent to Rome in 1214 by St Edmund's Abbey to seek papal support against King John over the election of Abbot Hugh (Thomson 1974, 32–43).

13. Matthew Paris, *La Vie de saint Edmund, arcevesque de Canterbire* [Dean 521], Prologue and Epilogue, London, British Library, MS Add. 70,513, ff. 85v–86r, 100r

Date of composition and provenance. As Matthew Paris states, he wrote the life of Edmund in two languages (*Escrit l'ay en deuz langages*, v. 100 below), translating into French his own Latin *vita* of Edmund Rich, archbishop of Canterbury (1234–40). The *vita* is datable to 1247–53, with the French text probably completed shortly after this, and before Paris's death in 1259.

Author, sources and nature of text. Matthew Paris (*c.* 1200–59), Benedictine monk of St Albans, was a prolific writer and illuminator. His abbey, a day's travel north from London, received frequent visitors (including King Henry III), and Matthew himself travelled and was active in court circles. He is best known for his *Chronica majora*, a universal chronicle, but his writing in both Latin and French and his drawing and painting explored many fields, including heraldry, cartography, and hagiography. He composed two saints' lives in Latin (the *Vita Stephani archiepiscopi Cantuariensis* and the *Vita Edmundi*), and four in French: the lives of Edmund, Thomas Becket, Edward the Confessor, and Alban. Of his four vernacular saints' lives, the life of Edmund is the only one not preserved in a copy with Paris's own illustrations or copies of them.

Matthew's *Vita Edmundi* is more sympathetic to Edmund in his conflict with the monks at Canterbury, and more openly critical of the papal legate Otto and the royal court, than he is in his *Chronica majora*. For the *vita* Matthew drew on accounts by those who knew Edmund personally, such as Richard, bishop of Chichester, Robert Bacon, and probably Edmund's brother, Robert of Abingdon, to supplement the earlier *vita* by Eustace of Faversham, Edmund's chaplain.

The fact that Matthew Paris wrote both a Latin and French version of the life allows a unique view of the differences in content and narrative technique he judged appropriate for each of these languages. For instance, Paris uses the same literary techniques of antithesis and word play in both the French and Latin lives (Lawrence 1960, 76–7; 1996, 100–17). In contrast, while the French translation generally follows the Latin *vita*, it adds more personal historical details about Edmund's life (as well as giving Paris's own name as author (*Maheu*, v. 1692). Most notable, however, are the addition of a prologue and epilogue, with details about his patroness and social-political-religious events at the time of writing, designed to maximise her significance for the creation of the text and the cult.

The opening rubric declares that the vernacular work was requested by the countess of Arundel (Isabel de Warenne, d. 1282). Isabel was also the patroness to whom Ralph of Bocking dedicated his *vita* of bishop Richard of Chichester, formerly archbishop Edmund's chancellor, and she was closely associated with both prelates during her long widowhood, 1243–82 (Russell, ed., 1995, 12, 135, 140). Matthew's presentation of Isabel's patronage provides a glimpse into the relationships between noblewomen and churchmen, between learned and vernacular texts, the laity and clergy, and competing dynastic expressions of piety.

Paris distinguishes the French life as an *escrit apert* (obvious; open, public; clear, unequivocal writing, v. 33): the vernacular life is, so to speak, popular history, the Latin *vita* is a learned academic work. Paris's threefold description of his relationship with his patroness makes it clear that the countess of Arundel was the prime mover for the translation into French from Latin; he argues that her motivation is the fact that everyone, both clergy and laity, uses and understands French more than they do Latin: she knows that only a text in French can permit all people, both clerical and lay, to learn of Edmund's virtues. The epilogue returns to this theme, but with the further claim that the countess commissioned both the French and Latin texts. This implies that a French text not based on a Latin source would not have much credibility, while a Latin text alone would have a limited audience.

But while Isabel of Arundel is first presented as the defender of 'popular' French history, she is also assimilated to the learned clerical world when Matthew uses the Benedictine topos of obedience to a religious superior. Because the countess has the advowson of the priory of Wymondham (a daughter house of St Albans, founded by the Arundel family in 1107, where Isabel's husband was buried), it is Paris's religious duty as a monk of St Albans to carry out her request. In the epilogue he formally makes a gift of his French text to her as his monastic superior.

Paris cites the countess's special relationship with Edmund as his most profound reason for accepting her commission: he is moved by her arduous pilgrimages to Edmund's shrine at Pontigny in France, and her service 'beyond the usual strength of women' (v. 58 and n.) to the saint, perhaps including help in the removal of a ban on women pilgrims there. In the epilogue, Paris further claims that Isabel has followed in the saint's footsteps (*suez la trace*, v. 108).

Paris also places Isabel's devotion to Edmund in the context of Plantagenet and Capetian dynastic rivalry (a rivalry Edmund himself embodies as a native-born prelate of England whose relics remained in France). The translation of Edmund's relics at Pontigny witnessed by Isabel in June 1247 took place in the presence of Louis IX, not Henry III, and Henry III's installation of the Holy Blood relic at Westminster Abbey in October 1247 was probably intended as a competitive response. In this way Henry could counter the prestige Louis gained through the presence of Edmund's relics at Pontigny, as well as outdo Louis's collection of passion relics at the Sainte-Chapelle in Paris. Both countries can claim blessing from the saint, Paris argues, but the balance of glory goes to England, since by Edmund's intervention the relic of the Holy Blood, holier still than any relics acquired by Louis IX, has come to England.

Paris deftly suggests that the countess is Edmund's agent in England's superior blessedness: by reclaiming her special relationship with Edmund at his shrine in France, she has also reclaimed Edmund's blessings to his country of origin. Her own tracing of Edmund's footsteps is amplified on a royal scale when Paris concludes his epilogue by citing Henry III's acquisition of Christ's own footprint, impressed in marble at the Ascension (vv. 128–33). The vernacular life demonstrates the influence wielded by an aristocratic widow living in the world, for Matthew Paris depicts his female patron as a baronial power (a patron of religious houses, a pilgrim gaining liberties for lay devotional practices), and as a monastic superior who provides for all people, not just the clergy, through her commissioning of both learned history in Latin and popular, accessible, written history in French.

Audience and circulation. The only known copy of the French life is found in the Campsey manuscript (BL Add. 70,513), written in the late thirteenth century (after 1276). Another copy, in London, BL Cotton Vitellius D.VIII, was destroyed by fire in 1731. It is possible (although there is no direct proof) that Isabel de Warenne was the patroness for whom the Campsey manuscript containing the life of Edmund was created (Russell 2003; Wogan-Browne 2003, 2001, ch. 5), but the earliest known owner of the manuscript is the aristocratic female convent of Augustinian canonesses at Campsey Ash, Suffolk. Campsey used the book at least into the fourteenth century for mealtime reading, and may well have been the original commissioners. The Life's lost London manuscript copy in BL Cotton Vitellius D.XVIII indicates that the Edmund Life also circulated beyond Campsey. There is a famous note in Paris's hand (on the flyleaves of his autograph copy of his Life of St Albans, MS Dublin Trinity College 177) which mentions the loan of his St Thomas and St Edward lives to the countess of Arundel, and requests that she pass them on to the countess of Cornwall: it is often cited as evidence for the popularity of Paris's saints' lives in French among aristocratic lay women, and suggests that his life of Edmund may also have circulated more widely in this social network. Paris's French hagiography seems to have been consumed both in monasteries, convents and among elite laypeople.

Manuscript source. BL Add. 70,513, ff. 85*v*–100*v*. The Campsey manuscript is a medium-size (250 × 175mm, 267 folios) elegant collection of saints' lives in French. Eleven lives were copied into the manuscript in the late thirteenth century and three more added in the early fourteenth century. An inscription in the manuscript states that it is for mealtime reading at Campsey. The manuscript is especially noted in modern scholarship for containing three saints' lives composed by women and providing a rich collection of British and other saints' lives for a female convent. In addition to Edmund, lives of Faith (**12**) and Becket (**11b**) are included in it, as are lives of the British abbess saints, Modwenna of Ireland, Scotland and Burton-on-Trent, and Osith of Chich, and the Barking Life of Edward the Confessor (**2**).

Bibliography. The French text is edited by Baker 1929 and the Campsey manuscript text is edited online by Russell at http://margot.uwaterloo.ca. For description and analysis of the manuscript (formerly Welbeck I C 1) with colour reproductions of its illuminated capitals, see Russell 2003; see also two at http://www.bl.uk/catalogues/illuminatedmanuscripts/record.asp?MSID=7165. For its possible uses and readerships see also Wogan-Browne 2003 and E. Campbell 2008. The Latin *vita Edmundi* is edited (1960), and separately translated (1996) by Lawrence. For the life and work of Matthew Paris see Vaughan 1958 and *ODNB*: Lewis 1987 discusses his illustrations to *Chronica majora*: the work is translated by Giles, repr. 1968. On Edmund in Paris's other works see Vaughan 1958, 166–7, 179; Lawrence 1996, 107, and for Paris's methods in the *vita*, Vaughan 1958, 164; Lawrence 1960, 74, 78–105. Isabel de Warenne is discussed in Gee 2002, 7–24 and Wogan-Browne 2001, 151–88. On the competitive pieties of Louis IX and Henry III see Vincent 2001. Paris's Life of Edward the Confessor is translated by Fenster and Wogan-Browne 2008 and his life of Alban by Wogan-Browne and Fenster 2010. For his Becket life, see Backhouse and De Hamel 1988. For Matthew Paris's maps and graphic pilgrimage itineraries see D. K. Connolly 2009.

TEXT AND TRANSLATION

Ici comence la vie saint Eadmund le confessur, arcevesque de Canterbire, translaté de latin en romanz par la requeste la cuntesse de Arundel

Here begins the life of St Edmund the Confessor, archbishop of Canterbury, translated from Latin into French at the request of the countess of Arundel.

Ki de un sul felun ad victoire
Mut pot aver joie e gloire;
E ki veint sul deus enemis,
Tant desert cil greignur pris;
Ki sul veint treis, cist plus desert
Que los eit en escrist apert.

He who wins victory over a single wicked enemy deservedly rejoices and wins renown; he who single-handedly defeats two evil opponents, by this act justly wins even greater esteem; but he who by himself alone conquers three evil-doers is the one who most deserves that his praise be recorded in an accessible written history.

Ces moz vus escrist e[n] sunt
Pur le arceveske saint Edmund,
De Canterbire le prelat,
Et de Engleterre fu primat,
Ki sul par sa vertu demene
Et [par] grace celestïene
Treis fors adversaries venqui:
Sa char, le mund, le Enemi;
Sa char, son enemi privé,
Par june e par chasteté;
Le mund, par [graunt] humilité
Et par sen de divinité;
Et si descunfist li diable

These words are written for you about the archbishop Edmund, the prelate of Canterbury and primate of England, who alone, by his own virtue, and with celestial grace, vanquished three strong adversaries: his own flesh, worldliness, and the Devil – his flesh, his own intimate enemy, through fasting and chastity; worldliness, by his humility and the wisdom of theology; and the Devil he defeated by his spirituality,

Par [son] penser espiritable,
[Et] par sa graunt devotïun,
Aumones e ou oraisun.

by his great devotion, his charity, and his prayers.

Bien dei de lui escrivere estoire [f. 86*ra*]
Et son nun mettre en memoire,
A ki Jhesus, rei de gloire,
Otreia si graunt victoire
Pur enhaucer son honur e fame.
Et [pur] vus, honuree dame,
Riche cuntesse de Arundele,
Et de Essexe dame Ysabele,
De saint Edmund le grant prelat
Icest' estoire vus translat
De latin en franceis apert;
Kar chascun est de ceo bien cert
[Ke] plus est use[e] et sue
Ke nule launge, et entendue
De clers e lais e la gent tute,
Ke le latins, ne mie dute.

I should indeed write about him, and record his name in history, he to whom Jesus, the king of glory, granted such a great victory, for the increase of his honour and fame. And for you, honoured lady Isabel of Essex, wealthy countess of Arundel, I have translated the history of St Edmund, the great prelate, from Latin into clear and understandable French. For everyone well knows that French is more used and known than any language, and without a doubt more understood by clerics, the laity, and all people, than Latin.

De vostre purpos la resun
Bien crei saver, e l'achaisun:
Ke ses beus vertuz e grace,
Clers e lays, chascuns le sache.
Bien i devez clamer dette
Ke a voz cumanz entente mette
A mun poer tut parfurmir!
La raisun vus en plest oïr?
Il est [ja] verité provee
Ke Wymundham est[es] awoee,
La summe est de ma sentence.
Porter vus dei reverence,
Et tute religiun,
Honur et subjectiun.

I believe that I understand well your intent and the reason [for this commission]: that everyone, both clergy and laity, may know Edmund's sweet virtues and grace. You should claim the credit for my attempts to implement, to the best of my abilities, your intentions for this work. Would you like to hear the reason why? It is, in all truth, because you are the vowess of Wymundham; this is the essence of my argument. I owe you reverence, honour and deference with all my monastic life.

De autre part, ke autant me mut,
Dunt la raisun dire me estut:
Jointe li est[es] par aliaunce,
Ke par pelerinage en France,
Par mer passers e lung chemins,
Et travail plus ke femenins, [f. 86*rb*]
Quis le avez e honuré
Et de servise enerré.
Priez le avez a vus entendre;
Fet l[i] avez un grant offrendre
De vostre alme e cors e vie.
Et ki bien aime, tart n'oblie:

There is another reason which equally moves me, which I must also state: you have been joined to Edmund by your particular allegiance, who, through pilgrimage to France, with sea-crossings and long travels, and with efforts beyond the usual strength of women, have sought him out and honoured him, and pledged him your service. You have prayed that he hear your pleas, and you have made him the great offering of your soul and body and life. He who has been well loved will not later forget: he will be close to, not

Procheins sera, ne mie loing,
A ses amis a grant bosoing.
Ore pri le creatur del mund,
[Et] le sen confessur Edmund,
[Ke] veirs me doint escrivre e dire
Sanz forveier de [la] matire.
A l'honur Deu e sun pleissir,
Ke de hel ne dei aver desir,
Entente i mettrai e travail.
De cest liveret le començail
Deu muster surt de Canterbire,
Dunt il m'apent a vus a dire
Ke par [tant] est si bien garnie
De plusurs seinz de haute vie
Ke a trespasser ne sunt pas:
Saint Eilphe e saint Thomas,
Saint Ainseme e saint Dunstan,
Et ki si bon clers fu, Lainfran.
Tut icist arceveskes furent
Ke a Deu pleire grant cure urent.
Ore est al vespre del mund
[Ke] sur[t] le confessur Edmund,
Kar nus conforte e nus visite,
Cum orét [en] la vie escrite.

far away from, his beloved when they are in great need.

I pray the creator of the world, and his confessor, Edmund, to grant that I write and compose truthfully, without straying from my subject. To honour and please God is my only desire, and I will put my mind and efforts to this task. The beginning of this life is from a book written in the church of Canterbury, which I must tell you was well furnished with many saints whose holy lives should not be overlooked: St Alphege and St Thomas, St Anselm and St Dunstan, and Lanfranc who was such a good theologian. All these were archbishops who sought to please God. Now, at the evening of the world, the confessor Edmund appears, for he comforts us and is present among us, as you will hear in the written life.

[Epilogue (lines 1964–2019)]

A genuiliuns e gointe meins [f. 100*ra*]
Pri Deu e les celestïens
Vertuz ke a m'alme profite
De seint Edmund [l']estoire escrite.
Espeir ke a m'alme sente
[...]
Seinz Deus en terre honurer
Et la gloire Deu enhaucer.
Unc ne començai pur el,
Ceo set tres bien le Rei de cel,
E ke chescun [en] seit plus sages,
Escrit l'ay en deuz langages
Pur vous cuntesse Ysabele
De Essex et de Arundele.
[Pur] ke me futes espurun
De cest treté, vous [faz] le dun;
Vous me estes avoee dame,
S[i] en surt de vous bone fame,
Ke vous par [la] devine grace

On bended knee and with clasped hands I pray God and the heavenly powers that writing the history of St Edmund will profit my soul. I hope that it [shows?] my soul the path [...] to honour God's saints on earth and exalt the glory of God. As the King of heaven well knows, I began this work for no other reason. And so that everyone may be wiser (because of it), I have written it in two languages for you, countess Isabel of Essex and Arundel. Since you were the spur for this work, I make it a gift to you. You are my lady vowess, from you springs good repute because you follow, by divine grace, in the

De saint Edmund suez la trace;
Ke Deu vous en face dun
De cel, cum il ad gerdun;
Si fra il sanz [nule] dotaunce
Kant deserte est, i a esperance.

footsteps of St Edmund. May God grant you the gift of heaven, as it is his reward to give; there is every hope that God will do this, when it is deserved.

Mut deit Engleterre aver
Gloire [et] joie demener
Ke cel seint de lui est issu,
Et France, ke l'ad receü.
Ore ad fet del Sauveür
A Engletere un autre honur,
Ki a Engleis est (si) large e franc: [f. 100rb]
Tramis nus ad de son seint sanc.
Ne puet, ço m'est avis, estre maire
Entre morteus [teu] saintuaire:
Non pas la croiz kar ele est seinte
Pur le sanc dunt ele est teinte,
Ne les clous ne la corune,
Kar li sanc seinté lur dune.

England, from which this saint comes, deserves great glory, and should rejoice, as, too, France, which has received him. Now Edmund, who is so generous and kind to the English, has made possible another honour to England from the Saviour: he has sent us a relic of his holy blood. In my view, there can be no greater relic given to mortal man than this: not the cross, for it is made holy by the blood with which it is stained; neither the nails, nor the crown (of thorns), for the blood gives them their sanctity.

Ke ge trespasse droit n'e[st] pas:
Ore nus ad Deus tramis le pas
K'enpreent est, cum en cire tendre,
En marbre, kant a cungé prendre
De tere munta sus en ceus,
Veiant et present [set] morteus,
Ke Deus [i] fist pur remembrance
De li, ke ne fust obliaunce.
Li reis Henriz ke ert fiz Johan
Eu trentime primer an
De son regne nus purchaça
Le sanc, ke a seint Edward dona,
Et pus le pas en l'an suant
Duna, u fist le sanc avant.
Omnipotent ki en ciel tune,
Teu biens a Engletere dune
K'i regne Reis celestïen
En tuz tens en gloire, amen.

It is not right that I overlook [another honour], for God has sent us the print of his foot set in marble, as if it were in soft wax, made when Jesus took leave of earth and ascended to heaven, in the presence and in sight of seven mortal men, which God did in remembrance of him, so that he not be forgotten. King Henry, who was the son of John, in the thirty-first year of his reign purchased for us the blood relic, which he gave to St Edward, and the following year he gave the footprint relic to the shrine where he had given the blood the year before. Almighty God who reigns in heaven gives such gifts to England so that the heavenly King may reign there in glory for ever, Amen.

Ici finist la vie saint Edmund de Pounteney, confessour e erceveske de Canterbieres.

Here ends the life of St Edmund of Pontigny, confessor, and archbishop of Canterbury.

Notes

7 **Ces** MS *Ceo* Only minor emendations are required to make sense of the line.

29–30 Isabel de Warenne (*c.* 1226–82) was the daughter of the count of Sussex, and grand-daughter of William Marshal through her mother Mathilda. She was married in 1234 to Hugh d'Albini, count of Arundel, and after his death in 1243 she remained a widow until her own death shortly before 1282. Matthew Paris's unusual reference to Isabel as countess of both Arundel and Essex (as opposed to Sussex) may be because Isabel also held the manor of Stanstead in Essex (Wogan-Browne 2001, 156 n. 8). The same double identity is used at 101–2.

36 **et** MS *ad* The correction is required by the sense.

41 **beus vertuz** (sweet virtues) Normally a feminine noun, *vertu* is treated as masculine, here, and at 90–1. Baker 1929 emends to *beles vertuz*.

48 **Wymundham** Isabel had the advowson, or patronage (the right to nominate the resident clergymen) of the priory (subsequently abbey) of Wymundham in Norfolk, the burial site for the counts of Arundel.

51–2 **religiun . . . subjectiun** Paris uses hexasyllabic lines on occasion: it is also possible that these two lines could be combined as an alexandrine.

56 **Par pelerinage en France** Isabel may have travelled to Pontigny with her cousin Henry III in 1254, or it may have been in 1247 in the company of her friend Richard of Chichester, to attend the translation of Edmund's relics to the new shrine.

58 **travail plus ke femenins** may suggest that the countess of Arundel was instrumental in obtaining the relaxation in 1255 of the church's ban on women at the shrine of Edmund (Baker 1929, 324; Wogan-Browne 2001, 168–9).

60 **enerré** MS *en erne*. *AND* gives the sense *reward* to the form *enerré*, quoted from this text only, using Baker's emendation (1929).

62–3 **Fet l[i] avez . . . vostre alme e cors e vie** could be taken to refer to Isabel's having taken a vow of chastity in her widowhood (but the suggestion of Baker 1929, 344 that she was a vowess is unlikely: Wogan-Browne 2001, 152–3, 169, and see further 105n. below). Such vows were, however, certainly known in the countess's circle: Eleanor, sister of Henry III, for instance, had taken vows of perpetual chastity in 1231 before archbishop Edmund and his chancellor, Richard of Chichester.

64 **ki bien aime, tart n'oblie** a proverb still in use in French as in the Middle Ages: it occurs, for instance, in some manuscripts of Chaucer's *Parliament of Foules*, at vv. 685–6 (Benson 1987, 1150, n. to 680–92), perhaps naming the tune of the poem's roundel.

69 [**ke**]; **doint** Baker 1929 emends the verb to third person plural, but the singular verb would also be possible in medieval usage; we add the conjunction.

70 **forveier** MS *forveire* the emendation is the standard form of this verb.

73 **i** MS [abbreviation for *et*]. The emendation is required for the sense.

74–5 **De cest liveret . . . de Canterbire**. This is a reference to Paris's written source, the earlier *vita* by Eustace of Faversham, Edmund's chaplain at Canterbury (Lawrence 1996, 109–10; see Lawrence 1960, 203–21, for an edition).

80–2 **Eilphe . . . Lainfran** A reference to five earlier archbishops. Dunstan (*c.* 909–88) was abbot of Glastonbury, then bishop of Worcester (957), London (959), and archbishop of Canterbury (960–88). Alphege (953–1012), archbishop 1005–12, was martyred by the Danes at Greenwich. Lanfranc (archbishop of Canterbury 1070–89) was first prior at the abbey of Bec (1045, where his fame as a teacher attracted Anselm to study at Bec); Lanfranc was the first archbishop appointed by William after the Norman Conquest. Anselm (1033–1109) succeeded Lanfranc as archbishop, 1093–1109. Thomas Becket (1118–70) was first chancellor for Henry II, then appointed archbishop in 1162. His conflicts with Henry II led to his murder in 1170 and his celebrated shrine at Canterbury (see further (**11b**)). Becket became an influential model for subsequent *vitae* such as Edmund's.

83 **Tut icist** MS *Tut cit* The emendation restores a plural subject 'all these', and an octosyllabic line.

85 **Ore . . . al vespre del mund** This is a reference to Matthew Paris's belief that the day of judgement would come in 1250 (*ODNB*, 14–15), a belief expressed dramatically in his chronicle leading up to 1250, but abandoned before his death in 1259.

94 There is a line, or lines, missing, marked by the absence of a line to rhyme with 92, and the gap in syntax. Baker 1929 suggests that *sente* is the final word of the missing line, added in error at the end of v. 93. There is a punctuation dot after *Seinz* in v. 95. Our translation is conjectural.

101–2 **Pur** MS *Par*; **cuntesse** MS *cuntasse*; on Isabel of Arundel see n. to 29–30 above.

104 **cest** MS *ceste* The adj. is emended to accord with *treté* (normally masculine), and the verb emended following Baker 1929.

105 **Vous me estes avoee dame** A reference to Isabel's advowson of Wymundham, rather than confirmation that she was a vowess (see n. to 62–3 above).

112 **i a** MS *e a* We emend for the meaning.

121–6 **Ne puet . . . lur dune** Paris's detailed account of Henry III's Holy Blood presentation to Westminster was requested of him by the king (Vincent 2001, 1–4). The unfavourable comparison between Henry's and Louis IX's competing relics here is repeated from a sermon preached at Westminster during the installation ceremony: fragments of the cross, or the crown of thorns are of secondary importance to the blood relic, since they are made holy only by the presence of the Holy Blood. Despite Matthew Paris's wish, however, these relics proved to be ineffective in increasing the prestige of the Plantagenets (Vincent 2001, 201).

132 [**set**] Baker 1929 suggests this correction, based on the seven disciples (mentioned in John 21:2) who were witnesses to the third appearance of Jesus to his disciples before his ascension. This passage (127–34) is also a reminder of the liturgy of the Eucharist, and connects the footprint with the blood relic. Moral conformity to the *vestigia Christi* – Christ's footsteps on earth – was an aspect of both actual and virtual medieval pilgrimage.

136 **Eu trentime primer an** Henry III presented the blood relic to the patron saints of Westminster Abbey, Edward the Confessor and St Peter, during the feast of the translation of Edward the Confessor's relics, 13 Oct. 1247.

14. Robert of Greatham, *Miroir ou Evangiles des domnees* [Dean 589], Prologue, excerpts: Nottingham University Library, MS MiLM4, ff. 57ra–60va

Karl Steel

Date of composition and provenance. Probably mid-thirteenth century, perhaps Shropshire or Northamptonshire.

Author, sources and nature of text. Robert of Greatham, who may have been from Greatham in Rutland, conceals his name until v. 634, so as to protect himself, he explains (in a topos also found in other works) from the envious who pervert moral works and speak ill of those who write them (vv. 137–50). He has been identified through lexicographical evidence with Robert the Chaplain who wrote *Corset*, a vernacular verse commentary on the seven sacraments. While writing the *Miroir*, Robert may have been engaged in one of several professions: full-time preacher; a Black Augustinian canon and conventual chaplain in the Arrouaisian abbey of the Blessed Virgin Mary at Lilleshall, Shropshire, under the patronage of the de Zouche family of Northamptonshire; or a chaplain in the household of his patrons, who were most probably Alan de la Zouche (d. 1270) and his wife Elena de Quincy (d. 1296). Lord Alan, to whom Robert dedicated *Corset*, held a number of important positions in Henry III's government; Elena de Quincy is possibly the *Dame Aline* (v. 1) of the *Miroir*'s dedication.

The *Miroir* is one of the largest Anglo-Norman sermon collections: more than 19,000 lines long, it has a substantial prologue (694 lines of flexible octosyllabic rhymed couplets) that is followed in the fullest extant manuscripts by fifty-four rhymed sermons on the Sunday Gospels following the Use of Sarum, together with some sermons on saint's feasts. The sermons follow older sermon structure rather than the new more complicated 'university' model: they consist of the Sarum readings plus exposition. The Gospel readings are fully translated into French, but the *Miroir* prologue's images of scriptural exegesis insist on the indispensability of an educated priesthood for their elucidation (vv. 245–362). Scripture is both a tree from which apples are shaken (vv. 197–214, a metaphor shared with Langland's allegory of the Tree of Charity) and a dark cloud which produces life-giving rain, i.e. priestly interpretation (vv. 215–54). Robert's exempla, which, like the prologue, concern themselves with the clergy's roles, are confined to narratives about hermits, monks, and other clergy, a narrower range than in many contemporary exempla collections (such as Bozon's early-fourteenth-century *Contes moralisés* (Dean 695)).

The first fifty-eight lines of the prologue argue that its reader should abandon chivalric narrative (*chançon de geste e d'estoire*, v. 5). The remainder can be understood as a sermon teaching the mutual responsibilities of laity and cleric. The laity must support the clergy materially, while the clergy must lead good lives and help the laity understand the scriptures. Although Robert credits the Holy Spirit with the *Miroir*'s felicities and his patron with the work's existence, he argues that even laypeople who read spiritual works require professional supervision (contrast Angier, **24a**). Several points in the prologue, such as Robert's remark that he has abridged his translations, seem designed to alert his patron that he kept some of his learning in reserve (see n. to 100 below).

The prologue's topographical, horticultural, and meteorological metaphors liken the priest to the arable land fundamental to the power of the nobility, a comparison that counteracts any conceptual model of a priest's subservience to his patron by arguing that without the sustenance provided by the land – the priest and his instruction – the patron would starve spiritually (For a different reading of the patronage relationship between Robert and Aline, see Ellis 2001, 35–8). At the same time, the act of interpreting in the vernacular also sees Robert aligning himself among those who find scripture difficult to understand (barely capable of paring the rind off the fruit, v. 628): responding appropriately to the Sunday Gospels is a common concern for him and his patron, Lady Aline, and one lived in the heightened awareness of the interdependence of lay and clerical languages.

Audience and circulation. Lady Aline (v. 1), if she is Alan de la Zouche's wife, was Elena de Quincy, third daughter of Roger de Quincy, earl of Winchester (d. 1264) and his first wife, Helen of Galloway (d. 1245). Robert envisages audiences and readers beyond the primary patronage circle (vv. 437–48, 609–34). The extant *Miroir* manuscripts show wide circulation and probably heavy use. Two of the ten are complete; four have some omissions: two consist of single leaves, and two contain only the *Miroir*'s exempla. The *Miroir* seems to have circulated among noble households and was often bound with various French spiritual works: but the work is suitable for public preaching as well as private reading and audition, and some manuscripts circulated in clerical milieux. The *Miroir* appears three times with William of Waddington's *Manuel des pechiez* (in CUL MSS Mm.6.4 (see (**24b**)); CUL Gg.1.1, and San Marino, Huntington Library, HM 903). It was translated into Middle English prose in the last quarter of the fourteenth century, probably in London and may have been known to the composer of the *Northern Homily Cycle* (Thompson 2008, Intro n. 37). Anglo-Norman copies of the text continued to circulate, to judge by fifteenth-century inscriptions in two of them (Huntington MS HM 903, from St Mary's Abbey, York, and Cambridge Trinity College MS B.14.39), as did the Middle English version.

14. Robert of Greatham, Miroir ou Evangiles des domnees

MANUSCRIPT SOURCE. Only Nottingham MiLM4 (s. xiii2/2) and CUL Gg.1.1 (after 1307) contain the prologue in its entirety. Aitken argues that the frequent unintelligibility of the Cambridge manuscript indicates that its scribe poorly understood what he copied (1922, 13). Our manuscript measures 270 × 180 mm (writing space 210 × 130 mm). The *Miroir* begins on f. 57^{r} with a six-line, flourished 'A', and is organised with alternating red and blue paraph markings (reproduced at http://mssweb.nottingham.ac.uk/document-viewer/medieval-women/theme7/document1/09-1111m-7-1_1.asp). The prologue is carefully copied and emended throughout: the corrections seem to be in the same hand as the text. The sparing use of abbreviations, occasional use of intralinear punctus for word separation, and clear hand suggests an effort to make the work easy to read, as do the red and brown marginal notations of 'Oml.' (for the start of sermon expositions), 'nota' (for exempla) and the red Latin rubrics and Gospel references.

BIBLIOGRAPHY. No complete edition has been published, although Nottingham MiLM4 has been previously edited in an unpublished Master's thesis (Marshall 1971) and, to line 4131, by Duncan and Connolly 2003. Hanna and Turville-Petre 2010, 93–4 describe MS MiLM4: for this and the other French and Middle English manuscript witnesses see Duncan and Connolly 2003, xxi–xxiii. Portions of the French *Miroir* have been edited in Aitken 1922 and Panunzio 1967; on the latter, see LeCoy 1971, Short 1972–3, Marshall and Rothwell 1970. Blumreich 2002 edits the Bodleian Holkham manuscript of the English *Mirror*: see Wogan-Browne 2005b. The French *Miroir* receives notice in Allen 1917, 452–3, Rothwell 1975–6, 463 and 1996, 191–2, and Wogan-Browne 2005a, 134–9 and 146–7. Hanna 2005, 177–202 is an important discussion of the French and Middle English versions. On the parallels between the *Miroir*'s model of scriptural exegesis and Langland see M. Connolly 2004. On Robert of Greatham's identity and possible occupations, see Marshall 1973; Duncan and Connolly 2003, lvii; Sinclair 1995, 20–1: for his patrons, Sinclair 1992 and 1995, 15–18; *ODNB*, *s.v.* 'Alan de la Zouche' and 'Roger de Quincy'. Aitken 1922, 27–53 discusses the *Miroir*'s exempla. On medieval French homilies see Robson 1952, on vernacular preaching and teaching, Waters 2003, 2015. On women as patrons, see Jambeck 1996, Gee 2002, Wogan-Browne 2009a. Anglo-Norman sermons are omitted from standard reportaria such as the *Typologie des sources*, but are listed in Dean 587–715, together with treatises, confessional interrogatories, etc.

TEXT AND TRANSLATION

A sa trechere dame Aline [f. 57ra]
Saluz en la vertu divine!
Ma dame, bien l'ai oï dire
Ke mult amez oïr e lire
Chançon de geste e d'estoire
E mult i metez la memoire.
Mais bien voil que vus sachez
Que ço [n']est plus ke vanitez,
Kar ço n'est rien fors controvure
E folie de vaine cure:
Si l'om i trove un bon respit,
Tut li altre valdra petit.
Ço est en vair le tripot
De chescun ki mentir volt:
Pur plus sourement mentir
Alcune rien dist a pleisir,

To his very esteemed dear Lady Aline, greetings in all-powerful God! My lady, I have indeed heard it said that you greatly love to hear and read songs about heroic deeds and history, and that you remember them well. But I want you to know that they are but empty trifles, for they are nothing but fictions and the foolishness of idle pursuit: even if one finds a good proverb in them, the rest will be worth little. They are in truth the ruse of anyone who wishes to lie: in order to lie more surely, he says anything to please, and says any seeming truth to make his falsehood heard. But it is not credible that all things said in fable are true, nor are those stories true that were written to be

E dist alcune verité
Pur feire oïr sa falseté.
E ço n'est pas chose creiable
Que tut seit vair k'est dit en fable,
Nun est ço vair quantk'est escrit
D'estoire ke l'em en chançun dist,
Kar cil ki chançuns controverent,
Sulum lur quiders les furmerent.
E l'om dist en respit pur vair
Ke quidance n'est pas savair.
Veez si ço pot estre vair
Que uns enfés oust poair,
Cum dist la Chançun de Mainet,
U del Orfanin Sansunnet,
U de la Geste Dan Tristram,
U del Bon Messager Balam.
Veez les altres ensement:
N'i ad celui ki trop n'i ment
Ne sunt forstrait d'escripture,
Mais chascun fait sa controvure.
Ore seit ke tut seit veritez,
Si est ço purquant vanitez
Tels escriz oïr e entendre,
U l'alme ne poet nul ben prendre:
Kar quanque a l'alme ne fait bien
Devant Dé ne valt nule rien.

told in song, because those who composed songs about history devised them according to what they believed. And as it is indeed said in the proverb, belief is not knowledge. Judge for yourself if it can be true that a child might have such power as the *Song of Mainet* says, or *Little Orphan Samson*, or *The Deeds of Sir Tristram*, or *The Good Messenger Balam*. Likewise, look at the others: there isn't one that doesn't lie enormously, nor are they taken from scripture: each one advances its own fiction. Now suppose that they are wholly true: it is nonetheless still a vain pursuit to listen to such writings, from which the soul derives no benefit: for whatever does not do good to the soul is worth nothing in God's eyes.

[*Lines 43–58 explain why or taking pleasure in reading secular works is dangerous: God wants everything to be turned to his purposes and has given us body and senses for that reason. We are all his stewards and have to look after these things, serving him with a good will or risking his vengeance for deliberate transgressions.*]

E pur ço que vus aim en Dé, [f. 57rb]
Tolir vus voil de vanité
Que vus li puissez rendre en bien
Quanque il demande a Crestïen.
Pur ço vus ai fait cest escrit,
U vus purrez lire a delit.
Ja nule rien n'i troverez
Dunt Jhesu Crist ne seit paez,
Dunt l'alme ne seit conforté,
E la char de mal turné.
Quant de lire vus prendra cure,
Traez avant cest escripture:
Les Ewangelies i verrez
Mult proprement enromancez,

And because I love you in God, I want to take you away from futility so that you may render to him in goodness whatever he asks of a Christian. For this reason, I have composed this text, where you can read to your delight. You will not find anything which Jesus might not be pleased with and which might not sustain the soul and turn the flesh away from wickedness. When you wish to read, take out this piece of writing: here you will see the Gospels accurately translated into the vernacular, followed by explanations, briefly interpreted according to the fathers of the church. For you may

E puis les exposicïuns
Brefment sulum les sainz expuns.
Kar sachez n'i ad nul mot dit
Que li sainz n'aient ainz escrit;
Jo l'ai excerpé e estrait
Des escriz ke li sainz unt fait.
Point de latin mettre n'i voil,
Kar ço resemblereit orgoil;
Orgoil resemble veraiement
Ço dire a altre qu'il n'entent,
E si est ço mult grant folie [f. 57*va*]
A lai parler latinerie;
Cil s'entremet de fol mester
Ki vers lai volt latin parler.
Chescun deit estre a raisun mis
Par la langue dunt il est apris.

be sure that there is no word said here that the church fathers have not previously written, for I have excerpted and extracted it from what the church fathers wrote. I do not wish to use any Latin here, because that would be pride; it is certainly arrogant to say to another what he cannot understand; hence it is a very great folly to speak Latin to laypeople: whoever speaks Latin to the laity engages in foolishness. Each person ought to be addressed in the language he has learned.

Ore vus pri, chere Dame Aline,
Pur Deu a ki tut le mund acline,
Ke vus priez escordrement
Que Deu me doint entendement
De si traiter e de si dire
Qu'il me pardoinst peché e ire;
Kar lealment sachez de fi
En vos prieres mult me fi,
Kar bien le sai k'a bon' entente
Deus s'abandune e presente,
E vus altre feiz m'avez dit
Que jo feisse cest escrit.

Now I pray you, my dear Lady Aline, for the sake of God to whom all the world bows, that you pray fervently that God give me the understanding so to compose and speak that he pardon my sins and spare me his wrath; and be assured that I rely greatly on your prayers, because I know that God makes himself present in good intention, and you have previously said to me that I should compose this work.

Pur ço sachez ne l'ai pas fait
Mais nostre entente ke Deu veit.
Vostre est li biens, vostre est li los,
Kar sanz vus penser ne l'os.
Si rien i ad d'amender
Del franceis u del rismeer
Nel tenez pas a mesprisiun,
Mais bien esguardez la raisun:
Deus n'entent pas tant al bel dit
Cum il fait al bon esperit.
Mielz valt vair dire par rustie
Que mesprendre par curteis[i]e;
Quanque s'acorde a verité,
Tut est bien dist pardevant Dé.
Dame, ne vus esmerveilliez
Que les lesçuns ai abriggez:
Jol faz pur vus ennui tolir

For this reason, know that I have done this only so that God may see our intention. The good is yours and yours is the praise, for without you I don't dare think of it. If there is anything to correct in the French or in the rhyming, do not consider it a fault, but think about the reason: God attends less to fine writing than he does to a good soul. It is better to speak the truth simply than to err through refinement; whatever is consonant with the truth is entirely well said before God. Lady, do not be surprised that I have abridged the readings: I do it to spare you boredom and to give you the desire to read, for it could all too quickly become tiresome. One grows bored with fine singing, and through boredom abandons the thing

E de lire duner desir,
Kar tost porreit trop ennuier.
L'em s'ennuie de bel chanter,
E par ennui poet l'em leisser
La rien ke plus doust aider;
Par ennui perd l'om suvent
La rien ke plus est a talent.
Purquant si tutdis puisse vivre, [f. 57vb]
E sanz nul entreleis escrivre,
E euse la buche trestut ferine,
E la lange tut ascerine,
E euse trestut la saveir,
Quanque nul home poet aver,
Ne purrai la maité dire
De ço k'apent a ma matire.
Mais mielz voil dire acune chose
De Deu que tenir buche close,
Kar suvent par petit bon dit
Tressalt li quors en grant delit.

that should help most; through boredom one often loses the thing most wanted. Nonetheless, if I could live for ever, and write without interruption, and if I had a mouth entirely of iron, and a tongue made entirely of steel, and if I had all the knowledge, as much as any man could have, I could not say the half of what pertains to my topic. But I would rather say something about God than keep my mouth closed, for often through some good, small tale the heart leaps with great delight.

[*In vv. 137–50 Robert refuses to name himself as yet, in order to put the envious off the scent: in 151–80 his mirror helps the soul while literal mirrors help only the body and its beauty; 181–8 anyone who reads the work should pray for its author; 189–96 the mirror of the prologue will show your cleanness and filth; looking closely in it you will see how to attire yourself for God: God grant that you conform to him from looking in it. 197–214 claims that the difficulty of interpreting scripture is like a tree whose fruit can be eaten only by shaking the tree: 215–54 adds that it is also a dark cloud that replenishes the earth with its rain (which stands for priests); 255–422 describe the divine establishment of the three orders and their duties. This discussion is devoted almost entirely to describing the duties of clerics, who ought to teach by word and example (see Bynum 1979); 423–8 explain that Robert has translated this work for each one to follow the example of the saints in giving themselves to Christ. Verses cited and used allegorically include Lam 4.4, Isa 24.2 (or Hos 4.9) and Ps 68.24*]

Kar enprés chascune lezçun [f. 59va]
Ki ad del Ewangelie nun
Ai mis tel exposicïun
Un poi pur mustrer la raisun
Ke hom le Ewangelie puisse entendre
E li nun lettrez bien aprendre.
E chascun ki siet lettr[e]üre
E de franceis la parleüre,
Lire i poet pur sei amender
E pur les autres endoctriner.

For after each reading from the Gospels I have added a homily, clarifying the meaning a little so that a person can understand the Gospel and teach the unlettered. And everyone who knows how to read their letters and how to speak French can read in this Gospel homily so as to improve themselves and to teach others.

[*Lines 439–50 use the compilatory topos of the flowery meadow to explain that Robert has provided only what he could, but not all that could be provided; 451–540 claim that he has not done this for praise but for the prayers of his audience and as penance for his sins. God gives him the authority to speak, just as the Holy Spirit (citing Ps 80.10 and Matt 10.20 or Mark 13.11), who inspires where He pleases, gave Balaam's ass the ability to speak; 541–58 develop a river metaphor, in which the Holy Spirit is both the river watering the earth of the learner and a channel running through a marsh; 559–90 argue that birth is not everything and that he who does good is worthy. None speaks the better for being rich, nor the worse for being poor: the spirit inspires where it will. If the rose is loved, its thorns must be loved too: the preacher must be cherished for his own sake, and still more for that of God.*]

Bien deit aver mundein aïe [f. 60va]
Ki al manger de ciel envie.
Bien deit aver chose terrestre
Ki pramet vie celestre.
Del ciel ert forsclos a estrus
Ki sun prechur leist busoignus.
Saint Pol commande veirement
Ke chascun home ki d'altre aprent
Od sun doctur deit comuigner
De tuz ses biens sanz demander.
Ore pri tuz cels que orrunt
Icest escrit e ki le lirrunt,
Qu'il prient Deu omnipotent
Ki de tuz mals me defent.
E doint cest ovre si parfeire
Qu'en dreite fei le puisse plaire,
E puis le curs de ceste vie
Od ses sainz seie en sa baillie.
Kar cest ovre faz verraiement
Pur mei e pur tute gent.

He who invites [others] to the banquet of Heaven must surely also be given help on earth. He who promises heavenly life ought to have terrestrial things. He who leaves his preacher needy will be entirely shut out from heaven. St Paul indeed commands that each man who learns from another must share with his teacher all his property without being asked. Now I pray that all who hear this work, and who read it, pray to God omnipotent that he keep me from all evils. And may he grant that this work be completed in such a way that I may be able to please him in true faith, and, after the course of my life, be with his saints in his kingdom. For truly I carry out this work for my own sake and for that of all people.

[*vv. 611–28 claim that this work was made for those who (like the author) cannot understand the meaning of scripture easily; 629–35 ask for forgiveness if anything is amiss in the work; the writer names himself ('Robert de Grettam') in 634; 636–60 cite the parable of the talents; 661–74 threaten with Hell those who do not support their preachers materially; 675–94 argue against despair since God loves anyone who repents and believes in the Trinity.*]

Notes

After line 120, prose summary numbering is from Connolly and Duncan 2003 for ease of reference.

1 **sa trechere Dame Aline** For the comparable dedication to Lord Alain see Sinclair 1995, vv. 1–3.

5 **chançon de geste e d'estoire** This becomes *romaunce and gestes* in the Middle English translation (see Part VI, §2.3).

7–10 **Mais bien voil . . . de vaine cure** Robert wishes Aline to know that pleasurable reading of secular fiction is not a harmless entertainment because it occupies the mind with idleness that distracts readers from what they owe God. Warnings of this sort are common: see, for example, the opening to the so-called *Traduction anonyme* of the Bible (ed. Szirmai 1985, vv. 3–12) and the *Bestaire* of

Guillaume le Clerc (see (**17**) and Reinsch 1892, vv. 564–8), Angier of Frideswide, *Dialogues* (**24a**, 141–2, 171–4) for topoi displacing *chanson de geste* figures in favour of spiritual reading.

23–4 **Kar cil ki chançuns . . . les furmerent** Robert denies secular writers a textual tradition by accusing them of creating works wholly from their own imagination. Several times in the prologue (see n. to 74, below), Robert attacks those who write without completely relying upon textual tradition.

26 **quidance n'est pas savair** A proverb unattested in Hassell 1982, Morawski 1925, or Schulze-Busacker 1985.

28 **uns enfés oust poair** Robert here refers to the *enfances* type of *chanson de geste*, which treat the hero's progress and extraordinary deeds from youth into manhood.

29 **Mainet** is the name taken on by the young Charlemagne in the *chanson de geste* of that name (Paris, ed., 1875).

30 The *chanson de geste* of **Sansunnet** (Samson) the Little Orphan is lost (Moisan 1986, II.5 843).

32 **Balam** is likely the father of Fierabras. The *chanson de geste* about this character is lost (Moisan 1986, II.5 817–18: on Fierabras, see (**18**)). In the Middle English *Miroir* translation these figures become 'Tristrem, other of Gy of Warrewyk' (Part VI, §2.3, p. 435, line 15).

46 **Quanque il demande a Crestïen** Robert frequently calls upon people to do the duty God gave them. He scolds ill-educated and wicked clerics who do not preach to the laity and, in the conclusion, laypeople who refuse to feed and clothe their clergy.

54 **Traez avant** suggests that Aline kept her books in an armoire: she is 'not only literate but libraried' (Hanna 2005, 184).

58 **sulum les sainz expuns** Robert authorises the *Miroir* by rooting it entirely in the textual traditions of the church fathers and professional exegesis. Aitken 1922, 39 cites the prologue of Bede's commentary on Luke: *Nihil sit dictum quod non sit dictum prius* (there is nothing said [here] that was not said before) (Bede *In Lucae* 1; see now Hurst, ed., 1960).

70 **Ki vers lai . . . latin parler** Although discussing his written translation, Robert briefly considers the folly of *speaking* Latin (or at least incomprehensible Latin) to the laity in preaching and pastoral work.

72 **Par la langue . . . apris** Like Latin, Robert implies, French is a language in which someone can be instructed. Cf. Grosseteste's *Chasteau* (**5**, 23–8).

73–80 **Ore vus pri, chere Dame Aline . . . mult me fi** Robert here requests Aline's prayers in particular, but also calls at several other points in the prologue (e.g. vv. 601–4), for the prayers of anyone who might come in contact with the work.

87 **Vostre est li biens** Robert assigns Aline responsibility for the work, and perhaps also in part removes guilt for any errors away from himself.

89–96 **Si rien i ad . . . par curteis[i]e** on this topos see also Part VI, §2.3, p. 436, lines 4–11.

100 **les lesçuns . . . abriggez** Robert translates the Gospel lections for each sermon, so his account of abridging the readings here, while conventionally demonstrating concern for ennui on the part of the patron, may suggest that Aline knows the original Latin texts, or perhaps that he has reserved some learning to himself. For advice to preachers on maintaining the distinction between themselves and their congregation as given, for instance, by Thomas of Chobham, see Waters 2003, 32–3.

104 **L'em s'ennuie de bel chanter** Variations of this proverb are attested in Hassell 1982, 64a, Morawski 1925, 9, and Schulze-Busacker 1985, 239.

109–15 **si tutdis . . . la maité dire** The *ferrea vox* version of the *occupatio* topos; e.g., *Aeneid*: *non mihi si linguae centum sint oraque centum / ferrea vox* (not even if I had a hundred tongues, a hundred mouths, and a voice of iron, VI vv. 625–6), which is quoted in such places as Jerome, *Letter* 66.5 653 and the *Cursor mundi*: 'for þouȝe my tunge were of steele', v. 20,023.

124 **Un poi** may be either a humility topos or an assertion that Robert has shared only a portion of his knowledge.

131–3 **Bien deit aver . . . chose terrestre** Requests for material assistance become increasingly frequent towards the prologue's conclusion.

137–40 **Saint Pol . . . demander** Gal 6.6.

139 **comuigner** A form of *communier*: see *AND*, *s.v.* 'communer' (3).

150 **pur tute gent** See 73–80 n.

15. Herman de Valenciennes, *Li Romanz de Dieu et de sa mere* [Dean 485], Prologue: London, British Library, MS Harley 222, ff. 9r–10r

Date of composition and provenance. Continental; after 1189–95? (Henry II '*rois d'Engleterre et quens de Normendie*' is cited at v. 5041 as an instance of mortality and transience, perhaps in an interpolation).

Author, sources and nature of text. The authorial persona Herman de Valenciennes presents to his readers is unusually detailed and personal. He states that he was a canon and a priest, born in Hainault: that he and all his family were baptised and raised in the town of Valenciennes and that Count Baldwin IX of Flanders (1171–1205), Countess Yolande (d. 1219?), and Bishop Oudars ('Dudars') were present at his baptism. He names his dead parents, Robers and Erambors, and seeks prayers for their souls and his own. In a typical modesty topos, he claims to be but a very young man and a cleric poor in intelligence, who has translated his work from Latin into French (Spiele 1975, v. 2012, 458). By his seeming haplessness and lack of experience, Herman emphasises his own youth and the newness of his ambitious undertaking, a vernacular handling of iconic material, with the Bible re-shaped around the Virgin. Herman's *Romanz* was widely popular in the thirteenth and fourteenth centuries, and has had modern praise for its lively writing. Many extant manuscripts of the *Romanz* are Anglo-Norman: it is possible that Herman wrote in England or spent time there.

Li Romanz de Dieu et de sa mere, also known as Herman's *Bible*, was composed at a period of intensified theological debate about the Virgin birth, the Assumption, and Mary's role in the redemption. The *Romanz* is a freely innovative translation and adaptation of canonical Old and New Testament and apocryphal material. Herman's originality lies in his exuberant transformation of the received corpus to intertwine the stories of Jesus and Mary, and, central to his *Bible*, the elevation of Mary to the position of co-redemptrix with her son. Although asserting a concern with truth and with not speaking amiss of God (Spiele 1975, vv. 4721–2), Herman takes what later might have been regarded as liberties. The *Romanz*'s metrical form (like that of Old French epic) is assonanced *laisses* of flexible alexandrines: it refers to itself as a *livre*, a *romanz*, a *sermon*, and a *chançun* (Spiele 1975, 3 and vv. 450, 398, 414, A545, A549) and also has some generic affiliations with hagiography. As with all these genres the work is vividly performative. Like many vernacular renderings of the Bible, the *Romanz* is not a continuous translation but a gathering of selected episodes. For canonical material Herman generally follows the Vulgate; for the Virgin's life, his principal source is the apocryphal *De Nativitate Mariae*, with material from the *Transitus beatae Mariae* (death and Assumption of Mary). The poem's shape and content are also influenced by liturgy. Herman uses Peter Comestor's biblical commentary, the *Historia scholastica* for Genesis, and Hebrew sources for the story of Moses and the crown. Wace's *Conception Nostre Dame* of *c.* 1150 was probably not used, but rather shares source material with Herman.

Like Adgar's miracle collection (11a), the *Romanz* is an important work in the proliferation of Marian literature and cult in Latin and in the vernaculars. In Herman's account, God summons the devil to announce that woman is to become God's own *amie*, and no longer, as in Eve's case, the devil's helper (Spiele 1975, v. 2730): the Virgin will heal the whole world (e.g. v. 2872). The *Romanz* concludes with an impressive death bed, attended by God and St Michael, in which the Virgin recapitulates, like a warrior-hero reciting his 'epic credo', or profession of faith, the important moments of Christ's life (Spiele 1975, 130–5; and see Labande 1955), before her own shining soul is taken directly to heaven and her body left for the apostles to bury in the Valley of Jehosaphat.

The account of the *Romanz*'s composition edited here is inserted into the story of Abraham, just after Sodom and Gomorrah (with its recommendation that 'natural sinning with women' (*naturel pechié des femes*, Spiele 1975, v. 396) is preferable) and before Isaac's near sacrifice by his father Abraham. Like the miracle tales in which Mary saves sinners, the *Romanz* originates as a form of healing and grace offered by the Virgin. Herman sins by drinking too much and giving way to anger and is quickly punished, but the Virgin's command to write her life offers work, hope and healing. Her patronage recalls the many women commissioners of doctrinal and devotional writing in England (see e.g. (**9**), (**11a**), (**11b**), (**13**), (**39**)).

In keeping with the Virgin's great powers, Herman maximises her role as patron. She is the creative force behind his work, her life is the matter of the book, she is its source (and possibly even dictates it to him): it is her book (*ton livre*, Spiele 1975, v. 560). It is also his cure: writing Mary's biography is her medicine for him (vv. 52–65).

Audience and circulation. Herman says that he has composed his work for those who do not know Latin (Spiele 1975, v. 5602). Formulas of address to the audience, like those in *chanson de geste*, argue that the *Romanz* is intended for public recitation (Nobel 1994, 119), and perhaps for instructive reading aloud at monastic meal times or in wealthy laypeople's houses (Spiele 1975, 3–4). Parts of the text are found in the well-known trilingual insular manuscripts Harley 2253 and Digby 86, believed to have served ecclesiastical and secular West Midlands households, as well as in bi-lingual insular and continental French and Latin manuscripts. Herman's *Bible* influenced French and English works: it was probably an important source for *Cursor mundi*, a major biblical adaptation in Middle English, and inspired the author of the Middle English poem *Iacob and Iosep*. It was a source for writers in French, such as Geoffroi de Paris (compiler of a Bible translation) and the fourteenth-century Anglo-Norman translator of the Harley 3775 rhymed Genesis (Dean 442: Nobel 2011 2.1, 130; Szirmai 2005, 56–62, 78–86).

Manuscript source. *Li Romanz de Dieu et de sa mere*, ff. 2–127, is the only work in BL Harley 222, a medium-size book (240 × 145 mm) of 128 folios, which, according to the colophon of the scribe, Robert (f. 127*v*) was copied in 1280. The Harley manuscript is one of thirty-five extant (of thirty-seven known). Nineteen are in Anglo-Norman; about half of all extant texts are partial copies, mostly thirteenth century, with a few from the fourteenth. Harley 222 is one of only two Anglo-Norman manuscripts to contain Herman's Old and New Testaments, the Passion, and the Assumption of the Virgin Mary (the other is Yale University Library 395): the Assumption often circulated independently, or sometimes with the *Romanz*'s Passion.

There is a legal text (perhaps of the fourteenth century) on f. 1, which was added as a flyleaf to the manuscript (with post-medieval foliation and title added later again). The poem is written in a single column, with each new *laisse* signalled by a larger lightly flourished initial letter in blue or red, some later painted over to form illuminated capitals. Rubrics are infrequent and appear in the margins, to the right of the text (see e.g. f. 44 at http://www.bl.uk/catalogues/illuminatedmanuscripts/). Appropriately for this cross-Channel text, the manuscript, though sometimes said to be of continental provenance, has many English palaeographic markers (Dean 485, Baswell private corr.)

Bibliography. The most recent edition of Herman's *Bible*, entitled *Li Romanz de Dieu et de sa mere* and based on BN fr. 20,039, is Spiele (1975). It was also edited earlier in a series of dissertations (Spiele 1975, xxx). There is as yet no critical edition of the shifting manuscript tradition: for an illustrative study of three groups of manuscripts, see Boulton 2005. Herman's autobiographical remarks are at Spiele 1975, v. 2019, 5610–11, 5612–15, 5617–18, 5622: see also 1 and nn. at 393. For an audio-visual reading from Herman, go to http://legacy.fordham.edu/academics/programs_at_fordham_/medieval_studies/french_of_england/audio_readings_94163.asp For literary composition as curative see further Olson 1982, esp. 39–89. On Herman's sources and influences, see Spiele 1975, 101–8, 150 (apocrypha), 5–15 (liturgy): Morey 1993, 17–18 (biblical commentary and Hebrew sources). On preceding traditions of Latin biblical versification see Dinkova-Bruun 2007. Relations or lack thereof with Wace are discussed by Spiele 1975, 71–5. Nobel 2011, II.1, 129–30 offers a succinct introduction to the poem and Bogaert 1992, 183, discusses it briefly among saintly verse histories. For its generic affiliations and performative qualities see Spiele 1975, 1, 130; de Mandach 1988, 1993, [with Roth] 1989, and for modern appreciations of Herman's writing, Nobel 2011; Spiele 1975, 4; Smeets 1968 I.1, 53. Style and the *Romanz* is discussed in Milland-Bove 2012, Boulton 2009 and van Coolput-Storms 2009. For parallels between Herman's Bible translation and *Cursor mundi* see Thompson 1997 and 1998. For foundational studies of medieval Bible translation into French, see Berger 1884 and Bonnard 1884, now much updated in Nobel 2011, I and II. For a general study of lives of Christ and the Virgin and other fictionalising devotional works in French, see Boulton 2015.

TEXT AND TRANSLATION

Seignurs, des ore dirai dunt en face la chançon
Pur qi jo l'ai estraite de si haute raison.
Jo la face de celui qui est e diex e hom,
Cum en terre fu nez, cum sustint Passïun,
Cum fu mort en terre e de sa Resurrecciun,
De lui e des apostels e de l'Asension,
Del jur de Pentecoste e de l'aparition,
Seignurs, cum nous venimes par li a raançun,
Cum avrum al derain jur de noz pechiez pardun.

Lords, here I'll begin telling you what I'm writing this song about and for whom I've composed it of such lofty matter. I am writing it about him who is both God and man: how he was born on earth and suffered the Passion; how he died on earth and about his Resurrection; about him and about the Apostles and about the Ascension at Pentecost and his manifestation – lords, about how we were saved by him, and how on the day of judgement we shall be pardoned for our sins.

Par fei si m'escultez! Raison orrez molt veire.
De bon quer l'escultez, qe Dieu nus doinst la gloire.
N'est pas controvee, escrit est en estoire.
Pur vus pur amur Dieu, bien l'aiez en memoire.
Ço vus dist dan Heremans, se vus le volez croire,
Qe par lui purrez venir a parmanable gloire.
Ne se deit Crestiens de bien oïr retreire;
Qi bien ot e mielz fait sempres vient a v[i]ctoire.

Listen to me, in faith! You shall hear a very true account. Listen to it wholeheartedly, so that God may give us glory. It is not false; it has a written source. For your sake, for the love of God, remember it. Master Herman is telling you this, if you choose to believe him, so that you may achieve everlasting glory through him. A Christian must not refuse to hear it; whoever hears a good thing and acts better earns victory.

Seignurs, ore escultez! Qe Dieu vus beneïe,
Car ço n'est pas fait de nul licherie.
Ele est faite de Dieu, le fiz seinte Marie;
De Jhesu e de sa mere vus dirrum mais la vie;
Del lignage sa mere bien est dreit qe jol die.
Si vus prie pur Dieu nel tenez a folie.
Si bien nel escultez, jol tenc a vilonie.

Lords, listen now! May God bless you, for this is not about lewdness. It is written about God, the son of St Mary. I'll tell you henceforth about the life of Jesus and his mother; it's right for me to tell you about his mother's lineage. I pray you, for God's sake, not to take it as foolishness. If indeed you do not listen to it, I hold that as an outrage.

Ne le tenez a gabeis iço que vus dirrai.
Ço fu a un Noel qe forment beivre amai.
Uns de mes clers me forfist, dunt molt me curuçai.
Un ardant tisun pris que le feu ne dutai.
Ars mun dei un petit, adunc nel gardai.
Ne feri pas le clers, ne pas ne l'adesai.
Culchai si m'endormi mais cum ge m'esveillai [f. 9v]
Ma main trouvai enflee si que murir quidai.

Don't laugh about what I'm going to tell you. It was one Christmas, when I liked to drink heavily. One of my clerics offended me, and I became enraged. I seized a burning log, for I did not fear the fire. I burned my finger a bit, but paid it no attention at the time. I did not strike the cleric or even touch him. I went to bed and fell asleep. But when I awoke I found that my hand was swollen, and I thought I would die.

Idunc mandai un prester, quant je quidai murir,
Pur mei faire confés, ne vus en quier mentir.
En sel dei ert l'anguisse que ne se volt partir;
Manda mires par tuit; ne me purent garir.
De .viii. jurs ne purrai mangier ne bivre ne dormir.

Since I thought I would die, I called for a priest so as to be shriven – I don't wish to lie to you. That finger caused me a suffering that refused to leave. I sent for doctors everywhere; they could not heal me. For a week I couldn't eat, drink, or sleep.

Si jo dunc oi pour, ne l'estuet demander.
Dunc quidai a estrus de cest siecle turner.
En mun lit u giseie me pris a purpenser
De la dame qui set la gent reconforter
Pur amur de sun fiz me deignast regarder.
Certes tut pecheur la deivent molt amer.

No need to ask whether I was afraid. I thought then, and for a fact, that I would depart from this world. In my bed where I lay, I began to think about the lady who knows how to comfort people and that, for love of her son, she should deign to think about me. Indeed, all sinners must love her a great deal.

Co fut seinte Marie, seignurs, que jo apelai
La nuit de la Tephaine, certes ne mentirai.
Qe dormi un petit iloec cum culchai,
Qe des .viii. jorz n'oi fait, idunc me reposai.
Vint a mei une dame e jo li demandai:

It was St Mary, lords, to whom I called out, the night of the Epiphany (I surely won't lie), when I slept a little, there where I lay, because for a week I had not, so I rested. A lady came to me and I asked her,

'Qui este vus, ma dame?' – Jo sui qui te garrai.
Jo ai a non Marie, jo nel te celerai.
Tu serras bien gari quant de tai turnerai.

Pareille en tes livres la vie si cum fui nee;
El temple divin cum je fui presentee,
E cum je fui de l'ang' en terre saluee;
De Josep mon espus cum jo fui espusee;
Cum fu en Bethleem de mun fiz deliveree;
Cum mon fiz fu requis, cum jo fui honuree
Des treis reis qui le requistrent d'aliene cuntree;
De la mort de mon fiz dunt la gent est salvee.
Garde la meie mort ne seit pas ublïe[e].
De latin en romanz seit tute tresturnee'.
[f. 10r]

'Dites, ma bele dame, u jo la troverai,
Unques ital mestier certes n'en commençai,
E si sui molt malades, ço quid que murrai'.
'Entenz tu que ai dit? Trestuit te guarrai.
Qant le commenceras ensemble o tei serrai.
Jo ere commencement e jo bien la finerai'.
Idunc fui jo molt liez par fei, si m'esveillai.
Si tost cum fui guarriz, cest livre commençai.
Si Dieu plaist e ma dame, tres bien l'esmerai.

'Who are you, my lady?' – 'I am she who will heal you. My name is Mary. I shall not conceal it from you. You will be completely healed when I leave here.

Prepare my Life in your book, how I was born; how I was presented in the holy temple, and how I was greeted on earth by the angel; about Joseph my spouse and how I was married; how I gave birth to my son in Bethlehem, how my son was sought out; how I was honoured by the three kings from a foreign country who sought him; about the death of my son, through which people have been saved. See that my death not be forgotten. Translate it all from Latin into French'.

'Do tell, my beautiful lady, where I will find it. I have certainly never undertaken such a task. And I am very sick and believe I shall die'.

'Do you understand what I've said? I shall heal you completely. When you begin it, I shall be with you. I shall be the beginning and I shall finish it'.

Then I was very happy, by my faith, and so I awoke. As soon as I was well, I began this book. If God is willing, and my Lady, I shall complete it successfully.

Notes

1 **Seignurs, chançon** The apostrophe to *Seignurs* and the use of the word *chançon* (but *romanz* in Spiele 1975, v. 398) hint at the epic style to follow, both in this passage and elsewhere in Herman's poem. Other verses also include a direct address to the audience (18 and 44). Note as well the frequent command to the audience to listen (*escultez*): 10, 11, 18, 24. Initial *S* of *Seignurs* is 3 lines high and is gold on a blue background. The text edited here corresponds to Spiele 1975, vv. 398–466.

1, 3 **face** Morphologically 3rd person subjunctive of *faire*, *face* in these lines functions as an indicative.

3–7 **Jo . . . aparition** As Herman indicates here, his poem is centred on Jesus and is informed by and organised according to the events of the liturgical year. Spiele's *de l'aparitïon*, v. 403, is undoubtedly the correct form and replaces *partisun* in Harley 222 (1975). In the canonical Gospels, Jesus's appearances are said to have occurred after his death, burial and Resurrection, but before his Ascension. See also note for *Tephaine*, Epiphany (v. 45).

12 **N'est pas . . . estoire** Herman's claim here is designed to reassure his audience that the astonishing episode he is about to recount is authentic. The assertion is commonplace, but it anticipates the

even more authoritative source that supersedes it, the Virgin's own account of her life.

17 **a v[i]ctoire** Spiele (1975): *en vitoire*, v. 412. In the word *uctoire* in the manuscript there is a red superscript letter between the *c* and the *t*, possibly a misplaced *i* meant to appear before *c*. The sentiment of this verse accords with Herman's expressed reason for writing the poem: *Por amor de Deu le faz, por amander la gent* 'I do it for love of God, in order to improve people', v. 5601).

19 **licherie** (lewdness) This assertion, using more pointed vocabulary than Herman's more conventional claim elsewhere that his book is not *fable* or *legerie* (Spiele 1975, v. 3213), links the passage to the immediately preceding destruction of Sodom and Gomorrah; God blames the cities' inhabitants – both men and women – for their homosexuality (Spiele 1975, vv. 352–3).

21 **dirrum** The form of the 4th person present tense can appear in French medieval literature with 1st person meaning, although it does so most often at the rhyme.

26–7 **Ço fu . . . curuçai** To medieval audiences accustomed to think that mental attitudes had somatic consequences, Herman's drinking and anger are not only evidence of sin but also predispose him to the burn he suffers and anticipate the ill-health he will experience afterward; see Olson 1982.

35 **En sel** (= **cel**); cf. Spiele 1975: *Si fu anflez mes doiz que il me dut partir*, v. 432.

37, 46–7 **De .viii. jurs . . . me reposai** Of this list, sleep in particular was regarded as essential to good health, as the narrator of Chaucer's *Book of the Duchess* famously points out (*The Riverside Chaucer*, 330, vv. 1–8). The reading of literature (as often happened after dinner) was undertaken to distract the listener from cares, if necessary, and as an aid to sleep (Olson 1982, 84–5).

39 **quidai a estrus** MS *quidai e a estrus* with *e* expuncted.

45 **Tephaine** Although the Epiphany refers to the manifestation of Jesus Christ after Christmas, mention of it here presages the appearance, on the very same night, of the Virgin Mary, thereby enhancing her importance, now equal to that of her son.

47 **Qe des .viii. jorz n'oi fait, idunc me reposai** Spiele 1975: *D'uit jorz dormi n'avoie, iluec me reposai*, v. 444.

52 **Pareille en tes livres . . . nee** Spiele 1975: *Fai la vie en .i. livre ensi com je fui nee*, v. 450.

67 **Jo . . . finerai** Herman refers to the Bible as source in only one extant manuscript, BN fr. 2162 (Spiele 1975, 393 n. 10).

69 **Si tost . . . commençai** Herman's statement here that he was healed before beginning to write, which assumes a kind of *quid pro quo* (his good health in exchange for writing Mary's Life), appears to contradict Mary's earlier assurance to him that he will be restored to good health by the time she leaves (v. 51).

16. Sir Thomas Gray of Heaton, *Scalacronica* [Dean 74], Prologue: Cambridge, Corpus Christi College, MS 133, f. 1*r–v*

Date of composition and provenance. *c.* 1355–64, Edinburgh and Northumberland.

Author, sources and nature of text. Sir Thomas Gray (d. 1369), a Northumbrian knight and warden of Norham Castle who had seen active service for Edward III and the Black Prince in Flanders and France, was captured in the Scottish Wars in 1355. He began his *Scalacronica* that year as a prisoner of the Scots in Edinburgh Castle (joining, on the one hand, a group of prison writers ranging from Boethius to Malory, Charles d'Orléans, Edward, duke of York, and King James I of Scotland, and, on the other, a second group of late-medieval lay writers of chivalric treatises and biographies, among them the Chandos Herald, Sir Geoffroi de Charny, and Christine de Pizan).

Gray's chronicle moves from creation to the Trojan Wars and down to 1364, drawing widely on its author's voluminous knowledge of chivalric romance, chronicle, and prophecy traditions, as well as his own and his father's careers. In its themes and preoccupations *Scalacronica* has many overlaps with chronicles composed for other elite and gentry families, which frequently combine the legendary origins of Britain in the Trojan diaspora with the timescales of universal chronicle and world history (see e.g. the *Mohun Chronicle* (**42**)).

Gray is often studied for his account of his own times, but also noteworthy is the range and distinctiveness of his treatment of Britain's legendary history, the *romans d'antiquité* and Alexander the Great, as well as his retelling of Genesis and other biblical material in the framing of his chronicle. His purview embraces not only 'Great Britain, formerly Albion, land of giants, now England' (lines *2–3*), but much of Europe. Gray's comments repeatedly suggest his independent consideration of his sources: the *Scalacronica*'s Arthur, for instance, is a composite from Wace and Geoffrey of Monmouth and later prose and verse romances, in which Gray accepts Arthur's historicity, praises him as the most effective opposition to the Saxons, and considers why Bede may have omitted such a figure, but nonetheless rejects many specific incidents told of Arthur. Gray also notes Bede's omission of British sources 'because he did not know the language' (*du dit langage n'avoit conisaunce*, Meneghetti 1979, 71) and himself takes a wider British perspective. In addition to Albina, foundress of Britain (ff. 29^{v}–30^{r}), Gray gives an account of Scota, foundress of Scotland (f. 191^{v}; Marvin 2001), and his Albina lands on the Mull of Galloway, not on the traditional south-west coast of England (see Rajsic forthcoming). He also reworks the Anglo-Norman *Brut*'s story of Haveloc (ff. 84^{r}–85^{v}: Moll 2008) as a Danish-British union (Goldesburgh is said to be the 'saxoun' form of a name that is Argentile 'en bretoun', f. 84rb). Gray's perspective on English and British histories and their authorities may well owe something to his Northumbrian borderland home as well as to his experiences in mainland Europe.

Gray remains distinctive on more recent events, presenting Becket's murder, for instance, as not what the king wanted (*noun pas au gree le roy*, f. 155vb: Thiolier 1993, 126). The breadth of Gray's reading (different from, but at least as broad as, Malory's for *Le Morte Darthure*) may owe something to the royal library in Edinburgh and to David II of Scotland's 1330 purchase of a large collection of books. Gray's is not, as Thiolier notes, 'un texte innocent' (1993, 147). Not only is Gray an acute reader of texts and traditions, but his prologue has a copious and artfully varied lexis for the processes of composition and for his authorities (see below and Glossary).

After posing the question of his own identity both as a matter of his habit (with a play on the notion of *habitus* and armorial bearings) and as a numerical acrostic, Gray lists trilingual materials *en latin, en fraunceis, et en englés* (line *21*) of several different historiographical types in verse and prose as what he initially *surveist* (looked over, line *19*), though he claims to have translated *de ryme en prose* (line *13*). His dream-vision prologue, in which the Sibyl guides Gray as narrator-dreamer through world and insular history and takes him to the authorities for his forthcoming *cronicles*, is remarkable. Gray images history as a ladder, with the *Brut* and the Bible as twin chocks keeping it upright against an orchard wall five storeys high. In the dream he climbs the ladder under the Sibyl's guidance to enter the various locations where his 'official' sources – historians from Bede to Ranulph Higden – are at work. Although the figure of the Sibyl is well established in insular culture (and Gray might well have known Virgil through the *romans d'antiquité* if not in the original), there is no known direct source for the architectural allegory of Gray's prologue, though the image of the ladder has analogues in medieval apocalypse illustrations of St John ascending a ladder to look into heaven with the guidance of an angel and in many allegories of spiritual ascent and intellectual quest. The ladder, which was, or became part of the family crest, may also have offered a pun on *gré*, which means 'stair' in both French and Middle English. Gray's historiographic ladder and his Sibyl guide witness to the medieval alliance between history and prophecy in which prophecy enables visions of the past as well as the future. Gray invokes prophecy as what should be left to masters of divinity, but deftly exemplifies his point with invocations of pro-British prophecies (lines *107–8*), before relinquishing vaticination to this higher authority. Indeed Gray's own dream-visits with the Sibyl to the writing desks of the authorities in his prologue are not unlike Merlin's own recurrent visits to his master Blaise, keeper of the record of Merlin's own life and events, in the Grail cycle's *History of Merlin* (for Grail cycles, see (**41**)).

AUDIENCE AND CIRCULATION. Among her other books, Gray's daughter Elizabeth Darcy willed 'unum librum de romans vocat Leschell de Reson', which was perhaps a copy of her father's chronicle (she left the book conditionally to Philip Darcy – probably her nephew – or, failing him, to her brother Thomas's son Sir Thomas Gray, who was executed in 1415 for plotting the assassination of Henry V; Moll 2003, 36, 246 n. 27). But the book must have been known among other families and to other gentry and nobility audiences: it is suggestive that the Gray family are not known to have borne the image of a ladder in their arms until a generation after the composer of *Scalacronica* (Moll 2003, 44; King 2005b), and possible that the chronicle is the cause rather than the result of this heraldic tradition. *Scalacronica* was the object of sixteenth-century interest: the antiquary Nicolas Wotton (d 1567?) transcribed extracts in BL Harley 902, the sixteenth-century manuscript of Rauf de Bohun's *Petit Bruit* of 1309 (*ODNB*, *s.v.* 'Thomas Gray'; Dean 52), and among the miscellaneous documents by Archbishop Parker's secretaries and others bound together in Cambridge, Corpus Christi College 119, item 124 is a sixteenth-century translation (probably after 1568) of the *Scalacronica* prologue into English.

MANUSCRIPT SOURCE. Cambridge, Corpus Christi College 133, f. 1^{r-v}. The manuscript is a relatively large (318 × 190 mm) professionally produced folio with the text of *Scalacronica* written in a formal book-hand in two columns, ff. 1^{a}–234^{d}, and the title page is decorated with a diapered initial and borders of leaves and flowers in gilt, orange, blue, green and pink. The book was in the library of the Fitzgeralds, Earls of Kildare, by the late Middle Ages (Byrne 2013, 131). An inscription of ownership, 'Si Dieu plet A moy cest livre partient G. vst. Kyldare' on f. viii^{v} may be that of Gerald, fifth earl of Kildare, and husband of the chronicler's granddaughter (Moll 2003, 36; King 2005a). *Scalacronica* is preceded on ff. i^{v} to iii^{r} by an Anglo-Norman rhymed *Algorism* (Dean 329) with lines 305–9 in Middle English and, on f. iii^{r}, rhymed notes on measurement of length and area (Wilkins 1993, 56), the former of which may have some bearing on Gray's use of cryptogram for his own identity (vv. 14–24 below), though the *Algorism* is more workaday in format. A sixteenth-century hand which may, according to James Carley, be Leland's annotates ff. 1–2 (King 2005a, 210). The manuscript lacks leaves 4–9 of its nineteenth quire (covering events in 1341–55), but since these are abstracted by Leland (King 2000a, 22), the missing leaves must have been present at least before 1535. No other manuscript is known: Cambridge, Jesus College Q.G.10 (58), ff. 1^{a}–70^{d} (cited in Dean 74) is a text of the Prose *Brut* (Meneghetti 1979, 49).

BIBLIOGRAPHY. *Scalacronica* has been partially edited and translated, initially in club and society editions (Stevenson 1836; Maxwell 1907); extracts appear in Meneghetti 1979: the first volume of King's complete edition and translation is available (2005a). The manuscript is digitised at http://parkerweb.stanford.edu/parker/actions/manuscript_description_long_display.do?ms_no=133

For studies of Gray's life and historical and political context see King 2000b, 2002, 2005b. On Gray's reading and on the Scottish royal library see Moll 2003, 37; Ditchburn 2000, I.120–1,125–8; King 2005a, xliv–liii. Most modern attention has so far been paid to Gray's account of fourteenth-century events, with particular interest in the relations between chivalric ideology and practice (Maxwell 1907; King 2000a, 2008). Moll 2003 is an important appreciation and discussion of the literary sophistication of Gray's prologue, as also of Gray's chivalric self-fashioning and Arthurian writing (31–63, 67–72): see also Meneghetti 1979, 69–71. On the sixteenth-century translation of Gray's prologue, see Thiolier 1993, 128–30. Anglo-Norman chronicle and genealogical writing is illuminated by Spence 2008a, 2008b, 2013: for the wider historiographical context see Ingledew 1994.

16. Sir Thomas Gray of Heaton, Scalacronica

TEXT AND TRANSLATION

Qe eit delite ou voet savoer coment le isle del Graunt Bretaigne (jadys Albeon, tere de geaunz, ore Engleter), fust primerment enhabité, et de quel gent, et de lour naissaunce, et la processe du ligné de rois qe y ount esté et lour conversacioun, solunc ceo qe cely qi cest cronicle emparla, et de la m[ati]er avoit trové en escript en divers livers en latin et en romaunce, pust il conoistre en party par cest estoir suaunt la processe de eaux. Et sy ne voet pas an plain nomer soun noume, qe cest cronicle translata de ryme en prose, mais prisoner estoit pris de guer' al hour q'il comensa cest tretice.

Si estoit de l'ordre enluminé de bons morez,
As veves, as pucelis, et a saint eglise succours:
Soun habite, sa droit vesture,
Estoit autretiel de colour,
Com est ly chape du cordeler,
Teynt en tout tiel maner.
Autre cote avoit afoebler
L'estat de soun ordre agarder,
Qe de fieu resemble la colour,
Et desus, en purtrature
Estoit li hardy best quartyner[e]
Du signe teynt de la mere,
Environ palice un mure,
De meisme peynt la coloure.
Soit .viii. joynt aprés .xix.
Si mettez .xii. aprés .xiiii.
Un et .xviii. encountrez,
Soun propre noun en saverez.
.vii. a .xvii. y mettez,
Le primer vowel au tierce ajoigniez, [f. 1b]
Soun droit surnoun entroverez
Solunc l'alphabet.
Le noun propre et surenoun portoit
Qe devaunt luy soun piere avoit:

Whoever has pleasure in or wants to know how the island of Great Britain (formerly Albion, land of giants, now England) was first inhabited and by what people and about their birth and about the succession in the line of kings who have been there and their way of life (according to him who has narrated this chronicle, having found the details of it written in various books in Latin and in the vernacular) may learn something through this history which follows the course of these matters. And he who translated this chronicle from verse to prose does not wish openly to name his name, but he was a prisoner taken in war at the time when he began this treatise.

And he was of an order made illustrious through good customs, a help to widows, maidens, and holy church: his habit, his own clothing, was of the same colour as the cape of a Franciscan, dyed in exactly the same way. In order to uphold the status of his order, he had another coat to put on, like fire in its colour, and on it, there was portrayed the bold beast quartered with the painted device of his mother, bordered about with a wall painted in the same colour. Let the eighth [=h] be joined after the nineteenth [=T], then place the twelfth [m] after the fourteenth [=o]; bring the first [a] and the eighteenth [=s] together, and you will know his personal name. Place the seventh there with the seventeenth [=Gr]; join the first vowel to the third [=ai], and you will find out the right surname for him, according to the alphabet. He bore the personal name and the surname that his father had before him:

Qe plus clerement le voet savoir
D'autre qe de moy l'estut avoir.
Sortez jettez, e divinez,
Sy ymaginez qe vous poez.

whoever wants to know in more detail must get it from someone other than me. Choose, cast lots and guess, and figure what you can.

Et coment ly surveint corage de cest matir atreter, l'estoir devyse qe com il fust prisoner en le opidoun Mount Agneth (jadys chastel de Pucelis, ore Edynburgh), surveist il livers de cronicles enrymaiez et en prose, en latin, en fraunceis, et en englés, dé gestez dez auncestres, de quoi il se mervailla: et durement ly poisoit qe il n'ust hu devaunt le hour meillour conisaunce du cours du siecle. Si deveint corious e pensive, com geris n'avoit en le hour autre chos a fair, a treter et a translater en plus court sentence lez cronicles del Graunt Bretaigne, et lez gestez dez Englessez.

And as to how the desire took him to deal with this matter, the story relates that while he was a prisoner in the dungeon of Mt Agned (formerly Castle of Maidens, now Edinburgh), he looked over books of chronicles both rhymed and in prose, in Latin, in French, and in English, about the deeds of ancestors, about which he greatly marvelled. And it weighed heavily on him that he had not previously had better knowledge of the course of the world. And as he had few other things to do at that time, he became concerned and preoccupied with composing and translating the chronicles of Great Britain and the deeds of the English in a more compact form.

Et com estoit du dit bosoigne plus pensive, ly estoit avys un nuyt en dormaunt qe Sebile la sage ly surveint, et ly dist q'el ly moustra voi a ceo q'il estoit en pensé: et ly fust avys q'el ly amena en un verger, ou, encountre un mure haut, sur un peroun, troverent un eschel de .v. bastouns adressez, et sur le peroun desoutz l'eschel .ii. livers au costé, et un frer cordeler suppuoillaunt od sa main dextre le dist eschele.

And while he was most preoccupied with this business, it seemed to him one night as he slept that Sibyl the prophet came to him and said to him that she would show him the way to what he was thinking about. And it seemed to him that she led him into an orchard where, propped against a high wall, they found a five-rung ladder standing on a block of stone, and on the stone underneath the ladder, two books, one at each side [of the ladder] and a Grey friar holding up this ladder with his right hand.

'Moun amy', ceo [f. 1v] disoit la viel Sebile, 'veiez cy sen et foly, le primer liver la bible, le secounde la gest de Troy, queux ne greverount a toun purpos a surveoir'. Et com ly fust avys ele ly amena outre, si mounterent l'eschel, qe au boute du primer bastoun du dist eschel au mayn dextre parmy le mure troverent un bele entree ou entrerent un graunt cité, ou dedenz un manoir en un sale troverent escrivaunt un mestre bien furré.

'My friend', said the ancient Sibyl, 'here you may see wisdom and folly: the first book is the Bible, the second the story of Troy, which it will not harm your project to look over'. And she led him further, as it seemed to him, and they climbed the ladder, where, at the end of the first rung of the ladder on the right-hand side, they found a fine entrance in the wall, through which they entered a great city, where, inside a room within a manor, they found a master dressed in furs, writing.

'Beaux amy', ceo dist Sebille, 'veez ycy

'Fair friend', said the Sibyl, 'You see

Gauter, erchedeken de Excestre, qe le *Brut* translata de bretoun en latin par ditz de Keile et de Gildas, dé ditz de qi poez avoir ensampler com de le *Bruyte*, lez gestz dé Bretouns, le primer liver de cronicles de cest isle'.

Puis ils sez realerent et remounterent le secound bastoun du dist eschel, au bout de quoi troverent autiel entree com devaunt; ou, dedens un priori, com ly fust avys, troverent un moigne noir escrivaunt en un estudy. Si disoit Sebille,

'Cesti est Bede en Wermouth, le reverent doctour q'escrit le liver *De gestis Anglorum*, de quoi doiez avoir a toun purpos graunt ensensement, com *De gestis Saxouns*, le secund liver du dit cronicle'.

Ils sez realerent, com fust avys, et remounterent le tierce bastoun du dit eschel, ou par tiel entree y troverent un autre moigne noir et chanu escrivaunt en un cloistre.

'Moun amy', fesoit Sebille, 'cesti est le moigne de Cestre qi escript le *Polecronicon*, de qoi doiez prendre graunt avisement du tierce liver dé ditz cronicles, ceo est assavoir de la uniement qe le roy Egbright fist de les .vii. realmes Saxouns, com par ditz dez autours avoit trové, c'est assavoir par Willam de Malmesbery, Henry de Huntyngdoun, Roger de Houdene, et Mariotus le Escot, entrepretours englessez'.

Ils sez realerent, com fust avys, et remounterent le quart bastoun du dist eschelle, ou au boute du dist bastoun troverent meisme un tiel entree, ou en un chambre dedenz un vilette devaunt un fort chastel troverent un chapelain escrivaunt sure un lettroun.

'Douce amy', ceo disoit Sebille, 'cesti est le vikeir de Tilmouth, qe escript le *Ystoria Auria*, dé ditz de qy tu poez avoir graunt enformacioun du quart liver dé ditz cronicles, c'est du primer venu Willam le

here Walter, Archdeacon of Exeter, who translated the *Brut* from British into Latin from the narratives of Keile and Gildas: from his narrative you will have a source for the *Brut*, the deeds of the Britons and the first book of this island's chronicles'.

Then they went back again and climbed up onto the second rung of the ladder, at the end of which they found an entry like the previous one, where, inside a priory, as it seemed to him, they found a Benedictine monk writing in a study. Then the Sibyl said,

'This is Bede in Wermouth, the venerated doctor, who wrote the book *About the Deeds of the English* from which you ought to have a great deal of instruction for what you mean to do by way of *The Deeds of the Saxons*, the second book of your chronicle'.

They went back again, as it seemed to him, and climbed the third rung of the ladder, where, through another such entrance, they found a second monk, a white-haired Benedictine, writing in a cloister .

'My friend', said the Sibyl, 'this is the monk of Chester who wrote the *Polychronicon*, from which you ought to take much information for the third book of your chronicle, that is to say about the union King Egbert made of the seven Saxon realms, as he had found in the narratives of authors such as William of Malmesbury, Henry of Huntingdon, Roger of Howden, and Marianus the Scot, translators of the English'.

They went back again, as it seemed to him, and climbed the fourth rung of the ladder, where at the end of the rung, they found just such another entrance, where, in a room in a village in front of a strong castle, they found a chaplain writing at a desk.

'Sweet friend', said the Sibyl, 'This is the vicar of Tynmouth, who wrote the *Golden History*, from whose narratives you can have much information for the fourth book of the chronicle, that is about how William the conquerour ensa: et beu sire', fesoit la viel Sebille, 'tu es ore mounté lez qatre bastouns de l'eschel, la droit voi as croniclis de cest isle, si bien lez voillez pursuyre. Mais le scinkisme bastoun ne poez mounter, qar il signify lez avenementz futurs qe dez ascuns est ymaginé dez auncienz ditz: com en *La Vie seint Edward* est trové dé ditz de un saint hom qe dist, '*Non solum de gente Francorum sed Scottorum quos Anglici vilissimos reputant* etc.' Et auxi par ditz du *Bruyt* – en englés, 'þat Cadwaladre sal on Conan cal etc' – par ditz de Merlyn. Mais pusqe les futures cheaunces ne sount pas en certain a de [f. 2r] terminer fors soulement au sen devyn, lessoms a lez devyns les chosis celestiens, lez hours et lez momentz qe a cel pussaunce sount reservez. Et si est', fesoit Sebille, 'le cordeler qe vous veistes suppuoillaunt l'eschel Thomas de Otreburn, un mestre de devinité et de l'ordre dé Frers Menours, qi dez cronicles de cest isle se entremist, qe si tu pusses en cas ateindre toutes houres a les propretés dé ditz bastouns du dist eschel, si cerchez lez cronicles du dist Thomas qe bien te mousterount ta droit voy, et si bien pussez acomplir cest tretice: tu lez doys appeller *Scalacronica*'.

Cesti qi cestz soungez avoist soungé sovenoit bien de toz lez propretez devisez, par ensamplere dé queuz comensa et pursuyst cest tretice en l'an de grace .mille. .ccc. .l. et synk. Et en le noun du Pier et Fitz et Saint Espirit comensa l'estoir de cest cronicle au comencement du siecle a nostre primer pier Adam et al ligné de ly, tanque al temps Enneas le proail Brutus, le primer roy qe cest isle poepla, la gest de qi et de sez successours il voet rementoyver del hour qe la genealogy veigne a ly.

Conqueror first came here: and, fair sir', said the venerable Sibyl, 'you have now climbed the four rungs of the ladder, the true paths to the chronicles of this island, if indeed you decide to pursue them. But you cannot climb the fifth rung, for it signifies the future events which are represented, according to some, in the ancient writings: as in the *Life of St Edward* there is found the pronouncement of a holy man who said, 'Not only the Frankish people, but the Scots, whom the English consider most worthless', etc. And also according to the sayings of the *Brut* – in English, 'Cadwallader shall call on Conan etc.' – in the sayings of Merlin. But since what happens in the future is not to be determined definitively except only by divine understanding, let us leave heavenly matters, and the hours and times which are reserved to this power, to the masters of divinity. And indeed', said the Sybil, 'the Francisan friar whom you saw holding up the ladder is Thomas of Otterbourne, a master of divinity and a member of the order of the Friars Minor, who took in hand the chronicles of this island, so that, if you are able in the event to give concentrated attention to the details of the rungs of the ladder, search the chronicles of this Thomas, which will show you your true path very well: and then you may be able to finish this composition: you must call them *Scalacronica*'.

He who had dreamed this dream remembered clearly all the matters related, through the example of which he began and continued with this treatise in the year of grace 1355. And in the name of the Father and the Son and the Holy Ghost, this chronicle's narrative will begin at the beginning of the world with our first father Adam and his lineage until the time of Aeneas the progenitor of Brutus, the king who first made this island known, the story of whom and of his successors he wishes to recall up to the time when the genealogy comes to his own self.

Notes

1 **Qe eit delite . . . savoer** a formula frequently used in historiographical texts (see e.g. 'Ki vult oïr e vult saveir/ de rei en rei . . .', the opening of Wace's *Roman de Brut* (Weiss 2002, 2, vv. 1–3).

7–8 **cely qi cest cronicle emparla, et de la m[an]er avoit trové en escript** This is most probably Gray himself, spoken of in the third person as is the convention of this prologue. But it may arguably refer to whoever supplied Gray with prison reading and found material for him.

8 **la m[ati]er** The manuscript is illegible at this point: the word may be *maner* or *matier.*

13 **de ryme en prose** None of the sources named in the prologue are in verse or in rhythmical cadenced prose. These named works certainly do not exhaust the list of Gray's sources (for vernacular and romance sources, see Moll 2003, 50–63; on Gray's use of further now unidentified Scottish chronicles and of oral accounts and newsletters, see King 2005a, xliv–lii). Gray's phrase may be a claim to stylishness and authenticity (on the wider fashion for prose history from the thirteenth century onwards and its association with truthful narration, see the discussion in Part VI, §1.2, pp. 426–8), or it may be simply the first action he associates with creating a new chronicle. An alternative explanation, that Gray's work is *dérimage* of an existing but now unknown verse compilation seems an unnecessary hypothesis, though see n. to *7–8* above. As is usual, the verse sections of Gray's prologue are written as prose in the manuscript.

1 **ordre** Gray puns on chivalric and religious orders: the protection of widows, young women and the church is part of the time-honoured functions of deacons and also of knights. On 'lay spiritual ambition' and fourteenth-century debates as to whether lordship can be a form of *imitatio clerici*, see Rice 2008. On Gray's chivalry, see further King 2000a; on its romance nature, Moll 2003, 39–40.

5 **cordeler** refers to the wearing of a rope girdle around a habit; hence to a Franciscan friar, a member of the order of Friars Minor (*Frers Menours*, line *117*), with the further possible pun here of 'Grey friar', after the colour of the friars' habit.

7 **autre cote** The second cape is constituted by Gray's arms. A diagram of these forms the frontispiece in Maxwell (1907), repr. Moll 2003, 39: the arms are *gules* (red, cf. *de fieu*, v. 9), a lion rampant (*li hardy best quartyner[e]*, v. 11), and a border engrailed argent.

10 **purtrature** MS *purturature.*

15 **joynt aprés .xix.** Counting *i* and *j* as one, *t* is the nineteenth letter of the alphabet.

27 **Sortez jettez** The use of an acrostic together with dicing metaphors may reflect the prophetic tradition of the Sibyls (n. to *32*) and the contemporary popularity of dicing prophecies: see Coote 2000, 196–7.

18 **Mount Agneth** Mynd Agned is a Gaelic name for Edinburgh, supplemented from at least 1142 by *Castellum Puellarum* (in the charters of King David I of Scotland), a name also used by Geoffrey of Monmouth as an alternative to 'oppidum montis Agned', and occurring in the romance *Fergus of Galloway* and the Breton lai *Doon* (see Blenner-Hassett 1942, Coates 2006). The name (unattached to Edinburgh) is also used in the *De ortu Waluuanii*, the *Prose Lancelot* and the *Queste del Sangreal.* For these details and the romance implications of Gray's naming of Edinburgh see Moll 2003, 40.

32 **Sebile le sage** These classical prophetesses and seers remained important in medieval historiography because of the prediction of Christ's birth by the Tiburtine Sibyl during emperor Augustus Octavian's reign (McGinn 1985, Holdenried 2006). Sibyls figure both in academic writings from Augustine onwards and in vernacular works, such as legendary histories of the cross. In Geoffrey of Monmouth and works deriving from his *Historia regum Britanniae*, agreement between Merlin's prophecies and the Sibyl's are considered to constitute very strong counsel (see e.g. Reeve and Wright 2007, 280–1 and the case of Cadwalader, lines *107–8*; also Layamon's *Brut*, ed. Brook and

Leslie 1978, 838, lines 16,063–6). All nine of the classical sibyls feature in the French of England in the *Livre de Sibile* (Shields 1979). Gray himself explains the Sibyl's name as a generic one belonging *al office dez femmes prophetessez* (f. 5*vb*). On Gray's Sibyl as a link between the historical and the prophetic see Moll 2003, 42 and Ingledew 1994, 665–8, and on prophecy in insular romance and historiography more generally Coote 2000.

35–6 **un mure haut . . . un eschel de .v. bastouns** There is no known direct source for Gray's image of historical sources and access to them via a ladder against an orchard wall. Contemporary libraries tended to use book chests and library 'wheel' desks: book fetching would be done by clerks for elite readers and Gray's image is unlikely to derive from the use of ladders in contemporary library organisation (one of the earliest and greatest dedicated secular libraries, the three storeyed library of Charles V of France in the tower of the Louvre would not be finished until 1368: d'Avril and LaFaurie 1968, 45–6). However, ladders were important structural metaphors in many discourses and lay people were not without experience of the mnemonic and meditative diagrams in which they often figure. At least two manuscripts of the late-thirteenth-century *Speculum theologiae* or *Orchard of Consolation* diagrams by the Franciscan John de Metz, circulating in elite lay as well as clerical books, were known in the north, one certainly from Durham (see Sandler 1999, 23–7, and 108–9. nos 1 and 9). For illustrations of these and other diagrams in a baronial psalter, see Sandler 1999, plates 2–4, 6–10, 14–15, 24: plate 25 and fig. 50 represent ladder-like steps as giving access to the multi-storied Tower of Wisdom). For Richard de Fournival, the author of the immensely popular thirteenth-century *Bestiaire d'amour* and his imaginary library imaged as a garden with three-stepped terraces (with books as plants), see Carruthers 1998, 273, and on the architectural allegorical background in which ladders are one trope, Carruthers 2008, 44–51; Whitehead 2003. In her *Chemin de longue étude* (1402), Christine de Pizan tours the firmament under the guidance of the Sybil by climbing a ladder into the sky (ed. Püschel 1974, v. 1584 ff.).

On ladder imagery in late-medieval pastoral books and imagery see Matsuda 1997; Brantley 2007. For the ladder on Philosophy's skirt in Boethius's notable work of prison-writing, *The Consolation of Philosophy* see Courcelle 1967, 90–9. Ladder images were also common in pedagogy (Carruthers 2008, 248, 251). Richard de Bury's account of metaphors for books in his *Philobiblon* includes 'scala Jacob' (Carruthers 2008, 160), an image with its own long history going back at least to the Benedictine Rule. In addition to Henry of Huntingdon's use of genealogy and lineage as prophetic material (see n. to *103–6*), Gray may have seen genealogical diagrams with their characteristic roundels branching off to allow detail within a systematic set of connections (see e.g. Carruthers 2008, 250–2; Spence 2008b; and (**20c**)): such diagrams may have been suggestive for the narrator's dream excursions through the wall to visit writers at work in their cells and studies.

37–8 **au costé** The books under the ladder *au costé* are usually taken as being under the feet of the ladder so that it rests on a dual foundation of ecclesiastical and Trojan history, but it is difficult to construe the French as meaning anything other than 'alongside, nearby' (see *AND*, *s.v.* 'costé'), with the books functioning as chocks to hold the ladder's feet in place. King's translation of *au costé* as 'expensive' seems less probable (2005a,1).

41 **sen et foly** For the argument (accepted here) that previous commentators have construed the Sibyl's terms as referring respectively to the Bible and the *Brut*, but that they must be taken as referring to what historical tradition contains, examples of wisdom and folly, see Moll 2003, 42.

52 **Gauter erchedeken de Excestre** The reference is to Geoffrey of Monmouth's *Historia regum Britanniae* or *De gestis Britonum*, but, like Gaimar in the *Estoire des Engleis* (see Short 1994, 325, vv. 6458–9), Gray refers to Geoffrey's work only by the name of Walter the Archdeacon (said erroneously here to be of Exeter rather than Oxford), the figure who, in the *Historia* itself is the provider of the ancient British book that is purportedly the *Historia*'s source (Reeve and Wright 2007, 5; see Moll 2003, 43 and nn. 82, 83 for a 'small tradition' of identifying Walter as the author). As King notes, Gray refers to *Gauter Archedeken de Oxenford* as the translator of the *Gest Bretoun* on f. 83^r, so Exeter here is probably due to confusion between *Exonie* and *Oxonie* (2005a, 210–11. n. 3).

54 **Keile** Moll suggests this may be an error for Wace's 'Aquile, le bon devin' (Weiss 2002, 372, line 14,814), a diviner cited alongside Merlin and the Sibyl by Gray from Wace on f. 95, line 2 and there spelled by him as 'Quyle' (Moll 2003, 43–4 and n. 86). For the Latin and French *Prophecy of the Eagle* collection often attributed to Merlin, see Putter 2009a, 94–5.

54 **Gildas** Romano-British historian of the defense of the Britons against the Picts and Saxons, author of the *De excidio et conquestu Britanniae* (*On the ruin and conquest of Britain*) of the late fifth or early sixth century. Gildas is later referred to by Gray as an authority on the Albina story (f. 29va).

55–6 **Lez gestz dé Bretouns** Gray's title is the one early used in the manuscript tradition of Geoffrey of Monmouth's *Historia* or the *De gestis Britonum* (Reeve and Wright 2007, vii–viii, lix).

64–5 **Bede en Wermouth . . . *De gestis Anglorum*** Now better known as *The Ecclesiastical History of England* (*Historia ecclesiastica gentis Anglorum*) by the Venerable Bede of Wearmouth and later Jarrow (d. 735). King suggests that the form of the title may mean that Gray used Durham's copy of Bede's *Historia* after his release, since both the late-medieval manuscript from Durham in which it is compiled (Durham Cathedral Library B.II.35) and the 1395 Durham catalogue name the work *Beda de gestis Anglorum* (2005a, 211 n. 5).

74–5 **le moigne de Cestre . . . *Polecronicon*** Ranulph Higden, a Benedictine at St Werburga's, Chester, composed his highly successful *Polychronicon* by 1340: it was translated into Middle English and circulated widely in the fourteenth to fifteenth centuries. Moll shows that Gray must have used the earlier, shorter version to which Higden's name was not always attached (2003, 253 n. 92).

78–9 **la uniement qe le roy Egbright fist** Ecgberht, king of Wessex 802–39 temporarily ended the Mercian supremacy over England and is himself called *Bretwalda* (Ruler of Britain) in the *Anglo-Saxon Chronicle* (see e.g. Irvine 2004, entries for 800–36); so too William of Malmesbury (Mynors *et al.*, ed. and trans., 1998–9 I, 14–16); Henry of Huntingdon (Greenway 1996, 260–4) and Roger of Howden (Stubbs 1868 I, 34).

81–3 **Willam de Malmesbery, Henry de Huntingdoun, Roger de Houdene, et Mariotus le Escot** William of Malmesbury (d. in or after 1142), Henry of Huntingdon (d. *c.* 1157) and Roger of Howden (d. 1201/2) are major figures of twelfth-century insular historiography: Marianus Scotus (d. 1082), author of a universal history, was known in England chiefly through John of Worcester's use of his text.

83 **entrepretours englessez** (translators of the English; see *AND*, *s.v.* 'entrepretur'). The word may here have historically specific aspects: these are writers dealing with the centuries of English domination of Britain after the British, and they 'carry over' the materials (and hence the deeds) of the English from the English people's own records into Latin, translating the English to their Anglo-Norman successors.

90 **sure un lettroun** (lectern, desk). *OED*'s earliest citation is 1325 in the sense 'reading or singing desk' (for use in church services: see also *AND*, *s.v.* 'leitrun'). The sense 'writing desk' is not cited until the early sixteenth century, principally from Scottish examples.

92–3 **le vikeir de Tilmouth . . . *Ystoria auria*** As King points out, Tilmouth (on the Tweed near the Grays' manor of Heaton) is probably a slip for Tynemouth (King 2005a, 211 n. 7). John of Tynemouth may have been the author of the *Golden History* which imitated Higden's *Polychronicon* in being a universal chronicle, and which is intercalated with the later part of *Polychronicon* in some manuscripts. King suggests Gray may have continued to work on his chronicle using the copy of the *Historia aurea* at Durham Cathedral Priory after his imprisonment ended in November 1356 (King 2005a, xx).

103–6 ***La Vie seint Edward*** **. . . 'Non solum de gente Francorum . . .'** As King has noted (2005a, 211 n. 8) this prophecy has a close verbal parallel in Henry of Huntingdon's *Historia Anglorum*, where the prophecy, ascribed to 'a man of God' continues 'eis ad emeritam confusionem dominaretur', i.e. the Scots as well as the Normans would 'lord it over [the English] to their well-merited confusion' (Greenway 1996, 340–1). It is not clear why Gray ascribes this prophecy to the life of Edward the Confessor (the phrase *La Vie seint Edward* here may be either a formal title or simply an allusion to a biography). The Confessor (r. 1042–66) is credited with a prophetic vision of a restored royal lineage-tree moving back to its roots: this dynasty prophecy is often cited in historical writing and so offers a parallel to the kind of apocalyptic prophecy invoked by Gray. But, unsurprisingly, in neither his pre- or post-Conquest biographies is Edward represented as prophesying Norman domination. At least two French lives of Edward are known, both based on the most influential of his Latin *vitae* (Aelred of Rievaulx' *Vita sancti Edwardi*: see PL195.771–4 for the prophecy): a late-twelfth-century life by the anonymous Nun of Barking (**2**) and Matthew Paris's version, based, like the Nun's, on Aelred's *vita*, and made for Eleanor of Provence and Henry III (Fenster and Wogan-Browne 2008). Henry of Huntingdon's account in his *Historia* of the union of Norman and Saxon lineages circulated separately as prophetic material in some thirteenth-century manuscripts (Coote 2000, 129), and Gray may have had access to variant traditions and sources among his unnamed Scottish sources (King 2005a, xliv–lii). For some examples of pro-Scots prophecies (French rubrics and English texts) see the request to Thomas of Erceldoune by 'La contesse de Dunbar' as to when 'la guere d'Escoce prendreit fyn' and Erceldoun's prophecy on Edward II and Bannockburn (ed. J. Dean 1996, 11–12).

107–8 **'þat Cadwaladre sal on Conan cal'** Gray invokes, this time in English, another prophecy of eventual British return and triumph against the English: 'Cadualadrus uocabit Conanum . . .' is one of the prophecies of Merlin, early incorporated by Geoffrey of Monmouth in his *Historia* as book VII. The prophecy continues 'et Albaniam in societatem accipet' (Cadwalader shall call on Conan and make Scotland his ally [against the Saxons]; see Reeve and Wright 2007, 149, line 110). At the end of the *Historia*, however, Cadwalader, the last British king, is instructed by an angelic voice to go to Rome for absolution: the Saxons will henceforth rule England, and the return of British rule is envisaged in a distant future when Cadwalader's body will return to Britain from Rome (Reeve and Wright 2007, 280–1). For another use of the Middle English phrase see 'When Rome is Removed', line 24 (ed. J. Dean 1996).

108 **ditz de Merlyn** Merlin's prophetic career dates from Geoffrey of Monmouth's *Historia*: although sometimes omitted by writers reworking the *Historia*'s narrative as a whole, the prophecies of Merlin were rapidly given separate and wide multilingual circulation throughout the Middle Ages (on the French versions, see J. Dean 1996 18–22, Blacker 2005, and more generally Coote 2000). On contemporary medieval use of chronicles for historical precedent (notably of the prose *Brut* by Edward I), see Taylor 1987, 56–8.

114–17 **le cordeler . . . Thomas de Otreburn . . . Frers Menours** A Thomas of Otterbourne (not to be confused with the fifteenth-century historian of that name) was lector of the Franciscans in Oxford *c.* 1350, and may be the same Thomas of Otterbourne who was licensed to hear confessions in the diocese of Durham in 1343 (King 2005a, 212 n. 10). He is the probable author of a continuation from 1297 of a Franciscan chronicle extensively used both by the *Lanercost* and the *Anominalle Chronicles* (*ODNB*, *s.v.* 'Thomas of Otterbourne'). Gray's remarks here constitute the evidence for the attribution.

123–4 **tu lez doys appeller** ***Scalacronica*** The plural object pronoun *lez* refers to the chronicles comprising Gray's treatise, the chronicle rungs of the ladder.

135 **rementoyver** see *AND*, *s.v.* 'amentiver', 'amentevoir'; *DMF*, *s.v.* 'ramentevoir'.

Part III. *Primes dirrum la dreyte fei*: The Conduct of Reading, Hearing and Seeing

Introduction

Part III is a long sub-division among our entries because it is concerned with the conduct both of texts and their audiences and hence also with the various modes of access envisaged by texts and adopted by users. Many French-language texts are vitally concerned with doctrine, exemplarity, memorability and value in reading, and hence with the performative efficacy, including the entertainment value of texts, and their ethical and devotional effects. *Primes dirrum la dreyte fey* ('*First* we will rehearse the true faith', 24.13): what ought to be in texts, how texts should be ordered, the politics of access – on the page, in the language, in the choice of text-, the relation of reader and text (visually, somatically, affectively, intellectually), the politics of style, questions of verse and prose, of orality, audition, visual literacies, and performance all contribute to a wide vocabulary of topoi for the realisation of text in various dimensions and in the reception and responses of audiences.

Texts often inscribe how they are to be narrated and responded to as endemic to their meaning and performance, and a further aspect of this performed 'situatedness' in audience-text relations is the existence of a vigorous lexis of reception. Alongside verbs for writing and composing, the envisaging of the audience who will read (**lirrunt**), hear read (**orrunt**) and see (**verrunt**) texts is recurrent. Audiences should hear **volontiers** and with **delit**, should **profiter, aprendre**, gain **amendement, savor** (spiritual nourishment), **moralité, divinité** and **essample, confort, desport, doctrine, enluminement, ensensement** (instruction), **joie, manger** (nourishment [*fig.*]) or **solaz** from texts, the right kind of which they should **aimer** and by which authors should not bore (**ennuier**) them: audiences may not have full **leisir** to **parlire** or **oïr** (read or hear) texts right through and texts, as well as being **beals** (beautiful, fine) and not peddling **arveire** (deception, illusion) or **mençonge** (lies), must often be **abriggez** and work **briefment** to avoid audience **ennui**, especially if they want to be **loez** (praised), **preisee** (valued) or to please (**pleire**) and to be **cher tenuez** (cherished). Audiences should read and hear texts to gain **saveir**, do so **souvent** (recurrently), and **retenir** worthy texts **en memoire:** they should **ymaginer** as the text prompts them, **despendre** time and **mettre sa cure** (give attention to) reading them: texts will **tolir** (take away) both **ennui** and **vanité**, and can provide alternatives to the **fables d'Artur de Bretaigne** and **les chançons de Charlemaigne.**

While audiences need to **entendre** and **oïr ententivement** and often **devotement**, books (especially in the thirteenth century) should be organised so that audiences can **eslire** the **chapitre** or **perograf** they seek (**quere**) or **desirer, sanz labor** and **sanz delai**, whether they are **lais** or **clerz.** For those who want their eyes to see what their ears hear, books should represent their narratives in illustrations, says Matthew Paris (*Ke oraille ot, voient li oil*).[1]

[1] Wallace, ed., 1983, 112, v. 3966. Bolded terms here are from the Glossary, below.

In addition to the expectation of engagement with text through reading or hearing, the material culture of the book and the visual, textual, and tactile interrelations it can generate (manuscript *mise-en-page*, finding aids, systems of images and diagrams) become increasingly important for readers in the vernacular. Allegorical and diagrammatic images (such as those of (**20a**, **c**, **d**)) abound in the mnemonic practices, often monastic in origin, developed in vernacular books (and as figural schemes in buildings, stained glass and wall-painting; as inscriptions in halls, tombs, on material objects etc.). Manuscript illustration provides crucial ways of reading in the medieval book, and contributes its own theorisations and practices to the idea of the book and the text.[2] The multi-dimensionality of medieval reading has been analysed by Sylvia Huot as 'active and inventive', involving associations with related graphic imagery and a trail or penumbra of virtual texts by association and memory prompts.[3]

Many entries in this volume are realised in significant *mise-en-page*: the *Destructioun de Rome* (**18**) and the *Roman de toute chevalerie* (**28**) for instance, are designed in some of their manuscripts with a frequency of illustration worthy of a graphic novel. (These, as with some other entries, need to be seen in the digital versions on the websites noted for them).[4] Our (**20a–d**) points to this visual culture with its examples of practice and discussion. The epigraph for this entry, *a dire devant la crucifix del muster u sur crucifix peint en livre* ('to be said before the cross in church or over a cross painted in a book') comes from a popular florilegium of prayers and sententiae ascribed variously to Anselm, Bernard, Augustine.[5] It is a reminder that particular sites and objects play a role in the realisation of text that is not only conceptual (as in the architectual allegory of (**5**) and (**16**), but material. Entry (**20**) offers less well-known examples of visual theory and practice than the vernacular *locus classicus*, the prologue discussion in the *Espurgatoire saint Patrice* accredited to Marie de France and the question (out of Gregory the Great) as to whether the tortured bodies seen on journeys to purgatory and hell are corporeally visible. Still more widely distributed in insular culture is the French prose apocalypse commentary frequently found in illustrated apocalypse books (the genre represented by (**20a**) here), through which lay as well as clerical audiences might become versed in the distinctions between corporeal, spiritual ('veue espiritel[e] ou ymagenerie') or intellectual vision.[6]

An analogous form is the combination of diagrammatic representation and narrative summaries in genealogical rolls (**20c**, **d**). The material roll offers a somatic correlative for moving down the generations: its visual organisation is complemented by brief textual reminders and formulaic shortenings of historiographical narrative brought down to present day kings. Roll audiences may well have brought with them a pre-existing aware-

2 For example, Coleman, Cruse and Smith 2013: see esp. Coleman 2013, 403–37; Kumler 2011; Sandler 2014.

3 Huot 2005.

4 Further on illustrated manuscripts, see, in addition to volumes in the invaluable Survey of Manuscripts Illuminated in the British Isles, the Survey of Manuscripts Illuminated in France and especially Stones 2013.

5 Dean 942, MS Arundel 288: see also Dean 981–4. For a translation of the Arundel prologue and the following meditation on the Passion (from Dublin, Trinity College MS 374), see Boulton 2013, 141–61, and compare Wogan-Browne *et al.* 1999, no 3.1. For further examples in French see Bliss, Hunt and Leyser, ed. and trans., 2010.

6 For a widely used Apocalypse commentary see Pitts, ed., 2010. This lacks the prologue, which can be read online in e.g. Corpus Christi College Cambridge MS 394, and see Dean 475.

ness of *Brut* and other narratives of British and European history which would have been evoked by the rolls. Performative narrative artefacts as they are, the rolls constitute vigorously political representations of lineage and wider textual communities in the English and related realms.

Sound and hearing are also important dimensions for the realisation of text. Wace's Life of St Nicholas (**25a**) insists throughout that celebration of the saint be a matter of good singing and good readings.[7] A striking example of sonic power is the nightingale poem for Eleanor of Provence (*Rossignos*, **21**). Theorised in its prose prologue as a nightingale-like harmony of disparate elements designed to enkindle love in the heart of the reader or hearer, the poem's monorhymed quatrains of unusually regular syllable count create a strong forward pulse, while its abundantly punning rhymes create sensuous and intellectual connections in the very texture and sound of human language.

Some 'secular' genres, such as that of *chanson de geste* (represented in (**18**), the *Destructioun de Rome*), use a double protocol of oral performance and written authority. The *Destructioun* conducts its *geste* through a vigorous inscribed oral narrative presence even as it authenticates its material as coming directly from compilers in the Parisian abbey of St Denis (often invoked as a repository of written authority for this genre).[8] The other manuscripts of the *Destructioun* repeat the opening *laisse* (with variation and underlining of its themes), and it is also re-used in the romance of *Fierenbras*. This suggests that highly competent oral performance (perhaps the chanting intonation of jonglaresque recitation) and the authority of the book were both perceived as appropriate support for such texts. *Chanson de geste* claims a high level of historical referentiality in its relation to the past, and both aspects of this double protocol perhaps secure that claim. At the same time, a present scene of noisy sociability is inscribed in the *Destructioun*'s vigorous injunctions to silence and attention. Comparably dramatic effects are chosen in less predictable places: Herman de Valenciennes's biblical retelling (**15**), for example, uses assonanced *laisses* of flexible alexandrines, as does the anonymous Commentary on the Song of Songs (*Chant des Chanz*, **26**). Such forms are considered more characteristic of sung or recited *chanson de geste* as with the *Destructioun de Rome* (**18**), but were in fact also widely used in religious narrative (the *Poème sur l'Ancien Testament* (**43**) is a further example, this time in decasyllabics). Performative dimensions might be expected in lyric verse and for texts categorised as drama (see *La Seinte Resurreccion* (**29**)), but the affect embedded in the *laisses* and alexandrines of para-biblical narrative and commentary speak to the intensity with which texts, most of them designed for predominantly oral delivery, reach for response in their audiences.

Chant des Chanz's careful theorisation of song and its own status (**26**) is an unusually explicit witness to how thoroughly aural poetics shape medieval texts, which are as much, or more often, supported by voice and performance as by codex and roll. The epic assonances and *laisses* of the *Poème sur l'Ancien Testament* (**43**) could be thought of as the equivalent of the manuscript page lay-out discussed by Michael Camille as a 'visual

7 Blacker, Burgess, Ogden, trans. (with facing page original text) 2013, vv. 225–6, 1110, 1043, 1092, 1172, and pp. 262–4.

8 See e.g. Short, ed., 1973, 32, lines 42–6.

vernacular': an inflection of the narrative that transfers it into the world of seignurial concerns and crusading, and a reminder that, for the Middle Ages, the Bible is a highly variegated library of different genres and is frequently presented in conventions familiar to lay people.[9] So too, for all its insistence that the Virgin is uniquely fitted to sing the Song, the interwoven voices in the verse Commentary on *Chant des Chanz* (26) are a form of polyphony, a form often associated with the concord of earth and heaven.

Scriptural interpretation is discussed with particular intensity in relation to Jewish tradition. In Guillaume le Clerc's *Bestiaire divin* (27) with its regrounding of the created world in the interpretation of Genesis, the Jew, unlike the Christian ant, fails to split the 'grains' of Hebrew scripture to extract Christian truth. In spite of knowing that Jewish allegoresis existed, Christians accused Jews of literal-mindedness; this, at least, was the reason given for Jews' refusal to accept the 'truth' of Christianity. That French, as noted above, made scripture *apert* to the laity must have made it even more obvious that Hebrew did not offer such access; worse, Hebrew stood in the way of what the Christian regarded as her or his own text. How could one take possession of what one did not understand? Perhaps it was in part frustration at always being at arm's length from sources and origins, that led to the feeling among Christians that Jews willfully withheld access to Scripture. This understanding of the Jews' relationship to their holy books becomes the excuse for the supersessionary narratives that repeatedly rewrite the books, as also for the normalisation of violence (**20b**). The responses of Christian laity, on the other hand, even in the wake of Lateran IV, are sometimes a less freighted concern than they would become in late-fourteenth-century England: Edmund of Abingdon's influential *Mirour de seinte eglyse* (22) recommends an austere prayer life focused on the Pater noster and filters lay access to contemplation, but is relaxed about the oral culture in which it expects and encourages the unlettered to pick up information about scripture. At the opposite end of the scale, the *Sermons on Joshua* (23) offer highly prescriptive, well practised readings and modes of interpretation. The pressure of an entire academic curriculum of exegetical aids and distinction collections can be felt behind the *Sermons*' reworking of its source's orthodox allegorical interpretations. This is prose of a demanding order, resonant with half-heard Latin intertexts. At the same time it has affective intentions shared with the more open style of (17) and (**20b**): its re-orientation of Origen serves its critique of Judaism.

None of these concerns, however, prevent the existence of a large body of highly performative, vigorous and sometimes playful presentation of scriptural and para-scriptural materials for lay audiences. Theological encylopaedias, teaching texts and texts of affective persuasiveness abound: this is a culture of dialogue and teaching, whose didactic concerns are both deeply serious and lively, engaging, and various. An array of approaches and strategies is at once apparent in the relatively small sample of thirteenth-century teaching texts here and in other Parts: at the turn of the century, Chardri outlines a theory of narrative as a better teaching mode than exegesis in his unusually abbreviated telling of Barlaam and Josaphaz (30); Edmund of Abingdon's early-thirteenth-century *Mirour* creates a dynamic scheme of approach to God, subsuming catechesis directly and lucidly into spiritual development in austerely and classically functional prose (22);

9 Camille 1988.

Pierre d'Abernon de Fetcham's *Lumere as lais* of 1267 (**19**) enacts its cultural transfer of scholasticism to the vernacular with an elaborate Aristotelian accessus and much new French lexis, yet d'Abernon's encyclopaedic enlightenment is aimed not at knowledge per se, but at the double 'illumination' (*enluminement*, **19**.147) of learning and love: this is knowledge (whether acquired by cleric or lay) to be taken into the heart (**19**.152). It is in pursuit of this internalisation of response that the early-fourteenth-century *Enfaunces de Jesu Crist* (**20b**) praises the beauty and efficacy of mingling visual and textual representation (extending this to further dimensions of material representation if, as seems likely, it is this manuscript instantiation of the *Enfaunces* that inspired the Tring wall tiles). A major goal in the *Enfaunces* (a work probably used for teaching children) is however, the inculcation of the wickedness of the Jews as key to the formation of Christian identity. In other texts, an apocalyptic or eschatological urgency drives the argument: thus sermon 4 on Joshua (**23**) says its text is designed to instruct us, who, in a haunting phrase, live in the last days (lit. 'evening') of the world: *nus, qui somes al vespree del siecle* (**23**, lines 1–2). Matthew Paris, who thought the end of the world was presaged by the thirteenth-century Mongol invasions of Europe and that it would come in 1250, presents his St Edmund in the same way: now, after the long succession of archbishops of Canterbury, when it is *al vespre del mund* (**13**.85), Edmund appears among us (the verb is *surdre*, which also means to arise) to our comfort.

Angier's *Dialogues de saint Gregoire* (**24a**) and Waddington's *Manuel des pechiez* (**24b**), will have had oral lives in this culture, but are here chosen for the explicitness of their concern with specifically textual access. These two thirteenth-century examples (*c.* 1212/1213 and 1260 respectively) are from a period when the interactive nature of lay and clerical reading and learning cultures is more than ever marked, and marked especially by the readerly agency that has always been sought by laypeople and which became a necessary consequence of Lateran IV's mandate on individual confession. Detailed engagement with the souls and penitential status of individual parishioners was the goal of much thirteenth-century pastoral care, and a narratorial and pedagogic presence remains an important aspect of these texts. Nevertheless, if penitents are to be sufficiently self-aware, the conduct of reading must allow for their own volition and choices. Angier of St Frideswide's preface to his reworking of Gregory's *Dialogues* (**24a**) is an under-recognised *locus classicus* of these concerns. The *mise-en-page* of the extant manuscript is explicitly discussed in the text as well as enacted in the codex: it forms part of Angier's injunctions to readerly choice and self-directed reading. In the *Manuel des pechiez* (**24b**), the text promises to show (*mustrer*) sin to a reader envisaged as looking at the book (*regarder*); the book's ordering of information is expounded (*Primes dirrum la dreyte fey* (**24b**, 13)), its arrangement into subdivisions and paragraphs stressed, and the book itself as object is focused on in the explanation of its name, *Manuel* (later reworked in Robert Manning's *Handlyng Synne*; see Part VI, §2.6), and the injunction that it should be carefully read through, twice (**24b**.53). Although frequently owned and used by clergy, the *Manuel* claims to be a book made for laypeople (the clergy, it suggests, should be seeing to the rigour of their own confessional practices).

Many different long thirteenth centuries can be presented through French of England texts – as Part VI, §3 suggests and as is represented in texts throughout this volume, it is, among other things, a period of great diversity in text-types and of widening response to the European, Mediterranean and Asian world. We have chosen here to present what might initially seem the more routine fare of insular Christian formation, instruction and preoccupation. However that may be, the long twilight of Anglo-Norman in literary histories as dully didactic dissolves immediately on contact with this living, performative, strategising, vocal and sensuous literary culture.

17. Guillaume le Clerc de Normandie, *Le Bestiaire divin* [Dean 702], Prologue and extracts: New Haven, Yale University Beinecke Library, MS 395, ff. 153ʳ, 158ʳ–159ʳ

Brenna Mead

Date of composition and provenance. 1210–11, England, in the diocese of Coventry and Lichfield. Datable by its mention of Pope Innocent III's interdict of England, begun in 1208: it also refers to King John's loss of Normandy as an English possession in 1204.

Author, sources and nature of text. Guillaume le Clerc (*fl.* 1210/11–1227 × 38) was a married secular clerk, who identifies himself as from Normandy (vv. 34–6 below). He lived in England, where his known patrons were ecclesiastics of the diocese of Coventry and Lichfield. He composed at least five other French biblical, hagiographic and homiletic works. 'Radalphus' (*Raoul*) the patron whom Guillaume names as his lord in the *Bestiaire* may have been Ralph of Maidstone, treasurer of Lichfield in 1215 (later Chancellor of Oxford *c.* 1231 and bishop of Hereford, 1234–8).

The *Bestiaire*'s principal source is the *Physiologus*. This early Latin compilation of Greek animal lore (perhaps made for a fourth-century Syrian Christian community) has a vigorous textual tradition in medieval Europe, drawing on or contributing to the materials of encyclopaedias, animal fable collections, exegetical tradition, and handbooks of medicine. New versions of the *Physiologus* proliferated in French and subsequently in other European vernaculars from the twelfth century onwards, the period from which *bestiaire* dates as a genre term. Bestiaries embrace secular love allegories (*bestiaires d'amour*) and heraldic texts, but Guillaume's follows in the tradition of Philippe de Thaon (writer of a bestiary for Henry I's queen, Adeliza of Louvain), who defined the bestiary as *un livre de grammaire*, essentially a book of learning for reading God's world. Guillaume's *Bestiaire divin* begins with the book of Genesis and a rapid summary of Biblical and apostolic events: its final items are parables of eschatological implication, the parables of the talents and of the labourers in the vineyard (Matt 25:14–20 and Luke 19:12–27; Matt 20:1–6). Between come accounts and moralisations of the animals, birds, insects, trees, stones (and selected hybrids such as the mermaid or the unicorn) in God's creation. These do not simply constitute a collection or viewing gallery, but aspire rather to a categorisation of animals and other species by which humans can assert and know their own place and nature. As with many bestiaries, Guillaume's offers a site for constructing and interpreting human relations with other species and with the natural world. Guillaume's own role as author is treated in the parable of the talents: he is obliged to use God's gift of speaking well (*De faconde m'a fet Deu riche*, v. 3565), since knowledge undeployed and unshared is lost (ed. Reinsch 1890, vv. 3588–92), and his audience should remember the *Bestiaire*'s demonstrations when they look at the world and human life.

The bestiary's preoccupation with interpretation revolves around the model of Jewish reading as benightedly literal (a foundational idea for Christian exegesis in spite of the existence of allegorical Jewish biblical commentaries). The nocturnal Owl (*niticorace*, v. 6) is said to represent the Jew (*le felon Jeue maleuré*, v. 610) and to signify a preference for darkness over the true light. In the account of the ant excerpted here, Guillaume takes up the *Physiologus*'s connection between hard working ants and Christian versus Jewish exegesis. The exegetical ants are textual Christians who are said to know how to divide their metaphorical grain – to separate the letter from the spirit, a supersessionary idea that makes Christians better readers of scripture than Jews. Guillaume does not go as far as the *Physiologus* which itself literalises the killing power of the letter to make the Jews killers of Christ. Merely literal reading is, however, repeatedly countered by injunctions to look beyond the *Bestiaire*'s stories for its spiritual and salvific depths (vv. 345–50, 1113–15, 1567–74): so too, secular tales of Arthur, Charlemagne or Ogier (*D'Arthur ou de Charle ou d'Oger*, v. 565) are not food for the soul for those who could be nourished by the pelican, i.e. Christ (vv. 521–614).

Audience and circulation. Guillaume mentions a mixed courtly audience of lords, ladies and nobles (*seignors e dames, gent nobire*, v. 3427), but otherwise addresses only *seignors*, who could have been clerical or lay readers. The combination of devotion, learning and exoticism in bestiaries gave them wide appeal: their audiences included secular clergy, monks, nuns, women in lay religious lives, members of court and urban elites. Finely illustrated Latin bestiaries, Old English versions of the *Physiologus* in verse and prose, and French verse bestiaries were produced, especially in England, from the eleventh to the late thirteenth century, and continued to circulate widely thereafter (although there is only one Middle English version of the *Physiologus*, extant in the early-thirteenth-century trilingual manuscript BL Arundel 292, many late-medieval English writers draw on bestiary materials and both insular and continental French-language bestiaries continue to circulate). Guillaume le Clerc's *Bestiaire*, the longest and most popular of the French bestiaries, is extant in at least twenty-two manuscripts, ten insular and twelve continental, from the thirteenth to the fifteenth centuries, in varied formats. Some copies are rich with miniatures, others have ink line drawings only or are without illustration.

Manuscript source. Beinecke MS 395 is a large (300 × 200 mm) parchment manuscript of 224 folios, made in the late thirteenth or early fourteenth century. Latin and Middle English glosses were added in the fifteenth century. The manuscript, written by six scribes, with blue and red initials and ink drawings, sometimes of animals, contains twelve French texts, including copies of Herman de Valenciennes's *Romanz de Dieu et de sa mere* (15); the *Poème sur l'Ancien Testament* (43), Wace's *Brut*, and the Anglo-Norman version of Petrus Alfonsi's *Disciplina Clericalis* (Dean 263). In the *Bestiaire* text's layout, each verse begins with a majuscule touched with red, and each item and its gloss (*moralité*) has its own decorated initial and opening rubric.

Bibliography. The *Bestiaire* is edited by Reinsch 1890 (based on BL Egerton 613: digitised at http://gallica.bnf.fr/ark:/12148/bpt6k229216k) and translated by Druce 1936. For the origins of the *Physiologus* see Diekstra 1985. The *Physiologus* is translated in Curley 2009 who discusses the complexities of the Latin tradition (for the version supplemented from Isidore of Seville which was probably used by Guillaume, see Carmody, ed., 1939, and Badke's account of BL Royal MS 2 C.XII: http://bestiary.ca/manuscripts/manu992.htm). Guillaume's other works are listed at Dean 468, 579, 703–5 (Guillaume le Clerc, author of the *Roman de Fergus* (Dean 167), is a separate figure; see Hunt, 'William the Clerk', *ODNB*). Ruelle 1973 edits Guillaume's *Besant de Dieu*: for Guillaume's Mary Magdalen life see Russell, trans., 2012. Rossi 2005 attempts an identification of Guillaume's secular patron as Ranulf, earl of Chester, rather than Ralph of Maidstone. The early Middle English *Physiologus* is edited by Faraci 1990 (with colour plates). Important studies of bestiaries include Hassig 1995, Yamamoto 2000, collections by Clark and McMunn 1989, and Hassig 1999. Bestiary audiences are discussed by Clark and McMunn (1989, 3–4) and Hassig (1995, 5). Crane 2013 is a notable study of medieval attitudes to animals. On the politics of skin and surface in bestiary manuscripts, see Kay 2014. Lewis 1986 explores anti-Jewish images in BN MS fr. 14,696, the most lavishly illuminated version of the *Bestiaire divin*. Beinecke MS 395 is described at http://brbl-net.library.yale.edu/pre1600ms/docs/pre1600.ms395.htm. For other medieval Latin and vernacular bestiary manuscripts see Badke, *The Medieval Bestiary: Animals in the Middle Ages*: http://bestiary.ca/manuscripts/manulocshelf.htm. On figurative Christian reading see Auerbach 1984 [1959], 11–78; on Christian constructions of Jewish reading see J. Cohen 1999, Biddick 2003, and for anti-semitism in the bestiary tradition, Hassig 1999.

TEXT AND TRANSLATION

Ci comence le bestiaire en franceis [f. 153ra]

Qui ben comence et ben define,
C'est verité seue et fine
En totes overaignes en deit
Estre loez, qui qu'il soit.
Livre de bon començaille
Qui avra bone definaille
E bon dit et bone matire
Velt Gillealme en romanz escrire
De bon latin ou il le trove.
Ceste overaigne fu fete nove
El tens ke Phelippe tint France,
El tens de la grant mesestance
K'Engleterre fu entredite,
Si k'il n'i avoit messe dite,
Ne cors mis en terre sacree.
De l'entredit ne li agree
K'a ceste foiz plus endie,
Por ço que Draiture mendie
E Lealté est povre et basse.
Tote ceste chose trespasse
Gillealme, qui forment s'en dolt
K'il n'ose dire ço qu'il velt
De la tricherie que cort
En l'une et en l'autre cort:
Mais a plus halt dire se prent,
Kar en cest livre nos aprent
Natures de bestes et mours,
Non pas de totes, mais de plusors;
Ou molt avera moralité
Et bon pas de devinité;
Ou l'em p[or]ra essample prendre
De ben faire et de ben aprendre.
Rimez ert par consonancie.
Li clers f[u] nez de Normandie
Qui auctor est de cest romanz.
Or oez que dist li Normanz.
[...]

The bestiary in French begins here

It is a known and certain truth that whoever begins well and ends well ought to be praised for it in all works, whoever he may be. William wants to write a book in French from the fine Latin where he finds it, a book with a good beginning, which will have a good ending, a good message and a good subject. This work was first written during the time when Philip held France, during the great suffering when England was under interdict, so that no Mass was said or body put in consecrated ground. It does not suit the author to speak further of the interdict right now, because justice goes begging and loyalty is poor and base. William, who on that score grieves so deeply that he does not dare say what he would like about the treachery in the one and the other court, passes over the entire matter. Rather, he is engaged in a nobler discourse, for in this book he teaches us about the natures of beasts and their habits – not all of them, but many. In it, there will be many moral lessons and a good measure of theology, and example may be found of doing well and learning much. It will be rhymed through the harmony of its sounds. The clerk who is the author of this French story was born in Normandy: now hear what the Norman says.

De la formie ci comence [f. 158*va*]

[. . .]

Seignurs, pernom garde al formi [f. 158*vb*]
Ke se travaille et porvoit si
K'en esté a tant travaillé
K'en iver en tot a eisié.
Encore fet il altre cointise
Ke ne deit estre en obli mise.
Kant son forment a ajosté,
Ke durement li a costé,
Chescun grain par miliu fent
E si les garde et defent
K'il n'e[n]pire ne ne porrist
Ne que nul germe ne norrist.

[. . .]

Here begins the account of the ant

Lords, let us consider the ant, who works and plans ahead, who in summer does so much work that in winter he is completely comfortable. He does yet another clever thing, which is not to be forgotten. When he has gathered in his wheat at the cost of great effort, he splits each grain in half and carefully keeps and guards it from damage, so that it does not rot or sprout a seed.

Moralité [f. 159*ra*]

O, tu, home, k'en Deu creis,
E l'escripture entenz et veis,
Fent et devise sagement
La lettre del Viel Testament:
C'est a dire et si a entendre
Que tu ne deis mie prendre
Solonc la lettre que ocist,
Mes solonc l'esperitel dist.
Fent e devise par grant cure
Hors de la lettre la figure.
Ben sés tu que l'apostre dit
Ke la lettre tue et ocist
E li esperiz vivifie:
Ço ne deis tu oblier mie.
Li Giu ki ne volent mettre
Ne sen ne figure en la lettre,
Sunt deçu molt laidement;
Ne voient pas parfondement.
Le grein gardent trestot enter
Tant k'il porrist en lor gerner
Molt a li formiz greinor sens
Ke se porvoit issi par tens
Ke de son grein a tot le pru
Kant vient en seison et en liu.

Moral

Oh you, mankind, who believe in God, and see and hear the scripture! Crack open and distinguish the letter of the Old Testament wisely: that is, we wish it to be said and understood that you must not take it according to the letter, which kills, but according to its spiritual meaning. Break it down with great care and locate the meaning beyond the letter. You know well what the apostle says: that the letter kills and murders, but the spirit gives life. You must not forget this. The Jews, who do not want to grant meaning or symbolism to the written word, are most basely deceived; they do not see deeply. They keep the grain entirely whole until it rots in their granary. The ant has much greater sense because he provides for himself in advance, so that when the season and opportunity come, he has all the profit from his grain.

Notes

R **bestiaire** Other manuscripts give the title as *Bestiaire en franceis divin* (McCulloch 1960, 57–8).

1 **Qui** A foliate initial 'Q', opposite which is the opening rubric in red. Text edited here corresponds to Reinsch 1890, vv. 1–36, 929–60. A flourish at the bottom of f. 153ra has been shaped into a small, dog-like animal.

1–9 **Qui ben comence . . . ou il le trove** This formula, a commonplace of rhetorical handbooks, is also used by Marie de France in the prologue to her *lais*.

11 **Phelippe tint France** In 1204 King John of England lost his lands in France, which included Normandy, to Philip II of France (Philip Augustus). This meant that Guillaume's birthplace was no longer part of England.

13; 16 **entredite; entredit** The interdict was designed to punish England for King John's refusal to accept the pope's choice of Stephen Langton as archbishop of Canterbury.

24 **l'une et en l'autre cort** Perhaps the English and papal courts if not the English and French courts.

28 **Non pas de totes** The full text presents thirty-four creatures and the Diamond, symbol of Christ.

34 **f[u]** *fu* is partially obscured.

38 **formi** For the exegetical traditions associated with the ant (sometimes mapped onto Christians and heretics as well as onto Christians and Jews), see Faraci 1990, 123–35 (52–5 for the early Middle English *Physiologus*'s ants, and colour plate Fig. 4 for Bodley 602's ants).

R ***Moralité*** This rubric appears in red above each interpretive section.

50 **O, tu, home** The reading in some other manuscripts is *Tu crestiens, qui* . . . (ed. Reinsch 1890, v. 941). The lack of religious specificity of *home* allows the text to be addressed to a broad audience, which could have included Jews. MS 395 also contains the *Disciplina clericalis* of Petrus Alfonsi, a convert who wrote to persuade other Jews to accept Christianity.

57–61 **Mes solonc . . . ocist** These lines do not appear in Reinsch's 1890 edition based on Egerton 613.

59 **figure** On *figura* and the reading of Old Testament stories and symbols as prefigurations of Christian tales, see Auerbach 1984, 11–76; Biddick 2003, 1–20.

60 **apostre** Paul, 2 Cor 3.6.

61 **la lettre tue et ocist** According to the *Physiologus* at this point, the Jews, 'regarding the letter alone, perished with hunger and became murderers of the prophets and God' (trans. Curley 2009, 21–2). Some Christian exegetes believed it was the misinterpretation of Hebrew prophesies that had led to the murder of Christ, with the result that exegetical practice could be used as justification for anti-semitic persecution (Hassig 1995, 147).

18. *La Destructioun de Rome* [Dean 82.1], Prologue: London, British Library, MS Egerton 3028, f. 64^{r-v}

Date of composition and provenance. Mid-thirteenth-century Anglo-Norman rewriting of a *chanson de geste* of the Charlemagne cycle; composed first on the continent.

Author, sources and nature of text. The discoverers, translators and revisers of the *Destructioun de Rome* are said to be Walter of Douai (v. 7), about whom nothing is known, and a deceased *roy Lawis* (v. 8), whose possible identity has provoked much speculation but little consensus. They are envisaged as working on a text kept in the abbey of St Denis, outside Paris. The Egerton manuscript text used here is an abridged version (990 verses) of the *Destructioun*, which in its only other extant copy (Hanover, Staatsbiliothek MS IV.578, also an insular manuscript), is 1507 verses long. In both the fuller Hanover manuscript and the shorter Egerton text the care to establish a written precedent for what the *Destructioun* presents as an oral performance is significant. Epic may offer a 'representation of orality [that] appears to be the voice of tradition speaking the past', but 'whatever its prehistory, the medieval epic as we have it is a written artifact, aware of itself as such in a highly literate world' (Stein 2006, 172).

In its prologue the *Destructioun* refers to itself as both a *chançon* (v. 3) and an *estoire* (vv. 6, 10). These suggest 'story', but *chançon* and *estoire* have additional valences: *chançon* can imply performance, whether sung or recited, and promises a tale at whose core is a conflict that will engender one or more military encounters. The term *estoire*, meaning both 'history' and 'story', buttresses the poem's claim to be a tale 'translated', 'put together' and initially 'written' at St Denis in France.

Like many *chansons de geste*, the *Destructioun* moves in a system of allusion and relation to other epic narratives and figures, focused around Charlemagne. The *Destructioun* is a prequel to the *Chanson de Fierabras* (*c.* 1170), perhaps the best known of the Charlemagne poems in England, and thus part of a sub-cycle on the Passion relics alongside *Fierabras* and *Le Voyage de Charlemagne à Jérusalem et à Constantinople* (the account of a fictional pilgrimage to bring the relics to Europe). In the *Destructioun*, the sultan Laban and his son Fierabras sack and destroy Rome, and flee with relics of the Passion: in *Fierabras* Charlemagne and his Franks recover the relics, and Fierabras converts to Christianity after being defeated by Oliver (companion of Roland in the *Chanson de Roland*). The effective leader in regaining the relics is the Saracen princess Floripas, who like others of her type, also marries the (Christian) man of her choice. (Kay 1995 showed that *chansons de geste* do not portray an all-male universe, and that love stories are not late entrants to *chanson de geste* from romance, since, with very few exceptions, both forms existed simultaneously). The prologue strategies of the epic inscribe a particular 'historic' relation to the matter the poems narrate, but this is not evidence that the *chanson de geste* is historically antecedent to romance, and the Saracen princess is found in both genres.

AUDIENCE AND CIRCULATION. The scant direct evidence for the *Destructioun*'s audience belies what was probably a relatively vigorous dissemination. The French texts survive in very few manuscripts (the *Destructioun* is extant in two, as is its sequel *Fierabras*, and the *Voyage de Charlemagne* in one, all of them Anglo-Norman copies of presumed continental originals). There is a significant reworking of French-language epic in Middle English narrative romances, however: the *Destructioun* becomes the *Sowdone of Babylone* and its *Fierabras* sequel is translated at least twice in the last quarter of the fourteenth century (the Ashmole and Fillingham *Fierabras* respectively). The possible copying of both the French and the Middle English Ashmole version of *Fierabras* in the south-west of England suggests relatively far flung dissemination. Epic has been perceived as an underrepresented genre in insular culture, but this may be because the capaciousness of Anglo-Norman romance accommodates the functions of epic. By the mid-thirteenth century, insular manuscripts cease to make codicological distinctions between romance and epic (Busby 2002, I. 502): the insular audience for the passion relics cycle is likely to have overlapped with that for romance.

The texts themselves inscribe secular oral and written transmission, with written transmission via monasteries, and in practice monasteries did own and copy *chansons de geste*. The *Destructioun* claims St Denis as its textual preserver and the sequel *Fierabras* was written under the influence of the monks of St Denis and disseminated by the abbey; it was declaimed by minstrels each year at the important commercial fair of Lendit (Le Person 2011, 225–6). Copies of *Fierabras* are recorded in the earl of Warwick's donation, *c.* 1305, of books to Bordesley Abbey and in Dover Priory (Sinclair 1993, 362–4). The French *Fierabras* had a continuing career in England: a continental version is included in the manuscript presented by John Talbot, earl of Shrewsbury to Margaret of Anjou for her marriage to Henry VI in 1445 (BL Royal MS 15 E.VI, ff. 25–85*v*, the 'Shewsbury Book').

Manuscript source. BL Egerton 3028, 197 × 121 mm, parchment, contains an acephalous text of Wace's *Roman de Brut*, continued to the time of Edward III and the Hundred Years War, the *Destructioun de Rome* and *Fierabras*. It was probably prepared 1338–40 (Busby 2011), possibly in the Gloucestershire-South Wales border area (Brandin 1938, n. 1). Fifty-three miniatures accompany the *Brut*: the *Destructioun* has twenty and *Fierabras* thirty-five. A full-page portrait of Fierabras (at f. 63^{v}) precedes the opening of the *Destructioun*, and one of Charlemagne (f. 83^{v}) prefaces that of *Fierabras* (f. 84^{r}), each text beginning with a similar large decorated blue initial and the text's call for silence. The illustrations, placed on the recto of each folio, are frequent enough to serve as a guide to the text, so that the manuscript may have been useful to people for looking at, hearing, or reading the narrative, or for combinations of these modes. The selection of works in the manuscript is aligned with the *chanson de geste*'s claims to historicity: they form a sequence of legendary British and crusading history, ending with Charlemagne's taking the relics back to Paris.

Bibliography. Brandin 1938 is the only modern edition of the Egerton *Destructioun de Rome*. The Hanover manuscript version has been edited three times: Formisano 1990 is a semi-diplomatic transcription; Formisano 1981 a reconstruction; Speich 1988 edits and translates into modern French and summarises scholarship. For the manuscripts of the other Anglo-Norman witnesses to the Passion relics cyle, see Dean 80, 82.2. Busby 2011 is a thorough dating and discussion of the Egerton manuscript and its illustrations. For the Egerton manuscript, see http://www.bl.uk/catalogues/illuminatedmanuscripts/ILLUMIN.ASP?Size=mid&IllID=11752

Boutet 1987 studies Egerton 3028 in comparison with its presumed continental original. For the question of *chanson de geste* in England see Ailes and Hardman 2008, Busby 2002, 500–9 and Short 2007a, 350–60. Smyser 1967 details the reworking of French epic into Middle English romances: for the Middle English *Sowdane of Babylon* and *Fierabras* (*Sir Ferumbras*); see Part VI, §2.4. The French *Fierabras* is edited in Le Person 2003, translated into modern French in Le Person 2012 and studied in Ailes 2003 and 2008 and Boutet 1987. On the interrelations of *chanson de geste* and romance see Kay 1995, Stein 2006, esp. 167, Ailes 2011; Busby 2002, I.370–1: for Christian-'Saracen' cultural conflict Camille 1989. On *chanson de geste* and monasteries see e.g. A. Taylor 2001, 2002, (**24a**) below, and for vernacular texts in monasteries, Pouzet 2004, 2009.

TEXT AND TRANSLATION

Seignurs, ore fetes pees, franke gent honoree!
Gardez qe il n'i ert noise ne corouce ne mellé,
Si orrez bone chançon, de bien enluminé;
N'i avera fable dit, ne mensonje prové.
Nuls de les autres jugelours qels le vous ont cuntee
Ne sevent de l'estoire vailliant un darré,
Mais Gauter de Doway od la chier membré
Et li roy Lawis dunt l'alme est trespassé –
Ke li face pardoun la virge honoré!
Par luy et par Gauter fu l'estoire auné
A Saint Denis de France escrit et translaté.

Lords, honoured noblemen, silence! See that there is no brawling or anger or quarreling and you'll hear a fine song, made luminous by its good content. It will be no fable, no patent lie. None of the other minstrels who have told it to you knew the story even a penny's worth, except wise Walter of Douay and King Louis, whose soul has passed on – may the revered Virgin grant him pardon! The story was compiled, written down and translated by him and by Walter at [the monastery of] St Denis of France.

Desormais vous dirray, seignurs, la verité
Com la cité de Rome fu destruit et guasté
Par Laban d'Espaigne, li soldan maleuré,
Et par Fierenbras, sun fiz, li vassals redouté.
Les relikes en robbierent Jhesu de majesté
Les clowes et la corone et l'ensigne honoré
Et la launce dunt Dieux out le queor percié.
Ellas! mar les pristrent, car chier ert comparé,
Kar pur cele bris fu puis mainte teste coupé
Mainte poigne et braz et maint membre trenché
Mainte alme as paiens hors de sun corps saché
Par le roy Charles de France, li fort coroné.

Starting now, lords, I shall tell you the truth about how the city of Rome was destroyed and laid waste by Laban of Spain, that wretched sultan, and by his son Fierabras, the redoubtable warrior. They stole the relics of sovereign Jesus, the nails and the crown and the honoured sign, and the lance that pierced his heart. Alas! it was to their misfortune that they took them. The theft was paid dearly, for many a head was severed on account of that destruction, many a wrist and arm and many a limb sliced off, and many a pagan's soul drawn from his body by King Charles of France, the powerful ruler.

Cil amena grant ost et mult beal assemblé,
Rollant et Oliver, qi tant furent preisé,
Duc Neimes de Baver et Ogier l'aduré
Danz Gy de Burgoine et Terri l'onuré,
Foukes et Alloris et Neiron li barbé,
Genes et Berard, qi sunt mult redouté, [f. 64b]
Et danz Brier de France et tote li douze pier.
Les relikes en recunquist, si les mena arere;
Par els fist maint eglise en France honurer.
Ore m'escotez, seignurs, barons et chivaler:
Si vous dirray coment le contek muet primer.

He brought a great host and a very fine army: Roland and Oliver, who were so highly valued, Duke Naimes of Bavaria and battle-hardened Ogier, Sir Guy of Burgundy, Alloris, and the honourable Terry, Fulkes and Neron the bearded, Genes and Berard, who are greatly feared, and Sir Brehier of France and all the twelve peers. They recaptured the relics and brought them back; through them many churches in France were honoured. Now listen to me lords, barons and knights: I shall tell you how the fighting first began.

Notes

1 **Seignurs . . . honoree** *Fierabras* begins with the same apostrophe to the audience; see Le Person 2003, 237.

5–6 **Nuls . . . darré** The second *laisse* of the Hanover manuscript insists on this point, saying that even if there were a gathering of ten thousand other jongleurs, the narrator would cheerfully dare to tell them that they know nothing of the story (Formisano 1990, vv. 44–6).

6–10 **estoire** The Hanover manuscript prologue, which continues into a second *laisse*, specifies that the *chanson* is *de droit estoire* (from a truthful story); this further stresses that the written poem preceded its oral recitation: Formisano 1990, v. 41.

7–11 **Mais Gauter . . . translaté** The prologue to *Fierabras* says that the story had been *drescie, esprise et alumee* (prepared and illuminated) from a scroll in the church of Denis (*rolles de l'eglise*), where it remained for one hundred and fifty years (Le Person 2003, 237, v. 6).

8 **roy Lawis . . . trespassé** Louis IX (St Louis) ruled from 1226 to 1270 and presumably was alive when the poem was first composed. Formisano (1981, 194) tentatively suggests *Lawis* as King Louis the Pious (d. 840), son of Charlemagne: the poem could plausibly be based on the sack of Rome in 846. Speich proposes Louis the Pious as one of the poem's authors and notes that *roi* was also used of the 'president' of a corporation of jongleurs (1988, 326, 233).

10 **Par luy et par Gauter** As against the *Destructioun*'s account of written and oral transmission, the Hanover prologue envisages a third layer when it mentions *cil que la chancon fist* (he who wrote the song) as a man who kept it safe for a long time, sought no gain, and never performed it in a noble court (Formisano 1990, vv. 14–19). For Hanover there is thus an author, possibly envisaged as a cleric who wrote in Latin; the editors and compilers, Louis and Walter; and, finally, the narrator of the *Destructioun*.

14 **Laban** The name Laban may be an echo of the biblical Laban of Gen 19–20, whose household gods are famously stolen by his daughter Rachel. Christian criticism of Muslims on the grounds of idolatry is a theme of the *Destructioun* and *Fierabras*; it is the subject of the illustration that appears as the *Destructioun* moves from the prologue to the story itself (at the bottom of f. 64^{v}). Column a shows four kings, identifiable by their crowns, making an offering of birds to their devil-like idols; just above the frame, the lines of text explain that Laban and his men have gone off to their temple to make an offering to Tervagant and Apollo: see (http://www.bl.uk/catalogues/illuminatedmanuscripts/ILLUMIN.ASP?Size=mid&IllID=11754).

17 **ensigne** Egerton 3028 is alone among French versions of the poem to give *ensigne*; elsewhere the fourth relic is a *signe*, sign, or *suaire*, shroud, which in the Hanover manuscript is the shroud in which Christ was enveloped when he was taken down from the cross (Formisano 1990, 3, vv. 26–7).

26 **Neimes de Baver et Ogier** The names of the Twelve Peers of France vary from text to text. Duke Naimes of Bavaria was one of the peers and Charlemagne's most trusted advisor; Ogier the Dane appears first in the *Chanson de Roland* and is later the subject of further adventures.

27 **Danz Gy de Burgoine et Terri** In *Fierebras* Guy is taken prisoner by the emir Balan, which is how Balan's daughter Floripas, sister to Fierabras, meets him. Terri is Tierri of Ardennes, who in the *Song of Roland* is sent by Charlemagne to Balan to claim the imprisoned Franks, among them Guy, but is himself taken prisoner.

28–30 **Foukes . . . Alloris . . . Neiron li barbé . . . Genes . . . Berard . . . danz Brier de France** These knights, not mentioned in the Hanover manuscript, appear to be idiosyncratically attached to the group of Charlemagne's most valued warriors.

19. Pierre d'Abernon de Fetcham, *Lumere as lais* [Dean 630], Prologue extract: Dublin, Trinity College MS 209 (B.5.1), ff. 111*ra*–112*ra*

Cathy Hume

Date of composition and provenance. Begun in Newark Priory and completed in Oxford, 1267, according to a colophon in the York manuscript of the text.

Author, sources and nature of text. The author names himself as 'Peris' (v. 20) in the extract below, and is described in two manuscripts of the *Lumere* as 'de Feccham' or 'de Pecchame'. In his two other known works, the *Secré de secrez* and the Life of St Richard, bishop of Chichester of 1276–7, he says that he is associated with the 'de Abernun' family. Accordingly, he is known as Pierre d'Abernon de Fetcham. Completion of the *Lumere* in Oxford is thought to suggest that the author was an Augustinian canon who received university training. He died in 1293, leaving a collection of canon and civil law books.

The extract given here comes from Pierre's 694-line Prologue to his vernacularised theological encyclopedia, which he entitles *Lumere as lais* (v. 140). It is named after his principal source, Honorius's *Elucidarium* of *c.* 1100 (identified as *Lucidarie*, v. 98). Pierre claims to have written primarily for lay readers (vv. 157–8), and in the passage immediately before the extract here, he laments the ignorance and impiety of many contemporary priests, whose crucial role in teaching Pierre describes. He goes on to explain that he wrote his book for people to learn the proper way to God by reading his work, or hearing it read. This allows for a lay audience independent of the priest – and it seems to be broadly conceived. At the end of the treatise Pierre even envisages his audiences as *veuz e joefnes, femmes e enfauntz* (old and young, women and children, v. 13,954). In the course of the text he treats many questions that might be presumed both to interest a general audience and to require answers from priests engaged in pastoral care. These include the gender of God (vv. 817–27), how the body can be in heaven (vv. 1725–84), whether childbirth would have been painful in Paradise (vv. 2109–10), the Augustinian question of whether sex in Paradise would have been pleasurable (vv. 2859–98), why children born Christian need baptism (vv. 2823–58), how pagans, Jews and Christians sin in different ways (vv. 2295–326), etc. Even though the questions are briskly dismissed with orthodox replies, they can be seen as indirect but vivid witnesses to lay concerns and to the points at which lay questioning exerted pressure on clergy.

The *Lumere* is remarkably different, however, from other contemporary treatises for direct or indirect audiences of laypeople, such as Edmund of Abingdon's *Mirour de seinte eglyse* (**22**), the *Manuel des pechiez* (**24b**) or Grosseteste's *Chasteau d'amour* (**5**). Not only does it extend to 13,960 lines, but Pierre takes an academic approach to his project. The *Lumere*'s question and answer format reflects the catechetical form of the *Elucidarium*, but also draws on the university disputations at Notre Dame in 1156–8 summarised in Pierre's other major source, Peter Lombard's *Sentences* (the standard text for university theological study in the thirteenth century). Although the *Sentences* spawned a host of abbreviations in prose and verse, the *Lumere* represents its first adaptation from Latin into French. Pierre makes use of other authorities beyond his two major sources, and indicates this with scholarly care, though not all his sources have yet been identified.

The *Lumere* opens with prayer to the God who made light on the first day and an account of creation, fall and redemption (vv. 1–404: cf. (**17**), *Le Bestiaire divin*), the transience of life on earth and the necessity of proper learning and teaching in finding the true path to heaven (vv. 405–530). The extract given here corresponds to vv. 531–694 in Hesketh 1996–2000, and demonstrates both Pierre's scholastic preoccupation with order, which he sees as divine in origin and as a crucial element of understanding texts, and his scholastic approach to literary theory. Pierre discusses his text in terms of the Aristotelian four causes – formal; efficient; material; and final, which he subdivides into general, special and personal – in a manner like that of academic Latin prologues of similar date, but much less common in the vernacular. Hesketh 1997 shows that Pierre's vernacular project requires him to innovate, borrowing many previously unattested words into the French language and coining some himself. (For an extended Aristotelian prologue in Middle English, see Bokenham *Legendys of Hooly Wummen*, Wogan-Browne *et al.* 1999, 1:11).

AUDIENCE AND CIRCULATION. The academic apparatus and tone of the work might suggest a crib for university students, or, especially given Pierre's emphasis on its usefulness for priests, a handbook for priests who were only semi-Latin-literate. The *Lumere* contains much information on the eucharist and penance arguably more directly useful to priests than to laity and in conformity with Grosseteste's requirements for the education of parish priests following the Fourth Lateran Council in 1215 and the Council of Oxford in 1222 (Hessenauer 1995, 384–5). Yet Pierre's major source, the *Elucidarium*, is a relatively simple work in Latin prose, written for ease of comprehension, and popular both in its original form and its many other translations and adaptations into vernaculars, and whatever Pierre's original intentions, his text reached lay and female readers as well as clerics. There are at least twenty manuscripts of the *Lumere*, including fragments, and it continued to be copied throughout the fourteenth century. One beautifully illustrated early-fourteenth-century manuscript, BL Royal 15 D.II (http://www.bl.uk/catalogues/illuminatedmanuscripts/) pairs the *Lumere* with a French prose *Apocalypse* (Dean 475), and was owned by Cecilia Welles (d. 1507), a daughter of Edward IV, and by her father-in-law John Welles before her. At least one monastic copy of the *Lumere* is recorded from the fifteenth century (see Legge 1929, 41 n. 4).

Unlike *Le Livre de Sydrac* and other adaptations of the *Elucidarium*, the *Lumere* was not later translated into Middle English (though it has a predecessor in a partial English translation of Honorius, extant in a mid-twelfth-century manuscript, ed. Warner 1917). As with the fact that the *Lumere* survives mainly in copies from monastic libraries, this contributes to the impression that it was mostly read or heard by an elite audience.

MANUSCRIPT SOURCE. Dublin Trinity College 209 (B.5.1) is a fourteenth-century manuscript in which the *Lumere* is paired in identical formatting with *Le Livre de Sydrac*, an enormously popular text, probably originally written around the end of the thirteenth century in France. *Sydrac*, too, is an encyclopedia in dialogue form, and, like the *Lumere*, it draws heavily on Honorius's *Elucidarium*, although it ranges over science as well as theology (see also (**22**), Manuscript Source). Though less systematic than the *Lumere*, many of *Sydrac*'s questions are of equally keen interest to laypeople and religious. The manuscript of these two encyclopedias may have been compiled for or commissioned by a nunnery: an inscription of *c.* 1400 states: 'Iste liber constat domine Johanne Kyngeston, abbatisse de Tarent', and Tarrant Keynston in Dorset, a wealthy Cistercian convent, did indeed have an abbess of that name in 1402 (Bell 1995, 210).

BIBLIOGRAPHY. The *Lumere* is ed. Hesketh 1996–2000, who does not, however, make use of this manuscript for his edition. Beckerlegge 1944 edits Pierre's *Secré* and Russell 1995 his *Vie de seint Richard Evesque de Cycestre.* On Pierre's career see Hesketh 1996–2000, III.1–5 and *ODNB*. Hesketh discusses Pierre's lexical innovations, which extend beyond the academic terminology found in this extract (Hesketh 1997). For the nature of the *Lumere*, its sources and contexts see Hesketh 1996–2000, III.15–18; Hessenauer 1989 (Hessenauer 1995 is an English-language summary). On the versions and dissemination of the *Elucidarium* see Flint 1988, esp. 179–83; Hartung 1967, III.741–2; Ruhe 1993; Rosemann 2004, 201–4. Minnis 1984 discusses the Aristotelian prologue: Latin examples are to be found in Minnis and Scott 1988. For an important study of the poetry of knowledge, including verse encyclopaedias and the *Lumere*, see Armstrong and Kay 2011. For the vivacity of the *Lumere* as didactic literature, see Waters 2012. Wogan-Browne 2005a discusses female audiences for the *Lumere*. For important studies of specific manuscripts of the *Lumere*, their images and audiences, see Sandler 2012a, 2012b. For Augustinian canons and their vernacular books and compositions see Pouzet 2004, 2009. For the multilingual dissemination of the *Elucidarium* see Sarah James and Huw Grange, 'Spreading the Light: Mapping the Vernacular *Elucidarium* in Medieval England': http://www.huwgrange.co.uk/elucidarium.html.

TEXT AND TRANSLATION

Cink choses sunt a enquere [f. 111ra]
Al comencement en livre fere:
Ky fust autour e l'entitlement,
E la matire, e la forme ensement,
E la fin; c'est par quel reson
Fust [faite] la composicion.

There are five things to ascertain, and to be done, at the beginning of a book: who was the author, the title and the subject matter, and, similarly, the form and the end: that is, for what reason it was composed.

De cel livre si est autour
Principalment Nostre Seignur,
Kar a ceo ne sui joe verraiment
For son notour e estruement,
Kar ceo k'en pensee me fist lire
Mis ai en ceste livre par escrire.
Ki qe veut enquere de mon noun,
Un clerk sui de petit renoun;
De poy de value verreiment
Endreit dul corps e d'entendement.
Mez pur ceo qe preere me puet valer
De bone gent, si me voil nomer,
Dunt jeo pri pur amur Jhesu Crist:
Pur Peris priez qi cest livere fist.
Quant l'en l'out, ne grevera mie
Pater noster dire e Ave Marie.

The author of this book is principally Our Lord, because as far as this is concerned, I am truly nothing but his scribe and instrument: what he directed my thoughts to read, I have put down in writing in this book. If anyone wants to ask my name, I am a cleric of little renown; of little value, in truth, in terms of my body and mind. But because the prayer of good people can assist me, I want to give my name and ask, for the love of Jesus Christ, that you pray for Peter who made this book. When the book is heard, it will not do any harm at all to say a Pater noster and an Ave Maria.

Le suget de cest livre, ou la matire –
Si puet home verreiment dire –
Ke est Jhesu Crist Nostre Seignur,
Ke est creature e creatour
Quant a la deité, quant a la nature.
Humeine si est creature,
Car cest livre est de Dieu verrement
E de sa creature ensement, [f. 111rb]
Pur ceo quant creature fuit savee
Par Jhesu Crist e rechatee
De lur pecché e de lur peine
Issi, come le livre enseigne,
Bien poum dunqe par reson dire
Ke Jhesu Crist en est matire,
Kar quanque est en cest livre trové
A luy, come a chief, est ordiné.
Kar pechez enseigne pur eschure;

The subject of this book, or the matter – as one may truly say – is Jesus Christ Our Lord, who is created and creator in terms of divinity and nature. As a creature, he is human, because, in truth, this book is at the same time about God and about his creation. But since creation was saved by Jesus Christ and redeemed from sin and suffering here, as the book teaches, we can therefore say correctly and with reason that Jesus Christ is the matter of it: because everything that is found in this book is ordered in relation to him as its origin; because it teaches about sins, for the sake of avoiding them; and man

E les biens q'enseigne deit home sure,
Dunt tut receit ordeinement
De Jhesu Crist, quanque al livre apent –
Dunt les pecheurs a derein punira
E as bons reguerdonera.

La forme, ou la cause formele,
En chesqun livre deit estre tele
Ke l'en deit la manere saver,
Come l'en poet faitement aver
Des parties noumbre e conisance:
De saver en ert plus asseurance.

Les parties principals nomez
Ai, en sis livrez ordinez.
Le premer est de Nostre Seignur,
Ke est verrei Dieu e creatour.
Le secund est de sa creature:
Ordre resemble e dreiture.
E pur ceo qe creature peccheit,
De pecchez est le tierz livre adreit.
E pur ceo qe tote nature humeyne
Par pecché perist, e alast en peine,
E de ceo fust nostre rechatour
Jhesu Crist, e nostre curour,
Dunt reson le doune e ordre dreit
Ke le quart livre de luy seit,
Come de sa seinte incarnacion
E de sa seintime passion
E de autre choses qe a luy apendent.
Sicome resons la se rendent.
E pur ceo qe Jhesu Crist Nostre Seignur
Est nostre mire e nostre curour,
E pus qe mire oevre par medicine,
Le quint livre est par ceste covine
De medicine des sept sacrementz, [f. 111*va*]
Dunt il cure qe bien creient gentz.
E pur ceo q'il veut les bons saver
E les maus peccheurs dampner
Al derein jour de jugement,
Pur ceo le derein livre verreiment,
Ke entre les autres est sime dit,
Est dul jour de juyse escript,
E dé peines, e dul turment
Ke averunt la dampné gent,
E de la joie q'en le ciel averunt
Ces qi avaunt deservi le unt.

ought to follow the virtues that it teaches, all of which are ordered by Jesus Christ, inasmuch as they are dealt with in the book – by these means he will punish sinners at the end and reward the good.

The form, or the formal cause, in every book should be such that one knows the mode, so that one can number the parts and understand them: in that way there will be a greater guarantee of knowledge.

I have named the principal parts and arranged them in six books. The first is about Our Lord who is true God and creator. The second is about his creation, which resembles order and justice. And, because creation sinned, the third book is properly about sin. And because all human nature would have perished and fallen into suffering through sin if Jesus Christ, who gave us reason and proper order, had not been our redeemer and healer, the fourth book should be about him, as it is about his blessed incarnation and his blessed Passion and other things that relate to him, insofar as explanations are given there. And because Our Lord Jesus Christ is our doctor and our healer, and since a doctor works through medicine, the fifth book is about the medicine of the seven sacraments, with which he saves the people who truly believe. And because he wants to save the good and damn the bad sinners on the final Day of Judgement, for this reason, truly, the last book (which is said to be sixth among the others) is written about the Day of Judgement, and about suffering, and about the torment that the damned people will have, and about the joy that those who have deserved it beforehand will have in heaven.

Les principales parties ai nomez
Ke en sis livres sunt distinctez,
Mez chesqun livre nepurquant en sei
Est destincté en bone fei
Par chapitres e distinctions,
Si come en rubriche demoustroms,
Dunt come disciple mout questions
E pus come mestre en faz respouns
Soulom ceo qe Dieu m'enseygne
Par ses escritures e reson meyne:
Car plus i ad solas, ceo semble,
Quant deus s'entredalient ensemble.

I have named the principal parts, which are divided into six books, but each book nevertheless is faithfully differentiated itself through chapters and subsections, as we show in rubrics where, as disciple, I pose the question and then, as master, I respond to them according to what God teaches me through his Scriptures and by means of reason: because there is more pleasure, it seems, when two debate together.

Le premer livre en alqun endreit
Est dul *Lucidarie* estreit.
Mes pus qe joe m'aparcevoie
Ke mesprist en pointz, ne voloie
Par fins de cest liveret treter.
Einz comencé ai en autres estudier,
E moveie les questions
Ke sunt escript, e les resons
Donai com Dieu m'enseigneit,
E come aillurs escript esteit.
Taunt suffist de la cause formele:
Ore fait a dire de la finele.

The first book is drawn in part from the *Elucidarium*. But because I realised that it was mistaken in some details, I did not want to write only within the limits of this little work. Rather, I started to study others and posed the questions that are written and gave the explanations as God taught me and as it had been written about elsewhere. That is enough of the formal cause: now it is time to speak of the final.

La fin est dit verraiment
Dieu meismes principalment,
Kar fin est e perfecion
De ceo q'en cest livre entendom.
Autre fins nepurquant ount,
Mez a ceste totes ordinez sunt:
Une fin i ad, bien sai e crei,
Ke est fermeté de nostre fey, [f. 111vb]
Kar nostre fei issi saunz dutaunce
Ver le ciel adresce nostre creaunce,
E cest livre verreiment
La veie enseigne qi garde en prent.

The end is said, indeed, to be God himself principally, because he is the end and the perfection of what we learn in this book. Nevertheless, there are other ends, but all are ordered to this: there is one end, I know well and believe, which is a certainty of our faith, because without a doubt our faith here directs our belief towards heaven, and this book truly teaches the way to him who pays attention to it.

Estre ceo une fin generale
I ad, e une autre especiale.
La tierce est propre entendue:
Dieu me doint qe me seit tendue.
La generale est, verraiment,
Ke jeo voudrai qe tote gent
En fussent trestouz amendez
Ke l'averunt oÿ ou regardez.
L'especial fin qe mon quoer sent

Apart from this there is a general purpose, and another known as the particular purpose, followed by the third, understood as the personal purpose: God grant that it be given to me. The general end is, indeed, that I wish that all people who will hear or see the book may be completely reformed by it. The particular end that my heart feels is the true ease and improvement of my particular

Est pur solaz e mendement
De mes especials amis:
C'est la reson pur quei le fiz.
La propre fin est q'entenge en sun
Ke Dieu me face remission
De mez pecchez, e qe meillure grace
En puisse aver de ver sa face.

De cest livre est l'entitlement –
Ceo m'est aviz assez proprement,
Soulom ma petite science –
'La lumere a lais ici comence.'
'Lumere a lais' l'ay nomé
Pur ceo q'en poent estre enluminé;
Ne mie pur ceo, verraiment,
Ke clers ne pount ensement
Estre enluminez par regarder,
Endreit de saver e endreit d'amer,
Kar duble i ad enluminement –
De saver e de amer ensement.
De saver, car meuz en savera
Choses qe avant aparceu ne a;
Enluminé puet estre d'amur
Ki en quoer le prent ver Nostre Seignur,
Pur ceo en pount, en veritez,
Clers e lais estre enluminez.
Mez pur ceo l'ai nomé sanz fable
'A lais' pur ceo qe fraunceis est entendable;
'La lumere a lais' car principaument
L'ay fait pur lais verraiment;
E pur ceo le fis en tiel langage [f. 112*ra*]
K'il en puissent estre le plus sage
E qe meuz conustre Nostre Seignur
Puissent, e aver ver luy amur.
Dieu lur doynt a ceo sa grace,
E a mei ausi le face.

friends: it is the reason for which I wrote it. The personal end is that I understand, all in all, that God may give me remission of my sins, and that through it I may have better grace to see his face.

The opening title of this book is – this is my view, quite personally, according to my poor understanding – '"The Light for Laypeople" begins here'. I have named it 'Light for Laypeople' because they can be illuminated through it: not, indeed, that clerics cannot be likewise illuminated by looking at it, in terms of knowledge and in terms of love, because there is double illumination – of knowledge and, similarly, of love. Of knowledge because through it one will have a better knowledge of things that one has not previously perceived; and he who takes it into his heart towards Our Lord can be illuminated by love, and, in truth, clerics and laypeople can be illuminated through it. But it's no lie that I have called it 'for Laypeople' for this reason: because French is comprehensible; and 'The Light for Laypeople' because I made it principally for the laity in truth; and therefore I made it in such language that they may be the wiser for it and that they may know Our Lord better, and love him. May God give them his grace for this, and also do the same for me.

Notes

1 **Cink choses** Pierre specifies five rather than the usual four causes found in the so-called Aristotelian prologue, which were the efficient cause (i.e. author), the matter, form, and final cause (Minnis 1984, 28). His addition is title – something that was found in the more elaborate prologue form often called Type C (Minnis 1984, 19–20). Pierre's approach reflects Minnis's observation that there were 'many possible permutations' of the exact terminology any given author used (Minnis and Scott 1988, 198). It also anticipates the hybrid approach Bokenham takes in the mid-fifteenth century, combining four causes with the questions 'what?' and 'why?' (see Wogan-Browne *et al.* 1999, 1:11).

6 **faite** MS *faire.*

7–8 **si est autour . . . Nostre Seignur** The assertion that God was the true author and the human author no more than the scribe spread from prologues to books of the Bible to other theological works. Similar assertions are made in Robert of Basevorn's *Forma praedicandi* (1322) and Pierre Bersuire's *Reductorium morale* (begun *c.* 1322; Minnis and Johnson 2005, 408–9).

10 **notour e estruement** St Bonaventure asserts, in his Commentary on Lombard's *Sentences*, that there are four ways of writing: someone who 'writes out the words of other men without adding or changing anything' is a *scriptor* (scribe), whereas someone who puts together material is a *compilator*; a *commentator* adds his own words to clarify those of others, while an *auctor* writes primarily in his own words (see Minnis and Scott 1988, 229). Pierre might properly be considered at least a commentator, making his description of himself as a scribe a conscious self-abasement. *Notour* (*notarie*) became an important new term for a writer in the thirteenth century: see (**8a**), (an adaptation of Brunetto Latini).

16 **dul** = enclitic *de le*, also found at vv. 80, 81, 98 below: on the archaic form of the article *lu* for *le* see Short 2013, §33.

23 **suget** This is one of Pierre's borrowings from Latin, which he helpfully glosses as *matire*, signalling that we have progressed to the second cause. The matter of biblical books was generally considered to be Christ (Minnis and Scott 1988, 70); Pierre here follows that model.

32 **e** A line appears above the letter *e* in the manuscript, which would normally indicate an abbreviation for *est*, but is here probably a scribal error.

38 **A luy . . . est ordiné** God is seen as controlling both the order of the creation and the order of the book.

45 **La forme . . . formele** These are two further neologisms. Pierre's discussion here covers both aspects of what was traditionally thought of as the formal cause: he devotes most space to the *forma tractatus*, i.e. arrangement or organisation, and finishes by discussing how he went about assembling his material, or the *forma tractandus*. Pierre's assertion of the importance of naming the *parties principals* and knowing their *noumbre* as a means to improving one's overall understanding reflects the contemporary scholastic emphasis on classification, described, for example, by Alexander of Hales (Minnis 1984, 122–3, 149).

57 **E pur ceo qe** Here and throughout this section Pierre is concerned to give his six-book form something akin to narrative logic – from creator to creation to sin, and so on. This seems to reflect a concern with natural order, which authorities such as Conrad of Hirsau (*c.* 1070–*c.* 1150?) described as 'the natural sequence of the matter narrated' (Minnis and Scott 1988, 45).

68 **rendent** MS rendunt

70 **nostre mire e nostre curour** The *Christus medicus* theme seems to have been first elaborated by St Augustine and was a commonplace by this period: Servasanto da Faenza, a rough contemporary, gives an elaborate explanation of how the sacraments work as medicines: see Ziegler 1998, ch. 4, esp. 196–7.

87–8 **Mez chesqun livre . . . destincté** Pierre again follows standard scholastic practice in considering the subdivisions of the text as important and the chapters as subordinate to the principal parts (Minnis 1984, 148–9).

91–2 **mout, en faz** The manuscript readings are *moud* and *enfanz*. Pierre's construction here seems to have confused scribes: *enfanz* is attested in Hesketh's base manuscript, which also shows these two lines initially interverted before being corrected, and Hesketh's base manuscript reads *muef* (= *moveir*, 1 pr) for *moud* (Hesketh 1996–2000, I.18,621–2). *Moud* (for *mout*, 3 pr *mover*) suggests in this reading that Pierre asserts that he scripts the questions in the role of the disciple, and then answers in the role of the master.

95 **solas** Interestingly for someone who has been called 'well-meaning but stupendously dull' (Legge 1950, 63), Pierre here presents his choice of dialogue form as directed towards entertaining the reader, rather than claiming the authority of the *disputatio* form for it. On the liveliness of this kind of teaching see further Waters 2012, 2015.

96 **entredalient** The verb's primary sense is 'argue, debate', but it has a secondary sense of 'embrace each other' (*AND*, *s.v.* 'entredalier'). For a comparable sense of playfulness and amorousness in literary performance cf. Piramus, *La Vie seint Edmund* (27), vv. 10–12.

98 ***Lucidarie*** i.e. Honorius's *Elucidarium*. Flint notes that manuscripts of this text were often owned by Austin canons (Flint 1988, 118).

100 **mesprist** This may be a reference to the controversy over Honorius's definition of free will. His definition in the original version of the *Elucidarium*, based on Anselm's earlier writings, was later revised in accordance with the development of Anselm's thought and the emerging orthodoxy – but the original version nevertheless circulated widely, especially in England (Flint 1988, 91–4 and 219–20).

105 **com Dieu m'enseigneit** Although in the body of the work Pierre will go on to specify his sources, here he does not do so, defining all that he has learned through his reading as directed by God.

109–10 **La fin . . . verraiment Dieu** The 'final cause' is the good that was intended to result from a work. It was possible to discuss this with more precision: for example, St Bonaventure argued at length that the final cause of Lombard's *Sentences* was 'that we should become good' (Minnis and Scott 1988, 226–8), and Pierre Bersuire saw his *Reductorium morale* as aimed at 'the cure of souls' (Minnis 1984, 163). But Pierre's more general designation of God as the final cause is shared with Robert of Basevorn's *Forma praedicandi* (1322) (Minnis and Johnson 2005, 408).

121 **une fin generale** Here Pierre introduces a further subdivision of the final cause into general, special and personal aims. This examination of the author's own motivations alongside the broader aims of the work has some parallel in prologues to classical authors: for example, in an early-fourteenth-century prologue, Giovanni del Virgilio considers Ovid's 'remote objective' of winning fame through writing his *Metamorphoses* (Minnis and Scott 1988, 364), but this is by no means universal practice and helps to make Pierre's prologue distinctive.

131 **mes especials amis** An immediate audience for the text is envisaged here: Pierre's particular friends are to be entertained and improved by it (cf. Bokenham, Wogan-Browne *et al.* 1999, 1:11). In the following line Pierre implies that this was the main reason for his writing the work. Two (possibly overlapping) groups of friends suggest themselves: Pierre's associates at university, perhaps in particular those at the Augustinian house in Oxford; or other Augustinians who are concerned with preaching to the laity and may welcome a convenient source of doctrine. Whichever is meant, this complicates Pierre's assertion that his text is for the laity – he does not, for example, here mention a lay patron.

138 **Ceo m'est . . . proprement** Pierre's humility about the distinctly authorial act of giving his work a title matches his earlier posture of modesty.

140 **'La lumere . . . comence'** The words that modern readers would consider the title, *La lumere a lais*, are followed by *ici commence*, the equivalent of *incipit* or opening rubric: it seems to have been conventional medieval practice to include 'incipit' or its vernacular equivalent whenever referring to a title (cf. Minnis and Scott 1988, esp. 18 and 20). Pierre makes a play on words, quoting the usual formula for an opening rubric, but also boldly claiming that this is the beginning of enlightenment of his lay readers, so that the formula here works at two levels.

146 **Endreit . . . d'amer** This assertion that a work of didactic instruction brings the reader closer to God both through knowledge and through love is presumably informed by the scholastic debate on whether theology appealed to the intellect or the affections. Alexander of Hales's 1245

Summa theologiae, for example, argued that theology primarily appealed to the affections, but later thinkers such as Aquinas thought of theology as intellectual (see Minnis 1983). Compare the approach in, for example, Edmund of Abingdon's *Mirour de seinte eglyse* (**22**), where the didactic material is no more than a first step to salvation, which should be followed by loving contemplation of God.

20. 'A dire devant la crucifix del muster u sur crucifix peint en livre': Visual Literacies

20a. *Apocalypse du manuscrit Lambeth: La Pénitente illustrée / The Lambeth Apocalypse: Penitence Diagram* [Dean 673], Lambeth Palace Library, MS 209, f. 53^{r}

Date of composition and provenance. Made, perhaps in London, probably in 1265–7 or 1271–4 for Lady Elena de Quincy (d. 1274), second wife of Roger de Quincy, earl of Winchester, widowed in 1264; or perhaps 1265–81 for Lady Margaret de Ferrers (d. 1281), wife of William Ferrers, earl of Derby, widowed in 1254.

Author, sources and nature of text. Illustrated apocalypses, which began as part of monastic rumination on the Bible, became a new genre of lay patronage in thirteenth-century England, customised and formatted for both clerical and lay users. The books are frequently multilingual, with varying combinations of (mostly) Latin, much French and later, English for their texts of the Apocalypse, or Revelation of John, and its commentaries. At the end of *Lambeth*'s lavishly illustrated Latin Vulgate apocalypse text and Berengaudus commentary, there are fourteen folios of customised illustrations and diagrams (ff. 40^{r}–53^{v}):

St Christopher bearing the Christ child (f. 40^{r})
Scenes from the life of John the Baptist (ff. 40^{v}–45^{r})
The Virgin as patroness of St Mercurius's killing of Julian the Apostate (f. 45^{v})
Theophilus, the cleric, saved by the Virgin from the charter signed with the Devil (ff. 46^{r}–47^{r}, with Anglo-Norman verse captions ff. 46^{v}–47^{r}, Dean 565)
John the Evangelist writing the Apocalypse after his exile (Latin caption and scroll) f. 47^{v}
The manuscript's patroness kneeling to the Virgin and Child (f. 48^{r})
Diagram of Alain de Lille's six-winged cherub, labelled in Latin (f. 48^{v})

Individual full-page colour-washed drawings (ff. 49^{r}–52^{v}):

Christ in the garden with Mary Magdalen
St Laurence, St Catherine, St Margaret, St Edmund of East Anglia, each full page
The Crucifixion
An archbishop saint (Thomas Becket?), a similar archbishop saint (Edmund of Abingdon?).

The penitence diagram (f. 53^{r}, labelled in Anglo-Norman) reproduced here is the penultimate item and is followed by a Veronica icon of Christ's face with Latin prayers and devotions, f. 53^{v}.

Though apparently marginal to the main Latin text and commentary, these additional leaves continue the work of apprehending the Apocalypse in visual and textual penitential discourses. They offer an exemplary response to the Apocalypse's eschatological urgency, tailored to the viewpoint of the book's female patron. Various meditative, devotional and protective possibilities are available through the images. Some, for instance, function as *memoriae* of the Passion and the saints, while the diagram representing the six-winged cherub of Alain de Lille's *De sex aliis* treatise may have served as a preparation for confession, perhaps used in conjunction with the patroness's chaplain (Morgan 1990, 60–1).

The penitential diagram on f. 53^r offers still more complex meditative possibilities. Rather like Langland's Tree of Charity in *Piers Plowman*, it is at once an account of the agents and processes of penitence and of their existential location and significance. As the Anglo-Norman labels explain, the figure of the lady sits under the tree of this world, assailed by the arrows of the devil, but with the flies of vain worldly thoughts brushed away by the *flabellum* of a guardian angel. Since the diagram's female penitent is 'repen*tant*' (present participle), she is not so much an allegorical figure of penitence as an image of its processes and practice. She defends herself with the shield of Trinitarian faith (an ingenious and dynamic icon for a complex doctrine). She is also directly under the angelic sword of anguish in the Last Judgement, with the dove of the Holy Spirit as expressed in scripture perched on her chair, the serpent of the devil's disturbance crushed under her foot, and the river of scripture as expounded by the preacher available to her gaze. Further tension arises in this already highly dynamic representation from the apparently hostile peasant-churl whose axe threatens the trunk of the lady's sheltering tree. This figure has to be read counter-intuitively, for he is in fact as much a part of God's plan as the lady herself: his axe is the sentence of judgement and the preaching of the Gospel and the tree he threatens represents the world. His social class, then, is the equivalent of the Gospel's disruptive vision and the *stylus humilis* in which it is represented. He is a graphic re-orientation of an elite penitent's priorities.

Audience and circulation. As with psalters and books of hours, women were notable patrons and readers of apocalypse books, alongside individual clerics and religious institutions. The heraldry on the Lambeth patroness's cloak on f. 48^r (reprod. Kumler 2011, 84) may be that of Roger de Quincy's daughter Margaret (d. 1281), married to William de Ferrers (d. 1254). The patroness wears de Ferrers arms on her dress (left side) and de Quincy on the cloak, and could be seen as a wealthy widow giving prominence to her father's arms over her late husband's. But the patroness may more probably be Eleanor de Quincy (d. 1274), daughter of William de Ferrers and married to Roger de Quincy (d. 1264), with prominence given to her husband's arms.

Each woman is the daughter of the other's husband: each is thus the other's step-daughter and step-mother, but this is not surprising, given the endogamous climate of baronial marriage strategies among the thirty or so families of this rank (see Waugh 1985, 189–91). The book's patron is thought to be herself represented in different ways in the book: recalled in the images of the crucifixion and the Magdalen with Christ in the garden (f. 49^r), represented as a patroness before the icon of the Virgin and Child (f. 48^r), alluded to in the penitence diagram (Morgan 1990, 59–60), she is at once an inscribed reader and exemplary penitent and subject.

The penitence diagram models silent individual reading, but in practice the book includes collective and oral modes as well. The Latinity of *Lambeth*'s text and commentary may have been explicated for the patron and her ladies by her clerics, and the *memoriae* and diagrams of the concluding sequence invite both collective and individual reading. The book is not large and the labels on the penitential diagram page require either turning it in one's hands to read what would otherwise be upside down, or, if all the labels are to be read, the presence of at least one other person. Hence the label for the churl's axe is not only an enactment of the challenge implicit in this figure – a peasant hacking down the lady's tree – but an injunction to read from a different position.

Manuscript source. The book is of parchment, and its dimensions convenient for individual and small group reading: 56 folios, 272×196 mm. The Apocalypse and commentary are accompanied by illuminated images: except for full painting in the images of the patroness with Virgin and child and the Veronica image, the concluding extra pages are colour-washed line drawings, quieter and more meditative. Folio 53 is a singleton, though its handwriting is very similar to that of the scribe who wrote ff. 1–19^v, and with whom the diagram captions hand probably shares training if not personal identity (Morgan 1990, 107–8, 112). Such miniatures are rare in Apocalypses (though the Burckhardt-Wildt Apocalypse has miniatures of a woman attacked by devils, Morgan 1990, figs. 47–8, reminiscent of Julian of Norwich's account of what she thought was to be her deathbed), so that Lambeth's sequence is a notable visual devotional and didactic addition.

BIBLIOGRAPHY. Morgan 1990 is a facsimile with accompanying volume of full transcription of the texts of Revelation and Berengaudus (127–246); on the patroness 73–82; on the added illustrations 247–60. Gee 2002, 46–7 argues for Margaret Ferrers's patronage. For f. 53^{r} together with its verso, see Kumler 2011, 76–96 (with colour reproductions of f. 53^{r-v} and ff. 48^{r}, 49r). Pitts 2010, 20–8 discusses women apocalypse patrons and readers: Wogan-Browne 2009a places the *Lambeth* diagram in the context of thirteenth-century women's reading; Bartal 2011 discusses women's apocalypse reading more widely. Morgan 1990, 49–50, 94–5, Carruthers 2008, 274–337, and Kumler 2011 discuss the teaching functions of apocalypse books and their illustrations and diagrams: see also (**20b**). Evans 1982 and Kumler 2011, 76–80 discuss the shield of faith. On apocalypses see Morgan 1990, 17–37, 92; further examples in Morgan 1982–8 and Dean nos. 473–8. Pitts 2010 edits the insular *Revelacion*. For a catalogue of apocalypses, see Emmerson and Lewis 1985, and on interpretation, Lewis 1995, Emmerson and McGinn 1992. The troping of spiritual warfare as chivalric is discussed by Kumler 2011, 80–3 (see also (**41**), *Estoire del saint Graal*): for women readers wielding such weapons, Wogan-Browne 2013, 185. Morgan 2006 discusses possible connections between a manuscript of Guillaume le Clerc's *Bestiaire divin* (**17**) illustrated by artists from *Lambeth* and Eleanor de Quincy. On women's material, visual, and literary patronage in the period see Gee 2002. For further diagrams and illustrated pages with vernacular inscriptions see e.g. the Delisle Psalter (Sandler 1999), the Holkham Bible picture book (Brown 2007; Baswell 2007).

TEXT AND TRANSLATION

[1]	
par le coc en l'arbre est signifié le precheur qui defule e le preie a despire.	*By the cock in the tree is signified the preacher who tramples on it and urges contempt for it.*
[2]	
par l'arbre, cest munde.	*By the tree, this world.*
[3]	
par l'angle remuant les musches od le muscher, le aide de l'angle qui est gardain de chescun home.	*By the angel moving the flies with the fly-swatter, the help of the angel who is the guardian of each human.*
[4]	
par les musches, les veines pensees qui desturbant le repentant orant.	*By the flies, the empty thoughts which hinder the penitent at prayer.*
[5]	
par l'angle od l'espee qui est pres de l' haterel, la destresce del devin jugement.	*By the angel with the sword which is close to the nape of the neck, the anguish of the divine judgement.*
[6]	
par le diable setant, les suggestions del diable.	*By the devil shooting, the arrows of diabolical promptings.*
[7]	
par la Dame est signifié repentant.	*By the Lady is signified repenting.*

[8]
par l'escu, lel fei.

By the shield, true faith.

[9]
par le columb, li Saint Espirit qui espunt la sainte escriture.

By the dove, the Holy Spirit which expounds holy scripture.

[10]
par le colovere agaitant al talon, le desturbement que le diable se aforce a faire as leals a l'issue de l'alme.

By the snake watching at the heel, the hindrance that the devil strives to exert on the faithful at the departure of the soul.

[11]
par l'ewe, devine escriture laquele le precheur demustre.

By the water, divine scripture which the preacher explicates.

[12]
par la coignée, la sentence del jugement ou le prechement de l'Ewangele.

By the axe, the sentence of the Judgement or the preaching of the Gospel.

[*Shield, outer rim*]
Pere: le Pere ne est le Saint Espirit
Saint Espirit: le Seint Espirit ne est le Pere
Fiz: le Fiz ne est le Pere

Father: the Father is not the Holy Spirit
Holy Spirit: the Holy Spirit is not the Father
Son: the Son is not the Father

[*inner*]
Deu: est Pere, est Saint Espirit, est Fiz

God: is Father, and Holy Spirit, and Son

Notes

5 **le muscher** The fly-swatter also had a role as a ceremonial liturgical fan (*flabellum*) for protecting the host at Mass.

10 **la destrece** has a legal sense, 'distress, distraint' (see *AND*, *s.v.* 'destrece'): cf. the Theophilus captions of f. 47^{r}, where the Virgin's 'Rendez la chartre, felun . . . Je vus cunjur par mun fiz pusant' in the same aristocratic register of legal and feudal power is associated with female protagonists.

11–12 **les suggestions del diable** also connotes a legal sense (see *AND*, *s.v.* 'suggestion': 'submissions'[in a court case]).

13 **repentant** The lady is not simply 'La Pénitente', but 'repenting'.

15 **le columb** The association of the dove with scripture was widely established and is also a figure much used in writings for women because of its associations with chastity: see e.g. Hugh of Fouilloy's *De avibus* in W. Clark, ed. and trans., 1992, 120–37 (134–6).

20 **l'ewe** For a similar gloss in a contemporary treatise for women in religion ('L'ewe senefie Escriture') see Hunt, ed., 1995, v. 264. The figure is of a mirror in which the shadow of the devil or other predators can be seen: it is found in Aelred's *De instructione inclusarum* for recluses as well as in bestiary entries on the dove: see Hunt, ed., v. 255n. and 207n.

Shield. The shield of faith (*scutum fidei*) diagram is traced in Evans 1982 to Hugh of St Cher, and in insular culture from 1240 or earlier: it is used by Grosseteste and painted in two St Albans manuscripts (including Matthew Paris's *Chronica majora*) and in the Abingdon Apocalypse (Morgan

Fig. 2. (20a) Lambeth Apocalypse: Penitential diagram (London, Lambeth Palace Library, MS 209, f. 53^r)

1990, 62–4): it is wielded by a knight in the famous diagram of Peraldus's treatise on the vices in BL Harley MS 3244 (http://www.bl.uk/catalogues/illuminatedmanuscripts/record.asp?MSID=8798&CollID=8&NStart=3244). The Virgin herself uses a shield in the Lambeth image of St Mercurius killing Julian the Apostate (f. 45^{v}). Morgan suggests the first and second canons of Lateran IV (on the indissoluable unity of the Trinity *contra* Abbot Joachim of Fiore's account of their individuality) as pertinent background to the high profile of the shield of faith (1990, 63 n. 62). The shield enables an intensely economical apprehension of complex doctrine by visual means (see Kumler 2011, 80).

24–6 *Shield, outer rim.* The absence of elision (*ne est ... ne est* etc.) perhaps deliberately inhibits swift reading and encourages meditation.

20b. *Les Enfaunces de Jesu Crist* [Dean 495], Second Epilogue: Oxford, Bodleian Library, MS Selden supra 38, f. 36^{r-v}

Date of composition and provenance. End of the thirteenth century, England.

Author, sources and nature of text. The second epilogue is found only in the unique insular French manuscript of the *Enfaunces de Jesu Crist*, dated to 1315–25. Here, a certain 'Johan' names himself (v. 39) and takes responsibility for both the text and its images (vv. 29–30). Whether Johan was the author or – most probably – the scribe (see Fig. 3), his claim advances an innovative view of what it meant to be the maker of a book in fourteenth-century England. The Selden *Enfaunces*, with its thirty-three episodes, is the most complete medieval compilation in French of Christ's apocryphal infancy. The manuscript's program of sixty images of infancy miracles is among the earliest extant, and when compared with the paucity or complete lack of images in other manuscripts, signals a fresh approach to the infancy.

Stories of Jesus's childhood, present from the early years of Christianity, often retold and supplemented Gospel accounts. The *Gospel of Pseudo-Matthew*, an eighth- or ninth-century translation into Latin of the conflated *Infancy Gospel of Thomas* and the *Protoevangelium of James*, was the source for most medieval redactions, but some episodes are found only in Armenian or Arabic infancy narratives. Heightened curiosity about Jesus's humanity in the thirteenth century contributed to translation of the infancy miracles into the vernacular languages, firstly in German, and in French from the mid- to late thirteenth century. Apocryphal accounts of the Virgin's early life were also popular; see Wace's *La Conception Nostre Dame* (Dean 489) and Herman de Valenciennes, *Li Romanz de Dieu et de sa mere* (**15**).

The Anglo-Norman *Enfaunces* closely resembles a continental version of the childhood miracles entitled, in its modern edition, the *Evangile de l'Enfance*, although there are enough differences between them in lexicon, structure, and prosody to argue for their independent production; the Anglo-Norman text also contains three more episodes than the *Evangile*. The *Enfaunces*' 2020 verses of Anglo-Norman flexible octosyllables are rhymed throughout in fours: the *Evangile* uses the more traditional couplet and respects the continental requirement for strictly counted octosyllables.

Slightly more than half of the *Enfaunces* episodes are non-canonical accounts of Jesus's interactions with other Jews. In some, Jesus is cast as either a teacher or a student, but he belittles his interlocutors in either case. In others he plays with fellow Jewish children, punishing them for perceived infractions. Sometimes he slyly leads his playmates to attempt deeds that only he can do, which results in their deaths. At his mother's intercession, he sometimes, but not invariably, returns them to life. Such *Enfaunces* episodes, centred on revenge for insult or trespass, are paralleled in Augustine's reinterpretation of the prophet Elisha's encounter with the 'boys of Bethel' (2 Kgs 2.23–4): Augustine rewrites Elisha as Jesus Christ punishing the boys with death for having teased him (Ziolkowski

2001, 36–43). But the stories also have contemporary inflections. In one of the most striking, Jesus, perceiving that Jewish parents have hidden their children in an oven, turns them into pigs and leaves the scene (Boulton 1985). This is said to explain why Jews treat pigs like brothers and do not eat pork. Christians had no ban on eating pork, but the narrative's hints at cannibalism and anxieties about ingesting human bodies may have echoed doubt surrounding the transubstantiation of bread and wine into Christ's flesh and blood (made doctrine in 1215). It can perhaps also be seen as a metaphorical warning against the incorporation of Jews into the English Christian communal body, even as 'converts'.

Modern criticism has sometimes ignored the anti-Judaic nature of *Enfaunces* episodes, or has minimised Jesus's actions by referring to them as pranks, perhaps taking at face value the epilogue's claim that the *Enfaunces* brings *solaz* (Boulton 1985, v. 12), that is, recreational play. The widespread conviction that Jews were a malevolent enemy would have invited the harshness of Jesus's actions, and Jesus's wizard-like cleverness could have afforded *solaz*, that is, both comfort and amusement. This is straightforwardly enunciated by Johan when he says he hopes Jesus will punish the Jews if they do not mend their evil ways (vv. 1991–4). Jesus's divine authority could have been invoked to explain his actions: that is, if Jesus put his playmates to death, they must have been evil. Nonetheless, there remains the troubling matter of his role as an example and its implications for the teaching of *imitatio Christi*. Some modern readers see in the *Enfaunces* a Jesus figure whose vengeful impulses and lack of charity constitute a disturbingly un-Christian template, and whose activities attract no disciples (see Vitz 2001, 130; Boulton 2007).

The second epilogue, edited here, sums up the qualities that make the manuscript of the *Enfaunces* especially attractive, first among them the book's *bele ... medlure* (fine mix, vv. 5–8) of text and image. The continuity between the *Enfaunces* images and those on the contemporary Tring tiles supports Johan's claim about the importance of his pictorial program and demonstrates his alertness to the fashionable requirements of story-telling. He claims that what he provides is both of *grant profit* and *bon respit* (great benefit, v. 9; good example, v. 10), and that it offers *beu desport* and *bon deliz* (fine entertainment, 10; delight, 11). The claim of *utilitas* no doubt extends to the *Enfaunces*' anecdotes about the Jews, a *male gent* (evil people; see vv. 13–25). The opening prologue to the *Enfaunces* further claims (as does the continental *Evangile*) that the instructive story to follow will please its audience as much as any *romaunz* (Boulton 1985, v. 14).

Audience and circulation. The enthusiasm of well-off francophone audiences in England for childhood stories of Jesus is shown by the existence of shortened versions of the *Enfaunces* and by the insertion of selected episodes into other works. An abridgement and another fragmentary manuscript from the early and the late fourteenth century include *Enfaunces* narrative; several of the *Enfaunces* miracles appear in prose in the *Bible Historiale* (late thirteenth to early fourteenth centuries: Dean 470), and in the form of captioned illustrations in the *Holkham Bible Picture Book* (Smith 2006). The Children in the Oven episode appears first in French versions of the *Enfaunces*, but is pictured only in Selden supra 38 and in other manuscripts prepared in England such as the Neville of Hornby Hours (Smith 2003, 277–8; Smith 2006, Fig. 2). Selden supra 38 may also have been the source of the Middle English poem entitled *Le Enfaunce Jesu Crist* in Bodleian MS Laud Misc. 108 (but see Boulton 1985, 17).

Selden supra 38 is a compellingly attractive book, small enough to be held easily in the hands. Among its later owners was John Raynzford of Great Tew (*c.* 1474–d. 1551), whose formula 'Jehan Raynzford me doit' (John Raynzford owns me) appears both at the end of the *Enfaunces*, under the image that follows the second epilogue, and at the beginning (f. 1^{r}), where Raynzford appears to have expunged the name of a previous owner. The effaced name is arguably that of Lady Joanna de Bishopsdon (or Bishopesdon, Bishopstone; Morgan 1990, 96), who may have been the Joanna recorded as the wife and widow of Thomas, son of Sir John de Bishopsdon (d. bf. 1339; Bartal 2006, 240–1). The manuscript's lavish presentation responds to contemporary taste for richly ornamented manuscripts of devotional literature, and its influence is shown in a set of contemporary earthenware tiles, possibly used on the wall of a parish church in Tring, Hertfordshire, for which the Selden images were plausibly the source (the tiles include the Children in the Oven episode).

That a text of the Apocalypse is the only other work in Selden supra 38 suggests strongly that the manuscript was designed for religious instruction. Apocalypse manuscripts rarely contain other works, and when they do, the works are likely to be didactic. Explicating abstract theological precepts through mnemonic images was an established practice in Latin and the vernaculars in the thirteenth century; cf. (**20a**). Images may also have functioned to teach the language of the text. Selden supra 38's memorable images could have been used together with its text to teach reading to those who already spoke French, whether children or adults. Perhaps the prologue's claim that the *Enfaunces* will add no *Glose* (learned commentary, Boulton 1985, v. 29), but will tell in detail (*destincterai*, v. 32) everything authenticated by the Latin writings (vv. 25–31) is made with the prospect of educating children in mind. But the manuscript could also have been used for teaching adults or by preachers requiring teaching aids. So too, the Tring tiles, which show no wear, are thought to have been wall rather than floor tiles and perhaps also served for instruction.

Manuscript source. Oxford, Bodleian Library, Selden supra 38, f. 36^{r-v}; 1315–25; unique second epilogue, vv. 1973–2020. The *Enfaunces de Jesu Crist* (ff. 1–36^{v}; title assigned by modern editor based on vv. 6–7) shares this small book (197 × 157 mm) with a complete French prose Apocalypse (ff. 37–129). The text of the *Enfaunces* is written two verses to a line, separated by a punctus, allowing each quatrain to be copied over two long lines. A later hand has written interlinear comments in (early-modern) English.

Most images are divided into two background blocks of undiapered colour, one red, one blue. Against these large and vivid stretches of colour, small figures, often in groups, are captured in motion and with careful detail to their physiognomy and to the folds of their beige garments. Jesus is identified by his halo, as well as by his sweet face and abundant curly hair, a figure seemingly inconsistent with the stern and punishing Christ of the text. Mary too has a halo, and the Jews, all male, can often be identified by the hats they wear and their hooked noses. The length of the text in Selden supra 38 argues for its having been prepared before the program of images. Images are not always placed near their parallel episodes (see Boulton 1985, 28; Boulton 1983, 59), and the promise in the second epilogue that the final illustration of the text will show Jesus raising his hand to bless the author is not fulfilled; instead, it shows the author kneeling, holding a scroll. These facts suggest that the program of images was not always required to function as an adjunct to the text, but may have also been used as a narrative in its own right.

Linguistic interference from English may account for the depiction of a wooden beam in the image for the tale of Jesus and the water pot. The pot is said in the text to hang on a *rai* (sunbeam, vv. 728, 744; Middle English *sonne beme*; see Boulton 1985, 12), reminding us that the manuscript was prepared in a trilingual culture.

Bibliography. Both the insular *Enfaunces* and the continental text have been edited by Boulton 1985 and 1984 respectively. For a translation of the Selden supra text, see Boulton 2013. A briefer redaction and a fragment of the *Enfaunces* remain unedited. Other apocryphal stories of Jesus as a child, or of Jesus and Mary, are listed in Dean 482, 484, 492, 496: for a prose version of the Infancy miracles see Dean 470. For the range of European vernacular *infantia Salvatoris* stories, see Dzon 2016 and Dzon and Kenney 2012. Armenian and Arabic infancy narratives are listed in Boulton 1985, 9, 10–16; on the greater western access to Arabic works in the twelfth and thirteenth centuries, see K. A. Smith 2003, 276–7; also Elliott 1993, 2006, Hennecke 1963, Akbari and Mallette, 2013. For German infancy narratives see Kauffmann 2003, 237. Bartal 2010 discusses the manuscript's illuminator. Selden supra MS 38's images are listed and the manuscript dated in Sandler 1986, 62–3, and Boulton 1985, 4–6; on contemporary taste for illustrated manuscripts and for visual literacies see Kumler 2011, Emmerson 2012, K. A. Smith 2003. For books teaching infancy material to children see K. A. Smith 2006 and 2003 (pl. 7, Fig.140 and 267–87). The foundational study of the Tring tiles is M. R. James 1923; see also Eames 1980; Casey 2000. For the 'narrative assault' on the Jews, see Rubin 1999; for the uses of anti-Judaism after the expulsion in 1290, see Bale 2006; Tomasch 2000; van Court 2000. Mundill 1998 is a historical analysis of the expulsion. For a history of the Jews in Britain, see Skinner 2003. Guillaume le Clerc, *Le Bestiaire* (17) gives a Christian account of Jewish literacies. For *Enfaunces* episodes and performance, Vitz 2001, 147 (but see also Kauffmann 2003, 239). Ziolkowski 2001 discusses evil children. For the narrative association between the Virgin, Jews, and children, see Rubin 1999, 7–27. On the visual stereotyping of Jews see Mellinkoff 1993 and Schreckenberg 1996. Fabre-Vassas 1997 discusses the Jews and the taboo against eating pork. On francophone lives of Christ, see Boulton 2015.

TEXT AND TRANSLATION: SECOND EPILOGUE (VV. 1973–2020)

La lettre k'avez avant oïe [f. 36r]
De Jesu est, le fiz Marie,
Des enfances k'il fist en vie
Ke de joie esteit replenie,
E dedenz veue la purtreture,
Ke mut dedeinz la lettre honure.
Mut est bele la medlure
De la lettre e la purtreiture,
Mut i a grant profit,
Beu desport e bon respit.
A cel entendre est bon deliz
E ne mie tener a enviz.

The story you have heard is about Jesus, son of Mary, about his human childhood, filled with joy; and you have seen the images within, which do honour to the story. The mixture of story and illustration is very lovely; there is great benefit in it, fine entertainment, and a good lesson. Hearing it is quite delightful and not to be begrudged.

De male gent vus voil conter
E en dit me veil pener
Ke lur doint mal encumbrer
A tuzjurs sant determiner:
De[s] Giuz ke aveient grant envie [f. 36v]
Vers Jesum le fiz Marie
Ma priere a Jesu crie
Ke lur confund e maudie
Si il ne se vunt amendant
De lur mefez, merci criant
A Jesu Crist k'est tut pussant,
A ki feseient mal si grant.

I have wanted to tell you about an evil people, and I have taken pains in the telling: may they be sorely afflicted for days on end. To Jesus I call out my prayer about the Jews, who were deeply jealous of Jesus, Mary's son: may he curse and destroy them if they do not set about correcting their misdeeds, begging for mercy from all-powerful Jesus Christ, to whom they did such great harm.

De[s] feluns Giuz ore lerrai
E d'autre chose vus dirrai.
Cest afere tost cesserai;
A bref parole vus lerrai
Pur celi ki la lettre escrist
E la purtreture dedeinz fist.
Par charité, a Jesu Crist
Priez ore de quer parfist

I'll now leave the evil Jews behind and tell you about something else. I'll end this account, leaving you with a brief word on behalf of the man who wrote the story and did the pictures. Out of charity, pray now to Jesus Christ wholeheartedly that God give

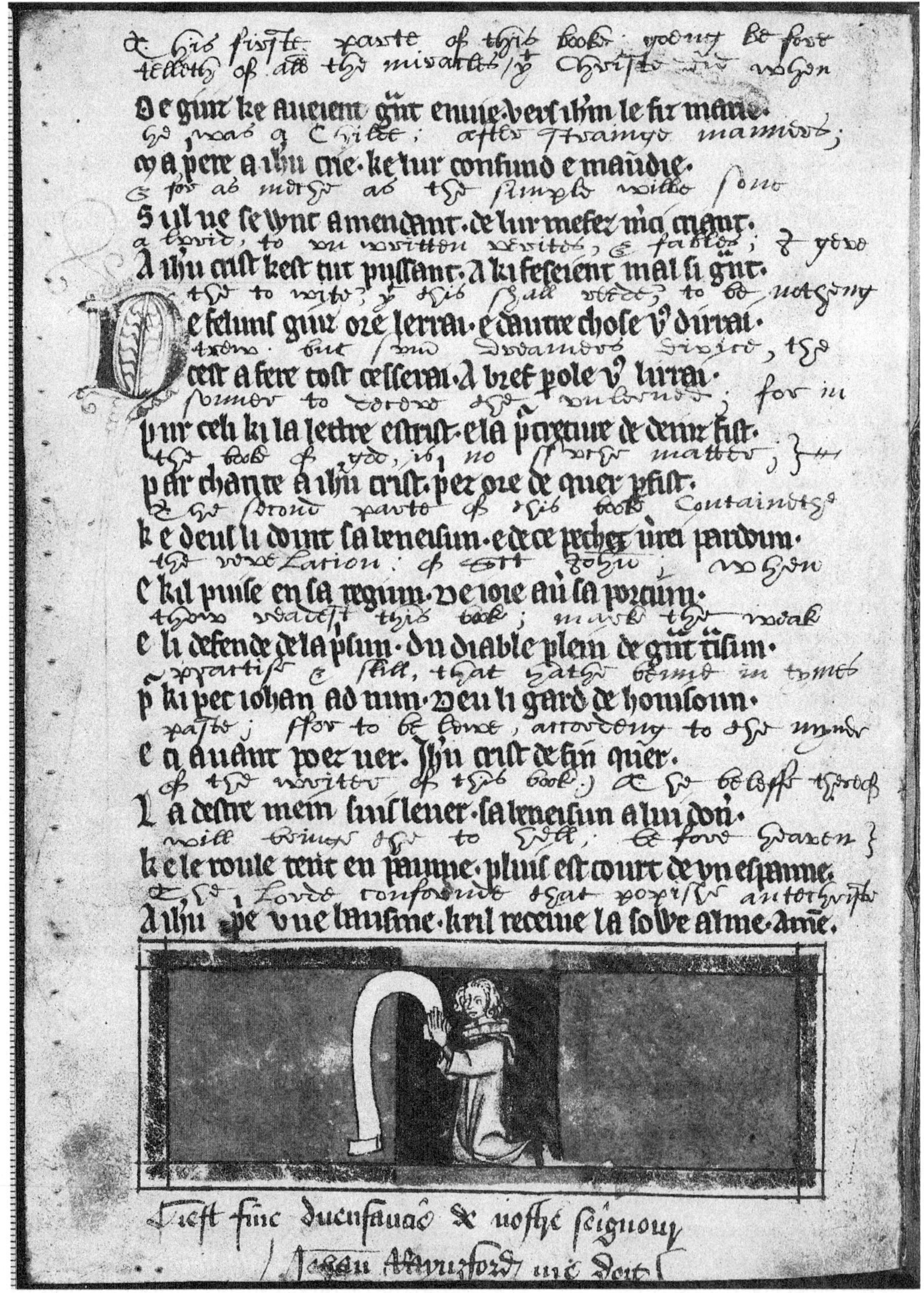

Fig. 3. (**20b**) *Enfaunces de Jesu Crist*: Johan, composer and/or scribe and/or artist? (Oxford, Bodleian Library, MS Selden supra 38, f. 36*v*)

Ke Deus li doint sa beneisun
E de ce[s] pechez verrei pardoun,
E k'il puise en la regïun
De joie aver sa porcïun.
E li defende de la prisun
Du diable plein de grant traisun.
Pur ki priét? Johan ad nun;
Deu li gard de honisoun.
E ci avant poez ver
Jesu Crist de fin quer
La destre mein suis lever,
La beneisun a lui doner
Ke le roule tent en paume;
Pluis est court de un espaune.
A Jesu prie une bausme,
Ke il receive la sowe alme. Amen

him his blessing and true forgiveness for his sins, and that he may have his portion of joy in heaven; and protect him from the prison of the devil, who is filled with great treachery.

The man for whom you are praying is named John; God keep him from disgrace. And below here you can see noble-hearted Jesus Christ raise his right hand to give his blessing to the holder of the scroll; it is narrower than a hand's breadth. He is praying to Jesus for the balm of receiving his soul. Amen.

Notes

1 **La lettre . . . oïe** The first and last words of a poetic line generally receive more stress than other elements in the line, making the pair consisting of *lettre*, meaning a written text, and *oïe*, referring to reading aloud, at once a clever contrast and a conceivably meaningful joining to denote something written that has been read aloud to an audience. Taken with *veue* of v. 5, referring to the illustrations, the three terms suggest how the manuscript was meant to be used.

3 **Des enfances k'il fist en vie** The *Enfaunces* will please its audience because it humanises Jesus and situates him in the sorts of interactions that children are universally seen to engage in.

4 **de joie . . . replenie** At the surface level, this is presumably the joy of insouciant childhood, although some modern scholars have been perplexed by this 'strangely malevolent and disturbing' little Jesus (Vitz 2001, 131). Joy also evokes the spiritual bliss Christians may experience thanks to Christ's incarnate presence.

5 **veue** Although modern French requires an *–e* of agreement on a past participle when it follows a feminine noun as direct object, it was not unusual in medieval French to add such an *–e* even when the past participle preceded a feminine noun; for the trio *lettre*, *oïe*, and *veue*, see n. to 1.

5, 30 **purtreture**, 8 **purtreiture** can refer both to the art of portraying and to the picture, or manuscript illustration, that results.

9–11 **profit . . . desport . . . bon respit . . . deliz** These reasons for reading a work such as the *Enfaunces* – it will be of benefit, it will entertain, there will be a lesson in it, and it will be a delight – became standard in many works of edification in the vernacular (see, e. g., Chardri, *La Vie de seint Josaphaz* (30), and see above).

15 **Ke lur doint** lacks a subject but presumably anticipates Jesus of vv. 19–20, of whom Johan asks that he destroy the Jews if they do not mend their ways

16 **sant**=*sans*

21–2 **Si il ne se vunt amendant / de lur mefez** This suggests that conversion would be an acceptable solution, but in fact, it is surely part of the point of the text that the Jewish parents, though grateful to Jesus for restoring their children, never seem to think of converting.

24 **a ki feseient mal si grant** Taken with *grant envie* (v. 17), this explains the *mefez* of v. 22, that is, the accusation that Jews, not Romans, crucified Christ.

25 An enlarged upper-case initial letter *D* in red ink appears here.

25, 28 **lerrai** *lerrai* of v. 25 is an emendation for the copyist's *lirrai* (= 'I will read'), possibly anticipating *dirrai* of the next line. The reading *lerrai* is 1 fut. of *laier*, leave behind or abandon.

27 **afere** The same word appears in v. 4 of the *Enfaunces* prologue, where the author says that he wants his audience to hear *cest afere*, which is glossed in *AND* from this very verse as topic or subject; used in another context, *AND* also offers 'matter'. The reference here is very generally deictic, indicating in v. 4 'what is to follow' and in v. 27 'what has preceded', allowing a reading for *afere* in both vv. 4, 27 as story, account, or matter.

29–30 **celi ki la lettre escrist / e la purtreture dedeinz fist** These lines offer an understanding of authorship that challenges clear distinctions between scribe and author, and, further, a model of book production that collapses the categories of scribe, author and illustrator to foreground the idea of a 'maker of the book'.

33 **beneisun** Cf. 34 *pardoun*, 35 *regïun*, 36 *porcïun*, 37 *prisun*, 38 *traisun*, 39 *nun*, 40 *honisoun*: in Anglo-Norman *–un*, *–oun*, and *–on* generally represented the same sound and the rhyme here covers eight verses.

35 **puise** = *puisse, 3 subj, pouvoir.*

35–6 **la regïun de joie** heaven; see also v. 4 and n.

40 **honisoun** can mean disgrace or shame, but also disadvantage or financial loss.

41 **ci avant** The portrait of the artist and scribe follows the last verse of the text and completes the column.

43 **suis** = sus.

45–6 **le roule ... pluis est court de un espaune** Even though Selden supra 38 was prepared as a book, in the illustration 'Johan' is depicted holding a scroll in his two hands, perhaps representing the Anglo-Norman use of *roule* for historical documents in the form of a handscroll, a narrow strip of parchment meant to be rolled up and carried. It could also have been envisaged as a speech scroll, used for teaching, or like the portable prayer rolls belonging to monks (Smith 2003, 228). As for the manuscript book, the emphasis given here to the small size of Selden supra 38, which in fact can be held in two hands, makes it easily portable.

20c and d. 'Par ceste figure l'en poet savoer': Two Genealogical Roll Chronicles: 20c [Dean 6]: Oxford, Bodleian Library, MS Ashmole Rolls 38

Date of composition and provenance. *c.* 1307 or 1310, or 1310 and later, provenance unknown.

Author, sources and nature of text. The authors and artists of genealogical rolls are mostly unknown. The genre emerged in England in the latter decades of the thirteenth century and flourished into and beyond the fifteenth, using texts in Anglo-Norman, Latin, and Middle English. The format and content of genealogical rolls differs widely, but many trace the lineage of the rulers of England from the West Saxon king Egbert (802–39), Brutus, the legendary founder of Britain, Noah, or Adam and Eve, usually in a tree diagram with interconnected roundels. The roundels name or portray rulers and are complemented by short paragraphs of text. Genealogical rolls therefore offer condensed and illustrated histories of England's kings. The tree diagram layout ultimately derives from Peter of Poitiers's late-twelfth-century *Compendium historiae in genealogia Christi*, originally designed as a teaching aid and widespread in England from the early thirteenth century.

Two main generations of genealogical rolls have been identified: those produced predominantly between 1271 and 1327, and the 'new kinds of royal pedigrees' written during the reigns of Henry VI (1422–61, 1470–1) and Edward IV (1461–70, 1471–83), which were influenced by the earlier rolls (De Laborderie 2008, 48–19). Scholars have been especially interested in them for their propagandist aims. In some cases, noble patrons commissioned genealogies in rolls and codices that tied their family's lineage together with that of the royal blood. The first generation of rolls have received less critical attention, but they met contemporary interests in the history of England and its kings (also serving as aides-memoire), and contributed to the shaping of Englishness during the late thirteenth and fourteenth centuries.

Ashmole Rolls 38 is a first-generation roll and, like many others, derives its content from *Li Livere de Reis de Brittanie* (Dean 13), a group of concise histories of England's kings, typically extending from Egbert or Brutus up to Henry III or Edward I, which is often referred to together with first-generation rolls as *Li Rei Engletere*: 'a miniature and eminently portable compilation of well-known texts, [*Li Rei*] offers an effective mechanism for manufacturing a (nearly) seamless English lineage that effaces rupture' (Goetz 2006, 39). Ashmole combines and adapts the prologues of versions three and four of *Li Rei Engletere* (thereby reminding us that the classification of texts according to versions is a modern approach, whereas authors and scribes would draw material from the exemplars to which they had access).

In the Ashmole roll, England's history goes from Brutus's conquest to the death of King Henry III, and the tree diagram stretches to his grandson, Edward II. A late-fourteenth-century continuer extends the roll's diagram to Richard II. Ashmole begins with an image of King Edward I enthroned (and captioned *Edwardus Rex pater istius regis*, Fig. 4) which appears above the circular diagram of the seven Anglo-Saxon kingdoms of England (see Fig. 5). This 'Heptarchy' diagram is characteristic of first generation rolls. It functions as a stylised map of Anglo-Saxon England, oversimplifying the geographical distribution of peoples, but embedding the genealogical narrative and tree diagram it introduces into an older England recognisable to contemporary readers. The diagram establishes territory as the organisational frame for the history: the land is the 'bloodline' between kings. British kings are thereby made 'English' (i.e. of England), insofar as they rule over territory recognisable as *Engletere* (Rajsic 2015).

A textual prologue follows the images of Edward I and the Heptarchy. It describes England's geography, political and ecclesiastical organisation, and select British and early Anglo-Saxon kings. Ashmole Rolls 38 and other *Li Rei Engletere* texts rapidly narrate the passage of dominion from British to Anglo-Saxon overlordship, and in the process they omit King Arthur (though some scribes made independent efforts to integrate him: Rajsic 2015, Spence 2013). Arthur is absent from the Ashmole prologue, but space is made for him in the account of Cnut's reign, where Cnut, in a comparison that assimilates him into English history, is said to be the most powerful ruler of *Engletere* since Arthur.

The Ashmole prologue ends with King Egbert (*Albrist*) of Wessex, claimed as the king who unites England and rules over the whole country. Egbert is also the starting-point of the genealogical diagram, so that the roll figures England's kings after Egbert as the rulers of a seemingly stable *Engletere*. The loss of British dominion is not denied in the narrative, but the roll's format emphasises continuity. A colourful pictorial gallery of England's kings runs down Ashmole's left and right margins, with Brutus (left margin) and Corineus (right margin) at the top (see Fig. 6). Thus all of England's rulers follow from the British founders, and here more strikingly than in other such rolls, mythical British kings are shown to be the founders and builders of the English nation and the forebears of an 'English' lineage that centres upon *Engletere*.

Audience and circulation. The audience for genealogical rolls in England ranged 'from country gentry to peers, possibly including the king himself' (de Laborderie 2008, 50). The rolls were also disseminated in monasteries across England (many first generation rolls were monastic productions). There, they could serve for learning England's past, helping, as William of Malmesbury put it in his *Gesta regum Anglorum*, to 'mend the broken chain of our history' (Mynors *et al.* 1998, 15). The audience of Ashmole Rolls 38 itself is uncertain. A Latin text drawn from Martinus Polonus's *Chronicon pontificum et imperatorum* and written on the dorse of membranes three and four in the hand of the continuer (Black 1845, 10) gives the succession of popes and Emperors up to Pope Urban VI and Holy Roman Emperor Frederick II. This suggests monastic production and readership (Polonus was usually known to lay readers, if at all, in translation; see (**42**), *Mohun Chronicle*), but nothing is known of the roll before it was acquired by Elias Ashmole in the seventeenth century. The practice of writing on the reverse of manuscript rolls was not uncommon. The dorse could contain a variety of texts, from an explanation of the game of chess (Hunt, ed., 1985) to a romance (*Amadas and Ydoine*: Wright 1872, xv; de Laborderie *et al.* 2000, 383), a heraldic treatise, a medical text, and so on (de Laborderie *et al.* 2000; Tyson 2001), and so can provide clues as to a roll's audience. Genealogical diagrams in the mode of the rolls are also found in the manuscript texts of chronicles (for example, the 'Wigmore Chronicle' in Chicago University Library MS 224 includes a diagram of the Mortimer family on ff. 51^{v}–52^{r}, showing their Trojan descent: Giffin 1951–2, pl. VI).

Manuscript source. Ashmole Rolls 38 is an attractive and colourfully decorated vellum roll, thirteen feet long and ten and half inches wide, with seven medieval membranes of varying length and an eighth modern canvas membrane at its top. Text from *Li Rei Engletere* is written on the recto in an early-fourteenth-century hand: there is nothing on the dorse. The opening illustration of King Edward I (membrane one, now partly torn), the Heptarchy diagram, the branches and roundel borders of the genealogical tree diagram, and the pictorial gallery of kings are each coloured in combinations of blue, green, yellow, orange and red ink. The names of England's kings appear in roundels in the centre of the roll and are written in red ink following a capital initial in blue. Names of persons appearing in roundels who do not rule, such as children or siblings, are written mostly in black ink (some in red), and their roundels are typically smaller. The roundels for Norman dukes Rollo, William Longsword, and Richard the Fearless, however, are large, thus drawing attention to William the Conqueror's Norman ancestry. In the Heptarchy diagram, the text giving the measurements of England is written in red ink, but the text written in all other circles appears in black. Capital initials in all Heptarchy circles are blue. Ornamentation, usually in red, fills spaces in the Heptarchy diagram and appears throughout the roll, especially around the genealogical tree diagram. Capital initials drawn in red and blue ink appear throughout the text. At the end of the roll, the number of regnal years for Edward I and Edward II are added by a later hand in black ink. The Hague Roll (*c.* 1272–4) is closely related to Ashmole Rolls 38, but does not have the opening illustration of Edward I or the pictorial gallery of kings, and ends with Henry III (text) and Edward I (tree diagram).

Bibliography. Ashmole Rolls 38 has never been edited. A black and white image of part of the prologue (*par ceste figure* to the bottom of King Bladud's roundel) appears in Meneghetti 1979, xxvi–xxvii. On its initial date see Watson 1984, 6; Pächt and Alexander 1973, no. 535 (1307) and Black 1845, 10 (1310). A few *Li Rei Engletere* texts and first-generation Anglo-Norman genealogical rolls are edited by Bovey *et al.* 2005 (a full-colour edition), Foltys 1962, Glover 1865, Koch 1886, Tyson 1975, and Wright 1872. For the Hague roll see Kooper and Kruijshoop 1989. For editions and study of *Li Rei* texts in connection with rolls, see Rajsic 2015, Spence 2013 and Goetz 2006. De Laborderie transcribed Ashmole Rolls 38 and all other first generation genealogical rolls that he identified (2002): his work on earlier and later rolls remains essential (2013, 2008, 2003, 2002, 2001, 1997). For other studies of first generation rolls see Rajsic 2013, Holladay 2010, Collard 2000, Monroe 1990, 1978–82, and Tyson 2001, 1975, and for the Hague Roll, Kooper and Kruijshoop 1989. Monroe 1978, 1990 discusses genealogical rolls of Christ. Fifteenth-century genealogies have received much scholarly attention: on their propagandist purposes see e.g. Allan 1979; for their patronage and ownership, see e.g. Griffiths 1986, P. Morgan 1998, Tscherpel 2003; for roll genealogies linking a noble to a royal family see e.g. Griffiths 1979, 1986; Given-Wilson 2003; Radulescu 2003: Wall 1919 and Tyson 1998 discuss rolls linking several families (the Maude Roll and the Adam and Eve Roll respectively). See also Cleaver (2014).

Text and Translation: Roundels (a) The Heptarchy (Fig. 5)

[C] Engletere contient en lungur [.]viij. cent lues, c'est a saver d'Escoce jesques a Totteneyse, et en laur, de Menevia en Gales jesques a Dovere, .CCC. lues. Et environ treys mil lues et sesaunte lues. Et si est bone tere et bele.

[C] England measures eight hundred leagues in length, that is from Scotland all the way to Totnes, and three hundred leagues in width, from Menevia [St David's] in Wales all the way to Dover, and three thousand and sixty leagues in circumference. It is also a good and beautiful land.

[1] *Le regne dé Eastsaxonis*: Ceste regne contient Suthfolk et Northfolke, et ileuk ad un eveské, cest de Northwiz, que fu jadis a Elymham ou a Tedford. Et si contient Grauntebregge, et illeuc le eveské de Ely.

[1] The kingdom of East Anglia: this kingdom includes Suffolk and Norfolk, and there is one bishopric, that of Norwich, which was formerly at Elmham or at Thetford. It also includes Cambridge, and the bishopric of Ely is there.

[2] Cest regne contient tut Eastsexe et Middelsexe et la moyté de Hertfordsyrre. Et illeuc a un eveské, cesty de Londres. Cest reaume ne dura mye lungement pur les reys qui se entrebaterent.

[2] This kingdom includes all of Essex and Middlesex and half of Hertfordshire, and there is one bishopric, that of London. This kingdom did not last long at all because of the kings who fought against each other.

[3] *Le regne de Kent*: Lé reys de Kent regnerent proprement en Kent. Et illeuke ad le see a l'erceveské de Caunterbery, qui jadis fu dist Dovere, et si ad un eveské, qui est dist a Rouecestre.

[3] The kingdom of Kent: the kings of Kent reigned rightfully in Kent. The see of the archbishopric of Canterbury is there, which was formerly said to be of Dover, and there is also one bishopric, said to be at Rochester.

[3b] Galerne

[3b] North-western wind

[4] *Le regne de Suthsexe*: Cest regne contient Suthsexe et illeuke a un eveské (de Cyscestre), et si contient Suthultesyre, et illeuke li eveské de Wyncestre, et si contient Somersete ou il ly ad le eveské de Baa, et si contyent Devenesyre [et] Cornwaylle.

[4] The kingdom of Sussex: this kingdom includes Sussex and one bishopric (of Chichester) is there, and it includes Southamptonshire, and the bishopric of Winchester is there. It also includes Somerset, where the bishopric of Bath is, and it further includes Devonshire and Cornwall.

[5] *Le regne de Westsexe*: Cest regne contient Wylteschyre [et] Barkeschire, et illeuke ad l'eveské de Salesbury, que jadis fu a Syrebourne ou a Rammescery, ou a Cilescestre, que ore est deserte. Cest regne fu tolet de autre rey.

[5] The kingdom of Wessex: this kingdom includes Wiltshire and Berkshire, and the bishopric of Salisbury is there, which was formerly at Sherborne, Ramsbury or Chichester, which is now deserted. This kingdom was seized by another king.

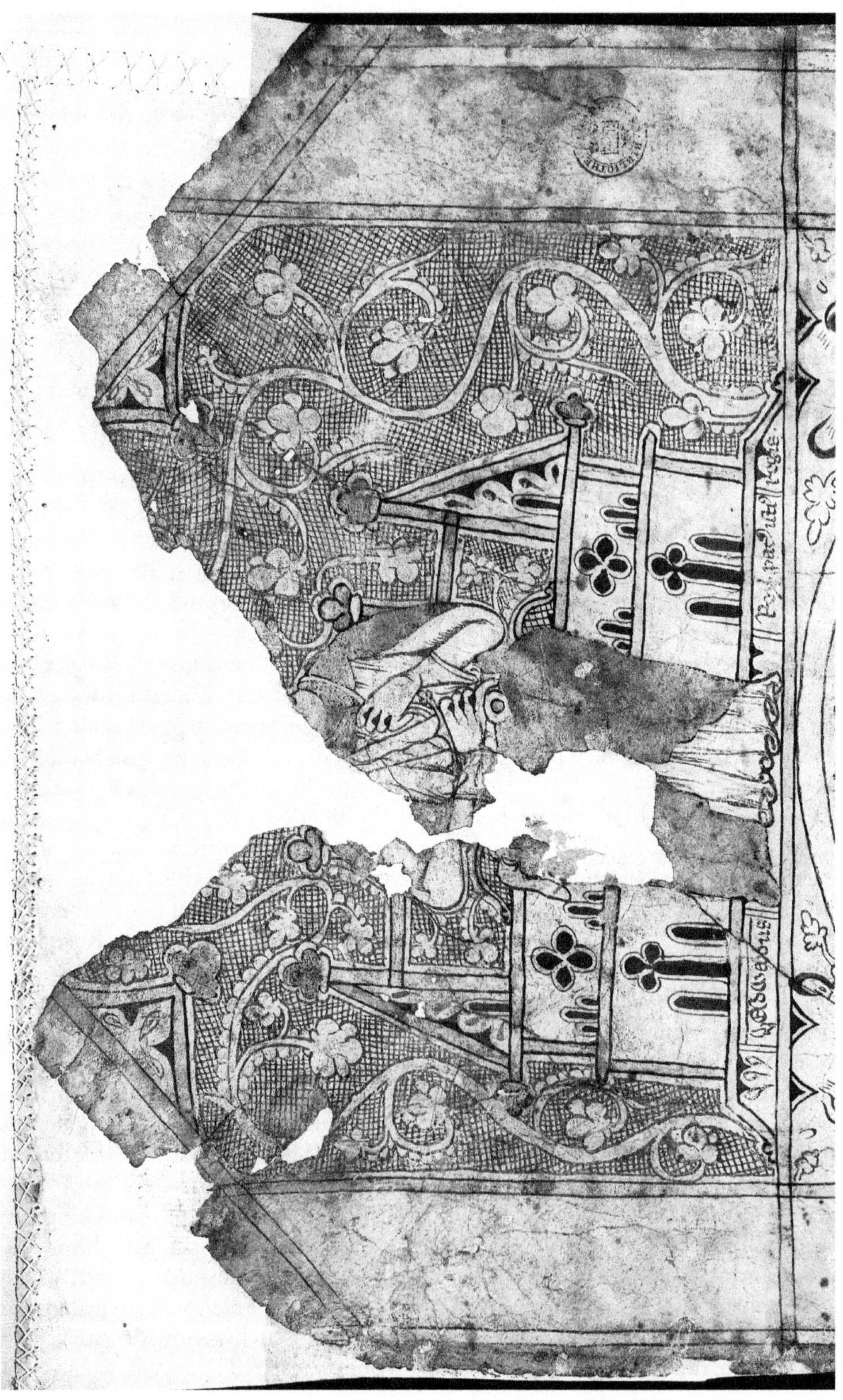

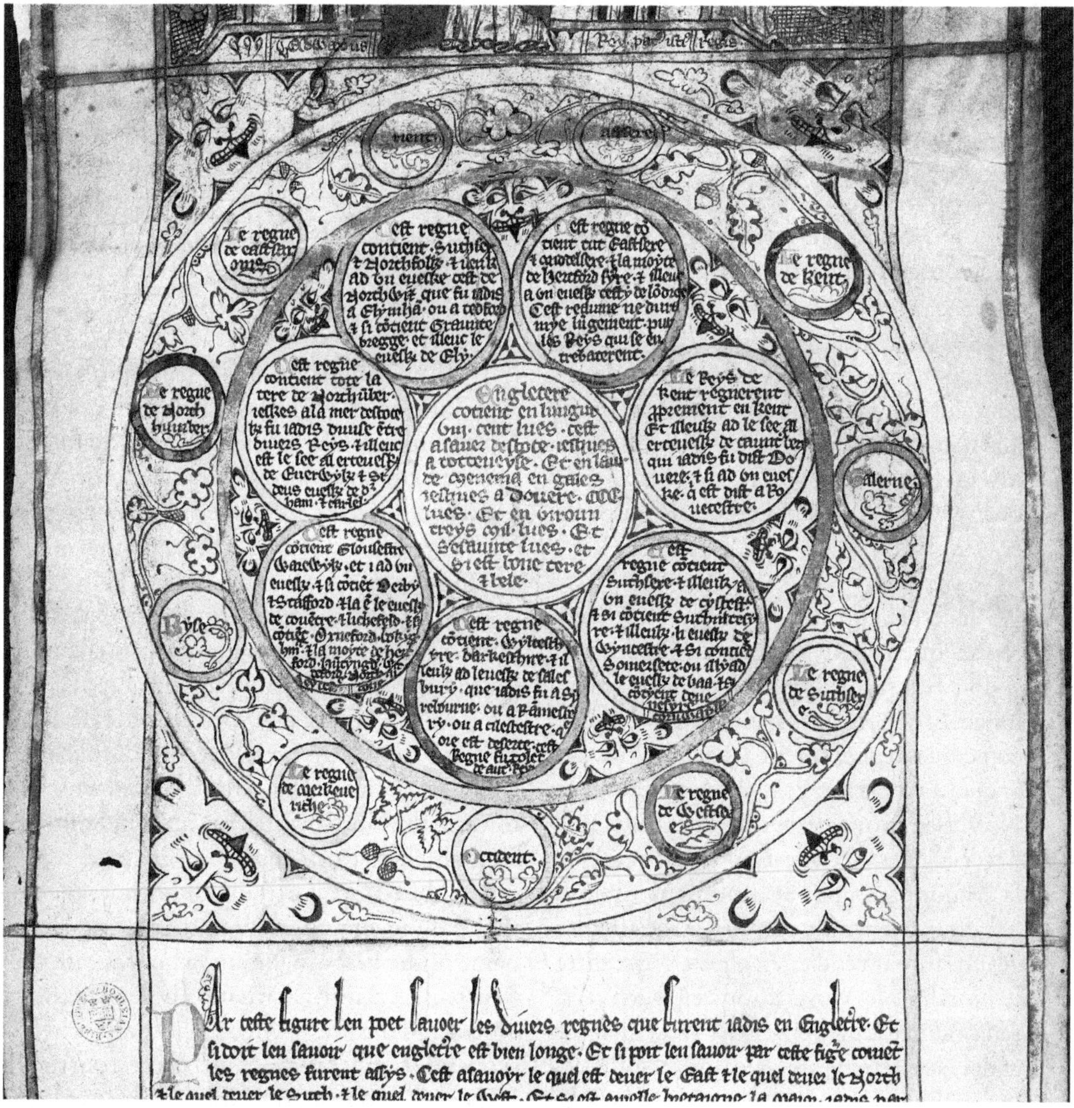

Fig. 5 (*above*). (20c) The Anglo-Saxon Heptarchy
(Oxford, Bodleian Library, MS Ashmole Rolls 38, membrane 1, detail)

Fig. 4 (*left*). (20c) King Edward I enthroned at the top of the genealogical roll
(Oxford, Bodleian Library, MS Ashmole Rolls 38, membrane 1, detail)

[5b] Occident

[6] *Le regne de Merkeneriche*: Cest regne contient Glousestre [et] Warewyke, et i ad un eveské. Et si contient Derby et Stafford, et la est le eveské de Coventre et Lichefeld. Et si contient Oxneford, Bokygham, et la moyté de Hertford, Huntyngdon, Bedeford, Northamtone, [et] Leycestre.

[6b] Byse

[7] *Le regne de Northhumber*: Ceste regne contient tote la tere de Northumber, jeskes a la mer d'Escoce, ke fu jadis divisé entre divers reys. Et illeuc est le see a l'erceveské de Everwyke et si deus eveské, de Durham et Carlel.

Par ceste figure l'en poet savoer les divers regnes que furent jadis en Engleterre. Et si doit l'en savoir que Engleterre est bien longe. Et si poit l'en savoir par ceste figure coment les regnes furent assys, c'est a savoyr le quel est dever le East et le quel dever le North, et le quel dever le Suth et le quel dever le West. Et si est appellé Bretaigne la Major jadis par le noun du premer habitour qui avoit noun Bruth, quaunt les geauns furent vencuz. Et ele est assise entre le North et le West, dount ele resseyt sa tempraunce, c'est a saver del West chalour et del North freydour. Mes ore lessums del sist de Engleterre, et parluns de cely Brut dount nous avums avaunt toché, par qui la tere fust premerement appellé Bretaigne la Major: et coment il la conquist, et sur queus gent, et dount il vynt quaunt il vynt en la tere pur gwerroyer.

Devaunt la Nativité Nostre Seignur .mil et .CC. anz, Brutus, le fuiz Silvius, et Corineus, soen frere, vindrent en Engletere oveskes graunt host de la bataylle de Troye sur un geaunt qui out noun Gogmagog. Et luy donerent bataille et l'occistrent et tous les geouns ke il troverunt en la tere. Et

[5b] West

[6] The kingdom of Mercia: this kingdom includes Gloucester and Warwick, and one bishopric is there. It also includes Derby and Stafford, and the bishopric of Coventry and Lichfield is there. It further includes Oxford, Buckingham, and half of Hertford, Huntingdon, Bedford, Northampton, and Leicester.

[6b] North-eastern wind

[7] The kingdom of Northumbria: this kingdom includes all the land of Northumbria, which was formerly divided between different kings, as far as the sea of Scotland. The see of the archbishopric of York is there, and also two bishoprics, those of Durham and Carlisle.

By this diagram you can find out about the different kingdoms that were once in England. Indeed, you should know that England is very long. And by this diagram you can also learn how the kingdoms were organised, that is, which was oriented towards the East, which towards the North, which towards the South, and which towards the West. England was once dubbed Great Britain, at the time when the giants were conquered, following the name of the first inhabitant, who was called Brutus. England is situated between the North and the West, whence she receives her moderate temperature, namely heat from the West and cold from the North. But now, let us set aside the matter of England's situation and speak instead about that Brutus whom we touched upon before, by whom the land was first called Great Britain: how he conquered it, and over which people, and whence he came when he arrived in the land to wage war.

Twelve hundred years before the birth of Our Lord, Brutus, son of Silvius, and Corineus, Brutus's brother, arrived in England with a great army from the battle of Troy, and went up against a giant who was called Gogmagog. They fought Gogmagog and killed him and all the giants they found

celuy Brutus fist fere la ville de Loundres. Et Corineus, son frere, regna en Cornwaille, et pur ceo que il out noun Corineus fist il appeller la tere Cornwaille. En cel tens Hely fust jugges des fuiz Israel.

Aprés Brutus regna son fuiz Sisillius graunt tens. [A]prés Sisillius regna Eboracus si fist fere Ewerwyke, et Aclud, et le Chastel des Puceles, et le Chastel de Mount Dolerous, de Mount Sorel. Et en cel temps regna David en Jerhusalem. Aprés Eborak regna Ruhudibraz soen fuiz et fist Caunterberi, et Wyncestre, et Septhone, Schaftebery. Aprés regna Leyr et fist Leycestre, et illeuke parla, adunke, un egle. Aprés Leyr regna Bladus et fist fere Baa, et fist les chaud bayns. Aprés Bladus regna Bellius, le fuiz Donewal, et fist quatre real voyez par Engletere: le une de Tottoneyse jeskes a Cateneyse, l'autre de Seynt David en travers jesques a Portemue, et les autres deus veyes cely Bellius fist fere en belif la tere. Et si fist fere a Loundres Billyngesgate. Icely rey prist Fraunce, Lombardie, et Rome. Aprés Bellius regna Cassibalan. Si jetta Julius Cesar hors de Engleterre deux fiez, mes a la terce fiez fu Cassibalan vencuz, si dona truez a Rome treys mil liveres de argent par an. Se fust devant la Nativité Nostre Seignur cent et quaraunte deus anz.

in the land. And Brutus built the city of London. Corineus, his brother, reigned in Cornwall, and because he was called Corineus he named the land Cornwall. At that time Ely was judge of the sons of Israel.

After Brutus his son Sisillius reigned for a long time. After Sisillius, Eboracus reigned and built York, Mound Agned, the Castle of Maidens, the Castle of Mount Dolorous, and Mountsorrel. At that time David ruled in Jerusalem. After Eboracus his son Rudhudibras reigned, and built Canterbury, Winchester, and Shaftesbury (once called Septhone). Afterwards Leir reigned and built Leicester, and there and then an eagle spoke. After Leir, Bladud reigned and built Bath, and made the hot baths. Belin, the son of Dunwallo, reigned after Bladud, and made four royal roads through England: the first from Totnes all the way to Caithness, the second from St David's across to Portsmouth; and Belin made the other two roads sideways across the land. He also built Billingsgate at London. This king took possession of France, Lombardy, and Rome. Cassibellan reigned after Belin. He cast Julius Caesar out of England two times, but the third time Cassibellan was defeated, so he gave tribute to Rome of three thousand pounds of silver per year. This was one hundred and forty two years before the birth of Our Lord.

Roundels (b) The Kings of England (Fig. 6)

[1] Le Rey Brutus fu le premer rey d'Engletere, qui unques i fust aprés la bataylle de Troye

[1] King Brutus was the first king of England, who lived after the battle of Troy

[2] Corineus fu le frere Brutus, et regna en Cornwaille aprés la bataylle de Troye

[2] Corineus was the brother of Brutus, and he reigned in Cornwall after the battle of Troy

[3] Aprés Brutus regna soen fuiz, Cisillius

[3] After Brutus his son Sisillius reigned

[4] Aprés Cisillius regna Eboracus

[4] Eboracus reigned after Sisillius

[5] Aprés Eborak regna Ruhudibras, soen fuiz

[5] After Eboracus his son Rudhudibras reigned

[6] [A]prés Ruhudibras regna Leyr

[6] Leir reigned after Rudhudibras

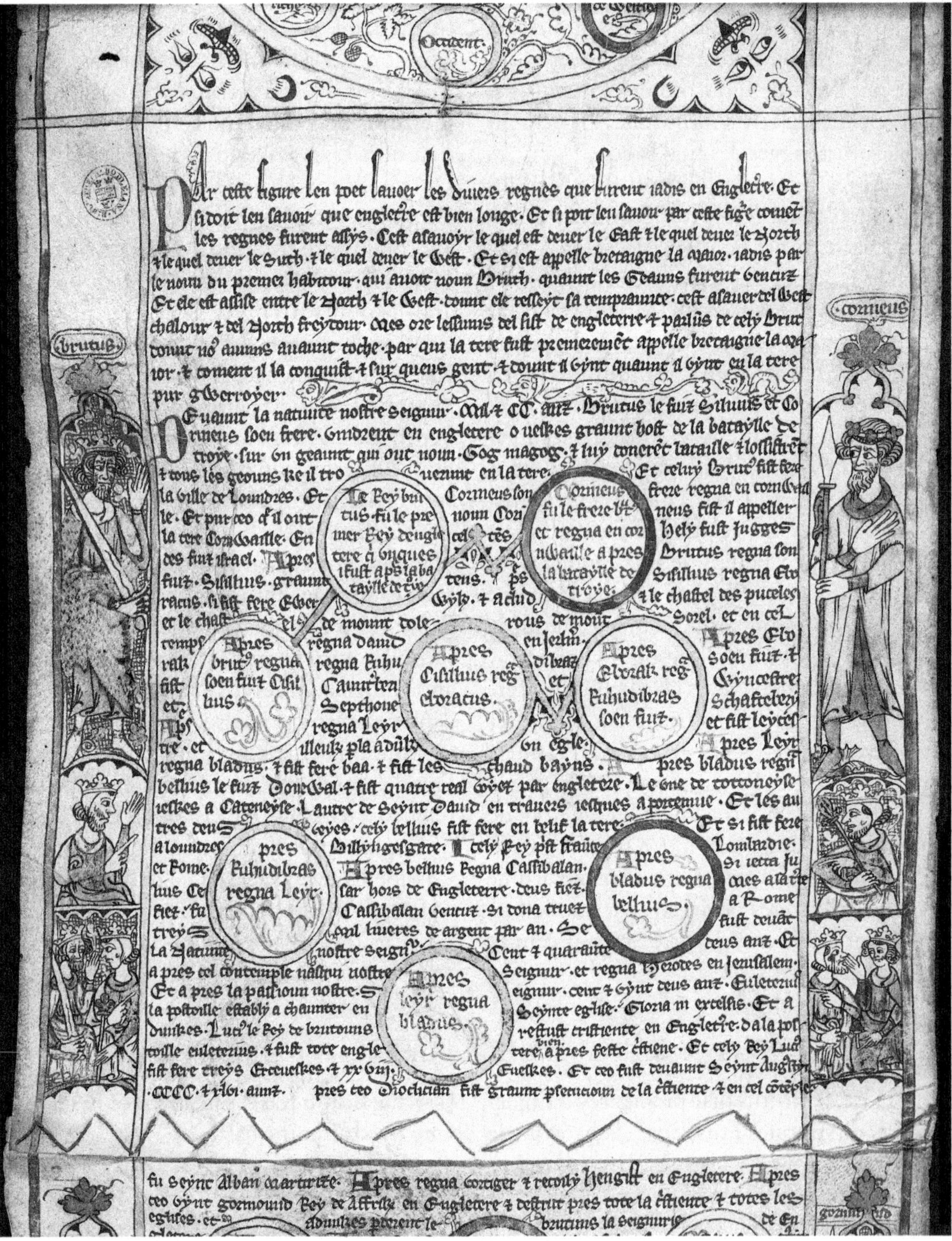

Fig. 6. (20c) Brutus, Corineus and the British founders of England (Oxford, Bodleian Library, MS Ashmole Rolls 38, membrane 1–2)

[7] Aprés Bladus regna Bellius
[8] Aprés Leyr regna Bladus

[7] Belin reigned after Bladud
[8] Bladud reigned after Leir

[Summary: *Jesus Christ was born and Herod reigned in Jerusalem; Pope Eleutherius ordered the singing of Gloria in excelsis in the holy church; British King Lucius ruled and all of England was made Christian; Lucius built three archbishoprics and twenty-eight bishoprics; Emperor Diocletian persecuted Christians; St Alban was martyred; Vortigern reigned and invited Hengist to England; the African King Gormund came to England and destroyed Christianity; the Britons lost lordship of England; and St Augustine arrived in England and restored the Christian faith to the land.]*

[9] Aprés Bellius regna Cassibalan
[10] Et pus regna Lucius le premer Cristien rey dé Brutouns
[11] Et pus regna le Rey Gormound de Affrike, qui destruit la Cristienté. Et fu la tere departie en set parties, et avoit de chescune un rey adunke, si cum la figure desus le monstre. Et pus ke lé regnes furent departies en set, les reys ke adunkes furunt et regnerent si comenserunt a batailler et a gwerroyer ensemble dount les uns furent vencuz, et furent les set regiouns resemblez en synk. Issi ke le premer rey regna taunt soulement en Kent auxi cum avaunt, saunz autre ajustement. Et ceo furunt lour nouns qui sunt issy escrites: [five roundels: Osmund fu Rey de Kent; Houne fu Rey de Estlinge; Wlstan fu Rey de Merkeneriche; Bern fu Rey de Northumbrelond; Bristrich fu Rey de Westsexe.] Le secund rey de Westsexe teneit Surreye, Suthsex, et les countés de Suthamthone et de Wyltone, Barkeschire, Somersete, Dorsete, Deveneschire, et Cornwaylle. Et avoit ces eveskés: de Cicestre et de Wyncestre; de Salesbury et de Baa, qui jadis fu a Welles; et le eveské de Excestre. Et en lu de cely furent jadis deux eveskés, le un si fu a Cridenthone et le autre a Seynt Germayn. Le tiers roy, c'est a saver de Merkeneriche, avoit ces countés: Gloucestre, Hereford, Wilecestre, Schalopesbury, Cestre, Stafford, Derby, Notyngham, Leycestre, Nichole, Northamthone, Warewyk, Oxeneford, Bokyngham, Hontyngdone, et la moyté

[9] Cassibellan reigned after Belin
[10] And then Lucius, the first Christian king of the Britons, reigned
[11] And then King Gormund of Africa reigned, who destroyed the Christian faith. At that time the land was divided into seven parts, and each had its own king, as the above diagram shows. After the kingdoms were divided into seven, the kings who then lived and ruled began to fight and wage war against one another until some were defeated, and the seven regions were reassembled into five. Thus the first king reigned as before only in Kent, without any change. And these were the names of the kings, which are written here: Osmond was king of Kent; Houne was king of East Anglia; Wulfhere was king of Mercia; Beorn was king of Northumberland; and Brithric was king of Wessex. The second king of Wessex held Surrey, Sussex, and the counties of Southampton and of Wilton (i.e. Wiltshire), Berkshire, Somerset, Dorset, Devonshire, and Cornwall. And he had these bishoprics: of Chichester and of Winchester; of Salisbury and of Bath, which was formerly at Wells; and the bishopric of Exeter. And in place of that [diocese] there were once two bishoprics: one was at Crediton and the other at St Germaine. The third king, that is, the king of Mercia, had these counties: Gloucester, Hereford, Worcester, Shropshire, Cheshire, Stafford, Derby, Nottingham, Leicester, Lincoln, Northampton, Warwick, Oxford, Buckingham, Huntingdon, and half of Bedford. And he had these bishoprics: of

de Bedeford. Et avoyt ces eveskés: de Hereford; Wylecestre; de Coventré, qui est dist de Cestre; et de Nichole. Le quart rey, c'est a saver de Eastsexe, teneyt Eastsexe, Middelsexe, Hertfordschyre, Suthfolke, Northfolke, Cauntebreggeschyre, et la moyté de Bedefordschire. Et avoit treys eveskés: de Loundres, de Ely, de Tedhford, que ore est a Northwyz. Le synqueme rey, c'est a saver de Northumber, avoyt tote la tere outre Humbre [jeskes a Escoce], si cum il pert desus en la figure, jeskes k'a duré la porole del suth d'Engletere. Ore lessums de ceo et dé princes que du tens as Bretouns urent seignurie, des queus les uns regnerent par dreit, et les autres par estrif et par bataille. Et turnums nostre matyre a ceus des queus nos reys natureus urent nessaunce. Et comensum a noble gwerreour Albrith, le fuiz Ailmound, qui conquist par bataille tote la seignurie d'Engletere sur tous les autres reys. Et regna en cel tens en Westsexe.

Hereford; of Worcester; of Coventry, which is said to be of Chester; and of Lincoln. The fourth king, that is, of Essex, held Essex, Middlesex, Hertfordshire, Suffolk, Norfolk, Cambridgeshire, and half of Bedfordshire. And he had three bishoprics: London, Ely, and Thetford, which is now at Norwich. The fifth king, that is, of Northumbria, had all the land beyond the Humber into Scotland, as is evident above in the diagram, for the time that the conflict of the south of England endured. Now let us set aside this subject and that of the princes, who from the time of the Britons had lordship, among whom some reigned rightfully and others through strife and battle. And let us change the subject to consider those from whom our rightful kings descend. Let us begin with the noble warrior Egbert, son of Ealhmund, who in battle conquered the lordship of all England over all the other kings. He reigned at that time in Wessex.

Notes

1–49 **Heptarchy diagram** The idea of the Heptarchy first appears in Henry of Huntingdon's *Historia Anglorum* (J. Campbell 1986; Bassett 1989; Greenway 1996, lx–lxi). As in *mappae mundi*, east is at the top (Tyson 2001, 109). In the outer shell of the circular 'map', small roundels identify six of the seven Anglo-Saxon kingdoms (Essex is not named), and give the names of two of the four cardinal winds (on medieval wind diagrams see Obrist 1997). These descriptions are drawn from William of Malmesbury's *Gesta regum Anglorum* (Mynors *et al.* 1998, 101, 147), but do not correspond exactly with his account. In the inner shell, seven larger roundels list shires, cities and bishoprics in each of the Anglo-Saxon kingdoms (labelled 1 through 7 here), beginning with the kingdom of East Anglia which appears at the top left of the Heptarchy diagram, and continuing clockwise from that point. Finally, in the centre of the circle, a single roundel (labelled C here), describes England as a whole.

R(a)C[entre].1 **contient** MS *cotient*

R(a)C.1–2 **Engletere contient en lungur [.]viij .cent lues** Bede gives the measurements of Britain as 800 miles long by 200 miles wide, and 4875 miles in circumference (Colgrave and Mynors, ed., 1969, i.i), and is followed by Henry of Huntingdon (Greenway 1996, i.i, 13). Ashmole Rolls 38 and other genealogical rolls give the dimensions as 800 × 300, with varying measurements for the circumference of England. Matthew Paris gives the measurements of *Anglia* as 800 miles by 300 miles in one of his maps of Britain (Cambridge, Corpus Christi College 16, f. iv[v]). With the switch of subject from Britain (in Bede) to England, the genealogical rolls join the *Historia Anglorum*, Anglo-Norman *Description of England* (*c.* 1139; see (1)), and other texts in representing England as the whole island. The borders of England in these genealogical rolls are elastic: England is at once

Anglo-Saxon England – made up of the seven kingdoms described in the Heptarchy diagram – and Britain.

R(a)C3 **de Menevia** is an earlier name for St David's. The *Li Rei* text found in BL Royal 13 A.XVIII (ff. 105^r–156^v) cites Menevia and St David's collectively: 'de Meneveya la cité Seynt David en Galis'.

R(a)8 **Suthfolk** MS *Suthsex*

R(a)22 **Galerne** (north-west wind) The scribe made a mistake here since south, not north, is the correct compass point.

R(a)39 **le eveské de Coventre et Lichefeld** From 1228 until the Reformation the usual title for the bishop of Coventry was 'bishop of Coventry and Lichfield' (Fryde *et al.* 1996, 253), hence Ashmole Roll 38's pairing of the sees here. Lichfield is the earlier of the two sees, but its bishop transferred his see to Chester in 1075, and the see was transferred again in 1102, this time to Coventry (ibid.).

R(a)43 **Byse** North-eastern wind. *Byse* can refer to north, north-east, or the north-east wind (*AND*).

70 **Devaunt la Nativité Nostre Seignur** Geoffrey of Monmouth, whose *Historia* or *De gestis Britonum* is the ultimate source for the history of the British kings in genealogical rolls, does not date Brutus's arrival in Britain (here England). However, chroniclers commonly dated events according to Christian chronology (see e.g. *Mohun Chronicle* (**42**); Given-Wilson 2004, 121–3).

72 **Corineus, soen frere** Brutus and Corineus are not brothers in the *Historia / De gestis Britonum*, but both are leaders of groups of Trojans, and Corineus collaborates with Brutus in conquering and naming Britain and Cornwall.

80–1 **En cel tens Hely fust jugges des fuiz Israel** This time scheme is first given in Nennius and also used in the *Historia / De gestis Britonum*; see Reeve and Wright 2007, 31. Such synchronicities are typical of medieval universal history writing.

90 **Septhone, Schaftebery** In the *Historia / De gestis Britonum* and many of its successors, Rudhudibras only builds Canterbury, Winchester and Shaftesbury; thus, the appearance of *Septhone* in Ashmole Rolls 38 is unusual. In *Castleford's Chronicle* (*c.* 1327), however, *Sephton* is said to be an earlier name for Shaftesbury (Eckhardt 1996, i, 85). The *Castleford* author's equation of the two cities is followed here.

20d. Genealogical Roll [Dean 10], Prologue: Oxford, Bodleian Library, MS Bodley Rolls 2

Date of composition and provenance. *c.* 1443, provenance unknown.

Author, sources and nature of text. In short paragraphs of text arranged in two vertical columns, Bodley Rolls 2 relates the history of the kings of England (right column) and France (left column) from their Trojan origins (Brutus and Priam respectively) to King Henry VI of England and King Charles VII of France. To the left of each textual column, an illustrated genealogical tree diagram (the author uses the term *a[r]bre*) provides a visual representation of royal descent. Because the history of England's kings appears in the right-hand column, the illustrated bloodline of those kings runs down the centre of the roll, while the illustrated lineage of the French kings occupies the left margin of the roll (Fig. 7). The pedigree of England's rulers thus achieves primacy.

The history in the left column of Bodley Rolls 2 is the only extant 'English' copy of a group of continental French genealogical chronicles, found in rolls and codices, known as *A tous nobles*. These recount the deeds of the kings of France from their Trojan forebears to contemporary rulers, concluding most often with King Charles VII, and were copied and continued into the sixteenth century. They drew material from *Les Grandes Chroniques de France*, a genealogical history of France's

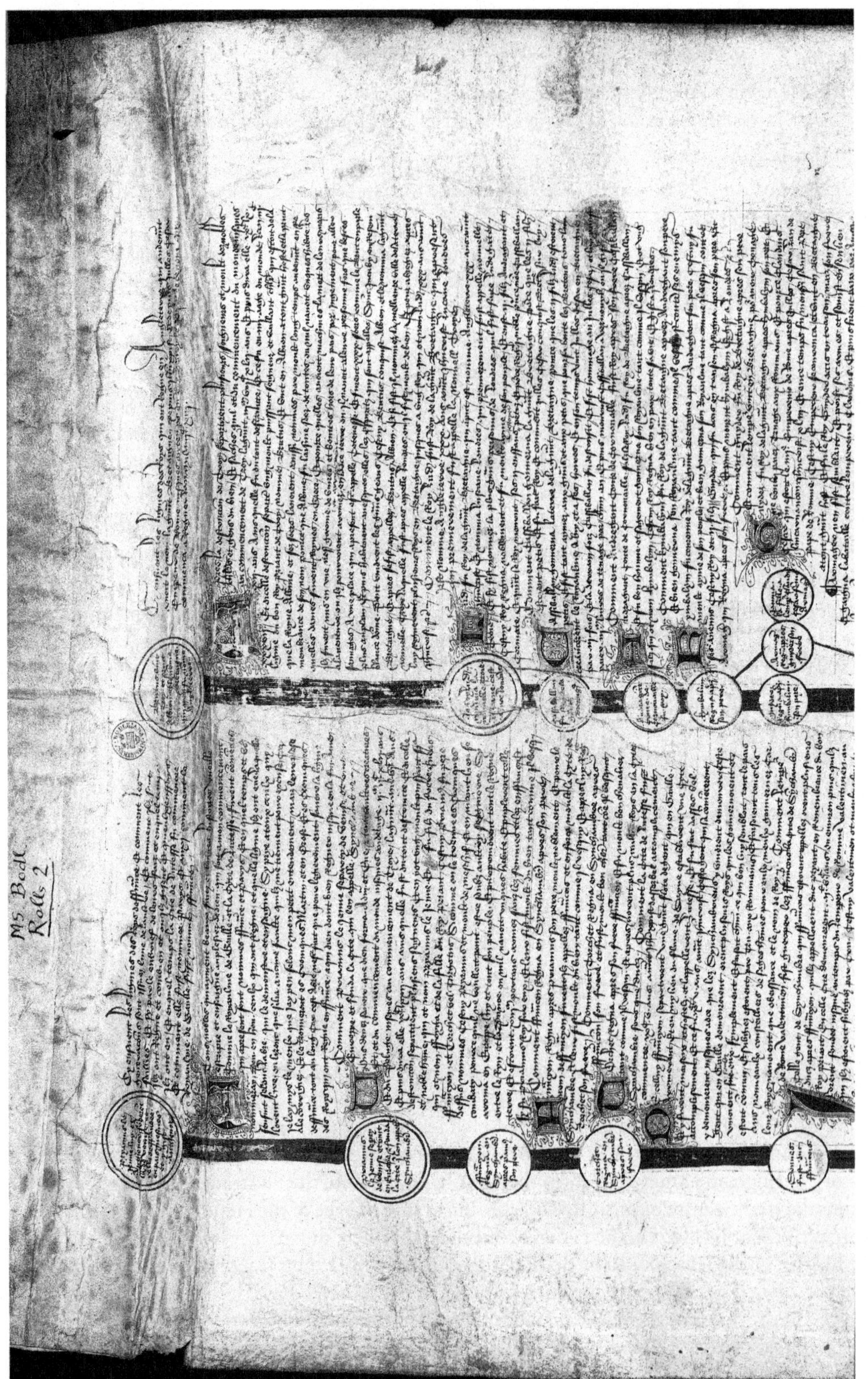

Fig. 7. (20d) The Kings of France (left) and England (right) (Oxford, Bodleian Library, MS Bodley Rolls 2, membrane 1)

rulers beginning with King Priam of Troy and compiled at various points between the thirteenth and fifteenth centuries. In the fifteenth century, 'a period when an emerging national sentiment rooted in the past was exacerbated by consequences of the rivalry between Valois and Plantagenet kings, *A tous nobles* served both to mould and to reflect the historical and political culture of its authors and audience' (Norbye 2007a, 317). Over sixty copies of *A tous nobles* in twenty-one different versions survive. *A tous nobles* may appear on its own; embedded within a universal chronicle showing the successions of popes and Emperors and of the kings of England; or alongside the genealogy of England's rulers only. Bodley Rolls 2 is not alone in the *A tous nobles* tradition in juxtaposing the pedigrees of French and English kings, but its version of history is unique.

Bodley Rolls 2 is remarkable for its pro-English sentiments. It leaves no doubt, for example, that King Edward III of England is the rightful claimant of the French throne through his mother Isabella of France. Moreover, its version of *A tous nobles* is one of only four to admit that the French succession of 1328 was contested, and one of two that allude to debates of female succession in relation to the 1328 crisis (Norbye 2007a, 314–15). The roll is also exceptional for its prologue of England's kings, where it incorporates a brief summary of the Albina myth into the Brutus story in order to explain the island's earliest name, Albion, and the origin of the giants that Brutus is said to overcome. The Albina myth credits the initial discovery and naming of Albion to Albina, the eldest of a band of some thirty sisters exiled from their Greek (sometimes Syrian) homeland for plotting to murder their husbands. Demons or spirits of the air copulate with the sisters, and the women thus give birth to the giants whom Brutus later defeats. No other genealogical history of England's kings coupled with *A tous nobles* includes the Albina story, and the myth rarely appears in genealogical rolls written in England. The account of England's kings found with *A tous nobles* usually begins with either Brutus or Lud. Brutus's story appears at the beginning of *Les Grandes Chroniques de France* (Viard 1920–53, 11).

The history of England's rulers in Bodley Rolls 2 includes more British kings than the prologue of Ashmole Rolls 38, among them Constantine and Arthur, and they are all fully integrated into the genealogical tree diagram. Directly or indirectly, Bodley Rolls 2 draws on romance as well as chronicle: we learn that Arthur killed Mordred by his own hand (*et la fu Morderd occis de la main Arthus*), a detail also found in the thirteenth-century continental French prose romance the *Mort Artu* and English versions thereof. The roll also makes the romance hero Guy of Warwick's defeat of the giant Colbron the chief event of King Athelstan's reign. Neither Guy nor Albina are made a part of the genealogical diagram, however, since they did not rule over England.

AUDIENCE AND CIRCULATION. The audience of Bodley Rolls 2 is uncertain. At its top is a post-medieval inscription, *Ex dono magistri Henrici Savilij* (the manuscript collector Henry Saville of Banke, 1568–1617, *ODNB*), suggesting possible acquisition ultimately from one of the dissolved northern monasteries. A genealogy of the kings of England from Noah to Edward III written on the dorse of the roll in a fifteenth-century hand reveals further interest on the part of Bodley Rolls 2's readers. Notes in the margins of the roll (on the recto side) signal the changes of peoples who rule in England (e.g. *Anglois, Danois*) and draw attention to other noteworthy events, such as battles.

MANUSCRIPT SOURCE. Oxford, Bodleian Library, Bodley Rolls 2. A vellum roll measuring about 18 feet and 8 inches in length by 21–3 inches, made up of ten membranes, of which one at the top of the roll is modern (Madan 1895–1953, 560, no. 2978). The roll is written predominantly in black ink. Rubrics introduce the short paragraphs of text about each ruler. Decorated red and blue capital initials begin each paragraph: several are illuminated. The main branch of each genealogical tree runs vertically down the roll, and roundels naming the French and English rulers appear along the appropriate branch. Roundels naming a ruler's children are drawn adjacent to the main line and connect to the parent's roundel (either by close proximity or via a thin red line).

On the English side, a tree diagram showing the lineage of Norman dukes from Rollo begins in the right margin next to the paragraph about King Edgar. This diagram soon turns into the centre

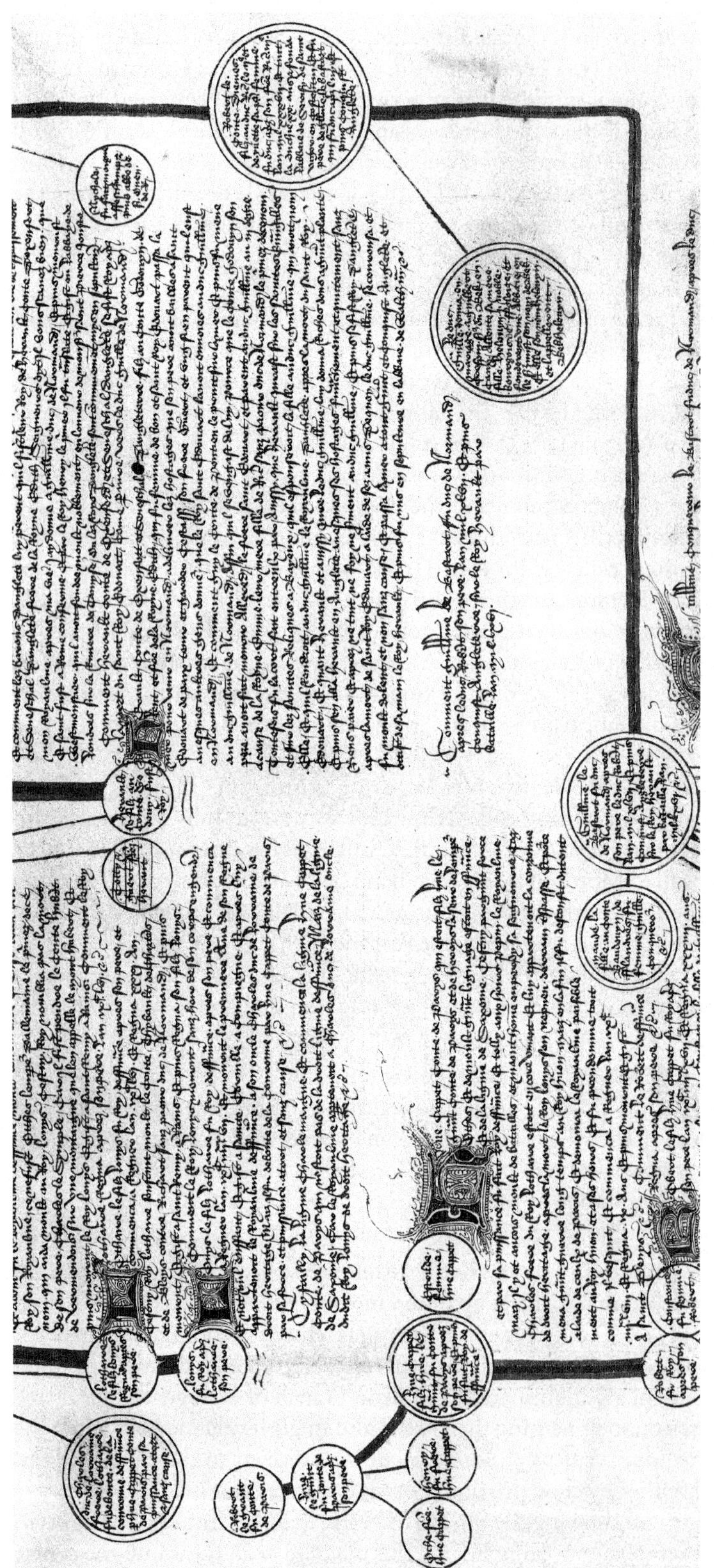

Fig. 8 (*above*). (20d) William of Normandy's ancestry (Oxford, Bodleian Library, MS Bodley Rolls 2, membrane 5, detail)

Fig. 9 (*below*). (20d) William of Normandy's lineage (Oxford, Bodleian Library, MS Bodley Rolls 2, membrane 5, detail)

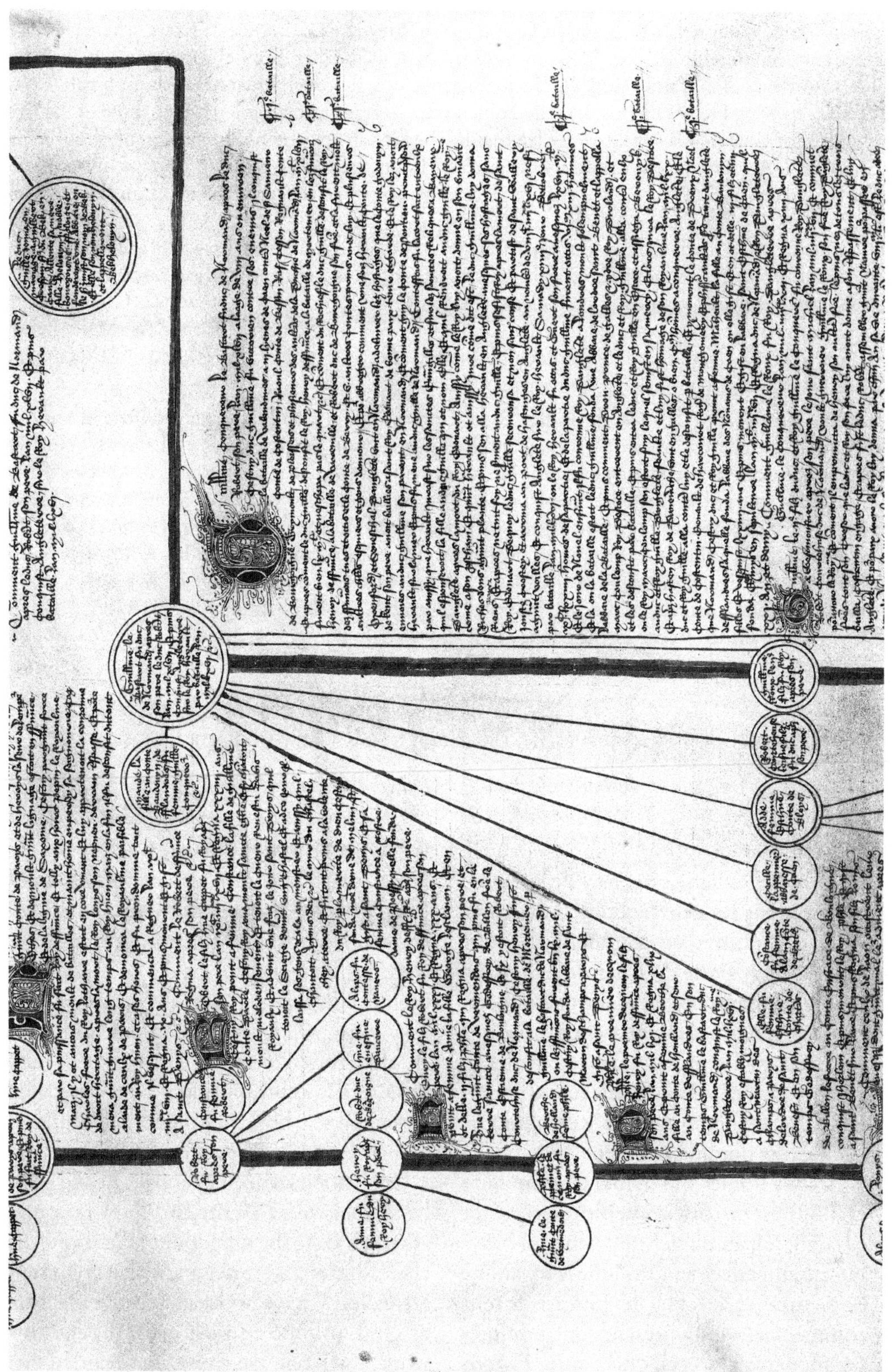

to connect to a roundel or William the Conqueror in the main genealogical branch. There is a large space between the roundels for William and Harold, and another roundel appears in the Norman line, below that of his father (Fig. 8). The main genealogical branch proceeds without breaks from William to King Henry VI (Fig. 9). The French tree diagram is incomplete, since three of the five roundels for Charles VII's children are left blank. The French text ends with a paragraph about King Charles VI. A rubric below introduces Charles VII, but there is no ensuing account of his reign. The illustrated lineages of French and English kings converge at several points from the reign of King Henry II of England onwards.

Other illustrations include an image of the True Cross between the main branch of the genealogical tree and the paragraph about King Constantius, father of Constantine, with an inscription *Sainte Helaine qui trouva la vraie croix* (St Helena who found the True Cross). Below, near Constantine's successors, a large circle outlined in red gives the names of nine cities in Brittany: St Malo, Leon, Rennes (*Resnes*), Nantes, Vannes, Cornouaille, Brest (*St Brys*), Tréguier (*Trigiez*), and Dol (Maximian is said to conquer Armorica, i.e. Brittany, during his reign).

Bibliography. No edition of Bodley Rolls 2 exists, and the roll has received little attention, though it is included in Tyson's survey and handlist (Tyson 2001 and 1994). Essays by Norbye (2007a and 2007b) and a study by Rajsic (2016) provide the only analyses to date. Norbye's work is essential for study of *A tous nobles* in roll or codex form (2007a, 2007b, 2008). For historiographical discussion see Hedeman 1991, Spiegel 1978. For universal chronicles inclusive of *A tous nobles* see Fagin Davis, ed., 2014, and 2009, 2006. Rolls with the Albina story include: BL Add. 24,342 and 27,342; Cambridge, Corpus Christi College 116 and 546; London, College of Arms 18/9, 20/2 (imperfect and damaged) and 20/6; and the 'Edward IV Roll', Philadelphia Free Library Lewis E 201 (on which see Visser-Fuchs 2002, 224)'. On the Albina myth see further (**42**), *The Mohun Chronicle*, Lamont and Baswell forthcoming, Johnson 1995.

Text and Translation: Left Column: The Kings of France

Pryamus le jeune, luy et Anthenor fonderent la regne de Venise et celle de Paudee en pais mesmes, et y gist Anthenor.

Cy ensuent les ligniés des roys de Fraunce: et comment les generaçouns sont issuez l'une de l'aultre, et comment ilz sont faillies. Et sy parle en brief de leurs faiz, et en quel temps ilz ont regné et combien, et ou ilz gisent, et quieulx enffans ilz ont eu, et en quel temps la cité de Lutesse fu commencee, et comment elle fust nommee Parys, et auxi comment le Royaulme de Gaulle fust nommé Fraunce.

A tous nobles qui ayment beaux faitz et bonnes histories vueille escripre et ensaigne[r], au plesier de Dieu, qui soit a mon commencement, comme le royaulme de Gaulle et la cyté de Lutesse furent commenciés, qui a present sont nommés Fraunce et Parys, et en quel temps. Et vous

Priam the young, he and Antenor founded the kingdom of Venice and that of Padua in the same kingdom, and there Antenor lies.

Here follow the lineages of the kings of France: how the generations descended from one another, and how the lineages were broken. It also speaks briefly about their deeds, at which time they ruled and for how long, where they lie buried, and what children they had, and at which time the city of Lutetia was begun, and how it was called Paris, and also how the kingdom of Gaul was named France.

To all nobles who like good deeds and good histories I wish to write and show how and at which time the kingdom of Gaul and the city of Lutetia were begun, which at present are called France and Paris, at the pleasure of God, may he be with me as I begin my work. I will tell you those who reigned one

nommeray d'on en hon ceulx qui ont regné, et quelle lignié ilz ont eue, la quelle s'ensuit, selonc l'a[r]bre qui le demonstre et ensaigne. Sy prye a toux ceulx quy l'orent lire ou liront que s'il i a aucune faulte qu'ilz me tiennent pour excusé, car je l'ay mys le meulx que j'ay peu selonc mon petit entendement, maiz leur plese a le corrigier. Et le trouveront es croniques Martin et en Orose, et es croniques de Fraunce tout au long. Car cest a[r]bre n'est fait que pour legierement savoir la lignié des roys qui ont regné en Fraunce, a qui Dieu doint bien regner jusque en la fin. Amen.

by one, what ancestry they had, and which lineage followed them, in accordance with the tree which demonstrates and teaches it. Also, I pray to all those who will hear it read or will read it that if there is any error they will excuse it, because I put it the best that I could, given my small understanding, but may it please them to correct it. And you will find it in the chronicles of Martin and in Orosius, and fully in the *Chroniques de France*. Indeed, this tree is only designed to easily learn the lineage of the kings who have reigned in France, whom may God allow to rule well all the way to the end. Amen.

Right column: the kings of England

Brutus vint de Troy et print Albion et le nomma Bretaigne qui aprés fu nommé Angleterre.

Cy ensuent les ligniés des roys qui ont regné en Angleterre, qui audevant avoit le nom la Graunt Bretaigne, depuis Jhesu Christus et depuis Julles Cesar, Empereur de Rome, jusques au temps du Roy Henry, le VI de ce nom, quy commenca a regner l'an mil. iiij.^{c} xiij.

Aprés la destructoun de Troy se partirent plusieurs seigneurs et moult dez nobles chevaliers et gens du bien. Et sachés qu'il ot du commencement du monde jusques au commencement de Troy la Graunt .iij.^{m} viij.^{c} xlij. ans, et puis dura elle .ix.^{c} lx.xij. ans ains qu'elle fu du tout destruitte. Et ce fu en .iiij. aage du monde, l'an iij.^{c} .xxxvij. Et d'icelle destructoun, se parti ung moult puissant seigneur et vaillant chevalier, qui estoit de la lignié du bon roy Priant de Troy, nommé Brutus. Et vint en Albion a tout graunt hoste et la print, que la royne Albine et sez soers l'avoient ainssi nommés par moult longtemps audevant en remembrance de son nom, pource que Albine fu l'aisnié soer de toutes, ou nul n'avoit unques habité. Les quelles dames furent roynes en Grece, et

Brutus came from Troy and took possession of Albion and named it Britain, which was afterwards called England.

Here follow the lineages of the kings who have reigned in England, which was formerly called Great Britain, from Jesus Christ and from Julius Caesar, Emperor of Rome, until the time of King Henry, the sixth of this name, who began to reign in the year 1413.

After the destruction of Troy several lords and many of the noble knights and good people departed. And know that there were 3842 years from the beginning of the world to the establishment of Troy the Great, and the city then stood for 972 years before it was completely destroyed. This was in the fourth age of the world, in the year 337. After the aforesaid destruction, one greatly powerful lord and valiant knight named Brutus, who was from the lineage of the good King Priam of Troy, left. He came with a great army and took possession of Albion, so named very long ago by Queen Albina and her sisters in remembrance of her name, because Albina was the eldest of all the sisters, and because no-one had ever lived there. The said ladies were queens in Greece,

pour ce qu'elles avoient machinés la mort de leurs maris, ilz furent mis en une nef garnie de vivres, et bouttés hors de leur païs par jugement pour aller a l'aventure ou ilz pourroient arriver. [Et arriverent] en la d[i]te terre, ou il n'avoit a l'eure personne fors que bestes sauvages, a une place qui a present est appellé Totenesse. Et furent .xxx. soers, comme le *Brut* en parle plus an plain. Et puis habitoient avesques elles lez espiritz, qui sont appellés Spirit incuby, en resemblance d'omme, dont vindrent les grauns geans. Cestuy Brutus conquist Albion et le nomma la Graunt Bretaigne, et aprés se fist appeller Brutus Albion. Et si fist il nommer la mellieure ville de la terre Nouvelle Troye, la quelle fust aprés appellé Londres, ou il fist moult de bien. Et pour abregier, aprés luy regnerent plusieurs roys en Bretaigne jusques a ung roy qui ot nom Lud .xxx. ans avaunt Jhesu Crist.

and because they had plotted the death of their husbands it was decreed that they be put into a boat provisioned with food, and be cast off from their country to take their chances wherever they might land. They arrived in the aforementioned land, where there was no-one at that time except for wild beasts, at a place that is now called Totnes. There were thirty sisters, as the *Brut* explains more fully. Then the spirits which are called incubi cohabited with them in the semblance of men, from which sprang the great giants. This Brutus conquered Albion and named it Great Britain, and afterwards called it Brutus's Albion. He also called the best city of the land New Troy, which afterwards was called London, where he did many good deeds. To summarise, several kings ruled in Britain after him, until the time of the king who was called Lud, thirty years before Jesus Christ.

Notes

Roundel 1a [left col.] 1 ***Pryamus le jeune . . . et Anthenor*** Priam was well-known in the Middle Ages as the last king of Troy. He was the youngest son of King Laomedon of Troy, and perhaps this is why he is here called 'the young'. Medieval audiences would have recognised Antenor as a Trojan elder and counsellor to King Priam before and during the Trojan War.

Roundel 1a [left col.] 2 **la regne de Venise et celle de Paudee** *Les Grandes Chroniques de France* make no mention of the kingdoms of Venice or Padua in relation to Priam and Antenor (see Paris 1836–8). According to Virgil's *Aeneid*, Antenor founded the city of Padua during the Trojan War.

29–30 **croniques Martin et en Orose** Martinus Polonus's *Chronicon pontificum et imperatorum* (Chronicle of Popes and Emperors) and Paulus Orosius's *Historiae adversus paganos* (History against the Pagans). Neither source is given in the prologue to the *Grandes Chroniques*, but both works were popular and influential in the later Middle Ages.

Roundel 1b [right col.] 37 **Bretaigne** MS *[ ] Bretaigne* (the word written before *Bretaigne* has been rubbed out).

40–1 **depuis Jhesu Christus et depuis Julles Cesar** The birth of Christ is a common chronological marker in chronicles of England. Julius Caesar's arrival in Britain is a frequent starting-point for a number of histories, including Bede's (Colgrave and Mynors, ed., 1969, i.2). There, Caesar's arrival follows the description of Britain and its earliest inhabitants.

42 **VI** The MS is difficult to read here. The original writing appears to have been rubbed out.

43–4 **l'an mil .iiij.^{c} xiij** [1413] The author gives the wrong date for King Henry VI's accession. Henry VI was born on 6 February 1421. After the unexpected death of his father, King Henry V, on 31 August 1422, an infant Henry VI succeeded to the throne of England (Griffiths 1981, 11).

51–2 **en .iiij. aage du monde** The organisation of events according to the six ages of the world was widespread in medieval history writing. The idea of the six ages ultimately derives from Augustine's Christian scheme for all history from the Creation of the world through to the Last Judgement (Given-Wilson 2004, 115). The seventh age denotes eternity. Augustine's scheme echoes the six days in which God created the world and the six stages of man's life cycle. In Augustine's view, the fourth age of the world encompasses the period from David to the Babylonian captivity of the Jews.

57–8 **la Royne Albine et sez soers** The Albina myth was first written in Anglo-Norman in the early fourteenth century, but was soon translated into Latin, Welsh, and Middle English (and Middle Dutch; see Ruch 2014, 91–2). It appears with or within historical texts in each of these languages. On the Albina myth in England's historiography, see Johnson 1995, Carley and Crick, ed., 1995, J. J. Cohen 1999, Ruch 2014, and for its texts, Lamont and Baswell forthcoming.

62 **Grece** Bodley Rolls 2 combines two main versions of the Albina story. In group A texts, Albina and her twenty-nine sisters are princesses of Greece and are unsuccessful in murdering their husbands. In group B texts the thirty-three royal sisters are Syrian and succeed in murdering their husbands (there is no youngest sister who reveals the murderous plot, as in A). In Bodley Rolls 2, Albina and her sisters are from Greece, but there is no mention of a youngest sister and the women seem to have successfully murdered their husbands. Some Middle English prose *Brut* texts also combine group A and B stories (Matheson 1998), as does Sir Thomas Gray in his *Scalacronica* (see (**16**)) and Jean de Wavrin in his fifteenth-century Burgundian history of England (Hardy 1864, 5–35), and further variations exist (see the *Mohun Chronicle* (**42**)).

64 **mis en une nef** The setting adrift theme is a common motif in medieval literature. See Schlauch 1927, and Reinhard 1941.

67–6 **[Et arriverent] en la d[i]te terre** MS *et arriv[ ]nt*, written above the line, is partly illegible. MS *dce* emended to *dite*.

69–70 **a une place qui a present est appellé Totenesse** Albina and her sisters here anticipate Brutus's conquest of Albion/Britain/England, since they disembark at the very place where Brutus famously lands (e.g. Reeve and Wright 2007, 27).

71–2 **comme le *Brut* en parle plus an plain** The author cites the *Brut* as his source for the Albina story. *Brut* could refer to the anonymous prose *Brut* chronicle, which together in Anglo-Norman and Middle English was the most popular secular vernacular text in later-medieval England (Matheson 1998, 9: Marvin 2006, 1). However, the term *Brut* could also refer to a history beginning with Brutus more generally. As in the prologue to *A tous nobles*, the author here draws attention to the brevity of his work. This occurs again in line 82. For a similar citation see *Waldef* (**6**).

77 **Brutus Albion** Brutus is most often identified with Britain and/or England. However, the Albina myth helped to shape the idea of Albion by providing the island with a history (previously, it was only a name, as in Bede, but see Crick 2008). In consequence, as Bodley Rolls 2 shows, the term Albion was sometimes detached from Albina and attached instead to Brutus (Rajsic 2012). Chaucer in his 'Complaint of Chaucer to his Purse' and Lydgate in his *Verses on the Kings of England*, *Troy Book*, and *Fall of Princes* also refer to 'Brutes Albion' (Benson 1987, 656; Gairdner 1876; Edwards 1998; Bergen 1924–7).

80–1 **Et pour abregier** The next ruler in the Bodley Rolls 2 narrative, also the next to appear in the genealogical diagram, is King Lud. The author here ensures that his readers know that Lud did not rule immediately after Brutus, and at the same time he shows his knowledge of mythical British history. Readers need only look on the back of the roll for a fuller genealogical diagram showing the descendants of Noah, and giving the mythical British kings between Brutus and Lud.

83 **avaunt Jhesu Crist** Something is written after *Jhesu Crist*, but it is difficult to read. It may be an *etcetera*. Other copies of *A tous nobles* paired with the genealogy of England's kings do not have similar writing and thus, unfortunately, do not shed light on the question.

21. John of Howden, *Rossignos* [Dean 626], Prologue, Extract and Explicit: Cambridge, Corpus Christi College, MS 471, ff. 1^r–1^v/4, 82^r/21–83^v/8, 110^r/13–111^r/4

Date of composition and provenance. Between 1273 and 1282; composed, most probably at the royal court, for Eleanor of Provence (d. 1291), queen of Henry III (r. 1217–72).

Author, sources and nature of text. The author is named at the opening of the prose prologue as *Johan de Houdene, clerc la roine d'Engleterre* (Prol. *1–2*): at the end of the poem he is God's mother's *menestrel* (minstrel), *Johan de Houdene*, who is sending his *chanzon* to King Edward's mother (vv. 5240–3, 5269–71). Howden is the largest medieval settlement in the East Riding of Yorkshire, with an important collegiate church: it produced at least one other author, the chronicler Roger of Howden (d. 1201/2). Several possible writers named John of Howden have been adduced, but the *Rossignos* author is now accepted as the John of Howden recorded as Queen Eleanor's clerk between 1268 and 1275, who was given a prebend in the royal gift at Bridgnorth, Shropshire, in 1275. John of Howden was an admired composer of Latin devotional poems, among them his *Canticum amoris*, *Viola*, *Quinquaginta salutationes* (to the Virgin) and others. Like Matthew Paris in the *Vie de saint Edmund* (**13**), Howden also reworked his own Latin writing in French for an elite woman patron: *Rossignos* is an expanded version of Howden's *Philomena* (1131 monorhymed quatrains on the Passion) for Eleanor of Provence, though the Latin and French versions are linked more closely by commonalities of theme and image than by direct translation.

The vernacular poem is 1318 monorhymed octosyllabic quatrains, including a verse epilogue and a prose prologue (possibly not authorial). The prologue claims that this intense poem of 5272 lines is a single thought or reflection (*pensee*, line *6*) which draws diverse materials into a single harmony (*acordaunce*, line *9*). Traditions concerning nightingales are long-lived, from the rape of Philomena in Ovid onwards: their medieval versions embrace the range of secular and divine passions, with the nightingale frequently representing both Christ and the believer's response, as well as the poet's voice. Structured meditations on Christ's death of the kind influentially modelled in Edmund of Abingdon's *Mirour de seinte eglyse* (**22**) were often equated with the nightingale's singing at the different canonical hours.

Rossignos consists of loosely sequential meditations on Christ's infancy (though without the apocryphal tales of *Les Enfaunces Jesu Crist*, (**20b**)), his life (briefly) and his passion (extensively). This narrative structure is framed by addresses to the Virgin. In her role of *virgo lactans* at the beginning of the poem, her milk is seen as the antidote to the 'poisoned apple' (vv. 76–82), her breast as a cellar of the wine of wisdom (vv. 97–100). At the end of the poem, she speaks at length on her own understanding of her son's life, the Old Testament prophets, and the natural and cosmological knowledge she has gained in the crucifixion (vv. 4199–4588). Here the nursing mother and the pietà figure combine in the iconography of the Virgin as a throne of wisdom, while Eleanor of Provence is farewelled as 'wise and spotless queen' (vv. 113–14 below).

The poem deploys the elaborate, often violent imagery associated both with the nightingale and with the affective devotion practised by the friars and some of the older orders, notably the Cistercians and the Victorines, in the thirteenth century. The imagistic density and the many sound effects of the Latin *Philomena* are not invariably reproduced line by line: *Rossignos* abounds in its own comparable vernacular effects (see e.g. vv. 29–32 below). Like many of the artistic works associated with Henry and Eleanor, the poem is a high-culture artefact, its polished aesthetic a tribute to the sacred nature of earthly as well as heavenly royalty. The poem's ardent spirituality shares their court's crusading militancy and embraces the personnel of the Grail quest, many of whom appear in *Rossignos* in a long list (vv. 3973–4048) of ancient and contemporary fighters (from the Maccabees to Lancelot to Eleanor's son Edward I and his crusading expeditions of 1270). All of these are outshone in battle by the heart emblazoned with the blood of *l'agneau sanz maille* (the spotless lamb, v. 3971, with a possible pun on 'lamb without [chainmail] armour'). The nine orders of angels are 'the Round Table of heaven' (v. 3547), a chivalric force armoured in 'pure light' (v. 3554).

Audiences such as Eleanor, her ladies, her clerics and her ecclesiastical friends and ministers may have read the poem, or heard it read, or both: the intensely literate awareness of its narrative persona and the frequency of the heart-as-book metaphor in the poem suggest the thirteenth-century development in which individual reading became a more prevalent mode. But the musico-lyrical effect of *Rossignos*'s monorhymed quatrains demands reading aloud, even if read in solitude, and the repeated announcement of its commencement in the prose prologue given here sounds like a call for attention to a listening audience. The poem moves in sections of different lengths, irregularly marked off by changing anaphora (*Amor, Mort, Quors, Jhesu, Lance, Tu moers, cest nom Jesu*, etc.). It is shot through with a deeply sensuous synaesthesia of blood, roses, scents, cosmology and the natural world, in which the evolution of one metaphor into another makes for a constantly alive and shifting texture. An exquisitely polished work of intricate, meaningful surfaces, the poem's meditative techniques and metaphysical imagery combine Donne-like strenuousness and delight with the Gothic aesthetic of high seriousness. This is startlingly rich allegorical material: it makes strong aesthetic and affective demands and implies highly cultivated mnemonic and meditative habits (see also the contemporary *Lambeth Apocalypse* (20a)).

AUDIENCE AND CIRCULATION. *Rossignos* is powerful, elegant, and consonant with the temper of Eleanor of Provence's reading circle and 'devotional community' among her ladies and clerics (see Howell 1998, 82–92 for this reading culture, where both romances and devotional books were owned). This piety is neither enclosed nor politically innocent. If the poem went with Eleanor to Amesbury, the royal Fontevrauldine nunnery which Eleanor entered in 1386, twelve years after her son's crowning, it would not, perhaps, have read very differently than at court. Unlike King Arthur's Guenevere, her legendary precedessor in retirement to Amesbury, Eleanor seems less to have been seeking refuge from the world than an alternative base from which to follow the interests of the crown.

Rossignos is strongly shaped by the idea of its regal recipient, but other readers are envisaged in the poem's explicit (see vv. 93–100 below) and the late date of the extant manuscript argues that the poem found them. Howden's *Philomena* remained even more influential, continuing to be read into the seventeenth century: John Pecham (d. 1292), Franciscan archbishop of Canterbury (who wrote in French for Eleanor of Provence's daughter-in-law, Eleanor of Castile, Edward I's queen) drew on Howden for his own *Philomela praevia* (translated into fourteenth-century French as *Rossignol*): the fourteenth-century Middle English *Meditations on the Life and Passion of Christ* is a free reworking of Howden, and *Philomena* influenced Rolle and other fifteenth-century writers. Charles d'Orléans borrowed a copy of *Philomena* from the Franciscans' London library during his English imprisonment, had it copied, and in 1440 took it back to France, where he composed an imitation of the poem. English-language nightingale poems were in vogue in the fifteenth century (see e.g. Wogan-Browne *et al.* 1999, no. 2.36; Glauning, ed., 1900).

MANUSCRIPT SOURCE. The extant manuscript, Cambridge Corpus Christi College MS 471, from the end of the fourteenth century and surviving in Archbishop Parker's own collection, contains only *Rossignos*. The manuscript is small (150 × 109 mm), professional and plain (cursiva Anglicana media script; unilluminated; written around occasional holes in the vellum). Red paraphs mark off the poem's quatrains in pairs. The manuscript layout was also intended to mark the poem into 43 sections (of varying length, but usually *c.* 124–6 lines): space is left for large initials throughout, though only the guide letters are entered (this may indicate that the work was understood as requiring slow meditative consumption over many sittings; see Hesketh 2006, 10). The text is occasionally annotated with Latin glosses and sometimes with French in a hand similar to the main scribe. An early-modern hand (Wilkins 1993, 146–7) translates *Rossignos*' prose prologue into English on a paper leaf paste-in (f. ii v). The title *Rosarium Johannis Howden* inscribed under this translation is suggestive, given the poem's meditative mode and its manuscript mark-up in paired quatrains, like so many rosary beads. On f. 6^{r} and f. 111^{v} are signatures of Francis Aldwyche, a Cambridge scholar *fl.* 1589–1608 (Hesketh 2006, 2). The modest quality of the manuscript is not incompatible with elite ownership: for devout patrons, devotional texts could be given deliberately humble and serviceable treatment as well as de luxe presentation. Nevertheless, a more glamorous presentation copy of *Rossignos* probably once existed (compare the beautifully illuminated copy of Pecham's *Philomela* in Glasgow Hunterian MS 231, privately owned by Roger of Waltham in the early fourteenth century: http://special.lib.gla.ac.uk/exhibns/month/june2008.html).

Bibliography. *Rossignos* has been partially published and studied by Stone (1946–7, 398 lines) and fully edited by Hesketh 2006 who discusses the poem's date at 10 and 220, n. to 4027, and the poet's career at 3–6: see also Rigg *ODNB*. Neave 1991 gives an account of medieval Howden and its educational opportunities. On Howden's *Philomena* and its influence see Rigg 1992, 208–15 and Blume 1930, who edits the poem: Raby 1939 edits Howden's other Latin poems. The Middle English reworking of Pecham's *Philomela* is edited by D'Evelyn 1921; see also her 1940 study. On Charles d'Orléans's version see Ouy 1959; Ouy 2000, 52–3. The Middle French version of Pecham's poem is edited by Baird and Kane 1978 and by Napoli 1979. On nightingale traditions see Rigg 1992, 157–239; Pfeffer 1985, Shippey 1970. Affective devotion has been re-examined by McNamer 2010 and Karnes 2011. On medieval models of the heart and their implications for reading see Jager 2000 and Webb 2010: for thirteenth-century individual reading see Saenger 1997, Millett 1996. Williamson 1998 discusses the iconography of the nursing Virgin. For Eleanor of Provence see the biography by Howell 1998: on Eleanor and Henry's tastes and patronage, Salter 2010, 82–92 (*Rossignos* succinctly characterised, 90), and on late thirteenth- and fourteenth-century sensibility Binski 2014. For a study of the poem and Eleanor as its dedicatee, see Wogan-Browne 2014.

TEXT AND TRANSLATION

(i) Prose Prologue and opening

Ci comence la pensee Johan de Houedene clerc la roine d'Engleterre, mere le roi Edward, de la neissance e de la mort et du relievement e de l'ascension Jhesu Crist e de l'assumpcion Nostre Dame. Et a non ceste pensee 'Rossignos', pur ce ke, sicome li rossignos feit de diverses notes une melodie, auci feit cestes livres de diverses matires une acordaunce. Et pur ce enkores a il non 'Rossignos' que il estoit fez e trové en un beau verger flori ou rossignol adés chauntoient. Et pur ce fu il faiz que li quor celi qui le lira soit esprys en l'amour Nostre Seignour. Benoit soit qui le lira! Ceste oevre comence. Ci comence li 'Rossignol'.

Here begins the meditation by John of Howden, clerk to the queen of England, mother of King Edward, on the birth and death and the resurrection and ascension of Jesus Christ and the assumption of Our Lady. And this meditation is called 'Nightingale' because just as the nightingale makes one melody out of different notes, so too this book makes different subjects into a single concord. And it is also called 'Nightingale' because it was made and composed in a beautiful flowering orchard where the nightingales were singing at the time. And it was made in order that the heart of whoever reads it should be enflamed with the love of Our Lord. Blessed be the reader. This is the beginning of this work. Here begins the 'Nightingale'.

[A]lme, lesse lit de peresse
E ta langor e ta tristesse;

Leave, soul, the bed of laziness, and your languor and your sadness: learn the depth

Apreng d'amour la parfondesse
E a penser d'amour t'adresse.
Oste de toi delivrement
De vaine amour le marrement;
Apreng d'amer entierement
Et parlier d'amor docement.

of love, and turn to thoughts of love. Swiftly remove from yourself the sorrow of foolish love; learn to love fully and to speak of love sweetly.

Jhesu, des saintz la drüerie,
Leur quor, leur amor, e leur vie
Fai a moun povre engin aïe
Que ta parole enpreigne et die.
Li seint feu de t'amour m'espreigne [f. 1v]
Si ke de toi penser m'enseigne,
Fai de ma langue riche enseigne
Que ta loange ben enpreigne!

Jesus, beloved of the saints, their heart, their love, and their life, give help to my poor craftsmanship so that I may learn and speak your word. Let the holy fire of your love enflame me so that it teaches me to think of you; make my tongue a noble banner so that it undertakes your praise well!

(ii) Reading with the heart [= Hesketh, vv. 3897–3956]

Par ceste mort bien remembree
Et einz eu quor encimentee
Est alme a Dieu droit mariee:
Il est l'espous, ele esposee.
Li queors ou cist penser repose [f. 82v]
Pur la vertu qu'i est enclose
Devient com une fresche rose
Devant Dieu overte e declose.
Cist pensers est droit alöé
Que quant eu coer est aloué,
Dieu mesmes i est lors vowé,
Com a l'offrende de Nöé;
Escrit est que Deus odora
Le don dont Nöé l'onora:
Mes cist penser tant de odor a
Que les sainz d'amor estora.
Cist pensiers est une chaëne
Que Dieu au quor droit enchaëne:
Il est respons, il est antenne
Qui gloire por löer desrenne.
Quoers, a touz les jours de ta vie
Cist pensiers soit ta melodie,
Tes matines e ta complie
Et tes heures, quoi que nul die.
Je di ke c'est chose provee
Que cist pensers est une espee
Dont la teste est adés trenchee
De la beste deffiguree.

By recollecting this death properly and setting it firmly in the heart, the soul is well and truly married to God: he is the spouse and she is the bride. The heart where this thought reposes becomes, through the power enclosed in it, a fresh rose opened and revealed before God. This thought is the true incense which, once placed in the heart, invokes God himself there: just as it is written of Noah's offering that God smelt the gift with which Noah honoured him. But this thought has so intense a fragrance that it provisions all the saints with love: this thought is a chain that tightly binds God within the heart. It is both response and antiphon, winning heaven's *gloria* for its praise. Heart, for all the days of your life let this thought be your melody, your matins, your compline and your hours, whatever may be said to you. I say that it is a proven thing that this thought is a sword with which the ugly beast's head can instantly be cut off.

Bien doit, pur voir, aver grant joie [f. 83r]
Li quors ou cist penser ombroie
Kar lors les felouns plus effroie
Que l'ostour par son vol sa proie.
Ne Judith qui le rei decire
Ne Davy quant sa funde vire
Ne poet tiels felons descomfire
Com cil qui cist pensee remire.
La memoire est abalsamee
Quant entient a ceste pensee.
Lors est li quors chambre acemee
Du Rei de Gloire enhabitee.
Cist pensers a la voiz si saine
Que, quant il chante a gorge plaine,
Li rossignos pur nient se paine
Chaunter a li, ne la siraine.
Si seint Pere out seint Jake estoie,
De cest penser messal ferroie,
Mon coer auter, e chaunteroie;
Lors jesqu'eu ciel oï seroie.
Qui en cest penser se delite
En son coer [a] la bible escrite:
Li reguarders est grant merite
Et la leson est joie eslite.
Qui a cest livre se prendra [f. 83v]
Devinité si aprendra,
Que quant a parler entendra
Li froissz quoers d'amor esprendra.
En cest trebieau livre a devise
Ont li saint sainteté aprise.
Voillez, doz livre, que je lise
En toi fine amor sanz feyntise.

Truly, the heart where this thought is harboured ought to experience great joy, for then it can terrify the wicked more than the goshawk's stoop does his prey. Neither Judith, when she beheaded a king, nor David in wielding his sling can overcome so many wicked enemies as can someone who contemplates this thought. Memory itself is made fragrant when it sets itself to this thought: then the heart is a chamber bedecked, inhabited by the King of Glory. This thought has a voice so wholesome that, when it sings with full throat, in vain do the nightingale and the siren strive to sing so well. If I were St Peter or St James, I would make a missal of this thought, an altar of my heart, and I would sing until I could be heard in heaven. Whoever delights in this thought has the Bible inscribed in their heart: contemplation of it is great merit, and the reading of it a rare joy. Whoever gives themselves over to this book learns divine knowledge thereby, for when it listens to what the book says, the cold heart takes fire. In this perfectly made book the saints learned their holiness: if only it could be your wish, sweet book, for me to read in you a courtly love without falseness!

(iii) Explicit [= Hesketh, vv. 5233–72]

Finir voil ma chanzon petite
Et pri Dieu pur sa grace eslite
Que cil eit joië e merite
Qui en oïr la se delite.
Reçoif en gré, virge Marie,
Ma chanzonete ja finie,
Et reguardez par cortoisie
Ton men[e]strel qui vers toi crie.
Miere de Dieu, meson e tente,

I will finish my little song and pray to God that, by his excellent grace, whoever takes pleasure in hearing it may have joy and reward. Virgin Mary, graciously receive my little song now it is finished, and look courteously upon your minstrel, who cries out to you. Mother of God, my house and my canopy, your writer John of Howden, presents to you by way of a true tribute this

Tes escrivains de droite rente,
Jehan de Houdene, te presente
Cest livret ou a mis entente.
[f. 110v] Et tot soit il de povr' afaire,
Preng lo, qui tant es debonaire,
Preng le e met en toun aumaire
Dont tote sainte eglise esclaire:
Et a trestoz a qui agree
D'oïr sovent ceste pensee,
Mostrez leur par droite soudee
En leur mort ta face esmeree.
Cist livret leur soit garantie
De toz mauz e signe de vie,
Sicom li rossignos quant crie
Est signe de sesoun jolie.

little book over which he has taken pains. And although it is a poor little thing, receive it, you who are so gracious; take it, and put it in your book-chest, which illumines all holy church; and give just repayment to all who find it pleasing to hear this meditation often, and look on them at their death with your sublime face. Let this little book be a protection against all evils for them, and an emblem of life, just as the nightingale's cry signals the lovely time of year.

Jhesu, des sainz joie enterine,
Ma chanzounete qui termine
T'envoie un salu d'amor fine:
Preng la, doz ami, e l'affine
Et quant mort me ferra finer,
Face t'amours por moi finer,
Et me voillez si affiner
Que soie o toi sanz diffiner.
A toi soit honor, Roi de Gloire,
Fine joie nient transitoire,
Loange, vertu, et victoire!
Einsi termine ceste estoire.

Jesus, joy entire of the saints, my little song which is ending sends you a greeting of true love: take it, sweet friend, and make it truer: and when death brings my end, make your love my ransom, and, if it is your will, refine my love so that I may be with you for ever. Honour to you, King of Glory, and true imperishable joy, praise, power, and victory! Thus this story ends.

[f. 111r] A la roïne, l'esmeree,
Mere au roi Edward, la senee,
Va, chanzon, e se li agree,
Li soiez leue e recordee.
Ci finist li 'Rossignos' Johan de Houdene

Go, little song, to the wise and spotless queen, mother of Edward the king, and if it pleases her, may you be read and remembered by her!

Here John of Howden's 'Nightingale' comes to an end.

Notes

1–16 **Ci comence . . . li 'Rossignol'** The Prologue is normally assumed to be authorial, but it may be a separate addition on the basis of a reading of the poem itself, added either in this manuscript or its exemplar.

8 **cestes livres** sic MS.

10–12 **fez e trové en un beau verger . . . chauntoient** *trové* (lit. 'found') can have the meaning of Latin *invenire*: the prologue locates inspiration or material as discovered (rhetorically) in an orchard of singing nightingales (a *chanson d'aventure* opening).

1 **[A]lme** Guide letter only in MS initial.

1–4 **[A]lme . . . t'adresse** This opening is close to that of the prologue to Anselm of Lucca's *Medita-*

tiones de gestis Domini Nostri Jesu Christi: Desere jam, anima, lectulum soporis; / Languor, torpor, vanitas excludantur foris. / Intus cor efferveat facibus amoris, / Recolens mirifica gesta Salvatoris (*Soul, leave now your drowsy bed, Send away laziness, sloth and vanity! / Within your heart let the firebrands of love be fervent,/ Remembering the wonderful deeds of the Saviour*, PL149.591A) and the *Meditationes* also continue with the same sequence of events as *Rossignos* (see Wilkins 1993). But apart from the metrical differences, there is so much elaboration and such different treatment in *Rossignos* that Anselm of Lucca is less a source than a prompt. So too (see below) Howden's own *Philomena* provides starting points, rather than *Rossignos*'s being a translation of it.

8 **parlier d'amor docement** On the rhetorical and affective force of sweetness see Carruthers 2006.

13 **seint feu de t'amour** A Pentecostal image of divine inspiration.

17–20 **Par ceste mort . . . esposee** Compare Howden's *Philomena* (Mortis huius dulci memoria/ Dum rubescunt cordis altaria/Digna Deo donatur hostia, Cuius scandit caelos fragrantia: *the sweet memory of this death is worthy to be given to God while the heart's altar reddens and the fragrance of the sacrifice rises to the heavens*, Blume 1930, 997). Although some of the principal themes developed in this passage are present in the Latin, they are freely treated and elaborated in consonant but different directions (see Blume 1930, 997–1020).

23 **fresche** MS *freche*.

25 **alöé** Hesketh 2006 (217, n. to 3905) suggests not *AND* 'juice of aloes' (cf. Chaucer's 'lign aloes and galle', in *Troilus* IV, 1109), but as in *Französchiches etymologisches Wörterbuch* 24, 345b, 'aromatic wood used to perfume the body, clothing and rooms'. He notes that T–L links the word with spices and incense. 'Incense' seems best to fit the context here. The annotating hand writes *alowe* in the right-hand margin as if the word needed elucidation.

26 **Que** MS *Qui*

27 **vowé** MS *vwoe* with marginal gloss *vowe*.

28 **l'offrende de Nöé** Gen 8.20–1.

29–34 **Deus odora /Le don . . . au quor droit enchaëne** For the argument that this passage depends on the medieval conception of the heart as porous and open to the passage of vital spirits (and of incense and voice), see Wogan-Browne 2014. On the relevant medieval model of the heart, see Webb 2010.

35 **antenne** Translated in its original sense of antiphon (cf. OE and ME 'antefne') since 'anthem' has become associated with optional special hymns or other compositions introduced into services, while the versicle and response, together making up the antiphon (*antenne*), remain basic elements of the office (*Oxford Dictionary of the Christian Church*, *s.v.* 'anthem').

36 **Qui gloire por löer desrenne** Another complex image of reciprocity and circular fulfilment in God's love and the love of God: the song of praise enacts the underlying assimilation of the believer to Christ, while the song itself can claim glory by praising Christ's glory, as in the antiphons of the office. As Hesketh (2006, 217 n. 3916) notes, *gloire* can mean heavenly glory and the *gloria* of the Mass (as translated here) and *desrenier* can mean both 'win by combat' and 'recite'.

39–40 **Tes matines . . . tes heures** Passion devotions are frequently seen as a version of the monastic office, with each of the hours denoting a different stage of Christ's torment and death.

41 **c'est** MS *ceste*

44 **la beste deffiguree** Probably the seven-headed beast of the Apocalypse, a figure in Anglo-Norman penitential thought for the seven deadly sins (Watson and Wogan-Browne 2004, 44). In the Trinity Apocalypse owned either by Eleanor of Provence or someone close to her, f. 14^{v} shows, unusually, a woman raising her sword against one of the heads of the beast as it destroys the saints (see McKitterick *et al.* 2005, pl. 11).

48 **par son vol** In modern English a raptor swooping down on its prey is said to stoop (*OED*, 'stoop' v. 1, I, sense 6).

49 **Judith** The slayer of King Holofernes and liberator of her people (Jth 13.2–8; Blume 1930, 1006).

49 **decire** MS *descire* with *s* expuncted.

50 **Davy** David, slayer of Goliath (1 Sam 17.49; Blume 1930, 1005).

52 **cist pensee** As Hesketh notes (2006, 218, 3932 n.), orthographic for *penser*, not a confusion of grammatical gender.

56 **Du** MS *Ou*

60 **la siraine** The Sirens of classical tradition lured sailors to shipwreck by their singing.

61 **seint Pere . . . seint Jake** St Peter and St James the Greater, apostles.

62, 65 **cest** MS *ceste.*

66 **En son coer . . . la bible escrite** On the heart as book, an important metaphor in much devotional tradition, see Jager 2000.

66 **En** MS *et*

72 **Li** MS *Les*

79 **cil** MS *celi*

87 **Jehan** possibly counts only as one syllable in the prosody of this line.

91 **toun aumaire** Hesketh glosses as (treasure) store (2006, vv. 1705, 1907) and reliquary (v. 3644) at other occurrences. Here the sense of book-case (*AND*, *s.v.* 'aumaire' 2) or more properly, given the furnishings of medieval libraries, book *chest* seems more appropriate and also picks up a metaphor of illumination at v. 1590. There is also perhaps a biblical echo, Luke 2.19 (But Mary stored all these things in her heart). Like other high-ranking women, the Virgin is frequently represented as learned in the later Middle Ages.

97 **livret** MS *lieuret*, first *e* expuncted.

106 **finer** Hesketh 2006 suggests the word may perhaps be *fuier*, but his reading as *finer*, 'pay a fine', makes good sense.

110 **transitoire** MS *transitory.*

22. St Edmund of Abingdon [ascribed], *Mirour de seinte eglyse* (*St Edmund's Mirror*) [Dean 629], Excerpts: London, British Library, MS Harley 1121, ff. 143^v–144^v, 149^r–151^r

DATE OF COMPOSITION AND PROVENANCE. Mid-thirteenth century, England.

AUTHOR, SOURCES AND NATURE OF TEXT. The *Mirour* is an anonymous translation of a *Speculum* composed by Edmund Rich of Abingdon, archbishop of Canterbury (1234–40, canonised 1247). Paris-trained, he was initially a master of arts and subsequently a doctor of theology at Oxford. He brokered a peace between Henry III and a baronial rebellion led from the Welsh Marches in 1232, upheld church rights against the royal courts throughout his archbishopric and died en route to Rome at Pontigny in 1240. His hagiographers customised his life as far as possible to the pattern of Becket's. The *Speculum* may have been written for the Augustinian canons at Merton with whom Edmund spent a year in 1213–14, or for the various communities (the University of Oxford, the canons of Salisbury) with whom he worked in the twenty years after the Lateran Council of 1215. Perhaps Edmund's two sisters, whom he installed as professed nuns at Catesby, Northamptonshire, had the vernacular translation done: according to Matthew Paris's verse life of Edmund (13), all the siblings were made to learn French by their mother. Although often referred to as *Speculum ecclesie*, the original Latin text was known as the *Speculum religiosorum*: *Speculum ecclesie* more properly applies to the re-translation of the *Mirour* into Latin in the latter half of the thirteenth century, presumably after Edmund's canonisation in 1247. The change in title from professed religious to the church in general epitomises the text's appeal for ever broader audiences.

An instant spiritual and pastoral classic, Edmund's *Speculum* draws substantially on Augustinian contemplative thought in the form of Hugh of St Victor's twelfth-century writings on knowledge of self and God, and on the work of the great pastoralist, Gregory the Great, in his *Moralities on Job* and *Homilies on Ezechiel*. The *Speculum* is initially offered as guidance for those already vocationally committed to the perfected life, i.e. professed religious, but its combination of contemplative and catechetical materials was a new synthesis, responsive to the energy of Lateran IV's pastoral initiatives for the whole church. The work's lucid organisation of doctrine in the service of spiritual growth made it attractive to many constituencies: monastic and secular clergy, and, as its modifications in the Anglo-Norman and *Speculum ecclesie* versions suggest, parish priests, spiritual directors and lay audiences. The *Speculum* outlines a comprehensive theory for reading the world and one's place in it (illuminating, among other things, the paradigms underlying the bestiary genre; see (17)).

Whether as a reminder to professed religious or as instruction for laypeople framed within an overarching spiritual rationale, the *Mirour*'s structure makes all its materials part of a dynamic process of spiritual development. Using only minor modifications and explications, the anonymous Anglo-Norman translator preserves the clarity of the source text's structure: a framing ascent from self-knowledge to knowledge of God through meditation on human wretchedness and God's generosity. After inward contemplation of what reason and revelation can give a human by way of self-knowledge, contemplation turns outwards to the created world and scripture, and finally to contemplation of God in various degrees. Edmund supplements scriptural contemplation with a concise presentation of the pastoral materials to be drawn from holy writings, such as were published after Lateran IV for parish priests to use with their parishioners: the catechetical sets of seven (deadly sins, sacraments, etc., with particular attention to the seven petitions of the *Pater noster*), the six works of mercy, ten commandments, four cardinal virtues and the pains of hell. The exemplary vehicle for human-divine contact is the Lord's prayer, and the *Speculum* presents the scriptural prose version as the only authoritative and cogent form. Unspecified elaborate verse versions (*verba ritmica et curiosa*) are decried as witness only to carnal partiality rather than true devotional feeling.

The *Speculum* supplements the contemplation of God in his humanity: it constructs a devotion by pairing events from Christ's passion with aspects of the incarnation and redemption, with each pair assigned to one of the seven canonical hours as subjects of meditation. In spite of the austerity with which Edmund hews to the text of the Vulgate Bible without the apocryphal details drawn on in later works such as ps-Bonaventura's *Meditationes vitae Christi*, his scheme remained popular as a separate devotion in its own right. The *Mirour*'s concluding account of God's divine Trinitarian nature draws distinctions between God's varying manifestations of himself to human understanding and it has been argued that different versions of the text divide around chapter 36, which outlines a three-fold model for contemplating God's trinitarian divinity. The full chapter is included for religious readers and omitted or abbreviated for lay audiences. Even so, in chapter 36 of the 'lay' version, for all its brevity in some manuscripts, the reader is given something of the final stages of raising the soul above itself to contemplate God, and encouraged to 'put every corporeal thing out of your heart, and let your living understanding fly beyond all human reason, and there you will find such great sweetness and such great intimacy that no-one can know who has not experienced it' (*metrez hors de vostre queor chascun ymagination corporele et lessez vostre vif entendement voler outre chascun humaine raisoun, et la troverez vous si grant douçour et si grant privetee qe nul ne sciet fors soul celuy qi l'ad esprouee*; f. 155rb).

The division between religious and lay is seldom stable or categorical in the *Mirour*'s vigorous manuscript transmission, but the work's combination of the contemplative and the pastoral undoubtedly creates what was to become an intensely negotiated and often contested frontier zone for medieval people's spiritual aspirations and anxieties: the question of where the boundaries between contemplative and active lives might be, and how to live a spiritually acceptable and fruitful life in the world. In its later, Middle English reworkings, the *Mirour* continues to fuel and serve a spectrum of views.

AUDIENCE AND CIRCULATION. Readily usable as basic instruction, as a convenient *summa* for fully developed spiritual programmes, and as a model for living that might apply to both professed and lay people, the *Mirour* travelled widely from the mid-thirteenth century to the sixteenth. It is witnessed in twenty-eight extant manuscripts, both insular and continental. Of all the didactic and devotional works composed in medieval England, perhaps only *Ancrene Wisse*, the celebrated early-thirteenth-century 'Guide for Anchoresses', has a comparably vigorous multilingual career throughout and beyond the Middle Ages. In addition to its mid-thirteenth-century translation from the Latin *Speculum religiosorum* into French and back again in the late thirteenth century as the *Speculum ecclesie*, the *Mirour* was translated into some eight late Middle English versions, and several fifteenth-century Latin versions, appearing eventually in print in the early sixteenth century. It circulated in manuscript until the end of the fourteenth century, travelling in monastic and clerical collections amidst Latin and French treatises (e.g. Oxford Bodleian, MSS Digby 20, 98) and in collections (equally multi-lingual) for lay households such as the *Fouke le Fitz Waryn* manuscript (**31**).

Sometimes the *Mirour* appears with other pastoral classics such as Grossteste's *Chasteau* (**5**) and Pierre d'Abernon de Fetcham's *Lumere as lais* (**19**), as well as with some of the prose treatises from the vast *compileisun* that is one of the French-language manifestations of *Ancrene Wisse* (Dean nos. 644–5, 654, 671, 678, 682), or with the continental *Livre de Sydrac* as here. In some manuscripts the *Mirour* is titled 'Sermon a dames religieuses': at least nine nunneries owned a copy. The *Mirour*'s seventeenth chapter on the *Pater noster* and how to pray was used as a separate text of the *explication du Pater* genre (this chapter is found on its own in, for instance, two nunnery books, a psalter from Wilton and a manuscript from Nuneaton). In some manuscripts the *Mirour* precedes instructions to laypeople for following the Mass in thought and prayer (Dean 720): it also sometimes includes the Middle English crucifixion lyric 'Nou goth sonne undir wode' (Boffey and Edwards 2005, 2320, *Digital Index of Middle English Verse* 3742, http://www.dimev.net).

MANUSCRIPT SOURCE. BL Harley 1121 is an elegantly presented, though not luxurious, smaller manuscript (152 × 232 mm) of the late thirteenth or early fourteenth century, in Gothic book hand in two columns, with rubrics, chapter tables, red and blue puzzle and other ornamented and flourished initials. The *Mirour* is preceded and followed by two other compendia of theological and related knowledge. The manuscript opens with a copy of the continental *Livre de Sydrac* (ff. 1^r–140^r, not in Dean) in an Anglo-Norman *scripta*. This encyclopaedia's prologue and *argumentum* advertises it as the fountain of all kinds of knowledge (*livere de la funtaine de totes sciences*, f. 1^r) for perfecting the bodies and souls of people living in the world, and gives its date as 1243 (f. 2va). The *Mirour* follows (ff. 141^r–155^v), with its opening rubric and table of chapters surrounded by a solid frame ending in trefoil leaves. A dog pursues a hare back up the bottom framing trefoil from right to left, and a small dragon looks up from the top of the capitulum towards the opening illuminated initial and its portrait of St Edmund as a bishop, holding up a mirror turned towards the viewer: http://www.bl.uk/catalogues/illuminatedmanuscripts/ILLUMINBig.ASP?size=big&IllID=26426

Grosseteste's *Chasteau d'amour* (**5**) is the other major work (ff. 156^v–168^r) in the manuscript, immediately preceded on f. 156^r by a brief note on the Virgin Mary's age at the various major occasions of her life (Dean 492). The *Mirour*'s elegant and dynamic opening *mise-en-page* is the most notable in the manuscript. High claims are also made in this 'lay' *Mirour*'s closing rubric: 'Here ends the *summa* of St Edmund of Pontigny which he calls *Speculum ecclesie*, that is to say *Mirror of the Church*, and it can well have that name, for a more valuable work cannot be found among all holy writings (*Issi finist la summe seynt Edmound de Pounteny quel il apelle* Speculum ecclesie, *ceo est a dire* Myreour de seintee eglise: *e bien peut aver cel noun, car plus especial ne pout estre trovee en toute seinte escr[ipt]ture*: ff. 155vb–156ra). There is no known evidence of provenance for the manuscript, but since its three main works were much read among laypeople as well as religious, the manuscript may be a commission by a lay person, or possibly a nunnery: for another manuscript copy of *Sydrac* belonging to a nunnery see (**19**).

BIBLIOGRAPHY. The *Mirour* is edited by Wilshere 1982: for the lay-religious distinctions around chapter 36 (originally proposed in Forshaw 1972a), see ix–xii. Dean 629 includes manuscripts not known to Wilshere. On the manuscript ownership of the *Sermon as dames religieuses* version see Gunn (forthcoming). The Latin *Speculum religiosorum* and *Speculum ecclesie* are edited in Forshaw 1973: see also Forshaw 1972a, 1972b. On the *Mirour*'s devotion structured on the canonical hours see Forshaw 1964. For the Middle English versions see Lagorio and Sargent 1993 (no. 72, 3116–17, 3460–2) and Goymer 1961–2: further study and editions are much needed. A generally illuminating study of the *Speculum* (with particular reference to the vernacular versions and the work's late-medieval impact) is Watson 2009a. For Matthew Paris's life of Edmund of Abingdon see Lawrence 1996: Paris reworked this *vita* in French for Countess Isabel d'Arundel (**13**). Gunn (2009) compares the two Latin versions of the *Speculum*. A *Mirour* manuscript illustrated by the Queen Mary Psalter group is discussed in Kumler (2011, 122–6 and fig. 37). For *Pater noster* commentaries, see Bliss, Hunt and Leyser 2010, and Dean 843–9: on prayer more generally, Reinburg 2012 is illuminating. Sand 2012 discusses an example of the devotional influence of Edmund's Anglo-Norman *Speculum* in books of hours. On the terrestial hierarchy of beings as between human and animal used in the *Speculum*, see Crane 2013.

22. *St Edmund of Abingdon [ascribed], Mirour de seinte eglyse*

TEXT AND TRANSLATION

[f. 143vb] *Le syme chapitre com homme deit veer Dieu en chascune creature.*

Treis maneres de contemplacioun sunt. La premere est en creatures, la secunde en escripture, la tierce en Dieu mesmes en sa nature. Contemplacioun n'est autre chose fors vewe de Dieu.

En ses creatures ly poez vous veer en ceste manere. Treis choses sount en Dieu: pusance, saver e bounté. Pussaunce est aproprié a Deu le Piere, saver a Dieu le Filz, bounté a Dieu le Seint Espirit. Par sa pussaunce sont toutes choses criez, par soun saver sount merveillousement ordinez, par sa bonté sount en ascune chose de vertue establiez et tut en jour multipliez. Sa pussaunce poez vous veir [f. 144ra] par lur grandour et par lur creacioun; soun saver par lur beauté e par lur dissposicioun; sa bounté par lur vertue et par leur multiplicacioun. Lur grandour poez vous veer par lur quatre dimensiouns, ceo est a saver par lur hautesce e par lur parfundesce e par lur largesce e par lur longesse. Soun saver poez vous veir si vous prenez bone garde coment il ad doné a chescune creature: estre sanz plus [come a pieres]; as autres estre et vivere, com as arbres; as autres estre et vivere et sentir, com as bestes; as autres estre et vivere et sentir et resoner, com a home et aungele. Car peres sunt, mes eles ne vivent ne sentent ne resounent; herbes sount et vivent, mes eles ne sentent ne resounont; bestes sount et vivent et sentent, mes eles ne resounent. Homes sount, vivent et sentent et resounent: sount, od les peres; vivent, od les arbrez, sentent od les bestes, resounent od les angles.

Issi devez penser la dignité de humayne nature, coment ele sourmonte chascune creature. Et pur ceo dist seint Augustin, 'Jeo [ne] voudrai aver le leu de un angle si

The sixth chapter on how one should perceive God in every creature.

There are three kinds of contemplation. The first is in the created universe, the second in scripture, the third in the nature of God himself. Contemplation is nothing other than the vision of God.

You can see him in his created beings in this way. There are three things in God: power, wisdom and goodness. Power is an attribute attaching particularly to God the Father, wisdom to God the Son, goodness to God the Holy Spirit. Through his power, all things are created, through his wisdom they are wondrously ordered, through his goodness they are daily multiplied. You can perceive his power in the magnitude [of all created things] and in their creation; his wisdom in their beauty and arrangement; his goodness in their excellence and their abundance. You can perceive their magnitude in their four dimensions, that is, in their height, depth, breadth and length. You can perceive his wisdom if you pay careful attention to how he has given to each creature what each should have and nothing more: to some, being and nothing further [as with stones]; and to others being and life, as with trees: to others, being, life, and sentience, as with animals; to others being, life, sentience and reason, as with men and angels. For stones exist but they do not live, feel or reason. Plants exist and live, but they do not feel or reason. Animals exist, live and feel, but they do not reason. Humans exist, live, feel and reason. With the stones, they exist; with the trees, they live; with the animals, they are sentient, and with the angels they can reason.

Thus you ought to consider the dignity of human nature and how it is above every creature. And for this reason St Augustine says: 'I would not wish for the place of

jeo puise aver le leu qi est purveu a home'. Pensez auxi com cel home est dingne de grant confusion qi ne veut vivere solom soun [f. 144rb] degré et solum sa condicioun.

an angel if I could have the place that has been prepared for humankind'. Think how deserving of shame is that human who does not wish to live according to their position and their state.

Car toutes les creatures de cest mound sunt criez pur home soulement. Les debonaireres sount criez pur home pur treis reisouns: pur nous aider de traveiller, si com boefs, vaches et chivas; pur nous vester et chaucer, si com lyn et leine et quir; pur nous pestre et sustenir, si com bestes, blé de terre, et pesshoun de meer. Les noissantes creatures, come sount les malurés [herbes] et les venimouses bestes, sount criez pur treis choses: pur nostre chastiement et pur nostre amendement et pur enseignement. Nous sumes puniz et chastiez quant nous sumes blescés, et ceo est grant misericorde quant il nous veut chastier temperaument qe nous ne eroms penés perdurablement. Nous sumes amende[z] quant nous pensoms qe tut ceo nous est avenu pur nostre pecché. Car quant nous veioms qe si petites creatures nous poount nu[i]re, dont pensoms de nostre freilleté et sumes humiliez. Nous sumes [a]pris pur ceo que nous veioms en celes creatures les merveillouses oeveres de nostre creatour. Car plus nous valent les oeveres de la fourmye quant a l'edificacion qe ne fet la force de l'ours, ou del lyoun. Auxi com jeo ay dist des bestes, auxi entendez des herbes.

For all the creatures of this world have been created for humankind alone. The beneficial ones have been created for humanity for three reasons: to help us with work, as with oxen, cows and horses; to clothe and put shoes on us, as with wool, linen and leather; to feed and sustain us, as with animals, corn from the earth, and fish from the sea. The harmful creatures, such as the poisonous plants and the venomous animals have been created for three reasons; for our punishment, our correction, and our instruction. We are chastised and punished when we are wounded, and it is a great mercy that he punishes us in the temporal world so that we are not punished eternally. We are corrected when we think that all this has happened to us through our sin, for when we see that such small creatures can harm us, then we think of our weakness, and we are humbled. We are taught by perceiving the marvellous works of our creator in these creatures, for the works of the ant are more edifying to us than the strength of the bear or the lion. What I have said about the animals can also be understood about the plants.

Quant avez entendu la manere, eiez garde de Dieu et ses oeveres en ses creatures et levez sus vostre queor a vostre createur et pensez com ceo est grant pussance de faire tiel chose de nient et doner [f. 144va] lur estre, et grant saver de ordeiner les en si grant beauté, et grant bounté de multiplier les chascun jour pur nostre utilité. A, Dieu! merci com nous sumes desnaturels! Nous dis[u]soums toutes les creatures et il les creia; et nous les confoundoums et il les guie; et nous les destruoums chascun jour et

Now that you have heard how, consider God and his works in his creatures and raise your heart up to your creator, and think what great power it is to create such things out of nothing and to give them their being: and what great wisdom to order them with such great beauty; and what great goodness to increase them daily for our use. Ah, God, mercy, how perverse we are! We misuse all creatures, and he created them; and we lead them astray, and he guides them; we destroy them daily, and he increases them. Therefore

il les multiplie. Dites pur ceo a luy en vostre queor, 'Pur ceo qe vous estes, pur ceo sount; pur ceo qe vous estes beaux, beaux sount; pur ceo qe vous [estes] bons, bons sount. A bon dreit vous loent, vous ahourent, vous glorifient toutes vos creatures, tres [de]bonaire Trinité, de qi sount toutes choses par sa pussance criez; par soun saver diversement en beauté ordinez; en qi sount toutes choses par sa bounté en ascune vertue multipliez. A lui seit honour et glorie en le siecle qe tut temps durra. Amen'.

say to him in your heart: 'Because you exist, they exist; because you are beautiful, they are beautiful; and because you are good, they are good. Rightly do all your creatures praise, adore, and glorify you, oh most gracious Trinity!, through whom all things are created by his power, by his wisdom ordained in variety and beauty, and in whom all things are increased in all their powers through his goodness. Amen'.

[f. 144va] *Le septime chapitre com vous poez veer Dieu en enscripture*

Le secund degré de contemplacioun est en escripture. Mes ore [me] demanderez vous, qi estes de simple lecture; 'Coment porra home jamés venir a contemplacioun de escripture?' Ore me entendez doucement e jeo vous dirray par aventure: quantq' est [f. 144vb] escrit si poet estre dit. Si vous ne savez mie entendre quantq' est escrist, oez volunters le bien qe l'em vous dist, quant vous oïez rien de seint' escripture, ou en saromon communement ou privé collacion. P[re]nez garde tantost si vous oyez rien qe vous valer pusse quant a l'edeficacioun de pecché hair e a vertue amer; a douter peine e joie desirer; a despire ceo mound e vers l'autre haster; quei vous devez faire e quei vous devez lesser; e quanqe enlumine vostre entendement en conoissance de verité; et quanqe enflambe vostre affectioun en fervour de charité. Car de ceo deus biens sert quanq'est escrist en privée ou en apert.

7. *The seventh chapter on how you can perceive God in Scripture*

The second stage of contemplation is in scripture. But those of you who have only basic literacy will ask me, 'How can anyone ever attain to contemplation in scripture?' Now listen to me gently and I will perhaps be able to tell you: whatever is written can be spoken. If you can't understand what is written, listen willingly to the good things that others tell you whenever you hear anything about holy scripture, whether in public discourse or private conversations. Pay attention immediately when you hear anything that can serve you as instruction in how to hate sin and love virtue; to fear pain and desire joy; to despise this world and to hasten towards the next; what you ought to do and what you should avoid; and whatever illumines your understanding in the knowledge of truth, and whatever kindles your affection in the fervency of charitable love. For whatever is written, whether in private or in public, serves these two goods.

[*The reader is then to go forward by taking from 'seint' escripture' (in the general sense of holy writing) knowledge of the catechetical lists: the seven deadly sins, the virtues, the commandments, etc.*]

[f. 149rb] *Le .xvii. chapitre dé sept prieres de la Pater nostre e coment l'en doit prier e en quele manere.*

Aprés ceo devez saver qex sount les sep[t] prieres de la Pater nostre qi oustent touz

17. *The seventeenth chapter about the seven petitions of the Pater noster and how one ought to pray and in what way.*

After this you need to know the seven petitions of the Pater noster, which remove maus et purchacent touz biens. E ces sept prieres sount communes en la douce Pater nostre qe Nostre Seignur Jhesu Crist aprist a ces desciples coment il deveient prier Dieu le piere et lur dit en tieu manere: 'Quant prierez, dites ensi: *Pater noster qi es in celis*, ceo est a dire, Nostre Piere qi es en ciel'.

all evils and obtain all good. And these seven prayers are contained in the sweet prayer Pater noster that Our Lord Jesus Christ taught to his disciples as the way they should pray to God the father, saying this to them: 'When you pray, say thus: *Pater noster, qui es in celis*, that is, Our Father, who art in heaven'.

[*The Lord's prayer follows with Latin phrases succeeded by French equivalents.*]

Cest orison surmounte [f. 149va] chascun orison en dignité et en utilité; en dingneté pur ceo qe Dieu meismes la fist. Et pur ceo fait celuy grant hounte et grant irreverence a Jhesu le filz Dieu qi se prent as paroles rimeiez [et curiouses] et lest la priere qe celui nous aprist qi sciet tut la volunté Dieu le piere et quel oreisoun plus li vient a pleiser et queux choses nous chaitifs avoums mester a prier. Car auxi com jeo vous ay dit, il soul sciet tote sa volunté et toute nostre necessité et pur ceo sount cent mile homes desceu par multiplicacion de oreisouns, car quant il quident q'il eyent devocion si ount une charnele affectioun pur ceo qe chascun charnel corage se delite naturelement en tiex tornez langages. E pur ceo seiez garny, car seurement ceo vous dy qe ceo est un ordre de lecherie pur deliter en tieu manere de goliardrie.

This prayer surpasses all prayers in worth and effectiveness: in worth because God himself composed it. And therefore dishonour and great irreverence is done to Jesus the son of God by anyone who turns to elaborate rhymed words and abandons the prayer taught us by him who knows the whole will of God the father and what prayer will most please him and for what things we wretches need to pray. For as I have said to you, he alone knows all his will and all our necessity. And because of this, thousands of people are deceived through the multiplication of prayers, for thinking they are being devout, they manifest a sordid carnal inclination, for every carnal heart naturally delights in such contorted rhetoric. And therefore, be warned, for I tell you for certain that it is a kind of lechery to take pleasure in such debauched language.

D'autre part seint Augustin et seint Gregoire et les autres seintz prierent aprés lur affectioun. Jeo ne blame point lur oreisouns. Mes jeo blame ceux qi lessent la priere qe Dieu mesmes fist et aprist et se prent a l'oreisoun de un simple seint ou qe il la troevent escrist. E pur ceo dit Nostre Seignur en l'Evvangelie, 'Quant vous volez prier, ne priez pas od moutz de paroles, mes priez en tieu manere: et dites issi *Pater noster qui es in celis*'.

On the other hand, St Augustine and St Gregory and the other saints prayed according to their feelings. I do not reproach their prayers. But I reproach those who abandon the prayer that God himself composed and taught, and turn to the prayer of a mere saint wherever they find it written. And because of this, Our Lord says in the Gospel: 'When you want to pray, do not pray with many words, but pray in this way, and say "Our Father which art in heaven . . . "'.

[*The bulk of the chapter is an exposition of the Pater noster, petition by petition, as all sufficient and containing all human needs, temporal and spiritual, for this life and the life hereafter.*]

[f. 150vb] Ce est la priere ke Nostre Seignur Jhesu Crist nous aprent en l'evaungelie. E

This is the prayer that Our Lord Jesus Christ teaches us in the Gospel. And do not assume n'entendez pas ke vous devez dire de bouche si come jeo ay escrist, mes dites soulement la lectre duwe de bouche, e pensez en vostre quor de ceo qe jeo ay ici mis seur chesqune parole par sey. E ne facez mie force de multiplier la Pater nostre, car miex vaut dire ove entendement une foiz qe mil foiz sanz entendement. Car issi dit seint Pol apertement: 'Jeo voil meix dire cink motz en mon queor devoutement qe cink mile de bouche sanz entendement.' En meme la manere devez faire a vostre office e queor. Kar issi dit le prophete, *psallite sapienter*, ceo est a dire, chantez e versaillez sagement. Sagement chanter, ceo est qe l'em dit de bouche, dire de queor. Car si vostre cors est en le quor, e vos leveres en le sauter, e vostre queor en le marchee, cheytivement estes devisee. E pur qe Nostre Seignur dit 'Primes querez le rengne Dieu, e tant come vous avez mester de temporels biens, vous serra doné sanz demander', por ceo devez saver que vous devez aver en la joie du ciel.

that you must say it with your mouth as I have written it here, but say only the naked letter with your mouth and think in your heart of what I have put here about each separate petition. And make no effort to say many Pater nosters, for it is better to say one with attention than a thousand without it. For as St Paul openly says: 'I would rather say five words devoutly in my heart than five thousand carelessly with my mouth.' And you should do the same with your office and your heart. For the prophet says: '*sing wisely*', that is to say, 'sing and chant wisely'. To sing wisely is that one ought to speak with the mouth what the heart says. For if your body is in the choir, and your lips on the psalter and your heart in the market, you are wretchedly distracted. And because Our Lord says 'Seek first the kingdom of God and whatever you need in earthly goods will be given to you without your asking', you can know by this what you should have in the joy of heaven.

[*Accounts of the seven gifts of body and spirit and the pains of hell in body and soul follow before the second degree concludes.*]

[f. 151ra, line 29] Atant finist le secund degree de contemplacion, ceo est contemplation en escripture, de la quele si vous prenez bone garde en vostre queor legier vous serreit chascun sermon a retenir. D'autre part vous avez matere de parler as clers ja ne sei[en]t [f. 151rb] si pruz et as lays ja ne seient si rudz. Quant vous parlez a plus sage de vous movez ascune de cestes materes e demandez et ensement quant vous parlez a simples gentz aprenez les volunters et doucement. Car assez avez dount penser e parler et coment vous devez vostre vie governer [e] autrui vie amender.

Thus ends the second stage of contemplation, that is contemplation of scripture, from which, if you pay careful heed in your heart, it will be easy for you to retain each word. And moreover, you have material to discuss with clerics, however learned, and with laypeople, however unlearned. When you speak to people wiser than yourself, raise any of these matters and ask about them, and likewise, when you speak with simple people, teach them gladly and gently. For you have enough with which to think and speak and to tell you how to direct your own life and improve that of others.

Notes

R2 **veer** Other manuscripts have *contempler* (Wilshere 1982, 16, 17). This is not the only example in this manuscript of the substitution of a less specialised word for an unfamiliar, theologically inflected one, and indeed the scribe's substitutions tend to confirm that the substituted words are new to him/her. The generation of new lexis in the Anglo-Norman version of Edmund's treatise (as also in Pierre d'Abernon de Fetcham's *Lumere* (**19**), and Hesketh 1997) is particularly strong: see Wilshere 1982, xxxv–xxxviii.

R 1–2 The concluding summary of the previous chapter is copied after the rubric for the current one: *Par ceste conissance de vous mesmes en ceste meditacioun devez venir a la conissance de Dieu par seinte contemplacioun* (Through this knowledge of yourself in this meditation you should come to the knowledge of God through holy contemplation). In accordance with modern reading order it is not included after the rubric in the extract here, but this is a frequent practice in this manuscript, as also in Wilshere's critical edition. Presumably the summary helps connectivity, but its dissociation from the visual device of the rubric in the manuscript may suggest that hearing the text was the default expectation.

4–5 **Contemplacioun . . . vewe de Dieu** Not in the Latin text. Wilshere 1982, 97, n. to 6.5 argues that the interpolation, run on into the next sentence in many manuscripts, garbles the threefold distinction clearly set out in the chapter's opening two lines, but it can be read as a helpful gloss, explaining that all three modes of contemplation are ways of seeing God, or as an explanation of the ultimate purpose and definition of *contemplatio*. This scribe (and sometimes the exemplar) is not a conventionally 'good text', but it is one that seems concerned to produce meaning.

12 **soun saver** MS *sount* with final *t* expuncted.

12 **saver** MS *saver saver.*

16 **creacioun** Identified by Wilshere (1982, 97, n. to 6.4, 5, 13) as a neologism, otherwise first used by Jean de Meung in 1265. He observes that the French text does not regularly use *creacioun* to translate *creatio*, but that it does separate out the Latin term's two senses (of creator, *natura naturans*, and created, *natura naturata*), translating *in creacione* here as *creacion* and *creacionis humane* (Forshaw 1973, 98.7) as *de humeyne nature* (Wilshere 1982, 29.4). This is at the cost of losing a distinction when the Latin *humana natura* (*Speculum ecclesiae: humane nature*, Forshaw 1973, 44.22 and 45.25) is translated by the same phrase (as here, lines 37–8 below).

22–36 **Soun saver . . . resounent od les angles** Forshaw 1973 (44, n. to 16–21) cites an analogous passage in Gregory's Homilies in Ezechiel II, hom. 5, *PL* 76.990.

24 **estre sanz plus** Manuscripts from both A and B traditions give the example *come as pieres.*

37–8 **la dignité de humayne nature** (Latin *humane nature*) Wilshere notes Gregory the Great's *Moralia in Job* 6.16 as an influential statement of terrestrial hierarchy (*PL* 75.740). On human exceptionalism and anthropocentric measures of value, see Crane 2013, Introduction (which also includes a valuable account of work in this field) and ch. 2.

40–1 **Jeo [ne] voudrai . . . purveu a home** cf. Ps-Augustine, *De angelis et eorum officio* VIII, ii: *Nollem habere locum angeli si possem habere locum qui providetur homini.*

42 **dingne** MS *dingne et.*

47 **criez pur home soulement** For the patristic doctrine that only humans have a use-value for the created world see Augustine, *PL* 40.19–20, trans. Mosher 1982, question 30 ('Has Everything Been Created for Man's Use?'), cited Crane 2013, 188 n. 10.

49–72 **pur nous aider . . . ou del lyoun** Forshaw (1973, n. to 44.28–46.13) notes that this passage combines ideas from Hugh of St Victor's *Didascalicon* VII c.14, *PL* 76.821–2 and his *De arca morali*, II. *c.* 4, *PL* 76.637.

50 **chivas** i.e. *chivaus* with graphemic reduction of *aus* to *as*.

59 **blescés** The scribe omits the reading of other B manuscripts *ou kuant nous dotoms d'estre blescez*, presumably through eye skip (Wilshere 1982, 19.44–21.45).

71 **la fourmye** For the ant as a source of edification see also *Bestiaire divin* (17).

74–6 **Quant avez entendu la manere, eiez garde . . . et levez** Other B manuscripts read *Quant en tele manere avez regardé* (Wilshere 1982, 21/56). The exemplar may have been faulty here, but the Harley scribe produces a fairly plausible reading.

79–80 **ordeiner les en si grant beauté**: *in tanta pulcritudine ordinare* (Forshaw 1973, 47.19). Wilshere notes (1982, 97, 6.58) that the French text translates Latin *species* in the sense of 'kind, species' as *especes*, but here takes *species* as 'appearance, form, beauty'.

81–96 **A Dieu! . . . multipliez** Uncompromisingly as the terrestrial hierarchy privileging humanity is set out in lines 46–73 above, it entails some respect for creatures and creation as God's plan.

83 **dis[u]soums** MS *dissoums* (*AND*, *s.v.* 'desuser').

R *Ore avez vous matire coment vous poez veer Dieu en chascune creature et ceo est le premer degré de contemplacioun* (Now you have material to enable you to perceive God in all created beings, and this is the first stage of contemplation). The summary of the previous chapter again appears after the visual cue for the following one (see R 1–2 above).

109 **P[re]nez** MS *puez*.

112 **douter** MS *deter*.

113 **vers** MS *vere* (a sign perhaps that the text was dictated to the scribe).

115 **enlumine** For Latin *illuminat*. Wilshere notes (1982, 97, 7.13) that the manuscripts of his B or 'lay' version select the ordinary term rather than the more precise *illumine* for the sense of Augustinian illumination.

117 **enflambe** Harley's reading here for *inflammat* (Forshaw 1973, 49.11–12) is the same as Wilshere's A or religious tradition and makes more obvious sense than *enblaunche* in other B or lay manuscripts (however *AND* accepts the sense of 'kindle to white heat' as a meaning of *enblaunchir*).

118–19 **deus biens sert** MS *Dieu bien sciet*. All versions struggle with the reading here: this sentence is not present in the Latin *Speculum* (Wilshere 1982, 98, 7.15 notes that the status of the reading *sert* is very uncertain). The A text reading is taken here as making better sense than the Harley scribe or the reading of other B manuscripts (B *sez bienz est*).

126–7 **Quant prierez . . . *Pater noster*** All literacy, lay or religious, began with learning the Latin alphabet, the credo and the Pater noster, so that the prayer's Latin phrases (rubricated in the manuscript) would not have been unfamiliar to most readers. They are translated into French in both the 'lay' and the 'religious' versions of St Edmund's *Mirour*, presumably to guarantee full comprehension, prior to the commentary on each of the seven petitions of the prayer with which the rest of the chapter is largely concerned.

133–4 **paroles rimeiez [et curiouses]** *et curiouses* occurs in a manuscript of Wilshere's A tradition: the Latin in *Speculum ecclesie* is *verba ritmica et curiosa* (Forshaw 1973, 75.2). We take *AND*'s definition 'rhymed words', but the Latin suggests rhythmical prose and/or prose with cursus. Old English texts in rhythmical prose were still being copied into the thirteenth century.

145 **en tiex tornez langages**: *in tali loquela curiosa* (B; Forshaw 1973, 75.9). A has *in carnali lingua* (ibid., 7.10).

147 **un ordre de lecherie** A and B manuscripts read *une orde lecherie* (Wilshere 1982, 48.33–4, 49.34). The Latin is *una turpis luxuria* (B) and *quaedam sordida luxuria* (A): see Forshaw 1973, 75.10–11, 74.11.

148 **goliardrie:** *guliardie* (Forshaw 1973, 75.11). *AND*, *s.v.* 'goliardie', gives 'loose living, debauchery', *DMF* 'Paroles grossières'. (Wilshere's gloss, 'mummery' is less forceful but suggests the performative element in goliardry).

154 **prent** MS *puent.*

156 **volez** MS *le volez.*

156–9 **'Quant vous volez prier . . . *in celis*'** Matt 6.7, 9.

160–84 This summing up on the Pater noster occurs in the manuscript immediately under the rubric for chapter eighteen (*Le xviii chapitre de .vii. dowaries en cors e .vii. en alme*), though nothing is said of the seven gifts until chapter nineteen.

163 **jeo ay escrist** B manuscripts: *je l'ay ci escrist* (Wilshere 1982, 55.147).

164 **la lectre duwe** ('the proper form', i.e. only the prayer's actual words). Both versions of the Latin read *nudam litteram* (Forshaw 1973, 74.28, 79), and vernacular manuscripts usually follow with *la nue lettre* or variants thereof.

169 **entendement** MS *faitzentendement*, with expunction of *faitz*. *sanz* is added in above.

170–2 **'Jeo voil meix dire . . . sanz entendement'** cf. 1 Cor 14.13.

173 **office e queor** B manuscripts: *office en quer* (Wilshere 1982, 55.155), but the reading makes sense without emendation. The Latin in B is *officium tuum in ecclesia* (Forshaw 1973, 79.38–81.1: A version *servicio divino*).

174 ***psallite sapienter*** Ps 46.8.

177 **de queor** MS *e de queor* with expuncted *cors* preceding *queor.*

179 **le marchee** cf. *Le Ménagier de Paris* in its advice on behaviour at Mass: 'quant li hom ou la femme est au moustier pour ouyr le service divin, son cuer ne doit mie estre en sa maison, ne es chanps . . .' (When a man or woman is at the minster to hear divine service, their heart must not be back at home nor out in the fields): see Brereton and Ferrier, ed., 1981, 12.I.iii. Henry of Lancaster's *Book of Holy Medicines* (*Livre des seyntz medicines*) has an extended passage on the heart as marketplace (Batt 2014, 117.9–123.23). Forshaw 1973 (81, n. to 3–5) prints verses added at this point in one of the Latin manuscripts (*Dum cor non orat / in vanum lingua laborat* etc., citing Walther 1969, II, 1 n. 6476 and II, 3 n. 18,723).

180 **devisee** The feminine form here suggests a female addressee, but the same spelling is used to indicate the sound in (masculine) *marchee* in the same line.

181–3 **'Primes . . . sanz demander'** An expanded version of Matt 6.33.

190 **matere** MS *materie.*

23. *Sermons on Joshua* [Dean 595], Extracts from Sermons 4 and 5: Paris, Bibliothèque nationale, fonds français, MS 19,525, ff. 180*vb*–181*va*, 185*ra*–185*va*

Date of composition and provenance. First half of the thirteenth century, England

Author, sources and nature of text. The five prose *Sermons on Joshua*, extant in three manuscript copies, are the vernacular tip of an enormous iceberg of Latin patristic writing that circulated in academic and clerical circles, but remained largely unknown to the unlettered. These *Sermons* have been called commentaries on (Zink 1976, 62) or works 'inspired by' (Hunt 1998a, 1) Origen's first eight homilies on Joshua. The *Sermons* follow Origen in the choice of opening biblical passage to be explicated, and the preacher translates into French selected exegetical passages, but departs from their Latin source by adding substantial independent commentary.

23. *Sermons on Joshua*

Origen (*c.* 185–254), a biblical scholar and school master from Alexandria, Egypt, was exiled to Caesaria, Palestine, in 231 and his homilies on Joshua were written near the end of his life, close to the period when he was imprisoned and tortured during the persecutions (*c.* 200–51) ordered by Decius, Roman emperor 249–51. Origen wrote some 574 homilies in Greek, examining most of the Bible (Longère 1983, 26), incuding his twenty-six homilies on Joshua, now preserved only in the Latin translation by Rufinus of Aquileia (*c.* 340–410). Jaubert (1960, 81–2) argues that while Rufinus adapts and paraphrases his Greek source text, his Latin recasting remains faithful to Origen's ideas.

The terms 'sermon' and 'homily' are often used interchangeably in modern English usage. In the patristic period both terms meant an exegesis, phrase by phrase, interpreting the meaning of a biblical excerpt (procope) read during the liturgy. During the thirteenth century the sermon developed a new structure in which the exegesis of a shorter biblical extract was a starting point for a longer (and freer) development of a related topic, using a variety of rhetorical devices, such as *distinctiones* or *exempla*.

The *Sermons on Joshua* remain close to the patristic model of a homily, in which a source text is followed by running commentary. Origen's homilies followed established patristic tradition, treating *Joshua* as an allegory in which Joshua, son of Navé, prefigures Jesus, son of Mary; in Hebrew the names Joshua and Jesus have the same written form, either transcription being valid. This prompted exegetes to propose the story of Joshua as an allegory for the life of Jesus. The interchangeability of Joshua/Jesus is frequently effaced in the *Sermons*, however, which often refer to Joshua only as *li fiz Navé* (the son of Navé) whereas the Origen/Rufinus text usually calls him Jesus, son of Navé.

Origen's major contribution to the exegesis of *Joshua* is his comprehensive interpretation of the whole text, in which he seeks to reveal the hidden meaning of all the narrative details, as well as the sense of the central allegory (Jaubert 1960, 10). In contrast, the *Sermons* are highly selective: they draw only on the first eight homilies of Origen/Rufinus (although the *Sermons* series may originally have been longer), and translate verbatim or paraphrase only limited passages of Origen's commentary, which are expanded by new interpretations offered by the vernacular preacher.

One such addition in the vernacular is the humility topos in Sermon 4 (lines 1–10) that draws on the standard request for inspiration from the Holy Spirit in order to interpret the hidden meaning of the text (not present in the source, Origen's Homily 4). The vernacular preacher's humility also includes a declaration of his sinful nature (lines 5–6) which makes him unworthy of receiving divine aid, but the declaration *qe puisse veraiement dire od le prophete* (line 7) preceding the citation from Ps 50 (line 8) both expresses his gratitude, and assures his audience that he has been divinely blessed with knowledge of hidden things. In this rhetorical stance the vernacular preacher contrives, then, to appear both truly humble and supremely confident in the knowledge that his understanding is blessed by the Holy Spirit.

If Origen's Homily 6 lacks a humility topos, his Homily 8 (the main inspiration for Sermon 5) does state the need for divine guidance, both for the preacher to explain, and for the audience to hear and understand, the true meaning of the brutal sacking of Ai (*Hom* 8.1, Jaubert 1960, 218), a story which Origen suggests his contemporaries (along with the Gnostic philosophers) found repugnant because of its cruelty. In Sermon 5, however, the vernacular text reduces Origen's explanation to the short initial declaration: *par la grace del Seint Espirit solum l'ordre esponderom ce que escrit trové avum* (lines 103–5). This single introductory reference in Sermon 5 to the technique of exegesis (*solum l'ordre esponderom*) is also a contrast to the proliferation of technical terms provided at the beginning of Sermon 4: in Sermon 4, the events in the narrative happen *par figure*; they have been *mis en escrit* to guide us in these latter days (*por asenser nus . . . en la vespree del siecle*); the preacher will *esclarzir la reson de cest escrit*, by removing *la coverture de la lettre*, uncovering the treasures hidden in the text (lines 1–10). This emphasis on the role of the exegete underlines the importance of reading and understanding sacred texts in the proper spiritual light, and consequently the importance of the role of the preacher in guiding lay people in moral understanding.

The attention paid at the beginning of Sermon 4 to the preacher's role in guiding reading may anticipate the passage in Sermon 5 (lines 110–48) deprecating classical learning in rhetoric, philosophy, law and poetry. This condemnation of polished worldly rhetoric, culminating in the mention of Gnostic philosophers who promulgated false beliefs (line 130), is not an addition by the vernacular writer, however, but is taken directly from Origen/Rufinus (7.7, Jaubert 1960, 215). One of the most striking aspects of the additions to the text made by the vernacular writer is his consistent criticism of Judaism, which is seen as recalcitrant in not accepting Jesus, son of Mary, as the messiah. In the opening commentary in Sermon 4, God, the celestial gardener, eradicator of the weeds of vice and sower of the seeds of belief (lines 26–8), works only in the field which is the heart of Christians (lines 22–4). The son of Navé recognises the man standing before him as both man and God (lines 48–68, 81–3), but the Jews and their leaders see Jesus, son of Mary, only as a man who is destroying their law (lines 35–8), not fulfilling it. Only a few Jews and other powerful worldly men eventually believe that Jesus Christ is bringing a new law (lines 64–70) to replace the old law. Similarly, in Sermon 5, the term *tote Synagogue* (line 106), introduced at the beginning of the commentary on the divine condemnation of all the tribes of Israel for the sin of one man (who took for himself golden objects from Jericho), establishes a conflictual relationship between the religious institutions of *Synagogue* (line 106) and *Seinte Iglise* (line 110). This opposition between Judaism and Christianity is not found in Origen/Rufinus, where the allegory is explained only in terms of moral references applicable to Christians (7.4 and 7.7; Jaubert 1960, 204–6, 214–16).

AUDIENCE AND CIRCULATION. Were these *Sermons* actually preached? Or were they written to be read? There is no mention of the identity of the author or patron, and little indication of the intended audience. The fact that each biblical citation in Latin is followed by a French translation, however, suggests that the author is addressing an audience for whom French was the preferred language of communication, not Latin (whether mixed lay and clerical, or learned and unlearned monastic). The sermons maintain the style of an oral performance, with direct apostrophes to the audience and the use of rhetorical questions to advance the argument. The preacher, using both a singular and plural first-person narrative voice, refers to his listeners with terms that suggest a mixed clerical and lay audience.

In Sermon 1 the listeners are addressed as *seigneurs* (my lords), *amis chers* (dear friends), *amis freres* (dear brothers, brother monks), *bone gent* (good people); in Sermon 2 as *treschers freres* (very dear brothers), *seinurs . . . les prudeshumes, freres pecchurs* (my lords, gentlemen and brother sinners); in Sermon 3 as *seinurs* and *cristien* (my lords and [fellow] Christians), in Sermon 4 as *bone gent* (good people), and in Sermon 5 as *seignurs* (my lords) and *freres* (brothers, monks). While the term *bone gent* used in Sermons 1 and 4 could refer to both men and women, all the other terms are usually limited to men. The absence of women is confirmed in the detailed inscription of the audience in Sermon 5, where the implied listeners are both clerical and lay, and of both high and low estate, but exclusively male: the monk in his cloister, the chaplain in his chapel, the knight at court, the peasant in the city. Unsurprisingly, the sermon also argues in favour of conserving the status quo of the social order by maintaining the feudal bonds of loyalty and trust between the prelate and his flock, and between the lord and his liegemen. This will be accomplished, the preacher suggests, by plain speaking (or clinging to orthodox beliefs) and by avoiding worldly learning, which is capable of deception and trickery.

Patristic homilies were routinely read in monastic settings, and adapted into the vernacular for homiletic use in parish preaching. For example, a well-known series of vernacular homilies attributed to Maurice of Sully, bishop of Paris (1160–96), a renowned preacher whose homilies have been preserved in both Latin (for the clergy) and French (addressed to lay audiences) circulated in England; see Robson 1952; Zink 1976, 171–80. Although there is no evidence apart from the rhetorical stance of the preacher that the *Sermons on Joshua* were initially delivered orally, their preservation in three mid-thirteenth-century manuscripts of English origin is proof that they circulated widely and were read, either privately or communally.

23. *Sermons on Joshua*

MANUSCRIPT SOURCE. The *Sermons* are extant in Cambridge, Trinity College O.2.14 (=C), Oxford, Bodleian Library, Douce 282 (=D), and Paris, BN fr. 19,525 (=P) (see Hunt 1998a, 1–3 for details), all from the mid-thirteenth century.

The text below is edited from the second section of manuscript P, a parchment manuscript of 204 folios, 227 × 150mm, which was copied in the style of the workshop of William de Brailles, Oxford, and is dated *c.* 1230–50 on art-historical grounds (Morgan 1982, 36 n. 35; Avril and Stirnemann 1987, 67–8, pl. xxxiv). The other texts in this part of the manuscript form a substantial anthology of religious writing. They include prose texts useful for pastoral work or private devotions (a prose treatise on confession, Dean 667, an exposition on the *Pater noster*, Dean 846, and the *Sermons*), as well as verse sermons such as the *Roman des romans*, a satire on ecclesiastical abuses (Dean 601), and narrative verse texts (including five works of Guillaume Le Clerc de Normandie; see (**17**)), Wace's *Vie de s. Marguerite* and other saints' lives, and the *Passion* and *Assumption* from the *Bible* of Herman de Valenciennes (**15**), all highly suitable for oral delivery.

Corrections and additions to the critical text (enclosed in square brackets) are based on manuscript D, the base manuscript in the edition by Hunt.

BIBLIOGRAPHY. The *Sermons on Joshua*, noted by James in 1902 and by Meyer in 1903, are discussed briefly by Zink 1976, in the context of preaching in French before 1300; Zink's is the most detailed study to date of vernacular preaching. The *Sermons* were first edited by Hunt in 1998, in the ANTS plain text series, with a brief introduction and minimal critical apparatus.

The manuscript used here is digitised at http://gallica.bnf.fr/ark:/12148/btv1b9062154g

Bataillon 1980 gives a succinct introduction to the field of medieval sermon studies; Longère 1983 gives a broad historical survey of preaching from the patristic period to the sixteenth century (for sermon structure see Bataillon 28 and Longère 26–7); D'Avray 1985 provides a useful introduction to preaching in his study focused on thirteenth-century Mendicant sermons emanating from Paris. See Briscoe and Jaye 1992 on the *Artes praedicandi* (rhetorical manuals for preaching). Robson 1952 provides the only edition of the vernacular homilies of Maurice of Sully, proposing that these are independent of his Latin homilies; Zink 1976, 171–80 argues that the vernacular sermons were adapted from Sully's Latin texts. Rufinus's Latin translation of Origen's homilies on Joshua are available in a modern edition by Jaubert 1960. On the thirteenth-century oppositional iconography of Ecclesia and Synagoga see Rowe 2011. For Gospel sermons on the older homiletic model see (**14**), Robert of Greatham's *Miroir*.

TEXT AND TRANSLATION: SERMON 4: JOSHUA WINS THE BATTLE OF JERICHO

[*Summary: following Origen, Homily 6, this sermon begins with the Latin text of Josh 5.13–16, and Josh 6.2, 16–18, 25, followed by a French translation. The narrative details cited are Joshua's encounter with the messenger of the Lord in the field outside Jericho (Josh 5.13); his interrogation, then worshipful adoration of the leader of God's army (Josh 5.14); the announcement that the Lord has delivered Jericho into the hands of Israel (Josh 6.2). Next follows a summary of the taking of the city: as commanded, every day for six days seven Israelite priests carried the ark of the covenant and sounded seven ram's horn trumpets as they marched once around the city walls. On the seventh day, they marched seven times around the city, the trumpet was sounded, and the people cried out that God had given them the city and that Jericho and all within it were condemned except for Rahab and her household (Josh 6.16–17). The people are warned to avoid the forbidden things within Jericho, in order that the house of Israel not be condemned and all Judaism destroyed (Josh 6.18). The trumpet was sounded, the people cried out, the walls fell down, and all of Jericho was destroyed, except for the household of Rahab, whose descendants to this day dwell with the tribes of Israel (Josh 6.25). Then the sermon proper begins with a detailed examination of the meaning of the text.*]

[f. 180vb, top line]

Tote ceste aventure avint par figure e fu mis en escrit por asenser nus qui somes en la vespree del siecle. E pur ceo que nus ne suffisons nient a esclarzir la reson de cest escrit, requerrons ententivement le Saint Esperit qu'il nus doinst sa grace en aie que dignement puissoms remuer la coverture de la lettre que le tresors que desoz tapist al preu de noz almes en la lumere del Seint Esperit seit esclarzi. Dont jeo pecchere plus que autre home qui nient ne sui digne d'enquerre la parfondesce de si grant segrei Damnedeu devant tuz autres rend graces a Deu de sa demostrance qe puisse veraiement dire od le prophete: *Ecce enim veritatem dilexisti incerta et occulta sapiencie tue manifestasti mihi.* C'est a entendre: 'Estevus verité veraiement amastes, les choses dotuses e celees demostré m'avez en apert.' Ceo dit en l'estoire que li fiz Navé vit eu champ de Jerico un home encontre lui qui tint un' espee nue. Cest champ signefiad les quers de ceus qui crurent qe Jesus ert a venir por le mond sauver. Quers de homes sont veirement ensement com champ dont Deus, qui cotefiur est celeste, esrace cardons de vices e de mescreance [e seme greins de vertu e de veire creance.] En cest champ devant ceo qu'il prist humanité fu Jesu Crist par desir de ses esliz es desirus quers de [f. 181ra] ceus solum la porveance de son pere en une manere ja formet home. Le vit le fiz Navé al regard de ses oilz espiriteus par creance e par entendement. Il le vit, ceo dit, ester encontre sei, car ceo fu avis al poeple Israel e a lur princes que Jesus Crist [e]stut contre eus quant il quiderent qu'il volsist lur lei abatre. Mes il ne la abati nient, ainz la parempli. E por ceo est escrit en l'estoire: li fiz Navé aprosmad a lui. Coment? Esmerveillant, enquerant, prophetizant, e dist: 'Es tu nostre, u de noz aversaries?' E il li respondi: 'Jeo sui prince de la chevalerie Deu. Ore vinc.' Par ceo

This whole book is an allegory, and was put down in writing to instruct us, we who live in these last days of the world. And because our own intellectual capacities are not sufficient to elucidate the meaning of this text, we fervently request that the Holy Spirit through his grace grant us help that we may remove the cover of the literal meaning so that the treasure hiding beneath may be made clear by the light of the Holy Spirit, for the benefit of our souls. Thus I, a sinner more than other men, who am not even worthy to enquire after the profound meaning of this, a secret of God greater than all others, give thanks to God for his revelation, so that I may say truly with the prophet: *Ecce enim veritatem dilexisti incerta et occulta sapiencie tue manifestasti mihi.* Which is to say: 'Verily, you have truly loved truth, you have shown me openly fearsome and secret things.' The scripture says that the son of Navé saw a man in the field outside Jericho coming towards him, carrying a naked sword. The field represents the hearts of those who believed that Jesus would come to save the world. The hearts of men are truly like a field in which God, the heavenly tiller, uproots the thistles of vice and unbelief, and sows seeds of virtue and true doctrine. Before he became incarnate as a human being, Jesus Christ was present in this field already in human form, in the hearts of his elect, because of their desire, according to the providence of his father. The son of Navé saw him through spiritual eyes, by means of his faith and his discernment. He saw him, says the scripture, coming to confront him, for the people of Israel and their princes believed that Jesus Christ stood against them when they thought he wished to abolish their law. But he did not abolish it, he fulfilled it. And for this reason it is written in scripture: the son of Navé went out to meet him. How? In marvelling, in seeking, and in prophesying, and he said: 'Are you with us, or devon entendre que tutdis se presente Deus a ceus qui por lui e por son dreit combatent e travaillent.

are you with our enemies?' And he replied: 'I have come here as the prince of the army of the Lord.' From this we must understand that the Lord always reveals himself to those who work and fight for him and his law.

Li fiz Navé regardad des oilz e vit un home. Dun[t] [n']out il anceis gardé e veu homes asez? Oïl, mes a cest regard vit il un hom d'autre vertu que ainz n'ot veu. Cest regard ert des oilz de quer qui sont apelé raison e entendement. De ces oilz vit il qu'il n'iert nient solement home com autre, ainz ert plains de vertuz. Mes uncore ne sout il lequel ces vertuz furent de Deu u de diable, e por ceo enquist ententivement e demanda umblement qui'l ert. E quant il fu acerté de lui memes, donc se lessa chair a ses piez e devotement l'aorad e dist: 'Sire, quei comandes tu [f. 181rb] a ton serf?' Estevus, jesqu'il conut qu'il fu veirs Deus e nient ainz, ert il prest de faire son comandement. Ensement avint de Jesu Crist nostre Salveor e de plusors Gius e d'autres poestifs homes del siecle. Il furent longes en dote del Salveor mes jesqu'il le conurrent en la lumere de ses granz miracles e qu'il paremplireit la lei espiritelment, donc a primes se covertirent il a lui e reçurent ses comandemenz.

The son of Navé looked, and his eyes saw a man. Had he not previously looked, then, and seen men sufficiently well with his eyes? Yes, but this time he looked and saw a man with strength different from what he had seen before. This gaze was with the eyes of his heart, which are called reason and understanding. With these eyes he saw that this was not just a man like other men, but instead one filled with great power. And yet he did not know if this strength was from God or from the devil, and for this reason he enquired fervently, and asked humbly, who the man was. And when he was assured by the man himself, he fell down at his feet and devoutly worshipped him, saying, 'Lord, what do you require of your servant?' Thus we see that, until he knew that he was the true God, and not before, was the son of Navé willing to do his commandments. A similar incident occurred with Jesus Christ our Saviour and several Jews and other powerful men of the world. For a long time they remained doubtful about the Saviour, but when they knew him in the light of his great miracles, and knew that he was spiritually fulfilling the law, then they converted to believe in him and followed his commandments.

Par ceste ententive enqueste somes nus apris qe nus ne devuns nient estre trop hardis de creire, ne ceo que l'em a l'oil veit ne ceo que l'om des orailles ot. Car il puet estre deceu par adobement u par fausine, u par fantesme, u par mençonge. De cest dit li apostre: *Nolite credere omni spiritui, sed probate spiritus si ex deo sunt.* Ceo fait a entendre: 'Ne creez nient ceo que chescun vus dit. Provez primes si ceo que le om dit vienge de bon esperit.' Le fiz Navé aorad

Through this sincere and careful questioning we learn that we must never be too quick to believe, neither that which we see with our eyes, nor that which we hear with our own ears. For we can be deceived by false show or forgery, by deception or by lies. The apostle speaks of this: *Nolite credere omni spiritui, sed probate spiritus si ex deo sunt.* This means: 'Do not believe what everyone tells you. First test it to see if what you are told comes from a good spirit.'

cel home nient por ceo qu'il ert de part Deu, mes por ceo qu'il ert memes Deus. Autrement ne l'eust il nient aorez, sil nel conuist e cert fuist qu'il ert vereis Deus. Veirement est Jesu Crist qi est veirs Deus e veirs hoem, prince de la chevalerie Deu, a qi [est] tote chevalerie celestiene: angles, archangles, vertuz e dominacions, poestez e principatés sont tutdis en la chevalerie Jesu Crist, car il est Prince des [f. 181va] princes e Poestif sor poestifs, e il done les poestez, si com il dit par essample: *Esto et tu potestatem habens supra decem civitates*, c'est: 'Tu aiez poesté sor dis citez.' Le espee qe nostre Prince tint traite e nue en sa main est la parole Deu. La waine de ceste espee fu la lettre de la lei. Ceste espee fud deswainé e desnué des icel hore q'en la lumere de vertuz e de miracles furent aparissantes totes les choses qe furent de Jesu Crist prophetizees en figure e en umbre.

The son of Navé worshipped this man not because he was sent by God, but because he was God himself. Otherwise he would not have worshipped him, had he not known and not been certain that he was the true God. In truth, he is Jesus Christ, who is truly God and truly man, prince of the army of the Lord, to whom belongs all the heavenly host: angels and archangels, powers and dominions of angels, realms and principalities are all members of the army of Jesus Christ, for he is Prince of princes and Ruler of rulers, and he is giver of realms as it is told in the following scripture: *Esto et tu potestatem habens supra decem civitates*, which is to say: 'may you have power over ten cities'. The sword that our prince holds drawn and naked in his hand is the word of God. The scabbard of this sword is the letter of the law. This naked blade was unsheathed at the moment that, through the light of his powers and miracles, all the things that were prophesied about Jesus Christ in figurative and hidden language were revealed and made apparent.

Sermon 5: The Taking and Sacking of Ai

[*Summary: inspired by Origen, Homily 8, with a reprise of part of Homily 7. The vernacular sermon begins by citing in Latin part of Josh 7.1, ending with 'et cetera', followed by a narrative summary of Josh 7.1–8, 11–13, 20–6 and 8.1–5, 10–12, 14–17, 19, 29. This includes the anger of the Lord with the people of Israel because they broke the anathema on taking treasure from Jericho; the first assault on the city of Ai, followed by the defeat of the Jews; the requirement that the Israelites atone for their disobedience; the confession by Achar of the theft from Jericho, and his execution; the successful taking of Ai using a military ambush, and the sacking of the city. Origen's Homily 8.1 begins with a more polished narrative summary, and does not use a direct citation from Joshua. The vernacular summary concludes: Issi avuns nus desque ça cunté l'ordre de l'estorie (Here we have recounted in order the events of the story), before beginning the exegesis, which follows.*]

[f. 185ra, line 5]

Ore par la grace del Seint Espirit solum l'ordre esponderom ceo que escrit trové avum. Ore enquerom donc por quei tote Synagoge fud escombré par si petit mesfait de un. Un home, ceo dit, emblad une riule de or, si la mist en miliu de son

Now, with the grace of the Holy Spirit we will explicate, step by step, the meaning of what we have found written in this scripture. First, let us ask why all Judaism was afflicted for such a small sin of one man. A single man, the scripture says, stole

tabernacle. Ceste chose avint en signefiance d'offense q'ert a venir en Seinte Iglise. Il i ad entre Crestiens science de rethoriens, de philosophes, de legistres, qui mult est luisante e doree par beles paroles, e dorees e colorees, qui totes sont de l'or de Jerico, c'est del saver de cest monde. Quant vus verrez tele science e si bien assises paroles escrites, u par boche d'autres les orrez dire, c'est la riule d'or, l'entredit de Jerico.

Donc vus covient qe cointement vus gardez qe la luisante doreure ne l'adobbé prove de la reisun seculere ne vus deceive. Derechief, si vus lisez les poetes qi descrivent lor deus e lur deuesses par beaus vers e colurez, ne vus delitez en lor eloquence, car c'est l'or de Jerico qe Deus maudist. Si vus les metez en vostre tabernacle, c'est en assiduele memorie de vostre quer, ceo dit seint Jerome, que [f. 185rb] vus soillez tute Sainte Iglise. Ceo firent li maleurez Valentins e Basilides e Marciaton, qi les errurs des philosophes voleient faire acreire as fiz de Sainte Iglise q'ele fuist tote soillee. E notez qe asquanz dient que cil larcin ert une riule, [asquanz une lange], asquanz une bou[ch]e de or, mes quel que ceo fust, home siet qe ceo fud por or, e signefie l'overaine que hoem fait purement por honte e nient al henur Deu. E resignefie la creance de ceus qi creient qe Jesu Crist est pur home e nient Deus. Redevez saver qe cel larcin, cel entredit de Jerico qui tant ert pur or e luisant signefie les guisches, les encusemenz, les artez e les boedies del siecle qe li seculer tricheur si adobent e planient par blanches paroles e dorees si qu'il les font luisanz com fin or. E ne porquant pleins sont de fausime ensement com le larcin de Jerico, tut fuist or fin, plein fud de felonie, car Deu l'ot maudit e si fud larcin. [Si] li home soeit entre les fiz Deu, qui ces

a golden rule and placed it in his tabernacle. The meaning of this incident is found in the offense committed against holy church. Among Christians there is the learning of the rhetoricians, the philosophers, and the lawyers, which is brilliant and enhanced by fine words, by many-coloured and gilded phrases, all of which are the gold of Jericho, that is to say, worldly learning. When you encounter such learning, and such well chosen, elegant written words, or hear them uttered by the mouths of others, this is the golden rule, the forbidden rule of Jericho.

Then it behooves you to watch yourself carefully so that you not be deceived by the brilliant gilding and the deceptive assurances of worldly reason. Above all, if you read poets who describe their gods and goddesses in fine and colourful verses, do not delight in their eloquence, for it is the gold of Jericho condemned by God. If you place them in your tabernacle, they will remain continually in your heart's memory; St Jerome says that by this you befoul all of holy church. This was done by wicked Valentinus, Basilides and Marciaton, who wished to make the sons of holy church believe in the errors of the philosophers, so that the church was wholly besmirched. And note that some say this theft was a rule, others a tongue, others a golden mouth, but whatever it was, we know that it was solid gold, and it signifies a shameful human endeavour which is not done for God's honour. Furthermore, it represents the belief of those who think that Jesus Christ is a man only, and not God. You should know that this theft, this anathema of Jericho, for all that it is pure and lustrous gold, signifies the ruses, the slander, the artifices and the deceits of the world which earthly tricksters so ornament and polish with innocent and golden words that they seem to shine like bright gold. Nonetheless, they are full of deception, just as the theft from Jericho, although pure gold, was full of wickedness, for God had

vices hante en Sainte Iglise, seit il moigne en son encloistre, seit il chapelein en sa chapele, seit chevaler en curt, seit vilein en vile, qui par encusement departe prelat de ses sugez, u par wische seignur de ses homes, cil ad muscé le maudit de Jerico el tabernacle, c'est en [f. 185va] la conversacion des feelz Deu, ne ja por tant com il i seit muscé n'averont les feelz Deu ja quiete ne victorie de lor enemis espiritels.

condemned it as theft. If, among the sons of God there be a man who practises these vices in holy church, be he a monk in his cloister, a chaplain in his chapel, a knight at court, or a peasant in the city, who by his accusations separates a prelate from his flock, or through his ruses separates a lord from his men, such a man has hidden the anathema of Jericho in his dwelling place, that is to say, it is hidden during his dealings with the faithful of God. As long as this forbidden vice is hidden, the faithful will never have respite nor gain victory over their spiritual enemies.

Notes

15–17 *Ecce enim . . . mihi* Ps 50.8; cf. 'Yet, though thou hast hidden the truth in darkness, through this mystery thou dost teach me wisdom' (New English Bible, Ps 51.6).

20–2 **Ceo dit . . . espee nue** A repetition of Josh 5.13 (cited in Latin and French at the beginning of the sermon, and also repeated at the beginning of *Hom 6.2* by Origen, Jaubert 1960, 184) as the theme that will be explicated by the sermonising gloss, which is independent of Origen.

34–5 **Il le vit . . . ester encontre sei** Another phrase repeated from Josh 5.13 (repeated also at the beginning of *Hom 6.2* by Origen, Jaubert 1960, 184), followed by independent commentary.

39–41 **E por ceo est escrit . . . aprosmad a lui** A phrase from Joshua 5.13 (cited at the beginning of the sermon, and repeated also at the beginning of *Hom* 6.2 by Origen, Jaubert 1960, 184), with independent vernacular commentary.

42–4 **'Es tu nostre . . . Ore vinc'** A repetition of Josh 5.13–14, cited at the beginning of this sermon, in Latin and in French (and repeated by Origen, *Hom* 6.2, Jaubert 1960, 186), before the explication of the allegory. The phrase *prince de la chevalerie Deu*, lit. 'prince of the knights of God', translates the Latin (from Rufinus) *princeps milicie Domini*.

58–61 **E quant il fu acerté de lui . . . a ton serf?'** a repetition of Josh 5.14, cited at the beginning of the sermon (and repeated by Origen, *Hom* 6.2, Jaubert 1960, 186), followed by independent vernacular commentary.

74–6 **Car il puet estre deceu par adobement u par fausine, u par fantesme, u par mençonge** Cf. the variant from MS D (Hunt 1998b): *kar oil pot estre deceu par adubement u par fantasme, oreille par mençunge* (the eye can be deceived by false show, by forgery or deception, the ear can be deceived by lies).

76–7 **De cest dit** Cf. the variant from MS D (Hunt 1998b): *De creance dist li Apostre* (on belief the Apostle says).

77–8 ***Nolite . . . sunt***: I John 4.1: 'But do not trust any and every spirit, my friends; test the spirits, to see whether they are from God' (New English Bible). The citation is used by Origen (*Hom* 6.2, Jaubert 1960, 186); the vernacular author adds the translation, lines 79–81.

81–95 **Le fiz Navé aorad cel home . . . sor dis citez.'** This section follows Origen, *Hom* 6.2, Jaubert 1960, 186.

87–8 **Deu, a qi [est] tote chevalerie** The syntax in this copy requires a verb; cf. the variant (MS D, Hunt 1998b), *Deu, kar tute la chevalerie*, which creates a run-on sentence.

87–93 **prince de la chevalerie . . . done les poestez** Drawn verbatim from Origen, *Hom* 6.2 (Jaubert 1960, 186), who paraphrases Col 1.16 and 2.10: 'Quis enim alius est princeps militiae virtutum Domini nisi Dominus [. . .] Omnis namque coeli militia, sive angeli, sive archangeli sive virtutes sive *dominationes sive principatus sive potestates* . . . qui largitur principibus principatus.'

93–4 ***Esto et tu . . . civitates*** Luke 19.17 (following Rufinus), and cited by Origen (*Hom* 6.2, Jaubert 1960, 186); cf. the Vulgate: *eris potestatem habens supra decem civitatem* ('you shall have charge of ten cities', New English Bible). The commentary (lines 95–102) is added by the vernacular writer.

101–2 **de Jesu Crist prophetizees en figure e en umbre** Lit.: prophesied about Jesus Christ in allegory and in shadow. This picks up the earlier reference to Ps 50.8 (see n. to lines 15–17 above), and 'truth hidden in darkness', concealed behind *figure* (allegorical meaning) and *umbre* (darkness of ignorance).

105–7 **por quei tote Synagoge fud escombré par si petit mesfait de un** This narrative transition from the summary of the event recounted in Josh 7.1 and 11–12, to the exegesis of the nature of the sin in question follows the text of Origen, at the end of Homily 7.6 and the beginning of 7.7 (Jaubert 1960, 214). Origen also discusses the meaning of the anathema in Homily 7.4, where it is equated with worldly things: 'sed anathema vobis sit omnis conversatio saecularis' (mais que vous soit anathème tout commerce avec le siècle, Jaubert 1960, 204–5).

107–8 **emblad une riule de or** Here the French does not follow Origen, who provides a Latin calque of the Hebrew, *linguam auream*, as opposed to the Vulgate: *regulamque auream* (Josh 7.21); cf. Jaubert 1960, 214–15.

111–29 **science de rethoriens . . . vus soillez tute Sainte Iglise** This condemnation of worldly learning and of the polished rhetoric of philosophers follows Origen closely (7.7), with the exception that the French text (lines 56, 58, 61) uses *l'or de Jerico* or *riule d'or* (based on the Vulgate *regula aurea*) as opposed to Origen's *lingua aurea* ('golden tongue').

129 **Ceo firent** MS *Ceo furent*; emended following D, Hunt 1998b.

130 **Valentins e Basilides e Marciaton** Valentinus, Basilides and Marcion are Gnostic philosophers, active in the second century AD, declared heretic by the church. Valentinus and Basilides were trained in Hellenistic learning at Alexandria; Marcion, son of a bishop from Asia Minor, was active in Rome, *c.* 140. Origen condemns them again, by name, in *Hom* 12.3, in particular for their misreading of Joshua (Jaubert 1960, 300). On Gnostic doctrines and their influence, see P. Healy, 'Valentinus and Valentinians', *Cath. En.* vol. 15 http://www.newadvent.org/cathen/15256a.htm; J. Arendzen, 'Basilides', *Cath. En.* vol. 2: http://www.newadvent.org/cathen/02326a.htm; idem, 'Marcionites', *Cath. En.* vol. 9: http://www.newadvent.org/cathen/09645c.htm.

134 [**asquanz une lange**] emendation based on D (Hunt 1998b). Origen refers to both a 'tongue and bracelets of pure gold' (*linguam auream et dextralia pura*; cf. *Homélies*, Jaubert 1960, 216), but does not specifically refer to a mouth; **bou[ch]e**; 'mouth' (cf. D *bou*) may have been suggested to the translator by the preceding 'tongue' of gold (see n. to 111–29 above); cf. also the reference to deceitful words spoken by others 'par boche d'autres les orrez dire' (line 117).

136 **home siet qe ceo fud por or, e signefie** The variant in D (*l'um set ben ke ço ert or pur e signefie*) supports the translation of *por or* as 'solid gold' rather than the possible 'for gold, [out of the lust] for gold'. This image is expressed less ambiguously as 'pure gold' using the adjective *fin* in line 146 (*luisanz com fin or*), describing the attraction of secular rhetoric, and in line 148 (*tut fuist or fin*), referring to the theft at Jericho.

24. Textual Ordering and Manuscript Layout

24a. Angier of St Frideswide, *Dialogues de saint Gregoire* [Dean 512], *Introductio* and *Prefatio-Proem*: Paris, Bibliothèque nationale, fonds français, MS 24,766, f. 3ra–b/1–17; ff. 9ra–10rb, extracts

Date of composition and provenance. According to an inscription in the extant manuscript, the *Dialogues* were completed on 29 November 1212 or 1213, most probably in Oxford, though possibly also worked on in France during the papal Interdict of England (1208–13).

Author, sources and nature of text. Angier is identified at the end of the *Dialogues* as 'Brother A. the subdeacon, the least of the servants of St Frideswide' and as 'the old sinner Angier, seven years young in the cloister' (Orengo 2013 II, *Explicit* and vv. 20,229–30). He may have been the magister Angerius who left Benedictine Durham for the Augustinian house of St Frideswide in Oxford shortly before the date of the *Dialogues*. Angier's only other known work, a much shorter verse translation of the Life of Gregory the Great (Dean 513), was added into the manuscript two years later: a Latin colophon notes the Life's completion in the ninth year of Angier's religious life and second year of his priesthood (f. 174r). The name Angier may reflect a continental origin, as some aspects of the texts' language have been thought to do, but there are also Anglo-Norman traits, and Angier is generally accepted as an Anglo-Norman writer.

Pope Gregory I 'the Great' wrote his *Dialogues* several years into his papacy (590–604). His account of the lives and miracles of the early Italian fathers (especially Benedict of Nursia, founder in 529 of Monte Cassino and the Benedictine order) was influential throughout the Western Middle Ages. In the insular context, Gregory has special importance as the instigator of the mission to Christianise the English. Angier's *Vie de saint Grégoire* includes the famous encounter in Rome between the pope and some English slave boys (represented by Angier as youths who still believe in Mahomet, *creient onqore en Mahon*, f. 156v, v. 15, ed. Meyer 1883, v. 504) which features in Bede's *Ecclesiastical History* (Bk II, ch 1) as inspiring the conversion of the English. The only known previous insular translation of Gregory is the Old English *Pastoral Care*, created by King Alfred and Bishop Wærferth in the ninth century (Schreiber 2003).

Angier's *Dialogues* form a substantial work (19,367 lines in octosyllabic couplets), and are supported by one of the most extensive and comprehensive discussions of writing and reading in any vernacular work. The *Dialogues* open with an *invocatio*, the *Veni, creator* hymn in Latin and monorhyme French quatrains, and a prayer in French to the Trinity in the same metre (Orengo 2013 II, 11–14), before the octosyllabic general introduction (*Introductio*, vv. 1–52 below). A table of chapters in parallel, colour-differentiated Latin and French columns follows on ff. 3v–8r (Orengo 2013 II, 16–27). Each of the four books of the *Dialogues* receives prefatory material: for Book II there is a *digressio* on Horace on combining utility and pleasure (vv. 3481–630): for Book III a digression on the merits of prose and verse and diversity in preaching (vv. 7535–822) and Book IV has a *prefatio* on writing and charity (vv. 14,185–306). At the end of the *Dialogues*, there is a French verse farewell to the text (vv. 20,189–232). This elaborate apparatus reveals Angier as an early experimenter in the creation of vernacular *accessus* to Gregory's authority and spiritual benefits. *Accessus* may embrace formal prologues describing the origins and procedures of a text, schematic guides to content such as chapter tables and manuscript layout and, more generally, levels and modes of access and the conception of access informing any text and its presentation. Angier exemplifies all of these, and even the addition of the *Vie de saint Grégoire* to the *Dialogues* can be seen as a portrait of a saintly *auctour* and a further form of access to Gregory's text: Angier's *proemium* to the *Vie* argues that Gregory's own example in his life should not be passed over in presenting the *Dialogues* (Meyer, ed., 1883, f. 153r, vv. 7–16).

The *Introductio* to the entire work discusses such topics as the ordering and rubrication of the text and its extensive table of contents. Angier emphasises the function of this latter aid (not at the time as routinely provided as it later became) as vital to the work of reading: whether lay or cleric (*lais ou clerz*, v. 1), you will be able to choose chapters at need and find 'whatever you seek ... to save your body and soul' (vv. 47–8). Chapter titles and the speaking personae of the *Dialogues* are carefully marked up in the text itself: everything possible is done to make the text searchable by readers, who, in consequence of this very concern, have to be entrusted with the exercise of their own choice and discretion in their use of Gregory's holy writings. No merely pragmatic convenience, being able to turn up the needed chapter at will is as essential to the work of salvation for lay audiences as for religious.

After the *Introductio* there follows the *Prefatio* of 130 lines in octosyllabic couplets and a *Proem* of a further 136 (both excerpted below). Here Angier considers the *commun profit* (v. 159 below) to be accrued through his work. Insisting on the benefits of community among the different estates and the translator cleric's indispensable role in it (cf. (**25**), Wace, *Vie de saint Nicolas)*, Angier contrasts the infinite growth of an economy of knowledge and wisdom powered by charity against the more finite modes of wealth and worldly knowledge. With these latter he aligns the 'fables of Arthur of Britain' and the 'songs of Charlemagne' (vv. 141–2 below): to them, he opposes his own work 'of truth' against the matter of Roland and Oliver (v. 171).

The themes of clerical utility and readerly activity continue throughout Angier's extensive apparatus. His digression between the *Dialogues*' first and second books (around, as noted above, Horace's 'Omne tulit punctum qui miscuit utile dulci', *Ars Poetica* v. 343) argues that highly ornamented verse is like an overdressed and made-up woman: whoever translates holy writings must not be too exalted nor too base (Orengo 2013, vv. 3603–4). Angier's second digression (partly based on Gregory's own account in the third book of his *Regula pastoralis*) elaborates Gregory's analogy of the musician to discuss the role of aesthetics and also that of the preacher-physician ('the soul has its spiritual physician as the body has a corporeal one', *alme a mire espirital / si com li cors le corporal*, vv. 7737–8), to discuss audience diversity. The preacher's remedies must be administered with a doctor's regard for time, season, region, individual constitution and circumstance, even, in Angier's account, for differences between the English and the Normans (*car li Englois e li Normant / sont de diverse qualité*, vv. 7694–5). For the prologue to the fourth and final book of the *Dialogues*, Angier returns to the theme of charity: Gregory and the common good inspire, as they had 'in the first prologue at the head of the first *Dialogue*' (vv. 14,275–6), the extension of the work of charity beyond the limits of the writer's personal ability, through grace and the audience's good will (cf. (**11a**), Adgar's *Gracial*). The final farewell to the text links deeds and words, inner and outer, teaching and speaking and performing what is good (20,189–232). A good book not put into practice by its audience is like a religion without a rule. As Cato (**37**) taught his son, reading and listening without attention and understanding is time spent in vain (vv. 20,203–8). Each can take the good of the *Dialogues* according to their ability so that understanding leads to spiritual health (*salu*, v. 20,223) and all should pray for the *translator* (v. 20,228) 'Angier, the old sinner' (*li vieil pecchierre, Angier*, v. 20,229).

In Angier's work newer textual modes co-exist with the older habits of monastic *ruminatio* as meditation and ritual practice. His presentation of the *Dialogues* several years before the fourth Lateran Council of 1215 has implications not only for the development of vernacular theology and its audiences, but for the construction of the reader and readerly self-consciousness in a society moving into increasingly systematic forms of textual organisation. Rivalled only by Robert of Greatham's *Miroir* (**14**) and Pierre d'Abernon de Fetcham's *Lumere as lais* (**19**) in the thirteenth century, Angier's remains among the most energetic and comprehensive vernacular discussions of the work of writers, texts, and audiences.

AUDIENCE AND CIRCULATION. Angier's careful presentation and concern for accessibility is compatible with the instruction of novices in a classic of spirituality such as the *Dialogues*, and many of the manuscript's features suggest a teaching work. But the Augustinians also had a pastoral mission and a strong engagement with vernacular texts, and Oxford was an established market and university town with large populations of both permanent and transient residents. The St Frideswide canons were responsible for various parish churches in the town and seem to have been a more pastoral and less university-oriented house than their neigbours, the Austin canons of Oseney Abbey. Angier's duties as subdeacon and, later, priest may thus shape his addresses to *lais ou clerz* (v. 1 below), and *seignurs et dames, laie gent* (v. 151 below) as also his preacherly articulation of occupational and personal diversity among audiences. Moreover, *pace* Angier's own contrast of Arthurian literature with the *Dialogues* noted above, there was considerable overlap between religious houses and their secular patrons in the taste for romance and *chanson de geste*, texts of these genres frequently being owned by monasteries as well as laypeople (the Oxford Augustinians at Oseney have been credited with copying the romance of *Gui de Warewic*, Wathelet-Willem 1975, 36–41). Angier's text and its manuscript seems designed for several possible readerships: serviceable for basic study within the Augustinian order, it could also be read to and by lay people.

Manuscript source. The extant manuscript, Paris, BN fr. 24,766, is a small (190 × 140 mm) parchment manuscript of 174 folios, written usually in two columns, in Gothic book hand and decorated only with blue and red, occasionally green, capitals and the 'hairpin' and other pen flourishings characteristic of the early thirteenth century. There is one hand throughout, usually accepted as Angier's own on the strength of the manuscript's colophons and the remarkably low incidence of corrections. The phrase *opus manuum mearum* (the work of my hands) in the colophon is usually taken to mean that Angier copied the text himself: Short 2011, 106–7 argues that it refers, rather, to his authorship and that the manuscript may have been copied by a book shop in Oxford's Catte Street, rather than, as has been previously accepted, at Angier's Priory of St Frideswide in Oxford. These questions, together with the poem's dating, are thoroughly considered in Orengo 2013 I, 159–64, 169–92 who opts for a holograph manuscript written at St Frideswide's. A great deal of care has been taken with the intelligibility of the text in the manuscript: the verse lines of both *Dialogues* and *Vie* are intensively marked off in black and red dashes above the words: Orengo 2013 I suggests that in addition to making distinctions (such as strokes over minims) and regulating metre by syllable count (*décompte des syllabes*), one set of the marks (aiming to mark tonic syllables, *tonicité*) may be an experiment in preparing the text for chant (Orengo 100–10, and see figs. 2–18 in colour). In Bk 1, ch. vi (on f. 16^{r}), as promised in the *Introductio* (vv. 43–4 below), translations of the Latin chapter rubrics begin to appear in red ink in the bas-de-page and occasionally in the margins: this is kept up throughout the *Dialogues*. Biblical quotations and other notes are added in the margins and bas-de-page sporadically.

Bibliography. The *Dialogues* are edited by Orengo 2013: the prologues and Angier's hymn and prayer were edited by Cloran 1901 (omitting the final 12 lines on f. 33vb of the first *digressio*). The argument of Pope 1904 for Anjou as Angier's place of origin has not been accepted (see Thomas 1904 for the form *Angerius* and Germany). On Angier's identity see Short 2014. Pope and Cloran both comment on the richness of Angier's lexis, especially in learned words. On the manuscript see Careri, Ruby and Short 2011, cat.74. The manuscript is digitised in colour at http://gallica.bnf.fr/ark:/12148/btv1b84522207n/f1.image; colour plates also in Orengo 2013 I, figs. 1–18. The *Vie de saint Grégoire* is edited in Meyer 1883: Meyer's dates for Angier are queried by Legge 1958, but see Short 2011, who also unsettles the received opinion that the manuscript is a holograph and suggests composition in France. Schreiber 2003 studies the Old English version. For the section of Gregory's *Regula pastoralis* used by Angier see Judic 1992, 116–20. On the Augustinians see Dickinson 1950: for their vernacular texts, Pouzet 2004, 2009, Hanna 2005: on St Frideswide's parishes *Victoria County History* Oxford ii, 99, and for nearby Oseney Abbey, A. Taylor 2011. Wathelet-Willem 1975 discusses the St Frideswide scriptorium; see also Walpole 1976, Weiss 1969, 2010, 52–4, Porcheddu 2001, 483–4. On *accessus* see Minnis 1988, 15–25, 46–63 and for its development in finding aids and *mise-en-page*, Rouse and Rouse 1979, 1–42 and 1982. Neither Angier's *Dialogues* nor his *Life of Gregory* have received much modern study: their significance in the history of reading and the book, and aesthetics and doctrine, prose versus verse (see Part VI, §1.2) and other questions remain to be further discussed (for a beginning, see Wogan-Browne 2009b).

TEXT AND TRANSLATION

(i)

Incipit introductio in librum sequentem
[f. 3ra]

Quiqe tu soies, lais ou clerz,
Qui de vertuz essamples querz-
Signe, miracle, moralité-
Por traire t'alme a sauveté,
Icest men document retien,
S'en avras prou, e feras bien:
Car, sans labor e sanz delai,
Quanq'as mestier t'enseingnerai.
Icest livre present lirras
Ou trovras quanqe desirras
De sens, de mours, e de vertu,
Od quanq'apent a ta salu.
Si ne soies pas en arveire
De quanq'i trovras escrit creire,
Car veirement cil l'endita
Qui li Seint Espirz espira.
Ço porras par l'escrit aprendre,
Si de tot quer i voelz entendre;
Q'onc ne fust taus ne tant parfit
Si nel feïst Seint Esperit.
E si seit qe n'aies laisir
De lu parlire ou paroïr,
Cest conseil feras soulement,
Sil savras tot a ton talent.
Des presenz chapitres notez
Si com en ordre sont nombrez,
Quelqe tu voudras eslirras,
E pués el livre lu querras.
Pués quant lu chapitre esleu
Avras parlit e entendu
Si ben te siet e il te plaise,
E ensemble as loisir e aise,
Tot en meïsme la maniere
Un autre chapitre regiere

Here begins the introduction to the following book

Whoever you may be, layperson or clerk, who seeks examples of virtue, miraculous signs, miracles and interpretations to draw your soul to safety, hold fast to my teaching from which you will benefit and do well, for without trouble and delay I will teach you whatever you need. You will read this present book where you will find whatever you desire of wisdom, of moral behaviour and virtue, together with whatever is relevant to your salvation. And do not have any doubt about believing whatever you find written here, for truly he who composed it was inspired by the Holy Spirit. You will be able to learn that from the text if you are willing wholeheartedly to attend to it, for there never was anything so perfect or so much of it unless the Holy Spirit brought it about.

And if it should happen that you do not have leisure to read or hear it all the way through, you have only to take this advice, and you will know everything according to your desire: you will be able to choose whichever you want among the chapters noted here and numbered in order as they are, and you will be able to look for it in the book. When you have thoroughly read and understood the chosen chapter, you can, if it suits and pleases you and at a time when you have leisure and ease, choose and examine another chapter with which you can delight your heart, in exactly the same way. Thus you

Porras eslire e porvoier, [f. 3rb]
Dont ton quer puesses apaier.
Einsi trovras legierement
Sanz tei grever tot prestement
Quanqe te plaist oïr ou lire,
Quel ore tis quers lu desire.
E si tis sens tant par est durs
Qe li latins lui seit oscurs,
En romanz en la marge escrit
Trovras quei li chapitre dit.
Einsi q'apertement verras
Tot mot a mot e pas por pas
Quanqe tu querz, sanz destorber,
A ton cors e t'alme sauver.
Por ço te lou, quiqe tu soies,
Icest conseil qe tu le croies,
E ço qe creiz, mostres en fait:
Car mar a conseil qui nel creit.

will easily find ready to hand and without wearying yourself whatever it pleases you to hear or read, at whatever hour your heart desires it. And if your intellect is so obdurate that it finds the Latin unclear, you will find written in the margin in French what each chapter says, so that you can clearly see word by word and step by step and without hindrance whatever you seek to save your body and soul. For this reason, I counsel you, whoever you may be, to believe this advice and display what you believe by your deeds, for whoever cannot trust to it has followed ill-advised counsel.

Explicit introductio.

Here the Introduction ends.

(ii)

Incipit prefatio Fratris A. in librum Dialogorum Beati Gregorii [f. 9ra]

Qui autrui voelt edefier
Soi meïsme entent heriter,
Car qui a autre en bien profite
Molt li rent Deu bien sa merite,
E sovent soi meïsme empiege
Icil qui fait a autrui piege,
Car molt voi avenir sovent
Qe meint home de son laz se pent.
Donc est li proeu tot asez mien
Quanqu' a mon proesme faz de bien,
E d'autrepart moie est la perte
Si mal li faz sanz sa deserte.
Mais li saive sa perte fuit.
E li fol la prent en deduit;
Li saive son sen multeplie,
E li fol acraest sa folie.
Ore entendon al sen, jol lou,
Si puesson amender le fou,
Car quiq'onc voelt le fou reprendre
Molt li covient a sen entendre.

Here the Preface of Brother Angier to the book of the Dialogues of Blessed Gregory begins:

Whoever wants to edify other people inherits his own intention, for God well repays the merit of any who enables others to profit in goodness. And often he who lays snares for others entraps himself, for I see it happen often that many a man hangs himself in his own noose. Thus the benefit is all mine when I do good to my neighbour, and on the other hand the loss is mine if I do him harm without his deserving it. But the wise man flees his loss and the foolish man takes it with pleasure. The wise man multiplies his understanding and the fool increases his folly.

Now let us listen to wisdom, I advise, so we may amend folly, for whoever wants to reprove folly must understand a great deal of wisdom. Wisdom seems equal to wealth

Sens semble a aveir parigal
E compaignon en un estal,
Car sens par avoir est apris,
E avoir par sens est conquis. [f. 9rb]
Hoem qui est sage marchëant
Son avoir craest en despendant;
Car quant plus despent en son proeu,
Plus li est sis avoir croeu:
E hoem qui bien e largement
Son sen e son savoir despent,
Plus li craest e plus i gäaigne,
Car miez le set quant plus l'enseingne.
Avoir souz terre empire tost,
E sens s'enfuit, s'il est rebost:
Avoir, quant l'en le baille, amende,
E savoir voelt q'om le despende.
Avoir quant est perdu revient,
E sens perist s'oem trop le tient:
Donc est li sens miez retenuz
Quant largement est despenduz.
Neporquant ne di pas de veir
Q'avoir vaille tant com saveir,
Car avoir fuit, savoir remaint:
Boer nasquit qui savoir ençaint.
Sens est noble possessïon,
Qui plus croist quant plus vient en don:
E por ço fait plus a cherir;
Quant par nul guast ne poet perir.

and its companion on an equal footing, for wisdom is acquired through wealth and wealth is conquered by wisdom. A man who is a wise merchant increases his wealth in spending it, for when he spends more to his profit, his wealth has grown greater for him; and a man who well and generously expends his wisdom and his knowledge increases it and wins more, for he knows it better the more he teaches it. Wealth in the ground quickly depreciates and wisdom goes away if it is left to rest; wealth, when one uses it, increases, and wisdom demands that one expend it. Wealth when it is lost, comes again, and wisdom perishes if one withholds it too much. So wisdom is retained better when it is freely expended. Nevertheless I do not really mean to say that wealth is worth as much as wisdom, for wealth is transitory, and wisdom permanent. He whom wisdom engenders is born blessed. Wisdom is a noble possession, which grows all the more the more it is given away, and it is to be the more intensely cherished because it cannot be lost by any waste.

Por tant dëust chasquns hoem sage
Son prou faire e son avantage
Tant com Deus li offre sa grace,
E done sen, tens, e espace:
Car sovent avient par deserte
A qui guäaingner ne voelt, perte.
Si com droiz est q'oem dirre soelt:
'Perte eit qui gäaigner ne voelt',
Hoem qui saive est pas ne porloingne
De faire en son tens sa besoigne,
Car qui son prou ne fait quant poet,
Ne le fera pas quant il voet.
Mais marchëanz sont molt divers: [f. 9va]
Li uns est francs, li autre fers,
Li uns dedenz, l'autre defors,
Li uns de l'alme, l'autre del cors.
Li uns fait tresor temporal,

Therefore each wise man ought to act more to his own benefit and advantage the more God offers him his grace and gives wisdom, time and space; for it often happens deservedly that whoever does not wish to gain, loses, so that what people are accustomed to say is right: 'he who does not wish to profit takes a loss'. A man who is wise does not postpone carrying out what he needs to in good time, for whoever does not act to his advantage when he is able will not do it when he needs to. But merchants are very varied: some are generous, some close-handed, some work indoors, some outdoors, some are merchants of the soul, some of the body, some create temporal wealth, and others heavenly: one has an

E li autre celestïal;
A lui est sis tresor durable,
A l'autre, veins e feible e lable.
Molt par est donc fel trichëour
Qui vent le pis por le meillour,
Car molt est plein de tricherie
Qui por lanterne vent vessie,
E cil rest trop fol marchëant
Qui a son oes le meins vaillant
Eslit, car molt est vice e vain
Qui prent la paille e laist le grain.
Por tant est bien q'oem sache eslire
Le bien del mal, car l'en selt dire:
'Fous est qui se prent en sa fin
Al sauze e guerpist saint Martin'.
E neporquant por voir le di,
Plus est hui icest jor oï
Cil qui enseingne vanité,
Mençonge, e fable, e falseté
Qe cil qui enseigne le voir,
Moralité, sen, e savoir,
Car vanité est escoutee,
E verité est reboutee.
Les fables d'Artur de Bretaigne
E les chançons de Charlemaigne
Plus sont cheries e meins viles
Qe ne soient les Evangiles;
Plus est escouté li jugliere
Qe ne soit saint Pol ou saint Piere;
E plus est hui cest jor li fol
Oïz qe saint Pierre ou saint Pol.
Li fous a par tot compaignie,
Li sage est soul e sanz aïe. [f. 9*vb*]

enduring treasure, and for another it is vain, weak and transitory. For this reason he who sells the worse for the better is a very great deceiver: for he who sells a bladder for a lantern is full of trickery; and he remains too foolish a merchant who chooses what is worth less in his eyes, for he who takes the chaff and leaves the grain is very foolish and empty-headed. Thus it is important that we know how to choose the good from the bad, for as the saying goes 'he is mad who at his ending takes to the willow and abandons St Martin'. And nevertheless I tell you truly that nowdays at the present time he who teaches vanity, lies, fable and falseness is more noticed than he who teaches truth, morality, understanding and wisdom, for vanity is listened to and truth is rejected. The fables of Arthur of Britain and the songs of Charlemagne are valued more highly and less reviled than are the Gospels. The minstrel is more readily listened to than is St Paul or St Peter, and the fool more readily heard nowdays than St Peter or St Paul. The fool has company everywhere, the wise man is alone and without help.

[*In spite of the prevalence of fools, the wise man should not be deterred: God is the final judge and among all the works of charity, drawing the sinner from sin is the greatest*]

Incipit proem

Seingnors e dames, laie gent,
Iceste acheison meismement
Me constraint a la chose enprendre,
Laquele a peine pues entendre:
Charité me fait commencer,
Comment qe soit de l'achever,
Od le mien e l'autrui besoing
Ço qe ultre ma vertu est loing:

Here the Proem begins:

Lords and ladies, lay people all, this reason particularly impels me to undertake something I can barely understand. Charity towards my own and others' need makes me begin, however the work (for it is well beyond my power) may turn out. For I want to translate to our common benefit some holy writing from Latin into the

Car a nostre commun profit
Tran[s]later voil un seint escrit
Del latin en lange romaine,
Qui plus est entendable e saine
A cels qui de sainte escriture [f. 10ra]
N'entendent pas la lettre oscure.
Ne me doit estre a mal torné
Si di ço q'autre a composé,
Car qui ne poet en soi trover
Q'om altre ou soi puesse amender
Saive est, e cointe e grant sen fait,
Sï il de son meillor la trait.

French language (which is more readily understandable and more beneficial for those who do not understand the obscure language of holy scripture). Nor should it be held against me if I narrate what another has composed, for he who cannot find within himself the wherewithal for improving himself or others is wise and knowledgeable and makes himself useful if he takes it from someone better than himself.

N'est de Rollant ne d'Olivier
Ne vos soit ja por ço meins chier!
Ainceis est de vertuz des sainz
Li livre, e sachez n'est pas fainz,
Ne trait de fause vanité,
Mais tot est pure verité.
D'iço pues bien ma foi plevir:
Cil qui le fist ne pot mentir,
Qu'il le fist par Seint Esperit
Qui onc a nuli ne mentit.
Ne vos doi pas celer son non,
Car molt par est de grant renon:
Ço est li pape saint Gregoire,
De seinte iglise flour e gloire.
Li livre est molt auctorizez,
Par totes terres renomez;
Clamez est as vals e as hoges
Li seint livre des *Dïaloges.*

It is not about Roland or Oliver: let it not be the less precious to you because of this! Rather, the book is about the miracles of the saints, and you may be sure that it is not false, not drawn out of false vanity, but is all pure truth. I can pledge my faith about this: he who made it could not lie about having made it through the Holy Spirit, which has never lied about anything. I must not conceal his name from you, for it is of very great renown: this is Pope St Gregory, the flower and glory of the church. The book is highly authoritative, famous in all lands; high and low it is called the holy book of *Dialogues*.

Or vos dirrei qe ço espeaut
Por q'oem le livre issi apeaut:
Dïaloge est veraiment
Entre deus fez li parlement
Quant uns respont e autre oppose.
Guaranz en truis d'iceste chose
Clers, devins e gramarïens,
E les dïaleticïens,
Meimement cels qui de lor nom
Entendent l'intrepreteison.
Les persones nomer redoi
Entre quels est la dite loi [f. 10rb]
Del dïaloge avant nomé:
Molt par est chasqun renomé.
Pierres a non li opposant,

Now I will tell you what this means, and why the book is so called. 'Dialogue' is truly the speech exchanged between two people over two points when one person responds and the other opposes the response. I find as witness for this clerics, theologians, grammarians and dialecticians, especially those who understand the meaning of their name. I must name again the people between whom is conducted the previously named procedure of dialogue; each is very well known. Peter is the name of the interlocutor, a deacon by profession, pleasing to God, and the one who responds is St Gregory, who composed this commemoration of miracles.

Deiacre en ordre, a Dé pleisant:
E cil qui sout est saint Gregoire
Qui des vertuz fait la memoire.
Quanqu' il en dit par ra[i]son proeve,
Qe la merveille nul ne moeve:
Par demonstrance espresse e certe
La verité fait tote aperte,
E totes les doutances sout.

Whatever he says, he, who is no mere promoter of wonders, proves by reason; by express and sure demonstration he makes the truth quite clear and solves all the puzzles.

E por ço soulement me plout
De totes les vertuz les titres
Destincter par divers chapitres,
E nis le non de la persone,
La ou l'une l'autre araisone,
De diverses colours noter.
Car tost porreit li lirre errer
S'il n'eüst sein qui li moustrast
Quoi de quoi, qui vers qui parlast.

And just because of this it pleases me to pick out the titles of all the miracles in different chapters and even to note the name of each person where he speaks to the other in different colours. For the reading can too easily go wrong if there were not a sign that showed what has been said against what and who has spoken against whom.

Li volume est de grant matire,
Mais por ço qu'il ne fust a lire
Grejous, e por ennui abatre,
Le partit saint Gregoire en quatre.
Por tant, si Deu me done vie,
Le chief de chasqune partie
E la fin vos esclarzirai.

The book is about important things, but so that it does not become burdensome to read and in order to eliminate boredom, St Gregory divided it into four. Wherefore, if God allows me to live so long, I will elucidate for you the beginning and the end of each part.

[*The concluding fifty lines elaborate the topos of envious detractors for the work and offer prayers for it to please God, and for the audience to remember what has been said about St Gregory*]

Notes

22 **lu** is an archaic form of the definite article and object pronoun: see Short 2013 §33. See also vv. 28, 29, 40.

26 **en ordre . . . nombrez** referring to the colour-coded table of chapters and their contents in Latin and French, ff. 3^{v}–8^{r}, which follows the *Introductio*.

27–35 **quelqe tu voudras eslirras . . . un autre chapitre . . . eslire** Anselm influentially promoted the notion of audience determination of reading pace and selections in his preface to his prayers and meditations (*c.* 1070–80: for the Anglo-Norman tradition of these prayers see Boulton 2013, 31–7 and Text 6a, and for Middle English versions Wogan-Browne *et al.* 1999, 3.2). Angier's specific linking with a particular manuscript formatting seems to be a new development.

28, 29 **pués, Pués** *Pués* is an adverb (for *puis*) in these uses and *1 pr ind* of *poeir* in the *Proem*, vv. 154,177.

29 **lu chapitre** an archaic form of the definite article and object pronoun, see n. to 22 above.

41 **si tis sens . . . est durs** This sounds like a remark made to monastic novices and in isolation would suggest an internal audience for the text. But Angier at other points also addresses laypeople and women (*Introductio* v. 1, *Proem*, v. 151 above).

52 **mar a conseil . . . creit** Like many of Angier's lines, this sounds like a proverb, but is not attested

in the standard proverbs dictionaries: Angier's proverbial quality may sometimes be a matter of using a particular register rather than of specific citation.

53 The *Prefatio* opens with 12 lines (not given here) on leading others into the right path as the way to go right oneself: see Orengo 2013 II, 27, vv. 1–12).

60 **meint home de son laz se pent** See n. to 52 above.

75–6 **sens par avoir est apris, E avoir par sens est conquis.** On topoi contrasting wisdom and wealth, see 2 Chron 1.10–12, also Eccles 7.11–12, Prov 8.20–1, and Nelson 1986, 34–7. On the development of quantifying discourses, see Kaye 2004.

111–12 **qui son prou . . . quant il voet** Proverbial: see Hassell 1982, F13.

123–4 **Car molt est . . . por lanterne vent vessie** Proverbial: see Hassell 1982, V80.

128 **prent la paille . . . laist le grain** Proverbial: see Hassell 1982, G46.

131–2 **'Fous est . . . saint Martin'** (Morawski 1925, 1312). Martin, bishop of Tours (d. 394) was intensely culted between the Loire and the Marne, and (through the abbey of Marmoutier and its fostering of Martin's patronal status for Angevins in the later twelfth century, Farmer 1991) was also known more widely. He provided an enduring model for pious deaths in his insistence on a bed of hair cloth and ashes in his last illness, according to the contemporary life by Sulpicius Severus (d. 425). Among the miracles credited to Martin, one concerns a flash flood while he and others are working in the fields. Those who cling to a willow to save themselves are carried away by the flood, those who cluster around the saint are saved (see Orengo 2013, I, 400, 91–2n.).

141–2 **Les fables d'Artur . . . les chançons de Charlemaigne** Wathelet-Willem suggests that Angier became disaffected with a putative production of *chansons de geste* copies at St Frideswide (1975, 51–2), but contrasts of romance and *chanson de geste* with devotional and doctrinal reading are a frequent topos (see e.g. (**39**), *Proverbes de Salemon*; (**14**), Greatham's *Évangile*; discussion in Russell 1991; A. Taylor 2011) and Angier's *Proem* v. 171 n).

145–6 **li jugliere . . . saint Piere** The saint is traditionally associated with a jongleur in the fabliaux.

150 There follow 26 lines, not given here, on the work of charity (Orengo 2013 II, vv. 111–34).

151 **Seingnors e dames . . .** Beside this line in the right-hand margin of f. 9^{v} is the rubric *Incipit proe[m]* (partially lost in the gutter of the page). It is conceivable that this might signal an alternative prologue to the *Dialogues*, perhaps specifically for use with lay audiences (if so, it would be most unlike Angier not to have pointed this out). Separate elements of the text's apparatus are normally signalled in the manuscript by a formal rubric within the text column.

161 **lange romaine** More usually *romanz*, with *romaine* reserved for 'Roman' (see *AND*, *s.v.* 'romaine'), but presumably dictated by the convenience of the rhyme here.

168 **Q'om** MS *Dom.*

170 **trait** MS *crait.*

171 **Rollant ne d'Olivier** The hero and his friend in the *Chanson de Roland*. The oldest extant copy of the *Chanson de Roland* was owned at the Oxford Augustinian house at Oseney (Taylor 2002). If Wathelet-Willelm (1975, I.46–50) and Walpole (1976, II.169) are right in identifying Angier's manuscript, the *Chanson de Guillaume* manuscript, and three constitutent booklets from the Edwardes manuscript as from the same scriptorium, it is possible that St Frideswide was producing in the mid-thirteenth century the oldest extant text of the romance *Gui de Warewic* (BL Add. 38,662); the continental version of the *Pseudo-Turpin Chronicle* patronised by Renaud de Beaujeu (BL Add. 40,142); and the *Chanson de Willelm* (BL Add. 38,663: Wathelet-Willem 1975, I.27–50, but see Weiss 1969 and 2010, 52–4). These three texts were bound together at an unknown date as part of the Edwardes MS and have been argued to be exemplars for the well-known Middle English Auchinleck MS (http://auchinleck.nls.uk/, Walpole 1976, 169–70; but see Weiss 1969,

Porcheddu 2001). The newly established book trade in Oxford's Catte St may be another possible provenance (Short 2011).

183 **li pape saint Gregoire** (Gregory the Great, d. 604: see headnote) MS 'la pape' has here been corrected by erasure to 'li'.

203 **Pierres** Gregory's interlocutor in the *Dialogues* is Peter, his deacon.

213–17 **les titres . . . diverse colours** The manuscript does in fact rubricate its chapter titles as well as picking out their initial letters in the chapter table (*li titre del present volume*, ff. 3^{v}–8^{r}), and it also marks the disputants as 'G' and 'P' in alternating red and blue.

218 **li lirre** MS *litre.*

24b. William Waddington, *Le Manuel des pechiez* [Dean 635], Prologue: Cambridge University Library, MS Mm.6.4, ff. 2^{r}–3^{r}

Date of composition and provenance. *c.* 1260; diocese of York

Author, sources and nature of text. The *Manuel des pechiez*, compiled to provide vernacular instruction in Christian dogma, is an important witness to the thirteenth-century efflorescence of pastoral literature in Anglo-Norman (and, later, also in English) that followed upon the work of the Fourth Lateran Council of 1215. The Council was determined to bring about reform of the clergy and, building upon intellectual trends of the twelfth century, it made annual confession to one's parish priest a requirement, along with communion every year at Easter. This was designed to bring laypeople into closer consultation with clergy, so that acts which might otherwise have remained unidentified as sins, or ignored, could be articulated and brought into view with the help of a priest. The clergy needed guidance in appropriate ways to make and hear confession, and although Latin guides to confession had been available for some time, not all parish priests could be depended upon to read Latin well. The greater number of clergy required for the church's 'outreach' program, and the increasing formalisation and systematisation of learning over the twelfth and thirteenth centuries, brought about the development of a searchable book.

The term 'Manuel', or 'handbook', hints at a well filled book which can nonetheless be held in two hands (v. 42), suitable for individual parish priests to own and use, not just for monastic libraries. Later in the book the author declares that it was expressly made in small format so that reading it would not be burdensome (*grevé*): it can be read without weariness (*ennui*) and remembered (*en memoyre bien retenu*; vv. 11,521–4; Schemmann 2000, 230). It reflects the contemporary shift in taste from individual books (such as books of the Bible), or parts or extracts, to whole books, perceived as carrying greater authority. This made separation into discrete units a necessity (Rouse and Rouse 1982, 221–3). Thus the *Manuel* author is eager to advise his readers, as early as the prologue, that his book is divided into *perograffes*, which are *destinctés* (v. 49).

Some manuscript copies include an epilogue naming William of Waddington as the author of the *Manuel*. But the epilogue is not thought to have been part of the original book, and Waddington could have been a scribe or redactor. The original *Manuel* was often varied and adapted in its history of vigorous use, containing, in its longest form, nine books and a prologue and epilogue. It can be thought of as a collectively produced text, even if, like most medieval treatises, it claims one or another authority figure. Some Middle English versions attribute the *Manuel* to Robert Grosseteste, bishop of Lincoln (see (5), *Chasteau d'amour*), a highly regarded writer of pastoral literature, though not of the *Manuel*.

In the early fourteenth century Robert Mannyng of Brunne translated, adapted and expanded the *Manuel* (see Part VI, §2.6). He named his book *Handlyng Sinne*, a title which fleshes out the implications of having a 'handbook' by allowing the reader to picture a book held open in the hands – open as sins should be. Like the author of the *Manuel*, for whom sin can be shown and seen (note the contrasting rhyme words *celer* and *mustrer*, vv. 65–6), Robert encourages the laity to 'shewe' sin, but one must also 'eschewe' sin.

Sources of the first five books of the *Manuel* are multiple and, not surprisingly, often repeat one another, which makes it difficult to specify a precise source. In addition to diocesan constitutions and episcopal articles, the *Manuel* seems to rely principally on the *Summa de vitiis* (begun *c.* 1236, completed, with a *Summa virtutis*, in 1249–50) by the French Dominican William Peraldus, and beyond that, on St Gregory's *Moralia* and on items from St Augustine.

AUDIENCE AND CIRCULATION. According to the prologue, the *Manuel des pechiez* was written for a francophone laity (v. 91), for whom it would provide instruction, to be taught through the local clergy. It was recopied and circulated to libraries, 'north to Durham, south all the way to the Isle of Wight, east to Bury, and west perhaps as far as Ludlow', which may be evidence that its circulation was the result of an organised effort at dissemination, perhaps emanating from York (Sullivan 1992–5, 241–2). The only illustrated manuscript of the *Manuel*, now Princeton University Library, Taylor Medieval MS 1, was made for a noblewoman, Joan de Tateshal, and includes Robert Grosseteste's *Chasteau d'amour* (5): it depicts her overseeing a clerk, representing either the author or scribe, in the production of the text (A. Bennett 1990, 166). Three further manuscript copies of the *Manuel* bear the name of a later, lay owner, Sir Thomas Tempest (1642–92; Sullivan 1992–5, 239–42; 1994). Many of its extant copies were for religious, as for instance a Bury St Edmunds manuscript of the mid-fourteenth century where the *Manuel* occurs together with an extract from Chrétien de Troyes's *Erec et Enide* (Busby 2007, and see (7c), p. 71). The *Manuel*'s exempla – short, lively illustrative stories – are a further innovation. Their variety and number, seventy by one count (Arnould 1940a, 110, 112), is unprecedented, arguing for a strong effort to capture a lay audience's good will and attention. The *Manuel* was reworked in Middle English in various ways: Robert Mannyng's amplified verse translation, *Handlyng Synne* as noted above; Book II of Peter Idley's mid-fifteenth-century rhyme royal verse *Instructions to his Son* (ed. D'Evelyn, 1935), and a prose fifteenth-century translation (see Part VI, §2.6b).

MANUSCRIPT SOURCE. MS CUL Mm.6.4 is the earliest example of the full nine-book *Manuel*. Small in format, 19 × 12.5 cm (261 ff.), it offers a table of contents for the longest version of the *Manuel*. The text of the *Manuel* is written in long lines, two verses to a line. The *Manuel* is the first work in the manuscript; the remaining folios feature Latin religious works, including one by Alain de Lille and a *Testament des douze patriarches* (Testament of the Twelve Patriarchs, Dean 479) attributed to Robert Grosseteste; see Arnould 1940a, 376–8 for a complete enumeration. At 178^r someone has written a curse against anyone who removes the book from its home in the armarium of a monastery.

BIBLIOGRAPHY. No critical edition of the *Manuel des pechiez* exists. Furnivall's *Manuel* texts accompanying his editions of *Handlyng Synne* (1862, 1901–3) are unreliable, owing to errors and numerous interventions. Thorough discussion of the text, including its sources, complex manuscript transmission, and sixty-four of the exempla, may be found in Arnould 1940a. For Peraldus, a major source for the *Manuel*, see The Peraldus Project: http://www.public.asu.edu/~rnewhaus/peraldus/. On the *Manuel*'s authorship see Sullivan 1992, 338; 1991, 155; 1990, 50–7, Biggar, *ODNB*. For manuscript transmission, see also Laird 1941, 1946 and Sullivan 1992 and further on readers, francophone and anglophone, Sullivan 1994. Barratt 2008a, 353–4 concisely surveys manuscripts and owners. Schemmann 2000 examines the *Manuel* as a practical guide to personal and social morality. For lists of the *Manuel*'s exempla, as they appear primarily in several Harley manuscripts, see Herbert 1910: see also Joan de Tateshal's manuscript (5). Allen 1916, 1917, 1918 offers three early readings of the *Manuel*. For similarities between the *Manuel* and Grosseteste's Constitutions, see D. W. Robertson 1945 and Arnould 1940a. On Lateran IV see Boyle 1985, and on Latin confessional guides Payer 2009, 5, Boyle 1982. An important collection of similar texts of vernacular instruction written in response to Lateran IV is Hunt, Bliss and Leyser 2010; the introduction by Leyser succinctly sets out essential background. In brief form Vitz 1989 explains how Christian doctrine after 1215 affected medieval literature. For Middle English versions see Part VI, §2.

TEXT AND TRANSLATION

Ore comence le prologe del lyvere apellé manuel dé pechez.

[L]a vertu del Seint Espirit
Nus seit eydaunt en set escrit
A vus teus choses cy mustrer
Dunt humme se put confesser,
E ausi en queu manere,
Ke ne fet pas bien a tere,
Kar ce est la vertu del sacrement
Dire le peché e coment.
Tuz pechez ne poum conter,
Mes par taunt se pot remembrer
E ses pechés mut amender
Ky cet escrit veut regarder.

Primes dirrum la dreyte fey
Dunt est fundé nostre lay,
Laquele ad .xii. poins provez
Ke sunt articles apellez.
Pus mettrum les comaundemenz
Ke garder deyvent tote genz,
Pus les .vii. pechés mortaus
Des queus surdent tant de maus.
Pus i troverét, se vus plest,
De seint' eglyse sacremens set
Par queus ele est governee
E del peple aoree.
La savrunt ky unt trespacez
Par sey amender de pechez.
Pus de sacrilege dirum
Cum de mestres apris avum.
E teus ne direy par trop treter
Mes sulement pechez cunter.
Ore me doynt Deu par sa pité
Confermer par auctorité
Les pechez ke yci mettray.
Si cum de seins estreit les ay.
Pur ce tut ert auctorité
Tut ne seient les seyns nomé.

Here begins the prologue to the book called the Handbook of Sins.

May the power of the Holy Spirit help us to show you in this book such things as one may confess, as well as how to confess them, because failure to mention them is not good, given that the strength of the sacrament comes from saying what the sin is and how it is committed. We shall not recount every sin but only as many as can be remembered, and such as can be repaired, by whoever wishes to examine this text.

First, we will tell about the true faith upon which our religion is founded, which has twelve verifiable tenets, called articles. Then we will add the commandments, which all people must keep; then the seven deadly sins, from which so much evil comes. Next, if you please, you will find the seven sacraments of holy church, by which it is guided and worshipped by the people. Those who have trespassed will learn there how to atone for their sins. Then we shall explain sacrilege, as we have learned it from our teachers; and I shall avoid treating whatever would be too much, describing only the sins. May God in his mercy now confirm by his authority the sins I shall enter here, as I have extracted them from the writings of the holy men; in that way they will be authoritative, even if
[2v] the saints are not named. I shall not add

Rien del mien ne y mettray
For si cum je apris les ay.
Nule fausine n'i troverét,
Plus volenters le lisét.

anything of my own but only what I have learned from them; no falsehood will you find –read it the more willingly.

'Le Manuel' serra apellé,
Kar en meyn deit estre porté.
L'alme aprent rectifier;
A chescun deit estre le plus chier.
Dé pechez iert le surnun,
Par ce apeller le devum
'Le Manuel dé pechez';
Seit dunkes issi baptizez!

It will be called 'the handbook', for it is to be carried in the hand. It teaches how to set the soul right and should be the dearest thing to all people. Its additional name shall be 'of sins'; we are to call it by that name. 'The Handbook of Sins': let it thus be baptised!

Par perograffes iert destinctés
Ke nus mustrent divers pechés.
Pur ce nul trop hastivement
Cet escrit lise nomeement;
Deu fez le deit rehercer
Ky s'alme vodra amender,
La ou il trovera divers peché,
Si cum il iert perograffé.
Ke plus en lisaunt seit delitus
Cuntes nus mettrum vus aucuns,
Si cum les seins nus unt cunté
Pur plus fere hayr peché.
De privetez n'i troverét rien,
Kar mal put fere ou poy de bien.

It will be divided into paragraphs that show us various sins. That is why no-one should read this particular book too hastily. Whoever would repair his soul should read it twice, there where he will find various sins, each in its own paragraph. So that reading it may be more enjoyable, we shall add some stories, just as the holy men have told them to us, to make sinning even more detestable. About intimate matters you will find nothing, for they can do harm or, at least, little good.

Nepurkant nul ne deit lesser
De privetez sey confesser:
Folie est pur hunte celer
Ke pus coveyne a tuz mustrer
A cel grant assemblement
Kaunt jugé serunt tote gent.
Pechez ke tuchent religiun
Entre privetez lerrum
Pur ce ne voil je traveyler
Ici lur pechez rehercer
Kar checun set serteinement
K'a religius meuz apent
Eus confesser plus menument
Ke ne funt la laye gent,
Kar tant cum sunt plus pres de Dé
Meus garder se deyvent de peché,
E les clers ke sunt bien lettré
Sevent kaunt cheunt en peché.
Pur ce de eus teray de gré

Nonetheless, no-one should desist from confessing his most secret sins: it is folly to hide in shame what will have to be shown to all at that great gathering when all people shall be judged. Sins that touch religious orders we shall leave in private – I do not wish to labour at enumerating their sins here because each of us surely knows that it is more fitting for men of religion to confess themselves in greater detail than laypeople do, for as long as they are closer to God they must do better at keeping themselves from sin. Well-educated clergy know when they fall into sin. That is why, willingly, I'll

Ke vers mey ne seyent curucé.
Mes tant lur di certaynement
Plus blamez sunt ke laye gent
Si eus pechent ausi sovent
Cum fet celi ke rens s'entent,
Kar plus est certes a blamer
Kant un humme ke veit clier
Trebuche en un ord fossé
Ke cil ke ad les eux crevé.
 Pur la laye gent iert fet;
Deu le parface si ly plest
K'eus ver pussent apertement
Kaunt eus trespassent e kaunt nient.
Si aukun de l'oyr seit amendé
Deu de cyel en seit gracié.
Beau fust unkes de mere né
Ke bien fust quites de peché!
 Mun nun ne voil ici cunter,
Kar de Deu sul je quer luer.
Bien say ke checun recevera
De Deu cum meus traveilera.
Ore par Deu la fey mettrum
Solum ce ke premis avum.

keep silent about them so that they won't be angry with me. But I shall surely say this much to them: they are more to be blamed than laypeople if they sin as often as does the person who understands nothing. For it is surely more blameworthy when a man who sees clearly stumbles into a filthy cesspool than a man who has lost his sight.

[3r] This book will be written for laypeople. May God see it through to completion, should it please him to do so, so that people may clearly recognise when they transgress and when not. If someone hearing this can be improved, God in heaven be thanked. One would look in vain to find a person born of mother who might be free of sin!

I do not wish to give my name here, for I seek praise only from God. I know that each person will receive more from God the better his deeds are. We shall now set out the tenets of God's faith, as we have promised.

Notes

1 **[L]**: a space two lines high remains where a letter **L** would have been entered.

9 **poum** Lit. 'we are not able'; the statement does not, however, refer to what the author is able to do but to what suits his purpose; once more, usability of the guide is foremost.

13–28 **Primes . . . avum** As these lines suggest, the original *Manuel* was most probably made up of the prologue and first five books (their subjects the Creed; Ten Commandments; Seven Deadly Sins; sacrilege; and Seven Sacraments: vv. 13–30; Sullivan 1992, 337; Arnould 1940a, 104). Book seven, on how to make confession, must also have been part of the original plan. Book eight, on the theory and practice of prayer, was, in the view of some, 'almost unquestionably' part of the original text, where it would have been the final book (Sullivan 1992, 339). The sixth book (on loving God and not sinning) and the ninth (prayers to Christ and the Virgin) are not found in the earliest manuscripts (Sullivan 1992, 337, 339; 1990, 39–49).

21 **troverét** MS *trovent*.

22 **sacremens set** Among the seven sacraments is that of confession and reconciliation which requires the penitent to confess his sins, express contrition, and propose amendment, whereupon the confessor suggests a penance and pronounces absolution.

25 **savrunt** This word is not entirely clear in the manuscript; Arnould 1940a, 403, transcribes as here, but with a question mark.

28 **mestres** According to Arnould 1940a, 193, *mestres* and *seins* (vv. 34, 59) refers to diocesan constitutions and episcopal articles.

34 **seins** See note 28 **mestres.**

49 **perograffes . . . destinctés** A paragraph could also denote a section or chapter of a book. The *distinctio* arose as a means of distinguishing the different meanings of a word in the Bible. It became standard in sermons throughout the thirteenth century, when preachers, engaged in the writing of sermons, required collections of *distinctio*. Over time it came to refer to divisions and subdivisions of books (Rouse and Rouse 1982, 213–14, 223–4).

59 **seins** See note 28 **mestres.**

61–2 **De privetez . . . poy de bien** Payer 2009, 3–4 studies the 'substantial position' occupied by sexual concerns in the literature of confession, as well as its 'sexual atmosphere'. Confessors were advised to exercise care in questioning penitents about sexual matters 'lest they [the penitents] learn what they had not known' before. Similar warnings were not issued for other sins, such as stealing or money lending.

79–80 **Et les clers . . . peché** Schemmann (2000, 56–7) notes that a passage in the *Manuel* dealing with the circumstances surrounding an offense is accompanied by a more detailed commentary in Latin which the cleric who reads the *Manuel* to 'you' will explain orally.

91 **iert** Although *iert* is found in the manuscript in this spelling, it is also possible to transcribe *i ert fet*, where *i* is (not unusually) a somewhat superfluous 'there'. Both *ert* and *iert*, 3rd pers. forms of the verb *être*, can be read as past imperfect or future indicative; the translation as future reads v. 91 as introducing the matter to come.

97 **Beau** It is difficult to produce a sure translation of this line, primarily because of its first word, which has given pause in other instances too; Arnould (1940a, 408) transcribes this word in British Museum manuscript Royal 20. B. XIV. as '[Bor]'.

99–100 **Mun nun . . . luer** Only in one manuscript (BL Royal 20 B.XIV) did the scribe remove these lines, perhaps thinking they presented a contradiction with the epilogue statement.

Part IV. *Ki veult oïr*: Forming Audiences and Creating Textual Communities

Introduction

The needs and responses of inscribed audiences are a frequent rationale for textual composition. Most vernacular works share a conceptualisation of audience-text relations as a face-to-face encounter with the people for whom a text is initially written, whether or not those specific relations were ever actualised or are pertinent to the version of the text in hand. Historical audiences are linked to but do not necessarily remain the same as production communities or textually inscribed communities. Nor are they defined by them as a single hypostasised community of one language or a particular social status. The audience for the 'Londonisation' of Brunetto Latini in the *Liber custumarum (*8a), for instance, probably identified itself not as a francophone community but as members of the occupational sub-groups of a highly variegated civic public: the court, plurilingual administrators, bureaucrats, merchants, urban dwellers of various kinds. So too the Crabhouse nunnery register (36), more concerned with verse and prose distinctions than its own trilinguality, testifies to the mixed and fluid socio-linguistics of female houses, witnessed in the linguistic ranges of their devotional, doctrinal, and administrative texts, and in their ecclesiastical and lay patronage networks.

Part IV's most explicit meditation on audiences and their formation as textual communities is Denis Piramus's prologue to his life of Edmund of East Anglia (27). As Ian Short has shown, this prologue offers considerable thought about vernacular writing (well worth consideration alongside more frequently discussed prologues such as those of Chrétien de Troyes or Marie de France).[1] Piramus's prologue plays with the assignation of literary genre to specific class or occupational groups and then transforms, redirects and complicates such correspondences together with the whole question of whether texts are to offer *sentence* or *solace* to their audiences. Wace's late-twelfth-century *Vie de saint Nicolas* (25a) adapts estates theory to form a cult community of audience and narrator. The anonymous thirteenth-century *Vie de seint Clement* (25b) outlines with mocking wit the usual parameters of academic writing and its ambitions in order to create narration and audience as joined in a textual community pursuing more useful and less well-known material and readings. A stylish piece of niche marketing, this prologue sets up a pace and intimacy sufficient to sustain with brio the succeeding 15,000 line vernacularisation of the *Clementine Recognitions*. As a genre, hagiography characteristically seeks widening textual communities in which successive circles of audience are brought in by the acts of reading, hearing, touching a written life or donating to a cult (as classically envisaged in Wace's own Life of St Margaret). Performing, singing, hearing, reading, seeing, touching the life makes contact with the saint the common point of a differentiated

1 Short, 2007b, 319–40.

but not exclusive community. The opposite strategy is made alluring in the anonymous early-thirteenth-century verse commentary on the Song of Songs (*Chant des Chanz*, **26**). As the commentary's prologue reviews sacred history and its songs, the biblical book that has required perhaps the most strenuous allegorisation of all to achieve its transformation from Jewish history into Christian is given a newly exclusive turn. Only the Virgin, mother and consort to Christ, can properly sing *the* Song. But through the lyric intensity of this verse commentary's very form, audience participation through listening and overhearing becomes a privileged form of incorporation into the poem's exclusive, courtly-erotic textual community.

The range of textual communities invoked and constructed in this Part defies easy summary. They include the powerful combination of a specific community, that of the Marches of Wales, with wider historiographical and romance communities when the *Brut* origin story is redeployed (*Fouke le Fitz Waryn* (**31**)) to take William of Normandy to Wales and stories of spectral encounters with the British past. Other textual commuities less specifically localised in Britain include audiences rendered global in perspective through their *francophonie*, and newly awakened to the world beyond by the range and glamour – and the exemplary limitations – of Alexander's mortal career (the *Roman de toute chevalerie* (**28**), from the turn of the thirteenth century). Such an audience is also created as a globally aware and specifically Christian textual community in Mandeville's *Livre* (**35**, 1356 or 57), and given the heritage of an entire Eurasian story world in Chardri's *Josaphaz* (**30**, turn of the thirteenth century). Jofroi de Waterford and Servais Copale's *Secré de secrez* (**33**, a vernacular encyclopaedic 'advice to kings' treatise), was produced by collaboration between a writer from Ireland, the far western edge of *francophonie*, and one from the European civic and artisanal hub of the Picard-speaking regions (Flanders, Hainault, northern France). It confidently addresses a transregional public, or at least, an audience encouraged to think of itself as the cosmopolitan inhabitants of a wide geographical and historical virtual community. In the *Miracle de Sardenai* ((**34**), thirteenth century), the story of a cult of the Virgin shared by Christians and Muslims is submitted to standard narrative templates and incorporated into *francophonie*: it leaves a dispersed trail of manuscripts across England and through Europe from south to north, and was presumably originally disseminated from francophone communities in Outremer. Textual faith communities are of course frequently constructed as each other's polar opposites in medieval texts, most notably in the role of the Jewish people as Christianity's others. *Sardenai*'s dual textual community is produced by a relic, the wonder-working statue of the Virgin which puts on flesh and exudes oil as the religious house originally founded by a solitary anchoress grows into a community. *Sardenai* does ultimately underline difference between Christians and Muslims and co-existence is, in effect, on Christian terms, but difference's re-inscription is at least benignly imagined as curative, a possibility not currently available to the medieval nunnery's daughter-house at Sardenaya in modern Syria.

Several prologues in Part IV show other kinds of complexities in the formation of textual communities. To exemplify texts categorised in modern terms as drama and to underline the importance of performance, we give both of the extant versions of the prologue to the *Seinte Resurrecion* (**29**). Less well known than the justly celebrated *Jeu d'Adam*, *Seinte Resurrecion* is presented as a large-scale staging of the Passion in the medium of *décor* *simultané* – the presence within the playing area of all the sites of the redemption narrative as 'mansions' (representations of Heaven, Christ's tomb, a jail, Hell etc.) on small stages probably a little larger than the pageant wagons of cycle drama. *Seinte Resurreccion*'s two manuscripts suggest the multi-directional relations between performance and textual communities brought to attention by Carol Symes.[2] Does the performance community – the guild, professional and amateur players, city dignitaries and citizens etc. – produce the text, which takes on the relation of record or notation to the performance? Or does the text produce the performance and its community? Medieval performances were given over a wide range of venues throughout urban and ecclesiastical spaces and less subject to censorship than, for instance, the Elizabethan enclosed stage: their texts may be less prescriptive than modern play-scripts.

If the relation between manuscript-text and performance event can be flexible and various, so too can the relation between inscribed and actual audiences. This is sharply exemplified in (**32a** and **b**), where an anonymous treatise on medicine and another on cosmetics both appear to be written for female audiences. But by drawing on the influential work of Monica Green and paying careful attention to the texts, it becomes likely that the texts are looking past their possible female audiences and their own association of the vernacular with modesty and self-help to an assumed but not explicitly invoked community of male readers – professional and vicarious conners of 'women's secrets'.

The final work in Part IV, the foundation story of Crabhouse nunnery in Norfolk (**36**), shows a female community creating its own historiography in a way that breaks down the boundaries between documentary and literary. The nuns' use of French verse to begin this story in their house's register is the equivalent of processional trumpets: before the sober history-writing of prose takes over the narrative, the presence and the story of Crabhouse is signalled with the kind of formal aural device more familiar from civic rituals (with a vestige remaining today in the town crier's 'Oyez!' and practised in the fifteenth century during the later stages of the Register's continuation). The nuns transfer the house's multilingual records and their relations with their episcopal and civil neighbours into the mythos of memory, creating a narrative that proposes their community as both worthy of any support given it and capable of withstanding secular and monastic depredation alike. This is creative record-making, not transparent documentation.

2 Symes 2002, 2011.

25a. Wace, *La Vie de saint Nicolas* [Dean 537.1], Prologue: Paris, Bibliothèque de l'Arsenal, MS 3516, f. 69*vb–c*

Date of composition and provenance. *c.* 1150 in Caen.

Author, sources and nature of text. Born on the island of Jersey about 1110, Wace identifies himself as a Norman and a master (*Nicolas*, vv. 35, 1546). After his schooling in Caen and then in the Île de France (perhaps in Paris or at Chartres), he returned to Caen where, as a *clerc lisant* (a clerk charged with reading and translating documents), he served from 1135 to 1170 under 'three kings named Henry'. He was given a prebend at Bayeux by Henry II between 1165 and 1169, and died perhaps in the mid-1170s. Wace is best known for his *Roman de Brut c.* 1155, an adaptation of Geoffrey of Monmouth's *Historia regum Britanniae*, dedicated to Henry II's queen, Eleanor of Aquitaine, and the first French text to transmit the Arthurian legend. Wace's *Roman de Rou* (see (3)) continues the *Brut* by recounting the deeds of the Normans as the Bretons' successors. These two major literary historical poems make Wace one of the most influential writers of the twelfth century, but he was also prolific in religious narrative and in (now lost) lyric poetry.

While at Caen, Wace wrote many *romanz*, including a life of St Margaret, followed by his *Vie de saint Nicolas* and the *Conception Nostre Dame* (a controversial subject, since the doctrine and church feast of the Immaculate Conception, though adopted in England in 1129 and in Normandy in 1145, was strongly opposed by Bernard of Clairvaux). A local personage in Caen and Bayeux, Robert Thiout, was the patron of *Nicolas*: Wace's patrons for his religious poems probably also included religious houses or members of the royal household.

St Nicholas, one of the most popular saints of the Middle Ages, was a fourth-century bishop of Myra in Asia Minor (south-western Turkey). Versions of his legend circulated in Greek from the early ninth century and in Latin from the third quarter of the ninth century. His relics were translated to Bari in 1087, after which time Nicholas was universally venerated in the West as patron of sailors, merchants and children. Wace's *Nicolas* is the earliest translation into French, and also the earliest example of a vernacular saint's life to combine the life with an account of posthumous miracles. The *Vie* is concentrated on Nicholas's deeds and miracles rather than on vernacular exposition of Christian doctrine: some twenty miracles show people of all classes and occupations as the subjects of Nicholas's mercy.

The miracles are narrated with a keen sense of their dramatic interest and their potential to show human weaknesses and foibles, as well as human gratitude and joy for the redemptive power of the saint's intercession. Nicholas's living miracles include a gift of gold to three impoverished young gentlewomen for their dowries, the resuscitation of three murdered clerks, and many more miracles involving sailors and children. In a posthumous miracle a Christian offers St Nicholas's image as surety for an unrepaid loan from a Jew, lies about the repayment, and is crushed under a cart. The Christian's secret cache of gold is revealed to the Jew, and in gratitude to St Nicholas, the Jew and his household become Christians (vv. 723–806). Almost two thirds of the poem (vv. 632–1562) concern the posthumous miracles, though Wace claims selectivity in his choices from oral and written sources (vv. 37–8, 1555–6).

Establishing the narrator's presence and authority via such claims is part of Wace's intense creation of textual community. The narrator's agency in *translatio studii* is to be complemented by the audience's attentive listening in a communally produced celebration of the saint. Wace articulates these mutual obligations in the prologue's exploration of the relationship between Latin and the vernacular: it is the moral duty of the cleric to instruct the unlettered about the saints and their feast days. Clerical indispensability in transmitting this knowledge is explained here in ways designed to lessen cultural gaps between the Latinate and the unlettered. Wace's list of people of all types (vv. 9–12) has been called an early vernacular example of estates theory (Le Saux 2005,

55), or a description of society (Uitti 1975, 400). It pairs opposite qualities: the well-known theory that the poor exist in order that the rich may exercise charity is here extended by Wace to explain all differences in abilities and status. Difference itself is celebrated as God-given: the world is made up of people of contrasting and opposing qualities, but harmony and balance are achieved when each person exercises their gifts for the good of others who lack them (vv. 17–21). This argument underlines the interdependence of all members of the saint's textual community – lay or learned, wise or foolish, noble or commoner, rich or poor, Christian or Jew, merchants, sailors, beggars and thieves – as Wace creates it in his prologue.

Audience and circulation. The *Vie de saint Nicolas* is extant in five manuscripts, all from the thirteenth century. Four of these are of English origin, the fifth (Arsenal MS 3516), used here, is Picard from north-west France. The manuscripts show that the text circulated between England, Normandy and Picardy, and that it appealed to a variety of patrons. Paris, BN MS fr. 902 is a mid-thirteenth-century collection made in England, consisting of biblical and hagiographic verse narratives, doctrinal works (including Grosseteste's *Chasteau* (**5**) and Guillaume le Clerc's *Bestiaire divin* (**17**)) and a play (*Seinte Resurreccion* (**29**)). The Picard manuscript is a luxury collection with many illuminations and a number of Anglo-Norman texts (see below). Oxford, Bodleian, Douce MS 270 (ff. 93^{v}–105^{v}) is a book made for a monastery at Durham; the Cambridge manuscript (Trinity College MS B.14.39) is a trilingual miscellany, probably for a cleric (Reichl 1973); Oxford, Bodleian, Digby MS 86 is a miscellany or common-place book made for a lay member of the Grimhill family from near Worcester (Tschann and Parkes 1996, lvii–lviii).

Manuscript source. Arsenal MS 3516 is a large (328 × 245 mm) parchment manuscript of 356 folios from the Artois region, dated to 1267–8. An extensive collection of, principally, religious poems, the manuscript includes a copy of Herman de Valenciennes's *Roman de Dieu* (**15**), the *Voyage de saint Brendan* (**9**), and all three of Wace's religious works (Dean 489, 571, and *Nicolas*). It is relatively luxurious, with 81 miniatures. The life of St Nicholas is preceded by an illumination sixteen lines high, showing Nicholas with bishop's mitre and crozier: see http://gallica.bnf.fr/ark:/12148/btv1b55000507q/f144.image

Bibliography. The *Vie de saint Nicolas* is edited in Ronsjö 1942: texts and translations of Wace's three religious narrative works are given in Blacker, Burgess and Ogden 2013, with substantial introduction. On the translation of Nicholas's relics see Geary 1990. For Wace's life and works see Le Saux 2005, also Blacker, *ODNB*, *s.v.* 'Wace'. Francis 1932 and Ronsjö 1942 discuss Wace's style. On Wace's narrator figures and textual community see Uitti 1975. Tschann and Parkes 1996 include a facsimile of Wace's *Nicolas* in a major trilingual insular manuscript (Bodleian, MS Digby 86): for the Cambridge manuscript, see Reichl 1973 (where the Middle English items are edited). Wace's *Vie de sainte Marguerite* and its iconography are studied in Keller, ed., 1990. Wace's *Rou*, excerpted in (**3**) above and used in (**42**) below, and the influence of his *Brut* is pervasive, alongside Geoffrey of Monmouth's *Historia regum Britanniae*, in medieval culture (see e.g. (**6**), (**16**), (**20c** and **d**), (**31**), (**42.64**) and Rajsic 2016).

TEXT AND TRANSLATION

Chi comenche li livres de saynt Nicolay.
[f. 69vb]

A ceus qui n'ont letres aprises,
Ne lor ententes n'i ont mises,
Doivent li clerc moustrer la loi,
Parler des sains, dire por koi
Chascune feste est celebree
E chascune a son jor gardee.
Cascun ne puet pas tout savoir,
Ne tout oïr, ne tout veoir.
Li .i. sunt lai, li autre letré,
Li un fol, li autre sené,
Li un petit, e li un grant,
Li un povre, l'autre manant.
Si done Dex diversement
Divers sens a diverse gent.
   Cascuns doit moustrer sa bonté
Del sens que Dex li a doné:
Qui plus est fort, plus doit porter,
Qui plus est haut, plus doit doner;
Qui miex set, miex doit enseingner
E qui plus peut, plus doit aider.
   Cascun doit moustrer son savoir,
E sa bonté e son pooir
Eu Dieu servir le creator,
E as barons sains por s'amor.
Qui bien l'amë e bien le sert,
Bon gueredon de lui desert.
Petit prendra qui sert petit,
Si cumme l'escripture dit:
'Qui petit seme, petit prent,
Qui auques a, auques atent'.
   Jou sui Normans, s'ai a nom Guace.
[f. 65vc]
Dist m'est, e prié que jou face
De saint Nicolas en romans,
Qui fist miracles biaus e grans.
En romans dirai de sa vie,
Des miracles une partie;
En romans veul dire .i. petit
De che que li latins nous dit
Que li lai peüsent entendre
Qui ne puent latin aprendre.

Here begins the book of St Nicholas

To those who have not learned to read, nor applied themselves to learning Latin, clerics must explain the laws of religion, speak to them about the saints, and say why each feast is celebrated, and why each has its own feast-day. No one person can know everything, nor hear everything, nor see everything. Some are lay people, others are learned clerics, some are foolish, others wise, some are born of high estate, others of low, some are poor and others wealthy. In this manner God bestows his gifts in many ways, giving different abilities to different people.

Each person must show the goodness of God through the use of his God-given talents. He who is the strongest must carry the heaviest burden; he who is nobly born must give the most generously; he who knows most should teach, and he who is able to do so must offer the most help.

Each person must exercise his knowledge, and his goodness and his power in serving God the creator and his saints, for his love of them. Whoever dearly loves and serves God well wins a good reward from him. He who serves God little will receive little in return, as the Scripture says: 'he who sows little, reaps little, but he who has sown more, may expect more'.

I am Norman, and my name is Wace. It was asked of me, and I was urged to write in French about St Nicholas, who accomplished great and wonderful miracles. I will recount his life and some of his miracles in French; I wish to relate in French a little of what the Latin tells us, so that lay people who cannot comprehend Latin may understand it.

Notes

9 **li autre** The other manuscripts have *li un*; it is possible that in the language of the Picard scribe either *li* or the final vowel of *autre* is elided to create an octosyllable.

12 **l'autre** Here the scribe elides the vowel of *li*; cf. the preceding note. The other manuscripts have *li un*. In vv. 9–12 the scribe retains the series *li un . . . li autre* as opposed to *li un . . . li un* found in the other manuscripts.

13–14 **Si done Dex diversement / Divers sens a diverse gent** These two lines could be an allusion to the statement of Paul in Rom 12.6–8 on the different gifts given by God's grace. The Pauline analogy of the different parts of the body, each with a different function or ability, yet each an essential part of the whole body, as similar to the differing talents of individuals within the body of the church, is developed more fully in 1 Cor 12.

14 **a** MS *e* is emended, based on the other manuscripts.

16 MSS B and D have six additional lines following 16: *Li chivaler et li burgeis / Et li vilein et li corteis / Deivent en Deu aver fiance / Et honurer de lur substance. / Bonement deivent esculter / Quant il oïent de Deu parler.* (Knights and bourgeois, peasants and courtiers must have faith in God, and honour him with all their being. They should listen attentively when they hear someone speaking of God.)

19 **Qui miex set** MS *Qui miex est*: in the manuscript *est* is written in abbreviated form. Only A has this variant, which may be a scribal misreading of an abbreviation for *set* in the exemplar. On the diversity of gifts and capacities envisaged here, see also n. to vv. 13–14.

29–30 **'Qui petit seme . . . auques atent'** The reference is to 2 Cor 9.6: 'Remember: sparse sowing, sparse reaping; sow bountifully, and you will reap bountifully'.

31 **Jou sui Normans, s'ai nom Guace** The epilogue (vv. 1546–56) in which Master Wace also names himself and his work (*Ci falt le livre mestre Guace*) is omitted in the Arsenal MS.

25b. Anon., *La Vie de seint Clement* [Dean 517], Prologue: Cambridge, Trinity College, MS R.3.46, ff. 122^r–123^v

Date of composition and provenance. Beginning to mid-thirteenth century, England. Provenance unknown.

Author, sources and nature of text. The anonymous, but presumably clerically produced *Vie de seint Clement* is an adaptation of the Latin text of the *Clementine Recognitions* translated by Rufinus of Aquilea (d. 410) from a third-century Greek text attributed to an anonymous Christian from Alexandria (Migne, *PG* I.1202–1474). *Clement* continues the narrative with the Epistle of Clement to James of Jerusalem (vv. 13,184–14,510), and adds additional material from the *Passio SS Petri et Pauli* of Pseudo-Marcellus; the text ends incomplete, at v. 14,994, in the middle of a discussion between Nero and Simon Magus.

Clement changes the source's first-person narrative to third person and re-orders the material into a chronological account. Born in a noble pagan Roman family, Clement is separated, first from his younger twin brothers and his mother: she leaves Rome with the twins to escape the sexual advances of Clement's uncle, only to be separated herself from the twins in a shipwreck. Clement is next separated from his father, who leaves Rome in search of his wife. Clement becomes a disciple of St Peter, and follows him in his preaching tours and debates with his rival Simon Magus. Throughout these tours, the debates systematically present competing views of the world, and gradually Clement, his brothers and his father are all converted to the Christian view, and the whole family is reunited. Clement becomes the successor to St Peter, who instructs him to write the 'Livre Clement' to record what he has learned in the process of his transformation from an orphaned pagan to a Christian family member and head of the church. The text's debates are experientially anchored in the dynamics of the family's loss and reconstitution of its identity: *pace* the prologue's protestations about how boring the debates are in the Latin source, they become dramatic speech acts in *Clement*. Since the debates involve some theologically inspired ethnography, ranging over the peoples of the world and their customs in the style of a verbal *mappa mundi*, the *Vie* can also be seen as responding to thirteenth-century encyclopaedic and compilatory impulses as the world beyond north-western Europe is explored. (The companion text in the manuscript, a life of St John the Almsgiver, is set in Cyprus and the Mediterranean).

The prologue's satirical account of academic writing as a closed self-promoting system of little use to laypeople also serves to define the text's own market share: it is to be in the vernacular so as to be of use to cleric and lay (except for those too rustic to know French, vv. 41–2), and not just to fellow clerics. Moreover, it will return to the values of earlier, divinely inspired writers in their valuable older books, and will vigorously abbreviate debates and sermons as necessary in order to avoid boredom. Equally tactical is the claim that astronomical detail will be omitted simply because of the author's ignorance. Astrology is one of Simon Magus's major tools in debating with St Peter; this science is shown to be inferior to theology in *Clement*, and was regarded with suspicion in the thirteenth century for its capacity to veer into necromancy. So too, the author's claims for the relative positions of Latin and French as written languages have a strategic element. Latin is represented as susceptible to refined expression and rhetorical embellishments, so that any opinion well written in Latin will be praised, whereas the same argument couched in the vernacular is ignored. But the author then deftly dismisses this superiority of Latin rhetoric (which, he asserts, is not only impossible to translate into the vernacular, but co-exists with boring transpositions in narrative chronology) with the claim that his version will avoid tedium, and translate only that which will delight and instruct his audience.

Audience and circulation. Nothing is known of *Clement's* provenance or circulation. However, an audience of clerics and laypeople is invoked at v. 39: *Clement* would be suitable both for use in monastic formation and as performative reading at feasts with visiting lay patrons, as well perhaps for pastoral work and those intending an ecclesiastical career. The corrections and variants in the manuscript suggest the existence of multiple exemplars. St Clement also has a Middle English life in the *South English Legendary*, but this is an independent reworking derived from the *Legenda aurea*; unlike the *Vie de seint Clement*, it includes the miracles of the sea which have particularly associated Clement's cult with mariners.

Manuscript source. Trinity College, MS R.3.46, ff. 122^r–356^r is a mid-thirteenth-century manuscript written in England; 372 leaves, 100 × 185 mm., with 32 lines in a single column per page. *Clement* is preceded by the *Vie de seint Jean l'Almodnier*, ff. 1^r–121^v (Dean 535) and followed by an excerpt from the Latin *Passio Petri et Pauli Apostolorum*. The manuscript was given to Trinity College Cambridge by Thomas Nevile, Master of Trinity (1593–1615) and Dean of Canterbury (Urwin 1980–1, II.3).

The text of *Clement* is the work of two scribes (Burrows 2007–9, III, 4) or three (Willson 1951). The quires normally have 12 leaves, but the last quire of *Clement* has 8, and the text stops in the middle of f. 356^r, incomplete (ff. 356^v–357^v are blank). The text is clearly written, with alternate colours of red and blue used in the large capitals marking section breaks. The Prologue begins with a decorated capital letter (four lines high), and smaller decorated capitals (two lines high) mark subdivisions at vv. 47, 57. The text has been revised and corrected by two hands in addition to those of the scribes, and the scribes have added a large number of variant readings to the text, presented as such (in the form of marginal or interlinear lines beginning with *uel* and the variant text).

Bibliography. The text has been edited by Willson 1951 and by Burrows 2007–9. On *Clement*'s complex relation to its sources and its date see Burrows 2007–9, III.40–56, 64. For a translation, see Burrows 2016. The companion life of St John the Almsgiver is edited in Urwin 1980–1 and the possibility of common authorship discussed in Burrows 2013. The manuscript is described in James 1901, §622, 117–19 and Burrows 2007–9, III.1–7. For literary discussion see Postlewate 2014 and Wogan-Browne 1994a.

TEXT AND TRANSLATION

La vie de seint Clement, pape

Li clerc d'escole ki apris unt [f. 122r]
Tant que aukes entendant sunt,
Mult se peinent de livres faire
E de sentences en lung traire,
Que pur mustrer lur saveir,
Que pur los del siecle aveir.
Livres funt tut de nuvel,
Sis adubbent asez bel;
Bel escrivent e bel les ditent,
Mes li lai poi i profitent;
E clerc i sunt poi amendé,
Ki en lettrure ne sunt fundé.
Li clerc meisme ki funt ces livres
Prest ne sunt ne delivres
De faire as nun lettrez aprendre,
E en vulgar cumun entendre
Que ceo seit que il unt dit
En lur livres que unt escrit;
Kar ceo lur suffist asez
Que de autres clers seient loez,
E que ceo peusse estre dit:
'Bon clers est ki si escrit'.

Pur ceo que fous est tel purpens
De si despendre en nient bon sens,
E pur ceo que livres sunt asez
Ki bien suffisent as lettrez,
Al mien avis mult mieuz serreit,
E a plus grant pru turnereit,
Si li livre de antiquité
Ki sunt fait de verité,
E dunt l'um ad bien entendu
Que li auctur sunt bien de Deu,
En tel language tresturné fussent [f. 122v]
Que plusurs genz pru en eussent.
Ne sui pas de ces lettrez
Ki en clergie sunt fundez,
Nepurquant cel poi que sai

The Life of St Clement, Pope

When clerks at the university schools have studied enough to know a little, they set out enthusiastically to write books full of lengthy discourses so they can show off their learning and win worldly praise. They write books on brand new topics and give them appealing titles. They write with flourish, and their books sound eloquent when they read them aloud, but laypeople profit little by them; nor are the clerics themselves much improved by these works, for they do not have a solid grounding in learning. Those who write these books are not themselves ready or eager to teach the uneducated, or to make understood in the common vernacular whatever it is they may have written. For them it is enough to be praised by other clerics, and to have said of them: 'He's a clever one, the clerk who writes that!'

But such an attitude is foolish, wasting talent to no good end, because there are already enough books written for the satisfaction of learned clerics. In my view it would be much better, and eminently more worthwhile, if the written works of antiquity – which are full of truth, and whose authors are well known to be righteous – were translated into a language such that many different types of people could profit from them. I am not one of these educated persons well-versed in higher learning. Nonetheless, it is my intention to write what little I know in such a fashion that both clerics and laypeople who hear my narrative will

De si escrivre en purpos ai
Que clerc e lai qui l'orrunt
Bien entendre le porrunt,
Si si vilains del tut ne seient
Que puint de rumanz apris n'aient.
Ki veut usdive eschiwir,
Mette entente de cest oïr,
Que ceo que dirrai de seint Clement
Turner li peusse a amendement.
Ki veut oïr de seint Clement,
Dunt il fud nez, e de quel gent,
De sun pere e de sa mere,
E de ses freres, en quel maniere
Li uns des autres departi furent,
E cument puis se recunuerent,
A seint Pierre cument turnerent,
Par ki tuz se entretruverent,
Ki tut cest saver vuldra,
Par cest rumanz bien le aprendra.

be able to understand it, unless they are so rustic that they have learned nothing of the French vernacular. Let those who wish to avoid idle chatter listen attentively to my story, so that what I say of St Clement may inspire them to mend their ways. Whoever wishes to hear the story of St Clement, of where he was born, of his family, his mother, father, and brothers, and of how they were separated one from the other; of how they were later reunited, of how they turned to St Peter, by whose agency everything happened, whoever wishes to know all this will learn it well from this French account.

Uns livres est, meis poi usez,
Ki 'Livre Clement' est apelez;
E si ad un autre nun,
Petri itinerarium,
Kar cel livre fist seint Clement,
E enz el livre descrit cument
Seint Pierre l'apostle par terre ala
E cument il de Jesu Crist parla,
Cument a Deu se cunvertirent [f. 123r]
Ki l'apostle preechier oïrent,
Cum il disputat od Symun,
Celui ki Magus out surnun;
Cument il meisme e si frere
Desputerent a lur pere,
E par la doctrine de seint Pierre
Tuz unt receu baptistere.

There is a book, but which is little read, called 'The Book of Clement'. It has another name: 'Petri Itinerarium', for this book was written by St Clement to describe the earthly travels of St Peter the Apostle, and how he talked about Jesus Christ, and how those who heard the Apostle preach were converted to God, and how he debated with Simon, whose surname was Magus. Clement tells of how he himself and his brothers debated with their father, and how, through the teaching of St Peter, they were all baptised.

Pur ceo que lungs sunt les sermuns,
E lunges les desputeisuns,
Tut tran[s]later ne puis mie,
Kar mult i ad de astronomie;
Jeo de cel art rien apris n'ai;
Ne puis espundre ceo que ne sai.
Mult lung serreit de escrivre
De chief en autre tut cel livre,
Kar bien comprent parchemin
Cel livre escrit en latin;

Because the sermons are lengthy, and the debates as well, I cannot translate them all, and moreover they often discuss astronomy. I am not learned at all in this art, and I cannot explain what I do not know. It would take too long to write out everything from beginning to end, for there is much parchment in this Latin book. As well, the narrative would be too boring and too long-winded if the whole of the debates was translated into

Tut ausi serreit li rumanz
Trop ennuius e trop granz,
Si tute la desputeisun
Fust mise en translatiun,
Kar cil ki latin unt en us
Asez seivent cum ceo est custus
De bel latin bien translater
E la beauté par tut guarder;
Kar tel sentence est mult preisee
Quant en latin est bel mustree,
Ki de asez legier pris serra
Quant autre language la dirra.
Pur ceo larrai les lungs sermuns
E les lunges desputeisuns,
E ceo mettrai en escrit [f. 123^{v}]
Que turner purrad a delit.

the vernacular. Those who are accustomed to using Latin know well how arduous it is to translate effectively its eloquence and rhetorical polish. For any thought, when well expressed in Latin, is highly praised, but the same thought will be little esteemed when expressed in another language. That is the reason I will leave aside lengthy sermons and long debates, and will put in writing only what will bring delight to my listeners.

De tut le livre ceo cuillerai
Dunt jeo nul ne ennuierai,
Meis mult deliter se porrunt,
E cil qui lirrunt e qui l'orrunt.
Le ordre e le cumencement
Ki est al livre seint Clement
Ne puis guarder pur les sermuns
K'i funt granz tresposiciuns,
Kar de grant tresposicium
Ne sout venir si ennui nun;
Pur ceo tel ordre i tendrai
Cum jeo mieuz i purverai
Qui primes la chose cumença
E en ordre avant ala.

From the whole book I will choose only that which will not bore anyone, so that both those who read this work, and those who hear it may delight in it. I will not follow the order of the first parts of the book of St Clement for the long speeches there contain many transpositions in the narrative, and such changes are nothing if not boring! For that reason I will see to the chronological order of the narrative as best I can, recounting first that which happened first, then later events in their proper order.

A ceo dire desore vendrum
Que en purpos par Deu avum.
Ki tut le mund fist de nient
Seit a nostre cumencement;
E il nus duinst a chief venir
Si cum li vendrat a pleisir.

We will now set out to accomplish what God has inspired us to do: may He who created the world out of the void be with us at the beginning of our task, and if it pleases Him, may He permit us to bring it successfully to an end.

Notes

1–2 **li clerc d'escole ... aukes entendant** The reference to university-trained clerics who have only a certain level of learning suggests that only the first three of the liberal arts, the *trivium* (grammar, rhetoric, dialectic), has been studied, and not the *quadrivium* (arithmetic, geometry, astronomy, and music). *Li clerc de scole* is given as the incipit by Meyer 1903a, Willson 1951, and in Dean 517, but the word division in the manuscript can be also be read as *d'escole*; all other occurrences of this word in the manuscript are written unambiguously *escole*.

4 **sentences**: 'judgement, opinion'; but here 'written discourse'; cf. also v. 91.

8 **adubbent**: 'give appealing titles to'; the *AND* (11b) gives 'deck out, adorn' for this passage. The word usually means to 'arm, equip, make ready' (a knight, or a ship, etc.), or to 'dub' a knight. It is also used in the pejorative sense 'arrange, trick out (with intent to deceive)' (*AND* 11b), here applied to sending a book out into the world.

12 **lettrure** The author claims that clerics who are not sufficiently grounded in learning cannot write morally improving works. *Lettrure* is a general term for learning, or simple competence in Latin. Advanced learning is called *clergie*, v. 36 (and sometimes, in other texts, referred to as *haute clergie*); this suggests training in theology as well, which could be studied after the *quadrivium*.

16 **vulgar cumun** An early use of *vulgar* applied to the common vernacular: T–L, *s.v.* 'vulgal', cites only this passage, and one other mid-thirteenth-century use (see Dean and Legge 1964, 8.33). *Rumanz* is the usual term used for the French language (see v. 42 below), although *franceis* also occurs.

32 **bien de Deu** The author seems to present these earlier writers as being directly inspired by God.

36 **clergie** See n. to 12, above.

42 **rumanz** (also 56, 83 and elsewhere in the text, 2785, 2794). The use of *rumanz* is ambiguous, since it could mean either simply the French language, or perhaps, in the context here, 'instructive narratives in French'.

43 **eschiwir** MS *eschewer*; *eschiwer* is an attested form but is emended here to preserve the rhyme.

57 **poi usez** in fact the 'Livre Clement' or *Petri Itinerarium* (the ps-Clement I of Rome *Recognitiones*) is extant in over a hundred manuscripts from the fifth to the fourteenth centuries (Burrows 2007–9, III, 41).

60 ***Petri Itinerarium*** The author deftly includes the Latin phrase in the metre and rhyme of his French text, and expands, vv. 62–3, on the literal meaning ('Peter's Itinerary') of the Latin title of his source.

106, 107 **tresposiciuns** Making transpositions in the chronological order, for rhetorical or thematic effect, was one of the standard medieval methods of narration (the 'artificial' method). The 'natural' method was to keep straight chronological order (cf. the well-known medieval rhetorical manuals of Geoffrey of Vinsauf, *Poetria nova*, or Matthew of Vendôme, *Ars versificatoria*).

111–15 **Qui primes la chose ... fist de nient** Burrows transposes the order of the lines in the manuscript so that 111–12 here follow 113 (2007–9, III, vv. 112–14 and III, 68) on grounds of sense: but the manuscript order seems intelligible and is let stand here.

113–18 **A ceo dire ... li vendrat a pleisir** The author ends by claiming for himself moral equality (if not superiority) to the Latin *auctores* which he earlier states to be 'right with God' (*bien de Deu*, v. 32), suggesting his work is also divinely inspired.

26. Commentary on the *Chant des Chanz* [Dean 461], Oxford, Bodleian Library, MS Rawlinson Poetry 234, ff. 57^r–59^v

Date of composition and provenance. Early thirteenth century, possibly York (Hunt 2004, 12)

Author, sources and nature of text. The Song of Songs is an epithalamium traditionally attributed to Solomon, but this anonymous verse Commentary interprets it as a wedding song sung by the Virgin when Jesus marries her (vv. 124, 171–3). The Commentary early announces itself as a *prophecie* (v. 2) or prefiguration, written by King Solomon, of the Virgin's entire life (v. 168), and in Christian liturgy the Song is indeed specially associated with the feast of the Virgin's Assumption into heaven. Early commentary on the Song, however, mainly interprets the work as an allegory of the union between God and the church and also (especially after St Bernard of Clairvaux's sermons of 1135 × 1153 on the Song) as the mystic union of God and the individual soul. It was in the twelfth century, following the work of Rupert of Deutz, Honorius of Autun and other exegetes, that a full Marian interpretation began to be applied to the entire Song in Latin commentaries. The insular Commentary is one of four Christian allegorical interpretations extant in medieval French, and it is the fullest of the four. The author, who may have been a canon at the Austin Friary in York (Hunt 2004, 15), based his work on the Cistercian-influenced Augustinian canon William of Newburgh (1135/5–1198), a writer today best known for his skeptical critique of Geoffrey of Monmouth's *Historia* and an unusually balanced account of the Jews in his own *History of English Affairs* (*Historia rerum Anglicarum*). Newburgh's *Explanatio sacri epithalamii in matrem sponsi* (*c.* 1190), a commentary on Mary's role as intercessor, was composed at the instigation of Roger, abbot of the Cistercian Byland in Yorkshire from 1143 to 1196 and a friend of St Bernard's (Gorman, ed., 1960, 22, 71, 364). In the earlier portion of its text in the extant manuscript, the Commentary is accompanied by quotations from Peter Riga's *Aurora*, a widely used Latin verse commentary on the Song, extant in over 250 manuscripts and known to Chaucer and Gower, as well as to French Bible versifiers (Beichner, ed., 1965, I, xlii–xlvi).

The Song offers a richly dramatic experience to its audiences. Its evocation of the mingled senses of taste, smell, sight, sound and touch encourage intense response. Exegesis from the eighth century onwards focused on how the Song was to be presented and performed. The work has a 'dramaturgy' all its own (Hunt 1981, 190) in the interplay of the three voices of the Song of Songs. The intermingling and merging of the male and female voices of Bride and Bridegroom and the chorus of 'daughters of Jerusalem' creates a vivid polyphonic experience. The Commentary is composed in striking twelve-syllable lines, more characteristic of sung or recited *chanson de geste*: the lines lyrically perform and comment on the love between Mary and Jesus (as they also capture the Virgin's life story in Herman de Valenciennes's *Bible* (**15**)).

Written at a moment of keen interest in the humanity of both Jesus and Mary, the Commentary, one of about seventy created in the twelfth and thirteenth centuries (Hunt 1981, 190), spiritualises love by reading the Song as Mary's love for God. The sensuous surface of the Song, its tactile and visual gorgeousness, is conjured in descriptions of gems, flora and fauna; these lent themselves to being rewritten in Christian allegorical terms and also allowed for the expression of intimate, often erotic, relationships with both Jesus and Mary. The Commentary makes full use of the tropes of erotic love discourse common across the range of contemporary poetry: the garden of the poem, for example, is also the *locus amoenus* of secular love poetry, and the metaphor of the *hortus conclusus*, or locked garden, evokes courtly literature's association of desirability and unattainability in women. As the voice of Mary, the female voice heard in the Song's own lush garden calls up a different *hortus conclusus*: Mary's fecund and inviolate virginity challenges the ideal of *fol amor* found in secular poetry (the *charnal amur* of v. 18) and redeems Eve's sin in an earlier garden.

The Commentary's prologue follows William of Newburgh's exegesis in offering an account of the Song's nature by explaining who may sing it and how it is to be heard. Adam, unable to sing with joy once cast out from Paradise, is disqualified. Although figures from the Hebrew Bible sang God's praises (Moses, Judith, Deborah, Samuel's mother Hannah and David), they are not among the redeemed of the church and cannot sing the Song, nor does David's 'new song', the Psalms, allow him to do so. So too, the new song of the 144,000 virgins who follow the lamb of the Apocalypse is exclusive to them. There is a yet more privileged song which the virgins and Mary sing; but the superlative song of songs can be sung only by Mary: 'she alone is both fertile as a virgin and virgin as one who has borne a child' (Fulton 2002, 436). In the end, the Commentary presents the Song as so intensely private that 'no-one can understand it but the singer and the one to whom the song is sung' (*... nul ne sent fors cil ke chante e a ki est chanté*, v. 164), a mystical experience fully knowable only to the participants (for William of Newburgh's complex treatment of this, see Fulton 2002, 438). The Song was usually regarded as advanced biblical reading, not to be studied before the Proverbs of Solomon (see (**39**)) and Ecclesiastes had been read. The anonymous Commentary proclaims mystical lyric ineffability in the Song, but seductively offers the promise of some participation in it through loving exegesis and intense listening, perhaps a version of the monastic practice of reading by hearing the *voces pagarum*, the 'voices of the pages', with 'the whole body and the whole mind' (Leclercq 1982, 15).

AUDIENCE AND CIRCULATION. The author frequently addresses his audience to remind them of earlier moments in the Commentary: much in the manner of *chanson de geste*, oral recitation or reading aloud is mimed by the text (and probably constituted the principal way in which this intensely lyrical and synaesthetic Commentary was received). The author claims to be writing for those who do not understand Latin (v. 7), as does Herman de Valenciennes, also writing about the Virgin ((**15**), Spiele 1975, v. 5602). Vernacular writings were produced and used in monasteries, and the Commentary was perhaps heard in private reading, group study or in a series of monastic refectory readings (Hunt 2004, 7). The Commentary's inscription of a listening audience and its insistently performative nature create a devotional textual community around the figure of the Virgin (cf. *tuz amans de seinte Marie*, v. 1183); its warning that carnal love must be abandoned (*de tut en tut deit estre guerpie*, v. 21) implies that it caters primarily to those by whom fleshly love has been renounced. Nevertheless, as the bridegroom says in his final thanks to Mary for her love song, 'Our friends are listening' (*Nos amis sunt escutant*, v. 5288), friends linked to the mystic partnership by ties of 'refined love' (*fin amur*, v. 5288). Like other works drawing on the tradition of erotic mysticism (see e.g. *Rossignos*, (**21**), or the *Eructavit* by Evrat dedicated to the countess of Champagne, Dean 705), the Commentary could also have appealed to the spiritual ambitions of lay people.

MANUSCRIPT SOURCE. Oxford, Bodleian Library, MS Rawlinson Poetry 234 'seems to date from the late thirteenth century' (Hunt 2004, 4); 225 × 150 mm, it shows much wear. The Commentary, ff. 57^r–105^r, is the work of two scribes. The verses in Latin from the 'Aurora' of Peter Riga (*c.* 1140–1209) appear below the writing blocks and are keyed to the text above. Other works in this manuscript are a *Vie de Tobie* thought to be the work of Guillaume le Clerc de Normandie (see (**17**), the prose *Roman de Barlaam et Josephat* (see (**30**)), and a brief work on the beatitudes (Dean 679); the Commentary is the final work.

BIBLIOGRAPHY. The edition is Hunt 2004; there is no English translation. William of Newburgh's *Explanatio* is edited by Gorman 1960: on William see also *ODNB*. Beichner 1965 is an edition of Peter Riga's *Aurora*. For the French 'Le Mans' commentary of *c.* 1200 (interpreting the Song as the relation between Christ and the church) see Pickford 1974 (with important corrections by Hunt 1980). A slightly later, French verse commentary, a set of short paraphrases of verses of the Song in the voice of the church, is edited by Paris 1866. Hunt 2006 edits *Les Cantiques Salemon*, a thirteenth-century verse commentary probably produced for beguines in north-eastern France. On *fol amour* see further Piramus (**27**). Important studies about or including the Song of Songs in medieval culture include Scheper 1971; M. H. Pope, trans. 1977, 112–31; Ohly 1958; Riedlinger 1958; Herde 1968; recent noteworthy discussions are Matter 1990 and Astell 1990. On Christian mimesis of the suffering Christ and his mother, including thorough discussion of the Song of Songs, see Fulton 2002. On Marian doctrines and devotions see Graef 2009; on the Virgin Mary see Rubin 2009. Pouzet 2009 surveys vernacular monastic holdings among the Augustinians in England: see also Hunt 2004, 12–15.

TEXT AND TRANSLATION

Ki vot leaument amer, primes se humilie, [f. 57r]
E ki de amur vot chanter, iteu chose die
Dunt il pot garant aver de seinte profecie:
De tut en tut deit lesser faus' ipocresie.
Le comaundement ke jo ay refuser n'os mie
Ke un lung chaunt fai d'amur de seinte Marie.
Mes iço me mot le quor ke lung chaunt ennuye,
Ja pur ceo nen os lesser, kar il ne enut mie
A ces ki la Dame unt cher et ki querent sa aÿe;
Mut est sutil icest chant e de haute clergie.
De si haut chant comencer pri Cil ke me aÿe
Ke lange de muz fet parler e dune a surz oÿe;
Cel Deu prie ke a sun voler sa grace me otrie
De si bele beau parler ke est sa cher' Amye,
U charité fist ordiner, u amaunz unt aÿe
E de leaument amer apernent sanz folie.
Treis amurs voyl destincter e en treis partie:
Le un est charnal amur ke a tuz maus se lie;
De li venent lecherie, orguyl e envie,
E tuz les autres pechez ke deske en enfer guie;
Cel amur de tut en tut deit estre guerpie.
Li autre amur est natural ki ad meudre partie:
Cel amur fet asaer ke il ne eit folie,

Whoever wants to love loyally first humbles himself, and whoever wants to sing about love should tell a story which is corroborated by holy prophecy: he must completely abandon false hypocrisy. I don't dare refuse the authority I have to write a long song about holy Mary's love, but I feel in my heart that a long song is tiresome. Yet that is no reason for me to dare refuse, since it does no harm to those who love the Lady and seek her aid. This song is very subtle, fine, and it expresses ineffable wisdom. I pray for help to the One who makes the mute tongue speak and gives hearing to the deaf; I beg God grant me his grace so I may speak fittingly about so beautiful a person as is his Beloved, in whom he ordained that charity should exist, from whom lovers receive help and learn to love loyally, without foolishness. I want to distinguish three loves, in three categories: the first is carnal love which is linked to every evil – from it come lechery, pride, envy and all the other sins that lead to Hell; that love must be completely renounced. The next kind of love is love of mankind, which is better: it is felt to guard against lust, thus

Adunc la deit home amer e tener a amie.
Le terz est espirital, cele ad la mestrie,
De cel e de tere tent la seignurie.
Au cel au paleis maur est sa voiz oÿe
Devant Deu Omnipotent, ki trestut otrie
Kanck'ele vot fere cum sa chere Amye.
Amur de cel en tere le tret e le guie,
Par amur s'enumbra en la Virgine Marie.
Amur est la corde ki al piler le lie,
Amur murut en la croyz pur nus doner vie.
De cel amur pri joe sucur, ke Seint Espirit m'aÿe [f. 57v]
Le chant dé chanz de amur chanter de seinte Marie,
E al glorie de Jhesu Crist en romanz le die
Pur ceus ke lettrure ne entendent mie,
Quey seit le Chant des Chanz e key signifie.

one ought to love it and consider it a friend. The third is spiritual; this love has dominion over all – it holds the lordship of heaven and earth. Its voice is heard in the highest hall of heaven, before omnipotent God, who grants whatever his dearly Beloved wants. Love led God from heaven to earth: through love, he was conceived in the Virgin Mary. Love is the tie that binds him to the pillar; Love died on the cross in order to give us life. From that love I beg for succor: may the Holy Spirit help me sing the Song of Songs about the love of sainted Mary. For those who do not understand Latin scripture, and to the glory of Jesus Christ, may I relate in French what the Song of Songs is and what it means.

Le Chant dé Chanz orrez ja, ke jo vus present.
Damnedeu le asela el Veu Testament:
De sun dei escrit l'ad, a Salomon le tent,
Ki en escrit le posa si sutillement
Ke al fiz Deu en mariage est fet le present.
De seinte eglise chante, ke est entre gent,
Ky est tant maumise e revilé forment.
Le fiz Deu l'ad receu deboneremeent,
Sun gage pur luy plie al Pere Omnipotent,
Pur sauver sa Amye la bataille enprent.
Or oez ke die le comencement!

You shall now hear the Song of Songs, which I present to you. Lord God sealed it in the Old Testament: he wrote it with his finger, then offered it to Solomon, who put it in writing so ingeniously that it was made a gift to the Son of God at his marriage. It sings of holy church, which is made up of all the people, yet is so mistreated and strongly reviled. The Son of God accepted it graciously; for the sake of the omnipotent Father, he threw down his gauntlet and took up the battle to save his Beloved. Listen now to what the beginning says.

Quant Deu al comencement le cel ad crié,
A tuz les angles dona franche volenté.
Kant li uns par orguyl eurent trepassé,
Trestuz ke asentirent a lur mauveisté
Enz enfernal umbrage les ad jus geté;
Ilokes sunt fermement e[n] lur mauveisté.
Les bons e lur frang voler ad si confermé
Ke en amurs sunt tuz jours e en charité.
Un' overe unt ke il ferunt, si n'ert ja chevé,
Honur e glorie chanterunt a Deu de majesté,
Loange a lur creatur ki les ad crié,

When in the beginning God created the heavens, he gave free will to all the angels. When some trespassed out of pride, God cast all those who consented to their evil into infernal darkness; there they remain steadfastly evil. He affirmed the good angels and their free will, so that they always exist in love and in charity. One task they will perform, never to be finished, is to sing honour and glory to Sovereign God, praise to their creator who made them and confirmed

En charité, en amur, en joye confermé.
Mes ce n'est pas le Chant des Chanz dunt vus ay preché.

in them charity, love and joy. But that isn't the Song of Songs I've been recommending to you.

Mes enquerum dunc avant de cest chant de pris,
A ki il est avenant, en quel buche asys,
E ki la pot chanter tut a sun devis.
De seint' escripture serchum les escriz [f. 58r]
E de totes veritez serum plus certifs.
Kant Adam engeté fu fors de paraÿs
En poverte e en dolur a tere fu mis,
De li ne trufs ne chansçun ne joye ne ris
Deske ad cel termine ke vindrent les dis
Ke par la deluvie furent tuz ossiz
Mes sul li bon Noé e od ly ses treis fiz
E lur femmes ke od eus sunt en le arche gariz.

But let us inquire further into this worthy song. Let us ask in whose mouth it is appropriately placed, and who may sing it freely. We shall seek in the writings of holy scripture and be more certain of all truths. When Adam was thrown out of paradise, he was placed on earth in poverty and pain; I find no song, no joy, no laughter from him, to the time of the coming of the days of flood, when everyone was killed except for good Noah, accompanied by his three sons and their wives who were spared, sustained in the ark with them.

Pus trovum ke Moysen, ke tant Deu ama
Ki al Munt Synai la ley li dona,
Le chant de loange a Dampnedeu chanta
Ki de servage de Egypte a pes l'amena.
Et chanterent amdu Judith e Delbora,
E la mere Samuel, e plusurs i a,
E les profetes plusurs, ke chanterent ja.
Le pussant Deu loerent ke trestut cria.
Mes le chant dunt jo vus di nul de eus ne sona.

And so we find that Moses, whom God loved so much that he gave him the commandments at Mount Sinai, sang a song of praise to Lord God, who brought him out of slavery in Egypt to peace. And Judith and Deborah both sang and Samuel's mother; many sang, including many prophets. They praised almighty God, who created everything. But as for the song I'm telling you about, none of them sang it.

Li prophete David, ke Deus out tant cher,
Ke en muz de vertuz fu si noble bier,
Deu si bon le trova tut solum sun quer
Ke dit ke de li istera ki pot tut sauver,
Et quant ke Adam trespassa tut pot amender.
Cil un novel chant chanta e fet convier
Tute gent de tere a cel chant chanter,
Kar le Roy de Glorie nus vout visiter
E de enfernal prisun nus vout rechater.
Ceo est le chant ke chante le salmistre el sauter:
'La misericor Deu voyl tuz jurz chanter'.

The prophet David, whom God cherished, who in many virtues was such a noble baron: God thought him so thoroughly good and to his liking that he said that the One who could save everyone would issue from him and he would make amends for whatever were Adam's trespasses. David sang a new song, and he invited all the people of the earth to sing that song because the King of Glory came to us and rescued us from the prison of Hell. This is the song the psalmist sings in the Psalter: 'I want to sing God's mercy for ever'.

La misericor Deu a nus se mustra
Dunc quant la Pucele le fiz Deu enfanta.

God's mercy was shown to us then, when the Virgin gave birth to the son of God. He

La racine Jesse Jhesum germina;
Ceo est le frut de vie ke nus rechata.
Le chant de redempciun cil chanter porra [f. 58*v*]
Od tute la comune ke Deu sauvera.
Mes certis le Chant dé Chanz plus haut se mustra.
Kar Chant dé Chanz n'es[t] mie, kant meillur i a.

caused Jesus to sprout from Jesse's roots; that is the fruit of life that saved us. He sings the song of redemption with all the common people whom God will save; but certainly the Song of Songs will be revealed as superior, for it is not the 'Song of Songs' if a better one exists!

Seint Johan le Evangelist, de Jhesu si privé
Ke sus sa peitrine al cene est cuché,
En le Apocalipse nus ad demustré,
De cent e quarante quatre mile i sunt numbré
Ke chanterent le chant Moysen, le serfs Dé,
E le chant a l'Agnel Deu ke ert crucifié
E ke nul ne pot chanter fors cele mesné.
Ceus de tere sunt ravi en virginité,
Cil sywent le Agnel Deu u k'il est alé.
Chantent il le Chant dé Chanz dunt vus ay preché?
Nanal, veir, kar ne purrunt, mes oez verité:
Icest chant est commun a virginité,
Cil ke pur le Agnel sunt morz e en sun sanc lavé.
Sanz per est li Chant des Chanz, sanz communité,
Autrement le Chant des Chanz ne serreit apelé.
Ne en cel ne en tere ne fu ne ert chanté
De nule creature ke tant eit poesté,
Fors sul de la Virgine ke Marie est nomé,
Ke utre creature munte sa bunté.
De totes creatures seit Cele lowé.
De luy seinte eglise est esluminé,
E al fiz Deu jointe, en grace espusé,
U les seintes almes sunt regeneré.
Par cel chant nus est venuz nostre sauveté.
Ore escutez si l'orrez, si il vus vent a gré!

St John the Evangelist, so much Jesus's confidant that he leaned on Jesus's breast at the Last Supper, showed us in the Book of Revelation that 144,000 sang the song of Moses, God's servant, as well as the song to the Lamb of God who was crucified and that none could sing but that group of supporters. Those on earth were swept up in ecstatic virginity and they followed the Lamb of God wherever he went. Did they sing the Song of Songs I've exhorted you about? No indeed, for they could not; but hear the truth: their song pertains to virginity, to those who died for the Lamb and were washed in his blood. The Song of Songs is without peer, not associated with any others; otherwise it could not be called the Song of Songs. Nor was it sung on this earth or in heaven, nor will it be by any being, however great his power, except by the Virgin, who is named Mary, whose goodness surpasses that of anyone else. May she be praised above all beings. She is the light of holy church and is joined to the son of God, married in grace, there where holy souls are saved. Our salvation came to us through this song. Now listen and you will hear it, should you be pleased to do so.

La parole Deu par ki les cels sunt fermé
E tuz les vertuz del cel par li governé,
La lumere dunt lumeres sunt esluminé,

The word of God by which the heavens are embraced and all the virtues of heaven governed, and the light by which lights

Purreit il fors en beu leu estre herbergé?
Ne Celi ke tut crea, le Deu de majesté, [f. 59r]
Char humeyne ne prist fors en grant purté,
Del comencement dil munde est apareylé,
Tuz les seins profetes l'unt avant preché.
Cum rose d'espine, des Jues engendré,
Virgine seinte Mere, sanz per de purté,
A[l] cel chante od angles al plus haut degré,
Kar la vie des angles ad tuz jurz mené.
Od Moysen e od David e od sun ligné
Chante loenge a Deu, ben l'avum trové,
E le chant des innocens de virginité.
E mut pase plus avant utre humanité,
Kar virgine chante od maternité;
E od les seintes meres ke Deus ad amé
Fecunde mere chante en virginité.
O! si grant merveille ne fust unkes trové!
Quanke Deu de grace al mund ad doné,
Par la meyn Marie nus ad dispensé,
De ki seinte eglise de crestienté
Grace de sa grace receit a pleinté,
Kar pleine grace trove ki n'ert amenusé.
Veez ci le Chant des Chanz dunt sumes sauvé,
Temple e sacrarie al Fiz Dampnedé,
En ki tuz les tresors Deu de sen sunt muscé.
De si trebele Dame esgardez verité,
Quel purté des angles ateint sa bunté,
Ke le mund ne pot prendre, tut l'ad enbracé;
Sur tutes creatures en ben est munté.
Ne est ele dunc ben digne ke ele seit lowé,
Ke al fiz Deu en mariage est predestiné?
Si comence le Chant des Chanz, s'il est escuté,
Ke en amur est plus chanté ke en voiz crié,
E nul ne sent fors cil ke chante e a ki est chanté.

are ignited: could that be lodged except in a beautiful place? And he who created everything, the God of majesty, took human flesh only from great purity, in which he has been clothed since the world's beginning: all the holy prophets preached about that before the fact. Like a rose among thorns, the Virgin holy Mary, without equal in purity, was born among the Jews, to the accompaniment of the angels' song in the highest, for she has always led an angelic life. With Moses and with David and all his lineage, she sings praises to God, as we have found, and the song of the virgin innocents. And she surpasses by far the rest of humanity, for she sings as a virgin mother; and with the holy mothers whom God has loved, the fecund mother sings in her virginity. Oh! never has so great a marvel been found! Whatever God in his grace has given us, he has dispensed to us with the hand of Mary, from whom the holy church of Christianity receives the abundant grace of his grace, for the church finds grace unending. Behold here the Song of Songs by which we are saved, temple and sanctuary of the Lord God's son, in whom all God's treasures of wisdom are hidden. Behold the truth about a very beautiful Lady whose goodness touches the purity of angels; what the world cannot grasp, she has embraced fully; she has risen above all other beings in goodness. Is she not then worthy of being praised, she who is predestined to marry the son of God? Thus I begin the Song of Songs, if you will listen to it, which is sung in love rather than declaimed, and which none experiences but the singer and the one to whom the song is sung.

OSCULETUR ME OSCULO ORIS SUI [f. 59v]

LET HIM KISS ME WITH THE KISS OF HIS MOUTH

Al comencement veum ke ço signefie
La duce parole ke en amur se plie,
Le dit dil Seint Espirist en la prophecie
Ke Salomon escrit, si ne l'overe mie.
Deus persones sunt parlans cum Ami e Amye,
E de espirital amur, de charnal ne e[s]t mye,
Mes est le chant de duçur epitalamye
Ke creit e chante de joie la Virgine Marie
Quant le fiz Deu par amur a li se marie,
Kar par femme vout sauver ke par femme ert perie.

At the beginning we see what the sweet word means that is enfolded in love, the Holy Spirit's statement in the prophecy Solomon writes about: I'm not inventing it. Two people are talking, like sweetheart to sweetheart, and about spiritual love. It's not about carnal love; rather, this is a song of epithalamic sweetness that the Virgin Mary joyfully accepts and sings when God's son marries her in love, for through a woman he wishes to save what was lost by a woman.

Notes

1 **se humilie** Humility is a trait required of both the courtly lover and the Christian seeking God. Hunt points out that this idea is also found in the gloss to a French prose translation of Ovid's *Ars amatoria*, 521–2; in Book II of *L'Art d'Amours* (thirteenth century, first third), the glossator claims that in Scripture can be found, *Orgueil chiet* ('Arrogance falls'), *Qui se humilie, il sera essauciés* ('Whoever humbles himself will be lifted up'), and *Par humilité peus tu conquerre amour* ('You can win love through humility'); Hunt 2004, 139; Roy 1974, 208.

In his notes to the text, Hunt (2004) documents specific parallels between it and William of Newburgh's *Explanatio*.

4 **ipocresie** MS *ipocrefie*, itself corrected from *apocrefie*. Cf. Eccles 1. 37, Matt 6. 5, 16; **seinte profecie** The Commentary emphasises Mary's role in salvation history by repeatedly referring to the Song as a *prophecie*, sometimes said to have been written by Solomon, e.g. vv. 167–8; or Mary's mercy leads Christians to the *tabernacle de seinte prophecie* (v. 588), *ceste prophecie* (v. 629), etc. On Christian typological prophecies of Mary in Genesis and Isaiah see Graef 2009, I.1–5.

5 Erasure after *jo*.

6 Erasure after *fai*.

7–9 **Mes iço me mot . . . querent sa aÿe** See Reinsch 1879, 211, lines 7–9 (Hunt 2004, 139).

17–26 **Treis amurs . . . seignurie** No Latin source for the triad of carnal, natural and spiritual love is known, though Hunt finds that Guiraut de Riquier, in his commentary on a poem by the troubadour Guiraut de Calanso, 'distinguishes *amors carnals*, *amors naturals* (love of mankind) and *amors celestials* (love of God)'; 2004, 139.

24 The *i* of *amie* appears over an erasure.

26 **tent** A space appears between *te* and *nt* where a letter has been expunged.

30 **tret** A space appears between *tre* and *t* where the letter *i* seems to have been expunged.

32 **piler** The Cross; further v. 974: 'Misericorde est la corde ke al piler le lie'; for a similar idea, see Hunt 2004, 23 (v. 1866).

36–8 **al glorie . . . signefie** An exegetical term, emphasised by being placed in line-final position; writing in the vernacular to explain religious doctrine and sentiment to the unlettered is a frequently expressed motivation; see e.g. Grosseteste's *Chasteau d'amour* (5), vv. 26–8.

37 **entendent** MS *attendent*.

40 **el** MS *del*; **asela**: *aseler* could refer both to sealing in the sense of closing up and to stamping or putting a seal upon something. As 'closing up', *asela* probably alludes to the Hebrew language of the Bible, often seen by Christians as a casing needing to be opened (see the *Proverbes de Salemon*, (39)). The term also denotes safekeeping and may thereby anticipate the principal Marian metaphor of the 'sealing' of the *hortus conclusus*, or walled garden, and Mary as *conclusa*. In Honorius of Autun's *Sigillum Sanctae Mariae* (The Seal of Blessed Mary) which appears to be the first interpretation of the Song based solely on Mary and which became a source for subsequent Marian theology and Marian liturgy (Carr 1991, 11–14), the *Sigillum* calls up the association between memory and the sealing of an impression upon wax; as Carr reads it, 'Christ's divinity is impressed on to the wax of humanity. Since his flesh is taken from the Virgin, Mary herself is the seal, or the instrument through which Christ appears. She is also wax, the human who has received the finest impression of divinity' (1991, 23).

41 **escrit** The letter *l* is erased before *escrit*; **De sun dei . . . Salomon** Exod 8. 15, 31. 18, Deut 9. 10 describe how the commandments were inscribed on the stone tablets which Moses brought down from Sinai. In Catholicism, miracles are caused by the finger of God, by 'the hand of the Lord' (1 Sam 5. 6), or 'the hand of our God' (Ezra 8. 31). In Luke 11. 20 Jesus suggests that he has cast out devils with the help of the finger of God. The mention of King Solomon, which makes him God's scribe and thereby argues for the poem's divine creation, differs from the conventional ascription of its authorship to Solomon, thought to explain how the Song became part of the canon.

49 vv. 1–4 of the 'Aurora' at bottom of page: *Omni plena bono Salomonis cantica regis / Christum commendant super omnia cantica legis. / Qui legit hoc et percipit hoc, cantare paratus / Tam solempne melos, hic dicitur esse beatus* (Beichner, ed., 1965, II, 703–4).

52 **orguyl** is followed by an erasure.

59–62 **Honur e glorie . . . Mes ce n'est pas le Chant des Chanz dunt vus ay preché** William of Newburgh distinguishes between the 'old song', sung by all 'creatures of intellect, including the angels' (cf. Ps 102. 22), and the 'new song', sung by earthly beings because Truth arose from earth when 'the Word became flesh and dwelt among us' (John 1. 14). The 'old song' is the song of Moses that John saw the angels singing (Rev 15. 2–3); the 'new song' is the song of the Lamb, sung only by those 'redeemed by the blood of the Lamb'. An even more privileged song is the song of the virgins, those who follow the Lamb 'wherever he goes', for they have retained not only the integrity of their minds but also that of their flesh (Fulton 2002, 436; the passage in Rev 14. 3–4, to which Fulton refers here, says that 'These are they who were not defiled with women', i.e. these virgins are men).

66 **seint'** MS *seinc*.

73–4 **ses treis fiz / E lur femmes** The wives of Shem, Ham and Japheth are not named.

75–83 . . . **Moysen, . . . ne sona** Exod 15. 1–18, Deut 32. 1–44; Hunt points out that in these verses the Commentary author comes close to St Bernard's first sermon on the Song of Songs (Hunt 2004, 140, n. to v. 72; see Leclercq *et al.*, 1955–77, vol. 6). Canticle translations [Dean 457] following some Anglo-Norman translations of the Psalter suggest that a loose grouping of songs in Anglo-Norman, to be used in devotions, existed as of the twelfth century. Like earlier writers of commentary in Latin such as Rupert of Deutz, Gregory the Great and Origen, the author here selects from such a collection, including some and rejecting others; see Hunt 2004, 140.

79–80 **Judith e Delbora . . . la mere Samuel** Jth 16. 1–17; Judg 5. 1–31; 1 Sam 2. 1–10; Samuel's mother was named Hannah or Chanah; see also Hunt 2004, 139–40, n. to v. 62.

93 **le chant** In MS these words are written above the line.

94 **La misericor . . .** Cf. Ps 100.1.

97 **La racine Jesse Jhesum germina** Isa 11. 1, 10; the farmer Jesse was the father of David, king of Israel, from whom Christians believe Jesus to have descended.

104 John 13. 23, 25.

105 Rev 15. 2–3.

108 **le chant a l'Agnel Deu** Rev 7. 4; after the phrase *l'Agnel Deu* the phrase *u kil est ale* has been crossed out; it appears later, in v. 112.

114–15 **virginité . . . en sun sanc lavé** Rev 14. 3–4 specifies an elite of 144,000 who alone can sing the new song and follow the Lamb. The link with the blood of martyrdom suggests virgin martyrs and hence the influence of the office for the Common of Virgins. Although virgins 'undefiled with women' are specified in the biblical verse, they were frequently reconceived as the female bridal procession of the Lamb: see further Bhattacharji 1995.

125 **regeneré**: *regenerer* can have a religious valence as causing to be reborn into the spiritual life, or saving, sometimes including baptism; see the *Dictionnaire du Moyen Français*, http://www.atilf.fr.

134 **dil** Sometimes used in this text as an alternative to **del** (Hunt 2004, 26).

162–4 **Si comence . . . a ki est chanté** On these key but syntactically challenging verses, Hunt states that the 'Song only makes sense when shared by a comprehending and loving reader and audience' (2004, 6 n. 9). What the 'sharing' probably meant is suggested by Fulton, commenting on William of Newburgh's subtle exegesis of the Song; for him, she says, it is 'a historical conversation between the bride and her bridegroom once actually spoken but now accessible only to the eyes, ears, and throat of the singing soul'; that is, 'it is not . . . a conversation that [the participating listener is] expected . . . to have experienced and so to understand. Rather, it is a record of a particular conversation "written wonderfully and mystically" by "the finger of the writing God" . . .' (2002, 436–8). On the importance of *hearing* Mass, see Zieman 2008, esp. 80–92.

164 **sent** MS has *s ent*, where it seems a letter has been expunged; 'Aurora' vv. 5–6 at foot of page: *Quatuor hoc carmen personas psallere cerno, / coniugium sacrum cantu celebrare quaterno.*

27. Denis Piramus, *La Vie seint Edmund le rei* [Dean 520], Prologue to Book One: London, British Library, MS Cotton Domitian A.XI, f. 3r–v

Date of composition and provenance. 1190–3, almost certainly at the Benedictine abbey of Bury St Edmunds, East Anglia.

Author, sources and nature of text. The author identifies himself as Denis Piramus (v. 16); as someone owing obedience to God, St Edmund and church seniors (Russell 2014, vv. 3289–98); and as a former court poet (v. 5 below). Whether he is the 'Magister Dionysus' (d. before 1214) who features in Jocelin de Brakelonde's *Chronicle* as the cellarer of the Benedictine abbey of St Edmund at Bury from 1173 to 1214 is unproven, but highly probable. Bury vigorously promoted the cult of Edmund of East Anglia, king and martyr (r. 855–70) during the twelfth century and later.

In this prologue to Book I of the *Vie seint Edmund*, Piramus presents the poem as a new departure in his career. He repudiates his youth as wasted in writing the sort of courtly poetry that, like an opportunistic sexual go-between, plays the game of bringing lovers together to fulfil their desires. Instead, his new Life of Edmund, a work both enjoyable and true, will establish bonds between present-day nobles and their predecessors, and provide the audience with virtuous examples. While he deprecates fables, *lais*, and *romans d'aventure*, Piramus advertises them persuasively in order to argue for the superiority of his own work as giving still more pleasure than secular poetry and as being morally and spiritually better. He freely concedes pleasure, skill and industrious labour to the writer of the courtly romance *Partenopeus de Blois*, and to Marie (de France?): their noble audiences 'love' them (vv. 33, 40, 41, 43, 49–52, 62) and the texts of secular leisure have relaxing, therapeutic functions (vv. 53–6). But if secular poetry both panders to its audiences and offers them recreation, sacred biography can form them in still more powerful ways, healing the spirit and safeguarding one's person from shame (vv. 64–5). The creation of collective monastic memory and its audiences is more authoritative, a powerful transmission of *virtu* from the past (vv. 72–6), and not, like secular courtly poetry, unverifiable (*pas de tut verais*, v. 38; Short 2007b, 331–6; more widely, Otter 1996).

The narrating persona, 'Piramus', is difficult to pin down. How far this figure of licentious youth and elderly *gravitas* is historically grounded, how far this is a virtuoso exploitation of prologue conventions in order to link secular and monastic audiences is unclear. Piramus's reference to *Partenopeus* has been thought to constitute an authorship claim (Legge 1950, 6–7), but since *Partenopeus* is a version of the Cupid and Psyche narrative of a mysterious night-time lover, the reference may equally stand for the lies and dreams (*menceonge*, *suonge*, vv. 29–30) with which the prologue identifies secular courtly literature. Similarly, 'Piramus' may be an ironic byname, evoking a figure of spectatorship, as in the anonymous *Piramus and Thisbe* lai of *c.* 1155–60.

The *Vie* consists of a prologue (vv. 1–94), a narrative (vv. 95–3271) of the life and martyrdom of King Edmund of East Anglia (d. 870), a prologue to the second part of the life (vv. 3271–98), an account of the miracles attributed to St Edmund and the attack upon England by King Swein of Denmark (vv. 3299–4981 in the longer of the two extant manuscript texts). The opening prologue's emphasis upon ancestry is present in the Life's sources, which were early identified as including Abbo of Fleury's *Passio Sancti Eadmundi*, Galfridus de Fontibus's *De Infantia Sancti Eadmundi*, Herman the archdeacon's *Liber de Miraculis Sancti Eadmundi*, probably Gaimar's *Estoire des Engleis* (10) and, possibly, Geoffrey of Monmouth's *Historia regum Britanniae* and Wace's *Roman de Brut*. The poem itself claims both Latin and English source materials (vv. 3269–70). The latter are not known, but Gaimar shows knowledge of Edmund material from the *Anglo-Saxon Chronicle*: so too, perhaps, Piramus. As the variety of source material suggests, modern generic categories of hagiography *versus* historiography do not adequately capture this text's concerns.

AUDIENCE AND CIRCULATION. Bury, a major Benedictine house, might fairly have bidden for a cult of its saint at the royal court, but over the late twelfth and thirteenth centuries Edward the Confessor became decisively established as the lineal saint of the Angevins and Plantagenets. Edmund was nonetheless an important saint in England, and in addition to Piramus's *Vie seint Edmund*, he is represented in another insular French life in quatrains (*La Passiun de seint Edmund*, Dean 519) and on the continent by a late-twelfth-century French prose *Vie seint Aymon*. His cult was vigorously propagated in the visual, aural and material culture of the abbey, its artefacts and liturgies. A Middle English version of Edmund's life by Lydgate survives in twelve manuscripts, including a spectacularly sumptuous presentation copy commissioned at Bury for the twelve-year-old Henry VI (London, BL Harley 2278).

The *Vie* is extant in two manuscripts, BL Cotton Domitian A.XI, ff. 3^{a}–26^{d} and Manchester, John Rylands University Library, Fr. 142, ff. 1^{a}–68^{b}, of which the first is an anthology suitable for use either in secular or monastic households and the second now contains an (illustrated) text of *Edmund* alone. Piramus's prologue invokes a noble audience directly (v. 57) and also implicitly by accumulative lists of aristocratic titles (vv. 42, 49–50, 83–4, 87–9): he also suggests appropriate reading matter for aristocrats (vv. 87–90). Since some noblemen became monks and elite laypeople were often present at the feasts of wealthy monasteries, aristocratic and monastic audiences could readily overlap (Rector 2012). Bury itself included lay members: being crucial to the defence of East Anglia, it was assigned forty knights by William I (Cownie 1998, 70), and in the later Middle Ages had a lay confraternity. Despite this, and despite the preservation of Marie de France's work in monastic manuscripts (notably BL Harley 978; see Taylor 2002), Piramus's references to *Dame Marie* (vv. 36–48) invoke distinctively secular courts where leisure reading has high status. In the more conventional prologue to the *Vie*'s second part, Piramus reveals that he has been instructed by church seniors (Russell 2014, vv. 3297–8) to translate the work and claims that by translating his source from Latin and English to French, he will make it accessible to all (Russell 2014, vv. 3277–80). The class range of shrine visitors and of persons experiencing saints' miracles in *miracula* narratives is characteristically wider than that of the proponents of saints' lives, so that this second audience is perhaps to be thought of as more inclusive than the courtly listeners invoked in the initial prologue.

Manuscript source. BL Cotton Domitian A. XI, ff. 3^{a}–26^{d}, a composite manuscript of which the first part is an early-fourteenth-century anthology of narrative lives in French, incomplete at the end (the Rylands manuscript of the *Vie*, incomplete at both beginning and end, lacks the prologue edited here, but includes some 900 extra lines and is illustrated). The Cotton anthology manuscript is 175 × 220 mm, without illustration, but with regular marking of sub-division by alternating red and blue capitals. The *Vie seint Edmund* is the first item, opening with a 5 line red and blue initial and followed by Guernes de Pont-Saint-Maxence's Becket life (**11b**). After these British saints' lives, there follows a verse life of Christ, the Assumption from Herman de Valenciennes's *Roman de Jesu Crist et de sa mere* (**15**), and the verse *Petit Sermon* on the Last Judgement (Dean 636). A legendary of nine female saints' lives by Nicholas Bozon (Dean 582) concludes the selection. The second part of the manuscript is slightly earlier and contains documents concerning the Benedictine abbey of Bec, written in another hand: it is not known when the parts of the manuscript were bound together.

Bibliography. The *Vie*, previously available in Kjellman 1935 (with a study by Rothwell 1977 of the subsequently discovered Rylands French 142 manuscript), has now been fully edited in Russell 2014, with a commentary on the Rylands images by Kathryn Smith (for the Ryland images see http://luna.manchester.ac.uk/luna/servlet/view/search?q=reference_number="French MS 142"). Russell 2014 gives a full account of the Life, its context and author: older studies are Haxo 1914, 1915 (sources, author, and language); Legge 1971 (the *Vie*'s style and sources), and see further on sources Hayward 2009. An audio-visual reading of the prologue is online at http://legacy.fordham.edu/academics/programs_at_fordham_/medieval_studies/french_of_england/audio_readings_94163.asp. Other French lives of Edmund are edited by Grant 1978 (*Passiun*), Richardson 1967 (prose *Aymon*), and listed in Porter and Baltzell 1954. For the *lai* of Piramus and Thisbe see Segre 1961; Burgess 1987, 14. The prologue to Piramus's *Edmund* is edited and discussed as literary criticism in an important study, together with consideration of its date and context, in Short 2007b. Hunt 1979 discusses the convention of the poet's defense of his writing. For Bury St Edmunds, see Cownie 1998 and Gransden 1964 and 2007: for the abbey's Latin rewritings of Edmund, Thomson 1974, Licence 2014. Edmund's cult in textual, visual and liturgical materials is studied in Bale, ed., 2009. The illuminated manuscript of Lydgate's Edmund is described and many folios reproduced at http://www.bl.uk/catalogues/illuminatedmanuscripts/record.asp?MSID=6643&CollID=8&NStart=2278.

TEXT AND TRANSLATION

La Vie Saint Edmund Le Rey [f. 3ra]

Mult ay usé cum[e] pechere
Ma vie en trop fole manere,
E trop ay use[e] ma vie
[E] en peché e en folie.
Kant court hantey[e] of les curteis,
Si fesei[e] les serventeis,
Chanceunettes, rymes, saluz
Entre les drues e les druz.
Mult me penay de tels vers fere

The Life of St Edmund the King

Like a sinner, I've spent my life in a very foolish way, and I've passed too much of it in sin and folly. When with courtly people I frequented the court, I composed *serventeis*, little songs, rhymes, and verse greetings between sweethearts and lovers. I worked hard to write those lines that might bring them together, so that they could be side by side to do as they wished. The devil made

Ke assemble les puise treire,
E k'ensemble fussent justez
Pur acomplir lur voluntez.
Ceo me fit fere le Enemy!
Si me tync ore a malbaily;
Jamés ne me burderay plus.
Jeo ay noun Denis Piramus.
Mes jurs jolifs de ma jofnesce
S'en vunt, si trey jeo a veilesce,
Si est bien dreit ke me repente.
En autre ovre mettrai m'entente,
Ke mult mieldre est e plus nutable.
Dieus me aÿde espiritable,
E la grace Seint Espirit
Seit of moy e si aÿt.

me do that! Now I see that I was misled; never again will I play those games! My name is Denis Piramus. The frivolous days of my youth are disappearing out of sight and I'm drawing towards old age. I should rightly repent. I'll direct my attention to better, more worthwhile work. May the Spiritual God help me, and may the mercy of the Holy Spirit be with me and help me.

Cil ki *Partonopé* trova,
E ki les vers fist e ryma,
Mult se pena [il] de bien dire.
Si dist bien de cele matire
Cum de fablë e de menceonge.
La matire resemble suonge,
Kar [i]ceo ne put unkes estre.
Si est il tenu pur bon mestre,
E les [suens] vers sunt mult amez,
E en ces riches curz loëz.
E Dame Marie autresi,
Ki en ryme fist e basti
E compassa les vers dé lays,
Ke ne sunt pas de tut verais,
E si en est ele mult loee,
E la ryme partut amee,
Kar mult l'ayment, si l'unt mult cher
Cunt[e], barun, e chivaler.
E si en ayment mult l'escrit, [f. 3rb]
E lire le funt, si unt delit,
E si les funt sovent retreire.
Les lays soleient as dames pleire.
De joye les oyent e de gré,
Qu'il sunt sulum lur volenté.

He who wrote *Partonopeus* and composed and rhymed its lines took great pains to express himself well. Indeed, he recounted the matter as one does fable and lie. The matter is like a dream, because it can never exist. He is considered a masterful teacher and his verses are greatly loved and praised in noble courts. Lady Marie is another such, who wrote and composed in rhyme, and planned out the verses of her lays, which are not at all true. And she is greatly praised for this and her poetry loved by all, for counts, barons, and knights love it dearly and cherish it greatly. They love it in its written form, and they have the lays read and are delighted, and they have them read over and over again. The lays please the ladies, who hear them joyfully and willingly, because they express their desires.

Li rey, li prince, e le courtur,
Cunt[e], barun, e vavasur
Ayment cuntes, chanceuns, e fables,
E bon diz qui sunt dilitables,
Kar hostent e gettent penser,
Doel, enuy, e travail de quer,

The kings, the princes and the courtiers, the counts, the barons, and the vavasours love stories, songs and fables, and good and pleasing tales, because they take away sorrow and cast out the heart's troubles. They cause ill-will to be forgotten and they lighten the

E si funt ires ublier,
E del quer hostent le penser.
Kant cil e vus, segnur, trestuit
Amez tel ovre e tel deduit,
Si vus volez entendre a mei,
Jeo vus dirray par dreit[e] fei,
Un deduit qui mielz vaut asez
Ke ces autres ke tant amez,
E plus delitable a oyr.
Si purrez les almes garir
E les cors garaunter de hunte.
Mult deit homme bien oyr tel cunte;
Hom deit mult mielz a sen entendre
Ke en folie le tens despendre.
Un dedut par vers vus dirray
Ke sunt de sen e si verray
K'unkes rien ne pout plus veir estre,
Kar bien le virent nostre ancestre,
E nus enaprés de eyr en eyr,
Avum bien veu que ceo est veyr,
Kar a nos tens est aveneu
De ceste oevre meynte verteu.
Ceo que hom veit, ceo deit hom crere,
Kar ceo n'est pas sunge ne arveire.

heavy heart. Since they and you, lords, all love such work and amusement, if you wish to listen to me I shall tell you, in good faith, an entertaining story worth a thousand times more than those others you so love, and more enjoyable to hear. You will be able to heal your souls and protect your bodies from shame. A man ought to hear such a story very gladly. A man should very much prefer listening to good sense than wasting his time in foolishness. I shall tell you a pleasing story in verses made of good sense and so true that nothing has ever been more true, for our ancestors saw it; afterward, from generation to generation, we too have seen the truth of it, for great virtue has come down to our times from this work. What a man sees, a man ought to believe, for this is neither dream nor illusion.

Les vers que vus dirray si sunt
Des enfances de seint Edmunt,
E dé miracles autresi;
Unkes hom plus beals ne oÿ.
Rei, duc, princë, e emperur,
Cunt[e], barun, e vavasur
Deivent bien a ceste oevre entendre, [f. 3*va*]
Kar bon ensample il purrunt prendre.
Rey deit bien oyr de autre rey,
E l'ensample tenir a sey,
E duc de duc, e quens de cunte,
Kant la reison a bien amunte.
Les bon[e]s genz deivent amer
De oïr retreire e recunter
De bons gestes e les estoyres,
E retenir e[n] lur memoyres.

The verses that I will recite to you concern St Edmund's youth and his miracles. No man has ever heard finer. Kings, dukes, princes and emperors, counts, barons and vavasours should indeed listen to this work, because they will be able to take good example from it. A king should hear about another king, a duke about another duke, a count about another count, and apply the example to himself, when the point made adds up to goodness. Good people ought to love to hear good deeds and histories retold and recounted, and hold them in their memories.

Notes

This extract was initially edited by Karen Trimnell as part of her graduate study. We thank her for her work.

La Vie . . . le rey MS title.

6–7 **serventeis / Chanceunettes, . . . saluz** All are forms of courtly love poems. The *saluz* or *saluz d'amor* is common to French and Provençal literatures. The appearance of *saluz* here seems to be the only known instance of a verse *saluz d'amor* in Anglo-Norman (for a *saluz d'amor* in Christ for women religious, see Dean 619, Wogan-Browne 2013). Wace lists the writing of *serventeis* amongst his other literary activities (*Roman de Rou*, 153; see (3)). On equivocal speech in *serventeis*, see Léglu 1997.

5 **court** MS courte

5–12 **Kant court hantey[e] . . . lur voluntez** Piramus casts himself and his verse in the role of go-between, facilitator, or procurer of the *fin'amors* tradition, a familiar Ovidian topos in Latin and vernacular writing, though rare outside lyric in the French of England.

9 **tels** MS teles

10 **assemble les . . . treire** The obj. pron. *les* may suggestively conflate the joining together of verses with the joining together of lovers.

15 **Jamés ne me burderay plus** vv. 13–19 reproduce the common medieval literary convention of later-life retraction of *juvenilia*. The use of the word *burde* (joke, game) recalls the *jocus amoris* of Baudri of Bourgueil (Bond 1995, 170.153–6), who uses the word *jocus* in a similar context. In Old and Modern French, *burde* carries the connotation of deception (*Trésor de la langue française*, *s.v.* 'bourde'), which it loses in Middle English, only to take on a sexual connotation in an idiomatic phrase 'to bourde in bed' (*MED*, *s.v.* 'bourde'), anticipated here in its contextual extension to 'debauch, prostitute myself'. See also Ovid: *Scis vetus hoc iuveni lusum mihi carmen, et istos,/ ut non laudandos, sic tamen esse iocos* ('You know that this poem [the *Ars Amatoria*] was written long ago, an amusement of my youth, and that those jests, though not deserving praise, were still mere jests'; *Tristia* I.ix, 61, 62: http://www.perseus.tufts.edu/hopper/text?doc=Perseus:abo:phi,0959,008:1:9

17 **jolifs** = frivolous; amorousness or even fickleness may also be implied.

25 ***Partonopé*** Presumably the popular late-twelfth-century romance *Partonopeus de Blois* (Dean 173), eventually translated into nine European languages.

25–48 Piramus's deprecation of the Partonopeus poet and Marie is distantly related to the twelfth-century literary commonplace of attacking the works of *vilains conteors* (Damian-Grint 1999, 102), of which the best known is probably that in the first 26 lines of Chrétien de Troyes's *Erec et Enide*. Piramus is distinctive in also noting their skill and hard work.

28 **dist** MS dist il

34 **curz** MS curtes

35 **Dame Marie** The most likely candidate is Marie de France, twelfth-century poet of the *lais*. For another possible case of poetic rivalry, see Adgar's *Gracial* and Guernes's *Thomas* (**11a** and **b**).

36–7 **fist . . . basti . . . compassa** MS *compensa*, an architectural metaphor for literary composition: cf. e.g. Geoffrey de Vinsauf, *Poetria Nova* (?1210), 1A 'Si quis habet fundare domum (If somene has to build a house)'; Luke 14.28–30; Boethius, *De Consolatione Philosophiae* IV, *prosa* 6 (Murphy 1964).

38 **de tut verais** Short argues that the sense here is not 'untrue', but 'unverified': Piramus distinguishes hagiography from secular poetry by its superior authority (2007b, 331–6).

41 **l'ayment . . . l'unt mult cher** The immediate antecedent of 'l'' seems to be 'verses' (*la ryme* of v. 41), but it is not impossible that Marie herself is meant.

48 **sulum lur volenté** Piramus may mean that ladies, having demanded to hear the *lais*, are gratified when this request is granted; or perhaps that the subject matter of the *lais* – most often concerning adulterous lovers, or lovers united despite seemingly insurmountable difficulties – reflects the desires of the hearers for similar adventures (cf. the heroine of Marie's *Yonec*, who is inspired by hearing of marvellous love adventures: *Yonec*, 101–4, Ewert 1995). The allusion to the demands of female literary patrons recalls the prologue to Chrétien de Troyes's *Chevalier de la Charette* (1–30), in which the narrator claims to suit his subject to the desires of his lady, Marie de Champagne.

53 **Kar** MS Kar il

53 **gettent penser** Kjellman 1935 argues that 'penser' is a scribal error (for examples supporting his reading *geter puer* see Godefroy, *s.v.* 'puer'). Short 2007b and Russell 2015 accept the MS reading.

54 **travail** MS travaile

53–6 **Kar hostent . . . le penser** Recreational literature is here seen to be physically beneficial. Cf. the *Regimen sanitatus salernitanum* (of vexed date, but *c.* 1200), two verses of which Piramus here virtually reproduces: *Si vis incolumen, si vis te reddere sanum,/ Curas tolle graves, irasci crede prophanum* ('If you want to be healthy, if you want to remain sound, take away your heavy cares, and refrain from anger'; http://www.accademiajr.it/bibvirt/regimen.html, vv. 2, 3: see more generally Olson 1982).

61–3 **Un deduit . . . a oyr** Piramus suggests that his work will fulfil Horace's famous dictum: *omne tulit punctum qui miscuit utile dulci,/ lectorem delectando pariterque monendo* ('He has won every vote who has blended profit and pleasure, at once delighting and instructing the reader': Fairclough, 1926, repr. 1978, *Ars poetica*, vv. 343–4).

61 **qui mielz vaut** MS q. milez valut

67 **Hom** MS Homme

72–3 **nostre ancestre . . . de eyr en eyr** Cf. Wace, *Roman de Brut*: 'De rei en rei e d'eir en eir' (Weiss 2002, 2): the topos is common in the *Brut* tradition from Wace onwards (Legge 1971, 84).

77 **hom** MS homme

77 **Ceo que hom veit, ceo deit hom crere** Rather than alluding to the authority of his sources, in this and in the immediately preceding lines Piramus emphasises the veracity of eyewitness account and experience. On twelfth-century vernacular histories deriving *auctoritas* and truthfulness from their authors' status as eyewitnesses, see Damian-Grint 1999, 193.

78 **sunge ne arveire** echoes vv. 30, 31, explicitly distinguishing Piramus's *Vie* from *Partenopeus de Blois*. *Arveire* may be translated either as illusion or deception (*AND*; T–L); with the sense of 'illusion' it appears elsewhere, as here, together with *songe* (*sunge*) (Godefroy, *s.v.* 'arvoire'). Gaimar (9) makes a similar claim: his *Estoire* is neither *fable ne sunge* but taken from an 'authentic historical source' (Short, ed., 2009, 354–5 A16–17).

80 **Des enfances de seint Edmunt** For Piramus's use of Galfridus de Fontibus's *De infantia Sancti Eadmundi* see Russell 2014, 3–4 and passim; Hayward 2009.

82 **hom** MS homme

86 **bon ensample** The idea that accounts of former times are valuable for their models of virtuous conduct is a topos of twelfth-century histories (Damian-Grint 1999, 94, 95, and see (3), (6), (41)).

28. Thomas of Kent, *Le Roman de toute chevalerie (Alexander the Great)* [Dean 165], Prologue: Paris, Bibliothèque nationale de France, fonds français, MS 24,364, f. 1ra

Katharine Handel

Date of composition and provenance. Late twelfth century (Foster and Short 1976–7, II, 73–6). Probably written at St Albans monastery, Hertfordshire.

Author, sources and nature of text. *Le Roman de toute chevalerie* retells the life of Alexander the Great (d. 323 BC) in rhymed alexandrine *laisses*, and includes a focus, often critical or ambivalent, on the glamour, excitement and riches of the substantial legendary material attached to Alexander in post-classical tradition. The *Roman* uses this pre-Christian space to explore the expanding limits of the known world. In common with medieval travel narratives and encyclopaedias, the *Roman* includes descriptions of the exotica Alexander encounters on his journeys, and it lingers over Alexander's meeting with the glamorous Queen Candace. The *Roman* looks back at the *romans d'antiquité* and forward to the preoccupation with Mediterranean and Eastern regions endemic to the crusades and later explored in, among other works, Mandeville's *Livre des merveilles du monde* (see **35**) and the *Secré de secrez* (**33**). In the *Roman*, as in some other texts, Alexander plays a role in sacred history and geography through his visit to Jerusalem, his journey to the Earthly Paradise, and his defeat of Gog and Magog. The *Roman* also allows for the articulation of contemporary political concerns in a safe space: the text is preoccupied with leadership, particularly the responsibilities of barons to the king and vice versa, and also with the corrupting effects of riches. The narrator displays some ambiguity towards the aspirations of his supposed aristocratic audience.

The author names himself as Thomas of Kent and Thomas (vv. P22 [Foster and Short, 1976–7, I, 120, f. 44^{d}], 6581, 6676), and at v. 6733 as 'Mestre Thomas', referring to his university education. This would almost certainly have meant that he had some ecclesiastical connections, perhaps some aristocratic sponsorship for his education, and possibly an ecclesiastical or clerical career before his entry into the cloister. Two manuscripts of the text show the author dressed as a Benedictine monk (f. 22^{r} in the Cambridge manuscript, f. 1^{r} in the Paris manuscript), and his use of many classical sources suggests that he was monastic. St Albans Abbey has been suggested as a likely location for the text's composition: one of the *Roman*'s sources is the *St Albans Compilation*, a prose Latin twelfth-century collection of Alexander material in the St Albans library. St Albans owned several vernacular Alexander manuscripts; one of the principal manuscripts of the *Roman* (Cambridge, Trinity College MS O.9.34) is thought to have been made there.

The *Roman de toute chevalerie* has contemporary continental as well as classical sources. It may have been written as a response to the *Roman d'Alexandre*, a twelfth-century continental French Alexander romance with different political concerns. Latin source material for the *Roman* largely comes from the Zacher *Epitome* (date uncertain, perhaps ninth century) and Justin's epitome of Trogus Pompeius's *Historiae Philippicae* (date unknown, but perhaps third century), the more fantastical sources for medieval Alexander material. Their use counterbalances that of the more negative views of Alexander from Orosius's *Historiae adversus paganos* (early fifth century), which is the major source for the *St Albans Compilation* and which presents a scathing view of Alexander as king. The *Epistola Alexandri ad Aristotelem*, a letter from Alexander to his tutor Aristotle describing his experiences in India, is also drawn on. Like the continental *Roman d'Alexandre*, the *Roman de toute chevalerie* incorporates the *Fuerre de Gadres* by Eustache: Foster and Short's edition (1976–7), as they explain, omits the *Fuerre de Gadres* and sections interpolated from continental Alexander material, and so does not represent the text as medieval readers of its extant manuscripts would have found it (the *Fuerre de Gadres* section alone is very large, from f. 28^{r} to f. 77^{v}, meaning that almost 50 folios are missing from the edited text). This inevitably underplays the interaction of continental and insular material in the text, which is an excellent example of the commonalities of interest between francophone audiences on both sides of the Channel.

The prologue surrounds the figure of Alexander with considerably more ambivalence than the continental version of the romance. Alexander's conquest of the world is framed both by Christian eschatology and by animadversions on envy, even as his life story is offered as source of comfort and joy. The following narrative opens by describing the world as measured by the ancients, its dimensions, times and seasons already known, and about which the narrator refuses to say more before moving to Nectanabus, sorcerer king of Libya, expert in reading and manipulating events with astrological knowledge. The opening of this encyclopaedic romance raises pertinent questions about the nature of the world and what can be known and achieved in it.

Audience and Circulation. The *Roman* is extant in three manuscripts: Cambridge, Trinity College O.9.34 (1446), mid-thirteenth century; Durham, Cathedral Library C. IV.27B, second half of the fourteenth century; Paris, BN fr. 24,364, early fourteenth century, in which it is the sole text. There are also two fragments (London, BL Add. 46,701, mid-thirteenth century, and Oxford, Bodleian Library, Latin misc. b.17 f. 140, early fourteenth century). The prologue addresses those who would like to alleviate their own sorrows by listening to a chivalrous tale. Given the roles of major monasteries like St Albans as overlords of their towns and places of accommodation for travellers, the *Roman* probably reached gentry and mercantile readers. Two of the extant manuscripts are lavishly illustrated and include blazons from aristocratic families. The frequency of illustration makes these books rather like graphic novels: they would have been suitable for audiences of various mixed literacies, aural and visual. The *Roman* need not be restricted to secular contexts, however: the Durham manuscript, which has no illustrations, but uses the image captions as headings for the text, is believed to have been made for the bibliophile Richard de Bury, bishop of Durham from 1334 to 1345. De Bury may have asked for a copy without illustrations: he was reputedly 'no admirer of pictorial art' (Foster and Short 1976–7, II.71). The Durham manuscript has many annotations naming the original sources of the material, which suggests it could have been used for study. The Paris manuscript's text shows signs of having been tailored for a continental French audience in its style and vocabulary (where, for instance, the text explains of the Plough constellation that 'the stars we call *Charle Wain*' are called *Char* by the French' (*Ces sunt les esteilles qe nos Charle Wain nomon. Char l'apellent Franceis*, vv. 4674–5), the Paris manuscript emends these to the (redundant) 'these are the seven stars we call *Char*: French people call them *Char*' (*Ces sont les set esteilles ke nus Char nomon, Char l'apelent Franceis*, f. 50[d]).

These different manuscript contexts show the text being adapted for various audiences and purposes, and suggest Alexander's breadth of appeal. The *Roman* is also the principal source of the fourteenth-century Middle English *Kynge Alisaundre* (where the prologue given here is much expanded; see Part VI, §2) and was used by Gower in his *Confessio amantis* (Bunt 1994).

Manuscript source. This edition is based on the Paris manuscript, BN fr 24,364, a moderately sized (320 × 225 mm) vellum manuscript with ii + 87 folios in 2 columns: dated 1308–12, it may have been produced in London for Jean d'Engaigne (Avril and Stirnemann 1987, 137), whose arms occur with the highest frequency in the manuscript. There are 311 illustrations (illuminated miniatures, tinted and grisaille drawings, not all finished) in the text and margins. This picture cycle is based on that in the (probably St Albans) manuscript, Cambridge Trinity College, MS O.9.34, digitised at http://sites.trin.cam.ac.uk/james/viewpage.php?index=981. The opening of the Paris text on f. 1 is lavishly bordered with individual figures of musicians and players in the bas-de-page, suggesting the courtly revelry noted in the prologue, while illuminated miniatures of the author as a Benedictine monk and of Alexander top each of the page's two framed and foliated columns (the author is framed in an 'O' rather than the 'M' of the text's incipit). Seven heraldic blazons occur in f. 1's borders, and further blazons occur in the first half of the manuscript. About

25 of them are the arms of contemporary knights called to Parliament in 1308–12: some are also applied to figures in the narrative. The Paris manuscript has been digitised: for f. 1r, see http://gallica.bnf.fr/ark:/12148/btv1b60002590/f13.image The *Roman* is preceded in the manuscript by five folios, with the arms (added in the fifteenth century) of the de Montigny family, both alone and impaled with those of the de Vendômes with whom they had several marriage alliances (Avril and Stirnemann 1987, 137).

Bibliography. *Le Roman de toute chevalerie* is edited by Foster and Short 1976–7 (with Durham as the base manuscript), and their text translated into modern French in Gaullier-Bougassas and Harf-Lancner 2003. On the Paris manuscript see Avril and Stirnemann 1987, 126–38; on the Durham and Cambridge manuscripts, Busby 2002, I, 322–38. For the *Fuerre de Gadres* interpolated in the Roman see Foulet and Armstrong 1942, repr. 1965. The continental *Roman d'Alexandre* is edited and translated into modern French in Harf-Lancner and Armstrong 1994. Gosman 1997 tabulates the contents of French Alexander romances and critiques Foster and Short's omission of passages from the continental texts (34–45, 290–2). For debates about Thomas of Kent, see Wind 1962, Foster 1955, and Legge and Ross 1955. Still informative for the uses of Alexander in medieval French writing are Meyer 1886 and (especially for the wide range of genres to which Alexander material contributes) Cary and Ross 1967. For a concise tabulation of Alexander texts, materials and traditions, see Stoneman 2008, Appendix II. Recent studies of francophone and insular Alexanders include Maddox and Sturm-Maddox 2002, Gaullier-Bougassas 1998 (for a comparison of the continental *Roman d'Alexandre* and the *Roman de toute chevalerie*), Stone 2013 (particularly important for the textual traditions of the sources), Handel 2015. On the illustration of the *Roman* manuscripts (on which further study is needed) see Ross 1963, 25–7. For a post-colonial reading of the *Roman*, see Akbari 2005. Baswell 2015 is important for its analysis of the cultural-political anxieties attached to Alexander. See also the Alexander project at http://mythalexandre.meshs.fr. For a generally illuminating discussion of an illustrated Alexander manuscript as a 'chivalric Bible' for 'secular veneration' of Alexander the Great, see Cruse 2011.

Text and Translation

Ci comence le prologe en la geste de Alisandre

Mult par est icest siecle dolenz e perilleus
Fors a icels qui servent le hault rei glorius,
Qui por nus delivra le seon sanc precïus.
Sicum mestier nus est, eiet merci de nus!
Car vie de homme est breve et cest mund laborus,
Decevables a tuz e a mulz envius.
Nequident n'ad el siecle [nul] si bosoingnus
Qe alcun delit n'i ait, itant meseurus.
Mult par poet estre dolent al jugement irus
Al jur que tant avera tristes e pour[u]s
Qi pur sa char norir est en icest mund penus.

Here begins the prologue to the deeds of Alexander

How sorrowful and dangerous is this world for all but those who serve the high king of glory who gave up his own precious blood for us. May he have mercy on us, for we are all in need of it! For the life of man is short and this world filled with toil, uncertain for all and a burden for many. Nevertheless, no-one in the world is so needy that he takes no pleasure in it at all, however unfortunate he may be. He who is eager to nourish his own flesh here below can [expect to be] very sorrowful at the wrathful day of judgement when there will be so many who are sad and fearful.

A ceo que homme entent est sis quors desirus.
Un deduit ai choisi qi mult est delitus,
As tristes [est] confort e joie as dolerus
E assuagement as mals des amerus.
Deliter si poent homme ben chevalerus
E tuit ceo qi de romanz sunt coveitus.
A l'enviouse gent sunt li bon vers custus
Car joie e enveisure est doel as envious.
Le mal le tient al quor dunt vient le dit custus;
Altrement creveroit car tut est verminus.
Si nul d'els me reprent, seigneurs, tant di a vous:
L'ume mesprent sovent en outre mal grevus.
Mult par serreit li homme en ses fez eurus
Si a la fiee n'est repris de l'envious.

Ore poet qui voelt oïr un vers merveillus
D'Alixandre le rei, de Darie l'orguillus,
Qi Babiloine prist, e sis uncles Cyrrus.
Alixandre conquist itanz isles hidus,
Ynde et Ethiope les regnes plentivus,
Par force de bataille en maint estur dotus.
Cum l'estorie dirrat fort fu et vig[o]rus,
Hardi e conquerant e enginnus.

A man's heart is eager for what preoccupies him: I have selected a pleasant tale that affords much delight, a solace to those who are sad and a joy to those who grieve, and relief for lovers' misfortunes. Chivalrous men may delight in it, as well as all those who want [to hear] a romance. To envious people these verses are irksome, for joy and lightheartedness spell grief to the envious man. Malice grasps him by the heart, from which hurtful speech springs out; if it were not so, his heart would burst, so full of venom is it. If anyone of them reproaches me, lords, I say this much to you: often more grievous sins are committed. Anyone would be quite happy with his own actions as long as he is not reproached by the envious.

Whoever wants to may now hear a wonderful story about Alexander the king, about Darius the Proud who captured Babylon, and his uncle Cyrus. Alexander conquered many fearsome islands and the fertile kingdoms of India and Ethiopia through battle and many a dangerous fight. As this story will relate, he was strong and energetic, bold and victorious and clever.

[*The text continues with a description of the earth's division into continents, the calendar months and seasons, etc., especially as understood by the astronomer Nectanabus.*]

Notes

R la geste de Alisandre Foster and Short chose an alternative, *Rumanz de tute chevalerie*, from the colophons in the Paris and Cambridge manuscripts to avoid confusion with the continental *Roman d'Alexandre* (Foster and Short, ed., 1977, II, 3).

1–6 **Mult par . . . e a mulz envius** This is a familiar topos expressing how Christian consolation is the only antidote to the troubles of the modern world; the narrator nevertheless identifies literature as a source of consolation later in the prologue (vv. 13–17).

1 **est icest** MS *est i icest.* The metrical variations analysed by Foster and Short (1976–7, II.24–9) indicate that the verse, characteristically of Anglo-Norman, is flexible in line length. We emend here to make two regular hemistichs within the line.

4 **eiet merci** *eiet* (*aiet*) is an archaic form of *ait*, 3 pr. subj. of *avoir* (= qu'il ait merci).

5 **cest mund laborus** MS *icest munde laborus.* The emendation makes two regular hemistichs.

9–10 **Mult par poet estre dolent . . . avera tristes e pour[u]s** Fear of the Day of Judgement was further heightened by the late twelfth- and early-thirteenth-century development of the Apocalypse (the earliest manuscripts of the six Anglo-Norman Apocalyptic texts [473–8 in Dean] date from the thirteenth century). The Apocalypses have much thematic material in common with Alexander narratives: both genres display an interest in fantastic beasts, geographical locations, precious stones, animal symbolism, the collision of classical and biblical history, and Gog and Magog.

13–15 **Un deduit ai choisi . . . as mals des amerus** The topos of literature as a source of consolation is common in Anglo-Norman literature and can be seen in many other prologues: see e.g. Piramus (27), Chardri (30).

17 **romanz** This term refers both to a literary mode and to the fact of composition in the vernacular.

17 **coveitus** The choice of this word to describe desire for romance may be significant, as it invokes negative connotations of gluttony and covetousness. This is striking, given that the prologue opens by insisting on Christian consolation but then moves to the secular comfort provided by chivalric tales. The clerical narrator may be implying criticism of the over-consumption of romance: there are several hints throughout the *Roman* that the author is critiquing the desires of the very audience to whom he is ostensibly catering.

18–19 **A l'enviouse gent . . . doel as envious** The narrator's version of envy's dangers plays on *enveisure* (joy, gladness, allurement) and *envious*. His many references to envy throughout the prologue suggest that envy is the worst sin, as it cancels out any pleasure or consolation that could be had from literature (represented here as a good, secular or not). It is envy of Alexander which motivates Antipater to murder him at the end of the text.

20 **le dit custus** Foster and Short note that this refers to 'the hasty ill-considered remark, affording relief to the heart of an envious person' (1976–7, II.20n.).

22 **seigneurs** MS *seignerus* with scribal metathesis.

24–5 **Mult par . . . n'est repris de l'envious** This third reference to envy within eight lines may allude to Alexander's death, and also to authorial envy: a suggestion that interference from others has prevented him from writing before now.

27, 29 **Alixandre** Expanded from MS *Alix.*

28 **Babiloine . . . e . . . Cyrrus** The Paris manuscript adds this line, which is not present in the Durham manuscript.

30 **Ynde et Ethiope** These places were often used to represent the limits of the known world to a medieval audience (see also *Secré de secrez*, 33).

32 **Cum l'estorie . . . et vig[o]rus** This is an extra line not present in the Durham manuscript (vig[o]rus for MS *vigrous*).

29. *La Seinte Resurreccion* (*La Résurrection du Sauveur*; *Anglo-Norman Resurrection*) [Dean 717], Prologues: a. Paris, Bibliothèque nationale de France, fonds français, MS 902, ff. 97*ra*–98*vd*; b. London, British Library, MS Add. 45,103, f. 215*rb*–*va*

Date of composition and provenance. *c.* 1200, England.

Author, sources and nature of text. This anonymous drama survives in two versions, both incomplete, and both apparently reworked from a now lost original. The Paris text of 371 verses is thought to be the earlier of the two and closer to the original than the British Library manuscript (originally from Canterbury) of 522 verses. The play summons into being a central moment of Christian religious history, Christ's resurrection, by freely adapting the Gospel narratives of Matthew, Mark and Luke, with some additions from the apocryphal *Acta Pilati* (part of the *Gospel of Nicodemus*). It begins with Joseph of Arimathea's request to Pilate to grant him Jesus's body; the Paris manuscript breaks off just as guards take up watch at the sepulchre, whereas the Canterbury text continues through the arrest of Joseph. The complete play, which probably included the Harrowing of Hell, may have been about 2,000 verses. Twelfth- and thirteenth-century concern with the incarnate Jesus and with affective reponse to his Passion must have made the performed crucifixion an exceptionally intense experience ('Slide the spear right through to the lungs, so we can know if he's dead', a soldier orders Longinus (P vv. 105–6, C121–2) as blood and water gush down onto Longinus's blind face). So too, the play's emphasis on the disposal of Christ's body and the large role played by Joseph of Arimathea must have created considerable suspense and drama en route to the triumph of the resurrection.

Precedents for *Seinte Resurreccion* are to be found in the *Quem quaeritis* (Whom do you seek?), an Introit trope to the Easter Mass consisting of a brief dialogue between attendant angels and the three Marys at Christ's sepulchre. In England, reforming provisions in Bishop Æthelwold's late-tenth-century *Regularis concordia* for Benedictine religious houses specified costuming and staging for *Quem quaeritis* (Kornexl 1993, §51, 104–7), elaborated the liturgy, and opened the conventual church to the laity for Sunday Mass (Butler and Given-Wilson 1979, 27). Latin and mixed Latin and French texts for Easter performances such as *Quem quaeritis* survive from at least six English and northern French nunneries and monasteries from the early twelfth century onwards, and some 830 such texts are known in medieval Europe from the twelfth to the sixteenth centuries (Pappano 2005, 49–54).

The prologues to both manuscript versions of *Seinte Resurreccion* contain notable stage instructions for the play's simultaneous or multiple setting (*décor simultané*), a staging technique whereby all the scenes are in view at the same time. Both prologue and play are in octosyllabic rhymed couplets, a seamless blend that may have helped the stage directions to survive (or perhaps to sustitute for physical staging in some performances). The play, with its several stage divisions, platforms and replicas of buildings, and an estimated 42 actors would have required a large space, perhaps in the open air before a church, but also perhaps within one. Stage locations are expressed as a syntax of visually meaningful juxtapositions rather than as precise positions in a fixed space. The prologue for (**29a**) (Paris manuscript) calls for five 'mansions': heaven, the crucifix, the 'monument' (Christ's sepulchre), a jail, and hell. (**29b**) (Canterbury) adds the Tower of David and possibly a separate structure for 'dan Tholomeu' (v. 22 and n.). Narrative movement would have occurred across the play space, against a visual panoply that offered oppositions (heaven and hell) and associations (heaven and the crucifix, the jail and hell), and episodes began and ended as actors moved from station to station.

Like many medieval plays or performance pieces, *Seinte Resurreccion* is not identified as a play in its prologue, nor is it clear whether the prologue itself was performed. The texts in both manuscripts look like scripts for actors or perhaps *metteurs en scène*: both make third-person references to the audience ((**29a**) Paris, v. 25; (**29b**) Canterbury, v. 35) that seem to tell performers when to begin the play. But instructions in the body of the play are given in the narrative past tense, supporting the argument that most extant medieval playtexts are not scripts for future enactments but postdate the performances to which they refer and that performances relied more on improvisation than on memorised scripts (Symes 2011). The *Resurreccion* texts may have been meant for a *meneur de jeu* (a kind of master of ceremonies) and may represent the text of a performance adapted for reading or recitation (Frank 1954, 89). But equally, the Paris scribe of the *Resurreccion* may have turned what was initially a verse narrative into a play: speeches are signalled by the characters' abbreviated names in the margins ('Jo' for Joseph, 'Pi' for Pilate, etc.), making the Paris version 'immediately recognisable as a text with parts allocated to more than one speaker' (Symes 2002, 805). The diversity of interpretation possible here argues against seeing the manuscript texts as single-purposed; rather, nothing in the manuscript prologues or the dramatic narrative they preface prevents each from being used variously. The play's structure accommodates full performance; reading aloud by several voices without stage setting; recitation; or simply reading aloud from the manuscript.

AUDIENCE AND CIRCULATION. The Canterbury text has the play performed *devant le puple* (v. 4), perhaps not surprisingly for a monastery that had become an important pilgrimage centre after Archbishop Becket's murder and burial there in 1172. The abbey had friends and wealthy patrons, both female and male, in France and England, including, at about the time the Canterbury text was first written down, King John (Dalton *et al.* 2011, 15). The audience for performances of the *Seinte Resurreccion* may therefore have included royalty and aristocracy, as well as local laity from various socio-economic groups. If, as some of its contents suggest, the mid-thirteenth-century Paris manuscript was compiled at Lincoln, its audience could have been quite similar to Canterbury's (and the text's scholastically inspired apparatus is a reminder that the learned and pastorally minded Robert Grosseteste, who had taught theology at Oxford, was appointed bishop of Lincoln in 1245). Whether or not those centres were directly involved in the production or dissemination of the play, their culture provides a plausible milieu for its reception.

MANUSCRIPT SOURCE. (**29a**), Paris, BN fr. 902, a manuscript of 233 × 166 mm written in two columns, may have been made in Lincoln *c.* 1255 (Symes 2002, 805); almost all its contents are in French verse. In addition to the *Resurreccion*, it contains the *Poème sur l'Ancien Testament* (i.e. versified books from the Hebrew Bible; see (**43**)), Grosseteste's *Chasteau d'amour* (**5**); saints' lives (among them Wace's St Nicholas (**25a**)); the story of Little St Hugh of Lincoln (Boulton, trans., 2013), and Guillaume le Clerc's *Bestiaire divin* (**17**). The play text adopts the new scholastic techniques of rubricating, indexing, glossing and crossreferencing used in Paris and Oxford universities (Symes 2002, 808; and see Rouse and Rouse 1982). In four places marginal instructions in Latin, presumably a reference device for clerical readers, repeat corresponding French instructions.

(**29b**), BL Add. 45,103, is a large (220 folios, *c.* 374 × 260 mm) vellum manucript. It may date from *c.* 1275 and was prepared in the monastery of Christ Church, Canterbury (Jenkins *et al.* 1943, x). Like BN MS fr. 902, it contains mostly Anglo-Norman works, including Wace's *Roman de Brut* (Dean 2), a *Prophecies* of Merlin (Dean 20), the *Petite Philosophie* (Dean 325) and *Quatre Filles Deu* (Dean 685), but without the scholastic apparatus of the Paris manuscript. *Seinte Resurreccion* begins with a 3-line high flourished blue and red initial, and a frame around the column sets off the beginning of the text from the end of the previous work, the *Brut*.

BIBLIOGRAPHY. The extant versions of *Seinte Resurreccion* are edited in Jenkins *et al.* 1943: both the editions and the accompanying discussion are unreliable and in need of fresh research and revision. Wright 1931 and Schneegans 1925 are earlier editions from the Paris manuscript. Differences between the two manuscript texts are listed by Jenkins *et al.* 1943 (cxxvi–cxxx) and discussed by Symes (2002, 805–9). For modern French translations of the Paris text see Sepet 1901, 145–59 and Jeanroy 1924, 62–8. The Paris text is translated into English by Freni in Hourihane 2009 and the Canterbury text by Wilkie 1978: Bevington 1975, 122–36 gives the Paris text with facing translation. On the *Acta* (or *Gesta*) *Pilati* see Hourihane 2009, 31–4 and Izydorczyk 1997. There has been no book-length study of the play, although comments about the *Seinte Resurreccion* by Frank (1954, 86–92), Hardison (1965, 253–83), Chambers (1903) and Young (1933) remain useful. For scholarship on the play see Kobialka 1999, 1–33. Symes (2011, 2009, 2002) reassesses approaches to medieval theatre and offers fresh observations; see also Perry (1978). On (slightly later) medieval staging and acting see Ogden 2001, 2002; Twycross 2008, 45–55, though focused on later, English place-and-scaffold staging, is enlightening. For the continuing use of French in early English plays (from the late thirteenth century onwards) see N. Davis, ed., 1970, cxi–cxv, 114–17 (for texts), N. Davis, ed., 1979 (manuscript facsimiles, nos 1 and 3) and D. Williams (2004), 67–85. BL Add. 45,103 is described at http://www.bl.uk/catalogues/illuminatedmanuscripts/record.asp?MSID=2934&CollID=27&NStart=45103 and there is a full list of BN fr. 902's contents on the BN's website.

TEXT AND TRANSLATION: (29A) (PARIS) BN F. FR. 902

En ceste manere recitom [f. 97ra]
La Seinte Resureccion.
Primerement apareillons
Tus les lius e les mansions:
Le crucifix primerement
E puis aprés le monument;
Une jaiole i deit aver
Pur les prisons enprisoner;
Enfer seit mis de cele part
Es mansions de l'altre part,
E puis le ciel; e as estals
Primes Pilate od ces vassals
Sis u set chivaliers avra.
Cayphas en l'altre serra,
Od lui seit la Juerie,
Puis Joseph d'Arimathie.
El quart liu seit danz Nichodens
(Chescons i ad od sei les soens),
El quint les deciples Crist,
Les treis Maries saient el sist.
Si seit purveu que l'om face
Galilee en mi la place;
Iemaus uncore i seit fait
U Jhesu fut al hostel trait.
E cum la gent est tute asise
E la pes de tutez parz mise,
Dan Joseph, cil de Arimathie,
Venge a Pilate, si lui die:
[...]

This is how we recount the Holy Resurrection. First, we prepare all the stations and the structures, the Crucifix first and after that the sepulchre. There must be a jail in which to imprison the prisoners. Let hell be placed on one side, the mansions to the other, and then heaven. And in the stations, first Pilate with his vassals – he'll have six or seven knights. Caïphas will be in the next; let all the Jews be with him. Then Joseph of Arimathea in the third, and let Sir Nicodemus be in the fourth: each has his own men with him. In the fifth, the disciples of Christ; let the three Marys be in the sixth. Provide for Galilee to be in the middle of the open space, and let Emmaus too be put there, where Jesus was invited into the inn. And when people have taken their seats and silence has fallen everywhere, let Sir Joseph of Arimathea come to Pilate and say to him [...]

NOTES: (29A) (PARIS)

1 **recitom**; 3 **apareillon*s*** Other translations are possible: subjunctives 'let us recount', 'let us prepare'; or the passive voice 'this is how [the Holy Resurrection] is recounted'. *4 pr* sometimes had *1 pr* meaning, but nothing indicates here that such a secondary reading prevails, which makes less plausible the interpretation advanced by Jenkins *et al.*, namely, recitation by a single actor or jongleur (1943, cxv).

1–2 **En ceste manere . . . Resureccion** Symes points to the unsystematic way in which medieval plays were recorded and the equally unsystematic habits of medieval scribes, both of which caused texts to lose their rubrics; tucking performance instructions 'within the fabric of the piece' would have offered a kind of 'protective colouring', assuring their preservation (Symes 2002, 779, 786; Symes 2011, 44). For a different treatment of stage directions, see the near-contemporary *Jeu d'Adam* (Dean 717).

4 **les lius e les mansions** *lius*, or stations, were raised platforms, with furniture as needed. There are six stations in the Paris text (Pilate, Caïaphas, Joseph of Arimathea, Nicodemus, the disciples

of Christ, and the three Marys). Some stations had no edifices: in the *Jeu d'Adam*, for example, the earthly paradise is to be built on a 'raised place' (*loco eminenciori*) set only with fruited trees, flowers, and foliage and surrounded by silk curtains that allowed the actors to be seen from the shoulders up (Van Emden 1999, 3). The *mansions* or structures, presumably also raised on scaffolding (five in (**29a**), Paris and six or more in (**29b**), Canterbury) could be small replicas of edifices, as, for example, Christ's sepulchre. Ogden (2002, 109) suggests that the prototype for a mansion emerged during the Crusades in imitation of the Holy Sepulchre in Jerusalem. See also *estals* v. 11 (Paris) and *estage* v. 15 (Canterbury). Mansions must have been supported by scaffolding, given the need to make all parts of the stage visible to spectators.

5 **primerement** This adverb makes the Crucifix the first and most important structure and signals its central place on the stage. Scholars have disputed whether the crucifix was the central mansion (Hardison 1965, 264–5) or the *monument*, i.e. sepulchre (Manly 1939; Nagler 1976, 4), the sepulchre perhaps sharing the position with the Tower of David in the Canterbury text (Jenkins *et al.* 1943, cxix).

9–11 **Enfer . . . ciel** If *Seinte Resurreccion* was performed in church, hell may have been at the west end of the nave and heaven towards the main altar at the church's east end: staging in the transept would also be possible with hell perhaps to the south (i.e. God's left-hand side in the Judgement).

11 **estals**: stations, in the sense of places to wait. Harris argues that a distinction beween *liu* and *estal* became the norm: *liu* was the place 'where things happen', *estal* denoted a platform where actors waited to perform (Harris 1992, 51: see n. 4 above and *estage*, v. 15 in the Canterbury manuscript).

12–13 **ces** = *ses*, his; **vassals . . . chivaliers**: examples of common medieval anachronisms.

16 **Joseph d'Arimathie** According to Mark 15.43, this Joseph was an 'honourable counsellor' who waited (or 'was searching') for the kingdom of God; this use of the term 'counsellor' is generally associated with the Sanhedrin, the Jewish court system, which suggests Joseph's important rank among the Jews. In Matt 27.57 he is not described as a counsellor but as a rich man and a disciple of Jesus. In John 19.38 he is secretly a disciple of Jesus: as soon as he hears the news of Jesus's death, he goes to Pilate and asks for the body of Jesus. He is given an important role in medieval Grail quest narratives (see e.g. (**41**)). The reading *Arunachie* in Jenkins *et al.* (1943) is erroneous.

17 **danz Nichodens** MS *Nichodem* plus a final superscript *–us* for the Latin name; a slight ambiguity in the written form makes possible something like *Nichodens* with the superscripted *–us* placed above a long *s*. The scribe anticipates the need for a rhyme with *soens*, v. 18; see Schneegans 1925. Following mention of Nicodemus, the Canterbury manuscript adds a verse giving a station to Longinus (**26b**, v. 18).

20 **treis Maries** In Mark 16.1 these are Mary Magdalene, Mary mother of James, and Salome, or Mary Salome. Other Gospels identify the women differently; see Matt 28.1; John 20.1. In spite of being mentioned in the prologue, this scene does not seem to have been included in the play as far as can be determined from the extant text.

22–3 **Galilee . . . Iemaus** The Sea of Galilee and the town of Emmaus would have been located at the front of the stage and in front of the stations and the mansions (Jenkins *et al.* 1943, cxix; Hardison 1965, 266).

24 **Jhesu fut al hostel trait** Although the MS form *Jh'c* is normally expanded by editors to 'Jhesu Crist', 'Jhesu' follows Jenkins *et al.*, who select this resolution for the Canterbury manuscript three times (1943, xx). They also argue that *fut* is to be read as *se fut*, 'took himself' (Jenkins *et al.* 1943, lxi, 44), but 'was drawn to' agrees with the Gospel story (Luke 24.28–9): Jesus, having met two of his disciples on the road, is persuaded to accompany them towards their lodging for the night.

TEXT AND TRANSLATION: (29B) (CANTERBURY) BL ADD. 45,103

Si vus avez devociun
De la Sainte Resurrectiun
En l'onur Deu representer
E devant le puple reciter,
Purveez ke il eit espace
Pur fere asez large place.
E si devez bien prover
Cum les lius devez aser
E les maisuns qui afferunt
Bien purveez [que i] serrunt:
Le crucifix premerement,
E puis aprés le monument;
Les serganz ke ja gueterunt
E les Maries ke la vendrunt,
Les disciples en lur estage
Se contenent cum sage.
Nichodemus i averat sun liu.
E dan Longins mendif et ciu.
E li dan Joseph de Arimathie.
E Pilat' od sa chevalerie,
Caïphas, Annas, et li Jeu,
La tur Davi et dan Tholomeu.
E une gaole mise i soit
Les prisuns mettre en destroit.
De l'une part i soit enfer mis:
Leinz serrunt les enemis
Ensemble od les anciens [f. 215*va*]
Ke la serrunt mis en liens.
Le cel ne devez ublier
U les angles deivent habiter;
Seit purveu ke l'un face
Galilee en mi la place
Et Emaus, un petit chastel
U li pelerin prendrunt hostel.
E quant la gent ert tut asise
E la peis de tutes parz mise,
Joseph de Arimathie
Vienge a Pilate, si die
[. . .]

If you are desirous of performing the Holy Resurrection to the glory of God and to tell it before the people, see that there is space to create a fairly wide area, and you must carefully designate how to place the platforms, and the appropriate structures will be provided: first, the crucifix, and after that the tomb; the soldiers who will be on watch there and the Marys who will come there; the disciples in their stall behave in the manner of wise people. Nicodemus will have a place there, as well as the needy and blind Sir Longinus, and Sir Joseph of Arimathea; and Pilate with his soldiers; Caiphas, Annas, and the Jews; the Tower of David and Sir Bartholomew. And let a jail be placed there to hold the prisoners. Let hell be placed to one side: in it will be the devil together with the Ancients, who shall be placed in chains. You must not forget heaven, where the angels are to live. Let Galilee and Emmaus, a small castle where pilgrims will seek shelter, be situated in the middle of the place. And when people have been seated and silence has fallen, let Joseph of Arimathea come to Pilate and say: . . .

Notes: 29b. (Canterbury)

3 **representer** This verb, derived from the standard Latin word for performance, *representatio*, comes closer to suggesting that the *Seinte Resurreccion* was performed than the Paris manuscript's *recitom*, v. 1, 'relate, tell'.

10 **Bien purveez [que i] serrunt**: can be translated as 'See that there will be' or 'See that there is'.

16 **Se contenent cum sage** Just how the disciples are to convey wisdom is unspecified; for discussion of gesture in medieval drama see Ogden 2001.

18 **Longins** Longinus: not a soldier or knight, as he was frequently represented later, but *mendif e ciu* (beggarly and blind, v. 18) and eager to accept money from Roman soldiers in exchange for plunging the lance into Christ's side. Although the Paris prologue does not mention a station for Longinus, his story is told in the play proper. *Danz* is an anachronism, like *serganz* in v. 13.

21 **Annas** The Paris manuscript omits this Jewish high priest but he appears in the Gospels (John 18.12–27; Luke 3.2) and in some Passion plays as the figure to whom Jesus is brought for judgement, before being taken to Pontius Pilate.

22 **La tur Davi . . . Tholomeu** Canterbury here calls for one or more stations than the Paris manuscript's five. The 'tower of David', part of the defensive wall around Jerusalem, may have been a familiar sight to travellers to Palestine and (by false etymology between the Syon of 2 Sam 5.7 and *specula*, watchtower) also figures in exegesis and devotional prose as the tower of Syon. Jenkins *et al.* reads MS *Tho[r]lomeu* as the apostle Bartholomew (1943, cxi–cxiii: cf. John 1.43–51). But it may be a corruption of Thomas and a following word; the doubting apostle Thomas is a frequent figure in later Resurrection Easter plays (Muir 1995, 141).

27 **Ensemble** MS *En semble*; **les anciens** The people of classical antiquity, especially writers and philosophers, who were born before Christ.

29 **purveu** MS *pur veu*.

33 **un petit chastel** What exactly appeared on the stage to represent the *chastel* is unclear. Galilee and Emmaus are downstage, and a small *chastel* replica could have impeded the audience's view of the *mansions* or *lius* detailed in the prologue. As in slightly later Resurrection plays, Emmaus could perhaps have been a simple platform with a chair (Ogden 2001, 30–1). The *castellum* of Emmaus (Luke 24.13) was usually represented in early plays as a *chastel*. Cf. the Paris manuscript's *hostel*, v. 24.

30. Chardri, *La Vie de seint Josaphaz* [Dean 532], Prologue: Oxford, Jesus College, MS 29, f. 223^{r-v}

Date of composition and provenance. Late twelfth or early thirteenth century, West Midlands (?)

Author, sources and nature of text. 'Chardri', plausibly an anagram of the name Richard, composed three narrative poems: the *Vie de seint Josaphaz*, a medieval retelling of the Barlaam and Josaphat story; the *Vie des set dormanz*, a tale of seven young men of Ephesus who escaped from the Roman emperor's persecution of Christians by falling asleep in a cave; and *Le Petit Plet*, a debate between an old man and a youth. Chardri identifies himself at the end of *Josaphaz* (v. 2954) and again in *Set dormanz* (v. 1892). Since the manuscripts of his known works are all from the West Midlands, Chardri may have known the Franco-Latinate literary community around Hereford cathedral and its secular canons, such as Gerald of Wales (1146–1223), Simund de Freine (*fl.* 1200, (38)), as well as Hue de Rotelande (late twelfth century, (4)) who lived close to Hereford. Chardri's choice of Eastern themes for two of his three poems could perhaps have been influenced by William de Vere (bishop of Hereford, 1186–98), who had been to the Holy Land and returned to England well aware of Mediterranean and Eastern cultures. De Vere was a significant literary patron and also encouraged pastoral writing for both lay and clerical devotion.

'Barlaam and Josaphat' originated in the East as a tale of Buddha's youth and his renunciation of the secular world in favour of an ascetic existence. At Josaphat's birth, it is predicted that he will convert to Christianity: his father shuts his son away, hoping to keep him from the knowledge of worldly evil that would drive him into an eremitic life. Josaphat nonetheless succeeds in leaving the palace briefly and sees disease and death. He is subsequently converted to Christianity by the desert-dwelling hermit Barlaam, and in a series of trickster-like episodes frees himself from his father, whom he ultimately converts. The earliest known Latin version was produced from the Greek in the mid-eleventh century (Sonet 1950, I.65): the narrative subsequently had a vigorous career in Latin and in most European vernaculars throughout the Middle Ages. Ten separate reworkings in Old French alone are included among the hundred extant versions. The narrative's Barlaam parables, the first collection of Indian parables to become popular in Christian Europe (Lach 1965–93, II.2, 101), were taken up by thirteenth- and fourteenth-century writers (Jacopo de Voragine, Vincent de Beauvais, Jacques de Vitry, Humbert of Romans, John Gower) and the Four Caskets parable was used by Shakespeare in his *Merchant of Venice*.

Chardri drastically abbreviates his source, the 'Vulgate' Latin Barlaam and Josaphat (*Bibliotheca Hagiographica Latina* 979; Sonet 1950, I.74–88) down to *c.* 2,950 verse lines. He shortens Barlaam's instruction of Josaphat and eliminates the source's parables, thus producing, in defiance of the thirteenth-century trend to compilation as a compositional principle, a work that is no longer a framed story-collection. Nevertheless, the prologue to *Josaphaz* argues strongly for the exemplary value of narrative, interpreting Josaphat's own story as an exemplum (*ensample*, v. 2) in itself. Unlike the doctrinal teachings of Augustine or Gregory (v. 7), the prologue argues, narrative always engages at least some part of its audience. Chardri's striking term here for intense response to narrative (*druerye*, v. 21) is more often used of passionate secular relationships in romance, but his claim is that the stirring effect of narrative rather than doctrine in matters of religion makes for easier remembering (*mettre en memorie*, v. 8) and readier entry into the community's shared religious culture.

In Chardri's prologue, God himself offers a renewed and passionate narrative when, unwilling to lose his creation, he responds to human shameful behaviour with the new story brought by Christ in the redemption (vv. 25–44). The prologue then traces the spread of this new religion (*la noeve lei*, v. 39) and its Good News (*la nuvele*, v. 45). Chardri's representation of Christian expansion proceeds not from the Middle East to the West and North, but from Western Europe (Lombardy, France, Spain, 'Bretaigne', England, and Ireland) to India, where the power of the Gospel news effects the kind of change and conversion of which Chardri's own narrative will provide an entertaining – and hence edifying – example.

Audience and circulation. *Josaphaz* survives in trilingual manuscripts, suggesting at least bilingual and possibly trilingual readers, such as secular clergy preaching to the laity or giving religious instruction, whether in a friary, monastic house, cathedral chapter, bishop's household or magnate's court. Chardri's emphasis on plots in which young men outsmart their elders (often in irreverent and amusing ways) may have been intended to appeal to the young in particular, and to encourage them in their spiritual, social and perhaps professional formation (the presence of Latin versions of Chardri's three poems in a manuscript recorded in Titchfield Abbey's medieval library catalogue would suggest their use in monastic formation). On the other hand, a manuscript containing works in more than one language could have been used by readers who did not necessarily read or hear every item, or who heard translated versions of some items. Households, whether episcopal or lay, could have included French- and Latin-speaking clerics with some English; anglophone estate managers or aspiring servants with some French; and elite lay speakers of French and/or English with a little recitational Latin. Chardri's works may have been directly known to religious, to those in their spiritual care, and to lay people.

MANUSCRIPT SOURCE. Oxford, Jesus College, MS 29 [J], ff. 223^{r}–244^{r}, known for its text of the early Middle English *Owl and the Nightingale*, is one of two trilingual manuscripts containing Chardri's three poems. Both manuscripts date from the second half of the thirteenth century, and although they share nine texts, neither is a copy of the other. BL Cotton Caligula A.IX [C; Merrilees 1977 L], is thought to be the older of the two. Manuscripts J and C were produced in the West Midlands, J probably in Herefordshire (Cartlidge 1997, 250). J is in two distinct parts, and part two, containing Chardri's work, has been dated between 1285 and 1300 (Hill 1963, 105; 2003, 273). Part one, copied in the fifteenth century, consists of an incomplete Latin chronicle of English kings. Part two of J includes mostly French and English writing, with some Latin and one macaronic work, *St Paul's Vision of Hell*, or *Seven Pains of Hell*, in which direct discourse is given in English and narration in French. *Doctrinal Sauvage* (Dean 244) is a courtesy text in manuscript J which would sit with the formation of young men in religious houses, or in bishops' or magnates' courts.

BIBLIOGRAPHY. Koch 1879 edits the *Vie de seint Josaphaz*, with manuscript C as base, but is highly interventionist: Rutledge 1973 re-edits from manuscript C. For Chardri's *Set Dormanz* see Merrilees, ed., 1977: *Petit Plet* is edited in Merrilees 1970. For an English translation of Chardri's works see Cartlidge 2015. On the Hereford writers see Frankis 2002 and on William de Vere's literary patronage, Barrow 1987. The most complete account of French versions of Barlaam and Josaphat is Sonet 1950: for editions after 1950 see Dean 533, Zotenberg and Meyer 1966. Recent discussions are Uhlig 2015; Lopez and McCracken 2014; Uhlig and Foehr-Janssens 2013. For hagiographic versions in the *Legenda aurea* and its translation by Jean de Vignay, see Sonet 1950, I.168–70. On the Champenois version made for Blanche of Navarre (copied in the same insular manuscript as *Chant des Chanz* (26)), see S. L. Field 2007. Ikegami, ed., 1999 provides background information on the legend in Europe and treats the Middle English versions in the *South English Legendary* and elsewhere. For Jesus College MS 29, see Hill 2003, 1975, 1963 and Cartlidge 2005, 1997. The Titchfield Abbey copy of Chardri's poems in Latin is noted in Cartlidge 1997, 251, and 2005, 32; Hill 1975, 103; and Wilson 1940, 271. On young men and ecclesiastical courts see Jaeger 2000.

TEXT AND TRANSLATION

Ici cumence la vie seynt Josaphaz

Ki vout a nul ben entendre [f. 223ra]
Par ensample peot aprendre
La dreyte veye de salu.
Ceo ad l'en sovente fé veu
Ke genz sunt par un respit
Amendez plus ke par le escrit
De Austyn u de seynt Gregorie.
Pur ceo voyl mettre en memorie
De un bel enfaunt la duce vie,
Pur estuper la graunt folye
U nus delitum e nut e jur.

Jeo crey en Deu ke cest labur
Ne serra pas de tut perdu,
Kar meyntefez est avenu

Here begins the life of St Josaphat

Whoever aims at good can learn the right way to salvation through an exemplum. It has often been seen that people are improved more by a moral story than by the doctrinal writing of Augustine or St Gregory. And so I want to put on record the pleasing life story of a fine youth, to put an end to the great foolishness in which we delight night and day.

By my faith in God, I believe that this work will not at all be wasted, for it has happened many a time that one man loves a

Ke uns eom eyme une geste
Dunt un autre ne fet ja feste.
Icel purra si akaïr:
Si l'un n'en vout nul plet tenir,
Un autre ert par aventure
Ke mut i mettra sa cure,
Tant l'amera par druerye
Ke il amendra sa sote vie.
Ki k'en die u mal u ben,
Pur Deu le faz, sanz autre ren.

story in which another takes no delight. That may be the case here, for if one man pays no heed, there will perhaps be another who will give it all his attention: so much will he love it, with a passionate love, that he will correct his foolish life. Whatever anyone may say about this, whether good or ill, I'm doing it for God and for no other being.

Quant Deu, ke fist tut le munde,
Cel e terre a la runde
E tute les choses ke i sunt,
En fu, en eyr, en mer parfunt,
Ne vout perdre sa feiture,
Tut sanz cunseil de nature [f. 223rb]
Nasqui de la Gloriuse,
Ke ly fu fylle, mere e espuse,
E suffri ceo ke dit le escrit,
Peyne e dolur ne mye petyt,
Pur ceo ke trop alout a hunte
La creature dunt plus tynt cunte:
Ceo est humené dunt jeo vus dy,
Pur ki Deu taunt mal suffry,
Si nus duna la noeve lei,
Si vus dirray ben pur quey:
Ne vout pas mettre a nunchaler
Tut ke ne vout sa part aver,
U tost u tart, quel ke ceo fust,
Si cum aprés ben i parut.

Since God, who made the whole world, heaven and earth round about and all the things in it, in fire, in air, in the deep sea, did not want to lose what he had created, he was born, without the help of nature, from the Blessed Woman who was his daughter, mother, and wife; and he suffered what Scripture says – no small pain and anguish – because the creation to which he attached the greatest importance was becoming very shameful. I'm talking about humankind, for whose cause God tolerated so much evil. He brought us the new law here, and I'll tell you why: he did not want to dismiss lightly all those who wanted no part of him, then or now, whoever they might be, as became clear later.

Par le mund ala la nuvele,
Ke mut esteyt e bone e bele,
E crurent ceus ke furent sage,
E vindrent en lur eritage,
Dunt furent essilez a primes
E pus jetez en abymes.
Car Jhesu lur mustra la veye
E voleyt taunt ke tute veye
Le sewyssent, sanz nule fable,
Deske a la vie pardurable.
E[n] meynte terre la folie
Plusur gwerpirent pur ceste vie,
E tuz jurs crut la creaunce
En Lumbardie deske en Fraunce,
Par Engletere e Normaundie,

This very good and fine news went throughout the world, and the wise believed it and came into their heritage, from which they had first been exiled, then thrown into the abyss. For Jesus showed them the way and so much wanted them to follow him in all things into everlasting life; and thus in many a land several abandoned foolishness for that life; and belief grew: from Lombardy to France, through England and Normandy,

Par Brutayne e Hungerye,
Par Burgoyne e Alemayne, [f. 223*va*]
Par Russye e par Espayne,
Par Loerenne e par Peytou,
Par Flaundres e par Angou
E de Auverne deske en Irlande.
Ki la avaunt terre demande
Qerre la purra avaunt ben,
Si trovera u poy, u ren.
Ja crut Crestienté itaunt
Ke ele vint en Ynde la graunt.
Teus en Ynde dunc tant firent
Ke lur folyes deguerpyrent
Pur la fey ke tant lur plout.
Tel i aveyt ke refusout
Terre e tresor tut en apert
Si s'en alout en desert
Pur Deu servyr ki les fist
E tel grace lur tramyst.

through Brittany and Hungary, through Burgundy and Germany, through Russia and through Spain, through Lorraine and through Poitou, through Flanders and through Anjou, and from Auvergne into Ireland. Whoever asks for more names of places will find little or nothing to add. So much did Christianity grow that it came to India. There were those in India who went so far as to give up their foolishness for the faith that so pleased them. There was one such who openly refused land and wealth and went into the desert in order to serve God, who made them and sent them such grace.

Notes

2 **aprendre** MS C *mut aprendre*.

2 **ensample** An *exemplum* is in the broadest sense an account or short story, fable, parable, moral lesson or description serving to support a doctrinal, religious or moral argument (Welter 1927, 1–2). Exempla were increasingly used in vernacular preaching after Lateran IV, and Gregory the Great's *Dialogues* (see (**24a**); Mosher 1911, 10–11) taken as a specially authoritative precedent for their use (Scanlon 1994, 58, 63).

5–7 **Ke genz . . . respit / . . . escrit / . . . seynt Gregorie** In Gregory the Great's *Dialogues*, the deacon Peter distinguishes between 'an explanation of holy Scripture', which 'teaches us how to attain virtue and persevere in it', and a 'description of miracles [which] shows us how this acquired virtue reveals itself in those who persevere in it', and he says that the 'lives of the saints are often more effective than mere instruction for inspiring us to love heaven as our home' (Zimmerman 1959, 6; *PL* 77.153). Chardri does not cite this precedent in his *Josaphaz* when mentioning Gregory (also cited with Augustine and St Paul in *Le Petit Plet*, vv. 797–9).

8 **mettre en memorie** could mean 'commit to memory', as well as 'put on record'. The wider context for Chardri's statement here would have to include the idea that he wishes to record the story *in the vernacular* for the first time, given the pre-emptive existence of his written Latin source. Implicit in his intention, therefore, is the desire to commit the story to a collective vernacular memory.

9 **un bel enfaunt** Youthful protagonists, reminiscent of the *puer senex*, or wise child, outwit an older male figure in each of Chardri's works: Josaphat outschemes his powerful father and goes off with Barlaam, a wiser 'father'; in the *Set Dormanz* the seven young men of Ephesus evade the murderous Roman emperor; and in *Le Petit plet*, the young man defeats the old man in debate. In *Le Petit Plet* the young man explains that the old resent the amusements of the young (vv. 111–18), a view also found in *Josaphaz* (vv. 575–85; and see Rutledge 1973, 30–1).

11–12 **U nus delitum . . . ke cest labur** This couplet, rhyming on *jur / labur*, is one of two examples in the prologue (the other is at vv. 65–6) of the *couplet brisé*, that is, a couplet that is 'broken' by beginning a new sentence or thought in its second line. The continental writer Chrétien de Troyes has been praised for his use of such couplets, and certain verses from Chrétien's *Erec et Enide* re-appear in *Josaphaz* (Rutledge 1973, 34–5).

14–19 **Kar meyntefez est avenu . . . Un autre ert par aventure** Adaptation of proverb structure: 'What is not good for one person is good for another' (Morawski 1925, no. 331).

15 **geste**, with its echoes of *chanson de geste*, *geste* had come to mean simply 'story' (cf. Chardri's emphasis on Josaphat's life story as entertainment). However, at the end of *Josaphaz* Chardri observes that stories such as that of Roland and Oliver are foolish – not because of what they contain but because of what they do not: they do not speak of God (vv. 2933–8). Similar topoi are found in e.g. (**14**) and (**24a**). In *Set Dormanz* Chardri condemns Ovid's 'fables', as well as stories about Galeron, Tristan, Renard, and Hersent (Merrilees 1977, vv. 51–7).

17 **akaïr** = *escheir*, to happen.

21 **druerye** See further on *druerÿe* in love poems and their audiences, Piramus (**27**), vv. 5–12.

26 **a la runde** The earth was well known to be spherical. Rendering the opening of the *Imago mundi* encyclopaedia, for instance, the early-thirteenth-century *Petite Philosophie* (Dean 325) gives *Li mund est rund cume pelote* ('The world is as round as a small ball, v. 253).

30 **nature** A figure often represented in medieval texts as authorised by God to create material human beings, but also as encouraging procreation: that Jesus was born without the *cunseil de nature*, without nature's help, or without the work of nature, alludes to the virgin birth. See further on the Nature figure White 2000, Newman 2003 (chs 2 and 3).

31 **la Gloriuse** = la Vierge Gloriuse.

37 **humené** See *AND*, *s.v.* 'humainé' (= humankind, humanity).

41–2 **Ne vout pas mettre . . . ke ne vout sa part aver** These verses parallel vv. 14–22 about those who do not take the religious point of Chardri's story.

48 **vindrent en lur eritage** The proclaiming of the Good News by Jesus also relates to the coming of the Kingdom of God ('The time is fulfilled, and the kingdom of God has come near; repent, and believe in the good news', Mark 1.14–15).

49–50 **Dunt furent essilez . . . jetez en abymes**: the expulsion from Paradise and putting into Hell of Adam and Eve.

58 **Lumbardie** The *Legenda aurea* was also known in the Middle Ages by its subtitle, 'The History of the Lombards', because of its penultimate section, 'St Pelagius, Pope; The History of the Lombards'. The 'History' concentrates on church doctrine (Ryan 1993, I.xiv and II.367–84).

58–64 **Fraunce . . . Normaundie . . . Brutayne . . . Peytou . . . Angou** France (the land belonging to the king of France), *c.* 1180, was a relatively small area centred around Paris. The western areas, Brittany, Poitou, and Anjou, were sites of struggle between England and France in the Middle Ages, and Normandy, which had belonged to the Norman kings of England ever since the Conquest, was captured by the French king, Philip Augustus, in 1204.

60 **Brutayne** Most probably Brittany (*AND*, *s.v.* 'Bretagne'): Chardri has already mentioned *Engleterre*, v. 59.

60 **Hungerye**, south and west of Russia, became a Catholic Apostolic Kingdom under King Stephen I (crowned 1000), who created a western feudal state upon which he imposed Christianity.

62 **Russye** or 'land of the Rus', was an East Slavic state that had adopted an Eastern form of Christianity towards the end of the tenth century, but by the mid-thirteenth century had fallen to the non-Christian Mongols.

66–8 **Ki la avaunt . . . u ren** The gist of these lines seems to be that however much one may look for lands where Christianity has not gone, few or none will be found, not, at least in Europe.

70–1 **Ynde la graunt, Ynde** In medieval usage, 'India' is often more or less synonymous with the modern 'Far East', but some schema are more specific, as in the prose legend of St Bartholomew (shortly before the mid-thirteenth century) found in Harley MS 2253 and elsewhere: '[Ç]oe cuntent cels qui sevent deviser les parties del munde que treis Indes sunt . . .' with the explanation that the first India stretches towards Ethiopia, the second towards *Mede* (the ancient Median empire, now parts of Iran and Turkey), the third at the end of all lands, bordered on one side by 'the kingdom of darkness' and on the other by 'the great ocean', *Saint Barthélemy* (ed. Russell 1989, 93, lines 1–6). The Apostle Thomas was believed to have preached in India among the Jews of Cochin in AD 52.

74–8 **Tel i aveyt . . . s'en alout . . . les fist . . . lur tramyst** The word *tel*, sg., of v. 74 hints at Josaphat himself, as does 3 pers. *s'en alout*, 'went', but the object pronouns of vv. 77–8 are plural, suggesting that Chardri has reverted to the plural of v. 71, or is perhaps thinking about Barlaam and Josaphat together.

31. *Fouke le Fitz Waryn* [Dean 156]: Prologue: London, British Library, MS Royal 12 C.XII, ff. 33ʳ–35ʳ (extracts)

Joshua Byron Smith

DATE OF COMPOSITION AND PROVENANCE. 1320–40, Hereford.

AUTHOR, SOURCES AND NATURE OF TEXT. The anonymous romance *Fouke le Fitz Waryn* incorporates elements of history, legend, folklore and the marvellous to form the tale of a minor baron's outlawry and the recovery of his rightful inheritance. At its core, *Fouke* relates the 1201 rebellion of Fouke III (d. *c.* 1258) against King John. The first third of the romance concerns the founding of Fouke's ancestral home of Whittington around the time of the Norman expansion along the Welsh borders and its subsequent loss in the vicissitudes of Marcher warfare. When King John refuses to restore his inheritance, Fouke renounces fealty and becomes an outlaw. Thereafter Fouke moves between outlaw life in England and periods of exile in increasingly distant places (the court of Llewellyn of Wales, the court of Philip Augustus of France, an unknown Western island, Iberia, the land of Barbary), everywhere performing feats of combat, conquest, trickery and disguise. On his final return to England, Fouke captures John in the New Forest and secures the return of his lands. In old age Fouke re-marries, repents his youth and becomes blind.

Fouke survives only in a single prose version, which is, however, a redaction of an earlier, octosyllabic French romance probably composed in the late thirteenth century. In several instances the original verse remains largely intact (e.g. vv. 1–18 below), especially towards the end of the text, which suggests that whoever converted the romance from verse to prose did not drastically alter the narrative. The text shows knowledge of local traditions about the Fitz Warin family, the town of Ludlow and the Welsh borderlands along Shropshire, so the author of the original verse romance was most probably a border dweller. That this author had close connections with the Fitz Warin family is uncertain. The family's recent history is somewhat garbled, with Fouke I and Fouke II being consolidated and Fouke III's wife misidentified, and critics troubled by this have looked to the nearby lordships of the central March for the poem's intended audience. Certainly, the romance's robust defense of Marcher rights against royal authority would have fallen on eager ears across many Marcher lordships. Nonetheless, historical inaccuracies do not disqualify a Fitz Warin audience or even patron: for medieval aristocratic families, distilling and reshaping historical traditions into compelling literary narratives remained one of the main ways – if not *the* main way – of constructing and conveying familial memory and identity. *Fouke* draws very widely on literary motifs (the narrative's resemblance to the outlawry of Robin Hood was already noted in Langtoft's French verse chronicle of Edward I's reign and in Robert Mannyng's early-fourteenth-century reworking of Langtoft (Benecke 1973; Kelly, trans., 1997, 689–90; Burgess 2005).

The prologue opens with the topos of spring as a time of remembrance and then proceeds to create ancestral and topographical cultural memory for the Marches. *Fouke*'s prologue skillfully frames Fitz Warin family history with Geoffrey of Monmouth's foundation narrative for Britain, the *Historia regum Britanniae* (or one of its vernacular adaptations, such as Wace's *Roman de Brut*). *Fouke* uses this material to anchor family history in Britain's ancient past: just as, in the *Historia*, the aboriginal giants must be defeated before Britain is settled, so must Geomagog, a resurrected giant straight out of the *Historia*, be slain before Whittington is settled. This foundational act is here credited to the reign of William the Conqueror, who is brought on stage in *Fouke*'s prologue solely to plant Marcher castles, towns and barons in the borders and then to return to London and die in Normandy. Under William's questioning, a 'Briton' (i.e. Welshman) recounts the haunting by Geomagog of *Castell Bran* (probably Dinas Bran, an impressive hill fort above the vale of Llangollen, still topped with the ruins of its thirteenth-century castle). William's knight Payn Peverel ends the haunting with a terrifying vigil at the site, before himself becoming a settler and castle builder in the region. In *Fouke* the invocation to remembrance and the 'remembered' narrative forms a fitting prologue to one of the most original and compelling French romances of England.

AUDIENCE AND CIRCULATION. The immediate audience for the original poem is thought to have been the Marcher aristocracy. Indeed, the poem's introduction calls into being a noble, chivalrous audience and asks them, in a common topos (see also (**42**)), to remember the deeds of their valorous ancestors (lines *1–11*). But the presence of merchants in the text suggests they too may have found a place in the audience: the focus on ancestral lands in the romance is complemented by an equally important socio-economic concern, the establishment and the commerce of Welsh border towns, under the Normans and later in the wake of Edward I's conquest of Wales (1277–83). Also of interest in determining the poem's audience is that it displays none of the common medieval English stereotypes for the Welsh. *Fouke* treats the Welsh in the even-handed manner that might be expected in border lordships where Welsh people were a common part of the social fabric (Lieberman 2009).

Up to about half a century may separate the audiences of the original verse text and the early-fourteenth-century prosification of the romance (the verse romance was probably written after Fouke III died *c.* 1258: it does not mention Fouke IV, d. 1265). Over the thirteenth century, prose had come increasingly to be associated with objectivity and verifiability, and *Fouke*'s change of form may seek to inflect the romance's materials in this direction.

The single surviving manuscript of *Fouke le Fitz Waryn* belies the popularity of medieval traditions of Fouke. There are two, possibly three, medieval witnesses to the original verse romance: the surviving prose redaction itself and a copy of a French romance seen by the antiquarian John Leland in the sixteenth century (Hathaway *et al.*, ed., 1975, xix–xxvi). Thomas Woodstock, duke of Gloucester, possessed a copy of *la gest de Fouke filtz Waryn* in 1397, perhaps the one that Leland saw (Hanna 2011b, 335), but if not, then Gloucester's copy is a third witness. In addition to French versions of Fouke's exploits, traditions of Fouke III's rebellion reached English and Welsh speakers, reflecting the trilingual milieu of the Marcher aristocracy: Leland also had access to an English poem about Fouke that seems to have been written in alliterative verse but which is no longer extant (Hathaway *et al.*, ed., 1975, xix–xxvi). Langtoft's *Chroniques*, and following him, Robert Mannyng's *Chronicle*, refer to the 'book' of 'Dan Waryn', and not only to his outlawry, but also, uniquely, to his madness, which suggests yet another variant tradition (Sullens, ed., 1996, lines 8203–9; Spence 2013, 158–9). Fourteenth-century Welsh court poets frequently cite Fouke ('Ffwg' in Welsh) as a positive symbol of martial prowess (Lloyd-Jones 1931–63, *s.v.* 'Ffawc'; Spence 2013, 159). Although no Welsh translation survives, Fouke's appearance alongside other romance heroes raises the possibility that a romance about him may have circulated in Wales. The prose *Fouke le Fitz Waryn* remains the only complete surviving witness to a popular medieval narrative tradition that reverberated in all three of the March's vernaculars – French, English, and Welsh.

MANUSCRIPT SOURCE. BL Royal 12 C.XII, ff. 33^r–60^v is a small (153 × 236 mm) vellum manuscript of 123 folios. A compilation of eight originally independent booklets, the manuscript contains Edmund of Abingdon's *Mirour de seinte eglyse* (**22**), a French treatise on the Mass (Dean 720), an Anglo-Norman copy of the *chanson de geste* version of *Amys e Amillyon* (Dean 157), the *Experimentarius* (an astronomical treatise attributed to Bernardus Silvestris), the *Short English Metrical Chronicle*, the liturgy for Thomas of Lancaster, indulgenced hymns, a miscellany on the conflicts of church and state, a miscellany on prognostication, and a final miscellany that includes recipes, puzzles, and prophecies. The manuscript is trilingual, though the English material is limited.

The early-fourteenth-century scribe of MS Royal 12 C.XII is well known for his compilation of the great trilingual collection of MS Harley 2253, for a second substantial collection of insular and continental French texts with some Irish and Latin, Harley 273, and some forty-one legal documents. MS Royal 12 C.XII dates from *c.* 1312 to *c.* 1340, though two different stages in the Harley scribe's Anglicana script can be discerned: the earlier from *c.* 1310–15 and the later from sometime after 1330. The first part of *Fouke* belongs to the earlier period, and the second part to the later, indicating that some time elapsed before the Harley scribe finished copying the romance. The Harley scribe worked in western Herefordshire, near the Welsh border, and seems to have had connections with the Mortimer family of Wigmore, the bishops of Hereford, the Talbots of Richard's Castle, and others. Whether or not Royal 12 C.XII was put together for one or more of these patrons has been the subject of debate.

BIBLIOGRAPHY. *Fouke le Fitz Waryn* has been edited by Michel 1840; Wright 1855; Stevenson 1875; Wood 1911; Brandin 1930; Hathaway *et al.* 1976, who provide a helpful map. It has been translated into English (Wright 1855; Stevenson 1875; Kemp-Welch 1904; Burgess 1997); German (Jordan 1906); and modern French (Guiton 1924). A partial English translation, focusing on the outlaw episodes, is available in Kelly 1997. For recent analyses of the Harley scribe see Fein 2007, O'Rourke 2005, and Revard 2000. The Fouke manuscript is described at http://www.bl.uk/catalogues/illuminatedmanuscripts/record.asp?MSID=19451&CollID=16&NStart=120312 The romance's political affiliations and relation with the Fitz Warin family are discussed by Brandin 1929, Painter 1935, Francis 1961, Hathaway *et al.* 1975, Meisel 1980; *ODNB* (Suppe 2004), and Stephenson 2002. On its historical accuracy see Painter 1935; Meisel 1980, 132–8; Stephenson 2002. Stephenson 2002, 29 and Hathaway *et al.* 1975, ix–x, xxix–xliii consider other possible Marcher affiliations for the text. Spence 2013, 153–61 gives a lucid account of these and other issues. The dating of the verse romance is discussed in Wright, ed., 1855, vi–viii; Brandin 1929, 24–5; Hathaway *et al.*, ed., 1975, xix–xxvi.

On Fouke's outlaw status and the romance's portrayal of King John see Benecke 1973; R. Allen 2003; Fletcher 2004; Burgess 2005, 2008; Price 2008. The romance's use of history and mythology is discussed in Jones 1994; Pensom 1994; Osborn 1998; A. J. Williams 2007; Coote 2008. For its Arthurian associations see Newstead 1939, 95–106; Loomis 1956, 42–52; Peele 1981; and Zink 1984. Burgess 2000 and Cavell 2010 study women in *Fouke*: Cavell 2007 treats the historical Marcher women. *Fouke* is explored as border literature in Otter 1991, Lieberman 2009, and Hanna 2011b. For the history and politics of the Welsh March, see e.g. Lieberman 2009 and on Welsh urban development, Fulton 2012. Leland's synopsis of the lost English version of the romance is in Hearne, ed., 1970, v. 1, 230–7, Michel, ed., 1840, 101–12, and Brandin 1929, 26–32. For the appearance of Fouke in Welsh poetry, see Lloyd-Jones 1931–63, *s.v.* 'Ffawc'; Bromwich 1982, 75–6 and O'Rourke 2000, 55–7. A full bibliography of scholarship is in Burgess 2009, 193–8. On *Fouke* and Anglo-Norman prose historiography see Spence 2013.

TEXT AND TRANSLATION

[f. 33r] En le temps de averyl e may, quant les prees e les herbes reverdissent e chescune chose vivaunte recovre vertue, beauté e force, les mountz e les valey[e]s retentissent des douce chauntz des oseylouns, e les cuers de chescune gent pur la beauté du temps e la sesone mountent en haut e s'enjolyvent, donqe deit home remenbrer des aventures e pruesses nos auncestres qe se penerent pur honour en leauté quere, e de teles choses parler qe a plusours purra valer.

Seygnours, vous avez oÿ eynz ces houres qe Willam Bastard, duc de Normaundie, vynt ou grant gent e pueple santz nounbre en Engleterre e conquist a force tote la terre, e ocist le roy Heraud, e se fist coroner a Loundres, e si estably pees e leys a sa volenté, e dona terres a diverse gentz qe ou ly vyndrent. En ycel temps Yweyn Goynez fust prince de Gales, e si fust vailaunt e bon guerreour, e le roy le dota mout le plus. Cesty Yweyn out guasté tote la marche, e tote fust voyde de Cestre tanqe al mont Gylebert. Le roy se apparilla mout richement, e vint ou grant ost en le countee de Saloburs, e trova tote les villes arses de Cestre desqe a Saloburs, quar le prince clama tote la marche pur la sue e aportenaunte a Powys. Le prince se retret, quar yl ne osa atendre le roy. Le roy fust mout sages, e pensa qu'il dorreit les terres de la marche as plus vaylauntz chevalers de tut le ost pur ce qu'il devereynt defendre la marche de le prince a lur profit e al honour lur seignour le roy. Ly roy apela Rogier de Belehealme, si li dona tote la counté de Saloburs mout franchement, e si fust apellee counte palays. Rogier funda dehors la vylle de Saloburs une abbeye de Seynt Piere, e la feffa mout richement, e tint le counté a tote sa vie. Si comença un chastiel a Brugge, e un autre chastel comença en Dynan, mes yl ne les parfist point.

In the season of April and May, when the meadows and the grass grow green again and every living thing regains vigour, beauty, and strength, the mountains and the valleys resound with the sweet songs of birds, and the heart of each man is uplifted and gladdened on account of the beauty of the weather and the season, then one should remember the adventures and noble deeds of our ancestors, who strove to seek honour in loyalty, and one should speak of such matters as could be profitable to many.

Lords, you have heard previously that William the Bastard, duke of Normandy, came with a great army and an uncountable number of people into England and conquered the entire land by force, and slew King Harold, and had himself crowned at London, and established peace and laws according to his will, and he gave lands to various people who came with him. At that time Owain Gwynedd was the Prince of Wales, and he was valiant and a good warrior, and the king feared him all the more. This Owain had ravaged all the March, and everything from Chester to Mount Gilbert was destroyed. The king equipped himself very richly and came with a great army into the county of Shrewsbury, and found all the towns from Chester to Shrewsbury burnt, because the prince claimed the entire March as his own and as belonging to Powys. The prince withdrew because he did not dare to wait for the king. The king was very wise, and thought that he would give the lands of the March to the bravest knights of all the army so that they could defend the March from the prince for their profit and for the honour of their lord the king. The king summoned Roger de Bellême, and gave him all of Shropshire in free tenure, and he was called earl palatine. Roger founded St Peter's Abbey outside the town of Shrewsbury and he endowed it very richly, and he held the county all of his life. He began a castle at Bridgnorth, and he began another castle in Dynan, but he did not complete them.

[*Afterwards, Roger's sons rebel against King Henry, who in turn disinherits them and grants Dynan to Sir Joce. Joce finishes the castle at Dynan which Roger Bellême had begun; Dynan is now called Ludlow. The narrative then returns to William the Conqueror's journey into Wales, where he sets up camp near a large town that lies in ruin. William asks a Briton what has happened.*]

'Sire', fet le Bretoun, 'je vous dirroy. Le chastiel fust jadys apellee Chastiel Bran, mes ore est apelee la Vele Marche. Jadys vindrent en ceste pays Brutus, un chevaler mout vaylaunt e Coryneus de qy Cornewayle ad uncore le noun, e plusours autres estretz du lignage troyene, e nul n'y habita ces parties estre tres lede gentz grantz, geans dount lur roy fust apelee Geomagog. Cyl oyerent de la venue Brutus, e se mistrent en la voye a l'encountre, e al dreyn furent tous lé geantz occys estre Geomagog, qe fust mervilous grant. Coryneus le vaylaunt dist que volenters luttreyt ou Geomagog pur esprover la force Geomagog. Le geant a la premere venue enbraça Coryneus si estroitement qu'il debrusa ces trois costees. Coryneus se coroça, si fery Geomagog del pee qu'il chay de un grant roche en la mer, e si fust Geomagog neyé. E un espirit del deble meyntenant entra le cors Geomagog, e vynt en ces parties, e defendy le pays longement qe unqe Bretoun n'osa habiter. E longement aprés, le Roy Bran fitz Donwal fist refere la cité, redresser les murs e afermer les grantz fosses, e fesoit burgh e grant marché. E le deble vint de nuyt e oost[a] quanqe leynz fust, e pus ensa unqe nul n'y habita.'

'Lord', said the Briton, 'I will tell you. The castle was once called Castle Bran, but now it is called The Old March. Long ago Brutus, a very valiant knight, and Corineus, from whom Cornwall still retains its name, came into this country, along with many others drawn from the lineage of Troy, and no-one dwelt in this region except great giants, a very vile people, whose king was called Geomagog. They heard about the arrival of Brutus, and they set off to meet him, and in the end all the giants were killed except Geomagog, who was wondrously large. Corineus the valiant said that he would be willing to fight with Geomagog in order to test Geomagog's strength. At once the giant gripped Corineus so tightly that he shattered three of his ribs. Corineus became enraged and kicked Geomagog so that he fell from a great rock into the sea, and thus Geomagog drowned. And a spirit of the devil immediately entered Geomagog's body, and came into this region, and for a long time he guarded the country so that no Briton ever dared to dwell there. And a long time afterwards King Bran fitz Donwal had the city rebuilt, the walls repaired, and the great moats strengthened, and he made it into a borough and a great market. And the devil came by night and took away all that lay inside, and afterwards no-one ever dwelt in that place'.

[*Payn Peverel, a bold knight and the king's cousin, arms himself and encamps at the highest point in the ruined city accompanied by fifteen men. As night falls, a fierce storm terrifies everyone but Payn, who prays to God for aid. [f. 34r] The Devil, in the guise of Geomagog, a giant who spits flame and wields a huge club, immediately attacks Payn. Supported by God, Payn is victorious, and when he has Geomagog at his mercy, he demands that the giant tell him who he is and why he dwells there.*]

La malfee comença counter de mot en autre come le Bretoun out eynz dit, e si dit qe quant Geomagog fust mort, meintenaunt il rendy l'alme a Belzebub lur prince, e si entrat le cors Geomagog e vynt en semblance de ly en ces parties pur garder le grant tresor qe Geomagog aveit amassé e mys en une mesone qe yl avoit fet desouth la terre en cele ville. Payn ly demaunda quele creature yl fust, e il ly dist que jadys fust aungle, mes or est par son forfet espirit de deble. 'Quel tresour', fet Payn, 'avoit Geomagog?' 'Buefs, vaches, cynges, poons, chevals e totes autres bestes tregettés de fyn or, e si avoit un tor d'or, qe parmy moy fust son devyn e en ly fust tote sa creance, e il ly dist ces aventures qe furent a venir. E deus foyth par an soleynt les geantz honorer lur dieu, ce fust le tor d'or, dont tant or est amassee q'a merveille. E pus avynt qe tote ceste countré fust apellee la Blaunche Launde, e moy e mes compaignons enclosames la launde de haut mur e parfounde fosse, yssi qe nul' entré fust si noun parmy cestre ville qe pleyne fust de mavoys espiritz, e en la lande feymes jostes e tornoyementz, e plusours vindrent pur vere les merveilles, mes unqe nul n'eschapa. Ataunt vynt un disciple Jhesu qe apelé fust Augustyn, e par sa predication nous toly plusors des nos. E baptiza gent, e fist une chapele en son noun, dount grant encombrer nous avynt'. 'Ore me dirrez', fet Payn, 'ou est le tresour dont avez dit'. 'Vassal', fait il, 'ne parlés mes de ce, quar yl [est] destyné as autres, mes vous serrez seignour de tut cet honour, e ceux qe vendrount aprés vous le tendrount ou grant estrif e guere.

The devil began to tell the story exactly as the Briton had told it before, and he said that when Geomagog was dead, he immediately delivered his soul up to Beelzebulb, their prince. And so he entered Geomagog's body and came into this region in his likeness in order to defend the treasure that Geomagog had amassed and placed in a lair which he had made underground in that town. Payn asked him what kind of being he was, and he told him that he once was an angel, but on account of his sin he was now a spirit of the devil. 'What kind of treasure', said Payn, 'did Geomagog have?' 'Oxen, cows, swans, peacocks, horses and all kinds of other animals cast in pure gold, and he also had a golden bull, which through my aid was his oracle, and he put all his faith in it, and it told him what would happen in the future. And twice a year the giants used to honour their god – that is the golden bull – from which such a marvellous amount of gold was amassed. And so it happened that this entire country was called the Waste Land, and I and my companions closed off the plain with a high wall and a deep moat so that there was no entrance except through this town which was full of evil spirits. And on the plain we held jousts and tournaments, and many people came in order to see these wonders, but no-one ever escaped. Thereupon, a disciple of Jesus whose name was Augustine arrived, and by his preaching he took many of our people away from us. And he baptised people and made a chapel in his name, which became a great hindrance to us'. 'Now you will tell me', said Payn, 'where the treasure is that you have spoken about'. 'Vassal', he said, 'speak no more about this, because it is destined for others, but you will be lord of all this domain, and those who come after you will hold it with great violence and war.

E de ta maunche issera [f. 34v]
Ly loup qe merveilles fra,
Q'avera les dentz aguz
E de tous serra conuz
E serra si fort e fer
Qu'il enchacera le sengler
Hors de la Blaunche Launde,
Tant avera vertue graunde.
Ly leopard le loup sywera
E de sa cowe le manacera.
Ly loup lerra boys e montz,
En ewe meindra ou peschons
E tresnoera la mer.
Environera cet ydle enter.
Au dreyn veyndra le leopart
Par son engyn e par son art.
Pus en ceste lande vendra;
En ewe son recet tendra.'

And from your sleeve will emerge the wolf that will do wonders, that will have sharp teeth and will be known by all, and he will be so strong and fierce that he will chase the boar out of the Waste Land – such great power will he have. The leopard will pursue the wolf and with his tail he will threaten him. The wolf will leave the forests and the mountains. He will live in the water with the fish, and he will cross the sea. He will travel around this entire island. Finally, he will conquer the leopard by his cunning and skill. Then he will come into this land; he will have his shelter in water.'

Quant l'espirit ou[t] dit ce, s'en issit du corps, e tiel puour avynt dont Payn quida dever, e quant passé fust, la nuyt enclarsyst e le temps enbely, e les chevalers e les autres q'enpourys furent s'enveylerent, e mout s'enmervelerent de l'aventure qe lur aveit avenu. L'endemeyn fust la chose mostré al roy e a tot l'ost, e le roy fist porter le cors Geomagog e gittre en un parfond put dehors la ville, e fist garder la mace, e la mostra longement a plusours pur la merveille q'ele fust si graunde.

When the spirit had said this, he left the body, and Payn was so frightened by that that he thought he would die. And when that had passed, the night grew brighter and the weather grew fairer, and the knights and the others who had been frightened recovered their wits and were astonished at the adventure that had happened to them. In the morning the matter was made known to the king and the entire army, and the king had Geomagog's body carried off and thrown into a deep pit outside the town. And he had the club kept, and for a long time he displayed it to many people on account of its wondrous size.

Ly roy s'en vet de yleqe e vent en une contré joygnant a la Blanche Launde qe jadys fust a un Bretoun, Meredus fitz Beledyns, e delees si est un chastelet q'est apellee Arbre Oswald, mes or est apellee Osewaldestré. Ly roy apela un chevaler Aleyn fitz Flael, e ly dona le chastelet ou tut l'onour qe apent, e de cely Aleyn vindrent tous les grantz seignours d'Engletere qe ount le sournoun de Fitz Aleyn. Pus cesti Aleyn fist enlarger mout le chastel.

The king left there and came into a country neighboring the Waste Land which a Briton, Maredudd ap Bleddyn, once held. And on its outskirts there is a small castle which is called Oswald's Tree, but now it is called Oswestry. The king summoned a knight, Alan fitz Flaald, and he gave him the small castle with all of the rights belonging to it. And from that Alan came all of the great lords of England who have the surname fitz Alan. This Alan then had the castle greatly enlarged.

Ly roys passa la ryvere de Salverne e vist le pays entour bon e bel, e apela un chevaler qe fust nee en Loreygne, en la Cyté de Mees, qe mout fust renounee de forte e de bealté e de corteysie, e sa enseigne fust de un samyt vermayl a deus poons d'or, e ly dona Alburburs, ou tot l'onour q'apent. E issi dona ly roys a ces meillour chevalers e plus afiez totes les terres, chaces e fees de Cestre desqe a Brustut.

Ly roy apela Payn Peverel, e ly dona la Blaunche Launde, e foreste, guastyne, chaces e tut le pays. E si aveit une mote environee de marreis e de ewe, e la fyst Payn un tour bel e fort, e fust la mote apelee Wayburs, e si court une ryvere delees qe de Payn Peverel tint le noun, e si est apelee Peverel, mes pus fust apellee Pevereye. Le roy, quant issi aveyt establie[s] ces terres, retorna a Londres, e de Loundres a Normandie, e yleqe morust. Pus reigna en Engletere Willam le Rous, son fitz, e aprés [f. 35r] ly Henri, son puysné frere, qe pus detint Robert Courtheose, son eyné frere en prisone tote sa vye. L'encheson ne vous serra ore dyte.

The king passed over the River Severn and saw that the land in that vicinity was good and fine, and he summoned a knight who was born in Lorraine, in the city of Metz, who was greatly renowned for his strength, his beauty, and courtliness, and his banner was of red samite with two golden peacocks. And the king gave him Alberbury and all the rights belonging to it. And so the king gave his best and most loyal knights all the lands, hunting grounds, and fiefs from Chester to Bristol.

The king summoned Payn Peverel and gave him the Waste Land, and its forest, wastes, hunting ground, and its entire country. And there was a hill surrounded by marshes and water, and Payn made there a fine and strong tower, and the hill was called Wayburs, and on its outskirts runs a river which takes its name from Payn Peverel, and so it was called Peverel. But later it was called Peverey. The king, when he had established these lands there, returned to London, and from London he went to Normandy, and there he died. Afterwards his son, William Rufus, reigned in England, and then Henry, his younger brother, who later held Robert Curthose, his older brother, in prison for all of his life. The circumstances of this will not be told to you now.

Notes

1–7 **En le temps . . . sesone** This opening passage is one of many in which the original verse romance and its *chanson d'aventure* topoi can be reconstructed: 'Quant prees e herbes reverdissent, / E mountz e valeyes retentissent, / Des douce chantz des oseylouns / Pur la beauté de la sesone' (Hathaway *et al.* 1975, 63).

13 **Willam Bastard, duc de Normaundie** This account of William the Conqueror corresponds closely to several verses in *The Shorter Metrical Chronicle*, which is also found in Royal 12 C.XII (Hathaway *et al.* 1975, 62–3 n. to 3.1). While William I never visited northern or central Wales, instead only making one journey to the country in his lifetime – a 'pilgrimage' to St David's in 1081 – his prominence in the romance's opening and his readiness to grant land to his subjects as they settle the borders starkly contrast with King John's behaviour. In this manner, *Fouke* reworks history in order to create a vivid and thematically appropriate foundation narrative for the Marcher lordships.

20 **Yweyn Goynez** Owain was the ruler of Gwynedd 1137–70, after William I's reign. As often happens in the first third of *Fouke*, people and events from the twelfth century, especially from Henry I's reign, anachronistically appear in the decades immediately after the conquest. Nonetheless, Owain would have been remembered as one of the most powerful Welsh leaders of the twelfth century. The romance's use of major historical figures such as Owain to craft a kind of personified history accurately captures the broad strokes of the violent struggles between the Welsh and Normans over border lordships, especially in the first half of the twelfth century. Even after Edward I's conquest, readers of *Fouke* would have been keenly aware of the March's political instability.

23 **la marche** The March of Wales comprised a series of Norman border lordships that were established to help quell and conquer the Welsh. In a looser sense, the March could simply refer to the Anglo-Welsh border. Not only does the crux of the narrative concern the rightful possession of a Marcher lordship, but much of the action occurs in and around the March.

24 **mont Gylebert** The Wrekin, a large hill in eastern Shropshire near Telford.

26–9 **trova tote les villes arses . . . e aportenaunte a Powys** Although the condition of the Welsh towns as discovered by William I is credited to Owain Gwynedd (see n. 20 above), the situation reflects the late-thirteenth-century revival of castles in Powys as centres of opposition to Edward I's conquest of north Wales (1282–3).

26 **SalobURS** For the unexpected final *s* in this word, see Hathaway *et al.* 1975, 64 n. to 3.18.

35–6 **Rogier de Belehealme** William the Conqueror granted the earldom of Shropshire to Roger de Montgomery (d. 1094, *ODNB*) sometime after 1071, and St Peter's Abbey in Shropshire's county town of Shrewsbury was founded by Montgomery in 1084. The memorable title Belehealme (Fine Helmet), though it in fact belonged to Roger's son and came originally from his wife's patronymic (Mabel de Bellême), resonates with the romance atmosphere of these early episodes which evoke the marvellous adventures of the grail quest.

43 **Dynan** For the foundation of the castle, see Renn 1987.

44 **dirroy** *1 fut* in place of expected *dirrai*. For the merger of the future and the conditional in *Fouke*, see Hathaway *et al.*, ed., 1975, xciii–xcvii.

45 **Chastiel Bran** Chastiel Bran is most often identified with Castell Dinas Brân (Castle of the City of Crows) near Llangollen in Wales, once the chief place of the ancient kingdom of Powys. For many of the 'new' towns of *Fouke* an explicit association is made in the landscape between planted or refounded towns and ancient sites of power in the region's many hillforts (Sarah Rees Jones, pers. comm.). Another possible location for *Chastiel Bran* is the iron-age hill-fort known as Old Oswestry in English and Hen Dinas (Old City) or Caer Ogyrfan (Gogyrfan's Castle) in Welsh (Wright, ed. and trans., 1855, 187; Brandin, ed., 1930, 89; Ross 1988). Whatever the audience's associations may have been, the text clearly implies that the castle is named after Bran fitz Donwal (lines *67–8*), that is, Brennius, son of Dunuallo, a famous king from Geoffrey's *Historia regum Britanniae* (Reeve and Wright, ed. and trans., 2007, §35–44). A figure in Arthurian legend, Bran's appearance further emphasises the Arthurian colouring of this episode (Newstead 1939, 95–106; Loomis 1956, 42–52; and Peele 1981).

46 **la Vele Marche** Often identified with the Latin name for the March of Wales, *Walliae Marchia*. However, 'the Old Border' could also refer to Wat's Dyke, which lies about a half mile north of Old Oswestry (Ross 1988).

47 **Brutus** The story of Brutus, Corineus, and Geogmagog is taken ultimately from Geoffrey of Monmouth's *Historia regum Britanniae* (Reeve and Wright, ed. and trans., 2007, §6–22).

51 **tres** MS *tre.*

81 **Payn** Payn [Peverel] was active in Henry I's reign, rather than that of William I (for the various Peverel settlers in the twelfth-century March, see Hathaway *et al.*, ed., 1975, 69 n. to 7.34; Burgess, trans., 1997, 186 n. 9). Payn ultimately wills Whittington (i.e. the *Blanche Lande*) to his nephew William, and William's niece Melette then marries Waryn de Metz, who becomes lord of Whittington. Waryn de Metz, in turn, is the grandfather of Fouke, the romance's eponymous hero.

87 **tor** In order to further connect Chastiel Bran to Arthurian legend, several scholars have assumed a scribal error here for *cor* (horn), the letters *t* and *c* being indistinguishable in several medieval scripts (Newstead 1939, 95–106; Loomis 1956, 42–52). However, medieval audiences would have easily connected the golden bull of *Fouke* with the golden calf that the wandering Israelites in *Exodus* make and revere (Exod 32) – both are symbols of pagan worship. There is also perhaps the further valence of buried unorthodox resources in Wales awaiting Norman and English development of border castles and towns and the releasing of the economic power of boroughs and markets.

93 **Blaunche Launde** The *Blanche Lande* (The Empty or Waste Land) evokes Arthurian romances, especially those concerning the Grail. Not only does the ancestral land of the Fitz Warins have a pedigree dating back to the beginning of British history, replete with Arthurian connotations, but Payn Peverel, the founding father of the dynasty, becomes an illustrious romance hero, in the mould of Perceval or Galahad, through his restoration of the Waste Land.

101 **Augustyn** St Augustine of Canterbury (d. 604) led the first Christian mission to the Anglo-Saxons.

1–18 **E de ta maunche . . .** The verse form of this prophecy has been left entirely intact in the prose. The end of the romance explains this prophecy for readers: Fouke, who is driven into exile overseas, is the wolf, and King John is the leopard. The boar, then, represents the unrightful holders of Whittington. Additionally, the text later identifies this particular prophecy as Merlin's, in yet another instance of the text's appropriation of Arthurian romance.

3 **les dentz aguz** The sharp teeth refer to Fouke's heraldic device which contains twelve teeth.

14 **ydle** For *d* instead of expected *s* before /l/ or /n/, see Short (2013), §23.4.

125–6 **Meredus fitz Beledyns** Maredudd ap Bleddyn (d. 1132), a prince of Powys, joined the rebellion of Robert de Bellême in 1102. His inclusion in this episode in *Fouke*, though anachronistic, succinctly illustrates the colonisation of southern Wales by the Normans.

127–8 **Arbre Oswald . . . apellee Osewaldestré** A walled medieval market town founded *c.* 1100 (Beresford 1988, 482–3), much celebrated in late-medieval Welsh poetry (Johnston 2012, 99–103).

129 **Aleyn fitz Flael** Alan fitz Flaad was a Breton knight who became sheriff of Shropshire and lord of Oswestry in 1101.

149 **Wayburs** Perhaps the Berth (< *burgh*), an iron-age hill fort near Baschurch in Shropshire (Hathaway *et al.* 1975, n. to 7.26), not the site of Whittington. *Fouke* later credits not Payn Peverel, but his nephew and heir, William (n. 81 above), with the building of *Blaunchetour* and *Blauncheville, e[n] englois Whytyntone* (the castle and town of Whittington) in the *Blanche Launde* (Hathaway *et al.*, ed., 1975, 7/38–8/3).

150 **de Payn** MS *de de Payn.*

151–2 **apelee Peverel . . . pus . . . Pevereye** The river Perry, a tributary of the Severn. The etymology of the name is more probably Welsh *pefr* (bright, radiant) + OE *ea* (river) (Hathaway *et al.* 1975, 69, n. to 7.27).

155 **Willam le Rous** William Rufus, king of England (1087–1100). This quick narrative of royal succession has much in common with similar passages in Geoffrey's *Historia* and Wace's *Brut.*

32a. *Sicom Aristotele nous dit* [Dean 423], Cambridge, Trinity College, MS O.2.5, ff. 123^r–124^v

Clarissa Chenovick

Date of composition and provenance. England, probably before the mid-fourteenth century.

Author, sources and nature of text. This brief Anglo-Norman treatise on menstruation consists of 188 verses in flexible octosyllabic couplets. The author begins by stressing the secret nature of the medical knowledge contained in the text (vv. 3–9), seemingly justifying the desire of women to keep secret those things which pertain to their particular 'illnesses' by claiming that he is writing in order to teach medical knowledge to women and girls so that they might help themselves without recourse to a doctor (vv. 10–14). However, the rest of the text refers consistently to women in the third person, suggesting the presence of a mediator who is not, in fact, a woman or girl.

The prologue details the humoral causes and potential malfunctions of menstruation, seen as comparable with male nocturnal emissions (v. 16). This material is loosely translated, via lost or unknown intermediaries, from the first redaction of the twelfth-century Latin *Liber de sinthomatibus mulierum* (also called *The Conditions of Women*), part of a group of texts often known as the *Trotula maior*, after Trota, the famous woman physician of twelfth-century Salerno. The *Liber de sinthomatibus* includes much discussion of menstruation and also deals with conception, childbirth, cures for the wandering and suffocation of the womb, and post-partum maladies. The text edited here focuses exclusively on menstrual disorders and their cures, but on ff. 103^v–106^v of the *Sicom Aristotele* manuscript an analogous prose treatise includes discussion of other ailments dealt with in the *Liber de sinthomatibus* and some cosmetic cures similar to those of the *Ornatus mulierum* (**32b**). It is possible that the compiler of *Sicom Aristotele* versified menstrual information from relevant portions of this prose treatise, but equally, the verse treatise may have had a separate existence and been included in the manuscript for its condensed and memorable treatment of a topic of special interest.

Menstruation stood at the intersection of several complex strands of medieval thought about the nature of the human body, the moral and social status of women, and the nature of the Incarnation. Because it was believed that men and women alike needed to be purged of their ill-humours, menstruation provided important support for theories of humoral balance and imbalance. Viewed as the female body's only inbuilt means of humoral purgation and as the prerequisite to conception, menstruation and its (mal)functions were not relegated to discussions of reproduction but rather constituted a woman's overall physical health or illness (Green 2005, 53). However, in non-medical scientific writings, menstrual blood was frequently viewed as poisonous and impure: following Plinian tradition, it was believed (by, among others, the church doctor Albertus Magnus) to kill crops, rust iron, make dogs rabid, to poison children (through poisonous vapors emitted by the menstruating woman's eyes), to cause stains to appear on mirrors, and to give leprosy or cancer to any man having intercourse with a menstruating woman (Green 2005, 58–9; 2008, 108; Lemay 1992, 60). More positively, menstrual blood could ward off locusts and disease, and its purgative value (*Mut purge ben lé mals humurs*, below, v. 34) suggested that women's bodies functioned more regularly than men's. Female 'bleeding and feeding' was also associated with 'Christ's bleeding on the cross, which purges our sin in the Atonement and feeds our souls in the eucharist' (Bynum 1991, 113–14). Menstrual blood could even be used in medicine, as was the liquid exuded by mummified bodies, which was known as the 'menstruation of the dead' (Pouchelle 1990, 74–5). As a purging of ill-humours, menstruation was viewed by theologians as a sign of woman's fallen nature, since a perfect body would have no need of purgation. However, it was also believed that menstrual blood provided the matter out of which infants were formed in the womb. This created a seemingly insoluable dilemma: if the Virgin Mary was truly without sin, then she would not have menstruated, but if she did not menstruate, Christ could not have truly taken on human flesh in the Incarnation.

The presence of this brief, rhymed treatise on menstruation in Trinity College MS O.2.5, a miscellany that includes, among many other items, a treatise on the nature of man, charts of eclipses, and astronomical works, places it within the context of greater questions about the nature of the human body and its place in the world. The role of the female body in this scheme, with its crucial yet only partly visible function in generation, motivated the almost obsessive interest in 'women's secrets' that fueled the popularity of the Trotula texts. *Sicom Aristotele nous dit* participates in the preoccupation with these kinds of 'knowing' both by virtue of its manuscript context and its subject matter, and allows us a point of entry into the kinds of questions medieval people asked not only about gender but about the ways in which their bodies were placed in relation to the cosmos.

Audience and circulation. *Sicom Aristotele* is the only known example of this version of the *Liber de sinthomatibus mulierum* material on menstruation, but this family of texts and the larger body of Trotula texts of which they form a subset enjoyed enormous popularity throughout the Middle Ages. Thirty-four medieval Latin and five vernacular Trotula manuscripts have evidence of English ownership (Green 2008, 325–44). Female ownership of medical books, however, was in general rare (Green 2008 counts only forty-four examples in Western Europe from the twelfth to the beginning of the sixteenth century).

Although the earliest twelfth-century Trotula texts would seem to have been composed in Latin for a female audience, most of the thirteenth-century Latin manuscripts were owned by men associated with universities, religious institutions, and professionalised medical practice. Books like the *Liber de sinthomatibus mulierum* are framed as works to be heard by a female audience of 'matrons' who could then treat their own disorders, but this requires a male mediation at odds with the texts' stated goals. Green notes that male copyists and translators of the Trotula texts frequently altered active verbs to passive and avoided first- and second-person pronouns when describing gynaecological treatments requiring hands-on physical intervention; she suggests that these grammatical choices suggest a hands-off approach to women's bodies although they are not systematic enough to suggest that these men thought through the implications of their role as intermediaries between medical texts authorised by feminine authority and a female audience (Green 2008, 80–5).

Manuscript source. Trinity College MS O.2.5 is a substantial (229 × 153 mm) vellum miscellany manuscript of 221+10 folios, datable *c.* 1330–60. Although the manuscript contains several French-language medical texts (see e.g. Dean 406, 414) and some Latin 'Secrets of Women' materials (Green 2008, 228 n. 84; Cadden 1993, 89–103) as well as the prose analogue on menstruation to *Sicom Aristotele* (ff. 103^{v}–106^{r}), it is not necessarily a professional medical miscellany. Its varied contents embrace illustrations of the wheel of fortune, a diagram of a labyrinth, treatises on medical herbs, chiromancy, physiology and astronomy, a Latin calendrical treatise, prognostications based on a child's date of birth, saints' lives, a penitential manual, works on natural philosophy (several invoking the letter of Aristotle to Alexander), a blessing for cattle, lunar and solar eclipse tables, and recipes for acqua vitae and Greek fire, and on f. 117vb, a French-titled charm in English. The handwriting throughout the manuscript is fourteenth century except for a table of contents in a fifteenth-century hand. The manuscript's evidence for the text's date of composition is ambiguous: a table of eclipses from 1330 to 1386 on f. 42^{v} suggests composition after 1330 (Meyer 1903b, 99), but if the book's first owner were Robert de Barry, rector of Bergelly, Pembrokeshire (attested in a deed of 1270 bound into the codex, Green 2008, 340 [78]), composition could be earlier. *Sicom Aristotele* is written in a mid-fourteenth-century anglicana cursiva script formatted in two columns of roughly 37–40 lines each. The text is accented by enlarged decorated capitals in red and blue, and the first letter in each line is usually capitalised and always accented with red. Although there is no punctuation, there are alternating red and blue paragraph marks throughout.

BIBLIOGRAPHY. *Sicom Aristotele* is unedited: for the first fourteen lines see Green 2008 (173 n. 24; 340–4): for other treatises in the same manuscript see Hunt, ed., 2014; on the manuscript see James 1902; Meyer 1903b, and for a longer and similar treatise see Dean 422. Meyer 1903b transcribes the first twenty lines. Hunt 1997 edits many associated materials, including a prose account of menstrual 'flowers' (Hunt 2011, 92–3). Green 2000a, 2000b, 2000c, 2000d, 2001 (ed.), 2008 are indispensable on the Trotula tradition and on women's medieval health care: on medical literacies see particularly Green 2000d, 2008. On the 'secrets of women' tradition, see Green 2000b, 147–78 and 2008; Park 2006 and Lemay 1992: Cadden 1993 also remains fundamental. On the physiology of menstruation see Green 2005, Pouchelle 1990; on theology, the Virgin Mary, menstruation and blood, see Wood 1981, L'Hermite-Leclerq 1999, Bynum 2007 and 1991. For comparable Middle English texts, see Green 1992, and on the importance of Anglo-Norman medical translation and its ties with southern Italy, Green 2009.

TEXT AND TRANSLATION

Sicom Aristotele nous dit
En Alisaundre en son escrit,
N'est pas reison ne afaitement
Que sues seient a tote gent
Lé maladies que aveinent
[E] en langor le cors teinent.
A homme icel[les] n'eut overé,
Ke femme cele, tant est coveré
Ke envis unkes a nul home.
Le voil mustrer, çoe [est] la sume,
Pur çoe aprendre medecine
E a dame e as meschine,
Par quei puse privément
Sei eider sanz asient.

As Aristotle tells us in his letter to Alexander, it is neither right nor fitting that the illnesses that come about and keep the body in a state of feebleness and decline should be known to all people. He [Aristotle] would not have revealed these maladies to a man, a topic a woman hides, so well that it is never willingly shown to a man. I want to show it, in short, in order to teach medicine to women and young girls alike so that they might help themselves in private, without specialised knowledge.

Des flours des femmes

Escrit est que par atele reson
Com vint al mal polucioun,
Tot est meme la manere
Avent icest mal a la muliere;
Çoe vint par habundance de humurs,
Si l'apele femme cez flours.
Naturement a femme avynt
Kant la quatorzime an de age tient,
E a duzime veraiment
Sout avenir bien sovent.

[*On the flowers of women*]

It is written that this trouble comes to the woman for exactly the same reason that ejaculation comes to the male; it comes about because of an excess of humours, and woman calls it her 'flowers'. By nature, it happens to a woman when she attains the fourteenth year of age, and, in fact, it is quite often wont to take place in the twelfth.

Mez celes sont a demesure
A ki se toust, nest pur chaude nature,
Dekes trente e cinc anz sout durer,

But for almost everyone, when it stops, it [menopause] brings on hot humours. Menstruation usually lasts for thirty-five

E[n] plusurs femmes, e pus cesser;
Dekes a caraunte ou cincante,
A plusurs dure dekes as sessante,
Quant vint a tupement e a drectoure.
A tut le cors sount mout secure,
Car sicom escrivent plusurs, [f. 123v]
Mut purge ben lé mals humurs.
Si çoe non, si seit certeine
Ke ne put pas durer seyne.

years for many women; for others it stops at forty or fifty, and for many others it lasts until sixty, when the flowers come to an end, and the body returns to a regular state. Flowers are a great help to the whole body, for as many write, they purge the ill-humours very well. Certainly, without this, the body cannot remain healthy.

Car çoe dit Galien en son escrit:
De beivre e de manger pert apetit,
Manger desire carbon ou tere
Ou altre chose de tiele manere.
Dolur de os e del chife vient,
Al col e dos sovent le tient:
Fevre ague sout avenir
Tele oure e vieult nusir.

For Galen says in his text [that without this purgation], a woman loses her appetite for food and drink and desires to eat charcoal or earth or another thing of this kind. Pain in the skull and in the head frequently result and often in the neck and back, and fever and ague habitually come about. These also do her a great deal of harm.

Sicum trowom en nos escriz,
Çoe vint de le vice de matriz,
Kant lé veines trop sanc tenent,
Ne l[e] poent suffrer, si en crevent.
E si avient tut autresi
De çoe que ele ad trop sanc quilli
Par beivre e manger a demesure,
E trop reposer si le put nu[i]re.

As we find in our sources, this comes from a malady of the womb. When the veins retain too much blood, they cannot withstand it, and they burst. It also comes about that the womb has collected too much blood as a result of drinking and eating an inordinate amount and resting too much, which is the way it nourishes itself.

Si avynt acune fé
De le sanc trop eschaufé
Par la colere que del fel vient,
Que l[e] sanc aerd e tient;
Tant le quit e fet boilir
Que lé veines ne le put tenir.

If it happens that the blood heats up too much because of the warmth that comes from bile, which ventilates and supports the blood, it cooks it so much and makes it boil so much that the veins cannot hold it.

Acune fé si est trové
La saucefleme, ou est mellé
Od le sanc, si le entremist,
Domke parmi lé veynes ist.

Sometimes salt phlegm is found, which mixes and mingles with the blood, causing it to flow out through the veins.

A la fé vint abortir
Dont la femme put tut morir,
E solum l'abunda[n]ce de homurs
Ad en sei deverse colurs.
De sanc turne a rugur;
De ruge colur a garnur;
De saucefleume a blanchur;
De veir colur a neirur.

Sometimes, hemorrhaging comes about, from which the woman may die. And according to the abundance of humours, it has various colours. From blood it turns to redness, from redness to more garnet-coloured, from salt phlegm to whiteness, from grey colour to blackness.

Femme qui ad surundeé
Sout estre mout descoluré.

A woman who has an overflow of blood is usually drained of colour. She is thin and

Megre est, la cher ad murne.
Au dropesie tel est atorne
Quant le fel sout refreidir,
Pur perte de sanc que dout norir
Ke ewe devent, si n'ad vertu,
Par quei le fel seit sustenu.

has a mournful appearance. In such cases, her condition turns to dropsy when the gall-bladder is chilled because of the loss of blood that should nourish it, but which has turned into useless water and does not have the virtues needed to nourish the gall-bladder.

Notes

1 **Sicom** Initial *S* executed in blue ink with fine red flourishes.

1–2 **Sicom Aristotele . . . Alisaundre en son escrit** Aristotle's authority in the Latin Alexander tradition varies (Aristotle sometimes deifies Alexander, sometimes teaches him humility). The tradition of letters between the two goes back to the early Middle Ages (there is a copy of the *Epistola Alexandri ad Aristotelem* in the late tenth to early eleventh century *Beowulf* manuscript for instance): by the thirteenth century the convention was well established (Gaullier-Bougassas 2002) and widely used to authorise texts of varying types (see e.g. (33), *Secré de secrez*).

7–9 **A homme icel[les] . . . unkes a nul home** A variant form of a shame topos common to the *De Sinthomatibus mulierum* in the '*Conditions of Women* tradition': women are ashamed to reveal their illnesses to a male physician because of the fragility of their 'secret parts'. *Sicom Aristotele* omits direct reference to shame, highlighting the (seemingly justified) secrecy of women instead. Framed as an aid to women who do not wish to reveal their diseases to men, the text will go on to speak of 'her' or 'their' illnesses (v. 85; see Green 2008, 48–53; 2001).

14 **sanz asient**: *without specialised knowledge*. Another possible reading is 'without trickery', referring either to the sick woman's vulnerability to the male doctor's 'trickery' or to anxieties in the male medical community about the 'trickery' of unregulated 'cunning' women practitioners.

14–15 a rubric is added in the MS margin between these two lines.

20 **Si l'apele . . . cez flours** In *De Sinthomatibus* texts, this euphemism is explained by the relationship between fertility and regular periods; like a tree or a plant, a woman must 'flower' in order to bear fruit. This explanation is influenced by the Arabic source text, which compares menstruation to the 'fluid excrescences of trees' but the vernacular use of the term 'flowers' was already in common usage amongst women (Green 2005, 52–3). The prose analogue gives the same explanation (f. 103^{r}).

38–9 **De beivre . . . carbon ou tere** One potential effect of a woman's inability to purge ill-humours. Several *De sinthomatibus* texts note that amenorrhea can lead to wanting to eat 'against nature', with charcoal and earth as examples (see Hunt 1997, 78, 117). For chalk as an example of this 'unnatural' appetite see Green 2001, 72–3.

45 **Sicum** *S* executed in blue with fine red lines and flourishes. As with the flourished capital *S* in v. 1 (also for *Sicom*), this embellishment introduces an appeal to authority, albeit not a specific one (*nos escriz*).

50 **ele ad . . . sanc quilli** the feminine pronoun here could refer to the woman herself, but contextually is more likely to refer to the womb.

55 **la colere que del fel vient** The type of bile referred to is presumably yellow bile, which is hot and dry. Although this heat is necessary to sustain the blood (and to facilitate the process of 'cooking' food into humours), an excess of heat leads to disease, in this case causing excess menses. The manuscript's prose analogue treatise has a similar explanation: 'Pur lez coler. que issent de chife e issi mellent ou le sanc si l'eschaufent sil fount boiler que les veinez ne pouent tenir si coe que en iste' (Concerning the forms of bile that arise in the head and there mingle with the blood, if they heat it

they make it boil so that the veins cannot hold [it], with the result that the blood flows out, f. 104^{r}).

57 **Tant le quit e fet boilir** The process of turning food into blood (the basic matter from which the rest of the body is formed) is considered to occur through a process of cooking that occurs within the body (Pouchelle 1990, 154–5). In the disorder described here, the natural cooking process becomes unbalanced, leading the veins to spill forth blood in a manner similar to a pot boiling over.

63 **abortir** Probably referring here to the expulsion of excess blood and humours from the womb, with abortion/miscarriage and hemorrhage being understood as analogous in medico-physiological terms. This reading is supported by the corresponding passage of the Latin *Liber de sinthomatibus mulierum*, which unambiguously uses the word *aborsum*. Thanks are due to Monica Green for this suggestion and for access to her transcription of the Latin text (labeled as LSM1 and described in Green 2000c). The analogous prose treatise in *Sicom Aristotele*'s manuscript has 'et le fetz avint cest mal [par] averter' (Hunt, ed., 2014, 18, 601).

67–70 **De sanc turne a rugur . . . De veir colur a neirur** These lines, which seem to comment on the significance of various colours of menstrual blood, correspond to the passage in the *Liber de sinthomatibus mulierum* on the humoral composition indicated by fluid's colour: 'If the blood which flows out turns into a yellowish colour, bile is the cause. If into a whitish colour, phlegm. If into a reddish colour, blood' (Green 2001, 81). However, the text edited here identifies only the red colour attributed to blood and the whitish colour attributed to 'saucefleume' or salt phlegm. This might suggest scribal error or textual corruption. The analogous prose text mentions only two possible colours: 'si cete de fleume si est de la blanc colur; si coe est de sanc si est rouge' (If it is of phlegm, it is white in colour; if it is of blood it is red, f. 104^{r}).

69 **saucefleume**: *salt phlegm*. This humour dries and thins the blood, causing it to issue forth from the veins (Green 2001, 81).

73 **cher** MS *cler*.

75 **fel**: *gall-bladder*. Perhaps a mistake for 'feie' (liver). The corresponding passage in the *Liber de sinthomatibus mulierum* describes the process through which the liver becomes chilled through a lack of blood, preventing it from preserving the organs in their natural heat or preventing the body from turning food into humours (Green 2001, 80–1). The analogous prose treatise in the *Sicom Aristotele* manuscript has: 'si li turne tost au dropesie que le feez est refreide par icoe sanc que ele pert coe que ele devereit tenir en sa naturel chalur ne peut le manger muer en naturel sanc ainz devient ewe' (It turns quickly to dropsy, for the liver is chilled by her loss of blood, which should maintain her in her natural heat, and [the liver] is unable to transform the food she eats into natural blood; it becomes water instead, f. 104^{v}).

32b. *Quant Deus out la femme fete / Ornatus mulierum* [Dean 426], Prologue: Oxford, Bodleian Library, MS Ashmole 1470, f. 276^r

Clarissa Chenovick

Date of composition and provenance. Composed in England during the thirteenth century, this treatise appears solely in the late-thirteenth-century manuscript from which the prologue is here edited. The predominance of Latin medical texts in this compendium, in which the *De Ornatu* is the only French item, suggests ownership by a monastery or a medical practitioner.

Author, sources and nature of text. This brief treatise on women's cosmetics consists of a verse prologue and three-and-a-half additional folios of prose 'cures'. The prologue is made up of twenty-three couplets in flexible octosyllabics. The anonymous author justifies the combination of verse and prose by declaring that it is simply not expedient to try to speak of medicine and to outline treatments in rhyme (vv. 39–42). Medical works were nonetheless frequently translated into verse both in England and on the continent, a practice designed to make them easier to recite and to remember.

The rubric *Incipit ornatus mulierum* signals the rubricator's familiarity with the Latin collection of cosmetic recipes widely circulated under the same name. This Latin *De ornatu* collection was attributed to 'Trota', the famous woman physician of twelfth-century Salerno. The Anglo-Norman *Ornatus* appears to have been composed independently of the Latin collection. There are few close parallels between the recipes in the two compilations, and their organising principles differ: the Latin *De ornatu* narrates a set sequence of beauty treatments – from a full-body depilatory treatment to soften the skin to local treatments for particular body parts like the teeth and lips – while the Anglo-Norman text lists cures by area of application but gives no instruction on ordering a beauty regime. It follows instead the conventional head-to-toe order common to some medical treatises and the rhetorical handbooks' conventions of *descriptio feminae*.

The Anglo-Norman *Ornatus* calls on a number of textual authorities – Galen, Constantinus Africanus, and Hippocrates – and on the ostensibly oral testimony of Trota and an unnamed female doctor identified only as a Saracen (vv. 31–8). However, borrowings from these authorities account for only a small number of recipes. A few analogous recipes are found in the works of Constantinus Africanus but none in Hippocrates and Galen's works (Ruelle 1967, 10–12).

The cosmetic recipes of the *Ornatus mulierum* might seem unconnected with medical concerns, but the treatise contains several cures related to medical conditions such as dermatological ailments and problems caused by parasites like fleas and lice (vv. 261–9, 296–304, 465–506). The prologue edited below, moreover, makes even surface-level cures (which include face-whitening powders and dyes to make the hair black or blonde, smooth or curly) a corrective for the corruption of female beauty associated with the Fall (v. 1–5). By associating the forfeiture of perfect beauty with original sin and the beginning of mankind's subjugation to death, the anonymous author strengthens the parallel between defects of appearance and physical illness. Adam, the perfect man, loses his humoral equilibrium and paradisal good health (Rawcliffe 2006, 71; Ziegler 2001), and Eve loses her perfect beauty. Casting cosmetic recipes as remedial rather than ornamental, the prologue legitimises what might be censored as meretricious artifice via a larger medical framework.

Notwithstanding the sophistication of this authorising strategy, the prologue is unlikely to have persuaded medieval moralists and theologians. The term *ornatus* was already highly freighted, and had appeared in commentaries on the dress and toilette of women from the church fathers onwards. In *De habitu muliebri* Tertullian uses *ornatus* to refer to the embellishment of the body, which he condemns as a result and cause of lust (I.4.1–2). Tertullian, whose assertions are echoed by Cyprian (ed. and trans. Keenan 1932, *De habitu virginum* 8.12) and taken up vigorously by medieval preachers (Polo de Beaulieu 1987), condemns several beauty treatments of the kind outlined in the Anglo-Norman *Ornatus mulierum*: skin-softening procedures; the use of cosmetics to redden the cheeks and of dyes to tint the hair; and artificial curling or straightening the hair (II.5.2–7.3). Instead, echoing 1 Tim 2.9–10 and 1 Pet 3.3–4, Tertullian – and a long line of preachers and moralists after him – urges Christian women to reject the ornaments of the earth for those of the heavens, taking on simplicity (*simplicitate*) instead of white face paints, and modesty (*pudicitia*) instead of rouge, adorning their eyes with shamefastness (*uerecundia*) and their mouths with silence (II.13.7; see also Cyprian VIII). Cosmetic practices were also associated with arrogance and sacrilege as well as lust: seeking to alter one's appearance denied the perfection of God's work in favour of self-creation (Tertullian II.5.2; Cyprian XV–XVII; Polo de Beaulieu 1987).

The long tradition of clerical opposition to female cosmetic practices stands alongside a male-authored literary tradition upholding a decidedly unnatural ideal of 'natural' beauty, touting, for example, the charming combination of blonde hair and dark eyebrows. These moral and literary discourses form part of a larger misogynist discourse in which male writers are in a real sense the creators as well as the critics of the cosmetic practices whose victims they claim to be (Martineau-Génieys 1987). By the thirteenth and fourteenth centuries men were the collectors and disseminators of the majority of cosmetic cures circulated in Western manuscripts. Medical and surgical compendia continued to include the arts of embellishment, often framing them with claims to disaffect the material at hand – attempts to specify a morally justifiable use (such as the conservation of beauty rather than the alteration of appearance; see vv. 18–20 below), or efforts to address a more 'honest' audience such as married women who wish to avoid becoming repulsive to their husbands (Moulinier-Brogi 2004, 62–6).

The prologue edited here is notable amongst those attached to works on women's cosmetics for its subtle engagement with these larger moral, theological, literary, and medical discourses. The more gynecologically focused *Liber de sinthomatibus mulierum* also grounds its discussion of female physiology in the Genesis account of creation (Green 2000c, 131), but cosmetic treatises of the day tend to present themselves as straightforward lists of beauty treatments (Gilleland 1988) or to suggest that the knowledge they contain will bring praise and fame to the practitioner (Green 2000c, 139, 141). In contrast, the Anglo-Norman *Ornatus* provides a sophisticated and carefully pitched rationale for itself and circumvents moral and theological critiques of cosmetics with a new Genesis narrative that gives cosmetic practices their own place in the work of restoring fallen female nature. The *Ornatus* also presents us with a male authorial persona who claims to empower women to gain and pass on medical knowledge even as he intervenes between them and the female authorities he cites. Thus, even in the process of carefully avoiding a direct engagement with the detractors of women's cosmetics, the prologue edited here brings into focus the numerous and highly fraught discourses that surround the text it advertises and introduces.

Audience and circulation. Little is known about the ownership and use of Bodleian MS Ashmole 1470, the only known witness of the Anglo-Norman *Ornatus*. There is an undated fourteenth-century Latin deed copied at the base of f. 278*v* in which Theobaldus, the son of Jowerth, the son of Madauc sells land known as 'tyden cadye' to John (Johanni) the son of Goronwey of Castellmarch, suggesting that the manuscript was in Wales at some point. The only other names associated with the manuscript are those found in the English and Latin medical receipts copied out in fifteenth-century cursive hands onto the front flyleaf and f. 316*r–v*. These include a 'Doctor Mychill' (three times on the front flyleaf, once at 316*r*), 'Master Doctor Kors', 'Master Wodroffe with Mylorde of Salsberi[?]', 'Master Phillip Feteplace', and 'William Boldre'. The name transcribed here (as also in Black 1845) as 'Salsberi' is partially over-written, but if it refers to the household of one of the Earls of Salisbury, and if the Philip Fettiplace mentioned is to be associated with the great Fettiplace family of Berkshire and Oxfordshire, this might suggest that the manuscript was being used in the south of England by the fifteenth century.

Although there is only one extant manuscript of this particular text, there was a strong revival of interest in cosmetic treatises in Europe from the twelfth century onwards and texts on the ornamentation of women circulated as part of popular surgical treatises (including Henri de Mondeville's *Chirurgie* and Guy de Chauliac's *Grande Chirurgie*), with authors protecting their market by emphasising the dangers of self-treatment (Moulinier-Brogi 2004). The audience of these texts steadily became male and professional (Green 2008).

The claims of the Anglo-Norman prologue are almost certainly less straightforward than they appear. Desire for the love and favour of women in exchange for the work (vv. 45–6), though a commonplace of secular verse, seems incongruous amidst the professional Latin medical texts of the *Ornatus* manuscript. And the *Ornatus*' ostensibly female audience, along with at least some of the supposedly female sources cited, may be an authorising fiction for a 'medical' text that contains very little treatment of actual diseases and that traverses the morally fraught territory of female cosmetics.

MANUSCRIPT SOURCE. Bodleian MS Ashmole 1470 is a medical miscellany of 314 folios, *c.* 270 × 195 mm, and three extra folios (1 and 315–16) of written material apparently composed on the flyleaves of the original manuscript. The folio size varies between the first and second half of the manuscript, and Ruelle suggests that it consists of two parts (ff. 1–219 and 220–314) perhaps copied around the same time by different scribes, possibly as part of a coherent whole commissioned by the same patron. Certainly the manuscript is rubricated throughout by a single hand roughly contemporary with that of the scribes. The manuscript displays fairly frequent annotation, and the pages are brittle, perhaps suggesting frequent use. The irregular shape of some folios might suggest that it was made with utilitarian purposes in mind.

The texts are primarily Latin medical treatises, including versions of Constantinus Africanus's Latin translations of Isaac Judaeus's *Liber febrium, Dietarum universalium*, and *Dietarum particularium*; the twelfth-century *Antidotarium Nicholai*; and the *Flores dietarum* frequently attributed to John of St Paul (d. 1214); (see Nicoud 2007, 37–45). The *Ornatus mulierum* is the only Anglo-Norman work: there are some English, including recipes on the front flyleaf and f. 316*r–v*, and on a slip of parchment bound in at folio 219*r*, with a table of contents in a later, fourteenth-century hand on the reverse (Ruelle 1967, 6). The manuscript is professionally executed, ruled throughout with wide side margins and deep bas-de-pages, and copied in several neat book hands. Space has been left for enlarged capitals (not executed). The text is written in two columns per page of roughly forty lines each. The fourteenth- and fifteenth-century recipes and annotations noted above (see Audience and Circulation) suggest that the manuscript may have been used professionally and that it had multiple owners and users over the course of the two centuries following its compilation.

BIBLIOGRAPHY. Ruelle 1967 edits the *Ornatus* with a Modern French translation. For a partial English translation see Garay and Jeay 2000 at http://mw.mcmaster.ca/scriptorium/ruelle.html. The manuscript contents are given in Black 1845. Grossel 1998 discusses the *Ornatus.* On medical verse, see Hunt 1996 and on the rhetorical *descriptio feminae*, V. Allen 1993. An Anglo-Norman cosmetics collection without the *Ornatus*' rationale is edited by Gilleland 1988. For medieval cosmetic practices, their contexts and condemnation, see Menjot 1987, Martineau-Génieys 1987, Moulinier-Brogi 2004, Polo de Beaulieu 1987. Ziegler 2001 discusses medicine and immortality. On Anglo-Norman medicine see Hunt, ed., 1997; on medicine for women, Green 2008, 2000a, 2000b, 2000c, 2000d are essential: on the historical status of Trota see Green 2008. For medieval and early-modern medicine see Nicoud 2007, Siraisi 1990.

TEXT AND TRANSLATION

Rubric: *Incipit ornatus mulierum* [f. 276ra]

The Adornment of Women begins

[Q]uant Deus out la femme fete,
De la coste Adam est traite.
Bauté la duna perdurable,
Mes ele le perdi par le deble;
Puis que ele out la pume gusté
Mult en fu disonuré.
E les dames que ore sunt,
Ke de ceo culpes ne hunt,
Pur ceo que Heve forfist tant
De lur bauté sunt mult perdant;
Kar tele i ad quant est pucele
Dunc est ruvente, blanche e bele:
Tant tost cum ele est marié
Li est colur remué.
Tele i ad que en sa vie
Unches de bauté unt ballie;
Pur ceo vus fas jeo cest livre,
Que tres bien seez delivre
Vus memes en bauté guarder,
E vos acuintes amender.

When God made woman, he took her from Adam's side. He gave her everlasting beauty, but she lost it by means of the Devil: once she had tasted the apple, she was greatly dishonoured. And women living today, who are not themselves guilty of this transgression, have highly perishable beauty because of Eve's great sin. For there are some who, when they are maidens, are rosy-cheeked, white and beautiful, but whose colour begins to fade as soon as they are married. There are others who have never in their lives possessed beauty. I am therefore making this book for you, so that you may become skilled at keeping yourselves beautiful and at helping your friends.

A prime des chevoilz dirai,
E par tut le cors decenderai.
Del frunt, des oilz, des surcilz dirum;
De la face, des dens, del mentun,
Des autre choses tut amunt,
De tut celes que mester unt.
A la mamele fin en frai;
De la marice aillurs dirai.

I will speak first about hair and will proceed downwards to the rest of the body. We will discuss the forehead, the eyes, the eyebrows, the face, the teeth, the chin, and other parts of the upper body, and of all those areas which need attention. I will finish with the breast and will speak of the womb in another place.

Les auturs trai a testemunie,
Verté dirai senz essuine.
Galien, Constantin, Ypocras;
Ne ublirai nul, seit ault seit bas,
Ne ceo que ai apris a medechine
D'une dame que ert Saracine
– Mires fu de sa lai;
Mut fust valiant si ust fei –
Ne que a Salerne oï de Trote;
Dame que li ne creit est sote.

I draw on the authorities as witnesses; I will speak the truth without making excuses. Galen, Constantine, and Hippocrates; I will not forget any of them, be he of greater or lesser renown. Nor will I forget what I learned about medicine from a Saracen woman who was a doctor according to the conventions of her country. She would have been very worthy if she had held the true faith. Nor will I forget what I learned at Salerno from a woman called Trota; any woman who does not believe her is a fool.

Ne dirai pas partut en rime
Kar hum ne pot pas de medecine

I will not tell all of it in rhyme because one cannot readily speak of medicine and set

En tuz lius prestement parler
Et les speces acunter.
Or pri Deu li rei celestre [f. 276rb]
Ke cest livre tel puisse estre
Que de dames en ai grez
Dunt en sei tutdis amez.

out whole remedies in rhyme. Now, I pray God the heavenly king that I may gain the favour of women with this book and that I may always be loved by them.

Notes

1 **[Q]uant Deus** Before the beginning of vv. 1–3 space is left for an enlarged capital that was never executed.

2 **de la coste Adam est traite** Eve's creation from Adam's rib in Gen 2.21–2 is the point of departure for volumes of moral and theological debate over the fundamental nature of woman (Formed in the image and likeness of God? An imperfect copy of Adam?) and her role (see e.g. d'Alverny 1977, Blamires 1997).

13–14 **Tant tost cum ele est marié / Li est colur remué** For ancient and medieval medical writers, 'complexion' referred literally to the mixture of humours in the patient's body (Siraisi 1990, 79, 101–4), which manifested themselves in his or her appearance. The loss of a woman's rosy complexion after marriage therefore points to a larger physiological and moral change presumably brought on by the onset of sexual experience (another implied consequence of the fall being the corruption of human sexuality).

15 **i** followed by expuncted *d* in MS.

20 **E vos acuintes amender** *amender* can mean to correct or cure but also to help or edify; thus the women whom the author ostensibly addresses are given the opportunity not only to help cure their female friends of their cosmetic ailments and imperfections but also to pass on medical knowledge. But women very rarely owned or had direct access to medical manuscripts such as the one in which this text appears (Green 2008, 19) and cosmetic knowledge was usually mediated by a male medical practitioner.

28 **De la marice aillurs dirai** This reference to the womb (which is in fact untreated in the text), perhaps signals the author's familiarity with the more predominantly medical *Liber de sinthomatibus mulierum* and *De curis mulierum*, which were also attributed to Trota and frequently circulated with the Latin *De ornatu*.

28 **aillurs** MS *alliurs*.

33 **medechine** MS has *me[?]chine* with a short abbreviation mark over the *m*. An alternative reading might be *meschine* (i.e. 'young woman') but a variant spelling of 'medicine' (*AND*, *s.v.* 'mescine') seems more probable.

36 **Mut fust valiant si ust fei** The phrase is used of Muslim knights in e.g. *La Chanson de Roland* (Brault, ed. and trans., 1984, vv. 899, 3164).

37 **Ne que a Salerne oï de Trote.** The use of *oï* suggests the oral transmission of knowledge directly from the renowned twelfth-century female medical practitioner to whom three separate treatises on the diseases of women came to be attributed. However, because the historical Trota was almost certainly not the author or primary source of the treatise on cosmetics attributed to her (Green 2008, 22), and because this treatise shares very little with the so-called *Trotula* texts, this is more likely a strategic ploy for asserting both firsthand acquaintance with an acknowledged authority and experiential knowledge gained through travel.

33. Jofroi de Waterford and Servais Copale, *Secré de secrez* [Dean 239], Extract and Prologue: Paris, Bibliothèque nationale de France, fonds français, MS 1822, ff. 84^{r-v}, 248^{vd}–249ra

Date of composition and provenance. 1266–1300; continental.

Author, sources and nature of text. The result of a collaboration between Jofroi de Waterford, probably an Irish Dominican, and Servais Copale, a Walloon, the *Secré de secrez* is a 'mirror for princes', a treatise on good government. Little is known about either man, but Jofroi would have lived in Waterford, an important royal city and port in the thirteenth century, at some point after the Dominicans arrived there in 1226 and established an influential priory. How he and Copale met and where they worked is unknown – perhaps they were at university in Paris together, or perhaps Jofroi was posted to the Picard-Walloon area. Equally unclear is how they apportioned their tasks: in the prologue Jofroi uses the first person singular, but the first person plural appears in the epilogue, where both Jofroi and Copale are named as responsible for the entire work. It seems that Copale was the scribe, given that the text is strongly marked for the area around eastern Picardy and western Wallonia and that all the manuscript's texts have been copied in the same hand. The two were also responsible for French prose translations of Dares (*La Guerre de Troie*, Dean 240) and Eutropius (*Le Regne des Romains*, Dean 241), both of which are found in the manuscript with *Secré*.

The *Secré* takes the form of a spurious letter from Aristotle in response to one from Alexander the Great: a number of such letters are attributed to the two (see also **32a**). *Secré* does not take Alexander and his chivalric deeds as its subject, but casts him as Aristotle's pupil, seeking the philosopher's advice about governing Persia. Like the verse version of the *Secré* composed about thirty years earlier by Pierre d'Abernun de Fetcham (Dean 236, and see (**19**)), the Waterford version is ultimately derived from Philip of Tripoli's Latin *Secretum secretorum* (*c.* 1220–30), itself traceable to the Arabic (*Kitab Sirr al-'asrar*). Authors such as Chaucer, Gower, Hoccleve and Lydgate knew and used the Latin *Secretum*, and Gower also drew material from the *Secré* itself for his *Confessio amantis* of *c.* 1390 (Beckerlegge 1944, xxiv).

The Waterford version of the *Secré* excises considerable amounts from its source in the *Secretum*, which had become a sprawling encyclopaedic work, acquiring sections on cosmology, astrology, and magic. These were suspect areas in thirteenth-century clerical culture (see (**25b**), headnote) and the prologue claim that Arabic writing is short on truth (line 64) may allude to Arabic expertise in these fields. (It may also be an example of a commonplace assertion made about both Arabic and Greek: S. J. Williams 2003, 18). Even so, the assertion may speak to Jofroi's (and perhaps Copale's) concept of the undertaking, a kind of 'deep translation' which aims to reach through the Latin to locate an authentic textual core, retained as the *meule*, the marrow, and the *veritei* (line 81).

Secré stays close to the Latin for the first twenty chapters, but the translating method is nevertheless fundamentally compilatory. As the text explains just before the first major interpolation, 'not everything is from the Latin of Aristotle's book on the governance of princes' because other, no less useful, materials in Latin have been found and added in, according to the initial promise that 'aucune bones choses' would be written in the book (f. 89^{v}, cited Monfrin 1964, 511). To each of the work's three parts – the moral education of princes, their physical health and the composition of a prince's entourage – the translator(s), as they re-iterate in their epilogue, have grafted (*entees*) materials from ancient history and philosophy (f. 143^{c}). After chapter 20, they incorporate into Part I a treatise on the four cardinal virtues, with a strong emphasis on prudence ('*visougetei* en romans') as the most important virtue in a king. This treatise is largely based on compendia by Martin of Braga (*c.* 570) and the Franciscan John of Wales's late-thirteenth-century *Breviloquium* (Monfrin 1964, 511–20). In Part II, Waterford and Copale extend the chapter on diet by translating 'des livres Ysaac qui sunt apellez Dietes universeles et particulers' (f. 143^{c}), i.e. the *De dietis universalibus et particularibus* of Ishak ben Soleiman or Isaac Judeus, *c.* 832–932. (The epilogue's careful sourcing of this material perhaps owes something to the difficulty of providing stably valid dietary advice for different regions.) In the third part they interpolate their translation of nearly all the Ps-Aristotelian *Physiognomica* produced by Bartholomew of Messina, chief translator, *c.* 1258–66, at the court of Manfred of Sicily (Monfrin 1964, 510), a work considered useful to princes in selecting advisors. The *Secré* is thus a good example of the flexibility, capaciousness and informativeness by which thirteenth-century encyclopaedic works were created and valued.

Audience and circulation. The number of extant manuscripts (one complete and one fragment, Hunt 2000) is not necessarily a guide to the text's popularity. In addition to Dominican and Franciscan clergy, who could have come to Ireland from Anglo-Norman England or France, the English colony at Waterford would have included military men, administrators, and officials, many accompanied by their families. Members of the aristocracy eager to have a part in government or to maintain their own perceived rights would have found support for their views in many parts of the *Secré*. The dialect of the *scripta* may mean that the Waterford *Secré* was also read on the continent: if it was also made or copied there, its later history nevertheless comes out of a network of Anglo-Irish and English connections. Among many other translations into Middle English from various versions of the text, Waterford and Copale's French was fully translated into English in 1422 by James Yonge of Waterford for James Butler, duke of Ormond, and King Henry V's representative in Ireland, with inserted passages on Ireland and the rights of Irish kings. The multilingual (Latin, French, English, and Irish) library of the Fitzgerald Earls of Kildare of the period (Byrne 2013) is further evidence of continued interest in French writings there.

Manuscript source. MS BN fr. 1822 is a vellum manuscript of the second half of the thirteenth century of 253 folios, *c.* 231 × 168 mm, written in two columns: see http://gallica.bnf.fr/ark:/12148/btv1b8425997k/f510.image.

A seventeenth-century hand has entered an index on a blank page at the beginning. The prologue has been placed at the end of the *Secré*, perhaps because a later re-binding of the manuscript did not follow the scribe's intended order (Pinchbeck 1948, 3). Each chapter of the *Secré* begins with a large illuminated capital in red and blue. The one hand used throughout the entire manuscript is a steady professional hand. There are twelve works, beginning with the *Sermons en prose*, followed by the Waterford-Copale translations of *L'Estoire des Troiens*, *L'Estoire des Romains*, and the *Secré*, maintained as a continuous grouping in the rebound book (but not, apparently, in the original; Pinchbeck 1948, 3); the manuscript also includes Gautier de Metz's encyclopedic *Image du monde*, Marie de France's *Fables* (*Fables d'Ysope*) and a continental French text of the *Elucidarium* (see (**19**)).

Bibliography. There is no complete published edition of *Secré*; Monfrin's 1947 dissertation remains unpublished and inaccessible, but his studies (1964, 1982) are indispensable. Henry 1986 edits chapters 57–64 (ff. 110*d*–113*d*), on wine. Schauwecker 2007 edits the Dietary. Parts of the prologue and epilogue are unreliably edited by Le Clerc 1847. Monfrin 1964, 510 transcribes part of the prologue (corresponding to vv. 13–29 below); for two longer extracts see Monfrin 1982, 100–1 (on largesse), 106–7 (on a sovereign's conduct upon awakening). Hunt's informative study of 2000 transcribes substantial passages (from Part II on diet and Part III from the Ps-Aristotle *Physiognomia*) discovered by him in cut-down fourteenth-century bi-folia re-used as flyleaves in London, Society of Antiquaries MS 101. Monfrin 1964, 510–23 discusses the additional sources used in translating *Secré*. Grignaschi 1977, 1981 gives essential background to the transmission history of the text from Arabic to Latin to the vernaculars: see further on sources Monfrin 1982, 74. Pinchbeck 1948 is an excellent description of the manuscript and its contents. On the advice genre see Ferster 1996. The religious houses of Waterford are described in Gwynn and Hadcock 1970. For Anglo-Norman in Waterford see Sinclair 1984 and for the late-medieval literary culture of Ireland see e.g. Byrne 2013; Justice and Kerby-Fulton 1997; O'Byrne 2012; Legge 1950, 78–80. For Yonge's translation see Part VI, §2.8. For a further unedited full French prose translation of the *Secreta secretorum* in BN fr. 571 variously provenanced to England (Monfrin 1982, Hunt 2000) and the Continent, see Dean 238 (a partial insular copy). For its Middle English versions see Keiser 1998, nos 6–22 and Part VI, §2.8; on that for Edward III see Escobedo 2011. For its European translations see Gaullier-Bougassas et al, 2015.

TEXT AND TRANSLATION (I)

[f. 84rb] Aristotles envoa pluisors epistles a Alixandre, des quez ceste est une, et fait a entendre tout le livre du governement des rois. L'oquoison de ceste epistle fu teile: quant Alixandres avoit Perse conquise, por ce que acun du peuple contre lui furent revelei, envoa ses epistles a Aristotle en ceste forme.

Aristotle sent several epistles to Alexander, of which this is one; and it explains the entire book of the government of kings. The occasion for this epistle was as follows: when Alexander had conquered Persia, he sent this epistle to Aristotle in these terms, because some of the people rebelled against him.

'A noble maistre de droiture, governeor de veritei, Aristotle, le sien desiple Alixandre salus. A ta cointise fai a savoir que je ai trovei en la terre de Perse une gent plainne de raison et de parfont entendement, et de perchant engin ke sur autres convoitent la signorie, por quoi les pensames toz destruire. Ce que toi iert avis sor chou nos fais a savoir par ces lettres.' A qui Aristotles ensi respondi: 'Se vos poez changier l'air [f. 84va] et l'ewe de celle terre, et surquetout l'ordenement des citeiz, parfaites vostre porpoz. Se ce non, governez les avoic bienvoilhance et debonairetei. Car se chou fachiés, avoir poez esperance avoic l'aide de Deu que tout serunt obeissans, et governer les porez en bone pais'.

'To the noble master of rectitude, keeper of the truth, Aristotle, greetings from your disciple Alexander. I appeal to your wisdom in saying that I have found in the land of Persia a people full of reason and profound understanding, and a cleverness at encroachment in that they covet lordship over others; which is why we have thought about destroying them all. Inform us in this exchange of letters what you would advise on this'. To which Aristotle answered as here: 'If you can change the air and the water of that land, and especially maintain good order in the cities, do what you wish. But if not, govern them with benevolence and fairness. For if you do that, you may, with God's help, expect that they will all be obedient, and you will be able to govern them in true peace'.

Et quant Alixandres out recheuwe l'espitre, fist solum son consel, par quoi ceus de Perse li furent sugés plus que nulle gent.

And when Alexander had received the epistle, he did according to Aristotle's counsel, by means of which the Persians submitted to him more thoroughly than any other people.

(II) *C'est li prologes de Secré de secrés*

This is the prologue to the Secret of Secrets

[f. 248d] A noble bers prouz et sages: freres Jofroi de Watreford del ordene az freres precheors le mendre, salus en Jhesu Crist et santei d'aulme et de cors. En une aprise acordent et une verité mostrent les plus

To a valiant and wise nobleman from Friar Jofroi of Waterford, of the Order of Preachers Minor, greetings in Jesus Christ, and health of soul and body. The wisest clerks and most renowned masters of those sages clers et maistres les plus renomez de ceus ki avant nos furent de cest siecle le clergie: ke la renomee, proeche et valor de toutes armeures, ou de emperriors ou de rois ou donque quel chevalerie, estoit estre gardee, sauvee et maintenue, non seulement par le garite des armes, ains par la visougetei et par l'aide de lois de sens, de savoir et de cointise, car force et grant poer sens cointise et savoir, forlingne en derverie. [f. 249ra] Et visougetei et savoir sens force et sens pooir seurement ne se guie, mais quant avoiques force de pooir s'aconpaingne sens et savoir, savoirs vat pooir conduisant, et donc soi puet princes juer et en tribous seur aler, ki ensemble li vont convoitant.

among the learned who have gone before us in this world unite in a single enterprise and demonstrate a single truth: that the renown, prowess and bravery of all bearers of arms, whether of emperors, kings, or any other knightly rank must be kept, preserved and maintained not only through a store of arms, but through prudence, and with the help of the laws of intelligence, of wisdom and knowledge. For strength and great power without knowledge and wisdom decline into destruction. And prudence and wisdom without strength and without power cannot lead the way. But when the force of power is accompanied by intelligence and wisdom, knowledge guides power; and thus, if these go with him, a prince may go forward into any troubles as a sure leader, in the company of superior men. [. . .]

[. . .]

[f. 249a] Entre les autres boens livres que vous aveiz, desireiz vous a avoir un livre Aristotle, le tres saichant philosophe, qui est apellez *Segrez des segrez* ou *Livre du governement des rois ou de princes*, et por ce moi priaste que cel livre, ki fu translatei de griu [f. 249b] en arabic, et derechief de arabic en latin, vos tran[s]lataisse de latin en franchois. Et je, a vous priieres, al translater ai mise ma cure, et avoiques le plus grant travail, k'en autres hautes et parfondes estudes sui enbesoingniés. D'autre part, savoir devez ke les Arabiiens trop ont de paroles en corte veritei, et les Grigois ont oscure maniere de parler; et il me convient de l'un et de l'autre langage translater: et por chou le trop de l'un oscurcirai, et l'oscurtei de l'autre esclarcirai, solonc ce ke la matire puet soffrir; car lur entente sievrai, ne mies lur paroles. Saichiés derechief que sovent i metterai autres bones paroles, les queus tot ne soient mie en cel livre, al mains sunt en autre livres d'autoritei, et ne sunt pas mains profitables ke celles ki en cel livre sunt escrites; et quanque je i metterai, a la matire acordant sera. A la parfin saichiés

[To place with] the other fine books that you have, you desire to have a book by Aristotle, the very skilled philosopher, which is called the *Secret of Secrets*, or the *Governance of Kings or of Princes*, and for that reason you asked me to translate this book – which had been translated from Greek into Arabic and then again from Arabic into Latin – from Latin into French. And I, at your urging, put my effort into translating it, and with the greatest toil, for I am busy with other studies, lofty and deep. And then, you ought to know that the Arabs have too many words that are short on truth, and the Greeks have an obscure way of speaking; and I have to translate from both languages. And so I shall hide the excess of the one and clarify the obscurities of the other, as the material permits, for I shall follow their meaning but not their words. Be advised that I shall often put in other, good words, ones that are not quite in the book but which come from other, authoritative books and are no less useful; and whatever I add will be perfectly in harmony with the subject. Finally, be advised that the books translated from Arabic into que les livres ki de arabic en latin furent translatei furent fausement translatei; et por ce lairai je pluisors choses ki ne sunt veritez ne profitables, et prenderai la meule et la veritei cortement.

Latin were translated incorrectly; that is why I shall omit many things that are not true or profitable and with fewer words seize the truthful marrow.

Notes

1 **Aristotles . . . pluisors epistles** Aristotle tutored Alexander III of Macedonia (Alexander the Great) from the age of 13 to 16. Stoneman (1994, xxv) writes that Alexander, having taken scholars with him to the East to report what they saw, 'certainly did correspond with Aristotle', who used some of the ethnographic information supplied by Alexander in his own studies. The earlier Anglo-Norman verse *Secré* explains that Aristotle became too old to travel to Alexander to counsel him and was also concerned to disseminate moral council (Beckerlegge 1944, vv. 1–36). The 'Epistola ad Aristotelem' is a source for many works, including (**28**).

5 **Perse conquise** For a decade from 334 BC Alexander campaigned against the Persian Empire, ultimately defeating its king, Darius III. At that point he ruled the land from the Adriatic Sea to the Indus River.

18–21 **Se vos poez changier l'air . . . parfaites vostre porpoz** Aristotle's advice perhaps reflects medieval theories of environmental influence on physiological and psychological make-up (see Bartlett 2001): unless he can change their environment, Alexander cannot change the Persians' dispositions.

20 **citeiz** *n*:*-ei* (instead of *–é*) is characteristic of some of the eastern dialects, including Walloon. See also 32 **santei** *n*; 41, 44 **visougetei** *n*; 52 **aveiz, desireiz** *5 pr*; 56, 78, 78 [sic] **translatei** *pp*; 64, 81, **veritei** *n*; 67 **oscurtei** *n*; 73 **autoritei** *n*.

34 **clers** The *s* is superscripted.

38 **estoit** < *estover, estovoir*, 'to be necessary'.

40 **garite** A turret, watchtower, gatehouse, movable shelter to protect soldiers; the context seems to call for 'store' or 'storehouse', with the idea of stockpiling.

41, 44 **visougetei** Prudence is further divisible into three parts, following the Ciceronian formula (*De Officiis*): memory, understanding or knowledge (*entendement*), and foresight (Monfrin 1964, 51). *Visougetei* is defined at f. 89^{r}: 'est ditte et clamee visougetei en romans qu'en latin est appellee prudentia' (what is called *visougetei* in French is *prudentia* in Latin). At f. 90^{r-v} *visougetei* is most often collocated with *savoir*, and Vegetius, Plato, Valerius Maximus, Seneca, and the biblical Solomon are all said to have recognised the value of *visougetei*. Iconographically, Prudence is often depicted holding a mirror and a book, or as having three eyes.

47 **savoir, savoirs** In the manuscript there is an illegible letter or perhaps pair of letters between the two words.

49 **juer** = *guier*, to guide. In his Middle English translation James Yonge appears to have been misled by the form *juer*, which he translates as 'play': 'But whan w*ith* Streynth and Powere, hym compaynyth witte *and* connynge, and witte dressith Powere, in goodnys may the Prynce Play, and w*ith* good men Surly walk' (Steele, ed., 1898, 121).

49 **tribous** from *tribuil* 'disturbance, trouble'.

50 **convoitant**, properly, 'coveting', is probably *conveer*, to accompany.

56–8 **moi priaste . . . ki fu translatei de griu en arabic, et derechief de arabic en latin** This statement was mistranslated by Seymour 1929, 32, who reads *fu translatei* incorrectly as 'I . . . translated'.

Kerns (2008, vi) reprints the mistaken translation and is thereby led to argue that Jofroi did not translate from those languages.

62–70 **D'autre part . . . paroles** This has sometimes been read as Jofroi's claim that he was translating from Arabic and Greek (Williams 2003, 17–18, observes that there is no extant Greek exemplar of the work; and see Pinchbeck 1948, 10). But it is more likely that by saying *et il me convient de l'un et de l'autre langage translater* (lines 65–6), Jofroi means that he is indirectly translating from those languages *through* the Latin, which transmits the flaws of earlier work. He will state a few lines further that *les livres ki de arabic en latin furent translatei furent fausement translatei* (lines 77–8), which implies that he saw his task as a correction of the Latin translator's failures. Criticism of one's predecessors both to establish the need for a new translation and to declare its superlativeness is a medieval literary commonplace.

34. *Le Miracle de Sardenai* [Dean 563], Prologue and Epilogue: Tours, Bibliothèque municipale, MS 927, ff. 217^{r}–218^{v}, 226^{v}–229^{v}

Date of composition and provenance. Early thirteenth century, provenance unknown.

Author, sources and nature of text. This legend concerns a hermitage at Sardenai, near Damascus, where an image of the Virgin grew flesh and exuded miraculous and curative oil. The legend arose in the last quarter of the twelfth century and spread simultaneously in Latin and Arabic accounts, making Sardenai a popular pilgrimage site. The convergence of different religious practices (of both Eastern and Western Christians, and Muslims) on a shared holy site is known elsewhere in Egypt and the Holy Land. Sardenai (or Saïadnaya) has continued to attract both Christian and Muslim pilgrims (for example, Syrian cosmonauts visited the shrine before and after their space flight in 1990, Kedar 2001, 92 n. 46).

Reports in Latin of the miraculous icon at Sardenai are found from the late twelfth century onwards: Burchard of Strasbourg mentions it in 1175, and Guy Chat recounts bringing relics from Sardenai to a church near Limoges in the early 1180s (Devos 1947). The story quickly becomes mainstream in western Europe: mention of the miraculous icon is found, for example, in Matthew Paris's and Roger of Wendover's Latin chronicles (at the date 1204: Devos 1947, 250); and in addition to the vernacular poem excerpted here, the legend figures in the *Miracles de Nostre Dame* by Gautier de Coincy (1177–1236; ed. Koenig 1970). Gautier, who lived in Soissons, affirms he spoke with a man from Soissons who brought back relics from a visit to the shrine at Sardenai.

At the time when the chapel which still houses the miraculous icon was founded by an ascetic nun from Damascus, Syria, according to the poem's narrator, was ruled by the Greeks and the Armenians. The first part of the legend occurs in this distant past: it recounts the foundation of the hermitage, then the miraculous means by which the icon of the Virgin, painted in Jerusalem, comes to be established at Sardenai. The last part of the narrative switches to the contemporary medieval period, when Sardenai is deep in Muslim territory, and the crusading knights Templar can visit the shrine only during periods of truce between the Christians and Saracens. This part of the poem relates the miraculous incarnation of the icon, which grows breasts that exude the copious thaumaturgic balm distributed through the agency of the Templars to both Western and Eastern pilgrims.

The narrator of *Sardenai* begins with the standard statement that he is translating into French from his authoritative Latin source, 'word for word' for the benefit of those who are unlearned, so that they may learn of the Sardenai icon. But his vernacular narrative is more than a simple linguistic transfer: in addition to providing a striking example of the convergence at Sardenai of Western and Eastern religions, the legend gives insight into Templar activities in the Holy Land, and the account is an early example of Western awareness of the use of religious icons in the East. The incarnation metamorphosis of the icon into a three-dimensional figure is itself a notable mediation between the Eastern tradition of icons painted on wooden tablets, and the Western artistic tradition of using statues to represent the Virgin.

The first scholars studying this legend believed that the Latin version of the legend was derived from a lost Greek original, but it is now accepted that the late-twelfth-century Latin text comes from an Arabic source, translated probably for (and perhaps by) a Templar. Peeters (1933) notes that, of the forty-odd Christian churches and monasteries at Sardenai, none preserve even traces of Hellenistic documents or religious rites. The Christian population of Sardenai would have spoken Arabic, facilitating their contact with the Sultans who also worship at the shrine at Sardenai. This peaceful interaction between the religions is reflected in the second part of the narrative.

The narrator is not completely, unabashedly partisan: the Christian view which initially marvels at the strength of the true faith healing even 'pagans', who formerly followed a 'fauce loi' but who now believe in the efficacy of the icon (vv. 445, 475–8), is tempered later by the admission that, because of their sins, God permits that the Christians be ruled by the Saracens (vv. 502–4). The Templars become part of this convergence of different religious practices at Sardenai, and, through their distribution of the relics and their probable patronage of the Latin translation, this doubly accredited miraculous shrine becomes well known in the West.

Audience and circulation. Although the poem has clear connections with the Templars, there is no overt statement of their patronage. To some extent, however, details of the audience and circulation of the *Miracle de Sardenai* can be inferred from the manuscript contexts in which the poem is preserved. These are all of English origin in the sense that, although the earliest surviving copy was made at Tours, the sources used by the scribes were of English origin and first written and circulated there, even if subsequently copied within the wide geographical range of Plantangenet courtly culture. The manuscripts are Tours, Bibliothèque municipale 927 [T], second quarter of the thirteenth century; London, BL Royal 4 C.XI [L], mid-thirteenth century; Oxford, Corpus Christi College 232 [O], mid-thirteenth century; Cambridge, Cambridge University Library, Mm.6.15 [C], second half of the thirteenth century.

T, the manuscript copied in the region of Tours, begins with Latin pieces for liturgical or musical performance (20 of 229 folios), but the rest of the contents are in French. *Sardenai* joins a number of major literary and religious works (such as the earliest known play in French, the *Jeu d'Adam*, found only in this manuscript, and Wace's *Conception Nostre Dame* and *Vie de sainte Marguerite*). The performative and literary nature of the manuscript's contents is evident, with a clear emphasis on vernacular texts designed for the entertainment of both lay and clerical audiences.

In manuscript L, *Sardenai* keeps largely historical company: along with Wace's *Rou* (3) and a vernacular translation of the *Pseudo-Turpin Chronicle*, it was appended to L in the thirteenth century, so that these vernacular texts follow a twelfth-century copy of Geoffrey of Monmouth's *Historia regum Britanniae*. The manuscript belonged in the fourteenth century to Battle Abbey (see (3) above), where, presumably, *Sardenai* was read and heard by the monks and their visitors as a literary-historical text, showing Western involvement in Outremer as a continuation of the historical narrative of the West.

Manuscript O was owned by the Benedictine abbey of St Augustine, Canterbury (Marx 1995, 166; Watson 1987, 13, 131), where the *Miracle de Sardenai* joins Robert Grosseteste's *Chasteau d'amour* (5) and the anonymous *Vie de sainte Marie l'Égyptienne*. A short requiem Mass in Latin for count William (ff. 65^r–66^v) follows *Marie l'Égyptienne* and precedes the *Miracle*. The last part of the manuscript (ff. 71–92) is Latin, in a later hand (Rigg 1978, 28). The main part of O, then, is in French, with two highly dramatic poems on women religious from the Holy Land set beside a popular literary-theological work by the well-known bishop of Lincoln. The inclusion of the requiem Mass for count William suggests that the manuscript was designed to appeal to a noble lay patron, perhaps a member of the late count William's family.

34. *Le Miracle de Sardenai*

The context of *Sardenai* in Manuscript C offers a vivid contrast to L and O: of unknown provenance, C is a utilitarian compendium of 219 leaves, gathered together from disparate quires, almost exclusively in Latin, dealing with theological or parochial subjects useful for the clergy (processionals, treatises on clerical orders, confession, the seven sins, vices and virtues, the ten commandments). There are only two works in French, a geographical tract with two diagrams (ff. 49^{v}–50, Dean 361), and *Sardenai* (ff. 105^{v}–108). *Sardenai* ends incomplete (at v. 502), at the end of the two-quire section in which it is found (ff. 87–108). The following section (five quires) is a collection of Marian miracles in Latin, one of which is the source text for the French poem.

To judge, then, from the evidence of its manuscript contexts, *Sardenai* had strong appeal to both clergy and laity, and circulated in varied cultural contexts, from utilitarian parochial Latin compilations to vernacular collections that were mainly literary and historical.

Manuscript source. The text below is from manuscript T: 229 folios, 148 × 108 mm, written in the region of Tours, in single columns of 18 lines per page, on paper, datable to 1225–50 (Keller 1990, 21–3). The *Miracle de Sardenai* is ff. 217^{r}–229^{v}, with lacunae created by a leaf missing between ff. 218–19, and ff. 222–3. In Dean's dating the four manuscripts of the *Miracle* are roughly contemporaneous. A comparison of the variants suggests, however, that manuscripts T and C give slightly earlier versions of the text than L and O; since T preserves a more regular text than C, it is used here as the base text.

Bibliography. *Sardenai* was first published (from manuscript O as an unidentified work, by Grosseteste) by Cooke 1852. The Tours manuscript was edited as a separate anonymous work in Raynaud 1882, and subsequently with variants and lacunae from L and O (Raynaud 1885). In both articles Raynaud discusses the Anglo-Norman nature of the work, and the Latin sources used both by this poet and by Gautier de Coincy in his version of the legend. For an argument that at least one section of the manuscript (containing Wace's *Conception Nostre Dame*) was copied for a community in the Mediterranean, see Ruini 2013.

On the cult of the Virgin at Sardenai and its cultural context, the creation and spread of the legend and the Templars' role see Kedar 2001. Minervini 1995 analyses the legend in its Arabic and Latin forms, and documents its diffusion in the East and the West. Baraz 1995 shows that the earliest Arabic account is 1183 and discusses the cultural differences behind the variations between the Arabic and Latin accounts (the Latin tradition is more popular, the Arabic more elitist). Devos 1947 examines earlier studies of the Latin and Arabic accounts and edits the 1186 Latin account of Guy Chat (a Templar who took Sardenai oil given to him by another Templar in Jerusalem to a church near Limoges). Peeters 1933, reviewing Zayat's history of Saïdanaya (published in Arabic, 1932), agrees that the original legend was in Arabic, renouncing his belief (Peeters 1906) in a lost Greek original. On transmission to the West of the painted icon as a mode of religious art see Carr 1986. Möhring 2008 is a useful starting point for the historical roles of Nur-ad-Din and Saladin. For *Sardenai*'s manuscripts, the most up to date descriptions are Keller 1990 for T, Marx 1995 for O; for L see (3), above; for C see Hardwick 1861, IV: 388–92.

TEXT AND TRANSLATION

(i) Prologue and Opening

El nom de sainte Trinité [f. 217r]
Si com vint en auctorité
E si cum en escrit trovai
Le miracle de Sardenai
De ma dame sainte Marie
Que plusors gens ne sevent mie,
De latin vueil en romanz metre,
Tot mot a mot selonc la letre,
Por ce que ici pora plus plaire
A ceaus qui n'entendent gramaire.
Li escrit dit qu'a cel termine
Que li Gresois e li Ermine
Teneient en lor seignorie
La sainte terre de Surie,
Vers Domas en un leu savage,
Loins del chemin e del passage
Une sainte feme abitoit
Qui abit de nonain portoit.
E por mener plus aspre vie [f. 217v]
Si estoit ileuques afuie
Hors dou peuple de la sité
Ou longement ot abité.
Quar se savez, qui viaut servir
Nostre Seignor a sun plaisir,
De mal faire l'estuet sesser
E le siecle del tot leisser.

In the name of Holy Trinity, because many people do not yet know about it, I want to translate the miracle of my lady St Mary of Sardenai into French, as it happened according to authoritative sources, and as I have found it in written Latin accounts. So that it may be more pleasing to those who do not know Latin, I will translate it all from Latin into French, word by word, according to its meaning. The history relates that when the Greeks and the Armenians ruled the holy land of Syria, a holy woman who wore a nun's habit lived near Damascus, in a desert region far away from people and their routes of passage. In order to live a more ascetic life she had fled to this place away from the crowds of the city where she had long lived. For, be assured, it behooves whoever wishes to serve Our Lord in a manner pleasing to him, to abstain from doing evil, and to completely abandon all worldly things.

.Vi. liues conte l'un petites
De Domas entre qu'as ermites
Qui convercent a Sardenai.
Par ceaus qui ont esté le sai,
Mais se sachés de verité,
Qu'encore n'avoit abité
A Sardenai ne home ne feme
Quant i vint sele sainte feme.
E quant elle vint a cel saint leu
El nom de Deu e el Deu veu
E de la çoe sainte mere [f. 218r]
A qui del tot ses pencez ere,
Establi un povre abitacle
Ou Deus fist puis mainte miracle,
E fait encore chascun jor,
Si com tesmoignent sil d'entor.

It is said that it was just six short leagues from Damascus to where the hermits lived at Sardenai. I know this from those who have been there, but in truth, no-one, man or woman, had yet lived at Sardenai when this holy woman came there. And when she arrived in this holy place, in the name of God and according to God's will and that of his sainted mother, to whom all of her thoughts were directed, she established a humble dwelling where God later accomplished many a miracle, and does still every day, as those who live nearby testify.

La dame qu'ileuc abitoit
En Deu servir se delitoit
E si qu'as povres pelerins,
As sofraitos, as orfenins
Qui veneient a l'ermitage
Prestoit por Deu le herbergage.
E par charité lor trovoit
Ce quë al jor lor covenoit.
Al termine d'ilors avint
Quë uns moines gresois la vint
Qui de Costantinople estoit
E en Jerusalem aloit
Au sepulcre en pelerinage [f. 218*v*]
E quist por Deu le herbergaje.
La sainte dame li trova
Aveuc se quë il [li] rova;
E quant ele encerché li ot
Dont il venoit e ou alot,
Quant elle sot de verité
Quë il a la sainte sité
De Jerusalem vout aler,
Si comença a lui parler,
E a preer por Deu amor,
Quant il se metroit el retor,
Qu'il revenist a l'herberjaje
E li aportast une ymage
De ma dame sainte Marie
En table painte e establie,
Que ele sor son autier meïst
E quë a li garde preïst
[Quant feroit ses afflictïuns,
Si encroistroit ses devotiuns.
Li moines sa proiere entent,
Qui justes ert; pitez en prent,
Si pramist quant repaireroit
Ke l'ymagë aporteroit.]

The lady who lived there rejoiced in her service to God, such that she granted shelter in the name of God to poor pilgrims, to the needy and to orphans who came to the hermitage. And through her charity she provided them what they needed every day.

During this period it happened that a Greek monk from Constantinople arrived there on pilgrimage to Jerusalem and to the Holy Sepulchre, and in the name of God, he sought shelter. The saintly lady provided him with what he asked of her; she then enquired of him where he came from and where he was going, and when she learned in fact that he wished to go to the holy city of Jerusalem, she spoke to him and asked him, for the love of God, to come back to the hermitage on his return journey, and bring her an image of Our Lady St Mary, made and painted on a wooden panel; she wanted to place it on her altar, to look at as she did penance, so that her devotions would be more fervent. The monk heard her entreaty, which was just. He was moved to pity, and promised to bring back the icon when he returned.

(ii) Ending and Epilogue

Graignor miracle i a encore [f. 226*v*]
Quar ne finerent tres qu'a ore
De creistre en char e d'engroisser
Les memeles e espesser.
Puis est tote muee en char,
E nel tenez pas a eschar,

There was yet a greater miracle, for the breasts now began to change into flesh, and to become larger and heavier: they changed completely into flesh. And do not scornfully dismiss this, for the man-made icon was changed into flesh and blood. People from

[Kar ymage de main ovree
Est en char e en sanc muee.]
Por veir le dit on a Domas,
Se tesmoigne maistre Tomas
Qui del Tenple fu chappelains,
E la senti o ses deus mains,
E plusors autres l'ont vëu
Qui bien en devent estre creu.
Li eule n'est pas en sejor,
Ains cort encore nuit e jor
E chiet en un vaisel de cuivre.
Li moines grec sont en grant cuivre,
Des malades ont a planté,
I vont por requerre santé.

Damascus state this is true, and it was witnessed by master Thomas, chaplain of the Templars, who felt it with his own two hands. And many others who are credible witnesses have seen it. The oil did not stop, but continues to flow down, night and day, into a copper vessel. The Greek monks hasten to deal with the sick, who go there in great numbers seeking cures.

Quant c'est chose que li crestien [f. 227r]
Sunt en triues o li paien,
Si [s'en]vont li frere do Temple,
E autres genz en sel contenple,
A oreisons, e eule querre,
Si en aportent en la terre
De Suriё en fioletes
De voire qui por ce sunt faites.
Sel tienent en grant saintuaire
Les gens, e bien le devent faire:
Nis li paien i ont crëance
E le tienent en reverence.
Jadis avint, se dit l'estoire
Qui mult est ancïene e voire,
Que Domas un sodans tenoit
Qui un des iaus perdu avoit;
Puis li est la maile creüe
E l'autre s'en pert la veüe.
Si li dist on qu'en l'ermitage [f. 227v]
De Sardenai ert une ymage
De ma dame sainte Marie,
Qui a toz seaus faiseit aïe
Qui par bone devocion
I aloient por garison.
Quant del miracle oï parler
Si s'atorne por la aler.
E quant il vint a l'ermitage
Onc ne fina tresqu'a l'ymage,
Puis se mist a genoil a terre.
Preer comença e requerre

When it happens that the Christians are granted safe passage by the pagans, on such occasions the Templar monks and other people go there together, prayerfully seeking the oil, and they carry it throughout Syria in glass phials made for that purpose. People consider this shrine to be a great sanctuary, as well they should: even the pagans believe in it, and hold it in great reverence. It happened formerly, as a very old and truthful account relates, that Damascus was ruled by a sultan who had lost the use of one eye. Then the leucoma spread, and he lost the sight in his other eye. He was told that in the hermitage of Sardenai there was an icon of Our Lady St Mary which gave relief to all those who went to it, devotedly seeking a cure. The sultan, when he heard the reports of this miracle, made preparations to go there. And when he came to the hermitage he went straight to the icon, knelt on the ground and began to pray

Damnedeu nostre verai pere,
E a la soe sainte mere,
Que par sa digne poesté
Li otroit en son euil santé.
Quant il ot s'oreison finee,
A orbetes e aclinee,
L'ymage mes plus ne tarda: [f. 228r]
Quant amont vers le siel garda
Si a une lampe ardant veue,
Lores a recovree sa veue.

Mot a grant chose en voire foi:
Quant sil qui ert de fauce loi,
Par la crëance qu'il ot eue
A tantost santé receüe.
Bien a la vertu esprovee
Quant sa veüe a recovree.
Asés ot entor lui de seaus
Que Deus sana de divers maus.
Lors dit qu'il seit de verité:
Mot est de grant autorité
La sainte dame en qui enor
Garisent [e] grant e menor.
E por ce que primes avoit
Veü la lampe qui ardoit
Si voa que tote sa vie [f. 228v]
Que en l'iglise fera aïe:
A Sardenai d'eule rendroit
.Lx. mesures tot droit.
L'estoire dit que sel vou tindrent
Il e sil qui aprés lui vindrent,
E desqu'al tens de Noradin
Rendirent bien li Sarasin
Sele rente a la sainte iglise.
Mais aprés fu en obli mise
Quant Salehadin pot rener,
Si ne l'osa nus desrener
Vers lui, ne jeunes ne ancïens,
Que auques mata les crestïens
Par lor peché e alenti,
Quar Damnedeus li concenti.
Mes je ne vueil ore plus dire,
Quar n'atient pas a [ma] matire.
Ains parlerai de Sardenai [f. 229r]
Si com en l'estoire trovai.
Moines i a si co[m] moi senble,

and beseech Our Lord the true Father and his holy mother, that through her worthy power God grant him health in his eye. When he had ended his prayer, bowed down and blindly feeling his way along, the icon was not slow to respond: when the sultan looked heavenward he saw a burning lamp, and he then recovered his sight.

True faith is a great thing: for he who formerly believed in a false religion immediately received health because he believed. The sultan experienced the power of faith when he recovered his sight: God also cured the various illnesses of many people present there with their ruler. The sultan then stated what he truly knew: the holy woman in whose honour both great and small were healed has great power. And because the burning lamp was what he saw first with his healed eyes, he vowed that during all his lifetime, he would send aid to the church: he would send sixty full measures of oil each year to Sardenai. History relates that the sultan and those who came after him kept this vow, and until the time of Nur-ad-Din, the Saracens faithfully sent this yearly tribute to the holy church at Sardenai. But the vow later was forgotten when Saladin gained power: no-one, neither young nor old, dared oppose the sultan who halted, and for a period, defeated the Christians, which God permitted because of their sin. But I do not want to speak longer about this, for it is not relevant to my story. Instead, I will speak of Sardenai, as I find it in my source. There were monks established there,

E nonains, mes non sont enssemble,
Quar a une part de l'iglise
Font li moines grec lor servise,
E d'autre part les nonains sunt
Qui del leu la seignorie ont.
E por ice raisons lor done
Que lor ancestre si fu none
Qui primes mist a l'ermitage,
Par qui eles orent l'ymage.
Por ce la seignorie en tienent.
Chascun jor miracles avienent
En l'enor de la sainte dame
Par qui est sauvee mainte arme:
Il s'est fait por sa sainte mere,
Li Fis, li Sirë, e li Pere
Qui vit e regne e regnera, [f. 229^{v}]
A qui parfaite amor sera,
Per seculorum secula. Amen

I believe, and nuns as well, but they did not live together, for in one part of the church the Greek monks perform their service, and the nuns who have the rule of the site are in the other part. It is right that the women have authority, for their ancestor was the nun who first lived in the hermitage, and through whom they received this icon. For this reason they have authority, and miracles are effected every day in honour of the holy lady through whom many a soul is saved. And this is accomplished for his holy mother by the Son, the Lord, our Father, who lives and reigns now and will reign, in whom love will be perfected, world without end. Amen.

Notes

Rejected readings have been emended following one, or all, of MSS LOC.

2 **com** MS *come.*

2 **vint** MS C has *vi* 'I saw', but *vint* can be short for *avint* 'happened', making the line 'and as happened, according to authoritative sources'.

5 **ma dame sainte Marie** Here we keep the singular form, 'my lady St Mary', but elsewhere (69, 119) the English plural 'Our Lady St Mary' seems a more accurate translation.

14–15 **sainte terre de Surie, vers Domas** Syria and Damascus were part of the Holy Land (taken in 1071 by the Seljuk Turks from the caliphs of Egypt), which the first crusade (1096–9) attempted to recapture. After the crusaders took Jerusalem in 1099 they established the Kingdom of Jerusalem, with dependent vassal states as far north as Edessa and Antioch. The re-capture of Edessa in 1144 by the emir of Mosul led to the second crusade (1147–9); part of this crusade was the unsuccessful Christian siege of Damascus (1148).

21 **sité**: the scribe frequently uses *s* for *c*: see also *sité=cité* 62; *se=ce* 23, 58, 88, 111; *sesser=cesser* 25; *sil=cil* 42, 158; *sil qui=cil qui* 140; *sel=cel* 102, 157; *sele=cele* 161. Conversely, the scribe sometimes uses *c* for *s*: *çoe=soe* 37, *pencez=pensees* 38.

56 **quist** MS *qui.*

58 **Aveuc** MS *E aveuc.*

63 **vout** MS *voleit.*

64 **parler** MS *aparler.*

70 **En table painte e establie**: 'made and painted on a wooden panel'; this is literally a wooden board, or tablet, on which the icon is painted.

73–8 Lacuna in T: the text here is from L.

74 **ses** MS *sa.*

85–6 These lines are found only in L.

86 **e en sanc** MS *e sanc.*

89 **del Tenple fu chappelains:** the religious order known as the Templars (*Pauperes commilitones Christi Templique Solomonici*: 'Poor Fellow-Soldiers of Christ and of the Temple of Solomon') was established *c.* 1120 under Baldwin II, king of Jerusalem, and confirmed by the Council of Troyes in 1128. The order was given space for its headquarters in the royal palace, built on what was thought to be the site of Solomon's Temple, on Temple Mount, and were known as the 'Ordre du Temple'. Their role was to protect pilgrims to Jerusalem crossing through parts of Outremer which were not held by the crusaders. Templars were exempt from local laws, allowing them to cross borders without taxes. They created a system of letters of credit, whereby pilgrims would deposit their money with Templars in the West, and redeem their wealth from Templars in the East, reducing the threat of bandits for travellers. In doing this, the Templars effectively created the first banking system and became increasingly influential in the Western economy. Their wealth led to their downfall: in 1307–12 Philip IV of France, to free himself from the enormous debts he owed the Templars, successfully arranged for the order to be tried and condemned for heresy and disbanded.

96 **en grant cuivre** The variants suggest that this passage is obscurely understood by the scribes. Raynaud 1882, 537 glosses as 'en grand souci' (an unusual sense). CO have *en(z) grant cur(r)e*, 'in a great hurry', but *curre* is a faulty rhyme with *cuivre* C, *cuvre* O. L changes both lines 95–6: . . . *en un vessel de marbre. / Li moine i sunt bien recevable* (marble vessel . . . very welcoming), although this meaning of *recevable* is unusual.

99 **c'est** MS *se est.*

100 **o li** MS *e li.*

101 **Si [s'en] vont:** *s'en* is missing in all the MSS.

104 **la terre** MS *la leur terre.*

122 **por** MS *par.*

123 **del miracle** MS *des miracles.*

134 **orbetes** Raynaud 1882, 537 glosses *a orbetés* 'dans l'aveuglement, à tâtons'. We take it as a spelling of *orbite* (<*orbita*), orbit. The line states that the bent-over sultan was moving around blindly in circles.

136–7 **vers le siel garda . . . une lampe** The Latin (Devos 1947, 256) indicates that the sultan looked upward after his prayer, and saw a lamp burning on an altar in front of the image of the Virgin: *Surgens ab oratione vidit ignem ardentem in lampade que ante Dei genitricis imaginem posita erat* (Rising up from his prayer he saw a flame burning in the lamp which was placed before the image of the mother of God). In failing to include this detail, the French text remains ambiguous.

145 **ot** MS *i ot.*

151–2 **que primes avoit / Veü la lampe** Because the lamp illuminating the icon was the first thing the sultan saw with his recovered sight, he vows to provide oil to keep the lamp burning at the shrine throughout his lifetime.

159 **Noradin** Nur-ad-Din (1118–74) first became ruler of the northern Syrian city of Aleppo (1146), then gained control of Damascus (1156), unifying his rule of Syria. He was active against the crusaders throughout his reign – he besieged the Templars at Bania in 1157, for example.

163 **Salehadin** The extra syllable in *Salehadin* makes this line octosyllabic. This is, in fact, a more accurate transliteration of the Arabic name, Salah-ad-Din, than the usual western form, *Saladin*, found in LC (making the line heptasyllabic); O also has *Saladin*, but adds *Kar* at the start of the line to make an octosyllable. Saladin or Salah-ad-Din (1137/38–1193), a Kurdish Muslim, was initially a military leader under Nur-ad-Din, whom he later defied, to become ruler of Egypt, then succeeded as ruler of Syria, reigning 1174–93. Saladin was the first to be sultan of both Egypt and Syria, and

he extended his rule into Mesopotamia. He unified the Muslim opposition to the crusaders in Outremer. Saladin took Jerusalem from the crusaders in 1187.

166–8 **mata les crestïens . . . li concenti** is a reference, presumably, to the failure of the third crusade (1189–92), the West's attempt to recapture Jerusalem. A truce in 1192 between Saladin and Richard Lionheart left Jerusalem in Muslim control but allowed Christian pilgrims access to the holy sites, but the Latin kingdom of the crusaders was reduced to a strip of land along the coast from Tyre to Jaffa.

169–70 **Mes je ne vueil . . . [ma] matire** A standard *occupatio* formula (here used to relegate the fall of Jerusalem and to revert to Sardenai).

176 **moines grec** Cf. the reading of O (*moine gent*: the monks, those who were monks). Although here and at v. 96 the narrator refers to Greek monks – as noted above, the Christians at Sardenai spoke Arabic.

177 **d'autre** MS *del autre.*

179–83 **E por ice . . . Por ce la seignorie en tienent** This careful explanation of the nuns' authority perhaps owes something to the ambivalence with which the double monasteries of the twelfth century, such as the Gilbertines in England or Robert d'Arbrissel's Fontevrauld in Anjou had been initially regarded.

184 **miracles avienent** MS *miracles i avienent.*

185 **En** MS *E en.*

35. Jean de Mandeville [?], *Le Livre des merveilles du monde* (Mandeville's Travels) [Dean 341], Epilogue: Oxford, Bodleian Library, MS Ashmole 1804, f. 42*rb*–42*va*

Date of composition and provenance. Most likely composed in 1356 or 1357, in England or France.

Author, sources and nature of text. In the exordium to the *Livre*, the author introduces himself as *Jeo Johan Maundeville chivaler* (I, John Mandeville, knight), born and raised in England, in the city of St Albans (Deluz 2000, 92). He says that he left England in 1322 and travelled for 35 years, and when he became old and arthritic and was forced to stay at home, he composed his travel book from memory. Important parts of this biography – the name Jean de Mandeville and the claim to have travelled – are thought to be largely fictional. No satisfactory historical author has been found and there is disagreement over whether Mandeville lived in England or on the Continent, and whether the *Livre* was first composed in Insular or Continental French. A manuscript discovery supports insular composition (M. J. Bennett 2006). Mandeville's use of nearly three dozen sources (travel and religious writings, histories, encyclopedias, and literary works seen as historical) suggests access to a large and well stocked library, perhaps a wealthy French monastery or St Albans Abbey (if Mandeville was associated with St Albans, his *Livre* may have been borrowing prestige from or paying tribute to the thirteenth-century monk Matthew Paris, whose *Chronica maiora* and maps of Palestine were created there). Whatever the author's identity or location, it is clear that his narrator is meant to be identified as an Englishman, but one who is French-speaking.

The *Livre* is thoroughly a product of the transregional French vernacular culture from which it sprang and which it in turn furthered, and also a striking example of textual *mouvance*, or *variance*. It survives in three versions, continental (31 manuscripts), insular (23–5 manuscripts), and the Liège, or Ogier version (7 manuscripts). The fact of composition in French and the author's reliance on French sources is conspicuously imbricated in the building of a francophone textual community with a shared Christianising and universalising vision. In his prologue, Mandeville explains that he writes in *romancz* so as to be understood by knights, lords, and other noblemen, whom he invites to supply whatever he may have forgotten (Deluz 2000, 93); this transforms the *Livre* from an 'act of individual memory' into a work that creates collective memory, 'requiring circulation, use, and even emendation to acquire its authority' (Higgins 1997, 55). Mandeville's principal source was the *Livre des Merveilles* by Jan de Langhe (Jean le Long) of Ypres, a monk of St Bertin in St Omer, which contained some of de Langhe's own French translations of William of Boldensele's *Liber de quibusdam ultramarinis partibus* (*Book of Certain Overseas Regions*, 1336, an account of its author's trip to Egypt and the Holy Land), Odoric of Pordenone's *Relatio* (1330, a report of ten years spent as a missionary in India and China), and the *Flor des Estoires de la terre d'Orient* (1307, *Flower of the Histories of the Orient*) by the Armenian monk and noble Hayton. Mandeville thus joins Jan de Langhe and other notable translators and compilers, such as Brunetto Latini and John Trevisa, and authors such as Philippe de Mézières, Christine de Pizan, and John Gower, in purposefully advancing vernacular lay culture.

Mandeville's claim to knighthood, whether true or not, places him among the privileged group tasked with ruling and defending the Christian community; Mandeville's writing hopes to extend that community eastward. To that end, the *Livre* brings together the biblical and the 'marvellous East' in two parts. The first, just under half the book, talks about the Holy Land and the Near East; the second recounts a journey through Turkey, Armenia, Tartary, Persia, Syria, Arabia, Egypt, Libya, Chaldea, Ethiopia, Amazonia, the islands around India, and Cathay (China). Mandeville urges his Christian readers towards better behaviour: the vision of universal dominion for Christianity was realisable if Christians would improve their ways. Conversion required tolerance, and Mandeville's is often mentioned in modern criticism; of all peoples, only the Jews, who had rejected Christ and resisted conversion were not welcome.

In making the claim that he is writing his *Livre* as a first-person, eye-witness account, Mandeville implicitly breaks with the medieval tradition of invoking written sources, especially Latin ones, as guarantors of truth. His ostensible rejection of the represented and the already written is equally a move away from the past, into the future and an earthly beyond, signalled in the epilogue below when the author points to future memories, those to be supplied by younger adventurers, and, repeatedly, to what is *par dela* (out there).

Audience and circulation. Nearly 300 manuscripts of Mandeville's *Livre* are extant: the work was extremely popular both in the Middle Ages and later. Monasteries, especially perhaps St Albans, played a role in the translation and diffusion of the *Livre*: it was rapidly translated into many other languages. Christine de Pizan consulted it for her *Chemin de longue étude*. Valentina Visconti, wife of King Charles V's younger brother Louis, duke of Orleans, owned a French copy of 1388, probably made in Italy from Michael Walser's German version (Higgins 2011, 6 n. 14; Morrall 1968, 185). King Charles VI borrowed the book from the Louvre library in 1392; his daughter, Isabella of Valois, second wife of Richard II of England, owned her own copy, as did the French poet Charles d'Orléans. By the early fifteenth century the bourgeoisie owned copies of the *Livre* (Deluz 1993, xvi). Columbus used it (Flint 1992; Greenblatt 1991, 26, 156–7 n. 1). Menocchio, an unlucky sixteenth-century Italian peasant, read a vernacular translation and was tried twice for heresy (Ginzburg 1980). The insular version is the ultimate source for an early and large series of translations into English and Latin (Deluz 1988, 26–7).

Manuscript source. Oxford, Bodleian Library, MS Ashmole 1804, produced 1400–50. The manuscript is comprised of 104 folios, 298 × 196 mm; two-columns, vellum; the hand is English, with chapter titles in red; initials in blue. The manuscript contains Mandeville, ff. 1–42^{v}; *Prophecies of John of Bridlington*, ff. 42^{v}–46^{v}; ff. 47–8 blank; a prose Albina story (Dean 41, Marvin 2001), ff. 49^{r-va}; *Le Cronique nommee le Brut* (Dean 46), ff. 49^{v}–end (stopping at the reign of Edward III). Ashmole 1804 ends with a dedication to King Edward III in Latin, rubricated in French as follows: *La copie de la lettre mande ovesque cest escript a tres noble prince monsire Edward de Wyndesore Roy dengleterre et de france par monsire John de Maundevill auctor suisdit* (Copy of the letter sent with this writing to the very noble prince, Edward of Windsor, king of England and France, by Sir John of Mandeville, the abovesaid author, f. 42v). The letter is found in a number of Mandeville manuscripts.

Bibliography. The *Livre* is edited in Deluz 2000; Deluz 1988 is a full study of Mandeville's geography, cultural and topographical. For Mandeville's sources, manuscripts and editions, see J. W. Bennett 1954; Deluz 1988, 39–58; Deluz 2000, 428–91. For medieval translations of the *Livre* see the important study by Higgins (1997, 2–23). On insular or continental authorship, see M. J. Bennett 2006 and Deluz 2000: on the first datable manuscript of the *Livre*, see Letts 1953. On Mandeville's audiences see Tzanaki 2003 and on his European reception, Bremer and Röhl 2007. For a review of scholars' interpretations of Mandeville's identity, see Deluz 1988, 3–24: Mandeville's possible identity as Jan de Langhe of St Bertin is discussed by Larner 2008 and Seymour 2007. On Mandeville's attitude towards the Jews see Braude 1996; Higgins 1997, 41–2 and Index 324; Greenblatt 1991, 50–1; for tolerance and intolerance in Mandeville, see Akbari 2004; Greenblatt 1991, 26–51. Higgins 2011 translates the early (continental) French text and Bale 2012 a Middle English one. Deluz, trans., 1993, is a modern French translation.

TEXT AND TRANSLATION

[f. 42rb] Il y a plusours autres diverses pays et multz d'autres merveilles par dela qe jeo n'ay mye tut veu, si n'en saveroie proprement parler. Et meisment el pays en quel j'ay esté y a plusurs diversités dont jeo ne face point de mençoun quar trop seroit long chose a tot deviser; et pur ceo qe jeo vous ay devisé d'ascuns pais vous deit soesfire quant a present. Quar si jeo devisoie tut quanqe y est par dela, un autre qe se peneroit et travailleroit le corps pur aler en celles marches et pur cerchier le pays seroit enpeschiez par mes ditz a recompter nuls choses estraunges qar il ne purroit rien dire de novelle en quoy ly oïantz y puissent prendre solatz. Et l'en dit totditz qe choses novelles pleisent, si m'en taceray ataunt sanz plus recompter nulz diversitees qe soient par dela a la fyn qe cys qe vourra aler en celles parties y trove assetz a dire.

There are many and varied other countries, and a multitude of other wonders out there, not all of which I've seen, and so I cannot rightfully talk about them. And even in the countries where I've been, there are many unusual things I should not mention, for describing them all would be a lengthy business. I have told you about some countries, and that must satisfy you for the present. For were I to describe everything out there, another person, who might give himself pain and cause his body hardship in order to reach those border places and explore the country, would be prevented by my stories from recounting anything wondrous, for he could not say anything new in which listeners might take pleasure. And since it is always said that new things please, I shall stop at that, without further reporting on anything unusual that may be out there, so that those who wish to go to those places may find enough to say.

Et jeo John [f. 42v] Maundevill desusdit qi m'en party de noz pais et passay la meer l'an du grace .mil.ccc.xxii. deqi meinte terre et meinte passage et meinte pays ay puis

And I, the abovesaid John Mandeville, who left our lands and crossed the sea in the year of grace 1322, and then searched many a land and many a sea passage and many a region;

cerchiez et qe ay esté en meinte compaignie et meint bele fait, come bien qe jeo ne feusse unqes, ne beal fait ne bele emprise. Et qi meintenaunt suy venu a repos maugré mien pur goutes artetiles qe moy destreignent. Empreignant en moun chetif repos en recordaunt le temps passé ay cestes choses compilés et mises en escript, si come il moy poait sovenir l'an de grace .mil.ccc.lvie., a xxxiiii^{te}. an qe jeo m'en partay de noz pays. Si prie a toutz les lisantz si lour plest q'ils veullent prier pur moy et jeo priera[i] pur eux. Et toutz cils qi pur moy dirront un *Pater noster* qe Dieu me face remissioun de mes pecchés, jeo les face parcenurs et lour ottroie part de toutz les bons pilgrimages et de touz les bienfaits qe jeo feisse unqes et qe jeo ferray, si Dieu plest, unqore jusqes a ma fyn. Et prie a Dieu de qi tout bien et tout grace descent qe il touts les lisantz et oïantz christens voille de sa grace reempler et lour corps et les almes salver a la gloire et loenge de luy qe est trinz et unz, saunz comencement et sanz fyn, sanz qualité bons, sanz qantité grauntz, en toutz lieux present et toutz choses continant, et qi nul bien poet ne amender ne nul male enpirer, qi en trinité parfet vit et regne par totz siecles et par totz temps.

Amen.

and who have been in many a company and present at many a worthy deed, even though I myself have never undertaken a noble feat or a noble enterprise; and who have now come to a state of inactivity in spite of myself, because of my arthritic gout, which handicaps me; I, finding comfort in my wretched repose by recording time past, have compiled these things and set them in writing, as I remember, in this year of grace, in the thirty-fourth year after I left our land. I beseech all those listening, if they please, to pray for me, and I shall pray for them. And for all those who will say a *Pater noster* for me, so that God may give me pardon for my sins, I make them my partners and grant them a portion of every good pilgrimage and of all the profits that I have ever earned and will ever earn, should it please God, until I die. And I pray to God, from whom comes every good and every grace, that he fill all Christian readers and listeners with his grace and save their souls to the glory and praise of him who is three and one, without a beginning and without an end, good without measure, whose greatness cannot be quantified, present in all places and containing all places, and whom no good thing can improve upon or any evil worsen, who lives in perfect trinity and reigns in all the world and in all time. Amen.

Notes

1–2 **diverses . . . merveilles; 5 diversités; 14 choses estraunges; 15 novelle; 18 diversitees** This piling up of a vocabulary for what is strikingly different is, in Higgins's view, a 'defamiliarisation' that serves the purpose of 'instructing, chastising, challenging and consoling' readers, while also 'entertaining and diverting them' (Higgins 1997, 267).

3–4 **jeo n'ay mye tut veu, si n'en saveroie proprement parler** A re-affirmation of Mandeville's eye-witnessing and its truth value.

16 **solatz** A multivalent word connoting comfort and solace; ease; pleasure, recreation; see Glossary and Olson 1982.

23 **deqi** Probably *deci*, 'until', though perhaps intended for *deqe* (= *desque*).

29 **artetiles** Arthritic: in various manuscripts, *artetikes*, *artecles*, and other spellings, frequently with k or c in the final syllable.

33 **sovenir**: the use of this verb rounds out Mandeville's invitation, in the prologue, to his special

group of readers, knights and other elite Christians who have been *outre mer* (beyond the [Mediterranean] sea) to correct any errors caused by memory lapse, 'for things seen long ago are forgotten, and human memory cannot retain or understand everything' (Deluz 2000, 93). For the importance of memory in medieval culture, see Carruthers 2008.

40 **pilgrimages** Readers have of course already shared Mandeville's pilgrimage vicariously, and they have been allowed to visualise pilgrimage sights with the mind's eye; see Higgins 1997, 93.

44–5 **lisantz et oïantz christens** Once more, Mandeville's inviting and inclusive embrace of his audience builds a specifically Christian community.

48–9 **sanz qualité bons, sanz qantité grauntz** Cf. St Anselm of Bec, bishop of Canterbury, *Meditatio* XIV, *PL* 158.780B: *Magnus es sine quantitate, et ideo immensus. Bonus sine qualitate, et ideo vere et summe bonus; et nemo bonus nisi tu solus.* (You are great without measure and immeasurable, good without measure and truly and supremely good: and no-one is good except you alone: cf. Luke 18.19).

36. *Coment la Mesun de Crabhus comencerunt* [not in Dean], London, British Library, MS Add. 4733 Vol. I, ff. 1r–2r

Rebecca June

Date of composition and provenance. Thirteenth? (Davis 1958), fourteenth and fifteenth centuries (Davis 2010); Wiggenhall parish, western Norfolk.

Author, sources and nature of text. *Once there was a maiden whose heart the Holy Spirit moved to seek a deserted spot* . . . The Crabhouse manuscript combines verse and a fairytale-like narrative of the nunnery's foundation for the unexpected opening to its collection of charters, land records and historical documents. Author(s) unknown, the manuscript is not included in Dean, and while Bateson (1892) refers to it as a *Register*, Davis (1958) lists it in the category *Other Registers Etc.*, in the pejorative sense that it was 'at some point wrongly described' as a cartulary (xii; the revised edition, 2010, includes Crabhouse with *Cartularies of Religious Houses*). As manuscripts containing copies of charters granting property and baronial privileges, cartularies and registers are quite similar to one another. For diplomatists, they can be distinguished by intended use and ownership, with registers compiled for grantors of properties or privileges, and cartularies for the grantees. This distinction breaks down in the labelling of individual manuscripts, however, as is apparent in Davis's own association of the Crabhouse document with what he calls 'chronicle-cartularies', those written in narrative form and intended for the 'general instruction' of a house's members (xii).

According to Davis, a cartulary's primary purpose is as a reference tool, but such a description fails to explain why cartularies omit some charters and include others, why they are ordered in particular fashions (not typically by chronology as one would expect), and why some include literary elements as does the Crabhouse manuscript. Bedos-Rezak (2002, 56–9) argues that cartularies were not meant to produce utilitarian copies of legal documents in order to organise and secure a house's claims; rather, cartularies construct original texts through 're-enactment'. For modern readers, cartulary re-enactments can be frustrating in their reshuffling of events and notorious lack of dates, but Bouchard (2002, 31) sees this reordering as 'deliberately [taking] the charters out of time'. Thus, the convoluted chronology of events in the Crabhouse foundation narrative, along with its formulaic beginning and verse form (sometimes viewed as charming but less than appropriately serious) may not signal an ignorance of documentary practice, but a desire to transform the community's archives into a coherent history – a task common to the chronicle, saint's life and even romance.

Whether cartulary or register, the Crabhouse manuscript creates an identity for the nunnery in its presentation of the community's foundation and history. Like the solitary maiden credited with founding Crabhouse, many nunneries – especially in East Anglia – were founded by or around an anchoress. Despite the large number of female houses and anchoresses, however (Gilchrist and Oliva count 73 anchoresses in the Norfolk diocese compared to only 32 male recluses; 1993, 77), very few cartularies and registers exist as witnesses of their histories (Thompson 1984, 132). Even fewer recluses are the subject of written histories, with Christina of Markyate's *Vita* the only female example. With conditions unfavourable for keeping extensive records (see n. to lines *5–12* below), a nunnery such as Crabhouse that kept a cartulary may have viewed that compilation as an opportunity to invent a more comprehensive textual identity for itself by adapting the standard legal documentary form to one that is sometimes more like a chronicle and at other times more like a saint's life. Furthermore, as the community's identity and needs changed over time, the same document could be adapted to fit those needs. This can be seen in the Crabhouse manuscript when a thorough and flattering record of Joan Wiggenhall's accomplishments as a fifteenth-century prioress is added to the already existing foundation legend and cartulary, aligning Joan with the nameless foundress and transforming the entire manuscript into a document leaning towards hagiography. The author of Joan's brief 'vita' is able to create a coherent account out of the works she undertook and the other documents in part because, more than introducing a list of legal claims, the manuscript's opening folios establish the community's identity in connection with its spiritual legacy, one earned through persevering to overcome natural, human, and diabolical adversity (see June 2009 and n. to line 20 below).

Audience and circulation. The Crabhouse author professes difficulty in sustaining a text in *rym*, and justifies writing in prose by stating that composing 'otherwise' (*altrement*) will allow the text to be understood *apertement*, meaning clearly or publicly (vv. 31–2). In using the word *apertement*, the author repeats an earlier stated desire for a wide audience: lords and ladies, old and young, free and bound, all who wish to hear and understand (vv. 7–9). The stated wish for a large audience must be weighed against the choice of French as the text's language, however, for English would have been the most accessible language in the region and time of the Crabhouse manuscript's production. The most common language employed for cartularies written in the thirteenth and fourteenth centuries was Latin, and it is likely that the women of Crabhouse could have had their cartulary and foundation narrative composed in that language, as evidenced by the use of Latin for a large portion of the manuscript written at a later date. Book clasps found at the Crabhouse site, records showing that the nuns owned two expensive antiphons, and figures of women reading in the iconography of a related parish church all indicate that the women of Crabhouse valued literacy, had some Latin liturgical books, and deliberately chose to record their history in the vernacular (Gilchrist 1995, 114; Oliva 1998, 65; Thompson 1991, 24).

The choice of French over Latin and English may be linked to the verse and legend-like literary forms of the text's opening folios. Verse had ceremonial functions in the Middle Ages and was employed in public ceremonies (Stevens 1979). Indeed, following the verse opening of the Crabhouse manuscript, two later entries also employ verse beginnings to create a sense of importance for the prose to follow – in one case for a donor who is to be held *devaunt tote gent ke unkes furunt fundours de ceo mesun* (before all those who ever were founders of this house) and in the other case as the introduction to a short discourse on the importance of securing one's assets in defense of difficulties (Bateson 1892, 37–8). Verse thus calls attention to what follows in the same way that a procession calls attention to a visiting dignitary.

Visiting dignitaries to medieval towns were also honoured through public readings of town charters – typically written in or translated into French, and civic organisations such as guilds read their foundational charters aloud during ceremonies for the installation of new leaders, creating a sense of collective identity through textual performance (Bedos-Rezak 1994, 40–1; Britnell 2009). Similarly, foundation charters were exhibited during ecclesiastical visitations of female houses (N.

Warren 2001, 14) and may have been read when new nuns entered a community. The Crabhouse manuscript's use of vernacular and literary form may thus indicate the community's familiarity with public ceremonial practices and a willingness to adopt those practices for the purpose of establishing their own collective identity. In this way, manuscripts such as the Crabhouse register, rather than exposing female illiteracy, demonstrate that the women were actually 'more up to date' than their male counterparts who stuck with the conventions of their 'conservative and traditional education' (Bell 1995, 77).

Manuscript source. BL Add. 4733 Vol. I is a small quarto vellum book in various, mostly informal hands; ff. 1^r–2^r are written in a neat, formal hand with rubricated initials, possibly as a presentation copy. Contents of Vol. I: f. i, Memorandum of wedding for Margaret Kervile and Thomas Hunston held at Crabhouse in 1476, English; f. ii, note of manuscript donation to BL by the Reverend Henry Robinson, Rector of Watlington, June 29, 1765; ff. 1–35, foundation legend and notes of early gifts, fees, etc., French and Latin; ff. 36–49, Terrarium (an inventory of property), with an introduction in neat, formal hand dedicated to Joan Wiggenhall, Latin; ff. 50^v–53, works under prioress Joan Wiggenhall 1420–44 – the hand matches Terrarium introduction; incomplete, English. Vol. II, ff. 55–64, contains *The survey of the late priory of Crabhouse and Westdereham*, made upon dissolution for Sir Edward Gage, 1556/7; English, written on paper. The manuscript may have been owned by antiquarian and author Sir Henry Spelman at one time (Bateson 1892, 2 and 14 note 1).

Bibliography. The only edition is Bateson (1892), which contains all but the fifteen Terrarium folios with accompanying introduction, index of names, and short glossary. On regional patronage, see Duffy 1997 and Thompson 1991, and for connections between nunnery location, architecture, living conditions and female piety, Gilchrist 1994 and 1995. Patronage, population, economic and physical conditions at Crabhouse and surrounding houses are discussed in Gilchrist and Oliva 1993; Oliva 1998. For connections with East Anglian eremetic tradition, see Coletti 2004. Although listed as a cartulary in Davis 1958 (rev. Breay 2010), Crabhouse has not been studied in relation to other cartularies, particularly those of nunneries. For an important parallel use of French at Godstow nunnery, see Amt 2012. On the cartulary as genre, see Bedos-Rezak 2002, Bouchard 2002, and Le Blévec 2006. N. Warren 2001, Bedos-Rezak 1994, and Stevens 1979 discuss textual identity and performance. On the creation of female memory and community through the retelling of foundation narratives, see June 2009.

TEXT AND TRANSLATION

Assit principio sancta Maria meo. [f. 1^r]

Jesu le Rey omnipotent
Seyt a ceste commencement,
Ke nasquyt de la virgine Marie
Et suffrit mort pur nus mener a vie,
Par ki totes choces sunt
Et ja furunt et serunt.
Seniurs et dames, veus et jones,
Francs et serfs et totes en communes
Ke voliunt oyer et entendre,
En cest escrit pount aprendre
Coment la mesun de Crabhus
Et de totes les fez et lus
Comencerunt, ke uncore sunt:

Aid my beginning, holy Mary.

May Jesus the all-mighty king be with this beginning, he who was born of the Virgin Mary and suffered death to lead us to life, through whom all things are and ever were and will be.

Lords and ladies, old and young, free and bound, and all in common who wish to hear and understand, in this book can learn how the house of Crabhouse and all its holdings and properties began and still remain: about donors who gave, and about lands and holdings, about rents and feoffments which

E de donurs ke donerunt,
E de terres et tenemens,
De rentes et de feffemens,
Ke a l'avauntdit Mesun parteynunt,
Coment et de queus don esteyunt.
Les uns don, les uns achat,
E mult diversement purchat.

pertained to the aforesaid house, how and by whom they were given, some donated, others bought and variously procured.

E pur ceo ke diversét est,
E la gent ci todis a mal atrest
Par coveyteyse ke lur destreyt
De tollir Seynt' Eglise sun dreyt,
Bon est tel ensurté fere,
Ke Seint Eglise deboneyre
Ne perde sa fraunchice avaunt euue,
Eyns le sustent et de plus seyt encrue.
Gref choce sereyt en rym poser;
Eynz serra pur moy mut aleger,
Esdira tut altrement,
Pur entendre apertement.

And because it is changed and the people here are always drawn to evil deeds through a covetousness that compels them to take from holy church her due, it is good to create such assurance as keeps blessed holy church from losing her previously held franchise, but rather sustains and enlarges it. It would be a difficult task to put it all in rhyme; instead, it will be expressed by me in a different, simpler fashion, so that it may be clearly understood.

[f. 1v] Jadis esteyt une pucele, le quer de ki li Seynt Espirit mova de quere lu de deserte, ou ele poeyt servir Deu saunz desturbaunce de terriene choce; si trova cest lu ke ore est apelee Crabhus, tut savagine et de graunt partie envirun de totes pars n'esteyt habitaciun de home, et unkore en les jours ke ore sunt si sunt acune gent ne mie de sessaunte anz, ke diunt ke lur peres lur desoyunt ke il poeyunt penser ke la ne fut nul mesun estaunt ne terre sayne ne habité de cest part Bustardesdole. Cele pucele avaunt dite trova cel lu a sun pleyser, si assembla oweske li altres puceles et se firunt aparalier une chapele en le honouraunce de Deu et sa chere mere et virgine Marie et Seyn Johan li Ewangelist: en quel lu meynt jour Deu servirunt. Mes li diable ki ne fine de abesser touz bons overaynes mist en le quers de ceus ke esteyunt ces ministres les avaunt dites puceles rober, ke issi feseyunt par quey le lu dekerpirunt ke ore est apelé en engleys le Gavelcroft; si firunt lur habitacion juste la rive ke uncore est, et pur estre le plus certeyn de aver lur lu et lur habitacion en pays, si lur firunt un chef

Once there was a maiden whose heart was moved by the Holy Spirit to seek a deserted spot where she could serve God without disturbance from anything worldly; and she found this place, which is now called Crabhouse, all completely wild and without human habitation for a large part of the region, in every direction; and even nowadays some people who are less than sixty years of age say their fathers told them they could remember when there was no house standing, nor reclaimed or inhabited land, on this side of Bustard's Dole. The aforesaid maiden found the place to her liking, so she gathered with her other maidens, and they had a chapel built in honour of God and his dear mother and virgin Mary and St John the Evangelist: in that place they served God many days. But the devil, who never ceases to detract from all good works, planted in the hearts of his servants the idea of robbing the religious women, and they did it successfully, so that the women abandoned the place which now is called in English Gavelcroft. So they made their dwelling place beside the river, which still exists; and seniur de ki il le poeyunt tener pur annual rente et de ki il poyeunt estre defendu et warrant; ke uncore dure.

to be more certain of possessing their place and their dwelling in peace, they appointed themselves an immediate lord upon whom they could depend in exchange for an annual rent and by whom they could be defended and guaranteed; this still endures.

Meynt an après si vinc une crestine de ewe ke surmunta lur habitacion [f. 2r] par quoy il se departirunt et n'ent plus repeyrerunt et coment ne ou enaprès vesquirunt n'ay entendu, fors soulement de l'une ke se fit recluse en le cymeterie de la Marie Magdaleyne de Wigenhale la quele out les monumenz de le avaunt dite lu de Crabhus, les queus ou en sa vie ou enaprès sun morir, furunt enport a la mesun de Chastelacre ou uncore sunt. Après ke le avaunt dite crestine de euwe esteyt chayue, li seniur ke il visent fet del tenement del avaunt dit lu de Crabhus si entra cum en sun achete, et li tint ben lung tens, si ke ataunt ke il le dona cum en mariage owoc sa sorur a un ke esteyt apelé Aylmer Kok le chapeleyn de Crabhus. Li noun de le seniur esteyt apelé Aleyn le fiz Richard de le paroz Nostre Dame de Wigenhale, en engleys Moder Cristes; sa sorur ke issi esteyt dou fut apelee Agneys, et de cest doun illia une chartre laquele pot tesmonier cele choce pur une certeyn rente de deus souz, ke uncore est don a deus termes par an. Cil avaunt dit Aylmer et Agneys donerunt demi le armitorie del avaunt dit lu de Crabhus owoc tote la demi terre plus pres la chapele a Roger le chanun et a touz ke serverunt Deu en meyme le lu en habit de chanoyne, pur duze deners par an de rendre a li et a ces heyrs, et de ceo il i a une chartre.

Many years later cresting flood waters inundated their dwellings, because of which they left and never again returned, and how and where they lived afterward I have not discovered, except for only one, who became a recluse in the cemetery of Mary Magdalene of Wiggenhall; and who kept the muniments of the aforesaid Crabhouse, which either in her lifetime or after her death were taken to the house at Castle Acre, where they are still. After the aforesaid flood waters had subsided, the lord whom they had chosen had the property of the aforesaid Crabhouse recorded as if it belonged to him, and he held it for himself for a long time, until he gave it in marriage, together with his sister, to a man called Aylmer Kok, the chaplain of Crabhouse. The lord was named Alan FitzRichard of the parish Notre Dame of Wiggenhall, in English the Mother of Christ; his sister who was thus gifted was called Agnes, and of this endowment there is a charter which can witness this through a fixed rent of two shillings, which is still paid twice per year. The aforesaid Aylmer and Agnes gave half of the hermitage of the aforesaid place of Crabhouse, with half the land nearest the chapel, to Roger the canon and to all who served God in the same place as canons for twelve deniers per year in rent to him and to his heirs, and for this there is a charter.

Notes

R The Latin incipit appears in the upper left-hand corner of the folio.

1–6 Lines 1–6 are metrically irregular and written together as four lines in the manuscript, ending with the words *commencement*, *suffrit*, *choces*, and *serunt*. Beginning with line 7, the remainder of the verse appears as individually written, rhyming octosyllabic couplets.

8 **et . . . et** Throughout the opening verse and narrative, the Tironian symbol consistently appears for *et*. In this line, however, a different symbol is used – one identified in Cappelli's dictionary of paleography as belonging to the fifteenth century (1990, 408). As yet, no-one has definitively dated the manuscript's opening folios, with suggested dates ranging from the thirteenth to the fifteenth centuries.

8 **totes en communes** Meaning here is ambiguous – *commune* eventually referred to a French governing body (see *OED*, *s.v.* 'commune') which would resonate with the political nature of the text; at the time of composition, however, *commune* indicated a general community or commoners as opposed to the nobility (see *AND*, *s.v.* 'commune'). Considering the disparate groups just listed, *totes en communes* seems to gesture summarily towards a wide and mixed communal audience: 'everyone'.

17 **avauntdit** This term appears repeatedly throughout the register's verse and narrative opening, and, along with numerous other legal terms, serves as a reminder that the author is working from original, authoritative documents. By making reference to other portions of the text, *avauntdit* also emphasises the manuscript's written form.

20 **purchat** MS *purchac* likely a scribal error.

31 **Esdira tut altrement** *AND* has but one example of *esdire*, in the meaning of 'contradict'. Here, *esdire* is simply a variant of *dire* (cf. *AND*, *s.v.* 'desdire').

1 **une pucele** Charters for Castle Acre Priory identify a Leva, daughter of Godric of Lynn, granted a hermitage south of Wiggenhall by William of Lesewis (see Dugdale's *Monasticon Anglicanum* 1846, V.69 and 70, items iv and v; note that *Leva* is incorrectly transcribed as *Lena*). Thompson (1991, 25) questions whether Leva is the maiden identified in the register, though others (e.g., Bateson 1892, 2–3; Oliva 1998, 25) accept the identification. The register's chronology is confusing; Gilchrist and Oliva (1993, 77) offer this history: Leva and her followers occupied the hermitage of Wiggenhall St Mary Magdalen until flooding forced them to leave. One woman, Joanna, remained behind when the others settled at Crabhouse, but the group retained the advowson of the Wiggenhall hermitage.

5–12 Wiggenhall parish, located in the marshy fenlands of western Norfolk, was mostly empty at Crabhouse's foundation, and the nuns' land was not reclaimed until the thirteenth century. Nunneries were often located on properties of poor quality, frequently bounded by water in the form of rivers or moats (Gilchrist 1995, 115–45, 155). These conditions could be thought to reflect the lower value assigned to women's houses or the desire to physically defend their chastity. Alternatively, the location and condition of nunneries – they were rarely afforded the same expenditure as male houses and were often unsanitary – could indicate the female communities' ascetic aspirations (Gilchrist 1994, 67–8, 126, 190).

5 **Crabhus** The area was referred to as Crawow in 1428 and is now known as Crabb's Abbey. Features of an archaeological survey of Crabb Abbey made in 1556 correspond to the register's description of construction at Crabhouse (Crabhouse manuscript vol. II; Gilchrist and Oliva 1993, 85–6).

8–10 **acune gent . . . poeyunt penser** The text later assures us that the house's foundational documents were kept by a recluse and transferred to Castle Acre (lines *34–40*), but here living witnesses take the place of written records. Only seventeen cartularies and registers are known to exist for women's houses due to a variety of impediments (fire, flood, difficulties obtaining chaplains and hiring scribes, and the instability of financing for smaller women's houses, etc.). Additionally, women's houses often developed over many years through a complicated process involving multiple donors and the oversight of various orders or male houses (Thompson 1984). Such a lengthy process could explain the lack of an original foundational document for Crabhouse and the subsequent need to create a story from memory.

20 **ces ministres** Though subsequent lines describe the move to Crabhouse as the result of flooding, this portion of the text introduces a predominant theme of the register: the perpetual struggle between the women and neighboring male religious houses over the rights to property and seigneurial privileges (see n. to lines *26–7*). The pressures of population growth in the eleventh century and the concurrent peak in monastic foundations led to increasing competition in the twelfth and thirteenth centuries for resources, including burial rights, rents, and grants from wealthy patrons (Venarde 1997, 54, 146–7). In the fifteenth century, a scribe added a memorandum to the Crabhouse manuscript's first folio, detailing a conflict with the vicar of St Magdalene over the right to perform marriages within the monastery and consequently reshaping the entire document as a defense against masculine encroachment (see headnote for another, hagiographic re-casting).

24 **juste la rive** Wiggenhall parish is located along the Ouse River which runs through western Norfolk, between Downham and King's Lynn (see n. to lines *5–12*), but the Great Ouse did not follow this course until 1236 when flooding diverted it from a more westerly path through Wisbech. The 1236 flood and change of course may have been the cause of the nuns' departure and subsequent conflicts over property rights (lines *30–61*); told retrospectively, however, the river dwelling and flood become a seamless part of the priory's narrative of tribulation and isolation (thanks to Niall and Grania Haigh of Crabb's Abbey for bringing the river's history to my attention).

26 **pays** This spelling is a variant of both *pais* (country, land) and *pes* (peace) and could be intended to connote both meanings. Bedos-Rezak (2002, 57–9) notes the 'appearance within diplomatic discourse of literary preambles which assert the use of writing as necessary to keep peace and memory . . .'.

26–7 **chef seniur** *AND* notes this as a legal term meaning *immediate lord*, indicating that the women may have wanted someone immediately available to protect their interests, rather than relying on ecclesiastical leaders who could be geographically and temporally unavailable and who often disagreeably intervened in the women's affairs. N. Warren (2001, 64) notes that by the fourteenth and fifteenth centuries women's houses tended to manage their own business rather than having an appointed administrator. The Crabhouse manuscript makes clear that the women have acted independently in hiring their own lord – even if that lord later treated the women's property as his own.

35 **recluse** The recluse Joanna, named in Castle Acre's charters as Johannes (Dugdale 1846, V.69, item 1), is the first of a number of anchorites associated with Crabhouse from the twelfth through the fifteenth centuries (Gilchrist and Oliva 1993, 77 and 99), indicating the continuing value of asceticism and seclusion for the community.

36 **Wigenhale** According to studies of English place names, *Wiggenhall* originates from the personal name *Wicga* and Old English *halh*, meaning a nook or small hollow. Because settlements in Wiggenhall were necessarily built on areas of raised ground, the term may refer to the lowest eminence on which building is possible; 'otherwise, it can only be suggested that *halh* was felt appropriate to the isolated situation of the Wiggenhalls' (Gelling 1984, 102). Thus the regional name further confirms the physical vulnerability of Crabhouse and the women's claim of seeking out a desolate location for their home.

36–49 **Marie Magdaleyne de Wigenhale . . . Nostre Dame de Wigenhale** Housed first at St Mary Magdalene, the nuns later seek help from Alan FitzRichard of St Mary the Virgin, another Wiggenhall parish church connected to Mary Magdalene in its iconography. Rood screens, bench carvings, and stained glass in St Mary the Virgin depict Mary Magdalene and other female saints, suggesting regional interest in contemplative devotion as well as community identification with the women of Crabhouse priory and other anchorholds in the vicinity (Coletti 2004, 58–72).

45–7 **en mariage owoc . . . le chapeleyne** 'Celibacy continued to be more and more enforced upon the English clergy during the next two centuries [following the conquest], but instances of married priests are to be met with in Norfolk as late as the middle of the thirteenth century, and the frequent occurrence of such examples indicates that in East Anglia the general feeling was rather in favour of the married men than the reverse' (Doubleday and Page 1906, 219).

46, 55 **Aylmer Kok, Agneys** Aylmer and his sons are mentioned in subsequent sections of the register. Agneys receives no further mention.

48 **Aleyn le fiz Richard** Pipe rolls during the reign of Henry II indicate that an Alan FitzRichard was living in the years 1179–81 (cited in Thompson 1991, 25). The remainder of the Crabhouse register documents the involvement of numerous individuals from the area, and like the majority of nunneries founded in this time and region, most individual support came from the lower gentry. The text also documents wider community involvement for Crabhouse, however, from sharing its chapel with the parish, to opening its doors to corrodians, guild members and guests, to accommodating burials and at least one wedding. Despite the nuns' wish for isolation, the women and lay community relied upon each other in an exchange of spiritual and physical support.

50 **dou** MS can be read either *dou*, meaning endowed, or *don*, meaning given. The *AND* gives similar meanings for both words, and while the terms are certainly related, the legal implications for property control can be quite different (i.e. is the property given to Agnes or is she given with the property to Aylmer? See n. to lines *46, 55*). The translation *gifted* is meant to retain the text's ambiguity.

59 **serverunt** Translated as *served* to suit the narrative sense, *serverunt* would normally indicate future tense; however, the manuscript's scribe consistently chooses the *–unt* ending where *–ent* would be expected (e.g., line 6 *furunt*, line 13 *comencerunt*, line 14 *donerunt*, etc.), making either reading possible.

Part V. *Si come en latyn trovay escrit*: The Lineage of the Text

Introduction

Latin's pervasive use as an authorising language is clear in our texts, and it is an important 'other' in French texts, as discussed in Part I above (pp. 10–11). Nevertheless, in Part V, as throughout the volume, the diversity with which the question of textual lineage is handled is striking. A number of other languages are invoked as part of textual lineage, including (as discussed above in Part I, pp. 10, 14) English and British. The Greek authorising figures of Aristotle and Alexander are unsurprisingly found in many works with eastward-turning textual communities in Part IV: not only the encyclopaedic romance of the *Roman de toute chevalerie* (**28**), or the *Secré de secrez* (**33**) with its mirror for princes, but (**32a**), a treatise on menstruation, deploy Aristotle. For its defence and prescription of cosmetic remedies, the *Ornatus mulierum* (**32b**) cites a still more complicated textual lineage: the written authority of ancient Greek medicine (Galen, Hippocrates), Latinised Arabic medicine (Constantinus Africanus) and the direct oral teaching of a Saracen woman and that of 'Trota' at Salerno. When Part V's Simund de Freine considers how linguistic diversity limits earthly fame (*Roman de Fortune* (**38**), late twelfth century), he ranges over Lombard, Greek, Hebrew, Latin, Spanish, Danish, Scots and English.[1]

The late twelfth and thirteenth century's intensified attention to the languages of the Mediterranean can be characterised by ambivalence or strategy. For all the power of Aristotle's name, in the late-thirteenth-century pseudo-Aristotelian *Secré de secrez* (**33**.31–6) both Greek and Arabic are treated as unreliable: Arabic is said to be too elaborate and unverifiable as to its truthfulness and Greek too obscure. (Waterford and Copale may not actually have translated from the Arabic or the Greek: these claims more probably concern the effects of these languages in the Latin source and thus serve to legitimate the Latin basis for the French-language translation, the Latin translator's competence, and the practice of making omissions or supplementing the translation (**33**.63–76)). These linguistic judgements of course also present the *Secré* as a work *au fait* with the new sources of knowledge in the thirteenth century's expanded world, and in spite of *Secré*'s claim of unreliability, Arabic is often used to code knowledge as both exotic and authentic. It may be the language of the written authority claimed for the *Miracle de Sardenai* (**34**.2). An Arabic 'King Evrax' is the authority for most of the French-language lapidaries of continental and insular culture, just as Hippocrates and Galen preside over the Greek learning of medical works alongside Aristotle (**32a** and **b**).[2]

1 Matzke, ed., 1909, vv. 947–90.

2 For the lapidaries see Dean 348–59 and Studer and Evans, ed., 1924 (repr. 1976), who also include early English-language lapidaries.

In Part V, our text selections are less exotic, but demonstate a great variety of approach. The first text, Cato's *Distichs* (37), is a foundational text of early schooling, and unsurprisingly presents Cato as a sage figure instructing his son in classical codes of mores and ethics. The Latin *Distichs* are deployed throughout the trilingual presentation here as an authorising source and anchor. But the first, bilingual prologue here also troubles to explain, in French and English, that Cato was pagan, although he taught nothing counter to the Christian faith. The grace of the Holy Spirit and the utility of Cato's teaching become part of a legitimated lineage of classical teaching, reframed into Christian use. The status of the Latin in the text moves between being the text's language of origin and being also perhaps a new language for at least some of its users in this largely English-language Vernon manuscript. The French version becomes part of this classical lineage for basic Latin grammatical teaching in that French seems to have had a long standing role as an oral teaching language in Latin classrooms.[3]

Simund de Freine's reworking of Boethius (38), on the other hand, is strikingly independent of Boethius's *gravitas* as the progenitor of the text. Boethius is transformed into a generic contemporary clerk, who comes before Simund's audience or readers to complain against Fortune and receive exemplary rebuke from Philosophy. Philosophy too, is transformed, moved into a lower, sharper, more proverbial register in the text. The vibrancy of Anglo-Norman didactic culture is already apparent here: authoritative textual lineages are freely transmuted into the key of contemporary, graspable, memorable teaching.

The role of Hebrew in the textual and cultural lineage of Christianity became an area of intense interest as Christian doctrine hardened into a collection of new rules for the laity around the fourth Lateran Council and as the church urged greater and better Christian education. Some writers pondered how Christianity differed from Judaism and how Christians were not like Jews. Both had complex histories of 'eating' or being nourished by the words of Scripture: Sansun de Nantuil's mid-twelfth-century commentary on Proverbs (39) exhorts his patroness to eat the 'bread' and split the nutshell of Scripture to find doctrine. For Sansun words are not just food; they are precious gems that provide wealth. But, at the same time, for the Christian, 'words of Scripture' and teaching (*la doctrine*) are hidden (*muciee*) in the Hebrew language (*en ebreu*, 39.105–6). Bede is the major source for Sanson's Commentary, but his prologue focuses on Jerome, the transitional figure between Hebrew and Latin who finds and transmits the riches of this food. Christian frustration produces scholarly investment and care, and Sansun's general concerns with Latin, Greek, and Hebrew origins make Jerome (*Cist prodes clers, cist bon devin* 39.119) a philological hero for him. Sansun's fascination with Hebrew and his concern for exactitude in originary language also ensure that he teaches his reader the Hebrew for different parts of the Bible (39.143, 155, 163). It may well have been fashionable for the aristocracy to know these few Hebrew words, as it was to know French. Certainly Jerome's widely circulating *Nomina hebraicorum* will have made most clerics feel they should know something of the Hebrew Bible, whether for exegetical or pastoral purposes.

3 Ingham 2012, 2015b, C. Cannon 2015.

What is surprising here is just how much detailed attention to the Bible's lineage Sansun feels able to supply for his patroness, Alice de Condet. His lengthy account of his Commentary's textual lineage not only gives learned etymologies, but creates an entire prestigious social milieu for the production of his text. Solomon's own name is etymologised as 'Peaceable God' (39.80): something his role as messenger from the supreme king enables him to signify. He is also noted as the son of a righteous king, David (39.52) and himself presented as a 'rich, wise and courteous king' (39. 50). His wisdom is extolled as carrying 'ninety-nine parts of Adam's understanding' (39.71–2), thus taking the text's lineage back to God's initial creation and plan for the world. Within Sansun's socio-cultural framing of his text, St Jerome emerges as a jeweller, polishing the gems of wisdom, and as, in effect, a household officer for Alice de Condet and Christianity at large: he is 'our steward and cook' (39.113–14). The vivdness of Sansun's socio-cultural translation and the affectivity of his metaphors in this long and complex Prologue signal a depth of engagement with the Bible's Judeao-Christian lineage that extends well beyond concern for authorising the text.

Rauf de Linham's concern with Jewish, Roman and Christian inheritances produces a different kind of engagement: in the text of his *Kalender* (40) he articulates the diversity of systems of time across the world: the Jews count the day from the evening because they found a rationale for doing so in the Bible (*Kalender*, ed. Hunt 1983, vv. 421–3). Christians, on the other hand, begin at midnight because Christ was born then (ibid., vv. 433–5), yet 'the common people' count the day as beginning at dawn when light first appears (vv. 437–42). Against this diversity of the world's peoples and their reckoning of time, Rauf produces a lineage for Christian time which begins with Rome and the establishment of time in Latin learning. He also alludes to Cato's *Distichs* (37), in a reminder that calendrical knowledge is foundational to medieval schooling and to the organisation of time and history. But he further guarantees his text by setting it firstly against a lineage in which it claims not to participate: that of vernacular literature. This will not be an account of knightly deeds or other fables, but of something verifiable (40.1–16).

These opening lines are couched as narratorial presence ('I don't want to sing about great deeds', 40.1), but the *Kalender* shares them with a late-thirteenth-century verse text, the *Marriage of the Devil's Nine Daughters* (Dean 686), a genealogically organised moral satire on sin dubiously attributed within the text itself to the great scholar-prelate Grosseteste (d 1253). It seems more likely that the *Mariage* borrows the prologue than that the *Kalender* does. But priority is in a way less interesting here than the fact of a floating prologue, found necessary and elegantly re-usable between texts. This speaks to the felt necessity of verse's social performance, even in an instructional treatise: the opening narratorial presence in Rauf's text also functions as part of its lineage, guaranteeing the text in the intentions of its presenter.

The *Estoire del saint Graal* (41) in effect accords the status of secular scripture to the French literature of chivalry. The characteristic authority of personal visionary experience for creating a direct textual lineage from God is deployed in its hermit narrator's account. In his solitude he receives, direct from the divine hand, a little book so powerful that it creates eco-catastrophe if recited with the language of the mouth rather than that of the heart (lines 125–30). The hermit pointedly suppresses his own lineage, partly by way of contrast with the extreme worthiness of the book with whose copying he has been entrusted, but heavily implies that he is in the lineage of the Grail keepers. The hermit is made still more qualified for his task by further visionary travel and a quest for a mysterious beast (unfortunately too lengthy to appear other than in summary here), as well as by the punctuation of his story with his observances of the liturgical hours and his storage of the powerful little book in the sacraments cupboard of his hermitage. In its all-out provision of a sacred lineage for chivalry, the *Estoire*'s prologue is a dazzling synthesis of *Vie des pères* traditions of vision, eremetic quest and apocalyptic urgency.

The lineage paradigm offered by the *Brut* is deployed in the baronial *Mohun Chronicle* (42), and is further enriched by the multiple traditions of later-medieval historiography, such as Martinus Polonus and perhaps Higden's *Polychronicon* (on which Sir Thomas Gray also draws in his *Scalacronica* (16)). Both Gray and the *Mohun Chronicle*, like the romance of *Fouke le Fitz Waryn* (31), exemplify what John Spence has argued is the confidence of French vernacular prose in the mid-fourteenth century.[4] In *Mohun*, French prose of apparent sparseness, but also of considerable resonance and efficiency, summons up and bolts together one historiographical template and topos after another from universal, European, papal, and lineal chronicle models, expecting audience response and recognition in yet another textual community founded initially round the *Brut*. This is not the prose of lack, but of confident functionality, combined with considerable rhetorical and affective power. Such writing may have helped tune Malory's fine ear to the ranging emotional effects he achieves in a prose that on the surface often seems to claim only the simplicity of paratactically organised record.[5]

Mohun is also a reminder of the origins of many texts in lay-clerical collaboration, where clerical access to theology and antiquity is given in exchange for patronage and placed at the service of households' and lineages' self-representation. At the period of the making of her chronicle in the mid-fourteenth century, the sonless Lady Joan de Mohun was busy making brilliant matches for her daughters: it is perhaps unsurprising that the *Mohun Chronicle*'s *Brut* variant traces British history back to Albina as the foundress of Britain in order to provide the text of the Mohun lineage.

We close Part V with a Bible translation, the Anglo-Norman *Poème sur l'Ancien Testament* (43), that remained current in England in the fourteenth century, its latest manuscript copy being late fourteenth or early fifteenth century. The *Poème sur l'Ancien Testament* (43) draws on the Vulgate Bible and on the Latinised version of Josephus's *Jewish Antiquities*. Like Sansun de Nanteuil's Commentary (39) it is preoccupied with the Hebrew foundations of the Bible, but in this case with its translation into a performable epic vernacular so as to create a historical song of Christian truth. In scholarship on the religious writings of late-medieval England, a tightly defined sense of the radicalism of English-language translation is being succeeded by the recognition of a more complex landscape in which orthodoxy is no more a single phenonenon than the heretical or the heterodox, and in which the vernacular, however often conceived as a single hypostasised

4 Spence 2013.

5 On Anglo-Norman curial prose, see Burnley 1986.

entity in opposition to the Latin of God's word, is also multiple.[6] As Nicholas Watson has argued, French religious writings in England are part of this landscape and they contribute to the complexity of a religio-cultural landscape in which the repression of biblical translation is an important, but not the only feature.[7] Presented as the lineage story of the holy prophets of antiquity, the *Poème*'s epic account of Jewish history and its self-presentation as a *chanson* 'de verité' and not just 'de geste' evidently retained its appeal from the time of its making in the late twelfth or early thirteenth century through to the end of the fourteenth century. As a work with much to say on kings and battle, it may have held for secular audiences the kind of interest that the *Roman de Thèbes* had for the fighting and would-be crusading Bishop Henry Despenser of Norwich, known for the violence with which he suppressed the Norwich revolt of 1381, and the owner of a copy of this originally twelfth-century text.[8] The *Poème* represents one of many possible strands in religious writing. As with almost all entries in the volume, a single example has to stand as a gateway to a multifarious literary scene of other texts and their audiences in the lineages of England's literary culture.[9]

The *Poème*'s verse *rifacimento* serves a further purpose here, however, as a pedagogical example of prosodic reconstruction (see p. 386, Notes, and p. 422 below). Both the texts and the varied and changing formal characteristics of francophone literary culture in England offer areas ripe for further exploration.

6 See for example Gillespie and Ghosh 2011.

7 Watson 2009b.

8 See Baswell 2002. Joan Ferrante and Robert Hanning are preparing a translation of the *Roman de Thèbes* based on Despenser's manuscript for the FRETS series.

9 For discussion of francophone prologues in religious writings, see Hasenohr 2000. A rough indication of francophone religious writing in England may be given by counting the fourteenth- and fifteenth-century items in Dean's categories: (i) s. xiv or later copies of Biblical translations 14/36 copies, Apocryphal 11/24, Hagiographic 39/82, Homiletic etc. 88/232, Devotional 116/266: total of later copies 267 (ii) s. xiv or later composition 268 items. The bulk of fourteenth-century composition is from the first half of the century, but composition of some items, and the copying and circulation of more, continues into the fifteenth century. There is currently no census of the continental French texts in circulation in this devotional landscape, but see Wogan-Browne (forthcoming) for an initial indication of their interest.

37. Everart, *Distichs of Cato* [Dean 255], Prologue: Oxford, Bodleian Library, MS Eng. Poet. a.1, f. 309^{va-c} (the Vernon Manuscript)

Maija Birenbaum

Date of composition and provenance. Late twelfth or early thirteenth century, England.

Author, sources and nature of text. The text edited here is the prologue to a version of the *Distichs of Cato* written by the monk Everart, once thought to be Everard de Gateley, a monk of Bury, who revised Adgar's *Gracial* (11a), but now not certainly identified.

The Latin text from which Everart's book of moral lessons derives is often credited in medieval sources to the third-century stoic philosopher Dionysius Cato (an attribution understood to be spurious by some commentators at least as early as the ninth century). Cato's text was Christianised, probably during the Carolingian period, when the *Disticha Catonis* was first used as a reader in church schools. The *Distichs* continued to be fundamental to medieval education, and remained one of the most widely used elementary texts into the eighteenth century. In addition to Everart's version of Cato, there are two other Anglo-Norman translations, one anonymous (Dean 256), and one by Elie of Winchester (Dean 254). All three date from the late twelfth or the earlier thirteenth century, but scholars have yet to reach agreement on the relative chronology of their composition. If the number of extant manuscripts is any guide, Everart's seems to have been the most widely used.

Everart's text is presented trilingually in the Vernon manuscript (ff. 309^{v}–314^{r}), where it includes 191 hexasyllabic tail-rhymed stanzas in French, and a prologue of 24 lines in the same metre (tail-rhyme is widely used in French-language texts in England, especially for works of instruction; see pp. 422–3 below). In Vernon, the *Distichs* open with two quatrains in Middle English, and each of Everart's prologue stanzas is thereafter followed by a Middle English summary of the French (in quatrains rhyming abcb). The prologue itself is in two parts, Everart's prologue as translator (vv. 1–52 in English and French in Vernon's version) followed by his translation of the original Latin prologue (vv. 53–94 in Latin, French, English). After the prologue, Vernon's text of the *Distichs* interleaves the French tail-rhyme stanzas with Latin distichs and more English quatrains, and the order of the languages is regular: first Latin, then French and then English.

Among the nine extant manuscripts of Everart's *Distichs*, only one (York, Minster Library 16 N 3) contains the poem in monolingual French. Six of the manuscripts have Latin text intercalated; the Simeon manuscript, like Vernon, is trilingual (and lacks Everart's prologue): the fragmentary Oxford, Bodleian Library Eng. misc. C291 is also trilingual (Horrall 1981b). The foundation of medieval literacy teaching is the Latin alphabet and primer, followed by grammatical schooling for some, and Latin grammar was the chief systematic grammar instruction until the late fourteenth and fifteenth centuries for those who had occupationally to write Latin and French (see (7e)). English with its variable orthography tended to be a third written language. Vernon's linguistic order in the second part of the prologue and the text itself thus follows one kind of expected linguistic order. Its bilingual presentation of Everart's translator's prologue suggests that English is beginning to adopt the role of access language often taken by French both before and after this date in relation to Latin, but in this case in relation to French. It has been argued that multilingual texts were included in Vernon only for their English content, and that the predominantly English manuscript was compiled for an audience unfamiliar or uncomfortable with French and Latin (Blake 1990). It seems more likely that these texts were included either because the intended audience was competent in reading all three languages or because they were interested in improving their reading and understanding of Latin and French, both important languages of learning in different ways. Latin texts of the *Distichs* were themselves taught with a varying density of glosses in both French and English. The Vernon

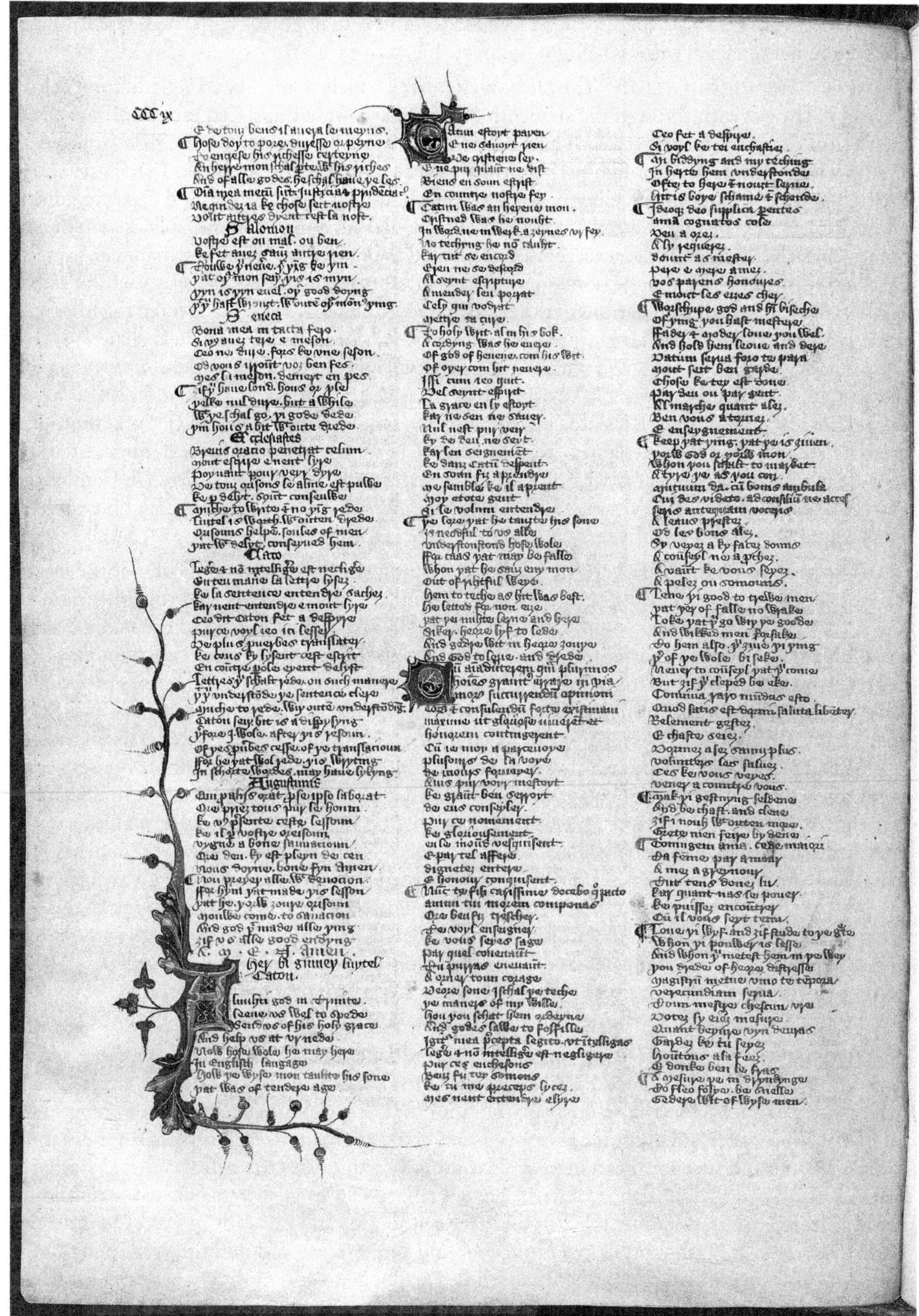

Fig. 10. (37) Tri-lingual Cato
(Oxford, Bodleian Library, MS Eng. Poet. a.1 (the Vernon Manuscript), f. 309*va–c*)

presentation of the *Distichs*, that is, can be seen as a testimony to linguistic contact and multilingual teaching rather than as a witness to rigid linguistic hierarchies.

Audience and circulation. The *Distichs* circulated widely in medieval England from at least the end of the eleventh through the sixteenth centuries and were translated into Old English (in the twelfth century), French (twelfth and thirteenth centuries), and Middle English (fourteenth and fifteenth centuries). Although perhaps early used as monastic library books (Treharne 2003), they became a staple of English schools, teaching boys grammar and rhetoric, and Caxton's edition of the *Distichs* was the first printed schoolbook. Vernacular versions were probably used in literate homes to teach children to read: excerpts are often used in books of courtesy and manners. Everart's *Distichs* is distributed in a range of manuscripts, suggesting adult readers as well as school use: in BN fr. 25,407, alongside explications of the creed and *Pater noster*, his text is collected together with the *Espurgatoire seint Patriz* (Dean 547), encylopaedias by Pierre d'Abernon de Fecham (19), and Gossuin de Metz (Dean 326), and a translation of Guillaume de Conches's *Moralium philosophia* (Dean 242), among other works. Like other texts from Vernon, Everart's translation is also found in the Simeon manuscript (BL Add. 22,283, with Everart's prologue omitted). Sometimes it is present in highly various miscellanies (York Minster 16 N 3, without the Latin text intercalated: BL Arundel 92), and once it occurs with Elie of Winchester's version of the *Distichs* (in Cambridge, Pembroke College 46). The Vernon audience for the *Distichs* may have been a lay household of some magnificence or a wealthy female religious house (Doyle 2013, 16).

Manuscript source. The Vernon manuscript, Bodleian Eng. Poet. a.1, is one of the largest extant collections of medieval English religious writings (377 texts on 355 – probably originally 426 – calf-skin leaves, 544 × 393 mm). Much scholarship has been devoted to the manuscript as a monument of Middle English literary culture, although the fact that Vernon also contains texts in French, as well as both bilingual and multilingual texts, is less often noted. Scase's proposal of William Beauchamp, the immensely wealthy younger brother of Thomas, earl of Warwick (d. 1401), as its patron locates the manuscript in a milieu of traditionally trilingual literacies in which English-language devotion and reading is rapidly joining the francophony of noble houses (Scase 2013). The *Disticha Catonis* is item 350 in the third and largest section of the manuscript. Everart's text immediately follows Bozon's *Proverbs of Prophets* (*Proverbes de bon enseignement*, Dean 252, in French and English), and precedes the *Stations of Rome*, in English. All these texts are copied in the main Vernon hand, which makes no distinction between the three languages of the manuscript's *Distichs* (see Fig. 10) and, as is not uncommon in Anglo-Norman texts, uses yogh for z. The first occurrence of each language in the prologue is marked with a decorated and flourished initial. The English opening of the poem is marked by a large initial framing the bottom left of f. 309*va*, and decorated with besants and trefoils: a much less extended gold initial follows at the top of column b as the French begins, with a plainer version for the start of the Latin in the middle of the column.

Bibliography. Everart's *Distichs* were first edited by Stengel 1886, based on the Arundel manuscript, and by Furnivall 1901, based on Vernon. On Everart's identity see Legge 1950, 15–17 and Hunt 1994, 2. Dean 255 lists the manuscripts. For the other Anglo-Norman *Distichs*, see Stengel 1886 for Elie of Winchester and Hunt 1994 for an edition of the anonymous Anglo-Norman translation, with a valuable and succinct introduction. Hazelton 1957 discusses the early-medieval Cato: see also Copeland and Sluiter, 2009. Treharne 2003 analyses Old English versions and manuscripts. For Middle English translations, see Horrall 1981a, and Boffey and Edwards 2005, 2. On the use of Cato's *Distichs* in English schools, see Hunt 1991 and Orme 2006 and on home schooling Orme 2006, 98. Cato in courtesy books is discussed in Parsons 1929 and Gillingham 2002. Hazelton 1960 considers Chaucer's parodic use of the *Distichs*; Caxton's fifteenth-century *Distichs* are edited in Kuriyagawa 1974. On Cato glosses, see Hunt 1991, I.59–79 and II.3–12 and for a comparison of the three Anglo-Norman versions, Hunt 1985 and 1994 (ed.). Hexasyllabic tail rhyme (French and English) is discussed in Purdie 2008, 32–65. Kristol 2000 discusses multilingual orthography and writing in Anglo-Norman and Latin. For a facsimile of the Vernon manuscript, see Doyle 1987 and Pearsall 1990, and for its digitisation, Scase 2011. The manuscript's structure and disposition of texts are discussed in Doyle 1987 and 1990; Blake 1990; Scase 2011 and 2013. Meale 1990 is an important early discussion of its possible *destinataires*: see more recently essays by Doyle and Horobin in Scase 2013, as well as Scase's own studies on the tradition of analogous large trilingual manuscripts and the Vernon patronage in Scase 2013.

TEXT AND TRANSLATION

Her biginneþ Luytel Caton. [f. 309va]

Her biginneþ Luytel Caton.

Almihti God in Trinite
Leeve us wel to spede;
Send us of his holy grace
And help us at ur need.
Now hose wole he may here (whoever)
In Englisch langage
How þe wyse mon tauhte his sone
Þat was of tendere age. (young)

[Middle English vv. 1–8]

Catun estoyt payen, [f. 309vb]
E ne savoyt rien
De cristiene ley:
E nepurquant ne dist
Riens en soun escrist
Encountre nostre fey.

[French: Cato was a pagan and did not know anything of the Christian religion. But nevertheless, he said nothing in his writing against our faith, vv. 9–14]

Catun was an heþene mon;
Cristned was he nouht.
In word ne in werk aȝeynes ur fey (faith)
No techyng he non tauht.

[ME vv. 15–18]

Kar tut se encord,
E ren ne se descord
Al seynt' escripture:
Amender l'en porrat
Cely qui vodrat
Mettra sa cure.

[French: For it is in complete accord with Holy Scripture and contradicts Scripture in nothing. Anyone who wants to give their attention can amend it, vv. 19–24]

To holy writ al in his bok
Acordyng was he evere.
Of God of hevene com his wit,
Of oþer com hit nevere.

[ME vv. 25–8]

Issi, cum jeo quit,
Del Seynt Espirit
La grace en ly estoyt,
Kar ne sen ne saver,
Nul n'est pur veir
Ky de Deu ne seyt:
Kar l'enseignement,

[French: So, as I believe, the grace of the Holy Spirit was in him, for truly there is no sense or wisdom or anything at all that doesn't come from God. For it seems to me

Ke dan3 Catun despent
En soun fi3 aprendre,
Me semble ke il aprent
Moy e tote gent,
Si le volum entendre.

that the teaching that Sir Cato dispenses for his son to learn, teaches me and everyone if we wish to pay heed to it, vv. 29–40]

Þe lore þat he tau3te his sone
Is neodful to us alle
Understond hose wole,
For caas þat may befalle. occurrence
Whon þat he sau3 eny mon
Out of rihtful weye,
Hem to teche as hit was best
He letted for non ei3e, trouble
Þat þei mihte lerne and here,
Siker heore lyf to lede, securely
And gedre wit in heore 3ouþe
And God to love and drede.

[ME vv. 41–52]

Cum animadverterem quam plurimo
homines graviter errare in via
morum, succurrendum opinioni
eorum et consulendum forte existimavi
maxime ut gloriose viverent et
honorem contingerent.

[Latin: When I noticed that most men go seriously astray on the road of morals, it occurred to me that it was important that I give assistance and counsel to their thinking, so that they should live in glory and achieve honour, vv. 53–8].

Cum je moy aparcevoye
Plusours de la voye
De mours forveyer,
Avis pur voyr m'estoyt
Ke graunt ben serroyt
De eus conseyler,
Pur ce noméme nt
Ke gloriousement
En le mound vesquisent,
Et par tel affere
Dignete3 en tere
Et honour conquisent.

[French: When I myself perceived many men going astray from the path of moral behaviour, I thought in all truth that it would be a great benefit to counsel them, especially so that they might live with glory in the world and thereby gain high offices and honour on earth, vv. 59–70]

Nunc te fili carissime docebo quo pacto
Animi tui morem componas

[Latin: Now, dear son, I will teach you how you may arrange the character of your understanding, vv. 71–2].

Ore, beu fiz tres cher,
Te voyl enseigner,
Ke vous seyés sage,
Par quel covenaunt
Tu purras enevaunt
Aorner toun corage.

[French: Now, my very dear fair son, so that you may be wise, I want to teach you the proper attitude which henceforth you should use to guide your behaviour, vv. 73–8]

Deore sone I schal þe teche

[ME vv. 79–82]

Þe maners of my wille
Hou you schal hem ordeyne
And godes lawe to folfille.
Igitur mea precepta legito ut intelligas:
legere et non intelligere est neglegere.

Pur ces enchesons,
Beuȝ fiȝ, tey somons
Ke tu mé preceps lyceȝ:
Mes nent entendre e lyre
Ceo fet a despire. [f. 309^{vc}]
Si voyl ke tei en chastieȝ.
Mi biddying and my teching
In herte hem understonde
Ofte to here and nouȝt lerne
Hit is boþe schame and schonde. waste

[Latin: Therefore, read my precepts in order that you may understand. To read and not to understand is to disregard, vv. 83–4]
[French: For these reasons, dear son, I urge you to read my precepts: but to read and not to pay heed to them is to scorn them, so I want you to correct yourself by them, vv. 85–90]
[ME vv. 91–4].

Notes

R ***Luytel Caton*** Although now, as in the Middle Ages, this collection of moral precepts is often referred to as the *Distichs of Cato*, the text is usually divided into two main sections, 'Parvus Cato' and 'Magnus Cato'; the former contains shorter aphorisms written in monostichs, while in the latter, the slightly longer snippets of advice are written in distichs (see Hunt 1994). A rubric at f. 310rb, v. 76 reads 'here endeth petyt Catoun', and v. 77 reads 'Incipit liber Catonis' marking the beginning of 'Magnus Cato'.

12 **nepurquant** Stengel 1886 reads *ne pourchant.*

13 **Riens** MS *Biens* (emended to *Ren* in Furnivall 1901, 554).

36 **danȝ Catun** Here, as elsewhere, the Vernon scribe adapts Middle English yogh for French *z*, as is common for *z* in insular French texts.

43 **Understond** MS *understondstond*

56 ***forte*** Boas gives *famae* in his critical text: however *forte* is the common reading of his Traditio vulgata manuscripts, including Vernon, of the thirteenth and fourteenth centuries (Boas, ed., 1957, 4, lxii).

65 **nomément** Stengel reads *memement*

69 **en tere** MS *entere*

69–70 **Digneteȝ en tere . . . honour conquisent** Unlike the Middle English (of which line 52 above is the last translated line from the relevant passage) Everart preserves the secularity of the Latin text.

81 **schal** MS *schat*

84 ***legere . . . est neglegere*** frequently cited as a proverb in medieval collections (cf. Vernon in Furnivall 1901, 552) (Boas, ed., 1957, 10).

87 **lyceȝ** sic MS: a variant spelling of *lisez*, which still here rhymes with *chastieȝ* in v. 90.

38. Simund de Freine, *Roman de philosophie* [Dean 243], Prologue: London, British Library, MS Add. 46,919, f. 107*ra–b*

Date of composition and provenance. Probably late twelfth century, Hereford.

Author, sources and nature of text. Simund [Simon de Fraxino], d. before 1228, was from a family connected with Sutton Freen, Herefordshire. He was a canon of Hereford by *c.* 1190, and his professional life remained centred on Hereford. Two of his Latin poems, addressed to his friend Gerald of Wales, defend the high reputation of the cathedral school at Hereford as a centre of learning, and he may have written his vernacular works under the patronage of William de Vere, bishop of Hereford, 1186–98. His two known Anglo-Norman works, the *Roman de philosophie* and the *Vie de saint Georges* (Dean 528), each have his name as an opening acrostic in the text, and were probably written before the poems addressed to Gerald of Wales, dated to 1194–7. Simund's interest in science and philosophy can be seen in the *Roman de philosophie*, an adaptation of Boethius's *Consolation of Philosophy* (AD 524) containing 1658 lines of heptasyllabic couplets. The poem includes additional material not present in the source on new advances in scientific study made at Hereford, often through its role as a centre for the absorption of Arabic thought at the time. Roger of Hereford, who compiled an astronomical table based on the meridian of Hereford in 1178, was a well-known astronomer, and Gerald of Wales called Hereford a place of joy for philosophers.

Boethius's *Consolation* was a standard text studied by clerics throughout the medieval period, and Simund's *Roman de philosophie* is part of a long-established intellectual tradition of commentary, glossing, translation and adaptation. The *Roman* itself is in the vanguard of French translations of Boethius's *Consolation* (of which there are at least thirteen, with continental versions beginning in the thirteenth century). In insular culture, Simund's is the first known vernacular reworking since the Old English prose and verse versions attributed to King Alfred (d. 899) and/or his clerks. The new emphases of Simund's text are partly summed up by the title given his work in one manuscript, *La romaunce Dame Fortunee*. An explicitly clerical narrator figure debates with Philosophy over the transience of riches and the whimsicality of Fortune, and where Boethius's Philosophy is accompanied by the Muses (whom she banishes from the narrator's company), Simund's Philosophy has the seven liberal Arts. This does not prevent her from using pungent similes and analogues in a much lower register than the *De consolatione*: riches are manure (*fermer*, v. 353), only useful when spread about (*esparpilez*, v. 355); the grasping man is like a chicken's foot, yanked by the tendon, compulsively clutching (vv. 669–78).

Solaz (comfort), in the Boethian tradition, is given as the primary reason for writing, and repeatedly invoked in the opening couplets of the poem as what a written work gives. *Solaz* as giver of comfort is immediately balanced by *solaz* as remover of sorrow in the opening line and this idea is expanded with the statement that one must not grieve over lost riches (vv. 5–6). While Fortune both gives and then takes riches, writing gives comfort but rather than later taking it away, it removes anguish, its opposite. The prologue proceeds by antitheses, enacting the wit and vigour of debate and the apparently counter-intuitive, paradoxical nature of arguing against riches (e.g. *dol aver* (v. 6, mourn), and *estre plus joius* (v. 8, rejoice), *fous* (v. 9, foolish) and *hom sage* (v. 12, wise person), *joier ou doler* (v. 10, rejoice or grieve). Simund does not make the instructive function of his writing an explicit term in these antitheses, but it is clearly implicit in the learned nature of his subject matter, in which the professional intellectual, the Clerk, debates with the allegorical figure of Philosophy. The prologue's general assertion that it is folly to strive after earthly riches is expressed in philosophical terms, but the subject of the debate, the clerkly lament about the sudden reversal of personal fortune, is from the outset presented as an untenable philosophical position (if one accepts the previous assertions of the folly of riches). It will be the role of Philosophy, with the aid of her seven daughters, the seven Arts of the trivium and quadrivium, to prove the Clerk is wrong to lament his treatment by Fortune.

38. Simund de Freine, Roman de philosophie

Audience and circulation. The *Roman de philosophie* is extant in three manuscripts (Simund's *Vie de saint Georges* survives only in one), and no doubt participated by association in the widespread popularity of the work by Boethius on which it draws. All three manuscripts are collections of largely religious and instructional writing. Simund's *Roman* inscribes an audience of clerks from the cathedral schools, well versed in both philosophy and the seven Arts of the curriculum: the extant manuscripts of the *Roman* suggest that it found this kind of audience and perhaps also that it could be used alongside more pastoral works in the late twelfth and thirteenth centuries' vivacious culture of teaching by debate.

Manuscript source. BL Add. 46,919 is a fourteenth-century vellum manuscript, ff. ii+211, measuring 230 mm x 170 mm, with many irregular leaves. Though written in several hands, the manuscript is an extensive trilingual compilation by the Franciscan theologian William Her(e)bert, who studied in Paris and Oxford, becoming regent master of the Franciscans at Oxford in 1317. Herbert retired to the Franciscan convent at Hereford, and is buried in Hereford (d. 1333/1337), where he was also probably born. At the foot of f. 107ra of his manuscript, he spells out the *Roman*'s acrostic 'Simund de freine me fist (Simund de Freine made me)'. The *Roman de philosophie* is also extant in two slightly earlier manuscripts: BL Royal 20.B.XIV, ff. 68^{v}–77^{r}, a large late-thirteenth- or early-fourteenth-century collection of pastoralia in French, and Oxford, Bodleian Library, Douce 210 (21,784), ff. 51^{v}–59^{v}, a more varied collection from the early fourteenth century that includes, for instance, the *Chevalier de Dieu* (Dean 684), a three estates treatise (Dean 625) and a poem against marriage (Dean 206) alongside its pastoralia.

Bibliography. The *Roman de philosophie* is edited from all three manuscripts in Matzke 1909, with discussion of the adaptation and its source text. Legge 1971 gives details on Simund's works and the intellectual context of Hereford: see now Burnett 1995, Frankis 2002, also *ODNB* Simund de Freine. Stevens 2009 is a preliminary attempt at more detailed study of the *Roman* and its contexts. For Simund's *Vie de saint Georges* (pre-dragon, but with a spectacular rhythm of torture and dismemberment, re-assembly and resurrection) see the translation by Russell 2012. For William Herbert, compiler of BL Add. 46,919 see *ODNB*; also Meyer 1884 and http://www.bl.uk/catalogues/manuscripts/. On William de Vere as literary patron, see Barrow 1987.

Text and Translation

Solaz doune e tout ire [f. 107ra]
Icest romanz ki l'ot lire.
Mult porte en sey grant deport,
Un escrit est de confort.
Ne deit hom, ce mustre bien,
Dol aver de perdre rien.
D'autre part, pur rien ke seit,
Estre plus joius ne deit.
Fous est ki pur nul avoir
Rien voet joier ou doler.
En poi de ure vet e vient,
Ia hom sage plet ne tient,
N'est aver fors chose veine
E ki lui aver se peine,
Mult le quert od grant dolur

This vernacular work will provide comfort to those who hear it read, and it will take away their anguish. It has the capacity within itself to give much solace, it is a written work which gives comfort. It shows clearly that no-one should mourn the loss of material wealth; nor, at the same time should anyone rejoice over any material possession. He who wishes either to rejoice or grieve over any earthly wealth is foolish: it comes or goes in a few hours. A wise man pays it no attention, earthly treasure is nothing but vanity, and whoever strives to gain it, seeks to gain it with great suffering, only to lose it in the

E tut pert a chef de tur.
Fous est ki aver desire,
Ia ne serra sanz martire.
Sanz tristur n'iert une hure
Tant li curent pensers sure.
  Pur mustrer ki rien ne vaut
Aver terriene ke faut,
E ke mes n'eit hume talent
De trop amer or ne argent,
Vient un clerc ki fet sa pleinte
De fortune fausse e feinte,
Ke le fit primes riche adés
E tut povre tost aprés.
Pus si vient Philosophie
Ki ad en sa compaynie
Ses set filles de set parz,
Ceo est a saver lé set arz,
E al clerk demustre bien
Ke sa pleynte ne vaut rien,
Ke richesce n'est fors sunge,
Chose pleyne de mensuynge,
Ore se vient, ore s'en vet
Cume flot ke munte e pus retret.
Oy avez la matire, [f. 107rb]
Ore oÿez le romanz lire.

end. He who wishes to gain wealth will never be without suffering, he will never be an hour without sadness, so assailed is he by his worried thoughts.

To demonstrate that earthly possessions, which in the end will fail one, are worth nothing, and so that people will no longer have the desire to love gold or silver excessively, here comes the Clerk who states his complaint against false and fickle Fortune, who made him first quite rich, then very poor immediately after. Next comes Philosophy who has in her retinue her seven daughters from seven regions, namely the seven Arts. And she proves clearly to the Clerk that his complaint is worthless, that riches are nothing but a dream, a thing filled with deception, which now comes and now goes away, like a flood which rises, and then subsides. You have now heard the subject matter [of my work], now listen to the reading of my vernacular tale.

Notes

Opening annotation: written in the top margin, across the two columns in one line, is the couplet *Kaunt je pens de ihesus crist la pensee mun quer enducist* (When I think of Jesus Christ, the thought sweetens my heart). The text has no opening rubric.

1–20 The acrostic SIMUND DE FREINE ME FIST ('Simund de Freine made/wrote me'), made by the first letters of each line, is also written out in the bottom margin of f. 107ra. We print these letters in bold to emphasise the acrostic.

1 The inital letter **S** is written over four line spaces.

1 **doune** The letter *o* has been added by a corrector.

1 **Solaz** the key function of *solaz* is given prominence by the inversion of the usual syntactic order (the stylistic device of hyperbaton). Two noun objects and two antithetical verbs are juxtaposed in the first line, with the two noun objects at the beginning and end of the line, *solaz* (comfort) and *ire* (anger, anguish), the two verbs, *doune* (gives) and *tout* (takes away, removes), balanced on the central conjunction *e* (and).

6 **Dol** MS *Del*. The confusion between *o* and *e* is common; we emend on the basis of *doler* (v. 10), but it could also be *doel*.

8 **joius** The letter *i* has been added by a corrector.

39. Sanson de Nantuil, *Les Proverbes de Salemon* [Dean 458], Prologue: London, British Library, MS Harley 4388, ff. 1*a*–2*b*

Date of composition and provenance. *c.* 1136–65 (Hunt 2012, 5); Lincolnshire?

Author, sources and nature of text. Sanson de Nantuil's translation from the biblical Book of Proverbs into nearly 12,000 octosyllables is both the earliest extant translation of Proverbs into French and the only medieval French verse translation of Proverbs to have a verse commentary. The work is incomplete (perhaps because as Sanson claims, he had an incomplete source copy, vv. 37, 88): it stops abruptly with Prov 19.27, omitting about 300 verses. Sanson says he has produced the work for Alice de Condet, who wished to have the text translated and commented upon (vv. 195–201), possibly for the instruction of her son, Roger de Condet (the first such known teaching text in French if so). Sanson's name does not appear in Alice's extant charters, and nothing is known of him from other sources. He was possibly her chaplain, and, although born across the Channel (in which particular Nanteuil is undetermined), is thought to have spent at least some years in England.

The principal source of the *Proverbes de Salemon* is Bede's *Super Parabolas Salomonis allegorica expositio*, some lines of which also appear in the *Glossa ordinaria*, a twelfth-century compilation of scriptural exegesis. Whether Sanson knew the *Glossa* or worked from a source common to both Bede and the *Glossa* is unclear. Some additional material comes from Jerome's preface to the biblical books of Solomon, and Sanson may also have used the *In Parabolas Salomonis expositio mystica* by Salonius, bishop of Geneva in the fifth century, and other sources.

Sanson divides his work into three parts: the prologue, vv. 1–218; the 'argumentum', or description of the subject matter, vv. 219–346; and the text, vv. 347–11,852. His treatment of the verses is also tripartite, beginning with the Latin text followed by the French (both titled *Litera*), and then by Sanson's commentary (the *Glose*), also in French. In his commentary, Sanson deploys religious references, maxims and sayings, and displays an extensive knowledge of classical Latin authors.

The prologue opens with a richly textured extended metaphor upon the 'food' of Proverbs as spiritual substance (vv. 1–26). Sanson's bread of wisdom, which may be tasted, eaten and savored, echoes an understanding, common from the patristic period, of the 'bread' that sermons were said to provide. Sanson's reference to living bread (*vif pain*, v. 85) gives his metaphor Eucharistic overtones. St Jerome, as the translator of the Bible from Hebrew into Latin, features as the loving cook (*cueus*, v. 114) and steward (*despenser*, v. 113) who nourishes the Christian generations.

At v. 40 Sanson introduces his second notable metaphor: God's words in *Proverbes* are precious gems. Later they are precious pearls (*precïoses margaries*) given by 'a priest' (vv. 89–90), St Jerome, who in translating them from Hebrew into Latin, has cleaned and polished them (vv. 108–12). Sanson develops, augments and customises his prologue well beyond Jerome's own prologue, but he paraphrases Jerome from vv. 143–76 in an early example of high-medieval use of material from Jerome to introduce commentary. The passage foregrounds the complex relationship between medieval Christian sacred culture and its Hebrew source, present here in the several metaphors by which Sanson describes how the Hebrew language both preserves scripture and keeps it hidden from Christians: it is a *coverture* (v. 187) that protects the sweet and edible nut of Scripture (vv. 183–8) but its prickly casing is difficult to penetrate. Just as Jerome translated the Bible from Hebrew into Latin at the request of two bishops, Alice de Condet's alleged insistence and the work of her writer Sanson are now deployed to translate Proverbs from Latin into French.

Audience and circulation. The highly laudatory nature of Sanson's dedication to Alice hints at her influence and reach as a member of a well-connected family. Her father, Ranulf le Meschin (d. 1129), was the hereditary viscount of the Bessin (Calvados) and son of the Hugh Lupus praised as a magnate in Gaimar's *Estoire* (10). After his brother Richard d'Avranches perished in the White Ship in 1120, Ranulf became the third earl of Chester. Alice's mother, Countess Lucy, supplied a further network of associations through her three marriages, and Alice herself made two advantageous marriages: first to a descendant of Duke Richard I of Normandy, Richard fitz Gilbert of Clare, killed in battle in 1136; next, to Robert de Condet, a Lincolnshire landholder, who soon died as well. The widowed Alice was ultimately able to retain her land and thereby her wealth and importance. Although Sanson presents Alice as long importuning him for the translation and commentary, her civil and social prominence could well have lent lustre to Sanson's reputation, an intangible provender that supplements whatever actual material reward Sanson receives from her. The lengthy food metaphor that informs Sanson's prologue may be read as the mirror reflection of his patron's material 'food', the agrarian-based wealth that sustained Alice, her household and estate staff, and her clerics and clergy (compare (14), Greatham's *Miroir*). In turn, Sanson offers figurative nourishment to his patron, who may thus have nourished members of her entourage, not to mention her own son, with scriptural translation and commentary.

Manuscript source. Only one manuscript survives: BL Harley 4388, ff. 1ra–86va, written *c.* 1200 (Isoz 1988, 3, 8). Beyond the reasonable conjecture that it was prepared in England, no more precise provenance can be offered. The *Proverbes de Salemon* is followed in the manuscript by three other Anglo-Norman texts of moral instruction which, as accompaniments to Proverbs, reinforce the suggestion that Alice sought Sanson's expertise for the purpose of her son's instruction: the *Sermon* of Guischart de Beaulieu (Dean 597); *Le Chastoiement d'un pere a son fils* (a translation of Petrus Alfonsi's *Disciplina Clericalis*, Dean 263); and the *Afaitement Katun*, Elie de Winchester's translation of Cato's *Distichs* (Dean 254), commonly used in the schoolroom (see (37) for a version of the *Distichs* by Everart).

Bibliography. The *Proverbes de Salemon* is edited in Isoz 1988, with substantial discussion of the patron and sources. Durnford's 1977 dissertation studies the work and summarises previous scholarship: see also Durnford 1981–2. See also entries in Hasenohr and Zink 1992 (Samson de Nanteuil, 1364, Bible au Moyen Âge, 174–8, and Bible française, 178–96) and Wogan-Browne 2005a. On Sansun's identity see Legge 1950, 121; Legge 1971, 40. For Alice de Condet's family, see Legge 1971, 36–42, Isoz 1988, also *ODNB* Ranulf I (Ranulf le Meschin). Lobrichon 2003, 158–70 and Giraud 2010 discuss the *Glossa Ordinaria*: on Jerome's own prologue to Proverbs and on its medieval uses, see Dahan 2009, 59–60. The three French treatments of the Book of Proverbs (Dean 458–60), are discussed by Hunt, ed., 2012, 5–19, who notes exegetical and other terms. On Christian children's formation in the alphabet and primer by ingestion of letters of bread and cake dipped in milk, see Alexandre-Bidon 1989: for the inscription of Ezekiel 3:3 on food in Torah learning for schoolboys in medieval Europe, see Marcus 1998.

TEXT AND TRANSLATION

A tort se lait murir de faim [f. 1ra]
Ki asez at e blé e pain.
Turner li pot l'um a peresce
Se ne s'en paist, u a feblesce
S'il fameillet e ne se paisse
E par desdeing murir se laisse.
De cels est dunc, si cum jeo crei,
Ki al mulin muerent de sei.
Pur nent irreit conquere en France
Ki suffraite at en habundance.
De bons mangers sui plenteïs;

It is a sin for the man who has sufficient wheat and bread to allow himself to die of hunger. If a man does not nourish himself he can be accused of sloth, should he, though he hungers, not eat and let himself die out of disdain. Those who die of thirst at the mill are in that group, I believe. He who suffers great deprivation goes conquering in France for nothing: I am abounding in good food; come hither, whoever is needy. If someone is slothful, I require only that he open his

Traiet sei ça ki est mendis.
S'est tels que perece le toche,
Ne li queor fors ovrir sa buche,
Ne li ruis plus a travailler
Fors a savurer e maschier.
N'est langueros s'il l'asavore
Ki ne delit meïsme l'ore.
A la buche rend grant dulçor
E mult i at seine savor.
L'espirit guarist, le cors reheite;
Trop est golis ki'n ad suffraite.
Molt est fols e prové vilain
Ki n'asavoret de cest pain,
Kar tut est fait de sapïence,
De grant doctrine et de scïence.

mouth, nor do I ask him further to exert himself, except to taste and chew. Any sick person who tastes it takes immediate delight. It brings great sweetness to the mouth and has a very healthy flavor. It heals the soul, it gladdens the body; he who deprives himself of it is quite frivolous. He's a great fool and a proven churl who does not taste of this bread, for it is made entirely of wisdom, great doctrine and knowledge.

Si l'ad tramis par son message
Cil ke de tute chose est sage.
Riches reis est, ne puet plus estre,
Në unches n'out ne per ne meistre.
Par un rei le nus ad tramis
Ki m[o]lt esteit de lui apris,
E molt aveit grant manantie
Dunt nus ad fait bele partie.
Mais cil ki'n unt a grant plenté
Unt l'aveir muciét e celé;
Molt grant partie en ai trovee
Dunt de mielz ert a ma contree.

He who is wise in everything sent it through his messenger. He is a rich king; there can be no richer, nor has he ever had an equal or better. He transmitted it to us through a king whom he had instructed well and who had many possessions, from which he gave us a generous portion: those who had a great deal of it hid their wealth, but I have found a large part, which will benefit my homeland.

Traient sei ça humes e femmes
Ki volent aveir chieres gemmes:
De molt precïoses en ai
E bon marchét lor en f[e]rai;
Ja mar le lairunt par muneie,
N'i ad nuls ki jeo ne creie,
Mais qu'il s'aquitent ben del pris,
Al terme li jur en ert mis.
Cil ki l'aveir ad endité,
E le pain dunt dis aporté,
N'ert pas frarin, ainz fut uns reis,
Riches e saives e curteis.
Salemon l'ad numé la geste,
Filz fut David, un rei honeste,
Ki out grace de prophecie
E traitét fist de psalmodie.
Cil Salemon out si grant sens
N'en out nul tant pus le son tens,

Let them gather round, the men and women who want to have valuable gems: I have many precious ones, and I'll sell them at a good price. Alas for those who leave them behind because of money! I extend credit to everyone, provided they pay the price by the day agreed upon. He who told us about the riches, and who brought the bread I talked about, was not a lowly person but rather a rich, wise, and courteous king. The story names him Solomon, son of David, a righteous king who had the gift of prophecy and wrote a treatise on psalmody. This Solomon had such great wisdom that there has been none like him since, except the son

Fors le fiz Deu ki de scïence
Est tresor e de sapïence,
Ne ainz si saives hom ne fut –
Ço ai des escriz entendut –
Fors l'ume que Deus fist premier,
Parfait de toz bens e plenier.
Parfitement fut saive e bels,
Forz e vig[o]ros e isneals,
Poëst[e]ïs, sains e hardiz,
Seürs, riches e repleneiz;
Ne de maior perfectïun
Ne pot aveir creatïun.
De cele grant perfectïun
Fist Deus sa grace a Salemon:
La nonante nueme part out
Del sens Adam, cume Deus vout,
E de tant est saive apelé [f. 1*va*]
Sur tuz cels ki el mund sunt nez.
Deus le fist escrire e traiter
Pur nus que voleit enseiner,
E pur testimonier sa lei
Par buche de si saive rei.

of God, who is a treasury of knowledge and wisdom. Nor was there ever such a wise man before him – I have understood this from Scripture – except for the first man whom God made, perfect and complete in all good things. He was thoroughly wise and fine, strong, vigorous and swift, powerful, healthy and bold, resolute, rich and endowed. No greater perfection could any created thing have. From that great perfection God gave his grace to Solomon: he had ninety-nine parts of Adam's understanding, as God wanted, and for that reason Solomon is called wise over all those who are born in the world. God caused him to write and teach because he wanted to instruct us and provide testimony to his religion through the mouth of a such a wise king.

Sis nuns par ethimologie
'Paisible Deu' nus senefie.
Cist ad Eglise saolee
De bons mangiers e confortee,
Dunt vos m'oïstes ainz parler,
Ke duz e sains sunt pur user.
Cist nos demustrat le vif pain
Dunt alme e cors sunt sauf e sain.
Cist out l'aveir, dunt ai parlé,
Dunt nos partie avum trové:
Les precïoses margaries
Kë uns prestres nos ad polies.
Ço fud escripture devine
U molt ad sens e grant doctrine.
Ço est li douz mangers e li pain
Dunt nostre espirit est forz e sain.
Se sovent peüt n'en esteit.
De grevose faim languireit,
Kar si com[e] cors est grevé
Se de manger n'est surtenté,
L'alme languist tot ensement
Se n'at devin enseignement.
Ço est li aveirs, ço sunt les gemmes

Etymologically, his name signifies to us 'Peaceable God'. He has satisfied and comforted the church with good food, about which you heard me speak earlier, which is sweet and beneficial to partake of. He showed us the living bread through which soul and body are safe and sound. He had the riches, about which I have spoken, of which we have found part: the precious gems, which a priest polished for us. That was holy scripture, in which there is much sense and great doctrine. It is the sweet food and bread which renders our spirit strong and healthy; were it not often fed, it would languish from grievous hunger, for as the body is harmed if it is not sustained by eating, so the soul languishes without divine teaching. Those are the goods, those are the gems which make men and women wealthy.

Dunt manant sunt omes e femmes.
Par ki est ço? Par Damledé,
E par celui ki l'at trové.
La doctrine nos ert muciee,
Kar en ebreu esteit traitee.
Reposte esteit tresque l'en traist
Sainz Jerommes ki nos en paist:
Ço est li prest[r]es ki poli
Les beles gemmes dunt vos di;
Les gemmes terst e neïat, [f. 1*vb*]
Q'en latin les translatat.
Cist en fud nostre despenser
E cueus del savoré manger,
Dunt les almes avront salu
De celx ki ben l'unt retenu.
Cist nos ad molt enmanantiz
E saolez de bels escriz.
Cist prodes clers, cist bon devin,
De ebreu translatat en latin
Les livres ke li Ebreu firent
E lor gestes quë il descristent.
Quant tot ot fait e asemblé
Ceo que ot escrit e translatét,
D'un ebrieu nun l'entitulat:
Son livre Bible en apelat,
Kar d'estoires ert l'assemblee
Qu'aveit escrit' e translatee.
Saint' Iglise molt resplendist
De ço que cist bons prestre escrist:
Quantqu'at traitét Jeronimus
Ad sainte eglise molt en us;
Peüe en ert tote sa vie,
Kar chascon jorn en est servie.
Tant en sumes tut amendé
Ne nos deit pas estre oblié
Icest escrit, dunt nos parlum,
Ke ad translaté del Salemon,
Ke treis voluns en aveit fait,
Si cum sainz Jerommes retrait,
Dunt en l'ebreu nos ad posez
Toz les titeles e enbrevez.
Maslot nos numad le premer,
Dun Paroles volt designer;
Li pueples Proverbes les cleimet
E les respeiz quë il molt aimet:

From whom does this come? From God, and from him who found it. The doctrine was hidden from us, for it was elaborated in Hebrew. It was kept in a hidden place until it was extracted by St Jerome, who nourishes us with it: he is the priest who polished the fine gems I have told you about: he cleaned and shined the gems by translating them into Latin. He was our steward and cook of the tasty food, which will save the souls of those who have kept it down. He has enriched us greatly and sated us with fine writing. This worthy clerk, this good theologian, translated into Latin the accounts the Hebrews wrote in Hebrew and the stories they recounted. When he had completely done and gathered together what they had written and translated it, he gave it a Hebrew name: he called his book Bible, for it was a gathering of stories that he had written and translated. Holy church is resplendent thanks to what this good priest wrote: whatever Jerome has written is much practised by holy church, which will be fed by it for all its life, for every day holy church is served by it. We are so much better for it that we must not forget the writing we are talking about, that he translated from Solomon, who divided his work into three volumes, as St Jerome recounts. He added and recorded all the titles in Hebrew. He named the first one Maslot, by which he meant 'Words'; people call them Proverbs and Sayings, which they love: we're talking

Ço sunt les Respeiz Salemon
E del Vilain dunt nos parlum.
Vilain en apelent la gent
Pur ceo qu'es dit apertement;
Cil de seculer corteisie
Li aturnent a vilanie,
Mais la raisun n'est pas vilaine
Ki vent de la cort suveraine.

about the Sayings of Solomon and of the Peasant. The people call them 'of the Peasant' because they are commonly known. Those who are of worldly courtliness interpret them as the common people's; but the proverb that comes from the sovereign court is not lowly.

Celeth nos numat le segunt
Dé voluns que Jeromme espont,
Ki en grezeise langue est ditz
Ecclesïastes e escriz,
E en latin Asemblëor
L'ethimologent li plusor;
Plaidëor resenefie
Solunc alt' ethimologie.
Li tierz vochat Syrasirim
Que de l'ebreu mist en latin;
En nostre langue est si trové:
Chaschons dé Chaschons l'at numé.
Par excellence issil nomout,
Plus haltement numer nel sout.

The second of the volumes that Jerome interpreted is named Celeth, which in Greek is called and written Ecclesiastes, and many etymologise it in Latin as *Assembler*. It also means 'Preacher', according to another etymology. The third that he rendered from Hebrew into Latin is called Syrasirin. It is found thus in our language, where it has been named Song of Songs. Jerome gave it that name for its excellence: he could not imagine any higher name.

Cist Jerommes dunt nos parlum,
Ki d'Eusebe ot le surnun,
Fud des Proverbes molt preiét
Ainz qu'en translatast le traitét;
Dui evesque l'en unt requis
Quë il nos numet, ço m'est vis:
Li uns ad nun Cromatïus
E li altre Helïodorus.
Des Proverbes quident alquant,
Ki ne sunt pas ben entendant,
Que Salemon par poëstez
Les ait escriz e comandez;
Mais mielz lor covent a enquerre,
Kar come l'or est quis en terre,
Et come le noël de noiz
Ki a manger est bon e doiz,
U de la chastaine herdue
Ki d'une schale est sorvestue,
Tot ensement de coverture
Fut reposte ceste escripture.
Enquerre i deit l'um ensement
Le devin sens plus haltement.
Ki ben en volt estre enqueranz,

This Jerome we're talking about, whose surname was Eusebius, was much sought after before he translated the treatise. Two bishops had asked him for a translation from Proverbs. He named them for us: one was Cromatius, the other Heliodorus. Some people of dim understanding believe that Solomon, through his own power, ordered and wrote them. But they would do better to seek their meaning in the way gold is sought in earth and meat in the nut, which is good and sweet to eat, or of the chestnut covered by a prickly case: in just that way this scripture was hidden by a covering. One must also attempt to find the holy meaning in more

Entendet dunc a cest romanz
Quë al loënge Damnedé
E a s'enor at translaté
Sanson de Nantuil, ki sovient
De sa dame qu'il aime e creient,
Ki mainte feiz l'en out preiéd
Que li desclairast cel traitéd.
Le nun de ceste damme escrist
Cil ki [la] translatïon fist:
Aëliz de Cundé l'apele,
Noble damme enseigné e bele.
Ne quident pas li losengier
Qu'ot eus se voille acompaigner,
Kar trestut cil de sa contree
Unt ben oï sa renumee,
E cil ki mentir l'en orreient,
Tot sun traitét en blasmereient.
Pur ço l'en fist translatïun
Qu'il conut sa devotïon,
Kar des escriz ad grant delit,
Molt volenters les ot e lit.
Nel pot laisser ne li traitast,
Coment que l'enui li grevast.
Tut cil l'en deivent bon gré rendre
Ki deliterat a entendre
La seinte escripture devine.
Atant li prologes define.

exalted places. And so, whoever agrees to seek it, listen to this story told in French, which Sanson de Nantuil translated to the praise and honour of God, and who remembers his lady whom he loves and fears, who asked him many a time to elucidate this treatise for her. He who has rendered this translation writes the name of this lady: she is called Alice de Condet, a noble and beautiful, educated lady. May lying sycophants not think he would want to be one of them, for everyone where she lives knows her reputation, and those who heard it lied about would blame the author's treatise entirely. He did this translation because he knows her devotion, for she takes great delight in writings of the faith and she hears and reads it with great pleasure. He could not avoid writing for her, although he is weighed down by weariness. All those who delight in hearing the divine, holy scripture must extend good will to him. Here the prologue ends.

Notes

2 **blé** The host could be made only of wheat (Rubin 1991, 38–9).

3 **peresce**; 13 **perece** *acedia, accidi*: sloth, one of the seven capital or deadly sins, is characterised by laziness and an aversion to work; hence Sanson's statement, vv. 13–16, that if a person is stricken with sloth, Sanson will not make him exert himself in order to receive the wisdom he is about to impart.

9–10 **Pur nent irreit conquere en France / Ki suffraite at en habundance** *conquere* may be figurative here: Isoz speculates that these lines allude to a resistance among writers in England to the *Glossa ordinaria*, disseminated from centres of learning in France, principally Laon and Paris (1988, 21). In v. 10 the mutually defining *suffraite* and *habundance* represent mild verbal play. For the view that Sanson took the Latin text of Proverbs from a Bible held in the Lincoln Cathedral Library, see Durnford 1977, 79–80, 100.

16 **a savurer** Recording this as two words rather than *asavurer* (Isoz 1988) draws out the parallel with *a travailler* in v. 15, allowing both to stand as likely complements of the verb *ruis*, which seems a more likely choice than the repetition that would occur with *n'asavoret*, v. 24.

20 **mult** This is the only instance in the prologue where this word is fully written; in other instances the abbreviation *mlt* appears, which, according to Isoz 1988, should be resolved as *molt*, on the

grounds that it is by far the more common spelling in the rest of the manuscript whenever this word is written out.

21 **espirit** Read as two syllables (and again at v. 94).

27–36 **Si l'ad tramis . . . celé** These lines seem further to qualify the ones preceding, i. e., the Hebrews for the most part kept this knowledge hidden, but Sanson (and Jerome) managed to locate a good part of it. Verses 37, *Molt grant partie en ai trovee*, and 88, *Dunt nos partie avum trové*, have been cited as suggesting that Sanson's translation is incomplete because his source was incomplete (Durnford 1981–2, 362).

31 **nus** Although in the prologue itself *nus, vus* are the most frequent fully written forms for these pronouns, Isoz 1988 observes that in the manuscript as a whole *nos* and *vos* are more frequent.

38 **Dunt de mielz ert a ma contree** This line may support vv. 9–10 in which Sanson advises the reader not to bother going to France for 'nourishment' (see n. to 9–10 above). Durnford suggests the reading, 'and better [yet] it was in my own country' (1981–2, 363).

44 **creie** *3 subj* **creire** to give, extend credit to.

51 **geste** this is one of Sansun's main terms for the narrative in Proverbs: he uses *escrit* still more frequently and occasionally *estoire, livre* and *traitét*. *Mester* is his word for the 'secret or mystery' of the text before commentary (v. 8118): his source text is a *continuel sermon* (v. 1762): see Hunt 2012, 5.

60 **Ço** Isoz: *Çö.*

68 **creatïun**, n. f. read as *creature* (cf. *AND, s.v.* 'creation').

71–2 **La nonante nueme part out / Del sens Adam** The source of this expression is not known (Isoz 1988).

80 **Paisible Deu** *Peaceable God* A common medieval misconception about the meaning of 'Solomon', arising from a confusion of terms. The name apparently comes from a Hebrew root meaning to be complete or sound. It is *shalom*, a derivative, that means peace.

89 **precïoses margaries** For the properties of precious stones in Anglo-Norman lapidaries, see Studer and Evans 1976.

90 **Kë uns prestres** Isoz 1998 emends MS *Ke uos prestres* to *Ke uns prestres.*

94 **espirit** see n. to v. 21.

103 **Damledé** MS *Damledeu*; emended to rhyme with *trové*, v. 104. See also v. 193 where MS *damnedeu* has been corrected to *damnede* through expunction of *u*.

106–8 **en ebreu esteit traitee / . . . l'en traist / Sainz Jerommes** In an important break from church tradition, which held that the Greek Septuagint, in Latin translation, was authoritative, Jerome believed that the Bible in Hebrew was a better guide to the coming of Christ. Although Augustine and others disagreed, over time Jerome's work came to replace the 'Old Latin'.

109 **Ço** Isoz: *Ço*, see n. 60.

122 **gestes** can refer to the 'deeds' of the Hebrews, as *gestes* referred to epic deeds in *chanson de geste*, but it also came to signify simply 'stories'.

125–6 **ebrieu nun . . . Bible** Sansun is mistaken. The origin of the word 'Bible' is in fact Greek *ta biblia*, 'the books', but instruction in Greek in twelfth-century England would have been even more difficult to obtain than instruction in Hebrew.

139 **treis voluns** 156 **voluns** Solomon was commonly thought to have composed three biblical books: Proverbs, Ecclesiastes, and the Song of Songs.

142 **titeles** Pronounce as two syllables.

143 **Maslot** Jerome (ed. Weber, 1983) says that 'Masloth' is the Hebrew for *Parabolas*, which is popularly called *Proverbia*.

144 **Paroles** Isoz: *paroles*

147–8 ***del Vilain*** refers to a collection of popular sayings known as *Proverbes au vilain*.

155–9 **Celeth . . . Asemblëor** *Coeleth* in Jerome (ed. Weber 1983). *Kohelet* may mean either 'one who gathers' or 'one among the gathering'. The title *Ecclesiastes* (v. 158) follows the Septuagint and is based on a Greek noun, *ecclesia*, denoting a gathering.

161 **Plaidëor** *the Preacher* Translation follows Jerome's suggested Latin title *Contionator* (ed. Weber 1983). This line is 7 syllables; a possible emendation is *E plaidëor resenefie*.

163 **Syrasirim** *Syrasirin*, Jerome: *Sirassirim*. The Hebrew name for the Song of Songs; also referred to as *Syrasirin Salomonis*.

170 **Eusebe** *Eusebius* St Jerome was known as Eusebius Sophronius Hieronymus.

175–6 **Cromatïus . . . Helïodorus** St Chromatius, bishop of Aquileia (d. 407) and Heliodorus, fourth-century bishop of Altimum, near Aquileia, are the original dedicatees of Jerome's prologue.

40. Rauf de Linham, *Kalender* [Dean 342], Cambridge University Library, MS Gg.1.1, f. 8r

Date of composition and provenance. According to its own statement (v. 1305), the *Kalender* was composed in 1256, but there is no evidence for the identity of its lay patron or the position of its author at the time.

Author, sources and nature of text. The author names himself as *Rau de Linham* (Hunt 1983, vv. 937, 1306). Lenham is a village close to the Canterbury Pilgrims' Way across the North Downs. The local knightly family of de Lenham seems to have consolidated its principal lands in Buckinghamshire by the late fourteenth century. Rauf is not mentioned in their land transactions (and was in any case probably a younger son and cleric), but he may be alluded to in some pipe rolls of Henry III. His patron is named only as *mun seignur* in the text (vv. 18, 1297) and remains unknown.

In the table of contents of the manuscript used here, Rauf's work is described as 'The Vernacular Art of the Calender' (*Art del kalendere en romance*, f. 6r). Medieval calendars are familiar preludes to psalters and books of hours, and many other texts, such as prognostications, lunaries and counsels for perilous days derive from them. The full art of computing the calendar was a complex ecclesiastical matter (Bede, Ælfric, Grossteste, Roger Bacon, Nicholas Trevet, among many others, produced computus treatises and commentaries), and calendrical knowledge was important to annalists and chroniclers. But calendars were also vital to laypeople and religious alike for devotions, for following the church year, running households, agricultural production, calculating provision for fast and feast days, and for identifying physiologically propitious times for humoral treatments such as medicinal bleeding. The first extant French calendrical treatise (Dean 346) is by Philippe de Thaon, composed between 1113 and 1119 for his uncle Honfroi de Thaon, a chaplain to Henry I's seneschal. In the form of household almanacs, calendars continued to be important well into the early-modern period.

The full *computus* of the calendar was reserved to specialists, but even so, the 1322 verse lines of Rauf de Linham's treatise contain much information on Roman and Christian systems of time, the calculation of Ides and Kalends, etymologies for the classical names of months, days and planets, the interrelations of the solar and Julian year, the complex but indispensable calculation of Easter and the other movable feasts of the liturgical *temporale*, the litany of saints and their fixed feasts, zodiacal and astronomical information, an account of the 'Egyptian' or 'dismal' days, and the interrelations of different seasons and individual physiological humours and their treatment. Some explicit treatment of cultural diversity is also part of the mix, as between Jewish, Roman and Christian calendrical calculations and customs. Explanations of the English name for Sunday are given (vv. 311–28), and February is made a short month because it is the time when heretics and unbelievers and their wives and children (*Li bougres e li mescreanz/ Od lur femmes, od lur enfanz*, vv. 183–4) sacrifice to Beelzebub and Pluto (vv. 185–6).

For all the developing vogue for prose in the thirteenth century, Rauf de Linham uses flexible Anglo-Norman octosyllabics for his *Kalender*. The treatise's vigorous verse narratorial presence helps hold together the diversities of the calendar as a single 'universal' system of reliable knowledge. The *Kalender*'s epilogue proposes *solas* and *delit* (v. 1316) as possible rewards for its audiences: across the spectrum of informational and imaginative thirteenth-century writing, there is no easy division between 'literary' and 'documentary' texts and audiences, and the pleasures of knowledge can be found in both.

Audience and circulation. The *Kalender* is extant in a large tri-lingual manuscript, CUL Gg.1.1 made after 1307 (see below), and in two other manuscripts of the same period. It was also present in BL Cotton Vitellius D.III before the Cottonian fire. The extant manuscripts suggest the text's usefulness to lay and religious alike. In Bodleian, MS Bodley 399, the *Kalender* text is datable to 1300 by its scribal colophon, which calculates the years since Christ's birth (ed. Hunt 1983, vv. 1323–30): this manuscript also includes Grosseteste's *Chasteau d'amour* (**5**) and the *Lumere as lais* ((**19**), with an exemplum incorporated from the *Manuel des pechiez* (**24b**), and Dean 635r). The text's rubric in the Bodley manuscript says that the *romauncé* (vernacular) *Kalender* is *pur simple gent lettré* (for non-clerical readers). But in Glasgow University Library, MS Hunter 467, a manuscript of computistical texts belonging to Dover Priory, the *Kalender* is in the early-fourteenth-century section of the manuscript, together with a Latin *Compotus*, *Algorismus* and a treatise on cosmology, and was presumably of use to the monks. Clerical administrators and religious professionals with pastoral duties must have had to explain the calendar to laypeople, especially as lay ownership of psalters and books of hours increased over the thirteenth and fourteenth centuries, and both the Bodleian and the Cambridge manuscript may have been useful for these purposes. Much less elaborate than Byrhtferth's well-known *Enchiridion* (a monastic Latin and English computus manual with some French compiled by Ramsey Abbey's schoolmaster, completed in 1011, and extant in three twelfth-century manuscripts), the *Kalender* is insufficiently technical for expert computation, but a good general guide. It may have been of value for teaching young novices and school children and possibly in the home schooling of the elite, as well as wanted for adult laypersons, such as its unknown patron. The *Kalender*'s prologue overlaps for 12 lines with that of a late-thirteenth-century verse text, ascribed to Grosseteste, the *Marriage of the Devil's Nine Daughters* (Dean 686), and as the latter is unlikely to be by Grosseteste, it may be that Rauf's handling of the prologue topoi of verification was imitated.

Manuscript source. CUL Gg.1.1 is a surprisingly small but very thick early-fourteenth-century manuscript (217 × 145 mm, writing space 156–63 × 110 mm) of 633 folios, made after 1307 by a single scribe and a single artist, possibly in Ireland or the West Midlands (McIntosh *et al.*, 1986, I.69). The manuscript's long and narrow shape suggests a holster (i.e. a portable) book, though one of almost impractical thickness. It contains some fifty-five items, mainly in French, but with some Latin and English: these are principally works of devotion and instruction, texts on prognostication and revelation, and some texts that might function as household entertainment – a debate as to whether it is better to love a cleric or a knight (*Quel vaut meuz a amer gentile*, ff. 474–6^{v}), the *Blasme des femmes*, ff. 627–8 (Dean 202) and some love lyrics. A library in itself, CUL Gg.1.1 could have served the chaplain of a large baronial household in Ireland or the West Midlands (compare the trilingual manuscripts BL Harley 2253 and Bodleian, Digby 86). It includes several theological encyclopaedias (the *Lumere as lais* (**19**), a continental copy of Gossuin de Metz's *Image du monde* (Dean 326), Robert of Greatham's *Miroir* (**14**), an Apocalypse (Dean 475), the *Manuel des pechiez* (**24b**), the Assumption from Herman de Valenciennes's *Bible* (**15**), Bibbesworth's *Tretiz* in English and French (7a), smaller pieces such as confessional interrogatories in French and Latin, a *Brut abregé* (Dean 43), Langtoft's *Chronicle* (Dean 66), the *Prophecies et les merveilles de Merlin* (Dean 18), the continental *Roman de sept sages* (Version A), and various other smaller works. The principal Middle English text is the *Northern Passion* (ff. 122–34^{v}). CUL Gg.1.1's Apocalypse is lavishly illustrated with small miniatures and its *Image du monde* has a full-page miniature of God blessing creation, and some diagrams (Binski and Zutshi 2011, Plates L and LI; Binski and Panayotova 2005, no. 151).

One of the book's three historiated initials is at the opening of the *Kalender* on f. 8^{r}. In the initial, a figure (Rauf de Linham as secular cleric, or the patron?) displays on a lecturn a large open book shaped like CUL Gg.1.1 itself, long, narrow and thick, and perhaps reads it aloud. He has curled hair and wears a pink gown and orange hat.

Bibliography. The *Kalender* is edited by Hunt (1983) and by Södergård (1989), both from Bodleian MS 399. On the author's identity see J. Russell 1936, 108. Petitions from the Lenham family are online at The National Archives (http://www.nationalarchives.gov.uk/), Ancient Petitions. On CUL Gg.1.1 see Binski and Zutschi 2011, no. 149. Lawrence-Mathers 2010 discusses medieval calendars and their early-modern descendants; see also Declercq 2000. Thorndike 1954 is a concise survey of computus treatises by medieval ecclesiastics and intellectuals; for vernacular works see Dean 366–79 and Keiser 1998 (Middle English). Wallis 2005 includes an overview of the scope of computus. For bibliography, glossary of computus terms and other resources, see her *The Calendar and the Cloister: Oxford St John's College MS 17*: http://digital.library.mcgill.ca/ms-17/.

Armstrong and Kay 2011 offer an argument on prose versus verse of significance for the *Kalender* and other informational texts.

TEXT AND TRANSLATION

De geste ne voil pas chaunter,
Ne veilles estories cunter,
Ne la vailance as chevalers,
Ke jadis estoient si fiers.
Mun sen, ce crem, pas nel saveroit
Lur valur escrivre a droit.
De dire poi crendrai mult;
D'autre part ausi redut
Ke taunt preisasse lur valur
Ke tenu fuisse a mentur,
Ke mut i ad cuntes e fables
Ke ne sunt pas veritables.
Pur ceo tels chose vous dirai
Dunt verité vous musterai,
E proverai de mun dité
Par resun la verité.

I don't want to sing about great deeds or tell old histories or recount the valour of knights who were once so brave. I'm afraid that my intelligence would not know how to describe their bravery properly. I'd fear too much that I'd say too little, and, on the other hand, worry that I'd so praise their bravery as to be held a liar, for there are many stories and fables that are not at all verifiable. Because of this I will tell you something whose truth I can show you, and I will prove the truth of my account through what I say.

De estudier en ceo labur
Bien sui tenu, kar mon seignur
Par ki amur ceste ouvre empris
Comandé me avoit e requis
De aprendre lui e enseigner
En romance l'art de[l] kalender.

I am obliged to give my attention to this task, because my lord, for love of whom I undertook this work, has required of me and commanded that I teach him and help him learn the art of the calendar in the vernacular: that is the reason, and I have no other, for

C'est l'acheson, autre n'en ai,
Ke cest dité comensai.
Mes nepurqant la laie gent
Asenser purrai bien sovent,
Ki ke les resons savera
Entendre; kar meint tel i a
Ke lunkes muser i porreit
E ja plus sages ne serreit:
Jeo di tel de la laie gent
Ke sunt de feble entendement.
Pur ceo, di jeo, ça entendez,
Vous ke saver le voilez,
Les resons de cest art, [f. 8rb]
Ou poi en ert la vostre part:
Kar une petite reson
En sun livret nus dit Catun:
'Li mestres en vein la lesson lit
Dunt ces disciples unt en despit,
E le cunte est pur rien cunté
Kant de nul est escoté.'
Pur ceo pensez de l'escoter
Kar mut harraie en vein counter.

beginning this treatise. But nevertheless, I will be able to instruct laypeople often enough, any capable of understanding my teaching (for there are many such who could mull it over for a long time and who would never be any the wiser – I'm talking about lay people of weak understanding). And therefore I call on you who want to know it to pay attention to the points of this art, or you'll know very little about it. Cato gives us a bit of good sense in his book: 'Pointlessly does the master expound upon a passage that his pupils hold in contempt, and the tale is told to no purpose when no-one is listening.' Therefore listen thoughtfully, for I would hate to tell it in vain.

A Roume al tens auncienur
Esteient clers de graunt valur;
Artilus erent de sens,
Bien ordeinerent tut le tens
Par les planetes e lur curs;
Acunterent houres e jours
E puis unt les jours assemblés
E par semaines ordeinés,
Et de semeines moys unt fet,
E de moys un an parfet.
Puis firent un kalender
Pur lur festes auctorizer;
Fet l'unt en lange de latin,
Dunt nul lai ne set la fin.
Mes jeo voil desoremés
Ke l'em sache tout adés,
Le viel e li enfauncenet,
Ky bien entendent cest livret.

In ancient Rome, there were clerics of great learning who were very subtle and clever. They reckoned all the different times according to the planets and their courses; they determined the hours and the days and then they grouped the days together and ordered them by weeks, and from weeks they made months, and from months, they completed a year. In this way they made a calendar to give authority to their feasts, and they did this in the Latin tongue which no layperson can understand fully. But from now on, I want laypeople, who can understand this book, both the young and the old, to know it all.

Notes

1–16 The opening lines overlap with the prologue to *The Marriage of the Devil's Nine Daughters* (Dean 686, who discusses the unlikeliness of this text's attribution to Grosseteste): see Meyer 1900, 61–72. On the implications of re-usable prologues, see p. 343 above.

12 **veritables** For the translation *verifiable*, see (27) and Short 2007b.

18 **sui** MS *su.*

19 **empris** MS *pris.*

24 **Cest** MS *cost.*

25 **nepurqant** MS *nepurgant*; **la laie** MS *le lai.*

31 **laie** MS *lai.*

33 **di jeo** MS *di ca.*

38 **Catun** Cato, the usual name of a school book, the anonymous *Disticha Catonis*, commonly used in teaching throughout the Middle Ages and beyond: see further (37).

44 **harraie** Emended from MS *araine*: the scribe perhaps tried to read 'avraie en vein counté', but failed to convince himself and compromised from his exemplar.

44 **counter** MS *counte*, apparently to preserve visually equal line lengths.

56 **festes** MS *fet.*

58 **set** Emended from MS *fet.*

61 **li** MS *lu*: the form exists as an archaic form of the masculine nominative article, but is probably a nonce form here.

61 **enfauncenet** The normal meaning 'little child' (see *AND*, *s.v.* 'enfançunet') may be pertinent here as children could encounter calendars early in their education when using the psalter as their primer.

41. [Robert de Boron, Walter Map, ascribed], *L'Estoire del saint Graal* (*The History of the Holy Grail*) [not in Dean], Prologue: London, British Library, MS Royal 19 C.XII, ff. 1r–v, 2r, 3r

Date of composition and provenance. *c.* 1220–30, northern France.

Author, sources and nature of text. The *Estoire* is one of the last thirteenth-century Arthurian prose prequels to be composed and subsequently included within the ensemble of five works now known as the *Lancelot-Grail Cycle* (formerly the 'Vulgate' cycle), where it is the opening branch. The unknown author of the *Estoire* – if single author there was – is currently not thought to have written the cycle's other branches. The *Lancelot-Grail Cycle* creates an apocryphal salvation history linking the Round Table into the universal Christian redemptive history of the world and supplies direct lineal connections to Christ's passion. After the fall of Jerusalem to Saladin (1187) and the final loss of the colonial Latin Kingdom of Jerusalem at Acre (1191), the Christianised Grail offered a seductive combination of fresh chivalric access to the power of Christ's blood, and a narrative that authenticated the transfer of holiness to the West as originary and continuingly valid.

Prequel to all prequels, the *Estoire del saint Graal* narrates how Joseph of Arimathea retrieves the Last Supper's serving vessel and gathers blood from the crucifixion in it. After Joseph has converted the mysterious Eastern kingdom of Sarras, he and his son Josephus bring the Grail to Britain. Joseph thus re-signifies the island of Britain as the holy territory of the Grail quest and himself becomes Britain's first evangelist. As in the Grail quest itself, narrative events and their exegesis are *demonstrances* or *merveilles* as well as *aventures*. The *Estoire* responds to and itself exemplifies the resonant allegorical and symbolic modes of reading which it shares with late-medieval religious and doctrinal writing for lay patrons and especially with the apocalypse.

In its long and complex prologue, the *Estoire* bids for the strongest possible authorisation of the Grail as scripture. Christ himself hands his own history in the shape of a little book the size of a man's hand to an anonymous hermit living 717 years after the Passion. When the book disappears (on the precedent of Christ's disappearance from his sepulchre), the hermit is commanded to follow a strange beast in quest of the book. After many adventures modelled both on chivalric romance and the ascetic Lives of the desert fathers, the hermit retrieves the book, and makes a copy of it with writing materials that mysteriously appear in the altar cupboard where he keeps the Eucharistic vessels. The book itself then vanishes again – with Christ – at the feast of the Ascension.

At the end of the *Estoire*, the French version of the hermit's Latin book is credited to *Messires Roberz de Borron qui cest'estoire translata de latin en françois* (ed. Ponceau 1997, II.478, 546). Sources used in the *Estoire* include the prose *Joseph d'Arimathie* ascribed to Robert de Boron as well as the three central members of the *Lancelot-Grail Cycle* itself, but de Boron's authorship of the *Estoire* is unlikely: the ascription reflects rather de Boron's originary prestige as the author of an earlier verse *Joseph d'Arimathie* that fed the prose thirteenth-century cycles. These multiple authorities – Christ, the hermit, de Boron – testify to the cycle's concern with origins and authority, just as the *Estoire* itself is largely concerned with providing holy lineages around the Grail for major Arthurian figures. The *Estoire* mystifies and multiplies its sources in launching the audacious 'secular scripture' of the *Lancelot-Grail* cycle, carefully sending its original source text back into heaven, but equating its own text with the resurrected body that returns in the Eucharist. It claims moreover to be not only divinely authenticated but historically scrupulous and well informed, noting of its own discrepancies with the *Brut* tradition that 'whoever translated [the *Brut*] into the vernacular knew nothing of the high *History of the Holy Grail*' (ed. Ponceau 1997, II.546, lines 14–18).

AUDIENCE AND CIRCULATION. The cycle survives in over two hundred manuscripts, of which at least nineteen were made or owned in England. From the early thirteenth to the sixteenth centuries, the cycle, sometimes as a whole, but also in its individual branches or varying combinations of them, circulated widely from northern France through Britain, the Netherlands, Portugal, Spain, Italy, Germany. De luxe versions of the Grail history had readerships often traceable over several generations, suggesting how greatly these books were valued. For example, BL Royal 14.E. III, a large (485 × 335 mm) and gloriously illustrated manuscript of the first quarter of the fourteenth century, passed from Charles V (1338–80, king of France), to Charles VI, was bought by John, duke of Bedford 1389–1485 and regent of France, later belonged to Sir Richard Roos of Gedney (d. 1482), and is further inscribed with the names of two daughters and a sister of Elizabeth Woodville (*c.* 1437–92), queen of Edward IV. The luxury market for the Grail was not the only one, however, and many manuscripts in England seem to have been plainer books, much read and annotated, perhaps by a readership similar to that for the prose *Brut*. The monks of Glastonbury Abbey formed a particular interest group among readers of the *Estoire*: its contradictions to their own originary history were met by making Joseph of Arimathea the leader of the disciples sent to Glastonbury by the apostles Philip and James (Scott 1981, 34–5, 46–7). The *Estoire* was also appropriated and adapted in John of Glastonbury's *Cronica sive Antiquitates Glastoniensis ecclesie* of the early 1340s (ed. and trans. Carley and Townsend 1985, 32–5, 47–55).

The *Lancelot-Grail Cycle* had a long francophone afterlife in later-medieval England and also moved into English. The London skinner Henry Louelich translated the *Estoire* into fifteenth-century English couplets (Furnivall, ed., 1861, 1874–8; M. Warren 2007a, 53–7). The *Lancelot-Grail* cycle influenced the *Scalacronica* (16) of Sir Thomas Gray, whose daughter owned two copies of *Lancelot-Grail* romances (Moll 2003, 36, 29–30), and was substantially reworked in Malory's *Morte Darthure*. Grail material partly shapes Langland's *Piers Plowman* (Zeeman 2008) and Joseph of Arimathea is given several late-medieval English hagiographic treatments (ed. Skeat 1871; see Lagorio 2001).

MANUSCRIPT SOURCE. BL Royal 19 C.XII is a large (340 × 230 mm) and somewhat battered manuscript of the first half of the fourteenth century, lacking four or five folios at the end. There are notes in possibly English cursive hands on the flyleaves and an inscription 'Jacob mathiis' on f. 84^{v}. It is chosen here as a text of the shorter version of the *Estoire* (see Ponceau 1997, xxv–xlviii) with a complete prologue, and also as a manuscript written either in England or France (the language is western and has far fewer Picard traits than the *Estoire*'s northern French continental manuscripts) but located in England after its writing (Middleton 2003, 223–4). It exemplifies the ready cross-Channel permeability of French texts in the later Middle Ages. The manuscript, being professionally executed, but among the plainer copies of the *Estoire*, also suggests a readership interested in the text itself (see Middleton 2003, 234 on 'utilitarian' manuscripts of the cycle). Royal 19 C.XII uses thin vellum, in gatherings of 12 leaves (sometimes torn or crumpled). The text (in two ruled columns) is usually not damaged, though f. 1^{r} is very worn, with the beginnings of lines often blurred or lost: a 16-line space has been left for an image at the top of column a, but remains blank. A handsome puzzle initial from f. 37^{r} is digitised at http://www.bl.uk/catalogues/illuminatedmanuscripts/ILLUMIN.ASP?Size=mid&IllID=48874

Alternating blue and red ink flourished initials of varying sizes mark divisions and sub-divisions of the text, and corrections are made via insertion in a smaller version of the text hand. Quire signatures and catchwords survive. A later reader has added a title 'Partie du saint Graal' on f. 11^{r}. The manuscript's text of the Prologue has many small differences from the published editions of the long and short versions of the *Estoire*.

BIBLIOGRAPHY. The *Estoire del saint Graal* is edited in its long version by Ponceau 1997, who extensively discusses the *Estoire*'s manuscripts, textual tradition and sources. For a prologue illumination of the hermit, his vision, and book, see Royal 14.E.III, f. 3^{r}, http://www.bl.uk/catalogues/illuminatedmanuscripts . The five *Lancelot-Grail* works were edited (as 'the Vulgate cycle') by Sommer 1909, together with the *Livre Artus* (now classified as a branch of the post-Vulgate cycle), using BL Add. 10,292–4 as base manuscript: for the *Estoire* see vol I. For the *Lancelot-Grail Cycle* and editions and translations of its other branches see Dover 2003, 255–6: for editions of the *Estoire* see Ponceau, ed., 1997, ix. Chase 2010 is a modern English translation of the long version of the *Estoire*. A modern French translation of the short version (with original text from the Bonn manuscript) is Gros 2001. Essays in Dover 2003 show the European dissemination of the *Lancelot-Grail* cycle: see Kibler 1994 for another collection on it. On the multiple lineages of texts and personnel in the cycle, see Baumgartner 1994; Burns 2010, 1985; on exegesis in romance see Trachsler 2003, Bruckner (forthcoming). The figure of Robert de Boron is discussed by Berthelot 1991, 437–49 and Gowans 2004. Among the few studies of the *Estoire*'s prologue are Pickens 1994 and Leupin 1982, 23–35. Szkilnik 1991 is a study of the whole work. On the *Lancelot-Grail Cycle's* manuscripts and circulation in England, see Middleton 2003: Cooper 2003 discusses its English afterlife. Valuable studies of vernacular Grail writing's affiliations and influence include Baldwin 1998, repr. 2013, and Zeeman 2008. For the iconography of the *Estoire*'s prologue in continental manuscripts, see Stones 2003 and the *Lancelot-Grail* Project, http://www.lancelot-project.pitt.edu/lancelot-project.html. The sumptuous illuminations of BL Add. 10,292 and BL Royal 14 E. III are online at http://www.bl.uk/catalogues/illuminatedmanuscripts, also *Arthurian manuscripts in the British Library: the French Tradition* at http://www.bl.uk/catalogues/illuminatedmanuscripts/TourArtProse.asp#OTHER

TEXT AND TRANSLATION

[f. 1r] Cil qui se tient e juge au plus petit e au plus pecheor de toz mande saluz el comencement de ceste estoire a touz ceuls qui lor cuers ont, e lor creance, en la Sainte Trinité, ce est el Pere, ce est el Fil, ce est [el] Saint Esperit. El pere par cui toutes choses sunt establies e reçoivent comencement de vie; el Fil par cui toutes choses sunt delivrees des poines d'enfer e ramenees a la joie qui dure senz fin; el Saint Esperit par cui toutes choses sunt oissues des mains au maligne esperit e raemplies de joie par l'enluminement de lui qui est verais enlumineres e verais confors. Li nons de cestui qui ceste estoire met en escrit n'est pas només ne esclairiez el comencement: mais par les paroles qui ci aprés seront dites, porreiz grant masse aperçoivre le non de celui e le païs [d]ont il fu nez e une grant partie de son lignage. Mais en cest comencement ne se vuelt pas descovrir e il i a trois raisons por quoi: la premere, por ce que [se] il se nomast e il deist que Dex eust descovert par lui si haute estoire com est cele del Saint Graal, qui est de toutes estoires la plus haute, li felon e li enviouz la torneroient en viulté. L'autre raisonz [est] por ce qe tels poist oïr son non qui le conoi[st e] si en prisast moins l'estoire por ce que tant povre persone l'eust mise en escrit. L'autre raisonz est por ce que s'il eust mis son non en l'estoire et il eust aucune chose mesavenant ou par lui ou [par] vice de malvais escrivain qui aprés la transla[tast] d'un leu en autre, touz li blasmes en fust sor son non. Quar il est ore a nos tens plus de boches [qui plus] mal dient que ben, e plus est uns home blasm[ez] d'un seul mal que loez de cent bens. Por ces trois choses ne vuelt que son non soit de tout en [tout] descovert, quar ja soit ce que il s'en voulsist [f. 1rb] conuz, si sera il plus aperceuz que il ne voldroit. Mais

At the beginning of this history, he who judges himself the lowest and most sinful in all the world sends greeting to all who place their belief and their heart in the Holy Trinity, that is, in the Father, the Son and in the Holy Spirit: in the Father through whom everything was created and given life; in the Son through whom creation was released from the pains of Hell and restored to joy everlasting; in the Holy Spirit through whom everything has emerged from the grasp of the evil spirit and is filled once more with joy through the illumination of him who is the true light and true comfort. The name of the one who put this history into writing is not given and revealed at the beginning: but through what is said further on from here, you will be able in large part to make out his name and the country where he was born and a great part of his lineage. But he does not want to reveal himself at the beginning, and he has three reasons for that: the first is that if he named himself and said that God had revealed through him so high a history as is that of the Holy Grail, the most exalted of all histories, the wicked and the envious would make this an occasion for shame. The second reason is that, if anyone who knew him were to hear his name, they might value the history less, since so wretched a person had put it into writing. The other reason is that if he were to put his name to the history and it had anything unfitting in it, whether through him or the mistakes of some wretched copyist and subsequent translator of the history from one place to the next, all the censure would fall on his name. For nowdays there are more mouths that speak evil than good, and a man is more condemned for a single evil than praised for a hundred good deeds. Because of these three things, he does not wish that his name should be completely revealed, for even had

il dira tout en apert come l'*Estoire del Saint Graal* li fu comandee a manifester.

Il avint aprés la passion Jhesu Crist .vij.c. e .xvii. anz que je, li plus pechierres de touz les autres pecheors, estoie en un leu le plus sauvage, que je ne vuell faire conoistre, et esloigniez de toutes gens crestienes. Mais itant puis je bien dire que li leus estoit moult sauvages, mais mult m'estoit delitables e plaisanz, quar hom qui est du tout en Deu, il a en contraire toutes les choses seculers. Ausint come je me gisoie en cel leu dont vus avez oï, si fu entre le juesdi absolu e le venredi beneoit, e si avoie, s'a Nostre Seignor plaist, dit le servise que l'en apele tenebres, e lors si me prist mult granz volentez de dormir. Si començai a someillier e ne demora pas que une voiz m'apela trois foiz par mon non, e me dist, 'Esvelle toi! e entent d'une chose trois, e de trois une, e autretant puet l'une come l'autre'. Atant m'esveillai e vi si grant clarté que je onques mais autresint grant ne vi, e puis si vi devant moi le plus bel home qui jamais soit. E quant je le vi, si fui si esbahiz que je ne soi que dire ne que faire. E il me dist, 'Entens tu la parole que je t'ai dite?'

E je li respondi en tremblant, 'Sire, je n'en sui mie encore ben certains'.

E il me dist, 'Ce est la reconoissance de la Trinité que je t'ai aportee, e ce est', dist il, 'por ce que tu avoies esté en doutance qu'en Trinité eust trois persones e si n'i avoit que une seule deité e une seule poissance'. (Ne onques n'oi doutance en ma creance que seulement en icel point).

E encores me dist-il, 'Pues tu encore parcevoir ne conoistre qui je sui?'

E je li dis que mi oill estoient mortel, si ne pooent pas esgarder si grant clarté, 'ne ne sui pas poissanz de dire ce dont toutes

he wished to be recognised, he would still be more noticed than he wanted. But he will narrate with complete openness how the *History of the Holy Grail* came to be entrusted to him to reveal.

It happened seven hundred and seventeen years after the passion of Jesus Christ that I, the most sinful of all sinners, was in a very wild place (I don't want to make known where), far away from all Christian people. But I can say this much, that the place was very wild, but very pleasing and delightful to me, for a man who is wholly concerned with God finds all worldly things inimical. In any case, when I was lying abed at the place you have heard about, between Maundy Thursday and Good Friday, and after having said, as it pleased Our Lord, the office called *Tenebrae*, a very strong desire to sleep overtook me. Then I began to sleep and it was not long before a voice called me three times by my name, and said to me: 'Wake up! And understand three things in one and one in three, and each as powerful as the other'. I awoke at once and saw light so intense that I have never since seen any other like it, and then I saw before me the most beautiful man that ever was. And when I saw him, I was so overcome that I did not know what to say or do. And he said to me: 'Did you hear what I said?'

And, trembling, I replied: 'Lord, I am not quite sure'.

And he said to me, 'I have brought you knowledge of the Trinity, and this', he said, 'is because you have been doubtful that there were three persons in the Trinity and yet only one godhead and one source of power'. (That was the one point of my faith on which I had ever had any uncertainty).

And again he said: 'Are you able to recognise who I am yet?'

And I said to him that my eyes were mortal and they could not look at so great a light, 'nor am I capable of saying what any mortal

les mortelx langues seroient encombrees de dire'.

tongue would be burdened by'.

E il se baissa vers moi, si me soufla enmi le vis. E lors me fu avis que je oi le sens a cent doubles plus cler que onques mais n'avoie eu, e puis si senti devant ma bouche une grant mervaille de langues. E il me dist, 'Puez tu encore conoistre qui je sui?' e quant je voil parler, si vi que uns brandonz come feu me sailli parmi la boche. Si avoie si grant paour que onques ne poi dire mot.

And he leaned down towards me and blew on my face. And then it seemed to me that my understanding was a hundred times clearer than ever before, and I felt a wonderful number of languages within my mouth. And he said to me, 'Can you recognise who I am yet?' and when I wanted to speak, I saw that a burning fiery coal leapt out of my mouth. Then I was so terrified that I could not say a word.

E lors me dist, 'N'aie mie paour, quar la fontaine de toute seurté est devant toi: e saches que je sui ça venus por toi aprendre ce de quoi tu doutes. Quar je sui de toutes doutances certains; je sui fontaine de sapience; je sui cil a cui Nichodemus dist, "Maistre, nos conoissonz qui vos estes". Je sui de cui l'escriture dist "tote sapience vient de Nostre Seignor". Je sui li parfez Maistres. Por ce sui je venus a toi, que je vuell que tu reçoives ensaignement de toutes iceles choses [f. 1va] dont tu seras en doutance. E si te ferai certain d'une chose nul home mortel ne fu onques certains, e par toi sera ele overte e esclairie a touz ceuls qui jamais l'orront contez'.

And then he said to me, 'Don't be afraid, for the fountain of all assurance is before you: you should know that I have come here to teach you about what you doubt. For I am the resolution of all doubt, I am the fountain of wisdom; I am he to whom Nichodemus said, "Master, we know who you are". I am he of whom scripture says "All wisdom comes from Our Lord". I am the perfect Master. I have come to you because I want to teach you all the things about which you are doubtful. And I will make you certain about something no mortal man was ever sure of, and through you it will be revealed and made clear to all those who hear it told.'

A ces mos me prist par la main, e me bailla un livre qui n'estoit pas plus granz en touz sens que la paume d'un home. E quant il le m'ot baillie, si me dist que il me bailloit dedenz si grant merveile que nus cuers mortelx nel porroit savoir, 'ne ja de chose ne seras en doutance que tu ne soies avoiez par cel livre. E si i sunt mi secré que nus hom ne doit veoir se il n'est avant espurgiez par veraie confession. Quar je meismes l'escris de ma main, e en tel maniere le dois dire que l'en le die par langue de cuer, si que ja icele de la boche n'i parot. Quar il ne puent estre nomé par langue mortel que tuit li quatre element ne soient meü, quar li ciels en plorra, li airs en troublera, la terre en crollera e l'eue en changera sa color. Tout

At these words he took me by the hand, and gave me a book no bigger in any of its dimensions than the palm of a man's hand. And when he had given it to me, he told me that within it he was giving me a great wonder beyond what any mortal heart could know, 'nor will you ever experience any uncertainty in which you cannot be guided by this book. In it there are my secrets, which no man should see unless he is first cleansed through true confession. For I wrote it myself with my own hand and it must be recited with the language of the heart, without that of the mouth having any role in it. For the things in it cannot be named by mortal tongues without all the four elements being disturbed: for the heavens will rain, the air

ce est en cest livret, e si i a plus que ja hom n'i gardera en parfaite creance, que il ne li vaille a l'ame e au cors: au cors que ja ne sera tant iriez, por tant que il gart ens que il ne soit erraument ploins de la grignor joie que nus cuers puisse penser: ne ja por pechié que il ait fait en cest siecle ne morra il de mort soubite – ce est la joie de l'ame'.

will become stormy, the earth will quake and water will change its colour. All this is in this little book and there is more there, in that if a man will maintain perfect belief in it, it will benefit him body and soul. Body, because he can never be so distressed that as long as he looks inside it he will not immediately be full of the greatest joy any heart is able to conceive: nor will he ever die a sudden death on account of any sin he has committed in this world – this is the joy of the soul'.

Et quant il ot ce dit, si cria une voiz ausint come une boisine e quant ele ot crié, si vint .i. si granz escrois de haut qu'il me fu avis que li firmamenz fu chaüs e que la terre fu fondue. E se la clartez fu granz devant, encor fu ele grignor a cent doubles. Quar je cuidai avoir la veue perdue, e si chaï a terre ausint com hom pasmez. E quant la vanitez du chief me fu alee, si ovri les ieux, mais je ne vi onques entor moi nule chose, ne ne vi onques rien de quanque j'avoie veu ançois. Ainçois tenoie tout a songe, quant je trovai en ma main le livret, ausint come li Granz Maistres le mi avoit mis. Lors me levai mult liez e mult joious, e lors fui en proieres e en oroisons et mult desirrai le jor que il venist. E quant il fu venus, si començai a lire, e trovai le comencement de mon lignage, que je desirroie tant a veoir. E quant je oi tant esgardé que il estoit prime, si n'oi je rienz esgardé, tant i avoit il letre. E si me merveillai mult coment en si petit livret pooit avoir tant letre. Ausint gardai el livre si que vers tierce tant que je oi veu grant plenté de mon lignage: e si vi la vie e les nons de tanz proudeshomes que a paine ousasse dire ne conoistre que je fusse d'aus descendus. E quant je vi lor bones vies e lor travals que il avoient en terre souffert por lor creator, si ne pooie pas tant penser coment je peusse m'ame tant amender que [f. 1vb] ele fust digne d'estre amenteüe avuec les lor, ne il ne m'estoit pas avis que je fusse home envers aus, mais faiture d'ome. E

And when he had said this, a voice like a trumpet cried out, and after it sounded, there came so great and loud a crash from on high that I thought the heavens had fallen and the earth split open. And if the brightness had been intense before, it was now a hundred times greater. I thought I had lost my sight, and fell to the ground like a man in a faint. And when my senses came back to me, I opened my eyes but I did not see anything near me, nor did I see anything of what I had previously seen. Rather, I thought it all a dream, until I found the little book in my hand, just as the great Master had placed it. Then I got up very relieved and joyful and said my prayers and entreaties and longed very much for day to come. And when it had come, I began to read, and found the origins of my lineage, which I was greatly wanting to see. And when I had looked at it for so long that the hour of prime was rung, it was as if I had looked at none of it, there were so many letters left. Then I marvelled greatly how there could be so many letters in such a small book. Then I looked at the book until, towards the third hour, I had seen a great deal about my lineage, and in that way I saw the lives and names of such worthy men that I hardly dared say or admit that I was descended from them. When I saw their worthy lives and the travails they had suffered on earth for their creator, I was unable so much as to think how I might amend my soul so that it could be worthy

quant je oi longuement esté en cel penser, si esgardai avant, e tant que je vi 'Ci comence le Saint Graal', e quant je oi leu tant que midiz fu passez, si trovai 'Ci comencent les Granz Paours'. E lui avant tant que je lui choses mult espoentables, e sache Dex que a grant doutance les veoie: ne ja veoir ne les osasse se cil ne le m'eust comandé par cui toutes choses sunt governees. E quant je oi ce veu, si commençai durement a penser.

of mention with theirs, nor could I see that I was truly a man in comparison with them, but a mere imitation of a man. When I had been preoccupied with these thoughts for a long time, I looked ahead until I saw, 'Here the Holy Grail begins'. And when I had read for so long that midday had passed, I found, 'Here the Great Fears begin'. I read on until I had read many very terrifying things, and God knows I saw them with great dread: nor would I ever have dared to look at them if he by whom all things are governed had not commanded it to me. And when I had seen all this, I began to think very hard.

[*A flash of lightning and more thunder cause the hermit to swoon again, but he is revived by sweet odours and the sound of singing. He says his Good Friday service but explains that he means to omit the Eucharist since there is no need for the sign of Christ's sacrifice on the day when it actually happens. At the point of the Mass when he would have received the host, an angel appears and takes the hermit to the third heaven and still higher. With spiritual rather than corporeal vision the hermit is able to see the three persons of the Trinity in one, and once he has assured the angel that he has no further doubt, his spirit is returned to his body and the angel leaves him as he wakes, apparently back into the same moment of his divine service as that in which his visionary journey began.*]

[f. 2*rb*, line 11] E je esgardai, si vi mon Sauveor devant moi ensint come je l'avoie veu en tel maniere com il estoit quant li angles m'emporta, e je lusai en bone creance. E je pris le livret si le mis el leu ou *Corpus Domini* estoit, quar mult i avoit beau leu e net. E quant je issi de la chapele si gardai que il estoit ja pres de nuit. E lors entrai en ma maisonete e mangai tele viande come Dex m'avoit aprestee.

Atant passa cel jor e que il vint au jor de la surrection au Sauveor e quant il li plot que je oi fait le servise icel jor qui est si haus come li jors de nostre sauvement, celui meismes qui le jor saintefia en trai a garant que je coru ainçois au livre por les bones paroles que je ne fis a la manne prendre. Quar tant estoient douces que eles me feisoient oblier la fain du cors. E quant je ving a la chasse ou je l'avoie mis e je la deffermai, si nel trovai pas. E quant je

And I looked around and saw my Saviour before me, exactly as I had seen him when the angel carried me away, and now I was radiant with true faith. And I took the little book and put it where the body of the Lord was kept, for that was a very beautiful and clean place. When I came out of the chapel, I saw that it was nearly night, and I went into my little house and ate whatever food God had provided for me.

So passed that day, and the next was the day of the Saviour's resurrection. When, as it pleased him, I had performed divine service for the day (which, being the day of our redemption is the most exalted feast), the one who himself sanctified this day is my witness that I ran more readily to the book for its good words than I would have to collect manna. For the words were so sweet that they made me forget bodily hunger. And when I came to the chest where I had put the book vi ce, si fui si dolans que je ne savoie que je fasoie. E me merveillai mult coment il peust estre hors de celi leu, quar ausint estoit il fermez come devant. Ensint come j'estoie en tel maniere si dist une vois, 'De quoi es tu esmaiez? En tel maniere issi Jhesu Cris[t] du sepulchre senz deffermer. Mais or te conforte e si va mengier, quar ainçois te covient poine sofrir que tu l'aies mais'.

and unlocked the chest, I didn't find it. I was so sorrowful when I saw this that I didn't know what I was doing. And I wondered very much how it could have left its place, for the chest was locked and undisturbed. As I was wondering, a voice said, 'What are you troubled about? In such a way Jesus Christ went out of the sepulchre without opening it. But now, comfort yourself and go and eat, since you will have to suffer trouble in order to have it again'.

E quant je oï qu'encore le ravroie je si me ting a ben paié. Lors alai mengier e quant je oi mengié si priai Nostre Seignor qu'il me donast avoiement de ce que je desiroie. Lors me dist une vois, 'Ce te mande li Haus Maistres que demain quant tu avras la messe chantee si mengeras e puis si t'en iras en la besoinge Jhesu Crist. E quant tu seras oissus de çaens, si enterras ou sentier qui te menra au grant chemin. Cil chemins te menra tant que venras au Perron de l'Aprise e lors lerras le chemin e torneras par un sentier qui moine el quarrefort de .vii. voies el Plain du Val Estot. E quant tu vendras a la Fontaine du Plor la ou la granz occisionz fu jadis, si trouverras une beste que onques ne veïs autretele. E si garde que tu la sives ausint come ele te menra, e quant tu l'avras perdue en la Tere de Negne, illuec achieveras ton erre, e savras por quoi li Granz Maistres ti envoie.' Atant leissa la voiz a parler. [f. 2v]

And when I heard that I would have the book once more, I was well content. Then I went to eat and when I had eaten, I prayed Our Lord that he would give me guidance towards what I desired. Then a voice said to me, 'The High Master commands that tomorrow, after you have sung Mass, you will eat and then depart on the business of Jesus Christ. And when you have left here, you will come onto a little track which will lead you to the great path. That path will lead you up to the Stone of Instruction, and then you will leave the path and turn down a track which leads to a crossroad of seven ways in the Valley of Obstinancy. And when you come to the Fountain of Weeping, where the great massacre took place long ago, you will find a beast such as you have never seen before. Be careful to follow where it leads you, and once you have lost it in the Realm of Snows, you will finish your journey and you will know why the Great Master sent you there'. Then the voice ceased speaking.

[*The hermit journeys from the Stone to the Valley of the Dead already familiar to him as the site of a battle between the two greatest knights of the world, and finds the beast at the seven ways crossroads. They journey on to another hermit's forest lodging (a humility contest on the model of the Vitae patrum ensues, each hermit sure he is less worthy of blessing the other): at a marvellous fountain under a pine tree a young squire gallops up to them with food sent by his lady; at a crossroads a knight and his company offer hospitality and escort them home; the hermit and the beast continue on to a nunnery where the hermit performs divine service, and on again to a block of stone with letters announcing the end of the hermit's mission: here the beast disappears. The hermit now finds in the forest a chapel with its holy man lying at the threshold, possessed by the devil: the possessed man partially responds to the sign of the cross made over his mouth, but the devil refuses to leave. Retrieving his little book from the chapel altar, the hermit uses its power in exorcism (the devil, being unable to come past the sign of the cross at the afflicted man's mouth, is forcefully ejected through his anus by the book's power). The hermit takes care of the devil's recovering victim, and heavenly fruit is delivered daily for their sustenance: the one sin during nearly thirty-five years of eremitism that had allowed the devil to possess the chapel's hermit is confessed to the narrator but not divulged to the reader. The two hermits part at the octave of Easter.*]

[f. 3rb, 1.32] Et errames tant que je ving au samadi au soir a mon herberjage e quant je i fui venus, si chantai vespres e complie, puis alai mengier ce que Deu plot. E puis m'alai coucher en mon lit, quar j'estoie mult travaillez. E quant je fui couchiez, si s'aparut li Haus Maistres ausint come il avoit fait a l'autre fois, e me dist: 'Au premier jor ovrable, escri ce du livret en un autre, e pren en l'aumaire quanque il covient a escrivain. E si ne t'esmaiez pas se tu ne seiz escrivre, quar tu le savras mult ben'. Au matin me levai e trovai ausint come il m'avoit dit, e trovai ce qu'il covenoit a escrivain, e pane e enque e parchemin e coutel. Et quant le diemenche fu passez e je oi au lundi la messe chantee e fait mon servise, si pris le livret e le parchemin tout droit a la quinzainne de Pasque; li commencemenz de l'escripture si fu pris du crucefiement Jhesu Crist.

And we went on until I came back to my hermitage on the Saturday evening, and when I got there I sang vespers and compline, then went to eat as God pleased. And then I went to sleep in my bed, for I was very weary. And when I got into bed, the High Master appeared as he had done on the previous occasion and said to me, 'On the first available working day, make a copy of the book. Take from the chest whatever a writer needs, and do not be dismayed if you do not know how to write, for you will find you do know very well'. In the morning I got up and found it was just as he had said to me, and I found a scribe's necessities: pen, ink and parchment, and a knife. And when Sunday was over, and I had sung Mass on Monday and said my office, then I took the little book and the parchment precisely on the fifteenth day after Easter: the writing began with the story of Jesus Christ's crucifixion.

Notes

3–8 **comencement de ceste estoire . . . commencement de vie** The Trinity is invoked as the beginning of creation and as presiding over the beginning of the *Estoire*.

6 **ce est [el] Saint Esperit** MS *ce est Saint Esperit.*

12 **oissues** MS for *eissus*, so also line 221 below. The scribe also uses *issi* (*1 pret* and *3 pret*) at 189 and 209, but *oissir* seems to be the prevailing dialectal form.

14 **de lui qui est** MS *quei* with *e* expuncted giving *qui.*

20 **son lignage** By the end of the *Estoire* a number of families are associated with the Grail: Alan, son of Bron receives the keeping of the Grail from Josephus and is the ancestor of a long line of Grail keepers: the descendants of Josephus's brother Josue become the Fisher Kings (*si furent tout apele en sornon [riche] pescheours*, Sommer 1909, 289.35–6), a name suggestively close to the hermit's identity as a sinner (*pecheor*, line 2 above). Celidone who defeats the Saxons is the ancestor of Lancelot. While most Grail families are descended from Joseph and his kin, in the *Estoire*, Lancelot's ancestors are Joseph's first converts (see further Chase 2003, 69–72).

22 **e il** MS *e li.*

46–7 **aprés la passion . . . vij.c. e .xvii. anz** the significance of the date is unclear. Leupin contrasts the auspiciousness of the numbers 1 and 7 with the wilderness setting in which the hermit is experiencing his religious doubt: Leupin 1982, 25–6.

59 **tenebres** *Tenebrae* (lit. 'shadows, darkness') the evening service before Maundy Thursday and Good Friday during which candles are gradually extinguished.

69 **que dire** MS line-end dittography *di | dire.*

91–5 **devant ma bouche . . . uns brandonz come feu** The hermit's experiences bear a general resemblance to the Pentecostal acquisition of many tongues by the apostles in Acts 2.2–4. To this is later added a divinely given ability to write as a copyist, lines 245–7 above.

103 **Nichodemus** the apocryphal *Gospel of Nicodemus* contributes much to the early part of the *Estoire* proper and its account of Joseph of Arimathea, but the prologue's Nichodemus is the sceptical Pharisee of John 3.1.

125–6 **langue de cuer . . . de la bouche** cf. St Edmund's *Mirour* (**22**: 163–80) and 1 Cor 14.13.

133–8 **au cors . . . joie de l'ame** For medieval theories of the power of text literally to re-create the psycho-physiology of readers, see Olson 1982.

138 **mort** MS *mort mort* with first *mort* expuncted.

139–40 **une voiz . . . come une boisine** cf. Rev 1.10.

158–62 **prime . . . tierce** Throughout the Prologue the hermit counts time liturgically: the hours by the monastic office (with the canonical hours of prime, matins, terce, nones, vespers, compline) and the days by the liturgical calendar.

177 **les Granz Paours** *Les Paours* refers to the section of the *Estoire* dealing with Mordrain, Nascien and others of God's servants and their dispersal and reassembly in the kingdom of Sarras before the evangelisation of Britain; see Ponceau 1997, I. xvi–xix.

183 **Sauveor** This may refer to the Eucharistic host (not normally consecrated on Good Friday: some of the consecrated host from Holy Thursday is processed to a ciborium and kept ready for the Good Friday service) or to Christ himself.

196–7 **nostre sauvement, celui meismes qui** In the complex syntax of this sentence, taking *sauvement* (salvation) as a personified abstract referring to Christ himself seems the best solution. In the long version, Ponceau notes some 'Sauveour' variants, but does not emend (Ponceau 1997, I.12).

199–200 **bones paroles . . . douces** Perhaps an echo of the sweetness of the book devoured by John in Rev 10.10. On sweetness as an aesthetic experience, see Carruthers 2006.

201 **eles** MS *oiels eles* with *oiels* expuncted.

210–11 **Mais or** Scribal insertion of *or.*

221 **oissus** See n. to line 12 above.

223–4 **Perron de l'Aprise** Stone of Instruction: Ponceau 1997, I.12 takes as *de la Prise* (Stone of the Capture). Given the mysteriousness of the Grail names (cf. *la granz occisionz*, lines 227–8 below), the definite article may not obviate the reading 'instruction' here. In the long version, the hermit's desert place of lines 48–9 above is specifically located in *la bloie Bretagne* (Ponceau 1997, I.2), so the hermit needs no sea-crossing in his quest for the book.

226 **Val Estot** Variants for this name include Walescot, Walestoch (cf. OE *wealh*, 'foreign'), Valestoc (Ponceau 1997, I.12), Val Estat (Gros 2001, 13), Val Estone (Sommer 1909, 8.27), but the literal sense of 'perverse, obstinate, stubborn' or even of 'stultified' is available and chosen here.

227–8 **la granz occisionz** The great slaughter. It is unclear to which incident this refers: perhaps to the mass crucifixion of Joseph's followers at Camelot, 'the richest of the Saracen cities of Great Britain' (Sommer 1909, 46.1–15, Ponceau 1997, I.xxi, §758–65; Chase 2010, 136–7), though this is chiefly associated with 'la croix Noire' because of the blackness of the bloodstained cross: or perhaps to the death of 150 of King Ganor's people who refuse to convert to Christianity (Sommer 1909, 225.26–32), the battle against the king of Northumberland at Galafort, scene of the first Christian victory in Britain (Sommer 1909, 229–30), or Nascien's battle against Crudel, king of Norgales (Sommer 1909, 240.26–4, 1.8).

228–9 **une beste ... autretele** When the hermit encounters the beast it is *diverse* (the head and neck of a sheep, the feet and thighs of a dog, the chest and body of a fox and the tail of a lion), but faithful to its task as guide (see Gros 2001, 14; Ponceau 1997, I.13; Sommer 1909, 9.1–6). The hermit's beast is distinct from the questing beast (*beste glatissante*) of subsequent Arthurian works: in the *Suite du Merlin* and Malory, for instance, the beast has parts from more aristocratic animals as well as the continual sound of baying hounds in its belly.

231 **la Tere de Negne** Variants for this name include Norvvage, Normaigne, Noreague, Norvagne (Ponceau 1997, I.13), Norweghe (Sommer 1909, 8 n. 5), all suggesting some meaning connecting Norway and snow (*neige*), but the place name Norway does not seem to have been recognised by the scribe here if it was indeed in the exemplar.

244 **l'aumaire** The term often means specifically book chest (though not used at lines 187–8 above, where the hermit says he put the book 'in the place where the Host was' (*el leu ou* Corpus Domini *estoit*) or at line 202 where the hermit expects to find the book in a *chasse*, the usual term for a reliquary.

250 **coutel** Medieval scribes kept a knife to hand for sharpening pens and scraping away any roughnesses in the parchment, and, occasionally, removing words or letters written in error.

42. Walter de la Hove (?), *The Mohun Chronicle* [Dean 65], Prologue: London, British Library, MS Add. 62,929, ff. 1r–2r

John Spence

Date of composition and provenance. Mid-fourteenth century (before 1350?); south-west England, Devon and Somerset.

Author, sources and nature of text. The author has been cautiously identified as Walter de la Hove, abbot of the Cistercian monastery of Newenham in Devon, which was founded by the Mohun family. In his prologue, the author lists what this chronicle will contain: the beginning of the world, the ages of the world until the Incarnation, how England was first inhabited, the emperors of Rome, the popes of Rome, the archbishops of Canterbury, the kings of France, the kings of England, and the arrival of the Mohun family in England and the family's history to the time of writing. What survives of the chronicle follows this outline – the only medieval manuscript breaks off while listing the popes, and parts of the chronicle's history of the Mohun family have survived in later copies.

The *Mohun Chronicle*'s accounts of emperors' and popes' lives are based on the Latin *Chronicon pontificum et imperatorum* (Chronicle of Popes and Emperors) written by Martinus Polonus (d. 1278), a Dominican friar who served as papal chaplain to Pope Nicholas III. The *Mohun Chronicle* also includes historical material on the Norman Conquest from Wace's *Roman de Rou* (3) and uses some version of the legend of Albina and her sisters, supposedly the first inhabitants of Britain, and perhaps also Ranulf Higden's *Polychronicon*.

The prologue interweaves material from major Angevin foundation traditions such as Wace's *Rou* (3) and the Pseudo-Turpin material deriving ultimately from the *Chanson de Roland* together with detail specific to the Mohun family. The *Mohun Chronicle* also compares its own role for its patrons with the legendary preservation of all knowledge on two pillars purportedly built by Adam (lines 1–13n.). Such boldness of reference for the cultural work of a single family's chronicle indicates the ambition with which insular historiographical tradition constructed identity for its patrons. In this, the *Mohun Chronicle* is comparable with other similarly accomplished prologues to historical works from the same period, such as *Fouke le Fitz Waryn* (**31**), Nicholas Trevet's *Cronicles*, Thomas Gray's *Scalacronica* (**16**) and the *Wigmore Abbey Chronicle*. Following the prologue, there is a five ages universal chronicle scheme and a prefatory narrative of Albina, foundress of Albion/Britain. Since in the *Mohun Chronicle* Albina eventually takes seisin of half the country from a base in Dartmouth and her sister the other half from a base in 'Hamtoun' (Southampton), this foundation narrative seems especially appropriate for a family with lineage and territorial concerns in south-west England, and moreover a family that, in the generation for which the *Chronicle* was made, produced no sons, but only daughters, two of whom made brilliant marriages.

Audience and circulation. The references to the Mohun family in the prologue (lines 48–58, 86–91) indicate that they were the author's immediate target audience, and it has been suggested that the *Mohun Chronicle* is identical with a 'Red Book' which contained historical information about the Mohuns, written by the abbot of Newenham for Lady Joan de Mohun between about 1330 and 1350. Joan de Mohun (d. 1404) was the daughter of Sir Bartholomew Burghersh the elder (d. 1355), a soldier and diplomatic envoy respected by Edward III. Her husband, John de Mohun (d. 1375), was lord of Dunster Castle in Somerset, a companion of the Black Prince and a founding member of the Order of the Garter. It has recently been suggested, however, that the marriage may have foundered by the mid-1340s.

The *Mohun Chronicle* does not seem to have reached a wide audience and only one medieval manuscript survives, but marginalia in the manuscript provide evidence for the responses of two readers. One fifteenth- or early-sixteenth-century reader, probably from a clerical background, noted developments in church history, especially the evolution of the Mass, by writing 'nota' in the margins beside information on this subject. A second, later reader, probably from the sixteenth century and with more Protestant leanings, went through the manuscript deleting the word *pape* and replacing it with *evec* (bishop). A cadet branch of the Mohun family at Boconnoc in Cornwall possessed a copy of the *Mohun Chronicle* in the sixteenth and seventeenth centuries, and this copy of the work was consulted by a number of antiquaries and historians, including John Leland and William Camden.

Manuscript source. BL Add. 62,929, ff. 1r–2r. This parchment quire of eight folios, which contains only the Prologue and the beginning of the *Mohun Chronicle*, is the sole extant medieval manuscript. It was copied by a single scribe who wrote in a mid-fourteenth-century Anglicana hand and made few errors. The manuscript has many decorated initials in red and blue ink. (Some early-modern transcriptions, probably made from *Mohun* passages now lost, are also extant).

The manuscript's early provenance is unclear. One possibility is that it passed into the Carew family when John de Mohun V's sister Margaret married John Carew (d. 1363). Since its earliest annotations are concerned with changes to the Mass, the manuscript might have been in clerical hands in the fifteenth century, perhaps even at Newenham Abbey itself. It is certain that in 1907 the manuscript was owned by Elizabeth and Beatrix Carew of Haccombe and remained in the possession of the Carew family until it was auctioned at Sotheby's in 1983, when it was bought by the British Library.

Bibliography. The prologue was first edited by Lega-Weekes 1906–7. For a complete edition and translation of the surviving parts of the *Mohun Chronicle* and its early-modern transcriptions, see Spence 2011. For Anglo-Norman prose chronicles and legendary histories see Spence 2008a, 2013. The dissemination of Martinus Polonus's *Chronicon* is discussed in Wolfram 2003. On Dunster castle, its muniments and the Mohun family, see the extensive study by Maxwell-Lyte 1909 and Payling 2011. On Joan de Mohun and her *Chronicle*'s Albina story, see Wogan-Browne 2011. For the Albina story see Lamont and Baswell forthcoming.

TEXT AND TRANSLATION

[f. 1r] *Ci comence le prologe en cesti livere.*

Adam, le premer homme qe unques fust, entendi et savoit bien de trois choses qe fussent a vener. C'est assavoir de deus jugementz par lesquels Dieux voleit le monde ajuger: le premer jugement par eve, qe vint en le tenps Noe; l'autre jugement par feu. Encontre cels deus jugementz il fist deus piliers: l'un de marbre, encontre l'eve, et l'autre de tighel ou de tai, encontre le feu. En lesquels pielers il escrit tote manere art, qe cels qe venissent aprés lui purroient savoir le cours de siecle et lui avoir plus frechement en memorie. La tierce chose qe Adam entendi bien fust qe totes choses tornerent en declin, et tote vif chose devoit morir, et herbes, foilles, et roses flestrier, tote manere beste trebouncher, homme porir, vestmentz et fer user, tote rien odve main feat perir. Par quel encheson il escrit tote manere art en ambesdeus piliers, a cels qe dussent vener aprés lui. Donques nous, que sumus plus frellez qe Adam ne fust, dussoms mettre en escrit les featz, les ditz, les nouns, les successions, et les bons mours de noz amis, et nomeement de noz fondours, qe de lour biens vivoms et joioms en terre, et els de ceo vivent et joient en ciel, et pur ceo qe moltz des choses fussent obliez par cours de longtenps, par grande age, par diverses gueres, et par sodeine mutacions des lignages, sanz ceo qu'els ne soient par gent de religion mis en livere.

Auxint com est trové plusours regions, villes, et surnons de grandz seignurs estre changez, com Engleterre, qe jadis fust apelé Albion, aprés Britaigne le grande; Southgalis fust apelé Demercia; et Northgalis Venodocia; Eschoce out a non jadis Aquitaigne; et Britaigne Amoriche; et Germaigne fust Alamaigne; Cologne aveit a non Agrippine; et Londres primes

Here begins the prologue to this book.

Adam, the first man that ever was, knew and understood well three things that were to come. That is, he knew of two judgements by which God wished to judge the world: the first judgement by water, which came in the time of Noah; the other judgement by fire. To guard against these two judgements he made two pillars; one of marble, to protect against the water, and the other of tile or of clay, against the fire. On these pillars he wrote all kinds of knowledge, so that those who came after him could know the course of the world, and to recall the knowledge more clearly in his own memory. The third thing that Adam understood well was that all things will come to an end, and every living thing must die, and plants, leaves and roses must wither, every kind of animal must die, man must decay, clothes and iron must wear out, and everything made by hand must perish. For which reason he wrote all kinds of knowledge on both pillars for those who should come after him. Therefore we, who are more frail than Adam ever was, must put into writing the deeds, the sayings, the names, the lines of succession and the virtues of our kin and particularly of our ancestors, since because of their good deeds we live and rejoice on earth and they live and rejoice in heaven, and because many things may be forgotten with the passage of time, old age, various wars, and sudden changes of lineage, unless they are put in a book by men of religion.

So, as one finds, several regions, towns, and surnames of great lords have been changed: for example, England, which was once called Albion, then Great Britain; South Wales was called Demercia; and North Wales Venodocia; Scotland once had the name Aquitaine; and Brittany Armorica; and Germany was Alamaigne; Cologne had the name of Agrippina; and London first

out a non Troie Nove, et aprés Trinovant; Everwik out a non [f. 1v] Eborak et aprés Kaer Ebrak. Et issint com les nons des regions et des grandes villes par passer de tenps sont changez, en meisme le manere les sournons des conquerours sont changez. Et nomeement les nons de la noble lignage des Mohuns par les susdistes enchesons sont changez. Qar les premers qe unqes estoient en ceste terre soleient estre apelez par sournon 'Moions', auxint com il est escrit eu livere des conquerours, et com il est trové par anceianz chartres qe la lignage ad feat a diverses abbeies et priories, jusqes a tenps le premer Johan de Mohun, lequil dil sournon 'Moion' osta un silable et fist apeler 'Mohun'.

Et pur teles mutacions nule people vivant greindre mester n'ad d'aprendre le cours du siecle et de seint esglise qe n'ont les grandz seignurs d'Engleterre, pur moltz d'enchaisons, et nomeement pur ceo qe Engleterre ad esté puis le tenps Brutus par guerre troblé sovent et enqore n'est ele pas bien establé, ne jamés serra, qar la figure de ceste siecle legerment passera.

Et ceo pust bien estre veu qui qe voille rewarder cestes petitez cronicles. Lesqueles primes touchent briefment del comencement del mond, enpursiaunt les ages jusqes a la Incarnacion; et coment Engleterre fust primes enhabitee; aprés ceo de les sodeines mutacions des emperours de Rome, coment celui qe malement vesquit, en pursiaunt seynte esglise, mal fin avoit. Puis aprés les changes de les papes de Rome et lour nons, et de quele nacion ils furrent, et combien de els suffrirent dure martirizacion pur l'amur de Dieux et seynte esglise meyntener. Aprés ceo les nons des archevesqes de Canterburi; puis aprés les nons des rois de France, qe sovent sont changez; aprés ceo des rois d'Engleterre et quantz [des] ans chescun regna en

had the name New Troy, and afterwards Trinovant; York had the name Eborak, and afterwards Kaer Ebrak. And so, just as the names of regions and of great towns have changed with the passage of time, in the same way the surnames of the conquerors have changed. And in particular the names of the noble lineage of the Mohuns have changed because of the reasons given above. For the first of them who were ever in this land were accustomed to be called by the surname 'Moion', as it is written in the book of the conquerors and as it is found in ancient charters which the family had made out to various abbeys and priories, until the time of the first John de Mohun, who removed a syllable of the surname 'Moion' and had himself called 'Mohun'.

And because of such changes no people living have a greater need to learn the history of the world and of holy church than the great lords of England have, for many reasons, and particularly because England has often been troubled by war since the time of Brutus, and still is not very stable, nor will it ever be, for the form of this world will readily pass away.

And that can be seen well by anyone who wishes to look at these little chronicles. They first touch briefly upon the beginning of the world; then the ages until the Incarnation; and how England was first inhabited; after that the abrupt overthrows of the emperors of Rome, how those of them who lived badly, persecuting holy church, came to a bad end. Then, after that, the succession of the popes of Rome and their names, and what people they were from, and how many of them suffered harsh martyrdom for the love of God and to maintain holy church. After that the names of the archbishops of Canterbury; then after that the names of the kings of France, which have often changed; after that the names of the kings of England and how many years each one reigned in England. And lastly how

Engleterre. Et au derain coment la noble lignage des Mohuns vint odve William, conquerour d'Engleterre, et combien des grandz seignurs William le Moion le veil aveit a sa retenance adonqes; et puis del decent des Mohuns jusqes a cesti jour.

Les[f. 2r]queles choses susdistes avoms escript com nous avoms oï, si deit estre cher tenuez et voluntiers oïez de touz hautz hommes. Qar pur ceo sont les bones vertues del siecle aukes defailliez et les queors des seignurages afebliez, qe hom n'out mes si volentiers com l'en soleit les oeveres des anciens ne les estoires ou les bons featz sont, qe enseinent coment l'en se deit avoir en Dieux et contener al siecle honoreement. Qar vivere sanz honur est morir.

Explicit prologus.

the noble family of the Mohuns came with William, Conqueror of England, and how many great lords William de Mohun the elder had in his retinue at that time; and then the line of descent of the Mohuns to this day.

These aforesaid things we have written as we have heard them, so that they should be cherished and gladly heard by all noble men. For the good qualities of the world have rather diminished, and the hearts of lords weakened, so that a man no longer hears as willingly as he used to the deeds of his ancestors, nor the stories that feature the great deeds, that teach how one should lead a Christian life and behave honourably in the world. For to live without honour is to die.

Here ends the prologue.

Notes

Thanks are due to Dr Michelle Brown and Dr Justin Clegg of the Department of Manuscripts, British Library for advice on the date of the handwriting of the later readers of the Mohun manuscript.

1–13 **Adam, le premer homme . . . frechement en memorie** The story of two pillars designed to preserve all knowledge was widely known in the Middle Ages, having first appeared in Josephus's *Antiquities*, Bk 1, Ch 2.3(70–1): 'And that their inventions [those of Seth's children, who invented astrology, according to this passage] might not be lost before they were sufficiently known, upon Adam's prediction that the world was to be destroyed at one time by the force of fire, and at another time by the violence and quantity of water, they made two pillars; the one of brick, the other of stone: they inscribed their discoveries on them both, that in case the pillar of brick should be destroyed by the flood, the pillar of stone might remain, and exhibit these discoveries to mankind; and also inform them that there was another pillar of brick erected by them. Now this remains in the land of Siriad to this day' (Thackeray *et al.* 1997 [1930], 32–3). The Josephus version, while probably not the direct source (since Adam himself builds the pillars in the *Mohun Chronicle*), is close to *Mohun* in the phrase 'the one of brick, the other of stone' describing the pillars. For discussion of earlier versions and analogues of the story, see Lega-Weekes, ed., 1906–7, 17–18; Horrall 1978–2000, I.366; Stephens 1989, 87, 364 nn. 64, 65.

14–19 **totes choses tornerent . . . odve main feat perir** These lines are adapted from the introduction to Wace's *Roman de Rou* (Holden 1970–3, part 3, vv. 131–6; and (3.131–6) above).

18 **vestmentz** MS *vestmeentz.*

27 **vivent** MS *viunt.*

28–32 **moltz des choses fussent obliez . . . par gent de religion mis en livere** A frequent topos in chronicles: on the interdependence of monastic writers and secular patrons in *Brut* historiography, see Marvin 2006, Introduction.

31–2 **sanz ceo . . . livere** Possibly indebted to Wace's *Rou* (Holden 1970–3, part 3, v. 141; (3.141) above).

35–44 **Engleterre . . . Kaer Ebrak** Examples from Wace's *Rou* (Holden 1970–3, part 3, vv. 15–20; (3.15–20) above).

37 **Demercia** Demetia is an early name for South Wales.

53 **livere des conquerours** Conceivably a reference to Domesday Book or possibly to the sub-genre of lists of those who came with the conqueror and other genealogical lists: see Dean 8, 9, 11 (2). However, it is most likely to refer directly to Wace's *Rou*: cf. Spence 2011, Extract 1, lines 6–8, where the phrase describes the source of the list of William de Moion I's companions during the Norman Conquest.

62–6 The earlier annotator of the MS has written *nota* in the margin beside this part of the text.

69 **petitez cronicles** As opposed to *grandes croniques*, i.e. universal chronicles. The *Mohun Chronicle* abridges the accounts of emperors' and popes' lives taken from Martinus Polonus's *Chronicon*.

70 **briefment** In the MS the *n* is written over the second *e*.

74–8 **emperours de Rome . . . les papes de Rome** These categories of lists are probably due to the influence of Martinus Polonus's *Chronicon* (Spence 2011, 159–60).

77 **papes** This word has been deleted, and *evc* written above it, by the second annotator of the MS.

85 **des** This word has been inserted above the line by the original scribe.

82–4 **archevesqes de Canterburi . . . rois de France . . . rois d'Engleterre** Such lists are found in French in the Newenham cartulary (Spence 2011, 166–8).

88–9 **combien des grandz seignurs** The chronicler may here have mistakenly viewed Wace's long list of persons immediately following William de Moion's name as a personal retinue (cf. Holden 1970–3, part 3, lines 8487–621 for the original).

93 **escript** In the MS the *p* is written over an *s*.

93–102 **si deit estre . . . est morir** This material is taken *verbatim* from the end of the prologue to an early-thirteenth-century French translation of the *Pseudo-Turpin* (Walpole 1976, I.130: Prologue lines 15–20).

97 **afebliez** In the MS the first *e* is written over a *b*.

43. *Poème sur l'Ancien Testament* (Poem on the Old Testament) [Dean 462], Prologue: London, British Library, MS Egerton 2710, f. 2*ra*

Date of composition and provenance. End of the twelfth or beginning of the thirteenth century, England.

Author, sources and nature of text. The author of this decasyllabic poem is unknown, and the title *Poème anglo-normand sur l'Ancien Testament* was created by Meyer (1889). The identity of the work's author and patron, if any, are unknown. It is an ambitious work, comprising (in its incomplete form) some 18,000 lines, based on the biblical books of Genesis, Exodus, Numbers, Joshua, Judges, Ruth, and Kings I-IV, with additional material from Flavius Josephus's *Jewish Antiquities*. The *Poème sur l'Ancien Testament* recounts only sacred history (unlike other translations based on the Bible which include non-biblical history), and draws moral lessons from the events, but does not expand these by allegorical interpretations or extensive theological glossing (Nobel 1996, I.158–9). The work is characterised by its focus on biblical kingship and warfare, and by its use of Josephus's *Antiquities* in the production of a lengthy but cohesive and compelling account of biblical history. Although the author does not name it as one of his sources, Josephus's *Jewish Antiquities* is used increasingly as the work progresses, becoming at times the sole source. The

Poème's composer draws on the narrative unity of the *Antiquities*, and on its more numerous details to heighten its own epic quality.

The *Poème* exploits the dramatic history of the Jews, while omitting biblical elements such as lengthy genealogies and presentations of Jewish law, or repetitive accounts of the same events. Although fast-paced, the *Poème* finds space to expand on characters' motivations by adding short explicative and moral glosses (sometimes anti-feminist and anti-Judaic). What dominates the whole, however, is the author's skilful adaptation of his sources to the concerns of a medieval audience interested in kingship and battle: biblical kings are seen to consult their baronial councils (who, for example, appoint Moses head of the army, or advise Saul to give his daughter in marriage to David, and later argue in favour of David naming Salomon his successor). In battle scenes, details of city fortifications are added, as well as descriptions of the heroic qualities of the defenders; the physical details of blows exchanged are expressed, as one would expect, using the stylistic formulae of the *chanson de geste*. The metrical form of the *Poème* also underlines its epic qualities, since decasyllabics are the *chanson de geste*'s traditional metre. The prologue is composed in sequences of monorhymed decasyllabic lines (of 6, 7, 13, 6, 6 lines, respectively, in vv. 1–38), similar to the *laisses* of the *chanson de geste*, but, after the first hundred lines, the work is written uniformly in decasyllabic rhyming couplets (a rare combination of metres in medieval poetry: Nobel 1996, I.51).

While the author does not expound in the body of his poem on Jewish history as the precursor to Christian history (the common medieval Christian view that the Old Testament is an allegorical prefiguring of the New), the prologue focuses on this relationship. The opening invocation to the all-powerful God of Judaism (vv. 1–6) is followed immediately by the author's dedication of his work to the Trinitarian Christian deity (vv. 7–9). His 'new poem of great deeds' (*de geste novel escrit*, v. 9) is at once both old and epic (the *geste*, based on Old Testament Jewish history) and new (*novel escrit*: the Christian interpretation of Jewish history). The linking of Judaism and Christianity is continued in the assertion of Jewish history's truth value (vv. 10–12): its biblical stories are not just oral tales (*de fable dit*, v. 10), but stories read publicly and cyclically in (Christian) churches. Their value is affirmed by Jerome, a church Father who understood these miraculous stories in the light of Christian doctrine, and who, as the source of the poem and the translator of the Vulgate Bible, guarantees their historical truth (Nobel 1996, I.293).

The poet's direct apostrophe to his listeners (*Oez, seignours*, v. 14) again draws attention to Christianity as the successor to Judaism. His *chançun de verité* (a poem in the epic style of the *chanson de geste*, but dealing with sacred history) portrays the patriarchs of antiquity in whose persons Christ and holy church were prefigured. Our 'pagan ancestors' (v. 27) first lived in ignorance of divine law, but after hearing of God, were among the most faithful. This enlightenment of the ancients is parallel to that of medieval clerics who already know this sacred history, for they 'see' (*veient*, v. 32) it often – a verbal echo back to Jerome who also 'saw' (*les merveilles vit*, v. 12), or understood, Jewish history in a new light. The author, as one of these clerics, offers his poem, then, to educate his lay audience, so that they, like the ancient Jews, may become among the most faithful once they have understood sacred history as recounted in the present work.

Audience and circulation. The narrative focus of the *Poème* suggests it was written for an audience interested in warfare and kingship, as well as biblical history; it is probable that the author was writing for members of one of the crusader orders of chivalry, such as the Templars or the Hospitallers (Short 1998, 82); the Templars are known to have commissioned a similar work, a translation of the book of Judges (Nobel 1996, I.9). The number of extant manuscripts demonstrates the *Poème*'s popularity in England among a wider range of audiences. It is found complete in four manuscripts, all of English origin: the *Poème* alone (Genesis to Ezekiel, MS BN fr. 898), and various doctrinal and devotional collections (BN. fr. 902; Oxford, Corpus Christi College 36; BL Egerton 2710), and it is also preserved as a fragment in five manuscripts (all of English origin, including two still in provincial English repositories in Lincolnshire and Wiltshire). In the late thirteenth or early fourteenth century the *Poème* was drawn on for one of the prose Anglo-Norman Bibles which continued to circulate in the fourteenth and fifteenth centuries (Dean 470: see also 463–5, 467, 469, 471) and in which the *Poème*'s concern with recuperating and amalgamating the historicity of the Jewish scriptures remains a key prologue concern.

Manuscript source. BL Egerton 2710 was written in England *c.* 1220–40: a vellum manuscript of 151 folios, 265 × 180mm (with varied writing spaces), it has red, blue and some gold initials in its double-columned text. The manuscript is a collection of some ten religious works, including extracts on the Passion and the Assumption from the *Bible* of Herman de Valenciennes (**15**) and the *Vie de saint Laurent*, along with other well-known works. With the exception of the *Poème*, all the works in Egerton 2710 are also found in BN fr. 19,525, which contains in addition other well-known works such as the *Vie de saint Alexis*, and the *Vie de sainte Marie l'Égyptienne*. MS BN fr. 19,525 was written at Oxford in the style of the workshop of William de Brailles *c.* 1230–50 (Morgan 1982, 36 n. 35; Avril and Stirnemann 1987, 67–8). Despite the close connection in contents between these two manuscripts, neither is copied from the other. Egerton 2710 belonged at the end of the fifteenth century to the Benedictine priory of nuns at Derby (f. 83[b], inscription in English); see digital images at http://www.bl.uk/catalogues/illuminatedmanuscripts/ILLUMIN.ASP?Size=mid&IllID=4174.

Bibliography. First noted by Abbé Lebeuf in 1751, the *Poème sur l'Ancien Testament* (and its later prose descendants) was referred to in passing by Berger (1967, 54–5), and was dismissed by Bonnard (1967, 92–104) as having no poetic merit. This view was countered by Meyer (1889), who drew attention to the popularity of this work in England, and to its interest as a biblical poem written for public recital in an epic style, in the rare metrical form of decasyllabic rhyming couplets. Meyer's notice on the Egerton manuscript also published a range of short extracts, and comments on the other manuscript copies. But it was more than two centuries after Lebeuf's notice that the first edition appeared (Nobel 1996), accompanied by a detailed study of the poem. Nobel provides extensive details on sources, on techniques of translation, on the scribal language of the two manuscripts used in his facing-page edition (B= Paris, BN fr. 902, E= London, BL Egerton 2710), and on the language of the author of the work (see also Nobel 1997). Ian Short's review (1998) provides a succinct overview of the work and of its context. The *Poème* and its prosified equivalents are taking their place in new work on francophone medieval Bible reading: see e.g. the valuable survey in Hoogvliet 2013; Waters (2015) and on late-medieval French biblical texts in England, Hanna 2005, Watson 2009b.

TEXT AND TRANSLATION

Al rei de glorie, [a] Deu omnipotent,
Qui meint sanz fin e sanz commencement,
Le mund governe tut par sun jugement,
E est a sons en chescun liu present,
A chescun socorable qui a lui se prent,
Honur, puissance sanz definement.
El nun del Pere, del Fiz, del Seint Espirit,
Des treis persones qui sunt un Deu parfit,
Comencerons de geste novel escrit.
L'estoire estrete n'est pas de fable dit,
Dë an en an en seint' eglise est lit,
Ço dit Jeroimes ki les merveilles vit.
N'est pas leaus qui cest tent en despit.

Honour and never-ending power to the King of Glory, God omnipotent, who is everlasting, without end and without beginning, who governs the whole world in his wisdom, who attends to his own everywhere and gives aid to each one who follows him. In the name of the Father, the Son, and the Holy Spirit, three persons who are one perfect God, we will begin a new poem of great deeds. The history that we have chosen to translate is not drawn from fables, but is read in holy church, year after year, as Jerome says, who understood these miracles. He who scorns

Oez, seignors, chançun de verité,
De veil' estoire estret sanz fauseté
Des patriarches devant que Deu fu né,
Des sainz prophetes qui furent d'antiquité,
De lur linage, de lur grant parenté.
En lur persones Jhesu fu figuré
E seint' eglise, qui puis nus fu mustré.
De la Deu vertu tant sunt enluminé
Qu'il ne saveient boidie, ne mauvesté
Ne vodreient fere. Ne fust aucun malfé
Ki la lei freinsist aprés qu'ele fu doné.
Qui la gardouent parvindrent a sauveté,
Qui la gerpirent grefment en sunt jugé.
   Nos ancessors trestoz paëns esteient,
Lei ne garderent kar Deu ne saveient.
Mes quant de Deu aparceu se aveient,
Ces furent cil ki en Deu melz creeient.
A lais escrif l'estoirë u qu'il seient,
Li clerc le sevent kar il sovent la veient.
   Al començail quant Deu creat le mund
E cel e tere e l'abime parfund,
Lumere, tenebres, li quel uncore sunt
La les fundat u il tut tens serrunt
Al premer jur si cum Moyses respunt
As fiz Jacob sur Syna[ï] le munt.

this is not loyal to his faith. Hear, my lords, a song of truth, based without falseness on the ancient history of the patriarchs from before the birth of Christ, the story of the holy prophets of antiquity, of their lineage and their ancestry. In their person Jesus and holy church were foreshadowed, which was later revealed to us. The prophets were so enlightened by the grace of God that they knew no treachery nor did they wish to do any evil. Not one of them was an evil man who broke the law after it was given: whoever kept the law well came to salvation, whoever abandoned it was severely punished.

Our ancestors were pagans; they followed no law for they did not know God. But when they had learned of God, they were the ones who believed the most in him. I write this history for laypeople, wherever they may be; clerics know it already for they often read it.

In the beginning, when God created the world, heaven and earth and the endless deeps, light and darkness, all which still exist, he created them on the first day, there where they will be eternally, as Moses explained to the sons of Jacob on mount Sinai.

Notes

The extract above is edited in an interventionist fashion, with the intention of providing a version of the text in regular decasyllabic rhythm, which usually breaks 4+6, or 6+4; the caesura can be masculine (4 + 6); epic (an unstressed –e in the fifth syllable is not counted in the rhythm: 4 +e +6); lyric (the 4th syllable is one containing an unstressed –e: 3 +e + 6), etc. In addition, within the hemistich, the scribe occasionally elides the final *–ent* syllable in verbal endings (*furent* 17, *saveient* 22, *vodreient* 23, *parvindrent* 25), or the final weak *–e* in nouns and pronouns (*geste* 9, *ele* 24, *lumere* 35, *tenebres* 35). The diaeresis is occasionally used to indicate vowels in hiatus which would normally be elided. The emendation on metrical grounds alone, of course, is not a tenable approach in general, since the metrics of the French written in England remain imperfectly understood. It is used in this extract alone as a pedagogical exercise to show the underlying decasyllabic structure of the work; using this approach to the complete poem would not be defensible, since it would be frequently arbitrary, and far removed from the extant manuscript evidence. The editorial stance used in this extract is in stark contrast, then, to Pierre Nobel's edition, which is very non-interventionist (in the extreme, according to Short 1998, 82–4). Most editors preparing an edition of this text would fall somewhere between these two editorial approaches – neither too interventionist, nor too respectful of the scribal forms in each manuscript copy.

1 **a Deu** Emended on the basis of MS B (Paris, BN fr. 902, printed in parallel page edition by Nobel). The epic caesura in this line means that *glorie* (=*gloire*) counts as one syllable.

3 **governe** MS *governez*: the syntax (and MS B) support the emendation.

5 **qui a lui** counts as two syllables, and could be emended to **qu'a lui**. The use of *que* (subject to elision) for *qui* is common in insular French.

6 **puissance** MS *puissant*: based on B, the emendation makes better sense of the line, where the use of *puissant* as an adjective qualifying *honur* is unlikely.

7 **del Fiz, del Seint** MS *del fiz e del seint*: emended on the basis of B.

8 **Des treis** MS E *des treis*; **un Deu** MS *en deu*: emended on the basis of B.

10 **estrete**, placed at the caesura, counts as two syllables.

11 **en seint' eglise est** MS *est en seint eglise*: the emendation makes a decasyllabic line by preserving the hiatus between the first two words, *Dë an*, and by placing *est* after *eglise*, the final e of *eglise* is elided. MS B has *D'an en an est en sante eglise lit* which has a very unlikely rhythm 3 + 7.

12 **Jeroimes** Jerome (*c.* 347–420, in Latin Sophronius Eusebius Hieronymus), an influential and prolific priest and theologian who translated (most of) the Bible into Latin (from Hebrew and Greek), in the version now known as the Vulgate. We adopt Nobel's view (that Jerome's statement in this line refers back to the content of vv. 10–11, rather than announcing the moral sentiment expressed in v. 13: Nobel, ed., 1996, I.293). Jerome in the prologue to his translation of the Pentateuch notes that his translation, written after Christ, has an historical view of biblical prophecy that differs from that of pre-Christian biblical writing (*Nos post passionem et resurrectionem eius, non tam prophetiam quam historiam scribimus. Aliter enim audita, aliter visa narrantur*; see the prologue to Genesis in Weber, ed., 1975, I.4).

12 **Ço** MS *Ico*: emended on the basis of B.

15 **De veil'** MS E *del v.*: emended following B.

16 **Deu** in this context obviously means Jesus, who is only explicitly mentioned at v. 19.

20 **E** MS *En*: based on B.

21 **De la Deu** presumably counts for two syllables: read either *D'la Deu vertu*, or emend to *De Deu vertu*.

23 **Ne vodreient fere** MS *Ne fere ne vodereit*.

24 The decasyllabic rhythm is possible if one reads *K'la lei freinsist aprés qu'el' fu doné.*

25 **Qui la gardouent parvindrent**: emended on the basis of B. Omitting *ben* restores the parallel syntactic structure of vv. 25–6.

27 **Nos** MS *Des*: the reading from B is better.

29 **se aveient** The pronoun would be elided, and the phrase counts for two syllables.

36 **La** MS *Ileuques*: emended to follow B.

37 **Moyses** counts for two syllables.

Postlude: *Honneurs . . . publiées en divers royaumes*

Introduction

Like some of the language treatises (**7a–e**) and the *Speculum ecclesie* of St Edmund (**22**), our final excerpt, the *Débat des hérauts* (**44**) is a work with both manuscript and print lives. Composed in France in probably the mid-fifteenth century, the *Débat* provoked a riposte in English in 1549 from John Coke, Clerk of the Staple under Edward VI, who encountered it in Flanders (see Part VI, §2.10). The *Débat* is chosen here for its review of late-medieval and early-modern cultural traditions, shared, across a patchwork of regional differences, between several adjacent and interlinked cultures, England, France and Flanders. These cultural overlaps are in some respects continuous with those of twelfth-century England and Britain and the vigorous diffusion of *Brut* materials in and beyond insular culture. England and France are represented in the *Débat* as pulling apart into oppositional identities, a process that cannot help but testify to all that is common to them (in the excerpt here, principally traditions around Brutus, but around many more cultural figures and resources in the text as a whole). The *Débat*'s imbrication of cultural traditions as between England and France can be compared with the *A tous nobles* genealogical roll of 1443 (**20d**). Here a version of the French royal genealogy is displayed, in order to assert superior English claims to the French throne through the female line, and the roll's account of continuity and succession reaches back behind Brutus to Albina.

It is important to resist teleology and not to see the *Débat* as an inevitable result of a developing sense of national identity, versions of which are invoked in varying ways on occasion in earlier literature. Socio-political communities in any case polarise identity around a variety of axes. Matthew Paris's thirteenth-century Life of St Edmund, archbishop of Canterbury (**13**) is an example where the focus is the realm and its access to the sacred, rather than the nation. Edmund died in France en route to Rome, and the Cistercians at Pontigny had the burying of his body, so that his cult is shared across the Channel. In his Epilogue to the life, even as he shows his patroness's pilgrimage journeys to and fro across the Channel to the saint, Matthew Paris connects Edmund's body into the question of which realm has the better passion relics, that of Louis IX (who built the Sainte Chapelle to house his holy thorn relic), or Henry III (who, through St Edmund's favour, has acquired for his rebuilt Westminster Abbey a holy blood relic, and through God's favour, a footprint of Christ preserved in marble). The cross-Channel cult polarises: if status is to be founded on the possession of relics, Henry's kingdom trumps Louis's, since, holy as the thorns or cross relics may be, it is Christ's blood that sanctifies them.

In the case of the *Débat*, the heralds of England and France discuss the various physical, cultural and military attributes of the two realms. How far this is a ludic version of the heralds' duty to declare the honours appropriate to disputants, how far polemic to a political end is hard to decide. The kingdom of England descends from Constantine, and Arthur and other valiant kings of the realm have often conquered the French, most recently at Crécy and Poitiers, asserts the English herald. *Au contraire*, claims the French herald, if you look at the Trojan diaspora, the realm that *à present* calls itself *Angleterre* was founded when Brutus defeated the giants and is properly *Bretaigne*: the origins of the *Anglois* lie in Saxon invaders, especially one called *Inglus*. Coke, whose riposte draws heavily on the Chronicle of Brabant, declares that Charlemagne was not French, but a Brabanter, and goes on to claim that Roland was 'of the nacion of England', his Breton homeland being held by the kings of Britain (VI §2.10, lines 112–15). Coke also, in the mid-sixteenth century, exacerbates competition over relics, claiming that the French holy chrism for coronations is not holy at all: it is *oyle olyve* whiche was brought out of *Espayne, very good for salettes . . . Of such fayned relyques they have in Fraunce . . .* (VI §2.10, lines 30–1). What may be ludic in the *Débat* is, however, politicised in other contexts. The debates between Cardinal Pierre d'Ailly and the English delegation at the Council of Constance in 1417–20 for instance, involve the same kinds of materials and arguments (with extra emphasis on Bede) in the effort to establish the independent validity of English religious tradition as that of a people and its church that can have a separate voice from the broader German delegation.[1]

Much else could have figured here, but the *Débat*'s reminder of the enduring nature of England's supraregional French-language literary culture, as instanced in the *Brut* narratives, does not come amiss in the later fifteenth century. This is a moment when French in many, if not quite all domains, is ceasing to be a language of insular record and literary culture, and finally, after its long insular career, beginning to be maintained, territorialised, and conceptualised as a foreign language in England, though one from which disengagement is still impossible.

44. *Le Débat des hérauts d'armes de France et d'Angleterre* [Not in Dean], London, British Library, G. 32, g. 4, ff. 2^v–5^r

Date of composition and provenance. 1453–61[?], France.

Author, sources and nature of text. In the fictional debate frame for this anonymous prose text one herald speaks for England and another speaks for France, in order to argue which Christian kingdom is the more honourable. Lady Prudence sets this question up with a visual image of the allegorical figure of Honour. Strolling in a meadow, she invites the debaters to imagine paintings and tapestries in which Honour sits in majesty, with canonical warrior heroes at her side who strive to move closer to her. Prudence asks *Qui est le royaume chrestien qui plus est digne d'estre approuché d'Onneur?* (Which Christian kingdom is the more worthy of approaching Honour?, Pannier and Meyer 1877, 2). Under their three rubrics, most of the categories for the ensuing debate are familiar from romance: *Plaisance* (beautiful women, hunting), *Vaillance* (battles and battle-worthiness on land and on sea, including ships and ports) and *Richesse* (the wealth of the land, both above and below ground, and of the sea; to which the French herald adds the excellence of the French clergy and nobility, and that of French workers and their workmanship). But it soon becomes apparent that the scales are tipped in favour of the French – the English herald's arguments are given short shrift, the English royal line is denigrated, and the herald himself is openly insulted, while the greatness of the French and their king is celebrated. From the deeply entangled materials of England and France's cultural and political traditions, the *Débat* quickly emerges as a pro-French polemical treatise.

1 See V. Gillespie 2011, Ruddick 2016.

The heralds of the *Débat* are meant to be authoritative, in keeping with the prestige heralds historically enjoyed: though originally minstrels or jongleurs of common background, they had gradually become 'dignified figures in the chivalric world' (Keen 1984, 134), participating more and more in medieval political life, thanks to their attachment to orders of chivalry and to princely houses. Prudence explains at the outset how by a herald's report, kings, ladies, princes and other great lords both judge and encourage the deeds that create worldly honour (Pannier and Meyer 1877, 1). Just as the worth of an individual nobleman depended in large part on lineage and martial prowess, so the worth of kingdoms is seen here to rest on myths of foundation and 'magnificent' wars of conquest. The *Débat* author sees the character of nationhood as best served by 'a single narrative' of foundation and lineage and by 'a single beginning' (Butterfield 2009, 391): when the English herald claims King Arthur and the Trojans for England, the French herald scornfully asserts that Arthur and Brutus were not English, but British. That 'discontinuous' English lineage which is not 'pure' (Beaune 1985, 233) contrasts with the stable and glorious French lineage, which can be traced to Clovis (*c.* 466–*c.* 511). Thus the *Débat* casts France as a single and unified contender against an opponent bound to lose the match in part because of a fractured lineage.

The *Débat* continued to arouse interest long after it was first composed. In the mid-sixteenth century it was rebutted in English by John Coke, then clerk to the merchant adventurers of England in Brussels, who went on to become clerk of the Staple at Westminster (a wool traders' monopoly licensed by the English crown). He answered the French herald's claims about the royal lineage in part by making Charlemagne a native of Brabant; Godfrey of Bouillon, born in Lorraine, was German; and the mythical Roland was implicitly English, having been born in Armorica (Brittany), conquered by Maximian of England (Pannier and Meyer 1877, 66–7). Coke's intervention pushes the boundaries east, into a triangulated English, French, and Dutch-Flemish area, further testing the 'unbroken monolingual identity for French' claimed, according to Butterfield, by modern historians and linguists; she envisages instead a historical 'bi-vernacularity' for the Anglo-French phenomenon (Butterfield 2009, 352–3). Coke's participation in the debate, however, may speak to situations more properly described as 'tri-vernacular' or 'multi-vernacular', with both the English and French involving still other linguistic cultures in their conversation.

Audience and circulation. The *Débat* participates in a tradition of polemical writings on the continent which envisaged a French public but without precluding other audiences; these writings include expressions of French pride from Alain Chartier, Christine de Pizan, and Jean Gerson. In its sympathies, the *Débat* recalls other pro-French writing and oral *fama*-making designed to encourage a sorely tested French population, as well as works that defamed adversaries and stigmatised traitors. Like these, the *Débat* may have been intended to bolster French self-identity by furnishing a wealth of flattering points about France, buttressed by reasons to disdain England. The *Débat* does not, however, appear to be an example of war propaganda, nor does it contain anything of direct relevance to the legal issues underlying the Hundred Years War (such as may be found in earlier writing by Jean de Montreuil and others intended for the use of royal officials and diplomats, or perhaps the king). The French herald claims to have been in England and to have inspected ancient and non-standard church vestments and has been thought a possible figure of the author, but remains unidentified if so (Pannier and Meyer 1877, 14, §38: Pyne 1870, 28–9).

The small number of the *Débat*'s extant manuscript witnesses suggests limited initial circulation, but its re-publication in at least four (possibly five) extant early printed books testifies to its afterlife, as does the rebuttal by John Coke and the much later translation of the French debate by Henry Pyne. Coke was a highly placed officer of the 'nacion of Englande', a 'clarke of the statutes of the Staple of Westmynster' who was in Brussels as secretary to the company of 'marchauntes adventurers'. He claimed to be well read in 'hystories' and 'cronycles' and said he had read the Anglo-Norman romance of Bevis of Hampton in French, English and Flemish (Pannier and Meyer 1877, 55–6, 74 §58 and n. 165); Coke's official documents are in Latin (Pannier and Meyer 1877, xxxi). Pyne suggests that the appearance of the *Débat* in print stimulated the printing of the earlier argument between the English and French delegations at the Council of Constance (1414–18) by Sir Robert Wingfield (*c.* 1464–1539), Henry VIII's ambassador to the Emperor Maximilian (Pyne 1870, xii–xiii), but this is purely speculative and further research is needed to trace the early-modern career of the *Débat*.

EARLY PRINTED EDITION. British Library G. 32, g. 4 is one of three prints of the *Débat*, this one printed in Rouen and called by Coke a 'lytell pamphelet' (Pannier and Meyer 1877, x, 55). On the first page is an engraving of a group of knights emerging from a forest encountering two knights coming in the opposite direction; the title of the work, *Le debat des heraulx d'armes de france et d'engleterre* is above the illustration, itself a re-used woodcut. In addition to BL G. 32, g. 4, there are three, or possibly four, printed editions located in England. The *Débat* also survives in four manuscripts. The only complete English translation (made from the print of the French text used here) is Henry Pyne's of 1870. Pyne thought the *Débat* had been written by the fifteenth-century French poet Charles d'Orléans, a rather wishful attribution that was immediately discredited (Pyne 1870, xi, 125–81; Pannier and Meyer 1877, vii–x).

BIBLIOGRAPHY. The only modern edition, based on Paris, BN fonds français manuscript 5839 with emendations from BN fr. 5837 and 5838, is Pannier and Meyer 1877: printed editions from England are discussed at xxl–xxii and the manuscripts at v and xxii; unusually for editions of the Société des Anciens Textes Français, it contains Coke's rebuttal in English (see Part VI, §2.10), which Meyer considered a necessary complement to the French debate. The work itself has not been the subject of sustained study since Meyer's early researches. For a dissenting view of the date of the *Débat* see Jones 1942, 14, 19. On medieval heralds, see especially J. D. D'A. Boulton 1987, Hiltmann and Israel 2007, Keen 1984, Lester 1990, Stanesco 1985 and Stevenson 2009; for heraldry and the *Débat* in particular, see Melville 2006, 1992. The classic study of chivalry is Keen 1984; see, more recently, Saul 2011; Taylor 2013. On the hero figures discussed in the *Débat*, see Schroeder 1971. On war literature, including legal issues and propaganda, see Lewis 1965, Grévy-Pons 1980, Pons 1982, 1990 and 1991, C. Taylor 2000 and ed., 2006, Contamine 1994. For a recent re-assessment of the Anglo-French nexus, see Butterfield 2009. For England and Flanders see Barron and Saul 1995.

TEXT AND TRANSLATION

[f. 2v] *Le herault d'Engleterre parle de vaillance du temps passé*

Dame Prudence, vous savez que de ce noble roiaume d'Engleterre saillit l'empereur Constentin, et par les Rommains fut mandé querir jusques en Engleterre, lequel fut obey et regna en grant honneur comme empereur universal. Maximianus, qui fut si noble chevalier et conquist les Gaules et les Lombardies, fut du royaulme d'Engleterre, et si fut le roy Artus qui fut si vaillant de sa personne et si grant conquereur que, pour ses grans vaillances, est en nombre l'un des Neuf Preux de son temps, et fist la Table Ronde, qui fut chose de si grant honneur et ou il y eut de si vaillans chevaliers, et qui firent tant de si haulx faiz que les rommans

The English herald talks about past valour

Lady Prudence, you know that the emperor Constantine was of this noble kingdom of England, and that the Romans sent him on a voyage of conquest all the way to England, which paid him obeisance, and where, as emperor of the world, he reigned in great honour. Maximian, who was so much a noble knight and conquered the Gauls and the Lombards, came from the kingdom of England. And so did King Arthur, who was so valorous in his person and so great a conqueror that, for his great acts of valour, he is numbered as one among the Nine Worthies of his time. He created the Round Table, which was a thing of such en sont encores par tout l'universal monde et en sera d'eulx memoire perpetuel. Et ainsi appert que du temps passé les vaillans ont esté d'Engleterre, et que nul a Engleterre ne se puet ne doit comparoir, et que c'est le royaume qui devant tous se doit aprocher d'onneur.

great honour, with such brave knights, who performed such high deeds that [their] stories are still told around the world and will remain perpetually in memory. And thus it seems that in the past the valorous came from England, that no other country could or can be compared with England, and it is the kingdom that above all must be honoured.

Dame Prudence, je dis que pour vaillance le royaume d'Engleterre vous devez aprocher d'Onneur devant tous roiaumes crestiens, et le vous monstreré par les vaillances faictes du temps passé que des vaillances faictes du temps moien, [f. 3r] dictes de memoire d'omme, que des vaillances du temps present.

Lady Prudence, I say that where valour is concerned, you must place the kingdom of England nearer to Honour above all Christian kingdoms, and I will show this to you through the brave deeds done in the past as well as those done within living memory and those of the present.

Du temps moien

Or parlons du temps moien, dit de memoire d'omme. C'est chose bien certaine que France, qui anciennement s'apelloit Gaules, c'est une des plus fortes nations de Crestienté. Or voions les batailles que les Anglois ont gaigné sur eulx de memoire d'omme: la grant bataille de Crissé qui fut a l'intencion des Anglois; la bataille de Poictiers, ou fut prins le roy de France, Jehan, et mené en Engleterre par les Anglois; et de neufve memoire, la tresgrande et honorable bataille de Quicourt, ou mourut tant de noblesse, et de si grant nombre des seigneurs de France du sanc de France furent pris; la bataille de Vernoil et plusieurs autres, et tout a l'intencion des Anglois; si dis, Dame Prudence, que tel roiaume doit on priser ou croissent si vaillans combatans. Et puis qu'ilz sont si victorieux sur la plus forte nation de Crestienté, on les doit bien priser et aprocher d'Onneur.

The recent past

Now let us talk about the recent past, said to be within living memory. It is very sure that France, which in the old days was called Gaul, is one of the strongest Christian nations. Now let us consider the battles the English have won against the French that are within living memory: the great battle of Crécy, which was won by the English; the battle of Poitiers, where John the king of France was captured and brought to England by the English; and of recent memory, the great and honourable battle of Agincourt, where so many of the nobility died and such a great number of princes of the royal blood of France were captured; the battle of Verneuil and several others; and all were won by the English. And so I say, lady Prudence, a realm like that, where such valiant warriors flourish, must be prized; and because they are victorious against the strongest nation in Christianity, we must prize them and have them approach Honour.

Du temps present

Item. Or disons du temps present. Le royaume d'Engleterre n'est pas si grant que le roiaume de France et si ont guerre

The present

Item. Now let us talk about the present. The kingdom of England is not as big as the realm of France and, indeed, the English are at war les Angloys o le roy de France, o le roy d'Espaigne, o le roy de Dannemarche et o le roy d'Escosse, qui est au dedens de l'isle d'Engleterre, et ainsi ont guerre o quatre roys. Et aussi ont guerre mortelle o les Iroys et Irelandois, et n'y a guere plus que une veue de mer a passer d'Engleterre en Irlande, et toutefois, Dame Prudence, ilz fournissent a tous les seigneurs dessus nommez, et n'est royaume fors Engleterre qui pourroit porter ung tel faiz. Si peut on bien veoir cuidamment la grant puissance dudit royaume d'Engleterre et la grant vaillance des Anglois qui fournissent a tant de roys.

Item. Et y a plus, car ilz sont les plus richement et les plus grandement montez a la mer de beaux et puissans navires que nation de Crestienté, et par ainsi sont roys de la mer, car nul ne peut a eulx resister; et qui se treuvent les plus fors a la mer se peuent dire roys [de la mer].

Item. Pour les raisons dessudictes, Dame Prudence, appert, tant du temps passé, moyen que present, que vostre question est solue et que vous devez aprocher d'Onneur le royaume d'Engleterre.

[f. 3v] *Le herault de France respond a Vaillance et dit*

Sire herault, vous dictes que Constantin l'empereur, Maximianus le vaillant chevalier, Artus le roy puissant et vaillant en armes, furent du royaume d'Engleterre, qui firent de vaillances en leur temps a merveilles, et tant que par leur moyen Engleterre en doit perpetuellement estre honnoree.

Ad ce je respons qu'il fault premierement savoir et veoir dont vindrent et furent extraiz les nobles chevaliers surditz par vous nommez. Croiez, Dame Prudence, s'il vous plaist le savoir, qu'ilz furent extraiz de la grant noblesse de Troye, et que aprés

with the king of France, with the king of Spain, with the king of Denmark, and with the king of Scotland, which is within the island of England. And so, they are at war with four kings. And also, the English have a deadly war against the Irish; and one catches scarcely more than a glimpse of water in going from England to Ireland; and nevertheless, Lady Prudence, the English do battle with all the said lords, and there is no kingdom except England that could shoulder such a burden. Thus is evident the great power of this kingdom of England, which does battle with so many kings.

Item. And there's more, for of any people in Christianity the English are the most richly and most grandly fitted out at sea, with fine, powerful ships. And that makes them kings of the sea, for no-one can oppose them. And those who find themselves the strongest at sea can call themselves kings of the sea.

Item. For the reasons above, Lady Prudence, it appears that your question, whether about the past, the present, or the time between, has been answered and that you should have the kingdom of England approach Honour, above all others.

The herald of France answers [on the matter of] Valour and says

Sir herald, you say that the emperor Constantine, the valiant knight Maximian, Arthur the king, powerful and brave at arms, who in their time performed valiant deeds marvellously, were from the kingdom of England; and by their agency England ought to be for ever honoured.

To that I answer that we must first examine and find out where the noble knights named by you above came from and what their lineage was. Do believe, Lady Prudence, if you would know this, that they were of the great line of the Trojan nobility,

la destruction faicte a Troye, ung vailiant chevaler nommé Eneas, troyen, acompaigné de plusieurs nobles, s'en vint ou pays de Romme; et de lui descendit subsecutement ung chevalier qui soy nomma Brutus, lequel Brutus descendit fort acompaigné en l'isle d'Albion, qui pour le present soy nomme Engleterre; et se combatit avecques plusieurs geans qui estoient en ladicte ysle, et a la parfin conquist l'isle et destruisit les gehans et [la] publia de ceulx qui estoient venuz avecques lui; et voulut e ordonna, pource qu'il avoit a nom Brutus, que ladicte ysle se appellast Bretaigne et non plus A[l]bion, et de cestuy Brutus et de sa generacion [sont sailliz les vaillans chevaliers dessus diz par] le dit herault d'Engleterre.

Or voyons, Dame Prudence, dont sont sailliz les Angloys et pour quoy ladicte ysle, qui pour lors se apelloit Bretaigne, se appelle maint[e]nant Engleterre. Et vous trouverez, s'il vous plaist l'enquerir, qu'ilz sont sailliz du pays de Soissonne, qui est une contree en Almaigne; et est bien vroy que pour une division qui fut entre les Brutz, lesditz Soissons furent mandez pour venir guerroier en Bretaigne, et firent de bien grans guerres. Puis par aucuns subtilz moiens, se voullurent atribuer a eulx apartenir le royaume, a quoy les Brutz resisterent par bien long temps. Et [par] le moien d'un qui s'appellot Gormond, qui fut filz de roy, mais il ne voulit suceder au royaume – ce fut celui qui dist qu'il n'estoit pas digne d'avoir royaume qui ne le savoit conquerir, si s'en alla triumphant parmy le monde et vint a l'aide desditz Soissons; et par son moyen ilz destruirent les Brutz et les geterent hors de leur pays, puis s'en passa [f. 4r] Gormand en Gaules et donna esditz Soissons sa conqueste.

Item. Pource qu'il y eut ung Soisson qui avoit nom Inglus qui avoit commencé la guerre du temps passé, et avant la venue dudit Gormand, tous les Soissons furent

and that after the destruction of Troy a valiant knight named Eneas the Trojan, accompanied by many nobles, came to the land around Rome. And subsequently, a knight named Brutus descended from him. Brutus came to the island of Albion, now called England, with a great company of men and fought many giants who were on the said island, and in the end conquered it. With those who had come with him he destroyed the giants and peopled the island with his companions; and because his name was Brutus, he ordered that the said island be called Britain and Albion no more, and from this Brutus and from his descendants sprang the valiant knights mentioned above by the herald of England.

Now let us see, Lady Prudence, where the English came from and why the said island, then called Britain, is now called England. You will find, should you want to look into it, that the English came from the area of Saxony, which is a region in Germany. And it is indeed the case that, because of a dispute between the British, the said Saxons were summoned to come to Britain to fight, and they fought fierce wars. Then, by craft, they claimed the kingdom belonged to them, which the British resisted for a long time. And by the craftiness of someone named Gormond, a king's son, except that he did not want to succeed to the throne – he was the one who said a man was not worthy of having a kingdom that he had not known how to conquer – so he went around the world winning battles, and he came to the aid of the said Saxons. Thanks to his help, they destroyed the British and threw them out of their country. Then Gormond left and went to Gaul, giving what he had conquered to the Saxons.

Item. Because there was a Saxon named Inglus who had begun the war in the past, before the arrival of the said Gormond, all the Saxons agreed that the said isle, which

d'acors que ladicte ysle, qui se nommoit Bretaigne, print le non de Inglus et qu'elle se apellast Engleterre. Et de la print son nom et ainsi sont recitees ces choses ou livre nommé le *Brut* et firent cel honneur lesditz Soissons audit Inglus long temps aprés son trespassement.

Item. Or voyons, Dame Prudence, comme le herault d'Engleterre mesprent et forfait grandement en son office, car il se veut parer et couvrir d'autruy robe et veult atribuer l'onneur des chevaliers dessus nommez, lesquelz furent de la nation de Bretaigne, a la nation de Soissonne, qui a present se nomme Angleteterre. Plus grans deshonneur ne plus grant reproche ne peut avoir ung chevalier que de soy atribuer l'onneur et la vaillance d'autruy; et vous avez dessu[s] dit, Dame Prudence, que nous, heraulx, devons departir les honneurs a ceulx a qui ilz appartienent.

Item. Et pour ce, sire herault, ne arguez point des vaillances des chevaliers susdiz, que l'on ne pourroit dire ne herauder les vaillances et honneurs grans qu'ilz firent de leurs temps, qui doi[ven]t estre raportee[s] a l'onneur de la nation de Bretaigne dont ilz furent et non pas a la renommee des Anglois.

Item. Mais parlez moy, sire herault, et dictes a Dame Prudence les grans vaillances et la guerre de manificence que les Englois, autrement diz Soissons, ont fait depuis la translation que l'isle de Brataigne cheut en generation ou dom[i]nation des Soissons par le moyen dudit Gormand. Et quant a moy, je n'ay sceu ne leu qu'ilz aient fait guerre fors guerre en eulx, que les Rommains apellent guerre civille, ou a leurs voysins; et de ce sont bien coustumiers. Et commencent voulentiers guerres, mais ilz ne les sçavent finer, ainsi que je monstreré cy aprés. Bien est vroy que ung roy d'Engleterre, nommé Richart, duc de Normendie, pour acquiter son fief

was called Britain, would take Inglus's name and be called England, and that is the source of the name. And these things are recounted in the book called *Brut*; the said Saxons honoured the said Inglus for many years after his death.

Item. Now let us see, Lady Prudence, how the English herald misrepresents and greatly transgresses in his office, for he wants to adorn and dress himself in borrowed colours, and he wants to attribute the honour of the above named knights, who were of the nation of Britain, to the Saxon nation, which is presently named England. A knight can have no greater dishonour, no greater reproach, than to impute to himself the honour and the valour of others. And you said above, Lady Prudence, that we heralds must bestow the honours upon those to whom they belong.

Item. And because of that, sir herald, do not argue the valorous deeds of the said knights, because the valorous deeds and great honours that they did in their time cannot be heralded for the glory of the English, but must be chalked up to the honour of the people of Britain, where the knights were from.

Item. Talk to me, sir herald, and recount to Lady Prudence the great and valorous deeds and wars of glory that the English, otherwise known as the Saxons, have undertaken since the transference by which the island of Britain, through the said Gormond, fell to the Saxon line of descent and Saxon domination. As for me, I have never known or read that they made war except war among themselves, which the Romans call civil war, or with their neighbors; they're quite used to that. They willingly start wars but don't know how to finish them, as I shall show shortly. It's indeed true that a king of England named Richard, duke of Normandy, to pay for his fief in Normandy, accompanied

de Normendie, acompagna le roy Philippe de France pour aller sur les Sarrazins, mais il n'y demeura point longuement, ny n'est chose qui se doye tourner a consequance car le cas n'est point avenu souvent.

Item. Sachez, sire herault, que je faiz grans difference entre guerre commune et guerre de grant magnificence. Car je [f. 4v] diz que guerre commune est en soy mesmes ou contre ses voisins et lignagers, et guerre de manificence est quant princes vont en ost concquerir en loingtain et estranges pais, ou soy combatre pour la foy catholicque deffendre ou eslargir.

Item. Et pour ce, Dame Prudence, a vostre bonne correction, parleré icy de la vaillance de France du temps passé. Clovis, roy de France, fut [le] premier roy crestien, que je repute a grant honneur. Et ung jour qu'il se combatoit avecques les Sarrazins, du ciel lui furent aportees ses armes o les fleurs de lis, et gaigna la bataille. La saincte empolle de quoy les roys de France sont enoings fut envoiee a Saint Remy par ung ange du ciel, laquelle est en l'abaye Saint Remy de Rains. La saincte baniere de l'orifflant lui fut aussi enveiee du ciel. Puisque Dieu lui fait si grant honneur, nous qui suimes en ce monde et mortelz lui devon bien porter honneur et [a] toute sa posterité et generation. Charles Mortel, roy de France, conquist [et] gaigna une grant bataille sur les Sarrazins auprés de Poictiers ou ilz estoient trois cens quatre vingtz et cinq mille combatans. Puis le dit Charles alla en Languedo[c] lever le siege que les Sarrazins tenoient devant la cité de Carcassonne. Et gaigna la bataille et desconfist trois roys Sareazins et tua et print des mescreans a merveilles.

Item. Le pape fut geté hors de Romme et perdit le demaine de l'eglise. Pepin, roy de France, le secourut et le remena a Romme et le mist en son siege, et fist le roy Extuple a soy tributaire. Charlemaine, filz de Pepin,

King Philip of France against the Saracens, but he did not remain there long, nor is this anything of consequence, for the situation has not come up often.

Item. Be advised, sir herald, that I make a great difference between an ordinary war and a war of glory. For I say that an ordinary war is internal or against one's neighbors and their relatives, and a war of glory is one in which princes go off to conquer armies in distant and foreign countries, or fight to defend or spread the Catholic faith.

Item. And so, Lady Prudence, saving correction from you, I shall here talk about the valour of France in the distant past. Clovis, king of France, was the first Christian king, which I count a great honour. And one day when he was fighting against the Saracens, his arms, figured with the lilies of France, were brought to him from the heavens, and he won the battle. The sainted vial from which the kings of France are anointed was sent to St Rémy by an angel from heaven; it is in the abbey of St Rémy in Reims. The holy banner of the oriflamme was also sent to him from heaven. Since God did him such great honour, we who are in this world and mortal must honour all his posterity and descendants. Charles Martel, king of France, won a great battle and conquered the Saracens, and near Poitiers, where they were five thousand three hundred and eighty soldiers. Then the said Charles went to Languedoc to raise the Saracen siege of the city of Carcassonne, and he won the battle and defeated three Saracen kings, and captured and killed a marvellous number of unbelievers.

Item. The pope was thrown out of Rome and lost the church's demesne. Pepin, king of France, saved him, brought him back to Rome, restored him to his seat, and forced King Astolphe to pay him tribute.

fut si noble roy et fist de si grans vaillances, et par especial sur les Sarazins, et mist toutes les Espaignes a la foy catholique et conquist tant de seigneuries, tant en Almaigne que es Lombardz; et remist une autre foiz le pape Adrien en son siege, et destrusit le roy Desir de Lombardie, ennemy du pape et des Romains, et recouvra tout le demaine de l'eglise et lui restitua, et lui en donna du sien propre, comme le recite maistre Brunet Latin en son *Livre de Tresor de sapience*; et aussi est recité ou *Livre du Songe du vergier* que par neuf foiz les rois de France ont remis le pape en son siege de Romme. Et puis ledit Charlemaine fut empereur, et vous mesmes d'Engleterre fustes en son obaissance, et pour ces [f. 5r] granns vaillances est mis ou nombre des Neuf Preux. Rolland et Olivier, qui firent tant de vaillances sur les Sarrazins, qui sont bien dignes de memoire, furent françoiz. Godeffroy de Billon, qui conquist Jherusalem et est l'un des Neuf Preux, fut de France et conte de Boullongne sur la mer. Et cecy sont guerres que je nomme de grant manificence et honneur, et que on doit bien reciter et en faire cronicques. Et ne sont pas guerres emprunctees d'autrui! Et des guerres communes que les François ont fait tant sur les Almans que sur autres leurs voysins, je m'en passe legierement, car ce seroit longue chose a reciter, et les romains et cronicques en font grans recits a merveilles; et telles guerres communes ne sont a reciter ne cronicquer o guerre de manificence.

Item. Sire herault, si voz rois d'Engleterre ou temps passé ont fait guerre[s] de manificence, vous feriez bien de les dire et reciter affin qu'on vous y peust respondre. Toutesfoiz, je vous advertiz, car voz cronicques n'en font nulle mention que voz predecesseurs ne vous feissez oncques guerre de manificence ne par mer ne par terre.

Charlemagne, Pepin's son, was a noble king who did extraordinary feats, especially against the Saracens, and he converted all of Spain to the Catholic faith; and he conquered so many lordships both in Germany and Lombardy; and then another time he restored Pope Adrian to his seat, and defeated King Desiderius of Lombardy, enemy of the pope and of the Romans, and recovered and returned the entire demesne of the church, and gave it some of his own, as master Brunetto Latini in his book *The Treasury of Wisdom* recounts; and it is also written in *The Dream of the Orchard* that the kings of France restored the pope to his seat in Rome nine times. Then the said Charlemagne was emperor, and you yourselves in England were obedient to him. For these great deeds Charlemagne was placed among the Nine Worthies. Roland and Oliver, who performed so many feats of valour against the Saracens, and who are indeed worthy of memory, were French. Godfrey of Bouillon, who conquered Jerusalem and is one of the Nine Worthies, was from France and count of Boulogne-sur-Mer. These are wars that I call wars of great glory and honour, and which we ought to recount and write chronicles about, and they are not wars borrowed from others! As for the ordinary wars which the French have waged as much against the Germans as against their other neighbors, I have no trouble passing over them, for it would take a long time to tell about all, and novels and chronicles marvellously provide great accounts of them; besides, ordinary wars like those should not be told about or chronicled alongside a war of glory.

Item. Sir herald, if your past kings of England have fought wars of glory, you would do well to say what they were and give an account of them so that we may respond. Nevertheless, I put you on notice, for your chronicles make no mention of you or your predecessors ever engaging in a war of glory, neither on land nor on sea.

Item, par les choses dessudictes, Dame Prudence, vous povez voir come les roys de France ont esté tousjours parfaiz en la loy, sans aucune var[i]ation, et comme ilz ont eslargi la Crestienté et deffendu les droiz de saincte Eglise. Et pour ce disent les Sarrazins et aussi tous les mescreans que c'est le grant roy des Crestiens; et chacun ne peut pas dire ainsi! Et sur ce je adresse ma parolle au herault d'Engleterre.

Item. By the above-mentioned things, Lady Prudence, you can see how the kings of France have always been firm in the faith without wavering, and how they have spread Christianity and defended the rights of holy church. And that's why Saracens and unbelievers say that [the French king] is the great king of the Christians; and not everyone can say as much! And now, I address my words to the herald of England.

Notes

Initial work on the *Débat* was done by Jade Bailey as part of her York MA: we thank her for her work. Emendations in brackets in the text have been taken from Pannier and Meyer, 1877.

3 **Constentin** (*c.* 272–337); as emperor, Constantine ruled Britain, Gaul, and Spain.

4 **lequel** There is a superfluous downstroke between *le* and *quel.*

6 **Maximianus** (*c.* 250–310); Maximian had been a Roman emperor and was a rival to Constantine; he was captured in Marseille and urged to commit suicide, which he did. In Geoffrey of Monmouth's *Historia regum Britanniae*, Maximian, having been invited to rule England, is said to desire more land and thus invades Gaul (Reeve and Wright 2007, 98–111).

12–13 **Table Ronde** The literary concept of the Round Table (Wace, *Roman de Brut*; Weiss 2002, 244, v. 9751) influenced extratextual history. King Edward III (r. 1327–77) determined to create a society of knights modeled 'directly and explicitly' on King Arthur's Round Table society, and he planned a 'House of the Round Table'. From the early thirteenth century, tournaments featured knights and ladies impersonating characters and reenacting scenes from Arthurian romance (J. D. D'A. Boulton 1987, 13, 106–7).

12, 250, 254 **Neuf Preux** The chivalric concept of the Nine Worthies elevated the three most admired representatives from among Hebrew, Classical and Christian antiquity: 1. Hector, Alexander, Caesar; 2. Joshua, David, Judas Maccabaeus; 3. Arthur, Charlemagne, Godfrey de Bouillon. These are the figures in Lady Prudence's visualisation of a painting or tapestry. The nine featured as part of an ever-growing 'cult of heroism', and by the end of the fourteenth century the Preux also included the names of great contemporary heroes (J. D. D'A. Boulton 1987, 2).

20 **se puet** G. 32, g. 4 *se puent.*

33 **anciennement** G. 32, g. 4 *aucunement.*

38 **Crissé** The battle of Crécy, 26 August 1346; sometimes spelled Cressy in English.

39 **Poictiers** the battle of Poitiers, 19 September 1356. See also n. to line 217.

43 **Quicourt** The battle of Agincourt, 25 October 1415, in which French forces were defeated by a smaller English infantry. Recent research has suggested that estimates of five to one, handed down by medieval chroniclers, are exaggerated.

46 **Vernoil** The battle of Verneuil, 17 August 1424, saw large losses by the French and their allies.

61 **Iroys et Irelandois** The term *Irois* may be a pun on the Middle French *irais*, angry (*MED*).

62 **veue** Given the frequent lack of clear difference between *n* and *u* in manuscripts and early printed books, this may also be *vene* (*veine*), 'narrow channel'.

64 **seigneurs** G. 32, g. 4 *signes*; **qui** G. 32, g. 4 *quil*, with very faint letter *i*.

68 **dudit** Throughout the text many occurrences of this compound appear with just one abbreviation for all forms of its second element; these have been resolved as agreement requires.

131 **qui ne le** G. 32, g. 4 *quil ne*.

128–36 **Gormond** In the *Débat* context, Gormond is implicitly an example of a leader who engages in a *guerre de manificence*, e.g. lines 191–9. 'Gotmundus', an African king, appears in Geoffrey of Monmouth's *Historia regum Britanniae*; Gormond also features in Geoffroi Gaimar's *Estoire des Engleis* (Short, ed., 2009). In Wace's *Roman de Brut* he leaves Africa and becomes king of Ireland. An early *chanson de geste*, *Gormond et Isembart* (*c.* 1130), in which Gormond is a rebellious vassal, survives in one (Anglo-Norman) manuscript (see Dean 81).

139–47 **Inglus . . . Inglus** In his *Brut* Wace puts this somewhat differently: 'Pur un lignage dunt cil furent / Ki la terre primes reçurent / S'i firent Engleis apeler / Por lur orine remenbrer, / E Englelande unt apelee / La terre ki lur ert dunee' ('After the name of the race who first received the land, they called themselves "English", in order to recall their origins, and called the land given to them "England"'; Weiss 2002, 343, vv. 13,643–8).

148 **son trespassement** G. 32, g. 4 *sont trepassez*.

175 **que l'isle** In G. 32, g. 4 a suspension for *–us* appears between these words.

185–7 **Richart . . . Philippe** King Richard I (r. 1189–99) accompanied King Philip of France (Philip Augustus, r. 1180–1223) and the Holy Roman Emperor Frederick I Barbarossa on the Third Crusade (1189–92); the Angevin kings of England were also dukes of Normandy. The French herald alludes to (and dismisses as of no consequence) Philip's return to France as soon as Acre had been taken; he does not mention that Richard remained.

203–17 **Clovis . . . generation** As king of the Franks (481–511), Clovis united the Frankish tribes under one ruler and was considered the founder of the French monarchy as well as the first Christian king; his memory conjured unity and peace. He was the first to bear the oriflamme (see n. to 212, *orifflant*). King Charles VII (r. 1422–61) enjoyed a reputation as a second Clovis for his 'seemingly miraculous expulsion of the English from the kingdom' (see further Beaune 1991, 70–89).

213 **orifflant** Displaying a red or orange-red silk field with gold flames and distinctive pointed ends, the oriflamme, given to kings preparing for battle by the bishop of St Rémi, was captured by the English at Poitiers and again at Agincourt and was not seen after Agincourt. The abbey of St Rémy, a *lieu de mémoire* named for the bishop thought to have converted Clovis to Christianity, was also a repository for the holy oil used to anoint French kings (lines 207–9). Along with Clovis's divinely sent shield, this collection of objects serves to reify the French royal lineage. The spelling *orifflant* may recall Roland's horn, the Olifant, in the *Chanson de Roland* (see Dufournet 1993, vv. 3093–5).

217 **Mortel** Charles Martel (b. *c.* 688, d. 741), grandfather of Charlemagne, led the Franks into the battle of Tours in 732 or 733, sometimes also known as the battle of Poitiers (not to be confused with the 1356 battle of Poitiers; see n. to line 39, **Poictiers**). 'Martel' (Martellus, 'the hammer'), a nickname bestowed on Charles because his victory was seen to be the result of God's favour, may also have been meant to recall the nickname given to Judas Maccabeus (the Hammerer), who was among the Nine Worthies (see n. to line 12, **Neuf Preux**). The unusual spelling of 'Martel' as 'Mortel' here may not be an error, but a pun; Charles delivers death (*mort*) to his enemies. Coke ripostes that Martel was the bastard son of Pepin and a mistress named Alpay (Pannier and Meyer 1877, 66).

219 **Sarrazins** The Franks defeated the Arabs in the battle of Tours in 732 or 733. Opinion has been divided over the significance of the battle, and thus over Martel's legacy; see Nicolle 2008, 7.

224 **Carcassonne** G. 32, g. 4 *Carrassonne*; a city in the region then known as Septimania, Carcassonne was taken by the Arabs in 725. In 759 Pepin the Short drove the Arabs out of Septimania.

227–31 **le pape . . . tributaire** Aistulph (d. 756), king of the Lombards, besieged Rome and was defeated by Pepin the Short.

232 **fut si noble roy** G. 32, g. 4 *qui fut si noble*; Charlemagne, who led an expedition into Spain but also marched into other lands, was known for his forceful conversion of conquered peoples.

236 **que** G. 32, g. 4 *qui*

237–8 **Adrien . . . Desir de Lombardie** G. 32, g. 4 *Adoien*; Pope Adrian (772–95) sought Charlemagne's help against Desiderius, king of the Lombards. Charlemagne restored the church's holdings.

242–3 **Brunet Latin . . . *Livre de Tresor de sapience*** Latini (1220–94), born in Florence, wrote his encyclopedia, *Tesoretto*, or *Livre du Trésor*, when he was a political exile in France (see (**8a**)).

243–4 ***Livre du Songe du vergier*** A long dialogue between a cleric and a knight debating the relationship between ecclesiastic and secular powers, written at the order of King Charles V. Completed in Latin in 1376 (*Somnium Viridarii*) by Evrard de Trémaugon, it was rapidly translated into French and put in the king's hands by 1378 (Schnerb-Lièvre 1982, xlix). Meyer states that he did not find in it any mention of the French kings restoring the pope to his seat (Pannier and Meyer 1877, 132 n. 35).

248 **en son obaissance** Charlemagne's empire did not include England.

250 **Rolland et Olivier** Fictitious characters created to support the narrative of the *Chanson de Roland*, itself an imaginative account loosely based on a very different expedition Charlemagne is known to have made into Spain.

266 **reciter** G. 32, g. 4 *recitez.*

266 **cronicquer** G. 32, g. 4 *cronicquez.*

271 **reciter** G. 32, g. 4 *recitez.*

Part VI. Essays and Resources

Part VI. 1. Two Essays

1. England and French

When, in the second eleventh-century conquest of England, William, duke of Normandy, led a coalition of Normans, Bretons, Flemings and other French speakers in the 1066 invasion, there was no question of his imposing a written French-language bureaucracy. The English court already included French among its languages, exchanges between clerics in England and in francophone areas of Europe had a long history and French-speaking landholders were present in England before the Norman Conquest.[1] But William retained the governance of the country by shires and hundreds and his initial writs were sent out in English drafted by the staff of the king's chapel, with greetings to all the king's people 'frencisce ⁊ englisce' (sometimes also 'englisce ge denisce'). In so far as William used a standard or 'official' language for establishing his rule, it rapidly became Latin: as Richard Sharpe argues, the most practical arrangement (in line with continental practice) was to have written Latin documents from which English and French (and Cornish, Irish, Welsh, and Gaelic, or, in continental domains, Norman, Breton and Flemish) translations could be given to differing groups of laypeople involved in government.[2] Certainly, spoken French quickly consolidated its elite status after the Conquest from being one among several languages used in the eleventh-century Anglo-Danish and Anglo-Saxon courts to being *the* vernacular of England's rulers. But French had as yet no full existence as a written language (some isolated texts from the ninth to the eleventh century survive, but they are specific to particular, usually para-liturgical or other ritual occasions, rather than part of a systematic use of French as a written language of secular culture or record).[3] In England the invaders encountered a different distribution of written and spoken language as between Latin and the vernaculars than in their home culture. Late Old English standardised West Saxon functioned much more like Latin, in that it was a written language used across historiography, law, biblical translation, pastoral care, science, learning, medicine, travel and romance.[4] For French-speaking elites accustomed to an

[1] On French-language settlement in England before 1066 see C. Lewis 1995: on the internationalism of English culture in the eleventh century see Tyler 2012b, 616–23; O'Donnell and Tyler (forthcoming).

[2] Sharpe 2011, 5–8 (also http://www.paradox.poms.ac.uk/redist/pdf/chapter1.pdf); a shorter version, focused on languages rather than charters, is Sharpe 2013 (on the formula 'frencisce 7 englisce' and the question of whether the Normans referred to themselves as *franci* or 'Northmen' (as in Wace's etymology of *c.* 1160–74, (3), vv. 47–80), see Sharpe 2011, 5 and nn. 14, 15, 17; p. 3 for continental linguistic practices in administration).

[3] 'Francien', the nineteenth-century name for French from the area of the modern French hexagon-shaped state centred on Paris, did not become a written standard until the thirteenth century: it provided no precedent in the twelfth century for conceptualising French as a written standard.

[4] Tyler 2009; Gretsch 2001.

almost exclusively Latin written culture, the encounter with prestige books written and consumed in the vernacular in England appears to have provided a decisive precedent for their own production of written vernacular texts.[5] At the same time, the Norman diaspora in Europe and the Mediterranean created an environment in which French-language texts from England were readily transmissible in many regions. French's early presence in England was thus of considerable importance in the European story of French as well as in the history of England.

The first secular French-language literary culture is found at the court of Henry I (r. 1100–35), following, and then continuing to be produced alongside, the earliest extant French-language versions of the psalter (the 'Oxford' psalter of *c.* 1100–15, the 'Cambridge' psalter of *c.* 1125–40, and others).[6] By the 1130s, the first French-language historical writing, Gaimar's *Estoire des Engleis* (10) was being produced in what can be seen as a dialogue between royal and magnate courts and between English, Danish, French and Latin cultural traditions. By the late twelfth century, French texts in historiography, hagiography, romance, sermon, biblical and para-biblical narrative and commentary, lyric and other genres were being composed, some at secular, some at ecclesiastical courts as well as in monasteries and civic contexts in England. In the thirteenth century the range of French-language writing widened: more people learned French as a language both of culture and for its use in various occupational registers and bureaucratic genres.[7] Increasing numbers of scientific, informational, pastoral and devotional texts were composed alongside continuing production in narrative and lyric genres, and French became a widely used language of record and administration.

Although French-language writing in England continued into the fourteenth and fifteenth centuries, composition in literary genres slowed in the later part of the fourteenth century. At the same time there was intensified learning and teaching of French, the continuing circulation of French-language works of internal and external composition, and the use of French in government, law, administration and bureaucracy alongside Latin. It was within this multilingual Franco-Latin environment of multiple and varying correlations between spoken and written registers that medieval English also became an established written vernacular in the later fourteenth and fifteenth centuries. In the first half of the fifteenth century, French's internal literary domains in England narrowed to a few forms of devotional writing and historiography, but there was a continuing circulation of French-language texts between England and European regions. A much greater number of French than of English-language works were printed in England in the fifteenth and sixteenth centuries.[8] The use of French in external cultural and political relations became if anything, more important in the fifteenth century, even as French became re-signified as a foreign language, now to be located outside England.[9] The habit of bringing up elite English children with early acquired French for cultural, political, and

5 Lusignan 2011. On Latin as a specialised language under pressure from lay users see Tyler 2009; Geary 2013.

6 Rector 2010, 2012.

7 Crane 1997; Ingham 2015b.

8 Butterfield 2010, 36, 54.

9 Machan, 2009; Lusignan 2016.

diplomatic purposes persisted through Henry VIII's and Elizabeth I's French masters to the UK Foreign Office and diplomatic corps for much of the twentieth century (when learning French was routinely part of elite English schooling).[10]

In contrast, English remained confined more or less to England until well into the early-modern period. It was not usually spoken by other Europeans and was rarely used by people from England in their dealings abroad, where French and Latin were the dominant contact languages. Writers of English were sometimes known through their Latin or vernacular European language contacts (as in Chaucer's case) but their work (as is true both of Chaucer and Shakespeare) remained almost entirely untranslated until the eighteenth century.[11] Throughout the Middle Ages (as also in the early-modern period), French continued as England's main vernacular of contact and exchange in Europe, the Mediterranean and the East.

These exchanges and contacts moved in multiple directions. The history of French-language works entering England from the continent is relatively well established (though still with some lacunae). The prose *Estoire del saint Graal* (**41**), for instance, is not routinely included in English-language histories of English Arthurian culture, but at least nineteen manuscripts are known to have been made or circulated in later-medieval England. A major work of twelfth-century Marian writing, Herman de Valenciennes's *Bible* or *Li Romanz de Dieu et de sa mere* (**15**), is known in thirty-seven thirteenth- and early-fourteenth-century manuscripts, of which nineteen are insular. As with the works of Christine de Pizan in the fifteenth century, the extremely influential *Somme le roi*, a royal confessional manual of *c.* 1279 written for Philip III of France, circulated in late-medieval England in French as well as in English-language reworkings.[12]

French literary influence used sometimes to be conceived as primarily inward-bound into England, but medieval literary exports *from* England, when not in Latin, were in French, travelling among francophone readers and writers who could have them copied in their own regional French *scriptae*, turn them into local vernaculars or command their translation.[13] Such exports continue across the medieval period, and were particularly important in the twelfth century when the Angevin kings commanded much more territory

10 Good single essay studies of French in England include Crane 1999, Ailes and Putter 2014.

11 Caroline Spurgeon discusses Dryden's claim that Mlle Scudéry (d. 1701) planned to translate Chaucer: she found no evidence in Scudéry's archive that the plan had been carried out (Spurgeon 1911, repr. 1972, 219–20). For a handful of rule-proving exceptions among royal nobles and bibliophiles see Coleman 2007; Clermont-Ferrand 2008; Rundle 2011, 280. The earliest known translation of a Shakespeare play is into German in 1741 (J. G. Robertson 1910) 322.

12 On French texts of de Pizan in England see Downes 2009. For *Somme le roi*, see É. Brayer and A. Leurquin Labie, ed., 2011, and on the English context, A. Barratt 2008a and b. Catherine Batt offers a new account of late-medieval religious multilingualism in England as part of her volume translating Henry of Lancaster (Batt, trans., 2014). Claire Waters studies French-language thirteenth-century pastoral and didactic works in England and the Continent (Waters 2015); Wogan-Browne (forthcoming) looks at the continuing use of French devotional and doctrinal works in fifteenth-century England.

13 M. Ailes, 'Coals to Newcastle? The Export of Anglo-Norman literature', paper for Fordham International Medieval Conference, March 2013, on 'Putting England in its Place: Cultural Production and Cultural Relations in the High Middle Ages', forthcoming. See more generally on the medieval circulation of French manuscripts Busby 2002.

than the Capetians did in the Île de France. Although the power of a realm cannot be straightforwardly correlated with its literary production, the diplomatic, dynastic, and administrative links along which cultural influence travelled were far-reaching under Henry I and Henry II of England, and twelfth-century French writing from England not only forms the earliest European French-language literary culture, but inspired writing and translation in other regions of Europe.[14] Cultural contacts with external Norse culture continued in the twelfth century, for example, but now principally in French and Latin rather than Danish, English and Latin (as had been the case when England was part of Swein and Cnut's Danish empire in the eleventh century). Some fifty works of mostly twelfth and thirteenth-century Angevin and Plantagenet literary culture – Marie de France's *lais*, the romance of Tristan, Charlemagne romances alongside Troy stories and other works – were translated from French into Norse.[15] Translations from English French texts were equally prevalent in the rest of Europe: they include the romance of *Boeve de Haumtone* (modern Southampton), translated into Dutch, German, Italian, Russian, Romanian and Yiddish, as well as Icelandic, Welsh, Irish and Middle English, and reworked in continental French versions.[16] Similarly, Mandeville's 'travels' (*Livre des merveilles du monde* (35)) now thought to have been initiated in French in England in the later fourteenth century (and extant in fourteen insular and ten continental manuscripts) is supplemented by vigorous European-wide translation.

From the later twelfth century onwards, Latin and French writings from England on the idea of Britain made Britain a cultural presence and imaginative domain for Europe as the land settled by Brutus after the fall of Troy and eventually as the territory of Arthurian kingship and the Grail. The importance of these *matière de Bretagne* (or *Brut*) perspectives in European narratives of origin can hardly be overestimated. The latest extant manuscripts of Wace's *Roman de Brut*, the most influential of the twelfth-century vernacular *Brut* writings, are continental fifteenth-century copies:[17] European historiography and romance continued to use this British imaginary throughout and beyond the medieval period.[18] The influence of the *Brut* in insular culture and its contacts is apparent throughout the present volume in works from the twelfth to the fifteenth centuries: *De Bretaine ki ore est* (1), *Roman de Rou* (3), *Roman de Waldef* (6), *Estoire des Engleis* (10), *Scalacronica* (16),

14 Careri, Ruby, Short *et al.* 2011 find some 66% of twelfth-century French-language manuscripts to be insular, while rightly insisting that insular and continental should not be opposed but seen as part of 'une francophonie médiévale' (xxxiv–xxxv).

15 For a list of insular and continental French romances and their Norse reworkings into sagas, rhymed verse and ballads, see Leach1921, 382–3: more generally, see Ríkharðsdóttir 2012. On eleventh-century cultural contacts between England and Scandinavia under Cnut, see M. Townend 2012.

16 See J. Weiss, trans., 2008; Fellows and Djordjević 2008, 1–6; Fenster and Behrend Valles 2016. Since Jews in England, like those in Germany, were unlikely to have their own copies of secular literature in the sacred language of Hebrew, it is possible that they too knew *Boeve* in French.

17 Blacker 1996, 185–6.

18 For example, in addition to the well-known European Arthurian works of the twelfth to fifteenth centuries, Girart d'Amiens's *Escanor* (1274 × 1290, its matter claimed to be supplied by 'la pluz vaillant roïne/ Qui onques fust d'Espaigne nee ... fenme ... au roi d'Engleterre' [Eleanor of Castile, 1244–90, queen of Edward I] (ed. Trachsler 1994, vv. 124,29), eventually makes Sir Kay king of Northumberland; *Perceforest* (1313 × 1344, trans. Bryant 2011) is a lengthy Arthurian prequel in which Britain is re-organised under Alexander the Great.

Genealogical Roll Chronicles (**20c and d**), *Fouke le Fitz Waryn* (31), *Estoire del saint Graal* (41), *Mohun Chronicle* (42), *Débat des hérauts d'armes* (44).[19] A history of appropriation and adaptation is signalled in the naming formulae of *Brut* texts: 'Bretagne, ore Engletere', 'Engleterre, jadis Bretagne, jadis Albion' and other variations echo through them, in the same way as Arthur is claimed for the British and for the English in varying cultural and political contexts.[20] Even before Trojan origins and Arthurian connections became fashionable in Europe, Britain's position had a certain ambiguous glamour as a land at the edge of the known world.[21] It was the venue from which the hugely popular *Le Voyage de saint Brendan* (9), composed in French in England about an Irish abbot *c.* 1121, took off on its European wide career. The Arthurian Empire, as Christopher Baswell argues, was based on the Roman Empire but inverts it to make England the point of origin: both Arthur and Brutus are the focus of great narrative congeries powerfully combining geographic marginality and narrative centrality for the British Isles.[22]

Movements of texts, ideas and talk about them were intra-regional and ran along particular networks of people and institutions: it is unhelpful to see them as the product of post-medieval geo-political formations such as nation states. The focus of this book is medieval England, but the literary texts that circulated there (and in Britain and Europe), cannot always be securely or usefully seen as belonging to a specific territory. A well-known example is the *Chanson de Roland*, adopted as the cornerstone of the modern French national canon, but first found in an insular manuscript of the twelfth century (1130 × 1170?). The language of the text of this earliest version is not definitively assignable to any region of modern England or modern France.[23] Twelfth-century genres such as the *romans d'antiquité* or the *chansons de geste* are not evenly represented in insular and continental manuscripts, but are nevertheless best thought of as mobile cross-channel genres.[24] The cultural mobility and varied origins of early francophone writers around Britain, the

[19] Arthur himself did not immediately become an independent figure. For a judicious assessment of Henry II and Eleanor of Aquitaine's knowledge of the *matière de Bretagne*, see Aurell 2007, and for Arthur's eventual French language career in insular *Brut* texts, see Marvin forthcoming. For an argument on the different insular and continental remodellings of Arthur as a function of different systems and histories of kingship see Ashe 2011.

[20] While the Anglo-Saxons knew Trojan origin stories, they treated them as fictional: see Tyler 2012a.

[21] Topographically Britain is self-evidently an archipelago of greater and smaller islands, but, imagined as a remote but desirable *insula felix* in whose mysterious and liminal territory marvels happened, and also as a fertile place for fresh colonisation, it was an important presence in origin stories from Bede to Geoffrey of Monmouth to Jean de Wavrin and beyond. See e.g. Lavezzo, 2006; Goodman 2006. On Wavrin's engagement with British origin legends in his 1471 *Recueil des croniques et anchiennes istories de la Grant Bretaigne*, see Rajsic forthcoming.

[22] Baswell 2005.

[23] Short 2007a, 352, 354–8. See also idem, 2006. The linguistic evidence is given in detail in Short's edition 2005, 13–42. On the modern reception of the work, see A. Taylor 2001, Gaunt 2003.

[24] Busby 2002, II, 485–635 (esp. 488–513) discusses western France and England as 'prime movers in the production of early French vernacular narrative manuscripts' (493), with dispersion to the north-east, Picardy, and the south-east and Italy. By the mid-thirteenth century, 'the Anglo-Norman literary public did not make a clear distinction . . . between romance and epic' (500). On *chansons de geste* in England, see Short 2007a, 2005 (for early echoes of *chanson de geste* in other texts in England); Ailes 2011. For *romans d'antiquité* in England and their continuing presence in the later Middle Ages, see Baswell 2002.

Channel, and continental regions can make their identification with a particular territory complicated: Wace (*c.* 1110–*c.* 1174), for instance, is a Jersey-born, Caen-trained cleric with a relation to the court of Henry II (see (3), (**25a**)) who writes about Normandy, Britain, and saints culted in both regions. The work of scribes, authors, illuminators may be mobile or take place in a number of regional centres: the late-twelfth- or early-thirteenth-century *Roman de toute chevalerie* (**28**) is a good example of a text that unites continental and insular French rewritings of material concerning Alexander the Great, while its early-fourteenth-century manuscript may have been produced in London for a continental French patron. Many literary patrons were cross-channel figures who would have found any canon of French literature that stopped at either side of the English Channel very surprising.[25]

Some texts can be seen as belonging to multiple places stretching from north-western Europe to the eastern Mediterranean.[26] The *Histoire de la guerre sainte* ascribed to 'Ambroise' is complete in one continental manuscript and fragmentary in one insular manuscript: it was probably composed by a Norman or Anglo-Norman in the entourage of the crusading Richard I.[27] The Anglo-Norman *Miracle de Sardenai* (**34**), an account of a shared Christian and Muslim cult in what is now Syria, is extant in one of its copies in a composite manuscript still at Tours, of which one section may have originally been made for a community in 'Outremer', the Mediterranean of northern European crusaders and traders.[28] French was the English crusaders and settlers' major language for text and book production and for military, diplomatic, commercial and cultural communication: it is thought, for instance, that a copy of Vegetius's *De re militari* in insular French was commissioned by Eleanor of Castile for Prince Edward (subsequently Edward I) in Acre, while both were on Edward's crusading expedition in 1271–2.[29]

The ways in which French was a language without borders is also visible internally in medieval England. French constituted a readier language of inter-regional exchange than English, since Middle English dialect differences were more marked than those of French. Chaucer and Caxton were not alone in their concern that 'the grete diversité' of English led to miscopying, and many texts speak of the need to be 'translat' whether from 'Northern tunge in to sutheren' or from 'southerin englis . . . till our aun/Langage of northrin lede [people]'.[30] Francophone regional cultures around particular monasteries or baronial and episcopal courts were readily mobile and French texts copied in one region could easily

25 A good example is the engagement of the Counts of St Pol with the figure of Edward the Confessor: see Russell 2009; S. L. Field 2010.

26 For examples inclusive of and ranging beyond insular French see the King's College project on Medieval Francophone Literary Culture Outside France and the textual trajectories discussed on its website: http://www.medievalfrancophone.ac.uk/.

27 See Dean 56.1 and Ailes and Barber, ed. and trans., 2003.

28 Ruini 2013. On Outremer and its French(es), see http://legacy.fordham.edu/academics/programs_at_fordham_/medieval_studies/french_of_outremer/index.asp; http://legacy.fordham.edu/mvst/conference14/index.html; Morreale and Paul 2016. On French literature and the Mediterranean see Kinoshita 2006 and Trotter 1988.

29 Dean 379: Morgan 1982–8, II, no. 150 (135–6); Legge 1953; McKendrick, Lowden, and Doyle 2011, no. 125 (360–1).

30 Chaucer *Troilus and Criseyde*, V, 1793–6; Caxton, prologue to *Eneydos*; Rolle, *Form of Living* (cited Gillespie 2008, 257, 267); *Cursor mundi* (Assumption), vv. 51–4, cited Corrie 2012, 120.

be read in another. The characteristic longevity of manuscripts also means that, alongside texts that continued to be re-copied, there were also early copies of French-language texts available for later readers. Continuity of cultural capital and inter-generational memory are at least as endemic to French-language writing as to English, if not more so, and this capacity is drawn on for some notable constructions of differing communities' memory (see, for example, *Fouke le Fitz Waryn* (**31**) and the Crabhouse Register (**36**)). The diachronic and regional range over which French texts could be exchanged remained large within England as well as outside it, and this makes French an importantly continuous mode of vernacular writing.[31]

A good example of both the regional and diachronic mobility of French within England is BL Harley MS 273, a composite manuscript of thirteenth-century texts assembled in its extant form by 1400 and written partly in the hand of the Ludlow scribe who copied both *Fouke le Fitz Waryn* (**31**) and parts of the well-known trilingual Harley MS 2253 in Shropshire between 1314 and 1328. Harley 273 contains a French calendar, psalter and hours, and a varied range of insular and continental texts, including Grosseteste's *Reules* for estate management, and the *Bestiaire d'amour* of Richard de Fournival of Amiens.[32] John Clark, the manuscript's late-fifteenth-century owner, was Warden of the Grocers Company in London 1467–75 and grocer and apothecary to Edward IV, whose town Ludlow was.[33] (Whether Clark read his manuscript or had it read to him, but by whichever means, the thirteenth-century French texts in his collection would have remained transparent.)

The multilingual culture of the West Midlands demonstrates the capacity of regional cultures to inform metropolitan culture. The contents of Harley 273 and other late-thirteenth- and early-fourteenth-century trilingual collections from the region, such as Harley MS 2253, BL Add. MS 46,919 (see **7a**), Oxford, Bodleian Digby 86 and Bodleian Poet A 1 [the Vernon manuscript; see (**37**)], exemplify this influence. As Ralph Hanna and Susannna Fein have shown, this regional literary culture contributed to the development of London literary culture in the later fourteenth century, and Fein has more recently shown how we might see a multilingual compiler and copyist such as the

[31] The precise nature of such continuities in England's multilingual culture has yet to be fully mapped: see, e.g. on romance, the valuable survey by Field 2010. Griffiths and Putter 2014 show, à propos romance, that one vector affecting the presence of French in multilingual insular manuscripts is text-type; see also C. Cannon 2015, Putter 2015.

[32] The manuscript's other main works are insular treatises on love and friendship, a poem on love by Bozon (Dean 690), works on penance (such as Waddington's *Manuel* (**24b**), the Purgatory of St Patrick (Dean 550), and meditative diagrams), a continental Pseudo-Turpin Chronicle (a continuation of the Roland story). See further http://www.bl.uk/catalogues/illuminatedmanuscripts/ILLUMINBig.ASP?size=big&IllID=15169. Clark may also have owned Harley 1628, with its prescriptions in French and Latin for Edward IV, Richard III and others at the royal court (P. M. Jones 2008).

[33] French was an important language for traders at least into the 1440s, especially those associated with the royal court. As the example of the Pui de Londres (**8a**) shows, successful London guildsmen included francophone cultural traditions in their social, political and cultural lives. Grocers handled spices which were often used in the preparation of medicines: there are Latin and French charms for wounds and fever in Clark's manuscript, and much of the vocabulary of grocery and the spice trade used in both food and medicine is itself French: see Rothwell 1999 and his bibliography in notes 1–7; Kowaleski 2009; Hsy 2013, Meale 1995.

main Harley 2253 scribe as a proto-Chaucerian writerly figure.[34] Tolkien's ardent vision of English continuity in the West Midlands, focused on the early-thirteenth-century English-language *Ancrene Wisse* and its related texts (with their hinterland of Parisian Victorine thought), is not a national literary story, but a small, if significant, part of a more complex regional culture – Latin, English, French and Welsh – flourishing from the twelfth century onwards.

There is still much further investigation to be done factoring in French-language records into the multilingualism of literary and administrative cultures in particular regions in England and Britain.[35] To continue the example of the West Midlands, it is also worth noting that, in a reversal of the usual east–west direction in which *translatio studii* is imagined in the medieval West, the western regions of England experienced cultural exchange and transfer from regions further west. The Shrewsbury School list of *c.* 1270, a leaf in Shrewsbury School MS 7, for example, names some 67 *lais* and other narrative works with Celtic and French titles, some of which resemble the titles of known *lais* (by Marie de France, for instance) and many others now unknown. This suggests a vigorous vernacular cultural traffic between Ireland, Wales, and the west of England to add to the literary and political contacts already well known through such figures as Gerald of Wales.[36] Contact with and awareness of regions to the south and east is also vigorous. Hereford, under Bishop William de Vere (d. 1198), for instance, was an early centre of Latin and Arabic learning, and a focus for the new learning and new monasticism of secular canons and friars.[37] Simund de Freine (38), author of the earliest French life of St George, and Hue de Rotelande (4), whose romances are set in southern Italy and Sicily are among the late twelfth and thirteenth-century writers from the region.[38] The cosmopolitan thirteenth-century poems of Chardri (30) and the brilliant early Middle English debate poem, *The Owl and the Nightingale* are found together in the same West Midlands manuscripts.[39] They share one manuscript with Layamon's early-thirteenth-century *Brut* (as innovative and multilingually aware a narrative poem as Gaimar's *Estoire des Engleis* (10) had been in early-twelfth-century Lincolnshire). A little north from Layamon's Severn, in Shropshire, the Marcher romance of *Fouke le Fitz Waryn* (31), with its own distinctive adaptation of *Brut* material, was composed in rhyme in the thirteenth century and given a prose *remaniement* in the early fourteenth century.

French was also used intra-regionally within England in various ways. Notably, it was a language with multiple functions for England's Jewish population, who came to settle

[34] Hanna 2005, repr. 2008, 1–43, and chs. 3 and 4; Fein 2007, 2014 and Plenary Lecture, Conference of the Early Book Society, Oxford, July 2015.

[35] For an excellent example of the value of seeing administrative and literary records together in a given region, see Kerby-Fulton 2015. A great deal of information on language and cultural contact is being generated by the *England's Immigrants 1330–1550: Resident Aliens in the Middle Ages* project and database: https://www.englandsimmigrants.com/

[36] Ed. Brereton 1950.

[37] Frankis 2007; Barrow 1987.

[38] Simund's Life of St George is translated in Russell 2012, who suggests (28) that the poem may have been composed in support of Archbishop Baldwin's 1188 preaching tour for the third crusade.

[39] For a translation of all Chardri's works see Cartlidge, trans., 2015.

following William of Normandy. Alongside the French spoken by Jews with each other in their communities and homes, and between Jews and Christian communities, Latin and Hebrew were used as languages of record. But for Jewish women and those Jewish men with limited Hebrew literacy, French would also have been an important reading and presumably written language in both scriptural and pragmatic domains. Written evidence drawn from the very few extant Hebrew books from medieval England is complicated to decipher, but extant Anglo-Norman glosses in Hebrew characters suggest that English Jews did sometimes transliterate French into Hebrew characters.[40] Twelfth- and thirteenth-century French-language texts, however, are an important source for the formation and propagation of Christian attitudes to Jews and Jewish scripture, and show Christianity's negotiation of its historical imbrication with the Judaic culture from which it sprang. Several selections in this volume reflect increasingly intense exploration by Christians of Jewish difference. This expressed itself through supersessionist writing (e.g., the overwriting of Jewish allegoresis of the Song of Songs, as in (**26**), reinforced by an insistence that Jews were literalists who could not plumb the meaning of their own books (**17**), and depictions of Jews as foolish, gullible,and physically repellent (**20b**). The more learned Sermons on Joshua (**23**) develop a contrast not present in their source homilies by Origen between Jewish and Christian responses to Christ as part of their criticism of Judaism. French pastoral and devotional writing in England from the twelfth and thirteenth centuries offers one of the largest bodies of evidence for attitudes to Jews before the 1290 expulsion, though one still relatively understudied in favour of the fourteenth-century post-expulsion Middle English texts.[41]

French has also long been regarded as a specialist koinē for common law in England, supposedly enduring because fixed. But, although technical terms of pleading are used as a professional vocabulary by men at law and law clerks, law French is essentially spoken and written French used for particular purposes (see further (**7d**) headnote), not a separate language. French in the domain of law was as alive and in contact with other languages as anywhere else. Terms used in the law were also part of the lexis of landowning, mercantilism, seafaring (maritime law being in French), crime, punishment, treason, etc. For example, when Albina lands in Albion as its foundress (see **20c** and **42**), she 'takes *seisin*' of the land, just as Anglo-Norman men and women did of their inheritances as discussed in Anglo-Norman law codes.[42] As Paul Hyams has shown, from the twelfth century on, the processes and many of the terms of trial, dispute resolution, lordship and warranty are deployed in narrative literature's representation of political and ethical dilemmas (*Roland*, *Tristan*, *Lanval* and others).[43] One insular witness to thirteenth-century European interest in vernacular law codes, the prose *Miroir des Justices* (*c.* 1285–90), is a jurisprudential account of English law that cites King Arthur and King Alfred as authorities and mingles

40 E. De Visscher 2013; Trotter 2015 (we thank Professor Trotter for a pre-publication copy of this article).

41 For examples of such French texts, see Boulton, ed. and trans., 2013.

42 Lamont and Baswell, ed. (forthcoming).

43 See Hyams 2011, 2010, 1983. For the thirteenth-century English development of spoken and written French law treatises and practices in its European context, see Kuskowski 2014. For the French-language law code *Britton*, see Nichols 1865.

law terms with the analysis of sin, and with historiography and ethical critique.[44]

Legal registers also figure in another important domain of French: urban regulation and civic culture. Collections of customary laws (**1**) interweave *Brut* origins and legal documents into civic identities, and the influential Brunetto Latini, notarial writer and teacher, having composed his *Tresor* in French, is also borrowed into the London *Liber custumarum* where the London elite mercantile association, the Pui de Londres, also has its own regulations in French (**8a**). A witty list of towns from the fourteenth century in another legal compilation offers a verbal *mappa mundi* of artisanal and cultural production in England:

> Rymeour de Wyrcestre, Furur de Cestre, Puteynes de Cherring, Chauces de Tikehull, Rovvours de Alton, Haraung de Gernemue, Morue de Grimesby (etc.).[45]

Town identities are often presented in French as well as Latin: in the Ipswich borough records, for instance, King Richard is shown in an elaborate historiated initial handing the burgesses his Latin charter for the town in 1378, but the mid-fourteenth-century *Customale Gippovicense* is in French with a highly decorative index to its collection of customary law.[46] In their rules for foreign merchants, civic legal compilations are a vivid reminder of French's function in further important domains, those of maritime and mercantile occupations, where French was both the language of regulation and frequently that of exchange between speakers from different places.[47] The range of London voices and terms in Gower's great estates satire, *Le Mirour de l'omme* (**8b**) draws on transregional as well as insular francophone traditions of satire in its savagely brilliant wordplay, but it also draws on a dense urban world where each profession has its own differently multilingual domain.[48]

As this discussion already begins to suggest, another cultural domain in insular culture enlarged by consideration of French-language writing is the border zone between literary and pragmatic writing, brought so alive in the work of Michael Clanchy. The extension of French-language writing across more domains in the long thirteenth century was in large part a bureaucratic, clerical expansion, in which a wider range of institutional contexts began to support the production of written texts, but clerks working for magnates of course also continued to produce texts within the bureaucracies of large households.[49] In their chapters on scientific, technical and medical writing, Ruth Dean and Maureen Boulton's *Guide to Anglo-Norman Literature* lists 115 treatises and encyclopaedias (about 200 if utilitarian works from their other categories are added), ranging from the twelfth

44 *Mirroir des Justices*, ed. and trans. Whittaker 1895: see further Trotter 2007. French, more suprisingly, played a role in written canon law, and here again both the law and the language interact with many other domains. The late-twelfth-century French version of Gratian's *Decretals* includes in its version of the *De consecratione* a musico-theological account of the angelic precedents for hymn singing and its regulation (ed. Löfstedt 1992–2001, vol. 4, 174–5 (the earlier association of this translation with Thomas Becket and his clerical staff in exile at Sens is not now accepted).

45 'Versifiers of Worcester, Furriers of Chester, whores of Charing [?Cross]; the Shoes of Tikehull, the Robbers of Alton Pass, Herrings of Yarmouth, Cod of Grimsby': text in Bonnier 1901.

46 Allen *et al.*, 2000, plates 1 and 2. See further Britnell 2009.

47 Kowaleski 2009: Hsy 2013.

48 On Gower's French see most recently R. and M. Ingham 2015 and other bibliography in (**8b**).

49 The fundamental study is Clanchy 2013. For recent work see K. Kerby-Fulton 2015.

to the fifteenth century, but mostly thirteenth and fourteenth century. This body of work may have been responsible for the older perception of Anglo-Norman as dull and didactic, or 'merely' utilitarian, but its diversity and energy belies such an account, as does its relation to form and use of literary topoi.

This corpus of texts and their manuscripts can be seen, rather, as a field of experimentation in the forms and modes of knowledge: in what literate culture can handle and make present to its various audiences and what kinds of knowledge can be subjectivised – i.e. known to be known.[50] The range of forms and subject matters in these texts is striking, even within a single area. Medicine, for instance, which at 35 items is the largest subfield, includes prose, verse, and mixed prose and verse treatises, and uses letters and other formal paradigms of organisation to create and perform a variety of relations to knowledge (see (**32a**) and (**32b**) for examples here).[51] This explosion of knowledge and vernacular textuality subsists alongside other copious and varied writings of the long thirteenth century: romance, saints' life, lyric, reworkings of biblical books and Bibles, historiography, devotional, pastoralia and preaching materials. This broadened literary culture where the literary, the literate and the bureacratic shade into each other made available more and more varied kinds of material to lay and cleric alike. Although vernacular writing and authorship continued to be frequently conceived as fundamentally occasional and useful for informational, ethical, or recreational purposes, the status of French-language writing, in England as elsewhere, became increasingly that of a language of the book and of learning, alongside the continuing use of French in still more pragmatic and documentary domains.

Much of this material draws on a shared range of literary topoi in its self-presentation, and we might therefore take it into account in considering such questions as the development of ideas of authorship in late-medieval vernaculars. In the expanding francophone textuality of England, many possible relations developed between a writer and the body of knowledge presented in the text, together with a spectrum of possiblities as to when knowledge shades into experience and vice versa. Mandeville's *Livre* (**35**) is the best-known earlier-fourteenth-century work to deploy these relations in a form where the writer's knowledge reaches further into the authorising of the text than, for example, Wace's performance of scrupulous narratorial fidelity to the record (**3**), and where, in spite of the letters to Edward III present in some Mandeville manuscripts, a patron does not seem to have been essential to the text's production. The medieval title of the work is also significant. The thirteenth century's increasingly laicised idea of the book (see

50 For further discussion see Armstrong and Kay: for an example discussed in this volume, see (**40**), Rauf de Linham's verse treatise on the *Kalender*, and p. 343 above. On the relations of prose and verse to knowledge see further the discussion in Part VI, §1.2.

51 Besides medicine, there are treatises – verse, prose, and mixed, framed and unframed – for a wide range of subjects: on geometry, chiromancy (prognostication by lines in the palm of the hand), geomancy (divination by signs derived from the earth), spatulamancy (what Chaucer's Parson called 'sweryng in the shuldre-boon of a shep', i.e. divination by animal bones), treatises on dreams, prophesy and prediction, *imago mundi* encylopaedias, geographies of the East and of the biblical lands: there are letter-treatises and books of travel, bestiaries, lunaries, lapidaries, treatises on computus and the calendar (see (**40**)), on cosmetics (**32b**), on falconry, on engraved gems, on alchemy, heraldry, and on the management of landed estates.

20a-d, **24a** and **b** for examples), replete with the finding devices of prologues, chapter tables, titles etc., allows personal experience to become encyclopaedic material, even as the personal figure of the writer serves as authentic witness to the book. Whether actually fictive or not, Mandeville's narratorial presence is a representative subjectivising anchor for a compilation of knowledge newly organised into chaptered books for newly 'global' textual communities.[52] Looking at the full range of French-language writing in England, that is, provides new matrices within which to view ideas of literacy and the literate as they develop in insular vernacular writing.

The spectrum from instructional to administrative and pragmatic also offers, as do the other kinds of French discussed here, all the complexities of different varieties, specific regional cultures and their interrelations. For all its status and mobility as a *lingua franca* and its relative transparency as a communicative medium, French itself was hardly a language without variations. Medieval cultural and political interactions were in practice not with, or in, a single unitary 'French' ('*l'unité du français*', as Serge Lusignan and others argue in their recent history of the language, is '*introuvable*').[53] The Frenches of Flanders, Hainault, Brittany, Gascony, central, southern and eastern Europe and of '*Outremer*' (a name that for insular medieval users can refer to French beyond the Channel, as well as to French in the Mediterranean) could communicate with each other, as with the French of England, but often did so in their own *scriptae* or regional accents.[54] The Cornish-born John Trevisa, writing his English-language reworking of Higden's Latin *Polychronicon* in Gloucestershire in 1385–7, claims that French is spoken more uniformly in England than is English, but that there is a diversity of dialect found in the French spoken in Europe:

> Hit semeþ a greet wonder how Englische [þat is þe burþe tonge of Englisshe] men and her [*their*] owne langage and tonge is so dyuerse of sown in þis oon ilond, and þe langage of Normandie is comlynge of anoþer londe, and hath oon manere soun among alle men þat spekeþ hit ariȝt in Engelond. Neuerþeles there is as many dyuers manere Frensche in the reem of Fraunce as is dyvers manere Englische in the reem of Engelond.'[55]

[52] Other less well-known users of French in England also turn exemplary lives and narratorial biography into conduits to cultural-geographical knowledge authorised by the writers' experience. The hospitaller-knight Roger de Stanegrave, for instance, was released from a Mameluke prison after, he says, 30 years, and sensationally returned to Edward II's court in 1320. In 1332, at the time of Edward III's crusading plans, Stangrave composed a treatise *Li charboclois d'armes du conquest precious de la terre sainte de promission* urging crusade, providing topographical, cultural and military information and offering the book in effect as a substitute for the ageing hospitaller in Edward's service ('si fortune ne voile soeffre qe je soie propre persone de la vostre retenance, a tout le mains membré y soit en parole', ed. J. Paviot 2008, 296). The extant manuscript is unfortunately fragmentary, but enough survives to make Stanegrave's work comparable with Mandeville's as a book, and as a book of experiential authority. We are grateful to Dr Nicholas Paul for the introduction of this text in the Fordham faculty and student Anglo-Norman Reading Group.

[53] Lusignan 2011.

[54] Lusignan 2012b. For a succint mapping of medieval European francophony, see Busby and Putter 2010, 7–10. Wallace 1997 considers Flanders. Gaunt 2015 is an important new approach: see also the materials at http://www.kcl.ac.uk/artshums/depts/ddh/research/projects/current/mflcof.aspx.

[55] Higden, ed. Babington 1869, vol 2, 161.

Central continental French developed increasing claims to status as a legal and literary standard from the late twelfth to the fourteenth centuries.[56] Yet this continental French 'standard' was itself only one of several north-western possibilities for French speakers: the prestige of Paris and the language of the Île de France developed amidst continuing production in other courts and cities in Artois, Picardy, Hainault, Flanders, the Burgundian Lowlands and Burgundy itself, Normandy, Champagne, Lorraine, etc. Before and alongside the French-language literate production of Paris, there are, for instance, large and significant Picard administrative and literary corpora from the twelfth century onwards.[57] For that matter there are Picard copies of French texts composed in England (**25a**, Wace's *St Nicolas*, for example) and insular copies of Picard texts: Picard and the French of England form a significant domain of cultural, commercial and diplomatic interchange (see e.g. **8a**, *Liber custumarum*).

The modern habit of thinking in terms of two discrete realms, England and France, each owning a distinctive language, English or French, thus fits remarkably few of the actual and imagined communities of medieval England or Europe from the eleventh to the fifteenth centuries. As Ardis Butterfield has shown in a subtle and powerful study, such constructions only begin to apply, with much particularity and complexity, to the period of the Hundred Years War and the English kingdom in France in the earlier fifteenth century.[58] As Butterfield points out, England became more, not less, aware of French in its efforts at conquest and colonisation (and French continued in its lingua franca function). Political and cultural narratives do not necessarily go hand in hand: the loss of King John's continental holdings in 1204, for instance, did not disrupt French-language commerce or cultural exchange, still less affect the status and widening use of French in thirteenth-century England.[59] Texts placing themselves as part of a national story are a sporadic and recurring feature of medieval literary culture, but not the whole of the variety and richness of French-language writing and use across the Middle Ages in and from England. The history of French in England and Europe in its combination of supra-regional permeability and local habitations makes for broad and diverse possibilities, to say nothing of great linguistic richness as the two main vernaculars in England re-lexify each other, and as medieval multilingual cultural production continues in realm, region, court, cloister, town, cathedral or gild alongside wider political communities. Whether purely insular or transregional, the texts offered in this volume are a small sampling from a vigorous, long-lived, and constantly changing literate culture.

[56] Lodge 2004.

[57] Lusignan 2012b. While Paris was a major centre of fourteenth and fifteenth-century book production (see e.g. R. M. and M. Rouse 2000), its late-medieval prestige has tended to be overgeneralised in modern literary histories. Important recent studies highlighting twelfth- and thirteenth-century regional cultures include Lusignan 2012a, Symes 2007. For transregional French (England and France), see now Lusignan 2016.

[58] Butterfield 2009. David Trotter argues that in England, distinctions between English and French as languages were often not only historically unavailable but less important in a culture where an ideologically pregnant conception of linguistic boundaries is not the default assumption (Trotter 2013).

[59] Trotter 2011a.

2. Poetry and Prose in the French of England

Does the French Poetry of Medieval England Count?

The 'vernacularisation of culture' initiated at the twelfth-century courts of Henry I and II in England produced many 'firsts' in French medieval literature, as Ian Short has observed. Among these is the first narrative poem in octosyllabic rhyming couplets; the earliest 'adventure narrative' and the first historiographic narrative; the first biblical translations; and the earliest 'significant examples of French prose'.[60] Henry II's court became a centre for literary creation which attracted writers as geographically disparate as the Norman Wace, the continental Benoit of Ste. Maure, and the Provençal troubadour Bernart de Ventadour, among others. In that early period, when Anglo-Norman poetry was creating patterns of rhythm and rhyme, verse was based on the strict counting of syllables, well suited to a language like French in which syllables are pronounced with uniform intensity and with phrasal stress. But as the number of native French speakers in England began to dwindle, a widening group of English speakers acquired French as a second language and French speakers increasingly spoke English.[61] In these circumstances Anglo-Norman would have come under the influence of the strong Germanic word stress of English, and verse appeared that was adjusted for stress and employed more flexible lines. On the continent, however, French poets continued to practise strict syllable count, so that two divergent prosodic practices developed. In the second half of the fourteenth century, writers such as Guillaume de Machaut, Jean Froissart, Eustache Deschamps, and Oton de Granson took continental French poetry in fresh directions. Their work came to the admiring attention of Geoffrey Chaucer and John Gower, and Gower wrote French verse following the techniques of continental scansion. As continental poets had once looked north and west, to the court of Henry II, insular poets now looked south and east.

For modern readers the extant evidence for the language and versification of medieval poetry is necessarily limited by the written form in which it has been transmitted. Orthography alone cannot tell us exactly how the sounds of a language are pronounced; yet medieval poetry was most fully realised when read aloud and shared.[62] Faced with not knowing how a particular grapheme might have been realised in the spoken language, modern linguists attempting to reconstruct its sound system have relied upon the evidence of syllable count and rhyme; but in the case of the French of England, the number of syllables in a verse is

[60] See Short 1992, 229. See also Short 2007a, 335–61, and Legge 1965, 327–49.

[61] According to R. Ingham, there would have been two important ruptures in the transmission of French: the first occurred when the number of continental native French speakers in England diminished following King John's loss of Normandy in 1204 (but see Trotter 2013 on the continuing French exchanges and trade relations), and the second occurred after the Black Death in the fourteenth century, which struck especially hard in the population centres where Anglo-Norman was spoken (Ingham 2012, 160–2).

[62] See the phonetic reconstruction of verses in Short and Merrilees, ed., 1979, 15–16. A selection of Anglo-Norman poetic texts, including Benedeit's *Voyage de saint Brendan* (9) Gaimar's *Estoire des Engleis* (10) Herman de Valenciennes's *Li Romanz de Dieu et de sa mere* (15), Denis Piramus's *Vie de seint Edmund rei* (27) and the Nun of Barking's *Romanz de saint Edward* (2) can be heard online at: http://legacy.fordham.edu/academics/programs_at_fordham_/medieval_studies/french_of_england/audio_readings_94163.asp.

often indeterminate, and both in England and on the continent rhymes frequently came from an understood common stock that could be used across dialects. Additional issues are raised by the manuscript copies in which we read texts, which are the work of at least two people, the poet who composed the work and one or more scribes who interpreted and recorded it, both when the poem was composed and when later recopied. Very few of the medieval works that have come down to us are *Ur*-texts, and present-day audiences are often reading a poem at several removes from its presumed original. A given *scripta*, the collection of orthographic forms learned by a scribe to record the perceivedly distinctive features of a dialect or language, may not be the same as the *scripta* in which an author's text was first set down, and *scriptae* may change over time. Many late-nineteenth and early-twentieth-century scholars understood strict syllable-timing to be the single standard for French poetry and they judged Anglo-Norman prosody harshly, dismissing poets as incompetent.[63] They did not take into account the transmission history of texts, the multilingualism of insular culture and the phonological changes that, although common to both insular and continental French, happened earlier in England.

More recently, the approximate syllable-timing of much French poetry composed in medieval England has been a focus of speculation and analysis, but no one explanation has achieved consensus.[64] There are many verse forms in England, and they draw in different ways on Latin, English and French traditions. In early English accentual verse, stressed syllables (usually four to a line) were primary, whereas the number of unstressed syllables freely varied, as in the later-fourteenth-century narrative poem *Sir Gawain and the Green Knight*:[65]

```
x (x) x   x   / x   x   / x  x x   /  /       12 (13)
Ande quen this Bretayn watz bigged bi this burn rych
              a        a           a  x
 x    /  x (x) /  / x x  x  /                  9 (10)
Such glaum ande gle glorious to here
    a        a a      x
```

Both these lines, varied as their syllable count may be, represent exactly the same metrical patterning, one of the most common of those used in Middle English alliterative poetry: two stresses on either side of the cesura, with alliteration across the cesura on the first three stresses. In the alliterative corpus, variant patterns of alliteration mark the stresses, the first half line is especially prone to have three stresses or two full stresses and one half stress, and there is variation, especially in the second half line, as to whether stresses 'clash' or are interspersed by unstressed syllables, but the principle of accentual, rather than syllabic, counting remains intrinsic to the line.

[63] Nonetheless, the theory that Anglo-Norman poetry was stress-timed was put forward almost from the beginning of the movement to edit medieval French works: R. Atkinson, for example, argued that in Matthew Paris's *Vie de seint Auban*, the 'general principle of three beats in each half [line] is unmistakeable' (Atkinson, ed., 1876, 61). J. Koch reached a similar conclusion in his edition of Chardri's poems (Koch, ed., 1879, xliv).

[64] Some studies have argued that individual texts show a detectable, uniform metrical scheme; see Johnston 1974, and Johnston, ed., 1981; and see Pensom 2006, 51–65, and Pensom 1998.

[65] Tolkien, Gordon and Davis, ed., 1967, lines 20, 46. For more nuance, see Putter *et al.* 2007, 1–4.

Alliterative verse in systems of stressed and unstressed syllables characterised not only later and earlier Middle English poetry, but also Old English, Old Norse and Old High German, all languages to which stress-timed poetry was naturally suited. In addition to apparently influencing the French verse of England, contact with English-language stress patterns led to loss of weak *–e* earlier in the French spoken in England than in that of the continent. That is, enhanced stress on tonic syllables meant there would be a corresponding diminution in the vowels of surrounding syllables; as a result many words lost final schwa (final weak *–e*), and this was accompanied by syncope (loss of weak *–e* word internally). In Martin Duffell's view, 'by the thirteenth century, poets of both [English and French] were composing four-beat verse that hovered on the margins of the iambic'.[66]

Metre as Message?

In both continental and insular French medieval poetry, the octosyllable was the most widely used metre. Benedeit's early-twelfth-century *Voyage de saint Brendan* (**9**), although not the earliest poem in octosyllables, was the earliest to use rhyming couplets of octosyllables, a configuration that became standard for a great variety of poetry.[67] Rhyming octosyllables came to be associated with the *roman*, initially denoting any composition in *romanz* (French), and subsequently courtly love stories in particular; but they were also used for history, legend, and chronicle; for social and moral works; homiletic, prayers, sermons, and apocrypha; for grammars, science, and medicine. Well adapted to oral performance, rhyming octosyllables were employed in the earliest vernacular drama, as in *La Seinte Resurreccion* (**29**), where they could have helped in memorisation.[68] The octosyllable may also have been a learning device.[69] The default description of the Anglo-Norman octosyllable, measured according to the standard of strict syllable counting, has been that it contains lines of 7–8–9 syllables, with some lines as short as six syllables or as long as ten. This formulation needs to be qualified by including changes that occurred over time and by the preferences of individual poets.

Because the octosyllable was used for so many compositional types, it was not identified with a specific kind of writing. But the decasyllable, the earliest French verse form for which there is extant evidence (in the ninth-century *Cantilène de sainte Eulalia*), could lend heroic *gravitas* to poetic works.[70] It was perhaps first fully formed in the eleventh-century *Vie de saint Alexis* [Dean 505], the first known copy of which was made in the twelfth century in England. It is the metre of the *Chanson de Roland* [Dean 76] and the *Poème sur l'Ancien Testament* (**43**). The twelve-syllable or alexandrine line, although first used in the parodic twelfth-century continental *chanson de geste*, the *Pèlerinage de Charlemagne*,

[66] Duffell 2008, 92.

[67] See Gros 2012, 99, 104. The earliest known octosyllabic couplets are said to be the continental *Vie de St Leger* and *La Passion de Jésus-Christ* (*Passion de Clermont*), both of the end of the tenth century; they use assonance.

[68] See Vitz 1999.

[69] On the octosyllable used as a learning device (in Philippe de Thaon's *Comput*, a verse treatise dating from 1113–19), see Gros 2012, 110.

[70] Gros 2012, 99.

appeared in otherwise elevated material, earning its name from a continental *Roman d'Alexandre*. It is the metre of the Anglo-Norman Alexander story, the *Roman de toute chevalerie* (**28**), and is one of two different metres used expressively in the *Roman de Rou* (**3**). That is, in two of the *Rou*'s three extant manuscript versions, the account of Rollo's foundation of the duchy is composed in monorhymed four- and six-line stanzas of alexandrines, whereas octosyllabic rhyming couplets are used to tell about the Scandinavian pirate Hastings.[71] Françoise Laurent observes that Wace's exaltation of the Anglo-Norman dynasty gains an 'epic tonality' from his metrical and strophic choices.[72] Guernes de Pont-Ste-Maxence uses alexandrines, arranged in five-line monorhymed stanzas, for his biography of St Thomas Becket, but when he describes the patronage of Mary Becket in his second epilogue, he changes to verses of sixteen syllables (**11b**). The twelve-syllable line also occurs in biblical narrative, as in Herman de Valenciennes's *Romanz de Dieu et de sa mere* (**15**), which consists of Hebrew Bible and New Testament stories, but also the Passion, apocrypha about the conception, birth and marriage of the Virgin Mary, and the Assumption. The Commentary on the *Chant des Chanz* (**26**), religious literature of a deeply spiritual nature, is also composed in alexandrines in the monorhymed *laisses* typical of *chanson de geste*.

Less frequent than other metres is the heptasyllable, which appears in this volume in Simund de Freine's *Roman de philosophie* (**38**), and the hexasyllable, found in the tail-rhymed stanzas of Everart's *Distichs of Cato* (**37**).

Counting Syllables, Counting Beats

Since earlier French poetry written in England, especially that of the twelfth century, tended towards the syllabic regularity that would become standard in continental French poetry, it may be helpful here to consider its technique. As a rule, it called for weak or unstressed *–e* to be pronounced before a consonant but elided before another vowel (although orthographically maintained), both in word-internal and word-final positions, e.g., *toute la journée, gouvernement* (these same instances of *–e* are silent in modern spoken French). In verse-final feminine rhymes (ending in *–e*, *–es*, or the 6 pers. *–ent* verb form), the *–e* does not count as a syllable, although it is pronounced as an off-glide. At the medial pause, the elision of *–e* is called a lyric cesura; where *–e* at the cesura is kept, it is an epic cesura.

The instability of vowel sounds such as *–e* in the always-evolving spoken language gave continental poets latitude in creating a fixed-syllable line, but only where syllable count for the rest of the line was stable. As discussed, weak *–e* was in the process of becoming silent in spoken French; in poetry, it was sometimes realised as a full syllable and sometimes not. For example, the elision of a vowel before another vowel could be disregarded (signalled with the tréma, e.g., *quë il*). Vowels in hiatus reduced over time to diphthongs or to simple vowels, and could be pronounced in two syllables or one. Word-internal

71 In the third manuscript, the section in octosyllabic rhyming couplets precedes the story of Rollo; see Holden, ed., 1970–3, III, 11.

72 Laurent 2012, 121–2.

hiatus could be evoked, especially where –*i* is followed by another vowel, as in the terminations –*ion*, –*iun*, –*ier* (*-ïon*, –*ïun*, –*ïer*) or in the combination –*ie*, as in *science* or *escience* (*scïence, escïence*), in all of which –*i* could be consonantalised as /j/ (yod) or not, as needed. Other combinations of vowels were also affected.

Sanson de Nantuil's *Proverbes de Salemon* (**39**), twelfth century, is seen to have been composed in strict octosyllables, once we allow for the fact that it is extant in a later copy. In its first thousand lines, for example, there are only thirteen verses that cannot be adjusted without the kind of editorial emendation that might now be seen as interventionist.[73] These lines from the prologue (**39**, vv. 11–30) scan as follows:

De / bons / man / gers / sui / plen / te / ïs;
Trai / et / sei / ça / ki / est / men / dis.
S'est / tels / que / pe / re / ce / le / toch*e*,
Ne / li / queor / fors / ov / rir / sa / buch*e*,
Ne / li / ruis / plus / a / tra / vai / ller
Fors / a / sa / vu / rer / e / ma / schier.
N'est / lan / gue / ros / s'il / l'a / sa / vor*e*
Ki / ne / de / lit / me / ïs / me / l'or*e*.
A / la / bu / che / rend / grant / dul / çor
E / mul / t i / at / sei / ne / sa / vor.
L'es / pirit / gua / rist, / le / cors / re / heit*e*;
Trop / est / go / lis / ki' / n ad / suf / frait*e*.
Molt / est / fols / e / pro / vé / vi / lain
Ki / n'a / sa / vo / rét / de / cest / pain,
Kar / tut / est / fait / de / sa / pï / enc*e*,
De / grant / doc / tri / n*e* et / de / scï / enc*e*.
    Si / l'ad / tra / mis / par / son / mes / sag*e*
Cil / ke / de / tu / te / cho / *se* est / sag*e*.
Ri / ches / reis / est, / ne / puet / plus / estr*e*,
Në / un / ches / n'out / ne / per / ne / meistr*e*.

In 39.11 the tréma indicates hiatus in *plenteïs*: verifiable both at the rhyme with *mendis* and by counting syllables; this prevents a reading of –*eis* as a diphthong. The word *meïsme* (Lat. *metipsimus*, Old French *medisme*) 39.18, which yields modern French *même*, could be employed with or without hiatus. *Traiet* in 39.12 and *savorét* in 39.24, in their unedited forms, may look as if they end on the same vowel sound (final *t* is silent in both). But *Traiet* is 3 pers. subjunctive and the –*e* is a weak –*e*, to be pronounced as an off-glide, whereas *savorét* is a past participle and its final –*e* is a full vowel, /e/; any ambiguity between them is obviated by the acute accent, *é*. In 39.21 *espirit* is an alternate spelling for *esprit*; that it is pronounced in two syllables and not three is shown by the total number of syllables in the verse. In 39.25 and 39.26, the tréma indicates hiatus in *sapïence* and *scïence*. Finally, in 39.30, because the *Proverbes* entry (and the poem as a whole) has proven to be reliably syllable-timed, *Në unches* is read as three syllables.

[73] Isoz, ed., 1988–94, III, 30–1.

Wace's use of syllable-timed verse in the *Roman de Rou* (3) allows us to determine that the French for 'Bayeux' should be pronounced in three syllables in v. 174:

> Ne / truis / gai / res / ki / rien / me / dunt,
> Fors / li / reis / Hen / ris / li / se / cunt:
> Cil / me / fist / du / ner, / Deus / lui / rend*e*,
> A / Ba / ï / eus / u / ne / pro / vend*e*,
> E / meint / au / tre / dun / me ad / du / né:
> De / tut / lui / sa / ce / Deus / bon / gré! (3, vv. 171–6)

Hiatus between a variety of vowel strings appears especially often in Angier of St Frideswide's *Introductio* and *Prefatio-Proem* to his *Dialogues de saint Gregoire* (**24a**). We find *gäaigne, guäaigner, gäaingner* (vv. 83, 106, 108), *deüst* (v. 101), *marchëant, marchëanz* (vv. 77, 113), *possessïon* (v. 97), *meïsme* (vv. 33, 54, 57) *trichëor* (v. 121), *gramarïens* (v. 195), *dïaleticïens* (v. 196), *dïaloge* (v. 201), eüst (v. 219); none of these is possible in modern French (and cf. English *gain, duty, merchant, possession, dialectician,* but *grammarian, dialogue*).[74]

Successive copying of texts and varying scribal orthographic habits had an effect on the presentation of French poetry in England. Thus the strict syllable-timing of early insular French poetry, almost all of which reaches us only through later manuscripts, is very often obscured by later scribal practice. This is true, for example, for Gaimar's *Estoire des Engleis* (**10**), and the Nun of Barking Abbey's twelfth-century *Romanz de saint Edward, rei e confessur* (**2**), which we read in an early-fourteenth-century manuscript.[75] Interference from English could affect a French-language *scripta*, as may be the case in what is now the first verse of the nun's prologue:

> Si / jo /e / l'or / dre / des / ca/ ses / ne / gart, 8
> Ne / ne / jui / gne / part / a / sa / part, 8
> Cer / tes / nen / dei / es/ tre / re / pris*e* 8
> Ke / nel / puis / fai / re en / nu / le / guis*e*. 8

The first line is only apparently formed of ten syllables. The form *joe* (*je*) in 2.1 is an insignificant alternative spelling of *jeo*, the orthography for the Anglo-Norman *je*, and counts as only one syllable regardless of its spelling. The word *cases* may well be a corrupt form of *cas*, the correct French form for both singular and plural, possibly under the influence of English. Once those two instances are accounted for, the line scans as eight syllables.

Denis Piramus wrote his life of *Edmund* (**27**) in the twelfth century but it is available to us only in two manuscripts of the first half of the fourteenth century. Without editorial intervention, the prologue in this volume would show greater 7–8 variation (**27**, vv. 1–8):[76]

[74] Orengo, ed., 2013; on Angier's use of accents to count syllables, see II, 102–4 (also Fig. 1–18); tableaux, 365–75.

[75] Short, ed., 2009, xxxv–xxxvii. Taking a broad view of Anglo-Norman syllable count, Short comments that 'certain discrepancies are less real than they seem, and function only at the level of orthography'; he attributes 'misleading impressions of hypersyllabism' to the scribal habit of adding letters or syllables (xxxvii). See also Short's very useful reconstruction of part of Marie de France's lai of *Lanval* as it might have looked copied by a scribe in continental French as compared with an actual Anglo-Norman transcription of the end of the thirteenth century; Short 2013, Appendix, 167.

[76] D. W. Russell comments that the text in Manchester, John Rylands University Library, French MS 142

Mult / ay / u / sé / cu / m [e] /pe / cher*e* 8
Ma / vi*e* / en / trop / fo / le / ma / ne / r*e*. 8
E / trop / ay / u / se / e / ma / vi*e* 8
[E] / en / pe / ché / e / en / fo / li*e*. 8
Kant / cour / t han / tey[*e*]/ of / les / cur / teis, 8
Si / fe / sei / [e] / les / ser / ven / teis, 8
Chan / ceu / net / tes, / ry / mes, / sa / luz 8
En / tre / les / dru /es / e / les / druz. 8

In v. 4 above, in the fourth syllable, the *e* is the conjunction and this never elides. Lines 1 and 6 are made into verses of eight syllables by emendation.

On the other hand, Chardri's *Vie de seint Josaphaz* (30) is an early-thirteenth-century composition available in a roughly contemporary manuscript; its verses show variation. Given that syllable count had become more flexible by this time, both authorial and scribal French usage may be the same (30, vv. 1–7).

Ki / vout / a / nul / ben / en / ten / dr*e* 7
Par / en / sam / ple / peot / a / pren / dr*e* 7
La / drey / te / ve / ye / de / sa / lu. 8
Ceo / ad / l'en / so / ven / te / fé / veu 8
Ke / genz / sunt / pa / r un / res / pit 7
A / men / dez / plus / ke / par / le es /crit 8
De Au / styn / u / de / seynt / Gre / go / ri*e*. 8

While it is perfectly possible to elide the *–e* of *le* in v. 6 and the *–e* of *De* in v. 7 to ensure the octosyllable, there seems no way to produce eight syllables in vv. 1, 2, and 5 without significant editorial intervention.[77]

By the late thirteenth century, as Richard Ingham observes, Anglo-Norman 'had diverged very significantly from continental Old French varieties', and poems like *Sicom Aristotele nous dit* (**32a**), a brief treatise on menstruation composed in the fourteenth century and transmitted in a fourteenth-century manuscript, shows a more flexible octosyllable than that found in most earlier poetry.[78] Given that the date of composition and the manuscript date are more or less contemporary, again scribe and author may share the same language (**32a**, vv. 15–20):

Es / crit / est / que / par / a / te / le / re / son 10
Com / vint / al / mal / po / lu / ci / oun, 8
Tot / est / me / me / la / ma / nere 7
A / vent / i / cest / mal / a / la / mu / liere; 9
Ço / e / vint / par / ha / bun / dan / ce / de / hu / murs, 11
Si / l'a / pe / le / fem / me / cez / flours. 8

presents greater metrical regularity than does the text of the slightly later Cotton manuscript in which this prologue is extant (Russell, ed., 2014, 37, with emendations to this passage at 67).

77 The first two lines in our example from (30) seem to the eye to be eight syllables long; however, vv. 1–2's line-final endings in *–dre* with weak *e* are pronounced as an off-glide, but not included in syllable count.

78 Ingham 2012, 70. In (**32a**), elision of weak –e in any position would reduce many seeming irregularities.

The poet John Gower wrote French verse that would become one of the 'canonical metres' of English verse, iambic tetrameter.[79] Scholarly opinion on whether Gower's French language was continental or Anglo-Norman has see-sawed over the years since Macaulay pronounced it to be Anglo-Norman.[80] There seems to be firm agreement on the nature of his verses, however, which, in his *Mirour de l'omme* (**8b**), are both syllable- and stress-timed. This can be seen by a comparison with the *Vers de la mort* by the continental poet, Hélinand de Froidmont, Gower's inspiration and from which he quotes:

Tex me couve / dessous ses dras.
Qui cuide estre / tous fors et sains.

Hélinand's verse shows phrasal stress (primary stress on *couve, dras, estre, fors and sains*). With a few adjustments, Gower instead writes a four-beat line:

Car tiel me couve soubz ses dras,
Q'assetz quide estre fortz et seins.[81]

While a number of other late-medieval English writers represented in this volume also write strict octosyllables, we know too little about them to understand their circumstances. These include John of Howden (**21**) and the authors of the *Miracle de Sardenai* (**34**) and the Crabhouse Register (**36**).[82]

Caesura

In the longer poetic lines, decasyllables and alexandrines, caesura is normally found. For Anglo-Norman poetry, maintenance of a medial break, which divides the line into two hemistichs each, is thought to be a more certain regulating principle than the number of syllables in each hemistich, classically 6 + 6 but sometimes 7 + 5 or, less often, 5 + 7. In the following verses from Herman de Valenciennes's *Romanz de Dieu et de sa mere* (**15**), final *–e* (in *estraite*, *terre*, *Pentecoste*, and *venimes*, respectively, in the second, fifth, seventh, and eighth lines) is not counted (**15**, vv. 1–9).

Sei / gnurs, / des / o / re / di / rai   dunt / en / fa / ce / la / chan / çon
Pur / qi / jo / l'ai / es / trai / *te*   de / si / hau / te / rai / son.
Jo / la / fa / ce / de / ce / lui   qui / est / e / diex / e / hom,

[79] Italian and French models also influenced Chaucer, whose iambic pentameter figures importantly in the canon of English metres (Duffell 2008, 92). Fifteen poems in a manuscript collection have the letters 'Ch' written next to them, suggesting that Chaucer may have composed poetry in Francien; see Wimsatt, 2009.

[80] Macaulay, ed., 1899–1902, I, xv. In her entry on Gower's *Cinkante balades*, Dean (707) thought that Gower's French was not 'distinctively Anglo-Norman'. B. Merrilees and H. Pagan have concluded that Gower's lexicon was in part Anglo-Norman and in part continental French (Merrilees and Pagan 2009, 123–4). R. Yeager believes that Gower Frenchified his Anglo-Norman (Yeager 2009, 141). Ingham 2015a states that Gower's language is Anglo-Norman with a slight continental colouring (we thank Professor Ingham for allowing us to see this essay before publication).

[81] Macaulay, ed., 1899–1902, I, xlvi.

[82] The editor of *Rossignos* states that, 'Plainly this is versification as correct as any to be found on the Continent, and which is clearly at pains to follow the same conventions of 'scansion' (Hesketh, ed., 2006, 28).

Cum / en / ter / r*e* / fu / nez,	cum / sus / tint / Pas / sï / un,
Cum / fu / mort / en / ter / r*e*	e / de / sa / Re / sur / rec / ciun,
De / lui / e / de / s a / pos / tels	e / de / l'A / sen / sion,
Del / jur / de / Pen / te / cos / t*e*	e / de / l'a / par / i / tion,
Sei / gnurs, / cum / nous / ve / ni / m*es*	par / li / a / ra / an / çun,
Cum / a / vrum / al / de / rain / jur	de / noz / pe / chiez / par / dun.

Other adjustments may be considered. In line 1, *ore* is flexibly *or*, and perhaps the final –*e* in words like *face* (etymologically, *faz*; v. 1, second hemistich, and v. 3, first hemistich) should not be counted. The final line here can be counted as twelve syllables if an elided –*e* is allowed in *derain* (*derain* > *d'rain*).

In the decasyllable of the *Poème sur l'Ancien Testament*, using the lyric caesura (**43**, vv. 1–6, and see further p. 386 above):

Al / rei / de / glo / rie,	[a] / Deu / om / ni / po / tent,	10 (4+*e* + 6)
Qui / meint / sanz / fin /	e / sanz / com / men / ce / ment,	10 (4 + 6)
Le / mund / go / vern*e*	/ tut / par / sun / ju / ge / ment,	10 (4+*e* + 6)
E / est / a / sons	/ en / ches / cun / liu / pre / sent,	10 (4 + 6)
		(4 + 4 + 2 perhaps also possible)
A / ches / cun / so / co / rabl*e*	/ qui a / lui / se / prent,	10 (6+*e* +4)
Ho / nur, / puis / san /	ce / sanz / de / fi / ne / ment.	10 (4 + 6)

In v. 1 *glorie* scans like *gloire* (*gloi* / *re*, but with lyric caesura, final –*e* has no syllabic value); [a] is added editorially for the sake of intelligibility, and that restores the decasyllable. In v. 5 the *i* of *qui* is elided; v. 6 has a weak caesura, mid-word.

Tail-Rhyme Stanzas

The term tail-rhyme essentially refers to a type of stanza that originated in Anglo-Norman literature of a 'spiritually or morally instructive' cast, 'whether directly so or obliquely through satire'; unlike other Anglo-Norman versification, however, it was '*not* used for less morally weighty material'.[83] Presented in saints lives, debate poems and the like, it was also associated with lyric, especially devotional lyric, which could be disseminated in sermons. Beneit's *Vie de Thomas Becket* [Dean 509] is both the earliest example of tail-rhyme structure and the first to portray a saint 'as a handsome romance hero with courtly manners in tail-rhyme'.[84] Tail-rhyme later figured in Middle English romance.

The French portion of Everart's *Distichs of Cato* (37), in octosyllabic stanzas that end on hexasyllabic tail-rhymes, is one of three Anglo-Norman translations of the work, all of which exemplify the use of tail-rhyme stanzas in moralising literature. In the Vernon manuscript Everart's French text (37) is presented macaronically, that is, with intercalated English quatrains and with distichs in Latin. The complete work is primarily a teaching text; Cato had long been used for instruction. But the tail-rhyme, in addition to bringing

[83] Purdie 2008, 32.

[84] In turn, the *Vie* may have influenced the first 474 lines of the later, Anglo-Norman romance of *Boeve de Haumtone*, whose 'accentual rendition' shows similarities to Beneit's poem (Purdie 2008, 44–5).

home the ethical dimension of the work, lends metrical diversity in a pointed way. In early Middle English literature, the tail-rhyme of the *Distichs* is paralleled by collections of proverbs and sayings, and a fifteenth-century tail-rhyme courtesy book shows that didactic literature continued to be produced in tail-rhyme stanzas even after the development of the Middle English romance.[85]

Assonance and Rhyme

The earliest documented rhymed composition in any kind of French was written in Provençal in the eleventh century (*Chanson de sainte Foy d'Agen*, monorhymed *laisses*), but Anglo-Norman poets or those writing in England were also among the first to pursue rhyme (the identity of vowels and any consonants following), abandoning the simple identity of the vowel alone that defines assonance. The octosyllabic couplet rhyming AABBCC etc. (*rime plate*) is of insular origin, its earliest practitioner, as noted above, being Benedeit, in his *Voyage de saint Brendan* (**9**), followed by Wace, Gaimar, and Sansun de Nantuil. The kind of rhyme Benedeit uses, however, is unusual. That is, in verses ending in feminine rhymes, contra the practice of not counting the weak final *–e* that would prevail in continental French poetry after Benedeit, the *–e* at the rhyme in verses 1–4 is counted (**9**, vv. 1–4):[86]

[Da]m / më / A / liz / la / re / ï / ne,
Pur / qui / ven / drat / lei / di / vi / ne,
Par / quei /crei / strat / lei / de /ter / re,
E / re / mein / drat / tu / te / guer / re

By contrast, the final rhyme-words of the two couplets following (vv. 5–8) are masculine rhymes simply by virtue of not ending in *–e.* Counting the number of syllables in each is straightforward.

Pur / le / s ar / mes / Hen / ri / le / rei, 8
Pur / le / cun / seil / ki / er / t en / tei, 8
Sa / lu / e / tei / mi / l e / mil / feiz 8
Li / a / pos / toil / les / dans / Be / neiz. 8

On the whole, authors comment less on their prosody than they do on their language or on the ethical purpose of their compositions. Guernes de Pont-Ste-Maxence, however, takes special pride in the uniqueness of his *Life of Thomas Becket* (**11b**), in part for his use of different metres. He boasts in his first epilogue about the 'five fives', saying that: *Li vers est d'une rime en cinc clauses coplez* (i.e. the verses are joined in five stanzas, each built on a single rhyme (**11b**, 9)). But William Waddington, writing in the mid-thirteenth century, claims deficiencies in what he calls *rimer*, which probably refers not only to his rhymes but also to his versifying as a whole.[87] At the end of his *Manuel des pechiez* (**24b**), Waddington says:

85 Purdie 2008, 56.

86 See Merrilees and Short, ed., 1979, 8 and n. 20.

87 For *rimer* the *AND* gives 'to rhyme'. The *DMF* gives both rhyme and metre (see under *rimer*, I, A and B),

De le franceis, ne del rimer,
Ne me dait nuls hom blamer[88]

(For my French and for my versifying no-one should blame me.)

The spirit of the Nun of Barking's now-famous protest, in the prologue to her life of Edward the Confessor (2), that she speaks a *faus franceis d'Angleterre*,[89] is countered by Matthew Paris, in his *Estoire de seint Aedward le Rei*. Laurent has cogently argued that Paris knew the nun's life of Edward but, unlike the nun, whom he mocks for seeming to apologise for her French, he 'validates' and 'legitimises' his own French, which those who speak the continental varieties of French are not able to correct.[90]

The Place of Prose

As Angier de St Frideswide translates Gregory the Great's *Dialogues*, he offers a *digressio* in octosyllabic couplets explaining how he will translate the Latin prose of the *Dialogues* into vernacular verse.[91] First, he invites any dissatisfied readers to make the text *cortois* (that is, to rewrite the verse), but he warns them not to make a mistake because *miez est qe la rime faille, / qu'en mençonge en vain soi travaille; / mielz vaut feiblement rimoier / q'estre prové a mençongier* (it is better for the rhyme to fail than for a person to work at a lie; it's better to rhyme poorly than be proved a liar). He then offers an extended metaphor comparing good writing with appropriate dress for a woman:

D'autre part, sache en verité:
Tant ai sentu e esprové
Qe qui translate autrui escrit
En autre lange qu'il n'est dit
Ne poet pas aler controvant
A son pleisir rime eslisant.
Car s'il voelt por chasqun bel dire
La rime a son pleisir eslire,
Sovent dirra, ço poet savoir,
Maleit gré soen al qe le voir,
Car quant del soen plus i mettra,
De l'autrui plus i mentira.

[f. 33ra] Moreover, know [this] in truth: I have myself felt and experienced that whoever translates someone else's writing into another language cannot go around inventing and choosing rhymes to suit himself. Because if he wants to suit himself with every fine utterance, he will often say, in spite of himself – and he can be sure of it – something other than the truth; for the more he puts in of his own thoughts, the more he will misrepresent the other's.

Por tant ne voeil rime choisir
Qe trop ne moi face mentir,
Mais simplement dirrai l'istoire
Si com la nos dit seint Gregoire,

That's why I don't want to write poetry that might make me lie overmuch, but I will tell the story simply, as St Gregory tells it to us, no matter how it might otherwise go with

noting that as a noun *rimer* meant the art of putting in verse or the practice of versification (*sub* III).

[88] See further Short 2010, 50.

[89] The Nun does not mention her rhymes or her prosody, but both may be implied in her comments about her French.

[90] Laurent 1998, 120–1.

[91] MS BN fonds français 24,766, online at http://gallica.bnf.fr/ark:/12148/btv1b84522070.r=dialogues+de+-saint+gregoire+le+grand.langFR; and see Orengo, ed., 2013, II, 141, vv. 3525–30.

Coment q'oel aut del rimoier,
Car sachez, mielz voeil apaier
Deu e ses sainz od verité
Q'offendre les od fauseté.

[f. 33rb] rhyme, for know that I prefer to satisfy God and his saints with the truth than offend them with falsehoods.

Derechief si jo bien voloie,
Apertement proveir porroie
Qe riche sentence eslosee
Ne doit pas trop estre aournee
De rhetorïenes colours,
Car dame qui desire amours
Sovent en devient orguillouse
Si sa robe est trop precïouse.
Mais s'ele est simplement vestue,
Non trop vilment ne del tot nue
Ne trop richement açaesmee,
Plus en ert bele e coloree.
E ço vos provrei par nature
Qe miez vient qe sa vesteüre
Soit auqes feible e bien soiante
Qe trop riche e desavenante,
Car povreté fera rougir
Sa color vive e refreschir,
E richesce la tendra pale
E desdeignante e desegale.

Furthermore, if I wanted to, I could prove clearly that a rich, honoured opinion should not be overly adorned with the colours of rhetoric, for a lady who desires love often becomes prideful if her dress is very costly, but if she is dressed simply – neither very poorly or revealingly or very richly – she will be more beautiful and radiant. And this I'll prove to you [by the effects of] nature, that it's better for her clothing to be a bit humble and appropriate than very rich and inappropriate, for poverty will bring out and refresh her lively colour, and wealth will keep her pale, disdainful, and inconstant.

De noble sentence ensement
Vos di q'oem la doit humblement
Aorner, q'el ne soit trop fiere;
Si doit tale estre sa chiere
Q'el soit de honte auqes rovente,
Si en ert plus bele e plus gente.

Similarly, I tell you that a man must clothe a noble opinion humbly, so that it doesn't seem too proud; its demeanor should be such that modesty gives it a rosy tinge and thus it will be more beautiful and noble.

D'autre part ne s'asiece pas
En tant vil liu ne en tant bas
Q'oem la desdeinge regarder,
Mais en tal liu s'auge soier
Q'oem l'apeauge avant a enor.
E si soit tale sa color
Qe ne soit de honte confuse,
Car sovent avient q'oem refuse
Icel qui est en robe sale
S'el est od tot confuse e pale;
Si tient hoem a grant vilenie
Quant dame trop s'enhumilie.

Moreover, may it not be found in such a vile or low place that someone may refuse to read it; rather, may it be lodged in such a place that people summon it forth honourably. And may its colour be such that it not be taken for shame, for it occurs often that a man may refuse she who is in a dirty dress [f. 33va] if she is, on top of that, pale and downcast; people hold it to be a great disgrace when a lady lowers herself unduly.

Por ço doit cil qui bien rimoie
Tenir la miliuëne voie
E faire sa rime entendable,

For those reasons, he who would versify well should hold to the middle road and make his poetry understandable, simple, pleasing, and beneficial. Thus it will be more

Legiere e douce e profitable,
S'en ert plus chier e eslosez
De tote gent e plus amez
Por q'ele soit pleisible a touz.
  Car 'qui le prou melle od le douz',
Ço dit Horace en *Pöeitrie*,[92]
Qe 'cil emporte la meistrie'.[93]

valuable and praised by everyone, and better loved, because it will please everyone.

For whoever blends what is profitable with what is sweet, as Horace says in his *Art of Poetry*, that person will carry away the honours.

In short, in Angier's view, verse not hewing to the *juste milieu* risks calling inordinate attention to itself (thus failing at the aim of pleasing God and his saints). Verse can provoke undue, immodest attention to the poet himself (vv. 11–12), either by highlighting his technical ingenuity to the point of distracting from the matter of the poem or by causing readers to disdain the matter because its form seems poor; by adding to the received matter something it did not originally contain, it misrepresents the original work and its author.

The background for Angier's comments lies in the long tradition of Christian thinking about the form in which religious doctrine should be written down. At least from the time of Augustine, prose was imagined as 'natural' and therefore suitable for contemplating the word of God, whereas the ornaments of poetry, including classical poetry, were thought to entice readers away from the truth. (Robert of Greatham too alludes to this idea when he says that, 'It is better to speak the truth simply than to err through refinement; whatever is consonant with the truth is entirely well said before God' (**14**, 93–6). More sternly, the translator of the *Mirour de seinte eglyse* says that it is a great shame and act of irreverence towards Jesus when someone takes to rhyme and abandons the actual prayer that Jesus taught him (**22**, 131–5).) Up to the twelfth century, religious doctrine intended to be imparted to the laity was generally elaborated in prose, whereas, as we have seen, secular and imaginative literature in medieval England and on the continent was composed in French verse, even in the case of translations from Latin prose. Thus it was in monasteries that psalters (such as the Oxford and Cambridge Psalters [Dean 445, 448]), commentaries on the psalters (Dean 451–2], and Bible translations in *romanz* such as *Li Quatre Livre des Reis* (*c.* 1170, Dean 444) and *Le Livre des Juges* (Dean 444.1), along with sermons such as the Sermons on Joshua (**23**) were prepared and preserved. As the unmarked category, French prose was also the language of juridical texts, charters, and letters and, as Serge Lusignan has shown, French, like Latin, was a language of exchange in the Middle Ages. The Anglo-Norman, Picard and Central French *scriptae*, travelling as major supralocal writing systems, were widely read and understood by scribes who had been schooled in the orthographic traits of each but who did not necessarily speak all three dialects. For such scribes, mastery of a *scripta* resembled the acquisition of a scholarly, literate language, such as Latin, more than it did a vernacular.[94]

It is generally assumed that the increasing use of prose starting in the late twelfth century reflects a 'new' concern for truth, but in reality truth claims were independent of any

92 A sign in the left margin next to v. 67 points to quotation of this line in Latin at the bottom of the column.

93 Orengo, ed., 2013, II, 141–3, vv. 3531–98, with minor adjustments.

94 Lusignan 2012b, 133. For a list of prose works in French up to the early thirteenth century, see Woledge and Clive, 1964.

specific type of writing. Verse entries in this volume repeatedly assure readers of their own verifiability, principally by invoking a respected Latin text as their source. Equally, the name of a prestigious religious institution said to house the Latin book, usually St Denis or Canterbury, could lend authenticity to the account. The *Destructioun de Rome* (**18**), for example, does both: the *bone chançon*, a rewriting in verse of a *chanson de geste* from the Charlemagne cycle, is neither *fable* or *mensonje*, according to its author (the word *fable* in this volume's entries is always pejorative): other *jongleurs* know not even a penny's worth of the truth. The inscribed poet-translators of the *Destructioun*, said to be 'King Louis' and Walter of Douai, found their Latin account in the abbey of St Denis, where they also worked to translate it into French (**18**, vv. 3–6, 10–11).[95] Guernes de Pont-Ste-Maxence implies that because he wrote his life of Thomas Becket at Canterbury, there never was a better *romanz*, nor does it contain a single falsehood (**11b**, vv. 6–8). When Bible translation/adaptation began to appear in verse, it too invoked its primary locus as 'holy church', where it was read 'year after year' (*Poème sur l'Ancien Testament*, (**43**, vv. 10–12). Further, eye-witnessing was valued early: Guernes, a Frenchman, travelled to England to interview people who had known Becket, anticipating the use of eye-witness evidence that would be the hallmark of later, prose chronicle-writing, most notably by Jean Froissart. And Wace, in his *Roman de Rou* (see (**3**)), tells us that he went to the forest of Brocéliande to look for the marvels alleged to have occurred there; he failed to find any and upon his return said that he felt like a fool.[96] In a related way, what could be seen with one's own eyes had special value: Rauf de Linham, writing octosyllables in his *Kalender*, eschews stories about knights and great deeds to underscore the need for verifiability instead – and still he writes in verse about 'something whose truth I can show you' (**40**, v. 14). Jean de Mandeville, writing in prose and eschewing any reference to a prior authority, hopes to persuade his readers that his *Merveilles du monde* (**35**) is the report of what he has seen with his own eyes – he says in his epilogue that he can't talk about what he hasn't seen (**35**, 1–3).

Scholars have long discussed whether and when prose became a dominant mode for perceivedly more objective and reliable writing than the nearly ubiquitous verse form. The postulated 'rise' of secular prose in the thirteenth century has provoked important scholarly work over the last few decades. In a study entitled *The Emergence of Prose*, J. Kittay and W. Godzich argued that, 'there are certain kinds of truth to which the signifying practice of performance no longer had the power to lend authority', and 'the crisis of authority that results from the fall of the signifying practice of performance (and written verse) is going to be solved in favor of prose'.[97] Gabrielle Spiegel, in *Romancing the Past*, claimed that 'the rise of prose' was linked to historiographic writing, and to one text and one group of patrons in particular: Nicolas de Senlis's vernacular rendering of the work known as the *Pseudo-Turpin Chronicle*, prepared for Yolande of Flanders and her husband Hugh IV and containing an expressed rejection of verse; according to Spiegel, *Turpin*

95 Herman de Valenciennes suggests that his tale of God and his mother can be trusted because it comes from a written source: *N'est pas controvee, escrit est en estoire* (**15**, 12).

96 Holden, ed., vv. 6395–8; cited in Short 2007b, 322.

97 Godzich and Kittay 1987, xviii, 77.

was the 'originating text of [vernacular] prose historiography'.[98] But these proposals have not gone unchallenged,[99] and entries in the present volume too offer counterexamples: Denis Piramus, in his *Vie seint Edmund le rei* (**27**), tells us that recitation was not the only kind of performance in the late twelfth century, for he notes that aristocratic book owners and their invited guests gathered in groups to hear Marie de France's *lais* read aloud to them.[100] Wace's *Roman de Rou* (**3**), Gaimar's *Estoire des Engleis* (**10**), and the *Destructioun de Rome* (**18**), to mention just those in this volume, are all milestone histories and all are in verse. Moreover, although some scholars draw a distinction between secular history and saints' lives, the two are not easily separable, given that their subjects also lived in and acted upon the secular, historical world and that both literary types share the criterion of exemplarity. In addition to Piramus's life of Edmund, the present volume includes the nun of Barking's life of King Edward the Confessor (**2**), Benedeit's *Brendan* (**9**), Guernes de Pont-Ste-Maxence's *Becket* (**11b**), Walsingham's *Vie de sainte Fey* (**12**), Paris's *Saint Edmund* (**13**), Wace's *Saint Nicolas* (**25a**), *Vie de seint Clement* (**25b**), and Chardri's *Vie de saint Josaphaz* (**30**), and all have in common that they claim to have been composed to serve as inspiring models of right thinking and right acting. When authors denigrated stories lacking a suitable ethic, it was not because they were composed in verse. Emmanuèle Baumgartner has observed that the adjective *verai* or *verur* designates 'une verité d'ordre moral, l'enseignement que ces récits peuvent délivrer aux lecteurs' (a truth of a moral kind, [that is] the teaching that these narratives can deliver to readers).[101] Thus when Piramus criticises *Partonopeus de Blois* for being a lying fable or dream and the *lais* of 'Lady Marie' (de France) for being not at all *verais* (v. 38), his target is not the practice of verse but rather the subject matter. What made Edmund's exemplarity was proven by 'our ancestors', passed down through the generations, and is still 'visible' (**27**, vv. 72–8).[102]

Marie de France herself, in *Guigemar*, also declared the truth of her *lais*, making herself the guarantor of their truth; they are, 'Les contes que jo sais verais, / dunt li Bretun ont fait les lais' (the tales I know to be true, from which the Bretons drew their *lais* (vv. 19–20).[103] For Piramus, then, Marie's poetry, explicitly not traceable to *nostre ancestre* (**27**, v. 72), fails 'to put examples of righteous behavior before its listeners, and bring their souls to salvation'.[104]

[98] Spiegel 1995, 63.

[99] Adrian Armstrong and Sarah Kay 2011, 29 believe that Kittay and Godzich weaken their thesis by misinterpreting the figure of the *acteur*; for their reservations about Spiegel see 33–5. Spiegel 1995, 79 argues that the composition of the *Pseudo-Turpin* can be atrributed to the resistance of Flemish nobility to the expansionist aims of King Philip Augustus. Simon Gaunt has more recently pointed out that 'many of the stylistic features and rhetorical moves concerning veracity that Spiegel regards as indices of the 'historical' nature of these texts, are also ubiquitous in texts she, along with many literary critics, regards as more properly 'fictional' or 'literary' (Gaunt 2015, 42–3).

[100] To the extent that prose is seen as adjunct to the 'rise of literacy', J. Coleman, in her influential 1996 study, argues against any loss of orality to literacy; see esp. ch. 5, 'Aural History', 109–47.

[101] Baumgartner 1998, 3.

[102] Short 2007b.

[103] Warnke and Harf-Lancner, ed., 1990, 26–7.

[104] Short 2007b, 331.

Verse or Prose, Prose or Verse

Just as in the choice of either prose or verse for a complete work, texts in this volume that deploy both verse and prose in the same piece of writing do not offer a consistent or collective reason for using one or the other form. Entries here range from conceivably accidental mixes of verse and prose to the brief use of one or the other by way of introduction or explanation. Only in the loosest sense are they examples of prosimetrum: they do not alternate prose and verse throughout, but some do depend for effect on a contrast between both their different content and their different form. Bibbesworth (**7a**) begins with a brief prose prologue and follows that with an equally brief prefatory 'letter' in prose, while he gives his French lesson in octosyllabic couplets, perhaps because verse can act more efficiently as a mnemonic. Both the *Ornatus mulierum* (**32b**) and the Crabhouse Register (**36**) begin with octosyllables and then move into prose. The Register explains that rhyming is arduous and prose makes meaning clearer, but the shift in time from the address in the present tense to the reader, in rhyme, to the past of Crabhouse's history, in prose, may have left the impression that prose was better suited to the account of past events. The *Ornatus* (**32b**), a treatise on cosmetics, claims in a verse prologue preceding the text's prose that one cannot easily talk about medecine or give remedies in verse, even though the writer must have known of the many other such medical texts in poetry.

The *Estoire del saint Graal* (**41**), part of the thirteenth-century *Lancelot-Grail Cycle*, is a well-known type of the *dérimage*, or de-rhyming (the process by which previously poetic narratives were redone into prose), although the new religious emphasis of the entire cycle was the occasion for considerable rewriting. In *Scalacronica* (**16**), a work influenced by the *Lancelot-Grail Cycle*, Sir Thomas Gray first uses prose to introduce his text, saying that he himself translated it from rhyme to prose; he goes on to write 34 lines in octosyllables into which he weaves an acrostic of his name, and then moves into the prose proper of his work. *Fouke le Fitz Waryn* (**31**) is a prosification of an earlier French romance in verse, which may help to explain why it contains occasional octosyllabic reminders of its earlier form as well as verse prophecy. Both *Fouke le Fitz Waryn* and *Scalacronica* also qualify to some extent as family histories, along with the *Mohun Chronicle* (**42**), and genealogical rolls (**20c** and **20d**), both in prose.

Pragmatic and utilitarian content such as customary practice (*Liber custumarum* (**8a**), or writing that purports to be the reproduction of speech, such as the *Manières de langage* (**7b**) or John Barton's *Donait françois* (**7e**) are given in prose. Lay letter-writing is done in French prose, as shown by Sampson's treatise on letter-writing (**7c**). This may also account for the prose of the *Secré de secrez* (**33**), which presents itself as a letter from Aristotle in response to one from Alexander the Great.

Evidence from entries in this volume therefore suggests that any search for a single, strictly uniform meaning or purpose for either verse or prose, generalised over the range of medieval literary, informational and documentary text types, should perhaps be re-thought as the developing, multifunctional and idiosyncratically inflected phenomenon it was. Each usage of one or the other needs to be seen in relation to its literary environment; this points to its existence as a choice, not a default or a requirement.

Part VI. 2. Middle English Versions of French Entries

Cathy Hume

Extracts from Middle English texts directly translated from French texts excerpted in this volume are presented here. The following conventions apply: thorn and yogh have been transliterated as 'th' and to 'y', 'gh' or 'g' respectively, and on occasion yogh to 'h'; u/v and i/j have been normalised; initial 'ff' has been represented as 'f'; and 'I' and its equivalents are given capitals, as are days of the week and languages. Capitals are supplied when space or guide letters allotted to them have not been fulfilled in the manuscripts. Textual notes have been kept to a minimum: we provide reading texts for comparison with French entries, and supply reference to editions and other reading for further information.

1. *Ipomadon*: Hue de Rotelande, *Ipomedon* (4)

There are three Middle English versions of *Ipomedon*. The tail-rhyme stanza version given here is generally a close translation of the French. However, the prologue takes quite a different tack to the source, and addresses the romance to an audience who will enjoy hearing about love, since it will give them hope that their own love affairs will turn out well: the French *Ipomedon*'s focus on wisdom is discarded altogether. The tail-rhyme *Ipomadon* appears only in one manuscript: Manchester, Chetham's Library, MS 8009, which is a large (*c.* 265 x 190 mm), late-fifteenth-century paper manuscript. There are no signs of its medieval provenance, but it might be thought of as a household anthology for communal reading and reference: it includes two other long romances, *Sir Torrent of Portyngale* and *Bevys of Hampton*, Russell's *Book of Carving and Nurture*, two saints' lives, the *Ballad of a Tyrannical Husband*, and other texts of moral instruction and devotion.

FURTHER READING. Purdie, ed., 2001.

Manchester, Cheetham's Library, MS 8009, f. 191^r

Here begynnyth a good tale of Ipomadon

Off love were *lykynge* of to *lere*, — pleasurable; learn
And joye tille all that wol *here* — listen
That *wote* what love may meane. — know
But whoso have grette haste to love
And may not com to his above,
That poynte dothe loveres *tene*. — pain, vexation

Fayre speche brekyth never bone,
That makythe these lovers ilkone
Ay hope of better *wone* — favourable outcome
And put themselffe to grete travayle,
Wheddyr it helpe or not avayle:
Ofte *sythes* this hathe be sene. — times

2. *The Castle of Love*: Grosseteste, *Chasteau d'amour* (5)

There are several English versions of the *Chasteau d'amour*, but the *Castle of Love*, composed *c.* 1300, is the most complete translation. It appears in three manuscripts, and the best text is found in the Vernon manuscript (Oxford, Bodleian Library, MS English Poetry a.1: see (37) above). This is a remarkably large manuscript, both in size (544 × 393 mm) and contents – its 377 items constitute a religious and didactic library. It is entitled 'Sowlehele', and collects together, largely in English, texts that offer a basic education in the Christian faith and texts of contemplation and spiritual ambition. It seems to be designed for lay readers or perhaps a female community. Copied by two scribes *c.* 1390, the manuscript is beautifully decorated and illustrated by several artists. The part of the manuscript where the *Castle of Love* appears contains only verse texts, such as two verse adaptations of the *Mirror of St Edmund* (see (22) above, no. 5 below) and a version of the story of Susannah. The rubric takes care to attribute the text to its francophone author, but in the body of the poem French is added to Grosseteste's list of learned languages the reader may not know, thereby justifying the need for an English poem.

FURTHER READING. Sajavaara, ed., 1967.

Oxford, Bodleian Library, MS English Poetry a.1, f. 293r, col. c

Her byginnet a tretys
That is yclept 'Castel off Love'
That Bisschop Grosteyght made, ywis,
For lewede mennes byhove.   to meet the needs of the unlettered

That good thenketh good may do,   whoever
And God wol helpe him therto: if
For nas nevere good werk wrought
Withoute beginninge of good thought,
Ne never was wrought non vuel thing   evil
That vuel thought nas the biginnyng.
God, Fader and Sone and Holi Gost,
That alle thing on eorthe sixt and wost,   sees; knows
That o God art, and thrillihod,   Trinity
And threo persones in onhod,   unity
Withouten ende and biginninge,
To whom we oughten over alle thinge
Worschupe him with trewe love,
That kineworthe kyng art us above,   royal
In whom, of whom, thorw whom beoth
Al the goodschipes that we here iseoth;   kindnesses
He leve us thenche and worchen so   may he allow; to think
That he us schylde from ure fo.
Alle we habbeth to help neode
That we ne beth alle of one theode   on account of the fact that; people
Ne iboren in one londe,
Ne one speche understonde,
Ne mowe we alle Latin wite,   know
Ne Ebreu ne Gru that beth iwrite,   written
Ne French, ne this other spechen   languages
That me mihte in world sechen   one may

To herie God, ure derworthe drihte, — praise; honoured lord
Ac[1] uche mon oughte with al his mihte — each
Loftsong syngen to God yerne — song of praise; eagerly
With such speche as he con lerne.
No monnes mouth ne be idut — closed up
Ne his ledene [be] ihud — speech; hidden
To serven his God that him wroughte
And maade al the world of noughte.
On Englisch I chul mi resun schowen
For him that con not iknowen
Nouther French ne Latyn.
On Englisch I chulle tellen him
Wherfore the world was iwrouht,
Theraftur how he was bitauht — it; entrusted
Adam, ure fader, to ben his
With al the merthe of paradys,
To wonen and welden to such ende — dwell; govern
Til that he scholde to hevene wende,
And hou sone he hit forles; — lost
And seththen hou hit forbouht wes — afterwards; redeemed
Thorw the heighe kynges sone
That here on eorthe wolde come
For his sustren[2] that were toboren — sisters
And for a prison that was forloren, — prisoner
And hou he made, as ye schul heeren,
That heo icuste and sauht weren; — kissed; reconciled
And to whuche a castel he alihte
Tho he wolde here for us fihte, — when
That the Marie bodi wes
That he alihte and his in ches. — inn
And tellen we schulen of Ysay
That us tolde trewely:
'A child ther is iboren to us
And a sone igiven us
Whos nome schal inempned beon — called
Wonderful, as me may iseon, — one may see
And God mihtful and rihtwys — righteous
Of the world that comen is, — to come
Lord the Fader
And Prince of Pes.'[3]
Alle theos nomen hou he wes — names
Ye schulen iheren and iwiten, — know
And of Domesday hou hit is iwriten
And of hevene we schulen telle,

[1] MS as

[2] In the *Chasteau*'s allegory, Christ's sisters are the 'Four Daughters of God' (see Ps.84.11), Peace, Mercy, Truth and Righteousness. He resolves their debate over the rightfulness of releasing imprisoned humanity from hell.

[3] MS lineation *sic.*

And sumdel of the pynen of helle.
Thauh hit on Englisch be dim and derk[4]
[f. 293*va*] Ne nabbe no savur bifore clerk, — has no attractiveness for clerks
For lewed men that luitel connen
On Englisch hit is thus bigonnen.
Ac who-se is witer and wys of wit, — wise
And yerne biholdeth this ilke writ,
And con that muchel of luitel unlouken, — much from little; extract
And hony of the harde ston souken
Alle poyntes he fynde may
Of ure beleeve and Godes lay — law
That bifalleth to Godes Godhede — belong
As wel as to his monhede.
Offte ye habbeth iherd ar this — before
Hou the world imaked is:
Forthi ne kep I nought to telle — I do not care
Bote that falleth to my spelle. — except what belongs; story
In sixe dayes and seve niht
God hedde al the world idiht — made
And tho al was derworthliche ido; — excellently
The sevethe day he tok reste and ro. — repose

3. Middle English *Mirror*: Robert of Greatham, *Miroir ou Evangiles des domnees* (14)

The Middle English *Mirror* is a prose adaptation of *Les Evangiles des domnees* extant in eight manuscripts. It was probably composed in the vicinity of London in the late fourteenth century. Oxford, Bodleian Library, Holkham MS Misc. 40 was written around the turn of the fourteenth and fifteenth centuries and is a plain, medium-sized manuscript (285 × 190 mm, ii + 260 ff.) which seems to have been put together more for practical ease of use than aesthetic beauty: there are a number of corrections to the text and marginal notes, for example, indicating where exemplary stories begin. There are additional sermons and other pieces at the end of the manuscript, which may suggest that it was used by a preacher. The prologue drops the French material about Lady Aline, who is obviously not the audience of the English text, and introduces some Latin scriptural quotations – meaning that the resulting text comes closer to conventional expectations of late-medieval sermons. Unlike the French *Evangiles*, where Robert of Greatham's name is initially withheld but later given, his name is never mentioned in this text, and nor is that of the translator.

FURTHER READING. Duncan and Connolly, ed., 2003.

Oxford, Bodleian Library, Holkham MS Misc. 40, f. 1*r*

Many men hyt ben that han wylle[5] to heren rede romaunces and gestes. That is more then ydelschyp [*idleness*]: and that I wol wel that alle men hit wyte, for they ben controved [*devised*] thorw mannes wytte that setten her [*their*] hertes to folyes and trofles, as the lyer doth. He maketh his speche queyntlyche [*elaborately*] that hit may ben delysious to mannes heryng, for that hit scholde be the better listened. For Salamon seyth he had

[4] Vernon highlights this line with an elegant illuminated letter thorn.

[5] MS wylleth.

enquered and sowght alle thyngus undur sunne, and then he fond in al nothyng but vanyte but [*except*] that thyng that falles to Goddes worschyp and to note [*benefit*] of mannes sowle.[6] And therefore Yche have sette my herte for to drawe owt a lytel tretyce of dyvynyte, that men that han wille for to here suche truyfles that they mow turne here hertes therfro and yeve hem to thyngus that is profitabul both to lyf and to soule: God hit me graunt gyf hit be hys swete wylle.

And for men seyn that al thyngus that ben ywryten hyt ben forto leven [*believe*], and they gabben [*lie*], for they that maken thes songes and these gestes they maken hem aftur wenyng [*opinion*]. And men sey on olde Inglysche that wenyng is no wysdom. Loke now to Tristrem, other of Gy of Warrewyk[7] or of ony other and thou ne schalt fynde non that ther nys many lesynges [*lies*] and gret [*great*]. For they ben nought drawen owt of holy wryt, but iche man that maketh hem enformeth hem [*informs himself*] aftur [*according to*] the wylle of his herte and thenketh that hit is al soth: and no forthan [*nevertheless*] al is vanyte forto here alle suche thyngus and undurstand hem that the sowle ne may no gode leren, for all thyng that doth no god to the sowle byfore God is nought [*nothing*] worth, and mychel he lest [*loses*] of his time that so settes his herte from God and trespaseth gretlyche, for God bit [*bids*] that he schal be al attendant unto hym. And alle he wol be tendant to hym, alle that he hath yeven to yche man: he hath yeve us body and life, sen [*seeing*] and heren, wytte and heryng [*the capacity for worship*] and undurstondyng in hert, and alle forto kepe us[8] from harm. We ben als his spensers [*stewards*] for to serve hym of his offices. Gyf we serve hym to wille [*willingly*], an hunduredfold schal be owre mede, and who that doth yvel by his wille, ful gret schal be the vengaunce that schal be taken of hym.

And for that we schul ben on [*one*] in God, Ichil fonde [*try*] to draw yow from vanyte, that we may yelde hym in god what that he asketh of cristenman and womman.

Forthey Iche have mad thys bok that ye may reden on. For nothyng ye schal fynde her but that God is wel payd [*pleased*] wythalle and that the soule mey be comforted wythalle and the body taught. Whan ye han wylle for to reden, draweth forth thys bok. The gode gospelles ye schul fynde herin: furst the tixt and then the undoyng [*interpretation*] schortlyche. Wyte ye wel ther nys nought a word wryten in that hit ne is in holy writte and owt [f. 1v] of the bokes that thys holy men that weren toforn us han mad[e] ydrawen. Latyn ne wol Ich sette non herin, for hit semeth as hit wer a pride for to telle another that he undurstondeth nought, and so hit is ful gret foli to speke Latyn to lewd folk, and he entermeteth [*undertakes*] h[im] of a fol mister [*foolish business*] that telleth to hym Latyne, for eche man schal be undurnome [*reproved*] and aresound [*called to account*] aftur the langage that he hath lered [*learned*].

Now Y byseche yow ententiflyche [*earnestly*] that ye byd [*pray*] to God that he gyve me undurstondyng so to drawe [*extract*] and wryte that he forgyve yow and me owre trespas: for undurstonde gyf ye wylle, Ich afye me [*entrust myself*] gretlyche in yowre biddynggus [*prayers*] that han gode wylle to here thys boke other [*or*] to reden hit.

6 Eccles 1:13–14

7 The translator replaces the French text's allusions to *chansons de geste* with romances (*Gui de Warewic* and *Tristan*) available in both English and French versions in the fourteenth century.

8 MS the

Ne gyveth no kepe [*heed*] to the lettur ne to the speche, but undurstondeth wel the resoun [*argument*]. Gode no geveth no kep to the feyre speche, ac to the spiryt he geveth kep. Bettur is to sey the soth buystuslyche [*roughly*] then for to sen fals thorw queyntyse [*ingenuity*], for alle that acordeth wyth sothnes [*truth*], al is wel seyde byfore God. Haveth no wondur thow Y speke as schortlyche as Y may, for Y hit do for to wythdrawen hem from grevaunces that hit heren other reden. For ofte longe redyng other heryng saddeth a mannes hert and maketh hym ful therof, they [*although*] the thyng lykened hym ful wel [*the matter was pleasing to him*]. Then gyf Y myght lyve til Domesday and wythouten lettyng [*hindrance*] alway wryten, and hadde the mowthe of yren and the tonge of stel and had al the wytte that alle men myght have, yet ne myght Yche nought halvendel [*half*] wryte this that falleth to my mater.[9] Ac better hit is to sey sumwhat of God then hold his mowth stylle, for ofte thorw lytel seggyng turneth the hert into delite.

My name ne wol Y not sey for the enmys that myten heren hit and myght drawe yowre hertes from God that hit wylle heren, for hit is the maner of the enmys to ben grochant [*disagreeable*] and noyus [*troublesome*] and wolen blethliche conjectin [*make inferences about*] the wordes of holy wryt and wolle tellen hit forth on her [*their*] maner and ne letten [*cease*] nought forto blame, other [*or*] the wycked weneth [*intend*] forto amenden it forto [*in order to*] blame the gode and conjecten hem.

[*There follows discussion of the* Mirror*'s title metaphor; of Scripture as an apple-bearing tree, needing shaking down for its sweetness to emerge; Scripture as a dark cloud from which refreshing rain comes; the three estates and the need for men in orders to provide the spiritual bread of the interpreted Gospel for laypeople etc.]*

[f. 3v] The gospelles of the Sonnendays and a partye of the seyntes that ben in heven Y have draw hem ought into Englys, fyrst after the lettur [*literally*] and then the ondoyng [*interpretation*] schortelyche, that men may wel undurstonden hem and for to schew ich man his lyf and how he schuld take ensampul of holy men, how he schal yelde God his soule and rede thys boke forto amenden himselven and forto teche other: wel Y wot [*know*] that alle may Y noght tellen.

[*The writer is able to gather only a few flowers from the endless resources of Scripture and charity, through which it is nonetheless possible for honey to come from the rock and for the ass to speak; a substantial account of the role of priests and the responsibilities of laypeople towards them is also given.*]

[f. 5r] *Dignus est operarius habere mercedem.*[10] Wele he ow to han wordeliche mete [*food*] the [*who*] bryngeth the mete of heven. Wel he ow to han wordlyche thynges that *byhoteth* [promises] the godes of heven. He schal be put out that letteth his prechour have nede. Seynt Poule hit seyth for sothe, that ich man that other lereth [*instructs*] or techeth he schal gyve hym of alle his godes wythouten askyng. *Communicent autem hiis qui catezyzant verbo* etc.[11]

9 Ultimately Virgil (Aeneas in Tartarus, *Aeneid*, book VI, vv. 625–6), influentially quoted by Jerome: see (14) n. to 109–15.

10 The labourer is worthy of his hire, Matt 10.10.

11 Variant of Gal 6.6: And let him that is instructed in the word communicate to him that instructeth him, in all good things.

75 Now Y beseche alle that hereth thys wryt or reden hit that they bysechen to God almyghty that he send me from alle yveles, and so forto make thys werk that hit may plesen hym in ryght byleve and aftur the passing owt of thys lyf be wyth his holy halwen [*saints*] in his company: for thys werk Y do forsothe [*truly*] for me and for al men.

[*A concluding discussion of the limits and the value of the writer's work in a world where (as in (5)) all do not have access to Scripture and learning, and an appeal to readers to lend the book of the* Mirror *and to exchange spiritual as well as bodily food.*]

4. *The Sowdane of Babylone and of Ferumbras his Sone who Conquerede Rome*: *Destructioun de Rome* (18)

The Sowdane is a late-fourteenth or early-fifteenth-century reworking into rhyming quatrains of the *Destructioun de Rome*: it is extant in a single manuscript of *c.* 1450, Princeton University Library, MS Garrett 140. The manuscript is 275 × 203 mm, and its 41 vellum leaves contain only the *Sowdane*. The poem is part of a loose congeries of Charlemagne materials, if not of a small cycle, in Middle English. The *Sowdane*'s narrative of how Ferumbras, son of Laban, seizes relics in Rome and takes them back to his father in Spain shares some incidents with the *Ferumbras* Middle English romances (these are extant in Oxford, Bodleian Library, MS Ashmole 33 (Herrtage, ed., 1879) and the Fillingham manuscript, now BL Add. MS 37,492 (*Firumbras and Otuel and Roland*, ed. O'Sullivan 1935). In reworking the *Destructioun*, the *Sowdane* freely alters conventions and registers: it compresses the *chanson de geste* authentication; abandons the inscription of oral performance in favour of invoking God's power, grace, and capacity for vengeance; and elaborates the narrative with the help of a rich store of Chaucerian reminiscences and allusions.

Further reading. Hausknecht, ed., 1881; Lupack, ed., 1990; http://d.lib.rochester.edu/teams/publication/lupack-three-middle-english-charlemagne-romances; for the manuscript http://libweb5.princeton.edu/visual_materials/mss/ME/Garrett_MS_140_OPT.pdf.

Database of Middle English Romance http://www.middleenglishromance.org.uk/

The Bodleian Ashmole (Middle English) *Fierabras* MS is discussed at http://medievalromance.bodleian.ox.ac.uk/A_rough_draft_and_fair_copy_of_Sir_Firumbras, and see S. H. A. Shepherd 1989.

Princeton, Princeton University Library, MS Garrett 140, f. 2^{r}

God in glorye of myghtes[12] moost,
That al thinge made in sapience
By vertue of woorde and Hooly Goost,
Gyvinge to man grete excellence,
And alle that is in erthe wroght
Subjecte to man and man to the,
That he shulde with herte and thought
To love and serve, and noon but the: — no-one except you
For yyfe man kepte thy comaundemente — if
In al thinge and loved the welle

[12] MS myghteste

And hadde [ne] synnede in his entente,   at his own will
Than shulde he fully thy grace fele.
But for the offences to God idoon   done
Many vengeaunces have befalle,
Whereof I wole you telle of oon-
It were to moch to telle of alle.
While that Rome was in excellence
Of all realmes in dignite,
And howe it felle for his offence,   its
Listinythe a while and ye shall see,
Howe it was wonen and brente   conquered; burnt
Of a Sowdon, that hethen was,
And for synne howe it was shente;   ruined
As King Lowes witnessith that cas,   Louis; matter
As it is wryten in romaunce   the vernacular
And founden in bokes of antiquyté
At Seinte Denyse Abbey in Fraunce,
There as cronycles remembrede be,   where; preserved
Howe Laban, the kinge of hie degre,
And syre and sowdon of hie Babilon,
Conquerede grete parte of Cristianté,
That was born in Askalon.
And in the cité of Agremare   city in Spain
Uppon the rivere of Flagote
At that tyme he sojorned there
Fulle roially, wel I wote,
With kinges twelfe and admyralles fourtene,   emirs
With many a baron and knightis ful boold,
That roialle were and semily to sene;
Here worthynesse al may not be told.
[f. 2v] But bifelle bytwyxte March and Maye
Whan kynde corage begynnneth to pryke,   natural desire
Whan frith and felde wexen gaye,   woodland and field
And every wight desirith his like;   mate
Whan loveres slepen with opyne yghe
As Nightyngalis on grene tre,
And for desire that thai cowde flye
That thay myghte with here love be,   their
This worthy Sowdon in this seson
Shope him to grene woode to goon . . .   prepared

5. *St Edmund's Mirror: Mirour de seinte eglyse* (22)

There are at least eight adaptations of the *Mirror of St Edmund* into English, either directly from French, from a Latin adaptation of the French, or from a combination of the two. This version, from MS Bodley 416, seems to be translated straight from the French, and is one of three extant manuscripts of a full prose version for laity (in Chapter One, the text is addressed to 'everi cristene man and woman that wol be saved'). Watson (2009a, 128–31) assigns this version to the late-medieval lay radicalism suspicious of monastic life and often associated with Wyclifism. At the beginning of the treatise (f. 109^{v}), the rubric attests to the popularity of the text by announcing that it has two alternative titles: 'the Myrour of Seint Edmund and somme clepen it the Myrour of Holi Chirche'. Bodley MS 416 is a collection of religious treatises, written *c.* 1400 in a Gothic textura. The manuscript (295 × 195 mm, 150 leaves) is plain but handsome, with titles and Latin quotations rubricated. Blue capitals flourished in red mark subdivisions in the text. It opens with *A Book to a Mother*, and includes a treatise that explains how women should behave on the Sabbath and holy days (which may suggest, along with the opening address in the *Mirror*, that it was produced for lay female readers).

FURTHER READING. Watson 2009a.

Oxford, Bodleian Library, MS Bodley 416, ff. 116^{v}–118^{v}, 127^{v}–128^{v}, 131^{r}–132^{r}

[f. 116^{v}, line 9] VI *capitulum*: Thre thinges ben in God, might, wisdom, and goodnes. Might is onlich [*uniquely*] to God the fadur, wisdom to God the sone, goodnes to God the Holi Gost. Bi his myght ben alle thinges formed. Bi his wisdom ben alle thinges ordeyned. And bi his goodnes ben thei stabled [*established*] in alle vertues, and everich dai thei ben multeplied. His myght thou myght sen bi here [*their*] gretnes [*extent*] and bi here forminge [*creation*]; his wisdom bi here feirnes [*beauty*] and bi here wel ordeynynge [*good ordering*]; his goodnes bi here vertu and here multepliinge. Here gretnes myghtow se bi here foure parties,[13] [f. 117^{r}] that is to seien bi here highnes and depnes, brodenesse and lengthe. His wisdom myghtow sen yif thou take good hede hou he hath yeven [*given*] everych creature beinge withoute more. For stones ben [*exist*] and wexen [*grow*] not, ne felen not. Trees and herbes ben and wexen, ne felen not. Bestes ben and wexen and felen. Men ben and lyven and felen and undirstonden. Thei have beinge with stones, wexinge with trees, felen with bestis and haven discrecioun and undurstondinge with angelis.

Thus shalt thou thenke of the dignite of mankinde, hou it is anhighed [*raised*] over alle creatures. And therfore seith Seint Austyn, 'I ne wolde not have the stude [*place*] of an angel yif Y myghte have the stude that is ordeyned for man.'

Thenk also hou gret is the dignite of man for wham alle creatures of the world were formed, principalli for thre skiles [*reasons*]: forte helpen us in traveile, as hors, chauvailes [*stallions?*][14] and oxen; and forte clothen us, as shep and net [*cattle*]; and forte susteyne us and fede us, corne of the erthe and fishes [f. 117^{v}] of the see. Allso the venemouse bestis ben mad for thre thinges: for oure chastisinge and amendinge [*correction*] and techinge. We ben ypurged and chastised whanne we ben of hem [*by them*] yhurt, and that is his [God's] grete mercie that he so sparinglich chastiseth us, that we no ben not put in peyne everelastinge. We ben amended whanne we thenke that all the anoy that we have is come to us for oure synnes, for whanne we seen that so litel creatures mowen greve us, thanne shulde we thenke on oure bretelenes [*frailty*] and be lowed [*humbled*].

We ben also taught that we shulde sen in thi creatures the wondur werkes of oure creature [*creator*]. More is worth to us the bisynes of the empte [*ant*] as to ensample than the strengthe of the bere or of the lioun. As Ich have iseid of bestis, undurstonde of erbes [*plants*]. And whanne thou hast undurstonde the maner, al aboute have lokinge to God

13 MS that [struck through]

14 See *AND*, *s.v.* 'cheval', for this sense.

and to his werkes in his creatures, and reise up thin herte unto thi creature [*creator*] and thenk how he hath [f. 118r] do gret myght to make suche thinges of nought and to yeven hem forte ben, and gret kounynge [*skill*] fort[e] ordeyne hem in here [*their*] feirnes, and great goodnes fort[e] multeplie hem everich dai.

A God, merci! hou unkynde [*unnatural*] we ben. We misusen alle thes creatures. He hem shop [*made them*] and we hem fordoth [*cause them to perish*]; and he hem gyeth [*guides*] and multeplieth; and we everich dei hem destrueth [*destroy*]. Therfore sei 'Jhesu merci!' And sei also to him [in][15] thin herte: 'Lord for [*because*] thou art, thei ben; for thu art feir, thei ben feir; for thou ert good, thei ben goode; for thou ert rightful [*righteous*], alle thyne blessud creatures worshupeth the, honoureth the and blessith the holi Trynite of wham ben alle thinges bi his might shapen [*formed*]; bi wham ben alle thinges bi his wisdom governed; in whom ben alle thinges bi his goodnes multeplied. To the, honour and blisse evere withoute ende. Amen.

[VII] Now hastow knowing hou thou shalt se God in his creatures. And this is the furste degre of contemplacioun. That other [*second*] degre is in holi writ. But now myght [f. 118v] thou asken, that ert of litel letterure [*knowledge of letters*], 'hou myghte ever ony lewede [*unlettered*] man come to contemplacioun of holi writ?' Now undurstond me swetlich and Y shal telle the. In cas as it is in holi writ, hit mai be seid: Yif thou ne canst not undurstonde, here bletheli [*hear happily*] the goode that men wollen seie the [*to you*] of al that thu herst of holi scripture in comune sermoun [*in open discussion*] or in prive colacioun [*private discourse*]. Tak yeme [*heed*] anon right yif thou herest ought [*anything*] that mai availen to thin amendement as to haten synne and to love vertue, forte doute [*fear*] peine and to desire joye, forte dispise this world and haste to that other, and what thou shalt don and what thou shalt leten [*leave aside*], and al that enlumineth thyn undurstondinge in knowinge of sothnes [*truth*], and al that enflameth thy affeccioun in strengthe of charite. [. . .]

[f. 127v, line 11] *Thes ben the sevene preiers of the Pater noster.*

Now shaltow wite which ben the sevene preieres of the Pater noster that don awei alle wickednes and purchaseth alle goodnes. And thes sevene preiers ben contained[16] in the swete Pater noster that oure swete lord Jhesu Crist taughte his disciples hou thei shulde preie to God the fadir and thus to hem seide: 'Whanne ye shulle preie, seie ye thus: '*Pater noster qui es in celis*, that is to seien, Fadur oure that art in hevene *Sancti* [f. 128r] *ficetur nomen tuum* halewed be thin name. *Adveniat regnum tuum* com thi kingdom *fiat voluntas tua sicut in celo et in terra* thi wil be don as wel in erthe as in hevene. *Panem nostrum cotidianum da nobis hodie*. Oure eche daies bred yif us todei. *Et dimitte vobis debita nostra sicut et nos dimittimus debitoribus nostris*. Foryef us oure dettis as we foryeven oure dettours. *Et ne nos inducas in temptacionem*. And ne led us not in to temptacioun. *Sed libera nos a malo*. But deliver us from yvel. *Amen*. That is to sey, so mot it be.

This orisoun passeth over alle other in worthynes and in profight, and for [*because*] God himself made hit: and therefore doth he gret shame to God and gret unworshup that taketh to him rimede orisouns [*prayers in verse*] and curiouse, and leteth be [*abandons*]

15 MS al

16 MS continued

the wordis and the preiere that he taughte us that wot al the wil of God the fadur and which orisoun plesith him most, and what thing wrecches hadde nede of to preie. For as Y seide [f. 128^{v}] afore, he allone knoweth bothe his fadur wil and thine nede also and therfore ben an hundred thousand disceyved thorugh multiplicacioun of orisouns. For whanne thei wene to have devocioun, thanne haven thei a foul fleshli desir. For euerich fleshli desir deliteth him [*takes delight*] kendeli [*naturally*] in such turned [*polished*] langagis, and therfore be war, for Y the seie [I tell you] sikerlich [*for certain*] hit is a foul lecherie to deliten in such maner curiositees.

Bi that other side seint Austin and seint Gregori and other seintis bisoughten [*prayed*] aftur here affectiouns [*according to their feelings*]. I ne blame nought here orisouns but I blame hem that [*those who*] leten the preiere that God himself made and taught and taketh hem to orisouns of a symple seint, though thei fynde hit write [*written*]. For oure Lord seith in the gospel, whanne ye preieth ne preie ye not with many wordis, but seieye thus: *Pater noster etc.* [f. 128^{v}, line 16] . . . [*Exposition of the Pater noster's petitions follows*]

[f. 131^{r}, line 8] That is the priere of oure Lord that he techithe in the gospel and ne undurstonde not [that] thou shalt seie with thi mouth al that Ich here have write, but sei onliche [*only*] the naked wordis, and thenk in thin herte of that other that here is write upon everich word bi himself.[17] And take non hede to multeplien many Pater nostres for better is to seien on [*one*] alone with a devocioun and undurstondinge than a thousand withoute undurstondinge. For seint Poul seith thus openlich, 'Ich hadde levere to seien five wordis in myn herte devoutliche than five thousand with my mouth withouten undurstondinge.' [f. 131^{v}] And therfore thou shalt do thin offis in thin herte devoutlich and so seith the prophet, 'Singeth wislich'. To synge wislich is that [*what*] men seien with mouth, seie also with herte: for <yif>[18] thi bodi be in the quer [*(church) choir*] and thi lippes in the sauter and thin herte in the stret or in the market, wrecchedlich artow thanne departed [*distracted*]. [. . .]

[f. 132^{r}, line 8] Here endeth the secunde degre of contemplacioun that is in scripture and therfore yif thou good yeme [*heed*] take, thou myght kepe [*hold onto*] everich sermoun, and bi that other half [*on the other hand*] thou hast mater to speken to clerkes, ben thei never so goode, and to the lewede [*unlettered*], ben thei never so boistouse [*ignorant*]. Whanne thou spekest to [*someone*] wiser than thou be, touche some of thes materis and aske of him, and whanne th[o]u spekest to semple folk, teche hem bletheli and swetli, for thou hast ynow whereof to speken and so thou shalt governe thi lif and other mennes amendi [followed by rubric *Contemplacioun in God self*].

[17] *thenk in thin herte of that other that here is write upon everich word bi himself*: i.e. use the other words written here on the Pater noster's petitions to meditate on each word individually.

[18] *yif* added in margin with *signe de renvoi* after '*for*'.

6. Robert Manning, *Handlyng Synne*; *The Manuel of Zynnes*: *Manuel des pechiez* (24b)

6a *Handlyng Synne*

This verse adaptation of the *Manuel des pechiez* by Robert Manning was begun in 1303 and its prologue probably composed between 1317 and 1330. Usually assumed to be a Gilbertine on the strength of his greetings to members of the order (see lines 57–76 below), Manning may have been an Augustinian (probably at the priory of Warter) at the time of writing *Handlyng Synne*. At lines 77–86, Manning makes a point of explaining how he has adapted his book and its title from its French source, and the French source (credited to Grosseteste) is obviously also the main concern of the rubricator in our manuscript, Oxford, MS Bodley 415. Manning nevertheless produces quite a free adaptation and amplification, departing from his source, for example, to declare that it does not matter where you pick up the book – where the French had emphasised its paragraph structure and the need not to read hastily. Manning also gives us an argument for the need to write a text in English to distract people from listening to idle chatter or 'trotovale', as well as implicitly criticising other 'clerkys' for not having done so previously.

There are nine extant manuscripts of *Handlyng Synne*, but Bodley MS 415, from which this text is taken, is one of only two that preserve the full text of the prologue. It is a nicely produced, though modest, medium-sized manuscript (290 × 190 mm), of *c.* 1400, with decorated initials – the opening one in purple and gold – which one might imagine to have been made for a friars' library.

FURTHER READING. Sullens, ed., 1983; Taubman 2009.

Oxford, Bodleian Library, MS Bodley 415, f. 1r

Here begynneth the boke that men clepen yn frenshe 'Manuele Pecche', the wheche boke made yn frenshe Roberd Grosteste, Bysshop of Lyncolne.

Fadyr and Sone and Holy Gost
That art o God of myghtys most,
At thy worshepe shul we begynne
To shame the fende and shewe oure synne.
Synne to shewe, us to frame, — profit
God to wrshepe, the fende to shame.
Shameful synne ys gode to lete:
Al that men do, bothe smale and grete,
The grete wythoutyn pryvyte — major [sins]; secrecy
That beyn commune to me and the –
Of hem wyle Y telle yow nede — as necessary
As Y have herd and red yn dede.[19]
Of thyse than ys my sawe:
The comaundementys of the olde lawe.
Thyse ten were fyrst us gevyn,
And fyrst we welyn of hem be schrevyn — confessed
Yn what poyntys that we falle
Yn opon synne ayen hem alle;
And sythyn of the sevene synnys — afterwards

[19] As in the *Manuel*, Manning distinguishes publically named and categorised sins and the secret sins (*pryvytees*) confessors are cautious about naming in case they inadvertently inform penitents about vices not already known to them.

Yn what thyng the fende us wynnys, — conquers
And sythyn of synne of sacrilage
That ys to holy cherche outrage,
And of the sacramentys sevene
That techyn us to the blysse of hevene.
Sythyn of the twelve poyntys of shryfte — confession
And of the twelve gracys of here gyfte:
Al that touchyth dedly synne
Yn any spyce that we falle ynne — variety
That ys oponly seen or wrought.
Of pryvytees speke Y nought:
The pryvytees wyle Y nought name,
For noun tharfore shuld me blame.
Lever ys me that they be hydde — I would rather
Than for me oponly were kydde. — made known
Notheles they mote be shrevyn — must
Yyf gyfte of grace shal be gevyn.
Of thys clerkys wyle Y nought seye –
To greve hem Y have grete eye – — fear
For they wote that ys to wetyn — what is to be known
And se hyt weyl before hem wretyn. — (they) see
[col b] That may be weyl on Englyssh told,
To telle yow that Y may be bold.
For lewed men Y undyrtoke — unlettered
On Englyssh tonge to make thys boke,
For many beyn of swyche manere
That talys and rymys wyle blethly here;
In gamys, yn festys, and at the ale
Love men to lestene trotovale, — idle tale-telling
That may falle ofte to velanye,
To dedly synne or outher folye.
For swyche men have Y made thys ryme
That they may weyl dyspende here tyme,
And theryn sumwhat for to here,
To leve al swyche foul manere,
And for to kun knowe therynne — to be able
That they wene no synne be ynne. — think
To alle Crystyn men undyr sunne
And to gode men of Brunne,[20]
And specyaly alle be name
The felaushepe of Sympryngham e,
Roberd of Brunne gretyth yow
Yn alle godenes that may to prow. — be profitable
Of Brymwake yn Kestevene,[21]

[20] *Brunne*: on the question of whether this is Nunburnholme in Yorkshire or Bourne in Lincolnshire, and the implications for Mannyng's career and affiliation when composing *Handlyng Synne*, see Taubman 2009.

[21] *Brymwake* (also Brunnewake, Bringwake in other manuscripts): Bourne Abbey, under the patronage of the Wake family, in Kesteven, a region of south-west Lincolnshire (Taubman 2009, 198).

Syxe myle besyde Symprynham evene,
Y duellyd yn the pryore
Ffyftene yer yn compayne,
Yn the tyme of gode Dan Jone
Of Cameltoun[22] that now ys gone.
Yn hys tyme was Y ther ten yers
And knew and herde of hys maners.
Sethyn wyth Dan Jone of Clyntone
Fyve wyntyr wyth hym gan Y wone.   live
Dan Felyp[23] was mayster that tyme
That Y beganne thys Englyssh ryme.
The yers of grace fyl than to be
A thousynd and thre hundryd and thre.
Yn that tyme tournede Y thys   translated
On Englyssh tonge out of Frankys,
Of a boke as Y fonde ynne:
Men clepyn the boke 'Handlyng Synne'.
[f. 1^v] Yn Frenshe ther a clerk hyt sees
He clepyth hyt 'Manuel de pecchees'.
'Manuel' ys handlyng wyth honde;
'Pecchees' ys synne to undyrstonde.
These twey wrdys that beyn otwynne,   apart
Do hem togedyr ys 'Handlyng Synne'!
And weyl ys clepyd for thys skyle,   named; reason
And as Y wote, yow shewe Y wyle.
We handyl synne every day
Yn wrde and dede, al that we may.
Lytyl or mochyl synne we do:
The fende and oure flesshe tysyn us tharto.   entice
For thys skyle hyt may be seyde,
Handlyng synne for oure mysbreyde.   wrongdoing
For every day and every oure
We synne: that shal we bye ful soure.   buy; sorely
Anouthyr handlyng ther shulde be,
Wyth shryfte of mouthe to clense the.
Handyl thy synne yn thy thoght,
Lytyl and mochyl what thou hast wroght,
Handyl thy synne to have drede   fear
Nothyng but peyne ys tharfore mede.   reward
Handyl thy synnys and weyl hem gesse   estimate
How they fordoun al thy godenesse.   destroy
Handyl thy synnys alle weyl and evene
Elles forbarre they the blysse of hevene.   obstruct
Handyl hem at onys everychone,

[22] *Cameltoun*, line 68, *Clyntone*, line 71: probably John de Camelton, Prior of Sempringham in 1298 and his successor John Clattone, prior 1298–1303 (see further Sullens, xxxix n. 2).

[23] *Dan Felyp*, line 73: Philip de Burton (or Barton), Prior of Sempringham and Master of the Order from 1298, succeeded by John de Glinton, elected 1332 (*Victoria County History* Lincs, II at http://www.british-history.ac.uk/vch/lincs/vol2/pp179–187).

Noght one be hymself alone. — itself
Handyl so to ryse from alle
That none make the eft to falle, — again
Wyth shryfte of mouthe and wyl of herte
And a party wyth penaunce smerte. — some
Thys ys a skyle that hyt may be tolde,
Handlyng synne many afolde.
Handlyng yn speche ys as weyl
As handlyng yn dede everydeyl.
On thys manere handyl thy dedys
And lestene and lerne wan any hem redys: — interprets them
Thou darst nevere recche whar thou begynne
For everywhare ys begynnyng of synne.
[col b] Whedyroutys thou wylt opene the boke — wherever
Thou shalt fynde begynnyng on to loke:
Overal ys begynnyng, overal ys ende,
Hou that thou wylt turne hyt or wende. — however; proceed
Many thynges theryn mayst thou here,
Wyth ofte redyng mayst thou lere. — frequent; learn
Thou mayst nought wyth onys redyng
Knowe the sothe of everythyng. — truth
Handyl hyt behovyth the ofte sythys
To many maner synnys hyt wrythys. — writes of
Talys shalt thou fynde therynne, — [exemplary] stories
And chauncys that have happyd for synne, — misfortunes
Merveylys some as Y fond wretyn,
And outhyr that have be seye and wetyn. — seen and known
None be therynne, more ne lesse,
But that Y fond wrete or hadde wytnesse. — except
Tharfore may hyt, and gode skyle why, — for good reason
'Handlyng Synne' be clepyd oponly, — called
For hyt touchyth no pryvyte
But opon synne that callyd may be. — may be named
Begynne we than to telle yn haste,
Wyth Fadyr and Sone and Hely Gaste
And yn wrshepe of Our Lady
And alle the halewys that beyn hem by, — saints
They gyve us grace ryth so to deme, — judge
Us to proffyte and God to queme. — please

6b *The Manuel of Zynnes*

This is a later English adaptation of the *Manuel des pechiez*, written in prose rather than verse, but otherwise far more faithful to the French. The author was probably unaware of the existence of *Handlyng Synne*. Although in his edition Bitterling entitles the text 'Of Shrifte and Penance', the author makes it clear in this passage that he considers 'The Manuel of Zynnes' to be his title: a straight translation of the French. The text appears only in Cambridge, St John's College, MS G.30, written in the second quarter of the fifteenth century, and it is the only text in this relatively small (263 × 150 mm) vellum manuscript. Such a close translation suggests that the author was concerned to reproduce the doctrinally important content of the original text for an audience who would not have been able to read French. At the text's conclusion he excuses his work, claiming that 'of the Vrenche nother of the ryme no man schulde blame me' since he was born 'in Ingelond . . . in a lytul town that is nat nemned nother burh ne cité', and he asks for prayers for 'William of Wytinde' (f. 82r).

FURTHER READING. Bitterling, ed., 1997.

Cambridge, St John's College, MS G.30, f. 1r

The vertu of the Holi Gost be helpynge to us in thys wrytinge to yow seche thynges to schewe wherof a man schulde schryue hym, and also in what manere that is gode to knowe: for that is the vertu of the sacrement to telle the synne and how. Alle synnes we mow nat telle, but as muche as we mowe thenke. And owre synnes wel to amende and so may he that wol byholde thys wrytynge.

First we wol sey of the ryghthful fey that is fundement of oure lawe, in the wheche ther be twelve pointes proved that articles ben callud. Zytthe [*then*] we schul putte the ten comandementes that alle men owen to kepe, zetthe the zefne dedly synnes of the weche ther sprynge many efles. After we schul putte the zefne sacrementes by the wheche confession is al governed and that in confession the[i][24] be nothyng helud [*concealed*]. Thanne he may se that hath trespassud and amende hys synnes. The doweries of holy chirche we schul nat foryete. Therefore of sacrilege we schul sey as of maistres we have lerned. We mowe notthynge ful [*fully*] touche, but only zynnes telle: he schulde make a gret boke that al thynge schulde telle. And therfore I leve hem to conferme hem by autorite the synnes that I schal here putte. Of seintes I have drawe hem owt:[25] therfore hyt schal be al autorite althow the se[intes] be nat nemned. Nothyng I schal nat putte of myn owne but as I have lerned. No falsehode ye schul nat fynde, therfore more wilfully [*eagerly*] red hyt.

The 'Manuel' hyt is called for in the honde hyt schulde be bore. Hyt maketh a mannes soule evene [*regular*]: to every man [f. 1v] hyt schulde be the more dere. The toname [*surname*] is of zynnes, and therfore we schul calle hyt 'The Manuel of Zynnes'. By parafes [*paraphs*] hyt is distincted [*divided*], the wheche yow schewe diverse zynnes: therfore no man rede hyt over hastly, but twyes atte leste, gyf he wol amende hys soule there that [*where*] he may fynde diverse zynnes as hyt is parafed. And that hyt be the more delicious [*delightful*], some talus we schul telle yow as seintes have tolde us the more to hate zynne. Of privites [*secret (sins)*] ye schul finde no thynge, ffor hyt mygthe do more evel than gode; natheles noman leve [*omit*] that he scryve hym [*confess*] of privites. Hyt schulde be folie a man to hele [*conceal*] for schame that that schal be schewed tofore alle folke at the grete day of dome. And [*if*] any man of the herynge be amendud,[26] God therof be thonked – in good tyme was he evere bore [*born*] that of zynne were quitte [*freed*]. I nel nat [*will not*] telle my name, ffor of God only I aske mede [*reward*]. Wel I wote that every man schal resceve of God aftur that he schal deserve. Therfore putte we the fey aftur that [*what*] we have byhote [*we have promised [above]*].

[24] Letters in square brackets are reconstructed with assistance from Bitterling: the manuscript is quite badly rubbed.

[25] 'I have extracted them from [the writings of] holy men'

[26] 'If anyone is improved by hearing it'

7. ***Kyng Alisaunder: Roman de toute chevalerie*** (28)

Kyng Alisaunder, a free adaptation of the *Roman de toute chevalerie*, was composed in the early fourteenth century, and is one of several English Alexander stories circulating in the Middle Ages. The freedom of the adaptation can be seen in this prologue. The English author no longer frames his audience as chivalrous: instead, he distinguishes them from drunks who enjoy 'ribaudrye', and gives his story a moral and learned context, as well as suggesting (as in the French) that it will be pleasurable. This extract is taken from MS Bodleian Laud Misc. 622, a large (376 × 262 mm) plain volume, written in the late fourteenth century in double columns of Anglicana script; *Kyng Alisaunder* takes up 8010 lines. The manuscript's contents interestingly accord with the tone struck in this prologue by mixing the exotic and the moral: *The Destruction of Jerusalem* (also known as *Titus and Vespasian*: titled *The Bataile of Jerusalem* on f. 71*v*) and a prose account of wonders in the Holy Land sit alongside content from the *South English Legendary* and Adam Davy's *Five Dreams about King Edward II*.

FURTHER READING. Smithers, ed., 1952 and 1957.

Oxford, Bodleian Library, MS Laud Misc. 622, f. 27*v* (new foliation), col a.

Divers is this myddellerde	Middle Earth
To lewed men and to lerede:	unlettered; educated
Bysynesse, care and sorough	
Is myd man uche morowghe	every day
Somme for sekenesse, for smert;	
Somme for defaut oither povert;	lack
Somme for the lyves drede	fear of mortality
That glyt away so floure in mede.	glides; meadow
Ne is lyves man non so sleighe[27]	
That [h]e ne tholeth ofte ennoyghe	suffer; tribulation
In many cas, on many manere,	
Whiles he lyveth in werlde[28] here.	
Ac is ther non, fole ne wys,	
Kyng ne duk ne knighth of prys	
That ne desireth sum solas	
Forto here of selcouthe cas.	marvellous
For Caton seith, the gode techer,	
'Othre mannes liif is oure shawer.'	mirror
Natheles, wel fele and fulle	a great many
Beeth yfounde in herte, and shulle,	
That hadden lever a ribaudye	rather; a rude story
Than here of God oither Seint Marie,	
Oither to drynk a copful ale	
Than to heren any gode tale.	
Swiche Ich wolde weren out bishett	shut

27 'There is no living man so ingenious'

28 'werlde', here, the 'ny' of 'knyth' in line 14, 'heren' in line 24 and the end of 'bishett' in line 25 are now very faint and hard to read. However, these readings, which Smithers records in his EETS edition, do seem to accord with the present appearance of the manuscript in normal light.

For certeynlich it were nett,	desirable
For hii ne habbeth wille, Ich woot wel,	know
Bot in the gut and in the barel.	except
Now: pes, listneth and leteth cheste.	leave off strife
Yee shullen heren noble geste	
[col b] Of Alisaundre the ric[he k]yng[29]	
That dude by hys mais[t]res teching	followed
And overcom, so I fynde,	
Darrye of Perce and P[o]re of Ynde,	Darius; Porrus
And many othere wighth and hende	powerful; distinguished
Into the Est Werldes ende,	
And the wondres of worme and beest:	serpent
Deliciouse it is to ylest.	delightful; listen to
Yif yee willeth sitten stylle	
Fulfylle ich wil al youre wille.	

8. James Yonge's *The Governaunce of Princes or Pryvete of Pryveteis*: *Secré de secrez* (33)

Oxford, Bodleian Library, MS Rawlinson B 490 ff. 28^{v}–72^{r} of *c.* 1470 is probably the earliest of the three extant texts of James Yonge's translation of Jofroi de Waterford's and Servais Copale's work. Yonge (*fl.* 1405–34), a notary public originally from Waterford, spent some time working for James Butler, earl of Ormond and Henry V's deputy lieutenant in Ireland, for whom he began the translation in 1422. It is a free rendering into which Yonge inserted passages about Ireland and the rights of Irish kings (Steele 1898, 1975, 121–248). Jofroi de Waterford's Irish connection and Yonge's translation link two expropriations of Ireland across the centuries: the Anglo-Normans and the English 'new men' and eventual Tudor colonisation of Ireland.

Further reading. *ODNB* James Yonge; Steele, ed., 1898; O'Byrne 2012, 67–70; H. E. Fox 2014.

Oxford, Bodleian Library, MS Rawlinson B 490, ff. 28^{v}–29^{r}

[f. 28^{v}, line 9] In oone techynge acordyth and in oone verite shewyth the moste wyse clerkes and maysteris of renoune that have beyn afor us in al tymys tretynge of prowes and worthynesse of emperours, kynges, and al othyr governors of chyvalry, that chyvalry is not only kepete, savyd, and mayntenyd by dedys of armes, but by wysdome and helpe of lawes, and of witte and wysdome of undyrstondynge. For streynth and powere without witte [*capacity for thought*] and connynge [*knowledge*] is but outrage and wodnys, and wysdome and connynge wythout streynth and powere surly hym gidyth [*directs itself*] not.[30] But whan with streynth and powere hym compaynyth witte and connynge and witte dressith [*adjusts*] powere, in goodnys may the Prynce play, and with good men surly walke.[31] This apperyth by many olde stories, for the connynge and grete witte of Arystotle lytill had avaylid to kynge Alexandyr, without the strenynth of the brut [*brutishness*] of his powere. And the olde Pryncis of Rome conquerid more al the worlde by connynge and study of

[29] A hole in the page here and in the line below largely obscures the reconstructed letters.

[30] Sentence underlined in MS.

[31] *In godnyss . . . walke* underlined in MS.

clergeable [*learned*] bokys than by assautes of battaill othyr streynth of pepill. And therfor Tully the grette clerke sayth, 'than were wel governette emperies and kyngdomes whan kynges wer phylosofors, and philosofy regnyd'. The whyche thynge, nobil and gracious lorde aforsayde, haith parcewid the sotilte of youre witte and the clernys [*clarity*] of youre engyn [*intelligence*],[32] and[33] therefore ichargid some good boke of governaunce of prynces out of Latyn othyr Frenche into youre modyr Englyshe tonge to translate. And for als moche as euer Y hame bounde for youre gracious kyndly gentilnesse onto youre comaundement to obey, now Y here translate to youre soverayne nobilnes the boke of Arystotle, prynce of phylosofors, of the governaunce of prynces, the whyche boke is called in Latyn *Secreta secretorum*: that is to say, *The Pryvete of Pryveteis*. The wych boke he makyd to his dysciple Alexandre the grete emperoure, conqueroure of al the worlde. This Arystotle was Alexandyres derlynge and wel belowid clerke, and therfor he made hym his maystyr and chyfe consailloure of his royalme. For Arystotle was a man of grete consaille, of profounde lettrure [*learning*] and percewynge [*perceptive*] undyrstondynge, and wel kowth [*knew*] the lawes; he was of hey nourtoure [*well brought up*], wel prowed [*experienced*] and ilerynyd of al sciencis, wyse, sotille, humbile, ever lowynge [*praising*] ryght and verité. And therfor many men helde hym a prophete. And as Y fynde writte [f. 29r], hit is founde in olde bokis of Grecanys [*Greeks*] that God sende His angill to hym, saynge, 'radyr I sholde cale the an angill than a man'.

Arystotle sende many pystelis that men callyth nowe lettres to Alexandre, of the whyche this presente boke is oone, of the governaunce of kynges and prynces. The cause that Arystotle makyd this pystill was this: whan Alexandyr hadd conqueride Perse, forthy that some of the pepyl ther weryn agaynys hym and dysobeiaunt, he sende to Arystotle this lettyr in this forme:

'To a nobyl Maystyr of ryght governoure and of verité,[34] Arystotle, sendyth gretynge his disciple Alexandre. To thy discrescioun I do to undyrstonde, that Y have founde in the londe of Perse a peple ful of reyson and of hey undyrstondynge and of parcewynge engyn, the whych afor al otheres coveytyth[35] dygnyte of lordshup, and therfor we purposyth to destru ham al. What the thynkyth up this matyr do us to witte [*let us know*] by thy lettres.'

With whych matyer, Arystotle answerid in this maner.

'Yf ye may chaunge the eyre and the wateris of that londe, and over that the ordyaunce of the Citteis, fulfill ye youre Purpos. And yf no, than governe ye hame wyth good woillaunce [*will*] and bonerté [*courtesy*], for yf ye so do, ye may have hoppe wyth Goddys helpe that al thay shal be to yow obeyaunt, and ye shall mow [*will be able*] tham governe in good pees.'

Whan Alexandyr hadd rescewid this lettyr, he did Arystotles consaille, wherefor thay of Perse were morre obieiaunt to Alexandre than any othyr pepill.

32 *Witte . . . and . . . engyn* are the subject of the sentence.

33 MS ~~subtilte~~

34 *of ryght . . . verité*: arbiter of rightfulness and truth

35 MS conveyteth

9. *The Book of Sir John Mandeville*: *Le Livre des merveilles du monde* (35)

This 'Cotton' version of *Mandeville's Travels* presents Mandeville as his own translator from French to English: 'I have put this boke out of Latyn into Frensch and translated it ayen out of Frensch into Englyssch that every man of my nacioun may vnderstonde it' (f. 3v). The writer seems to have taken the widely circulating English 'Defective' version and revised it to bring it closer to the French text. However, in this passage the reviser retains an innovation found in the English versions of the text: a paragraph that tells how the pope authorised the book, which interestingly suggests the greater importance of ensuring orthodoxy for a work written in English prose and perhaps indicates something about the sceptical reception of the original work. BL Cotton Titus C.XVI is an early-fifteenth-century manuscript of a small and portable size (218 × 142 mm), containing only *Mandeville's Travels* and written in a highly abbreviated style. It has been well annotated in the margins by a later hand.

FURTHER READING. Higgins 1997, 1–41; Higgins 2011, Appendix A.3; Bale, trans., 2012.

London, British Library, Cotton MS Titus C.XVI, f. 132r–v.

[f. 132] Ther ben manye other dyverse contrees and manye other merveyles beyonde that I have not seen, wherfore of hem I cannot speke propurly to tell you the manere of hem. [f. 132v] And also in the contrees wher I have ben ben manye mo dyversitees of many wondirfull thinges thanne I make mencoun of, for it were to longe thing to devyse [*describe*] you the manere. And therfore that that I have devysed you of certeyn contrees that I have spoken of before, I beseche youre worthi and excellent noblesse that it[36] suffise to you at this tyme. For yif that I devysed you all that is beyonde the see, another man peraunter [*perhaps*] that wolde peynen him and travaylle his body for to go into tho marches [*regions*] for to encerche [*investigate*] tho contrees myghte ben blamed be my wordes in rehercynge manye straunge thinges, for he myghte not seye nothing of newe in the whiche the hereres myghten haven outher [*either*] solace or desport [*relaxation*] or lust [*pleasure*] or lykyng in the herynge. For men seyn allweys that newe thinges and newe tydynges ben plesant to here, wherfore I wole holde me stille withouten ony more rehercyng of dyversiteez or of mervaylles, that whoso wil gon into tho contrees, he schall fynde ynowe to speke of that I have not touched of in no wyse.

And yee schull undirstonde yif it lyke [*please*] you that at myn homcomynge I cam to Rome[37] and schewed my lif to oure holy fadir the Pope and was assoylled [*absolved*] of all that lay in my conscience of many a dyverse grevous poynt, as men mosten nedes that ben in company dwellyng among so many a dyverse folk of dyverse secte and of beleeve, as I have ben. And amonges all I schewed hym this tretys that I had made after [*according to*] informacoun of men that knewen of thinges that I hadde seen myself, as fer as God wolde yeve me grace, and besoughte his holy fadirhode that my boke myghte ben examyned and corrected be avys of his wyse and discreet conseill. And oure holy fader of his special grace remytted my boke to ben examyned and proved be the avys of his seyd conseill, be the whiche my boke was preeved for trewe, in so moche that thei schewed

36 MS is

37 Words underlined here are underlined in red in the manuscript.

me a boke that my boke was examynde by that comprehended full moche more be an hundred part, be the whiche the Mappa Mundi was made after. And so my boke, all be it that many men ne list not to yeve credence to nothing but to that that thei seen with hyre eye, ne be the auctour ne the persone never so trewe, is affermed and proved be oure holy fader in maner and forme as I have seyd.

And I John Maundevyll knyght aboveseyd, allthough I be unworthi, that departed from oure contrees and passed the see the yeer of grace a .mille. ccc. and .xxij. [*1322*], that have passed many londes and manye yles and contrees, and cerched [*explored*] manye full straunge places, and have ben in many a full gode honourable companye and at many a faire dede of armes, all be it that I dide none myself for myne unable insuffisance [*inadequacy*]. And now I am comen hom mawgree myself [*against my will*] to reste, for gowtes artetykes [*arthritic gout*] that me distreynen [*afflict*], that diffynen [*bring to a conclusion*] the ende of my labour ayenst my will, God knoweth. And thus takynge solace in my wrecched reste, recordynge the tyme passed, I have fulfilled theise thinges and putte hem wryten in this boke, as it wolde come into my mynde, the yeer of grace a .mille. ccc. and .lvj. [*1356*] in the .xxxiiij. yeer that I departed from oure contrees, wherfore I preye to all the rederes and hereres of this boke, yif it plese hem, that thei wolde prayen to God for me, and I schall praye for hem. And all tho that seyn for me a Pater noster with an Ave Maria that God foryeve me my synnes, I make hem parteneres [*partakers*] and graunte hem part of all[38] gode pilgrymages and of all the gode dedes that I have don, yif ony ben to his [*God's*] plesance – and noght only of tho, but of all that evere I schall do unto my lyfes ende. And I beseche almyghty God, fro whom all godeness and grace cometh fro, that he vouchesaf of his excellent mercy and habundant grace to fullfylle hire soules with inspiracoun of the Holy Gost in makynge defence of all hire gostly [*spiritual*] enemyes here in erthe, to hire salvacoun bothe of body and soule, to worschipe and thankynge of him that is three and on withoute[n be]gynnynge and withouten endyng, that is withouten qualitee good, withouten quantytee gret, that in alle places is present, and all thinges conteynynge, the whiche that no goodness may amende, ne non evell empeyre [*diminish*], that in parfyte Trynytee lyveth and regneth, God be alle worldes and be all tymes. Amen. Amen. Amen.

10. *The Debate betwene the Heraldes of Englande and Fraunce, compiled by Johnn Coke . . . vulgerly called clarke of the statutes of the Staple of Westmynster / Débat des hérauts d'armes de France et d'Angleterre* (44)

In his prologue of 1549 (printed 1550), Coke presents himself as having been in Brussels in employment as secretary to 'the ryght worshipfull and famous company of marchantes adventurers of the nacion of Englande'. In a printer's shop, he comes across the *Débat* as a pamphlet in French, and soon perceives it as compiled out of 'harty malyce' and pro-French bias, which he answers with a 'small treatyse', drawing, he claims, on 'Etropius, Colman, Bede, Guilda, Orose [Orosius], Lucan, *Cronica cronicarum*, the *Cronycles of Lytel Britayne*, the cronycles of Brabant, *La Mere des histories*, Frosart, Engram de Monstrelet, Gagwyne [Robert Gaguin], Hardyng, Fabyan, and other auctors'.

38 There is an indecipherable smudge at this point, which perhaps obscures the word 'the'.

Coke presents his treatise as a labour of virtue, eschewing idlenes and giving pleasure to those who delight in the exemplary work of historiography and its repertoire of noble men's virtous deeds and chivalric acts. His riposte uses the French text as a starting point only: Coke freely supplements the English case by adding passages of extended invective against the French herald's arguments.

FURTHER READING. Coke's response is printed in full in Pannier and Meyer, ed., 1877, 53–122 (their paragraphing is followed below for ease of reference). A fascinating enterprise with something to say of early printing as well as English polemics, Coke's work has so far been the object of little research since the 1877 edition.

The heralde of Englande declareth when England was fyrst christened, and then answereth to valyaunce of tyme past.

27. Syr Heralde, fyrste where you say how Fraunce was christened .c.vij. yeres before Englande, I say, lady Prudence, howe the Frenche heralde offendeth greatlye, in that he declareth not the truth accordyng to his offyce. For Arvyragus, kyng of England, was christened and all his realme by Josephe of Baromathy [*Arimathea*], the thre score and syxe yere after the deth of Christ, beyng long before any Hungarien, nowe Frenchemen, reygned in Fraunce. Clowes [*Clovis*] was the fyrst kyng of Fraunce that was baptyzed, which was the yere of Our Lord .cccc.lxxxviij., as yourselfe, Syr Heralde, have declared before, beyng, yf you accompt wel, .cccc.xij. yere after England was christened, and as appereth by the Brytayne cronycles, Saynt Bede, Guylda [*Gildas*], *Cronica cronicarum*, and other. And afterwarde the people of Englande, not beynge fully enstructed in the christen fayth in the tyme of Lucius kynge of Englande, they were by Fagan and Duven, .ij.holy men, baptyzed the yeare of Christ .c.lxxxx. Eleutherius, beynge byshop of Rome, as reherseth Petrus Picta[v]iensis [*Peter of Poitiers*] and other; beyng also before Fraunce was baptyzed .cc.lxxxxviij. yeres.

28. And albeit that the Romaynes, Affricanes, Danes, Saxons, beyng then paynymes, with the comforte and helpe of the Galles, then lykewyse paynymes, dyd many tymes assay clerely to extynguyshe out of Englande the catholyque fayth, yet, God be thanked, they had never the powre so to do, for Wales, Cornwall and many other shyres of Englande (albeit they were longe persecuted by those nacions barberous) continued in theyr fayth, even from the begynnyng unto this present day.

29. And, lady Prudence, as for theyr thre flower de lyces which the Frenche heralde sayth was sent to Clowes from heaven, I answere, it was sent hym from Sathan, for the sayd Clowes, his ancetours and people out of Sacambria [*Sicambria*], a shyre in Hungary, as shalbe more playnly declared herafter, gave in theyr armes the vyle blacke poysoned spralyng [*sprawling*?][39] todes [*toads*], who, beynge therof most ashamed, and for pryde to avaunce his glory, devysed and caused a payntour to make in a baner thre flower de lyces, common flowres in every felde, which armes the Frenche kynges have ever sythen borne, and yet bere unto this present tyme.

30. Lykewyse for theyr holy oyle, it is great superstición to gyve credyte to it, or to any suche fayned thynges invented by Sathan to blynde [*deceive*] the symple people. Theyr

39 *Sprawling*, hence resembling the shape of the *fleur-de-lys*. The poisonous quality of the toads may rather suggest ME *spraien* (used here in a sense – 'spraying' – attested in *OED* only from the sixteenth century, but antedated by Coke). There is no equivalent passage in the French.

oyle is oyle olyve whiche was brought out of Espayne, very good for salettes.

Of suche fayned relyques they have in Fraunce, yet at this daye, without nombre, to whom they give devine honour; whether they be good christyans or not, I remyt to the descrete judgementes of the readers hereof.

31 Item, the Sarasyns with whom kyng Clowes fought were his neyghbours, of Flaunders, Arthoys [*Artois*], Picardy, Champayne, Bourgoygne, Normandy, Guyan [*Guienne*], Poytou, Angeou [*Anjou*], and other shyres nere adjoynyng, beyng poore labouring men not accustomed to the warres, right easye to be subdued, whiche warres he made onely to robbe and spoyle them of goodes, landes, and possessions, and for no zeale he had to the augmentacyon of the Chrystyan fayth.

32. Item, where you say Charles Martell, kynge of Fraunce, wan a great battayle agaynst the Sarasyns beyng in nombre .ccc.lxxx.v.m. fyghtynge men, lady Prudence, this is not true, so innumerable of fyghtynge men to be on the one parte: truth it is the Cronycles of Brabant[40] declareth how he most cruelly slewe a great nombre of men, women and chyldren wherby he grevously displeased God, for they were poore people of Espayne and Gascoyne sekynge waste [*uncultivated*] countres to inhabyte in. And as Eucherius, bysshop of Orlyence, wryteth, he was therfore, and [for] other thynges, by the just judgement of God dampned. And where you call them Sarasyns, it shoulde thereby appeare, howe they were better Chrystyans then you, whiche scarsely be yet good at this daye.

33. Also this Charles Martell was a Dowcheman, and the fourth duke of Brabant, and no Hungarien, or Frencheman, as you cal your selves. Nor was ever kynge of Fraunce, but hured [*hired*] by Hyldericus theyr kynge to defende hym and his poore Hungariens, After, they perceyvynge the valyaunce of the sayde Charles Martell the Brabander, wolde have desposed Hyldericus to have made hym kynge, whiche he refused, syenge he wolde be no kynge, but a ruler, and above kynges. So that after the death of Hyldericus, he made Dagobert, Lothary, Cylparycke [*Chilperic*], and Diederycke [*Theodoric*] kynges over the sayde Hungariens, one after another, as in the dowche Brabant Cronycle, the .XV. chapitre, doth more playnely appere, where is wrytten of hym these verses folowyng:

Iste Brabantinus dux quartus in orbe triumphat,
Malleus in mundo specialis[41] victor ubique,
Dux dominusque ducum, comitum quoque, rex fore spernit;
Non vult regnare, sed regibus[42] imperat ipse.[43]

34. Item, to that you say, Charlemayne, kyng of Fraunce, a Frencheman, wan many battayles agaynst the Almaynes [*Germans*], and Lombardes, and subduyng al Espayne, brought them to the catholyque fayth, and after was Emperour and kyng of England,

[40] On this chronicle, first printed in 1498, see J. Tigelaar (2006), http://dspace.library.uu.nl/handle/1874/18829, and Pannier and Meyer 1887, 161–2, n. to §33.

[41] Corrected from *specialiter* in Coke's text against the *Cronyke van Brabant* (pr. Anvers 1497) in the BN by Meyer (Pannier and Meyer 1877, 161–2).

[42] Corrected from *regulis* by Meyer as above.

[43] 'This fourth duke of Brabant triumphs over the globe/ the unique hammer and victor throughout the world, / leader and lord of dukes, as also of counts, he rejects becoming king: he does not want to reign, but himself to command kings.'

I say, lady Prudence, how the Frenche heralde talketh at adventure, as the facion of his contremen, whiche customably use subtely and untruly to set forth with their tonges and writinges that which they can not atcheve with theyr handes. But nowe, lady Prudence, to declare unto you the truth, you shall understande how this Charlemayne was a Dowcheman, and the .vj. duke of Brabant, whose grandfather was Charles Martell before mencioned, as appereth in the Cronycles of Brabant the .xvij. chapitre, where is wrytten of hym these verses folowynge

Hic rex Cesar erat, dux sextus Lotariensis,
Atque Brabantinus, in cujus jure quiescit.[44]

35. Then to procede, how Charlmayne came to the crowne of Fraunce, the truth is howe his tresaioul [*great-great-grandfather*], named Pepyn, duke of Brabant, beyng hured to be governer of the house of Chyldebartus, kyng of the Hu[n]gariens now Frenchemen, and defendeur of his people, had to his wyfe a lady named Plectrude, doughter of the kyng of Burgoyne, yet he kepynge to his paramoure a poore woman called Alpay, had by her a bastard sone named Charles Martel of whom I spake before. This Charles was duke of Brabant, and had issue a sone named Lytell Pepyn, also duke of Brabant, whiche was father to Charlemayne, nowe by the Frenchemen called Charles the Great. This Lytell Pepyn, Charlemaynes father, was retayned by Chyldericus, then kyng, to defende hym and his people agaynst other nacions; whiche Hungariens founde meanes most trayterously to depose hym, and crowned Lytell Pepyn kyng, the yere of Our Lorde God .vij.cl. Of whom in the Brabant Cronycle is wrytten these verses:

Iste Brabantinus dux quintus Lothariensis,
Ex duce rex primus sit tandem germinis hujus.[45]

After whose deth Charlmayne his sone, the .vj. duke of Brabant, lykewyse toke upon hym the crowne. Wherfore, lady Prudence, yf any contrey shulde be honoured by Charlemayne, it shulde be of reason Brabant his natyfe countrey, and not Fraunce. And concernyng his battayles agaynst the Almaynes, Lombardes and other, although Charlemayne were conductor of the armye, yet had he ayde of the kynges of England, Denmarke and other nacions; for all the world knoweth that the Hungariens or Sacambriens, now Frenchemen, be not able to make battayle agaynst a poore duke with theyr owne wretched people, but havyng wares (as they be never in peace) they retayne Souches [*Swiss*], Hygh Dowche, Italiens, Spanyardes, Albanoys [*Albanians*], Scotes, and other nacions to fyght for them. And when they lose .xx. or .xxx.m. men in a batayle, then there is bokes and ballets craftely devysed, makyng therby the myserable Frenchemen beleve how they have vanquysshed and won all. And as to the subduynge of Espayne, it is truth howe there was dyvers battayles betwene Charlemayne and the Espaynyerdes, but yet for the most part the Espaynyerdes had the victorie, as appered by the batayle of Ronceaulx, where they slewe Richard of Normandy, Rolande, Olyver, and al the chiefe capytaynes of Fraunce, so that they had ever as moche or more losse then wynnynge.

44 'This king was Caesar, the sixth duke of Lotharingia/ And of Brabant, in whose domain he died.'

45 'This duke of Brabant, the fifth of Lotharingia/ is at last the first king of this seed from the duke.'

36. And for bostynge yourselves, Syr Heralde, how you brought them to the fayth, I say that lyeth not in the strength of man, but in God and by his vocacion. And yet within .lx. yeres passed, some parte of Espayne was not christened, as the realme of Garnatho [*Granada*], Tholoso [*Tolosa*], and other. And where you say further howe Charlemayne was kyng of England, that I report me to your owne cronycles, the Dowche cronycles, the cronycles of Lytel Brytayne, *Cronica cronicarum*, and to al writers of histories, for yf he had, I trust it shulde not have ben forgotten, but remembred in a thousande fayned [*fictive*] bokes. Thus, I, John Coke, compyler of this small treatyse, conclude for Charlmayne, that Brabant ought of ryght to have the glory, honour and fame mondayne of his hygh enterpryses, for that he hym selfe and his ancitours were al Brabanders borne, and that all the victorious actes whiche he atcheved, was by the onely strength, force and puissaunce of the noble Brabanders, with some ayde of England and Denmarke, and not of the Hungaryens.

37. Item, Syr Heralde, touchyng Roulande and Ogier le danoyes,[46] which you say were Frenchemen, and by whom Fraunce ought the more to be honoured, I saye, lady Prudence, under your correction, Roulande the noble knyght was of the nacion of England, and no Hungaryen or Frencheman, for he was borne in Armorica, whiche beyng conquered by Maxymian kyng of England, gave the same to Conan Mereodoke his cosyn and to his heyres, to holde of the kynges of Englande for ever, namyng it Lytel Brytayne. And, as Galfryde and *Policronica*[47] witnesseth, the sayd Conan and his knyghtes dysdaynyng to mary with the Galles (beyng many hundredes of yeres before the Hungaryens came into Fraunce), sent mesengers unto Devotus, duke of Cornwall and ruler then of Englande, for his doughter Ursyla with .xj.m. in nombre of virgyns to be kopled with hym and his knyghtes in maryage, whiche virgynes, in the tyme of Marcianus emperour, were by Guames and Malgo, tyrantes paynymes, cruelly martered. Yet after, they copled them with other noble mens doughters of Englande, wherby Lytell Brytayne multiplied in people and contynued doyng theyr homage and dutye to England from the yere of Our Lord God .ccc.xx. unto the yere of Our Lorde God .m.cc.lxxii., as Hardyng[48] and other cronycles wytnesseth; so it is apperant that the sayd Rowlande was lyneally extracted of the nacion of Englande, and not of the Hungariens now Frenchemen.

[46] *Ogier le danois*: a knight of Charlemagne's in the *Chanson de Roland.*

[47] Geoffrey of Monmouth and Ranulf Higden.

[48] John Hardyng (d. *c.* 1464, *ODNB*), author of a verse *Brutus* chronicle (a minor source for Malory and Spenser, among others).

Part VI. 3. Alternative Arrangements of the Entries

Names and titles occurring in manuscript texts or their rubrics etc. are given in bold.

1. By Date of Text

c. 1121	***Vita sancti Brendani*** [*Voyage de saint Brendan*] (9 *Incipit*)
1136–50	*L'Estoire des Engleis* (10)
c. 1150	*Les Proverbes de Salemon* (39)
	Li Livres de saynt Nicolay (25aR)
Late C12th	*Roman de philosophie* (38)
	Le Roman de toute chevalerie, ***La Geste de Alisandre*** (28R)
1160–74	*Roman de Rou* (3)
1163–70	***Le Romanz de saint Edward rei et [confessur]*** (2aR)
1165–80?	***Le Gracial*** (11a.35, 45)
1170–4	***Vita sancti Thomae Archiepiscopi et martiris Canturiencis*** (11b *Explicit*)
1175–90	***La Vie seint Edmund le rey*** (27R)
After 1180	*Ipomedon* (4)
Late C12th–early 13th	***Her biginneþ Luytel Caton*** [*Distichs of Cato*] (37R)
	La Vie seynt Josaphaz (30R)
	Poème sur l'Ancien Testament (43)
c. 1190–1210	*Waldef* (6)
After 1189–95	*Li Romanz de Dieu et de sa mere* (15)
Late C12th	***De Bretaine ki ore est apelé Engletere*** (1.1)
c. 1200	***La Seinte Resureccion*** (29a.2), ***La Sainte Resurrectiun*** (29b.2)
Early C13th	Commentary on the *Chant des Chanz* (26)
	Le Miracle de Sardenai (34.4)
	La Vie sainte Fey, virgine et martire (12R)
1200–50	***La Vie de seint Clement, pape*** (25bR)
	Sermons on Joshua (23)
1210–11	***Le Bestiaire en franceis*** (17R)
1212	***Dïaloges*** [***de saint Gregoire***] (24a.188)
1220–30	*L'Estoire del saint Graal* (41)
1230–53	*Chasteau d'amour* (5)
Mid-C13th	*La Destructioun de Rome* (18)
	Miroir ou Evangiles des domnees (14)
	Mirour de seinte eglyse (22)
1240–50	***Tretyz . . . ke vous aprendra le fraunceys de plusour choses de ce mound*** (7aR)
1248–59	***La Vie seint Eadmund le confessur, arcevesque de Canterbire*** (13R)

1256	***L'Art de[l] kalender*** (40.22)
c. 1260	***Le Manuel*** (24b.41), ~ ***dé pechez*** (24b.47)
1265–74	The Lambeth Apocalypse (20a)
1266–1300	***Secré de secrés*** (33R), ***Segrez des segrez*** **ou** ***Livre du governement des rois ou de princes*** (33.54-5)
1267	***La Lumere a lais*** (19.140. 141, 156)
After 1271	***Coment la Mesun de Crabhus . . . comencerunt*** (36.11–13)
1273–82	***Rossignol*** (21.*16*), ***Rossignos*** (21.Prol.*6*, *10*, *Explicit* 117)
	Ornatus mulierum (32bR): ***Quant Deus out la femme fete***, (32b.1)
Late 13th	*Les Enfaunces de Jesu Crist* (20b)
Late C13th–early C14th	Prose *remaniement* of *Romanz de saint Edward* (2b)
1307 or 1310	***Par ceste figure l'en poet savoer*** Genealogical Roll Chronicle (20c.50)
After 1321	*Liber custumarum*: ***Qui veut bone electioun faire*** (8aR); ***La Feste royale du Pui*** (8a.65)
1320–40	*Fouke le Fitz Waryn* (31)
Before mid-14th	***Sicom Aristotele nous dit***: Treatise on menstruation (32a.1)
Mid C14th	*The Mohun Chronicle* (42)
1355–64	***Scalacronica*** (16.*124*)
1356 or 1357	***Le Livre des merveilles du monde*** (35)
1360–79	*Mirour de l'omme* (8b)
1396, 1415	*Manières de langage* (7b)
Late C14th	***De modo dictandi letteras . . . in gallicis*** (*7c*R): ***Ore fait a dire quant vus frez . . . en manere de lettre*** (7c.*1-2*)
	Iam incipiunt regule cartarum (7dR): Treatise on conveyancing
c. 1400	***Donait françois*** (7e.19)
c. 1443	Genealogical Roll Chronicle (20d)
1453–61	*Le Débat des hérauts d'armes de France et d'Angleterre* (44)

2. By Text's Patron, *commanditaire*, *destinataire*, etc.

Abbot Samson, d. 1211 (12)
Abbess of Barking (1173-5), ***l'abesse suer saint Thomas*** (11b.26)
Adeliza of Louvain, *c.* 1103–51, ***Aliz la reïne*** (9.1)
Alice de Condet, 1099–1152, ***Aëliz de Cundé*** (39.201)
Aline (possibly Elena de Quincy, d. 1274), ***Dame Aline*** (14.1, 73)
Arundel, countess of (Isabel de Warenne), d. 1282, ***La cuntesse de Arundel*** (13R.3), ~ ***et de Essexe, dame Ysabele*** (13.30).
Barton, John, *fl.* 1417 (possibly author), ***Johan Bartoun*** (7e.*16*)
Constance, wife of Ralph Fitz Gilbert, early-mid 12th century (10)
Dionysia de Munchensi, d. 1304?, ***ma dame Deonyse de Mountchensy*** (7aProl.*2-3*)
Eleanor of Provence, d. 1291, ***Roine d'Engleterre, mere le roi Edward*** (21Prol.*2-3*), ***mere au roi Edward*** (21.114)

Elena de Quincy, d. 1274 (20a?)
Gregory, late 12th century? (11a), *see also* ***Mahaut***
Henry II (*destinateur*, possibly patron) (3)
Joan de Mohun, d. 1404 (42)
Kirvyngton (7b, 1396 recension, Headnote)
Mahaut, dame, late 12th century? Abbess of Barking? (11a.65)
Margaret de Ferrers, d. 1281 (20a?)
Odo, Prior of Canterbury, 12th century, ***Oede li buens priurs*** (11b.41)
Raoul (Radalphus, [?] Ralph of Maidstone), early 13th century (17)
Templars, ***li frere do Temple*** (cult sponsors) (34.101)
Thiout, Robert, 12th century (25a)
Vere, William de, bishop of Hereford 1186–98 (38?)

3. By Authors, Compilers, Translators, etc.

Adgar (also known as William), late 12th century? (11a)
Angier of St Frideswide, *fl.* 1212 ***li vieil pecchierre, Angier*** (24a, Headnote)
Anon (1), (6), (18), (20a), (20c) (20d), (23), (25b), (26), (29), (31), (32a and b), (34), (43), (44).
Barton, John, *fl.* 1417 (possibly patron), ***Johan Bartoun*** (7e.*16*)
Benedeit, early 12th century, ***li apostoilles Dans Beneiz*** (9.8)
Bibbesworth, Walter of, 1235–70, ***Gautier de Biblesworth*** (7aProl.*1-2*)
Chardri, late 12th/early 13th century (30)
Copale, Servais (collaborator? scribe?) later 13th century (33)
Denis *see* Piramus
Edmund of Abingdon, St, 1175–1240 (22)
Everart, late 12th /early 13th century (37)
Gaimar, Geffrei, *fl.* 1136–7 (10)
Gauter *see* Walter
Gillealme *see* Guillaume
Gilliam Scrivener *see* William Kingsmill
Gower, John, *c.* 1330–1408 (8b)
Gray, Sir Thomas (Jr), d. 1369 (16.16–28, cryptic verse)
Grosseteste, Robert, *c.* 1168–1253, ***seint Robert . . . Eveske de Nichole*** (5.*1-2*)
Guace see Wace
Guernes de Pont Sainte Maxence, 12th century, ***Guarniers li clerc del Punt*** (11b.1)
Guillaume le Clerc de Normandie, *fl.* 1210/11–1227 × 38, ***Gillealme*** (17.8), ***li Normanz*** (17.36)
Herman de Valenciennes, late 12th century, ***Dan Heremans*** (15.14)
Horn, Andrew (compiler), *c.* 1275–1328 (8a)
Hue de Rotelande, *fl.* 1175–90 ***Hue de Rotelande*** (4.33)
Jofroi de Waterford, *fl.* 1300 (patron? collaborator?), ***Jofroi de Watreford*** (33.*30*)
Johan, late 13th-early 14th century (scribe? artist? author?), ***Johan*** (20b.39)

John of Howden, *fl.* 1268–75, ***Johan de Houedene*** (21Prol.*1*)
Lawis, li roy [?] (18.8)
Mandeville, Sir John, fictional (?), 14th century, ***John Maundevill*** (35.*21*)
La Mesun de Crabhus (as collective producer) (36.11)
Nun (Clemence?) of Barking, 12th century, ***Une ancele al dulz Jhesu Crist*** (2a.80), ***Une des anceles Jhesu Crist*** (2b.18–19)
Paris, Matthew, *c.* 1200–59 (13)
Pierre d'Abernon de Fetcham, d. 1293, ***Peris*** (19.20)
Piramus, Denis, *fl.* 1150–early 13th century, ***Denis Piramus*** (27.16)
Rauf de Linham, 13th century (40)
'Robert de Boron', late 12th to early 13th century (41)
Robert Grosseteste, *seint Robert* see Grosseteste
Robert of Greatham, early-mid 13th century (14)
Sanson de Nantuil, 12th century, ***Sanson de Nantuil*** (39.195)
Simon of O[xford, Osney, Offord?], *fl.* 1420 (7d)
Simon of Walsingham, early 13th century, ***Symon de Walsingham*** (12.99)
Simund de Freine *fl.* 1190, d. before 1228, (acrostic) (38.1–14)
Thomas of Kent, late 12th century (28)
Thomas Sampson, *c.* 1340–1409, ***Thomas Sampson*** (7c.99)
Wace, *c.* 1110–74, ***maistre Wace*** (3.158), ***Guace*** (25a.31)
Walter de la Hove, 14th century (42)
Walter of Bibbesworth, *see* Bibbesworth
Walter of Douai, ***Gauter de Doway*** (18.7)
William Kingsmill, *fl.* 1415, ***Gilliam Scrivener*** (7b.73)
William Waddington, 13th century (24b?)

4. By Place, Provenance/Region

Barking Abbey, Middlesex (2a), ***l'abeie de Berkinges*** (2b.18), (11b)
Bayeux, Normandy (3?)
Bury St Edmunds, Suffolk, East Anglia (12), (27)
Caen, Normandy (25a)
Canterbury, Kent (11b), (29b?)
Continent and England (3), (15), (18), (20d), (25a), (33), (34?), (41), (44)
Coventry and Lichfield diocese (17)
Crowland Abbey, Lincolnshire (6?)
Devon (42, see also Somerset)
Edinburgh and Northumberland (16)
England (place uncertain) (9), (20b), (20c and d), (22), (23), (25b), (32a), (32b), (34), (37), (40), (43)
Hereford, Herefordshire, West Midlands (4), (30?), (31), (38)
Hertfordshire (7a? or Essex?)
Lincolnshire (6?), (10), (29a?), (39?)

London (1), (7e?), (20a?), (21?)
London, Guildhall (8a)
London and Southwark (8b)
London (East London, modern Middlesex) (2a)
London (St Paul's Cathedral) (11a)
Ludlow, Herefordshire (31?)
Newark Priory and Oxford (19)
Norfolk (Crabhouse and parish of Wiggenhall) (36)
Normandy (34?)
Normandy and England (2b)
Northern France (41), (44)
Oxford (5?), (7b), (7c), (7d?), (7e?), (19), (23?)
Oxford, St Frideswide's Augustinian house (24a)
Picard-Walloon area (33?, see also Waterford)
St Albans, Hertfordshire (13), (28?), (35?)
Shropshire or Northamptonshire: (14?)
Somerset (42, see also Devon)
Valenciennes, Northern France (15?)
Waterford, Ireland (33?)
West Midlands (30?)
York, North Yorkshire (26?), York diocese (24b)

5. By Genre

Apocryphal:
Enfaunces de Jesu Crist (20b)
Romanz de Dieu et de sa mere (15)
Biblical and Bible commentary:
Chant des Chanz (26)
Lambeth Apocalypse (20a)
Miroir ou Evangiles des domnees (14)
Poème sur l'Ancien Testament (43)
Proverbes de Salemon (39)
Chanson de geste:
Destructioun de Rome (18)
Custumal/Civic Records/Cartulary:
De Bretaine, ki est ore apelé Engletere (1)
Liber custumarum (8a)
Coment la Mesun de Crabhus . . . comencerunt (36)
Devotional:
Chant des Chanz (26)
Chasteau d'amour (5)
Enfaunces de Jesu Crist (20b)

Le Gracial (11a)
Lambeth Apocalypse (20a)
Miracle de Sardenai (34)
Mirour de seinte eglyse (22)
Mirour de l'omme (8b)
Rossignos (21)
Seinte Resurreccion (29)

Hagiography and miracles:
Dialogues de saint Gregoire (24a)-miracle collection
Le Gracial (11a)-miracle collection
Miracle de Sardenai (34)
Romanz de saint Edward, rei e confessur (2)
Vie de seint Clement (25b)
Vie seint Edmund le rei (27)
Vie de saint Edmund, arcevesque de Canterbire (13)
Vie de sainte Fey, virgine e martire (12)
Vie de seint Josaphaz (30)
Vie de saint Nicolas (25a)
Vie de saint Thomas Becket (11b)
Voyage de saint Brendan (9)

Historiography:
Coment la Mesun de Crabhus . . . comencerunt (36)
De Bretaine ki ore est apelé Engletere (1) – chronicle, legal compilation
Destructioun de Rome (18) – epic, romance
Estoire des Engleis (10) – chronicle
The Mohun Chronicle (42) – chronicle
Roman de Rou (3) – history, romance
Scalacronica (16) – chronicle
Two Genealogical Roll Chronicles (20c and d) – visual literacy

Pastoral/Ethical:
Bestiaire divin (17) – doctrinal
Chant des Chanz (26) – Bible commentary/devotional
Chasteau d'amour (5) – devotional/theological
Distichs of Cato (37) – ethics and education
Lumere as lais (19) – theological encyclopaedia
Manuel des pechiez (24b) – confessional
Miroir ou Evangile des domnees (14) – homiletic commentary
Mirour de l'omme (8b) – estates satire/devotional
Mirour de seinte eglyse (22) – doctrinal/devotional
Proverbes de Salemon (39) – Bible commentary
Sermons on Joshua (23)

Romance:
Estoire del saint Graal (41) – legendary history, romance
Fouke le Fitz Waryn (31) – legendary history, romance

Ipomedon (4)
Roman de toute chevalerie (28)
Voyage de saint Brendan (9)
Waldef (6)

Linguistic and Compositional Manuals:
Tretiz de langage (7a)
Manières de langage (7b)
Pur ceo que j'estoie: Treatise on conveyancing (7d)
Quant vous frez as seignours (dictaminal) (7c)
Donait françois (7e)

Travel Literature.:
Livre des merveilles du monde (35)
Voyage de saint Brendan (9)

Treatise/Commentary:
Chant des Chanz (26) –devotional
Débat des hérauts d'armes de France et d'Angleterre (44)
Kalender (40)
Mirour de seinte eglyse (22)
Proverbes de Salemon (39)
Quant Deus out la femme fete: *Ornatus mulierum* (32b)
Roman de philosophie (38)
Sicom Aristotle nous dit: Treatise on menstruation (32a)
Secré de secrez (33) – mirror for princes

Visual Literacy:
Lambeth Apocalypse (20a)
Enfaunces de Jesu Crist (20b)
Two Genealogical Roll Chronicles (20c and d)

6. By Form (Metrical/Prose/Pictorial)

Prose:
Coment la Mesun de Crabhus . . . comencerunt (36) (with prologue in octosyllables)
Débat des hérauts d'armes de France et d'Angleterre (44)
De Bretaine ki ore est apelé Engletere (1)
Donait françois (7e)
Estoire del saint Graal (41)
Fouke le Fitz Waryn (31) (from verse source and some prophetic verse)
Lambeth Apocalypse (20a) prose, pictorial
Livre des merveilles du monde (35)
Liber custumarum (8a)
Manières de langage (7b) prose (with some versified dialogue)
Mirour de seinte eglyse (22)
Mohun Chronicle (42)

Pur ceo que j'estoie requis: Treatise on conveyancing: (7d)
Quant Deus out la femme fete: *Ornatus mulierum* (32b) prose recipes (prologue couplets)
Quant vous frez as seignours: Dictaminal Training (7c)
Romanz de saint Edward, rei e confessur (2b) prose *remaniement*
Secré de secrez (33)
Sermons on Joshua (23)
Two Genealogical Roll Chronicles (20c and d) prose, pictorial

Metrical (octosyllables in couplets unless otherwise noted):
Bestiaire divin (17) octosyllables
Chant des Chanz (26) monorhymed alexandrine *laisses*
Chasteau d'amour (5) octosyllables
Coment la Mesun de Crabhus . . . comencerunt (36) prologue in octosyllables
Destructioun de Rome (18) monorhymed alexandrine *laisses*
Dialogues de saint Gregoire (24a) octosyllables
Distichs of Cato (37) hexasyllabic tail-rhymed stanzas
Enfaunces de Jesu Crist (20b) monorhymed quatrains, octosyllables
Estoire des Engleis (10) octosyllables
Le Gracial (11a) octosyllables
Ipomedon (4) octosyllables
Kalender (40) octosyllables
Lumere as lais (19) octosyllables
Manuel des pechiez (24b) octosyllables
Miracle de Sardenai (34) octosyllables
Miroir ou Evangiles des domnees (14) octosyllables
Mirour de l'omme (8b) octosyllables in 12-line stanzas: aab aab bba bba
Poème sur L'Ancien Testament (43) decasyllables in monorhymed sequences, then rhymed couplets
Proverbes de Salemon (39) octosyllables
Quant Deus out la femme fete: *Ornatus mulierum* (32b) prol. couplets
Roman de Rou (3) octosyllables
Roman de philosophie (38) heptasyllabic couplets
Roman de toute chevalerie (28) alexandrine *laisses*
Romanz de Dieu et de sa mere (15) monorhymed alexandrine *laisses*
Romanz de saint Edward, rei e confessur (2a) octosyllables
Rossignos (21) octosyllables in monorhymed quatrains (marked as huitain pairs)
Seinte Resurreccion (29) couplets, quatrains (drama)
Sicom Aristotle nous dit: Treatise on menstruation (32a) octosyllables
Tretiz de langage (7a) octosyllables
Vie de seint Clement, pape (25b) octosyllables
Vie de saint Edmund, arcevesque de Cantorbire (13) octosyllables
Vie seint Edmund le rei (27) octosyllables
Vie de sainte Fey (12) octosyllables
Vie de seint Josaphaz (30) octosyllables
Vie de saint Nicolas (25a) octosyllables

Vie de saint Thomas Becket (11b) 1. 5-line monorhymed alexandrine stanzas
2. 16-syllable verses rhymed at the eighth and sixteenth syllables
3. 12-syllable lines, with internal rhyme at the sixth and line-end rhyme
Voyage de saint Brendan (9) octosyllables
Waldef (6) octosyllables

Mixed: Verse, Prose, Pictorial:
Coment la Mesun de Crabhus . . . comencerunt (36) verse prologue, prose
Enfaunces de Jesu Crist (20b) verse, pictorial
Fouke le Fitz Waryn (31) prose (from verse source): verse prophecy
Lambeth Apocalypse (21a) prose, pictorial
Manières de langage (7b) prose with some versified dialogue
Quant Deus out la femme fete: *Ornatus mulierum* (32b) prose, verse prologue
Romanz de saint Edouard, rei e confessur (2b) prose *remaniement*
Scalacronica (16) prose with a section of rhymed couplets
Two Genealogical Roll Chronicles (20c and d) prose, pictorial

7. By Manuscript (as used for French texts; see also Index of Manuscripts)

Cambridge
Corpus Christi College, 133 (16)
Corpus Christi College, 471 (21)
Trinity College, O.2.5 (1109) (32a)
R.3.46 (622) (25b)
University Library, Add. 3035 (8b)
Gg.1.1 (40)
Ee.iv.20 (7c)
Mm.6.4 (24b)

Cologny-Geneva
Bibl. Bodmeriana, Bodmer 168 (formerly Phillipps 8345) (6)

Dublin
Trinity College, 209 (B.5.1) (19)

Durham
Cathedral Library, C.IV.27 (10)

London
British Library, Add. 4733 Vol 1 (36)
Add. 14,252 (1)
Add. 38,664 (11a)
Add. 45,103 (aka Penrose, Wakefield, Canterbury MS) (29b)
Add. 46,919 (formerly Phillipps 8336) (7a,) (38)
Add. 62,929 (formerly Haccombe MS, in Carew family) (42)
Add. 70,513 (2), (12), (13)
Cotton Domitian A.XI (27)
Cotton Vespasian A.VII (4)

Egerton 745 (2b)
Egerton 2710 (43)
Egerton 3028 (18)
G.32, g.4 (early print) (44)
Harley 222 (15)
Harley 1121 (22)
Harley 3988 (7b)
Harley 4388 (39)
Harley 4971 (7d)
Royal 4 C.XI (3)
Royal 12 C.XII (31)
Royal 19 C.XII (41)
City Corporation of London Records Office COL/CS/01/006 (8a)
Lambeth Palace, Lambeth Palace Library 209 (20a)
New Haven
Yale University, Beinecke Library, 395 (formerly Phillipps 4156) (17)
Nottingham
Nottingham University Library, MiLM4 (formerly at Wollaton Hall) (14)
Oxford
All Souls College, All Souls 182 (7e)
Bodleian Library, Ashmole 1470 (7005) (32b)
Ashmole 1804 (25,174) (35)
Ashmole Rolls 38 (20c)
Bodley Rolls 2 (2978) (20d)
Eng. Poet. a.1 (3938–42) (the Vernon MS) (37)
Latin misc. e. 93 (7b)
Rawlinson poet. 234 (26)
Selden supra 38 (3426) (20b)
Jesus College, 29 (30)
Paris
Bibliothèque de l'Arsenal, 3516 (25a)
Bibliothèque nationale de France, f. fr. 902 (29a)
f. fr. 1822 (33)
f. fr. 13,513 (11b)
f. fr. 19,525 (23)
f. fr. 24,364 (28)
f. fr. 24,766 (24a)
nouv. acq. fr. 4503 (9)
Princeton
Princeton University Library, Taylor Medieval MS 1 (formerly Phillipps 2223) (5)
Tours
Bibliothèque Municipale, 927 (Marmoutier 237) (34)
Vatican City
Biblioteca Apostolica Vaticana, MS Reg. lat. 4

Timeline: England and French

This necessarily eclectic chart emphasizes the unstable collocation of insular and other territories associated with the English crown and the various Frenches in and affecting insular culture

REIGNS AND TERRITORIES	PEOPLES, EVENTS, LANGUAGES	LITERARY/TEXTUAL PRODUCTION
Cnut r. 1017–35, m. Emma of Normandy (d. 1052), previously m. to King Æthelræd (d. 1016). Cnut rules England, Norway, Denmark.	Edward and Alfred, Emma of Normandy's sons by Æthelræd, brought up in exile in Normandy. French is a language of the English court alongside Danish, Latin, English. Ramsey, Fleury and other insular-continental monastic exchanges. *Togail Troí,* Irish version of Dares Phrygius' *De excidio Troiae Historia.*	English and Latin writing continues from Æthelræd's reign (Bishop Wulfstan, homilist, d. 1023), O.E. *Apollonius of Tyre* (copied). Skaldic production for Cnut, patronage by him and Emma of religious book and material culture. Law codes. Arabic learning (e.g. the astrolabe) in England.
1035–42 Danish rule continues under Harold (d. 1040) and Harthacnut (d. 1042)	Norman and Lotharingian clerics and secular elite bring French to court and church.	Latin and English-language text and book production
Edward 'the Confessor', r. 1042–66, rules England. M. Edith (d. 1072), Godwin's daughter. Harold II, Edith's brother, r. Jan–Oct 1066, m. (i) Eadgifu (ii) as consort, Ealdgyth (d. after 1066?), daughter of the Earl of Mercia, widow of Gruffudd ap Llywelan, Welsh king.	English court continues to include francophony: Edward brings Norman, French and Lotharingian francophones with him, and he and his queen, Edith, have some French.	*Cambridge Songs,* collected in German imperial court, copied in England. *Vita Edwardi* commissioned by Edith. Exeter Book of Old English verse donated 1072 by Edward's adherent, Bishop Leofric, from francophone Lotharingia. Includes OE *Physiologus*

REIGNS AND TERRITORIES	PEOPLES, EVENTS, LANGUAGES	LITERARY/TEXTUAL PRODUCTION
William of Normandy, r. 1066–1087, m. Matilda of Flanders (d. 1083). Rules England, Normandy, Maine. Scotland remains an independent kingdom. Norman conquests in Wales resisted, some Norman control of the Welsh marches asserted. rule of Welsh provinces continues under Welsh kings. (Isle of Man under Norse suzerainty until 1266).	Governance in Latin documents with translation into English and French. From 1085, Domesday Book. Churchmen from Europe (Lanfranc, d. 1089) Many from the continent probably become bilingual in English and French within a couple of generations. Jewish communities, bi-lingual in French and Hebrew, arrive in England from Rouen. Gaelic, Norse, Inglis spoken in Scotland with increased French and Anglo-French interchange.	Anglo-Saxon chronicles continue. Other genres in English and Latin, e.g. Goscelin of St Bertin's Latin 1080s-90s hagiography of English saints for Ely, Barking, St Augustine's Canterbury, Ramsey. Saints from Normandy (Nicholas, Giles) given English-language lives in later C11th. Copying and anthologizing of English materials, especially homiletic and hagiographic works, continues.
William Rufus, r. 1087–1100, England (Normandy and Maine pass to his brother Robert Curthose)	Consolidation of French as a spoken court language in England, though French is probably not a first language for very long outside the royal household.	French glosses and notes in Latin and Old English manuscripts from *c.* 1100
Henry I, r. 1100–35, m. (i) Edith-Matilda of Scotland (d. 1118) (ii) Adeliza of Louvain (d. 1151) in 1121. Rules England, Normandy (after 1106), Maine, Anjou, Ireland	Churchmen from Europe (Anselm, d. 1109). Interest in insular pasts; influential late C11th to early C12th Latin monastic historians, e.g. Orderic Vitalis, Henry of Huntingdon, William of Malmesbury (with patronage of Edith-Matilda). Earliest extant Scottish law text (*Leges inter Brettos et Scottos*) composed, in French.	French courtly literature production (*Brendan,* and other texts) for, principally, Henry's Lotharingian queen Adeliza. Early French versions of the psalter. Earliest *Vie st Alexis* text in St Albans Psalter, 1120s–1130s. *Leis Willelme*, earliest French law code.

Timeline: England and French

REIGNS AND TERRITORIES	PEOPLES, EVENTS, LANGUAGES	LITERARY/TEXTUAL PRODUCTION
Stephen, r. 1135–54, m. Matilda (d. 1152) of Boulogne, at the time part of Flanders. Rules England, Boulogne, initially Duke of Normandy (lost by 1144). Northumbria ceded in 1149 to David of Scotland (r. 1124–53).	Struggle for throne with Matilda, daughter of Henry I, mother of Henry II, widowed Empress of the Holy Roman Empire, wife of Geoffrey of Anjou, declared Henry I's heir. Under David of Scotland (d. 1153), Inglis and French at court: Gaelic declines in southern Scotland.	Gaimar *Estoire des Engleis* *c.* 1136/7. Geoffey of Monmouth, *Historia* (medieval title sometimes *De gestis Britonum)* by 1139. Wace *Roman de Brut* finished 1155.
Henry II, r. 1154–89, m. Eleanor of Aquitaine (d. 1204). Rules England, Northumbria (regained), Normandy, Anjou, Touraine, Aquitaine by marriage: the 'Angevin Empire'. 1169- invasions of Ireland. Youngest son John invested as Duke of Ireland 1177. William I ('the Lion') reigns as king of Scotland, 1165–1214, defeated by Henry II, 1174.	Increased bureaucracy and the beginnings of wider access to French, acquired for clerical and administrative careers. 1170 murder of Archbishop Thomas Becket. Southern French troubadours at the English court. Joanna, Henry and Eleanor's third daughter, m. William II of Sicily, 1177. French used in administration and literary genres among Anglo-Norman elites in Ireland.	Large corpora of insular French hagiography (eventually some 70 lives), historiography, romance, devotional and doctrinal French-language writing composed: includes Thomas' *Tristan*, 1150–70. Biographies of Becket, 1172 onwards. Jordan Fantosme *Chronique* (of Anglo-Scots war, 1173–4). *Roman de Horn c.* 1180. Hue de Rotelande's 'Sicilian' romances, *c.* 1180–90. *La Geste des Engleis en Yrlande*, *c.* 1190–1200.
Richard I, r. 1189–99 (partly in absentia on crusade), m. Berengaria of Navarre (d. 1230)	Intensified relations with the Mediterranean and the Latin Kingdom (conducted in Latin and the French of Outremer).	Ambroise, *Histoire de la guerre sainte* (by 1196). French texts across literary and informational genres. Late C12th lapidaries from 'King Evrax' of Arabia.

REIGNS AND TERRITORIES	PEOPLES, EVENTS, LANGUAGES	LITERARY/TEXTUAL PRODUCTION
John I, r. 1199–1216, m. (i) Isabella of Gloucester, d. 1217 (ii) as consort, Isabella of Angoulême, d. 1246. Rules England, Gascony, Channel Islands, Aquitaine: over 1202–5 loses the Angevin heartlands (Anjou, Maine, Normandy, Poitou, Touraine) to Philip Augustus of France. Stronger controls over Ireland and king of Scotland, weaker crown control of Wales. 1216 claim to English crown by Louis of France, London briefly captured .	Quarrel with papacy leads to interdict 1208–14. *Magna carta* issued first in 1215, dissemination in Latin with French translation. Francophone trade and other relations continue cross-Channel, though some families concentrate their land-ownership on one or other side instead of both. Expansion of French for social and meritocratic purposes ongoing and increasing. *Mabinogi* and other C12th–13th Welsh Arthurian romances, reworking earlier local traditions and French materials. Welsh court poetry continues.	French-language treatises on scientific and technical matters. Guillaume le clerc's *Bestiaire divin* 1210–11. Around and after Lateran IV in 1215, many pastoralia produced in French. Early C13th romances with wide-ranging continental settings (*Waldef, Gui de Warewic, Boeve de Haumtone*). *Fergus* [of Galloway] early C13th French verse romance in Scotland. *Guillaume d'Angleterre* (early C13th continental French verse romance).
Henry III, r. 1216–71, m. Eleanor of Provence (d. 1291). Rules England, Ireland (against successful local insurgencies), Wales, Gascony: loss of Maine. Scotland remains an independent kingdom. 1254 papal offer of Sicilian throne accepted. Title to Normandy and Anjou ceded 1259 (as also Maine, Touraine, Poitou). Baronial rebellions, notably Simon de Montfort (d. 1265), married to king's sister. 1266 Scottish rule of Isle of Man. Llewellyn recognised as Prince of Wales 1267.	Regency (and later, French-language biography) of William Marshal (d. 1219). Friars in England from 1221 to 1224. French and Latin pastoralia by Grosseteste (d. 1253) and others. 'Bracton' (ascribed), law code 1230s to 1240s. Poitevin and Savoyard factions at court. Insular French the language of royal and crown letters.. Documentary, administrative, professional French materials. Late C13th to C15th is apogee of French documents in England and its external communications.	French-language writing continues, alongside some C13th English-language writing: hagiography, homiletic, devotional, doctrinal texts, lyric, estates satire, verse and prose historiography. Matthew Paris of St Albans (d. 1259) composes hagiography, historiography and cartography in Latin and French. French- language encyclopaedias and travel writings, pilgrimage itineraries. Illustrated Apocalypses in various Latin/French combinations. *c.* 1240–50 first guide to spoken French, Bibbesworth's *Tretiz de langage.*

REIGNS AND TERRITORIES	PEOPLES, EVENTS, LANGUAGES	LITERARY/TEXTUAL PRODUCTION
Edward I, r. 1272–1307, m. Eleanor of Castile (d. 1290). Rules England, lordship of Ireland, dukedom of Aquitaine. Conquest of Wales 1282–3 Conquest of Scotland 1292 (continued Scottish resistance in Scottish Wars of Independence 1296–1328). Creation of 'empire' of *Engleterre.* War with France 1294, Franco-Scottish alliance against England 1295. Isle of Man variously under English and Scottish suzerainty until 1794.	Continued use of French in law reports, with long term records in Latin. Oral use of insular French in court proceedings until probably the later C14th. Latin continues to be frequently taught through French in schools. Some clerks and bureaucrats learn French when young enough to achieve considerable mastery. 1290 Expulsion of the Jews First French statutes and Year Books. *Britton* French law code 1290s? French used in municipal administration from the late C13th-15th. Marco Polo, *Le Devisement dou monde*, 1298; other trade/travel works.	Continued French-language hagiography, historiography, homiletic, devotional and doctrinal, scientific, technical, French texts. *Brut* historiographic genres sometimes deployed in services of Edward I's *imperium.* Gascon and other continental Frenches familiar in English royal and other administrative offices. Though Latin remains a fundamental administrative language until Henry VIII's reign, Anglo-Norman becomes an important crown administrative language.
Edward II, r. 1307–27, m. Isabella of France (d. 1358). Rules England, lordship of Ireland, duke of Aquitaine (continuingly disputed). Isabella governs after Edward's death. Scots win Bannockburn 1314, independence recognised 1328, Bruce, then Stewart dynasties.	Court continues to read and listen in insular and continental Frenches (Queen Isabella is a noted owner of romance, beast epic and other texts). 1315–22 British and Northern European famine.	*Brut* writings in verse (e.g. Langtoft *Chronicle* from Brutus to 1307) and prose continue. Large early C14th trilingual miscellany manuscripts produced for baronial/episcopal households, notably in W.Midlands (e.g. BL Add. 46,919 and others).

REIGNS AND TERRITORIES	PEOPLES, EVENTS, LANGUAGES	LITERARY/TEXTUAL PRODUCTION
Edward III, r. 1327–77 (personal rule from 1333), m. Philippa of Hainault (d. 1369). Rules England, France (claimed, from 1340), Gascony. Lordship of Ireland restricted to the Pale. Scots independence continues. 'Hundred Years War' with France, 1337–1443 English victories at Crécy (1346) and Poitiers (1356), capture of John II of France. Calais English-controlled from 1346.	Some English used at court, and hospitality to the new English-language writing by Chaucer and others. French continues as the dominant regal language in England and NW Europe. John II's captivity increases court's centrality to Northern European affairs. Close political and diplomatic exchanges in NW France: Picard *scriptae* familiar in English governmental offices. 1348–9, 1361 Black Death (continuing sporadic outbreaks into C15th). Plague has disproportionate effects in towns and perhaps therefore on transmission of bureaucratic French among clerks and administrators.	Nicole Bozon, fl. 1320, prolific Franciscan writer of French pastoralia, lyric, homily, estates satire. Sir Roger de Stanegrave's proposal for recapturing the Holy Land (*Li Charboclois d'armes*), *c.* 1331. Oxford school of French from mid-C14th produces guides for speaking French (for business and professional people). More specialized legal training in French in London. Continued production and circulation of earlier French texts and manuscripts, insular and continental, including biblical translations. Increasing numbers of English texts produced alongside insular and continental French texts.
Richard II, r.1377-deposed 1399, m. (i) Anne of Bohemia (d. 1394) (ii) Isabella of France (d. 1409). Rules England, Ireland (partially), Wales, Aquitaine.	Close relations between English and French courts. C14th development of Parisian book and literary production becomes newly influential: Flanders also continuingly important. European interchange between English and continental writers intensified: southern as well as northern Europe (e.g. Chaucer's engagement with Italian writing).	Late C14th, early C15th increased attention to French as a formal written language, on which handbooks and treatises are produced. *Anominalle Chronicle* (French) (Brutus-1381) and other historiographic production in insular French. 1370s-*c.* 1400 John Gower writes in French, Latin, English.

REIGNS AND TERRITORIES	PEOPLES, EVENTS, LANGUAGES	LITERARY/TEXTUAL PRODUCTION
Henry IV, r. 1399–1413, m. Mary Bohun (d. 1394), then Joan de Navarre (d. 1437). Rules England, Ireland, duke of Aquitaine, partial rule of Wales. Owain Glyndŵr's rebellion, 1400–1410. Oldcastle's 'Lollard' uprising, 1415.	First king of England formally to use English (in Parliament etc), though continuing diplomacy, administration and some literary commissioning in French. 'Lancastrian' court writing in English.	First fully grammaticalised guide to French 1409: continental French guides are later. Grammar treatises viewing English as a formal written vernacular begin to be composed. Some Anglo-Norman and French Bible translations continue to circulate.
Henry V, r. 1413–22. m. Catherine de Valois (d. 1420). Scottish–French alliances. Normandy and other territories regained. Title of heir and regent of France from 1420 (Treaty of Troyes). Scottish-French alliances against England.	France invaded and Agincourt victory 1415 won by Henry V. English kingdom in France won (and lost over following thirty years). Wider use of French by English people of various occupations (soldiers and their commanders, colonists). Continued Anglo-French, Anglo-Flandrian, Burgundian and other contacts. Council of Constance 1414–18 ends schism. 1417–41 sporadic plague and famine in Britain and Europe.	French and Latin maintained in varying proportions in administrative genres. English replaces French as the language of some crown letters from early C15th. English joins Latin and French as a language of civic and other chronicling. Continental French texts continue to participate in insular literary culture (e.g. Henry is presented in 1420 with Jean de Galupe's French version of Bonaventura's *Meditationes vitae Christi,* subsequently reworked by Lydgate in English).

REIGNS AND TERRITORIES	PEOPLES, EVENTS, LANGUAGES	LITERARY/TEXTUAL PRODUCTION
Henry VI, r. 1422–61, m. Margaret of Anjou 1445. Rules England, lordship pf Ireland, duke of Aquitaine. English defeated at Orleans 1429, Charles VII of France crowned in Rheims 1429, Henry VI crowned in Paris 1431. 1445 surrender of Maine promised by Henry VI. 1449–50 French take over Normandy. 1453 Gascony lost to French. 1455 dynastic wars for English throne (later called Wars of the Roses).	Shifting English, French and Burgundian alliances. Flemish/ Burgundian contact influential for books and texts. Cultural contact, cross-Channel exchange and creation of fine books if anything intensified by war. The duke of Bedford (regent of France, d. 1435) acquires the huge French royal library which is largely sold and scattered in England and France. High literary Scottish writing in 'Inglis' flourishes alongside Latin and continuing French contacts on into late C15th and early C16th.	The poet Hoccleve's French and Latin formulary for letters and documents, *c.* 1420–6. English begins to be used by the privy seal in the 1440s. The range of text types composed in insular French contracts (mainly now genealogical rolls, some *Brut* texts, prayers, devotions, psalters): continuing circulation of older French texts from England and Europe. England remains a culture of translations and multilingualism alongside its greatly expanded range of English-language writing.
Edward IV, r. 1461–70, m. Elizabeth Woodville (d. 1492). Rules England and has lordship of Ireland. Alliance with Burgundy and marriage (1468) of Edward's sister, Margaret of York (d. 1503) to Charles of Burgundy.	Edward significantly enlarges royal library with French texts in de luxe manuscripts from Flanders and from Burgundian book-makers.	English documents more frequent in general administration alongside French. French remains the vector of supra-regional exchange and literary culture.
Henry VI, r. 1470–1		
Edward IV, r. 1471–83. Some Lancastrian reconciliation, increased control of Scotland and Wales until war with Scotland 1482.	1477 Caxton begins printing in French in England, having previously tried printing his English-language Troy translation from Le Fèvre in Bruges. 1479–80 plague in England.	Waurin, *Chroniques* (Brutus 1471) and other continuing French-language engagement with the matter of Britain in Europe and England, alongside English-language *Bruts*. Latin expands its range in administration and in the 1480s takes over functions earlier taken over by English from French.
Edward V, r. April–June 1483		

REIGNS AND TERRITORIES	PEOPLES, EVENTS, LANGUAGES	LITERARY/TEXTUAL PRODUCTION
Richard III, r. 1483–5, m. Anne Neville (d. 1485). Rules England, lord of Ireland. Truce with Scotland 1484.	Continued royal ownership of fine French books.	Little is composed in insular French apart from law texts and some documents. French-language literary culture continues in England in Anglo-French.
Henry Tudor, r. as Henry VII, 1485–1509, m. Elizabeth of York (d. 1503). Rules England, lord of Ireland. Scottish, Spanish, Netherlands alliances.	Royal library remains largely French into early C16th. Latin, French, English court poets. Elite/meritocratic children continue to be taught French, with English sometimes the teaching language (as in Barclay's 1521 *Introductory to Write and to Pronounce French*).	Margaret Beaufort (d. 1509), mother of Henry VII, commissions a French romance from Caxton in 1483. Later she herself translates French devotional material into English.

Bibliographic addenda of importance for language:

Carruthers, M., ed., 2014. *Language in Medieval Britain. Networks and Exchanges, Proceedings of the 2013 Harlaxton Symposium* (Donington).

Durkin, P. 2013. *Borrowed Words: A History of Loanwords in English* (Oxford).

Nissille, C., 2014. *'Grammaire floue' et enseignement du français en Angleterre au XVe siècle: Les leçons du manuscrit Oxford Magdalen 188* (Tübingen). [With thanks to Serge Lusignan for this reference]

Ormrod, W. M. 2003. 'The Use of English: Language, Law, and Political Culture in Fourteenth Century England', *Speculum* 78: 750–87.

Glossary

Introduction

Language History and the Lexis of Literary Discussion

A very high proportion of English lexis comes from Anglo-Norman, and, given the long career of French as a prestigious literary vernacular and language of record in England, it is not surprising that Anglo-Norman has strongly contributed to the lexicon of literary discussion and practice in English.[1] In this Glossary alone, words that entered English from Anglo-Norman (with or without reinforcement from Middle French or Latin) include

accusative, art, author, authority, beauty, cases (grammatical),
chronicle, entitle, interpreters, exemplar, grammar, image,
imagine, language, letter (as written word and as epistle),
manual [handbook], [subject] *matter, missal, music, nominative,*
notary, oeuvre, parchment, poet, precept, preach, preacher,
prologue, prose, psalmody, recite (verb), *record* [verb], *rehearse* [verb],
remembrance, remember, render, represent, rhyme (noun and verb),
romance [language], *rubric, psalmist, science* [i.e. knowledge], *sermon, signify, statutes, treatise.*[2]

The role of England's French in the development of English and of French at large has greatly increased in visibility over recent decades. Studies by Anglo-Norman scholars and lexicographers have long demonstrated the importance of the insular French words not so much 'borrowed' as adapted or shared by early and later Middle English.[3] Online dictionaries now co-operate more closely than ever before, and both the electronic Oxford English Dictionary and the *Dictionaire étymologique de l'ancien français* at Heidelberg take increasingly full account of insular French. Although the online Anglo-Norman

[1] In the first fifty lines of Langland's *Piers Plowman*, for example, W. Rothwell counts 32 important French words ('Introduction to the electronic edition' *AND*). These particular examples of the resources of a multilingual environment are not signalled as 'French' by Langland in the passage, but for illuminating studies of his and other writers' marked code-switching between languages and between varieties of language, see Putter 2011, Machan 1994. The *AND* online estimates that 'Romance vocabulary (which largely means Anglo-Norman) makes up probably 50% of the word-stock of modern English'.

[2] Words also move from Middle English into Anglo-Norman: this is a much smaller category than the traffic from Anglo-Norman into English, though still significant (see e.g. Ingham 2009, Trotter 2012, Trotter 2011b, and http://anglonormandictionary.blogspot.co.uk/2015_02_01_archive.html). For words moving from Anglo-Norman into continental use see Trotter 2008.

[3] Pope (1944, 1–14) cites many fundamental terms from the fields of administation, government, law, land-tenure, social hierarchy, sports, literature and music, church hierarchy and organisation, education, science and arts, architecture, civic organisation, trade, commerce and handicrafts, agriculture, sea-faring, military matters, place names. Further detailed studies from among the hundred-odd articles published by W. Rothwell are available at http://www.anglo-norman.net/articlesA: it is to be hoped that the large bibliography of the late Professor Trotter will join them on the site.

Dictionary (*AND*) is not yet fully revised from a semantic to a historical and etymological dictionary, its citations often antedate older dictionary attestations (sometimes by as much as a century or more).[4] The *AND* thus helps scholars and students of Middle English, Old French and insular Latin to see the nature of the lexis in their texts with more nuance than ever before, and perhaps also to recapture more of the familiarity many French terms must have had for writers and audiences in England and related regions from the twelfth to the fifteenth centuries. The *Middle English Dictionary* (which uses AF for French-derived words and marks some entries as specifically Anglo-Norman, but identifies small proportions of insular to continental or assumed continental French lexis), can also be nuanced through the use of the *AND*.

To say this is to ignore the fuzziness of lexicon, and the way words flow between socio-linguistic networks and have individual histories of naturalisation. Linguists and lexicographers have argued for some time that labelling words as 'French' or 'English' obscures how language behaves, especially in multilingual systems.[5] 'English' or 'French' is what many words have become in subsequent linguistic history, not necessarily how French lexis behaved or was thought of in medieval England. Many of the terms in this Glossary are shared with those of the analogous Middle English glossary in Wogan-Browne *et al.* 1999, which contains a very high proportion of French lexis from varying sources.[6] (A new project, the Bilingual Thesaurus of Medieval England is much to be welcomed as a vehicle for looking at both languages together).[7]

Lists such as the one given above simplify the actualities of lexical history. Merely adding other lists from our Glossary complicates the picture. Some words were present in Old English from Latin, but later borrowed again in their Anglo-Norman form: examples include

> *dialogue, epistle, history, memory, note* (verb), *psalter,*
> *school* (AN *escole*), *scholar* (AN *escolier*), *verse* (OE *fers*).

Other words have not yet had full study, and may eventually have their current

[4] See further Rothwell 1991. In his article on the making of medieval English and Anglo-Norman dictionaries, Rothwell gives detailed exemplification from the letter A of the changes to older dictionaries' etymologies and citations necessitated by Anglo-Norman (Rothwell 2001, 542–53). In an experimental project invited by the *OED* on its 1933 edition, D. W. Russell found that of the 34,729 words entering English between 1100 and 1500, some 32,837, or 95%' were explained as 'derived from French'. Of these, the 32% that continued on into early-modern (continental) French were listed as OFr and about 5% were specifically labelled Anglo-French (Russell 1993). That is, *OED* began to make discriminations between insular and continental French before work on the first electronic edition began, though it tended to underestimate the role of insular French in favour of continental lexis (the earliest attestations of at least some of the 32% extracted by Russell and his team could well have been in insular texts). *OED* currently has a continuing program for revising its French etymologies and distinguishing between Anglo-Norman and continental varieties of French.

[5] See further Rothwell 1998. Trotter 2010 argues for the inadequacy of the term 'loan word' and the inappropriateness of modern concern with language boundaries in the light of the frequently unmarked lexical switches in medieval usage. See also Trotter 2013 for the retrospective nature of our labels 'French' and 'English'.

[6] Of the 40 entries under A in Wogan-Browne *et al.* 1999, for example, 32 are French-derived, or derived from Latin with French reinforcement, and ten of these directly overlap with the present glossary: *abredge, affeccion, adresse, amende, antiquite, assemble, auctor, auctorite, aunter/aventure, avised/avisement.*

[7] Directed by Richard Ingham with Louise Sylvester at Birmingham Central University, UK.

etymologies from continental French (or French and Latin) replaced or supplemented with Anglo-Norman. Possible examples in the Glossary, all of which have earlier attestations in insular than in continental French, include:

> *bible, clerk, compile, compose, composition, devotion, doctrine, document, eloquence, exemplar, exposition, fable, figure* (noun), *grammar, ink, sentence, solace, study* (noun and verb: *estudy* and *estudier), title, translate, translation, volume, vowel.*

Or again, some words circulated in both continental and insular French and in English, including:

> *chapitre, dialectician, doctur, paragraph, rhetorician, scrivener, title*

while still others, such as *scripture, ethimologie, maistre, primer, significance*, are taken into Middle English from Latin but also circulated in the French of England; or, they are reinforced in English by French. For writers of French or English, trained initially in Latin letters and bi-lingual in the vernacular, and/or using French and English for different domains, language difference will have been a matter of fluid shifts and overlaps in registers and code-switches rather than movement from one clearly bounded language to another.[8]

Moreover, a word's subsequent life in a new or shared linguistic system is as important as its origin and moment of adoption.[9] Semantic shifts away from the first meaning(s) of adopted items are frequent, sometimes taking place interlingually through language contact.[10] Many terms in this Glossary, given that they no longer operate within the medieval religio-cultural network, no longer signify in the same way in the modern English with which, in insular culture, they were eventually identified. Although the forms *auctour, auctorité, auctorizer* occur, for example, only once does a vernacular writer refer to himself as an 'author' in our texts (17.35), and he does so as a translator from a Latin bestiary. As is well established for medieval literate production in general, the lexis of author-ity leans rather to source traditions (e.g., the 'Latin book') or to God (see under *Deu, Deus, Dieu, Dieux*), than to individual writers, and the French of England is no exception.

The present Glossary of course makes no claim to full accounts of medieval vernacular lexis in England (on which much research in any case remains to be done). In listing literary and literate lexis, however, it shows, among other things, something of the history of such terms and of the literary preoccupations of their users.

8 Discussing London's Frenches in the fourteenth century, David Burnley argues that 'it is more revealing when considering French influence to attend to the social circumstances in which [French words] were used', and that shifts betweeen English, French, Latin in London documents were not 'considered to be comparable to translation between foreign languages', but were seen rather 'as a code shift': (Burnley 2001, repr. 2003, at 18 and 28).

9 Trotter 2010 notes that first appearances of lexemes have been scholars' predominant focus, while their naturalisation histories have been relatively neglected.

10 The introductions to ANTS editions reveal many varieties of lexical innovation within and between languages: see e.g. Russell 2014, 34–7 for an account of Denis Piramus's borrowings from English and adaptations and resignifications of French of many domains in his *Vie seint Edmund* (see (27)).

The nature and Scope of Vernacular Literary Terms and Discussion

The Glossary can also be used to get a sense of the paradigms and parameters of medieval literate culture, which includes many terms not now deemed part of literary theory and criticism proper. Firstly, in accordance with medieval literary production's highly situated nature (see Introduction, pp. 3–5), the Glossary includes lexis from the social relations and contexts within which medieval texts are produced, performed, and transmitted (terminology which features repeatedly and prominently in our extracts). Secondly, clerical training and practice is important as the formative domain of the professional writers who, together with their patrons, are chiefly responsible for literary as also for all written production. Text-types across the high literary to the documentary and the pragmatic often share terms and tropes in their self-presentation. Administration and bureaucracy are domains to which Anglo-Norman has contributed strongly whether in basic concepts of governance (itself a French term), the lexis of record and memory (both documentary and affective), or the particularities of ink and parchment. Thirdly, the domains of pastoral instruction and practice are important. As clerical productions, texts of this type sometimes overlap administrative technical lexis as for instance the term *notarie*, common both to the material from Brunetto Latini in the London *Liber custumarum* (**8a**) and the *Lumere as lais* (**19**), or words such as *suget* (in the sense of subject matter), *rubriche*, *composiciun*. But insular texts also contribute prolifically to vernacular theology and devotion, often providing lexis that supplements or replaces Old English's reworkings of Latin texts. The *Lumere* (**19**) alone uses, in its entirety, some 161 neologisms,[11] including such important terms as *contempler*, *ymaginer*, and (from the lexis of sin) *capital*, *cardinal*, *circumstance*, *commisiun*, *concupiscence*, *coruptible*, *omissiun*, *reconciliaciun*. Other texts in this volume are equally prolific, notably (**14**), (**22**), (**24a** and **b**), (**39**).[12]

The question of who participates in textual culture, and how, arises sharply around devotional and doctrinal texts: we include terms for the laity's various ways of engaging with texts and authors and for the learning of clerics, the more so as this lexis can have a socio-political edge in medieval use. Devotional texts are strong theorists of the necessity and virtues of translation (see especially Grosseteste, (**5**) for an implied democracy of devotion). Moreover, as St Edmund's *Mirour* (**22**) makes explicit in its discussion of scriptural understanding, talk about texts is an important aspect of how they are known and who knows them. This aspect, as well as the more meritocratic clerisy of bureaucratic and literate culture particularly visible from the thirteenth century onwards, needs remembering alongside the aristocratic aspirations of much of the pervasive discussion of patronage in these texts: as noted in the Introduction, French is both a prestige language and a language of access.

Reading across the Glossary illuminates the vectors of this literary culture. 'Grace', for instance, is no longer part of our literary terminology, but in accounting for his work,

11 See Hesketh 1997 for the complete list of neologisms in literate and technical, theological, devotional, and musical lexis he finds in the *Lumere* (some can now be seen to be further antedated in Angier's *Dialogues* (**24a**)).

12 For the *Mirour de seynte eglyse*'s lexis, see Wilshere 1982, 36–8 (his argument prefers to see the French as inadequate Latin rather than new possibilities in vernacular lexis, but nonetheless provides interesting material on the creation of French contemplative vocabulary).

Adgar/Willelm, writer of the first vernacular miracles of the Virgin (**11a**), sees it as vitally important. A circuit of grace provides both miraculous events and the proper stylistic level of the text presenting them: grace also constitutes the infusing medium uniting the community gathered around the text of the *Gracial*. Pierre de Fetcham shares the model in his large theological encyclopaedia (**19**), as does the anonymous author of the Sermons on Joshua (**23**), who seeks the Holy Spirit's grace for uncovering textual meaning in appropriate Bible exposition. The luminous verse commentary on the Song of Songs (**26**) locates its own existence in the *grace de sa grace* (**26**.151), God's grace manifested through the Virgin. For Angier of St Frideswide, in one of the most extended literary theoretical discussions sampled in this volume (**24a**), an economy of grace is infinite in comparison with that of mercantile exchange, and he seeks as a writer to become a merchant of grace. Grace informs letter salutations (**7c**) and is refracted linguistically in French as 'the most gracious language', designed by God himself (in the claims of the 1396 *Manière de langage* (**7b**)). It is through grace, whether directly from God or as manifested in their relations with each other, that writers, audiences and patrons get their reward for literary, devotional, and other labour, whether material or spiritual (*gueredon*), salvific (*guarison*), or (a pervasive concern and rationale of historical writing), that of being recorded and remembered (*mettre en memoire, en remembrance*). The circuit of grace between clerical writer and institutional or aristocratic commissioner thus provides a model for textual communities constructed around ancestral and lineage pieties as well as hagiographic commemoration.

The Glossary's silences have to be allowed for, as much as its inclusions. The word 'patron', for instance, does not appear: although it entered English from Anglo-Norman, *patron*'s primary medieval senses are 'model, pattern (etymologically a metathesised form of the same word), *plan, design, ecclesiastical land or other owner, captain*' (*AND, s.v.* 'patron'). The word's application to those who accept the dedication of a literary work is a development of the seventeenth and eighteenth centuries. Yet, precisely because patronage is so ingrained a socio-political and cultural relation for medieval texts, its lexis is found in the vocabulary of rank and in salutations addressed to patrons (*dame, ma dame, seignour*) rather than in a category name for patrons of text.

There is also the question of whether there are elements that, as later readers, we might find lacking in this literary discourse. A purely aesthetic sense of literary value might seem unlikely in texts couched in grace, or in the service of God, the patron, the lineage, the institution or community, for instance. Yet pleasure and aesthetics are often present, even if only in order to be dismissed or co-opted (notably in Piramus's *Edmund* (**27**) with its performed replacement of courtly leisure and pleasure with hagiographic textual community). The importance of the aesthetic is confirmed by the hostility of some other texts: Edmund of Abingdon's *Mirour* (**22**), for instance, is stern about elaborate language and the superfluity of all prayer outside the Pater noster (its lucid articulation of the divinely supervised existence within which all human perception and effort is located provides a rationale for this sternness, as much as it does for the anthropocentrism by which it firmly aligns all other creatures to human use). The allegorical sermons on Joshua (**23**) are equally forbidding, but less austere, reprehending pagan and Jewish writings in a luxuriant rhetoric. For sermon 5, these are glittering theft, the gold of Jericho that is both *riwle*, *lange* and *bouche d'or*. Here, not only classical poets and pagans (as in (43)) but rhetoric, philosophy and law are all presented as potentially too seductive.

In our texts then, beauty (*beauté*) is frequently subsidiary to *bonté* (the goodness of God as distributed in creation and other gifts). Yet joy (*joie*), pleasure (*pleisir*), delight (*delit*) and comfort (*confort, solatz*), both earthly and heavenly, are attributes of Christ, his saints, his passion, and audiences' responses to these, and of the texts focused on him, as well as of courtly *lais*, songs, and romance narratives.[13] A single text, the *Enfaunces Jesu* (20b), offers its audiences *profit, desport, bon respit* and *deliz* in its combination of text and images. Desire for more of these things is bred by reading and hearing, especially desire for the unlimited joy of heaven. There could hardly be a more elaborately crafted, aesthetically self-aware and exquisite poem than the expanded passion meditation of John of Howden's *Rossignos* (21), a more inventive, playful and daring re-orientation of the biblical narrative than the *Roman de Dieu et de sa mere* of Herman of Valenciennes (15), or a more thoughtful practice of the relation between style and meaning than the *Poème sur l'Ancien Testament*'s *chanson de geste* vision of the past and its relation to the present (43). While never an independent or self-sufficient good in this literature, aesthetic considerations still play a variety of roles.

The Glossary is necessarily only a selection, and many more terms and meanings of interest are to be found in *AND* (see e.g. entries for 'langage, lettre', 'lettré', 'lettrel', 'lettrure', 'literature'). Reading through the Glossary at large, or pursuing the lexis of particular themes and aspects, nonetheless offers a close-textured experience of literary culture's continuities and changes as well as an indication of the lexical history and significance of England's French.

Glossary Conventions

The Glossary includes all vernacular words in the text selections that could be deemed literary/literate according to the expansive medieval paradigms discussed above. Names of patrons, writers, and titles of works are included in the Lists of Alternative Arrangements of the Entries. Other proper nouns, such as literary and doctrinal authorities or sources, and selected figures referenced in the texts, such as Arthur and Brutus, are included in the Glossary. Latin literary/literate terms follow in a separate list.

Given the orthographic variation of medieval French, Glossary entries usually take as headword the first spelling given in the online *AND* (so, for instance, *loange* (praise) is entered under 'loenge', which also occurs in our texts). Verbs are always listed first in infinitive form; italics indicate that the infinitive does not occur in our selections, and is supplied from *AND*'s principal infinitival spelling. Where relevant, reference to the *DMF* is also noted. Only meanings in which words occur in our texts are given: for further meanings, see *AND* and *DMF*. Verbal nouns are included under present participles and not given separate entries: past participles used adjectivally are likewise normally included under past participles.

[13] On 'joy', an important term in our texts, see further Hans Diller, who argues that the increased lexical distinctions between the state of the experiencer and the nature of the cause by which Anglo-Norman extends English lexis for joy testify to 'the growing importance of the human subject' (Diller 2011, 28).

Citations are by Entry and line numbers, except for (**20a**, **c** and **d**) where numbers in square brackets refer to rubrics or roundels.

1, 2, 3, 4, 5, 6	persons of the conjugated verb	*imper*	imperative
act	active	*n*	noun
adj	adjective	*n pl*	noun plural
adv	adverb	*pass*	passive
adv phr	adverbial phrase	*pp*	past participle
dem pron	demonstrative pronoun	*pr*	present tense
fig	figurative	*pret*	preterite tense
fut	future	*pr p*	present participle
fut imper	future imperative	*refl*	reflexive
imp	imperfect	*subj*	subjunctive
imp subj	imperfect subjunctive	*v*	verb

Glossary of French Literary Terms

abalsamee *see* ***enbalsamer***.

abatre *v* eliminate 24a.223.

abeïe *n* abbey (as production community) 2a.77, **abeie de Berkinges** 2b.18.

abesse *n* abbess (as literary patron) 11b.26.

abregier *v* summarise 20d.82, **abriggez** *pp* abridged (of work of writing) 14.100n.

abuvrer *v* infuse (with knowledge) 7b.*18*.

achaisun *n* reason, occasion (of patron's commission) 13.40, **encheson** circumstances (of context of a narrative) 31.*158*, reason (for writing) 42.19; **enchesons** *n pl* 37.85, 42.49.

achever *v* finish (writing a work) 24a.156.

acordant *adj* in harmony with (of translator's additions to subject matter) 33.76, **acordaunce** *n* concord (unity of a work's sections) 21.*9*.

acquietancez *n pl* acquittals (testifying to acquittance) 7d.5.

acrestre v add to: **acrestrai** (of amplifying literary work) *1 fut* 4.41.

acunter *v* enumerate 32b.42, **acunterent** *6 pret* determined, ~ **houres e jours** (work of computus) 40.50.

acusatif *adj* accusative, **romanz** ~ (of vernacular accusative case as issue of translation) 2a.6.

adeprimes *adv* first, ~ **en latyn** 7d.22. *See also* **primes.**

adrescement *n* list (as part of chronicling) 10.16.

adresser v address: **adresse** *1 pr* (of speech in debate) 44.285.

adubber *v* adorn: **adubbent** *6 pr* (of work with appealing title) 25b.8n.

Aelof Aelof (purported romance about King Horn's father) 6.49.

affectioun *n* affection (aroused by reading or talk about Scripture) 22.117, (as source of prayer) 22.151, **charnele** ~ substitute for devotion (in overly elaborate prayer) 22.143.

afere *n* story, account 20b.27n.

afferir *v* appertain: **afferunt** (of appropriate stage settings) 6 fut 29b.9.

agreer *v* be pleasing: **agree** *3 pr* (of song) 21.93, 115, be pleased 17.16.

aïe *n* help (in composition) from the Virgin 2a.13, (Christ) 21.11, **aie** (the Holy Spirit) 23.6.

aise *n* ease, **loisir e** ~ (for reading) 24a.32.

ajuster *v* gather, assemble: **ajosté** (of verses) *pp* 17.44.

Albine Albina, exiled queen and foundress of Albion, 20d.61, **la royne** ~ 20d.58n.

Alisandre Alexander the Great, 3.107n., 28.R, **Alisaundre** 32a.2, **Alixandre le rei** 28.27n., **Alixandre** 28.29n., 33.2, 11, **Alixandres** 33.5, 26.

alme *n* the soul (writer's) 11a.25, 13.91, 20b.48, (audience's) 14.40, 41, (sustained by spiritual food) 39.86, (languishing without divine teaching) 39.99, ~ **amender** (reader's purpose in using handbook) 24b.54, **l'** ~ . . . **rectifier** (purpose of handbook) 24b.43, **marchëanz**

de l' ~ (purveyors of spiritual meaning) 24a.116, (to be saved by reading) 24a.4, **ton cors e t'** ~ (to be saved by reading) 24a.48, **ame** (its needs met by reading composition) 5.*5*; **almes** *n pl* (of patrons, to be rewarded) 11b.34, (audiences', benefitted by spiritual reading) 39.115, ~ **garir** (purpose of text) 27.64, **noz** ~ (of textual community's) 23.9, ~ **salver** (writer's prayer for audience) 35.46.

amendement *n* (self) improvement (through attention to literary work) 11a.2, 25b.46, (through contemplation of God's world) 22.57. *See also* **mendement.**

amender *v* amend (purpose of devotional information) 22.198, (the soul, through reading) 24b.54, 41.169, (friends, through book) 32b.20, (text) 37.22, improve (writer and audience through writing text) 24a.70, 168, (sin, through reading) 24b.11, 26, (French language or rhyme) 14.71, ~ **sei** improve oneself (purpose of reading) 14.129, **amendez** *5 imper* correct (audience to correct writer's language) 2a.10, **amenderent** *6 pret* improved (narratives) 6.62, **amendé** *pp* improved (by penitential manual) 24b.95, (by writing) 25b.11, (through Jerome's translation) 39.135, **amendez** (audience, by narrative), 19.127, (audience, by proverb) 30.6, (audience to correct narrative) 11b.7.

amer *v* love (of proper response to good narratives and histories) 27.91, ~ **or ne argent** (discouraged by philosophical text) 38.24, **leaument** ~ (learned from Song of Songs) 26.16, (after looking at text) **saver et** ~ 19.146, 148, **vertue** ~ (result of edification) 22.112, **aim** *1 pr* 14.43, **aime** *3 pr* (of cleric's relation to patroness) 39.196, **aimet, molt** ~ (of proverbs) 39.146, **eyme** (narrative) 30.15, **amez** *5* (of audience and secular verse) 14.4, 27.58, 62, **ayment** *6 pr* (response to poetry) 27.41, 43, (response to different genres) 27.51, (fine things) 20d.14, **amera** *3 fut* 30.21, **amee** *pp* loved (of French language) 7b.*25*, (of a story) 6.33, 36, (of Marie [de France?]'s poetry) 27.40, **amees** (of stories) 6.46, **amez** (of lines of verse) 27.33, (text, by ostensibly female addressees) 32b.46.

amerus *see* **mals (des amerus).**

amiable *adj* aimable (of French language) 7b.*26*.

ami *n* friend, **doz** ~ (of Christ as textual *destinataire*) 21.104, **amie** beloved, **ma duce** ~ (of patroness) 6.75, **amye** (speaking person of Song) 26.169; **amis** *n pl*, **mes especials** ~ (writer's target audience) 19.131, **mes tres doulz** ~ (address by writer to audience) 7b.*47–8*, **noz** ~ (kin, whose virtues to be recorded), 42.25.

amor *n* love, ~ **fine** (read in book of heart) 21.103, **amur** (as owed between writer and patron) 40.19, (of God, through text) 19.151, (subject of Song) 26.2, 35, (mode of angelic song) 26.61, **en** ~ (mode of Song) 26.163, 166, **charnal** ~ (not mode of Song) 26.18, 21, **espirital** ~ (mode of Song) 170, ~ **natural** (legitimate love, not mode of Song) 26.22, 23, **par** ~ **en compaigne** love of community (as reason for writing) 12.88, **amurs** (mode of angelic song) 26.57; **amurs** *n pl* **treis** ~ (possible modes of Song) 26.17n.

amunter *v* add up to: **amunte, a bien** ~ *3 pr* (effect of hearing appropriate examples) 27.90.

ancele *n* handmaiden, **cele Deu** ~ (as translator) 2a.99, **une** ~ **al dulz Jhesu Crist** (as translator) 2a.80; **anceles** *n pl* **une des** ~ **Jhesu Crist** (as translator) 2b.18–19.

ancessors *see* **ancestre.**

ancestre *n* ancestor 34.180, (subject of literary commemoration) 27.72; **auncestres** *n pl* 31.*9*, **ancessors** (pagan) 43.27, **auncestres, gestez dez** ~ deeds of ancestors 16.21–2, **ancesurs** 3.1. *See also* **ancienes, foundours, lignage, ligne.**

ancienes *n pl* the ancients 6.55n., **anciens** (of pre-Christian people) 29b.27, ancestors 42.99.

ancïene *adj* (of story) ancient 34.112, **anciens,** ~ **escriz** 1.34n., **remenbrance es** ~ **escriz** 38n., ~ **tens** 4.5.

antiquité *n* antiquity, **livre de** ~ works of classical antiquity 25b.29.

apaier *v* please: **ton quer . . .** ~ (effect of reading) 24a.36.

apareiller *v* prepare: **apareillons** *4 imper* (of stage locations) 29a.3.

apeler *v* name: **apeller** call (of name of book) 16.123, 24b.46, **apelent** *6 pr* (of proverb collection) 39.149, **apelat** *3 pret* **son livre Bible** ~ 39.126, **apeaut** *3 pr subj* 24a.190, **apelerez** *5 fut imper* (of specific title for a work) 11a.46, **apelé** *pp* titled (of Song) 26.117, **apelez** (of book) 25b.58, **apellé** (of a handbook) 24b.R, 41.

apendre *v* belong: **apent** *3 pr* (to a theme or subject) 5.40.

apert *adj* clear, open, **escrist** ~ accessible history 13.6, **franceis** ~ (of French contrasted with Latin) 13.33, **aperte, verité fait tote** ~ completely open (of text's teaching) 24a.210, **apert, en** ~ *adv phrase* openly (how text written) 22.119, (of knowledge revealed) 23.20, **tout en** ~ completely openly (of narration) 41.44, **tut en** ~ 30.75.

apertement *adv* clearly (of *Brut* narration) 6.18, (requirement of translating) 6.80, (of prose's intelligibility), ~ ... **escrite** (correctly written) 8a.82n., 36.32, (of reading well-laid-out text) 24a.45, openly (of St Paul on sincerity) 22.170, **dit** ~ commonly known (of popular sayings) 39.150.

aporter v bring: **aporté** *pp* (of figurative bread of Solomon's teachings) 39.48.

aprendre *v* learn (from stories) 4.2, (a story) 6.81, (French) 7b.*20*, (impossible without God) 11a.17, (Latin) 12.94, (the illiterate may learn) 14.126, (from book) 17.32, (from written text) 24a.17, (by example) 30.2, (from document) 36.10, (of Cato's son) 37.37, (the course of history) 42.60, comprehend (Latin) 25a.40, 25b.15, (of patron's requirement of writer) 40.21, (teach of Christ) 41.100, ~ **medicine** 32a.11, **aprent** *3 pr* (from Latin source) 14.108, (from another person) 14.138, teaches 17.26, 24b.43, 37.38, (prayer) 22.161, **apreng** *2 imper* (to soul) 21.*10, 14*, **aprenez** *5* teach (by dialogue) 22.195, **aprist** *3 pret* (prayer) 22.124, 135, 153, **aprendra** *3 fut* learn 25b.56, (from book of the heart) 21.70, teach 7a.*R.3*, **apris** *pp* learned (French) 2a.9, 7b.*78*, 81, (of King Alfred) 10.32, (by interviewing) 11b.13, (language) 14.72n., 88, (from authorities) 24b.28, 38, (Latin) 25b.1, 42, 77, (medicine) 32b.33, instructed 23.72n., 24a.75n., 39.32, **aprise** (from book of the heart) 21.74, **aprises, letres** ~ (of the Latinate) 25a.1, **aprys** 7a.Pref.let.*11*, **apryz** instructed (in speaking French) 7a.27.

aprise *n* instruction 33.32, **apryse,** ~ **de fraunceys** (teaching text for French) 7a.Pref.let.*10*.

arabic *n* the Arabic language 33.57, 58, 77.

Arabiiens *n pl* the Arabic people 33.63.

araisuner v address, speak to: **araisone** *3 pr* (in a formal dialogue) 24a.216.

arcesveske *n* ~ archbishop, ~ **de Cantebire** (about whom work written) 13.R, (for whom work intended) 13.8.

arguer v argue: **arguez** *5 imper* (in debate) 44.163.

a[r]bre *n* tree [diagram], 20d.31, **l' ... qui ... demonstre et ensaigne** 20d.24. *See also* **figure.**

Aristotele 32.a.1n., **Aristotle** 33.7, 10, 53, **Aristotles** 33.1, 18.

art *n* (academic) discipline, body of knowledge 25b.77, ~ **de kalender** 40.22, 35, **art** *n pl* knowledge 42.11, **artez** arts, ~ ... **del siecle** worldly artifices 23.143, **arz, lé set** ~, the seven liberal arts of the trivium and quadrivium 38.32.

artilus *adj* clever (of clerks) 40.47.

Artur *n* King Arthur 24a.141 (subject of merely fictive stories), **Artus** (king of England) 44.9, (as British, not English historical king) 44.85.

arveire *n* illusion, deception (of poetic subject matter) 27.78.

asavurer v taste: **asavore** *3 pr* (spiritual nourishment) 39.17, **asavoret** 39.24.

ascerine *adj* of steel (quality of speech) 14.112.

asela *see* **ensealer.**

Asemblëor Assembler, Gatherer (refers to Ecclesiastes) 39.159.

asenser *v* instruct 23.2.

aser *v* place (of platforms, in drama) 29b.8.

asient *see* **escient.**

asmer v complete: **esmerai** *1 fut* (the book of the Virgin's life) 15.72.

assembler v assemble: **asemblant** *pr p* compile (of chronicles) 10.18, **asemblé** *pp* gathered 39.123.

assemblee *n* a gathering (of the stories of the Hebrew Bible) 39.127.

assises *adj* expressed, **si bien** ~ (of written words) 23.116.

assuagement *n* relief (of love sickness, through romance narrative) 28.15.

astronomie *n* astronomy (one of seven liberal arts), [**art**] **de** ~ 25b.76.

aturner v interpret: **aturnent** *6 pr* 39.152.

auctor *n* author 17.35, **autour** 19.3, 7; **auctur** *n pl* (canonical Latin) writers 25b.32, **autours** 16.*80*, **auturs** (written authorities) 32b.29.

auctorité *n* authority (God's, for text) 24b.32, authoritative (of well-sourced text) 24b.35, written source (here perhaps both Arabic and Latin) 34.2, **autorité** power 34.148, **autoritei, livres d'** ~ 33.73.

auctorizer *v* authorise (through calendar) 40.56, **auctorizéd** *pp* (of the Anglo-Saxon Chronicle) 10.19, **auctorizez** (of book) 24a.185.

Augustin Augustine (of Hippo) 22.39, 149, **Austyn** 30.7, **Augustyn** (of Canterbury) 31.*101*n.

aumaire *n* chest or cupboard for books and writing materials 41.244n., (*fig.* the Virgin's memory) 21.91n.

auner *v* gather together: **auné** *pp* compiled 18.10.

Austyn *see* **Augustin.**

avant *adv* above (of place in text) 20b.1.

avantdite *adj* (of language) 7e.25, **avauntdite** 8a.88.

aveir *n* wealth (metaphor for spiritual riches) 39.36, 47, 87; **aveirs** *n pl* 39.101.

avenementz *n pl* ~ **futurs** future events (sub-genre of historiography) 16.*101*.

aventure *n* adventure 20d.67, (allegorical narrative) 23.1, **par** ~ perhaps (writer can or will tell story) 22.103, 30.19n.; **aventures** *n pl* deeds 31.*8*, (future) events 4.4, 31.*89*, (worthy of memory or record) 6.32, 57, 73, (subject of historiography) 10.34.

aver *v* have: **orent** *6 pret*, ~ **bone manere** (of the custom of remembering) 6.56, **averunt** *6 fut* possess (a text) 12.91n.

averyl *n* April, ~ **e may** (springtime opening of text) 31.*1*. *See also* **temps.**

aveyement *n* information (gained by seeing text) 8a.63, **avoiement** *n* guidance (for finding book) 41.216.

avisement *n* information (source material) 16.*76*.

avoier *v* guide: **avoiez** *pp* (by book) 41.120.

baptizer *v* baptise: **baptizez** *pp* (of naming handbook) 24b.48.

barnarges *n pl* deeds of noblemen (among subjects for history writing) 3.4.

baron *n* baron (rank to be addressed in letters) 7c.69, (audience for hagiography) 27.84, **la tumbe al** ~ (of saint's tomb, as place for recital of biography) 11b.3, **bier, si noble** ~ (of David) 26.85; **barons** *n pl*, ~ **sains** (of saints, as objects of textual community's service) 25a.24, **seignurs,** ~, **et chivaler** (inscribed audience for chanson de geste) 18.33, **barun** noble (or worthy) man, (as audience for lais) 27.42, 50, **pur le** ~ (commissioned biography in Becket's honour) 11b.26, (as audience for songs and fables) 27.50, **baruns** (source of reward for historians) 3.147, **bers, a noble** ~ (address in prologue) 33.29.

baronesse *n* baroness (address to be used in letters) 7c.69.

bass *adv* softly (of singing) 8b.14.

bastir *v* construct: **basti** *3 pret* structured (of verse) 27.36.

batailles *n pl* battles (subject for historiography) 10.9.

beals *adj* beautiful (quality of hagiographic narrative) 27.82, **bel** (of French language) 7b.*22*.

beauté *n* (rhetorical) beauty, elegance 25b.90, **biaultee** (of French language) 7b.*30*.

Bede Bede the Venerable d. 735 ~ **en Wermouth, . . . q'escrit le liver *De gestis Anglorum*** 16.*65*.

bers, bier *see* **baron.**

besoing *n* need, **le mien e l'autrui** ~ (addressed by the charity of composing a text) 24a.157, **busuin** task (of writing about the Virgin) 11a.74.

bestiaire *n* bestiary 17.Rn.

bible *n* Bible 16.*42*, (of Jerome's translated narratives) 39.126n., ~ **escrite** (in heart of Passion meditator) 21.66n.

bien de Deu *see* **Deu.**

bien *n* value (in literary work) 2a.90, **biens** good deed (done by patroness) 14.87n., property (what a person must share with teacher) 14.140.

bille *n* formal document (complaint about a third person sent to a non-ecclesiastical superior) 7c.3, 12, 24, (document sent by man of no rank to a superior) 7c.94. *See also* **letre, supplicacion.**

blamer *v* blame, **plus est certes a** ~ (of clergy who should know handbook's proscriptions) 24b.87, **blasmer** (of writer) 9.16, **blame** *1 pr* 22.151, 152, **blamez** *5 imper*, **ne me** ~ (of writer, for mistakes in French) 12.34, **blamez** *pp* (clergy more than laity) 24b.84, **blasmereient** *6 cond* (audience's response if writer makes false claims about patron) 39.208. *See also* ***emblasmer***.

Blaunche Launde *n* Waste Land 31.*93*n.

blé *n* wheat (for the host, as spiritual nourishment) 39.2.

boedies *n pl* deceptions, ~ **del siecle** learned rhetorical conceits 23.143.

bonté goodness 22.13 (God's, in creation), 25a.15, 22, **bunté** (God's, to saint's textual community) 2.65, 106, (of monastic patrons) 11b.46, (of Virgin) 26.121, 157.

bourder *v* jest: **burderay** *1 fut* (of poet's work) 27.15.

bretoneis *n* the British language 1.30n.

bretoun *n* the British language, **de ~ en latin** 16.*53*.

briefment *adv* briefly (manner of treating story of world's beginning) 42.70n., concisely 8a.20.

Bruit *n* Brutus (of Wace's *Roman de Brut*) 6.18, 47, 31.47n., ***Brut*** 6.24, 16.*52*, 20d.72, 44.146, **Bruth** 20c.59, **Bruyt** (generic title of histories of Britain) **Bruyt** 16.*107*, **Bruyte** 16.*55*.

Latin *Livre de Tresor de sapience* Brunetto Latini's *Book of the Treasury of Knowledge* 44.242–3n.

Brutus *n* Trojan refugee, legendary founder of Britain 16.*133*, 20c.72, 78n., 83, 109, 112, 114, 20d.36, 57, 76, 78, 31.*47*, *53*, 42.64, 44.101, 101, 108, 110.

busoignus *adj* needy (as condition of preacher) 14.136.

busuin *see* **besoing.**

caroler *v* dance: **carolloie** *1 imp* 8b.5.

cases *n pl* (grammatical) cases 2a.1.

Catun *n* Cato (teaching authority) 37.9, 36, 40.38.

cause *n* cause (of writing, according to Aristotelian literary theory) 19.45, 107.

cel *n* staged representation of Heaven 29b.29, **ciel** 29a.11.

celer *v* conceal: **celé** *pp* hidden (of meaning) 11a.12.

Celeth *n* the Hebrew word for Ecclesiastes 39.155.

cels *dem pron pl* those, **~ que orrunt** (of audience for text) 14.141, (those who do not understand holy scripture) 24a.163, (of those who do not partake of spiritual nourishment) 39.7, **qe ~ qe venissent aprés** (of audience for inscription) 42.11, **a ~ qe dussent vener aprés** 42.21.

cercher *v* search: **cerchez** *5 pr* search (scrutinise source material) 16.*120*.

Cesar Julius Caesar 3.113, 127, **Julles ~** 20d.42n., **Julius ~** 6.7, 20c.103, **Julius de Rome** 6.9.

cesser *v* bring to an end: **cesserai** *1 fut* cease (writing) 20b.27.

chäaine *n* book-chain 10.24n.

chambre *n* chamber (scene of chaplain's writing) 16.*88*, **~ acemee** bedecked (*fig.* of heart, memory) 21.55.

chançon *n* song 8b.11, 15.1n., 18.3, **~ cordial** song from or of the heart 8b.15, **~ de geste e d'estoire** song about heroic deeds and history 14.5n., **chançonal** 8b.23, **chançun** 14.22, 43.14, 26.70, **chanzon** 21.77, 115, **chaunçoun** 8a.80, 86, 94, **~ reale** 8a.84, 95, **chansoun** 8a.68; **chanceuns** *n pl* 27.51, **chançons,** narrative songs **~ de Charlemaigne** 24a.142, **chaunçons,~ roiaus** 8a.70, **chaunçouns** 8a.89, **chançuns** 14.23, **Chaschons, ~ dé Chaschons** Song of Songs 39.166. *See also* **chant, chanzonete.**

changer *v* change: **changerunt** *6 pret* **les languages si ~** 6.44.

chanoines *n pl* secular clergy, **~ de abeies** (as writers of historiography) 10.7.

chant *n* song 8a.90, 26.10, 83, 93, 114, 126, etc., **~ a l'Agnel Deu** 26.108, **Chant des Chanz** 26.38, 62, 116, 117, 153, **Chant dé Chanz** 26.39, 101, 102, 112, **~ de loange** 26.77, **~ de pris** 26.63, **~ de redempciun** 26.99, **haut ~** 26.11, **novel ~** 26.89, **~ Moysen** 26.107, **chaunt** lyrics (of song) 8a.9n., 91, 93, **lung ~** 26.6. *See also* **chançon, chanzonete.**

chanter *v* sing 8b.12, 26.65, (of love) 26.2, 35, (all people on earth) 26.90, (of psalmist) 26.94, (of redeemed community) 26.99, (only by virgins) 26.109, **~ e lire** 12.13n., **en communal ~** 8b.22–3, **chante** *1 pr* 8b.14, **chante** *3 pr* 26.164, (of Solomon) 26.44, (of psalmist) 26.93, (of Virgin) 26.141, 144, 146, 172, **chantent** *6 pr* 26.112, **chauntoient** *6imp* (of nightingales, as locus of poetic invention) 21.*12*n., **chantai** *1 pret* **~ vespres e complie** 41.237, **chanta** *3 pret* (of Moses) 26.77, (of Christ) 26.89, **chanterent** *6 pret* (of figures in Hebrew scriptures) 26.79, 81, (of virgins in Revelation) 26.107, **chanteray** *1 fut* 8b.11, **chanterunt** *6* 26.59, **chanté** *pp* 26.118, 163, 164, **chantee, la messe ~** 41.219, 251, **chaunter** sing 8a.84, 40.1, **chantant** *pr p* 8b.5, 24, **chanter** *n* singing, **bel ~** 14.104n.

chanteur *n* singer (of God's praise) 5.20.

chanzonete *n* little song 21.82, **chanzounete** 21.102, **chanceunettes** *n pl* short songs 27.7.

chapelain *n* chapelain (image of a writer) 16.*89*.

chapitre *n* chapter, 22 opening R, R after 97, R before 120, 24a.29, 34, 44, **chapiters** *n pl* 8a.29, **chapitres** 19.89, 24a.25, **par … ~** 24a.214.

charité *n* charity (audience's in praying for writer) 20b.31, motive for writing 24a.155, **fervour de ~** (effect of religious teaching) 22.118.

Charlemaigne *n* Charlemagne 24a.142, **Charlemaine** 44.231, 246, **Charles, ~ de France** 18.23.
chartre *n* charter 7d.23, 36.*52*, *61*, **chartes** *n pl* 7d.4, **chartres** 42.54, **chartours** 7d.26.
chartuarie *n* cartuary 7d.2n.
Chaschons *see* **chançun.**
chastaine *n* chestnut, *fig.* casing for nut (of wisdom) 39.185.
chaunter *see* **chanter.**
chemin *n* path (of line of narration) 11b.19.
cher *adj* expensive (of poet's reward) 11a.52, **~ tenuez** (how written records should be treated) 42.94, **unt mult ~** cherish (of Marie's lais) 27.41n **cheries** valued, **plus ~ qe . . . les Evangiles** (of romances and *chansons de geste*) 24a.143–4.
cheval *n sg* horse (as reward from patron) 11a.52.
chevaler *n* knight (hypothetical patron) 11a.51, **chevalier** (as recipient of letters) 7c.70, **chivaler** *n pl* (as audience) 18.33, 27.42, **chivalers** (as recipients of letters) 7c.73.
chief *n* beginning of a section in text 24a.226, chapter heading 25b.80, conclusion 25b.117.
chose *n* thing, subject 11a.21, **long ~ a tot deviser** account 35.7, subject matter 26.2, **choses** *n pl* items, subjects 3.9, 7a.R.*4*, Pref.let.*14*, 7c.115, 7d.7, 7e.9, 8a.6, 36, 43, 19.1, 67, 150, 23.19, 24b.3, 31.*10*, 32b.25, 33.79, 35.31, 44.13, 14, 92, 144, 276, **~ novelles** accounts of new things 35.16–17, **toutz ~ continant** containing all places 35.50, **eschoses** 7c.17.
clauses *n pl* lines of verse, **en cinc ~ coplez** five line stanzas 11b.9.
clamer *v* call, name: **cleimet** *3 pr* 39.145.
Clement, seint *n* (subject of biography) 25b.45, 47, 61, 104, ***Livre Clement*** *Clementine Recognitions* 25b.58n.
clerc *n* clerk, cleric 8a.61, 10.16, 25b.1, 11, 13, 39, 38.33, literate person 3.141, (writer's profession) 21.*2*, (*vagans*) 11b.1, (of cathedral school) 38.25, **~ lisant** clerk of record 3.180, **clers** cleric 3.8, 103, 17.34, 24a.195, 25b.20, 22, theologian 13.82, **clerz** (as audience) 24a.1; **clerc** *n pl* (educated persons) 25a.3, clerics 43.32, **~ e lai** clerics and laypeople 4.32, **li bon ~** 10.38, **clercs** 8b.43, 48, **clers** 40.46, **~ e lais** clergy and lay people 13.37, **~ e lays** 13.42, **~ sages** wise clerics 4.21.
clergie *n* learning 5.28, advanced learning, theology 25b.36n, wisdom **de haute ~** 26.10.
cloistre *n* cloister (location for writing) 16.*73*.
coer *n* heart (as organ and site of meditation) 21.26, 63, 66n., **de tot ~** (of full attention in reading) 24a.18, (how one should listen) 15.11, **quer, memorie de vostre ~** (of reading about gods and goddesses) 23.127; **quers** *n pl*, **~ de homes** (as metaphorical field for God's weeding) 23.24–5, **quoers, li froissz ~** (cold heart warms at reading book) 21.72, **quor** 21.10, *12*, 18, 34, **de bon ~** wholeheartedly (how one should pray) 11a.70, **quors** 21.46, 55, **tressalt li ~** (heart's reaction to story) 14.120.
coillir *v* select (from literary source): **cuillerai** *1 fut* 25b.99.
cointise *n* shrewdness (ant's symbolic cleverness) 17.42.
collacion *n* discussion (of sacred writings) 22.109.
colours *n pl* colours (used in manuscript text) 24a.217.
comander *v* order (commission): **cumandas** *2 pret* (by patron) 9.9, **comandé** *pp* required, asked (of writer by patron) 12.83, 40.20, (a work) **comandez** 39.180.
comaundement *n* commandment (to compose) 26.5. *See also* **cumanz.**
començail *n* beginning (of a text) 13.74, **començaille** 17.5.
comencement *n* beginning (of narrative or text) 26.49, 165, 41.3, 8, 17, **al ~ en livre** incipit 19.2, **commencement** (of the act of writing) 15.69, 36.2, **commencemenz** 41.254.
comencer *v* begin (a work) 26.11, **comence** *1 pr* 26.162n., **comence** *3* (a text) 2a.R, 13.R, 17 opening R, 17.1n., R before 38, 19.140n., 41.174, (a poem) 21.1n., 15x2, 24b.R, 42.R, **commençai** *1 pret* 15.71, **comencé** *pp* 12.89, 19.102, **commencer** 24a.155, **commenceras** *2 fut* 15.68.
commun *see* **cummun.**
communal *adj* together, **en ~** mode of singing 8b.22, **cumunal** available to all 11a.36.
communement *adv* communally, publicly (of heard discourse) 22.109.
compaignie *n* company (of writer's conventual companions) 2.31, 12.88, **cumpaignie, sainte ~** (of convent as production site for text) 2a.98.
compasser *v* construct: **compassa** *3 pret* 27.37.

compiler *v* compile: **compilés** *pp* 35.32.
composer *v* compose: **composé** *pp* 24a.166.
composicion *n* composition 19.6.
confession *n* confession (precondition of reading holy history) 41.123.
confort *n* solace, ~ **as tristes** (property of romance narrative) 28.14, **un escrit de** ~ (of philosophical work) 38.4.
conforter *v* comfort: **conforté** *pp* sustained (state of spirit after reading) 14.51, **confortee** (of church, after Proverbs written) 39.82.
conisaunce *n* knowledge, ~ **du course du siecle** (benefit of reading or hearing chronicles) 16.*24*.
conoistre *v* know (through reading chronicle) 16.*10*, **conustre, meuz** ~ **nostre Seignur** (purpose of experiencing text) 19.161, ***se conoistre en***: be an expert in, **se conoisent en** *6 pr* (lyrics and music) 8a.90n.
conseyler *v* give advice (in writing) 37.64.
consonancie *n* rhyme, resemblance of sounds 17.33.
contemplacioun *n* contemplation 22.1, 4, 98, 101, **contemplation** 22.186.
contenir *v* contain: **se cuntenge** *3 subj refl* set within a space 11a.78.
conter *v* narrate 8b.39n., tell, relate 20b.13, 24b.9, **conte** *3 pr* 6.18, 34.27, **contez** *pp* 41.113, **counter** compose (accounts) 7b.80n., 41.44n., **cunter** 3.106n., 11a.31, 24b.30, (writer's name) 24b.99, 40.2, **cunté** *pp* 24b.59, 40.41, **cuntee** recited (of minstrels) 18.5.
controvee *adj* false (of narrative without a written source) 15.12.
controver *v* compose: **controverent** *6 pret* (of narratives) 14.23.
controvure *n* fiction 14.9, 36.
conustre *see* **conoistre**.
cordial *see* **chançon**.
corouner *v* crown 8a.67, **corouné** *pp* 8a.72, **corounee** (with literary-musical prize) 8a.86, 95.
coroune *n* crown (for prince of Puy) 8a.76.
corrigier *v* correct (audience's role in response to text) 20d.28.
cors *n* body, **le** ~ **reheite** (of spiritual food of scripture) 39.21, **par tut le** ~ **decenderai** 32b.22 (ordering principle for information), **cors** *n pl* ~ **garaunter de hunte** (property of saint's life) 27.65. *See also* **alme, primes**.
corteisie *n* courtliness, ~ **seculer** (viewpoint for aesthetic judgement) 39.151, **curteis[i]e** refinement (of language or breeding) 14.96n.
cortement *adv* in brief (of concise translating) 33.81.
counter *see* **conter**.
coupler *v* link together: **coplez** *pp* (of lines of verse) 11b.9.
cours *n* way, ~ **de siecle** 42.12, **du siecle** 16.*24–5*, **et de seint esglise** history of the world and of the holy church 42.61.
esglise history of the world and of holy church 42.61.
court *n* court (as literary venue) 27.5; **curz, riches** ~ *n pl* 27.34.
courtur *n pl* courtiers (as audience) 27.49.
coutel *n* (scribe's) knife 41.250n.
couvenans *n* promise (of audience prayers) 2b.15, **cuvenant** condition (of audience prayers) 2a.73.
coveitus *adj* desirous, **de romanz** . . . ~ (audiences for romance) 28.17.
coverir *v* cover up: **coveré** *pp* (of women's knowledge) 32a.8.
coverture *n* covering (shell of a nut, *fig.* for Hebrew of Bible) 39.187, surface (*fig.*), ~ **de la lettre** metaphorical image, concealing meaning 23.7–8.
creance *n* belief, **parfaite** ~ (appropriate attitude towards holy narrative) 41.4, 79.
Creator *n* Creator (to be served by saint's textual community) 25a.23, **Creatour** (God, as subject matter) 19.54, (in his creatures) **Creatur, al loenge le** ~ (purpose of translation) 2a.11, **loer lor** ~ (task of human language) 5.19, **loange a lur** ~ (of angels) 26.60.
creature *n* creation, the created 19.26, 28, 30, 31, (what book is about) 19.55, 57, (what chapter is about) 22.R, **creatures** *n pl* (subject for contemplation) 22.2, 6, 46, 54, 65, 68, etc.
creire *v* believe (of a text) 24a.14, **creis** *2 pr* (belief in God as pre-requisite for proper reading habits) 17.50, **creit** *3 pr* 26.172, **croiez** *5 imper* 44.94.
crier *v* declaim: **crié** *pp* (of song, sung not declaimed) 26.163.
Cromatïus *n* (bishop) 39.175n.
cronicle *n* chronicle 16.7n., *12, 68, 130*, **[C]ronike** [the *Anglo-Saxon*] *Chronicle* 10.17, **cronicles** *n pl* 16.*20, 77, 117*, ~ **de cest isle** 16.*56–7*, **dé ditz** ~ *77*, ~ **del Grant Bretaigne** 16.*28*, ~ **enrymaiez et en prose** 16.*20*, ~ **petitez**

42.69n., **cronicles** *n pl* **liver de** ~ 16.*56*, ~, **cronicques,** 44.273, **en faire** ~ write chronicles about 44.258, **romains et** ~ 44.264, ~ **Martin** chronicles of Martin 20d.29n., ~ **de Fraunce** 20d.30, **croniclis** 16.*98*.

cronicquer *v* chronicle, **ne sont a reciter ne** ~ 44.266n.

crucifix *n* crucifix (of stage prop representing it) 29a.5, 29b.11.

cueus *n* cook (*fig.* of St Jerome as provider of text) 39.114.

cumanz *n* command (of patron) 9.11; **cumanz** *n pl* commands (of patron) 13.42. *See also* **comander, comaundement.**

cummun *adj* available to all 11a.39. *See also* **communal.**

cumunal *see* **communal, communement.**

cunte *n* count (rank, as exemplary narrative protagonist for other counts) 27.89; **cunt[e]** *n pl* (as audience for narratives) 27.50, 84. *See also* **quens.**

cunte *n* narration 27.66, 40.41; **cuntes** *n pl* 24b.58, 27.51, 40.11, **countes***n pl* **bons** ~ 4.1.

cure *n* attention (of audience to narrative) 30.20, effort (of writing) 33.29.

curteisie *see* **corteisie.**

curteis *n pl* courtly people 27.5.

custus *adj* (intellectually) arduous 25b.88, annoying (property of text) 28.20.

dame *n sg* lady 11a.53, (address to patron) 14.1, 3 (the Virgin, as subject matter) 8b.31, 33, 11a.68, (the Virgin, as destinatrix of text) 8b.37, 40 (the Virgin, as presider over text) 11a.29, 61, 15.72, (the Virgin, as recipient of text) 11a.59, (the Virgin, as intercessor for writer) 11a.82, (the Virgin, visiting writer) 15.48, (as audience for Trota's medicine) 32b.38, ~ **Aline** (patron) 14.1, 73n., ~ **Ysabele** (patron) 13.30, ~ **Mahaut** (leading destinatrix) 11a.65, ~ **Marie** (writer) 27.35n., ~ **Prudence** (allegorical presider over debate) 44.1, 23, 48, 63, 114, 149, etc., **avoee** ~ 13.104n., **ma** ~ **Deonyse de Mountchensy** (destinatrix of text) 7a.R.*2–3*, ~ **que ert Saracine** (as a source of writer's knowledge) 32b.34, **et a** ~ **e as meschine** (as students of medicine) Dame, **honuree** ~ (patron) 13.28, **riche** ~ (hypothetical patron) 11a.53, **nostre** ~ (of the queen of England) 7c.64, **Nostre Dame** (opening prayer to) 7b.*9*, 21.5, **sa** ~ (writer's patron) 39.196, **damme** 39.199, ~ **enseigné e bele** 39.202; **dames** *n pl* (as recipients of letters) 7c.60, (as senders of letters) 7c.75, 107, 7e.10, (conventual ladies, as patrons) 11b.32, (as audience for vernacular doctrine) 24a.151, (as audience for lais) 27.46, (as audience for document) 36.7, (as recipients of text) 32b.45, **nobles** ~ (patrons for history writing) 3.148. *See also* **abesse, femme, seignour.**

Damledé *n* God (as source of scripture) 39.103, **Damnedé** *n* God, **al loënge** ~ **e a s'enor** (purpose of text) 39.193–4, **segrei Damnedeu** 23.13, **Dampnedeu** *n* ~ . . . **et sa mere** (recipients of text) 11a.47. *See also* **Deu.**

declaracioun *n* statement (narration of a story, with legal undertones) 8b.46.

deduit *n* pleasure, (audience's) 27.58, 61, a pleasant tale 28.13, **dedut** (audience's) 27.69. *See also* **delit.**

defendre *v* defend against: **defent** *2 imper,* ~ **ne seit gabét** (of patron's duty to protect writer) 9.14.

defesance[s] *n pl* anulments (legal deed annulling another document) 7d.5.

definaille *n* ending (of a text) 17.6.

definer *v* end: (text) **define** *3 pr* 17.1.

dei *n* finger, **de sun** ~ (how God wrote the Song of Songs) 26.41.

delit *n* delight (for listener from text) 25b.98, 28.8, **a** ~ 14.48, (patron's) 39.211, (from Dame Marie's *lais*) 27.44, **en grant** ~ (heart's reaction to tale) 14.120, **delite** pleasure (in learning British history) 16.*1*n., **deliz** delight 20b.11. *See also* **deduit.**

delitable *adj* delightful, **plus** ~ **a oyr** (superiority of author's text) 27.63, **dilitables** pleasurable (of poems) 27.52.

deliter *v* take delight in (ribald narrative) 22.147, (in narrative) 28.16, **delit** *3 pr* (in spiritual food) 39.18, **deliterat** *3 fut* (in hearing scripture) 39.216, **deliter, se** *v refl* be delighted, 25b.101, **se delite** *3 pr* (with literary work) 21.65, 80, (with contorted rhetoric) 22.144.

delitus *adj* enjoyable (of reading of text) 24b.57, (property of narrative) 28.13.

delivre *adj* skilled (as a result of consulting treatise) 32b.18, **delivres** eager (to teach) 25b.14.

deliz *see* **delit.**

demonstrance *n* demonstration (by text, of truth), ~ **espresse e certe** 24a.209.

demustrer *v* explain 1.41, (reveal patron's name) 6.92n., **demustre** *3 pr* explicate (scripture) 20a.21, prove (by discourse) 38.33.

deport *see* **desport.**

desclairer *v* elucidate: **desclairast** *imp subj 3* (of clerk to patron) 39.198.

descorder *v* be discrepant: **se descord** *3 pr refl* (of separate texts) 37.20.

descrire *v* describe 5.39, 7a.24, 12.14, **descriere** 7b.82, **descrit** *3 pr* 4.34, 25b.62, **descrivent** *6 pr* 23.122, **descristent** *6 pret* (in recounting) 39.122, **descrit** *pp*, **en latin . . .** ~ 4.26.

deshonour *n* (done by inappropriate salutation) 7c.133.

designer *v* signify 39.144. *See also* **resignefier, signifier.**

desir *n* desire (writer's, to compose) 13.72, **de lire duner** ~ give the desire to read 14.102.

desirer *v* desire, **joie** ~ (result of religious teaching) 22.113, **desireiz** *5 pr* (of patron's desire for book) 33.52, **desirroit** *2 imperf* (of knowledge of writer's identity) 2b.7, **desirras** *2 fut* (of reader) 24a.10, **desiranz** *pr p* (for knowledge of writer's identity) 2a.69.

desirus *adj* (of heart, for spiritual meaning of narrative) 28.12.

despendre expend *v*: **despent** *3 pr* (of intelligence) 11a.1, 24a.82, dispense, give (of teaching) **dan Catun** ~ 37.36.

despenser *n* steward (*fig.* of St Jerome as translator) 39.113.

despire v denigrate (of audience response), **despire** *3 pr* 2.89n., (feel contempt for) 20a.2, (of scorn for teaching) 37.89, ~ **ceo mound** (object of studying scripture) 22.113.

despit *n* contempt, **tent en** ~ (of audience reaction) 43.13, **unt en** ~ 40.40.

desport *n* entertainment 20b.10, **deport** solace (given by vernacular text) 38.3.

desputeisun *n* (formal) debate, argument 25b.85; **desputeisuns** *n pl* 25b.74, 25b.96.

desputer *v* debate (with): **disputat (od)** *3 pret* 25b.67, **desputerent (a)** *6 pret* 25b.70.

dessudictes *adj* above-mentioned (in document), **les raisons** ~ 44.78, **les choses** ~ 44.277.

destincter *v* distinguish 26.17, pick out, adorn (elements of text) 24a.214, **destincté** *pp* separated into chapters or parts 19.88, **destinctés** 24b.49.

Deu *n* God (as object of audience's prayers for writer) 2a.74, (as object of clerics' good deeds) 4.18, (as implied entity (patron) who orders writer's work to be done) 5.4, 8, 10, 21n., 25, (writer takes God's seventh-day rest as end of his poem) 5.41, (what scripture says) 9.25, (to whom work should lead audience) 11a.4, 8, (as punisher of a man who does not share his knowledge through writing) 11a.11, 14n., 19, 22, (as source of writer's knowledge) 11a.16, (of being present for writer) 11a.60, (of audience believing in God) 12.1, (as object of writer's prayers for self and/or text) 12.34, 74, 90, 95n., 98, 101, etc., 13.90, 108, 14.86, 90, 92, 20b.40 (to whose honour writer writes) 12.86, 13.71, 96, (about whom writer must speak) 14.118, 134, (as object of audience's prayers for writer) 14.74, 76, 143, (as entity in whom audience necessarily believes) 17.50, 24a.56, 32b.43, (as control over writer's life) 24a.225, (as source of writer's reward) 24b.102, (as source of what writer knows) 24b.31, (as being who makes writing possible) 24b.96, 26.13, (as presider over text) 24b.92, 43.1, (from whom writer seeks praise) 24b.100, **a** ~ **atrere** (purpose of text) 11a.4, **a** ~ **mener** 11a.8, **bien de** ~ (of righteous authors) 25b.32n., (of writer and audience together praising God) 26.59, **a l'honur de** ~ (aim of writing) 12.86, 13.71, ~ **le Pere e** ~ **le Fiz** 5.7, **l'onur** ~ (purpose of staging) 29b.3, ~ **loer** (purpose of speech) 5.21, **la gloire** ~ **enhaucer** (purpose of work) 13.95, **par** ~ (how text to be realised) 24b.103, 25b.114, **la parole** ~ (as metaphorical sword) 23.97, **pur** ~ (purpose of writing) 30.24, **seint** ~ (God's, subject of poem) 9.19, **Deus** (author entreats God to reward his patron(s) or benefactor(s)) 3.173, 176, 10.39, 11b.33, 34, 42, (author wishes God to show him how to exalt his saints) 13.94, (as rewarder of patroness's prayers) 14.82, (as appreciator of a fine spirit over fine writing) 14.93, (in author's prayer) 20b.33, (as source of text's improvement or completion) 24b.96, (as source of King Solomon's writing) 39.75, **deus** *n pl* pagan gods, **lor** ~ **e leur deuesses** 23.123, **Dex** (author's expatiation on humankind's various gifts, to explain why he's writing) 25a.13n., 16, **Dieu** (in whose honour author writes) 2b.1, (to whom author exhorts audience to pray) 2b.16, 27, (as presider over

enough money to hire a scribe) 3.155, (of grant of heavenly life) 2a.101, 11a.84, (writer asks God for abundant food for abbey residents) 11b.35, (may God grant that writer completes work) 25b.117, **dunast** *3 imp subj* (of hypothetical gift from knightly patron) 11a.52, (of hypothetical gift from lady patron) 11a.54.

doulce *adj* sweet (of French language) 7b.*26*, **douces** (of words in book) 41.200, **doulz, ~ françois** 7b.*5*, *21–2*, **doiz** (of scripture) 39.184, **doz** (of book) 21.75n., **duce, ~ amie** (of poet's patroness) 6.75, (of Mary, as a subject of poem) 11a.44, **duces . . . a escuter** (to listen to) 11a.32, **duz** (of spiritual writing) 39.84. *See also* **douçour.**

douçour *n* sweetness (of melody) 8a.96, **dulçur** 11a.50.

doutances *n pl* puzzles 24a.211.

douter *v* fear, **~ peine** (effect of devotional reading) 22.112.

Douze pier *n phr* Charlemagne's twelve peers 18.30.

droitement *adv* correctly (of text for public display) 8a.82.

druerye *n* passionate love, **par ~** (response to text) 30.21.

druz *n pl* sweethearts (as consumers of poetry) 27.8.

dun *n* gift (of work presented by writer to patron) 13.103, (from patron to writer) 11a.55, 11b.32, **dun** *n pl* (gifts from patron to writer), **meint autre ~** 3.175, **duns, beaus ~** 3.148.

duz *see* **doulce.**

ebreu *n* Hebrew (language) 5.18, 39.106, **de ~ translat en latin** 39.120, **l'ebreu** 39.141, 164, **li Ebreu** the Hebrew people 39.121.

ebrieu *adj* Hebrew 39.125.

Ecclesïastes *n* Ecclesiastes 39.158.

edefïer *v* edify 24a.53.

edificacion *n* edification (from God's created world) 22.71.

eloquence *n* eloquence 23.124.

em *see* **hom.**

emblasmer *v* blame: **emblasmez** *5 imper* (audience to attribute textual faults to writer) 2a.95.

enbalsamer *v* make fragrant: **abalsamee** *pp* (of devotional memory) 21.53.

embosoigner *v* to be busy: **enbesoingniés** *pp* (author engaged in other work) 33.62.

emparler *v* tell about: **emparla** *3 pret* 16.7n.

emprise *see* **enprendre.**

enbrever *v* write down, record: **enbrevez** *pp* 39.142.

encheson *see* **achaisun.**

encorder *v* rope around: **se encord** *3 pr refl* (of agreement between texts) 37.19.

encusemenz *n* slander 23.143.

endentures *n pl* indentures (what children will learn to prepare in French) 7d.4, 24.

endire *v* narrate: **endie** *1 pr subj* 17.17.

enditer *v* compose (documents) 7b.80, **endita** *3 pret* 24a.15, **endité** *pp* told 39.47.

endoctriner *v* instruct: **~ autres** (purpose of reading) 14.130.

enfance *n* childhood (of beginning of learning) 10.32, **enfances** *n pl* youth (narrative of), **~ de seint Edmunt** 27.80, (of Christ) 20b.3; **enfantz** *n pl* children (as pupils) 8a.26, **enfés** *n* child (hero of chanson de geste) 14.28n.

enfauncenet *n* the young (of audience for text) 40.61.

enfer *n* hell (stage prop) 29a.9.

enformacion *n* instruction (in clerkship of charters) 7d.29, **enformacioun** 8b.47, (source material) 16.*94*.

enfourmer *v* instruct (in the French language) 7a.R.*5*, **enformer** (in Latin and French charter writing) 7d.3.

engin *n* craftsmanship (writer's) 21.11.

engleis *n* English (language) 1.30, 3.59n., 6.53, **en ~ . . . fetes** (language of stories) 6.41, (of language of book) 10.33n., **englés** 16.*21*, *107*, **engleys** 7a.*7*, 36.*23*, *49*, **engloys** 7b.87.

Engleis *n pl* people 3.53, (appreciators of story) 6.36, (should know French) 7e.13, **Englés** (who loved story) 6.34n.

enhaucer *v* raise higher (saint's fame, through hagiography) 13.27, (God's glory) 13.95, **eshalcerai** *1 fut* (poet's promise regarding patron's name) 11b.30, **enhaunsiee** *pp* raised in esteem (effect of song at feast) 8a.68.

enluminement *n* enlightenment (purpose of text) 19.147.

enluminer *v* illuminate (with knowledge) 7b.*18*, **enluminé** *pp* (song made luminous by exalted subject matter) 18.3, enlightened (by text) 19.142, 151, **enluminez** 19.145, 154.

enmanantir *v* enrich: **enmanantiz** *pp* (with spiritual goods) 39.117.

ennui *n* boredom (effect of reading or hearing read) 14.105, 107, (in reading) 24a.223, (caused by transposed narrative order) 25b.108, ~ **tolir** (purpose of abridging) 14.101.
ennuier *v* bore (what some types of reading do) 14.103, **ennuierai** *1 fut* (author selecting what does not bore) 25b.100, **s'ennuie** *3 pr* (of fine singing) 14.104.
ennuius *adj* boring (of translation) 25b.84.
enprendre *v* undertake 12.43, 24a.153, **enprenge** *1 pr subj* 12.85, **enpreigne** *3 pr subj* undertake (praise of God in composition) 21.12, 16, **empris** *1 pret* undertake (of composition) 40.19, **emprise** *pp* 11a.23, **enpris** (literary commission) 9.9, 12.78.
enque *n* ink 41.249.
enquerre *v* seek (spiritual understanding) 39.189, ~ **la parfondesce** deep meaning 23.12, **enquerum** *4 pr* 26.63, **enqueranz** *pr p* (for divine wisdom) 39.191.
enqueste *n* enquiry, **ententive** ~ fervent questioning 23.71.
enregistrer *v* register: **enregistré** *pp* (of statutes) 8a.60n.
enromancer *v* educate in French: **enromancé** *pp* **poverement** ~ of author, poorly skilled in French 12.38n., **enromancez** translated into the vernacular 14.56.
[enrymer?] put in rhyme: **enrymaiez** *pp* 16.*20*.
ensaigne[r] *see* **enseigner.**
ensample, ensampler *see* **essample.**
ensealer *v* seal: **asela** *3 pret* (of God's placing of Song in Hebrew scripture) 26.40n.
enseigner *v* teach 37.74, (writer's duty to patron) 40.21, **ensaigne[r]** 20d.16, **enseiner** 39.76, **enseigne** *3 pr* 24a.137, **enseingne** *3 pr* 24a.84, 135, (function of book) 19.34, 39, 40, 120, **enseinent** *6 pr* (function of historiography) 42.100, **enseigneit** *3 imp* (of God's instruction of writer) 19.105n., **enseingnerai** *1 fut* 24a.8, **enseignera** *3 fut* (of book's teaching) 7b.*4*, **enseigné** *pp* (of pupil) 7b.*67*, 79, (of patroness) 39.202.
enseigne *n* banner (*fig.*, language) 21.15.
enseignement *n* teaching (of Cato) 37.35, **devin** ~ divine 39.100.
ensensement *n* instruction 16.*67*.
entendable *adj* comprehensible (quality of French) 19.156, (quality of vernacular writing) 24a.162.
entendanz *n* those who understand (Latin) 4.29.
entendement *n* understanding 40.32, **petit** ~ (writer's modesty topos) 20d.28.
entendre *v* hear 4.1n., 20b.11, understand 12.92, 25a.39, 36.9, 32, 39.216, (French) 7e.3, (something read aloud) 14.39, 125, heed 24a.18, listen (to text) 12.93, (scripture) 17.54, 27.59, 67, 85, 37.40, 88, (written matter) 22.105, ~ **a** be attentive to 4.1, **i** ~ 24a.18, **clerc e lai** . . . ~ 25b.40, **lai** . . . ~ (of lay understanding), **a peine** . . . ~ hardly understand (author's modesty) 24a.154, **faire** ~ make understood (of the laity) 25b.15–16, **fait a** ~ explain 33.2–3, **entenz** *2 pr* 17.51, **entendent** *6 pr* 4.22, **bien** ~ (of laypeople) 40.62, **entendez** *5 imper* listen 11a.82, 12.17 **entendrunt** *6 fut* 4.32, **entendant** *pr p* 25b.2n., **entendant** (of audience attention to text) 12.32, **ben** ~ (able to understand scripture) 39.178, **entendu** *pp* 25b.31, **entendue, plus** . . . ~ (of French contrasted with Latin) 13.36, **entendre** *v* intend (of audience) 30.1.
entente *n* estimation (of author) 2b.21, effort (of author) 13.44, 73, intention (of author and patroness) 14.81, 86, (of author) 21.88, 25b.44, 27.20, meaning (of a text) 33.69, mind (applied to composition) 13.73, **ententes** *n pl* efforts (to learn Latin) 25a.2.
entitlement *n* title 19.3, 137.
entituler *v* give a name to: **entitulat** (of text) *3 pret* 39.125.
entrecomuner *v* communicate (by letter) 7e.4n.
entreduyr *v* introduce (to the French language) 8a.20.
entreleis *n* interruption (in writing) 14.110.
entremetre *v* work hard: **entremis** *1 pret* (at literary composition) 11b.12, **s'entremet** *3 pr refl* concern oneself with 11a.9, **se entremist** *3 pret* (undertook writing) 16.*118*.
entrepretours *n pl* translators, ~ **englessés** 16.*83*.
entrer *v* record: **entra** *3 pret* (of property ownership) 36.*43*.
entrescrivent *see* **escrivre.**
enveier *v* send: **envoie** *3 pr* (of song's greeting to God) 21.103.
enveisures *n pl* amusing tales 4.3.
enviouse *adj* envious, ~ **gent** literary detractors 28.18; **enviouz** *n pl* **li felon e li** ~ detractors (of textual work) 41.26–7.
epistle *n* letter 33.4, **epistles** 33.1n., 7, **espitre** 33.27.

epitalamye *n* epithalamium 26.171.
Ercevesqe *n* archbishop (addressee of petition) 7c.49.
errer *v* go astray (in reading) 24a.218.
eschoses *see* **choses.**
eschoteis *n* Scots (language) 1.30.
escient *n* knowledge (women's, of a secret nature) 32a.8, **asient, sanz** ~ specialised knowledge (by-passable with aid of book) 32a.14n.
esclarer v shed light on: **esclairie** *pp* (of revelatory knowledge transmitted through narrator) 41.112, **esclairiez** (of revealing writer's name) 41.16. *See also* **esclarcir.**
esclarcir v make clear: **esclarcirai** *1 fut* (how writer will translate from Greek) 33.68, **esclarzir** *v*, ~ **la resun** 23.4, **esclarzirai** *1 fut* 24a.227, **esclarzi** *pp* 23.10. *See also* **esclarer.**
escole *n* school, **latin d'** ~ educated Latin 7b.*24*, **clerc d'** ~ (of university scholars) 25b.1n., **oscolle** 7b.73n.
escoler *n* scholar (of letter-writer) 7c.28, 98, **escolier,** ~ **de Paris** (how author characterizes himself) 7e.16, **escoliers** *n pl* students 7b.*17*.
escoter *see* **escuter.**
escrier *see* **escrivre.**
escripture *n* holy scripture 17.51, 39.188, scripture 22.3, 99, 187, 25a.28n., writing (the Grail) **seint'** ~ holy scripture 26.66, 41.254, accounts 3.7n., written work 14.35, 54, ~ **devine** 39.91, 217, **escriture, devine** ~ 20a.20, **sainte** ~ 20a.16, 24a.163, **seynt' escripture** 37.21, **l'Escriture** the Gospel 41.105, **escritures** *n pl* writing (God's) 19.94.
escrist *n* a written history 13.6, 24a.14, 37.13, **cest** ~ **orrez** (of recital of text) 12.33, **Escrit** *n* Scripture 30.33, **escript, en** ~ in writing 16.*8*n., **escrit** a written work 11a.27, 46, 47, 12.73n., 89, 14.142, 24a.17, 160, 32a.2, 37, 38.4, 39.137, writing 11a.46, 47, 78n., 26.42, 27.43, 30.6, written source (Latin, possibly and/or Arabic?) 34.11, 36.10, (the work in hand) 24b.2, 12, 52, ~ **seint** holy writing 24a.160, **novel** ~ new (poetical) record 43.9, **escripts** *n pl* writs 7d.4, **escriptz** 7d.23, **escriz** written texts (secular) 3.88, 14.39, (holy writings) 14.62, 26.66, scripture 39.60, 211, **anciens** ~ 1.34n., 38n., **en nos** ~ (of textual sources) 32a.45, **esguardai tuz les** ~ (inspect texts) 6.84n.
escrire *n* writing 19.12.
escrite *adj* written 13.88, 92.
escriture *see* **escripture.**
escrivain *n* writer 41.34, 245, 249, **escrivains** 21.84.
escrivre *v* 1.7, ~ **e dire** write and recount 13.69, 14.110, 25b.38, 79, **fist** ~ cause to be written 10.33, put down in writing 40.6, make a copy 41.246, **escriveré** *5 fut* 7c.31, **escripre** *v* write 20d.15, **escrier** (documents) 7b.79, **escrire** 7e.3, (books) 3.152, 159, 17.8, (French) 3.152, **droit** ~ 7b.*21*, . . . ~ write correctly 7b.*4*, **eust feit** ~ caused to be written down 3.84n., **fist** . . . ~ (caused to be written) 10.37, 39.75, **escrivere,** ~ **estoire** write the history (of someone) 13.23, **escrif** *1 pr* (of composing a history) 43.31, **escrit** *3 pr* 26.168, **escrivent** *6 pr* 25b.9, 32a.33, **escris** *1 pret* 11b.14, ~ **de ma main** (of Christ) 41.123–4, **escrit** *3 pret* 16.*65*, 25b.22, inscribed (on pillar) 42.11, **escript** 16.*75*, *92*, **escrist** 13.7, 20b.29n., **escristrent** *6 pret* 3.103, 10.8, **escrist** *pp* 22.105, 119, 155, 163n., ~ **eu livere** 42.53, **escript** 42.93, **escrit** 2a.84, 3.130, 13.99, 14.21, 60, 15.12, 18.11, 24a.43, 25b.18, 82, 26.41n., 42, (by unspecified authorities) 32a.15, **escrite** (of song text) 8a.82n., ~ **en son coer** (of Bible) 21.66n., 33.75, **escrites** (of king's names) 20c.136, 23.117, 33.75, **escrist** 13.7, **escrivaunt** *pr p* 16.*49*, 62, 72, 89. ***entrescrire, se*** *v* write to one another: **s'entrescrivent** *6 pr refl* 7e.12.
escuter *v* listen to 11a.32, 4.3, (to text being recited) 6.26, **escutez** *5 imper* 11a.63, 26.127, **escuté** *pp* 26.162, **escoter** (task of audience) 40.43, **escotez** *5 imper* 18.33, 4.48, **escoté** *pp* 40.42, **escoulter** 8b.13, **escoulte** *2 imper* 8b.14, **escultez** *5 imper* (author to audience) 15.10, 11, 18, **escouté** *pp* 24a.145, **escoutee** 24a.139.
esdire v express : **esdira** *3 fut* 36.31.
esgarder *v* look at 41.84, **esgardai** *1 pret* (at book or text) 41.174, **esguardai** inspected (of texts) 6.84n., **esgardé** *pp* 41.158, 159. *See also* **garder, regarder.**
eshalcer see **enhaucer.**
eslire *v* choose (in reading) 24a.35, **eslirras** *2 fut* 24a.27, **esleu** *pp* 24a.29.
eslite *adj* rare (of joy in reading) 21.68.
espace *n* space (on the stage) 29b.5.
espaune *n* handsbreadth (as measure of scroll's width) 20b.46.
espeaut *see* **espeleir.**
especial *adj* particular (used of a writer's specific aim in writing a text, i.e., a local objective), ~

fin 19.129, **especiale** 19.122, **especials**, ~ **amis** (for whom text is intended) 19.131.
espeleir v: **espeaut** *3 pr* signify (of work's title) 24a.189.
esperit *n* spirit 41.12, **Saint Esperit** ~ (object of prayer for grace in discerning meaning) 23.5–6, 41.6, 11, **Seint** ~ as power behind composition 5.8, 24a.20, 179, **esperiz li** ~ **vivifie** 17.62, **Seynt** ~ as source of writing's validity 37.30, **Saint Espirit** 20a.15, **Espirz** 24a.16, **la lumere del Seint** ~ 23.9–10.
esperitel *adj* spiritual (of non-literal meaning) 17.57.
espirer v inspire: **espira** *3 pret* inspired (of text) 24a.16.
espitre *see* **epistle.**
esprendre v set fire to: **espreigne** *3 pr subj* 21.16, **esprys** *pp* ~ **en l'amour** (inflamed as result of reading) 21.*13*.
espundre *v* explain 25b.78, **espunt** *3 pr* 20a.15, **espont** (Jerome interpreted) *3 pret* 39.156.
espurun *n* spur (of patron in regard to writer) 13.102; **esperun** *n pl* (to complete writer's gift from patron) 11b.27.
essamplaire *n* source 11a.76.
essample *n* example (lesson learned from texts) 17.31; **essamples** *n pl* 24a.2, **essanple** *n* exemplar 11a.77, **ensampler** *n* exemplar 16.*55*, **ensamplere** 16.*127*, **ensample** *n* example 27.88, exemplum 30.2, ~ **prendre** to take an example (what audience should do) 27.86n.
essuine *n* excuse, **senz** ~ (author will speak truth without giving excuses) 32b.30.
estage *n* stall (in staging) 29b.15.
estals *n* station (in staging) 29a.11n.
Estatuz *n pl* statutes (of London Puy) 8a.50.
estoir *n* chronicle 16.*17*, *130*, story 16.*10*, **estoire** 6.23, 25, 33, 63, 13.23, 32, 92, 22, 18.6n., 10, 21.112, 157, 41.3n., 5, 43.10, 15, 31, 23.40, written source 15.12n., (as a genre of writing) 14.5n., 22, history book 3.149n., ~ **amee** 6.33, ~ . . . **anciene e voire** history, ancient and true 34.111–12, **dreite** ~ 10.21n., **d'une** ~ . . . **parler** narrate a history 6.25, ~ **savoir** 6.23, **si haute** ~ . . . **cele del Saint Graal** 41.24–5, **veil'** ~ ancient history 43.15; **estoires** *n pl* 3.6n., 146n., 39.127, 41.26, 42.99, **granz** ~ 6.40n., **estorie** 4.23, 34n., 6.79, 85n., 28.32n., **estories, veilles** ~ 40.2, **estoyres** histories 27.93, **histories, bonnes** ~ (subjects for genealogical rolls) 20d.15.
estraire v draw out, extract: **estrait** *pp* 2a.72, 14.61, **estraite** 15.2**estret** 11a.37, 43.15, **estrete** (of sources) 24b.34, 43.10n., **estreite** composed (of text) 6.28n., 11a.41.
estudes *n pl* studies, **hautes et profondes** ~ (abandoned in order to carry out commissioned translation) 33.61–2.
estudier *v* give attention to (literary task) 40.17, **estudianz** *pr p* studying (in a book) 7b.*17*.
estudy *n* study (location for writing, perhaps a carrel) 16.63.
estoper v stop: **estuperfolye** (function of narrative) 30.10.
estuper *see* ***estoper***.
ethimologer v etymologise: **ethimologent** *6 pr* (biblical names) 39.160.
ethimologie *n* etymology (of biblical name) 39.162.
Eusebe *n* Eusebius (Jerome) 39.170.
Evangiles *n pl* Gospels 24a.144, **Evvangelie** *n* 22.156, **Ewangele** 20a.23, **Ewangelie** Gospel homily 14.122, 126, **Ewangelies** *n pl* Gospels 14.55.
eveske bishop, ~ **de Nichole** 5.*2*, **evesqe** (as addressee of petition) 7c.16, (how to address in a letter) 7c.106; **evesque** *n pl* **dui** ~ (as *commanditaires* of Jerome's translation) 39.173, **evesques** (as addressees of women's letters) 7c.108, (as subjects of historiography) 10.15.
eveské *n* bishopric (as nodal point in cartography of early England) 20c.9, 11, 14, 20, 24, 26, etc.; **eveskés** *n pl* 20c.145, 148, 156, 163.
excerper v excerpt: **excerpé** *pp* (from Gospel expositions) 14.61.
exposicïun *n* explanation (of Gospel homily) 14.123, **exposicïuns** *n pl* (patristic, of Gospels) 14.57.
expuns *n pl* commentaries, **sainz** ~ sacred commentaries 14.58n.
eyme *see* **amer.**

fable *n* (pejorative) fabulous or untrue story, 14.20, (of chanson de geste) 18.4, 24a.136, **fable** 27.29, (of biblical stories) 43.10, **a** ~ . . . **tenu** (of Pictish language) 1.36n., **fables** *n pl* 40.11, ~ **d'Artur** 24a.141n., 27.51.
faim *n* hunger (absence of spiritual nourishment) 39.1, 96.
fainz *adj* false, **n'est pas** ~ (of book) 24a.174.
faire *v* make 11a.75, 22.77, (what author cannot

do) 2a.4, ~ **rumanz et serventeis** 3.153n., ~ . . . **chartuarie** 7d.2n., ~ **chartes** 7d.4, **ben** ~ 17.32, **bien** ~ (by writing) 8b.25, **livres** ~ 25b.3, teach (cause to learn) ~ . . . **aprendre** 25b.15, (make known) ~ **conoistre** 41.50, 93, 165, ~ **cronicques** 44.258, **fere** create (on the stage) 29b.6, **faz** *1 pr* 11a.27, 56, 59, 12.46, 14.101, 149, 19.92n., 24a.62, 64, 30.24, **fait** *3 pr* 24a.206, 210, **fait a** ~ (of Aristotle) 33.2–3, **face** *1 pr subj* 2a.75, compose 7d.15, 15.1, 3n., 25a.32, (of stage placement) 29.21, (of what writer should not do) 35.6, **face** *3 pr subj.* 11b.5, 12.69, **feisse** *1 imper subj* 14.84, **fist** *3 pret* 2a.76, 79, 2b.14, 17, 19.20, 20b.3n., 24a.178, 179, ~ **lire** 19.11, **en ryme** ~ composed in verse 27.36, **priere qe Dieu** . . . ~ 22.153, **frez** *5 fut* 7c.1n., **fait** *pp* 14.85, (what text made of) 15.19, (of stage placement) 29a.23, 39.25, 123, 139, **faite** (what story is about) 15.20, **fet** 11b.7, **feite** 6.27, **fetes** 6.41, **fez** 11b.6, 21.*10*.

faitz *n pl* deeds, **beaux** ~ (matter for genealogical rolls) 20d.14, **featz** 42.23, **bons** ~ great deeds 42.99. *See also* **gest.**

falseté *see* **fauseté.**

fameiller *v* hunger: **fameillet** *3 pr* (for spiritual knowledge) 39.5.

fausement *adv* incorrectly (of translation) 33.78.

fauseté *n* falseness 43.15, **falseté** falsehood (in literature) 14.18, (of teaching) 24a.136.

fausine *n* falsehood (what reader will not find in the book) 24b.39.

faz, feite, fetes, fez *see* **faire.**

featz *see* **faitz.**

feble *adj* weak (of lay understanding) 40.32.

femme *n* (as translator) 2a.88, (as proprietor of gynaecological knowledge) 32a.8; **femmes** *n pl* (to be given greater reverence than men in letter salutations) 7c.86, 90, **humes e** ~ (as consumers of spiritual wisdom) 39.39, **omes e** ~ 39.102. *See also* **abesse, dame.**

fendre *v* separate (grains of wheat, the spirit and letter of the text): **fent** *3 pr* 17.46, **fent** *2 imper* 17.52, 17.58.

fere *see* **faire.**

ferine *adj* made of iron (quality of speech or writing) 14.111.

feste *n* feast ~, **ne fet ja** ~ pay no attention (to narrative poetry) 30.16; **festes** *n pl* feasts (as sites of narrative performance) 3.6n.

figure *n* symbolism 17.59n., (non-literal) meaning 17.65, diagram 20c.50, 53, **par** ~ allegory 23.1, **prophetizees en** ~ prophesied in figurative language 23.101–2n. *See also* **umbre.**

figuré *adj* foreshadowed (i.e. allegorically prefigured) 43.19.

fin *n* end (of book) 11b.15, (of a sub-section in book) 24a.227, purpose (of book) 19.5, 109, (of God, who perfects book's meaning) 19.111, **une** ~ (of faith in heaven as purpose of book) 19.115, **une** ~ **generale** 19.121, ~ **especiale** (of a particular purpose for book) 19.129, **la propre** ~ (of personal purpose for book) 19.133, **fins** *n pl* 19.113.

finele *adj* final (of the final cause, i.e., the aim of a text) 19.108.

finer *v* bring to an end: **fine** *3 pr* (of narrative) 11b.1, **finerai** *1 fut* (of Virgin's participation in book) 15.69n.

fist *see* **faire.**

fondours *n pl* founding ancestors (to be commemorated in writing) 42.26.

forme *n* form (of work) 19.4, 45.

formi *n* ant (figure of Christian reader) 17.38n., **formie** 17.R.2, **formiz** 17.70n., **fourmye** (useful for edification) 22.71n.

formele *adj* formal, **la cause** ~ formal cause (text's form) 19.45.

forstraire *v* extract: **forstrait,** ~ **d'escripture** *pp* 14.35.

forveer *v* stray: **forveier** (from subject matter) 13.70n.

franceis *n* the French language 3.60n., 6.54, 86, 7b.80, 87, (as used in writing) 14.90, 17.R, **france[is]** 7e.23, **franceis,** (translation from Latin) 13.33, ~ **la parleüre** speak French 14.128, **faus** ~ faulty French 2a.7, **francés** French (language) 1.32, **franceys, en** ~ **dire** 7b.81n., **en latyn [et]** . . . **ensemblement** 7d.6–7n., **en latyn et puis en** ~ 7d.28n., **franchois** (translated into) 33.59, **fraunceis** 16.*21*, 19.156, **fraunceys** 7a.*R.4*, *R.6*, *Pref.let.10*, **françois** 7e.9, ***Donait*** ~ (title) 7e.19, **droit** ~ correct French 7e.3–4, **droite nature de** ~ 7e.13–14 **fraunczoys** 7a.23, **Franceis** *n pl* the French (people) 3.70, 75n.

frechement *adv* freshly (of maintaining cultural memory) 42.13n.

frer *n* friar ~ **cordeler** Grey friar, Franciscan (image of a writer) 16.*38*.

funder *v* ground: **fundé** *pp* grounded (in learning), well educated 25b.12, **fundez** 25b.36.

fourmer *v* devise: **furmerent** *6 pret* (a literary work) 14.24.

gabeis *n*, **ne le tenez a** ~ don't laugh about (possible audience response) 15.25.

garantie *n* protection (function of devotional work) 21.97.

garder *v* look at: **gardai** *1 pret,* **gart** *3 pr subj* 41.134, (at book) 41.161, **gardast** *3 imp subj* (at book) 10.25, **gardera** *3 fut* 41.132. *See also* **esgarder, regarder.**

garir *v* heal: **almes** ~ (function of narrative) 27.64, **guarist** *3 pr* (what spiritual nourishment does) 39.21.

gemmes *n pl* gems (of knowledge, wisdom) 39.40, 101, 110, 111.

genealogy *n* lineage, **la** ~ history 16.*136*.

generale *adj* general (used of a text's general aim) 19.121.

gent *n* people (of audience) 29a.25, (about what people call proverbs) 39.149, ~ **de religion** (who write books) 42.32n., **bone** ~ (people who will pray for author) 19.18, (who will be improved by book) 126, **tote** ~ (who pay attention to writing) 37.39, for whom book intended 14.150, (audience for play) 29a.25, 29b.35, **bone** ~ **senee** audience 11a.63, **franke** ~ **honoree** 18.1, 14. 610n., **laie** ~ of audience 24a.151, 40.25, 31, **laye** ~ for whom work was written 24b.91, **male** ~ subject of text (the Jews) 20b.13, **la riche** ~ book patrons 3.163, **tute** ~ (who understand French better than Latin) 13.37, (who should be edified by writing) 19.126; **genz** *n pl* people (improved by book) 25b.34, (those improved by moral story) 30.5n., **petites** ~ **e des granz** greater and lesser people (as appreciators of text) 6.37, **bon[e]s** ~ (who should like edifying stories) 27.91.

geste *n* narration of great deeds 40.1, poem 43.9, story 30.15n., (Solomon named in) 39.51n., tale, narrative 3.82, 104, 145, **chançon de** ~ **e d'estoire** 14.5n., ~ **de Alexandre** 28.R, **Geste Dan Tristram** Deeds of Sir Tristram 14.31, **gest** set or account of events 16.*134*, ~ **de Troy** 16.*42*, **gestes** *n pl* 3.5n., 82, 104n., 145n., histories 27.93, stories (the Hebrew people's) 39.122n., histories 6.53n., **gestez** memorialised deeds, ~ **dez auncestres** events in lineage histories 16.*21*, ~ **des Englessez** 16.*29*, **gestz dé Bretouns** deeds of the Britons 16.*55–6*n. *See also* **estoir, histories.**

geter *v* throw: **gettent** *6 pr* ~ **penser** to cast out sorrow (therapeutic function of poems) 27.53.

Giu *see* **Jues.**

goliardrie *n* debauched language 22.148.

governeor *n*, ~ **de veritei** (address to Aristotle) 33.9.

grace *n* grace, (God's, needed for text to succeed) 19.163, ~ . . . **cumunal** (in textual and other communities of miracles) 11a.36, ~ **fine** (attribute of Virgin and writing about her) 11a.42, **la Deu** ~ 11a.43, **la** ~ **del Seint Espirit** (needed for appropriate exposition of text) 23.103, **la** ~ **Seint Espirit** (needed by writer) 27.23, ~ **seinte** (ultimate source of writing on miracles) 11a.37.

Gracial *n* title of work refracting grace 11a.35, '**Graciel**' (as spelled in text itself) 11a.45.

gracious *adj* gracious, **la plus** ~ (of French language) 7b.*22*, **graciouse** epithet in letter salutations 7c.26, **tresgracious** 7c.97.

gramaire *n* Latin 34.10.

gramarïens *n pl* grammarians 24a.195.

gré *n* will 39.215, **a** ~ willing (of audience, to listen) 26.127, **de** ~ willingly 27.47, **en** ~ graciously (how Virgin should receive song) 21.81, **grez** grace, favour (as a return for literary labour) 32b.45.

Gregoire *n* Pope Gregory the Great, d. 604 (patristic authority), 22.150, 24a.183, 224, (authority in dialogue) 24a.205, **Gregorie** 30.7.

grejous *adj* burdensome (of reading) 24a.223.

grezeise *adj* Greek 39.157.

Grigois *n pl* Greek people (obscure in their way of speaking) 33.31.

griu *n* the Greek language 33.27, **gru** 5.18.

guarder *v* preserve (beauty of Latin) 25b.90, keep (narrative order) 25b.105, (beauty of women who are audience) 32b.19.

guarisun *n* reward (from saint to hagiographer) 11b. 37.

guarist *see* **garir.**

gueredun *n* (what patroness will receive through poet's praise of her) 11b.29, **gerdun** reward (God's, to hagiographic patron) 13.109, **gueredon** (God's, for poetic and other service) 25a.26, **guerredun** (to soul of writer 11a.25, **mal** ~ (for unused talents) 11a.13.

guereduner *v* reward: **guerredunast** *3 subj* (of literary devotional labour) 11a.72.
guisches *n pl* (rhetorical) ruses 23.142.

hair *v* hate (of sin) 22.111, **hayr** (of exempla) 24b.60.
hastivement *adv* hastily (how not to read) 24b.51.
hautes *adj* ~ **et parfondes** lofty (of studies) 33.60.
Helïodorus *n* bishop 39.176n.
herdue *adj* prickly (of chestnut casing, in metaphor for knowledge) 39.185.
Higden, Ranulf *see* **moigne de Cestre**.
histories *see* **estoir**.
hom *n* man, **sains** ~ (subject of biography) 2b.10, **em** 5.*4* (reader), **home** (as subject of treatise subdivision) 19.24, **bon** ~ **de maistre** (apprentice master of a child with some French) 7b.*66*, **grant** ~ (subject of biography) 2b.22, **saint** ~ **noble** 2b.3, **O, tu** ~ (apostrophe to audience) 17.50, **homme** (as contemplator of God) 22.R.1, (audience for improving narrative) 27.66, 67, (excluded from gynaecological knowledge) 32a.7, ~ **ben chevalerus** (audience for Alexander narrative) 28.16, **simple homme** 7c.91, ~ **ove petit enformacion** (as audience of treatise) 7d.30, **hommes, jeofnes** ~ **de savoir** (modesty topos of treatise writer) 7d.8, **home** *n pl* **fiz de gentyls** ~ (object of language instruction in French) 7a.R.*5*, **hommes, touz hautz** ~ all noble men (appropriate audience for chronicles) 42.94, **humes,** ~ **e femmes** (consumers of spiritual wisdom) 39.39, **omes,** ~ **e femmes** 39.102.
honor *n* honour (to Christ, at poem's end) 21.109, **honur** (creator's, as object of translation) 2a.12, 13.71, (honouring of saint) 12.47, (of God) 12.86, (from monastic writer to patron) 13.52, (to God, in angelic song) 26.59, (to God, in biblical paraphrase) 43.6, **onour,** ~ **d'estiel** style (of a rank's title) 7c.95, **onur, en l'**~ **Deu** purpose of dramatic representation 29b.3, **pur s'** ~ (of Becket's sister's commission to biographer) 11b.26, **honneurs** *n pl*, **departir les** ~ (mode of debate) 44.161, **honours** (to spiritual daughter in archbishop's lettter) 7c.113. *See also* **deshonour**.
honourable *adj* ~ **seignour** (salutation to archbishop of Canterbury) 7c.48, (to Chancellor of Oxford University) 7c.51, (to Prince Edward) 7c.80, (to a bishop) 7c.105.
honurer *v* do honour to (saint, through writing) 12.51, (God and saints) 13.94, **honure** *3 pr* (of images in relation to text) 20b.6. **honouré** *pp* (letter salutation to pope) 7c.45, **honoré** (a function of song at feast) 8a.68, **honoree, franke gent** ~ (in opening address to audience) 18.1, **honuree,** ~ **dame** (address to patron) 13.28, **onuré** (of writers of historic deeds) 3.143, **tres** ~ **mere** (letter salutation from prince to mother) 7c.88, **treshonoré** 7c.100, 109.
hoster *see* **oster**.
houche *n* chest (for documents): **la commune** ~ company's record chest 8a.61n.

***image*, ymage** *n* icon 34.68, 78, 126, 135, 182, ~ **de main ovree** man-made 34.85, ~ **de . . . sainte Marie** icon of the Virgin 34.68–9, 118–19.
imaginer *v* imagine: **ymaginé** *5 imper* figure forth (audience response) 16.*102*.
incarnacion *n* incarnation (Christ's, as subject matter) 19.65.
intrepreteison *n* meaning (of what it is to conduct formal dialogue) 24a.198.

jaiole *n* gaol (stage prop) 29a.7.
Jerome Saint Jerome, d. 420, **seint** ~ 23.128, **Jeroimes** 43.12, **Jeromme** 39.156, **Jerommes, sainz** ~ 39.108, 140, 169.
Jesu *n* Jesus (as subject matter) 20b.2, **a** ~ **prie** (activity of writer/artist in image) 20b.47, **Jhesu** (prayed to for pardon by writer) 11b.5, (to be prayed to for writer/artist) 19.19, 20b.31, (greeted by writer in conclusion) 101, (dishonoured by elaborate language) 22.133 (figured by holy prophets) 43.19, ~ **Crist** Jesus's handmaiden, as translator) 2.*19*, (prayed to for textual community by writer) 11b.21, (whom text seeks to please) 14.50, (as subject matter and source of text's organisation) 19.25, 36, 42, (as subject matter) 21.*4*, (as teacher of the Pater noster) 22.124, (glorified in vernacular poem) 26.36, ~ **et de sa mere** (as subject of biography) 15.21.
joie *n* joy (to be shared by saint's textual community) 2a.67, (what reading of book is) 21.68, (Jesus, destinataire of song) 21.110, (through reading Christ's book) 41.10, 13, 136, ~ **as dolerus** (property of romance narrative) 28.14, **de** ~ (how the Virgin will sing) 26.172, ~ **de**

l'ame 41.138n., ~ **desirer** (outcome of Bible study) 22.113, ~ **plenere** (writer to share with saint) 12.70, **joye**, (response to poetry) 27.47, ~ **espirital** (response to song) 8b.18.
Juerie *n* group of Jews on stage 29a.15.
Jues *n pl* Jews 26.136, **Giu** (as subject of text) 17.64, **Giuz** 20b.17, 25.
jugliere *n* minstrel 24a.145, **jugelours** *n pl* minstrels 18.5.
juger *v* judge, **chaunçouns** ~ (of song contest) 8a.89.
justez *pp* joined (of verses) 27.11.

kalender *n* calendar 40.22, 55.

labur *n* (textual) task 40.17, work (effort of writing) 30.12n.
lai *n* laypeople (not to be addressed with Latinity) 14.68, 70n., 25b.10, **lai** *n pl* (illiterate) lay people 25a.9, 39, **clerc e** ~ 4.32, **lais** (intended audience of text) 19.140, 157, **a** ~ (element of title) 19.156, **clers e** ~ 13.37, 19.154, ***la Lumere a*** ~ (title) 19.140, 141, 157, ~ **ou clerz** (address to audience) 24a.1, **pur** ~ (target audience) 19.158, (not Latin literate) 43.31, (of audience for doctrinal text) 24a.1, **leis, plus i ad** ~ **ke lettrez** 4.27.
laie *adj see* **gent.**
laisir *n* leisure (for the work of reading) 24a.21, **loisir** 24a.32.
lairai *see* **lesser.**
langage *n* language 3.53, 5.23, 7a.R.*6*, 19.159, 33.32, **langgage, prendre . . . a** ~ begin to learn a language 7a.22, **language** 7b.*23*, 7e.22, 25, 25b.33, 94, **droit** ~ **du Paris** 7e.20–1, **maniere de** ~ language manual 7b.*3*, **languages** 11b.10; **langage** *n pl* 5.17, **langages** *n pl* 4.22, 13.99, 22.145, **languages** 6.44.
lange *n* tongue 26.12, language ~ **de latin** 40.57, ~ **romaine** romance language 24a.161n., ~ **tut ascerine** tongue of steel (of author) 14.112, **langue** tongue 21.15, **langue** language 14.72n., 39.165, ~ **de cuer** (for narrating holy book) 41.125, ~ **icele [langue]de la boche** (of the mouth, inadequate for holy book) 41.126, ~ **de romance** French 8b.45n., **grezeise** ~ Greek 39.157, **launge** 13.36; **langues** *n pl* **mortelx** ~ 41.86, **une grant mervaille de** ~ 41.92.
languir *v* languish (spiritually): **languist** *3 pr* (of soul, without divine instruction) 39.99, **languireit** *3 cond* (consequence of lacking spiritual food) 39.96.
larrai *see* **lesser.**
larrun *n* thief (of one who conceals knowledge) 11a.14n.
latin *n* Latin (language) 2a.5, 72, 4.26, 28, 35n., 5.18n., 11b.19, 12.94, 108, 13.*R*, 33, 14.63, 70n., 86n., **de** ~ **en romanz . . . tresturnee** (translated from Latin into French) 15.63, 25a.40, 25b.82, 87, 89, 92, 33.58x2, 39.112, 120, 159, 164, (as target language of translation) 16.*53*, ~ **d'escole** (acquired through formal schooling) 7b.*24*, **de arabic en** ~ 33.57–8, **en** ~ 16.*9, 21*, **leur** ~ (as specialised professional language) 8b.44, **metre de** ~ **en romanz** translate from Latin into French 34.7, **latins** 13.38, 24a.42, 25a.38, **latyn** 7d.6, 28.
latineis *n* Latin (language) 1.31.
latinerie *n* Latin (words or phrases) 14.68n.
launge *see* **lange.**
leçoun *n* reading 8b.43, **leson** 21.68, **lesson** 40.39, **lezçun** 14.121, **lesçuns** *n pl* readings 14.100n.
lectre *see* **letre.**
lectrure *see* **lettrure.**
legierement *adv* easily (of audience learning) 20d.32.
legistres *n pl* lawyers, **science . . . de** ~ legal learning, laws 23.112.
lei *n* law ~ **de la cité de Lundres** (what writer will show) 1.8, (God's, as witnessed by Solomon) 39.77, (God's as witnessed by Christ) 23.68, **lettre de la** ~ (of Hebrew scriptures, imaged as scabbard to sword of God's word) 23.98, **la noeve** ~ the New Testament 30.39, **loi** procedure, ~ **del dïaloge** (how to be conducted) 24a.200–1, (of religious doctrine and practices) 25a.3; **leis** *n pl* ~ **de la cité de Lundres** 1.42–3, (what King Alfred has put into writing) 10.35.
lerrai *see* **lesser.**
lesçuns, leson, *see* **leçoun.**
lesser *v* leave (abandon writing) 26.8, **lairai** *1 fut* omit 33.79, **larrai** leave out (material from source text) 25b.95, **lerrai** abandon 20b.25, 28n., **lerrum** *4 fut* (of what will not be talked about) 24b.70.
letre *n* meaning (of written source) 34.8, **en** ~ **mis** put into writing 9.10, 12, **lettre** letter (as opposed to bill or petition) 7c.2n., (man of lowly status writing) 7c.94, **manere de . . .** ~

(how letter to be written) 7c.122–3, **la dos de la** ~ (as place to inscribe monastic house of recipient) 7c.127–8, story 20b.1, 29, (text honoured by images) 20b.6, ~ **oscure** (of text of scripture) 24a.164, literal meaning (of Hebrew scriptures) 17.53, 56, 58, 61, 65n., **coverture de la** ~ (literal meaning) 23.7–8, ~ **de la lei** (of the Hebrew scriptures as metaphorical scabbard to the sword of God's word) 23.98, **lectre, la** ~ **duwe** (what the mouth says) 22.164n., **letre** *n pl* letters (of text) 41.159, 161, **letres, qui n'ont** ~ **aprises** 25a.1, **lettres** (general term for written communications to specific people) 7c.18, (from lords) 7c.71, (from ladies) 7c.75.

letré *n pl* literate person (educated in Latin) 25a.9, **lettré** *adj* 24b.79, **guere** ~ (writer's modesty topos) 12.37n., **lettrez** *n pl* 4.27, 25b.26, 35, **nun** ~ (illiterate) laypeople 14.126, 25b.15. *See also* **clerc, lai.**

lettroun *n* writing desk 16.90n.

lettrure *n* learning 25b.12n., 26.37, **lectrure** Latin (literacy in) 5.28, **lettr[e]üre** ability to read letters 14.127.

leüe *see* **lire.**

lezçun *see* **leçoun.**

lignage *n* family (as commissioners of charters) 42.48.

lire *v* read 10.25, 14.4, 48, 53, 102, 129, 20d.25, 24a.39 (King Alfred's chained book) 10.38, 14.53, 118, (in God-directed research) 19.11, 41.156, ~ **a delit** (of Gospel expositions) 14.48, ~ **a festes** 3.6, **a** ~ **grejous** (of potential boredom in reading) 24a.222, **aprendre e** ~ 6.81, **chanter e** ~ (about saint) 12.13n., ~ **et escrire** (French) 7e.3, ~ **le funt** (cause to be read aloud) 27.44 **oïr e** ~ 14.4, **oïr ou** ~ 24a.39, **ot** ~ (hear read aloud) 38.2, **oyez . . . lire** 38.40, **quy l'orent** ~ 20d.24–5, ~ **l'orrunt** 11a.86, **lyre, entendre e** ~ 37.88, **lise** *2 imper* 24b.52, **lit** *3 pr*, **la lesson** ~ 40.39, **ot e** ~ 39.212, **lisum** *4 pr* 3.118, **lisét** *5 pr* 24b.40, **lisez,** ~ **les poetes** 23.122, **quant vus mun nun** ~ (writer to audience) 12.101, **lyceȝ** *5 imper*, **mé preceps** ~ (Cato to son) 37.87n., **lisaunt** *pr p* 24b.57, **list** *3 pret*, ~ **a la tumbe al barun** (of biography read aloud at Becket's tomb) 11b.3, **leue** *pp* (of song) 21.116, **lit** 2.83, (annually, in the church) 43.11, **litte** 3.8, **lirras** *2 fut* 24a.9, **lira** *3 fut* 21.*13*, *14*, **liront** *6 fut* 20d.25, **lirrunt,** ~ **e . . . l'orrunt** 25b.102, **orrunt . . . e . . . lirrunt** ~ 14.141–2, **lise** *1 pr subj* 21.75.

lirre *n* reader 24a.218.

lisant *n* reading 3.126, **clerc** ~ 3.180n., **lisantz** *n pl* readers 35.35, ~ **et oïantz christens** 35.44–5.

liu *n* place (station in drama) 29a.17, space (of composition) 11a.2n., **sun** ~ (of a book) 10.26, 29b.17, **lius** *n pl* stations (in drama) 29a.4n., 29b.8.

livre 2a.83, 2b.14, 25, 3.141, 165, 7b.*17*, 17.5, 10.17, 11a.33, 35, 19.2, 7, 12, 23, 29, 24a.9, 32b.17, etc., **enregistré en un** ~ 8a.60n., ~ **fet par dulçur** (of devotional writing) 11a.50n., (Latin as source text) 25b. 61, 62, 80, 82, 99, 104, 33.52, 187, 243, 252, **livre Aristotle** 33.52–3, ~ **Bible en apelat** 39.126, ~ ***Clement*** 25b.58, ~ ***du governement des rois ou des princes*** 33.*54–5*, (of *Mirror for Princes* genre), ~ ***du Songe du vergier*** 44.244n., ~ ***de Tresor de sapience*** 44.242–3, **meint** ~ 10.33, 36, ~ **nommé le Brut** 44.145, **seint** ~ 24a.188, **un** ~ **Aristotle** 33.25, **un** ~ **engleis** (about the English) 10.7, **livres, cestes** ~ 21.*8*n., **uns** ~ 25b.57, ***li . . . de saynt Nicolay*** 25a.R; **livre** *n pl*, ~ **d'antiquité** (patristic learning) 25b.29, **livres** 3.5, 104, 152, 15.54, 19.86, 25b.3, 7, 13, 18, 25, 33.25, ~ **d'autoritei** 33.35, ~ **escrire e translater** 3.152, ~ **ke li Ebreu firent** 39.121, **livrez, en sis** ~ **ordinez** 19.52, **liver** *n* book 16.*41*, *56*, *65*, *68*, *77*, *94*, 17.26, ~ **de cronicles** 16.*56*, **livere** literary work 6.89, 19.20, (of chronicle) 42.R, 32, ~ **des conquerors** 42.53, **livers** *n pl* 16.*9*, *37*, ~ *de cronicles 20*.

livret *n* little book 21.88, 97n., 40.38, 62, 41.131, 151, 161, 187, 243, 252, **liveret** *n* little book (of source) 19.101, written history 13.74n.

loange *see* **loenge.**

loer *v* praise, 5.19, 21, **loee** *pp* (of Marie de France) 27.39, **loez** 25b.20, **loëz** 27.34.

loenge *n* praise 11a.49, (of God, reason for writing) 12.86, 26.141, ~ **le creatur** (motive of composition) 2a.11, ~ . . . **de Dieu** 2b.1, (of the French language, designed by God in his own honour) 7b.*27–8*, **loange** (of God by poet) 21.16.

loi *see* **lei.**

los *n* praise (for written work) 14.87, ~ **del siecle** worldly praise 25b.6.

loyer *n* **luier** (as writer's reward) 11a.74.

luer *n* (desired by writer from God) 24b.100n.

luier *see* **loyer.**
lyre *see* **lire.**
maistre *see* **mestre.**
maisuns *n pl* buildings or divisions of the stage 29b.9, **mansions** 29a.4, 29a.10.
mals *n pl* misfortunes, ~ **des amerus** (of love troubles relieved by narrative) 28.15n.
manant *adj* wealthy (through textual feeding of spiritual goods) 39.102.
manantie *n* possessions (of a spiritual nature) 39.33.
manere *n* mode (in which a text is arranged) 19.47, (in which story is told) 29a.1n., **maniere, oscure ~ de parler** way (how writer sees writing by Greeks) 33.65.
manger *n* nourishment (from holy books) 39.98, 114, **mangers** 39.11, 93, **mangiers** 39.82.
manger *v* eat (wisdom of holy books) 39.184. *See also* **maschier.**
maniere *see* **manere.**
manifester *v* reveal (of text) 41.45.
manuel *n* handbook, **Le ~** (of book to be held in the hand) 24b.41, ***Le ~ dé pechez*** 24b.47.
marchëant *n* merchant (metaphor for didactic writer) 24a.125, **marchëanz** *n pl* 24a.113.
margaries *n* pearls (of wisdom) 39.89.
marge *n* margin (of page), **en la ~ escrit** 24a.43.
Marie *n* Mary (mother of Christ, dedicatee of poem) 21.81, (as singer of Song on her marriage to Christ) 26.172, **Ave ~** to be said by audience 19.22, **Dame ~** (writer's name [Marie de France?]) 27.35n., **la miracle de . . . ~** subject matter 34.5, **seinte ~** (her love as subject of poem) 26.6, 35, **une ymage de ~** 34.69, 119, (as mother of Christ in opening invocation) 36.3, **Virgine . . . ~** 26.120, **Virgine ~** 26.172, **Maries** *n pl* (the Marys) 29b.14, **les treis ~** (in dramatic representation) 29a.20n.
Martin, croniques ~ chronicles of Martin (Martin Polonus, Martin of Opava, Dominican and chronicler, d.1278) 20d.30n.
maschier *v* chew (texts of spiritual nourishment) 39.16.
Maslot *n* Proverbs (Hebrew) 39.143.
master *n* master (teacher) 7b.79n.
matire subject matter (of written work) 5.40, 13.70, 19.4, 23, 36, 24a.221, 27.28, 30, 33.33, 36, 38.39, theme 17.7, topic 14.116, **hastiver la ~** move the story along 4.39, **m[ati]er** 16.8n., **matere** 22.190, **matir** matter (of material for text) 16.*16*; **materes** *n pl* 22.193n., **matires** subject matter, ~ 21.8.
may *n* May, **averyl et ~** (Springtime opening of text) 31.*1*.
medlure *n* mixture, **bele ~** (of text-image relations) 20b.7.
melodies *n pl* melodies (as necessary part of song) 8a.96.
memoire *n* memory (record of supporters for written work) 3.150, (of the passion) 9.53, **aiez en ~** remember 15.13, **des vertuz . . . la ~** (of the recorded version of miracles) 24a.206, **dignes de ~** (worthy of chronicling) 44.252, **en ~ metoient** committed to memory 6.59n., **~ d'omme** (within living memory) 44. 29, 37, **~ perpetuel** (of Round Table) 44.17, **metez la ~** memorise (narratives) 14.6, **mettre en ~** (of recording written history) 13.24, **neufve ~** (recent memory) 44.41, **memore, . . . venent en ~** (come to mind) 7a.Pref.let.*12*, **memorie, veignent en ~** 7d.13, **frechement en ~** (of inscribed pillars to remind the future and Adam) 42.13, **en** (in the (collective) memory ~ 4.24, **~ de vostre quer** (heart's memory) 23.127, **mettre en ~** put on record 30.8n.; **memoires** *n pl* record(s), subject of biography 10.22, **memoyres** (of audience) 27.94.
menceonge *n* falsehood (of *Partenopeus de Blois*) 27.29, **mençonge** 24a.136, **mençunge** (of biography) 11b.15.
mençoun *n* mention, **point de ~** (of omissions for brevity's sake) 35.6, **mention, n'en font nulle ~** (English chronicles, of King Arthur) 44.273.
mendement *n* improvement (of audience) 19.130. *See also* **amendement.**
mendis *adj* in need (of nourishing wisdom) 39.12.
mener *v* lead 11a.8 (of writer guiding audience), ~ **vie penuse** (of writer's toil at writing) 11a.24.
men[e]strel *n* minstrel, **ton ~** (of poet's relation with Virgin) 21.84.
mention *see* **mençoun.**
mentir *v* lie (of authors of *chansons de geste*) 14.14, 16, (author's claim to audience) 15.34, 24a.178, 39.207, **ment** *3 pr* (in literary composition) 14.34, **mentirai** *1 fut* (of writer) 15.47.
mentur *n* liar (discredited writer) 40.10.
mere *n* mother (of Edward I) 21.*2*, **signe teynt de la ~** heraldry of Sir Thomas Gray's mother

(part of cryptogram) 16.12, (of Christ, in text's second invocation after Trinity) 7b.*10*, (as mother to the true faith) 8b.35, (co-receiver with Christ of text presented by author) 11a.48, (co-dedicatee) 11a.57, (as maternal and virginal singer) 26.146, **de Jhesu e de sa ~** (subject matter) 15.21, **del lignage de sa ~** (subject matter) 15.22, **~ Jesu** 11a.81, **~ e . . . duce amie** (source, with Christ, of grace in poem) 11a.44, **~ Marie** (destinatrix of audience's prayer for writer) 12.103, **Miere, ~ de Dieu** presented with poem as rent 21.85; **meres** *n pl*, **les seintes ~** (as Old Testament singers of Song) 26.145.

merite *n* merit (from looking at a book) 21.65, 77; **merites** *n pl* (of Saint Edward) 2b.5.

merveille *n* wonder (as opposed to miracle, unworthy subject matter) 24a.208, (of Virgin birth) 26.147; **merveilles** *n pl* (of subject of book) 35.2, **a merveilles** *adv phrase* marvelously (how stories are told) 44.265.

meschine *n* young woman (hypothetical patron) 11a.53, 32a.12.

mesprisiun *n* fault (of style) 14.91.

message *n* messenger (of Solomon and God's word) 39.27.

messal *n* missal 21.62.

mester *n* need (of the soul) 5.*5*.

mestier *n* task (of writing Virgin's life) 15.65.

mestre *n* master of letters or theology (representation of author) 16.*50*, **~ de devinité** 16.*116*, **come ~** (of author) 19.92, **mestres** 40.39, **maistre** (title for writer) 3.158, 44.241, **bon home de ~** good professional man 7b.*66*, **noble ~ de droiture** (address to Aristotle) 33.9, **~ Tomas** (witness to miracle of Sardenai) 34.88, **Granz Maistres** (who placed book) 41.152, **mestres** *n pl* teachers (diocesan constitutions, as authorities on what writer records) 24b.28n., **sages clers et ~** (the learned) 33.34.

mettre *v* place, put (into written composition), **~ en escrit** (in writing) 42.23, **~ . . . en estoire** (in historical writing) 3.149n., **~ en memoire** 13.24, **en memorie** 30.8n, **latin ~** 14.63, **met** *3 pr* **~ en escrit** 41.16, **metterai** *1 fut* (into the text), 13.73, 33.34, 36, **mettrai, ~ en escrit** 25b.97, **mettray** (said of what will be put in the book, or not) 24b.33, 37, **mettrum** *4 fut* 24b.17, 58, 103, **mist** *3 pret* translate 39.164, **mis** *pp* 11b.4, 8, **~ en escrit** 23.*2*, **en livere** 42.32, **~ son non** 41.32, **mise, ~ en escrit** 41.31, **~ en translatiun** 25b.86, **mises en ~** 35.32, **misez, ~ en françois** 7e.9.

meule *n* marrow (authentic core of work) 33.38.

mi, en ~ *prep* in the middle (where Galilee should be situated on stage) 29b.32.

miracle *n* miracle (example of virtue for readers) 24a.3, (subject matter) 34.4, **miracles** *n pl* (subject matter) 11a.67, 25a.36, 27.81.

moigne *n* **moigne de Cestre qi escript le *Polecronicon*** Ralph of Higden(Benedictine author of *Polychronicon*, d. 1364) 16.*75*n., **~ noir** Benedictine (image of an writer) 16.*62*, *72*, **moines** *n pl* monks (as writers of historiography) 10.7.

montrer *v* show: **monstreré** *1 fut* (one character to another) 44.26. *See also* **moustrer**.

monument *n* representation of Christ's tomb (stage prop) 29a.6, 29b.12.

monumenz *n pl* muniments 36.*37*, **munimentz** 7d.27.

moralité *n* interpretation (of event or text) 24a.3, 138, **moralité** *n* moral lesson 17.29.

mot *n* word, **~ a ~** (way of translating) 34.8, **~ a ~** (mode of searching a book) 24a.46, **motz** *n pl* words (of text), **biau ~** fine words 4.40, **moz** 13.7.

mours *n pl* customs, habits (of animals, as moral lessons) 17.27, **bons ~** virtues (exemplary matter for historiography), **~ de noz amis** (of our ancestors, as material for book) 42.25, moral behaviour (learned in books) 24a.11, 37.61.

moustrer *v* demonstrate, **~ sa bonté del sens** (of writer's responsibility to use intelligence given him) 25a.15, **~ son savoir** 25a.21, **~ la loi** (explain the law) 25a.3, **mustrer** tell 1.11, 3.101, 6.6310.10, clarify 14.124, show 24b.66, show off (learning) 25b.5, demonstrate 38.21, tell 6.63, (set out history of Britain) 1.19, expound 32a.10, **mustre (bien)** shows clearly *3 pr* 38.5, **mustrent** *6 pr* (what the book shows) 24b.50, **mustrasse** *1 imp subj* 6.80, **moustrast** *3 imp subj* (how to read) 24a.219, **musterai** *1 fut* 1.7, 40.14, **mustree** *pp* 25b.92. *See also* **demustrer**.

mucier *v* hide: *pp* **muciee** (of wisdom) 39.105, **muciét** (of wisdom) 39.36.

muement *n* changes (of language) 3.12.

mu[e]t *adj* mute (writer's state if knowledge unused) 11a.10.

munimentz *see* **monumenz.**
muser *v* mull over (difficult material) 40.29.
musike *n* music (knowledge of, for Pui judge) 8a.90n.

nature *n* nature, **droit** ~ true nature (of French) 7e.13–14.
neïer v clean: **neïat** *3 pret* (of gems representing spiritual knowledge) 39.111.
noble *adj* noble (of French language) 7b.23, (of patroness) 39.202.
nobles *n pl* noble people, ~ **qui ayment beaux faitz . . .** (of audience) 20d.14.
noël *n* kernel, ~ **de noiz** *n* meat of the nut (spiritual knowledge) 39.183.
nombrer v number: **nombrez** *pp* ~ **en ordre . . .** (of chapters) 24a.26.
nominatif *adj* nominative, ~ **en latin** Latin nominative case 2a.5.
non *n* name (writer's) 2a.10, **nons** 2b.21, **num, sun** ~ **ne vult dire** (of writer's preferred anonymity) 2a.81, **nun** 11a.35, 24b.99, 39.125, **nouns** (name of treatise) 5.3, **nouns** *n pl* names (material for historiography) 20c.136, 42.24. *See also* **numer.**
normand *n* Norman (as language) 1.32, **normonde** *n* 7b.87.
Normans *n* Norman, **jou sui** ~ (writer's self-identification) 25a.31, **Normanz, li** ~ (soubriquet of writer) 17.36; **Normant** *n pl* (etymologised as coming from the North) 3.65, 73.
norreis *n* Norse (language) 3.59.
note *n* melody 8b.16, **notes** *n pl* notes (of song) 8a.91.
noter *v* make marginal *notae* 24a.217, **notez** *pp* noted (in *capitulum*) 24a.25.
notour *n* scribe, notary 19.10.
numer *v* name 39.168, **ne me vuel . . .** ~ *refl* (of writer's preference for anonymity) 6.87, **numet** *3 pr* 39.174, **numad** *3 pret* 39.143, **numat** 39.155, **nomout** *3 imp* 39.167, **numé** *pp* 39.166, **numez** 11a.45.
numpueir *n* (writerly) inadequacy 2a.95.
num *see* **non.**
nutable *adj* noteworthy 27.21.

obli *n* state of forgetting, **en** ~ **mise** forgotten 17.43, **ubli, ne me mettez en** ~ (writer's request to audience) 12.96.
oblier *v* forget (lessons taught) 17.63, **ublier, funt ires** ~ (function of entertaining verse) 27.55: **ublié** *pp* 3.129, **ubliees** (events not recorded) 3.9.
obligacions *n pl* bonds (documents) 7d.4.
oelz *n pl* equivalencies (corresponding words in French) 4.37n.
oïantz *n* listeners *n pl* 35.15, **lisantz et** ~ **christens** 35.44–5, **oïanz** 2a.85.
oilz *n pl* eyes, ~ **de quer** *lit* eyes of the heart (compassion) 23.52, ~ **espiriteus** *lit* spiritual eyes (spiritual discernment) 23.33.
oïr *v* hear 4.46n., 6.52, 11a.33, 11b.17, 12.12, 13.46, 14.4, 18, 39, 15.16, 21.94, 25a.8, 25b.47, 28.26, ~ **retreire e recunter** 27.92, ~ **ou lire** 24a.39, listen to 25b.44, **oyer,** ~ **et entendre** 36.9, **oyr** 4.6, 27.63, 66, 87, **out** *3 pr* 42.97, **ot,** ~ **lire** (hears read aloud) 38.2, 39.212, **oyez** *5 pr* (of listening for scriptural discussions) 22.110, ~ **le romanz lire** 38.40, **oez** *5 imper* 17.36, **oï** *1 pret* 41.213, **oïstes . . . parler** *5 pret* (heard said) 39.83, **oïrent** *6 pret* 25b.66, **orras** *2 fut* (song) 8b.16, **orét** 13.88, **orra** *3 fut* (a text or story) 6.24, **orrez** *5 fut* 12.15, 31, 33, 15.10, 18.3, 26.127, **orront** *6 fut* 41.113, **orrunt** *6 fut* 2a.86, 2b.24, 11a.86, 11b.16, 25b.39, 102, **oï** *pp* 5.37, (as a manner of gathering material) 41.56, 42.93, **oïe** 20b.1, **oiez** 42.94, **oÿ** 19.128, ~ **avez la matire** 38.39.
oïr *n* hearing (of literary work) 21.80, **oyr, si de l'**~ **seit amendé** (of text) 24b.95.
Olivier *n* Oliver (in the *Song of Roland*) 24a.171n., 44.250n.
onour, onuré *see* **honor, honurer.**
opposant *n* interlocutor (in formal dialogue) 24a.203.
opposer v put questions: **oppose** *3 pr* 24a.193.
or *n* gold (metaphor for Hebrew wisdom) 39.182, **riule d'**~ golden rule (stolen) 23.108n., worldly learning 118, 140, **l'**~ **de Jerico** classical poetry (despised by God) 125, **une bou[ch]e de** ~ golden mouth (what may have been stolen) 23.135, **por** ~ 136, **pur** ~ 142, **fin** ~ 146, ~ **fin** 148.
ordeinement *n* ordering (God's, of world and book) 19.41.
ordener v reckon: **ordeinerent** *6 pret* (systematising of time) 40.48.
ordiner v order: **ordiné** *pp* (of book) 19.38, **ordinez** (of book's purposes) 19.114, **en sis livrez** ~ 19.52.

ordre *n* (chronological) order 25b.103, 109, 112.
orent *see* **aver.**
oreisoun prayer *n* 22.136, 154, **orison** 22.129, 130; **oreisons** *n pl* 34.103, **oreisouns** 22.152, **multiplicacion de** ~ 22.141–2.
Orose *n* Orosius d. 420, priest and historian 20d.30n.
oscurcir *v* hide: **oscurcirai** *1 fut* (how writer will translate perceived verbosity) 33.67.
oscure *adj* difficult (quality of text) 24a.164, **oscurs** (quality of language) 24a.42.
oscurtei *n* obscurity (of Greek writing) 33.67.
oser *v* dare: **osa** *3 pret* (of female writer) 2b.29.
oster *v* delete (from literary work) 11b.15, **hostent** *6 pr* (of text's therapeutic action on sorrow) 27.53, 56, **ostai** *1 pret* (of errors in text) 11b.14.
overaigne *n* literary work 17.10; **overaignes** *n pl*17.3, **overaine** 12.85, **uvraine** 11a.23.
overtement *adv* 7d.28 clearly (of writing documents).
ovre *n* literary work 2a.12, 4.43, 12.78, 27.20, 58, **oevre** 21.*15*, 27.76, 85, **overe** 5.3, 26.58, **ouvre** 40.19, **uvre** (of sharing one's knowledge) 11a.3; **oeveres** *n pl* deeds (of ancestors) 42.98.
ovrir *v* create: **overe** *3 pr* explain 26.168, **overé** *pp* 32a.7 revealed, **overte** (of textual mystery) 41.112.

paier *v* to be pleased: **paez** *pp* (of Christ's approval of text) 14.50 (*see MED, s.v.* 'pai(e)').
pain *n* (bread as spiritual nourishment) 39.2, 24, 48, 93, **vif** ~ living bread (the host?) 39.85.
paistre, paist etc. see pestre.
palefrei *n* palfrey (poet's reward) 11b.27. *See also* **cheval.**
pane *n* writing pen 41.249.
pape *n* pope (as addressee of letter) 7c.15, 41, 43, (of St Gregory) 24a.183n., (of St Clement) 25b.R, **papes de Rome** *n pl* (as subject of chronicle) 42.77–8n.
parcenurs *n pl* partners (of audience) 35.39.
parchemin *n* parchment 25b.81, 41.249, 252.
pareiller *v* prepare: **pareille** *2 imper* (write the Virgin's story) 15.54.
paremplir *v* fulfil: **parempli** *3 pret* (of Christ and the old law) 23.39, **paremplireit** *3 cond*, ~ **la lei espiritelment** 23.68–9.
parfere *v* complete: **livere** ~ (of text) 6.89, **parfeire** 14.145.
parfondement *adv* deeply (below surface of text) 17.67.
parfondes *adj* deep (of study writer engaged in) 33.29.
parlement *n* speech exchanged (in formal dialogue) 24a.192.
parler *v* speak (write about) 2b.11, 3.105, 4.8, 6.25, 7b. *21*, *80*, 8b.*31*, 70n., 21.71, 22.190, 197, 26.12, 31.*11*, 32b.41, 39.83, 41.94, 235, (French) 7e.3, (about the saints) 25a.4, (about Mary) 26.14, (of the Greek way of speaking) 33.*65*, **droit** ~ speak (good French) 7b.*4*, ~ **latinerie** use Latin 14.68, ~ **de** speak about 4.8, 35.4n., **oï** ~ heard about 34.123, **parle** *3 pr* 44.R, **parlons** *4 pr imper* 44.31, **parluns des gestes** 3.82, **parlans** *pr p* 26.169, **parleré** *1 fut* 44.201, **parlerai** 34.171, **parlast** *3 imp subj* (in formal dialogue) 24a.220.
parler *n* speech (French) 7b.*23*, (the angels') 7b.*29*.
parleüre *n* manner of speaking 14.128.
parlire *v* read through 24a.22, **parlit** *pp* 24a.30.
paroïr *v* hear (text) to the end 24a.22.
parole *n* word, (Christ's) 21.12, (petition of the Pater noster) 22.166, (divine voice in dream) 41.70, **a bref** ~ 20b.28, **cest** ~ **'salutz'** 7c.132, **duce** ~ 26.166, **en** ~ speech 7a.27, **la** ~ **Deu** 26.128, (in metaphor, naked sword) 23.97; **paroles** *n pl* 7a.Pref.let. *12*, 33.64, 41.17, ~ **rimeiez** 22.134n., **Paroles** (meaning of Hebrew title) 39.144n., **bones** ~ 33.71, **bones** ~ . . . **douces** (in Christ's little book) 41.199–200n., **breves** ~ 7a.Pref.let.*10*, **metterai autres bones** ~ (translator's protocol) 33.71, **moutz de** ~ (not good in prayer) 22.157, **ne mie lur** ~ (of not translating literally) 33.69–70, ~ **beles e dorees e colorees** (of pagan learning) 23.113–14, **si bien assises** ~ (of pagan eloquence) 23.116, ~ **en corte veritei** (of Arabic language) 33.64n.
part *n* part (of speech) 2a.2, **de l'une** ~ *prep phr* on one side (of stage) 29b.25.
Partonopé *n* romance of *Partenopeus de Blois* 27.25n.
partie *n* part (of text) 19.49, part (of a book) 24a.226, (of hidden wisdom found by writer) 39.37, 88, **bele** ~ generous portion (of learning) 39.34; **parties** *n pl*, 19.49, ~ **principals** principal parts (of a book) 19.51, 85.
partir *v* divide: **partit** *3 pret* (a book) 24a.224.

pas *n* step, ~ **por** ~ step by step (of reading) 24a.46.

passer, se passer de *v refl* do without: **je m'en passe** *1 pr* pass over (subject matter) 44.262.

passiun *n* saint's martyrdom (as subject matter) 12.21, 109, **passion** (Christ's, as subject matter) 19.66, **passïun** (Becket's, as subject for versifying) 11b.36.

paume *n* palm (of writer holding book) 20b.45, ~ **d'un home** (size of book) 41.116.

Pater nostre *n* Lord's prayer (subject matter of chapter) 22.R before 120, 121, **la douce** ~ 22.123–4, 127, **multiplier la** ~ (unnecessarily elaborate praying) 22.167, ***Pater noster***, ~ **dire** (said for writer) 19.22, (audience's reciprocation for virtual participation in writer's pilgrimage) 35.38.

patriarches *n pl* patriarchs (history of) 43.16.

pecché *n* sin 19.33, 22.64, ~ **hair** (aim of edification) 22.111, **peché** (subject matter) 24b.55, **dire le** ~ 24b.8, **hayr** ~ (what exempla teach) 24b.60, (clerical knowledge of) 24b.78, 80, **pecchez** (subject matter of book) 19.58, **pechez** *n pl* ~ (subject of manual) 24b.30, **pechez** ~ **enseigne** (of teaching sins in order to avoid them) 19.39, (inexhaustible) subject matter 24b.9, (sins pardoned as writerly reward) 20b.34, subject matter to be authorised 24b.33, content of text 24b.45, **amender de** ~ fruit of using manual 24b.26, ***manuel de*** ~ title 24b.R, **Manuel de** ~ title 24b.47, ~ **rehercer** 24b.72, **pechés** (content of particular paragraphs) 24b.50, ~ **amender** object of reading 24b.11, ~ **mortaus**(subject matter) 24b.19, **pechiez** (pardon for, sought as writerly reward) 11a.26.

pecchere *n* sinner, ~ **plus que autre** (of writer) 23.10–11, **pecheor, au plus** ~ **de toz** (of writer) 41.2, **pecheur** (of writer) 12.39, 15.44, **pechur** (of writer) 11a.82, **pechere** (of writer's youth) 27.1, **freles et** ~ (condition of hagiographer) 12.39; **pecheors** *n pl* 41.48, **pecheurs** 19.43, **pechierres,** *adj* **li plus** ~ (of writer) **de touz** 41.47.

pees *n* quiet (required of audience)18.1, **peis** (established among spectators) 29b.36.

pelice *n* cloak (writer's reward) 11a.54.

pener *v* strive (through writing) 11a.7, **se pener** *v refl* take pains to, **me . . . pener** ~ (to write) 20b.14, **me penay** *1 pret* 27.9, **se pena** *3 pret* 27.27.

pensee *n* thought 19.11, meditation (as genre of poem) 21.*1*, *6*, passion meditation 21.52n., 54, 94; **pensees** *n pl* 20a.7.

penser *n* passion meditation 21.21, 31, 44, 60, 63, *etc.*, **gettent** ~ (function of poems) 27.53, **hostent le** ~ 27.56n.

penser *n* 12.41, 21.2, 19, 41.173, **pensers** 21.25, (as a sword) 40, (as singing) 55, **pensiers** 21.31.

penser *v* think (at length prior to writing) 3.151, (*v* or *n*, precondition of writing) 5.2n., **sanz vus** ~ **ne l'os** (work unthinkable without patron's support) 14.88, (instruction to audience) 22.37, 196, (of recall) 36.*10*n., 41.136, **pensez,** *5 pr* ~ **de l'escoter** (injunction to audience) 40.43.

pensive *adj* preoccupied (writer's state prior to dream vision) 16.*25*, *31*.

penuse *adj* painful, ~ **vie** life of toil (in writing) 11a.24.

perograffer *v* arrange in paragraphs: **perograffé** *pp* 24b.56.

perograffes *n pl* paragraphs 24b.49.

persone *n* persona (in a dialogue) 24a.215; **persones** *n pl* 24a.199, (of voices, in the Song) 26.169.

pestre *v* nourish: **paist** *3 pret* 39.108, **peüt** *pp* sated 39.95, **peüe** (with what Jerome wrote) 39.133, ***se paistre de*** *v refl* partake of: **s'en paist** *3 pr* (spiritual nourishment) 39.4, **se paisse** *3 pr subj* (partake in spiritual nourishment) 39.5.

philosophe *n* philosopher (of Aristotle) 33.53, **philosophes** *n pl* 23.112, **les errurs de** ~ 23.131, **philosophre** *n* philosopher, **le sage** ~ 7b.*44*n., **Philosophie** *n* personification 38.29.

picteis *n* Pictish (language) 1.30, **Picteis** (people) 1.17, 34.

pielers *n pl* pillar (as textual medium) **piliers** 42.8, 10, 20.

piere *n* 7c.44, 48, 110 term of address to a holy father, **Deu le Piere** God the Father 22.9, **Dieu le** ~ 22.125–6, 136, **Nostre** ~ (words of prayer) 22.128.

Piere *n* St Peter (Apostle), **saint** ~ 24a.146, **Pierre, saint** ~ 24a.148, **seint** ~ 25b.53, 63, 71.

Pierres *n* Peter the Deacon (junior partner in St Gregory's Dialogues) 24a.203.

place *n* space (a cleared space centre stage) 29a.22, 29b.6, 32.

Plaidëor *n* Preacher (refers to Ecclesiastes) 39.161.

plaire *v* please (of author pleasing God) 14.146, 34.9, **pleire** (female audience) 27.46, **plaist** *3 pr* **qu'il luy** ~ (of God and enlightenment of students) 7b.*15*, **si Dieu** ~ (of book's completion) 15.72, **quanque te** ~ (of reader's choice) 24a.39, **plest,** ~ **oïr** (of audience) 13.46, **si lour** ~ (of listeners, politeness formula) 35.35, **se vus** ~ (of audience) 24b.21, **si Dieu** ~ (of book's completion) 35.42, **si ly** ~ 24b.92, **pleisent** *6 pr* (of new subjects of writing) 35.17.

pleinte *n* lament (discourse of) 38.25, **pleynte** 38.34.

pleisir *n* pleasure **a** ~ as much as (he) pleases (of writer's invention) 14.16, **vient a** ~ if it pleases you (of audience preference) 12.11.

plesance *n* pleasure **a ta** ~ (to Virgin as presiding over text) 8b.37.

plet *n* attention ~ **tenir** pay heed to (narrative) 30.18.

poetes *n pl* poets (of classical antiquity) 23.122.

pointz *n pl* points (of argument) 8a.R.3, details (of subject matter) 19.100, **poins** tenets (of doctrine in treatise) 24b.15, **poinz** notation (of song) 8a.91.

Pol St Paul (Apostle), **saint** ~ 14.137n., 24a.146, 148, **seint** ~ 22.169.

Polecronicon *see* Higden.

polir *v* polish: **poli** *3 pret* (of gems of wisdom) 39.109, **polies** *pp* 39.90.

porrir *v* rot: **porrist** *3 imp subj* (of grains of wisdom) 17.48, 68.

poursuivre v follow: **enpursuiant** *pr p* (manner of organising successive periods in chronicle) 42.71.

porter *v* carry: **porté** *pp* (of handbook) 24b.42.

porveoir *v* provide: **porvoit** *3 pr* (spiritually, by reading the text properly) 17.39, 70.

porvoier *v* examine (text) 24a.35.

poser *v* put, **en rym** ~ (put in rhyme) 36.29, **posez** *pp* **en l'ebreu . . . ad** ~ 39.141.

preceps *n pl* precepts (as set out in writing) 37.87.

prechement *n* preaching, ~ **del Ewangele** (of the Gospel) 20a.23.

precher *v* exhort: **preché** *pp* (what writer does) 26.62, 112, 135.

precheur *n* preacher (signified by cock in tree) 20a.1, 21, **prechur, sun** ~ (owed support of patron) 14.136, **precheors** *n pl* **freres** ~ Dominicans (writer's order) 33.15.

precïoses *adj* precious (gems of wisdom) 39.41, 89.

predication *n* preaching (of St Augustine of Canterbury, d. 604) 31.102.

preez *see* **prier**.

preier *v* entreat: **proia** *3 pret* (patron, to writer) 6.78. *See also* **prier**.

preiser *v* praise: **preisasse** *1imp subj* 40.9, **preisé** *pp* **mult** ~ (of writers) 3.144, **preisee** (of Latin) 25b.91.

prendre *v* take (meaning from the text) 17.55, take up (a language) 7a.22, ~ **garde** consider, **pernom** *4imper* 17.38, **prenderai,** ~ **la meule** (seize the marrow of the text) *1 fut* 33.38, **se prendra** *3 fut* (give oneself to the book) 21.69.

present *n* gift (of book) 11a.59.

presenter *v* present: **presente** *3 pr* (literary work) 21.87, **presentase** (the book) *imp subj 1* 11a.51.

presompcion *n* presumption (ascribed to woman writer) 2b.29, **presumptiun** 2a.92n.

prestement *adv* readily, ~ **parler** (rhyme as deterrent to speaking readily) 32b.41.

Preux, Neuf *n* the Nine Worthies 44.12, 250, 254n.

prier *v* pray 22.157n., (for writer) 35.36, **coment . . .** ~ **Dieu le piere** (subject matter) 22.125n., **pri** *1 pr* (writer to audience) 12.34, 95n., 19.19, (writer to God) 13.67, 90, 14.141, 26.11, 34, 32b.43, (writer to patron) 14.73n., **prie** 35.35, (writer to God) 26.13, 35.43, **prie** *3* (writer to audience) 2b.26, (of illustrated figure) 20b.47, **priera[i]** *1 fut* (writer for audience) 35.36, **prierez** *5* (of audience) 22.127n., **prieront** *6 fut* (for writer) 2b.30, **prie** entreat *1 pr* 15.23, **priét** *5* (of audience) 20b.39, **priez** (audience for writer) 2b.15, (patron for writer) 14.75, 19.20n., 20b.32, 22.158, **priums** *4 imper* (audience and writer, to Jesus), **preez** *5 imper* (writer to Virgin for intercession) 11a.83, **prient** *6 pr subj* (audience for writer) 2b.27, 14.143, **prieent remedie** (of petition to ecclesiastical superior) 7c.15, **priant** *pr p* (writer to audience) 7d.13, **prierons** *6 pr* (audience and writer, to God) 7b.*8*, **priaste** *5 pret* (writer of patron's request) 33.27, **prié** *pp* (of request to writer) 25a.32.

priere *n* prayer (saint's, for hagiographer) 12.69, (saint's, for hagiographic community) 12.105, (author's, to Jesus), 20b.19, (taught by God) 22.134, 153, 160, **prieres** *n pl* (of patron) 14.80,

les sep[t] ~ de la Pater nostre (subject matter) 22.R before 120, 121, 123.
prime *n* prime (monastic office) 41.158n.
prime *adj* first, **a ~ des chevoilz dirai** (of head to toe ordering of information) 32b.21.
primes *adv* first, **~ dirrum la dreyte fei** (ordering principle) 24b.13, **~ en fraunczoys** 7a.23, **~ . . . cumença** (of writing in chronological order) 25b.111, **~ se humilie** (first act in loving) 26.1, (order of chronicles) 42.70. *See also* **adprimez.**
primer *n* first, **~ liver de cronicles** (of *Brut*) 16.*56*, **~ vowel** 16.20, **premer** (of book, first of several) 39.143.
privetez *n* private matters (of sins not to be treated in manual) 24b.61, 64, 70.
prodhommes *n pl* **~ et mesnés hommes** (audience of text) 7d.9, (users of text) 7d.14, **prodeshommez** (commissioners of text) 7d.2n.
profecie, profetes *see* **prophecie, prophetes.**
proffrir *v* offer (of song) 8a.85.
profit *n* benefit (from writing) 12.74, 90, (to audience) 20b.9, **commun ~** (of writer and audience) 24a.159n., **profite** (for writer) 13.91.
profitables *adj* useful (of writer's textual additions) 33.35, profitable 33.38.
profiter *v* benefit (morally) from: **profite** *3 pr* (from reading) 24a.55, **profitent** *6 pr* (of lay people) 25b.10.
preier *see* **prier.**
prologe *n* prologue 24b.R, 28.R, (to chronicle) 42.R, **prologes** 33.R.before 29, 39.218.
promesse *n* promise (by which writer's lady enjoins translation) 6.76.
promettre *v* promise: **premis** *pp* (of writer's agenda for text) 24b.104.
prophecie *n* prophecy 26.167, **grace de ~** (capacity of David the psalmist) 39.53, **profecie** 26.3.
prophetes *n pl* prophets, **sainz ~** (of Israel) 43.17, **profetes** 26.81, 135.
propre *n* something personal (writer's own purpose in writing) 19.123.
propre *adj* personal, **~ fin** personal purpose (of writer) 19.133.
propretez *n pl* names 7a.*13*, matters (material of a dream vision) 16.*126*.
prose *n* prose, **en ~** 16.*13*n., *20*.
provende *n* prebend (as clerk's reward) 3.174.
prover *v* prove, realise (of stage settings) 29b.7, **proverai** *1 fut* (truth of *Kalender*) 40.15, **provez** *pp* verifiable (of articles of faith) 24b.15.
Proverbes *n* Book of Proverbs 39.145, 171, 177.
pru *n* (moral) benefit 4.20, 25b.28, 34.
pruesses *n pl* valorous deeds, **~ nos auncestres** (of our ancestors, to be remembered) 31.*9*.
psalmodie *n* **traitét . . . de ~** (of psalter of David) 39.54.
Pui *n* literary group 8a.45n., **gentil compaignoun du ~** 69, **feste roiale du ~** 65, **~ graunt feste du ~** 73, **la feste du ~** 76, 78, 85, **Puy** 50. *See also* **Estatuz du Pui.**
puple *n* audience (of dramatic performance) 29b.4.
purpens *n* purpose (of writer) 25b.23.
purpenser *v* resolve to: **purpensé** *pp* (writer's resolve) 11a.20.
purpos *n* (patron's) intent 13.39, **aveir en ~** intend (of writer's intention) 25b.38, 114.
purtreture *n* illustration 20b.5n, 30n, **purtreiture** 20b.8.
purveer *v* see to: **purveez** *5 imper* (peformance space) 29b.5, 10, **purverai** *1 fut* (order of narrative) 25b.110, **purveu** *pp* (of performance space) 29a.21, 29b.31.
puselles *n pl* young girls (as pupils), **tresdoulcez ~** sweet young girls 8a.26–7n.

quer *see* **coer.**
quere *v* seek, **ailurs ~** (to learn French) 2a.8, **quer** *1 pr* (of writer, to have praise) 24b.100, **querz** *2 pr* (of reader wanting examples of virtue) 24a.2, 47, **querras** *2 fut* (look for in the book) 24a.28.
quidance *n* imagination (of literary invention) 14.26.
quiders *n* **solum lur ~** (writing without authority) 14.24.
quor *see* **coer.**

raconter *v* recount (a saint's life) 2b.2, **recompter** (marvelous stories) 35.13, 18, **recunter, oïr ~** hear recounted 27.92.
raison *n* matter (of substance of book) 15.2, (matter, as recounted) 15.10, **raisun** proverb 39.153, **la veire ~** the true record 10.10, **reison** discourse 5.26, point made (in narration) 27.90, (what is right or just) 32a.3, **reisun, ~ seculere** worldly reason 23.121, **reson** (why book written) 19.5, (reason, what writer uses)

19.94, meaning 23.4, ~ **enditee** (of words to song) 8a.92–3, **par** ~ (of Christ's being subject matter of book) 19.35, (what Cato gives) 40.37, **resons** (of author's teaching) 40.27, **resun** (for book's commissioning) 13.39, **par** ~ (prove truth through reason) 40.16, **resons** *n pl* 19.68, explanations 19.104, ~ **de cest art** (points of calendar art) 40.35.

recevoir *v* receive: **receive** *3 pr subj* ~ **en gré** (of God's response to work) 2a.15, **recevez** *5 imper* **en vos bienfaz me** ~ (writer's injunction to readers) 12.102.

reciter *v* tell of 44.263, (great wars) 44.258, (lesser wars) 44.266, **dire et** ~ (what herald should do) 44.270, **devant le puple** ~ (of dramatic performance) 29b.4, **recite** *3 pr* (of Brunetto Latini) 44.241–2, **recitom** *4 pr* 29a.1, **recité** *pp* (the *Livre du Songe du vergier*) 44.243–4, **recitees** (what is in the *Brut*) 44.144.

recits *n pl* narrative accounts (of wars) 44.264.

reclamer *v* invoke: **reclaiment** *6 pr* (by audience) 11a.70.

recompter *see* **raconter**.

recorder *v* record: **recorderent** *6 pret* (of adventures) 6.61, **recordaunt** *pr p* (past time) 35.31, **recordee** *pp* (of story) 6.34n., (of poem) 21.116.

regarder *v* look at (text) 19.145, (parts of the book) 24b.12, **regardai** *1 pret* (of text or book) 6.85, **regarde** *3 subj pr* (written guidance) 8a.R.*3*, **regardez** *pp* (of book) 19.128, **rewarder** *v* look at (chronicles) 42.69. *See also* **esgarder, garder**.

reguarders *n* act of looking (at text) 21.67.

rehercer *v* read, **deu fez le deit** ~ (of need to read book twice) 24b.53, enumerate (sins) 24b.72.

rei *n* king (King Edward, subject of story) 2a.R, (in stories about Alexander) 28.27, (King Solomon as transmitter of God's message) 39.31, 39.78, ~ . . . **de majesté** (as intended recipient of work) 11a.56, **reis, li** ~ **Elvred** (as proprietor of book) 10.23, (King Solomon) 39.49, **riches** ~ (of Solomon as God's messenger) 39.29, **reis** *n pl* kings (as audience for story) 6.35, (as subjects of historiography) 10.8, 11, 21, 10.11, **rois** (subjects of story) 6.28n.

remembrance *n* reminder (to clerics, as aim of writing) 8b.48, **remenbrance** (found in old writings) 1.37n.

remembrer *v* remember (deeds found in books) 3.1n, **remenbrer** *v* call to mind (stories of ancestors) 31.*8*.

rementoyver *v* recall (genealogy, so as to write about it).

remistrent *6 pret of **remaindre*** remain or of ***remettre*** revive, restore (a tradition) 6.40n.

remuer v remove (covering of literal meaning) 23.7, **remuast** *3 pret* (a chained book) 10.26.

rendre *v* render (uses of one's intellect to others) 11a.18, (to God, as writer teaches) 14.45, **bon gré** ~ (what users of writer's translation should do), 39.215, **rend** *1 pr*, ~ **graces** (to God, for Holy Spirit's help in writing) 23.14–15, **rend** *3 pr*, ~ . . . **dulçor** (of sweetness yielded by ruminating on Scripture 39.19, **rent** (of saint's rewards for work of hagiography) 11b.37.

renommer *v* make known: **renomez** *pp* (of book) 24a.186.

reposte *adj* hidden (scriptural knowledge, because in Hebrew) 39.107, 188.

reprendre *v* hold to account (of hagiographer) 12.44, **reprise** *pp* reproach (for language use) 2a.3.

representer *v* perform 29b.3.

repruver *n* reproach (God's, against writer's composition) 11a.22, **repruvé** *pp* (writer, by God) 11a.11.

requeste *n* request (by patron to writer) 13.R.3.

requere *v* require: **requist** *3 pret* (patron requests writer) 6.75, **requis** *pp* (for translation) 39.173, (by patron of writer) 40.20.

resignefier *v* have an additional meaning: **resenefie** *3 pr* 39.161.

reson, resons, resoun, resun *see* **raison**.

respit *n* lesson 20b.10n., moral story 30.5n, proverb (in frivolous stories) 14.11, 25, **respeiz** *n pl*, ~ **Salemon / E del Vilain** *Proverbs of Solomon and the Peasant* 39.147–8.

respondre *v* answer (in debate) 44.271, **respont** *3 pr* respond (in formal dialogue) 24a.193.

retenir *v* retain (words as way of reading scripture) 22.189, keep, ~ **en lur memoyres** (of audience response) 27.94, **retien** *2 imper* (book's teaching) 24a.5, **retindrent** *6 pret* 6.58, **retenu** *pp* kept ('kept down', of fully ingested scripture) 39.116, **retenuz** (of wisdom) 24a.91.

rethoriens *n pl* rhetoricians, **science de** ~ 23.111.

retraire *v* recount: **retrere** 4.4, **a mal** ~ criticise 4.36, **retreire, funt** ~ cause to be recounted

27.45, **oïr** ~ hear recounted 27.92, **retrait** *3 pr* 39.140, **retrait** *pp* retold 3.166, **retraite** 3.8n, **retret** spoken of 4.17.

reverence *n* reverence (writer's for patron) 13.50.

rewarder *see* **regarder**.

rime *n* rhyme 11b.9, 32b.39, **rym** 36.29, **ryme** poetry 27.40, **en** ~ in verse 27.36, **de** ~ **en prose** 16.*13*n., **rymes** *n pl* verses 27.7n.

rimeier *v* compose a work in rhyme 11b.36, **rimeiez** *pp* 22.134n.

rimer v rhyme: **ryma** *3 pret* 27.26, **rimez** *pp* 17.33.

rismeer *n* prosody 14.90.

Robert, seint n Lord Robert, bishop of Lincoln 5.*1*.

Rolland Roland (eponymous chanson de geste hero), ~ **et Olivier** 44.250n., **Rollant,** ~ **et Olivier** 18.25, ~ **ne d'Oliver** 24a.171.

romaine *adj* vernacular, French, **lange** ~ French language 24a.161n.

romanz *n* French language 2a.6, 4.30, 35, 5.26, 9.12, 11b.19, 13.R3, 15.63, 17.8, 24a.43, 26.36, 34.7, **romance** 7e.12, 8b.45, 40.22, **romans** 25a.33, 35, 37, **romaunce** 16.*9*, **roumans** 2.7, **rumanz** 2.70, 3.63, 67, 25b.42n., **romanz** a narrative in French 2.R, 5.2–3n., 11b.6, 12, 12.35, 93, 17.35, 28.17, 38.2, 40, 39.192, **rumanz** 3.153n, 25b.56, 83, **soen** ~ (the writer's) 2a.86, **romains** *n pl* narratives in French 44.264, **rommans** 44.15.

romaine *adj* French, **lange** ~ 24a.161n., **roumans** 2b.14.

roule *n* speech scroll (represented in manuscript image) 20b.45.

rubriche *n* rubric 19.90.

rustie *n* simplicity, **par** ~ simply (of writing the truth, opposed to **curteis**[**i**]**e**, refinement) 14.95.

sacrarie *n* sanctuary ~ **al fiz Dampnedé** (of poem) 26.154. *See also* **temple**.

sage *adj* wise (of philosopher) 7b.*44*n., **estre le plus** ~ (result of experiencing text) 19.160, (how actors portraying disciples should behave) 29b.16n., (result of writer's teaching) 37.75, (of Solomon) 39.28, **sages** 11a.15, **plus** ~ (reader, after reading text) 13.98, **sages** (of clerks who wrote in Latin) 4.21, (of dedicatee) 33.15, **les plus** ~ (of clerks of old) 33.17, (what a segment of audience cannot be) 40.30.

saine *adj* beneficial (of French language) 24a.162, **sains** (of text) 39.84.

saintez *n pl* saints, **toutz les** ~ **de paradis** (in whose honour text is written) 8a.15–16.

sale *n* room (location for writing) 16.*49*.

Salamon King Solomon 8a.14n., **Salemon** 39.51, 55, 70, 138, 179, **Respeiz** ~ (proverb collection) 39.147, **Salomon** 26.41, 168.

salmistre *n* psalmist 26.93.

salu *n* salvation (goal of reading) 24a.12, **dreyte veye de** ~ (what reader learns from an exemplum) 30.3, **salu** *n* greeting, **un** ~ **d'amor fine** (of poem to Christ) 21.103, **salus** *n pl* greetings (in letter) 33.6, (in book's prologue) 33.16, (in letters) 7c.121, (not to be used if of lower rank) 131, 132, **salutz** (not to be used if angry) 7c.140, **saluz** (to patron) 14.2, verse greetings (between lovers) 27.7n., 41.2.

saluer v greet: **salue** *3 pr* (author to patron) 9.7, **saluant** *pr p* ~ **son degré** (in letters) 7c.126.

salutaciones *n pl* (greetings, in letters) 7c.123.

saoler v sate: **saolez** *pp* (with fine writing) 39.118.

sauter *n* psalter (to be read attentively) 22.178, 26.93.

sauver *v* save: **ton cors e t'alme** ~ (through reading) 24a.48.

saveir *v* know (what audience should know) 1.27, 2.71, (what author should not hide) 11a.12, (author's wish to have) 14.113, knowledge (clerical showing off of) 25b.5, **saver** (of languages learned) 5.17, (author understands patroness) 13.40, (of pupils) 7a.*13*, 19.47, 50, (of audience) 22.184, 25b.55, 40.34, **savoer** (audience's attitude) 16.*1*n., **savoir** (of audience's desire) 2b.13, (of the *Brut*) 6.23, (of letter-writing) 7c.19, 7d.8, (of audience) 16.25, 20c.52, 53, (what one learns from genealogy tree) 20d.32, 25a.7, (what human heart can know) 41.119, (what interlocutor must know) 44.91, 94, **fais a** ~ (make known) 33.11, 17, **savera** *3 fut* 19.149, **sout** *3 pret* (of St Gregory) 24a.205, **sachez** *5 imper* 7c.5, 31, 84, 122, 11a.16, 14.59, 24a.174, 44.191, **sue** *pp*, **plus** . . . ~ better known (French as against Latin) 13.35, **sues** (of Aristotle's advice to Alexander) 32a.4. *See also* **saver**.

saveir *n* knowledge 11a.12, (writer's) 14.113, (clerical writers showing off) 25b.5, **saver** *n* knowledge, 19.149, **de** ~ . . . **d'amer** 19.146, 148, (quality of God) 22.8, 9, 12n., 22, 79, 93, etc., 37.32, ~ **de cest monde** worldly learning 23.115, **saveir** wisdom (good to possess)

24a.94, **savoir** (of author's youth) learning 7d.17, 19, wisdom 24a.82, 88, 138, 33.42, 43, 44, 47n., **savoirs** wisdom 33.47n.
saver v be able: **sievent** *6 pr* (audience ability with Latin) 12.94, **savera** *3 fut* (of audience) 40.27, **saverai** *1 fut* (of writer) 6.92n., **saveroie** *1 cond* (of writer) 35.3n., **saveroit** *3 cond* (of writer's intelligence) 40.5.
savor *n* flavour (of spiritual nourishment) 39.20.
savoré *adj* tasty (of spiritual food) 39.114.
savoir *see* **saveir.**
savurer *v* taste (spiritual nourishment) 39.16.
schale *n* shell (what the Hebrew scriptures are encased in) 39.186.
science *n* learning 23.111n., 116, (writer's understanding) 19.139.
scripture *n* scripture 9.23. *See also* **escripture.**
Scrivener *n* scrivener 7b.73.
Sebile *n* Sibyl the prophet (as guide to writer), ~ **la sage** 16.*32*n., **la viel** ~ 16.*40–1*, **Sebille** 16.*51, 63, 74, 97*. ***Secré des secrés*** Secret of Secrets (title) 33.R, ***Segrez des Segrez*** 33.26, **segrei,** ~ **Damnedeu** (of hidden scriptural meaning) 23.13.
seculer *adj* worldly, ~ **corteisie** (of one audience for Proverbs) 39.151.
seignour *n* lord (as addressed in letters) 7c.25, 27x2, 32, 49, etc., **en l'amour nostre Seignour** (love of God inspired by text) 21.*14*, **onour del** ~ (of formal title for use in letters) 7c.37, **seignur** (of saint, as hagiographer's lord and patron) 11b.35, **mon** ~ (writer's patron) 40.18, **Nostre** ~ (as writer of book) 19.8, (as subject matter of book) 19.25, 53, (as teacher of the Pater noster) 160, 180, (title for Jesus as teacher of disciples) 22.124, (what book enables better knowledge of) 19.161; **seigneurs** *n pl* (as audience) 28.22, **seigniurs** (as audience) 12.95, **seignors** (as audience) 43.14n., **seingnors,** ~ **e dames** lords and ladies (apostrophe to audience) 24a.151, **seygnours** (apostrophe to audience) 31.*12*, **seignours** (as recipients of letters) 7c.1, 39, (as senders of letters) 7c.70, 76, **seignurs** 15.1n, 8, 18, 44, 17.38, 18.1, 12, 33, **li covenz des** ~ (of monastery, as patron) 11b.42. *See also* **dame.**
sein *n* sign (on page) 24a.219, **signe** numinous manifestation (sought by audience) 24a.3.
sen *n* wisdom 4.19, (writer's) 9.10, ~ **de divinité** (spirituality) 13.18, (what reader should listen to) 24a.69, 72, ~ **et foly** (what reader may see exemplified in historiography) 16.*41*n., ~ **devyn** divine understanding (as interpretive authority) 16.*111*, meaning 4.47n, (what Jews refuse to see) 17.65, **sens** (reader will find in text) 4.6, 8, 15, intelligence (implied, of reader) 11a.1, 17, 24a.11, 41, ~ **naturel** innate understanding 7b.*20*, **sens** *n pl* abilities 25a.14.
senee *adj* wise 11a.63.
senefie *see* ***signifier.***
sentence *n* meaning (writer's) 13.49, opinion 25b.91, discourse, **en plus court** ~ in more compact form 16.*27*; **sentences** *n pl* discourses, ~ **en lung traire** lengthy discourses 25b.4n.
sermun *n* exposition 11b.1, sermon 25b.73; **sermuns** *n pl* 25b.95, 105.
servant *n* servant (writer as servant of patron) 9.16.
serventeis *n* lyric poem 3.153, 27.6.
servir v serve: **servi** *pp* (of hagiographer's work on saint's life) 11b.35, **servie** *pp* served (church, by Jerome's translation) 39.134.
sievent *see* **saveir.**
sievrai *see* **suivre.**
signe *see* **sein.**
signefiance *n* meaning 23.109.
signifier *v* signify: **signefie** *3 pr* 26.165, **senefie** 39.80, **signifié** *pp* 20a.1, 13.
sire n salutation in letter 7c.45, ~ **herault** (form of address) 44.83, 162, 170, 191, 268, **syre, mon** ~ **Gautier de Biblesworth** (secular, aristocratic writer) 7aR.*2*.
soer *n* sister, **chere** ~ (address to commanditaire) 7a.Pref.let.*1*.
soffrir *v* permit 33.33.
solatz *n* pleasure, **prendre** ~ **a** take pleasure in 35.16n., **solaz** (mental) comfort 38.1n., ease (as result of experiencing text) 19.130.
soloir *v* be accustomed to: **soel[ei]nt** (writers formerly praised) 3.143.
soner *v* sound, **bien** ~ pronounce correctly 7b.*21*, **sona** *3 pret* sang (of biblical songs) 26.83.
songe *n* dream 41.150 (writer's impression of material for book), **soungez** dream-vision 16.*125*, **sunge** 27.78n, **suonge** (matter of poem) 27.30.
(sor)vestir *v* cover: **sorvestue** *pp* (of Hebrew writing) 39.186.
sounger *v* dream: **soungé** *pp* (how writer obtained material) 16.*125*.

sout *see* **savoir.**
sovenir *v* remember 35.33n, **suveigniez** *5 imper* ~ **vus de mei** writer's injunction 12.98.
successions *n pl* lines of succession (within a lineage) 42.24.
sue, sues *see* **savoir.**
suffiçance *n* ability (in composing) 8b.38.
suffraite *n* deprivation (audience's, of spiritual nourishment) 39.10n, 22.
suget *n* subject (of text) 19.23n.
suggestions *n pl* promptings (of devil, figured as arrows) 20a.11n.
suivre *v* follow: **suez** *5 imper* ~, **la trace** (follow the example) 13.107, **sievrai** *1 fut* (of adhering to source's meaning) 33.33.
summe *n* essence (of writerly intention) 13.49.
supplicacione *n* petition 7c.3, 16, ~ **de temporaltee** civil petition 7c.8.
supportacion *n* support (for composition) **vostre benigne** ~ 7d.21.
surnun *n* additional name (of title of work) 24b.45.
surveoir *v* look over (source material) 16.*43*, **surveist** *3 pret* 16.*19*.
susdistes *adj* aforesaid (of placement in text) 42.49, 92.
sutil *adj* fine (of song) 26.10.
sutillement *adv* ingeniously (how the song was put in writing) 26.42.
Symun (Magus) *n* Simon the Magician 25b.67–8.

table *n* ~ **painte** (for devotional icon of Virgin) 34.70.
Table Ronde *n* Round Table 44.12–13.
taire *v* keep silent: **teray** *1 fut* 24b.81, ***se taire*** *v reflex* fall silent (end the story), **m'en taceray** *1 fut* 35.17.
talent *n* desire (of audience to listen) 4.46n, (of audience) 11a.40, (what audience desires to know) 24a.24.
temple *n* temple (metaphor for Song of Songs) ~ **et sacrarie** 26.154.
temps *n* season (spring topos as opening) 31.*1*, *6*. *See also* **averyl, may.**
tenir *v* hold (writer should not keep silent about God) 14.118, (fig.) **l'ensample** ~ 27.88, **tent** *3 pr* 20b.45, **tenu** *pp* (reputed, of poet) 27.32, (writer obliged to patron) 40.18, **tenuez, cher** ~ cherished (of material of chronicles) 42.93.
tens *n pl* (verb) tenses 4.38.
terminer *v* end: **termine** *3 pr* (of literary work) 21.112.
tesmonier *v* testify 36.*52*, **testimonier** provide testimony 39.77.
testemunie *n* testimony, **trai a** ~ adduce authorities 32b.29.
titeles *n pl* titles 39.142, **titres** 24a.213.
tolir *v* take away, **ennui** ~ spare (audience) boredom 14.101, ~ **de vanité** take away from worldly things (purpose of translation) 14.44.
toucher *v* touch upon: **touchent** *6 pr* (subject matter) 42.70, **toché** *pp* (alluded to) 20c.65.
traire *v* compose, **en lung** ~ draw out at length 25b.4, **trai** *1 pr* (adduce) 32b.29, **trait** *3 pr* 24a.170n., **traez** *5 imper*, ~ **avant** take out (a book) 14.54, **traist** *3 pret* (how Jerome translated from Hebrew) 39.107, **trait** *pp* extracted 24a.175, **treites** 6.42.
traitéd *n* book 39.198, **traitét** 39.172, 208, ~ **de psalmodie** Book of Psalms 39.54, **treté** *n* composition 13.103.
traiter *v* compose 14.77, 12.42, 39.75, **treiteient** *6 imp* 3.146, **traitast** *3 imp subj* 39.213, **traitee** *pp* 39.106n, **traitét** 39.131, **treiter** *v* narrate 11a.21, 62, 73, 75, 84, **treter** treat (in composition) 16.*27*, (talk about) 24b.29, **treitié** *pp* 11b.18. *See also* **traire.**
tramettre *v* send: **tramis** *pp* (of writing) 39.27, 31.
transecrist *n* copy 8a.62, **transecrit** 8a.64.
translater *v* translate 2a.14, 93, 2b.29, 4.43, 16.*27*, 24a.160, 25b.75, 89, 33.29, 32, **translat** *1 pr*, **estoire vus** ~ translate a history (from Latin to French) 13.32, **tran[s]lataisse** *1 pr subj* 33.58, **translatast** *3 imp subj* 39.172, **translatasse** *1 imp subj* 6.79, **translatai** *1 pret* **franceis** ~ 6.86, **translata** *3* 2b.19, *26*, 16.*13*, *53*, **transla[tast]** 41.35, **translatat** 39.112, 120, **translaté** *pp* 2a.78, 88, 13.R3, 18.11, 39.138, 194, **translatee** 2b.17, 39.128, **translatees** 6.45, 54, **translatei** 33.56, 78x2, **translatét** 39.124, **translatez** 4.28.
translatïon *n* translation 39.200, **translatïun** 39.209, **translatiun, mise en** ~ translated 25b.86.
travail *n* (literary) labour 2a.15, **travail** efforts (at composition) 13.73, toil 33.29.
travaillier *v* work: **traveyler** *v* labour at (writing) 24b.71, **travaille** *3 pr* (the work of splitting the letter from the spirit of the text) 17.39, **travaillé** *pp* 17.40.
treiter *see* **traiter.**

treitiz *n* treatise 5.*1*, *4*.
trespasser *v* omit in narration 13.79, **trespasse** *3 pr* 17.20, **trespasse** *1 pr subj* 13.126, **trespassees** happened (of events worthy of being recorded) *pp* 3.10.
tresposiciuns *n pl* shift (in chronological order) 25b.106, **tresposicium** 25b.107.
tresturner *v* translate: **tresturné** *pp* 25b.33, **tresturnee** 15.63.
treté *see* **traitéd.**
tretice *n* treatise 16.*15*, *123*, *128*.
trier *v* assess, **les notes . . . del chaunt . . .** ~ (of song contest) 8a.91.
tripot *n* (literary) ruse 14.13.
Tristram *n* Tristan (title of romance) 6.47.
trop *n* excess (of words) 33.30.
trover *v* find (material for writing) 24a.167, **troverai** *1 fut* (a source for the Virgin's story) 15.64, **trovras** *2 fut* (material for reading) 24a.10, 14, 37, 44, **troverét** *5 fut* (what readers can expect in book) 24b.21n, 39, 61, **trova** *3 pret* wrote 27.25, **trové** *pp* 21.5 (of source material) 16.*8*, *80*, ~ **par anceianz chartres** (proved by ancient charters) 42.54, **trovez** composed (in verse) 11b.6.
turner *v* turn: **turné** *pp* ~ **de mal** from wickedness (effect of reading) 14.52.

ubli, ublier *see* **obli, oblier.**
us *n* use, **aveir en** ~ (read, write, speak) 25b.87.
usage *n* vernacular idiom 3.54.
usdive *n* idleness (preventd by listening to text) 25b.43.
user *v* use (partake of) 39.84, **use[e]** *pp* 13.35, **usez** (read) 25b.57n.
uvraine, uvre *see* **overaigne, ovre.**

vailance *n* valour, ~ **as chevalers** (as textual material) 40.3.
valer *v* be of value to, **vaille** *3 pr* (wealth not as valuable as wisdom) 24a.94, **vaille** *3 pr subj* benefit (of reading), ~ **a l'ame e au cors** 41.133.
vair *adj* true (of literary works) 14.20, 21, 27, **pur** ~ as truth 14.25, ~ **dire** speak truly 14.95, **veir** (quality of narrative) 27.71, **verais** (of secular verse) 27.38, **veyr** (quality of narrative) 27.74.
vanité *n* false teaching 24a.135, 139, 175, futility 14.60, **vanitez** *n pl* trifles (worth of secular literature) 14.8.
veoir *v* see 25a.8, (of divine secrets) 41.122, (of author reading in book) 157, 179, **ver** (behold image of writer) 20b.41, **voir** 44.277, **veis** *2 pr* (scripture) 17.51, **veum** *4 pr* 26.165, **voyons** 44.113, **veient** *6 pr* read 43.32, **veoie** *1 imp* 41.179, **vi** *1 pret* 41.65, 67x2, 68, 94, 148, etc., **veïs** *2 pret* 41.229, **verras** *2 fut* see (in a book) 24a.45, **veu** *pp* 41.182, 184, **veue** (of manuscript) 20b.5.
verais *see* **vair.**
verger *n* orchard, **un beau** ~ **flori** (represented site of composition) 21.*10*.
veritables *adj* verifiable 40.12n.
veritei *n* truth, **paroles en corte** ~ (of writer's view of Arabs) 33.64.
verité *n* truth 11b.4, 13, 17, 20, 14.17, 113, 17.2, 25b.30, 40.14, 16, truthful teaching 24a.140, 176, 210, **de** ~ **. . . feite** (based on truth) 6.27n, **veritei** (of text, garnered in translation) 33.31, 38, **verrour** 4.41, **verté** 32b.30, **veritez** 11b.8, 14.37; **veritez** *n pl* 33.38.
verrour *see* **verité.**
vers *n* metrical line, verse 11b.9, poem 28.26, **un dedut par** ~ 27.69, **vers** *n pl* verses 27.26, 33, 37, 79, 28.18, strophes 27.9, **par beaus** ~ **e colurez** (fine and beautiful) 23.123.
verseiller *v* chant: **versaillez** *5 imper* 22.175.
vertu *n* virtue 24a.11, power of writing 24a.158; **vertuz** *n pl* miracles 11a.31, 24a.206, 213, virtues 12.14, 82, 13.41n, ~ **des sainz** subject of book 24a.173.
Veu Testament *n* Old Testament 26.40, **Viel** ~ 17.53.
vice *n* mistake (of scribe) 41.34.
vie *n* life *2a.14*, 78, 93, 100, 103, 2b.2, 17, 22, 27, 30, ~ **pardurable** (eternal life for author and convent-dwellers) 2b.32, (biography of the Virgin) 15.54, (of Christ and his mother) 15.21, (of saint) 11b.16, 12.R, 21, 23, 28, 65, 13.R.1, R.2, 88, *Explicit*, 25a.35, 25b.R, 27.R, 30.R, (writer's putative biography) 27.2, 3, **la** ~ **. . . de tanz proudeshomes** (of lineal ancestors in Grail) 41.164, *la* ~ *Seint Edward* 16.*103*n., ~ **nuvele** 2a.100, ~ **et la passiun** 12.21; **vies** *n pl* biographies of kings 10.8, 10.22, **lur bones** ~ (of ancestors) 41.166.
viel *n* the old (people, of audience for treatise) 40.61.
vilain *n* churl 39.23, ***Vilain, Respeiz . . . del*** ~ (what people call proverbs) 39.148–9.
vilains *adj* rustic (non-francophone) 25b.41.

viles *adj* lowly 24a.143.
Virgine seinte Mere (of Mary as singer of praises to God) 26.137.
vit *see* **veoir.**
visougetei *n* key term for rulership recommended by wise clerics 33.41, 44n.
voir *n* truth (in text) 24a.137, **por** ~ *adv phrase* truly 24a.133, **pur** ~ 21.45.
voiz *n* voice **en** ~ **crié** declaimed 26.163.
voloir *v* want: **voil** *1 pr* (writer's intention) 1.6, 2b.2, 11, 4.30, 47n., 5.39, 11a.21n, 31, 73, 75, 14.7n., 44, 63, 117, 19.18, 20b.13, 21.77, 24a.161, 24b.71, 99, 32a.10, 40.1, **voilez** *5 pr* 40.34.
voluntiers *adv* willingly, ~ **oiez** (manner of hearing text) 42.94, **volentiers, n'out mes si** ~ no longer hears so willingly (audience attitude) 42.98.
volume *n* volume 24a.221; **voluns** *n pl* volumes 39.139, 156.
voucher *v* call (a text): **vochat** *3 pret* 39.163.
vulgar *n* vernacular ~ **cumun** common vernacular 25b.16n.

Willam William of Normandy, William I of England, d. 1087, ~ **Bastard, duc de Normaundie** 31.*12*, ~ **le conquerour** 16.*95–6*, **William** ~, **conquerour d'Engleterre** 42.87–8.

ymage, ymaginez *see* ***image, imaginer***.

Glossary of Latin Literary Terms

aptum *adj* appropriate (of text for laypeople) 5R.30.
articuli *n* points, ~ **fidei** *n pl* the articles of faith 5R.33.
Ave n hail, **Ave Marie** (may also be French) 19.22.

billas *n pl* bills (formal documents of complaint, *see* **billes** above) 7c.R.1.

consulere v counsel: **consulendum** *fut pass part* 37.56.
coram *prep* in the presence of ~ **clericis** (of how romance tongue sounds to clerics) 5R.28.

docere v teach: **docebo** *1 fut* 37.71.
dominum R. lincolniensem episcopum, secundum ~ Lord Robert, bishop of Lincoln 5R.6–8.
dulcedine *n* sweetness, ~ **coelesti** (fig.) divine quality of religious writing 5R.33.

explicare v explain: **Explicit** *pp abrev* 'here finishes' or 'it is finished' (conventional signal that text has ended) 11b.colophonn., 24a.R after 52, 42 after 102.

Fratris A. Brother Angier, translator of Gregory's *Dialogues* 24a.R at 52.

gallicis *adj* French, ***in*** ~ 7c.R.3.

honorem *n* honour, ~ contingerent (of obtaining honour as result of text's teaching) 37.58.

incipere v begin: **Incipit** 'here begins' (conventional signal of text's beginning) *3 fut* 9.R, 24a.R at 1, 53, 151, 32b.R, ***incipiunt*** *6 pr* 7d.R.
intelligere *v* understand 37.84, ***intelligas*** *2 pr subj (active)* 37.83, **intelligunt** *6 pr*, **minus** ~ (of lay people) 5.R.29.
Introductio *n* introduction 24a.R at 1, 53.
item *n* item 5.R.17, 25, 26, 44.53, 71, 78, 137, 148, 162*etc.*

laicis *n pl* laypeople 5.R.29.
lector *n* reader, **prudens** ~ 'the wise reader' 5.R.31.
legere *v* read 37.84, **legito** *2 sg fut imper* 37.83.
letteras *n pl* letters 7c.R.1.
Librum *n* book, ~ **sequentem** (the following book) 24a.R at 1, ~ ***Dialogorum*** *The Book of Dialogues* 24a.R at 52.
lingua *n* language, ~ **romana** French 5.R.6, 27.

mel *n* honey, ~ **de petra** honey from the rock (*fig.* for reader's extraction of religious meaning) 5.R.31.
modo *n* method, ~ **dictandi** *n* art of letter writing 7c.R.1.
morem *n* habit, **animi tui** ~ **componas** (of addressee's making a guide for behaviour in response to text's teaching) 37.72.

negligere *v* pass over, disregard (not to be done with reading) 37.84.

oleum *n* oil, ~ . . . **de saxo** oil from stone (*fig.* for reader's extraction of religious meaning) 5.R.12.
opusculum *n* (literary) work (diminutive) 5.R.30.
ornatus mulierum (*title*) *The Adornment of Women* 32b.R.

Pater noster n Our Father (prayer taught by Christ to his disciples) 19.22, 22.127, 35.38. **Pater nostre.**
precepta *n pl* precepts 37.83.
prefatio *n* preface 24a.R before 53.
principio *n* beginning, **assit** ~ **meo** (injunction to Virgin at text's opening) 36.R.n.
Proem *n* preamble 24a.R (before 151).
prologus *n* prologue 42 after 102.
psallite *imper* sing ~ **sapienter** sing wisely 22.174.

regule cartarum *n* protocol for charter writing 7d.R.

salutatore *n* treatise on salutations 7c.R.2.
sancta Maria *n* Holy Mary (opening invocation) 36.R.
sancti Brandani *n* St Brendan (as subject of biography) 9.R.
sancti Thome archiepiscopi et martiris canturiencis *n* (Becket as subject of biography) 11b. *Explicit.*
saporem *n* flavour ~ **suavitatis** (*fig.* of text) sweet tasting 5R.28.
scriptum *n* written text 5.R.32.
succurendum *fut pass part* help (to men in error, function of precept-writer) 37.55.
suggere *pres inf act* produce (meaning from text) 5R.31.
supplicaciones *n pl* petitions 7c.R.2.

tractatus *n* treatise 5.R.6.

usum *n* custum, **secundum novum** ~ (of new charter protocol) 7d.R.

vita *n* life (biography of saint) 9.R at *Incipit*, 11b.
vivere *v* live: **viverent** *6 imp subj act*, ~ ***gloriose*** (living with glory as result of text's teaching) 37.57.

Bibliography

Primary Sources

Note. Manuscripts used for this volume's texts are listed in Part VI, §3.7: see also Index of Manuscripts.

Ailes, M., and M. Barber, ed. and trans. 2003. *The History of the Holy War: Ambroise's* Estoire de la guerre sainte, 2 vols. (Woodbridge).

Aitken, M. Y. H. 1922. *Étude sur* le Miroir: *ou* Les Évangiles de domnees *de Robert de Greatham, suivie d'extraits inédits* (Paris).

Allen, D., with G. Martin and F. Grace, ed. 2000. *Ipswich Borough Archives, 1255–1835*, Suffolk Record Society 43.

Arnold, T., ed. 1965 [1890]. *Jocelini de Brakelonda Cronica*, in *Memorials of St Edmund's Abbey*, Rolls Series 96 (London), I, 209–336.

Atkinson, Robert, ed. 1876. *Vie de seint Auban: A Poem in Norman French* (London).

Aungier, G. J., ed. 1844. *Croniques de London, depuis l'an 44 Hen. III. jusqu' à l'an 17 Edw. III.*, Camden Society OS 28 (London).

Baird, J. L., and J. R. Kane, ed. 1978. *Rossignol: An Edition and Translation with Introductory Essay on the Nightingale Tradition by J. L. Baird* (Kent, OH).

Baker, A. T., ed. 1907–8. 'Fragment of an Anglo-Norman Life of Edward the Confessor', *Modern Language Review* 3.4: 374–5 [publication of fragment, now lost].

—— ed. 1929. 'La Vie saint Edmond, archevêque de Cantorbéry', *Romania* 55: 332–81.

—— ed. 1940–1. '*Vie anglo-normande de sainte Foy* par Simon de Walsingham', *Romania* 66: 49–84.

Baldwin, S., and P. Barrette, ed. 2003. *Brunetto Latini, Li Livres dou Tresor*, Medieval and Renaissance Texts and Studies 257 (Tempe).

Bale, A., trans. 2012. *Sir John Mandeville: The Book of Marvels and Travels* (Oxford).

Barrette, P., and S. Baldwin, trans. 1993. *Brunetto Latini, The Book of the Treasure (Li Livres dou tresor)* (New York).

Barron, W. R. J., and G. S. Burgess, ed. 2002. *The Voyage of Saint Brendan: Representative Versions of the Legend in English Translation* (Exeter).

Bateson, M. B. 1892. 'The Register of Crabhouse Nunnery', *Norfolk Archaeology* 11: 1–71.

—— 1902a. 'A London Municipal Collection of the Reign of John', *English Historical Review* 17.67: 480–511.

—— 1902b. 'A London Municipal Collection of the Reign of John (continued)', *English Historical Review* 17.68: 707–30.

Batt, C., trans. and intro. 2014. *Henry of Grosmont, First Duke of Lancaster: The Book of Holy Medicines*, FRETS 8, Medieval and Renaissance Texts and Studies 419 (Tempe).

Beckerlegge, O. A., ed. 1944. *Le Secré de secrez by Pierre d'Abernun of Fetcham, from the Unique Manuscript B.N. f. fr. 25407*, ANTS 5 (Oxford).

Beichner, P. D., ed. 1965. *Aurora: Petri Rigae Biblia versificata*, 2 vols. (Notre Dame), II.

Bell, A. 1993. 'The Anglo-Norman *Description of England*: An Edition', in Short, ed., pp. 31–47.

—— ed. 1960. *L'Estoire des Engleis by Geffrei Gaimar*, ANTS 14–16 (Oxford).

Beltrami, P. G. *et al.* [P. Squillacioti, P. Torri and S. Vatteroni], ed. 2007. *Brunetto Latini, Tresor* (Torino).

Benson, L. D. *et al.*, ed. 1987. *The Riverside Chaucer*, 3rd edn (Boston).

Bergen, H., ed. 1924–7. *Lydgate's Fall of Princes*, 4 vols., EETS ES 121–4 (London).

Bevington, D., ed. and trans. 1975. 'The Holy Resurrection', in *Medieval Drama* (Boston), pp. 122–36.

Bitterling, K., ed. 1997. *Of Shrifte and Penance, the Middle English Prose Translation of the* Manuel des péchés, METS (Heidelberg).
Blacker, J., ed. 2005. *Anglo-Norman Verse Prophecies of Merlin*, *Arthuriana* 15.1: 1–125.
Blacker, J., G. S. Burgess and A. V. Ogden, trans. 2013. *Wace, The Hagiographical Works: The* Conception Nostre Dame *and the Lives of St Margaret and St Nicholas* (Leiden).
Bliss, J., trans. 2014. *La Vie d'Edouard le Confesseur, by a Nun of Barking Abbey*. Exeter Medieval Texts and Studies (Liverpool).
Bliss, J., trans., T. Hunt, ed., and H. Leyser, intro. 2010. *Cher alme: Texts of Anglo-Norman Piety*, FRETS OPS 1, Medieval and Renaissance Texts and Studies 385 (Tempe).
Blume, C., ed. 1930. *Johannis de Hovedene 'Philomena'*, Hymnologische Beiträge IV (Leipzig).
Blumreich, K. M., ed. 2002. *The Middle English 'Mirror': An Edition Based on Bodleian Library, MS Holkham misc. 40*, Medieval and Renaissance Texts and Studies 182, Arizona Studies in the Middle Ages and Renaissance 9 (Tempe).
Boas, M., ed. 1957. *Disticha Catonis* (Amsterdam).
Boulton, M. B. M., ed. 1984. *The Old French* Evangile de l'enfance, Studies and Texts 70 (Toronto).
—— ed. 1985. *Les Enfaunces de Jesu Christ*, ANTS 43 (London).
—— ed. and trans. 2013. *Piety and Persecution in the French Texts of England*, FRETS 6, Medieval and Renaissance Texts and Studies 420 (Tempe).
Bovey, A., O. de Laborderie and M. A. Norbye, ed. 2005. *The Chaworth Roll: A Fourteenth-Century Genealogy of the Kings of England* (London).
Brandin, L., ed. 1930. *Fouke fitz Warin: Roman du XIVe siècle*, Classiques français du Moyen Âge 63 (Paris).
—— 1938. '*La Destruction de Rome* et *Fierabras*: MS. Egerton 3028, Musée Britannique, Londres', *Romania*, 64: 18–100.
Brault, G. J., ed. and trans. 1984. *La Chanson de Roland: Student Edition, Oxford Text and English Translation* (University Park).
Brayer, É., and A. Leurquin-Labie, ed. 2011. *Somme le roi*, Société des Anciens Textes Français (Paris).
Brereton, G. 1950. 'A Thirteenth-Century List of French Lays and Other Narrative Poems', *Modern Language Review* 45: 40–5.
Brereton, G. E., and J. M. Ferrier, ed. 1981 [1846]. *Le Menagier de Paris* (Oxford [Paris]).
Briggs, H. M., with H. Jenkinson, ed. 1936. *Cy poet un juvenes home ver Coment il deit sotylement parler en Court* (London).
Brook, G. L., and R. F. Leslie, ed. 1978. Laȝamon, *Brut*, EETS os 277 (London), II.
Brown, M. P. 2007. *The Holkham Bible: A Facsimile* (London).
Bryant, N., trans. 2011. *Perceforest: The Prehistory of King Arthur's Britain* (Cambridge).
Burgess, G. S. 2009 [1997]. *Two Medieval Outlaws: Eustace the Monk and Fouke Fitz Waryn* (Cambridge).
—— trans. 2004. *The History of the Norman People: Wace's* Roman de Rou [with commentary by E. van Houts] (Woodbridge).
Burrows, D., ed. 2007–9. *La Vie de seint Clement*, 3 vols., ANTS 64–5, 66, 67 (London).
—— trans. 2016. *The Life of St Clement*, FRETS 10, Medieval and Renaissance Texts Series 488 (Tempe).
Burton, T. L., ed. 1998–9. *Sidrak and Bokkus*, EETS os 311–12 (Oxford).
Camargo, M., ed. 1995. *Medieval Rhetorics of Prose Composition: Five English* artes dictandi *and Their Tradition*, Medieval and Renaissance Texts and Studies 115 (Binghamton).
Carley, J. P., and J. Crick, ed., 1995. 'Constructing Albion's Past: An Annotated Edition of *De origine gigantum*', *Arthurian Literature* 13: 41–114.
Carley, J. P., ed., and D. Townsend, trans. 1985. *The Chronicle of Glastonbury Abbey: An Edition, Translation and Study of John of Glastonbury's* Cronica sive antiquitates Glastoniensis ecclesie (Woodbridge).

Carlson, D. R., ed. and A. G. Rigg, trans. 2011. *John Gower, Poems on Contemporary Events: The* Visio Angliae *(1381) and* Cronica tripertita *(1400)* (Toronto).
Carmody, F., ed. 1939. *Physiologus Latinus: Editions préliminaires, versio B* (Paris).
—— ed. 1948. *Li Livres dou tresor* (Berkeley).
Carpentier, É., G. Pon and Y. Chauvin, ed. 2006. *Rigord, Histoire de Philippe Auguste* (Paris).
Carr, A., trans. 1991. *The Seal of Blessed Mary by Honorius Augustodunensis* (Toronto).
Cartlidge, N., trans. 2015. *The Works of Chardri: The Life of the Seven Sleepers, The Life of St Josaphaz* and *The Little Debate*, FRETS 9, Medieval and Renaissance Texts and Studies 462 (Tempe).
Cazelles, B. 1991. 'The Life of Saint Faith' [a translation of vv. 1–894], in *The Lady as Saint: A Collection of French Hagiographic Romances of the Thirteenth Century* (Philadelphia), pp. 182–203.
Chase, C. J., trans. 2010 [1992–6]. *The History of the Holy Grail*, vol. 1 of *Lancelot-Grail: The Old French Arthurian Vulgate and Post-Vulgate in Translation*, gen. ed. N. J. Lacy (Cambridge).
Chaucer, G. 1987. *The Book of the Duchess*, in Benson *et al.*, pp. 329–46.
Christiansen, E., trans. 1998. *Dudo of St Quentin: History of the Normans* (Woodbridge).
Clark, W. B., ed. and trans. 1992, *The Medieval Book of Birds: Hugh of Fouilloy's Aviarium*, Medieval and Renaissance Texts and Studies 80 (Binghamton).
Clermont-Ferrand, M., ed. 2008. *Jean d'Angoulême's copy of 'The Canterbury Tales': An Annotated Edition of the Bibliothèque nationale's 'fonds anglais' 39* (Paris).
Cloran, T, ed. 1901. *The Dialogues of Gregory the Great: Translated into Anglo-Norman French by Angier* (Strassburg).
Coke, J. 1877 [1550]. 'The Debate between the Heralds of England and France', in Pannier and Meyer, pp. 53–125.
Colgrave, B., and R. A. B. Mynors, ed. and trans. 1969. *Bede's Ecclesiastical History of the English People* (Oxford).
Cooke, M., ed. 1967 [1852]. *R. Grossetete Carmina Anglo-Normannica: Robert Grossetete's* Chasteau d'amour (London, repr. New York).
—— ed. 1852. [*Miracle de Sardenai*, published without title], in Cooke, *R. Grosseteste Carmina*, pp. 114–31.
Copeland, R., and I. Sluiter, trans. 2009. *Medieval Grammar and Rhetoric: Language Arts and Literary Theory, AD 300–1475* (Oxford).
Curley, M. J., trans. 2009. *Physiologus* (Chicago).
D'Evelyn, C., ed. 1921. *Meditations on the Life and Passion of Christ, from British Museum Addit. MS. 11307*, EETS OS 158 (London).
—— ed. 1935. *Peter Idley's Instructions to his Son*, MLA Monograph Ser. 6 (Boston and London).
Dalby, A., trans. 2012. *The Treatise,* Le Tretiz, *of Walter of Bibbesworth: Translated from the Anglo-Norman with the Anglo-Norman Text as Established by William Rothwell and Published by the Anglo-Norman Online Hub* (Totnes).
Davis, N., ed. 1970. *Non-Cycle Plays and Fragments*, EETS SS 1 (London).
—— ed. 1979. *Non-Cycle Plays and the Winchester Dialogues: Facsimiles of Plays and Fragments in Various Manuscripts and the Dialogues in Winchester College MS 33* (Leeds).
Dean, J. M., ed. 1996. *Medieval English Political Writings* (Kalamazoo).
Dean, R. J., and M. D. Legge, ed. 1964. *The Rule of St Benedict: A Norman Prose Version* (Oxford).
Deluz, C., trans. 1993. *Jean de Mandeville: Voyage autour de la terre* (Paris).
—— ed. 2000. *Jean de Mandeville, Le Livre des merveilles du monde*, Sources d'histoire médiévale 31 (Paris).
Doyle, A. I., ed. and introd. 1987. *The Vernon Manuscript: A Facsimile of Bodleian Library, Oxford, MS. Eng. Poet. a.1* (Cambridge).
Druce, G. C., trans. 1936. *The Bestiary of Guillaume le Clerc Originally Written in 1210–11: Translated into English* (Ashford).

Dufournet, J., ed. 1993. *La Chanson de Roland* (Paris).

Dugdale, W., and R. Dodsworth, ed. 1846. *Monasticon Anglicanum* (London), V.

Duggan, J. J., ed. 2005. *La Chanson de Roland: The Song of Roland: The French Corpus* (Turnhout).

Duncan, T. G., and M. Connolly, ed. 2003. *The Middle English* Mirror*: Sermons from Advent to Sexagesima*, Middle English Texts 34 (Heidelberg).

Eckhardt, C. D., ed. 1996. *Castleford's Chronicle or The Boke of Brut*, 2 vols., EETS OS 305, 306 (Oxford).

Edwards, R. R., ed. 1998. *John Lydgate, Troy Book: Selections* (Kalamazoo).

Ewert, A., ed. 1995 [1944]. Marie de France, *Lais*, rev. G. S. Burgess (Oxford).

Fagin Davis, L., ed. 2014. *La Chronique anonyme universelle: Reading and Writing History in Fifteenth-Century France*, Studies in Medieval and Early Renaissance Art History 16 (Turnhout).

Fairclough, H. R., trans. 1978 [1926]. *Horace: Satires, Epistles and Ars poetica* (Cambridge, MA).

Faraci, D. 1990. *Il bestiario medio inglese: MS Arundel 292 della British Library* (Rome).

Fenster, T. S., and J. Wogan-Browne, trans. 2008. *The History of Saint Edward the King by Matthew Paris*, FRETS 1, Medieval and Renaissance Texts and Studies 341 (Tempe).

Foltys, C., ed. 1962. *Kritische Ausgabe der anglonormannischen Chroniken: Brutus, Li Rei de Engleterre, Le Livere de reis de Engleterre* (Berlin).

Formisano, L., ed. 1981. *La Destructioun de Rome: Version de Hanovre* (Florence).

—— ed. 1990. *La Destructioun de Rome*, ANTS PTS 8 (London).

Forshaw, H. P., ed. 1973. *Edmund of Abingdon, Speculum religosorum and Speculum ecclesie* (Oxford).

Foster, B., with assistance from I. Short, ed. 1976–7. *The Anglo-Norman Alexander (Le Roman de toute chevalerie), by Thomas of Kent*, 2 vols., ANTS 29–31, 32–3 (London).

Foulet, A., and E. C. Armstrong, ed. 1942, repr. 1965. *The Medieval French Roman d'Alexandre* (Princeton, repr. New York), IV.

Francis, E. A., ed. 1932. Wace, *La Vie de sainte Marguerite*, Classiques français du Moyen Âge (Paris).

Freni, G., trans. 1842, repr. 2009. 'Appendix B: *The Holy Resurrection*', in Hourihane, pp. 383–9.

Furnivall, F. J., ed. 1861. *Seynt graal, or the Sank ryal. The History of the Holy Graal, partly in Engl. verse, by H. Lonelich, and wholly in Fr. prose, by Robiers de Borron*, Roxburghe Club, 2 vols. (London).

—— ed. 1862. *Robert of Brunne's 'Handling Synne', with those parts of the Anglo-French Treatise on which it was founded, William of Waddington's 'Manuel des Pechiez'* (London).

—— ed. 1874–8. *The History of the Holy Grail by Henry Lovelich*, 4 vols., EETS ES 20, 24, 28, 30 (London).

—— ed. 1901. *The Minor Poems of the Vernon Manuscript*, EETS OS 117 (London), II.

—— ed. 1901–3, repr. 1975. *Robert of Brunne's 'Handlyng Synne', A. D. 1303, with those parts of the Anglo-French Treatise on which it was founded, William of Waddington's 'Manuel des Pechiez'*, EETS OS 119, 123 (London).

Gairdner, J., ed. 1876. 'Lydgate's Verses on the Kings of England', in *The Historical Collections of a Citizen of London in the Fifteenth Century*, Works of the Camden Society, New Series 17 (London), pp. 49–54.

Garay, K., and M. Jeay, trans. 2000. *L'Ornement des dames*, translation of Ruelle 1967, pp. 32–9, 43, 45, 47, 53, 59, 71, 73. http://mw.mcmaster.ca/scriptorium/ruelle.html.

Gaullier-Bougassas, C., and L. Harf-Lancner, ed. 2003. *Thomas de Kent, Le Roman d'Alexandre ou Le Roman de toute chevalerie* (Paris).

Gerald of Wales. 1868. *Itinerarium Kambriae*, ed. J. F. Dimock, Rolls Series 21, vol. 6 (London).

Gessler, J., ed. 1934. *La Manière de langage qui enseigne à bien parler et écrire le français. Modèles de conversations composés en Angleterre à la fin de XIVe siècle* (Brussels).

Giles, J. A., trans. 1968 [1852–4]. *Matthew Paris's English History, from the Year 1235 to 1273*, 3 vols. (New York [London]).

Gilleland, J. R. 1988. 'Eight Anglo-Norman Cosmetic Recipes: MS Cambridge, Trinity College 1044', *Romania* 109:50–67.

Glauning, O., ed. 1900. *Lydgate's Minor Poems: The Two Nightingale Poems (A.D. 1446)*, EETS ES 80 (London).

Glover, J., ed. 1865. *Le Livere de Reis de Brittanie e Le Livere de Reis de Engletere*, Rolls Series 42 (London).

Goering, J., and F. A. C. Mantello, ed. and trans. 2010. *The Letters of Robert Grosseteste, Bishop of Lincoln* (Toronto).

Gorman, J. C., ed. 1960. *William of Newburgh's Explanatio sacri epithalamii in matrem sponsi* (Fribourg).

Gouttebroze, J., and A. Queffélec, trans. 1990. *Guernes de Pont-Sainte-Maxence, La Vie de saint Thomas Becket, traduite en français moderne* (Paris).

Goymer, C. R. 1961–2. 'A Parallel-Text Edition of the Middle English Prose Version(s) of *The Mirror of St Edmund* Based on the Known Complete Manuscripts' (Unpublished MA dissertation, University of London).

Gransden, A., ed. and trans. 1964. *The Chronicle of Bury St Edmunds, 1212–1301* (London).

Grant, J., ed. 1978. *La Passiun de seint Edmund*, ANTS 36 (London).

Green, M. H., ed. and trans. 2001. *The Trotula: A Medieval Compendium of Women's Medicine* (Philadelphia).

Greenway, D., ed. and trans. 1996. Henry Archdeacon of Huntingdon, *Historia Anglorum: The History of the English People* (Oxford).

Greenway, D., and J. Sayers, trans. 1989. Jocelin of Brakelond, *Chronicle of the Abbey of Bury St Edmunds* (Oxford).

Gregory the Great (Saint Gregory, Gregory I). *Dialogues*, in *Patrologia Latina* 77.149B–431A.

Gros, G., ed. and trans. 2001. 'Joseph d'Arimathie', in *Le Livre du Graal*, ed. D. Poirion *et al.* (Paris), I, pp. 1–567.

Guiton, P. A, ed. and trans. 1924. *Histoire de Foulques Fitz Garin, Edited and Annotated* (London).

Hardy, W., ed. 1864. Jehan de Waurin, *Recueil des croniques et anchiennes istories de la Grant Bretaigne, a present nomme Engleterre*, Rolls Series 39, I (London).

Harf-Lancner, L., and E. C. Armstrong, trans. and ed. 1994. *Le Roman d'Alexandre* (Paris).

Hassell, J. W., ed. 1991. 'Thomas Sampson's Dictaminal Treatises and the Teaching of French in Medieval England: An Edition and Study' (unpublished Ph.D. dissertation, University of Toronto).

Hathaway, E. J., *et al.* [P. T. Ricketts, C. A. Robson and A. D. Wilshere], ed. 1976. *Fouke le Fitz Waryn*. ANTS 26–8 (Oxford).

Hausknecht, E. 1881, repr. 1969. *The Romaunce of the Sowdone of Babylone and of Ferumbras his sone who conquerede Rome*, EETS ES 38 (London).

Hearne, T, ed. 1970 [1774]. *Johannis Lelandi Antiquarii de rebus Britannicis collectanea, cum Thomae Hearnii praefatione notis et indice ad editionem primam, editio altera*, 6 vols. (Westmead [London]).

Hemming, T. D., ed. 1994. *La Vie de saint Alexis: Texte du manuscrit A (B.N. nouv. acq. fr. 4503)* (Exeter).

Hennecke, E. 1963. *New Testament Apocrypha*, ed. W. Schneemelcher and R. M. Wilson, vol. 1: *Gospels and Related Writings*, 3rd edn (Philadelphia).

Henry, A. 1986. 'Un texte oenologique de Jofroi de Waterford et Servais Copale', *Romania* 107: 1–37.

Herrtage, S. J., ed. 1879. *Sir Ferumbras*, EETS ES 34 (London).

Hesketh, G., ed. 1996–2000. *La Lumere as lais by Pierre d'Abernon of Fetcham*, 3 vols., ANTS 54–8 (London).

—— ed. 2006. *Rossignos by John of Howden*, ANTS 63 (London).

Higden, Ranulf. 1869. *Polychronicon*, ed. C. Babington, Rolls Series 41, vol. 2 (London).

Higgins, I. M., trans. 2011. *The Book of John Mandeville with Related Texts* (Indianapolis).

Hippeau, C., ed. 1859, repr. 1969. *La Vie de saint Thomas le martyr, archevêque de Canterbury, par Garnier de Pont-Sainte-Maxence, poète du XIIe siècle* (Paris, repr. Geneva).

Holden, A. J., ed. 1970–3. *Le Roman de Rou de Wace*, 3 vols. (Paris).

—— ed. 1979. *Ipomedon, poème de Hue de Rotelande (fin du XIIe siècle)*, Bibliothèque française et romane B 17 (Paris).

—— ed. 1984. *Le Roman de Waldef (Cod. Bodmer 168)* (Cologny-Genève).

—— ed. 1991–3. *Protheselaus by Hue de Rotelande*, 3 vols., ANTS 47–9 (London).

Horrall, S. M. 1981a. 'Christian Cato: A Middle English Translation of the *Disticha Catonis*', *Florilegium* 3: 158–97.

—— 1981b. 'An Unknown Middle English Translation of the *Distichs* of Cato', *Anglia* 99: 25–37.

—— gen. ed. 1978–2000. *The Southern Version of* Cursor Mundi, 5 vols. (Ottawa).

Hourihane, C., ed. 2009. *Pontius Pilate, Anti-Semitism and the Passion in Medieval Art* (Princeton).

Hunt, T., ed. 1983. *Rauf de Linham, Kalender*, ANTS PTS 1 (London).

—— ed. 1985. *Les Gius partiz des eschez: Two Anglo-Norman Chess Treatises*, ANTS PTS 3 (London).

—— ed. 1994. *Le Livre de Catun*, ANTS PTS 11 (London).

—— ed. 1995. 'An Anglo-Norman Treatise on Female Religious', *Medium Aevum* 64.2: 205–31.

—— ed. 1997. *Anglo-Norman Medicine, Vol. 2: Shorter Treatises* (Woodbridge).

—— ed. 1998a. *Sermons on Joshua*, vol. I: Sermon 1, ANTS PTS 12 (London).

—— ed. 1998b. *Sermons on Joshua*, vol. II: Sermons 2–5, ANTS PTS 13 (London).

—— ed. 2000. 'A New Fragment of Jofroi de Waterford's *Segré de Segrez*', *Romania* 118: 289–314.

—— ed. 2004. *Le Chant des Chanz*, ANTS 61–2 (Oxford).

—— ed. 2006. *Les Cantiques Salemon: The Song of Songs in MS Paris BNF fr. 14966*, Medieval Women Texts and Contexts 16 (Turnhout).

—— ed. 2011. *Old French Medical Texts* (Paris).

—— ed. 2012. *Les Paroles Salomun*, ANTS 70 (London).

—— ed. 2014. *An Anglo-Norman Medical Compendium (Cambridge, Trinity College MS O.2.5 (1109))*, ANTS PTS 18 (Oxford).

Hurst, D., ed., 1960. Bede, *In Lucae Evangelium expositio*, Corpus Christianorum, Series Latina 120 (Turnhout).

Hyatte, R., trans. 1997. *The Prophet of Islam in Old French: The Romance of Muhammad (1258) and the Book of Muhammad's Ladder (1264)*. (Leiden).

Ikegami, K., ed. 1999. *Barlaam and Josaphat: A Transcription of MS Egerton 876 with Notes, Glossary and Comparative Study of the Middle English and Japanese Versions* (New York).

Irvine, S., ed. 2004. *The Anglo-Saxon Chronicle: A Collaborative Edition, Vol. 7, MS E* (Cambridge).

Isoz, C., ed. 1988–94. *Les Proverbes de Salemon by Sanson de Nantuil*, 3 vols., ANTS 44, 45, 50 (London).

Jaubert, A., ed. and trans. 1960. *Origène, Homélies sur Josué*, Sources chrétiennes 71 (Paris).

Jeanroy, A., ed. 1924. *Le Théâtre religieux en France du XIe au XIIIe siècles* (Paris).

Jenkins, T. A., J. M. Manly, M. K. Pope and J. G. Wright, ed. 1943. La Seinte Resurreccion *from the Paris and Canterbury MSS*, ANTS 4 (Oxford).

Johnston, R. C., ed. and trans. 1981. *Chronique de la guerre entre les Anglois et les Ecossais en 1173 et 1174*. In English as *Jordan Fantosme's Chronicle*. (Oxford).

Jordan, L., trans. 1906. *Das Volksbuch von Fulko Fitz Warin*, Romanische Meistererzähler 7 (Leipzig).

Judic, B., ed. 1992. Grégoire le grand, *Règle pastorale*, Sources Chrétiennes 381 (Paris).

Keenan, A. E., ed. and trans. 1932. 'Thasci Caecili Cypriani, *De habitu virginum*: A Commentary, with an Introduction and Translation' (Ph.D. Dissertation), CUA Patristic Studies 34 (Washington, DC).

Keller, H., ed. 1990. *Wace, La Vie de sainte Marguerite*, Beihefte zur Zeitschrift für Romanische Philologie 229 (Tübingen).

Kelly, T. E., trans. 1997. *Fouke le Fitz Waryn*, in *Robin Hood and Other Outlaw Tales*, ed. S. Knight and T. Ohlgren (Kalamazoo), pp. 687–723.

Kemp-Welch, A., trans. 1904. *The History of Fulk Fitz-Warine, Englished by Alice Kemp-Welch with an Introduction by L. Brandin Ph.D.* (London).

Kerns, L. 2008. *The Secret of Secrets (Secretum secretorum): A Modern Translation, with Introduction, of the Governance of Princes* (Lewiston).

King, A., ed. and trans. 2005a. *Sir Thomas Gray, Scalacronica 1272–1363*, Surtees Society 209 (Woodbridge).

McKitterick, D., ed. 2005. *The Trinity Apocalypse (Trinity College Cambridge, MS R.16.2)* (London).

Kjellman, H., ed. 1977 [1922]. *La Deuxième Collection anglo-normande des miracles de la sainte Vierge* (Geneva [Paris]).

—— ed. 1974 [1935]. *La Vie seint Edmund le Rei: Poème anglo-normand du XIIe siècle par Denis Piramus* (Gothenburg, repr. Geneva).

Koch, J., ed. 1879. *Chardri's* Josaphaz, Set dormanz *und* Petit Plet: *Dichtungen in der anglo-normannischen Mundart des XIII Jahrhunderts*, Altfranzösische Bibliothek 1 (Heilbronn).

——ed. 1886. *Li Rei de Engleterre: ein anglo-normannischer Geschichtsauszug* (Berlin).

Koenig, V. F., ed. 1970. *Les Miracles de Nostre Dame par Gautier de Coinci* (Geneva), 'De l'ymage Nostre Dame de Sardanei', IV, 378–411.

Kölbing, E., and E. Koschwitz, ed. 1889. *Hue de Rotelande's* Ipomedon: *Ein französischer abenteuerroman des 12. jahrhunderts* (Breslau).

Kornexl, L., ed. 1993. *Die* Regularis concordia *und ihre altenglische Interlinearversion* (Munich).

Kristol, A. M., ed. 1995. *Manières de langage (1396, 1399, 1415)*, ANTS 53 (London).

Kunstmann, P., trans. 1981. *Vierge et merveille: Les miracles de Notre-Dame narratifs au moyen âge* (Paris).

—— ed. 1982. Adgar, *Le Gracial* (Ottawa).

Kuriyagawa, F., ed. 1974. *Parvus Cato, Magnus Cato* (Tokyo).

Lafont, R., ed. and trans. 1998. *La Chanson de sainte Foi* (Geneva).

Lagomarsini, C. 2011. 'The Prose *Description of England*: A Hitherto Unedited Anglo-Norman Text from BL Additional MS 14252', *Medium Aevum* 80: 325–35.

Lawrence, C. H., ed. 1960. *St Edmund of Abingdon: A Study in Hagiography and History* (Oxford).

—— trans. 1996. *The Life of St Edmumd by Matthew Paris* (Stroud).

Leclercq, J., H. Rochais and C. H. Talbot, ed. 1955–77. *S. Bernardi Opera*, 8 vols. (Rome).

Lega-Weekes, E. 1906–7. 'The Mohun Chronicle at Haccombe', *Devon Notes and Queries* 4: 17–22.

Legge, M. D., ed. 1941. *Anglo-Norman Letters and Petitions from All Souls MS 182*, ANTS 2 (Oxford).

Lemay, H. R. 1992. *Women's Secrets: A Translation of Pseudo-Albertus Magnus's* De secretis mulierum *with Commentaries* (Albany).

Le Person, M., ed. 2003. *Fierabras: Chanson de geste du XIIe siècle*, Classiques français du Moyen Âge 142 (Paris).

—— trans. 2012. *Fierabras: chanson de geste du XIIe siècle* (Paris).

Letts, M., ed. and trans. 1953. *Mandeville's Travels: Texts and Translations*, 2 vols. (London).

Lewis, C. S. 1952. *The Voyage of the Dawn Treader* (London).

Löfstedt, L., ed. 1992–2001. *Gratiani Decretum: La traduction en ancien français du Décret de Gratien: édition critique*, 5 vols. (Helsinki).

Luard, H. R., ed. 1861. *Roberti Grosseteste episcopi quondam Lincolniensis epistolae*, Rolls Series 25 (London).

Lupack, A., ed. 1990. *Three Middle English Charlemagne Romances* (Kalamazoo). http://d.lib.rochester.edu/teams/publication/lupack-three-middle-english-charlemagne-romances

Macaulay, G. C., ed. 1899–1902. *The Complete Works of John Gower*, 4 vols. (Oxford).

Mackie, E. A., ed. 2002. 'Robert Grosseteste's *Chasteau d'amur*: A Text in Context' (unpublished Ph.D. dissertation, University of Toronto).

Mackie, E. A., trans. 2003. 'Robert Grosseteste's Anglo-Norman Treatise on the Loss and Restoration of Creation, Commonly Known as *Le Château d'amour*: An English Prose Translation', in *Robert Grosseteste and the Beginnings of a British Theological Tradition, Papers Delivered at the Grosseteste Colloquium Held at Greyfriars, Oxford on 3rd July 2002*, ed. M. O'Carroll (Rome), pp. 151–79.
Marie de France. 1994. *Fables*, ed. and trans. H. Spiegel (Toronto).
Marshall, L. 1971. 'A Lexicographical Study of Robert of Greatham's *Miroir*' (unpublished MA thesis, University of Manchester).
Martin, C. F. J., trans. 1996. Robert Grosseteste, *On the Six Days of Creation: A Translation of the* Hexaëmeron (Oxford).
Martin, C. T., ed. 1882–5. *Registrum epistolarum fratris Johannis Peckham, archiepiscopi cantuariensis*, 3 vols., Rolls Series 77 (London).
Marvin, J., ed. and trans. 2006. *The Oldest Anglo-Norman Prose* Brut *Chronicle: An Edition and Translation* (Woodbridge).
Matzke, J. E., ed. 1909. *Les Oeuvres de Simund de Freine, publiées d'après tous les manuscrits connus* (Paris).
Maxwell, H., ed. and trans. 1907. *Scalacronica: The Reigns of Edward I, Edward II and Edward III as recorded by Sir Thomas Gray* (Glasgow).
Meneghetti, M. L., ed. 1979. *I fatti di Bretagna: Cronache genealogiche anglo-normanne dal XII al XIV secolo* (Padua).
Merrilees, B. S., ed. 1970. *Le Petit Plet*, ANTS 20 (Oxford).
—— ed. 1977. *La Vie des set dormanz by Chardri*, ANTS 35 (London).
Merrilees, B., and B. Sitarz-Fitzpatrick, ed. 1993. *Liber Donati: A Fifteenth-Century Manual of French*, ANTS PTS 9 (London).
Meyer, P., ed. 1883. 'La *Vie de Saint Grégoire le Grand*', *Romania* 12: 145–208.
Michel, F., ed. 1840. *Histoire de Foulques Fitz-Warin, publiée d'après un manuscrit du Musée Britannique* (Paris).
Minnis, A. J., and A. B. Scott, ed. 1988. *Medieval Literary Theory and Criticism c. 1100–c. 1375: The Commentary Tradition* (Oxford).
Monfrin, J. 1947. 'Le "Secret des secrets": Recherches sur les traductions françaises suivies du texte de Jofroi de Waterford et Servais Copale' (unpublished, and apparently unavailable, dissertation, École des Chartes).
Morgan, N. J. 1990. *The Lambeth Apocalypse, Manuscript 209 in Lambeth Palace Library: A Critical Study* [facsimile and commentary with palaeographic contribution by M. Brown], 2 vols. (London).
Morrall, E. J., ed. 1968. 'The Text of Michel Velser's "Mandeville" Translation', in *Probleme mittelalterlicher Überlieferung und Textkritik: Oxforder Colloquium 1966*, ed. P. F. Ganz and W. Schröder (Berlin), pp. 183–96.
Mosher, D. L., trans. 1982. *Eighty Three Different Questions*, Fathers of the Church 70 (Washington).
Mullally, E. 2002. *The Deeds of the Normans in Ireland = La Geste des Engleis en Yrlande: A New Edition of the Chronicle Formerly Known as the Song of Dermot and the Earl* (Dublin).
Murray, J., ed. 1918. *Le Chateau d'amour de Robert Grosseteste, Évêque de Lincoln* (Paris).
Mynors, R. A. B., R. M. Thomson and M. Winterbottom, ed. and trans. 1998–9. *William of Malmesbury, Gesta regum Anglorum: The History of the English Kings*, 2 vols. (Oxford).
Napoli, C., ed. 1979. *Le Livre du Rossignolet: Une traduction médiévale de la* Philomena praevia, Le moyen français 4 (Palermo).
Neuhaus, C., ed. 1886, repr. 1968. *Adgar's* Marienlegenden, *Nach der Londoner Handschrift Egerton 612* (Heilbronn, repr. Wiesbaden).
Neuhaus, C., ed. 1887. *Das Dulwich'er Adgar-Fragment* (Aschersleben).
Nichols, F. M. 1865. *Britton: The French Text Carefully Revised with an English Translation, Introduction and Notes*, 2 vols. (Oxford).

Nobel, P., ed. 1996. *Poème anglo-normand sur l'Ancien Testament: édition et commentaire*, vol. I: *Étude, notes, glossaire*, vol. II: *Texte et variantes*, Nouvelle bibliothèque du Moyen Âge 37 (Paris).

O'Sullivan, M. I, ed., 1935. *Firumbras and Otuel and Roland*. EETS os 198 (London).

Orengo, R., ed. 2013. *Les Dialogues de Grégoire le Grand traduits par Angier, publiés d'après le manuscrit Paris, BNF, Fr. 24766*. 2 vols. (Paris).

Owen, A., ed. 1977 [1929]. *Le Traité de Walter de Bibbesworth sur la langue française* (Geneva [Paris]).

Pannier, L., and P. Meyer, ed. 1877. *Le Débat des hérauts d'armes de France et d'Angleterre*, with *The Debate between the Heralds of England and France by John Coke*, Société des Anciens Textes Français (Paris).

Pantin, W. A., ed. 1929. 'A Medieval Treatise on Letter-Writing, with Examples, from the Rylands Latin MS 394', *Bulletin of the John Rylands Library* 13.2: 326–82.

Panunzio, S., ed. 1967. *Miroir, ou Les Évangiles des domnées* (Bari).

Paris, G., ed. 1866. 'Fragment d'un petit poème dévot du commencement du XIIe siècle', *Jahrbuch für romanische und englische Literatur* 6: 362–9.

—— ed. 1875. *Mainet: fragments d'une chanson de geste du XIIe*, *Romania* 4: 305–37.

Paris, P. M., ed. 1836–8. *Les Grandes Chroniques de France, selon que elles sont conservées en l'église de Saint-Denis en France*, 6 vols. (Paris), I.

Parsons, H. R., ed. 1929. 'Anglo-Norman Books of Courtesy and Nurture', *Publications of the Modern Language Association of America* 44: 383–455.

Paviot, J., ed. 2008. *Li Charboclois d'armes du conquest precious de la Terre saint de promission*, Documents relatif à l'histoire des croisades, publiées par l'Académie des Inscriptions et Belles Lettres, XX (Paris).

Pickford, C. E. 1974. *The Song of Songs: A Twelfth-Century French Version* (Oxford).

Pitts, B. A., ed. 2010. *Revelacion: (BL Royal 2. D. XIII)*, ANTS 68 (London).

Ponceau, J., ed. 1997. *L'Estoire del Saint Graal*, 2 vols. Classiques français du Moyen Âge 120, 121 (Paris).

Pons, N., ed. 1990. *'L'Honneur de la couronne de France': Quatre libelles contre les Anglais (vers 1418–vers 1429)* (Paris).

Pope, M. H., trans. 1977. *Song of Songs: A New Translation with Introduction and Commentary*, The Anchor Bible 7C (New York), pp. 112–31.

Pope, M. K., ed. 1955–64. *The Romance of Horn*, 2 vols. ANTS 9–10, 12–13 (Oxford).

Purdie, R., ed. 2001. *Ipomadon*, EETS os 316 (Oxford).

Püschel, R. ed 1974 [1887]. *Le Livre du chemin de long estude* (Geneva [Berlin]).

Pyne, H., trans. 1870. *England and France in the Fifteenth Century: The Contemporary French Tract entitled 'The Debate between the Heralds of France and England'* (London).

Raby, F. J. E., ed. 1939. *Poems of John of Howden*, Surtees Society 154 (London).

Raynaud, G., ed. 1882. 'Le Miracle de Sardenai', *Romania* 11: 519–37.

—— 1885, ed. 'Le Miracle de Sardenai (article complémentaire)', *Romania* 14: 82–93.

Reeve, M. D., ed. and N. Wright, trans. 2007. *Geoffrey of Monmouth, The History of the Kings of Britain: An Edition and Translation of* De gestis Britonum *(Historia regum Britanniae)* (Woodbridge).

Reichl, K., ed. 1973. *Religiöse Dichtung im englischen Hochmittelalter. Untersuchung und Edition der Handschrift B. 14. 39 des Trinity College in Cambridge* (Munich).

——ed. 1975. 'An Anglo-Norman Legend of Saint Margaret (MS BM. Add. 38664)', *Romania* 96: 53–66.

Reinsch, R., ed. 1879. 'Guillaume le Clerc, *Les Joies Nostre Dame*', *Zeitschrift für romanische Philologie* 3:200–31.

——ed. and trans. 1892 [1890]. *Le Bestiaire: Das Thierbuch des Normannischen Dichters Guillaume le Clerc* (Leipzig).

Richardson, H. G, ed. 1942. 'Letters of the Oxford *Dictatores*', in *Formularies which Bear on the History of Oxford, c. 1204–1420*, ed. H. E. Salter, W. A. Pantin and H. G. Richardson (Oxford), II, 329–450.

Richardson, L. B., ed. 1967. '*La Vie seint Aymon*: The Old French Prose Version of the Life of St Edmund, King of East Anglia' (unpublished Ph.D. dissertation, Columbia University).

Rigg, A. G., ed. 1978. *The Poems of Walter of Wimborne*, Studies and Texts 42 (Toronto).

Riley, H. T., ed. 1859–62. *Munimenta Gildhallae Londoniensis*, 3 vols. in 4, Rolls Series 12 (London).

Ronsjö, E., ed. 1942. *La Vie de saint Nicolas par Wace, Poème religieux du XIIe siècle, publié d'aprés tous les manuscrits*, Études romanes de Lund 5 (Lund).

Rothwell, W., ed. 1990. *Walter de Bibbesworth, Le Tretiz*, ANTS PTS 6 (London).

—— ed. 2005. *Femina (Trinity College, Cambridge MS B. 14. 40)*(Aberystwyth). Online edition: http://www.anglo-norman.net/texts/femina.pdf.

—— ed. 2009. *Walter de Bibbesworth, Le Tretiz* (Aberystwyth). Online edition: http://www.anglo-norman.net/texts/bibb-gt.pdf.

Roy, B., ed. 1974. *L'Art d'amours* (Leiden).

Ruelle, P., ed. 1967. *L'Ornement des Dames (Ornatus mulierum): Texte anglo-normand du XIIIe siècle* (Brussels).

—— ed. 1973. *Le Besant de Dieu de Guillaume le clerc de Normandie* (Brussels).

Russell, D. W., ed. 1989. *Légendier apostolique anglo-normand* (Montreal).

—— ed. 1995. *La Vie seint Richard evesque de Cycestre by Pierre d'Abernon of Fetcham*, ANTS 51 (London).

—— trans. 2012. *Verse Saints' Lives Written in the French of England*, FRETS 5, Medieval and Renaissance Texts and Studies 431 (Tempe AZ).

—— ed. 2014. *La Vie seint Edmund le Rei, by Denis Piramus*, with an art-historical excursus by K. A. Smith, ANTS 71 (Oxford).

Rutledge, T. J. S. 1973. 'A Critical Edition of *La Vie de Seint Josaphaz*, a Thirteenth-Century Poem by the Anglo-Norman Poet Chardri' (unpublished Ph.D. dissertation, University of Toronto).

Ryan, W. G., trans. 1993. *Jacobus de Voragine, The Golden Legend: Readings on the Saints*, 2 vols. (Princeton).

Sajavaara, K., ed. 1967. *The Middle English Translations of Robert Grosseteste's* Chateau d'Amour, Mémoires de la Société Néophilologique de Helsinki 32 (Helsinki).

Sandler, L. F. 1999. *The Psalter of Robert de Lisle in the British Library* (London).

Scase, W., ed. 2011. *A Facsimile Edition of the Vernon Manuscript, Oxford, Bodleian Library,MS. Eng. Poet. A. 1* (Oxford).

Schauwecker, Y. 2007. *Die Diätetik nach dem 'Secretum secretorum' in der Version von Jofroi de Waterford: Teiledition und lexikalische Untersuchung* (Würzburg).

Schneegans, F. E., ed. 1925. *La Résurrection du Sauveur: Fragment d'un Mystère anglo-normand du XI–I[e] siècle, publié d'aprés le manuscrit 902 du fonds français de la Bibliothèque nationale* (Strasbourg).

Schnerb-Lièvre, M., ed. 1982. *Le Songe du vergier: édité d'après le manuscrit Royal 19 C IV de la British Library* 2 vols. (Paris).

Scott, J., ed. 1981. *The Early History of Glastonbury: An Edition, Translation and Study of William of Malmesbury's* De Antiquitate Glastonie Ecclesie (Woodbridge).

Sepet, M., trans. 1901. *Origines catholiques du théâtre moderne* (Paris).

Sheingorn, P., ed. and trans. 1995. '*Passio*: The Passion of Sainte Foy'; '*Translatio*: The Translation of Sainte Foy, Virgin and Martyr, to the Conques Monastery', in *The Book of Sainte Foy*, trans. P. Sheingorn and R. L. A. Clark (Philadephia), pp. 33–8, 263–74.

Shields, H., ed. 1979. *Le Livre de Sibile by Philippe de Thaon*, ANTS 37 (London).

Shirley, J., trans. 1975. *Garnier's Becket, translated from the 12th-century* Vie saint Thomas le martyr de Cantorbire *of Garnier of Pont-Sainte-Maxence* (London).

Short, I., ed. 1973. *The Anglo-Norman Pseudo-Turpin Chronicle of William de Briane.* ANTS 24 (Oxford)

—— ed. and trans. 1994. 'Gaimar's Epilogue and Geoffrey of Monmouth's *Liber vetustissimus*', *Speculum* 69: 323–43.

—— ed. 2005, *La Chanson de Roland: The Song of Roland: The French Corpus*, gen. ed. J. J. Duggan, I (Turnhout), pp. 8–338.

—— ed. and trans. 2009. *Geffrei Gaimar, Estoire des Engleis / History of the English* (Oxford).

—— trans. 2013. *A Life of Thomas Becket in Verse*, Mediaeval Sources in Translation 56 (Toronto).

Short, I., and B. Merrilees, ed. 1979. *Benedeit, the Anglo-Norman Voyage of St Brendan* (Manchester).

Short, I., B. Merrilees and D. Tixhon. 1999. *Le Voyage de saint Brendan*: http://saintbrendan.d-t-x.com/

Sinclair, K. V., ed. 1995. *Corset by Robert le Chapelain: A Rhymed Commentary on the Seven Sacraments*, ANTS 52 (London).

Skeat, W. W., ed. 1871. *Joseph of Arimathie: Otherwise Called the Romance of the Seint Graal or Holy Grail*, EETS OS 44 (London).

—— ed. 1906. 'Nominale Sive Verbale', *Transactions of the Philological Society* (London), pp. 1*–50*.

Smithers, G., ed. 1952 and 1957. *Kyng Alisaunder*, EETS OS 227 and 237 (London).

Södergård, Ö., ed. 1948. *La Vie d'Édouard le Confesseur: Poème anglo-normand du XIIe siècle* (Uppsala).

—— ed. 1989. *Art de kalender de Rauf de Lenham: Poème anglo-normand de l'année 1256*, Acta Universitatis Lundensis 47 (Stockholm).

Sommer, H. O., ed. 1909. *The Vulgate Version of the Arthurian Romances: Volume I, Lestoire del saint graal* (Washington).

Speich, J. H., ed. 1988. *La Destructioun de Rome (d'après le ms. de Hanovre IV, 578)*, European University Studies 135 (Berne).

Spence, J. 2011. 'The *Mohun Chronicle*: An Edition and Translation', *Nottingham Medieval Studies* 55: 149–216.

Spiegel, H., ed. 1994. Marie de France, *Fables* (Toronto).

Spiele, I., ed. 1975. *Li Romanz de Dieu et de sa mère d'Herman de Valenciennes, chanoine et prêtre (XIIe siècle)* (Leiden).

Steele, R., ed. 1898, repr. 1975. *Three Prose Versions of the* Secreta Secretorum, EETS ES 74 (London, repr. New York).

Stengel, E., ed. 1879. 'Die ältesten Anleitungsschriften zur Erlernung der französischen Sprache', *Zeitschrift für neufranzösische Sprache und Literatur* 1: 1–40.

—— ed. 1886. *Elie's de Wincestre, eines Anonymus und Everarts Übertragungen der* Disticha Catonis (Marburg).

Stevenson, J., ed. 1836. *Scalacronica by Sir Thomas Gray of Heton, Knight: A Chronicle of England and Scotland from A.D. MLXVI to A.D. MCCCLXII* (Edinburgh).

—— ed. and trans. 1875. *The Legend of Fulk Fitz-Warin*, in *Radulphi de Coggeshall Chronicon anglicanum*, Rolls Series 66 (London), pp. 275–415.

Stone, L. W., ed. 1946–7. 'Jean de Howden: poète anglo-normand du XIIIe siècle', *Romania* 69: 496–519

Stubbs, W., ed. 1868. *Chronica magistri Rogeri de Houedene*, Rolls Series 51 (London), I.

Suchier, H. 1909 Transcription of *Le Roman de Waldef*, given to the University of Göttingen in 1952 (Holden, ed. 1984, n. 1).

Sullens, I., ed. 1983. Robert Mannyng of Brunne, *Handlyng Synne* (Binghamton, NY).

—— ed. 1996. Robert Mannyng of Brunne, *The Chronicle*, Medieval and Renaissance Texts and Studies 153 (Binghamton, NY).

Szirmai, J. C., ed. 1985 *La Bible anonyme du Ms. Paris BN.f.fr. 763: édition critique* (Amsterdam).

—— ed. 2005. *Un Fragment de la Genèse en vers (fin XIIIe-début XIV siècle): Edition du MS Brit. Libr. Harley 3775* (Geneva).

Tanquerey, F. J., ed. 1916. *Recueil de lettres anglo-françaises 1265–1399* (Paris).
Taylor, C., ed. 2006. *Debating the Hundred Years War*: Pour ce que plusieurs (la loy salicque) *and* A declaration of the trew and dewe title of Henry VIII (Cambridge).
Taylor, E., trans. 1837. *Master Wace: His Chronicle of the Norman Conquest from the* Roman de Rou (London).
Thackeray, H., R. Marcus and A. Wikgren, ed. and trans. 1997 [1930]. Josephus, *Jewish Antiquities* (Cambridge MA) [London].
Thomas, J. T. E., ed., 2002. *Guernes de Pont-Sainte-Maxence, La Vie de saint Thomas de Canterbury*, 2 vols. (Louvain).
Thomson, R. M., ed. and trans. 1974. *The Chronicle of the Election of Hugh, Abbot of Bury St Edmunds and Later Bishop of Ely* (Oxford).
Tolkien, J. R. R., E. V. Gordon and N. Davis, ed. 1967. *Sir Gawain and the Green Knight*, 2nd ed. (Oxford).
Trachsler, R., ed. 1994. *Escanor: Roman arthurien en vers de la fin du XIIIe siècle*, 2 vols. (Geneva).
Troendle, D. F., ed. 1960. 'John Gower's *Mirour de l'omme*' (unpublished Ph.D. dissertation, Brown University).
Tschann, J., and M. B. Parkes, intro. 1996. *Facsimile of Oxford, Bodleian Library, MS Digby 86*, EETS ss 16 (Oxford).
Turcan, M., ed. and trans. 1971. *Tertullien, La Toilette des femmes (De cultu feminarum)*, Sources Chrétiennes 173 (Paris).
Tyson, D. B., ed. 1975. 'An Early French Prose History of the Kings of England', *Romania* 96: 1–26.
Urwin, K., ed. 1980–1. *The Life of Saint John the Almsgiver*, 2 vols., ANTS 38–9 (London).
Van Emden, W., ed. 1999. *Le Jeu d'Adam*, 2nd edn, British Rencesvals Publications 1 (Edinburgh).
Van Houts, E. M. C, ed. 1992–5. *The* Gesta Normannorum ducum *of William of Jumièges, Orderic Vitalis and Robert of Torigni*, 2 vols. (Oxford).
Viard, J., ed. 1920–53. *Les Grandes Chroniques de France: publiées pour la Société de l'histoire de France*, 9 vols., Société de l'histoire de France 395 (Paris), I.
Walberg, E., ed. 1922, repr. 1936. *La Vie de saint Thomas le martyr, par Guernes de Pont-Sainte-Maxence: poème historique du XIIe siècle (1172–74)* (Lund) [1936 repr. Paris, shortened critical apparatus]. Electronic version: http://www.anglo-norman.net/sources/.
—— ed. 1975 [1929]. *La Tradition hagiographique de saint Thomas Becket avant la fin du XIIe siècle: Études critiques* (Geneva [Paris]).
Wall, A., ed. 1919. *Handbook to the Maude Roll, Being a XVth Century MS Genealogy of the British and English Kings from Noah to Edward IV, with a Marginal History* (Auckland).
Wallace, K. Y., ed. 1983. Matthew Paris, *La Estoire seint Aedward le rei*, ANTS 41 (London).
Walpole, R. N., ed. 1976. *The Old French Johannes Translation of the* Pseudo-Turpin *Chronicle: A Critical Edition* [2 vols, includes supplement] (Berkeley).
Warnke, K., ed. 1990 [1900]. *Lais de Marie de France* with introduction and notes by L. Harf-Lancner. Lettres Gothiques (Paris).
Warner, R. D-N., ed. 1917. *Early English Homilies from the Twelfth Century MS. Vesp. D. XIV*, EETS OS 152 (Oxford).
Waters, E. G. R., ed. 1928. *The Anglo-Norman Voyage of St Brendan by Benedeit, a Poem of the Twelfth Century* (Oxford).
Weber, R., ed. 1975 [1969]. *Biblia sacra iuxta vulgatam versionem*, 2 vols. (Stuttgart).
—— ed. 1983. *Biblia sacra iuxta vulgatam versionem*, 3rd edn [emended], 2 vols. (Stuttgart), II.
Weiss, J., ed. and trans. 2002 [rev. ed. of 1999]. *Wace's* Roman de Brut: *A History of the British* (Exeter).
Weiss, J., trans. 2008. *Boeve de Haumtone and Gui de Warewic: Two Anglo-Norman Romances*, FRETS 3, Medieval and Renaissance Texts and Studies 332 (Tempe).
Whittaker, W. J., ed. and trans. 1895. *Mirroir des Justices*, Selden Society 7 (London).

Wilkie, E. C., trans. 1978. 'Anglo-Norman Resurrection (C Text)', *Allegorica* 3.2: 127–61.
Willson, N. K., ed. 1951. 'Critical Edition of the "Vie de Saint Clement Pape"' (unpublished Ph.D. dissertation, University of Cambridge).
Wilshere, A. D., ed. 1982. *Mirour de seinte eglyse (St Edmund of Abingdon's Speculum Ecclesiae)*, ANTS 40 (London).
Wilson, W. B., trans., N. W. Van Baak, rev. and R. F. Yeager 1992. John Gower, *Mirour de l'omme (The Mirror of Mankind)* (East Lansing).
Wimsatt, J., ed. 2009. *Chaucer and the Poems of 'Ch'* (Kalamazoo, MI); repr. of *Chaucer and the Poems of 'Ch' in University of Pennsylvania MS French 15*, ed. Wimsatt 1982, Chaucer Studies 9 (Cambridge).
Wogan-Browne, J., and G. S. Burgess, trans. 1996. *Virgin Lives and Holy Deaths: Two Exemplary Anglo-Norman Biographies for Women* (London).
Wogan-Browne, J., and T. Fenster, trans. 2010. *The Life of Saint Alban by Matthew Paris*. FRETS 2, Medieval and Renaissance Texts and Studies 342 (Tempe).
Wood, A. C., ed. 1911. *Fulk Fitz-Warin: Text and a Study of the Language* (London).
Wright, J. G., ed. 1931. *La Résurrection du Sauveur, fragment de jeu* (Paris).
Wright, T., ed. and trans. 1855. *The History of Fulk Fitz Warine, an Outlawed Baron in the Reign of King John* (London).
Wright, T., ed. 1872. *Feudal Manuals of English History: A series of popular sketches of our national history, compiled at different periods, from the thirteenth century to the fifteenth, for the use of the feudal gentry and nobility* (London).
Wunderli, P., ed. 1968. *Le Livre de l'Eschiele Mahomet: Die französischen Fassung einer alfonsinischen Übersetzung* (Bern).
Zimmerman, O. J., trans. 1959. *Saint Gregory the Great: Dialogues*, Fathers of the Church 39 (Washington).
Ziolkowski, J., ed. 1986. *Nigel of Canterbury, Miracles of the Virgin Mary, in Verse* (Toronto).
Zotenberg, H., and P. Meyer, ed. 1966 [1864]. *Barlaam und Josaphat: französisches Gedicht des dreizehnten Jahrhunderts von Gui de Cambrai* (Amsterdam [Stuttgart]).

Secondary Sources

Ailes, M. J. 2003. 'La Réception de *Fierabras* en Angleterre', in *Le Rayonnement de* Fierabras *dans la littérature européenne*, ed. M. Le Person, CEDIC 21 (Lyon), pp. 177–89.
—— 2008. 'Fierabras and Anglo-Norman Developments of the Chanson de Geste', *Olifant* 25.1–2: 97–109.
—— 2011. 'What's in a Name? Anglo-Norman Romances or *Chansons de geste*?', in *Medieval Romance, Medieval Contexts*, ed. R. Purdie and M. Cichon (Cambridge), pp. 61–75.
—— 2013. 'Coals to Newcastle? The Export of Anglo-Norman Literature', paper delivered at Fordham University Conference: Putting England in its Place: Cultural Production and Cultural Relations in the High Middle Ages.
Ailes, M., and P. Hardman 2008. 'How English are the English Charlemagne Romances?', in *Boundaries in Medieval Romance*, ed. N. Cartlidge (Cambridge), pp. 43–56.
Ailes, M., and A. Putter 2014. 'The French of Medieval England', in *European Francophonie: The Social, Political and Cultural History of a Prestige Language*, ed. V. Rjéoutski, G. Argent, D. Offord (Bern), pp. 51–78.
Akbari, S. C. 2004. 'The Diversity of Mankind in *The Book of John Mandeville*', in *Eastward Bound: Travel and Travelers, 1050–1550*, ed. R. Allen (Manchester), pp. 156–76.
—— 2005. 'Alexander in the Orient: Bodies and Boundaries in the *Roman de toute chevalerie*', in *Post-colonial Approaches to the European Middle Ages: Translating Cultures*, ed. A. J. Kabir and D. Williams (Cambridge), pp. 105–26.

Akbari, S. C., and K. Mallette, ed. 2013. *A Sea of Languages: Rethinking the Arabic Role in Medieval Literary History* (Toronto).

Alexandre-Bidon, D. 1989. 'La Lettre volée. Apprendre à lire a l'enfant au Moyen Âge', *Annales. Histoire, Sciences Sociales* 44.4: 953–92.

Allan, A. 1979. 'Yorkist Propaganda: Pedigree, Prophecy and the "British History" in the Reign of Edward IV', in Ross, pp. 171–92.

Allen, H. E. 1916. 'Two Middle-English Translations from the Anglo-Norman', *Modern Philology* 13.12: 741–5.

—— 1917. 'The *Manuel des Pechiez* and the Scholastic Prologue', *Romanic Review* 8: 434–62.

—— 1918. 'The Mystical Lyrics of the *Manuel des Pechiez*', *Romanic Review* 9: 154–93.

Allen, R. 2003. 'The Loyal and Disloyal Servants of King John', in *The Court Reconvenes: Courtly Literature Across the Disciplines. Selected Papers from the Ninth Triennial Congress of the International Courtly Literature Society, University of British Columbia, 25–31 July, 1998*, ed. B. K. Altmann and C. W. Carroll (Cambridge), pp. 265–74.

Allen, V. 1993. 'Portrait of a Lady: Blaunche and the Descriptive Tradition', *English Studies* 74.4: 324–42.

Amt, E. 2012. 'The Foundation Legend of Godstow Abbey: A Holy Woman's Life in Anglo-Norman Verse', in *Writing Medieval Women's Lives*, ed. C. N. Goldy and A. Livingstone (New York), pp. 13–31.

Anderson, R. 1978. 'Waldef', in *Le Roman jusqu'à la fin du XIIIe siècle*, ed. J. Frappier and R. R. Grimm, 2 vols., Grundriss der romanischen Literaturen des Mittelalters 4 (Heidelberg), I, 283–91.

Armstrong, A., and S. Kay 2011. *Knowing Poetry: Verse in Medieval France from the* Rose *to the* Rhétoriquers (Ithaca).

Arnold, I. 1937. 'Thomas Sampson and the *Orthographia Gallica*', *Medium Aevum* 6.3: 193–209.

Arnould, E. J. 1969 [1939]. 'Les Sources de *Femina Nova*', in *Studies in French Language and Mediaeval Literature Presented to Professor Mildred K. Pope by Pupils, Colleagues and Friends* (Freeport [Manchester]), pp. 1–9.

—— 1939. 'On Two Anglo-Norman Prologues', *Modern Language Review* 34: 248–51.

—— 1940. *Le Manuel des péchés: Étude de littérature religieuse anglo-normande (XIIIe siècle)* (Paris).

Ashe, L. 2007. *Fiction and History in England, 1066–1200* (Cambridge).

—— 2011. 'The Anomalous King of Conquered England', in *Every Inch a King: Kings and Kingship in the Ancient and Medieval Worlds*, ed. L. Mitchell and C. Melville (Leiden).

Ashley, K., and P. Sheingorn 1999. *Writing Faith: Text, Sign and History in the Miracles of Sainte Foy* (Chicago).

Astell, A. W. 1990. *The Song of Songs in the Middle Ages* (Ithaca).

Auerbach, E. 1959, repr. 1984. '*Figura*', in *Scenes from the Drama of European Literature* (New York, repr. Minneapolis), pp. 11–78.

Aurell, M. 2007. 'Henry II and Arthurian Legend', in *Henry II: New Interpretations*, ed. C. Harper-Bill and N. Vincent (Woodbridge), pp. 262–94.

Avril, F., and J. Lafaurie 1968. *La Librairie de Charles V* (Paris).

Avril, F., and P. D. Stirnemann 1987. *Manuscrits enluminés d'origine insulaire, VIIe–XXe siècle* (Paris).

Backhouse, J., and C. De Hamel 1988. *The Becket Leaves* (London).

Bahr, A. 2013. *Fragments and Assemblages: Forming Compilations of Medieval London* (Chicago).

Bainton, H. 2009. 'Translating the "English" Past: Cultural Identity in the *Estoire des Engleis*', in Wogan-Browne *et al.*, *Language and Culture*, pp. 179–87.

Bainton, H., 2012. 'Literate Sociability and Historical Writing in Later Twelfth-Century England', *Anglo-Norman Studies* 34: 23–40.

Baker, J. H. 1990. *Manual of Law French*, 2nd edn (Aldershot).

Baker, J. H. 1999. 'Oral Instruction in Land Law and Conveyancing, 1250–1500', in *Learning the Law: Teaching and the Transmission of English Law, 1150–1900*, ed. J. A. Bush and A. Wijffels (London), pp. 157–73.
Baker, J. H., and J. S. Ringrose 1996. *Catalogue of English Legal Manuscripts in Cambridge University Library* (Woodbridge).
Baldwin, J. W. 2013 [1998]. 'From the Ordeal to Confession: In Search of Lay Religion in Early Thirteenth-Century France', in P. Biller and A. J. Minnis, ed., *Handling Sin: Confession in the Middle Ages* (York), pp. 191–209.
Bale, A. 2006. *The Jew in the Medieval Book: English Antisemitisms, 1350–1500* (Cambridge).
—— ed. 2009. *St Edmund King and Martyr: Changing Images of a Medieval Saint* (York).
Baraz, D. 1995. 'The Incarnated Icon of Saidnaya Goes West: A Re-examination of the Motif in the Light of New Manuscript Evidence', *Le Muséon* 108: 181–91.
Barlow, F. 1986. *Thomas Becket* (Berkeley).
Barratt, A. 1997. 'Books for Nuns: Cambridge University Library MS Additional 3042', *Notes and Queries* 242, n.s. 44.3: 310–19.
—— 2008a. 'Spiritual Writings and Religious Instruction' in *The Cambridge History of the Book in Britain*, ed. N. J. Morgan and R. M. Thomson (Cambridge), II, pp. 340–66.
—— 2008b. 'Women Translators of Religious Texts', in *The Oxford History of Literary Translation in English, Vol. 1 to 1550*, ed. R. Ellis (Oxford), pp. 284–95.
Barron, C. M. 2004. *London in the Later Middle Ages: Government and People 1200–1500* (Oxford).
Barron, C. M., and N. Saul, ed. 1995, *England and the Low Countries in the Late Middle Ages* (Stroud).
Barrow, J. 1987. 'A Twelfth-Century Bishop and Literary Patron: William de Vere', *Viator* 18: 175–89.
Bartal, R. 2006. 'A Note on Bodleian Library MS Selden Supra 38, Jehan Raynzford and Joanna de Bishopsdon', *Bodleian Library Record* 19.2: 239–45.
—— 2010. 'The Illuminator of Bodleian Library MS Selden Supra 38 and his Working Methods', *Pecia* 13: 387–404.
—— 2011. 'The Pepys Apocalypse (Cambridge, Magdalene College, MS Pepys 1803) and the Readership of Religious Women, *Journal of Medieval History*, 37:4, 358–77, DOI: 10.1016/j.jmedhist.2011.09.001
Bartlett, R. 2001. 'Medieval and Modern Concepts of Race and Ethnicity', *Journal of Medieval and Early Modern Studies* 31.1: 39–56.
Bassett, S., ed. 1989. *The Origins of Anglo-Saxon Kingdoms* (London).
Baswell, C. 2002. 'Aeneas in 1381', *New Medieval Literatures* 5: 7–58.
—— 2005. 'Troy, Arthur, and the Languages of "Brutis Albyon"', in *Reading Medieval Culture: Essays in Honor of Robert W. Hanning*, ed. R. M. Stein and S. P. Prior (Notre Dame), pp. 170–97.
—— 2007. 'Multilingualism on the Page', in Strohm 2007, pp. 38–50.
—— 2010. 'The Manuscript Context', in *Matthew Paris: The Life of St Alban*, trans. J. Wogan-Browne and T. Fenster, FRETS 2, Medieval and Renaissance Texts and Studies 346 (Tempe), pp. 169–94.
—— 2015. 'Fearful Histories: The Past Contained in the Romances of Antiquity', in *Romance and History: Imagining Time from the Medieval to the Early Modern Period*, ed. J. Whitman (Cambridge), pp. 23–39.
Bataillon, L. 1980. 'Approaches to the Study of Medieval Sermons', *Leeds Studies in English*, n.s. 11: 19–35.
Batt, C. 1991. 'Clemence of Barking's Transformations of Courtoisie in *La Vie de sainte Catherine d'Alexandrie*', *New Comparison* 12: 102–23.
Baumgartner, E. 1993. 'Figures du destinateur; Salomon, Arthur, Le Roi Henri d'Angleterre', in Short, ed., pp. 1–10.
—— 1994. 'From Lancelot to Galahad: The Stakes of Filiation', in Kibler, pp. 14–30.

Baumgartner, E. 1998 . 'Le Choix de la prose', *Cahiers de recherches médiévales et humanistes*, 5, http://crm.revues.org./1322, 2–7, 3; hard copy: 7–13.

Bazin-Tacchella, S., D. de Carné and M. Ott, ed. 2011. *Le Souffle épique: L'Esprit de la chanson de geste: Études en l'honneur de Bernard Guidot* (Dijon).

Beaune, C. 1985. *Naissance de la nation France* (Paris). Trans. 1991 as *Birth of an Ideology: Myths and Symbols of Nation in Late-Medieval France*, trans. S. R. Huston, ed. F. L. Cheyette (Berkeley).

Bedos-Rezak, B. 1994. 'Civic Liturgies and Urban Records in Northern France, 1100–1400', in *City and Spectacle in Medieval Europe*, ed. B. A. Hanawalt and K. L. Reyerson, Medieval Studies at Minnesota 6 (Minneapolis), pp. 34–55.

—— 2002. 'Towards an Archaeology of the Medieval Charter: Textual Production and Reproduction in Northern French *Chartriers*', in Kosto and Winroth, pp. 43–60.

Bell, A. 1962. 'Notes on Walter de Bibbesworth's *Treatise*', *Philological Quarterly* 41.2: 361–72.

Bell, D. N. 1995. *What Nuns Read: Books and Libraries in Medieval English Nunneries* (Kalamazoo).

Benecke, I. 1973. *Der gute Outlaw: Studien zu einem literarischen Typus im 13. und 14. Jahrhundert*, Studien zur Englischen Philologie, neue Folge 17 (Tübingen).

Bennett, A. 1990. 'A Book Designed for a Noblewoman: An Illustrated *Manuel des péchés* of the Thirteenth Century', in *Medieval Book Production: Assessing the Evidence*, ed. L. L. Brownrigg (Los Altos), pp. 163–81.

Bennett, J. W. 1954. *The Rediscovery of Sir John Mandeville*, Modern Language Association of America Monograph Series 19 (New York).

Bennett, M. 1982. 'Poetry as History? The 'Roman de Rou' of Wace as a Source for the Norman Conquest', *Anglo-Norman Studies* 5: 21–39.

Bennett, M. J. 2006. '*Mandeville's Travels* and the Anglo-French Moment', *Medium Aevum* 75: 273–92.

—— 2009. 'France in England: Anglo-French Culture in the Reign of Edward III', in Wogan-Browne *et al.*, pp. 320–33.

Benoit, J. 2012. Le Gracial *d'Adgar: Miracles de la Vierge: Dulce chose est de Deu cunter* (Turnhout).

Bérat, E. 2010. 'The Patron and her Clerk: Multilingualism and Cultural Transition', *New Medieval Literatures* 12: 23–45.

—— 2012. 'The Authority of Diversity: Communal Patronage in *Le Gracial*', in Brown and Bussell, pp. 210–32.

Beresford, M. 1988 [1967]. *New Towns of the Middle Ages: Town Plantation in England, Wales and Gascony* (Gloucester [London]).

Berger, S. 1967 [1884]. *La Bible française au Moyen Âge: Étude sur les plus anciennes versions de la Bible écrites en prose de langue d'oïl* (Paris, repr. Geneva).

Berthelot, A. 1991. *Figures et fonction de l'écrivain au xiii*[e] *siècle* (Montreal).

Bestul, T. H. 1993. 'Gower's *Mirour de l'omme* and the Meditative Tradition', *Mediaevalia* 16: 307–28.

Bhattacharji, S. 1995. '*Pearl* and the Liturgical "Common of Virgins"', *Medium Aevum* 64.1: 37–50.

Bibliotheca hagiographica Latina antiquae et mediae aetatis. 1898–1901. Subsidia hagiographica 6 (Brussels).

Biddick, K. 2003. *The Typological Imaginary: Circumcision, Technology, History* (Philadelphia).

Binski, P. 2014. *Gothic Wonder: Art, Artifice and the Decorated Style 1290–1350* (New Haven).

Binski, P., and S. Panayotova. 2005. *The Cambridge Illuminations: Ten Centuries of Book Production in the Medieval West* (London).

Binski, P., and P. Zutshi, with S. Panayotova 2011. *Western Illuminated Manuscripts: A Catalogue of the Collection in Cambridge University Library* (Cambridge).

Black, W. H. 1845. *A Descriptive, Analytical and Critical Catalogue of the Manuscripts Bequeathed unto the University of Oxford by Elias Ashmole, Esq., MD, FRS, Windsor Herald. Also of some*

additional manuscripts contributed by Kingsley, Lhuyd, Borlase and Others (Oxford).
Blacker, J. 1996. 'Will the Real Brut Please Stand Up? Wace's *Roman de Brut* in Anglo-Norman and Continental Manuscripts', *Text: Transactions of the Society for Textual Scholarship* 9: 175–96.
—— 1997. '"Dame Custance la gentil": Gaimar's Portrait of a Lady and her Books', in Mullally and Thompson, pp. 109–20.
Blake, N. F. 1990. 'Vernon Manuscript: Contents and Organisation', in Pearsall, pp. 45–59.
Blamires, A. 1997. *The Case for Women in Medieval Culture* (Oxford).
Blanton, V., V. O'Mara and P. Stoop, ed. 2013. *Nuns' Literacies in Medieval Europe: The Hull Dialogue* (Turnhout).
Blenner-Hassett, R. 1942. 'Geoffrey of Monmouth's *Mons Agned* and *Castellum Puellarum*', *Speculum* 17: 250–4.
Bliss, J. 2012. 'Who Wrote the Nun's Life of Edward?', *Reading Medieval Studies* 38: 77–98.
Bloch, R. H. 1983. *Etymologies and Genealogies: A Literary Anthropology of the French Middle Ages* (Chicago).
Boffey, J., and A. S. G. Edwards 2005. *A New Index of Middle English Verse* (London).
Bogaert, P. M. 1992. 'Bible française', in Hasenohr and Zink, pp. 179–96.
Bolens, G., and L. Erne 2011. *Medieval and Early Modern Authorship* (Tübingen).
Bond, G. A. 1995. *The Loving Subject: Desire, Eloquence and Power in Romanesque France* (Philadelphia).
Bonnard, J. 1884, repr. 1967. *Les Traductions de la Bible en vers français du Moyen Âge* (Paris, repr. Geneva).
Bonnier, C. 1901. 'List of Towns', *English Historical Review* 16.63: 501–3.
Bouchard, C. B. 2002. 'Monastic Cartularies: Organizing Eternity', in Kosto and Winroth, pp. 22–32.
Boulton, D'A. J. D. 1987. *The Knights of the Crown: The Monarchical Orders in Later Medieval Europe, 1325–1520* (Woodbridge).
Boulton, M. B. M. 1983. 'The "Evangile de l'Enfance": Text and Illustration in Oxford Bodleian Library Selden Supra 38', *Scriptorium* 37.1: 54–65.
—— 2005. 'La *Bible* d'Herman de Valenciennes: texte inconstant, texte perméable', in *Mouvances et jointures: du manuscrit au texte médiéval*, ed. M. Mikhaïlova (Orléans), pp. 85–96
—— 2007. 'Anti-Jewish Attitudes in Anglo-Norman Religious Texts: Twelfth and Thirteenth Centuries', in *Christian Attitudes toward the Jews in the Middle Ages: A Casebook*, ed. M. Frassetto (New York), pp. 151–65.
—— 2009. 'The Lives of the Virgin by Wace and Herman de Valenciennes: Conventions of Romance and Chanson de Geste in Religious Narrative', in *The Church and Vernacular Literature in Medieval France*, ed. D. Kullman (Toronto), pp. 109–23.
—— 2015. *Sacred Fictions of Medieval France: Narrative Theology in the Lives of Christ and the Virgin, 1150–1500* (Cambridge).
Boureau, A. 1997. 'The Letter-Writing Norm, a Mediaeval Invention', in *Correspondence: Models of Letter-Writing from the Middle Ages to the Nineteenth Century*, ed. R. Chartier, A. Boureau, and C. Daúphin (Princeton), pp. 24–58.
Boutet, D. 1987. 'Le *Fierabras* anglo-normand du manuscrit Egerton 3028 du British Museum: Style épique et remaniement', in *Au Carrefour des routes d'Europe: la chanson de geste: Xᵉ Congrès international de la Société Rencesvals, Strasbourg 1985, Senéfiance* 20–1 (Aix-en-Provence), pp. 283–99.
Boyle, L. E. 1982. '*Summae confessorum*', in *Les Genres littéraires dans les sources théologiques et philosophiques médiévales: Définition, critique et exploitation: Actes du Colloque international de Louvain-la-Neuve, 25–27 mai 1981*, Publications de l'Institut d'Études Médiévales, 2nd series: Textes, Études, Congres 5 (Louvain-la-Neuve), pp. 227–37.
—— 1985. 'The Fourth Lateran Council and Manuals of Popular Theology', in *The Popular Literature of Medieval England*, ed. T. J. Heffernan, Tennessee Studies in Literature 28 (Knoxville), pp. 30–43.

Brand, P. 1992. *The Making of the Common Law* (London).
—— 2000. 'The Languages of the Law in Later Medieval England', in *Multilingualism in Later Medieval Britain*, ed. D. A. Trotter (Cambridge), pp. 63–76.
—— 2003. *Kings, Barons and Justices: The Making and Enforcement of Legislation in Thirteenth-Century England* (Cambridge).
Brandin, L. 1929. 'Nouvelles recherches sur *Fouke Fitz Warin*', *Romania* 55: 17–44.
Brantley, J. 2007. *Reading in the Wilderness: Private Devotion and Public Performance in Late Medieval England* (Chicago).
Braude, B. 1996. '*Mandeville*'s Jews among Others', in *Pilgrims and Travelers to the Holy Land*, ed. B. F. Le Beau and M. Mor (Omaha), pp. 133–58.
Bremer, E., and S. Röhl, ed. 2007. *Jean de Mandeville in Europa: Neue Perspektiven in der Reiseliteraturforschung* (Munich).
Briscoe, M. G., and B. H. Jaye 1992. *Artes praedicandi. Artes orandi*, Typologie des Sources du Moyen Âge Occidental 61 (Turnhout).
Britnell, R. 2009. 'Uses of French Language in Medieval English Towns', in Wogan-Browne *et al.*, *Language and Culture*, pp. 81–9.
Broadhurst, K. M. 1996. 'Henry II of England and Eleanor of Aquitaine: Patrons of Literature in French?' *Viator* 27: 53–84.
Bromwich, R. 1982. 'Cyfeiriadau Dafydd ap Gwilym at Chwedl a Rhamant' [Dafydd ap Gwilym's References to Legend and Romance], *Ysgrifau Beirniadol* 12: 57–76.
Broun, D. 2007. *Scottish Independence and the Idea of Britain: From the Picts to Alexander III* (Edinburgh).
Brown, A. L. 1972. 'The Latin Letters in MS All Souls 182', *English Historical Review* 87.344: 565–73.
Brown, J. N. 2012. 'Body, Gender and Nation in the Lives of Edward the Confessor', in Brown and Bussell, pp. 145–63.
Brown, J. N., and D. A. Bussell, ed. 2012. *Barking Abbey and Medieval Literary Culture: Authorship and Authority in a Female Community* (Woodbridge).
Brown, M. C. 2011. '"Lo, Heer the Fourme": Hoccleve's *Series*, *Formulary*, and Bureaucratic Textuality', *Exemplaria* 23.1: 27–49.
Bruckner, M. T. (forthcoming). 'Weaving a Tapestry from Biblical Exegesis to Romance Textuality: Caught in the Web of Chrétien's *Conte du Graal*', in *Thinking Romance*, ed. K. C. Little and N. F. McDonald (Oxford).
Bunt, G. H. V. 1994. *Alexander the Great in the Literature of Medieval Britain* (Groningen).
Burgess, G. S. 1981. *Court and Poet: Selected Proceedings of the Third Congress of the International Courtly Literature Society* (Liverpool).
—— 1987. *The Lais of Marie de France: Text and Context* (Athens).
—— 2000. 'Women in the *Fouke le Fitz Waryn*', in *'Por le soie amisté': Essays in Honor of Norris J. Lacy*, ed. K. Busby and C. M. Jones (Amsterdam), pp. 75–93.
—— 2005. 'I kan rymes of Robyn Hood, and Randolf Erl of Chestre', in *'De sens rassis': Essays in Honor of Rupert T. Pickens*, ed. K. Busby, B. Guidot and L. E. Whalen (Amsterdam), pp. 51–84.
—— 2008. 'Fouke Fitz Waryn III and King John: Good Outlaw and Bad King', in Phillips, pp. 73–98.
Burgess, G. S., and C. Strijbosch, ed. 2006. *The Brendan Legend: Texts and Versions*, The Northern World 24 (Leiden).
Burnett, C. 1995. 'Mathematics and Astronomy in Hereford and its Region in the Twelfth Century', in *Medieval Art, Architecture and Archaeology at Hereford*, ed. D. Whitehead (Leeds), pp. 50–9.
Burnley, J. D. 1986. 'Curial Prose in England', *Speculum* 61.3: 593–614.
—— 2003 [2001]. 'French and Frenches in Fourteenth-Century London', in D. Kastovsky and A. Mettinger, ed., *Language Contact in the History of English* Frankfurt am Main), pp. 17–32.

Burns, E. J. 1985. *Arthurian Fictions: Rereading the Vulgate Cycle* (Columbus).
—— 2010. 'Introduction', in Chase, trans., pp. xiii–xxxvi.
Burrows, D. 2013. 'Die anglonormannischen *Life of St John the Almsgiver* und *Vie de seint Clement*: Werke ein und desselben Autors?', *Zeitschrift für romanische Philologie* 129: 3–23.
Busby, K. 2002. *Codex and Context: Reading Old French Verse Narrative in Manuscript*, 2 vols., Faux Titre 221, 222 (Amsterdam).
—— 2007. 'Erec, le Fiz Lac (British Library, Harley 4971)', in *People and Texts: Relationships in Medieval Literature, Studies Presented to Erik Kooper*, ed. T. Summerfield and K. Busby (Amsterdam), pp. 43–50.
—— 2011. 'Texte et image dans le manuscrit de Londres (British Library, Egerton 3028) de la *Destructioun de Rome* et *Fierabras*', in Bazin-Tacchella *et al.*, pp. 215–24.
—— 2017. *French in Medieval Ireland, Ireland in Medieval French: The Paradox of Two Worlds*, Medieval Texts and Cultures of Northern Europe, vol. 27 (Turnhout).
Busby, K., and C. Kleinhenz, ed. 2010. *Medieval Multilingualism: The Francophone World and its Neighbours* (Turnhout).
Busby, K., and A. Putter 2010. 'Introduction: Medieval Francophonia', in Busby and Kleinhenz, pp. 1–13.
Butler, L., and C. Given-Wilson 1979. *Medieval Monasteries of Great Britain* (London).
Butterfield, A. 2003. 'Articulating the Author: Gower and the French Vernacular Codex', *Yearbook of English Studies* 33: 80–96.
—— 2006. *Chaucer and the City*, Chaucer Studies 37 (Cambridge).
—— 2009. *The Familiar Enemy: Chaucer, Language and Nation in the Hundred Years War* (Oxford).
—— 2010. 'National Histories', in *Cultural Reformations: Medieval and Renaissance in Literary History*, ed. B. Cummings and J. Simpson, Oxford Twenty-First Century Approaches to Literature (Oxford), pp. 33–55.
Bynum, C. W. 1979. *Docere verbo et exemplo: An Aspect of Twelfth-Century Spirituality*, Harvard Theological Studies 31 (Missoula).
—— 1991. *Fragmentation and Redemption: Essays on Gender and the Human Body in Medieval Religion* (New York).
—— 2007. *Wonderful Blood: Theology and Practice in Late Medieval Northern Germany and Beyond* (Philadelphia).
Byrne, A. 2013. 'The Earls of Kildare and their Books at the End of the Middle Ages', *The Library: Transactions of the Bibliographical Society* 14.2: 129–53.
Cadden, J. 1993. *Meanings of Sex Difference in the Middle Ages: Medicine, Science and Culture* (Cambridge).
Cahn, W. 1989. 'Ascending to and Descending from Heaven: Ladder Themes in Early Medieval Art', in *Santi e demoni nell'alto medioevo occidentale (secoli V–XI)* (Spoleto), II, 697–724.
Calin, W. 1988. 'The Exaltation and Undermining of Romance: *Ipomedon*', in *The Legacy of Chrétien de Troyes*, ed. N. J. Lacy, D. Kelly and K. Busby, Faux Titre 37 (Amsterdam), II, 111–24.
—— 1994. *The French Tradition and the Literature of Medieval England* (Toronto).
—— 2014. *The Lily and the Thistle: The French Tradition and the Literature of Scotland* (Toronto).
Camargo, M. 2007. 'If You Can't Join Them, Beat Them; or, When Grammar Met Business Writing (in Fifteenth-Century Oxford)', in Poster and Mitchell, pp. 67–87.
Camille, M. 1988. 'Visualising in the Vernacular: A New Cycle of Early Fourteenth-Century Bible Illustrations', *Burlington Magazine* 130.1019: 97–106.
—— 1989. *The Gothic Idol: Ideology and Image-making in Medieval Art* (Cambridge).
Camp, C. T. 2013. 'Osbern Bokenham and the House of York Revisited', *Viator* 44.1: 327–52.

Campbell, E. 2004. 'Sacrificial Spectacle and Interpassive Vision in the Anglo-Norman Life of Saint Faith', in *Troubled Vision: Gender, Sexuality and Sight in Medieval Text and Image*, ed. E. Campbell and R. Mills (New York), pp. 97–115.

—— 2008. *Medieval Saints' Lives: The Gift, Kinship and Community in Old French Hagiography* (Woodbridge).

Campbell, E., and R. Mills., ed. 2012. 'Introduction', in their *Rethinking Medieval Translation: Ethics, Politics, Theory* (Cambridge), pp. 1–20.

Campbell, J. 1986. 'Some Twelfth-Century Views of the Anglo-Saxon Past', in *Essays in Anglo-Saxon History* (London), pp. 209–28.

Cannon, C. 2014. 'From Literacy to Literature: Elementary Learning and the Middle English Poet', *Publications of the Modern Language Association of America* 129.3: 349–64.

—— 2015. 'Vernacular Latin', *Speculum* 90.3: 641–53.

Cannon, D. 2003. 'London Pride: Citizenship and the Fourteenth-Century Custumals of the City of London', in *Learning and Literacy in Medieval England and Abroad*, ed. S. R. Jones (Turnhout), pp. 179–98.

Cappelli, A. 1990 [1928]. *Lexicon abbreviaturarum*, 6th edn (Milano [Leipzig]).

Careri, M., C. Ruby and I. Short, with T. Nixon and P. Stirnemann 2011. *Livres et écritures en français et en occitan au XIIe siècle: Catalogue illustré* (Rome).

Carr, A. W. 1986. 'East, West and Icons in Twelfth-Century Outremer', in *The Meeting of Two Worlds: Cultural Exchange between East and West during the Period of the Crusades*, ed. V. P. Goss and C. V. Bornstein, Studies in Medieval Culture 21 (Kalamazoo), pp. 347–59.

Carruthers, M. 1998. *The Craft of Thought: Meditation, Rhetoric and the Making of Images, 400–1200* (Cambridge).

—— 2006. 'Sweetness', *Speculum* 81: 999–1013.

—— 2008 [1990]. *The Book of Memory: A Study of Memory in Medieval Culture*, 2nd edn (Cambridge).

Cartlidge, N. 1997. 'The Composition and Social Context of Oxford Jesus College MS 29 (II) and London, British Library, MS Cotton Caligula A.IX', *Medium Aevum* 66.2: 250–69.

—— 2005. 'Imagining X: A Lost Early Vernacular Miscellany', in Kelly and Thompson, pp. 31–44.

—— 2011. 'Masters in the Art of Lying? The Literary Relationship between Hugh of Rhuddlan and Walter Map', *Modern Language Review* 106.1: 1–16.

Cary, G., with D. J. A. Ross 1967 [1956]. *The Medieval Alexander* (Cambridge).

Casey, M. 2000. 'Conversion as Depicted on the Fourteenth-Century Tring Tiles', in *Christianizing Peoples and Converting Individuals*, ed. G. Armstrong and I. N. Wood, International Medieval Research 7 (Turnhout), pp. 339–52.

Cate, J. L. 1937. 'The English Mission of Eustace of Flay, 1200–1201', in *Études d'histoire dédiées à la mémoire de Henri Pirenne* (Brussels), pp. 67–89.

The Catholic Encyclopaedia, 1907–22. Ed. C. G. Herberman *et al.*, 15 volumes (New York). http://www.newadvent.org/cathen/

Catto, J. 1981. 'Andrew Horn: Law and History in Fourteenth-Century England', in *The Writing of History in the Middle Ages: Essays Presented to Richard William Southern*, ed. R. H. C. Davis and J. M. Wallace-Hadrill (Oxford), pp. 367–91.

Cavell, E. 2007. 'Aristocratic Widows and the Medieval Welsh Frontier: The Shropshire Evidence', *Transactions of the Royal Historical Society* 6th s. 6 17: 57–82.

—— 2010. '*Fouke le Fitz Waryn*: Literary Space for Real Women?' *Parergon* 27.2: 89–109.

Chambers, E. K. 1903. *The Mediaeval Stage*, 2 vols. (London).

Chase, C. J. 2003. 'The Gateway to the *Lancelot-Grail Cycle: L'Estoire del Saint Graal*', in Dover, pp. 65–74.

Clanchy, M. T. 2011. 'Did Mothers Teach their Children to Read?', in *Motherhood, Religion, and Society in Medieval Europe, 400–1400: Essays Presented to Henrietta Leyser*, ed. C. Leyser and L. Smith (Farnham), pp. 129–53.

——2013 [1993, 1979]. *From Memory to Written Record: England, 1066–1307*, 3rd edn (Chichester).

Clark, W. B., and M. T. McMunn, ed. 1989. *Beasts and Birds of the Middle Ages: The Bestiary and its Legacy* (Philadelphia).

Cleaver, L. 2014. 'From Codex to Roll: Illustrating History in the Anglo-Norman World in the Twelfth and Thirteenth Centuries', *Anglo-Norman Studies* 36: 69–90.

Coates, R. 2006. 'Maiden Castle, Geoffrey of Monmouth and Harun al-Rasid', *Nomina* 29: 5–60.

Cohen, J. 1999. *Living Letters of the Law: Ideas of the Jew in Medieval Christianity* (Berkeley).

Cohen, J. J. 1999. *Of Giants: Sex, Monsters and the Middle Ages*, Medieval Cultures 17 (London).

Coleman, J. 1996. *Public Reading and the Reading Public in Late Medieval England and France* (New York).

—— 2007. 'Philippa of Lancaster, Queen of Portugal – and Patron of the Gower Translations?' in *England and Iberia in the Middle Ages, Twelfth to Fifteenth Century: Cultural, Literary, and Political Exchanges*, ed. M. Bullón-Fernandez (New York), pp. 135–65.

—— 2013. 'The First Presentation Miniature in an English Language Manuscript', in Coleman, Cruse and Smith, 403–37.

Coleman, J., M. Cruse and K. A. Smith, ed. 2013. *The Social Life of Illumination: Manuscripts, Images, and Communities in the Late Middle Ages*, MTCNE 21(Turnhout).

Coletti, T. 2004. *Mary Magdalene and the Drama of Saints: Theater, Gender and Religion in Late Medieval England* (Philadelphia).

Collard, J. 2000. 'Gender and Genealogy in English Illuminated Royal Genealogical Rolls from the Thirteenth Century', *Parergon* 17: 11–34.

Connolly, D. K. 2009. *The Maps of Matthew Paris: Medieval Journeys through Space, Time and Liturgy* (Woodbridge).

Connolly, M. 2004 online [2003]. 'Shaking the Language Tree: Translating the Word into the Vernacular in the Anglo-Norman *Miroir* and the Middle English *Mirror*', in *The Medieval Translator 8*, ed. R. Voaden *et al.* (Turnhout), pp. 17–27.

Constable, G. 1976. *Letters and Letter-Collections*, Typologie des sources du Moyen Âge occidental 17 (Turnhout).

——1977. 'The Structure of Medieval Society According to the *Dictatores* of the Twelfth Century', in *Law, Church, and Society: Essays in Honor of Stephan Kuttner*, ed. K. Pennington and R. Somerville (Philadelphia), pp. 253–67.

Contamine, P. 1994. 'Aperçus sur la propagande de guerre, de la fin du XIIe au début du XVe siècle: les Croisades, la Guerre de Cent Ans', in *Le forme della propaganda politica nel due e nel trecento*, ed. P. Cammarasano (Rome), pp. 5–27.

Cooper, H. 2003. 'The *Lancelot-Grail Cycle* in England: Malory and his Predecessors', in Dover, pp. 147–62.

——2006. 'London and Southwark Poetic Companies: "Si tost c'amis" and the *Canterbury Tales*', in *Chaucer and the City*, ed. A. Butterfield, Chaucer Studies 37 (Cambridge), pp. 109–24.

Cooper, L. H. 2007. 'The Poetics of Practicality', in Strohm, pp. 491–505.

Coote, L. A. 2008. 'Prophecy, Genealogy and History in Medieval English Political Discourse', in Radulescu and Kennedy, pp. 27–44.

——2000. *Prophecy and Public Affairs in Later Medieval England* (York).

Copeland, R. 1995. *Rhetoric, Hermeneutics and Translation in the Middle Ages: Academic Traditions and Vernacular Texts* (Cambridge).

Cornelius, I. 2010. 'The Rhetoric of Advancement: *Ars dictaminis, Cursus*, and Clerical Careerism in Late Medieval England', *New Medieval Literatures* 12: 289–330.

Corrie, M. 2012. 'Middle English: Dialects and Diversity', in *The Oxford History of English*, ed. L. Mugglestone (Oxford), pp. 106–46.
Courcelle, P. 1967. *La Consolation de philosophie dans la tradition littéraire: Antécédents et postérite de Boèce* (Paris).
Cownie, E. 1998. *Religious Patronage in Anglo-Norman England, 1066–1135* (Woodbridge).
Crane, S. 1997. 'Social Aspects of Bilingualism in the Thirteenth Century', in *Thirteenth Century England VI*, ed. M. Prestwich *et al.* (Woodbridge), pp. 103–16.
—— 1999. 'Anglo-Norman Cultures in England, 1066–1460', in *The Cambridge History of English Literature*, ed. D. Wallace (Cambridge), pp. 35–60.
—— 2013. *Animal Encounters: Contacts and Concepts in Medieval Britain* (Philadelphia).
Crick, J. 2008. 'Edgar, Albion and Insular Dominion', in *Edgar, King of the English, 959–975: New Interpretations*, ed. D. Scragg (Woodbridge), pp. 158–70.
—— forthcoming. 'Albion before Albina: The Scottish Question', in Lamont and Baswell.
Crooks, P., D. Green and W. M. Ormrod, ed. 2016. *The Plantagenet Empire, 1259–1453: Proceedings of the 2014 Harlaxton Medieval Symposium* (Donington).
Cruse, M. 2011. *Illuminating the* Roman d'Alexandre, *Oxford, Bodleian Library, MS Bodley 264: The Manuscript as Monument* (Cambridge).
D'Alverny, M. 1977. 'Comment les théologiens et les philosophes voient la femme', *Cahiers de civilisation médiévale* 20.2–3: 105–29.
D'Avray, D. L. 1985. *The Preaching of the Friars: Sermons Diffused from Paris before 1300* (Oxford).
D'Evelyn, C. 1940. '"Meditations on the Life and Passion of Christ": A Note on its Literary Relationships', in *Essays and Studies in Honor of Carleton Brown* (New York), pp. 79–90.
D'Evelyn, C., and F. A. Foster 1970. 'Legends of Individual Saints', in *A Manual of the Writings in Middle English* (New Haven), II, 553–649.
Dahan, G. 2009. *Lire la Bible au Moyen Âge: Essais d'Hermeneutique médiévale* (Geneva).
Dalton, P. 2007. 'The Date of Geoffrey Gaimar's *Estoire des Engleis*, the Connections of his Patrons and the Politics of Stephen's Reign', *Chaucer Review* 42.1: 23–47.
Dalton, P., C. Insley and L. J. Wilkinson, ed. 2011. *Cathedrals, Communities and Conflict in the Anglo-Norman World* (Woodbridge).
Damian-Grint, P. 1997. '*Estoire* as Word and Genre: Meaning and Literary Usage in the Twelfth Century', *Medium Aevum* 66.2: 189–206.
—— 1999. *The New Historians of the Twelfth-Century Renaissance: Inventing Vernacular Authority* (Woodbridge).
Davis, G. R. C. 1958. *Medieval Cartularies of Great Britain: A Short Catalogue* (London) rev. 2010 by C. Breay *et al.*, as *Medieval Cartularies of Great Britain and Ireland* (London)].
de Laborderie, O. 1997. 'Les Généalogies des rois d'Angleterre sur rouleaux manuscrits (milieu XIIIe siècle-début XIVe siècle): Conception, diffusion et fonctions', in *La Généalogie entre science et passion*, ed. T. Barthélemy and M. Pingaud (Paris), pp. 181–99.
—— 2001. 'Élaboration et diffusion de l'image de la monarchie anglaise, XIIIe–XIVe siècles', in *Histoires d'outre-Manche: Tendances récentes de l'historiographie britannique*, ed. F. Lachaud, I. Lescent-Giles and F. Ruggiu (Paris), pp. 37–56.
—— 2002. '"Ligne de reis": culture historique, représentation du pouvoir royal et construction de la mémoire nationale en Angleterre à travers les généalogies royales en rouleau du milieu du XIIIe siècle au début du XVe siècle' (unpublished Ph.D. dissertation, EHESS, Paris).
—— 2003. 'La Mémoire des origines Normandes des rois d'Angleterre dans les généalogies en rouleau des XIIIe et XIVe siècles', in *La Normandie et l'Angleterre au Moyen Âge, Colloque de Cerisy-la-Salle (4–7 octobre 2001)*, ed. P. Bouzet and V. Gazeau (Caen), pp. 211–32.
—— 2008. 'A New Pattern for English History: The First Genealogical Rolls of the Kings of England', in Radulescu and Kennedy, pp. 45–61.

de Laborderie, O. 2013. *Histoire, mémoire et pouvoir: les généalogies en rouleau des rois d'Angleterre (1250–1422)* (Paris).

de Laborderie, O., J. R. Maddicott and D. A. Carpenter 2000. 'The Last Hours of Simon de Montfort: A New Account', *English Historical Review* 115.461: 378–412.

de Mandach, A. 1988. 'Comment éditer un mystère inséré dans un texte biblique? Le "Jeu des Trois Rois" de Herman de Valenciennes', *Fifteenth-Century Studies* 13: 597–613.

—— 1993. '*The Creation* of Herman de Valenciennes: An Unpublished Anglo-Norman Mystery Play of the Twelfth Century', in Short, pp. 251–72.

de Mandach, A., with E. Roth 1989. 'Le "Jeu des trois rois" de Herman de Valenciennes: Trois cycles anglo-normands inédits du XIIe siècle', *Vox Romanica*, 48: 85–107.

De Visscher, E. 2013. 'Hebrews, Latin, French, English: Multilingualism in Jewish-Christian Encounters', in Jefferson and Putter, pp. 89–103.

Declercq, G. 2000. *Anno Domini: The Origins of the Christian Era* (Turnhout).

Deluz, C. 1988. *Le Livre de Jehan de Mandeville: Une 'géographie' au XIVe siècle*, Publications de l'Institut d'Études Médiévales: Textes, Études, Congrès 8 (Louvain-la-Neuve).

Dennison, L. 1990. '"Liber Horn", "Liber Custumarum" and other Manuscripts of the Queen Mary Psalter Workshops', in *Medieval Art, Architecture and Archaeology in London*, ed. L. Grant (Leeds), pp. 118–34.

Derolez, A. 2006. *The Palaeography of Gothic Manuscript Books: From the Twelfth to the Early Sixteenth Century* (Cambridge).

Devos, P. 1947. 'Les Premières Versions occidentales de la Légende de Saïdnaia', *Analecta Bollandiana* 65: 245–78.

Dickinson, J. C. 1950. *The Origins of the Austin Canons and their Introduction into England* (London).

Diekstra, F. N. M. 1985. 'The *Physiologus*, the Bestiaries and Medieval Animal Lore', *Neophilologus* 69: 142–55.

Diller, H. J. 2011. 'Why *anger* and *joy*? Were *tene* and *bliss* not good enough?', in J. Fisiak and M. Bator, ed., *Foreign Influences on Middle English* (Frankfurt-am-Main), pp. 213–30.

Dinkova-Bruun, G. 2007. 'Biblical Versification from Late Antiquity to the Middle of the Thirteenth Century: History or Allegory?', in *Poetry and Exegesis in Premodern Christianity: The Encounter between Classical and Christian Strategies of Interpretation*, ed. W. Otten and K. Pollmann (Leiden), pp. 315–42.

Ditchburn, D. 2000. *Scotland and Europe: The Medieval Kingdom and its Contacts with Christendom, c. 1215–1545*, I (East Linton).

Dodd, G. 2014. 'Kingship, Parliament and the Court: The Emergence of "High Style" in Petitions to the English Crown, *c.* 1350–1405', *English Historical Review* 129.538: 515–48.

Doubleday, H., and W. Page, ed. 1906. *Victoria County History Norfolk*, II (London). http://www.british-history.ac.uk/report.asp?compid=38296.

Dover, C., ed. 2003. *A Companion to the Lancelot-Grail Cycle*, Arthurian Studies 54 (Cambridge).

Downes, S. 2009. 'A "French booke called the Pistill of Othea": Christine de Pizan's French in England', in Wogan-Browne *et al.*, pp. 457–68.

Doyle, A. I. 1990. 'The Shaping of the Vernon and Simeon Manuscript', in Pearsall, pp. 1–13.

—— 2013. 'Codicology, Palaeography, and Provenance', in Scase, pp. 3–25.

Duffell, M. 2008. *A New History of English Metre* (London).

Duffell, M. J., and D. Billy 2004. 'From Decasyllable to Pentameter: Gower's Contribution to English Metrics', *Chaucer Review* 38: 383–400.

Duffy, E. 1997. 'The Parish, Piety and Patronage in Late Medieval East Anglia: The Evidence of Rood Screens', in *The Parish in English Life 1400–1600*, ed. K. L. French, G. G. Gibbs and B. A. Kümin (Manchester), pp. 133–62.

Duggan, A. 2004. *Thomas Becket* (London).

Dunbar, H. O. 2001. 'Gesture and Characterization in the Liturgical Drama', in *Gesture in Medieval Drama and Art*, ed. C. Davidson, Early Drama, Art and Music Monograph Series 28 (Kalamazoo), pp. 26–47.
Durnford, T. J. 1977. 'A Critical Study of *Les Proverbes de Salemon* by Sanson de Nantuil' (unpublished Ph.D. dissertation, University of Connecticut).
—— 1981–2. 'The Incomplete Nature of *Les Proverbes de Salemon*', *Romance Notes* 22.3: 362–6.
Dutton, E., J. Hines and R. F. Yeager 2010. *John Gower, Trilingual Poet: Language, Translation and Tradition* (Cambridge).
Dzon, M. 2016. *The Quest for the Christ Child in the Later Middle Ages* (Philadelphia).
Dzon, M. C., and T. M. Kenney, ed. 2012. *The Christ Child in Medieval Culture: Alpha es et O!* (Toronto).
Eales, R., and S. Tyas, ed. 2003. *Family and Dynasty in Late Medieval England: Proceedings of the 1997 Harlaxton Symposium* (Donington).
Eames, E. S. 1980. *Catalogue of Medieval Lead-Glazed Earthenware Tiles in the Department of Medieval and Later Antiquities, British Museum*, 2 vols. (London).
Egbert, D. D. 1936. 'The So-called "Greenfield" *La Lumiere as Lais* and *Apocalypse*, Brit. Mus., Royal MS 15 D II', *Speculum* 11.4: 446–52.
Eley, P. 2000. 'The Subversion of Meaning in Hue de Rotelande's *Ipomedon*', *Reading Medieval Studies* 26: 97–112.
Elliott, J. K. 1993. *The Apocryphal New Testament: A Collection of Apocryphal Christian Literature in an English Tradition* (Oxford).
—— 2006. *A Synopsis of the Apocryphal Nativity and Infancy Narratives* (Leiden).
Ellis, R. 2001. 'Figures of English Translation, 1382–1407', in *Translation and Nation: Towards a Cultural Politics of Englishness*, ed. R. Ellis and L. Oakley-Brown (Clevedon), pp. 7–47
Emmerson, R. K. 1999. 'Reading Gower in a Manuscript Culture: Latin and English in Illustrated Manuscripts of the *Confessio Amantis*', *Studies in the Age of Chaucer* 21: 143–86.
—— 2012. 'Visual Translation in Fifteenth-Century English Manuscripts', in *Medieval Poetics and Social Practice: Responding to the Work of Penn R. Sittya*, ed. S. Chaganti (New York), pp. 11–32.
Emmerson, R. K., and S. Lewis 1985. 'Census and Bibliography of Medieval Manuscripts Containing Apocalypse Illustrations, ca. 800–1500, II', *Traditio* 41: 367–409.
Emmerson, R. K., and B. McGinn, ed. 1992. *The Apocalypse in the Middle Ages* (Ithaca).
Escobedo, L. K. 2011. *The Milemete Treatise and Companion* Secretum Secretorum*: Iconography, Audience, and Patronage in Fourteenth-Century England* (Lewiston, NY).
Evans, M. 1982. 'An Illustrated Fragment of Peraldus's *Summa* of Vice: Harleian MS 3244', *Journal of the Warburg and Courtauld Institutes* 45: 14–68.
Fabre-Vassas, C. 1997. *The Singular Beast: Jews, Christians and the Pig* [Trans. of *La Bête singulière: les juifs, les chrétiens, le cochon*, trans. C. Volk (Paris 1994)] (New York).
Fagin Davis, L. 2006. 'Scrolling through History: *La Chronique universelle*, Boston Public Library MS Pb. Med., 32', in *Secular Sacred: 11th–16th Century Works from the Boston Public Library and the Museum of Fine Arts, Boston*, ed. N. Netzer (Chestnut Hill), pp. 43–50.
—— 2009. 'The First and Second Recensions of the "Chronique Anonyme Universelle": Houghton MS Typ 41 and MS Fr 495', *Harvard Library Bulletin* 20.1: 1–33.
Faraci, D. 1990. *Il bestiario medio inglese (MS Arundel 292 della British Library)* (Rome).
Farmer, S. 1991. *Communities of St Martin: Legend and Ritual in Medieval Tours* (Ithaca).
Fein, S. 2007. 'Compilation and Purpose in MS Harley 2253', in *Essays in Manuscript Geography: Vernacular Manuscripts of the English West Midlands from the Conquest to the Sixteenth Century*, ed. W. Scase (Turnhout), pp. 67–94.
—— 2014. 'The Fillers of the Auchinleck Manuscript and the Literary Culture of the West Midlands', in *Makers and Users of Medieval Books: Essays in Honour of A. S. G. Edwards*, ed. C. M. Meale and D. Pearsall (Cambridge), pp. 60–77.

Fellows, J., and I. Djordjević, ed. 2008. Sir Bevis of Hampton *in Literary Tradition* (Cambridge).
Fenster, T. 2012. '"Ce qu'ens li trovat, eut en sei": On the Equal Chastity of Queen Edith and King Edward in the Nun of Barking's *La Vie d'Edouard le confesseur*', in Brown and Bussell, pp. 135–44.
Fenster, T., and D. Smail, ed. 2003. *Fama: The Politics of Talk and Reputation in Medieval Europe* (Ithaca, NY).
Fenster, T., and M. Behrend Valles 2016. 'Elia Levita's Bovo Bukh: Pulp Fiction for Women?', in *The Epic Imagination in Medieval Literature: Essays in Honor of Alice M. Colby-Hall*, ed. P. Bennett, L. Z. Morgan and F. F. Psaki. Romance Monographs (s-05 University, MI), pp. 161–77.
Ferster, J. 1996. *Fictions of Advice: The Literature and Politics of Counsel in Late Medieval England* (Philadelphia).
Field, R. M. 2000. '*Waldef* and the Matter of/with England', in *Medieval Insular Romance: Translation and Innovation*, ed. J. Weiss, J. Fellows and M. Dickson (Cambridge), pp. 25–39.
—— 2004. 'What's in a Name? Arthurian Name-Dropping in the *Roman de Waldef*', in *Arthurian Studies in Honour of P. J. C. Field*, ed. B. Wheeler (Cambridge), pp. 63–5.
—— 2010. 'Patterns of Availability and Demand in Middle English Translations *de romanz*', in *The Exploitations of Medieval Romance*, ed. L. Ashe, I. Djordjević, J. Weiss (Cambridge), pp. 73–89.
—— 2011. '"Pur les francs homes amender": Clerical Authors and the Thirteenth-Century Context of Romance', in *Medieval Romance, Medieval Contexts*, ed. R Purdie and M. Cichon (Cambridge).
Field, S. L. 2007. 'From *Speculum anime* to *Miroir de l'âme*: The Origins of Vernacular Advice Literature at the Capetian Court', *Mediaeval Studies* 69: 59–110.
—— 2010. 'Marie de St Pol and her Books', *English Historical Review* 125.513: 255–78.
Fisher, J. H. 1964. *John Gower: Moral Philosopher and Friend of Chaucer* (New York).
Fletcher, C. D. 2004. 'Narrative and Political Strategies at the Deposition of Richard II', *Journal of Medieval History* 30.4: 323–41.
Flint, V. I. J. 1988. *Ideas in the Medieval West: Texts and their Contexts* (London).
—— 1992. *The Imaginative Landscape of Christopher Columbus* (Princeton).
Forshaw, H. P. (as Mother Mary Philomena, SHCJ) 1964. 'St Edmund of Abingdon's Meditations before the Canonical Hours', *Ephemerides liturgicae* 78: 35–57.
—— 1972a (for 1971). 'New Light on the *Speculum ecclesie* of Saint Edmund of Abingdon', *Archives d'histoire doctrinale et littéraire du Moyen Âge* 38: 7–33.
—— 1972b (publ. 1973). 'Saint Edmund's Speculum: A Classic of Victorine Spirituality', *Archives d'histoire doctrinale et littéraire du Moyen Âge*, 39: 7–40.
Foster, B. 1955. 'The *Roman de toute chevalerie*: Its Date and Author', *French Studies* 9.2: 154–8.
Fox, H. E. 2014. 'Langlandian Economics in James Yonge's *Gouernaunce*: Translation and Ethics in Fifteenth-Century Dublin', in Kerby-Fulton, Thompson and Baechle, pp. 251–70.
Fox, J. 1974. *A Literary History of France: The Middle Ages* (London).
Francis, E. A. 1961. 'The Background to "Fulk FitzWarin"', in *Studies in Medieval French Presented to Alfred Ewert in Honour of his Seventieth Birthday* (Oxford), pp. 322–7.
Frank, G. 1954. *The Medieval French Drama* (Oxford).
Frankis, J. 2002. 'Towards a Regional Context for Lawman's *Brut*: Literary Activity in the Dioceses of Worcester and Hereford in the Twelfth Century', in *Laȝamon: Contexts, Language and Interpretation*, ed. R. Allen, L. Perry and J. Roberts, King's College London Medieval Studies 19 (London), pp. 53–78.
—— 2007. 'Languages and Cultures in Contact: Vernacular Lives of St Giles and Anglo-Norman Annotations in an Anglo-Saxon Manuscript', *Leeds Studies in English*, 38: 101–33.
Freeman, M. A. 1976. 'Chrétien's *Cligès*: A Close Reading of the Prologue', *Romanic Review* 67.2: 89–101.
Friis-Jensen, K., and J. M. W. Willoughby 2001. *Peterborough Abbey*, Corpus of British Medieval Library Catalogues 8 (London).

Fryde, E. B. *et al.*, ed. 1996. *Handbook of British Chronology*, 3rd edn, with corrections (Cambridge).
Fulton, H., ed., 2012. *Urban Culture in Medieval Wales* (Cardiff).
Fulton, R. 2002. *From Judgment to Passion: Devotion to Christ and the Virgin Mary, 800–1200* (New York).
Galderisi, C., and V. Agrigoroaei, ed. 2011. *Translations médiévales: cinq siècles de traductions en français au Moyen Âge (XIe–XVe): Étude et répertoire*, 2 vols. (Turnhout).
Galloway, A. 2006. *The Penn Commentary on Piers Plowman*, vol. 1 (Philadelphia). 1, C Prologue-Passus 4; B Prologue-Passus 4; A Prologue-Passus 4 (Philadelphia).
—— 2011. 'The Account-Book and the Treasure: Gilbert Maghfeld's Textual Economy and the Poetics of Mercantile Accounting in Ricardian Literature', *Studies in the Age of Chaucer* 33: 65–124.
Gaullier-Bougassas, C. 1998. *Les Romans d'Alexandre: Aux frontières de l'épique et du romanesque* (Paris).
—— 2002. 'Alexander and Aristotle in the French Alexander Romances', in *The Medieval French Alexander*, ed. D. Maddox and S. Sturm-Maddox (Albany), pp. 57–73.
——, M. Bridges, and Y. Tilliette, ed. 2015. *Trajectoires européens du Secretum secretorum du Pseudo-Aristote (XIIIe-XVIe siècle)* (Turnhout).
Gaunt, S. 1995. *Gender and Genre in Medieval French Literature* (Cambridge).
—— 2003. 'The *Chanson de Roland* and the Invention of France', in *Rethinking Heritage: Cultures and Politics in England*, ed. R. S. Peckham (London), pp. 90–101.
—— 2015. 'French Literature Abroad: Towards an Alternative History of French Literature', in *Interfaces: A Journal of European Medieval Literatures* I (2015): 25–61 (at http://riviste.unimi.it/interfaces/index)
Geary, P. J. 1990. *Furta sacra: Thefts of Relics in the Central Middle Ages*, rev. edn (Princeton).
—— 2013. *Language and Power in the Early Middle Ages* (Lebanon, NH).
Gee, L. L. 2002. *Women, Art and Patronage from Henry III to Edward III: 1216–1377* (Woodbridge).
Gelling, M. 1984. *Place-Names in the Landscape* (London).
Giancarlo, M. 2007. 'Property, Purchase and Parliament: The Estates of Man in John Gower's *Mirour de l'omme* and *Cronica Tripertita*', in his *Parliament and Literature in Late Medieval England* (Cambridge), pp. 90–128.
Giffin, M. E. 1951–2. 'A Wigmore Manuscript in the University of Chicago Library'. *National Library of Wales Journal* 7: 316–25.
Gilchrist, R. 1994. *Gender and Material Culture: The Archaeology of Religious Women* (Abingdon).
—— 1995. *Contemplation and Action: The Other Monasticism* (London).
Gilchrist, R., and M. Oliva. 1993. *Religious Women in Medieval East Anglia: History and Archaeology c. 1100–1540* (Norwich).
Gillespie, A. 2006. *Print Culture and the Medieval Book: Chaucer, Lydgate, and their Books, 1473–1577* (Oxford).
Gillespie, V. 2008. 'Religious Writing', in *The Oxford History of Literary Translation in English, vol. 1: 700–1550*, ed. Roger Ellis (Oxford), pp. 23–53.
—— 2011. 'Chichele's Church', in Gillespie and Ghosh, pp. 3–42.
Gillespie, V., and K. Ghosh, ed., 2011. *After Arundel: Religious Writing in Fifteenth Century England* (Turnhout)
Gillingham, J. 2000. *The English in the Twelfth Century* (Woodbridge).
—— 2002. 'From *Civilitas* to Civility: Codes of Manners in Medieval and Early Modern England', *Transactions of the Royal Historical Society* 6th s. 12: 267–89.
Ginzburg, C. 1980. *The Cheese and the Worms: The Cosmos of a Sixteenth-Century Miller*, trans. J. Tedeschi and A. Tedeschi (Baltimore).
Giraud, C. 2010. *Per verba magistri: Anselme de Laon et son école au XIIe siècle*, Bibliothèque d'histoire culturelle du Moyen Âge 8 (Turnhout).

Given-Wilson, C. 2003. 'Chronicles of the Mortimer Family, *c.* 1250–1450', in Eales and Tyas, pp. 67–86.

—— 2004. *Chronicles: The Writing of History in Medieval England* (London).

Godzich, W., and J. Kittay 1987. *The Emergence of Prose: An Essay in Prosaics* (Minneapolis).

Goetz, S. K. 2006. 'Textual Portability and its Uses in England, *ca.* 1250 to 1330' (unpublished Ph.D. dissertation, University of California, Berkeley).

Goodman, A. 2006. 'The British Isles Imagined', in *The Fifteenth Century, VI*, ed. L. Clark (Woodbridge), pp. 1–14.

Gosman, M. 1997. *La Légende d'Alexandre le Grand dans la littérature française du 12e siècle* (Amsterdam).

Gouttebroze, J. 1991. 'Pourquoi congédier un historiographe: Henri II Plantagenêt et Wace (1155–1174)', *Romania* 112.3–4: 298–311.

—— 1995. 'Entre les historiographes d'expression latine et les jongleurs, le clerc lisant', *Senéfiance* 37: 215–30.

Gowans, L. 2004. 'What did Robert de Boron Really Write?' in *Arthurian Studies in Honour of P. J. C. Field*, ed. B. Wheeler (Cambridge), pp. 15–28.

Graef, H. 2009. *Mary: A History of Doctrine and Devotion, with a New Chapter Covering Vatican II and Beyond by Thomas A. Thompson, S. M.* (Notre Dame).

Gransden, A. 2007. *A History of the Abbey of Bury St Edmunds, 1182–1256: Samson of Tottingham to Edmund of Walpole*, Studies in the History of Medieval Religion 31 (Woodbridge).

Green, M. H. 1992. 'Obstetrical and Gynecological Texts in Middle English', *Studies in the Age of Chaucer* 14: 53–88.

—— 1996b. 'The Development of the *Trotula*', *Revue d'histoire des textes* 26: 119–203.

—— 2000a. *Women's Healthcare in the Medieval West: Texts and Contexts* (Aldershot).

—— 2000b. [1998] '"Traittié tout de mençonges": The *Secré des dames*, "Trotula" and Attitudes toward Women's Medicine in Fourteenth- and Early-Fifteenth-Century France', VI, in Green 2000, pp. 146–78.

—— 2000c.[1996] 'The Development of the *Trotula*', V in Green 2000a, pp. 119–203.

—— 2000d. 'The Possibilities of Literacy and the Limits of Reading: Women and the Gendering of Medieval Literacy', first published in Green 2000a, pp. 1–76.

—— 2005. 'Flowers, Poisons and Men: Menstruation in Medieval Western Europe', in *Menstruation: A Cultural History*, ed. A. Shail and G. Howie (Hampshire), pp. 51–64.

—— 2008. *Making Women's Medicine Masculine: The Rise of Male Authority in Pre-Modern Gynaecology* (Oxford).

—— 2009. 'Salerno on the Thames: The Genesis of Anglo-Norman Medical Literature', in Wogan-Browne *et al.*, pp. 220–31.

Greenblatt, S. 1991. *Marvelous Possessions: The Wonder of the New World* (Chicago).

Gregory, S., and C. Luttrell 1993. 'The Manuscripts of *Cligès*', in *The Manuscripts of Chrétien de Troyes*, ed. K. Busby *et al.*, 2 vols. (Amsterdam), I, 67–96.

Gregory, S., and D. A. Trotter, ed. 1997. *De mot en mot: Aspects of Medieval Linguistics: Essays in Honour of William Rothwell* (Cardiff).

Gretsch, M. 2001. 'Winchester Vocabulary and Standard Old English: The Vernacular in Late Anglo-Saxon England', *Bulletin of the John Rylands University Library of Manchester* 83.1: 41–87.

Grévy-Pons, N. 1980. 'Propagande et sentiment national pendant le règne de Charles VI: l'exemple de Jean de Montreuil', *Francia* 8:127–45.

Griffiths, G., and A. Putter 2014. 'Linguistic Boundaries in a Multilingual Miscellany: The Case of Middle English Romances', in *Middle English Texts in Transition: A Festschrift Dedicated to Toshiyuki Takamiya on his 70th Birthday*, ed. S. Horobin and L. Mooney (York), pp. 116–24.

Griffiths, R. A. 1979. 'The Sense of Dynasty in the Reign of Henry VI', in Ross, pp. 13–36.

Griffiths, R. A. 1981. *The Reign of King Henry VI: The Exercise of Royal Authority, 1422–1461* (Berkeley).
—— 1986. 'The Crown and the Royal Family in Later Medieval England', in *Kings and Nobles in the Later Middle Ages: A Tribute to Charles Ross*, ed. R. A. Griffiths and J. Sherborne (Gloucester), pp. 15–26.
Grignaschi, M. 1977. 'L'Origine et les métamorphoses du "Sirr-al-Asrâr"', *Archives d'histoire doctrinale et littéraire du Moyen Âge* 43 [for 1976]: 7–112.
—— 1981. 'La Diffusion du *Secretum secretorum* (Sirr-al-Asràr) dans l'Europe occidentale', *Archives d'histoire doctrinale et littéraire du Moyen Âge* 47 [for 1980]: 7–70.
Gros, G. 2012. 'Octosyllabe et rime plate: à la recherche d'une forme et d'un genre', *Deuxième journée d'études anglo-normandes*, ed. A. Crépin and J. Leclant (Paris).
Grossel, M. 1998. 'Entre médecine et magie, les gestes de beauté (l'*Ornatus mulierum*)', *Senéfiance* 41: 255–72.
Gunn, C. 2009. 'Reading Edmund of Abingdon's *Speculum* as Pastoral Literature', in Gunn and Innes-Parker, pp. 100–14.
—— (forthcoming). 'Anonymous Then, Invisible Now: The Readers of the *Sermon a dames religieuses*', in *Nuns' Literacies in Medieval Europe: The Antwerp Dialogue*, ed. V. Blanton, V. O'Mara and P. Stoop, MWTC 20 (Turnhout).
Gunn, C., and C. Innes-Parker, ed. 2009. *Texts and Traditions of Medieval Pastoral Care: Essays in Honour of Bella Millett* (York).
Gwynn, A., and R. N. Hadcock 1970. *Medieval Religious Houses: Ireland* (London).
Ham, E. B. 1935. 'The Language of the *Roman de Waldef*', *Medium Aevum* 4: 176–94.
Hamesse, J., ed. 2000. *Les Prologues médiévaux: Actes du Colloque international organisé par l'Academia Belgica et l'Ecole française de Rome avec le concours de la FIDEM (Rome, 26–28 mars 1998)* (Turnhout).
Hamel, M. 1990. 'Arthurian Romance in Fifteenth-Century Lindsey: The Books of the Lords Welles', *Modern Language Quarterly* 51.2: 341–61.
Handel, K. 2015. 'French Writing in the Cloister: Four Texts from St Albans Abbey featuring Thomas Becket and Alexander the Great, *c.* 1184 – *c.* 1275' (Unpubl. Ph.D. dissertation, University of York).
Hanna, R. 2008 [2005]. *London Literature, 1300–1380* (Cambridge).
—— 2011a. 'Images of London in Medieval English Literature', in *The Cambridge Companion to the Literature of London*, ed. L. Manley (Cambridge), pp. 19–33.
—— 2011b. 'The Matter of Fulk: Romance and History in the Marches', *Journal of English and Germanic Philology* 110.3: 337–58.
Hanna, R and T. Turville-Petre, ed. 2010. *The Wollaton Medieval Manuscripts: Texts, Owners and Readers* (York).
Hanning, R. W. 1966. *The Vision of History in Early Britain: From Gildas to Geoffrey of Monmouth* (New York).
—— 1974. '*Engin* in Twelfth-Century Romance: An Examination of the *Roman d'Enéas* and Hue de Rotelande's *Ipomedon*', *Yale French Studies* 51: 82–101.
Hardison, O. B. 1965. *Christian Rite and Christian Drama in the Middle Ages: Essays in the Origin and Early History of Modern Drama* (Baltimore).
Hardwick, C., *et al.*, ed. 1861. *A Catalogue of the Manuscripts Preserved in the Library of the University of Cambridge* (Cambridge), IV.
Harris, J. W. 1992. *Medieval Theatre in Context: An Introduction* (London).
Hartung, A. E., ed. 1967–2005. *A Manual of the Writings in Middle English, 1050–1500*, 11 vols. (New Haven).
Hasenohr, G. 2000. 'Les Prologues des textes de dévotion en langue française (XIIIe–XVe siècles): formes et fonctions', in Hamesse, ed, pp. 593–638.

Hasenohr, G., and M. Zink, ed. 1992 [1964]. *Dictionnaire des lettres françaises: le Moyen Âge* (Paris) [1964 edn, ed. R. Bossuat, L. Pichard, G. R. de Lage].

Hassell, J. W. 1982. *Middle French Proverbs, Sentences and Proverbial Phrases* (Toronto).

Hassig, D. 1995. *Medieval Bestiaries: Text, Image, Ideology* (Cambridge).

—— 1999. *The Mark of the Beast: The Medieval Bestiary in Art, Life and Literature* (New York).

Haxo, H. E. 1914. 'Denis Piramus: "La Vie Seint Edmunt"', *Modern Philology* 12.6: 345–66.

—— 1915. 'Denis Piramus: "La Vie seint Edmunt": Language of Denis Piramus (concluded)', *Modern Philology* 12.9: 559–83.

Hayward, P. A. 2009. 'Geoffrey of Wells' *Liber de infantia sancti Edmundi* and the "Anarchy" of King Stephen's Reign', in Bale, pp. 63–86.

Hazelton, R. 1957. 'The Christianization of "Cato": The *Disticha Catonis* in the Light of Late Mediaeval Commentaries', *Mediaeval Studies* 19: 157–73.

—— 1960. 'Chaucer and Cato', *Speculum* 35.3: 357–80.

Hedeman, A. D. 1991. *The Royal Image: Illustrations of the Grandes Chroniques de France, 1274–1422*, California Studies in the History of Art 28 (Berkeley).

Herbert, J. A. 1903. 'A New Manuscript of Adgar's Mary-Legends', *Romania* 32: 394–421.

—— 1910. *Catalogue of Romances in the Department of Manuscripts in the British Museum*, 3 vols. (London), III, 272–303.

Herde, R. 1968. *Das Hohelied in der lateinischen Literatur des Mittelalters bis zum 12. Jahrhundert* (Spoleto).

Hesketh, G. 1997. 'Lexical Innovation in the *Lumere as lais*', in Gregory and Trotter, pp. 53–79.

Hessenauer, M. 1989. *La Lumière as Lais: Pierre de Peckhams Vermittlung scholastischer Theologie* (Wiesbaden).

—— 1995. 'The Impact of Grosseteste's Pastoral Care on Vernacular Religious Literature: *La Lumière as lais* by Pierre de Peckham', in *Robert Grosseteste: New Perspectives on his Thought and Scholarship*, ed. J. McEvoy (Turnhout), pp. 377–91.

Higgins, I. M. 1997. *Writing East: The 'Travels' of Sir John Mandeville* (Philadelphia).

Hill, B. 1963. 'The History of Jesus College, Oxford MS 29', *Medium Aevum* 32.3: 203–13.

—— 1975. 'Oxford, Jesus College MS 29: Addenda on Donation, Acquisition, Dating and Relevance of the "Broaken Leafe": Note to "The Owl and the Nightingale"', *Notes and Queries* 220, n.s. 22.3: 98–105.

—— 1977. 'The Twelfth-Century *Conduct of Life*, Formerly the *Poema morale* or A Moral Ode', *Leeds Studies in English* n.s. 9: 97–144.

—— 2003. 'Oxford, Jesus College MS 29, Part II: Contents, Technical Matters, Compilation and its History to *c.* 1695', *Notes and Queries* n.s. 50.3: 268–76.

Hiltmann, T., and U. Israel 2007. '"Laissez-les aller": Die Herolde und das Ende des Gerichtskampfs in Frankreich', *Francia* 34:1, 65–84.

Hobbins, D. 2009. *Authorship and Publicity before Print: Jean Gerson and the Transformation of Medieval Learning* (Philadelphia).

Høgel, C., and E. Bartoli, ed. 2015. *Medieval Letters: Between Fiction and Document* (Turnhout).

Holdenried, A. 2006. *The Sibyl and her Scribes: Manuscripts and Interpretations of the Latin* Sybilla Tiburtina, *c. 1050–1500* (Aldershot).

Holladay, J. A. 2010. 'Charting the Past: Visual Configurations of Myth and History and the English Claim to Scotland', in *Representing History, 900–1300: Art, Music, History*, ed. R. A. Maxwell (University Park), pp. 115–32.

Hoogvliet, M. 2013. 'The Medieval Vernacular Bible in French as a Flexible Text: Selective and Discontinuous Reading Practices', in *Form and Function in the Late Medieval Bible*, ed. E. Poleg and L. Light (Leiden), pp. 283–306.

Hourihane, C. 2009. *Pontius Pilate, Anti-semitism, and the Passion in Medieval Art* (Princeton).

Howell, M. 1998, repr. 2001. *Eleanor of Provence: Queenship in Thirteenth-Century England* (Oxford).

Hsy, J. 2013. *Trading Tongues: Merchants, Multilingualism and Medieval Literature* (Columbus, OH).

Hunt, T. 1979. '"Prodesse et delectare": Metaphors of Pleasure and Instruction in Old French', *Neuphilologische Mitteilungen* 80.1: 17–35.

—— 1980. 'The O. F. Commentary on the *Song of Songs* in MS Le Mans 173', *Zeitschrift für romanische Philologie* 96: 267–97.

—— 1981. 'The *Song of Songs* and Courtly Literature', in *Court and Poet*, ed. G. S. Burgess (Liverpool), pp. 189–96.

—— 1982. '"The Four Daughters of God": A Textual Contribution', *Archives d'histoire doctrinale et littéraire du Moyen Âge* [for 1981] 48: 287–316.

—— 1985. 'Anecdota Anglo-Normannica', *Yearbook of English Studies* 15: 1–17.

—— 1991. *Teaching and Learning Latin in Thirteenth-Century England*, 3 vols. (Woodbridge).

—— 1996. 'The Poetic Vein: Phlebotomy in Middle English and Anglo-Norman Verse', *English Studies* 77.4: 311–22.

Huot, S. 1987. *From Song to Book: The Poetics of Writing in Old French Lyric and Lyrical Narrative Poetry* (Ithaca).

—— 2005. 'Polytextual Reading: The Meditative Reading of Real and Metaphorical Books', in *Orality and Literacy in the Middle Ages*, ed. M. Chinca and C. Young, Utrecht Studies in Literacy 12 (Turnhout), pp. 203–22.

Hyams, P. 1983. 'Henry II and Ganelon', *Syracuse Scholar* 4.1: 22–35.

—— 2010. 'Thinking English Law in French: The Angevins and the Common Law', in *Feud, Violence, and Practice: Essays in Medieval Studies in Honor of Stephen D. White*, ed. B. S. Tuten and T. L Billado (Farnham), pp. 175–96.

—— 2011. 'The Legal Revolution and the Discourse of Dispute in the Twelfth Century', in *The Cambridge Companion to Medieval English Culture*, ed. A. Galloway, pp. 43–65.

Ingham, R. 2009. 'Mixing Languages on the Manor', *Medium Aevum* 78.1: 80–97.

—— 2010. *The Anglo-Norman Language in its Contexts* (York).

—— 2012. *The Transmission of Anglo-Norman: Language History and Language Acquisition* (Amsterdam).

—— 2015a. 'John Gower, poète anglo-normand', in *Anglo-français: linguistique et philologie/ Anglo-francese: filologia e linguistica*, ed. O. Floquet and G. Giannini (Paris).

—— 2015b. 'The Maintenance of French in Later Medieval England', *Neuphilologische Mitteilungen* 115/4: 623–45.

Ingham, R., and M. Ingham 2015. 'Pardonetz moi qe jeo de ceo forsvoie': Gower's Anglo-Norman Identity', *Neophilologus* 2015: 667–84.

Ingledew, F. 1994. 'The Book of Troy and the Genealogical Construction of History: The Case of Geoffrey of Monmouth's *Historia regum Britanniae*', *Speculum* 69.3: 665–704.

Iogna-Prat, D., E. Palazzo and D. Russo, ed. 1996. *Marie: le culte de la Vierge dans la société médiévale* (Paris).

Izydorczyk, Z. 1997. *The Medieval Gospel of Nicodemus: Texts, Intertexts and Contexts in Western Europe*, Medieval and Renaissance Texts and Studies 158 (Tempe).

Jaeger, C. S. 2000. *The Envy of Angels: Cathedral Schools and Social Ideals in Medieval Europe, 950–1200* (Philadelphia).

Jager, E. 2000. *The Book of the Heart* (Chicago).

Jambeck, K. K. 1996. 'Patterns of Women's Literary Patronage: England, 1200–*ca.* 1475', in *The Cultural Patronage of Medieval Women*, ed. J. H. McCash (Athens GA), pp. 228–65.

James, M. R. 1901–2. *The Western Manuscripts in the Library of Trinity College, Cambridge: A Descriptive Catalogue*, II, 1901; III, 1902 (Cambridge).

—— 1923. 'Rare Medieval Tiles and their Story', *Burlington Magazine for Connoisseurs* 42.238: 32–7.
Jefferson, J., and A. Putter, ed. 2013. *Multilingualism in Medieval Britain (c. 1066–1520): Sources and Analysis* (Turnhout).
Johnson, L. 1993. 'The Anglo-Norman Description of England: An Introduction', in Short, pp. 11–30.
—— 1995. 'Return to Albion', *Arthurian Literature* 13: 19–40 (repr. in Lamont and Baswell, forthcoming)
Johnson, P., and B. Cazelles 1979. *Le Vain Siecle guerpir: A Literary Approach to Sainthood through Old French Hagiography of The Twelfth Century* (Chapel Hill).
Johnston, D. 2012. 'Towns in Medieval Welsh Poetry', in Fulton, ed., pp. 95–115.
Johnston, R. C. 1974. *The Versification of Jordan Fantosme* (Oxford).
Jones, E. J. 1942. 'The Date of the Composition of the *Débat des hérauts d'armes de France* et d'Angleterre', *Comparative Literature Studies* 5:13–21; 6/7:14–20.
Jones, P. M. 2008. 'Witnesses to Medieval Medical Practice in the Harley Collection', *Electronic British Library Journal* 6–7.
Jones, T. 1994. 'Geoffrey of Monmouth, *Fouke le Fitz Waryn* and National Mythology', *Studies in Philology* 91.3: 233–49.
June, R. 2009. 'The Languages of Memory: The Crabhouse Nunnery Manuscript', in Wogan-Browne *et al.*, pp. 347–58.
Justice, S., and K. Kerby-Fulton, ed. 1997. *Written Work: Langland, Labor and Authorship* (Philadelphia).
Kaeuper, R. W. 1999. *Chivalry and Violence in Medieval Europe* (Oxford).
Kappler, C., and S. Thiolier-Méjean 2009. *Le Plurilinguisme au Moyen Âge: Orient – Occident: De Babel à la langue une* (Paris).
Karnes, M. 2011. *Imagination, Meditation, and Cognition in the Middle Ages* (Chicago).
Kauffmann, C. M. 2003. *Biblical Imagery in Medieval England 700–1550* (London).
Kay, S. 1995. *The Chansons de geste in the Age of Romance: Political Fictions* (Oxford).
—— 1997. 'Who was Chrétien de Troyes?', *Arthurian Literature* 15: 1–35.
—— 2001. *Courtly Contradictions: The Emergence of the Literary Object in the Twelfth Century* (Stanford).
—— 2007. *The Place of Thought: The Complexity of One in Late Medieval French Didactic Poetry* (Philadelphia).
—— 2014. 'Surface and Symptom on a Bestiary Page: Orifices on Folios 61^v–62^r of Cambridge, Fitzwilliam Museum, MS 20', *Exemplaria* 26: 127–47.
Kaye, J. 2004. 'Money and Administrative Calculation as Reflected in Scholastic Natural Philosophy', in *Arts of Calculation: Quantifying Thought in Early Modern Europe*, ed. D. Glimp and M. R. Warren (New York), pp. 1–18.
Kedar, B. Z. 2001. 'Convergences of Oriental Christian, Muslim and Frankish Worshippers: The Case of Saydnaya and the Knights Templar', in *The Crusades and the Military Orders: Expanding the Frontiers of Medieval Latin Christianity*, ed. Z. Hunyadi, J. Laszlovszky (Budapest), pp. 89–100 [also published, with slight variation in *De Sion exibit lex et verbum domini de Hierusalem: Essays on Medieval Law, Liturgy and Literature in Honour of Amnon Linder*, ed. Y. Hen, Cultural Encounters in Late Antiquity and the Middle Ages 1 (Turnhout), pp. 59–69].
Keen, M. 1984. *Chivalry* (New Haven).
Keene, D. 2008. 'Text, Visualization, Politics: London, 1150–1250', *Transactions of the Royal Historical Society* 18: 69–99.
Keiser, G. R. 1998. 'Works of Science and Education', in *A Manual of the Writings in Middle English, 1050–1500*, X (New Haven).
Kelly, S., and J. J. Thompson, ed. 2005. *Imagining the Book*, Medieval Texts and Cultures of Northern Europe 7 (Turnhout).

Kempshall, M. 2011. *Rhetoric and the Writing of History, 400–1500* (Manchester).
Kennedy, K. E. 2003. '*Le Tretiz* of Walter of Bibbesworth', in *Medieval Literature for Children*, ed. D. T. Kline (New York), pp. 131–42.
—— 2009. *Maintenance, Meed and Marriage in Medieval English Literature* (New York).
Kenney, J. F. 1929. *The Sources for the Early History of Ireland: An Introduction and Guide* (New York).
Ker, N. R. 1985 [1954]. '*Liber custumarum* and Other Manuscripts Formerly at the Guildhall', in *Books, Collectors and Libraries: Studies in the Medieval Heritage*, ed. A. G. Watson (London), pp. 135–42. [repr. from *The Guildhall Miscellany* 1. 3: 37–45].
—— 1964 [1941]. *Medieval Libraries of Great Britain: A List of Surviving Books* (London).
Kerby-Fulton, K. 2006. *Books under Suspicion: Censorship and Tolerance of Revelatory Writing in Late Medieval England* (Notre Dame, IN).
—— 2014. 'The Clerical Proletariat: The Underemployed Scribe and Vocational Crisis', *Journal of the Early Book Society* 17 (2014).
—— 2015. 'Office Vernaculars, Civil Servant Raconteurs, and the Porous Nature of French during Ireland's Rise of English', *Speculum* 90.3: 674–700.
Kerby-Fulton, K, J. J. Thompson and S. Baechle, ed. 2014. *New Directions in Medieval Manuscripts Studies and Reading Practices* (Notre Dame).
Kibbee, D. A. 1991. *For to Speke French Trewely: The French Language in England, 1000–1600, its Status, Description and Instruction*, Studies in the History of the Language Sciences 60 (Amsterdam).
Kibler, W. W., ed. 1994. *The Lancelot-Grail Cycle: Text and Transformations* (Austin).
King, A. 2000a. 'A Helm with a Crest of Gold: The Order of Chivalry in Thomas Gray's *Scalacronica*', in *Fourteenth Century England 1*, ed. N. Saul (Woodbridge), pp. 21–35.
—— 2000b. 'Englishmen, Scots and Marchers: National and Local Identities in Thomas Gray's *Scalacronica*', *Northern History* 36.2: 217–31.
—— 2002. '"According to the custom used in French and Scottish Wars": Prisoners and Casualties on the Scottish Marches in the Fourteenth Century', *Journal of Medieval History* 28.3: 263–90.
—— 2005b. 'Scaling the Ladder: The Rise and Rise of the Grays of Heaton, *c.* 1296–*c.* 1415', in *North-East England in the Later Middle Ages*, ed. C. D. Liddy and R. H. Britnell (Woodbridge), pp. 57–73.
—— 2008. 'War and Peace, a Knight's Tale: The Ethics of War in Sir Thomas Gray's *Scalacronica*', in *War, Government and Aristocracy in the British Isles c. 1150–1500: Essays in Honour of Michael Prestwich*, ed. C. Given-Wilson, A. J. Kettle and L. Scales (Woodbridge), pp. 148–62.
Kinoshita, S. 2006. *Medieval Boundaries: Re-thinking Difference in Old French Literature* (Philadelphia).
Kinoshita, S., and P. McCracken. 2014 [2012]. *Marie de France: A Critical Companion* (Cambridge).
Knowles, D. 1970. *Thomas Becket* (London).
Knowles, D., and R. N. Hadcock 1971. *Medieval Religious Houses: England and Wales* (London).
Knox, P. 2013. 'The English Glosses in Walter of Bibbesworth's *Tretiz*', *Notes and Queries* n.s. 60.3: 349–59.
Kobialka, M. 1999. *This is My Body: Representational Practices in the Early Middle Ages* (Ann Arbor).
Koch, J. 1886. *Li Rei de Engleterre: ein anglo-normannischer Geschichtsauszug* (Berlin).
Kooper, E., and A. Kruijshoop, ed., 1989. 'Of English Kings and Arms', in *In Other Words: Transcultural Studies in Philology, Translation and Lexicology Presented to Hans Heinrich Meier on the Occasion of his Sixty-Fifth Birthday*, ed. J. L. Mackenzie and R. Todd (Dordrecht), pp. 45–56.
Kosto, A. J., and A. Winroth, ed. 2002. *Charters, Cartularies and Archives: The Preservation and Transmission of Documents in the Medieval West* (Toronto),
Kowaleski, M. 2009. 'The French of England: A Maritime *lingua franca*?' in Wogan-Browne *et al.*, *Language and Culture*, pp. 103–17.
Kristol, A. M. 1990 'L'Enseignement du français en Angleterre (XIIIe–XVe siècles): Les sources

manuscrites', *Romania* 111: 289–330.

Kristol, A. M. 1990–1. 'Un nouveau fragment de manière de langage: Lincoln, Linc. Arch. Off., Formulary 23', *Vox Romanica* 49/50: 311–41.

—— 2000. 'L'Intellectuel "anglo-normand" face à la pluralité des langues: le témoignage implicite du MS Oxford, Magdalen Lat. 188', in Trotter, pp. 37–52.

Krueger, R. L. 1987. 'The Author's Voice: Narrators, Audiences and the Problem of Interpretation', in *The Legacy of Chrétien de Troyes*, ed. N. J. Lacy, D. Kelly and K. Busby, Faux Titre 31 (Amsterdam), I, 115–40.

—— 1990. 'Misogyny, Manipulation and the Female Reader in Hue de Rotelande's *Ipomedon*', in *Courtly Literature, Culture and Context: Selected Papers from the 5th Triennial Congress of the International Courtly Literature Society*, ed. K. Busby and E. Kooper (Amsterdam), pp. 395–409.

Kumler, A. 2011. *Translating Truth: Ambitious Images and Religious Knowledge in Late Medieval France and England* (New Haven).

—— 2012. 'Translating ma dame de St Pol', in *Translating the Middle Ages*, ed. K. L. Fresco and C. D. Wright (Burlington, VT), pp. 35–53.

Kuskowski, A-M. 2014. 'Lingua Franca legalis? A French Vernacular Culture from England to the Levant', in *Reading Medieval Studies* 40, special issue, *Law's Dominion: Medieval Studies for Paul Hyams*, ed. M. C. Escobar-Vargas, pp. 140–58.

L'Engle, S., and G. B. Guest, ed. 2006. *Tributes to Jonathan J. G. Alexander. The Making and Meaning of Illuminated Medieval and Renaissance Manuscripts, Art and Architecture* (London).

Labande, E. 1955. 'Le "Credo" épique: a propos des prières dans les chansons de geste', in *Recueil de travaux offert à M. Clovis Brunel, membre de l'Institut, directeur honoraire de l'Ecole des chartes, par ses amis, collègues et élèves* (Paris), II, 62–80.

Lach, D. F. 1965–93. *Asia in the Making of Europe*, 9 vols. (Chicago), II.

Ladd, R. A. 2010. 'The *Mirour de l'omme* and Gower's London Merchants', in his *Antimercantilism in Late Medieval English Literature* (New York), pp. 49–75.

Lagorio, V. M. 2001. 'The Evolving Legend of St Joseph of Glastonbury', in *Glastonbury Abbey and the Arthurian Tradition*, ed. J. Carley (Woodbridge), pp. 55–81.

Lagorio, V. M., and M. G. Sargent 1993. 'XXIII. English Mystical Writings', in *A Manual of the Writings in Middle English 1050–1500*, ed. A. E. Hartung (New Haven), IX, 3049–3137, 3405–71.

Laird, C. G. 1941. 'Manuscripts of the *Manuel des Pechiez*', in *Stanford Studies in Language and Literature*, ed. H. Craig (Stanford University), pp. 99–123.

—— 1946. 'Character and Growth of the *Manuel des pechiez*', *Traditio* 4: 253–306.

Lamont, M., and C. Baswell, ed. (forthcoming). *The Albina Casebook* (Toronto).

Larner, J. 2008. 'Plucking Hairs from the Great Cham's Beard: Marco Polo, Jan de Langhe and Sir John Mandeville', in *Marco Polo and the Encounter of East and West*, ed. S. C. Akbari and A. Iannucci (Toronto), pp. 133–55.

Laurent, F. 1998. *Plaire et édifier: Les récits hagiographiques composés en Angleterre aux XIIe et XIIIe siècles.* (Paris).

—— 2012. '"Mises en roman" et faits de style: Le *Roman de Rou* de Wace et l'*Estoire des ducs de Normandie* de Benoît de Sainte-Maure', *Effets de style au Moyen Âge*, ed. Chantal Connochie-Bourgne and Sébastien Douchet. *Senefiance* 58, Aix-en-Provence, pp. 115–24; 121–2.

Lavezzo, K. 2006. *Angels on the Edge of the World: Geography, Literature, and English Community, 1000–1534* (Ithaca, NY).

Lawrence-Mathers, A. 2010. 'Domesticating the Calendar: The Hours and the Almanac in Tudor England', in *Women and Writing c. 1340–1650: The Domestication of Print Culture*, ed. A. Lawrence-Mathers and P. Hardman (York), pp. 34–61.

Le Blévec, D., ed. 2006. *Les Cartulaires méridionaux* (Paris).
Le Clerc, V. 1847. 'Jofroi de Waterford, Dominicain', in *Histoire littéraire de la France* (Paris), XXI, 216–29.
Le Person, M. 2011. 'Le Souffle épique religieux dans *Fierabras* et la *Destruction* [sic] *de Rome*: une hagiographie, une histoire des reliques et la sacralisation de la fonction royale', in Bazin-Tacchella *et al.*, pp. 225–32.
Le Saux, F. H. M. 2005. *A Companion to Wace* (Cambridge).
—— 2006. 'Wace as Hagiographer', in *Maistre Wace: A Celebration. Proceedings of the International Colloquium Held in Jersey, 10–12 September 2004*, ed. G. S. Burgess and J. Weiss (St Helier), pp. 139–48.
—— 2009. 'The Languages of England: Multilingualism in the Work of Wace', in Wogan-Browne *et al.*, pp. 188–97.
Leach, H. G. 1921. *Angevin Britain and Scandinavia* (Cambridge, MA).
Lebeuf, M. 1751. 'Recherches sur les plus anciennes traductions en langue françoise', in *Mémoires de littérature tirés des registres de l'Académie Royale des Inscriptions et Belles Lettres* (Paris), XVII, 709–61.
Leclercq, J. 1982. *The Love of Learning and the Desire for God: A Study of Monastic Culture* (New York).
LeCoy, F. 1971. Review of Panunzio, ed., 1967, *Romania* 92: 429–30.
Lees, C. A., ed. 2012. *The Cambridge History of Early Medieval English Literature* (Oxford)
Legge, M. D. 1929. 'Pierre de Peckham and his "Lumiere as Lais"', *Modern Language Review* 24: 37–47, 153–71.
—— 1939. 'William of Kingsmill – A Fifteenth-Century Teacher of French in Oxford', in *Studies in French Language and Mediæval Literature: Presented to Professor Mildred K. Pope by Pupils, Colleagues and Friends* (Manchester), pp. 241–6.
—— 1950. *Anglo-Norman in the Cloisters: The Influence of the Orders upon Anglo-Norman Literature* (Edinburgh).
—— 1953. 'The Lord Edward's Vegetius', *Speculum* 7: 262–5.
—— 1958. 'La Date des écrits de Frère Angier', *Romania* 79: 512–14.
—— 1965. 'La Précocité de la littérature anglo-normande', *Cahiers de Civilisation Médiévale*, 8:327–49
—— 1971 [1963]. *Anglo-Norman Literature and Its Background* (Oxford).
Legge, M. D., and D. J. A. Ross 1955. 'Discussions: Thomas of Kent', *French Studies* 9.4: 348–51
Léglu, C. 1997. 'Negative Self-Promotion: The Troubadour "Sirventes Joglaresc"', in Mullally and Thompson, pp. 47–56.
Lemay, H. R. 1992. *Women's Secrets: A Translation of Psuedo-Albertus Magnus's* De secretis mulierum *with Commentaries* (Albany).
Lester, G. A. 1990. 'The Literary Activity of the Medieval English Heralds', *English Studies* 71.3: 222–9.
Leupin, A. 1982. *Le Graal et la littérature: étude sur la Vulgate arthurienne en prose* (Lausanne).
Levi, E. 1925. 'Troveri ed Abbazie', *Archivio storico italiano* 7th s. 83.3.1: 45–81.
Lewis, C. 1995. 'The French in England before the Norman Conquest', *Anglo-Norman Studies* 17: 123–44.
Lewis, P. S. 1965. 'War Propaganda and Historiography in Fifteenth-Century France and England', *Transactions of the Royal Historical Society* 5th s. 15:1–21.
Lewis, S. 1986. '*Tractatus adversus Judaeos* in the Gulbenkian Apocalypse', *The Art Bulletin* 68.4: 543–66.
—— 1987. *The Art of Matthew Paris in the* Chronica majora (Berkeley).
—— 1995. *Reading Images: Narrative Discourse and Reception in the Thirteenth-Century Illuminated Apocalypse* (Cambridge).
L'Hermite-Leclerq, P. 1999. '*Le Sang et la lait de la Vierge*', in *Le Sang au Moyen Âge*, Les Cahiers

du CRISIMA 4 (Montpellier), pp. 145–62.
Licence, T., ed. 2014. *Bury St Edmunds and the Norman Conquest* (Woodbridge).
Lieberman, M. 2008. *The March of Wales 1067–1300: A Borderland of Medieval Britain* (Cardiff).
—— 2009. 'The English and the Welsh in *Fouke le Fitz Waryn*', in *Thirteenth-Century England 12*, ed. J. Burton, P. Schofield and B. Weiler (Woodbridge), pp. 1–11.
Lindenbaum, S. 1999. 'London Texts and Literate Practice', in *The Cambridge History of English Medieval Literature*, ed. D. Wallace (Cambridge), pp. 284–310.
Livingston, C. H. 1942. 'Manuscript Fragments of a Continental French Version of the *Roman d'Ipomedon*', *Modern Philology* 40.2: 117–30.
Lloyd-Jones, J. 1931–63. *Geirfa Barddoniaeth Gynnar Gymraeg* [*A Dictionary of Early Welsh Poetry*], 2 vols. (Cardiff).
Lobrichon, G. 2003. *La Bible au Moyen Âge* (Paris).
Lodge, A. R. 2004. *A Socio-Linguistic History of Parisian French* (Cambridge).
Longère, J. 1983. *La Prédication médiévale* (Paris).
Loomis, R. S. 1956. *Wales and the Arthurian Legend* (Cardiff).
Lopez, D., and P. McCracken 2014. *In Search of the Christian Buddha: How an Asian Sage became a Medieval Saint* (New York).
Lowes, J. L. 1914. 'Spenser and the *Mirour de l'omme*', *Publications of the Modern Language Association of America* 29.3: 388–452.
Lusignan, S. 1987 [1986]. *Parler vulgairement: les intellectuels et la langue français aux XIIIe et XIVe siècle*, 2nd edn (Paris).
—— 2004. *La Langue des rois au Moyen Âge: le français en France et en Angleterre* (2nd edn, Paris).
—— 2009. 'Brunei Latin et la pensée politique urbaine dans le nord de la France', in *Scientia valescit: Zur Institutionalisierung von kulturellem Wissen in romanischem Mittelalter und früher Neuzeit*, ed. E. Eggert, S. Gramatzki and C. O. Mayer (München), pp. 217–36.
—— 2011. 'La Naissance d'une littérature en franceis en Angleterre au XII siècle', in *L'Introuvable Unité du français: Contacts et variations linguistiques en Europe et en Amérique (XIIe–XVIIIe siècle)*, ed. S. Lusignan, F. Martineau, Y. C. Morin and P. Cohen (Laval), pp. 16–27.
—— 2012a. *Essai d'histoire sociolinguistique: le français picard au Moyen Âge* (Paris).
—— 2012b. 'Á chacun son français: La communication entre l'Angleterre et les régions picardes et flamandes (xiiie et xive siècle)', *Deuxième journée d'études anglo-normandes: Approches techniques, littéraires et historiques*, ed. A. Crépin and A. Leclant (Paris), pp. 117–33.
—— 2016. 'Communication in the Later Plantagenet Empire: Latin and Anglo-Norman as Regal Languages', in Crooks, Green and Ormrod, pp. 271–87.
MacBain, W. 1958. 'The Literary Apprenticeship of Clemence of Barking', *AUMLA: Journal of the Autralasian Universities Language and Literature Association* 9: 3–22.
—— 1988. 'Some Religious and Secular Uses of the Vocabulary of *fin' amor* in the Early Decades of the Northern French Narrative Poem', *French Forum* 13.3: 261–76.
—— 1993. 'Anglo-Norman Women Hagiographers', in Short, pp. 235–50.
MacColl, A. 2006. 'The Meaning of "Britain" in Medieval and Early Modern England', *Journal of British Studies* 45.2: 248–69.
Machan, T. W. 1994. 'Language Contact in *Piers Plowman*'. *Speculum* 69.2: 359–85.
—— 2006. 'Medieval Multilingualism and Gower's Literary Practice', *Studies in Philology* 103: 1–25.
—— 2009. 'French, English and the Late Medieval Linguistic Repertoire', in Wogan-Browne *et al.*, pp. 363–72.
Madan, F. *et al.*, ed. 1895–1953. *A Summary Catalogue of Western Manuscripts in the Bodleian Library at Oxford which have not hitherto been catalogued in the Quarto series*, 7 vols. (Oxford).
Maddicott, J. R. 1994. *Simon de Montfort* (Cambridge).
Maddox, D., and S. Sturm-Maddox 2002. *The Medieval French Alexander* (Albany).

Maitland, F. W., and W. P. Baildon, ed. 1891. 'The Manner of Holding Courts', in *The Court Baron: Being Precedents for Use in Seignorial and Other Local Courts*, Selden Society 4 (London), pp. 93–106.
Manly, J. M. 1939. 'The Penrose MS of *La Résurrection*', *Modern Philology* 37.1: 1–6.
Marcus, I. G. 1998. *Rituals of Childhood* (New Haven).
Marshall, L. 1973. 'The Authorship of the Anglo-Norman Poem, *Corset*', *Medium Aevum* 42.3: 207–23.
Marshall, L., and W. Rothwell 1970. 'The *Miroir* of Robert of Greatham', *Medium Aevum* 39.3: 313–21.
Martineau-Génieys, C. 1987. 'Modèles, maquillage et misogynie, à travers les textes littéraires français du Moyen Âge', in Menjot, pp. 31–50.
Marvin, J. 2001. 'Albine and Isabelle: Regicidal Queens and the Historical Imagination of the Anglo-Norman Prose *Brut* Chronicles', *Arthurian Literature* 18: 143–91.
Marvin, J. (forthcoming). *The Construction of Vernacular History in the Prose 'Brut' Tradition* (York).
Marx, C. W. 1995. *The Devil's Rights and the Redemption in the Literature of Medieval England* (Cambridge).
Matheson, L. M. 1998. *The Prose Brut: The Development of a Middle English Chronicle*, Medieval and Renaissance Texts and Studies 180 (Tempe).
Mathey-Maille, L. 2005. 'L'Étymologie dans le *Roman de Rou* de Wace', in '*De sens rassis:' Essays in Honor of Rupert T. Pickens*, ed. K. Busby *et al.* (Amsterdam), pp. 403–14.
Matsuda, T. 1997. *Death and Purgatory in Middle English Didactic Poetry* (Woodbridge).
Matter, E. A. 1990. *The Voice of My Beloved: The Song of Songs in Western Medieval Christianity* (Philadelphia).
Maxwell-Lyte, H. C. 1909. *A History of Dunster and of the Families of Mohun and Luttrell*, 2 vols. (London).
McCulloch, F. 1960. *Mediaeval Latin and French Bestiaries* (Chapel Hill).
McDannell, C., and B. Lang 1988, repr. 2001. *Heaven: A History* (New Haven).
McEvoy, J. 2000. *Robert Grosseteste* (Oxford).
McGinn, B. 1985. '*Teste David cum Sibylla*: The Significance of the Sibylline Tradition in the Middle Ages', in *Women of the Medieval World: Essays in Honor of John H. Mundy*, ed. J. Kirshner and S. F. Wemple (Oxford), pp. 7–35.
McIntosh, A., M. Benskin, M. Laing, M. L. Samuels and K. Williamson 1986. *A Linguistic Atlas of Late Medieval English* (Aberdeen).
McKendrick, S., J. Lowden and K. Doyle, ed. 2011. *Royal Manuscripts: The Genius of Illumination* (London).
McNamer, S. 2010. *Affective Meditation and the Invention of Medieval Compassion* (Philadelphia).
Meale, C. M. 1984. 'The Middle English Romance of *Ipomedon*: A Late Medieval "Mirror" for Princes and Merchants', *Reading Medieval Studies* 10: 136–91.
—— 1990. 'The Miracles of Our Lady: Context and Interpretation', in Pearsall, pp. 115–36.
—— 1995. ' The "Libelle of Englyshe Polycye" and Mercantile Literary Culture in Late-Medieval London', in *London and Europe in the Later Middle Ages*, ed. J. Boffey and P. King (London), pp. 181–228.
—— ed. 1996 [1993]. *Women and Literature in Britain, 1150–1500*, 2nd edn (Cambridge).
Meisel, J. 1980. *Barons of the Welsh Frontier: The Corbet, Pantulf and Fitz Warin Families, 1066–1272* (Lincoln).
Mellinkoff, R. 1993. *The Outcasts: Signs of Otherness in Northern European Art of the Late Middle Ages*, 2 vols. (Berkeley).
Melville, G. 1992. 'Hérauts et héros', in *European Monarchy: Its Evolution and Practice from Roman Antiquity to Modern Times*, ed. H. Duchhardt, R. A. Jackson and D. Sturdy (Stuttgart), pp. 81–97.
—— 2006. 'Pourquoi des hérauts d'armes ? Les raisons d'une institution', *Revue du Nord* 88: 491–502.

Ménard, P. 1969. *Le Rire et le sourire dans le roman courtois en France au moyen-âge (1150–1250)* (Geneva).

Meneghetti, M. L., ed. 1979. *I fatti di Bretagna: Cronache genealogiche anglo-normanne dal XII al XIV Secolo* (Padua).

Menjot, D., ed. 1987. *Les Soins de beauté: Moyen Âge, début des temps modernes, Actes du IIIe Colloque international, Grasse (26–28 avril 1985)* (Nice).

Merrilees, B. 1986. 'Teaching Latin in French: Adaptations of Donatus' *Ars minor*', *Fifteenth-Century Studies* 12: 87–98

—— 1993. 'Donatus and the Teaching of French in Medieval England', in Short, pp. 273–91.

Merrilees, B., and H. Pagan 2009. 'John Barton, John Gower and Others: Variation in Late Anglo-French', in Wogan-Browne *et al.*, pp. 118–34.

Meyer, P. 1884. 'Notice et extraits du MS. 8336 de la Bibliothèque de Sir Thomas Phillipps à Cheltenham', *Romania* 13: 497–541.

—— 1886. *Alexandre le Grand dans la littérature française du Moyen Âge*, 2 vols. (Paris).

—— 1889. 'Notice du ms. Egerton 2710 du Musée Britannique', *Bulletin de la Société des anciens textes français* 15: 72–97.

—— 1900. 'Notice du ms. Rawlinson Poetry 241 (Oxford)', *Romania* 29: 54–72.

—— 1903a. 'Notice d'un manuscrit de Trinity College (Cambridge) contenant les vies, en vers français, de saint Jean l'Aumônier et de saint Clément, Pape', *Notices et extraits des manuscrits de la Bibliothèque nationale* 38: 293–339.

—— 1903b. 'Les Manuscrits français de Cambridge', *Romania* 32: 18–120.

—— 1910. 'Notice du MS. Egerton 745 du Musée Britannique', *Romania* 39: 532–69.

—— 1911. 'Notice du MS. Egerton 745 du Musée Britannique (2e article)', *Romania* 40: 41–69.

Meyer-Lee, R. 2013. Review of G. Bolens and L. Erne, *Medieval and Early Modern Authorship* (Tübingen, 2011), and S. Partridge and E. Kwakkel, ed., *Author, Reader, Book: Medieval and Early Modern Authorship in Theory and Practice* (Toronto, 2012), in *Studies in the Age of Chaucer* 35:387–93.

Michael, M. A. 1985. 'A Manuscript Wedding Gift from Philippa of Hainault to Edward III', *The Burlington Magazine* 127.990: 582, 584–99.

Middleton, A., 1990. 'William Langland's "Kynde Name": Authorial Signature and Social Identity in Late Fourteenth-Century England', in *Literary Practice and Social Change in Britain, 1380–1530*, ed. L. Paerson (Berkeley and Los Angeles), 15–82.

Middleton, R. 2003. 'Manuscripts of the *Lancelot-Grail Cyle* in England and Wales: Some Books and their Owners', in Dover, pp. 219–36.

Milland-Bove, B. 2012. 'Le Style épique dans le *Roman de Dieu et de sa Mere* d'Herman de Valenciennes: langue de soi ou langue de l'Autre?', in *Langue de l'autre, langue de l'auteur. Affirmation d'une identité linguistique et littéraire aux XIIe et XVIe siècles*, ed. M. Masse and A. Pouey-Mounou (Geneva), pp. 167–82.

Millett, B. 1996. 'Women in No Man's Land: English Recluses and the Development of Vernacular Literature in the Twelfth and Thirteenth Centuries', in Meale, pp. 86–103.

Minervini, L. 1995. 'Leggende dei cristiani orientali nelle letterature romanze del medioevo', *Romance Philology* 49: 1–12.

Minnis, A. J. 1983. 'Affection and Imagination in "The Cloud of Unknowing" and Hilton's "Scale of Perfection"', *Traditio* 39: 323–66.

—— 1988 [1984]. *Medieval Literary Theory of Authorship: Scholastic Literary Attitudes in the Later Middle Ages*, 2nd edn (Aldershot [London]).

Minnis, A., and I. Johnson, ed. 2005. *The Cambridge History of Literary Criticism*, vol. 2: *The Middle Ages* (Cambridge).

Möhring, H. 2008. *Saladin: The Sultan and his Times, 1138–1193*, trans. D. S. Bachrach (Baltimore).

Moisan, A. 1986. *Répertoire des noms propres de personnes et de lieux cités dans les Chansons de Geste françaises et les ouevres étrangères dérivées*, 5 vols. (Geneva).

Moll, R. J. 2003. *Before Malory: Reading Arthur in Later Medieval England* (Toronto).
—— 2008. '"Nest pas autentik, mais apocrophum": Haveloks and their Reception in Medieval England', *Studies in Philology* 105.2: 165–206.
Monfrin, J. 1964. 'Sur les sources du *Secret des Secrets* de Jofroi de Waterford et Servais Copale', in *Mélanges de linguistique romane et de philologie médiévale offerts à M. Maurice Delbouille*, ed. J. Renson (Gembloux), II, 509–30.
—— 1982. 'La Place du *Secret des secrets* dans la littérature française médiévale', in *Pseudo-Aristotle, Secret of Secrets: Sources and Influences*, ed. W. F. Ryan and C. B. Schmitt (London).
Monroe, W. H. 1978. 'A Roll-Manuscript of Peter of Poitiers' Compendium', *The Bulletin of the Cleveland Museum of Art* 65.3: 92–107.
—— 1978–82. 'Two Medieval Genealogical Roll-Chronicles in the Bodleian Library', *The Bodleian Library Record* 10: 215–21.
—— 1990. 'Thirteenth- and Early Fourteenth-Century Illustrated Genealogical Manuscripts in Roll and Codex: Peter of Poitiers' "Compendium", Universal Histories and Chronicles of the Kings of England' (unpublished Ph.D. dissertation, University of London).
Montoya Martínez, J. 1981. *Las colecciones de Milagros de la Virgen en la Edad Media (El Milagro Literario)*(Granada).
Mooney, L. R., and E. Stubbs 2013. *Scribes and the City: London Guildhall Clerks and the Dissemination of Middle English Literature, 1375–1425* (Woodbridge).
Morawski, J., ed. 1925. *Proverbes français antérieurs au XVe siècle*, Classiques français du Moyen Âge 47 (Paris).
Morey, J. H. 1993. 'Peter Comestor, Biblical Paraphrase and the Medieval Popular Bible', *Speculum* 68.1: 6–35.
Morgan, N. J. 1982–8. *Early Gothic Manuscripts*, 2 vols., A Survey of Manuscripts Illuminated in the British Isles 4 (London).
—— ed. 1990. *The Lambeth Apocalypse: Manuscript 209 in Lambeth Palace Library, a Critical Study* [Commentary and Text Volume to the Facsimile Edition] (London).
—— 2006. 'Pictured Sermons in Thirteenth-Century England', in L'Engle and Guest, pp. 323–40.
Morgan, P. 1998. '"Those were the Days": A Yorkist Pedigree Roll', in *Estrangement, Enterprise and Education in Fifteenth-Century England*, ed. S. D. Michalove and A. C. Reeves (Stroud), pp. 107–16.
Morreale, L., and N. Paul 2016. *The French of Outremer: Communities and Communications in the Crusading Mediterranean* (New York).
Mosher, J. A. 1911. *The Exemplum in the Early Religious and Didactic Literature of England* (New York).
Moulinier-Brogi, L. 2004. 'Esthétique et soins du corps dans les traités médicaux Latins à la fin du Moyen Âge', *Médiévales* 46: 55–72.
Muir, L. 1995. *The Biblical Drama of Medieval Europe* (Cambridge).
Mullally, E. 1988. 'Hiberno-Norman Literature and Its Public', in *Settlement and Society in Medieval Ireland: Studies Presented to F. X. Martin, OSA*, ed. John Bradley (Kilkenny), pp. 327–43.
Mullally, E., and J. Thompson, ed. 1997. *The Court and Cultural Diversity: Selected Papers from the Eighth Triennial Congress of the International Courtly Literature Society, Queen's University of Belfast, 26 July – 1 August 1995* (Cambridge).
Mundill, R. R. 1998. *England's Jewish Solution: Experiment and Expulsion, 1262–1290* (Cambridge).
Murphy, J. J. 1964. 'A New Look at Chaucer and the Rhetoricians', *Review of English Studies* 15.57: 1–20.
Nagler, A. M. 1976. *The Medieval Religious Stage: Shapes and Phantoms* (New Haven).
Neave, D. 1991. *Howden Explored: A Guide to the Town and its Buildings* (Howden).
Nègre, E. 1990. *Toponymie générale de la France: Etymologie de 35.000 noms de lieux, 1* (Geneva).
Nelson, J. L. 1986. 'Wealth and Wisdom: The Politics of Alfred the Great', in *Kings and Kingship*,

ed. J. Rosenthal (Binghamton), pp. 31–52.
—— 1993. 'The Political Ideas of Alfred of Wessex', in *Kings and Kingship in Medieval Europe*, ed. A. J. Duggan (London), pp. 125–58.
Newman, B. 2003. *God and the Goddesses: Vision, Poetry and Belief in the Middle Ages* (Philadelphia).
Newstead, H. H. 1939. *Bran the Blessed in Arthurian Romance* (New York).
Ní Mhaonaigh, M. 2013. 'Of Bede's "five languages and four nations": The Earliest Writing from Ireland, Scotland and Wales', in Lees, pp. 99–119.
Nicolle, D. 2008. *Poitiers AD 732: Charles Martel Turns the Islamic Tide* (Oxford).
Nicoud, M. 2007. *Les Régimes de santé au Moyen Âge: Naissance et diffusion d'une écriture médicale (XIIIe–XVe siècle)*, 2 vols. (Rome).
Nobel, P. 1994. 'Epopée et traduction biblique', in *La Chanson de geste: Écriture, intertextualités, translations*, ed. F. Suard, Littérales 14 (Nanterre), pp. 105–24.
—— 1997. 'Mots anglo-normands dans une traduction de la Bible', in Gregory and Trotter, pp. 147–59.
—— 2011. 'La Traduction biblique' and 'Bible d'Herman de Valenciennes', in Galderisi and Agrigoroaei, I, 207–23 and II, 129–30.
Nolan, M. 2013. 'Agency and the Poetics of Sensation in Gower's *Mirour de l'omme*', in *Answerable Style: The Idea of the Literary in Medieval England*, ed. F. Grady and A. Galloway (Columbus), pp. 214–43.
Norbye, M. A. 2007a. 'Genealogies and Dynastic Awareness in the Hundred Years War: The Evidence of *A tous nobles qui aiment beaux faits et bonnes histoires*', *Journal of Medieval History* 33.3: 297–319.
—— 2007b. 'A Popular Example of "National Literature" in the Hundred Years War: *A tous nobles qui aiment beaux faits et bonnes histoires*', *Nottingham Medieval Studies* 51: 121–42.
—— 2008. 'Genealogies in Medieval France', in Radulescu and Kennedy, pp. 79–101.
O'Brien, B. R. 1999. *God's Peace and King's Peace: The Laws of Edward the Confessor* (Philadelphia).
O'Byrne, T. 2012. 'Dublin's Hoccleve: James Yonge, Scribe, Author and Bureaucrat and the Literary World of Late Medieval Dublin' (Unpublished Ph.D. thesis, University of Notre Dame).
O'Donnell, T. 2011. 'Anglo-Norman Multilingualism and Continental Standards in Guernes de Pont-Sainte-Maxence's *Vie de Saint Thomas*', in *Conceptualizing Multilingualism in England, 800–1250*, ed. E. M. Tyler (Turnhout), pp. 337–56.
—— 2012a. '"The Ladies have made me quite fat": Authors and Patrons at Barking Abbey', in Brown and Bussell, pp. 94–114.
O'Donnell, T. (with M. Townend and E. M. Tyler) 2012b. 'European Literature and Eleventh-Century England', in *The Cambridge History of Early Medieval English Literature*, ed. C. Lees (Cambridge), pp. 607–36 (625–36).
O'Donnell, T., and E. Tyler (forthcoming). 'From the Severn to the Rhine: Some Unexamined Geographies and Social Networks of English Literary Culture, ca. 1000–1150'.
O'Rourke, J. 2000. 'Literary and Political Culture in Wales and the English Border Country, 1300–1475', Unpubl. Ph.D. Dissertation, Queens University, Belfast.
—— 2005. 'Imagining Book Production in Fourteenth-Century Herefordshire: The Scribe of British Library, MS Harley 2253 and his "Organizing Principles"', in Kelly and Thompson, pp. 45–60.
Obrist, B. 1997. 'Wind Diagrams and Medieval Cosmology', *Speculum* 72.1: 33–84.
Ogden, D. H. 2001. 'Gesture and Characterization in the Liturgical Drama', in *Gesture in Medieval Drama and Art*, ed. C. Davidson, Early Drama, Art and Music Monograph Series 28 (Kalamazoo), pp. 26–47.
—— 2002. *The Staging of Drama in the Medieval Church* (Newark, DE).]
Ohly, F. 1958. *Hohelied-Studien: Grundzüge einer Geschichte der Hohenliedauslegung des Abendlandes bis um 1200* (Wiesbaden).
Oliva, M. 1998. *The Convent and the Community in Late Medieval England: Female Monasteries in the Diocese of Norwich, 1350–1540* (Woodbridge).

Olson, G. 1982. *Literature as Recreation in the Later Middle Ages* (Ithaca).
——2005. 'The Profits of Pleasure', in Minnis and Johnson, pp. 275–87.
Orme, N. 2006. *Medieval Schools: From Roman Britain to Renaissance England* (New Haven).
Osborn, M. 1998. 'The Real Fulk Fitzwarine's Mythical Monster Fights', in *Words and Works: Studies in Medieval English Language and Literature in Honour of Fred C. Robinson*, ed. P. S. Baker and N. Howe, Toronto Old English Series 10 (Toronto), pp. 271–92.
Otter, M. 1991. '"Gaainable tere": Symbolic Appropriation of Space and Time in Geoffrey of Monmouth and Vernacular Historical Writing', in *Discovering New Worlds: Essays on Medieval Exploration and Imagination*, ed. S. D. Westrem (New York), pp. 157–77.
—— 1996. *Inventiones: Fiction and Referentiality in Twelfth-Century Literature* (Chapel Hill).
Ouy, G. 1959. 'Un poème mystique de Charles d'Orléans: le "Canticum Amoris"', *Studi Francesi* 7: 64–84.
—— 2000. 'Charles d'Orléans and his Brother Jean d'Angoulême in England: What their Manuscripts have to tell', in *Charles d'Orléans in England (1415–1440)*, ed. M. Arn (Cambridge), pp. 47–60.
Owen, D. D. R. 1997. *William the Lion, 1143–1214: Kingship and Culture* (East Linton, Scot.)
Pächt, O., and J. J. G. Alexander 1973. *Illuminated Manuscripts in the Bodleian Library, Oxford*, vol. 3: *British, Irish and Icelandic Schools; with an addenda to volumes 1 and 2* (Oxford).
Painter, S. 1935. 'The Sources of *Fouke Fitz Warin*', *Modern Language Notes* 50.1: 13–15.
Pappano, M. A. 2005. 'Sister Acts: Conventual Performance and the *Visitatio Sepulchri* in England and France', in *Medieval Constructions in Gender and Identity: Essays in Honor of Joan M. Ferrante*, ed. T. Barolini, Medieval and Renaissance Texts and Studies 293 (Tempe), pp. 43–67.
Paradisi, G. 2003. '"Par muement des languages:" Il tempo, la memoria e il volgare in Wace', *Francofonia* 45: 27–47.
Park, D. 1987. 'Wall Painting', in *Age of Chivalry: Art in Plantagenet England 1200–1400*, ed. J. Alexander and P. Binski (London), pp. 125–30, 313.
Park, K. 2006. *Secrets of Women: Gender, Generation and the Origins of Human Dissection* (Brooklyn).
Partridge, S., and E. Kwakkel, ed. 2012. *Author, Reader, Book: Medieval Authorship in Theory and Practice* (Toronto).
Paulsson Lash, A. 2012. 'Gender and Social Positioning in French Language Manuals, 1396–1605' (unpublished French of England MA essay, Fordham University).
Payer, P. J. 2009. *Sex and the New Medieval Literature of Confession, 1150–1300* (Toronto).
Payling, S. J. 2011. 'Legal Right and Dispute Resolution in Late Medieval England: The Sale of the Lordship of Dunster'. *English Historical Review* 126.518: 17–43.
Pearsall, D., ed., 1990. *Studies in the Vernon Manuscript* (Cambridge).
Peele, M. 1981. 'Dinas Bran in Legend', *Notes and Queries* 226, n.s. 28.4: 293–5.
Peeters, P. 1906. 'La Légende de Saïdnaia', *Analecta Bollandiana* 25: 137–57.
—— 1933. Review of Habib Zayat, 1932, *Histoire de Saidanaya* [in Arabic], *Analecta Bollandiana* 41: 434–8.
Pensom, R. 1994. 'Inside and Outside: Fact and Fiction in *Fouke le Fitz Waryn*', *Medium Aevum* 63.1: 53–60
—— 1998. *Accent and Metre in French: A Theory of the Relation between Linguistic Accent and Metrical Practice in French, 1100–1900* (Bern).
—— 2006. 'Pour la versification anglo-normande', *Romania* 124: 51–65.
Perry, A. A. 1978. 'An Early Historical Play: The *Seinte Resurreccion*' [sic], *Indiana Social Studies Quarterly* 31: 39–45.
Pfeffer, W. 1985. *The Change of Philomel: The Nightingale in Medieval Literature* (New York).
Phillips, H., ed. 2008. *Bandit Territories: British Outlaws and their Traditions* (Cardiff).
Pickens, R. T. 1994. 'Autobiography and History in the Vulgate *Estoire* and in the *Prose Merlin*', in

Kibler, pp. 98–116.

Pinchbeck, C. 1948. 'A Mediaeval Self-Educator', *Medium Aevum* 17: 1–14.

Polo de Beaulieu, M. 1987. 'La Condamnation des soins de beauté par les prédicateurs du Moyen Âge (XIIIe–XVe siècles)', in Menjot, pp. 297–309.

Pons, N. 1982. 'La Propagande de guerre française avant l'apparition de Jeanne d'Arc', *Journal des savants* 2:191–214.

—— 1991. 'La Guerre de cent ans vue par quelques polémistes français du XVe siècle', in *Guerre et société en France, en Angleterre et en Bourgogne XIVe–XVe siècle*, ed. P. Contamine, C. Giry-Deloison and M. H. Keen (Lille), pp. 143–69.

Pope, M. K. 1904. *Étude sur la langue de Frère Angier, suivie d'un Glossaire de ses Poèmes* (Paris).

—— 1944. 'The Anglo-Norman Element in our Vocabulary: Its Significance for our Civilization', Deneke Lecture, Oxford (Manchester), pp. 1–14.

Porcheddu, F. 2001. 'Edited Text and Medieval Artifact: The Auchinleck Bookshop and "Charlemagne and Roland" Theories, Fifty Years Later', *Philological Quarterly* 80.4: 463–500.

Porter, M. E., and J. H. Baltzell 1954. 'The Old French Lives of Saint Edmund, King of East Anglia', *Romanic Review* 45: 81–8.

Poster, C., and L. C. Mitchell, ed. 2007. *Letter-Writing Manuals and Instruction from Antiquity to the Present: Historical and Bibliographic Studies* (Columbia).

Postlewate, L. 2015. 'Turner a pru: Conversion and Translation in the *Vie de seint Clement*', in *Telling the Story in the Middle Ages: Essays in Honor of Evelyn Birge Vitz*, ed. K. A. Drus, E. Emery and L. Postlewate (Cambridge), pp. 187–203.

—— (forthcoming). *Selected Works of Nicolas Bozon*, FRETS.

Pouchelle, M. 1990. *The Body and Surgery in the Middle Ages*, trans. R. Morris (Oxford).

Pouzet, J.-P. 2004. 'Quelques aspects de l'influence des chanoins augustins sur la production et la transmission littéraire vernaculaire en Angleterre (XIIIe–XVe siècles)', *Académie des Inscriptions et Belles-lettres, Comptes rendues* 148: 169–213.

—— 2009. 'Augustinian Canons and their Insular French Books in Medieval England: Towards an Assessment', in Wogan-Browne *et al.*, pp. 266–77.

Power, E. 1922. *Medieval English Nunneries c. 1275 to 1535* (Cambridge).

Press, A. R. 1981. 'The Precocious Courtesy of Geoffrey Gaimar', in Burgess, pp. 267–76.

Price, A. 2008. 'Welsh Bandits', in Phillips, pp. 58–72.

Purdie, R. 2008. *Anglicising Romance: Tail-Rhyme and Genre in Medieval English Literature* (Cambridge).

Putter, A. 2009a. 'Gerald of Wales and the Prophet Merlin', *Anglo-Norman Studies* 31: 90–103.

—— 2009b. 'The French of English Letters: Two Trilingual Verse Epistles in Context', in Wogan-Browne *et al.*, 397–408.

—— 2011. 'Code-Switching in Langland, Chaucer and the *Gawain* Poet: Diglossia and Footing', in *Code-Switching in Early English*, ed. Schendl and Wright, pp. 281–302.

—— 2015. 'The Organisation of Multilingual Miscellanies: The Contrasting Fortunes of Middle English Lyrics and Romances', in *Insular Books: Vernacular Manuscript Miscellanies in Late Medieval Britain*. Ed. M. Connolly and R. Radulescu (Oxford), pp. 81–100.

Raby, F. J. E. 1935. 'A Middle English Paraphrase of John of Howden's "Philomena" and the Text of his "Viola"', *Modern Language Review* 30.3: 339–43.

Radulescu, R. 2003. 'Yorkist Propaganda and *The Chronicle from Rollo to Edward IV*', *Studies in Philology* 100.4: 401–24.

Radulescu, R. L., and E. D. Kennedy, ed. 2008. *Broken Lines: Genealogical Literature in Medieval Britain and France* (Turnhout).

Rajsic, J. 2013. 'Britain and Albion in the Mythical Histories of Medieval England', unpubl. D.Phil. thesis (Oxford).

Rajsic, J. 2015. 'Looking for Arthur in Short Histories and Genealogies of England's Kings'. [under revision for *Review of English Studies*].

—— 2016. '"Cestuy roy dit que la couronne de Ffraunce luy appartenoit": Reshaping the Prose *Brut* Chronicle in Fifteenth-Century France', in Crooks, Green, Ormrod, pp. 126–47.

—— (forthcoming). '"Eles arryverent la ou or est apellé lez Rennes de Galeway": The Albina Myth in Sir Thomas Gray's *Scalacronica*', in Lamont and Baswell.

—— (forthcoming). 'Jean de Wavrin's *Recueil des croniques et anchiennes istories de la Grant Bretaigne*', in Lamont and Baswell.

Rawcliffe, C. 2006. *Leprosy in Medieval England* (Woodbridge).

Rector, G. 2010. 'The Romanz Psalter in England and Northern France in the Twelfth Century: Production, *Mise-en-page* and Circulation', *Journal of the Early Book Society for the History of Manuscripts and Printing* 13: 1–38.

—— 2012. '*En sa chambre sovent le lit*: Literary Leisure and the Chamber Sociabilities of Early Anglo-French Literature (*c.* 1100–1150)', *Medium Aevum* 81.1: 88–125.

Reeves, A. 2015. *Religious Education in Thirteenth-Century England: The Creed and the Articles of Faith* (Leiden).

Reinburg, V. 2012. *French Books of Hours: Making an Archive of Prayer, c. 1400–1600* (Cambridge).

Reinhard, J. R. 1941. 'Setting Adrift in Mediaeval Law and Literature', *Publications of the Modern Language Association of America* 56.1: 33–68.

Renn, D. A. 1987. '"Chastel de Dynan": The First Phases of Ludlow', in *Castles in Wales and the Marches: Essays in Honour of D. J. Cathcart King*, ed. J. R. Kenyon and R. Avent (Cardiff), pp. 55–73.

Revard, C. 2000. 'Scribe and Provenance', in *Studies in the Harley Manuscript: The Scribes, Contents and Social Contexts of British Library MS Harley 2253*, ed. S. Fein (Kalamazoo), pp. 21–109.

Rice, N. R. 2008. *Lay Piety and Religious Discipline in Middle English Literature* (Cambridge).

Richardson, H. G. 1939. 'An Oxford Teacher of the Fifteenth Century', *Bulletin of the John Rylands Library* 23.2: 436–57.

—— 1941. 'Business Training in Medieval Oxford', *American Historical Review* 46.2: 259–80.

Riddy, F. J. 1996. '"Women talking about the things of God": A Late Medieval Sub-culture', in Meale, pp. 104–27.

Riedlinger, H. 1958. *Die Makellosigkeit der Kirche in den lateinischen Hoheliedkommentaren des Mittelalters* (Münster).

Rigg, A. G. 1992. *A History of Anglo-Latin Literature 1066–1422* (Cambridge).

Ríkharðsdóttir, S. 2012. *Medieval Translations and Cultural Discourse: The Movement of Texts in England, France and Scandinavia* (Cambridge).

Robertson, D. 1996. 'Writing in the Textual Community: Clemence of Barking's Life of St Catherine', *French Forum* 21.1: 5–28.

Robertson, D. W. 1945. 'The *Manuel des Péchés* and an English Episcopal Decree', *Modern Language Notes* 60.7: 439–47.

Robertson, J. G. 1910. 'Shakespeare on the Continent, 1660–1700', in *The Drama to 1624*, *The Cambridge History of English and American Literature*, ed. A. W. Ward and A. R. Waller, vol. 5 (Cambridge), pp. 315–43.

Robson, C. A. 1952. *Maurice of Sully and the Medieval Vernacular Homily* (Oxford).

Rosemann, P. W. 2004. *Peter Lombard* (Oxford).

Ross, C., ed. 1979. *Patronage, Pedigree and Power in Later Medieval England* (Gloucester).

Ross, D. J. A. 1963. *Alexander Historiatus: A Guide to Medieval Illustrated Alexander Literature* (London).

—— 1988. 'Where did Payn Peverell Defeat the Devil? The Topography of an Episode in *Fouke le Fitz Waryn*', in *Studies in Medieval French Language and Literature Presented to Brian Woledge in Honour of his 80th Birthday*, ed. S. B. North (Geneva), pp. 135–43.

Rossi, C. 2005. 'Identificazione del dedicatorio del "Bestiaire Divin" di Guillaume le Clerc de Normandie', *Medioevo romanzo* 29: 442–62.

Rothwell, W. R. 1975–6. 'The Role of French in Thirteenth-Century England', *Bulletin of the John Rylands Library* 58: 445–66.

—— 1977. 'The Life and Miracles of St Edmund: A Recently Discovered Manuscript', *Bulletin of the John Rylands Library* 60: 135–80.

—— 1982. 'A Mis-Judged Author and a Mis-Used Text: Walter de Bibbesworth and his "Tretiz"', *Modern Language Review* 77.2: 282–93.

—— 1991. The Missing Link in English Etymology: Anglo-French. *Medium Aevum* 60:173–96. Online at http://www.anglo-norman.net/articlesA/missinglink.xml?

—— 1994. 'The Tri-lingual England of Geoffrey Chaucer', *Studies in the Age of Chaucer* 16: 45–67.

—— 1996. 'Playing "Follow My Leader" in Anglo-Norman Studies', *French Language Studies* 6.2: 177–210.

—— 1998. 'Arrivals and Departures: The Adoption of French Terminology into Middle English', *English Studies* 79: 144–65.

—— 1999. 'Sugar and Spice and All Things Nice: from Oriental Bazaar to English Cloister in Anglo-French', *Modern Language Review* 94: 647–59. Online at http://www.anglo-norman.net/articlesA/s_and_s.xml?

—— 2001. '*OED*, *MED*, *AND*: The Making of a New Dictionary of English', *Anglia* 119 (2001): 527–53.

Rouse, R. H., and M. A. Rouse 1979. *Preachers, Florilegia and Sermons: Studies on the Manipulus florum of Thomas of Ireland* (Toronto).

—— 1982. '*Statim invenire*: Schools, Preachers and New Attitudes to the Page', in *Renaissance and Renewal in the Twelfth Century*, ed. R. L. Benson, G. Constable and C. D. Lanham (Cambridge, MA), pp. 201–25.

—— 2000. *Manuscripts and their Makers: Commercial Book Producers in Medieval Paris, 1200–1500*, 2 vols. (Turnhout).

Rowe, N. 2011. *The Jew, the Cathedral and the Medieval City: Synagoga and Ecclesia in the Thirteenth Century* (New York)

Rubin, M. 1991. *Corpus Christi: The Eucharist in Late Medieval Culture* (Cambridge).

—— 1999. *Gentile Tales: The Narrative Assault on Late Medieval Jews* (New Haven).

—— 2009. *Mother of God: A History of the Virgin Mary* (New Haven).

Ruch, L. M. 2014. *Albina and her Sisters: The Foundation of Albion* (Amherst).

Rudd, W. R. 1929. 'The Priory of Horsham St Faith', *Norfolk Archaeology* 23: 68–73.

Ruhe, E. 1993. *Elucidarium und Lucidaires: Zur Rezeption des Werkes Honorius Augustodunensis in der Romania und in England* (Wiesbaden).

Ruini, D. 2013. 'Una redazione d'*Outremer*' della '*Conception Nostre Dame*' di Wace (ms. Tours, BM, 927)?', *Medioevo romanzo* 37 (2013): 296–326.

Rundle, D. 2011. 'English Books and the Continent', in *The Production of Books in England 1350–1500*, ed. A. Gillespie and D. Wakelin (Cambridge), pp. 276–91.

Russell, D. W. 1991. 'The Secularization of Hagiography in the Anglo-Norman "Vie Seinte Osith"', *Allegorica* 12: 3–16.

—— 1993 'The New *OED* Project and Anglo-Norman Lexicography', in Short, ed., pp. 327–36.

—— 2003. 'The Campsey Collection of Old French Saints' Lives: A Re-Examination of its Structure and Provenance', *Scriptorium* 57.1: 51–83.

—— 2009. 'The Cultural Context of the French Prose *remaniement* of the Life of Edward the Confessor by a Nun of Barking Abbey', in Wogan-Browne *et al.*, pp. 290–302.

—— 2012. '"Sun num n'i vult dire a ore": Identity Matters at Barking Abbey', in Brown and Bussell, pp. 17–34.

Russell, J. C. 1936. *Dictionary of Writers of Thirteenth Century England* (London).

Sabapathy, J. 2014. *Officers and Accountability in Medieval England 1170–1300* (Oxford).
Saenger, P. R. 1997. *Space between Words: The Origins of Silent Reading* (Stanford).
Salter, E. 2010 [1988]. *English and International: Studies in the Literature, Art and Patronage of Medieval England*, ed. D. Pearsall and N. Zeeman (Cambridge).
Sand, A. 2012. '*Cele houre memes*: An Eccentric English Psalter-Hours in the Huntington Library', *Huntington Library Quarterly* 75: 171–211.
Sandler, L. F. 1986. *Gothic Manuscripts, 1285–1385*, 2 vols., A Survey of Manuscripts Illuminated in the British Isles 5 (London).
—— 2012a. 'The *Lumere as lais* and its Readers: Pictorial Evidence from British Library MS Royal 15 II D', in *Thresholds of Medieval Visual Culture: Liminal Space*, ed. E. Gertsman and J. Stevenson (Woodbridge), pp. 73–94.
—— 2012b. 'Scribe, Corrector, Reader: The Marginal Drawings of the Morgan Library *Lumere as lais* and their Maker', in *English Manuscripts before 1400*, ed. A. S. G. Edwards and O. Da Rold, *English Manuscript Studies 1100–1700* 17 (London), pp. 107–39.
—— 2014. *Illuminators and Patrons in Fourteenth-Century England: The Psalter and Hours of Humphrey de Bohun and the Manuscripts of the Bohun Family* (London).
Saul, N. 2011. *For Honour and Fame: Chivalry in England, 1066–1500* (London); *Chivalry in Medieval England* (Cambridge, MA).
Scafi, A. 2006. *Mapping Paradise: A History of Heaven on Earth* (Chicago).
Scanlon, L. 1994. *Narrative, Authority and Power: The Medieval Exemplum and the Chaucerian Tradition* (Cambridge).
Scase, W., ed. 2013. *The Making of the Vernon Manuscript: The Production and Contexts of Oxford, Bodleian Library, MS Eng. Poet. a.1* (Turnhout).
Schemmann, U. 2000. *Confessional Literature and Lay Education: The* Manuel dé Pechez *as a Book of Good Conduct and Guide to Personal Religion*, Studia Humaniora 32 (Düsseldorf).
Schendl, H., and L. Wright 2011. 'Introduction' and 'Code-switching in Early English: Historical Background and Methodological and Theoretical Issues', in their *Code-switching in Early English* (Berlin), pp. 1–14, 15–45.
Scheper, G. L. 1971. 'The Spiritual Marriage: The Exegetic History and Literary Impact of the Song of Songs in the Middle Ages' (unpublished Ph.D. dissertation, Princeton University).
Schlauch, M. 1927. *Chaucer's Constance and Accused Queens* (New York).
Schreckenberg, H. 1996. *The Jews in Christian Art: An Illustrated History* (New York).
Schreiber, C. 2003. *King Alfred's Old English Translation of Pope Gregory the Great's* Regula pastoralis *and its Cultural Context* (Frankfurt am Main).
Schulze-Busacker, E. 1985. *Proverbes et expressions proverbiales dans la littérature narrative du moyen âge français* (Paris).
Schroeder, H. 1971. *Der Topos der Nine Worthies im Literatur und bildender Kunst* (Göttingen).
Segre, C. 1961. 'Piramo e Tisbe nei Lai di Maria di Francia', in *Studi in onore di Vittorio Lugli e Diego Valeri* (Venice), II, 845–53.
Severin, T. 1978. *The Brendan Voyage* (London).
Seymour, M. C. 2007. 'More Thoughts on Mandeville', in Bremer and Röhl, pp. 19–30.
Seymour, St J. D. 1929. *Anglo-Irish Literature 1200–1582* (Cambridge).
Sharpe, R. 2001 [1997]. *A Handlist of the Latin Writers of Great Britain and Ireland before 1540* [Additions and Corrections 2001] (Turnhout).
—— 2011. 'Peoples and Languages in Eleventh and Twelfth-Century Britain and Ireland: Reading the Charter Evidence', in *The Reality behind Charter Diplomatic in Anglo-Norman*, ed. D. E. Broun (Glasgow), pp. 1–119. http://paradox.poms.ac.uk/redist/pdf/chapter1.pdf.
—— 2013. 'Addressing Different Language-Groups: The Evidence of Charters from the Eleventh and Twelfth Centuries', in Jefferson and Putter, pp. 1–40.

Shea, J. 2007. 'Adgar's *Gracial* and Christian Images of Jews in Twelfth-Century Vernacular Literature', *Journal of Medieval History* 33.2: 181–96.
Sheingorn, P. 1993. '"The Wise Mother": The Image of St Anne Teaching the Virgin Mary', *Gesta* 32.1: 69–80.
Shepherd, S. H. A. 1989. 'The Ashmole *Sir Ferumbras*: Translation in Holograph', in *The Medieval Translator 1*, ed. Roger Ellis (Cambridge), pp. 103–21.
Shippey, T. A. 1970. 'Listening to the Nightingale', *Comparative Literature* 22.1: 46–60.
Short, I. 1972–3. Review of Panunzio, ed., 1967 *Romance Philology* 26:732–5.
—— 1977. 'An Early Draft of Guernes' *Vie de Saint Thomas Becket*', *Medium Aevum* 46.1: 21–34.
—— 1980. 'On Bilingualism in Anglo-Norman England', *Romance Philology* 33.4: 467–79.
—— 1987. 'The Patronage of Beneit's *Vie de Thomas Becket*', *Medium Aevum* 56.2: 239–56.
—— 1992. 'Patrons and Polyglots: French Literature in Twelfth-Century England', *Anglo-Norman Studies* 14: 229–49.
—— ed. 1993. *Anglo-Norman Anniversary Essays*, ANTS OPS 2 (London).
—— 1994. 'Gaimar's Epilogue and Geoffrey of Monmouth's *Liber vetustissimus*', *Speculum* 69.2: 323–43.
—— 1998. Review of P. Nobel, ed., 1996, in *Cahiers de civilisation médiévale* 41: 82–4.
—— 2005. 'Une généalogie hybride des rois de France', *Romania* 123: 360–83.
—— 2006. 'The Song of Roland and England', in *Approaches to Teaching the Song of Roland*, ed. W. Kibler and L. Morgan (New York), pp. 133–8.
—— 2007a. 'Literary Culture at the Court of Henry II', in *Henry II: New Interpretations*, ed. C. Harper-Bill and N. Vincent (Woodbridge), pp. 335–61.
—— 2007b. 'Denis Piramus and the Truth of Marie's *Lais*', *Cultura Neolatina* 67.3–4: 319–40.
—— 2009a. 'L'Anglo-normand au siècle de Chaucer: un regain de statistiques', in *Le Plurilinguisme au Moyen Âge: Orient – Occident: De Babel à la langue une*, éd. C. Kappler and S. Thiolier-Méjean (Paris), pp. 67–78.
—— 2009b. '*Anglice loqui nesciunt*: Monoglots in Anglo-Norman England', *Cultura Neolatina* 69: 245–62.
—— 2010. 'Another Look at "le faus franceis"', *Nottingham Medieval Studies*, 54, 35–55.
—— 2011. 'Frère Angier: Notes and Conjectures', *Medium Aevum* 80.1: 104–10.
—— 2013. *Manual of Anglo-Norman*, 2nd edn, ANTS OPS 8 (Oxford).
—— 2014. 'Sur l'identité de Frère Angier', *Romania* 132: 222–6.
Sinclair, K. V. 1984. 'Anglo-Norman at Waterford: The Mute Testimony of MS Cambridge, Corpus Christi College 405', in *Medieval French Textual Studies in Memory of T. B. W. Reid*, ed. I. Short (London), pp. 219–38.
—— 1992. 'The Anglo-Norman Patrons of Robert the Chaplain and Robert of Greatham', *Forum for Modern Language Studies* 28: 193–208.
—— 1993. '*Fierabras* in Anglo-Norman: Some Cultural Perspectives', in Short, pp. 361–77.
Siraisi, N. G. 1990. *Medieval and Early Renaissance Medicine: An Introduction to Knowledge and Practice* (Chicago)
Skemer, D. C., *et al.* [A. Bennett, J. F. Preston and W. P. Stoneman] 2013. *Medieval and Renaissance Manuscripts in the Princeton University Library*, 2 vols. (Princeton), I.
Skinner, P., ed. 2003. *The Jews in Medieval Britain: Historical, Literary and Archaeological Perspectives* (Woodbridge).
Smeets, J. R. 1968. 'Les Traductions, Adaptations et Paraphrases de la Bible en vers', in *Grundriss der romanischen Literaturen des Mittelalters*, ed. H. R. Jauss and E. Köhler, 2 vols. (Heidelberg), I, 48–57.
Smith, J. B. 2012. 'An Edition, Translation, and Introduction to Benedict of Gloucester's *Vita Dubricii*', *Arthurian Literature* 29: 53-100.

Smith, K. A. 2003. *Art, Identity and Devotion in Fourteenth-Century England: Three Women and their Books of Hours* (London).
—— 2006. 'Accident, Play and Invention: Three Infancy Miracles in the Holkham Bible Picture Book', in L'Engle and Guest, pp. 357–69.
Smith-Bernstein, D. 2007. 'Finding Faith: An Edition of the "Vie de Sainte Fey, Virgine et Martire", and a Study of the Cult of St Faith in Post-Conquest East Anglia' (unpublished Ph.D. dissertation, City University New York).
Smyser, H. M. 1967. 'Charlemagne Legends', in *A Manual of the Writings in Middle English 1050–1500*, gen. ed. J. Burke Severs (New Haven), 1, pp. 80–100, 256–66.
Somerset, F., and N. Watson 2003. *The Vulgar Tongue: Medieval and Postmodern Vernacularity* (University Park, PA).
Sonet, J. 1950. *Le Roman de Barlaam et Josaphat*, 2 vols. (Namur).
Southern, R. W. 1958. 'The English Origins of the "Miracles of the Virgin"', *Mediaeval and Renaissance Studies* 4: 176–216.
—— 1992 [1986]. *Robert Grosseteste: The Growth of an English Mind in Medieval Europe* (Oxford).
Spearing, A. C. 2005. *Textual Subjectivity: The Encoding of Subjectivity in Medieval Narratives and Lyrics* (Oxford).
—— 2012. *Medieval Autographies: The 'I' of the Text* (Notre Dame, IN).
Spence, J. 2008a. 'Anglo-Norman Prose Chronicles and their Audiences', in *Regional Manuscripts*, ed. A. S. G. Edwards, English Manuscript Studies 1100–1700 14 (London), pp. 27–59.
—— 2008b. 'Genealogies of Noble Families in Anglo-Norman', in Radulescu and Kennedy, pp. 63–77.
—— 2013. *Reimagining History in Anglo-Norman Prose Chronicles* (York).
Spiegel, G. M. 1978. *The Chronicle Tradition of Saint-Denis: A Survey*, Medieval Classics 10 (Brookline).
—— 1995 [1993]. *Romancing the Past: The Rise of Vernacular Prose Historiography in Thirteenth-Century France* (Berkeley).
—— 1997. *The Past as Text: The Theory and Practice of Medieval Historiography*. (Baltimore).
—— 2005. *Practicing History: New Directions in History Writing after the Linguistic Turn* (New York).
Spurgeon, C. F. E. 1911, repr. 1972. *Chaucer devant la critique en Angleterre et en France depuis son temps jusqu'à nos jours* (New York).
Stanesco, M. 1985. 'Le Héraut d'armes et la tradition littéraire chevaleresque', *Romania* 106: 233–53.
Staunton, M. 2006. *Thomas Becket and his Biographers* (Woodbridge).
Stein, R. M. 2006. *Reality Fictions: Romance, History and Governmental Authority, 1025–1180* (Notre Dame).
Stephens, W. 1989. *Giants in Those Days: Folklore, Ancient History and Nationalism* (Lincoln).
Stephenson, D. 2002. 'Fouke le Fitz Waryn and Llywelyn ap Gruffydd's Claim to Whittington', *Transactions of the Shropshire Archaeological and Historical Society* 77: 26–31.
Stevens, K. 2009. 'An Investigation of the "Roman de philosophie" by Simund de Freine' (unpublished MA thesis, University of York).
Stevens, M. 1979. 'The Royal Stanza in Early English Literature', *Publications of the Modern Language Association of America* 94.1: 62–76.
Stevenson, K., ed. 2009. *The Herald in Late Medieval England* (Woodbridge).
Stock, B. 1983. *The Implications of Literacy: Written Language and Models of Interpretation in the Eleventh and Twelfth Centuries* (Princeton).
Stone, C. R. 2013. *From Tyrant to Philosopher-King: A Literary History of Alexander the Great in Medieval and Early Modern England*, Cursor Mundi 19 (Turnhout).
Stoneman, R. 1994. *Legends of Alexander the Great* (London).
—— 2008. *Alexander the Great: A Life in Legend* (New Haven).
Stones, A. 2003. '"Mise en page" in the French *Lancelot-Grail*: The First 150 Years of the Illustrative Tradition', in Dover, pp. 125–44.

—— 2013. *Gothic Manuscripts: 1260–1320* Pt One. A Survey of Manuscripts Illuminated in France (London).

Strijbosch, C. 2000. *The Seafaring Saint: Sources and Analogues of the Twelfth-Century Voyage of Saint Brendan* (Dublin).

Strohm, P. 1992. 'The Textual Vicissitudes of Usk's "Appeal"', in *Hochon's Arrow: The Social Imagination of Fourteenth-Century Texts* (Princeton), pp. 145–57.

Strohm, P. ed. 2007. *Middle English*, Oxford Twenty-First Century Approaches to Literature (Oxford).

—— 2014. *The Poet's Tale: Chaucer and the Year that Made* The Canterbury Tales (London).

Studer, P., and J. Evans. 1976 [1924]. *Anglo-Norman Lapidaries* (Geneva [Paris]).

Suggett, H. 1946. 'The Use of French in England in the Later Middle Ages'. *Transactions of the Royal Historical Society* 28: 61–83.

Sullivan, M. 1990. 'The Original and Subsequent Audiences of the *Manuel des péchés* and its Middle English Descendants' (unpublished Ph.D. dissertation, University of Oxford).

—— 1991. 'The Author of the *Manuel des péchés*', *Notes and Queries* 236, n.s. 38.2: 155–7.

—— 1992. 'A Brief Textual History of the *Manuel des péchés*', *Neuphilologische Mitteilungen* 93.3–4: 337–46.

—— 1992–5. 'Readers of the *Manuel des péchés*', *Romania* 113: 233–42.

—— 1994. 'Historical Notes on Some Readers of the *Manuel des péchés* and its Middle English Descendants', *Scriptorium* 46 (1992): 84–6.

Sutton, A. F. 1992. 'Merchants, Music and Social Harmony: The London Puy and its French and London Contexts, circa 1300', *The London Journal* 17.1: 1–17.

Symes, C. 2002. 'The Appearance of Early Vernacular Plays: Forms, Functions, and the Future of Medieval Theater', *Speculum* 77: 778–831.

—— 2007. *A Common Stage; Theater and Public Life in Medieval Arras* (Ithaca, NY).

—— 2009. 'The History of Medieval Theatre / Theatre of Medieval History: Dramatic Documents and the Performance of the Past', *History Compass* 7.3: 1032–48.

—— 2011. 'The Medieval Archive and the History of Theatre: Assessing the Written and Unwritten Evidence for Premodern Performance', *Theatre Survey* 52.1: 29–58.

—— 2013. 'A Mirror for Merchants and Minstrels: The Influence of Arras on the Political and Literary Culture of London', Invited paper delivered at Fordham University Conference: Putting England in its Place: Cultural Production and Cultural Relations in the High Middle Ages.

Szkilnik, M. 1991. *L'Archipel du Graal: Étude de l'Estoire del Saint Graal* (Geneva).

Taubman, A. 2009. 'New Biographical Notes on Robert Mannyng of Brunne', *Notes and Queries* 56.2: 197–201.

Taylor, A. 2001. 'Was there a Song of Roland?' *Speculum* 76.1: 28–65.

—— 2002. *Textual Situations: Three Medieval Manuscripts and their Readers* (Philadelphia).

—— 2011. 'Can an Englishman Read a *chanson de geste*?' in Tyler, pp. 321–36.

Taylor, C. 2000. 'War, Propaganda and Diplomacy in Fifteenth-Century France and England', in *War, Government and Power in Late Medieval France*, ed. C. T. Allmand (Liverpool), pp. 70–91.

—— 2013. *Chivalry and the Ideals of Knighthood in France during the Hundred Years War* (Cambridge).

Taylor, J. 1987. *English Historical Literature in the Fourteenth Century* (Oxford).

Thaon, B. 1983. 'La Fière: The Career of Hue de Rotelande's Heroine in England', *Reading Medieval Studies* 9: 56–69.

Thiolier, J. 1993. '*La Scalacronica*: Première approche (MS 133)', in *Les Manuscrits français de la bibliothèque Parker, Actes du Colloque 24–27 mars 1993*, ed. N. Wilkins (Cambridge), pp. 121–55.

Thomas, A. 1904. Review of M. K. Pope, 'Étude sur la langue de frère Angier', 1903 (thesis), *Romania* 33: 440–3.

Thomas, H. M. 2003. *The English and the Normans: Ethnic Hostility, Assimilation and Identity, 1066–c. 1220* (Oxford).
Thompson, A. B., ed. 2008. *The Northern Homily Cycle* (Kalamazoo).
Thompson, J. J. 1997. 'The Governance of the English Tongue: The *Cursor Mundi* and its French Tradition', in *Individuality and Achievement in Middle English Poetry*, ed. O. S. Pickering (Cambridge), pp. 19–37.
Thompson, J. J. 1998. *The Cursor Mundi: Poem, Texts and Contexts*, Medium Aevum Monographs n.s. 19 (Oxford).
Thompson, S. 1984. 'Why English Nunneries had no History: A Study of the Problems of the English Nunneries Founded after the Conquest', in *Medieval Religious Women: Distant Echoes*, ed. J. A. Nichols and L. T. Shank, Cistercian Studies Series 71 (Kalamazoo), pp. 131–49.
—— 1991. *Women Religious: The Founding of English Nunneries after the Norman Conquest* (Oxford).
Thomson, R. M. 1974. 'Two Versions of a Saint's Life from St Edmund's Abbey: Changing Currents in XIIth Century Monastic Style', *Revue Bénédictine* 84: 383–408.
Thorndike, L. 1954. 'Computus', *Speculum* 29.2: 223–38.
Tigelaar, J. 2006. *Brabants historie ontvouwd: Die alder excellenste cronyke van Brabant en het Brabantse geschiedbeeld anno 1500* (MA thesis, University of Utrecht, published online at http://dspace.library.uu.nl/handle/1874/18829).
Tomasch, S. 2000. 'Postcolonial Chaucer and the Virtual Jew', in *The Postcolonial Middle Ages*, ed. J. J. Cohen (New York), pp. 243–60.
Townend, M. 2006. 'Contacts and Conflicts: Latin, Norse and French', in *The Oxford History of English*, ed. L. Mugglestone (Oxford), pp. 61–85.
—— 2012. 'European Literature and Eleventh-Century England', in O'Donnell, Townend, Tyler, pp. 607–36 (609–15).
Trachsler, R. 2003. 'A Question of Time: Romance and History', in Dover, pp. 23–32.
Treharne, E. M. 2003. 'The Form and Function of the Twelfth-Century Old English *Dicts of Cato*', *Journal of English and Germanic Philology* 102.4: 465–85.
Trotter, D. A. 1988. *Medieval French Literature and the Crusades (1100–1300)* (Geneva).
—— 1994. 'L'Anglo-français au Pays de Galles: une enquête préliminaire', *Revue de linguistique romane* 58: 461–88.
—— ed. 2000. *Multilingualism in Later Medieval Britain* (Woodbridge).
—— 2003a. 'Not as Eccentric as it Looks: Anglo-French and French French', *Forum for Modern Language Studies* 39: 427–38.
—— 2003b. 'L'Anglo-normand: variété insulaire, ou variété isolée?', *Médiévales* 45: 43–54.
—— 2007. 'Language and Law in the Anglo-French *Mirror of Justices*', *L'Art de la philologie: Mélanges en l'honneur de Leena Löfstedt*, ed. J. Härmä, E. Suomela-Härmä and O. Välikangas (Helsinki), pp. 257–70.
—— 2008. 'L'Anglo-normand en France: les traces documentaires', *Comptes rendus des séances de l'Académie des Inscriptions et Belles-Lettres* 152: 893–905.
—— 2010 'Language Labels, Language Change, and Lexis', in Busby and Kleinhenz, pp. 43–61.
—— 2011a. '(Socio)linguistic Realities of Cross-Channel Communication in the Thirteenth Century', *Thirteenth-Century England 13*, ed. J. E. Burton, pp. 117–31.
—— 2011b, 'L'Anglo-normand et le français, et les emprunts en anglais', in *Actes du colloque international 'Les Emprunts lexicaux au français dans les langues européennes', Craiova, 10–12 novembre 2011*, ed. M. Illiescu *et al.* (Craiova: Editura Universitaria), pp. 299–309.
—— 2012 'L'Anglo-normand à la campagne', in *Comptes-rendus de l'Académie des Inscriptions et Belles-Lettres, Paris, juin 2012*, II (avril–juin), 1113–31.
—— 2013. 'Deinz certeins boundes: Where does Anglo-Norman Begin and End?', *Romance Philology* 67: 139–77.

Trotter, D. A. 2015. 'Peut-on parler de judéo-anglo-normand? Textes anglo-normands en écriture hébraïque', *Médiévales* 68: 25–34.

Tscherpel, G. 2003. 'The Political Function of History: The Past and Future of Noble Families', in Eales and Tyas, pp. 87–104.

Turner, Marie 2014. 'Guy of Warwick and the Active Life of Historical Romance in *Piers Plowman*', *Yearbook of Langland Studies* 28: 3–27.

Turner, Marion 2013. *A Handbook of Middle English Studies* (Chichester).

Twycross, M. 2008. 'The Theatricality of Medieval English Plays', in *The Cambridge Companion to Medieval English Theatre*, ed. R. Beadle and A. J. Fletcher, 2nd edn (Cambridge), pp. 26–74.

Tyler, E. M. 2009. 'From Old English to Old French', in Wogan-Browne *et al.*, pp. 164–78.

—— ed. 2011. *Conceptualizing Multilingualism in England c. 800–c. 1250* (Turnhout).

—— 2012a. 'Trojans in Anglo-Saxon England: Precedent without Descent', *Review of English Studies* online n.s.: 1–20. doi: 10.1093/res/hgs083

—— 2012b. 'European Literature and Eleventh-Century England', in O'Donnell, Townend, Tyler, pp. 607–36 (616–25).

—— 2016. *England in Europe: English Royal Women and Literary Patronage c. 1000 – c 1150* (Toronto).

Tyson, D. B. 1979. 'Patronage of French Vernacular History Writers in the Twelfth and Thirteenth Centuries', *Romania* 100.2: 180–222.

—— 1994. 'Handlist of Manuscripts Containing the French Prose *Brut* Chronicle', *Scriptorium* 48.2: 333–44.

—— 1998. 'The Adam and Eve Roll: Corpus Christi College Cambridge MS 98', *Scriptorium* 52: 301–16.

—— 2001. 'The Manuscript Tradition of Old French Prose *Brut* Rolls', *Scriptorium* 55: 107–18.

Tzanaki, R. 2003. *Mandeville's Medieval Audiences: A Study on the Reception of the Book of Sir John Mandeville (1371–1550)* (Aldershot).

Uhlig, M. 2015. 'The Hagiographical Legend Challenged by Poetry: The French Metrical Versions of *Barlaam et Josaphat* (13th Century)', in *Barlaam and Josaphat: Neue Perspektiven auf ein europäisches Phänomen*, ed. C. Cordoni and M. Meyer (Berlin) pp. 433–55.

Uhlig, M., and Y. Foehr-Janssens, ed. 2013. *D'Orient en Occident: Les recueils de fables enchâssées avant les* Mille et une nuits *de Galland*, Cultural Encounters in Late Antiquity and the Middle Ages 16 (Turnhout).

Uitti, K. D. 1975. 'The Clerkly Narrator Figure in Old French Hagiography and Romance', *Medioevo Romanzo* 2.3: 394–408.

Van Coolput-Storms, C. 2009. 'Démarche persuasive et puissance émotionnelle: *Li Romanz de Dieu et de sa Mere* d'Herman de Valenciennes', in *Lors est ce jour grant joie nee: Essais de langue et de littérature françaises du Moyen Âge*, ed. M. Goyens and W. Verbeke, Mediaevalia Lovaniensia, Series 41(Leuven), pp. 71–96.

Van Court, E. N. 2000. 'Socially Marginal, Culturally Central: Representing Jews in Late Medieval English Literature', *Exemplaria* 12.2: 293–326.

Van Houts, E. M. C. 1984. 'The Adaptation of the *Gesta Normannorum Ducum* by Wace and Benoît', in *Non nova, sed nove: Mélanges de civilisation médiévale dédiés à Willem Noomen*, ed. M. Gosman and J. van Os (Groningen), pp. 115–24.

—— 1999. *Memory and Gender in Medieval Europe, 900–1200* (Basingstoke).

—— 2004. 'Wace as Historian', in Burgess, trans., pp. xxxv–lxii.

Vaughan, R. 1958. *Matthew Paris* (London).

Victoria County History http://www.victoriacountyhistory.ac.uk/counties.

Victoria County History Essex II (ed. W. Page and J. H. Round, 1907) and http://www.british-history.ac.uk/vch/essex/vol2

Venarde, B. L. 1997. *Women's Monasticism and Medieval Society: Nunneries in France and England, 890–1215* (Ithaca).

Vincent, N. 2001. *The Holy Blood: King Henry III and the Westminster Blood Relic* (Cambridge).
Vising, J. 1923. *Anglo-Norman Language and Literature* (London).
Visser-Fuchs, C. T. L. 2002. 'Warwick and Wavrin: Two Case Studies on the Literary Background and Propaganda of Anglo-Burgundian Relations in the Yorkist Period' (unpublished Ph.D. dissertation, University College London).
Vitz, E. B. 1989. '1215, November, the Fourth Lateran Council Prescribes that Adult Christians Confess at Least Once a Year: The Impact of Christian Doctrine on Medieval Literature', in *A New History of French Literature*, ed. D. Hollier, *et al.* (Cambridge, MA), pp. 82–8.
—— 1999. *Orality and Performance in Early French Romance* (Cambridge).
—— 2001. 'The Apocryphal and the Biblical, the Oral and the Written in Medieval Legends of Christ's Childhood: The Old French *Evangile de l'Enfance*', in *Satura: Studies in Medieval Literature in Honour of Robert R. Raymo*, ed. N. M. Reale and R. E. Sternglantz (Donington), pp. 124–49.
Wallace, D. 1997. 'In Flaundres', *Studies in the Age of Chaucer* 19: 63–91.
Wallis, F. 2005. '"Number Mystique" in Early Medieval Computus Texts', in *Mathematics and the Divine: A Historical Study*, ed. T. Koetsier and L. Bergmans (Amsterdam), pp. 179–200.
—— *The Calendar and the Cloister: Oxford St John's College MS 17*: http://digital.library.mcgill.ca/ms-17/ accessed July 2015.
Walther, H. 1969. *Initia carminum ac versuum Medii Aevi posterioris Latinorum: Alphabetisches Verzeichnis der Versanfänge mittellateinischer Dichtungen* (Göttingen), II.
Ward, B. 1987. *Miracles and the Medieval Mind: Theory, Record and Event, 1000–1215*, rev. edn (Philadelphia).
Warner, L. 2014. *The Piers Plowman Myth* (Cambridge).
Warren, M. R. 2000. *History on the Edge: Excalibur and the Borders of Britain, 1100–1300* (Minneapolis).
—— 2007a. 'Translation', in Strohm, pp. 51–67
—— 2007b. 'Translating in the Zone', *New Medieval Literatures* 9: 191–8.
Warren, N. B. 2001. *Spiritual Economies: Female Monasticism in Later Medieval England* (Philadelphia).
Waters, C. M. 2003. 'Talking the Talk: Access to the Vernacular in Medieval Preaching', in Somerset and Watson, pp. 31–42.
—— 2012. 'Loving Teaching: Status, Exchange and Translation in Pierre d'Abernon's *Lumere as lais*', *Medium Aevum* 81.2: 303–20.
—— 2015. *Translating 'Clergie': Status, Education, and Salvation in Thirteenth-Century Vernacular Texts* (Philadelphia).
Wathelet-Willem, J. 1975. *Recherches sur La Chanson de Guillaume*, 2 vols. (Paris).
Watson, A. G. 1984. *Catalogue of Dated and Datable Manuscripts, c. 435–1600 in Oxford Libraries*, 2 vols. (Oxford), I.
Watson, A. G., ed. 1987. *Medieval Libraries of Great Britain: A List of Surviving Books, edited by N. R. Ker: Supplement to the Second Edition* (London).
Watson, N. 2009a. 'Middle English Versions and Audiences of Edmund of Abingdon's *Speculum Religiosorum*', in Gunn and Innes-Parker, pp. 115–31.
Watson, N. 2009b. 'Lollardy: The Anglo-Norman Heresy?' in Wogan-Browne *et al.*, pp. 334–46.
Watson, N., and J. Wogan-Browne 2004. 'The French of England: The *Compileison*, *Ancrene Wisse*, and the Idea of Anglo-Norman', *Journal of Romance Studies* 4: 35–59.
Waugh, S. L. 1985. 'Marriage, Class and Royal Lordship in England under Henry III', *Viator* 16: 181–207.
Webb, H. 2010. *The Medieval Heart* (New Haven).
Weiss, J. 1969. 'The Auchinleck MS and the Edwardes MSS', *Notes and Queries* 214, n.s. 16.12: 444–6.
—— 2002. 'Emperors and Antichrists: Reflections of Empire in Insular Narrative, 1130–1250', in

The Matter of Identity in Medieval Romance, ed. P. Hardman (Cambridge), pp. 87–102.

Weiss, J. 2010. 'The Exploitation of Ideas of Pilgrimage and Sainthood in *Gui de Warewic*', in *The Exploitations of Medieval Romance*, ed. L. Ashe, I. Djordjević, J. Weiss (Cambridge), pp. 43–56.

Welter, J. T. 1927. *L'Exemplum dans la littérature religieuse et didactique du Moyen Âge* (Paris).

White, H. 2000. *Nature, Sex and Goodness in a Medieval Literary Tradition* (Oxford).

Whitehead, C. 2000. 'A Fortress and a Shield: The Representation of the Virgin in the *Château d'amour* of Robert Grosseteste', in *Writing Religious Women*, ed. D. Renevey and C. Whitehead (Cardiff), pp. 109–32.

—— 2003. *Castles of the Mind: A Study of Medieval Architectural Allegory* (Cardiff).

Wilkins, N. 1993. *Catalogue des manuscrits français de la bibliothèque Parker (Parker Library) Corpus Christi College, Cambridge* (Cambridge).

Williams, A. J. 2007. 'Manipulating the Past for the Sake of the Future: Optimistic Perspectives in the Outlaw Romance *Fouke le Fitz Waryn*', *New Zealand Journal of French Studies* 28.1: 19–31.

Williams, D. 2004. *The French Fetish from Chaucer to Shakespeare* (Cambridge).

Williams, S. J. 2003. 'The Vernacular Tradition of the Pseudo-Aristotelian *Secret of Secrets* in the Middle Ages: Translations, Manuscripts, Readers', in *Filosofia in volgare nel Medioevo*, ed. N. Bray and L. Sturlese (Louvain-la-Neuve), pp. 451–82.

Williamson, B. 1998. 'The Virgin *Lactans* as Second Eve: Image of the Salvatrix', *Studies in Iconography* 19: 105–38.

Wilson, R. M. 1940. 'The Medieval Library of Titchfield Abbey', *Proceedings of the Leeds Philosophical and Literary Society* 5: 150–77, 252–76.

—— 1952. *The Lost Literature of Medieval England* (London).

Wind, B. H. 1962. 'Faut-il identifier Thomas, auteur de *Tristan*, avec Thomas de Kent?' in *Saggi e ricerche in memoria di Ettore Li Gotti*, 3 vols., Bollettino (Centro di studi filologici e linguistici siciliani) 6–8 (Palermo), III, 479–90.

Wogan-Browne, J. 1994a. '"Bet . . . to . . . rede on holy seyntes lyves . . .": Romance and Hagiography Again', in *Readings in Medieval English Romance*, ed. C. M. Meale (Cambridge), pp. 83–97.

—— 1994b. 'The Apple's Message: Some Post-Conquest Hagiographic Accounts of Textual Transmission', in *Late-Medieval Religious Texts and Their Transmission: Essays in Honour of A. I. Doyle*, ed. A. J. Minnis (Cambridge), pp. 39–54.

—— 1994c. 'Wreaths of Thyme: The Female Translator in Anglo-Norman Hagiography', in *The Medieval Translator 4*, ed. R. Ellis and R. Evans, Medieval and Renaissance Texts and Studies 123 (Binghamton), pp. 46–55.

—— 1996. '"Clerc u lai, muïne u dame": Women and Anglo-Norman Hagiography in the Twelfth and Thirteenth Centuries', in Meale, pp. 61–85.

—— 2001. *Saint's Lives and Women's Literary Culture c. 1150–1300: Virginity and its Authorizations*: (Oxford).

—— 2003. 'Powers of Record, Powers of Example: Hagiography and Women's History', in *Gendering the Master Narrative: Women and Power in the Middle Ages*, ed. M. C. Erler and M. Kowaleski (Ithaca), pp. 71–93.

—— 2005. '"Our Steward, St Jerome": Theology and the Anglo-Norman Household', in *Household, Women and Christianities in Late Antiquity and the Middle Ages*, ed. A. B. Mulder-Bakker and J. Wogan-Browne, Medieval Women: Texts and Contexts 14 (Turnhout), pp. 133–65.

—— 2005b. Review of Blumreich 2002, *Speculum* 80.2: 518–20.

—— 2009a. '"Cest livre liseez . . . chescun jour": Women and Reading *c.* 1230–*c.* 1430', in Wogan-Browne *et al.*, pp. 239–53.

—— 2009b. 'Time to Read: Pastoral Care, Vernacular Access and the Case of Angier of St Frideswide', in Gunn and Innes-Parker, pp. 62–77.

Wogan-Browne, J. 2011. 'Mother or Stepmother to History? Joan de Mohun and her Chronicle', in *Motherhood, Religion and Society in Medieval Europe, 400–1400: Essays Presented to Henrietta Leyser*, ed. C. Leyser and L. Smith (Surrey), pp. 297–316.
—— 2013. 'What Voice is that Language?/What Language is that Voice? Multilingualism and Identity in a Medieval Letter-Treatise', in Jefferson and Putter, pp. 171–94.
—— 2014. 'The Tongues of the Nightingale: "hertely redying" at English Courts' in Kerby-Fulton, Thompson, and Baechle, pp. 78–98.
—— 2015. 'Invisible Archives? Later Medieval French in England', *Speculum* 90.3: 653–73.
—— (forthcoming). 'Parchment and Pure Flesh: Elizabeth de Vere, Countess of the Twelfth Earl of Oxford and her Book', in *Women's Objects: Essays in Honor of Carolyn P. Collette*, ed. N. Bradbury and J. Adams (Ann Arbor).
Wogan-Browne, J. *et al.* [C. Collette, M. Kowaleski, L. Mooney, A. Putter, D. Trotter], ed. 2009. *Language and Culture in Medieval Britain: The French of England c. 1100–c. 1500* (York).
Wogan-Browne, J. *et al.* [N. Watson, A. Taylor and R. Evans], ed. 1999. *The Idea of the Vernacular: An Anthology of Middle English Literary Theory, 1280–1530* (University Park, PA).
Woledge, B. 1951. 'Notes on Wace's Vocabulary', *Modern Language Review* 46.1: 16–30.
Woledge, B., and H. P. Clive 1964. *Répertoire des plus anciens textes en prose française depuis 842 jusqu'aux premières années du XIIIe siècle* (Geneva).
Wolfram, H. 2003. 'Martin of Troppau', in *New Catholic Enyclopedia*, ed. B. L. Marthaler, 2nd edn, 15 vols. (Detroit), IX, 220, 222.
Wood, C. T. 1981. 'The Doctor's Dilemma: Sin, Salvation and the Menstrual Cycle in Medieval Thought', *Speculum* 56.4: 710–27.
Wooding, J. M. 2000. *The Otherworld Voyage in Early Irish Literature: An Anthology of Criticism* (Dublin).
Worley, M. 2003. 'Using the *Ormulum* to Redefine Vernacularity', in Somerset and Watson, pp. 1–23.
Wright, L. 1996. *Sources of London English: Medieval Thames Vocabulary* (Oxford).
—— 2000. 'Bills, Accounts, Inventories: Everyday Trilingual Activities in the Business World of Late Medieval England', in Trotter 2000, pp. 149–56.
—— 2012. 'On Variation and Change in London Medieval Mixed-Language Business Documents', in *Language Contact and Development around the North Sea*, ed. M. Stenroos, M. Mäkinen and I. Særheim (Amsterdam), pp. 99–115.
—— 2013. 'Mixed-Language Accounts as Sources for Linguistic Analysis', in Jefferson and Putter, pp. 123–36.
Yamamoto, D. 2000. *The Boundaries of the Human in Medieval English Literature* (Oxford).
Yeager, R. F. 1990. *John Gower's Poetic: The Search for a New Arion* (Cambridge).
—— 2006. 'Gower's French Audience: The *Mirour de l'omme*', *Chaucer Review* 41.2: 111–37.
—— 2009. 'John Gower's French and his Readers', in Wogan-Browne *et al.*, pp. 135–45 (repr. in Dutton *et al.*, pp. 304–14).
Yeager, R. F., M. West and R. L. Hinson 1997. *A Concordance to the French Poetry and Prose of John Gower* (East Lansing).
Young, K. 1933. *The Drama of the Medieval Church*, 2 vols. (Oxford).
Zatta, J. 1997. 'Gender, Love, and Sex as Political Theory? Romance in Geffrei Gaimar's Anglo-Norman Chronicle', *Mediaevalia* 21.2: 249–80
—— 1999. 'Gaimar's Rebels: Outlaw Heroes and the Creation of Authority in Twelfth-Century England', *Essays in Medieval Studies* 16: 27–37.
Zeeman, N. 2008. 'Tales of Piers and Perceval: *Piers Plowman* and the Grail Romances', *Yearbook of Langland Studies* 22: 199–26.
Ziegler, J. 1998. *Medicine and Religion c. 1300: The Case of Arnau de Vilanova* (Oxford).

Ziegler, J. 2001. 'Medicine and Immortality in Terrestrial Paradise', in *Religion and Medicine in the Middle Ages*, ed. P. Biller and J. Ziegler, York Studies in Medieval Theology 3 (York), pp. 201–42.

Zieman, K. 2008. *Singing the New Song: Literacy and Liturgy in Late Medieval England* (Philadelphia).

Zink, M. 1976. *La Prédication en langue romane avant 1300* (Paris).

Zink, M. 1984. 'Le Rêve avéré: La mort de Cahus et la langueur d'Arthur du *Perlesvaus* à *Fouke le Fitz Waryn*', *Littératures* 9–10: 31–8.

Ziolkowski, E. J. 2001. *Evil Children in Religion, Literature and Art* (Basingstoke).

Useful Websites

(other than individual manuscript sites, located in Entries: see also Abbreviations)

Anglo-Norman Dictionary, sources and articles on Anglo-Norman:
www.anglo-norman.net/

Audio-visual Readings in the French of England:
http://legacy.fordham.edu/academics/programs_at_fordham_/medieval_studies/french_of_england/audio_readings_94163.asp

British History:
http://www.british-history.ac.uk/search/series/rymer-foedera.
www.victoriacountyhistory.ac.uk/counties
https://www.englandsimmigrants.com/
http://www2.le.ac.uk/projects/impact-of-diasporas/

French Manuscripts: Institut d'histoire et recherche des textes, Paris
http://aedilis.irht.cnrs.fr/manuscrit/litteraires.htm

French of Outremer:
http://legacy.fordham.edu/academics/programs_at_fordham_/medieval_studies/french_of_outremer/index.asp and conference abstracts at http://legacy.fordham.edu/mvst/conference14/program.html

Medieval English Romance:
http://www.middleenglishromance.org.uk/

Medieval Francophone Literary Culture Outside France:
http://www.medievalfrancophone.ac.uk/
http://www.kcl.ac.uk/artshums/depts/ddh/research/projects/current/mflcof.aspx

Medieval French Literature: Bibliography:
http://www.arlima.net/

General Index

Page numbers in **bold** indicate edited texts and translations

Index of Manuscripts